W9-BLU-273

GLO-BUS – *Developing Winning Competitive Strategies.*
It calls for participants to test their strategy-making and decision-making skills by running a company that competes in the global digital camera industry. **GLO-BUS**, also a totally automated online simulation that is delivered at **www.glo-bus.com**, takes somewhat less time for students to play (due to fewer decision variables) and features a 3-year strategic plan option, an option for company managers to make quarterly updates for some decisions as the year progresses, strategic group maps, company strengths/weaknesses, and benchmark and competitive data.

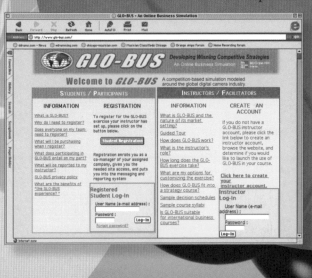

Gregory G. Dess
University of Texas at Dallas

G. T. Lumpkin
University of Illinois at Chicago

Alan B. Eisner
Pace University

Strategic Management

text and cases

3e

McGraw-Hill
Irwin

Boston   Burr Ridge, IL   Dubuque, IA   Madison, WI   New York
San Francisco   St. Louis   Bangkok   Bogotá   Caracas   Kuala Lumpur
Lisbon   London   Madrid   Mexico City   Milan   Montreal   New Delhi
Santiago   Seoul   Singapore   Sydney   Taipei   Toronto

McGraw-Hill
Irwin

STRATEGIC MANAGEMENT: TEXT AND CASES

Published by McGraw-Hill/Irwin, a business unit of The McGraw-Hill Companies, Inc., 1221 Avenue of the Americas, New York, NY, 10020. Copyright © 2007 by The McGraw-Hill Companies, Inc. All rights reserved. No part of this publication may be reproduced or distributed in any form or by any means, or stored in a database or retrieval system, without the prior written consent of The McGraw-Hill Companies, Inc., including, but not limited to, in any network or other electronic storage or transmission, or broadcast for distance learning.

Some ancillaries, including electronic and print components, may not be available to customers outside the United States.

This book is printed on acid-free paper.

1 2 3 4 5 6 7 8 9 0 WCK/WCK 0 9 8 7 6 5

ISBN-13: 978-0-07-310246-7
ISBN-10: 0-07-310246-6

Editorial director: *John E. Biernat*
Senior sponsoring editor: *Ryan Blankenship*
Developmental editor II: *Natalie J. Ruffatto*
Editorial coordinator: *Allison J. Clelland*
Senior marketing manager: *Lisa Nicks*
Producer, Media technology: *Damian Moshak*
Project manager: *Harvey Yep*
Production supervisor: *Gina Hangos*
Senior designer: *Adam Rooke*
Lead media project manager: *Susan Lombardi*
Cover design: *Pam Verros*
Interior design: *Pam Verros*
Typeface: *10/12 Times Roman*
Compositor: *GTS–New Delhi, India Campus*
Printer: *Quebecor World Versailles Inc.*

Library of Congress Cataloging-in-Publication Data

Dess, Gregory G.
    Strategic management : text and cases / Gregory G. Dess, G.T. Lumpkin, Alan B. Eisner.—3rd ed.
        p. cm.
    Includes bibliographical references and indexes.
    ISBN-13: 978-0-07-310246-7 (alk. paper)
    ISBN-10: 0-07-310246-6 (alk. paper)
    1. Strategic planning. I. Lumpkin, G. T. II. Eisner, Alan B. III. Title.
HD30.28.D4746 2007
658.4'012—dc22   2005056295

www.mhhe.com

Brief Contents

Dedication

To my family, Margie and Taylor;
my parents, Bill and Mary Dess;
and the late Wayne D. Bodensteiner
—Greg

To my wife, Vicki, and my colleagues at the
University of Illinois at Chicago
—Tom

To my family, Helaine,
Rachel, and Jacob
—Alan

Contents

Cases

About the Authors

Gregory G. Dess is the Andrew R. Cecil Endowed Chair in Management at the University of Texas at Dallas. His primary research interests are in strategic management, organization–environment relationships, and knowledge management. He has published numerous articles on these subjects in both academic and practitioner-oriented journals. In August 2000, he was inducted into the Academy of Management Journal's Hall of Fame as one of its charter members. Professor Dess has conducted executive programs in the United States, Europe, Africa, Hong Kong, and Australia. During 1994 he was a Fulbright Scholar in Oporto, Portugal. He received his PhD in Business Administration from the University of Washington (Seattle).

G. T. (Tom) Lumpkin is Associate Professor of Management and Entrepreneurship at the University of Illinois at Chicago. He received his PhD in management from the University of Texas at Arlington and MBA from the University of Southern California. His research interests include entrepreneurial orientation, opportunity recognition, strategy-making processes, and innovative forms of organizing work. He has published numerous research articles and book chapters. He is a member of Editorial Review Boards of *Entrepreneurship Theory & Practice* and the *Journal of Business Venturing*. Professor Lumpkin also conducts executive programs in strategic and entrepreneurial applications of e-commerce and digital business technologies.

Alan B. Eisner is Associate Professor of Management and Graduate Management Program Chair at the Lubin School of Business, Pace University. He received his PhD in management from the Stern School of Business, New York University. His primary research interests are in strategic management, technology management, organizational learning, and managerial decision making. He has published research articles and cases in journals such as *Advances in Strategic Management, International Journal of Electronic Commerce, International Journal of Technology Management, American Business Review, Journal of Behavioral and Applied Management,* and *Journal of the International Academy for Case Studies.* He is the Associate Editor of the Case Association's peer reviewed journal, *The CASE Journal.*

Preface

Welcome to the Third Edition of *Strategic Management: Text and Cases!* We are very pleased with the positive response that our two earlier editions have received, and we are very grateful for the constructive and extensive feedback that we have obtained from the many professionals who took the time to review and critique our work. Much of this input has been invaluable and has led to what we feel are many improvements that we will summarize below. We are happy to acknowledge these important contributors later in the Preface.

We'd first like to briefly address what is, perhaps, the most obvious question: Why did we write the book? We would all agree that there are already many good strategy textbooks on the market. We felt that there was still a need for a book that students would find relevant and readable as well as rigorous. In striving for such goals, we endeavored to "cover all of the traditional bases" and to integrate some central themes throughout the book that are vital to understanding strategic management in today's global economy. These include such topics as globalization, technology, ethics, and entrepreneurship. And, to bring the concepts to life, we have included short examples from business practice to illustrate virtually every concept in the book, and we have provided over 100 Strategy Spotlights—more detailed examples—to drive home key points. We also have included four separate chapters that other strategy texts typically don't have. These chapters focus on timely topics about which all business students should have a solid understanding: the role of intellectual assets and knowledge in value creation (Chapter 4); the key role of the Internet and digital business strategies in creating competitive advantage (Chapter 8); the value of fostering entrepreneurship in established organizations (Chapter 12); and the creation of new venture start-ups (Chapter 13). We also provide an excellent set of cases to help students analyze, integrate, and apply strategic management concepts.

In developing *Strategic Management* and the support materials, we did not, of course, forget the instructors. You certainly have a very challenging (and rewarding) job. And we want to do our best to help you. We provide you with a variety of supplementary materials that should help you in class preparation and delivery. We did not, like many texts, simply summarize the material in the chapters. Instead, we focused our efforts on where we felt that we could add value to your pedagogy. We worked hard to provide you with a complete package that should make your classes relevant, rigorous, and rewarding for both you and your students. We felt it was important to develop all of the supplementary materials ourselves and not farm them out to others as some other textbook authors do. We feel this has helped to ensure a consistent level of quality and consistency in all of the materials.

What Remains the Same: Key Features from Earlier Editions

Before we discuss some of the most important changes that we have made to improve *Strategic Management* and keep it fresh and up-to-date, let's briefly address some of the exciting features that remain from the earlier editions.

- *Traditional organizing framework with four other chapters on timely topics.* Crisply written chapters cover all of the strategy bases and address contemporary topics. First, the chapters are divided logically into the traditional sequence: strategy analysis, strategy formulation, and strategy implementation. Second, we include four chapters on such timely topics as intellectual capital/knowledge

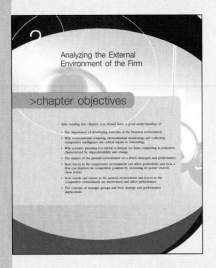

Analyzing the External
Environment of the Firm

>chapter objectives

After reading this chapter you should have a good understanding of

- The importance of developing forecasts of the business environment
- Why environmental scanning, environmental monitoring, and collecting competitive intelligence are critical inputs to forecasting.
- Why scenario planning is a useful technique for firms competing in industries characterized by unpredictability and change.
- The impact of the general environment on a firm's strategies and performance.
- How forces in the competitive environment can affect profitability, and how a firm can improve its competitive position by increasing its power vis-à-vis these forces.
- How trends and events in the general environment and forces in the competitive environment are interrelated and affect performance.
- The concept of strategic groups and their strategy and performance implications.

management, Internet and digital strategies, innovation within the corporation, and new ventures.

- *Chapter opening cases.* What can go wrong? To enhance student interest, we begin each chapter with a case that depicts an organization that has suffered a dramatic performance drop, or outright failure, by failing to adhere to sound strategic management concepts and principles. We believe that this feature serves to underpin the value of the concepts in the course and that it is a preferred teaching approach to merely providing examples of outstanding companies that always seem to get it right! After all, isn't it better (and more challenging) to diagnose problems than admire perfection? As Dartmouth's Sydney Finkelstein, author of *Why Smart Executives Fail,* notes: "We live in a world where success is revered, and failure is quickly pushed to the side. However, some of the greatest opportunities to learn—both for individuals and organizations—come from studying what goes wrong."[1] We'll see how, for example, Coca-Cola's performance has suffered from an overbearing and intrusive board of directors and because they largely ignored the trend to non-carbonated drinks; why Jaguar has been quite a flop for its parent, Ford Motor Company; and how Charles Schwab and Company's acquisition of U.S. Trust, a financial services firm that caters to wealthy clients, has not worked out as planned.

- *Consistent chapter format and features to reinforce learning.* We have included several features in each chapter to add value and create an enhanced learning experience. First, each chapter begins with an overview and a set of bullets pointing to key learning objectives. Second, as previously noted, the opening case describes a situation in which a company's performance eroded because of a lack of proper application of strategy concepts. Third, at the end of each chapter there are four different types of questions/exercises that should help students assess their understanding and application of material:

(1) Experiential exercises.

(2) Summary review questions.

(3) Application questions and exercises.

(4) Ethics questions. Given the emergence of Internet and e-commerce, each chapter contains at least one exercise that involves the use of the Internet.

- *Clear articulation and illustration of key concepts.* Key strategy concepts are introduced in a clear and concise manner and are followed by timely and interesting examples from business practice. Such concepts include value-chain analysis, the resource-based view of the firm, Porter's five forces model, competitive advantage, boundaryless organizational designs, digital strategies, corporate governance, ethics, and entrepreneurship.

- *Extensive use of sidebars.* We include 110 sidebars (or about eight per chapter) called Strategy Spotlights. The Strategy Spotlights not only illustrate key points but also increase the readability and excitement of new strategy concepts.

[1]Personal communication, June 20, 2005.

- *Integrative themes.* The text provides a solid grounding in ethics, globalization, and technology. These topics are central themes throughout the book and form the basis for many of the Strategy Spotlights.
- *Implications of concepts for small businesses.* Many of the key concepts are applied to start-up firms and smaller businesses, which is particularly important since many students have professional plans to work in such firms.
- *Not just a textbook but an entire package. Strategic Management* features the best chapter teaching notes available today. Rather than merely summarizing the key points in each chapter, we focus on value-added material to enhance the teaching (and learning) experience. Each chapter includes dozens of questions to spur discussion, teaching tips, in-class group exercises, and about a dozen detailed examples from business practice to provide further illustrations of key concepts.
- *BusinessWeek subscription.* Students can subscribe to *BusinessWeek* for a special rate in addition to the price of the text. Students will receive a passcode card shrink-wrapped with their new text. The card directs students to a Web site where they enter the code and then gain access to *BusinessWeek*'s registration page to enter their address information and set up their print and online subscription. Please ask your McGraw-Hill/Irwin representative for more information.
- **Case Studies** We have selected an outstanding collection of current and classic cases for this edition, carefully including a wide variety of cases matched to key strategic concepts and organized to create maximum flexibility. We now have a balance of short, concise and longer, comprehensive cases while maintaining currency and name recognition of our cases with many new and updated classroom-tested cases. We have two new industry cases on the express package industry and the casino industry. We also have updated many of the favorites from the Second Edition such as Southwest Airlines, General Motors, World Wrestling Entertainment, and many others to further engage students. New cases include: Sears–Kmart Merger, Kroger, Readers Digest, and QVC. We are once again pleased to include several cases from The Harvard Business School and *The Harvard Business Review,* including Crown, Cork, and Seal; Zara; and Philips versus Mashusita.
- We offer a balance of short, medium-length, and comprehensive cases that provide a variety of classic and contemporary industry settings.
- Teaching notes for all cases are available on the Instructor's Resource CD-ROM. And finally, several of the cases have supplemental student and teacher resources to cultivate research skills, provide additional background, and encourage critical thinking. These enhanced case studies have a variety of features such as case PowerPoint slides, Web links, discussion questions, and videos with teaching notes.

Standard & Poor's Educational Version of Market Insight. McGraw-Hill/Irwin is proud to partner with Standard & Poor's to offer access to the Educational Version of Standard & Poor's Market Insight©. This rich online resource provides six years of financial data, key ratio summary reports, and S&P's exclusive "Industry Surveys" that offer an in-depth look at industry trends, projections, and competitive analysis for 500 top U.S. companies in the renowned COMPUSTAT ® database. The password-protected Web site is the perfect way to bring real data into today's classroom for use in case analysis, industry analysis, and research for team and individual projects. Learn more at www.mhhe.com/edumarketinsight.

What's New: Highlights of the Third Edition

Now, let's briefly summarize some of exciting topics and changes that we have made in the Third Edition to enhance the value of *Strategic Management* for both instructors and students.

- Ten of the 13 opening "minicases" that lead off each chapter are totally new. And the three others have been carefully updated. As we noted, we believe that it is better to analyze things that can go wrong when strategy concepts aren't followed than to observe perfection. Approximately half of the 110 Strategy Spotlights are new, and most of the others have been updated. We will address, for example, how the Sarbanes-Oxley Act has been a boon for the accounting profession, the implications of the global market for talent (especially for people in professional services industries), how VoodooPC has developed a successful differentiation focus strategy in an industry (personal computers) that is usually associated with cut-throat price competition, and how Sony develops its video games by using outsourced talent.

- **Chapter 1** expands the section on stakeholder analysis to include a more detailed discussion of social responsibility and environmental sustainability. We build on Rosabeth Kanter's advocacy that social innovation should address community needs not merely as financial donations and volunteer work but as opportunities to develop new ideas and demonstrate business technologies as well as find and serve new markets. We also reinforce the notion that organizations are becoming more sensitive to how their operations affect the physical environment and the benefits of incorporating a "triple bottom line," which includes financial, social, and environmental performance, when assessing their firm's performance.

- **Chapter 2 (external analysis)** now includes a discussion of the dynamic nature of industries. Such a perspective has important implications for strategy, and we build on Anita McGahan's work. She suggests that an industry may follow one of four possible evolutionary trajectories that are based on two types of obsolescence: core activities and core assets. These range from radical change which occurs when both core activities and core assets face threats of obsolescence (for example, the overnight delivery industry) to progressive change when neither core assets nor core activities face imminent threats of obsolescence (e.g., commercial airline industry).

- **Chapter 3 (internal analysis)** builds on the foundation of Kaplan and Norton's balanced scorecard and introduces the strategy map concept. Strategy maps are helpful in providing a stronger link between a firm's improvements in a given area (financial, customer, internal business, learning and innovation) and the desired outcomes of an organization, helping employees see how their jobs are tied to the overall objectives of the firm, and providing insights as to how an organization can convert its assets, both tangible and intangible, into tangible outcomes. We illustrate how to develop a strategy map by using ExxonMobil as an example.

- **Chapter 4 (analysis of intellectual assets)** incorporates a discussion of electronic teams (or e-teams). More and more managers at all levels in firms are working on e-teams. We address how e-teams incorporate the three central concepts in this chapter—human capital, social capital and technology—and how their effective use can enhance a firm's performance. In addition, we address the benefits of a diverse workforce as well as the important roles of both human capital and social capital in achieving such an outcome.

- **Chapter 5 (business-level strategy)** addresses the dynamic nature of competition and how competitive advantages can be only temporary. Our presentation builds on the path-breaking work of Clayton Christensen and discusses the impact of disruptive technologies on an industry and their implications for strategy. We will discuss how resources, processes, and values help to determine whether or not a firm is able to successfully embrace an innovation.

- **Chapter 6 (corporate-level strategy)** provides a more comprehensive discussion of the trend toward consolidation in many industries, ranging from high-tech industries such as telecommunications and software to low-tech industries such as roofing supplies. In addition, we extend our prior discussion on real options analysis to address some of its potential downsides such as managerial conceit (that is, a manager's escalating commitment to a prior decision and overconfidence). This, we believe, helps to provide a more balanced discussion of this important concept.

- **Chapter 7 (international strategy)** addresses some of the potential benefits and pitfalls of offshoring (that is, when existing jobs in one country are outsourced to another country). Our discussion centers on the impacts on competitiveness, loss of jobs, and broader economic effects. Clearly, there are not many issues in business today that evoke such strong emotions!

- **Chapter 8 (Internet and digital business strategies)** discusses the role of competitive disruption in advancing economic progress and growth. Although the impact of the Internet and digital technologies has been highly disruptive, it has also created opportunities that have important strategic implications. We address the technology-driven Napster phenomenon and show that, even though its business model was unsustainable, Napster's efforts led to business development and positive change in the music industry for both new and incumbent firms.

- **Chapter 9 (strategic control and corporate governance)** extends our discussion of corporate governance to incorporate an international perspective. Here, we point out that there are many differences in corporate governance across regions and nations. For example, problems arise when there is concentrated ownership, along with extensive family ownership, business group structures, and weak protection for minority shareholders. The resulting serious conflicts tend to exist between two classes of principals—controlling shareholders and minority shareholders—giving rise to principal-principal conflicts (as opposed to principal-agent conflicts).

- **Chapter 10 (organization structure and design)** addresses how organizations can cope with the inevitable trade-offs associated with exploring new opportunities and the exploitation of existing resources and capabilities. Such dilemmas give rise to the creation of what are called "ambidextrous organizations" in which operations may become decentralized with effective means of coordination and integration at the corporate office. We also address a relatively recent phenomenon—global start-ups. They have been facilitated by an increase in the globalization of economies throughout the world and technologies associated with the Internet.

- **Chapter 11 (strategic leadership, learning organizations, and ethics)** provides a balanced perspective on one of the most popular concepts in leadership today—emotional intelligence (EI). For example, leaders can use EI to grasp what people want only to pander to such desires to gain more authority and influence. And, if leaders begin to have too much empathy for others, it may prevent them from making difficult decisions.

- **Chapter 12 (managing innovation and corporate entrepreneurship)** addresses the challenges that larger firms face when trying to foster a viable innovation strategy. We introduce a promising approach known as the "blue ocean strategy" based on the work of Chan Kim and Renee Mauborgne. Rather than outperforming competitors, the essence of a blue ocean strategy is to make them irrelevant by capturing uncontested markets. By offering innovative products and services that break down traditional industry boundaries, blue ocean strategies provide new value to both the customer and the company.

- **Chapter 13 (recognizing opportunities and creating new ventures)** addresses the important role that strategic alliances provide to young and small firms. Not only are many established firms interested in expanding their reach by partnering with entrepreneurial firms, but also young firms can use the market knowledge and resources of larger firms to overcome some of the "liability of newness" problems that often prevent new ventures from thriving.
- **Chapter 14 (case analysis)** addresses the problems that team members often face when attempting to concentrate on a problem and reach a team decision. Suggestions for managing case analysis meetings and avoiding time-wasting activities are presented.

Acknowledgments

Strategic Management represents far more than just the joint efforts of the three co-authors. Rather, it is the product of the collaborative input of many people. Some of these individuals are academic colleagues, others are the outstanding team of professionals at McGraw-Hill/Irwin, and still others are those who are closest to us—our families. It is time to express our sincere gratitude.

First, we'd like to acknowledge the thorough, constructive reviews that we received from our superb team of reviewers and symposia participants. Their input was very helpful in both pointing out errors in the manuscript and suggesting areas that needed further development as additional topics. We sincerely believe that the incorporation of their ideas was critical to improving the final product. These professionals and their affiliations are:

Reviewers for the 3rd Edition

Moses Acquaah, *University of North Carolina–Greensboro*

Joyce Beggs, *University of North Carolina–Charlotte*

Naomi A. Gardberg, *Baruch College, City University New York*

J. Michael Geringer, *Orfalea College of Business–Cal Poly*

Yezdi H. Godiwalla, *University of Wisconsin–Whitewater*

David J. Lemak, *Washington State University–Tri-Cities*

Donald L. Lester, *Arkansas State University*

John Mezias, *University of Miami*

Jeffrey R. Nystrom, *University of Colorado*

Karen L. Page, *University of Wyoming*

Matthew R. Rutherford, *Gonzaga University*

Jeremy Short, *Utah State University*

Andrew Spicer, *University of California–Riverside*

John Stanbury, *George Mason University and the Inter-University Institute of Macau, SAR China*

Symposia Participants

Moses Acquaah, *University of North Carolina–Greensboro*

Todd Alessandri, *Syracuse University*

Kathy Anders, *Arizona State University*

William Bogner, *Georgia State University*

Jay Dial, *Ohio State University*

David Flanagan, *Western Michigan University*

Sandy Gough, *Boise State University*

Donald Hatfield, *Virginia Polytechnic Institute*

Helaine Korn, *Bernard M. Baruch College*

Jim Kroeger, *Cleveland State University*

John Logan, *University of South Carolina*

Kevin Lowe, *University of North Carolina–Greensboro*

Catherine Maritan, *State University of New York at Buffalo*

Sarah Marsh, *Northern Illinois University*

Doug Moesel, *University of Missouri–Columbia*

Carolyn Mu, *Baylor University*

Anil Nair, *Old Dominion University*

Steve Porth, *Saint Joseph's University*

George Redmond, *Franklin University*

Ron Rivas, *Bentley College*

David Robinson, *Texas Tech University*

Simon Rodan, *San Jose State University*

Terry Sebora, *University of Nebraska–Lincoln*

John Seeger, *Bentley College*

Jamal Shamsie, *Michigan State University*

Chris Shook, *Auburn University*

Anne Smith, *University of Tennessee*

Linda Teagarden, *Virginia Tech*

Andrew Watson, *Northeastern University*

Laura Whitcomb, *California State University–Los Angeles*

Marta White, *Georgia State University*

Second, the authors would like to thank several faculty colleagues who were particularly helpful in the review, critique, and development of the book and supplementary materials. While Greg was at the University of Kentucky, faculty in the strategic management area were extremely generous with their time. They provided many excellent ideas and contributions for the book's first edition. Accordingly, he would like to thank Wally Ferrier, Gordon Holbein, Dan Lockhart, and Bruce Skaggs. His colleagues at the University of Texas at Dallas also have been helpful and supportive. These individuals include Joe Picken, Kumar Nair, Paul Gaddis, Seung-Hyun Lee, Tev Dalgic, and Jane Salk. His administrative assistant, Yung Hua, has been extremely helpful. Former MBA student Naga Damaraju, along with two doctoral students, Ted Khoury and Muthu Subbiah, have provided many useful inputs and ideas. He also appreciates the support of his dean and associate dean, Hasan Pirkul and Varghese Jacob, respectively. Tom would like to thank Gerry Hills, Abagail McWilliams, Darold Barnum, Mike Miller, Rod Shrader, James Gillespie, Lou Coco, and other colleagues at the University of Illinois at Chicago, for their support and patience throughout the process. Tom also extends a special thanks to Benyamin Lichtenstein for his support and encouragement. Both Greg and Tom wish to thank a special colleague, Abdul Rasheed at the University of Texas at Arlington, who certainly has been a valued source of friendship and ideas for us for many years. He provided many valuable contributions to the Third Edition. Alan thanks his colleagues at Pace University and the Case Association for their support in developing these fine case selections. Special thanks go to Jamal Shamsie at Michigan State University for his support in developing the case selections for this edition.

Third, we would like to thank the team at McGraw-Hill/Irwin for their outstanding support throughout the process. This begins with John Biernat, Editorial Director, who signed us to the contract. John was always available to provide support and valued input during the entire process. In editorial, Ryan Blankenship and Natalie Ruffatto kept things on track, responded quickly to our never-ending needs and requests, and offered insights and encouragement. Once the manuscript was completed and revised, project manager Harvey Yep expertly guided us through the production process. Cathy Tepper and Susan Lombardi did an outstanding job in helping us with the supplementary materials. Designer Adam Rooke and freelance designer Pam Verros provided excellent design and art work. And finally, we thank Ellen Cleary, Lisa Nicks, and Dana Woo for their energetic, competent, and thorough marketing efforts.

Finally, we would like to thank our families. For Greg this includes his parents, William and Mary Dess, who have always been there for him. His wife Margie and daughter, Taylor, have been a constant source of love and companionship. Greg would also like to acknowledge the professional collaboration and friendship that he enjoyed with the late Professor Wayne D. Bodensteiner. Wayne was a remarkable leader—a Rear Admiral in the United States Navy and a combat pilot during the Vietnam War—who also served as the Dean of the College of Business at the University of Texas at San Antonio. Greg learned a lot from him and really misses him. Tom thanks his wife Vicki for her constant love and companionship. Tom also thanks Lee Hetherington and Thelma Lumpkin for their inspiration, as well as his mom Katy, and his sister Kitty, for a lifetime of support. Alan thanks his family—his wife Helaine and his children Rachel and Jacob—for their love and support. He also thanks his parents, Gail Eisner and the late Marvin Eisner, for their support and encouragement.

Strategic Analysis

Chapter 1
Introduction and Analyzing Goals and Objectives

Chapter 2
Analyzing the External Environment

Chapter 3
Analyzing the Internal Environment

Chapter 4
Assessing Intellectual Capital

Strategic Formulation

Chapter 5
Formulating Business-Level Strategies

Chapter 6
Formulating Corporate-Level Strategies

Chapter 7
Formulating International Strategies

Chapter 8
Digital Business Strategies

Strategic Implementation

Chapter 9
Strategic Control and Corporate Governance

Chapter 10
Creating Effective Organizational Designs

Chapter 11
Strategic Leadership Excellence, Ethics and Change

Chapter 12
Fostering Corporate Entrepreneurship

Chapter 13
Strategic Leadership Creating New Ventures

Case Analysis

Chapter 14
Case Analysis

Strategic Analysis

Chapter 1
Introduction and Analyzing Goals and Objectives

Chapter 2
Analyzing the External Environment

Chapter 3
Analyzing the Internal Environment

Chapter 4
Assessing Intellectual Capital

Strategic Formulation

Strategic Implementation

Chapter 5
Formulating Business-Level Strategies

Chapter 9
Strategic Control and Corporate Governance

Chapter 6
Formulating Corporate-Level Strategies

Chapter 7
Formulating International Strategies

Chapter 10
Creating Effective Organizational Designs

Chapter 11
Strategic Leadership Excellence, Ethics and Change

Chapter 8
Digital Business Strategies

Chapter 12
Fostering Corporate Entrepreneurship

Chapter 13
Strategic Leadership Creating New Ventures

Case Analysis

Chapter 14
Case Analysis

Strategic Analysis

1

Strategic Management:

Creating Competitive Advantages

After reading this chapter, you should have a good understanding of:

- The definition of strategic management and its four key attributes.

- The strategic management process and its three interrelated and principal activities.

- The vital role of corporate governance and stakeholder management as well as how "symbiosis" can be achieved among an organization's stakeholders.

- The importance of social responsibility, including environmental sustainability, and how it can enhance a corporation's innovation strategy.

- The key environmental forces that are creating more unpredictable change and requiring greater empowerment throughout the organization.

- How an awareness of a hierarchy of strategic goals can help an organization achieve coherence in its strategic direction.

$\mathcal{W}$e define strategic management as *consisting of the analyses, decisions, and actions an organization undertakes in order to create and sustain competitive advantages.* At the heart of strategic management is the question: How and why do some firms outperform others? Thus, the challenge to managers is to decide on strategies that provide advantages that can be sustained over time. There are four key attributes of strategic management. It is directed at overall organizational goals, includes multiple stakeholders, incorporates short-term as well as long-term perspectives, and recognizes trade-offs between effectiveness and efficiency. We discuss the above definition and the four key attributes in the first section.

The second section addresses the strategic management process. The three major processes are strategy analysis, strategy formulation, and strategy implementation. These three components parallel the analyses, decisions, and actions in the above definition. We discuss how each of the 13 chapters addresses these three processes and provide examples from each chapter.

The third section discusses two important and interrelated concepts: corporate governance and stakeholder management. Corporate governance addresses the issue of who "governs" the corporation and determines its direction. It consists of three primary participants: stockholders (owners), management (led by the chief executive officer), and the board of directors (elected to monitor management). Stakeholder management recognizes that the interests of various stakeholders, such as owners, customers, and employees, can often conflict and create challenging decision-making dilemmas for managers. However, we discuss how some firms have been able to achieve "symbiosis" among stakeholders wherein their interests are considered interdependent and can be achieved simultaneously. We also discuss the important role of social responsibility, including the need for corporations to incorporate environmental sustainability in their strategic actions.

The fourth section addresses three interrelated factors in the business environment—globalization, technology, and intellectual capital—that have increased the level of unpredictable change for today's leaders. These factors have also created the need for a greater strategic management perspective and reinforced the role of empowerment throughout the organization.

The final section focuses on the need for organizations to ensure consistency in their vision, mission, and strategic objectives which, collectively, form a hierarchy of goals. While visions may lack specificity, they must evoke powerful and compelling mental images. Strategic objectives are much more specific and are essential for driving toward overall goals.

One of the things that makes the study of strategic management so interesting is that struggling firms can become stars, while high flyers can become earthbound very rapidly. For example, consider Coca-Cola—a firm that has experienced a hard fall from consistently being recognized as one of *Fortune* magazine's "Most Admired Firms."

As late as the 1990s, the Coca-Cola Company was one of the most respected companies in the world—a master of brand building and management in the dawning global era.[1] Under Chief Executive Officer (CEO) Roberto Goizueta's legendary leadership from March 1981 to October 1997, Coca-Cola's stock price soared an amazing 3,500 percent. He was rewarded very handsomely, becoming the first professional manager to break the $1 billion pay barrier during his 16-year tenure! However, in recent years, things have not gone well. Coke has endured many struggles, including a stale and outdated strategy that has suppressed innovation, an insular culture focused on the past, an aging and overbearing board of directors, and ineffective leadership at the top. The bottom line: Between 1990 and 1997, Coke's net income growth averaged 18 percent per year, but in recent years, it has averaged only 4 percent. And since its stock price peaked at $88 in 1998—shortly after Mr. Goizueta's death—it has dropped over 50 percent (as of mid-2005, it was selling at around $40 a share).

Part of the problem has been the erosion in Coca-Cola's marketing strategies. Goizueta's replacement, Doug Ivester, had previously served as a highly respected and talented Chief Financial Officer.[2] However, he made some serious marketing missteps. Almost immediately after becoming CEO, Ivester began shifting resources away from advertising and blanketing the world with as many vending machines, refrigerated coolers, and delivery trucks as Coke and its bottlers could muster. In his goal to strengthen market share, Ivester ignored the subtleties of brand building. Recalls one former executive: "There was no vision, no marketing. It was all growth through distribution."

Coca-Cola's core problem is that it has been stuck in a mind-set that was formed during its heyday in the 1980s, when Goizueta transformed Coke into a growth story that captivated the world. In effect, the "Goizueta Way" focused on emphasizing Coke's market share in terms of "share of stomach," as though, with the right amount of marketing, people could be persuaded to give up coffee, milk, and even water in favor of Coke. Unfortunately, an unwillingness to tamper with the structures and beliefs formed during those glory years created a culture that has left the company unable to adapt to new consumer tastes and demands. As noted by Tom Pirko, president of BevMark LLC, a consulting firm, "The whole Coke model needs to be rethought. The carbonated soft-drink model is 30 years old and out of date."

Coca-Cola has stuck to an unwavering focus on its aging group of soda-pop brands, especially Coca-Cola, Diet Coke, Sprite, and Fanta (carbonated beverages account for 82 percent of its worldwide beverage sales). Unfortunately, Coca-Cola has not been in tune with changes in consumer tastes. In recent years, demand has shifted from sodas to an array of sports drinks, vitamin-fortified waters, energy drinks, herbal teas, coffee, and other noncarbonated products. Some of these products are growing as much as *nine times* faster than cola, which has experienced a per capita decline in consumption in the United States every year since 1998.

Why has Coca-Cola been so resistant to change? A good share of the blame can be directed at the board of directors. Ten of the 14 members date back to the Goizueta era. Many of them wield enormous power. These include Warren Buffett, who is CEO of Berkshire Hathaway (Coke's largest shareholder), and Donald Keough, who was Goizueta's longtime number two executive. Consider an example of how such power was exercised. When Doug Daft (who was CEO from February 2000 to May 2004) tried to push Coke to become a "total beverage company," he met strong resistance from Coke's board. The reactions of two members were as follows:

- "That's all fine and good, but I still believe that getting the four core (soda) brands right is 85 percent of the equation."
- "[Bottled water is] something I guess we have to carry. But the fact is we're still the kings of carbonation—always have been, always will be."

Daft's credibility and confidence was severely shaken when the board of directors—urged on by Warren Buffett—vetoed his bid in November 2000 to acquire Quaker Oats Company (which included Gatorade sports drinks). Daft had, in fact, earlier assured Quaker Oats' CEO that the acquisition would be finalized! John Nash, a board consultant and former president of the National Association of Corporate Directors contends that, "The board has to challenge management's plan but should not challenge its authority." Coke's board has not only made clear its opposition to product diversification and acquisitions, but also they have been involved in many operational decisions. For example, board member Keough offended some marketing staffers in 2004 when he personally killed an edgy TV ad.

Many feel that Coke's board is responsible for the numerous rejections that it received from executives who it tried to hire to replace Doug Daft, who resigned under pressure early in 2004. Among those who passed on the opportunity to lead one of the world's most recognized brands were GE's recently retired CEO Jack Welch, James Kilts of Gillette, Robert A. Eckert of Mattel Inc., and Carlos M. Gutierrez of Kellogg. Some well-known executives were annoyed by press leaks committed by the board. One said, "It was like the search was playing out on CNN." Publicity surrounding the search was not positive. For example, A. G. Lafley, Procter and Gamble's CEO, called the search "one of the strangest processes we've ever seen," and executive recruiter Joseph D. Goodwin said, "If I were associated with that search, I would be embarrassed."

The result of the search for a new "outside" CEO resulted in the selection of Neville Isdell, a retired Coca-Cola executive with 35 years of service. Will some needed changes occur soon? It doesn't appear to be likely. As *BusinessWeek* writer Nanettte Burns puts it, "Isdell seems to have fallen into lockstep with the reigning Coke orthodoxy." Isdell says that the company's future will be directed at improving the soda operations and capitalizing on existing brands. He told Wall Street analysts in November 2004, "We are not talking about radical change in strategy. We are talking about a dramatic change in execution."

Today's leaders, such as those at Coca-Cola, face a large number of complex challenges in the global marketplace. In considering how much credit (or blame) they deserve, two perspectives of leadership come immediately to mind: the "romantic" and "external control" perspectives.[3] First, let's look at the romantic view of leadership. Here, the implicit assumption is that the leader is the key force in determining an organization's success—or lack thereof.[4] This view dominates the popular press in business magazines such as *Fortune, BusinessWeek,* and *Forbes,* wherein the CEO is either lauded for his or her firm's success or chided for the organization's demise. Consider, for example, the credit that has been bestowed on leaders such as Jack Welch, Andrew Grove, and Herb Kelleher for the tremendous accomplishments of their firms, General Electric, Intel, and Southwest Airlines, respectively.

More recently, Carlos Ghosn has been lionized in the business press for turning around Nissan's fortunes in the worldwide automobile industry. He transformed huge losses into a $7 billion profit, eliminated $23 billion of debt, and made Nissan the world's most profitable volume producer.[5] And, in the world of sports, managers and coaches, such as Bill Belichick of the New England Patriots in the National Football League, get a lot of credit for their team's outstanding success on the field.

On the other hand, when things don't go well, much of the failure of an organization can also, rightfully, be attributed to the leader. For example, when Carly Fiorina was fired as CEO of Hewlett Packard, the firm enjoyed an immediate increase in its stock price of 7 percent—hardly a strong endorsement of her leadership! And the failures of the CEOs at Coca-Cola (who followed the legendary Roberto Goizueta) to change their firm's strategies to become more consistent with dramatic changes in consumer tastes and preferences reflect shortcomings in their leadership. Coca-Cola has seen their market position and share values substantially erode.

However, this reflects only part of the picture. Consider another perspective of leadership called "external control." Here, rather than making the implicit assumption that the leader is the most important factor in determining organizational outcomes, the focus is on external factors that may positively or negatively affect a firm's success. We don't have to look far to support this perspective. For example, Coca-Cola's core business in carbonated beverages (soda) has been eroded by a shift in consumer preferences toward other beverages. The soft drink industry has been hurt by rising raw material costs, intense competition in some international markets, and price erosion. Such factors have caused *Value Line* to rate the soft drink industry 88th out of 98 industries in terms of "timeliness"—hardly an enviable industry in which to compete.[6]

The point, of course, is that, while neither the romantic nor the external control perspective is entirely correct, we must acknowledge both in the study of strategic management. Our premise is that leaders can make a difference, but they must be constantly aware of the opportunities and threats that they face in the external environment and have a thorough understanding of their firm's resources and capabilities.

In contrast to Coca-Cola, PepsiCo has leveraged its financial, marketing and distribution resources, and capabilities to aggressively diversify beyond carbonated beverages and has created many strong brands. Pepsi has been able to avoid sinking into a slow-growth pit as its core soda pop and potato chip products age.[7] As noted by Robert van Brugge of Sanford C. Bernstein & Co., "They have been early to see trends and aggressive in targeting them." For example, its Tropicana juice, Gatorade sports drinks (part of Quaker Oats which Coca-Cola failed to acquire), and Aquafina water have all become billion-dollar brands. Its CEO, Steve Reinemund, was recently named one of *Business-Week*'s "Best Managers."[8] His approach: "Being outside of carbonated (soft drinks) makes sure we're growing in the areas where there is growth." Not surprisingly, PepsiCo's recent performance is far stronger than Coke's. While Coke's stock price has declined slightly over the most recent five-year period, PepsiCo's is up about 60 percent.

Before we move on, we'd like to provide a rather dramatic example of the external control perspective at work: the terrorist attack on the twin towers of the World Trade Center in New York City and the Pentagon building in Arlington, Virginia, on September 11, 2001. The loss of life and injuries to innocent people were immense, and the damage to property was enormous. Wall Street suffered a loss of about $1.4 trillion in the five trading sessions after the market opened on September 17. The effect on many industries was devastating. Strategy Spotlight 1.1 looks at some high-technology industries that have recognized opportunities and benefited from the terrorist attacks and from subsequent developments such as the creation of the Department of Homeland Security, the Iraq War, and the "War on Terror."

>>What Is Strategic Management?

Given the many challenges and opportunities in the global marketplace, today's managers must do more than set long-term strategies and hope for the best.[9] They must go beyond what some have called "incremental management," whereby they view their job as making a series of small, minor changes to improve the efficiency of their firm's operations.[10] That is fine if your firm is competing in a very stable, simple, and unchanging industry. But there aren't many of those left. As we shall discuss in this chapter and throughout the book, the pace of change is accelerating, and the pressure on managers to make both major and minor changes in a firm's strategic direction is increasing.

Rather than seeing their role as merely custodians of the status quo, today's leaders must be proactive, anticipate change, and continually refine and, when necessary, make

STRATEGY SPOTLIGHT

Terrorism and U.S. Business

The terrorist attacks on September 11, 2001, paralyzed the U.S. economy for a few days. Their aftermath can still be felt in several industries, including airlines and tourism. Consumers, businesses, schools, and colleges have all significantly cut their technology spending. There is, however, a major purchaser of the latest technology: the federal government.

With the 2003 Iraq War and the creation of the Department of Homeland Security, government spending has become a bright spot in the technology arena. For example, according to the Morgan Keegan Investment firm, for the first half of 2004, the 13 companies related to homeland security enjoyed a 25 percent average price gain in stocks. And in the 90 days following 9/11, the same group averaged a 200 percent gain before settling down. Homeland security legislation has been passed that allocates money for homeland security to individual states, but not a lot has been spent yet, according to Michael Hoffman, a security analyst. Two firms that are likely to benefit from increased security spending are:

- Verint Systems Inc. is a maker of analytic software used in security for airports, public buildings, financial institutions, retail stores, and corporate sites. It has a large potential for growth based on future terrorist threats. Verint upgrades communication through interaction of video, voice, e-mail, and the Internet.

Sources: Kerstetter, J., Crock, S., & Hof, R. D. 2003. More bang for the bite. *BusinessWeek*, April 7: 39–40; Rae-Dupree, J. 2003. A target for tech, *U.S. News & World Report*, January 13: 30–32; Lawrence, S. 2001. Defense spending may be the mother of all invention. *Red Herring*, December 11: 17–18; www.sgi.com; and, Luckey, A. 2004. Security stocks ride fears about terrorism. *Sun-Sentinel Times*, June 20: np.

- Drexler Technology, is a maker of LaserCard optical memory cards and chip-ready Smart/Optical cards. Its cards are used in inspection procedures for immigration, border crossing visas, cargo manifests, motor vehicle registration, and identification cards.

Not all tech firms do business with the government directly. When Lockheed Martin became the prime contractor on the $200 billion Joint Strike Fighter program, it chose Silicon Graphics, Inc. (SGI) to design, evaluate, and simulate the aircraft. Similarly, when General Dynamics was asked to develop the Navy's Area Air Defense Commander Capability System—a real-time, three-dimensional view of the tactical area around the ship—high-end SGI computers were a natural fit. Apart from this, SGI now does ballistic missile defense; training systems; command, control, and surveillance systems; and weather and climate forecasting. All this has meant that for SGI, which traditionally had generated less than 28 percent of its revenues selling supercomputing defense systems, government contracts now represent 35 percent of its $1.3 billion annual revenue.

At times, high-profile success on the battlefield can provide a powerful boost for new technology that carries over to the commercial world. For example, in 1990 tiny Trimble Navigation Ltd., based in Sunnyvale, California, sold 10,000 handheld devices with global positioning systems to the military for the first Gulf War. The devices were a success in the war and a boon to Trimble and the commercial GPS market. Now Trimble is a $466 million firm, with just 3 percent of its sales from the military.

---

dramatic changes to their strategies. The strategic management of the organization must become both a process and a way of thinking throughout the organization.

Defining Strategic Management

As we stated at the beginning of this chapter, strategic management consists of the analyses, decisions, and actions an organization undertakes in order to create and sustain competitive advantages. This definition captures two main elements that go to the heart of the field of strategic management.

First, the strategic management of an organization entails three ongoing processes: *analyses, decisions,* and *actions.* That is, strategic management is concerned with the *analysis* of strategic goals (vision, mission, and strategic objectives) along with the analysis of the internal and external environment of the organization. Next, leaders must make strategic decisions. These *decisions,* broadly speaking, address two basic questions: What industries should we compete in? How should we compete in those industries? These questions also often involve an organization's domestic as well as its international operations.

And last are the *actions* that must be taken. Decisions are of little use, of course, unless they are acted on. Firms must take the necessary actions to implement their strategies. This requires leaders to allocate the necessary resources and to design the organization to bring the intended strategies to reality. As we will see in the next section, this is an ongoing, evolving process that requires a great deal of interaction among these three processes.

Second, the essence of strategic management is the study of why some firms out-perform others.[11] Thus, managers need to determine how a firm is to compete so that it can obtain advantages that are sustainable over a lengthy period of time. That means focusing on two fundamental questions: *How should we compete in order to create competitive advantages in the marketplace?* For example, managers need to determine if the firm should position itself as the low-cost producer, develop products and services that are unique and will enable the firm to charge premium prices, or some combination of both.

Managers must also ask how to make such advantages sustainable, instead of highly temporary, in the marketplace. That is: *How can we create competitive advantages in the marketplace that are not only unique and valuable but also difficult for competitors to copy or substitute?*[12,13]

Ideas that work are almost always copied by rivals immediately. In the 1980s, American Airlines tried to establish a competitive advantage by introducing the frequent flyer program. Within weeks, all the airlines did the same thing. Overnight, frequent flyer programs became a necessary tool for competitive parity instead of a competitive advantage. The challenge, therefore, is to create competitive advantages that are sustainable.

Michael Porter argues that sustainable competitive advantage cannot be achieved through operational effectiveness alone.[14] Most of the popular management innovations of the last two decades—total quality, just-in-time, benchmarking, business process reengineering, outsourcing—all are about operational effectiveness. Operational effectiveness means performing similar activities better than rivals. Each of these is important, but none lead to sustainable competitive advantage for the simple reason that everyone is doing them. Strategy is all about being different from everyone else. Sustainable competitive advantage is possible only through performing different activities from rivals or performing similar activities in different ways. Companies such as Wal-Mart, Southwest Airlines, and IKEA have developed unique, internally consistent, and difficult-to-imitate activity systems that have provided them with sustained competitive advantage. A company with a good strategy must make clear choices about what it wants to accomplish. Trying to do everything that your rivals do eventually leads to mutually destructive price competition, not long-term advantage.

The Four Key Attributes of Strategic Management

Before discussing the strategic management process in more detail, let's briefly talk about four attributes of strategic management.[15] In doing so, it will become clear how this course differs from other courses that you have had in functional areas, such as accounting, marketing, operations, and finance. Exhibit 1.1 provides a definition and the four attributes of strategic management.

First, strategic management is *directed toward overall organizational goals and objectives.* That is, effort must be directed at what is best for the total organization, not just a single functional area. Some authors have referred to this perspective as "organizational versus individual rationality."[16] That is, what might look "rational" or most appropriate for one functional area, such as operations, may not be in the best interest of the overall firm. For example, operations may decide to schedule long production runs of similar products in order to lower unit costs. However, the standardized output may be counter to what the marketing department needs in order to appeal to a sophisticated

Exhibit 1.1
**Strategic
Management
Concepts**

> **Definition:** Strategic management consists of the analyses, decisions, and actions an organization undertakes in order to create and sustain competitive advantages.
>
> **Key Attributes of Strategic Management**
>
> *   Directs the organization toward overall goals and objectives.
> *   Includes multiple stakeholders in decision making.
> *   Needs to incorporate short-term and long-term perspectives.
> *   Recognizes trade-offs between efficiency and effectiveness.

and demanding target market. Similarly, research and development may "overengineer" the product in order to develop a far superior offering, but the design may make the product so expensive that market demand is minimal. Therefore, in this course you will look at cases and strategic issues from the perspective of the organization rather than that of the functional area(s) in which you have had the most training and experience.

Second, strategic management *includes multiple stakeholders in decision making.* Managers must incorporate the demands of many stakeholders when making decisions.[17] Stakeholders are those individuals, groups, and organizations who have a "stake" in the success of the organization, including owners (shareholders in a publicly held corporation), employees, customers, suppliers, the community at large, and so on. We'll discuss this in more detail later in this chapter. Managers will not be successful if they continually focus on a single stakeholder. For example, if the overwhelming emphasis is on generating profits for the owners, employees may become alienated, customer service may suffer, and the suppliers may become resentful of continual demands for pricing concessions. As we will see, however, many organizations have been able to satisfy multiple stakeholder needs simultaneously. For example, financial performance may actually be greater because employees who are satisfied with their jobs make a greater effort to enhance customer satisfaction, thus leading to higher profits.

Third, strategic management *requires incorporating both short-term and long-term perspectives.* Peter Senge, a leading strategic management author at the Massachusetts Institute of Technology, has referred to this need as a "creative tension."[18] That is, managers must maintain both a vision for the future of the organization as well as a focus on its present operating needs. However, as one descends the hierarchy of the organization from executive to middle-level managers to lower level managers at the level of operations, there tends to be a narrower, short-term perspective. Nonetheless, all managers throughout the organization must maintain a strategic management perspective and assess how their actions impact the overall attainment of organizational objectives. For example, laying off several valuable employees may help to cut costs and improve profits in the short term, but the long-term implications for employee morale and customer relationships may suffer, leading to subsequent performance declines.[19]

Fourth, strategic management *involves the recognition of trade-offs between effectiveness and efficiency.* Closely related to the third point above, this recognition means being aware of the need for organizations to strive to act effectively and efficiently. Some authors have referred to this as the difference between "doing the right thing" (effectiveness) and "doing things right" (efficiency).[20] While managers must allocate and use resources wisely, they must still direct their efforts toward the attainment of overall organizational objectives. Managers who are totally focused on meeting short-term budgets

STRATEGY SPOTLIGHT

Amgen's CEO Discusses the Challenge of Managing at "Different Altitudes"

A CEO must always be switching between what I call different altitudes—tasks of different levels of abstraction and specificity. At the highest altitude you're asking the big questions: What are the company's mission and strategy? Do people understand and believe in these aims? Are decisions consistent with them? At the lowest altitude, you're looking at on-the-ground operations: Did we make that sale? What was the yield on the last lot in the factory? How many days of inventory do we have for a particular drug? And then there's everything in between: How many chemists do we need to hire this quarter? What should we pay for a small biotech company that has a promising new drug? Is our production capacity adequate to roll out a product in a new market?

You have to be working at all of these levels simultaneously, and that's not easy. . . . But most CEOs tend to gravitate toward the altitude where they are most comfortable. That's natural. Someone might choose to operate almost exclusively at the highest possible altitude: "I'm going to be responsible for the company's strategic vision." Another might choose to operate mainly at a lower altitude: "I'm going to pick the curtains in that hotel." Both altitudes are important. But most CEOs who get in trouble do so because they get stuck at a particular altitude.

Source: Reprinted by permission of *Harvard Business Review.* Excerpt from "A Time for Growth: An Interview with Amgen CEO Kevin Sharer," by Paul Hemp, July–August 2004. Copyright © 2004 by The Harvard Business School Publishing Corporation; all rights reserved.

and targets may fail to attain the broader goals of the organization. Consider the following amusing story told by Norman Augustine, former CEO of defense giant, Martin Marietta (now Lockheed Martin):

> I am reminded of an article I once read in a British newspaper which described a problem with the local bus service between the towns of Bagnall and Greenfields. It seemed that, to the great annoyance of customers, drivers had been passing long queues of would-be passengers with a smile and a wave of the hand. This practice was, however, clarified by a bus company official who explained, "It is impossible for the drivers to keep their timetables if they must stop for passengers."[21]

Clearly, the drivers who were trying to stay on schedule had ignored the overall mission. As Augustine noted, "Impeccable logic but something seems to be missing!"

Successful managers must make many trade-offs. It is central to the practice of strategic management. At times, managers must focus on the short term and efficiency; at other times the emphasis is on the long term and expanding a firm's product-market scope in order to anticipate opportunities in the competitive environment. Some authors have written on the concept of "ambidexterity"; that is, managers need to both align resources to take advantage of existing product markets and proactively exploit new opportunities.[22] We address this concept in greater detail in Chapter 10. There are other trade-offs such as how to prioritize various stakeholder needs that must be satisfied in a given situation. Strategy Spotlight 1.2 addresses an interesting top management perspective associated with managing at "different altitudes." It is provided by Kevin Sharer who is CEO of Amgen, the world's largest biotechnology company with $8.4 billion in revenues.

>>The Strategic Management Process

We've identified three ongoing processes—analyses, decisions, and actions—that are central to strategic management. In practice, these three processes—often referred to as strategy analysis, strategy formulation, and strategy implementation—are highly interdependent. Further, these three processes do not take place one after the other in a sequential fashion in most companies.

Exhibit 1.2   **Realized Strategy and Intended Strategy: Usually Not the Same**

Source: From Mintzberg, H. & Waters, J. A., "Of Strategies: Deliberate and Emergent," *Strategic Management Journal,* Vol. 6, 1985, pp. 257–272. Copyright © John Wiley & Sons Limited. Reproduced with permission.

Henry Mintzberg, a very influential management scholar at McGill University, argues that conceptualizing the strategic management process as one in which analysis is followed by optimal decisions and their subsequent meticulous implementation neither describes the strategic management process accurately nor prescribes ideal practice.[23] In his view, the business environment is far from predictable, thus limiting our ability for analysis. Further, decisions in an organization are seldom based on optimal rationality alone, given the political processes that occur in all organizations.

Taking into consideration the limitations discussed above, Mintzberg proposed an alternative model of strategy development. As depicted in Exhibit 1.2, decisions following from analysis, in this model, constitute the *intended* strategy of the firm. For a variety of reasons, the intended strategy rarely survives in its original form. Unforeseen environmental developments, unanticipated resource constraints, or changes in managerial preferences may result in at least some parts of the intended strategy remaining *unrealized.* On the other hand, good managers will want to take advantage of a new opportunity presented by the environment, even if it was not part of the original set of intentions. For example, consider the wind energy industry.[24] In September 2004 the United States Congress renewed the wind tax credit. Legislation in 19 states now requires that electricity providers offer a certain percentage of "green" (i.e., renewable) energy. Such legislation, combined with falling clean energy costs and rising prices for coal, oil, and gas, have created a surge in demand for competitors such as GE Wind Energy, which makes large turbines and fan blades. Not surprisingly, such businesses have increased hiring and research and development, as well as revenue and profit forecasts. The final *realized* strategy of any firm is thus a combination of *deliberate* and *emergent* strategies.

In the next three subsections, we will address each of the three key strategic management processes: strategy analysis, strategy formulation, and strategy implementation. We also highlight brief examples from business practice that are based on the opening vignettes for each chapter. Throughout the book, they serve to demonstrate that effective strategic management poses complex challenges and that sometimes things can go wrong.

Exhibit 1.3 depicts the strategic management process and indicates how it ties into the chapters in the book. Consistent with our discussion above, we use two-way arrows to convey the interactive nature of the processes.

Strategy Analysis

Strategy analysis may be looked upon as the starting point of the strategic management process. It consists of the "advance work" that must be done in order to effectively formulate and implement strategies. Many strategies fail because managers may want to

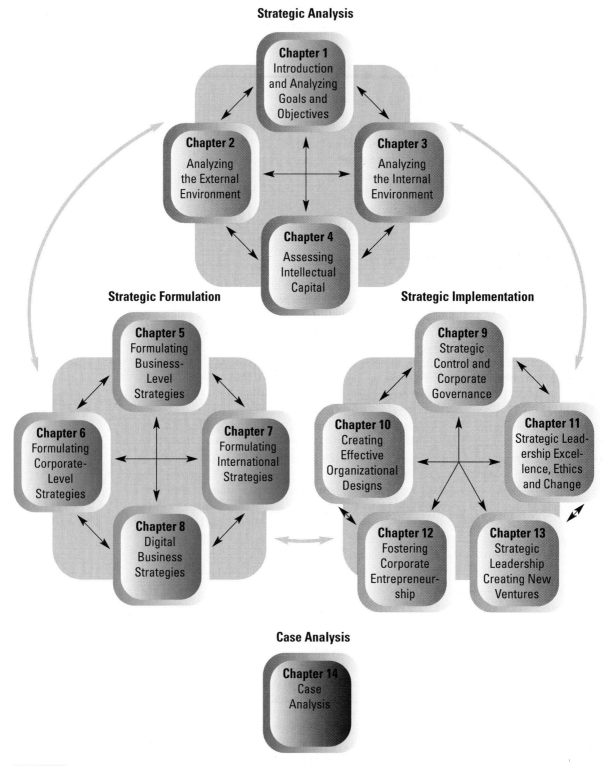

Exhibit 1.3   **The Strategic Management Process**

formulate and implement strategies without a careful analysis of the overarching goals of the organization and without a thorough analysis of its external and internal environment.

Analyzing Organizational Goals and Objectives (Chapter 1)   Later in this chapter, we will address how organizations must have clearly articulated goals and objectives in order to channel the efforts of individuals throughout the organization toward common ends. Goals and objectives also provide a means of allocating resources effectively. A firm's vision, mission, and strategic objectives form a hierarchy of goals that range from broad statements of intent and bases for competitive advantage to specific, measurable strategic objectives.

As indicated in Exhibit 1.3, this hierarchy of goals is not developed in isolation. Rather, it is developed in concert with a rigorous understanding of the opportunities and threats in the external environment (Chapter 2) as well as a thorough understanding of the firm's strengths and weaknesses (Chapters 3 and 4). The opening incident in Chapter 1 describes how Coca-Cola has failed to adapt to changes in customer tastes and demands, largely because of its outdated culture and mindset, an overbearing and entrenched board of directors, and ineffective CEO leadership.

Analyzing the External Environment of the Firm (Chapter 2)   Managers must monitor and scan the environment as well as analyze competitors. Such information is critical in determining the opportunity and threats in the external environment. We provide two frameworks of the external environment. First, the general environment consists of several elements, such as demographic, technological, and economic segments, from which key trends and events can have a dramatic impact on the firm. Second, the industry environment consists of competitors and other organizations that may threaten the success of a firm's products and services. We discuss how Interstate Bakeries Corporation (IBC) (makers of such American icons as Wonder Bread, Twinkies, Zingers, and Ding Dongs) was forced into bankruptcy. The problem was that IBC was unable to adjust its product mix to reflect the market's move away from high carbohydrate products and sugary snacks. Clearly, recent concerns about childhood obesity didn't help either.

Assessing the Internal Environment of the Firm (Chapter 3)   We provide some useful frameworks for analyzing a firm's internal environment. Such analysis helps to identify both strengths and weaknesses that can, in part, determine how well a firm will succeed in an industry. Analyzing the strengths and relationships among the activities that constitute a firm's value chain (e.g., operations, marketing and sales, and human resource management) can be a means of uncovering potential sources of competitive advantage for the firm. We discuss how Ford's Jaguar products have stumbled in the marketplace. Poor product styling, marketing, and the use of interchangeable parts with less expensive nameplates have eroded the brand. Heavy rental sales and huge rebates also have caused image problems.

Assessing a Firm's Intellectual Assets (Chapter 4)   The knowledge worker and a firm's other intellectual assets (e.g., patents, trademarks) are becoming increasingly important as the drivers of competitive advantages and wealth creation in today's economy. In addition to human capital, we assess how well the organization creates networks and relationships among its employees as well as its customers, suppliers, and alliance partners. We also address the need for organizations to use technology to enhance collaboration among employees as well as provide a means of accumulating and storing knowledge. We discuss how a small advertising and marketing firm, Wildflower, stumbled when it hired a "star" professional from a large, blue chip firm. The person's skills and attitude didn't fit in well at a small firm like Wildflower, and soon office morale became a serious problem. Clearly, any skills and talents the new hire could have offered were more than offset by how adversely relationships among colleagues were affected.

Strategy Formulation

A firm's strategy formulation is developed at several levels. First, business-level strategy addresses the issue of how to compete in given business environments to attain competitive advantage. Second, corporate-level strategy focuses on two issues: (1) what businesses to compete in and (2) how businesses can be managed to achieve synergy; that is, they create more value by working together than if they operate as stand-alone businesses. Third, a firm must determine the best method to develop international strategies as it ventures beyond its national boundaries. Finally, the growing importance of the Internet has increased the necessity for firms to explore the ramifications of this new strategic platform and formulate Internet and e-business strategies.

Formulating Business-Level Strategy (Chapter 5)   The question of how firms compete and outperform their rivals and how they achieve and sustain competitive advantages goes to the heart of strategic management. Successful firms strive to develop bases for competitive advantage. These can be achieved through cost leadership and/or differentiation as well as by focusing on a narrow or industrywide market segment. We'll also discuss why some advantages can be more sustainable (or durable) over time and how a firm's business-level strategy changes with the industry life cycle—that is, the stages of introduction, growth, maturity, and decline. We discuss how Sharper Image erroneously based its competitive advantage on a product—an air purifier—that was easily imitated by rivals. Gains in profitability and market position became short-lived.

Formulating Corporate-Level Strategy (Chapter 6)   Whereas business-level strategy is concerned with how to create and sustain competitive advantage in an individual business, corporate-level strategy addresses issues concerning a firm's portfolio (or group) of businesses. That is, it asks (1) What business (or businesses) should we compete in? and (2) How can we manage this portfolio of businesses to create synergies among the businesses? In this chapter, we explore the relative advantages and disadvantages of firms pursuing strategies of related or unrelated diversification. In addition, we discuss the various means that firms can employ to diversify—internal development, mergers and acquisitions, and joint ventures and strategic alliances—as well as their relative advantages and disadvantages. We describe how a leading discount broker, Charles Schwab and Company, erred when it acquired U.S. Trust, a financial services firm that catered to wealthy clients.

Formulating International Strategy (Chapter 7)   When firms expand their scope of operations to include foreign markets, they encounter many opportunities and potential pitfalls. They must decide not only on the most appropriate entry strategy but also how they will go about attaining competitive advantages in international markets. Many successful international firms have been able to attain both lower costs and higher levels of differentiated products and services through the successful implementation of a "transnational strategy." We describe some of the problems experienced by Volkswagen as it tried to enter the luxury segment of the U.S. car market.

Formulating Digital Business Strategy (Chapter 8)   Digital technologies such as the Internet and wireless communications are changing the way business is conducted. These capabilities present both new opportunities and new threats for virtually all businesses. We believe that when firms formulate strategies, they should give explicit consideration to how digital technologies add value and impact their performance outcomes. The effective use of the Internet and digital business strategies can help an organization improve its competitive position and enhance its ability to create advantages by enhancing both cost leadership and differentiation strategies. We describe how Agillion, Inc., an application service provider founded in 1999, went bankrupt in just three years not because the Internet bubble burst, but because its product could easily be imitated. Further, it did not use digital technologies in a way that customers valued.

Strategy Implementation

As we have noted earlier in the chapter, effective strategies are of no value if they are not properly implemented. Strategy implementation involves ensuring that a firm has proper strategic controls and organizational designs. Of particular importance is ensuring that the firm has established effective means to coordinate and integrate activities within the firm as well as with its suppliers, customers, and alliance partners. In addition, leadership plays a central role. This involves many things, including ensuring that the organization is committed to excellence and ethical behavior, promotes learning and continuous improvement, and acts entrepreneurially in creating and taking advantage of new opportunities.

Strategic Control and Corporate Governance (Chapter 9)   To implement strategies, firms must exercise effectively two types of strategic control. First, informational control requires that organizations continually monitor and scan the environment and respond to threats and opportunities. Second, behavioral control involves the proper balance of rewards and incentives as well as cultures and boundaries (or constraints). In addition to effective informational and behavioral controls, successful firms (those that are incorporated) practice effective corporate governance. That is, they must create mechanisms to ensure that the interests of the managers are consistent with those of the owners (shareholders) of the firm. These include an effective board of directors, actively engaged shareholders, and proper managerial reward and incentive systems. We also discuss the important role played by various external mechanisms such as the market for corporate control, auditors, banks, analysts, and the financial press in ensuring good governance. We discuss how Lantech, a $100 million manufacturing company, suffered when it implemented an ineffective reward system. The pay incentive program pitted one division against another, which resulted in intense rivalries and destructive "gamesmanship."

Creating Effective Organizational Designs (Chapter 10)   To succeed, firms must have organizational structures and designs that are consistent with their strategy. For example, firms that diversify into related product-market areas typically implement divisional structures. In today's rapidly changing competitive environments, firms must design their companies to ensure that their organizational boundaries—those internal to the firm and external—are more flexible and permeable. In many cases, organizations should consider creating strategic alliances in order to capitalize on the capabilities of other organizations. We discuss how the National Health Service in Great Britain experienced inefficiencies and wasted resources when its various units failed to coordinate properly.

Creating a Learning Organization and an Ethical Organization (Chapter 11)   Effective leaders must engage in several ongoing activities: setting a direction, designing the organization, and developing an organization that is committed to excellence and ethical behavior. In addition, given the rapid and unpredictable change in today's competitive environments, leaders need to create a "learning organization." This ensures that the entire organization can benefit from individual and collective talents. We describe how Krispy Kreme's fortunes sunk when it expanded too rapidly and its top leadership engaged in self-interested behavior in granting and managing its franchises.

Fostering Corporate Entrepreneurship (Chapter 12)   Today's successes do not guarantee success in the future. With rapid and unpredictable change in the global marketplace, firms must continually improve and grow as well as find new ways to renew their organizations. Corporate entrepreneurship and innovation provide firms with new opportunities, and strategies should be formulated that enhance a firm's innovative capacity. Within corporations, proactiveness and autonomous entrepreneurial behavior by product champions and other organizational members are needed to turn new ideas into corporate ventures. We present the case of Polaroid, a company that grew from a revolutionary technology—instantly developing film. However, it fell behind when it was slow to adapt to a new way of developing pictures instantly—digital photography.

Creating New Ventures (Chapter 13)   New ventures and small businesses represent a major engine of economic growth. Although the challenges they face are unique, especially for start-up firms entering into business for the first time, many of the concepts that we address in the text can be applied to new ventures and small businesses. Viable opportunities must be recognized, effective strategies must be implemented, and entrepreneurial leadership skills are needed to successfully launch and sustain these enterprises. We discuss the fate of Rosen Motors, a young firm with an innovative, hybrid automobile drive train that could save millions in energy costs. However, Rosen did not recognize critical market forces when implementing its start-up strategy—including the power of its most important buyers, the big automakers—and failed as a result.

We've discussed the strategic management process. In addition, Chapter 14, "Analyzing Strategic Management Cases," provides guidelines and suggestions on how to evaluate cases in this course. Thus, the concepts and techniques discussed in these 13 chapters can be applied to real-world organizations.

Let's now address two concepts—corporate governance and stakeholder management—that are critical to the strategic management process.

>>The Role of Corporate Governance and Stakeholder Management

Most business enterprises that employ more than a few dozen people are organized as corporations. As you recall from your finance classes, the overall purpose of a corporation is to maximize the long-term return to the owners (shareholders). Thus, we may ask: Who is really responsible for fulfilling this purpose? Robert Monks and Neil Minow, in addressing this issue, provide a useful definition of corporate governance as "the relationship among various participants in determining the direction and performance of corporations. The primary participants are (1) the shareholders, (2) the management (led by the chief executive officer), and (3) the board of directors."[25] This relationship is illustrated in Exhibit 1.4.

The directors on the board of directors (BOD) are the elected representatives of the shareholders. They are charged with ensuring that the interests and motives of management are aligned with those of the owners (i.e., shareholders). In many cases, the BOD is diligent in fulfilling its purpose. For example, Intel Corporation, the giant $34 billion maker of microprocessor chips, is widely recognized as an excellent example of sound

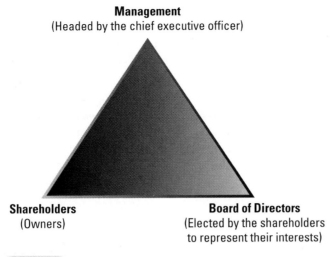

Management
(Headed by the chief executive officer)

Shareholders
(Owners)

Board of Directors
(Elected by the shareholders
to represent their interests)

Exhibit 1.4   **The Key Elements of Corporate Governance**

governance practices. Its BOD has established guidelines to ensure that its members are independent (i.e., not members of the executive management team and do not have close personal ties to top executives) so that they can provide proper oversight; it has explicit guidelines on the selection of director candidates (to avoid "cronyism"); and it provides detailed procedures for formal evaluations of both directors and the firm's top officers.[26] Such guidelines serve to ensure that management is acting in the best interests of shareholders.

Recently, there has been much criticism as well as cynicism by both citizens and the business press about the poor job that management and the BODs of large corporations are doing. We only have to look at the recent scandals at such firms as Arthur Andersen, WorldCom, Enron, Tyco, and ImClone Systems.[27] Such malfeasance has led to an erosion of the public's trust in the governance of corporations. For example, a recent Gallup poll found that 90 percent of Americans felt that people leading corporations could not be trusted to look after the interests of their employees, and only 18 percent thought that corporations looked after their shareholders. Forty-three percent, in fact, believed that senior executives were in it only for themselves. In Britain, that figure, according to another poll, was an astonishing 95 percent.[28] To drive home the point, consider the humorous perspective of Russell T. Lewis, CEO of the New York Times Company, in a recent speech:[29]

> Not long ago, CEOs were regarded as captains of industry—among the country's best and brightest talents—at least that's what I've been telling my parents, and they seem to have bought the line. Today, however, CEOs and their CFOs are highly reviled defendants in felony criminal proceedings. And their companies are the subjects of billion-dollar shareholder lawsuits. Things have gotten so bad that any day now I expect *Fortune* Magazine to come out with its list of "Most Wanted CEOs." No doubt this will soon be followed by a spin-off of a popular TV program. I can see the promo now: "Tonight at 8 PM—Help us catch America's Most Wanted CEOs . . . they could be hiding in our hometown."
>
> But, folks, the final indignity for this particular CEO concerns my own parents: my loving 87-year-old mother—a former public school teacher and my unfailingly supportive 94-year-old father. They no longer brag about me to the clerks at the Lake Worth, Florida, Publix supermarket. Yes, folks, it has gotten that bad.

STRATEGY SPOTLIGHT

Italy's Parmalat: Europe's Enron?

On December 15, 2003, Parmalat's founder, chairman, and CEO Calisto Tanzi resigned. And later that month on December 27, the $7.2 billion firm filed for bankruptcy. Parmalat is one of the world's largest dairy firms with headquarters in Italy and operations in 13 other countries, including the United States. Parmalat did not fail due to market and economic factors such as declining market demand, intensifying competition, or problematic foreign exchange rates. Instead, it is a textbook case of management fraud and poor corporate governance.

The defrocked Tanzi has spent 2004 and much of 2005 fighting the law. He denies prosecutors' charges of market-rigging, falsifying accounts, and obstructing Italy's stock market regulator, Consob. He is now awaiting trial on those charges, and he has confessed to siphoning off $665 million from the milk giant to a family-owned travel company. Parmalat was found to have $18 billion missing from its accounts early last year, making it one of the biggest corporate frauds in history. Italian prosecutors have discovered that managers simply invented assets to offset liabilities and falsified accounts over a 15-year period. It is uncertain whether the missing funds were used to plug operating losses, pay creditors, or illegally enrich top managers, who come from the founding family.

Several criminal and civil trials are set to get under way soon involving Tanzi and other top Parmalat executives, banks, auditing companies, and others. Tanzi, who suffers from ill health and is now under house arrest, faces up to 15 years in prison if convicted.

Prior to the outbreak of the scandal, Parmalat was already known for its poor corporate governance. Its big investors had utterly failed to use their leverage to alter the behavior of Tanzi and his executives. It is not yet clear, however, if investors made any real effort to demand better disclosure and to end "overly creative financing." Respected multinational banks such as Citigroup, J. P. Morgan, and Deutsche Bank were all too eager to construct the derivative deals by which Parmalat was able to transfer funds offshore. Although Parmalat failed to disclose a lot of information to Standard & Poor's (S&P), the agency was still content to issue investment-grade ratings on its bonds. It was only when the firm entered crisis mode that it became clear how wrong S&P had been.

Italy's government is drafting a new law on financial regulation that will overhaul both institutions and laws, forcing greater disclosure, granting regulators more investigative powers, and tightening control over accounting practices. Although leading proponents of corporate governance in Italy agree that it is still too early to see what will eventually develop, they remain confident that the once lax attitude toward self-compliance with the country's code has changed dramatically in the wake of Parmalat.

Sources: Anonymous. 2005. The worst managers. *BusinessWeek*, January 10: 74–77; Anonymous. 2005. A curious delay. *The Economist*, April 9: 52; Capell, K. et al. 2004. Europe's old ways die fast. *BusinessWeek*, May 17: 54–57; Déjà vu all over again? 2003. *The Economist*, December 20: 95–96; Turning sour. 2004. *The Economist*, January 3: 8–9; and Edmonson, G. 2004. How Parmalat went sour. *BusinessWeek*, January 12: 46–48. We would also like to thank Yi Jiang and Michael W. Peng, both of Ohio State University, for their useful input.

At times, BODs have become complacent and, in many cases, incompetent. They have often been accused of rubber stamping strategies and actions proposed by top management, and they have clearly not acted in a manner consistent with shareholder interests.

Clearly, there is a strong need for improved corporate governance, and we will address this topic in greater detail in Chapter 9. We focus on three important mechanisms to help ensure effective corporate governance: an effective and engaged board of directors, shareholder activism, and proper managerial rewards and incentives.[30] In addition to these internal controls, a key role is played by various external control mechanisms. These include the auditors, banks, analysts, an active financial press, and the threat of hostile takeovers.

Not surprisingly, the United States does not have a monopoly on executive malfeasance and poor corporate governance. For example, Strategy Spotlight 1.3 discusses the case of Italy's Parmalat. Here's a firm that has been called Europe's Enron—a label that is well deserved.

Generating long-term returns for the shareholders is the primary goal of a publicly held corporation. As noted by former Chrysler vice chairman Robert Lutz, "We are here to serve the shareholder and create shareholder value. I insist that the only person who owns the company is the person who paid good money for it."[31]

Despite the primacy of generating shareholder value, managers who focus solely on the interests of the owners of the business will often make poor decisions that lead to negative, unanticipated outcomes. For example, decisions such as mass layoffs to increase profits, ignoring issues related to conservation of the natural environment to save money, and exerting excessive pressure on suppliers to lower prices can certainly harm the firm in the long run. Such actions would likely lead to negative outcomes such as alienated employees, increased governmental oversight and fines, and disloyal suppliers.

Clearly, in addition to *shareholders,* there are other *stakeholders* that must be explicitly taken into account in the strategic management process.[32] A stakeholder can be defined as an individual or group, inside or outside the company, that has a stake in and can influence an organization's performance. Although companies can have different stakeholders, each generally has five prominent stakeholder groups:[33]

- customers
- employees and managers
- suppliers (of goods, services, and capital)
- the community at large
- owners

Zero Sum or Symbiosis? Two Alternate Perspectives of Stakeholder Management

There are two opposing ways of looking at the role of stakeholder management in the strategic management process.[34] The first one can be termed "zero sum." In this view, the role of management is to look upon the various stakeholders as competing for the attention and resources of the organization. In essence, the gain of one individual or group is the loss of another individual or group. That is, employees want higher wages (which drive down profits), suppliers want higher prices for their inputs and slower, more flexible delivery times (which drive up costs), customers want fast deliveries and higher quality (which drive up costs), the community at large wants charitable contributions (which take money from company goals), and so on. This zero-sum thinking is rooted, in part, in the traditional conflict between workers and management, leading to the formation of unions and sometimes ending in adversarial union–management negotiations that can lead to long, bitter strikes.

Although there will always be some conflicting demands placed on the organization by its various stakeholders, there is value in exploring how the organization can achieve mutual benefit through *stakeholder symbiosis,* which recognizes that stakeholders are dependent upon each other for their success and well-being.[35] That is, managers acknowledge the interdependence among employees, suppliers, customers, shareholders, and the community at large, as we will discuss in Chapter 3 in more detail. Sears, for example, has developed a sophisticated quantitative model that demonstrates symbiosis. With this model, Sears can predict the relationship between employee satisfaction, customer satisfaction, and financial results.[36] The Sears model found that a 5 percent improvement in employee attitudes led to a 1.3 percent improvement in customer satisfaction, which, in turn, will drive a 0.5 percent improvement in revenue.

Social Responsibility, Social Innovation, and Environmental Sustainability: Moving Beyond the Immediate Stakeholders

Organizations must acknowledge and act upon the interests and demands of stakeholders such as citizens and society in general that are beyond its immediate constituencies—customers, owners, suppliers, and employees. That is, they must consider the needs of the broader community at large and act in a socially responsible manner.[37]

Social responsibility is the expectation that businesses or individuals will strive to improve the overall welfare of society.[38] From the perspective of a business, this means that managers must take active steps to make society better by virtue of the business being in existence.[39] Similar to norms and values, actions that constitute socially responsible behavior tend to change over time. In the 1970s affirmative action was a high priority and firms responded. During the 1990s and up to the present time, the public has been concerned about the quality of the environment. Many firms have responded to this by engaging in recycling and reducing waste. And in the wake of terrorist attacks on New York City and the Pentagon as well as the continuing threat from terrorists worldwide, a new kind of priority has arisen: the need to be responsible and vigilant concerning public safety.

Today, demands for greater corporate responsibility have accelerated from a number of stakeholders.[40] These include corporate critics, social investors, activists, and, increasingly, customers who claim to assess corporate responsibility when making purchasing decisions. Such demands go well beyond product and service quality.[41] They include a focus on issues such as labor standards, environmental sustainability, financial and accounting reporting, procurement, supplier relations, environmental practices, and supply chain management.

Recent corporate scandals have intensified significant public concern about corporate responsibility, transparency, and accountability.[42] External critics reinforce the reputational damage, as Nike, Levi Strauss, Gap, Adidas, and other global brands recently found when activists directed attention to abusive labor and human rights practices in their developing-nation suppliers. Such global brands were forced to implement new systems for managing their supply chain companies in order to ensure that they were consistent with their own codes of conduct. And many large brand-name companies are adopting internal responsibility management systems to avert similar criticisms.

A key stakeholder group that appears to be particularly susceptible to corporate social responsibility (CSR) initiatives is its customers.[43] Surveys indicate a strong positive relationship between CSR behaviors and consumers' reactions to a firm's products and services. For example:

- the 2002 Corporate Citizenship poll conducted by Cone Communications found that "84 percent of Americans say they would be likely to switch brands to one associated with a good cause, if price and quality are similar."[44]
- a 2001 Hill & Knowlton/Harris Interactive poll reveals that "79 percent of Americans take corporate citizenship into account when deciding whether to buy a particular company's product and 37 percent consider corporate citizenship an important factor when making purchasing decisions."[45]

Such findings are consistent with a large body of research that confirms the positive influence of CSR on consumers' company evaluations and product purchase intentions across a broad range of product categories.

From Social Responsibility to Social Innovation   Rosabeth Moss Kanter, of the Harvard Business School, and her colleagues have recently found that many leading-edge companies are creating a new paradigm: moving beyond social *responsibility* to social *innovation*.[46] Such companies consider community needs not as, in effect, social ills that require "Band-Aid" solutions such as financial donations and volunteer work. Rather, they see them as valuable opportunities to develop ideas and demonstrate business technologies as well as ways to find and serve new markets.

Such innovations have both community and business payoffs. When companies approach social needs in this manner, they have a stake in the problems and they treat the effort in the same way that they would address any other project that is central to the company's operations. They deploy their best talent and their core skills. They direct their efforts to invent sophisticated solutions through a hands-on approach. Such initiatives are not viewed as charity. Rather it is R&D that strengthens their capabilities—a strategic business investment. Consider, for example, IBM's efforts in public education:

> Under the personal leadership of CEO Louis V. Gerstner, Jr., IBM began its Reinventing Education program in 1994. The program was designed to develop new tools and solutions for systemic change and now operates at 21 locations in four countries. Several product innovations, which benefit both the schools and IBM, have resulted from this initiative. For example, as part of the Wired For Learning program in four new schools in Charlotte-Mecklenburg, North Carolina, IBM created tools to connect parents to teachers digitally. This enables parents to view their children's schoolwork from home or a community center and compare it with the district's academic standards. Also, new tracking software is facilitating the introduction of flexible scheduling in Cincinnati, Ohio, including a new year-round high school. In Broward County, Florida—the fifth largest school district in the United States—IBM's data-warehousing technology provides teachers and administrators with access to extensive information on students. And, in Philadelphia, IBM created a voice recognition tool to teach reading that is based on children's high-pitched voices and speech patterns.[47]

The Triple Bottom Line: Incorporating Financial as well as Environmental and Social Costs   To remain viable in the long run, many companies are measuring what has been called a "triple bottom line." This technique involves assessing financial, social, and environmental performance. Shell, NEC, and Procter & Gamble, among other corporations, have recognized that failing to account for the environmental and social costs of doing business poses risks to the company and the community in which it operates.

The environmental revolution has been almost four decades in the making.[48] It has changed forever how companies do business. In the 1960s and 1970s, companies were in a state of denial regarding their firms' impact on the natural environment. However, a series of visible ecological problems created a groundswell for strict governmental regulation. In the United States, Lake Erie was dead, and in Japan, people were dying of mercury poisoning.

Stuart Hart, writing in the *Harvard Business Review,* addresses the magnitude of problems and challenges associated with the natural environment:

> The challenge is to develop a *sustainable global economy:* an economy that the planet is capable of supporting indefinitely. Although we may be approaching ecological recovery in the developed world, the planet as a whole remains on an unsustainable course. Increasingly, the scourges of the late twentieth century—depleted farmland, fisheries, and forests; choking urban pollution; poverty; infectious disease; and migration—are spilling over geopolitical

STRATEGY SPOTLIGHT

1.4

Productivity Improvement and Environmental Sustainability

Chad Holliday, CEO of DuPont, articulates his firm's innovative approach to productivity improvement:

> Many companies consider productivity to be a cost-saving operational issue. We at DuPont have elevated productivity to the strategic level because we believe that it is central to our efforts in sustainability. As a sign of our commitment in this area, we have adopted six-sigma methodology, a stringent approach that strives to reduce manufacturing defects to just several per million. At the end of last year, we had 1,100 black belts and 1,700 green belts (employees who have undergone weeks of training in the six-sigma methodology) working on 4,200 projects....
>
> Altogether, our projects using six-sigma methodology are responsible for savings of more than $1 billion a year, and these efforts to improve productivity invariably result in less waste, both in energy and raw material. For example, a six-sigma team enabled a DuPont plant in Old Hickory, Tennessee, that manufactures medical gowns made of Sontara, a high-strength durable cloth, to slash its defect rate, saving the equivalent of 760,000 gowns per year. By reducing waste, our six-sigma projects connect directly to sustainable growth.

Source: Holliday, C. 2001. Sustainable growth, the DuPont way. *Harvard Business Review*, 19(9): 129–134.

borders. The simple fact is this: in meeting our needs, we are destroying the ability of future generations to meet theirs . . . corporations are the only organizations with the resources, the technology, the global reach, and, ultimately, the motivation to achieve sustainability.[49]

Environmental sustainability is now a value embraced by the most competitive and successful multinational companies.[50] The McKinsey Corporation's survey of more than 400 senior executives of companies around the world found that 92 percent agreed with former Sony President Akio Morita's contention that the environmental challenge will be one of the central issues in the 21st century.[51] Virtually all executives responding to the survey acknowledged their firm's responsibility to control pollution, and 83 percent agreed that corporations have an environmental responsibility for their products even after they are sold.

For many successful firms, environmental values are now becoming a central part of their cultures and management processes. And, as noted earlier, environmental impacts are being audited and accounted for as the "second bottom line." Such environmental impacts are not always measured in financial terms. However, they have a special value that companies are finding increasingly difficult to ignore.

> Chad Holliday, CEO of DuPont, is one executive who heads a multinational corporation that has taken a proactive approach to sustainable environmental strategies. He also chairs the World Business Council for Sustainable Development, a coalition of 150 companies from more than 30 countries that is committed to environmental protection, social equity, and economic growth. In Strategy Spotlight 1.4, Holliday shares his perspective on DuPont's strategic approach to productivity improvement that is also environment friendly.[52]

>>The Strategic Management Perspective: An Imperative Throughout the Organization

As we have noted in this chapter, strategic management requires managers to take an integrative view of the organization and assess how all of the functional areas and activities fit together to help an organization achieve its goals and objectives. This cannot be accomplished if only the top managers in the organization take an integrative, strategic perspective of issues facing the firm and everyone else "fends for themselves" in their independent, isolated functional areas. Marketing and sales will generally favor broad, tailor-made product lines, production will demand standardized products that are relatively easy to make in order to lower manufacturing costs, research and development will design products to demonstrate technical elegance, and so on. Instead, people throughout the organization need to be striving toward overall goals.

The above argument clearly makes sense. However, the need for such a perspective is accelerating in today's increasingly complex, interconnected, ever-changing, global economy. In this section, we will address some major trends that are making the need for a strategic perspective throughout the organization even more critical. As noted by Peter Senge of MIT, the days when Henry Ford, Alfred Sloan, and Tom Watson (top executives at Ford, General Motors, and IBM, respectively) "learned for the organization are gone." He goes on to say:

> In an increasingly dynamic, interdependent, and unpredictable world, it is simply no longer possible for anyone to "figure it all out at the top." The old model, "the top thinks and the local acts," must now give way to integrating thinking and acting at all levels. While the challenge is great, so is the potential payoff. "The person who figures out how to harness the collective genius of the people in his or her organization," according to former Citibank CEO Walter Wriston, "is going to blow the competition away."[53]

In this section we will first address some of the key forces that are driving the need for a strategic perspective at all levels as well as greater participation and involvement in the strategic management process throughout the organization. Then, we will provide examples of how firms are engaging people throughout the organization to these ends.

Some Key Driving Forces

There are many driving forces that are increasing the need for a strategic perspective and greater involvement throughout the organization.[54] Among the most important of these are globalization, technology, and intellectual capital.[55] These forces are inherently interrelated and, collectively, they are accelerating the rate of change and uncertainty with which managers at all levels must deal. The implication of such unpredictable change was probably best captured by former AOL Time Warner Chairman Stephen M. Case, in a talk to investors and analysts:

> I sometimes feel like I'm behind the wheel of a race car. . . . One of the biggest challenges is there are no road signs to help navigate. And . . . no one has yet determined which side of the road we're supposed to be on.[56]

Globalization The defining feature of the global economy is not the flow of goods—international trade has existed for centuries—but the flow of capital, people, and information worldwide. With globalization, time and space are no longer a barrier to making deals anywhere in the world. Computer networks permit instantaneous transactions, and the market watchers operate around the clock on a 24/7 basis.

Along with the increasing speed of transactions and global sourcing of all forms of resources and information, managers must address the paradoxical demand to think globally and act locally. They have to move resources and information rapidly around the world to meet local needs. They also face new challenges when formulating strategies: volatile political situations, difficult trade issues, ever-fluctuating exchange rates, unfamiliar cultures, and gut-wrenching social problems.[57] Today, managers must be more literate in the ways of foreign customers, commerce, and competition than ever before.

As markets become more open—as evidenced by free trade agreements between nations—more foreign firms are likely to enter domestic markets. This increases the amount of competition. Further, since firms are operating in global markets, competitive moves in a domestic economy may negatively impact the firm in another segment of the international market. This places pressure on firms to move into international markets in order to maintain their competitiveness in areas where they already operate. Clearly, globalization requires that organizations increase their ability to learn and collaborate and to manage diversity, complexity, and ambiguity. Top-level managers can't do it all alone.

Technology   Technological change and diffusion of new technologies are moving at an incredible pace. Such development and diffusion accelerate the importance of innovation for firms if they are to remain competitive. David de Pury, former cochair of the board of Asea Brown Boveri, claimed that "innovate or die" is the first rule of international industrial competition. Similarly, continuous technological development and change have produced decreasing product life cycles. Andrew Grove, chairman of Intel, explained the introduction of a new product at his company. Recently, the firm introduced a sophisticated product in which it had invested considerable funds. However, later in the same year, Intel introduced a new product that would cannibalize its existing product. Thus, the firm had only 11 months to recoup that significant investment. Such time-intensive product development involves the efforts and collaboration of managers and professionals throughout the organization.

From videoconferencing to the Internet, technology has made our world smaller and faster moving. Ideas and huge amounts of information are in constant movement. The challenge for managers is to make sense of what technology offers. Not all technology adds value. In the coming years, managers in all organizations will be charged with making technology an even more viable, productive part of the work setting. They will need to stay ahead of the information curve and learn to leverage information to enhance business performance. If not, they risk being swallowed in a tidal wave of data, not ideas.

In addition to its potential benefits, technology can raise some important ethical issues that need to be addressed. Strategy Spotlight 1.5 raises the issue of "designer babies."

Intellectual Capital   Knowledge has become the direct source of competitive advantage(s) for companies selling ideas and relationships (e.g., professional services, software, and technology-driven companies) as well as an indirect source of competitive advantage for all companies trying to differentiate themselves from rivals by how they create value for their customers. As we will note in Chapter 4, Merck, the $52 billion pharmaceutical company, has become enormously successful because its scientists discover medicines, not because of their skills in producing pills in an efficient manner. As noted by Dr. Roy Vagelos, Merck's former CEO, "A low-value product can be made by anyone anywhere. When you have knowledge no one else has access to—that's dynamite. We guard our research even more carefully than our financial assets."[58]

Creating and applying knowledge to deliver differentiated products and services of superior value for customers requires the acquisition of superior talent, as well as the ability to develop and retain that talent.[59] However, successful firms must also create an environment with strong social and professional relationships, where people feel strong ties to their colleagues and their organization. Gary Hamel, one of today's leading strategic management writers, noted, "As the number and quality of interconnections between individuals and ideas go up, the ability to combine and recombine ideas accelerates as well."[60]

STRATEGY SPOTLIGHT

Designer Babies

No one would dispute that it's all right to custom-design some products and services. Given individual tastes, it's only natural that people will want customization. But customization, and its associated technology, can go too far.

James D. Watson and Francis H. C. Crick's discovery of the DNA molecule in 1954 made customizing human children technologically feasible. Watson and Crick probably never foresaw this. But nearly a half century later, the potential to genetically alter babies before birth is actually here.

This raises a host of ethical questions. Imagine designer babies, children born to parents who have the financial resources to create the "perfect" child. Without a doubt, DNA experimentation has led to scientific advances, such as treatment of certain diseases, that are valuable and ethical. But when it comes to customizing a human being, the line between right and wrong can become blurry. The Honorable Michael Kirby, Justice of the High Court of Australia and a member of the International Ethics Committee of United Nations Educational, Scientific and Cultural Organization (UNESCO), raises some thought-provoking ethical questions:

> Fundamental questions are raised about the long-term effects of genetic alteration of the human species. For example, we have identified the genes that express themselves in Huntington's disease. Should the law permit, encourage, or forbid the elimination of a fetus which manifests these genes? Elimination of a fetus with likely intellectual impairment is now not uncommon, but how far do we go down that track in the quest of the "perfect" child? Should we eliminate obesity, baldness, and heart disease (if that turns out to be, at least in part, genetic)? Not to regulate these characteristics is, effectively, to permit them all. . . . When it becomes possible to eliminate particular genes and transplant others, what will prevent the attempted creation of a superspecies? Or an underspecies? Or an altered human species? We must be ready with our answers to these questions. It should not be assumed that sermons, political press releases, and the solemn resolutions of corporate ethics committees will have the power to prevent developments deemed undesirable by most of humanity.

Technology, with all its benefits, must also be considered in light of these and other ethical considerations.

Source: Licking, E. 2000. Ten technologies that will change our lives. *BusinessWeek*, Spring; and Kirby, M. 2000. The human genome project in the dock. *Medical Journal of Australia*, 173: 599–600.

Technologies also must be used effectively to leverage human capital to facilitate collaboration among individuals and to develop more sophisticated knowledge management systems.[61] The challenge and opportunity of management is not only to acquire and retain human capital but also to ensure that employees develop and maintain a strategic perspective as they contribute to the organization. This is essential if management is to use its talents to effectively help the organization attain its goals and objectives.

Strategy Spotlight 1.6 discusses the global market for talent. It illustrates how forces of globalization, technology, and intellectual capital can be related.

Let's now look at what some companies are doing to increase the involvement of employees throughout the organization in the strategic management process.

Enhancing Employee Involvement in the Strategic Management Process

Today's organizations increasingly need to anticipate and respond to dramatic and unpredictable changes in the competitive environment. With the emergence of the knowledge economy, human capital (as opposed to financial and physical assets) has become the key to securing advantages in the marketplace that persist over time.

STRATEGY SPOTLIGHT

The Global Market for Talent

Globalization today involves the movement of not only goods and investments across borders, but also people and information. Many American technology-strategy consultants, who make about $150,000 annually, today are blissfully unaware of the challenge posed by the likes of Ganesh Narasimhaiya.

Ganesh is a 30-year-old Indian who enjoys cricket, R&B music, and bowling. He has a bachelor's degree in electronics and communications, and he can spin out code in a variety of languages: COBOL, Java, and UML (Unified Modeling Language), among others. Ganesh has worked on high-profile projects for Wipro, a $1 billion Indian software giant, all over the world. He has helped GE Medical Systems roll out a logistics application throughout Southeast Asia. He proposed a plan to consolidate and synchronize security solutions across a British client's e-business applications. He developed a strategy for transferring legacy system applications onto the Web for a company in Norway. He works up to 18 or 19 hours a day at a customer site and for that he may earn as much as $7,000 a month. When he's home in Bangalore, his pay is about one-quarter of that—$21,000 a year. But by Indian standards, this is a small fortune.

Ganesh is part of Wipro's strategy of amassing a small force of high-level experts who are increasingly focused on specific industries and can compete with anyone for a given consulting project. Wipro's Trojan horse is the incredibly cheap offshore outsourcing solution that it can provide. The rise of a globally integrated knowledge economy is a blessing for developing nations. What it means for the U.S. skilled labor force is less clear. This is something strategy consultants working for Accenture or EDS in the United States need to think about. Why? Forrester Research has predicted that at least 3.3 million white-collar jobs and $136 billion in wages will shift from the U.S. to low-cost countries by 2015. With dramatically lower wage rates and the same level of service, how is the American technology professional going to compete with the likes of Ganesh and his colleagues?

Sources: Hammonds, K. H. 2003. Smart, determined, ambitious, cheap: The new face of global competition. *Fast Company*, February: 91–97; Engardio, P., Bernstein, A., & Kripalani, M. 2003. Is your job next? *BusinessWeek*, February 3: 50–60.

To develop and mobilize people and other assets in the organization, leaders are needed throughout the organization.[62] No longer can organizations be effective if the top "does the thinking" and the rest of the organization "does the work." Everyone needs to be involved in the strategic management process. Peter Senge noted the critical need for three types of leaders.

- Local line leaders who have significant profit and loss responsibility.
- Executive leaders who champion and guide ideas, create a learning infrastructure, and establish a domain for taking action.
- Internal networkers who, although they have little positional power and formal authority, generate their power through the conviction and clarity of their ideas.[63]

Sally Helgesen, author of *The Web of Inclusion: A New Architecture for Building Great Organizations,* made a similar point regarding the need for leaders throughout the organization. She asserted that many organizations "fall prey to the heroes-and-drones syndrome, exalting the value of those in powerful positions while implicitly demeaning the contributions of those who fail to achieve top rank."[64] Culture and processes in which leaders emerge at all levels, both up and down as well as across the organization, typify today's high-performing firms.[65]

Now we will provide examples of what some firms are doing to increase the involvement of employees throughout the organization. Top-level executives are key in setting the tone. Consider Richard Branson, founder of the Virgin Group, whose core businesses include retail operations, hotels, communications, and an airline. He is well known for creating a culture and an informal structure where anybody in the organization can be involved in generating and acting upon new business ideas. In an interview, he stated,

> [S]peed is something that we are better at than most companies. We don't have formal board meetings, committees, etc. If someone has an idea, they can pick up the phone and talk to me. I can vote "done, let's do it." Or, better still, they can just go ahead and do it. They know that they are not going to get a mouthful from me if they make a mistake. Rules and regulations are not our forte. Analyzing things to death is not our kind of thing. We very rarely sit back and analyze what we do.[66]

To inculcate a strategic management perspective throughout the organization, many large traditional organizations must often make a major effort to effect transformational change. This involves extensive communication, training, and development to strengthen a strategic perspective throughout the organization. Ford Motor Company is one such example.

Ford instituted a major cultural overhaul and embarked on a broad-based attempt to develop leaders throughout the organization. It wanted to build an army of "warrior-entrepreneurs"—people who have the courage and skills to reject old ideas and who believe in change passionately enough to make it happen. A few details of Ford's effort follow.

> Ford sent about 2,500 managers to its Leadership Development Center during the year for one of its four programs—Capstone, Experienced Leader Challenge, Ford Business Associates, and New Business Leader—instilling in them not just the mind-set and vocabulary of a revolutionary but also the tools necessary to achieve a revolution. At the same time, through the Business Leaders Initiative, all 100,000 salaried employees worldwide will participate in business-leadership "cascades," intense exercises that combine trickle-down communications with substantive team projects.[67]

We'd like to close with our favorite example of how inexperience can be a virtue. It further reinforces the benefits of having broad involvement throughout the organization in the strategic management process (see Strategy Spotlight 1.7)

>>Ensuring Coherence in Strategic Direction

To be successful, employees and managers throughout the organization must strive for common goals and objectives. By specifying desired results, it becomes much easier to move forward. Otherwise, when no one knows what the firm is striving to accomplish, they have no idea of what to work toward. As the old nautical expression puts it, "No wind favors the ship that has no charted course."

Organizations express priorities best through stated goals and objectives that form a *hierarchy of goals.* The hierarchy of goals for an organization includes its vision, mission, and strategic objectives. What visions may lack in specificity, they make up for in their ability to evoke powerful and compelling mental images. On the other hand, strategic objectives tend to be more specific and provide a more direct means of determining if the organization is moving toward broader, overall goals. We will now address visions, missions, and strategic objectives in the next subsections.[68]

Organizational Vision

The starting point for articulating a firm's hierarchy of goals is the company vision. It is often described as a goal that is "massively inspiring, overarching, and long term."[69] A vision represents a destination that is driven by and evokes passion. A vision may or may not succeed; it depends on whether everything else happens according to a firm's strategy.

STRATEGY SPOTLIGHT

Strategy and the Value of Inexperience

Peter Gruber, chairman of Mandalay Entertainment, explained how his firm benefited from the creative insights of an inexperienced intern.

Sometimes life is all about solving problems. In the movie business, at least, there seems to be one around every corner. One of the most effective lessons I've learned about tackling problems is to start by asking not "How to?" but rather "What if?" I learned that lesson from a young woman who was interning on a film I was producing. She actually saved the movie from being shelved by the studio.

The movie, *Gorillas in the Mist,* had turned into a logistical nightmare. We wanted to film at an altitude of 11,000 feet, in the middle of the jungle, in Rwanda—then on the verge of a revolution—and to use more than 200 animals. Warner Brothers, the studio financing the movie, worried that we would exceed our budget. But our biggest problem was that the screenplay required the gorillas to do what we wrote—in other words, to "act." If they couldn't or wouldn't, we'd have to fall back on a formula that the studio had seen fail before: using dwarfs in gorilla suits on a soundstage.

We called an emergency meeting to solve these problems. In the middle of it, a young intern asked, "What if you let the gorillas write the story?" Everyone laughed and wondered what she was doing in the meeting with experienced filmmakers. Hours later, someone casually asked her what she had meant. She said, "What if you sent a really good cinematographer into the jungle with a ton of film to shoot the gorillas. Then you could write a story around what the gorillas did on film." It was a brilliant idea. And we did exactly what she suggested: We sent Alan Root, an Academy Award–nominated cinematographer, into the jungle for three weeks. He came back with phenomenal footage that practically wrote the story for us. We shot the film for $20 million—half of the original budget!

This woman's inexperience enabled her to see opportunities where we saw only boundaries. This experience taught me three things. First, ask high-quality questions, like "what if?" Second, find people who add new perspectives and create new conversations. As experienced filmmakers, we believed that our way was the only way—and that the intern lacked the experience to have an opinion. Third, pay attention to those with new voices. If you want unlimited options for solving a problem, engage the what if before you lock onto the how to. You'll be surprised by what you discover.

Source: Gruber, P. 1998. My greatest lesson. *Fast Company* 15: 88, 90.

Developing and implementing a vision is one of a leader's central roles. In a survey of 1,500 senior leaders, 870 of them CEOs from 20 different countries, respondents were asked what they believed were the key traits that leaders must have. Ninety-eight percent responded that "a strong sense of vision" was the most important. Similarly, when asked about the critical knowledge skills, the leaders cited "strategy formulation to achieve a vision" as the most important skill. In other words, managers need to have not only a vision but also a plan to implement it. Regretfully, 90 percent reported a lack of confidence in their own skills and ability to conceive a vision for their organization. For example, T. J. Rogers, CEO of Cypress Semiconductor, an electronic chipmaker that faced some difficulties in 1992, lamented that his own shortsightedness caused the danger, "I did not have the 50,000-foot view, and got caught."[70]

One of the most famous examples of a vision is from Disneyland: "To be the happiest place on earth." Other examples are:

- "Restoring patients to full life." (Medtronic)
- "We want to satisfy all of our customers' financial needs and help them succeed financially." (Wells Fargo)
- "Our vision is to be the world's best quick service restaurant." (McDonald's)

Although such visions cannot be accurately measured by a specific indicator of how well they are being achieved, they do provide a fundamental statement of an organization's values, aspirations, and goals. Such visions go well beyond narrow financial objectives, of course, and strive to capture both the minds and hearts of employees.

The vision statement may also contain a slogan, diagram, or picture—whatever grabs attention.[71] The aim is to capture the essence of the more formal parts of the vision in a few words that are easily remembered, yet evoke the spirit of the entire vision statement. In its 20-year battle with Xerox, Canon's slogan, or battle cry, was "Beat Xerox." Motorola's slogan is "Total Customer Satisfaction." Outboard Marine Corporation's slogan is "To Take the World Boating." And Chevron strives "To Become Better than the Best."

Clearly, vision statements are not a cure-all. Sometimes they backfire and erode a company's credibility. Visions fail for many reasons, including those discussed in the following paragraphs.[72]

The Walk Doesn't Match the Talk   An idealistic vision can arouse employee enthusiasm. However, that same enthusiasm can be quickly dashed if employees find that senior management's behavior is not consistent with the vision. Often, vision is a sloganeering campaign of new buzzwords and empty platitudes like "devotion to the customer," "teamwork," or "total quality" that aren't consistently backed by management's action.

Irrelevance   A vision that is created in a vacuum—unrelated to environmental threats or opportunity or an organization's resources and capabilities—can ignore the needs of those who are expected to buy into it. When the vision is not anchored in reality, employees will reject it.

Not the Holy Grail   Managers often search continually for the one elusive solution that will solve their firm's problems—that is, the next holy grail of management. They may have tried other management fads only to find that they fell short of their expectations. However, they remain convinced that one exists. Visions support sound management, but they require everyone to walk the talk and be accountable for their behavior. A vision simply cannot be viewed as a magic cure for an organization's illness.

Too Much Focus Leads to Missed Opportunities   Clearly, one of the benefits of a sound vision statement is that it can focus efforts and excite people. However, the downside is that in directing people and resources toward a narrow perspective, exciting and innovative opportunities can be missed. Consider, for example, Komatsu:[73]

> Faced with the challenge of rival Caterpillar's entry into Komatsu's protected home market, Ryoichi Kawai, then CEO of Komatsu, focused the whole company on beating Caterpillar. "Maru-C" became the rally cry which meant "Encircle Caterpillar." And, to make the enemy visible and omnipresent, Kawai purchased the largest Caterpillar bulldozer available and placed it on the roof of Komatsu headquarters. The story is well-known of how Kawai leveraged his aggression against Caterpillar into a highly disciplined and effective process of building up Komatsu's strengths and market position. (In fact, it became the most-used Harvard case study.)
>
> However, there was a lesser-known downside. The two decades of focusing on a "life-and-death battle" with Caterpillar prevented Komatsu from identifying new opportunities in related areas of business and from pursuing genuine breakthrough innovations in its core earthmoving-equipment business. Eventually, Tetsuya Katada took over and formally abolished the "Maru-C" slogan and removed all of the symbols Kawai had built to represent the Caterpillar battle. The result was successful expansion into related areas, such as robotics, and several fundamentally different and highly innovative products, such as earthmoving equipment for undersea operations.

An Ideal Future Irreconciled with the Present   Although visions are not designed to mirror reality, they do need to be anchored somehow in it. People have difficulty identifying with a vision that paints a rosy picture of the future but takes no account of the often hostile environment in which the firm competes or ignores some of the firm's weaknesses. As we will see in the next section, many of these same issues can apply to mission statements.

Mission Statements

A company's mission differs from its vision in that it encompasses both the purpose of the company as well as the basis of competition and competitive advantage.

Exhibit 1.5 contains the vision statement and mission statement of WellPoint Health Networks, a $21 billion managed health care organization. Note that while the vision statement is broad based, the mission statement is more specific and focused on the means by which the firm will compete. This includes providing branded products that will be tailor-made to customers in order to create long-term customer relationships.

Effective mission statements incorporate the concept of stakeholder management, suggesting that organizations must respond to multiple constituencies if they are to survive and prosper. Customers, employees, suppliers, and owners are the primary stakeholders, but others may also play an important role in a particular corporation. Mission statements also have the greatest impact when they reflect an organization's enduring, overarching strategic priorities and competitive positioning. Mission statements also can vary in length and specificity. The two mission statements below illustrate these issues.

- To produce superior financial returns for our shareholders as we serve our customers with the highest quality transportation, logistics, and e-commerce. (Federal Express)
- To be the very best in the business. Our game plan is status go . . . we are constantly looking ahead, building on our strengths, and reaching for new goals. In our quest of these goals, we look at the three stars of the Brinker logo and are reminded of the basic values that are the strength of this company . . . People, Quality and Profitability. Everything we do at Brinker must support these core values. We also look at the eight golden flames depicted in our logo, and are reminded of the fire that ignites our mission and makes up the heart and soul of this incredible company. These flames are: Customers, Food, Team, Concepts, Culture, Partners, Community, and Shareholders. As keeper of these flames, we will continue to build on our strengths and work together to be the best in the business. (Brinker International, whose restaurant chains include Chili's and On the Border)[74]

Few mission statements identify profit or any other financial indicator as the sole purpose of the firm. Indeed, many do not even mention profit or shareholder return.[75] Employees of organizations or departments are usually the mission's most important

Exhibit 1.5

Comparing WellPoint Health Network's Vision and Mission

Vision

WellPoint *will redefine our industry:*
Through a new generation of consumer-friendly products that put individuals back in control of their future.

Mission

The WellPoint companies provide health *security* by offering a *choice* of quality branded health and related financial services *designed* to meet the *changing* expectations of individuals, families, and their sponsors throughout a *lifelong* relationship.

Source: WellPoint Health Network company records.

NextJet's Change of Mission

The dot-com crash was only the first blow to NextJet, Inc., a Dallas-based business launched in 1999 to ship packages overnight. The bigger blow came with the September 11 terrorist attacks, when passenger airlines were forced to add security and reduce flights. One of NextJet's strengths was its nationwide network of local courier services that got packages to and from airports, all coordinated through their proprietary software that could determine the optimal routing. However, the company's business model fell apart when it could not rely on the airlines to get packages between cities quickly enough to make the added cost for same-day delivery worthwhile.

Rather than give up, NextJet reinvented the business around the idea that its most important asset was the software itself. The company's new mission received almost immediate validation when its software was deployed successfully at United Parcel Service (UPS). NextJet's software provides Atlanta-based UPS with tools for setting online rates and tracking packages. While a lot of same-day business did evaporate when corporations tightened the reins on spending, some things can't wait overnight to be shipped. For example, makers of hospital equipment may need to ship critical parts within a few hours. NextJet's software can help shippers make important decisions in less than a second, finding the fastest and most economical route among air, truck, and courier operations. In addition to UPS, its customers include FedEx, Greyhound, and Menlo Worldwide.

NextJet serves a very large industry segment—Service Parts & Logistics (SPL). The annual expenditures for spare parts in the United States are estimated to be $500 billion. And managers have increased their focus on the importance of effective logistics operations, given its potential impact on a firm's income. After all, whether or not a production line is running can often depend on the quick and effective installation of relatively inexpensive spare parts.

NextJet currently has 50 employees and four offices in the United States, and it seems to be on the right track with its new mission. Although executives at the privately held company will not disclose financial results, they say they are about to complete their third consecutive profitable quarter.

Sources: Goldstein, A. 2002. NextJet is hoping that its software can deliver. *Dallas Morning News*, December 4: 1–3; industry.java.sun.com/javanews/stories/story2/0,1072,34986,00.html; Nelson, M. G. 2001. NextJet network adds wireless. *Information Week*, April 30: 34; Anonymous. 2004. Who's who in e-logistics. www.americanshipper.com, September; Hudspeth, B., & Jones, J. 2004. Service parts and logistics: Should you in-source or outsource. *3pl line*, www.inboundlogistics.com, October.

audience. For them, the mission should help to build a common understanding of purpose and commitment to nurture.

Profit maximization not only fails to motivate people but also does not differentiate between organizations. Every corporation wants to maximize profits over the long term. A good mission statement, by addressing each principal theme, must communicate why an organization is special and different. Two studies that linked corporate values and mission statements with financial performance found that the most successful firms mentioned values other than profits. The less successful firms focused almost entirely on profitability.[76] In essence, profit is the metaphorical equivalent of oxygen, food, and water that the body requires. They are not the point of life, but without them, there is no life.

Although vision statements tend to be quite enduring and seldom change, a firm's mission can and should change when competitive conditions dramatically change or the firm is faced with new threats or opportunities. Strategy Spotlight 1.8 provides an example of a firm, NextJet, that changed its mission in order to realize new opportunities.

Strategic Objectives

Thus far, we have discussed both visions and missions. Statements of vision tend to be quite broad and can be described as a goal that represents an inspiring, overarching, and emotionally driven destination. Mission statements, on the other hand, tend to be more specific and address questions concerning the organization's reason for being and the basis of its intended competitive advantage in the marketplace. Strategic objectives are used to operationalize the mission statement.[77] That is, they help to provide guidance on how the organization can fulfill or move toward the "higher goals" in the goal hierarchy—the mission and vision. As a result, they tend to be more specific and cover a more well-defined time frame.

Setting objectives demands a yardstick to measure the fulfillment of the objectives.[78] If an objective lacks specificity or measurability, it is not very useful, simply because there is no way of determining whether it is helping the organization move toward its mission and vision.

Exhibit 1.6 lists several strategic objectives of corporations, divided into financial and nonfinancial categories. While most of these strategic objectives are directed toward generating greater profits and returns for the owners of the business, others are directed at customers or society at large.

For objectives to be meaningful, they need to satisfy several criteria. They must be:

- *Measurable.* There must be at least one indicator (or yardstick) that measures progress against fulfilling the objective.
- *Specific.* This provides a clear message as to what needs to be accomplished.
- *Appropriate.* It must be consistent with the vision and mission of the organization.
- *Realistic.* It must be an achievable target given the organization's capabilities and opportunities in the environment. In essence, it must be challenging but doable.
- *Timely.* There needs to be a time frame for accomplishing the objective. After all, as the economist John Maynard Keynes once said, "In the long run, we are all dead!"

When objectives satisfy the above criteria, there are many benefits for the organization. First, they help to channel employees throughout the organization toward common goals. This helps the organization concentrate and conserve valuable resources and work collectively in a more timely manner.

Second, challenging objectives can help to motivate and inspire employees throughout the organization to higher levels of commitment and effort. A great deal of research has supported the notion that individuals work harder when they are striving toward specific goals instead of being asked simply to "do their best."

Exhibit 1.6
Strategic Objectives

Strategic Objectives (Financial)

- Increase sales growth 6% to 8% and accelerate core net earnings growth to 13% to 15% per share in each of the next 5 years. (Procter & Gamble)
- Generate Internet-related revenue of $1.5 billion. (AutoNation)
- Increase the contribution of Banking Group earnings from investments, brokerage, and insurance from 16% to 25%. (Wells Fargo)
- Cut corporate overhead costs by $30 million per year. (Fortune Brands)

Strategic Objectives (Nonfinancial)

- We want a majority of our customers, when surveyed, to say they consider Wells Fargo the best financial institution in the community. (Wells Fargo)
- We want to operate 6,000 stores by 2010—up from 3,000 in the year 2000. (Walgreen's)
- We want to be the top-ranked supplier to our customers. (PPG)
- Reduce greenhouse gases by 10 percent (from a 1990 base) by 2010. (BP Amoco)

Sources: Company documents and annual reports.

Third, as we noted earlier in the chapter, there is always the potential for different parts of an organization to pursue their own goals rather than overall company goals. Although well intentioned, these may work at cross-purposes to the organization as a whole. Meaningful objectives thus help to resolve conflicts when they arise.

Finally, proper objectives provide a yardstick for rewards and incentives. Not only will they lead to higher levels of employee motivation but they will also help to ensure a greater sense of equity or fairness when rewards are allocated.

There are, of course, still other objectives that are even more specific. These are often referred to as short-term objectives—essential components of "action plans" that are critical in implementing a firm's chosen strategy. We will discuss these issues in Chapter 9.

Summary

We began this introductory chapter by defining strategic management and articulating some of its key attributes. Strategic management is defined as "consisting of the analyses, decisions, and actions an organization undertakes to create and sustain competitive advantages." The issue of how and why some firms outperform others in the marketplace is central to the study of strategic management. Strategic management has four key attributes: It is directed at overall organizational goals, includes multiple stakeholders, incorporates both short-term and long-term perspectives, and incorporates trade-offs between efficiency and effectiveness.

The second section discussed the strategic management process. Here, we paralleled the above definition of strategic management and focused on three core activities in the strategic management process—strategy analysis, strategy formulation, and strategy implementation. We noted how each of these activities is highly interrelated to and interdependent on the others. We also discussed how each of the 13 chapters in this text fits into the three core activities, and we provided a summary of the opening vignettes in each chapter.

Next, we introduced two important concepts—corporate governance and stakeholder management—which must be taken into account throughout the strategic management process. Governance mechanisms can be broadly divided into two groups: internal and external. Internal governance mechanisms include shareholders (owners), management (led by the chief executive officer), and the board of directors. External control is exercised by auditors, banks, analysts, and an active business press as well as the threat of takeovers. We identified five key stakeholders in all organizations: owners, customers, suppliers, employees, and society at large. Successful firms go beyond an overriding focus on satisfying solely the interests of owners. Rather, they recognize the inherent conflicts that arise among the demands of the various stakeholders as well as the need to endeavor to attain "symbiosis"—that is, interdependence and mutual benefit—among the various stakeholder groups. Managers must also recognize the need to act in a socially responsible manner which, if done effectively, can enhance a firm's innovativeness. They also should recognize and incorporate issues related to environmental sustainability in their strategic actions.

In the fourth section, we discussed three interrelated factors—globalization, technology, and intellectual capital—that have accelerated the rate of unpredictable change that managers face today. These factors, and the combination of them, have increased the need for managers and employees throughout the organization to have a strategic management perspective and to become more empowered.

The final section addressed the need for consistency among a firm's vision, mission, and strategic objectives. Collectively, they form an organization's hierarchy of goals. Visions should evoke powerful and compelling mental images. However, they are not very specific. Strategic objectives, on the other hand, are much more specific and are vital to ensuring that the organization is striving toward fulfilling its vision and mission.

Summary Review Questions

1. How is "strategic management" defined in the text, and what are its four key attributes?

2. Briefly discuss the three key activities in the strategic management process. Why is it important for managers to recognize the interdependent nature of these activities?

3. Explain the concept of "stakeholder management." Why shouldn't managers be solely interested in stockholder management, that is, maximizing the returns for owners of the firm—its shareholders?

4. What is "corporate governance"? What are its three key elements and how can it be improved?

5. How can "symbiosis" (interdependence, mutual benefit) be achieved among a firm's stakeholders?

6. What are some of the major trends that now require firms to have a greater strategic management perspective and empowerment in the strategic management process throughout the firm?

7. What is meant by a "hierarchy of goals"? What are the main components of it, and why must consistency be achieved among them?

Experiential Exercise

Using the Internet or library sources, select four organizations—two in the private sector and two in the public sector. Find their mission statements. Complete the following exhibit by identifying the stakeholders that are mentioned. Evaluate the differences between firms in the private sector and those in the public sector.

Name				
Mission Statement				
Stakeholders (✓ = mentioned)				
1. Customers				
2. Suppliers				
3. Managers/employees				
4. Community-at-large				
5. Owners				
6. Others?				
7. Others?				

1. Go to the Internet and look up one of these company sites: www.walmart.com, www.ge.com, or www.fordmotor.com. What are some of the key events that would represent the "romantic" perspective of leadership? What are some of the key events that depict the "external control" perspective of leadership?

2. Select a company that competes in an industry in which you are interested. What are some of the recent demands that stakeholders have placed on this company? Can you find examples of how the company is trying to develop "symbiosis" (interdependence and mutual benefit) among its stakeholders? (Use the Internet and library resources.)

3. Provide examples of companies that are actively trying to increase the amount of empowerment in the strategic management process throughout the organization. Do these companies seem to be having positive outcomes? Why? Why not?

4. Look up the vision statements and/or mission statements for a few companies. Do you feel that they are constructive and useful as a means of motivating employees and providing a strong strategic direction? Why? Why not? (*Note:* Annual reports, along with the Internet, may be good sources of information.)

1. A company focuses solely on short-term profits to provide the greatest return to the owners of the business (i.e., the shareholders in a publicly held firm). What ethical issues could this raise?

2. A firm has spent some time—with input from managers at all levels—in developing a vision statement and a mission statement. Over time, however, the behavior of some executives is contrary to these statements. Could this raise some ethical issues?

1. Byrnes, N. 2004. Gone flat. *BusinessWeek,* December 20: 76–82; Foust, D. 2004. Things aren't going better at Coke. *BusinessWeek,* August 16: 38; Trent, B. 2005. Succession screw-ups. *BusinessWeek,* January 10: 84; Morris, B. The real story. *Fortune.* May 31: 84–98; and Foust, D. 2005. Shaking up the Coke board. *BusinessWeek.* April 4: 46.

2. As CFO, Doug Ivester was responsible for the spinoff of Coke's U.S. bottling operations in 1986. This removed $2.4 billion of debt from its balance sheet. At the same time, Coca-Cola was able to maintain a 49 percent stake (and six board seats, which it packed with current and former Coke executives) in the new company, Coca-Cola Enterprises. Coke was thus able to have effective control of pricing of its concentrate as well as what the new entity charged its distributors. Interestingly, when Ivester tried to sustain profits by imposing an enormous 7.6 percent price hike on the distributors, the animosity that he created was a key factor that led to his forced resignation in 1999. Refer to Byrnes, op. cit. and Foust, 2005, op. cit. for insightful discussions of this issue.

3. For a discussion of the "romantic" versus "external control" perspective, refer to Meindl, J. R. 1987. The romance of leadership and the evaluation of organizational performance. *Academy of Management Journal* 30: 92–109; and Pfeffer, J., & Salancik, G. R. 1978. *The external control of organizations: A resource dependence perspective.* New York: Harper & Row.

4. A recent perspective on the "romantic view" of leadership is provided by: Mintzberg, H. 2004. Leadership and management development: An afterword. *Academy of Management Executive,* 18(3): 140–142.

5. Anonymous. 2005. Face value: The 10 billion dollar man. *The Economist.* February 26: 66. Interestingly, this article speculated that Mr. Ghosn could add approximately $10 billion to the market value of Ford or General Motors if he were to sign on as Chief Executive Officer. Such a perspective is clearly consistent with the "romantic view" of leadership. For an insightful perspective on the challenges faced by Mr. Ghosn as he assumes the roles of CEO for both Nissan and Renault (which owns 44 percent of Nissan), refer to: Edmondson, G. 2005. What Ghosn will do with Renault. *BusinessWeek,* April 25: 54.

6. Sanborn, S. 2005. Soft drink industry. *Value Line,* February 4: 1541.

7. Brady, D. 2004. Pepsi's thousand and one noshes. *BusinessWeek online,* June 14.

8. Anonymous. 2005. The best managers. *BusinessWeek,* January 10: 56–57; and Byrnes, op. cit.

9. For an interesting perspective on the need for strategists to maintain a global mind-set, refer to Begley, T. M., & Boyd, D. P. 2003. The need for a global mind-set. *MIT Sloan Management Review* 44(2): 25–32.

10. Porter, M. E. 1996. What is strategy? *Harvard Business Review* 74(6): 61–78.

11. See, for example, Barney, J. B., & Arikan, A. M. 2001. The resource-based view: Origins and implications. In Hitt, M. A., Freeman, R. E., & Harrison, J. S. (Eds.), *Handbook of strategic management:* 124–189. Malden, MA: Blackwell.

12. Barney, J. 1991. Firm resources and sustained competitive advantage. *Journal of Management,* 17(1): 99–120.

13. Much of Gary Hamel's work advocates the importance of not focusing on incremental change. For example, refer to Hamel, G., & Prahalad, C. K. 1994. *Competing for the future.* Boston: Harvard Business School Press; see also Christensen, C. M. 2001. The past and future of competitive advantage. *Sloan Management Review,* 42(3): 105–109.

14. Porter, M. E. 1996. What is strategy? *Harvard Business Review,* 74(6): 61–78; and Hammonds, K. H. 2001. Michael Porter's big ideas. *Fast Company,* March: 55–56.

15. This section draws upon Dess, G. G., & Miller, A. 1993. *Strategic management.* New York: McGraw-Hill.

16. See, for example, Hrebiniak, L. G., & Joyce, W. F. 1986. The strategic importance of managing myopia. *Sloan Management Review,* 28(1): 5–14.

17. For an insightful discussion on how to manage diverse stakeholder groups, refer to Rondinelli, D. A., & London, T. 2003. How corporations and environmental groups cooperate: Assessing cross-sector alliances and collaborations. *Academy of Management Executive,* 17(1): 61–76.

18. Senge, P. 1996. Leading learning organizations: The bold, the powerful, and the invisible. In Hesselbein, F., Goldsmith, M., & Beckhard, R. (Eds.), *The leader of the future:* 41–58. San Francisco: Jossey-Bass.

19. For another interesting perspective on this issue, refer to Abell, D. F. 1999. Competing today while preparing for tomorrow. *Sloan Management Review,* 40(3): 73–81.

20. Loeb, M. 1994. Where leaders come from. *Fortune,* September 19: 241 (quoting Warren Bennis).

21. Address by Norman R. Augustine at the Crummer Business School, Rollins College, Winter Park, FL, October 20, 1989.

22. For an excellent theoretical and empirical contribution on this subject, refer to Gibson, C. B., & Birkinshaw, J. 2004. The antecedents, consequences, and mediating role of organizational ambidexterity. *Academy of Management Journal,* 47(2): 209–226.

23. Mintzberg, H. 1985. Of strategies: Deliberate and emergent. *Strategic Management Journal,* 6: 257–272.

24. Carey, J. 2005. Tax credits put wind in the sails of renewables. *BusinessWeek.* January 10: 94.

25. Monks, R., & Minow, N. 2001. *Corporate governance* (2nd ed.). Malden, MA: Blackwell.

26. Intel Corp., www.intel.com/intel/finance/corp_gov.html.

27. For example, see The best (& worst) managers of the year, 2003. *BusinessWeek,* January 13: 58–92; and Lavelle, M. 2003. Rogues of the year. *Time,* January 6: 33–45.

28. Handy, C. 2002. What's a business for? *Harvard Business Review,* 80(12): 49–55.

29. From Lewis, Russel T., "The CEO's Lot is Not a Happy One . . ." *Academy of Management Executive: The Thinking Manager's Source,* 16(4): 38–39, Copyright © 2002 by Academy of Management. Reproduced by permission of Academy of Management via Copyright Clearance Center.

30. For an interesting perspective on the changing role of boards of directors, refer to Lawler, E., & Finegold, D. 2005. Rethinking governance. *MIT Sloan Management Review,* 46(2): 67–70.

31. Stakeholder symbiosis. 1998. *Fortune,* March 30: S2.

32. For a definitive, recent discussion of the stakeholder concept, refer to Freeman, R. E., & McVae, J. 2001. A stakeholder approach to strategic management. In Hitt, M. A., Freeman, R. E., & Harrison, J. S. (Eds.). *Handbook of strategic management:* 189–207. Malden, MA: Blackwell.

33. Atkinson, A. A., Waterhouse, J. H., & Wells, R. B. 1997. A stakeholder approach to strategic performance measurement. *Sloan Management Review,* 39(3): 25–38.

34. For an insightful discussion on the role of business in society, refer to Handy, op. cit.

35. Stakeholder symbiosis. op. cit., p. S3.

36. Rucci, A. J., Kirn, S. P., & Quinn, R. T. 1998. The employee-customer-profit chain at Sears. *Harvard Business Review,* 76(1): 82–97.

37. An excellent theoretical discussion on stakeholder activity is Rowley, T. J., & Moldoveanu, M. 2003. When will stakeholder groups act? An interest- and identity-based model of stakeholder group mobilization. *Academy of Management Review,* 28(2): 204–219.

38. Thomas, J. G. 2000. Macroenvironmetal forces. In Helms, M. M. (Ed.), *Encyclopedia of management.* (4th ed.): 516–520. Farmington Hills, MI: Gale Group.

39. For a strong advocacy position on the need for corporate values and social responsibility, read Hollender, J. 2004. What matters most: Corporate values and social responsibility. *California Management Review,* 46(4): 111–119.

40. Waddock, S. & Bodwell, C. 2004. Managing responsibility: What can be learned from the quality movement. *California Management Review,* 47(1): 25–37.

41. For a discussion of the role of alliances and collaboration on corporate social responsibility initiatives, refer to Pearce, J. A. II., & Doh, J. P. 2005. The high impact of collaborative social initiatives. *MIT Sloan Management Review,* 46(3): 30–40.

42. Ibid.

43. Bhattacharya, C. B., & Sen, S. 2004, Doing better at doing good: When, why, and how consumers respond to corporate social initiatives. *California Management Review,* 47(1): 9–24.

44. Cone Corporate Citizenship Study, 2002, www.coneinc.com.

45. Refer to www.bsr.org.

46. Kanter, R. M. 1999. From spare change to real change. *Harvard Business Review,* 77(3): 122–132.
47. Ibid.
48. This section draws on Hart, S. L. 1997. Beyond greening: Strategies for a sustainable world. *Harvard Business Review,* 75(1): 66–76, and Berry, M. A. & Rondinelli, D. A. 1998. Proactive corporate environmental management: A new industrial revolution. *Academy of Management Executive,* 12(2): 38–50.
49. Hart, op. cit., p. 67.
50. For a creative perspective on environmental sustainability and competitive advantage as well as ethical implications, read Ehrenfeld, J. R. 2005. The roots of sustainability. *MIT Sloan Management Review,* 46(2): 23–25.
51. McKinsey & Company. 1991. *The corporate response to the environmental challenge.* Summary Report, Amsterdam: McKinsey & Company.
52. Holliday, C. 2001. Sustainable growth, the DuPont way. *Harvard Business Review,* 79(9): 129–134.
53. Senge, P. M. 1990. The leader's new work: Building learning organizations. *Sloan Management Review,* 32(1): 7–23.
54. Barkema, G. G., Baum, A. C., & Mannix, E. A. 2002. Management challenges in a new time. *Academy of Management Journal,* 45(5): 916–930.
55. This section draws upon a variety of sources, including Tetenbaum, T. J. 1998. Shifting paradigms: From Newton to chaos. *Organizational Dynamics,* 26(4): 21–33; Ulrich, D. 1998. A new mandate for human resources. *Harvard Business Review,* 76(1): 125–135; and Hitt, M. A. 2000. The new frontier: Transformation of management for the new millennium. *Organizational Dynamics,* 28(2): 7–17.
56. Garten, J. E. 2001. *The mind of the C.E.O.* New York: Basic Books.
57. An interesting discussion on the impact of AIDS on the global economy is found in Rosen, S. 2003. AIDS *is* your business. *Harvard Business Review,* 81(2): 80–87.
58. Weber, J. 1996. Mr. nice guy with a mission. *BusinessWeek,* November 25: 137.
59. Ulrich, D. 1998. Intellectual capital: Competence × commitment. *Strategic Management Journal,* 39(2): 15–26.
60. Stewart, T. A. 2000. Today's companies won't make it, and Gary Hamel knows why. *Fortune,* September 4: 390.
61. Rivette, K. G., & Kline, D. 2000. Discovering new value in intellectual property. *Harvard Business Review,* 78(1): 54–66.
62. For an interesting perspective on the role of middle managers in the strategic management process, refer to Huy, Q. H. 2001. In praise of middle managers. *Harvard Business Review,* 79(8): 72–81.
63. Senge, 1996, op. cit., pp. 41–58.
64. Helgesen, S. 1996. Leading from the grass roots. In Hesselbein, F., Goldsmith, M., & Beckhard, R. (Eds.), *The leader of the future:* 19–24. San Francisco: Jossey-Bass.
65. Wetlaufer, S. 1999. Organizing for empowerment: An interview with AES's Roger Sant and Dennis Blake. *Harvard Business Review,* 77(1): 110–126.
66. Kets de Vries, M. F. R. 1998. Charisma in action: The transformational abilities of Virgin's Richard Branson and ABB's Percy Barnevik. *Organizational Dynamics,* 26(3): 7–21.
67. Hammonds, K. H. 2000. The next agenda. *Fast Company,* April: 140.
68. Our discussion draws on a variety of sources. These include Lipton, M. 1996. Demystifying the development of an organizational vision. *Sloan Management Review,* 37(4): 83–92; Bart, C. K. 2000. Lasting inspiration. *CA Magazine,* May: 49–50; and Quigley, J. V. 1994. Vision: How leaders develop it, share it, and sustain it. *Business Horizons,* September–October: 37–40.
69. Lipton, op. cit.
70. Quigley, op. cit.
71. Ibid.
72. Lipton, op. cit. Additional pitfalls are addressed in this article.
73. Bruch, H., & Ghoshal, S. 2004. *A bias for action.* Boston: Harvard Business School Press.
74. Company records.
75. Lipton, op. cit.
76. Sexton, D. A., & Van Aukun, P. M. 1985. A longitudinal study of small business strategic planning. *Journal of Small Business Management,* January: 8–15, cited in Lipton, op. cit.
77. For an insightful perspective on the use of strategic objectives, refer to Chatterjee, S. 2005. Core objectives: Clarity in designing strategy. *California Management Review,* 47(2): 33–49.
78. Ibid.

Analyzing the External Environment of the Firm

>chapter objectives

After reading this chapter, you should have a good understanding of:

- The importance of developing forecasts of the business environment.

- Why environmental scanning, environmental monitoring, and collecting competitive intelligence are critical inputs to forecasting.

- Why scenario planning is a useful technique for firms competing in industries characterized by unpredictability and change.

- The impact of the general environment on a firm's strategies and performance.

- How forces in the competitive environment can affect profitability, and how a firm can improve its competitive position by increasing its power vis-à-vis these forces.

- How trends and events in the general environment and forces in the competitive environment are interrelated and affect performance.

- The concept of strategic groups and their strategy and performance implications.

*S*trategies are not and should not be developed in a vacuum. They must be responsive to the external business environment. Otherwise, your firm could become, in effect, the most efficient producer of buggy whips, leisure suits, or slide rules. To avoid such strategic mistakes, firms must become knowledgeable about the business environment. One tool for analyzing trends is forecasting. In the development of forecasts, environmental scanning and environmental monitoring are important in detecting key trends and events. Managers also must aggressively collect and disseminate competitor intelligence. The information gleaned from these three activities is invaluable in developing forecasts and scenarios to minimize present and future threats as well as to exploit opportunities. We address these issues in the first part of this chapter. We also introduce a basic tool of strategy analysis—the concept of SWOT analysis (strengths, weaknesses, opportunities, and threats).

In the second part of the chapter, we present two frameworks for analyzing the external environment—the general environment and the competitive environment. The general environment consists of six segments—demographic, sociocultural, political/legal, technological, economic, and global. Trends and events in these segments can have a dramatic impact on your firm. The competitive environment is closer to home. It consists of five industry-related factors that can dramatically affect the average level of industry profitability. An awareness of these factors is critical in making decisions such as which industries to enter and how to improve your firm's current position within an industry. This is helpful in neutralizing competitive threats and increasing power over customers and suppliers. We also address industry analysis from a dynamic perspective, which reflects the rapid, unpredictable changes that are taking place in many industries. In the final part of this section, we place firms within an industry into strategic groups based on similarities in resources and strategies. As we will see, the concept of strategic groups has important implications for the intensity of rivalry and how the effects of a given environmental trend or event differ across groups.

Having well-known brands for generations will not necessarily provide a company with a permanent guarantee of success. Such firms can run into trouble if they do not effectively respond to changes in customer demands and preferences. Consider, for example, the case of the $3.5 billion Interstate Bakeries Corporation (IBC).[1] The firm has been delivering sliced bread and other bakery products since the 1930s, and many of their brands have become American icons. These include snack foods such as Twinkies, Ding Dongs, and Zingers as well as Wonder Bread. For the recent fiscal year ending May 29, 2004, IBC had a loss of $25.8 million compared to a profit of $69.8 million over the previous 2 years. Unfortunately, along with the losses, a heavy debt load of more than $1.3 billion forced the company into bankruptcy in September 2004. What went wrong with Interstate Bakeries?

> Perhaps, IBC's major shortcoming was its seeming inability to keep its brands alive. "To not innovate is a death sentence, and nostalgia won't carry you through this," says Rick Bozzelli, merchandising manager for McCaffrey's Markets, a regional supermarket in Langhorne, Pennsylvania. Enamored with its past glory, IBC never really reinvented itself. Instead, it continued to flood the baked-goods aisle with its low-priced Wonder Bread, even as consumers were turning toward fresh-baked supermarket or specialty breads. Many of its rivals' products were focused on the consumer trend toward low-carbohydrate alternatives, made popular in recent years by the Atkins diet. It is estimated that 32 million American adults follow low-carb diets such as Atkins and South Beach. It wasn't until late 2004 that IBC introduced a line of low-carb breads under the "Home Pride Carb Action" name. By then, as the old cliché goes, it was "too little too late."
>
> IBC faced similar problems with its line of snack foods. Products like Twinkies are viewed as junk foods—a sugary snack that few adults would indulge in and one lacking in appeal to a generation of children who snack on products such as Gogurt (a popular children's yogurt product). As noted by Wendell Perkins, chief investment officer at Johnson Asset Management, "I look back on Dolly Madison and Twinkies fondly and romantically from my childhood, but a lot has changed since then, and the company had a difficult time keeping up with the times." And the growing concern about child obesity in the United States certainly hasn't helped sales. Concerning IBC's bankruptcy, Kelly Brownell, director of the Yale Center for Eating and Weight Disorders contends, "I don't think there's a nutritionist in America who will shed a tear over this."
>
> IBC also failed to cut its overhead costs. Thus, it was unable to offer bargain-basement prices that would have enabled the firm to push more aggressively into mass-market channels such as Wal-Mart Stores, Inc. and Target stores. In recent years there has been a greater consolidation in the grocery industry. As some large grocery and retail chains grow in size and become more dominant, their buying power increases. This places greater pricing power on manufacturers. Thus, IBC's unfavorable cost structure put them at a significant disadvantage.

To be a successful manager, you must recognize opportunities and threats in your firm's external environment. You must be aware of what's going on outside your company. If you focus exclusively on the efficiency of internal operations, your firm may degenerate into the world's most efficient producer of buggy whips or carbon paper. But if you miscalculate the market, opportunities will be lost—hardly an enviable position for you or your firm.

In their award-winning book *Competing for the Future,* Gary Hamel and C. K. Prahalad suggest that "every manager carries around in his or her head a set of biases, assumptions, and presuppositions about the structure of the relevant 'industry,' about how one makes money in the industry, about who the competition is and isn't, about who the customers are and aren't, and so on."[2] Environmental analysis requires you to continually question these assumptions. Peter Drucker labeled these interrelated sets of assumptions the "theory of the business."[3]

A firm's strategy may be good at one point in time, but it may go astray when management's frame of reference gets out of touch with the realities of the actual business situation. This results when management's assumptions, premises, or beliefs are incorrect or when internal inconsistencies among them render the overall "theory of the business" invalid. As Warren Buffett, investor extraordinaire, colorfully notes, "Beware of past performance 'proofs.' If history books were the key to riches, the Forbes 400 would consist of librarians." And Arthur Martinez, former chairman of Sears, Roebuck & Co., states, "Today's peacock is tomorrow's feather duster."

In the business world, many peacocks have become feather dusters or at least had their plumage dulled. Consider the high-tech company Novell, which has undergone hard times.[4] Novell went head-to-head with Microsoft and bought market-share loser WordPerfect to compete with Microsoft Word. The result was a $1.3 billion loss when Novell sold WordPerfect to Corel. And today we may wonder who will be the next Wang, Kmart, or *Encyclopaedia Britannica.*

>>Creating the Environmentally Aware Organization

So how do managers become environmentally aware?[5] We will now address three important processes—scanning, monitoring, and gathering competitive intelligence—that managers must use to develop forecasts. Exhibit 2.1 illustrates relationships among these important activities. We also will discuss the importance of scenario planning in anticipating major future changes in the external environment and the role of SWOT analysis.[6]

The Role of Scanning, Monitoring, Competitive Intelligence, and Forecasting

Environmental Scanning   Environmental scanning involves surveillance of a firm's external environment to predict environmental changes to come and to detect changes already under way.[7] Successful environmental scanning alerts the organization to critical trends and events before the changes have developed a discernible pattern and before competitors recognize them.[8] Otherwise, the firm may be forced into a reactive mode instead of being proactive.[9]

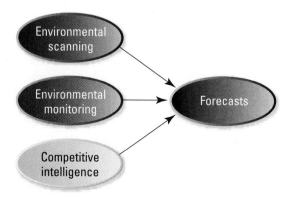

Exhibit 2.1   **Inputs to Forecasting**

Sir John Browne, chief executive officer of petroleum company BP Amoco, described in a speech the kind of environmental changes his company was experiencing.

> The next element of the change we've experienced is the growth in demand, and the changing nature of that demand. The world uses eight million more barrels of oil and 30 billion more cubic feet of natural gas every day than it did in the spring of 1990. The growth of natural gas in particular has been and continues to be spectacular, and I believe that change can legitimately be seen as part of a wider, longer-term shift to lighter, cleaner, less carbon-intensive fuels.[10]

Consider how difficult it would be for BP Amoco to develop strategies and allocate resources if it did not scan the external environment for such emerging changes in demand.

At times, your company may benefit from studies conducted by outside experts in a particular industry. A. T. Kearney, a large international consulting company, identified several key issues in the automobile industry, including:[11]

- *Globalization.* This is not a new trend but it has intensified, with enormous opportunities opening up in Asia, central and eastern Europe, and Latin America.
- *Time to Market.* Although some improvements have been made, there's still a gap between product development cycles in the United States and Europe compared to Japan. This gap may be widening as Japanese companies continue to make improvements.
- *Shifting Roles and Responsibilities.* Design responsibility, purchasing, and even project management and systems engineering are shifting from original equipment manufacturers to integrators/suppliers.

Consider how disadvantaged you would be as an executive in the global automobile industry if you were unaware of such trends.

Environmental Monitoring   Environmental monitoring tracks the evolution of environmental trends, sequences of events, or streams of activities. These are often uncovered during the environmental scanning process. They may be trends that the firm came across by accident or ones that were brought to its attention from outside the organization. Consider the automobile industry example. While environmental scanning may make you aware of the trends, they require close monitoring, which involves closer ongoing scrutiny. For example, you should closely monitor sales in Asia, central and eastern Europe, and Latin America. You should observe how fast Japanese companies and other competitors bring products to market compared with your firm. You should also study trends with your own suppliers/integrators in purchasing, project management, and systems engineering. Monitoring enables firms to evaluate how dramatically environmental trends are changing the competitive landscape.

One of the authors of this text recently conducted on-site interviews with executives from several industries to identify indicators that firms monitor as inputs to their strategy process. Examples of such indicators included:

- *A Motel 6 executive.* The number of rooms in the budget segment of the industry in the United States and the difference between the average daily room rate and the Consumer Price Index (CPI).
- *A Pier 1 Imports executive.* Net disposable income (NDI), consumer confidence index, and housing starts.
- *A Johnson & Johnson medical products executive.* Percentage of gross domestic product (GDP) spent on health care, number of active hospital beds, and the size and power of purchasing agents (indicates the concentration of buyers).

Such indices are critical for managers in determining a firm's strategic direction and resource allocation.

Competitive Intelligence *Is* . . .	Competitive Intelligence *Is Not* . . .
1. **Information** that has been analyzed to the point where you can make a decision.	1. **Spying.** Spying implies illegal or unethical activities. It is a rare activity, since most corporations do not want to find themselves in court or to upset shareholders.
2. **A tool** to alert management to early recognition of both threats and opportunities.	2. **A crystal ball.** CI gives corporations good approximations of short- and long-term reality. It does not predict the future.
3. **A means to deliver reasonable assessments.** CI offers approximations of the market and competition. It is not a peek at a rival's financial books. Reasonable assessments are what modern entrepreneurs need and want on a regular basis.	3. **Database search.** Databases offer just that—data. They do not massage or analyze the data in any way. They certainly don't replace human beings who make decisions by examining the data and applying their common sense, experience, and intuition.
4. **A way of life, a process.** If a company uses CI the way it should be used, it becomes everyone's job, not just the strategic planning or marketing staff's. It is a process by which critical information is available to those who need it.	4. **A job for one smart person.** A CEO may appoint one person as the CI ringmaster, but one person cannot do it all. At best, the ringmaster can keep management informed and ensure that others become trained to apply this tool within their business units.

Exhibit 2.2
What Competitive Intelligence Is and Is Not!

Sources: Imperato, G. 1998. Competitive intelligence—Get smart! *Fast Company,* April: 26–29; and Fuld, F. M. What competitive intelligence is and is not! www.fuld.com/whatCI.html.

Competitive Intelligence   Competitive intelligence (CI) helps firms define and understand their industry and identify rivals' strengths and weaknesses.[12] This includes the intelligence gathering associated with collecting data on competitors and interpreting such data for managerial decision making. Done properly, competitive intelligence helps a company avoid surprises by anticipating competitors' moves and decreasing response time.[13]

Examples of competitive analysis are evident in daily newspapers and periodicals such as *The Wall Street Journal, BusinessWeek,* and *Fortune.* For example, banks continually track home loan, auto loan, and certificate of deposit (CD) interest rates charged by peers in a given geographic region. Major airlines change hundreds of fares daily in response to competitors' tactics. Car manufacturers are keenly aware of announced cuts or increases in rivals' production volume, sales, and sales incentives (e.g., rebates and low interest rates on financing). They use this information to plan their own marketing, pricing, and production strategies. Exhibit 2.2 provides some insights on what CI is (and what it isn't).

The Internet has dramatically accelerated the speed at which firms can find competitive intelligence. Leonard Fuld, founder of the Cambridge, Massachusetts, training and consulting firm Fuld & Co., specializes in competitive intelligence.[14] His firm often

STRATEGY SPOTLIGHT

Ethical Guidelines on Competitive Intelligence: United Technologies

United Technologies (UT) is a $28 billion global conglomerate composed of world-leading businesses with rich histories of technological pioneering, such as Otis Elevator, Carrier Air Conditioning, and Sikorsky (helicopters). It was founded in 1853 and has an impressive history of technological accomplishments. UT built the first working helicopter, developed the first commercially available hydrogen cells, and designed complete life support systems for space shuttles. UT believes strongly in a robust code of ethics. In the last decade, they have clearly articulated their principles governing business conduct. These include an antitrust guide, an ethics guide when contracting with the U.S. government and foreign governments, a policy on accepting gifts from suppliers, and guidelines for proper usage of e-mail. One such document is the Code of Ethics Guide on Competitive Intelligence. This encourages managers and workers to ask themselves these five questions whenever they have ethical concerns.

1. Have I done anything that coerced somebody to share this information? Have I, for example, threatened a supplier by indicating that future business opportunities will be influenced by the receipt of information with respect to a competitor?

2. Am I in a place where I should not be? If, for example, I am a field representative with privileges to move around in a customer's facility, have I gone outside the areas permitted? Have I misled anybody in order to gain access?

3. Is the contemplated technique for gathering information evasive, such as sifting through trash or setting up an electronic "snooping" device directed at a competitor's facility from across the street?

4. Have I misled somebody in a way that the person believed sharing information with me was required or would be protected by a confidentiality agreement? Have I, for example, called and misrepresented myself as a government official who was seeking some information for some official purpose?

5. Have I done something to evade or circumvent a system intended to secure or protect information?

Sources: Nelson, B. 2003. The thinker. *Forbes*, March 3: 62–64; and The Fuld war room—Survival kit 010. Code of Ethics (printed 2/26/01).

profiles top company and business group managers and considers these issues: What is their background? What is their style? Are they marketers? Are they cost cutters? Fuld has found that the more articles he collects and the more biographies he downloads, the better he can develop profiles.

One of Fuld & Co.'s clients needed to know if a rival was going to start competing more aggressively on costs. Fuld's analysts tracked down articles from the Internet and a local newspaper profile of the rival firm's CEO. The profile said the CEO had taken a bus to a nearby town to visit one of the firm's plants. Fuld claimed, "Those few words were a small but important sign to me that this company was going to be incredibly cost-conscious." Another client retained Fuld to determine the size, strength, and technical capabilities of a privately held company. Initially, it was difficult to get detailed information. Then one analyst used Deja News (www.dejanews.com), now part of Google, to tap into some online discussion groups. The analyst's research determined that the company had posted 14 job openings on one Usenet group. That posting was a road map to the competitor's development strategy.

At times, a firm's aggressive efforts to gather competitive intelligence may lead to unethical or illegal behaviors.[15] Strategy Spotlight 2.1 provides an example of a company, United Technologies, that has set clear guidelines to help prevent unethical behavior.

A word of caution: Executives must be careful to avoid spending so much time and effort tracking the actions of traditional competitors that they ignore new competitors. Further, broad changes and events in the larger environment may have a dramatic impact on a firm's viability. Peter Drucker, whom many consider the father of modern management, wrote:

> Increasingly, a winning strategy will require information about events and conditions outside the institution: noncustomers, technologies other than those currently used by the company and its present competitors, markets not currently served, and so on.[16]

Consider the fall of the once-mighty *Encyclopaedia Britannica*.[17] Its demise was not caused by a traditional competitor in the encyclopedia industry. It was caused by new technology. CD-ROMs came out of nowhere and devastated the printed encyclopedia industry. Why? A full set of the *Encyclopaedia Britannica* sells for about $2,000, but an encyclopedia on CD-ROM, such as Microsoft *Encarta*, sells for about $50. To make matters worse, many people receive *Encarta* free with their personal computers.

Environmental Forecasting   Environmental scanning, monitoring, and competitive intelligence are important inputs for analyzing the external environment. However, they are of little use unless they provide raw material that is reliable enough to help managers make accurate forecasts. Environmental forecasting involves the development of plausible projections about the direction, scope, speed, and intensity of environmental change.[18] Its purpose is to predict change. It asks: How long will it take a new technology to reach the marketplace? Will the present social concern about an issue result in new legislation? Are current lifestyle trends likely to continue?

Some forecasting issues are much more specific to a particular firm and the industry in which it competes. Consider how important it is for Motel 6 to predict future indicators, such as the number of rooms, in the budget segment of the industry. If its predictions are low, it will build too many units, creating a surplus of room capacity that would drive down room rates. Similarly, if Pier 1 Imports is overly optimistic in its forecast of future net disposable income and U.S. housing starts, it will order too much inventory and later be forced to discount merchandise drastically.

A danger of forecasting is that managers may view uncertainty as black and white and ignore important gray areas. Either they assume that the world is certain and open to precise predictions, or they assume it is uncertain and completely unpredictable.[19] The problem is that underestimating uncertainty can lead to strategies that neither defend against threats nor take advantage of opportunities. In 1977 one of the colossal underestimations in business history occurred when Kenneth H. Olsen, then president of Digital Equipment Corp., announced, "There is no reason for individuals to have a computer in their home." The explosion in the personal computer market was not easy to detect in 1977, but it was clearly within the range of possibilities that industry experts were discussing at the time. And, historically, there have been underestimates of the growth potential of new telecommunication services. The electric telegraph was derided by Ralph Waldo Emerson, and the telephone had its skeptics. More recently, an "infamous" McKinsey study in the early 1980s predicted that there would be fewer than 1 million cellular users in the United States by the year 2000. Actually, there were nearly 100 million.[20]

At the other extreme, if managers assume the world is unpredictable, they may abandon the analytical rigor of their traditional planning process and base strategic decisions on gut instinct. Such a "just do it" approach may cause executives to place misinformed bets on emerging products or markets that result in record write-offs. Entrepreneurs and venture capitalists who took the plunge and invested in questionable Internet ventures in the late 1990s provide many examples.

A more in-depth approach to forecasting involves scenario analysis. Scenario analysis draws on a range of disciplines and interests, among them economics, psychology, sociology, and demographics. It usually begins with a discussion of participants'

STRATEGY SPOTLIGHT

Scenario Planning at Shell Oil Company

Preparing to cope with uncertainty is one of the biggest strategic challenges faced by most businesses. There are few tools for coping with strategic uncertainty, especially over medium- to long-term horizons. One technique that has proved its usefulness is scenario planning.

Scenario planning is different from other tools for strategic planning such as trend analysis or high and low forecasts. The origins of scenario planning lie with the military, which used it to cope effectively with multiple challenges and limited resources.

In the 1960s and 1970s, Shell combined analytical tools with information to create scenarios of possible outcomes. The result of the 1973 oil embargo was a sharp increase in crude oil prices, short supplies of gasoline for consumers, and a depressed world economy. However, Shell's strategic planning, including the use of scenarios, had strongly suggested that a more unstable environment was coming, with a shift of power from oil companies to oil producers. As a result of the precautionary actions it took, Shell was in a better position than most oil companies when the 1973 embargo occurred. Shell also uses scenario planning to plan major new oil field investments because elements of risk can be identified and explored over a considerable period of time.

The Shell process of scenario planning involves the following stages:

1. Interviews with people both inside and outside the business, using an open-ended questioning technique to encourage full and frank answers.

2. Analysis of interviews by issue in order to build a "natural agenda" for further processing.

3. Synthesis of each agenda to draw out underlying areas of uncertainty/dispute and possible interrelationships among issues.

4. A small number of workshops to explore key issues to improve understanding and identify gaps for further research. These generate a wide range of strategy options.

5. A workshop to identify and build a small number of scenarios that may occur in the next 10 to 15 years or even later.

6. A testing of strategy options against the scenarios in order to assess robustness (i.e., whether or not a given strategy is effective under more than one scenario).

Other practitioners of scenario planning include Levi Strauss, which uses scenario planning to consider potential impacts of everything from cotton deregulation to the total disappearance of cotton from this planet. Also, a German insurance company anticipated the fall of the Berlin wall and made plans to expand in central Europe. And in 1990 when Nelson Mandela was released from a South African prison, he met with a panel that helped him create scenarios to chart out the country's future. Scenario planning helps by considering not just trends or forecasts but also how they could be upset by events and the outcomes that may result.

Sources: Martin, R. 2002. The oracles of oil. *Business 2.0*, January: 35–39; www.touchstonerenard.co.uk/Expertise/Strategy/Scenario_Planning/scenario_planning.htm; and Epstein, J. 1998. Scenario planning: An introduction. *The Futurist*, September: 50–52.

thoughts on ways in which societal trends, economics, politics, and technology may affect the issue under discussion.[21] For example, consider Lego. The popular Danish toy manufacturer has a strong position in the construction toys market. But what would happen if this broadly defined market should change dramatically? After all, Lego is competing not only with producers of similar products but also on a much broader canvas for a share of children's playtime. In this market, Lego has a host of competitors, many of them computer based; still others have not yet been invented. Lego may end up with an increasing share of a narrow, shrinking market (much like IBM in the declining days of the mainframe computer). To avoid such a fate, managers must consider their future in a wider context than their narrow, traditional markets. They need to lay down guidelines for at least 10 years in the future to anticipate rapid change. Strategy Spotlight 2.2 provides an example of scenario planning at Shell Oil Company.

SWOT Analysis

To understand the business environment of a particular firm, you need to analyze both the general environment and the firm's industry and competitive environment. Generally, firms compete with other firms in the same industry. An industry is composed of a set of firms that produce similar products or services, sell to similar customers, and use similar methods of production. Gathering industry information and understanding competitive dynamics among the different companies in your industry is key to successful strategic management.

One of the most basic techniques for analyzing firm and industry conditions is SWOT analysis. SWOT stands for strengths, weaknesses, opportunities, and threats. SWOT analysis provides a framework for analyzing these four elements of a company's internal and external environment. It provides "raw material"—a basic listing of conditions both inside and surrounding your company. The strengths and weaknesses portion of SWOT refers to the internal conditions of a firm—where your firm excels (strengths) and where it may be lacking relative to competitors (weaknesses). We will address strengths and weaknesses again in Chapter 3. Opportunities and threats are environmental conditions external to the firm. These could be factors in the general environment, such as improving economic conditions, that cause lower borrowing costs or trends that benefit some companies and harm others. An example is the heightened concern with fitness, which is a threat to some companies (e.g., tobacco) and an opportunity to others (e.g., health clubs). Opportunities and threats are also present in the competitive environment among firms competing for the same customers.

>>The General Environment

The general environment is composed of factors that can have dramatic effects on firm strategy.[22] Typically, a firm has little ability to predict trends and events in the general environment and even less ability to control them. When listening to CNBC, for example, you can hear many experts espouse totally different perspectives on what action the Federal Reserve Board may take on short-term interest rates—an action that can have huge effects on the valuation of entire economic sectors. Also, it's difficult to predict future political events such as the ongoing Middle East peace negotiations and tensions on the Korean peninsula. In addition, who would have guessed the Internet's impact on national and global economies in the past decade or two? Such dramatic innovations in information technology (e.g., the Internet) have helped keep inflation in check by lowering the cost of doing business in the United States at the beginning of the 21st century.

We divide the general environment into six segments: demographic, sociocultural, political/legal, technological, economic, and global. First, we discuss each segment and provide a summary of the segment and examples of how events and trends can impact industries. Second, we address relationships among the general environment segments. Third, we consider how trends and events can vary across industries. Exhibit 2.3 provides examples of key trends and events in each of the six segments of the general environment.

The Demographic Segment

Demographics are the most easily understood and quantifiable elements of the general environment. They are at the root of many changes in society. Demographics include elements such as the aging population,[23] rising or declining affluence, changes in ethnic composition, geographic distribution of the population, and disparities in income level.

The impact of a demographic trend, like all segments of the general environment, varies across industries. The aging of the U.S. population has had a positive effect on the health care industry but a negative impact on the industry that produces diapers and

Exhibit 2.3
General
Environment: Key
Trends and Events

Demographic

- Aging population
- Rising affluence
- Changes in ethnic composition
- Geographic distribution of population
- Greater disparities in income levels

Sociocultural

- More women in the workforce
- Increase in temporary workers
- Greater concern for fitness
- Greater concern for environment
- Postponement of family formation

Political/Legal

- Tort reform
- Americans with Disabilities Act (ADA) of 1990
- Repeal of Glass-Steagall Act in 1999 (banks may now offer brokerage services)
- Deregulation of utility and other industries
- Increases in federally mandated minimum wages
- Taxation at local, state, federal levels
- Legislation on corporate governance reforms in bookkeeping, stock options, etc. (Sarbanes-Oxley Act of 2002)

Technological

- Genetic engineering
- Emergence of Internet technology
- Computer-aided design/computer-aided manufacturing systems (CAD/CAM)
- Research in synthetic and exotic materials
- Pollution/global warming
- Miniaturization of computing technologies
- Wireless communications
- Nanotechnology

Economic

- Interest rates
- Unemployment rates
- Consumer Price Index
- Trends in GDP
- Changes in stock market valuations

Global

- Increasing global trade
- Currency exchange rates
- Emergence of the Indian and Chinese economies
- Trade agreements among regional blocs (e.g., NAFTA, EU, ASEAN)
- Creation of WTO (leading to decreasing tariffs/free trade in services)

2.3 STRATEGY SPOTLIGHT

Older Employees: An Increasingly Important Demographic Segment of Today's Workforce

The U.S. Bureau of Labor Statistics states that only 13 percent of American workers were 55 and older in 2000. However, by 2006 that figure will increase to 15 percent, and by 2015, 20 percent, or one in five, of all U.S. workers will be 55 or older. At the same time, the United States is expected to experience a significant drop in the percentage of younger workers ages 25 to 44, making it increasingly important for employers to find ways to recruit and retain older workers. Similarly, the National Association of Manufacturing estimates that as baby boomers continue retiring and the economy grows, the United States will have 7 million more jobs than workers by 2010. Some firms have discovered an important part of the answer to this labor shortfall: luring older workers back into their ranks.

Home Depot, the $65 billion retailer, has been partnering with the American Association of Retired Persons (AARP) to recruit more than 700 older employees—not for menial jobs, but as sales associates and managers who can help customers navigate Home Depot's towering, intimidating shelves. "We want them to have technical depth," says Cindy Milburn, Home Depot's senior hiring director. "That means plumbers, carpenters, electricians, people with millwork backgrounds, and people with design skills."

Home Depot says that there are many advantages to hiring older workers. The firm says that they stay on the job longer and don't take as many sick days as younger workers. More than two dozen companies—including Anheuser-Busch, Barnes & Noble, and Sears—are now exploring similar partnerships with the AARP.

Sources: Warner, M. 2004. Home Depot goes old school. *Business 2.0,* June: 74; and, O'Brien, S. 2005. Over 50 and looking for work? www.seniorliving. about.com.

baby food. Rising levels of affluence in many developed countries bode well for brokerage services as well as for upscale pets and supplies. However, these same trends may have an adverse effect on fast food restaurants because people can afford to dine at higher-priced restaurants. Fast-food restaurants depend on minimum-wage employees to operate efficiently, but the competition for labor intensifies as more attractive employment opportunities become prevalent, thus threatening the employment base for restaurants. Let's look at the details of some of these trends.

The aging population in the United States and other developed countries has important implications. With the graying of baby boomers, the demand for homes for "active elders" (as home developers refer to retirees) is bound to soar. The National Association of Home Builders estimates that people in the 55 to 74 age group will buy 281,000 homes in 2010, up from 189,000 in 1995.[24] This provides an opportunity for developers who focus on that segment of the construction industry. Another long-term projection is that by the year 2025, nearly one-fifth of the American population will be 65 or older. This may be good news for baby boomers, because there is always strength in numbers (especially in the political arena). It's also good news for drugstores, which see older patients seven times more often than younger ones.[25] Strategy Spotlight 2.3 addresses the important implications of older workers for today's workforce.

Another demographic trend is the shift in the geographic population of the United States. Although the population increased by about 13 percent (from 248 million to 281 million) during the 1990s, this growth was not evenly distributed.[26] Strong growth in the South and West—spurred in large part by an increase in the Hispanic population and relocation to economic hot spots such as Atlanta and Las Vegas—was offset by slowing growth in the North and Midwest. The resulting redistribution affects two other environmental segments: the economic well-being of those regions and the political/legal population-based representation in the U.S. House of Representatives.

The Sociocultural Segment

Sociocultural forces influence the values, beliefs, and lifestyles of a society. Examples include a higher percentage of women in the workforce, dual-income families, increases in the number of temporary workers, greater concern for healthy diets and physical fitness, greater interest in the environment, and postponement of having children. Such forces enhance sales of products and services in many industries but depress sales in others. The increased number of women in the workforce has increased the need for business clothing merchandise but decreased the demand for baking product staples (since people would have less time to cook from scratch). A greater concern for health and fitness has had differential effects. This trend has helped industries that manufacture exercise equipment and healthful foods but harmed industries that produce unhealthful foods.

The trend toward increased educational attainment by women in the workplace has led to an increase in the number of women in upper management positions. U.S. Department of Education statistics show that women have become the dominant holders of college degrees. Based on figures of a recent graduating class, women with bachelor's degrees will outnumber their male counterparts by 27 percent. By the class of 2006–2007, the gap should surge to 38 percent. Additionally, throughout the 1990s the number of women earning MBAs increased by 29 percent compared to only 15 percent for men.[27] Given these educational attainments, it is hardly surprising that companies owned by women have been one of the driving forces of the U.S. economy; these companies (now more than 9 million in number) account for 40 percent of all U.S. businesses and have generated more than $3.6 trillion in annual revenue. In addition, women have a tremendous impact on consumer spending decisions. Not surprisingly, many companies have focused their advertising and promotion efforts on female consumers. We address this issue in Strategy Spotlight 2.4.

The Political/Legal Segment

Political processes and legislation influence the environmental regulations with which industries must comply.[28] Some important elements of the political/legal arena include tort reform, the Americans with Disabilities Act (ADA) of 1990, the repeal of the Glass-Steagall Act in 1999 (banks may now offer brokerage services), deregulation of utilities and other industries, and increases in the federally mandated minimum wage.

As with many factors in the general environment, changes that benefit one industry may damage others. For example, tort reform (legislation designed to limit the liability of defendants in the litigation process) may be good for industries such as automobile and tire manufacturers. Witness the litigation associated with Firestone tires and Ford Explorers, for example. However, tort reform will be bad for law firms, whose fees are often linked to the size of a settlement. Many have argued that without significant tort reform, large jury awards are a constant threat to companies and lead to higher consumer prices. On the other hand, the possibility of large judgments influences companies to act in a more ethical manner. The Americans with Disabilities Act has had a profound impact on industries. Companies with more than 15 employees must provide reasonable accommodations for employees and customers, which increases their construction and maintenance costs, but companies manufacturing elevators, escalators, and ramps have benefited from such legislation.

Government legislation can also have a significant impact on the governance of corporations. The U.S. Congress passed the Sarbanes-Oxley Act in 2002, which greatly increases the accountability of auditors, executives, and corporate lawyers. This act was a response to the widespread perception that existing governance mechanisms have failed

STRATEGY SPOTLIGHT

The Impact of Women on Consumer Spending Decisions

Although women may be paid less than men and may make it to the CEO suite less often, the U.S. economy is more and more female-driven. U.S. women account for about $3.3 trillion in annual consumer spending and $1.5 trillion more in business expenditures, according to Tom Peters's latest book, *Re-Imagine*. Women also comprise 47 percent of individuals with assets over $500,000 and 51.3 percent of the private wealth in the United States. According to Peters, ". . . women are not a niche. At 51 percent of the population, women are the majority. Second, in most households, the real story is that even though they're 'only' 51 percent of the population, women represent more like 80 percent of the purchasing power." Most consumer companies know that women are the key decision makers for household goods: 80 percent is the rule of thumb used by many consumer goods companies as the percentage of purchases made by women. According to Martha Barletta, CEO of Trendsight Group, women decide 92 percent of vacation plans, 62 percent of car purchases, and 52 percent of home-improvement projects.

Not surprisingly, many traditional male-oriented industries are getting in touch with their feminine sides.

Home Depot, for example, spent $1 billion in 2004 to add softer lighting and brighter signs in 300 stores. Why? It is an effort to match rival Lowe's long-standing appeal to women. And Best Buy, recognizing that women purchase 55 percent of electronics items, will add personal-shopping assistants in some stores to explain "geek speak" with which some women (and, of course, some men as well!) may not be familiar.

Companies, however, need to make sure they don't overplay the gender card. "A very important part of the home-improvement business is still more down-market, more male," says Geoff Wissman, an analyst at Retail Forward, a retail consultancy in Columbus, Ohio. After all, one-fourth of sales at home-improvement retailers come from contractors, who are predominantly male. The key is to figure out a balance between men's and women's interests.

Wilkesboro (North Carolina)-based Lowe's has found that women prefer to do larger home-improvement projects with a man—be it a boyfriend, husband, or neighbor. As a result, in addition to its "recipe card classes" (that explain various projects that take only one weekend), Lowe's offers co-ed store clinics for projects like sink installation. "Women like to feel they're given the same attention as a male customer," states Lowe's spokesperson Julie Valeant-Yenichek, who points out that most seminar attendees, whether male or female, are inexperienced.

Sources: Tsao, A. 2005. Retooling home improvement. *Businessweek.com*. February 14; Grow, B. 2004. Who wears the wallet in the family? *BusinessWeek*, August 16: 10.

---

to protect the interests of shareholders, employees, and creditors. Perhaps it is not too surprising that Sarbanes-Oxley has also created a tremendous demand for professional accounting services. We address this trend in Strategy Spotlight 2.5.

Legislation also helps companies in the high-tech sector of the economy by expanding the number of temporary visas available for highly skilled foreign professionals. For example, a bill passed in October 2000 allows 195,000 H-1B visas in each of the next three years, up from the cap of only 115,000 in 2000. The allotment for the year 2000 was used up by March, and the cap decreased to 107,500 for 2001 and a mere 65,000 each year thereafter (at least through 2005). Almost half of the visas are for professionals from India, and most of them are computer or software specialists.[29] For U.S. labor and workers' rights groups, however, the issue was a political hot potato.

The Technological Segment

Developments in technology lead to new products and services and improve how they are produced and delivered to the end user. Innovations can create entirely new industries and alter the boundaries of existing industries.[30] Examples of technological developments and trends are genetic engineering, Internet technology, computer-aided design/computer-aided manufacturing (CAD/CAM), research in artificial and exotic

STRATEGY SPOTLIGHT

The Sarbanes-Oxley Act: A Boon for Accountants

Government regulation is often prompted as elected officials respond to voters' expectations. When faced with a crisis, voters often demand a solution and expect elected officials to provide one. If the politicians fail to deliver, they suffer in the next election. Consider some of the historical examples of how the U.S. government has reacted to ethical disasters with the blunt force of increased legislation.

- The creation of the Securities and Exchange Commission (SEC) and other legislation following the stock market crash of 1929.

- The Foreign Corrupt Practices Act of 1977, which followed Lockheed's bribes to government officials.

- In the wake of the Enron, WorldCom, and Andersen debacles, Congress passed the Sarbanes-Oxley Act on July 30, 2002. (The law was passed just 35 days after WorldCom announced that it had overstated its revenues by at least $3.8 billion.)

Sources: Arndt, M. 2004. A boon for bean counters. *BusinessWeek*, November 22: 13; Thomas, T., Schermerhorn, R. R., Jr., & Dienhart, J. W. 2004. Strategic leadership of ethical behavior in business. *The Academy of Management Executive*, 18(2): 56–68.

Accounting firms have really benefited from the Sarbanes-Oxley Act. They had lobbied hard to keep the act from being passed. But, fortunately for them, they lost!

Companies are working hard to comply with Section 404 of the act. The provision requires publicly traded corporations to vouch for internal financial controls and remedy problems. A recent survey by Financial Executives International (FEI) finds that, on average, companies will spend $3.1 million and 30,700 hours to comply—nearly double the estimates of an earlier poll.

Much of that expense goes to privately held accounting firms. Audit fees are expected to surge more than 50 percent, according to FEI. To deal with the increased business, the Big Four accounting firms are in a hiring frenzy and logging lots of overtime. For example, KPMG has added 850 auditors in 2004, while PricewaterhouseCoopers (PWC) has hired 400 people from English-speaking foreign countries as temporary employees. "It's a scramble," say Dennis Nally, PWC's U.S. senior partner. It seems every cloud has a silver lining.

---

materials, and, on the downside, pollution and global warming. Firms in the petroleum and primary metals industries incur significant expenses to reduce the amount of pollution they produce. Engineering and consulting firms that work with polluting industries derive financial benefits from solving such problems.

Another important technological development is the combination of information technology (IT) and the Internet. By the end of 2000, productivity in the United States was increasing at an annual rate of 5.7 percent. This represents the fastest pace in 35 years—double the historical average of 2 to 3 percent per year. According to a study conducted jointly by Harvard University and the Federal Reserve, IT is responsible for almost half of the rapid productivity gains in recent years. It also has helped offset the inflationary effects of wage increases.[31]

The Internet has reduced the cost of getting information and increased its availability, boosting company profits. How are these costs reduced? Consider two examples. The National Association of Purchasing Managers pinpoints the cost of an average in-store purchase to be $79. However, Commerce One believes the proper use of the Internet can cut it to $6. Similarly, Fidelity Investments has found that it costs $15 to handle a transaction over the phone but less than a cent to perform that same transaction on the Web.

Nanotechnology is becoming a very promising area of research with many potentially useful applications.[32] Nanotechnology takes place at industry's tiniest stage: one billionth of a meter. Remarkably, this is the size of 10 hydrogen atoms in a row.

Researchers have discovered that matter at such a tiny scale behaves very differently. While some of the science behind this phenomenon is still shrouded in mystery, the commercial potential is coming sharply into focus. Familiar materials—from gold to carbon soot—display starting and useful new properties. Some transmit light or electricity.

Exhibit 2.4
**Nanotechnology:
Some Future
Applications**

Groundbreaking advances in nanotechnology are expected to spread through the economy, shaking up entire industries.

	Vision	Prognosis
FIGHT CANCER	Sensors will be able to detect a single cancer cell and will help guide nanoparticles that can burn tumors from the inside out, leaving healthy cells alone.	Diagnostics will hit the market within three years, but treatments carry far higher risk. Testing and government approvals will delay them for the next decade.
TRANSFORM ENERGY	Nano-enhanced solar panels will feed cheap electricity onto supercon-ducting power lines made of carbon nanotubes.	Next-generation panels will emerge this decade in Japan, which leads in the technology and suffers from higher energy prices.
REPLACE SILICON	Carbon nanotubes will take over when silicon peters out, leading to far faster chips that need less power than today's.	IBM has built working nanocircuits. But in the factory, chipmakers must be able to make billions of them. The transition is unlikely before 2015.
TRAVEL TO SPACE	Podlike crawlers will carry cargo thousands of miles up a carbon-nanotube cable to a space station for billions less than rocket launches.	Today the longest nan-otubes are mere millime-ters. To make miles of cable, scientists must learn how to weave these into threads. A working cable is at least 20 years away.

Source: From Baker, S., & Aston, A. 2004. "Universe in a grain of sand." *BusinessWeek,* October 11: 138–140. Reprinted with permission.

Others become harder than diamonds or turn into potent chemical catalysts. What's more, researchers have found that a tiny dose of nanoparticles can transform the chemistry and nature of far bigger things, creating everything from stronger fenders to superefficient fuel cells. Exhibit 2.4 addresses some of the promising future applications of this emerging science.

There are downsides to technology. In addition to ethical issues in biotechnology, there are threats to our environment associated with the emission of greenhouse gases. To combat such problems, some firms in the petroleum industry take a proactive approach. BP Amoco plans to decrease its greenhouse gas emissions by giving each of its 150 business units a quota of emission permits and encouraging the units to trade them. If a unit cuts emissions and has leftover permits, it can sell them to other units that are having difficulty meeting their goals. For example, Julie Hardwick, manager at the Naperville, Illinois, petrochemical division, saved up permits by fast-tracking a fur-nace upgrade that allowed elimination of a second furnace.[33]

The Economic Segment

The economy has an impact on all industries, from suppliers of raw materials to manufacturers of finished goods and services, as well as all organizations in the service, wholesale, retail, government, and nonprofit sectors. Key economic indicators include interest rates, unemployment rates, the Consumer Price Index, the gross domestic product, and net disposable income. Interest-rate increases have a negative impact on the residential home construction industry but a negligible (or neutral) effect on industries that produce consumer necessities such as prescription drugs or common grocery items.

Other economic indicators are associated with equity markets. Perhaps the most watched is the Dow Jones Industrial Average (DJIA), which is composed of 30 large industrial firms. When stock market indexes increase, consumers' discretionary income rises and there is often an increased demand for luxury items such as jewelry and automobiles. But when stock valuations decrease, demand for these items shrinks.

Despite the recent mediocre stock market and overall economic performance in the United States, the housing sector continued to be one of the bright spots. This is mainly due to a series of interest rate cuts by the Federal Reserve which, by mid-2003, led to the lowest mortgage rates since World War II.

The Global Segment

There is an increasing trend for firms to expand their operations and market reach beyond the borders of their "home" country. Globalization provides both opportunities to access larger potential markets and a broad base of factors of production such as raw materials, labor, skilled managers, and technical professionals. However, such endeavors also carry many political, social, and economic risks.

Examples of important elements in the global segment include currency exchange rates, increasing global trade, the economic emergence of China, trade agreements among regional blocs (e.g., North American Free Trade Agreement, European Union), and the General Agreement on Tariffs and Trade (GATT) (lowering of tariffs). Increases in trade across national boundaries also provide benefits to air cargo and shipping industries but have a minimal impact on service industries such as bookkeeping and routine medical services. The emergence of China as an economic power has benefited many industries, such as construction, soft drinks, and computers. However, it has had a negative impact on the defense industry in the United States as diplomatic relations between the two nations improve.

Few industries are as global as the automobile industry. Consider just a few examples of how some of the key players expanded their reach into Latin America during the 1990s. Fiat built a new plant in Argentina, Volkswagen retooled a plant in Mexico to launch the New Beetle, DaimlerChrysler built a new plant as a joint venture with BMW to produce engines in Brazil, and General Motors built a new car factory in Brazil. Why the interest? In addition to the region's low wage rates and declining trade barriers, the population of 400 million is very attractive. But the real bonus lies in the 9-to-1 ratio of people to cars in the region compared to a 2-to-1 ratio in developed countries. With this region's growth expected to be in the 3 to 4 percent range for the first part of the century, sales should increase at a healthy rate.[34]

The extent of globalization is illustrated by the Norwegian shipping industry. Despite a small population of only 4.5 million, Norway developed the world's third-largest merchant fleet. And as the world's second-largest oil exporter, it has the vessels and equipment needed to service oil fields off its storm-swept coast. When the warship *USS Cole* was severely damaged by terrorists on October 12, 2000, it was returned to the United States from Yemen aboard a giant Norwegian-owned transport ship, the *Blue Marlin*. According to Frederik Steenbuch, manager of Oslo-based Offshore Heavy Transport, which owns the *Blue Marlin,* "This has nothing to do with Norway. It is purely international. The *Blue Marlin* was built in Taiwan, flies a Panamanian flag, and has a crew from Latvia. The key machinery on board was built in Korea under a Danish license."[35]

Relationships among Elements of the General Environment

In our discussion of the general environment, we see many relationships among the various elements.[36] For example, two demographic trends in the United States, the aging of the population and regional population shifts, have important implications for the economic segment (in terms of tax policies to provide benefits to increasing numbers of older citizens) and the political segment (because the redistribution of seats in the U.S. House of Representatives among the states increases the power of some states and reduces the power of others). Another example is the emergence of information technology as a means to increase the rate of productivity gains in the United States and other developed countries. Such use of IT results in lower inflation (an important element of the economic segment) and helps offset costs associated with higher labor rates.

Maquiladoras are manufacturing and exporting assembly plants located in Mexico that are typically owned by United States, Japanese, and European companies. Their emergence, decline, and reemergence over time illustrate how many elements of the general environment can be highly interrelated. We address this issue in Strategy Spotlight 2.6.

The effects of a trend or event in the general environment vary across industries. Governmental legislation (political/legal event) to permit the importation of prescription drugs from foreign countries is a very positive development for drugstores but a very negative event for drug manufacturers in the United States. Exhibit 2.5 on page 59 provides other examples of how the impact of trends or events in the general environment can vary across industries.

>>The Competitive Environment

In addition to the general environment, managers must also consider the competitive environment (also sometimes referred to as the task or industry environment). The nature of competition in an industry, as well as the profitability of a firm, is often more directly influenced by developments in the competitive environment.

The competitive environment consists of many factors that are particularly relevant to a firm's strategy. These include competitors (existing or potential), customers, and suppliers. Potential competitors may include a supplier considering forward integration, such as an automobile manufacturer acquiring a rental car company, or a firm in an entirely new industry introducing a similar product that uses a more efficient technology.

In the following sections, we will discuss key concepts and analytical techniques that managers should use to assess their competitive environments. First, we examine Michael Porter's five-forces model that illustrates how these forces can be used to explain low profitability in an industry.[37] Then, we address the concept of strategic groups. This concept demonstrates that even within an industry it is often useful to group firms on the basis of similarities of their strategies. As we will see, competition tends to be more intense among firms *within* a strategic group than between strategic groups.

STRATEGY SPOTLIGHT

Maquiladoras: Staging a Comeback

Maquiladoras originated in Mexico in the 1960s. *Maquiladora* is a Spanish word that refers to manufacturing and export assembly plants that are owned by U.S., Japanese, and European companies. Maquiladoras primarily produce electronic equipment, clothing, plastics, furniture, appliances, and auto parts, and today 80 percent of the goods produced by maquiladoras in Mexico are shipped to the United States. The plants are quite prevalent in Mexican cities such as Tijuana, Ciudad Juarez, and Matamoros that lie directly across the border from the interstate highway–connected U.S. cities of San Diego and El Paso and Brownsville, Texas.

By the late 1990s, the number of plants peaked at about 3,000 and employed over a million Mexican workers. However, from 2000 to 2003, employment declined as the competition for cheaper labor elsewhere in the world, especially China, intensified. In 2004, the sector began showing a dramatic increase. In June 2004, for example, the country's maquiladoras exported goods worth $7.72 billion—a figure that is 20 percent higher than a year earlier and an all-time monthly record. And 55,000 new maquila jobs were created in 2004.

What has caused the revitalization? There are several factors that demonstrate the interdependence between political–legal, economic, and global elements of the general environment.

First, there is the recovery in the U.S. economy. Also, the cheaper peso—down 8 percent against the dollar during a recent 1-year period—has enhanced Mexico's allure for companies looking to cut costs.

Second, there are important logistical factors that are associated with the large distance between the United States and China. Although much of the production that has been relocated to China is not expected to return, many manufacturers are favoring Mexico because they believe that the lower Chinese wages do not compensate for the logistical difficulties of supplying the U.S. market from such a great distance. According to consultant Richard N. Sinkin of Inter-American Holdings Co., "Yeah, China's great for that dollar-a-day labor, but I can't wait 30 days to get my product to a customer." And for large goods, such as cars and side-by-side refrigerators, shipping costs from China can outrun savings on labor.

Third, political issues also come into play. Heeding investor complaints, the government of Mexican president Vicente Fox has postponed until 2008 a new fiscal regime that would require maquiladora owners to pay corporate taxes in Mexico. Custom procedures also have been streamlined. Mexico recently got a boost from the U.S. Department of Commerce when it increased duties on Chinese-made TV sets to as much as 78 percent to combat "dumping" of foreign products. This measure is a boon for Japanese, Korean, and Mexican TV manufacturers based in Tijuana and Ciudad Jaurez. Another factor favoring Mexico cited by many high-tech companies is that China has weak protection of intellectual property rights.

Sources: Smith, G. 2004. Made in the maquilas—Again. *BusinessWeek*, August 16: 45; and Brezosky, L. 2004. Border factories stage a comeback in Mexico. *Dallas Morning News*, December 28: 6A.

Porter's Five-Forces Model of Industry Competition

The "five-forces" model developed by Michael E. Porter has been the most commonly used analytical tool for examining the competitive environment. It describes the competitive environment in terms of five basic competitive forces.[38]

1. The threat of new entrants.
2. The bargaining power of buyers.
3. The bargaining power of suppliers.
4. The threat of substitute products and services.
5. The intensity of rivalry among competitors in an industry.

Each of these forces affects a firm's ability to compete in a given market. Together, they determine the profit potential for a particular industry. The model is shown in Exhibit 2.6 on page 60. As a manager, you should be familiar with the five-forces model for several reasons. It helps you decide whether your firm should remain in or exit an industry. It provides the rationale for increasing or decreasing resource commitments. The model helps you assess how to improve your firm's competitive position with regard to each of

Segment/Trends and Events	Industry	Positive	Neutral	Negative
Demographic				
Aging population	Health care	✓		
	Baby products			✓
Rising affluence	Brokerage services	✓		
	Fast foods			✓
	Upscale pets and supplies	✓		
Sociocultural				
More women in the workforce	Clothing	✓		
	Baking products (staples)			✓
Greater concern for health and fitness	Home exercise equipment	✓		
	Meat products			✓
Political/legal				
Tort reform	Legal services			✓
	Auto manufacturing	✓		
Americans with Disabilities Act (ADA)	Retail			✓
	Manufacturers of elevators, escalators, and ramps	✓		
Technological				
Genetic engineering	Pharmaceutical	✓		
	Publishing		✓	
Pollution/global warming	Engineering services	✓		
	Petroleum			✓
Economic				
Interest rate increases	Residential construction			✓
	Most common grocery products		✓	
Global				
Increasing global trade	Shipping	✓		
	Personal service		✓	
Emergence of China as an economic power	Soft drinks	✓		
	Defense			✓

Exhibit 2.5
The Impact of General Environmental Trends on Various Industries

the five forces. For example (and looking ahead a bit), you can use insights provided by the five-forces model to create higher entry barriers that discourage new rivals from competing with you.[39] Or you may develop strong relationships with your distribution channels. You may decide to find suppliers who satisfy the price/performance criteria needed to make your product or service a top performer.

The Threat of New Entrants   The threat of new entrants refers to the possibility that the profits of established firms in the industry may be eroded by new competitors.[40] The extent of the threat depends on existing barriers to entry and the combined reactions

General Environment
Demographic
Sociocultural
Political
Technological
Economic
Global

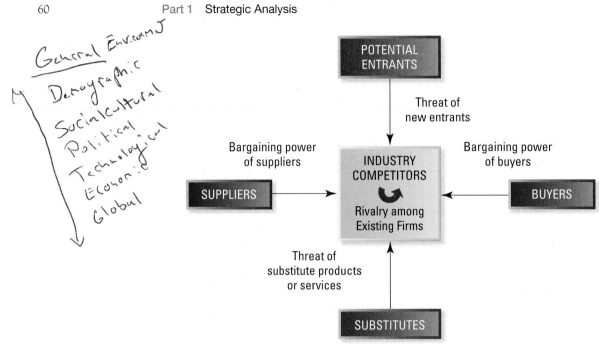

Exhibit 2.6   Porter's Five-Forces Model of Industry Competition

Source: Reprinted with permission of The Free Press, a division of Simon & Schuster Adult Publishing
Group, from *Competitive Strategy: Techniques for Analyzing Industries and Competitors* by Michael
E. Porter. Copyright © 1980, 1998 by The Free Press. All rights reserved.

from existing competitors. If entry barriers are high and/or the newcomer can anticipate
a sharp retaliation from established competitors, the threat of entry is low. These circumstances discourage new competitors. There are six major sources of entry barriers.

Economies of Scale Economies of scale refers to spreading the costs of production over
the number of units produced. The cost of a product per unit declines as the absolute
volume per period increases. This deters entry by forcing the entrant to come in at a
large scale and risk strong reaction from existing firms or come in at a small scale and
accept a cost disadvantage. Both are undesirable options.

Product Differentiation When existing competitors have strong brand identification and
customer loyalty, differentiation creates a barrier to entry by forcing entrants to spend
heavily to overcome existing customer loyalties.

Capital Requirements The need to invest large financial resources to compete creates a
barrier to entry, especially if the capital is required for risky or unrecoverable up-front
advertising or research and development (R&D).

Switching Costs A barrier to entry is created by the existence of one-time costs that the
buyer faces when switching from one supplier's product or service to another.

Access to Distribution Channels The new entrant's need to secure distribution for its
product can create a barrier to entry.

Cost Disadvantages Independent of Scale Some existing competitors may have advantages that are independent of size or economies of scale. These derive from:

•   Proprietary product
•   Favorable access to raw materials

- Government subsidies
- Favorable government policies

In an environment where few, if any, of these entry barriers are present, the threat of new entry is high. For example, if a new firm can launch its business with a low capital investment and operate efficiently despite its small scale of operation, it is likely to be a threat. One company that failed because of low entry barriers in an industry is ProCD.[41] You probably never heard of this company. It didn't last very long. ProCD provides an example of a firm that failed because it entered an industry with very low entry barriers.

The story begins in 1986 when Nynex (a Baby Bell company) issued the first electronic phone book, a compact disk containing all listings for the New York City area. It charged $10,000 per copy and sold the CDs to the FBI, IRS, and other large commercial and government organizations. James Bryant, the Nynex executive in charge of the project, smelled a fantastic business opportunity. He quit Nynex and set up his own firm, ProCD, with the ambitious goal of producing an electronic directory covering the entire United States.

As expected, the telephone companies, fearing an attack on their highly profitable Yellow Pages business, refused to license digital copies of their listings to this upstart. Bryant was not deterred. He traveled to Beijing and hired Chinese workers at $3.50 a day to type every listing from every U.S. telephone book into a database. The result contained more than 70 million phone numbers and was used to create a master disk that enabled ProCD to make hundreds of thousands of copies. Each CD sold for hundreds of dollars and cost less than a dollar each to produce.

It was a profitable business indeed! However, success was fleeting. Competitors such as Digital Directory Assistance and American Business Information quickly launched competing products with the same information. Since customers couldn't tell one product from the next, the players were forced to compete on price alone. Prices for the CD soon plummeted to a few dollars each. A high-priced, high-margin product just months earlier, the CD phone book became little more than a cheap commodity.

The Bargaining Power of Buyers   Buyers threaten an industry by forcing down prices, bargaining for higher quality or more services, and playing competitors against each other. These actions erode industry profitability.[42] The power of each large buyer group depends on attributes of the market situation and the importance of purchases from that group compared with the industry's overall business. A buyer group is powerful under the following conditions:

- *It is concentrated or purchases large volumes relative to seller sales.* If a large percentage of a supplier's sales are purchased by a single buyer, the importance of the buyer's business to the supplier increases. Large-volume buyers also are powerful in industries with high fixed costs (e.g., steel manufacturing).
- *The products it purchases from the industry are standard or undifferentiated.* Confident they can always find alternative suppliers, buyers play one company against the other, as in commodity grain products.
- *The buyer faces few switching costs.* Switching costs lock the buyer to particular sellers. Conversely, the buyer's power is enhanced if the seller faces high switching costs.
- *It earns low profits.* Low profits create incentives to lower purchasing costs. On the other hand, highly profitable buyers are generally less price sensitive.
- *The buyers pose a credible threat of backward integration.* If buyers are either partially integrated or pose a credible threat of backward integration, they are typically able to secure bargaining concessions.

- ***The industry's product is unimportant to the quality of the buyer's products or services.*** When the quality of the buyer's products is not affected by the industry's product, the buyer is more price sensitive.

At times, a firm or set of firms in an industry may increase its buyer power by using the services of a third party. FreeMarkets Online is one such third party.[43] Pittsburgh-based FreeMarkets has developed software enabling large industrial buyers to organize online auctions for qualified suppliers of semistandard parts such as fabricated components, packaging materials, metal stampings, and services. By aggregating buyers, FreeMarkets increases the buyers' bargaining power. The results are impressive. In its first 48 auctions, most participating companies saved over 15 percent; some saved as much as 50 percent.

The Bargaining Power of Suppliers   Suppliers can exert bargaining power over participants in an industry by threatening to raise prices or reduce the quality of purchased goods and services. Powerful suppliers can squeeze the profitability of firms in an industry so far that they can't recover the costs of raw material inputs.[44] The factors that make suppliers powerful tend to mirror those that make buyers powerful. A supplier group will be powerful in the following circumstances:

- ***The supplier group is dominated by a few companies and is more concentrated (few firms dominate the industry) than the industry it sells to.*** Suppliers selling to fragmented industries influence prices, quality, and terms.
- ***The supplier group is not obliged to contend with substitute products for sale to the industry.*** The power of even large, powerful suppliers can be checked if they compete with substitutes.
- ***The industry is not an important customer of the supplier group.*** When suppliers sell to several industries and a particular industry does not represent a significant fraction of its sales, suppliers are more prone to exert power.
- ***The supplier's product is an important input to the buyer's business.*** When such inputs are important to the success of the buyer's manufacturing process or product quality, the bargaining power of suppliers is high.
- ***The supplier group's products are differentiated or it has built up switching costs for the buyer.*** Differentiation or switching costs facing the buyers cut off their options to play one supplier against another.
- ***The supplier group poses a credible threat of forward integration.*** This provides a check against the industry's ability to improve the terms by which it purchases.

When considering supplier power, we focus on companies that supply raw materials, equipment, machinery, and associated services. But the supply of labor is also an important input to businesses, and labor's power varies over time and across occupations and industries. As we enter the 21st century, the outlook is not very good for semiskilled and unskilled laborers. Annual wage gains before inflation is taken into account—typically a good measure of workers' bargaining clout in the labor market—have remained in the 3 percent range for much of the 1990s.[45] When the CPI averaged around 2 percent, that provided employees with pay increases that exceeded inflation. With higher consumer prices, however, real wage gains (wage increases above the inflation rate) have been virtually nonexistent recently.

Workers with the right skills and jobs have enjoyed the spoils of the New Economy and will likely continue to do so. However, many other employees face the same forces that kept wages flat in the early 1990s: high immigration, deunionization, and globalization. For example, steel imports surged in 2000, threatening the jobs of many U.S. steelworkers. Not surprisingly, members of the United Steel Workers (USW) have been

Enhancing Supplier Power: The Creation of Delta Pride Catfish

The formation of Delta Pride Catfish in 1981 is an example of the power that a group of suppliers can attain if they exercise the threat of forward integration. Catfish farmers in Mississippi had historically supplied their harvest to processing plants run by large agribusiness firms such as ConAgra and Farm Fresh. When the farmers increased their production of catfish in response to growing demand in the early 1970s, they found, much to their chagrin, that processors were holding back on their plans to increase their processing capabilities in hopes of higher retail prices for catfish.

What action did the farmers take? They responded by forming a cooperative, raising $4.5 million, and constructing their own processing plant, which they supplied themselves. Within two years, ConAgra's market share had dropped from 35 percent to 11 percent, and Farm Fresh's market share fell by over 20 percent.

By the late 1980s, Delta Pride controlled over 40 percent of the 280-million-pound-per-year U.S. catfish market. It has continued to grow by including value-added products such as breaded and marinated catfish products. Recently it introduced Country Crisp Catfish Strips, a bakeable, breaded product with country-style seasoning. By 2005, Delta Pride had more than 500 employees. Its approximately 100 shareholders are mostly catfish farmers who own more than 60,000 acres of catfish production ponds and produce more than 200 million pounds of live catfish each year.

Source: Cargile, D. 2005. Personal communication. (Vice President of Sales, Delta Pride Catfish, Inc.), February 2; Anonymous. 2003. Delta Pride Catfish names Steve Osso President and CEO. www.deltabusiness.journal.com, February; and Fritz, M. 1988. Agribusiness: Catfish story. *Forbes*, December 12: 37.

forced to accept below-inflation pay increases. On September 1, 2000, 900 USW members at AK Steel Corp.'s Ashland, Kentucky, facility approved a pay hike of only 2.6 percent a year for the next five years. Said Roy Murray, a USW official, "We didn't want to be out there demanding more money when the industry is on its heels."

Strategy Spotlight 2.7 discusses how catfish farmers were able to enhance their bargaining power vis-à-vis their customers—large agribusiness firms—by banding together to form a cooperative.

The Threat of Substitute Products and Services   All firms within an industry compete with industries producing substitute products and services. Substitutes limit the potential returns of an industry by placing a ceiling on the prices that firms in that industry can profitably charge. The more attractive the price/performance ratio of substitute products, the tighter the lid on an industry's profits.

Identifying substitute products involves searching for other products or services that can perform the same function as the industry's offerings. This is a subtle task, one that leads a manager into businesses seemingly far removed from the industry. For example, the airline industry might not consider video cameras much of a threat. But as digital technology has improved and wireless and other forms of telecommunication have become more efficient, teleconferencing has become a viable substitute for business travel for many executives.

Teleconferencing can save both time and money, as IBM found out with its "Manager Jam" idea.[46] Currently, with 319,000 employees scattered around six continents, it is one of the world's largest businesses (including 32,000 managers) and can be a pretty confusing place. The shift to an increasingly mobile workplace means many managers supervise employees they rarely see face-to-face. To enhance coordination, Samuel Palmisano, IBM's new CEO, launched one of his first big initiatives: a two-year program exploring the role of the manager in the 21st century. "Manager Jam," as the project was nicknamed, was a 48-hour real-time Web event in which managers from 50 different countries swapped ideas and strategies for dealing with problems shared by all of them, regardless of geography. Some 8,100 managers logged on to the company's intranet to participate in the discussion forums.

The Intensity of Rivalry among Competitors in an Industry   Rivalry among existing competitors takes the form of jockeying for position. Firms use tactics like price competition, advertising battles, product introductions, and increased customer service or warranties. Rivalry occurs when competitors sense the pressure or act on an opportunity to improve their position.

Some forms of competition, such as price competition, are typically highly destabilizing and are likely to erode the average level of profitability in an industry.[47] Rivals easily match price cuts, an action that lowers profits for all firms. On the other hand, advertising battles expand overall demand or enhance the level of product differentiation for the benefit of all firms in the industry. Rivalry, of course, differs across industries. In some instances it is characterized as warlike, bitter, or cutthroat, whereas in other industries it is referred to as polite and gentlemanly. Intense rivalry is the result of several interacting factors, including the following:

- *Numerous or equally balanced competitors.* When there are many firms in an industry, the likelihood of mavericks is great. Some firms believe they can make moves without being noticed. Even when there are relatively few firms, and they are nearly equal in size and resources, instability results from fighting among companies having the resources for sustained and vigorous retaliation.
- *Slow industry growth.* Slow industry growth turns competition into a fight for market share, since firms seek to expand their sales.
- *High fixed or storage costs.* High fixed costs create strong pressures for all firms to increase capacity. Excess capacity often leads to escalating price cutting.
- *Lack of differentiation or switching costs.* Where the product or service is perceived as a commodity or near commodity, the buyer's choice is typically based on price and service, resulting in pressures for intense price and service competition. Lack of switching costs, described earlier, has the same effect.
- *Capacity augmented in large increments.* Where economies of scale require that capacity must be added in large increments, capacity additions can be very disruptive to the industry supply/demand balance.
- *High exit barriers.* Exit barriers are economic, strategic, and emotional factors that keep firms competing even though they may be earning low or negative returns on their investments. Some exit barriers are specialized assets, fixed costs of exit, strategic interrelationships (e.g., relationships between the business units and others within a company in terms of image, marketing, shared facilities, and so on), emotional barriers, and government and social pressures (e.g., governmental discouragement of exit out of concern for job loss).

Rivalry between firms is often based solely on price, but it can involve other factors. Take Pfizer's market position in the impotence treatment market. Pfizer was the first pharmaceutical firm to develop Viagra, a drug that treats impotence. International sales of Viagra were $332 million during a recent quarter. There are currently 30 million prescriptions for the drug. Pfizer would like to keep competitors from challenging this lucrative position.

In several countries, the United Kingdom among them, Pfizer faced a lawsuit by Eli Lilly & Co. and Icos Corp. challenging its patent protection. These two pharmaceutical firms recently entered into a joint venture to market Cialis, a drug to compete with Viagra. The U.K. courts agreed and lifted the patent.

This opened the door for Eli Lilly and Icos to proceed with challenging Pfizer's market position. Because Cialis has fewer side effects than Viagra, the drug has the potential to rapidly decrease Pfizer's market share in the United Kingdom if physicians switch prescriptions from Viagra to Cialis. If future patent challenges are successful, Pfizer may see its sales of Viagra erode rapidly. With projected annual sales of Cialis at $1 billion, Pfizer has reason to worry. With FDA approval, sales of Cialis could cause those of Viagra to plummet in the United States, further eroding Pfizer's market share.[48] But Pfizer is hardly standing still. It recently doubled its advertising expenditures on Viagra.

Using Industry Analysis: A Few Caveats   For industry analysis to be valuable, a company must collect and evaluate a wide variety of information from many sources. As the trend toward globalization accelerates, information on foreign markets as well as on a wider variety of competitors, suppliers, customers, substitutes, and potential new entrants becomes more critical. Industry analysis helps a firm not only to evaluate the profit potential of an industry, but also to consider various ways to strengthen its position vis-à-vis the five forces.

Five-forces analysis implicitly assumes a zero-sum game, determining how a firm can enhance its position relative to the forces. Yet such an approach can often be shortsighted; that is, it can overlook the many potential benefits of developing constructive win–win relationships with suppliers and customers. Establishing long-term mutually beneficial relationships with suppliers improves a firm's ability to implement just-in-time (JIT) inventory systems, which let it manage inventories better and respond quickly to market demands. A recent study found that if a company exploits its powerful position against a supplier, that action may come back to haunt the company if the position of power changes.[49] Further, by working together as partners, suppliers and manufacturers can provide the greatest value at the lowest possible cost. Later chapters address such collaborative relationships and how they can be made most effective.

The five-forces analysis also has been criticized for being essentially a static analysis. External forces as well as strategies of individual firms are continually changing the structure of all industries. The search for a dynamic theory of strategy has led to greater use of game theory in industrial organization economics research and strategy research. Based on game-theoretic considerations, Brandenburger and Nalebuff recently introduced the concept of the value net,[50] which in many ways is an extension of the five-forces analysis. It is illustrated in Exhibit 2.7. The value net represents all the players in the game and analyzes how their interactions affect a firm's ability to generate and appropriate value. The vertical dimension of the net includes suppliers and customers. The firm has direct transactions with them. On the horizontal dimension are substitutes and complements, players with whom a firm interacts but may not necessarily transact. The concept of complementors is perhaps the single most important contribution of value net analysis and is explained in more detail below.

Complements typically are products or services that have a potential impact on the value of a firm's own products or services. Those who produce complements are usually referred to as complementors. Powerful hardware is of no value to a user unless there is software that runs on it. Similarly, new and better software is possible only if the hardware on which it can be run is available. This is equally true in the video game industry, where the sales of game consoles and video games complement each other. Nintendo's success in the early 1990s was a result of their ability to manage their relationship with their complementors. They built a security chip into the hardware and then licensed the right to develop games to outside firms. These firms paid a royalty to Nintendo for each copy of the game sold. The royalty revenue enabled Nintendo to sell game consoles at

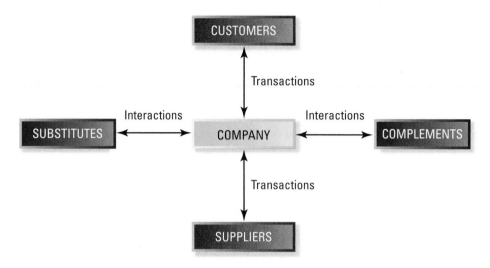

close to their cost, thereby increasing their market share, which, in turn, caused more
games to be sold and more royalties to be generated.

Industry Analysis: A Dynamic Perspective

One of the criticisms often leveled against traditional industry analysis is that it is static
in nature. As we are all aware, the competitive landscape in most industries is undergoing very rapid changes due to changes in technology and customer preferences. While
this does not diminish the value of the five-forces analysis at a given point in time, we
need additional tools and frameworks to understand and analyze the rapid changes taking
place in most industries. One very useful framework for the analysis of industry evolution
has been proposed by Professor Anita McGahan of Boston University.[51] Her analysis is
based on the identification of the *core activities* and the *core assets* of an industry and
the threats they face. She suggests that an industry may follow one of four possible
evolutionary trajectories based on two types of threats of obsolescence.

First is the threat of obsolescence faced by the *core activities* of the firm. Core activities are activities that historically have generated profits for the industry. For example,
because consumers today can find all information they need to make a purchasing decision on an automobile, such as price, performance, reliability, and technical characteristics,
by going online, the core selling activities of a car dealership are no longer of great value
to the customer. Second is the threat of obsolescence faced by an industry's *core assets.*
These refer to the resources, knowledge, and brand capital possessed by firms in an industry. For example, in the video rental industry, the core assets were traditionally locations
and a wide selection. In an era of video downloads, location is of little value and typical
rental outlets cannot begin to match the enormous selection offered by firms such as
Netflix. The four change trajectories followed by industries based on possible combinations
of threats to core activities and core assets are described in the following paragraphs.

Radical change occurs when both core activities and core assets face the threat
of obsolescence. For example, the overnight letter delivery industry is beginning to experience this problem. The availability of cheap but instantaneous means of document
delivery through fax machines and the Internet has made the core assets (delivery trucks,

airplanes, and a central hub) and core activities (document tracking) of firms such as Federal Express suddenly less relevant. A similar situation was faced by typewriter manufacturers two decades ago when relatively inexpensive PCs became widely available.

Intermediating change occurs when core assets are not threatened but core activities are under threat. An example of an industry facing intermediating change is automobile dealerships. This occurs for a variety of reasons. First, as mentioned earlier, prospective customers can get all the information they need online. Second, as the quality and longevity of cars improve, individual purchases have become less frequent. Third, car manufacturers are now sharing the task of customer relations with the dealers. In some cases, they have even completely taken over this function. Finally, inventory management and financing are now subject to significant economies of scale that only large, integrated companies can take advantage of.

When core assets are threatened, but core activities are not, industries tend to follow the *creative change* trajectory. Examples of industries experiencing creative change include the film production industry, pharmaceuticals, oil and gas exploration, and prepackaged software. In each of these cases, there is rapid asset turnover but relatively stable relationships with suppliers and customers. For example in the pharmaceutical industry, patents for some drugs expire while new drugs get FDA approval, but the core activities of commercialization and marketing continue to be relevant.

Finally, *progressive change* occurs in industries where neither core assets nor core activities face imminent threat of obsolescence. Change does occur, but it is within the existing framework of the industry. At any given moment, changes may be incremental, but over time they cumulate to substantial changes. The commercial airline industry and the discount retailing industry are examples of two industries where progressive change has been occurring. The suppliers and the customers are, by and large, the same. The core assets and activities have changed only incrementally in any given year, but over the last decade both these industries have experienced significant changes.

Exhibit 2.8 presents the four evolutionary trajectories and the conditions under which they are likely to occur.

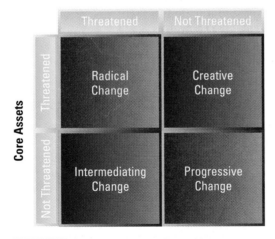

Exhibit 2.8   Four Evolutionary Trajectories of Industry Change

Each of the above four change trajectories unfolds over many years, sometimes even decades. This gives firms within an industry time to respond to the changes. Fighting change, on the other hand, seldom succeeds. When faced with *radical* or *intermediating changes,* it is wise to aggressively pursue profits in the near term while avoiding investments that could reduce strategic flexibility in the future. Another response is alliances, often with rivals, to protect common interests and defend against new competition from outsiders. For firms facing *radical change,* one option is diversification. FedEx's acquisition of Kinko's fits into this category. In order to succeed, firms facing *intermediating change* must find unconventional ways to extract profits from their core assets. For example, threatened by eBay, traditional auctioneers have responded by capitalizing on their appraisal expertise. That is, for a fee, they will certify the value of the items being sold online.

Strategies for firms facing *creative change* include spreading the risk of new-project development over a portfolio of assets as well as outsourcing project management and development tasks. Successful companies in *progressive change* industries carve out distinct positions based on geographic, technical, or marketing expertise. They also develop a system of interrelated activities that are defensible against competitors. Wal-Mart and Southwest Airlines are excellent examples of this approach. Their strategies are entirely observable and easy to understand. But they are the result of hundreds of incremental changes compounding over time and thus are difficult for rivals to match.

Industries also can change as a result of specific actions by individual firms. In Chapter 5, we will be revisiting this topic when we discuss how innovations can change the competitive landscape of an industry.

Strategic Groups within Industries

In an industry analysis, two assumptions are unassailable: (1) No two firms are totally different, and (2) no two firms are exactly the same. The issue becomes one of identifying groups of firms that are more similar to each other than firms that are not, otherwise known as strategic groups.[52] This is important because rivalry tends to be greater among firms that are alike. Strategic groups are clusters of firms that share similar strategies. After all, is Kmart more concerned about Nordstrom or Wal-Mart? Is Mercedes more concerned about Hyundai or BMW? The answers are straightforward.[53]

These examples are not meant to trivialize the strategic groups concept. Classifying an industry into strategic groups involves judgment. If it is useful as an analytical tool, we must exercise caution in deciding what dimensions to use to map these firms. Dimensions include breadth of product and geographic scope, price/quality, degree of vertical integration, type of distribution (e.g., dealers, mass merchandisers, private label), and so on. Dimensions should also be selected to reflect the variety of strategic combinations in an industry. For example, if all firms in an industry have roughly the same level of product differentiation (or R&D intensity), this would not be a good dimension to select.

What value is the strategic groups concept as an analytical tool? First, strategic groupings help a firm identify barriers to mobility that protect a group from attacks by other groups.[54] Mobility barriers are factors that deter the movement of firms from one strategic position to another. For example, in the chainsaw industry, the major barriers protecting the high-quality/dealer-oriented group are technology, brand image, and an established network of servicing dealers.

The second value of strategic grouping is that it helps a firm identify groups whose competitive position may be marginal or tenuous. We may anticipate that these competitors may exit the industry or try to move into another group. This has been the case in recent years in the retail department store industry, where firms such as JCPenney and Sears have experienced extremely difficult times because they were stuck in the middle,

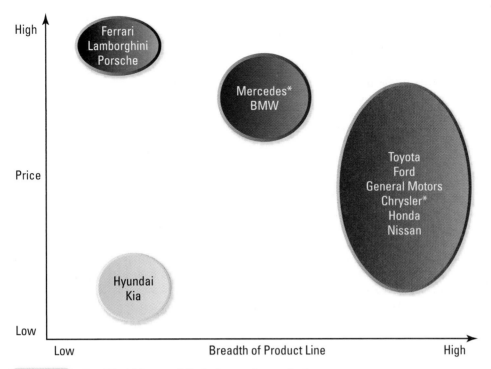

Exhibit 2.9   The World Automobile Industry: Strategic Groups

*Chrysler and Mercedes (part of DaimlerChrysler) are separated for purposes of illustration.

Note: Members of each strategic group are not inclusive, only illustrative.

neither an aggressive discount player like Wal-Mart nor a prestigious upscale player like Neiman Marcus.

Third, strategic groupings help chart the future directions of firms' strategies. Arrows emanating from each strategic group can represent the direction in which the group (or a firm within the group) seems to be moving. If all strategic groups are moving in a similar direction, this could indicate a high degree of future volatility and intensity of competition. In the automobile industry, for example, the competition in the minivan and sport utility segments has intensified in recent years as many firms have entered those product segments.

Fourth, strategic groups are helpful in thinking through the implications of each industry trend for the strategic group as a whole. Is the trend decreasing the viability of a group? If so, in what direction should the strategic group move? Is the trend increasing or decreasing entry barriers in a given group? Will the trend decrease the ability of one group to separate itself from other groups? Such analysis can help in making predictions about industry evolution. A sharp increase in interest rates, for example, would tend to have less impact on providers of higher-priced goods (e.g., Porsches) than on providers of lower-priced goods (e.g., Dodge Neons). The Dodge Neon customer base is much more price sensitive.

Exhibit 2.9 provides a strategic grouping of the worldwide automobile industry.[55] The firms in each group are representative; not all firms are included in the mapping. We have identified four strategic groups. In the top left-hand corner are high-end luxury automakers who focus on a very narrow product market. Most of the cars produced by the members of this group cost well over $100,000. Some cost many times that amount. The Ferrari F50 costs roughly $550,000 and the Lamborghini L147 $300,000[56] (in case you were wondering how to spend your employment signing bonus). Players in this market have a very exclusive clientele and face little rivalry from other strategic groups. At the other extreme, in the lower left-hand corner is a strategic group that has low-price/quality attributes and targets a narrow market. These players, Hyundai and Kia, limit competition from other strategic groups by pricing their products very low. The third group (near the middle) consists of firms high in product pricing/quality and average in their product-line breadth. The final group (at the far right) consists of firms with a broad range of products and multiple price points. These firms have entries that compete at both the lower end of the market (e.g., the Ford Focus) and the higher end (e.g., Chevrolet Corvette).

The auto market has been very dynamic and competition has intensified in recent years. Many firms in different strategic groups compete in the same product markets, such as minivans and sport utility vehicles. In the late 1990s Mercedes entered the fray with its M series, and Porsche has recent entry as well with its Cayenne, a 2004 model. Some players are also going more upscale with their product offerings. Recently, Hyundai introduced its XG300, priced at over $25,000 for a fully loaded model. This brings Hyundai into direct competition with entries from other strategic groups such as Toyota's Camry and Honda's Accord. Hyundai is offering an extensive warranty (10 years, 100,000 miles) in an effort to offset customer perceptions of their lower quality. Perhaps Ford has made the most notable efforts to go upscale. Not content to rely solely on the Lincoln nameplate to attract high-ticket buyers, Ford, like other large players, has gone on an acquisition binge. It recently acquired Volvo, Land Rover, Jaguar, and Aston Martin. Ford is aggressively accelerating its forecasted sales for each of these brands.[57] To further intensify competition, some key automakers are providing offerings in lower-priced segments. Mercedes and BMW, with their C-class and 3-series, respectively, are well-known examples. Such cars, priced in the low $30,000s, compete more directly with products from broad-line manufacturers like Ford, General Motors, and Toyota.

These new products are competing in an industry that has experienced relatively flat unit sales in the first half of this decade.[58] In addition, high-incentive–laden offerings appear to be losing some of their appeal to consumers, and there are higher levels of inventory at dealerships. Further, since manufacturers have maintained, if not increased, production schedules and plant capacity, overall competition should intensify. Don't be surprised, therefore, if rebates and discounting continue on most models.

Summary

Managers must analyze the external environment to minimize or eliminate threats and exploit opportunities. This involves a continuous process of environmental scanning and monitoring as well as obtaining competitive intelligence on present and potential rivals. These activities provide valuable inputs for developing forecasts. In addition, many firms use scenario planning to anticipate and respond to volatile and disruptive environmental changes.

We identified two types of environment: the general environment and the competitive environment. The six segments of the general environment are demographic, sociocultural, political/legal, technological, economic, and global. Trends and events occurring in these segments, such as the aging of the population, higher percentages of women in the workplace, governmental legislation, and increasing (or decreasing) interest rates, can have a dramatic effect on a firm. A given trend or event may have a positive impact on some industries and a negative, neutral, or no impact at all on others.

The competitive environment consists of industry-related factors and has a more direct impact than the general environment. Porter's five-forces model of industry analysis includes the threat of new entrants, buyer power, supplier power, threat of substitutes, and rivalry among competitors. The intensity of these factors determines, in large part, the average expected level of profitability in an industry. A sound awareness of such factors, both individually and in combination, is beneficial not only for deciding what industries to enter but also for assessing how a firm can improve its competitive position. The limitations of five-forces analysis include its static nature and its inability to acknowledge the role of complementors. Given the rapid, unpredictable change that is occurring in many industries, we also discussed industry analysis from a dynamic perspective. Although we addressed the general environment and competitive environment in separate sections, they are quite interdependent. A given environmental trend or event, such as changes in the ethnic composition of a population or a technological innovation, typically has a much greater impact on some industries than on others.

The concept of strategic groups is also important to the external environment of a firm. No two organizations are completely different nor are they exactly the same. The question is how to group firms in an industry on the basis of similarities in their resources and strategies. The strategic groups concept is valuable for determining mobility barriers across groups, identifying groups with marginal competitive positions, charting the future directions of firm strategies, and assessing the implications of industry trends for the strategic group as a whole.

Summary Review Questions

1. Why must managers be aware of a firm's external environment?
2. What is gathering and analyzing competitive intelligence and why is it important for firms to engage in it?
3. Discuss and describe the six elements of the external environment.
4. Select one of these elements and describe some changes relating to it in an industry that interests you.
5. Describe how the five forces can be used to determine the average expected profitability in an industry.
6. What are some of the limitations (or caveats) in using five-forces analysis?
7. Explain how the general environment and industry environment are highly related. How can such interrelationships affect the profitability of a firm or industry?
8. Explain the concept of strategic groups. What are the performance implications?

Select one of the following industries: personal computers, airlines, or automobiles. For this industry, evaluate the strength of each of Porter's five forces as well as complementors.

Experiential Exercise

Industry Force	High? Medium? Low?	Why?
1. Threat of new entrants		
2. Power of buyers		
3. Power of suppliers		
4. Power of substitutes		
5. Rivalry among competitors		
6. Complementors		

Application Questions Exercises

1. Imagine yourself as the CEO of a large firm in an industry in which you are interested. Please (1) identify major trends in the general environment, (2) analyze their impact on the firm, and (3) identify major sources of information to monitor these trends. (Use Internet and library resources.)

2. Analyze movements across the strategic groups in the U.S. retail industry. How do these movements within this industry change the nature of competition?

3. What are the major trends in the general environment that have impacted the U.S. pharmaceutical industry?

4. Go to the Internet and look up www.kroger.com. What are some of the five forces driving industry competition that are affecting the profitability of this firm?

Ethics Questions

1. What are some of the legal and ethical issues involved in collecting competitor intelligence in the following situations?

   a. Hotel A sends an employee posing as a potential client to Hotel B to find out who Hotel B's major corporate customers are.

   b. A firm hires an MBA student to collect information directly from a competitor while claiming the information is for a course project.

   c. A firm advertises a nonexistent position and interviews a rival's employees with the intention of obtaining competitor information.

2. What are some of the ethical implications that arise when a firm tries to exploit its power over a supplier?

References

1. Grow, B. 2004. Can Wonder Bread rise again? *BusinessWeek,* October 18: 108, 110; Horovitz, B. 2004. Twinkie maker files for protection, gets new CEO. *USA Today,* September 22: 3B; Goglo, P. 2004. Interstate Bakeries' Twinkie defense. *BusinessWeek Online,* September 23: np; and Higgins, K. T. 2003. The world's top 100. *Food Engineering,* October: 58, 64–70.

2. Hamel, G., & Prahalad, C. K. 1994. *Competing for the future.* Boston: Harvard Business School Press.

3. Drucker, P. F. 1994. Theory of the business. *Harvard Business Review,* 72: 95–104.

4. The examples of Novell and Silicon Graphics draw on Pickering, C. I. 1998. Sorry . . . Try again next year. *Forbes ASAP,* February 23: 82–83.

5. For an insightful discussion on managers' assessment of the external environment, refer to Sutcliffe, K. M., & Weber, K. 2003. The high cost of accurate knowledge. *Harvard Business Review,* 81(5): 74–86.

6. Charitou, C. D., & Markides, C. C. 2003. Responses to disruptive strategic innovation. *MIT Sloan Management Review,* 44(2): 55–64.

7. Our discussion of scanning, monitoring, competitive intelligence, and forecasting concepts draws on several sources. These include Fahey, L., & Narayanan, V. K. 1983. *Macroenvironmental analysis for strategic management.* St. Paul, MN: West; Lorange, P., Scott, F. S., & Ghoshal, S. 1986. *Strategic control.* St. Paul, MN: West; Ansoff, H. I. 1984. *Implementing strategic management.*

Englewood Cliffs, NJ: Prentice Hall; and Schreyogg, G., & Stienmann, H. 1987. Strategic control: A new perspective. *Academy of Management Review,* 12: 91–103.

8. Elenkov, D. S. 1997. Strategic uncertainty and environmental scanning: The case for institutional influences on scanning behavior. *Strategic Management Journal,* 18: 287–302.

9. For an interesting perspective on environmental scanning in emerging economies see May, R. C., Stewart, W. H., & Sweo, R. 2000. Environmental scanning behavior in a transitional economy: Evidence from Russia. *Academy of Management Journal,* 43(3): 403–27.

10. Browne, Sir John. The new agenda. Keynote speech delivered to the World Petroleum Congress in Calgary, Canada, June 13, 2000.

11. Bowles, J. 1997. Key issues for the automotive industry CEOs. *Fortune,* August 18: S3.

12. Walters, B. A., & Priem, R. L. 1999. Business strategy and CEO intelligence acquisition. *Competitive Intelligence Review,* 10(2): 15–22.

13. Prior, V. 1999. The language of competitive intelligence, Part 4. *Competitive Intelligence Review,* 10(1): 84–87.

14. Zahra, S. A., & Charples, S. S. 1993. Blind spots in competitive analysis. *Academy of Management Executive* 7(2): 7–27.

15. Wolfenson, J. 1999. The world in 1999: A battle for corporate honesty. *The Economist* 38: 13–30.

16. Drucker, P. F. 1997. The future that has already happened. *Harvard Business Review,* 75(6): 22.

17. Evans, P. B., & Wurster, T. S. 1997. Strategy and the new economics of information. *Harvard Business Review,* 75(5): 71–82.

18. Fahey & Narayanan, op. cit., p. 41.

19. Courtney, H., Kirkland, J., & Viguerie, P. 1997. Strategy under uncertainty. *Harvard Business Review,* 75(6): 66–79.

20. Odlyzko, A. 2003. False hopes. *Red Herring,* March: 31.

21. For an interesting perspective on how Accenture practices and has developed its approach to scenario planning, refer to Ferguson, G., Mathur, S., & Shah, B. 2005. Evolving from information to insight. *MIT Sloan Management Review,* 46(2): 51–58.

22. Dean, T. J., Brown, R. L., & Bamford, C. E. 1998. Differences in large and small firm responses to environmental context: Strategic implications from a comparative analysis of business formations. *Strategic Management Journal,* 19: 709–728.

23. Colvin, G. 1997. How to beat the boomer rush. *Fortune,* August 18: 59–63.

24. Grant, P. 2000. Developing plans to serve a graying population. *Wall Street Journal,* October 18: B12.

25. Walgreens, Inc. 2000. Annual report, 20.

26. Armas, G. C. 2000. Census figures point to changes in Congress. washingtonpost.com/wpdyn/articles/A58952Dec28. html.

27. Challenger, J. 2000. Women's corporate rise has reduced relocations. *Lexington* (KY) *Herald-Leader,* October 29: D1.

28. Watkins, M. D. 2003. Government games. *MIT Sloan Management Review* 44(2): 91–95.

29. Davies, A. 2000. The welcome mat is out for nerds. *BusinessWeek,* October 16: 64.

30. Anonymous. Business ready for Internet revolution. 1999. *Financial Times,* May 21: 17.

31. The Internet example draws on Bernasek, A. 2000. How the broadband adds up. *Fortune,* October 9: 28, 30; and Kromer, E. B2B or not B2B? *UW Alumni Magazine:* 10–19.

32. Baker, S., & Aston, A. 2005. The business of nanotech. *BusinessWeek,* February 14: 64–71.

33. Ginsburg, J. 2000. Letting the free market clear the air. *BusinessWeek,* November 6: 200, 204.

34. Smith, G., Wheatley, J., & Green, J. 2000. Car power. *BusinessWeek,* October 23: 72–80.

35. Mellgren, D. 2000. Norwegian ships relied on in global disasters. *Lexington* (KY) *Herald-Leader,* November 6: A8.

36. Goll, I., & Rasheed, M. A. 1997. Rational decision-making and firm performance: The moderating role of environment. *Strategic Management Journal,* 18: 583–591.

37. This discussion draws heavily on Porter, M. E. 1980. *Competitive strategy:* Chapter 1. New York: Free Press.

38. Ibid.

39. Fryer, B. 2001. Leading through rough times: An interview with Novell's Eric Schmidt. *Harvard Business Review,* 78(5): 117–123.

40. For a discussion on the importance of barriers to entry within industries, read Greenwald, B., & Kahn, J. 2005. *Competition demystified: A radically simplified approach to business strategy.* East Rutherford, NJ: Portfolio.

41. The ProCD example draws heavily upon Shapiro, C., & Varian, H. R. 2000. Versioning: The smart way to sell information. *Harvard Business Review,* 78(1): 106–114.

42. Wise, R., & Baumgarter, P. 1999. Go downstream: The new profit imperative in manufacturing. *Harvard Business Review,* 77(5): 133–141.

43. Salman, W. A. 2000. The new economy is stronger than you think. *Harvard Business Review,* 77(6): 99–106.

44. Mudambi, R., & Helper, S. 1998. The "close but adversarial" model of supplier relations in the U.S. auto industry. *Strategic Management Journal,* 19: 775–792.

45. Bernstein, A. 2000. Workers are doing well, but will it last? *BusinessWeek,* October 9: 48.

46. Tischler, L. 2002. IBM: Manager jam. *Fast Company,* October: 48.

47. For an interesting perspective on the intensity of competition in the supermarket industry, refer to Anonymous. 2005. Warfare in the aisles. *The Economist,* April 2: 6–8.

48. Marcial, G. 2000. Giving Viagra a run for its money. *BusinessWeek,* October 23: 173.

49. Kumar, N. 1996. The power of trust in manufacturer-retailer relationship. *Harvard Business Review,* 74(6): 92–110.

50. Brandenburger, A., & Nalebuff, B. J. 1995. The right game: Use game theory to shape strategy. *Harvard Business Review,* 73(4): 57–71.

51. McGahan, A. M. 2004. How industries change. *Harvard Business Review,* 82(10): 87–94.

52. Peteraf, M., & Shanley, M. 1997. Getting to know you: A theory of strategic group identity. *Strategic Management Journal,* 18 (Special Issue): 165–186.

53. An interesting scholarly perspective on strategic groups may be found in Dranove, D., Peteraf, M., & Shanley, M. 1998. Do strategic groups exist? An economic framework for analysis. *Strategic Management Journal,* 19(11): 1029–1044.

54. This section draws on several sources, including Kerwin, K. R., & Haughton, K. 1997. Can Detroit make cars that baby boomers like? *BusinessWeek,* December 1: 134–148; and Taylor, A., III. 1994. The new golden age of autos. *Fortune.* April 4: 50–66.

55. Csere, C. 2001. Supercar supermarket. *Car and Driver,* January: 118–127.

56. Healey, J. R. 1999. Groomed so as not to marry. *USA Today,* August 6: B1.

57. Csere, op. cit.

58. Smith, J. A. 2005. Auto & Truck Industry. *Value Line,* March 4: 101.

3

Assessing the Internal Environment of the Firm

>chapter objectives

After reading this chapter, you should have a good understanding of:

- The benefits and limitations of SWOT analysis in conducting an internal analysis of the firm.

- The primary and support activities of a firm's value chain.

- How value-chain analysis can help managers create value by investigating relationships among activities within the firm and between the firm and its customers and suppliers.

- The resource-based view of the firm and the different types of tangible and intangible resources, as well as organizational capabilities.

- The four criteria that a firm's resources must possess to maintain a sustainable advantage and how value created can be appropriated by employees and managers.

- The usefulness of financial ratio analysis, its inherent limitations, and how to make meaningful comparisons of performance across firms.

- The value of recognizing how the interests of a variety of stakeholders can be interrelated.

*t*wo firms compete in the same industry and both have many strengths in a variety of functional areas: marketing, operations, logistics, and so on. However, one of these firms outperforms the other by a wide margin over a long period of time. How can this be so? This chapter endeavors to answer that question. We begin with two sections that include frameworks for gaining key insights into a firm's internal environment: value-chain analysis and the resource-based view of the firm. In value-chain analysis, we divide a firm's activities into a series of value-creating steps. We then explore how individual activities within the firm add value, and also how *interrelationships* among activities within the firm, and between the firm and its suppliers and customers, create value.

In the resource-based view of the firm, we analyze the firm as a collection of tangible and intangible resources as well as organizational capabilities. Advantages that tend to be sustainable over time typically arise from creating *bundles* of resources and capabilities that satisfy four criteria: they are valuable, rare, difficult to imitate, and difficult to substitute. Not all of the value created by a firm will necessarily be kept (or appropriated) by the owners. We discuss the four key factors that determine how profits will be distributed between owners as well as employees and managers.

In the closing sections, we discuss how to evaluate a firm's performance and make comparisons across firms. We emphasize both the inclusion of financial resources and the interests of multiple stakeholders. Central to our discussion are the concepts of the balanced scorecard and the strategy map, which recognize that the interests of different stakeholders can be interrelated. We also consider how a firm's performance evolves over time and how it compares with industry norms and key competitors.

Jaguar has *not* been a star in Ford Motor Company's automotive arsenal. In fact, it has been referred to in the press as CEO "Bill Ford's recurring nightmare."[1] It appears that over the 15 years that Ford has owned the British luxury marquee, each time that it seems to turn the corner, the unit begins to lose money. Jaguar's estimated losses over the past 3 years are $1.5 billion. In fact, a recent *BusinessWeek* article included a cartoon with two customers looking at a Jaguar at a dealership with the seemingly appropriate caption: "Does it come in any color other than red ink?" Let's take a look at Jaguar's recent history and the source of its problems.

In early 2002, Bill Ford vowed that Ford's Premier Automotive Group (PAG)—consisting of Land Rover, Volvo, Aston Martin, and Jaguar—would contribute nearly a third of $7 billion in pre-tax profits by 2006. Ford has recently abandoned that profit goal, in part due to Jaguar's continuing slide. For example, Jaguar's problems dragged PAG down to a $342 million loss during the first half of 2004. If Ford can't turn Jaguar around, it will be very difficult to meet the corporation's reduced profit targets.

First, the good news: Factory efficiency and quality have improved significantly in recent years. However, there is far more bad news, including some huge mistakes. A major stumble was the rollout of the Jaguar X-Type compact. Many viewed it as a poorly executed entry-level car, known as the Baby Jag, that alienated Jaguar loyalists. The share of owners who stayed with the brand when they bought new vehicles has plunged from 85 percent to 38 percent in the past few years, according to an automotive consultant. Jaguar can also be criticized for an overly ambitious expansion, a one-size-fits all marketing strategy, and stale styling. Not surprisingly, it becomes rather easy to see why Jaguar has had to discount heavily to try to meet its global sales target of 125,000 units in 2004. (With sales of 118,918 units—down one percent from 2003—it still fell short.)

Let's briefly elaborate on some of these shortcomings:

- Jaguar based the X-Type on the mass market Ford Mondeo, which cheapened the brand. Jim Sanfilippo, executive vice president of the automotive consultancy AMCI Inc. of Bloomfield Hills, Michigan, said that the X-Type "turned Jaguar into a Ford with a Jaguar badge on it."
- Sales of the revamped XJ model, Jaguar's flagship, were hurt because it looked too much like the replacement model. Perhaps, people who pay $70,000 want everyone to know they have a new Jag!
- There were major problems with Jaguar's marketing approach. It adopted a mass marketing approach and then changed it too frequently. Its current "Born to Perform" slogan emphasizes horsepower, not looks. However, style is the main reason owners cite for purchasing a Jaguar!
- Jaguar's image has been tarnished by heavy rental-car sales and large rebates. For example, in late-2004, Jaguar's U.S. sales incentives were nearly $5,000 per car. This compared to $464 and $552 for Lexus and Mercedes, respectively. This partly explains Jaguar's low resale values. In fact, the only luxury brand with lower resale values was Jag's PAG stablemate, Land Rover. Hopefully, improved products and an appealing marketing strategy will help Jaguar cut back on expensive financial sales incentives.

Under Ford, Jaguar has made great strides in operational efficiency and overall product quality. These strengths, however, do not seem to offset weaknesses in a number of areas, including marketing, engineering and styling. In addition, Jaguar has suffered from an erosion of brand image that has occurred during the past decade due to such factors as fleet sales, huge cash incentives, and the introduction of entry-level models.

Before moving ahead to value-chain analysis, let's briefly revisit SWOT analysis to discuss some of its benefits and limitations. As discussed in Chapter 2, a SWOT analysis consists of a careful listing of a firm's strengths, weaknesses, opportunities, and threats.

While we believe SWOT analysis is very helpful as a starting point, it should not form the primary basis for evaluating a firm's internal strengths and weaknesses or the opportunities and threats in the environment. Strategy Spotlight 3.1 elaborates on the limitations of the traditional SWOT approach.

We will now turn to value-chain analysis. As you will see, it provides greater insights into analyzing a firm's competitive position than SWOT analysis does by itself.

>>Value-Chain Analysis

Value-chain analysis views the organization as a sequential process of value-creating activities. The approach is useful for understanding the building blocks of competitive advantage. Value-chain analysis was described in Michael Porter's seminal book *Competitive Advantage.*[2] In competitive terms, value is the amount that buyers are willing to pay for what a firm provides them. Value is measured by total revenue, a reflection of the price a firm's product commands and the quantity it can sell. A firm is profitable to the extent that the value it receives exceeds the total costs involved in creating its product or service. Creating value for buyers that exceeds the costs of production (i.e., margin) is a key concept used in analyzing a firm's competitive position.

Porter described two different categories of activities. First, five primary activities—inbound logistics, operations, outbound logistics, marketing and sales, and service—contribute to the physical creation of the product or service, its sale and transfer to the buyer, and its service after the sale. Second, support activities—procurement, technology development, human resource management, and general administration—either add value by themselves or add value through important relationships with both primary activities and other support activities. Exhibit 3.1 illustrates Porter's value chain.

To get the most out of value-chain analysis, you need to view the concept in its broadest context, without regard to the boundaries of your own organization. That is, place your organization within a more encompassing value chain that includes your firm's suppliers, customers, and alliance partners. Thus, in addition to thoroughly understanding how value is created within the organization, you must become aware of how value is

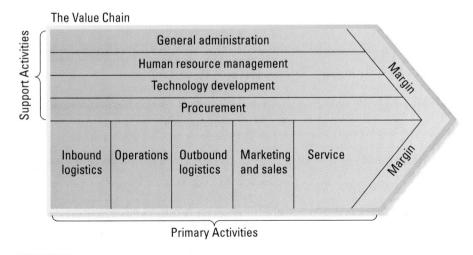

Exhibit 3.1   The Value Chain: Primary and Support Activities

Source: Adapted with the permission of The Free Press, a division of Simon & Schuster Adult Publishing Group, from *Competitive Advantage: Creating and Sustaining Superior Performance* by Michael E. Porter. Copyright © 1985, 1998 by Michael E. Porter. All rights reserved.

The Limitations of SWOT Analysis

SWOT analysis is a tried-and-true tool of strategic analysis. SWOT (strengths, weaknesses, opportunities, threats) analysis is used regularly in business to initially evaluate the opportunities and threats in the business environment as well as the strengths and weaknesses of a firm's internal environment. Top managers rely on SWOT to stimulate self-reflection and group discussions about how to improve their firm and position it for success.

But SWOT has its limitations. It is just a starting point for discussion. By listing the firm's attributes, managers have the raw material needed to perform more in-depth strategic analysis. However, SWOT cannot show them how to achieve a competitive advantage. They must not make SWOT analysis an end in itself, temporarily raising awareness about important issues but failing to lead to the kind of action steps necessary to enact strategic change.

Consider the ProCD example from Chapter 2, page 61. A brief SWOT analysis might include the following:

Strengths	Opportunities
First-mover advantage	Demand for electronic phone books
Low labor cost	Sudden growth in use of digital technology

Weaknesses	Threats
Inexperienced new company	Easily duplicated product
No proprietary information	Market power of incumbent firms

The combination of low production costs and an early-mover advantage in an environment where demand for CD-based phone books was growing rapidly seems to indicate that ProCD founder James Bryant had a golden opportunity. But the SWOT analysis did not reveal how to turn those strengths into a competitive advantage, nor did it highlight how rapidly the environment would change, allowing imitators to come into the market and erode his first-mover advantage. Let's look at some of the limitations of SWOT analysis.

Strengths May Not Lead to an Advantage A firm's strengths and capabilities, no matter how unique or impressive, may not enable it to achieve a competitive advantage in the marketplace. It is akin to recruiting a concert pianist to join a gang of thugs—even though such an ability is rare and valuable, it hardly helps the organization attain its goals and objectives! Similarly, the skills of a highly creative product designer would offer little competitive advantage to a firm that produces low-cost commodity products. Indeed, the additional expense of hiring such an individual could erode the firm's cost advantages. If a firm builds its strategy on a capability that cannot, by itself, create or sustain competitive advantage, it is essentially a wasted use of resources. ProCD had several key strengths, but it did not translate them into lasting advantages in the marketplace.

SWOT's Focus on the External Environment Is Too Narrow Strategists who rely on traditional definitions of their industry and competitive environment often focus their sights too narrowly on current customers, technologies, and competitors. Hence they fail to notice important changes on the periphery of their environment that may trigger the need to redefine industry boundaries and identify a whole new set of competitive relationships. Reconsider the example from Chapter 2 of *Encyclopaedia Britannica,* whose competitive position was severely eroded by a "nontraditional" competitor—CD-based encyclopedias (e.g., Microsoft *Encarta*) that could be used on home computers.

SWOT Gives a One-Shot View of a Moving Target A key weakness of SWOT is that it is primarily a static assessment. It focuses too much of a firm's attention on one moment in time. Essentially, this is like studying a single frame of a motion picture. You may be able to identify the principal actors and learn something about the setting, but it doesn't tell you much about the plot. Competition among organizations is played out over time. As circumstances, capabilities, and strategies change, static analysis techniques do not reveal the dynamics of the competitive environment. Clearly, ProCD was unaware that its competitiveness was being eroded so quickly.

SWOT Overemphasizes a Single Dimension of Strategy Sometimes firms become preoccupied with a single strength or a key feature of the product or service they are offering and ignore other factors needed for competitive success. For example, Food Lion, a large grocery retailer, paid a heavy price for its excessive emphasis on cost control. The resulting problems with labor and the negative publicity led to its eventual withdrawal from several markets.

SWOT analysis has much to offer, but only as a starting point. By itself, it rarely helps a firm develop competitive advantages that it can sustain over time.

Sources: Shapiro, C., & Varian, H. R. 2000. Versioning: The smart way to sell information. *Harvard Business Review,* 78(1): 99–106; and Picken, J. C., & Dess, G. G. 1997. *Mission Critical.* Burr Ridge, IL: Irwin Professional Publishing.

created for other organizations that are involved in the overall supply chain or distribution channel in which your firm participates.[3]

Next, we'll describe and provide examples of each of the primary and support activities. Then, we'll provide examples of how companies add value by means of relationships among activities within the organization as well as activities outside the organization, such as those activities associated with customers and suppliers.[4]

Primary Activities

Five generic categories of primary activities are involved in competing in any industry, as shown in Exhibit 3.2. Each category is divisible into a number of distinct activities that depend on the particular industry and the firm's strategy.[5]

Inbound Logistics	Operations	Outbound Logistics	Marketing and Sales	Service
• Location of distribution facilities to minimize shipping times. • Excellent material and inventory control systems. • Systems to reduce time to send "returns" to suppliers. • Warehouse layout and designs to increase efficiency of operations for incoming materials.	• Efficient plant operations to minimize costs. • Appropriate level of automation in manufacturing. • Quality production control systems to reduce costs and enhance quality. • Efficient plant layout and workflow design.	• Effective shipping processes to provide quick delivery and minimize damages. • Efficient finished goods warehousing processes. • Shipping of goods in large lot sizes to minimize transportation costs. • Quality material handling equipment to increase order picking.	• Highly motivated and competent sales force. • Innovative approaches to promotion and advertising. • Selection of most appropriate distribution channels. • Proper identification of customer segments and needs. • Effective pricing strategies.	• Effective use of procedures to solicit customer feedback and to act on information. • Quick response to customer needs and emergencies. • Ability to furnish replacement parts as required. • Effective management of parts and equipment inventory. • Quality of service personnel and ongoing training. • Appropriate warranty and guarantee policies.

Source: Adapted with permission of The Free Press, a division of Simon & Schuster Adult Publishing Group, from *Competitive Advantage: Creating and Sustaining Superior Performance* by Michael E. Porter. Copyright © 1985, 1998 by Michael E. Porter. All rights reserved.

Exhibit 3.2   **The Value Chain: Some Factors to Consider in Assessing a Firm's Primary Activities**

Inbound Logistics   Inbound logistics is primarily associated with receiving, storing, and distributing inputs to the product. It includes material handling, warehousing, inventory control, vehicle scheduling, and returns to suppliers.

Just-in-time (JIT) inventory systems, for example, were designed to achieve efficient inbound logistics. In essence, Toyota epitomizes JIT inventory systems, in which parts deliveries arrive at the assembly plants only hours before they are needed. JIT systems will play a vital role in fulfilling Toyota's commitment to fill a buyer's new car order in just five days.[6] This standard is in sharp contrast to most competitors that require approximately 30 days' notice to build vehicles. Toyota's standard is three times faster than even Honda Motors, considered to be the industry's most efficient in order follow-through. The five days represent the time from the company's receipt of an order to the time the car leaves the assembly plant. Actual delivery may take longer, depending on where a customer lives. How can Toyota achieve such fast turnaround?

- Its 360 key suppliers are now linked to the company by way of computer on a virtual assembly line.
- Suppliers load parts onto trucks in the order in which they will be installed.
- Parts are stacked on trucks in the same place each time to help workers unload them quickly.
- Deliveries are required to meet a rigid schedule with as many as 12 trucks a day and no more than four hours between trucks.

Operations   Operations include all activities associated with transforming inputs into the final product form, such as machining, packaging, assembly, testing, printing, and facility operations.

Creating environmentally friendly manufacturing is one way a firm can use operations to achieve competitive advantage. Shaw Industries (now part of Berkshire Hathaway), a world-class competitor in the floor-covering industry, is well known for its strong concern for the environment.[7] It has been successful in reducing the expenses associated with the disposal of dangerous chemicals and other waste products from its manufacturing operations. Its environmental endeavors have multiple payoffs. Shaw has received numerous awards for its recycling efforts—awards that enhance its corporate reputation.

Additional examples of environmentally friendly manufacturing include: EcoSolution Q®, the industry's first nylon covering containing recycled content, which was the most successful product launch in the company's history. Shaw's residential staple polyester carpet, made from virtually 100 percent petroleum-based materials, keeps one billion plastic containers out of landfills each year through recycling. Shaw is also pioneering other innovative recycling solutions, including recycled nylon for automotive under-hood applications and ground-up carpet as an ingredient in road materials and fiber-reinforced concrete.

Strategy Spotlight 3.2 discusses how Canon was able to improve its operations by applying the principles of the Toyota Production System.

Outbound Logistics   The activities of outbound logistics are associated with collecting, storing, and distributing the product or service to buyers. They include finished goods, warehousing, material handling, delivery vehicle operation, order processing, and scheduling.

Campbell Soup uses an electronic network to facilitate its continuous-replenishment program with its most progressive retailers.[8] Each morning, retailers electronically inform Campbell of their product needs and of the level of inventories in their distribution

STRATEGY SPOTLIGHT

3.2

Improving Operations at Canon

Canon, the $30 billion Japanese consumer electronics firm, dramatically improved its operational effectiveness by implementing the Toyota Production System (TPS). Could automobile manufacturing systems improve the operations of an electronics manufacturer? At the core of TPS's just-in-time manufacturing system is the elimination of waste and absolute concentration on consistent high quality by a process of continuous improvement.

In 1997, Canon hired TPS consultant Hiroshi Yamada, a one-time journalist who founded a TPS training company. Yamada advised Canon to rip the conveyor belts out of its manufacturing plants and replace them with production "cells," in which groups of employees build entire products. As might be expected, productivity declined during the first few years of the change as workers had to learn to take responsibility for the finished product instead of a single function. According to Canon CEO Fujio Mitarai, "When there were problems in the line, the production manager responsible would get an earful from our account reps."

However, believing that cell production would pay off, Mitarai stuck with it, telling subordinates he would take responsibility for problems. "As a leader, you have to remove fear," he says. Such persistence paid off. Converting 13 domestic plants and 54 overseas facilities to cells, Canon reclaimed 7.5 million square feet of space and the labor equivalent of 35,000 workers. Those workers were redeployed to increase production of key competitive components like CMOS sensors, used in digital cameras. Over the past five years, these efforts, along with research and development advances, have resulted in $2 billion in savings.

Sources: Anonymous. 2005. The car company in front. *The Economist*, January 29: 65–67; and Migliorato, P. 2004. Toyota retools Japan. *Business 2.0*, August: 39–41.

---

centers. Campbell uses that information to forecast future demand and to determine which products require replenishment (based on the inventory limits previously established with each retailer). Trucks leave Campbell's shipping plant that afternoon and arrive at the retailers' distribution centers the same day. The program cuts the inventories of participating retailers from about a four- to a two-weeks' supply. Campbell Soup achieved this improvement because it slashed delivery time and because it knows the inventories of key retailers and can deploy supplies when they are most needed.

The Campbell Soup example also illustrates the win–win benefits of exemplary value-chain activities. Both the supplier (Campbell) and its buyers (retailers) come out ahead. Since the retailer makes more money on Campbell products delivered through continuous replenishment, it has an incentive to carry a broader line and give the company greater shelf space. Campbell found that after it introduced the program, sales of its products grew twice as fast through participating retailers as through all other retailers. Not surprisingly, supermarket chains love such programs. For example, Wegman's Food Markets in upstate New York has augmented its accounting system to measure and reward suppliers whose products cost the least to stock and sell.

Marketing and Sales   Marketing and sales activities are associated with purchases of products and services by end users and the inducements used to get them to make purchases.[9] They include advertising, promotion, sales force, quoting, channel selection, channel relations, and pricing.[10] It is not always enough to have a great product.[11] The key is to convince your channel partners that it is in their best interests not only to carry your product but also to market it in a way that is consistent with your strategy. Consider Monsanto's efforts at educating distributors to improve the value proposition of its line of Saflex® windows.[12] The products introduced in the early 1990s had a superior attribute: The window design permitted laminators to form an exceptional type of glass by sandwiching a plastic sheet interlayer between two pieces of glass. This product is not only stronger and offers better ultraviolet protection than regular glass, but also when cracked, it adheres to the plastic sheet—an excellent safety feature for both cars and homes.

Despite these benefits, Monsanto had a hard time convincing laminators and window manufacturers to carry products made with Saflex. According to Melissa Toledo, brand manager at Monsanto, "Saflex was priced at a 30 percent premium above traditional glass, and the various stages in the value chain (distributors and retailers) didn't think there would be a demand for such an expensive glass product." What was Monsanto's solution? Subsequently, it reintroduced Saflex as KeepSafe® and worked to coordinate the product's value propositions. By analyzing the experiences of all of the players in the supply chain, it was able to create marketing programs that helped each build a business aimed at selling its products. Said Toledo, "We want to know how they go about selling those types of products, what challenges they face, and what they think they need to sell our products. This helps us a lot when we try to provide them with these needs." Thus, marketing is often a key element of competitive advantage.[13]

At times, a firm's marketing initiatives may become overly aggressive and lead to actions that are both unethical and illegal.[14] For example:

- *Burdines.* This department store chain is under investigation for allegedly adding club memberships to its customers' credit cards without prior approval.
- *Fleet Mortgage.* This company has been accused of adding insurance fees for dental coverage and home insurance to its customers' mortgage loans without the customers' knowledge.
- *HCI Direct.* Eleven states have accused this direct-mail firm with charging for panty hose samples that customers did not order.
- *Juno Online Services.* The Federal Trade Commission brought charges against this Internet service provider for failing to provide customers with a telephone number to cancel service.

Service   This primary activity includes all actions associated with providing service to enhance or maintain the value of the product, such as installation, repair, training, parts supply, and product adjustment.

Internet-based retailers (e-tailers) provide many examples of how superb customer service is critical for adding value. Nearly all e-tailers have faced a similar problem: They figured that the Web's self-service model would save them millions in customer service costs. But that was the last place they could afford to shave costs.[15] According to market researcher Datamonitor, 7.8 percent of abandoned online shopping carts could be salvaged through an effective customer service solution—an impressive $6.1 billion in lost annual sales. Bill Bass, senior vice president of e-commerce at catalog retailer Lands' End, Inc., claimed, "If there's a train wreck to happen, it's going to be around customer service."

Let's see what two retailers are doing to provide exemplary customer service. At Sephora.com, a customer service representative taking a phone call from a repeat customer has instant access to, for example, what shade of lipstick the customer likes best. This will help the rep cross-sell by suggesting a matching shade of lip gloss. CEO Jim Wiggett expects such personalization to build loyalty and boost sales per customer. Nordstrom, the Seattle-based department store chain, goes even a step further. It offers a cyber-assist: A service rep can take control of a customer's Web browser and literally lead her to just the silk scarf that she is looking for. CEO Dan Nordstrom believes that such a capability will close enough additional purchases to pay for the $1 million investment in software.

STRATEGY SPOTLIGHT

Virgin Atlantic's High-Flying Service

On June 14, 2004, Virgin Atlantic's chairman and extreme sports enthusiast Richard Branson broke a 40-year-old world record for crossing the English Channel in an amphibious vehicle. He piloted a Gibbs Aquada across the 22-mile strait in an hour and 40 minutes. This might be good news for Sir Richard, but it is even better news for U.K.-based Gibbs Technologies. Orders for the sports cars have doubled since the feat. And Branson himself plans to buy a fleet of the three-seat Aquadas to ferry his Virgin Atlantic first-class passengers down the Thames River from London to Heathrow International Airport.

After setting the record, Branson said "for many years our Upper Class passengers have enjoyed our complimentary limousines to and from the airport. Some people prefer our chauffeured motorbikes, but we are now planning to go one step further by introducing the chance to experience a Gibbs Aquada. This new service follows in our tradition of product innovation and fun. Using the Gibbs Aquada, we will be able to cut thirty minutes off the journey between Heathrow and The City, giving our travelers extra time for meetings or relaxation."

The Gibbs Aquada is not the only car/boat hybrid ever made, but it is by far the fastest. A 175 horsepower V-6 engine powers the three-seater at up to 100 miles per hour on land. And at sea, the same engine drives a jet that expels water out the back at high speeds to propel the boat like a jet-ski. The price is $250,000.

Source: Copeland, M. V., & Thomas, O. 2004. A new sales Channel. *Business 2.0,* August: 134; Pidcock, K. (Ed.). 2004. Virgin boss sets new record. *Orange Aero Club News,* September: 2; and Anonymous. 2003. The best of what's new. *Popular Science* (www.popsci.com).

Strategy Spotlight 3.3 discusses a very innovative approach to customer service: Virgin Atlantic's use of amphibious vehicles to ferry their "Upper Class" passengers to London's Heathrow International Airport.

Support Activities

Support activities in the value chain are involved with competing in any industry and can be divided into four generic categories, as shown in Exhibit 3.3. As with primary activities, each category of the support activity is divisible into a number of distinct value activities that are specific to a particular industry. For example, technology development's discrete activities may include component design, feature design, field testing, process engineering, and technology selection. Similarly, procurement may be divided into activities such as qualifying new suppliers, purchasing different groups of inputs, and monitoring supplier performance.

Procurement   Procurement refers to the function of purchasing inputs used in the firm's value chain, not to the purchased inputs themselves.[16] Purchased inputs include raw materials, supplies, and other consumable items as well as assets such as machinery, laboratory equipment, office equipment, and buildings.[17]

Microsoft is a company that has enhanced its procurement process (and the quality of its suppliers) by providing formal reviews of its suppliers. One of Microsoft's divisions has extended the review process used for employees to its outside suppliers.[18] The employee services group, which is responsible for everything from travel to 401(k) programs to the on-site library, outsources more than 60 percent of the services it provides. Despite all the business it was doing with suppliers, the employee services group was not providing them with enough feedback on how well Microsoft thought they were doing. This was feedback that the suppliers wanted to get and that Microsoft wanted to give. The evaluation system that Microsoft developed helped clarify its expectations to suppliers. An executive noted: "We had one supplier—this was before the new system— that would have scored a 1.2 out of 5. After we started giving this feedback, and the

Exhibit 3.3

The Value Chain: Some Factors to Consider in Assessing a Firm's Support Activities

General Administration

- Effective planning systems to attain overall goals and objectives.
- Ability of top management to anticipate and act on key environmental trends and events.
- Ability to obtain low-cost funds for capital expenditures and working capital.
- Excellent relationships with diverse stakeholder groups.
- Ability to coordinate and integrate activities across the "value system."
- High visibility to inculcate organizational culture, reputation, and values.

Human Resource Management

- Effective recruiting, development, and retention mechanisms for employees.
- Quality relations with trade unions.
- Quality work environment to maximize overall employee performance and minimize absenteeism.
- Reward and incentive programs to motivate all employees.

Technology Development

- Effective research and development activities for process and product initiatives.
- Positive collaborative relationships between R&D and other departments.
- State-of-the art facilities and equipment.
- Culture that enhances creativity and innovation.
- Excellent professional qualifications of personnel.
- Ability to meet critical deadlines.

Procurement

- Procurement of raw material inputs to optimize quality and speed, and to minimize the associated costs.
- Development of collaborative "win–win" relationships with suppliers.
- Effective procedures to purchase advertising and media services.
- Analysis and selection of alternate sources of inputs to minimize dependence on one supplier.
- Ability to make proper lease-versus-buy decisions.

Source: Adapted with permission of The Free Press, a division of Simon & Schuster Adult Publishing Group, from *Competitive Advantage: Creating and Sustaining Superior Performance* by Michael E. Porter. Copyright © 1985, 1998 by Michael E. Porter. All rights reserved.

supplier understood our expectations, its performance improved dramatically. Within six months, it scored a 4. If you'd asked me before we began the feedback system, I would have said that was impossible."

Technology Development   Every value activity embodies technology.[19] The array of technologies employed in most firms is very broad, ranging from technologies used to prepare documents and transport goods to those embodied in processes and equipment or the product itself. Technology development related to the product and its features

An Interesting Technological Innovation: A Seaworthy Foldable Boat

When people think of foldable products, they are likely to think of lawn chairs, tables, and fans but not boats. However, last year Sandy Kaye, owner of Porta-Bote in Mountain View, California, sold nearly 10,000 dinghy-size boats for up to $1,600 each. The boat folds to 4 inches in height and it is made from a resin developed by NASA that gets stronger with each folding. With its flat design, the Porta-Bote fits on the side of a recreation vehicle, the hull of a larger boat, or even a yak! Britain's Royal Air Force Mountain Rescue Service strapped it (it only weighs about 60 pounds) on the scruffy animal for a trek up Mt. Everest and used it to cross a lake. A company spokesperson said that they have submitted an application for the Porta-Bote to appear in the *Guinness Book of World Records* as the first and only boat in to world to have "sailed" on a lake 20,000 feet above sea level.

The men from the RAF Mountain Rescue service took the folding Porta-Bote as a precaution against being stranded by melting glaciers. They expected to find the lake frozen. However, it had thawed slightly and they were able to break the ice and "set sail." Expedition leader Flight Lt. Ted Atkins said his crew used shovels as paddles to cross a glacier lake high above the Himalayas. He joked, "I've flown an RAF Nimrod at 20,000 feet before but I've never paddled a boat at that altitude."

Many might ask how a boat can be folded not just once, but many times and still have seams strong enough to never leak. Although the exact answer remains a proprietary secret of the firm, the technique is used in the aerospace industry. It involves the complex welding of the four pieces together via staple wires and some type of sealant material injected in between the panels. Whatever the exact method of welding is, it certainly does a superb job of holding the Porta-Bote together.

Sources: Anonymous. 2004. Porta-Bote. A completely collapsible watercraft that transforms from surfboard dimensions into a full-fledged boat. *TackleTour*, April 19 (www.tackletour.com); Chambers, E. Seaworthy. *BusinessWeek*, January 25: 12; and www.porta-bote.com.

supports the entire value chain, while other technology development is associated with particular primary or support activities.

The 2000 merger of Allied Signal and Honeywell brought together roughly 13,000 scientists and an $870 million R&D budget that promises to lead to some innovative products and services in two major areas: performance materials and control systems. Some of the possible innovations include:

- **Performance materials.** The development of uniquely shaped fibers with very high absorption capability. When employed in the company's Fram oil filters, they capture 50 percent more particles than ordinary filters. This means that cars can travel further with fewer oil changes.
- **Control systems.** Working with six leading oil companies, Honeywell developed software using "self-learning" algorithms that predict when something might go wrong in an oil refinery before it actually does. Examples include a faulty gas valve or hazardous spillage.[20]

Strategy Spotlight 3.4 addresses a unique use of technology—a foldable boat!

Human Resource Management Human resource management consists of activities involved in the recruiting, hiring, training, development, and compensation of all types of personnel.[21] It supports both individual primary and support activities (e.g., hiring of engineers and scientists) and the entire value chain (e.g., negotiations with labor unions).

Like all great service companies, JetBlue Airways Corporation is obsessed with hiring superior employees.[22] But they found it difficult to attract college graduates to commit to careers as flight attendants. JetBlue developed a highly innovative recruitment program

STRATEGY SPOTLIGHT

SAS and Employee Turnover

Jeffrey Pfeffer, professor of organizational behavior at Stanford University, asked a managing partner at a San Francisco law firm about its employee turnover rate. Turnover had increased from 25 percent to 30 percent over the last few years. The law firm's solution was to increase recruitment of new employees. Pfeffer's response was, "What kind of doctor would you be if your patient was bleeding faster and faster, and your only response was to increase the rate of transfusion?"

It's not difficult to calculate the cost of a new hire, but what does it cost a firm when employees leave? Software developer SAS Institute puts the cost at around $50 million. David Russo, director of human resources at SAS, suggested that keeping employees is not just about caring for your employees—it also provides a strong economic advantage to the company.

Consider Russo's example: Average employee turnover in the software business is 20 percent per year. SAS's turnover rate is 4 percent. SAS has 5,000 employees earning an average of $60,000 a year. The difference between turnover in the industry and turnover at SAS is 16 percent. Multiplying 16 percent by SAS's 5,000 employees at $60,000 a year, SAS has a cost savings of nearly $50 million. SAS estimates the total cost of turnover per employee to equal the employee's annual salary.

What can a firm do with an extra $50 million? SAS spends a large portion of this sum on its employees. The SAS gym, cafeteria (with pianist), on-site medical and child care, flexible work schedules, employer retirement contributions of 15 percent of an employee's pay, and a host of other family-friendly programs help keep SAS's employee turnover level well below the industry average. Even after all these perks, SAS still has money left over.

Russo's message? "This is not tree-huggery. This is money in the bank." The bottom line is it pays to retain employees.

Sources: Levering, R., & Moskowitz, M. 2003. "The 100 Best Companies to Work For. *Fortune*, January 20: 127–152; and Webber, A. M. 1998. Danger: Toxic Company. *Fast Company*, November: 152–161.

for flight attendants—a one-year contract that gives them a chance to travel, meet lots of people, and then decide what else they might like to do. They also introduced the idea of training a friend and employee together so that they could share a job. With such employee-friendly initiatives, JetBlue has been very successful in attracting talent.

Employees often leave a firm because they reach a plateau and begin to look for new opportunities and challenges.[23] AT&T strives to retain such people with Resource Link, an in-house temporary service that enables employees with diverse management, technical, or professional skills to market their abilities to different departments for short-term assignments. This not only enables professionals to broaden their experience base but also provides a mechanism for other parts of the organization to benefit from new sources of ideas.

Strategy Spotlight 3.5 describes how SAS Institute's innovative approach to human resources provides an insightful financial justification for the broad array of benefits it provides to employees.

General Administration General administration consists of a number of activities, including general management, planning, finance, accounting, legal and government affairs, quality management, and information systems. Administration (unlike the other support activities) typically supports the entire value chain and not individual activities.

Although general administration is sometimes viewed only as overhead, it can be a powerful source of competitive advantage. In a telephone operating company, for example, negotiating and maintaining ongoing relations with regulatory bodies can be among the most important activities for competitive advantage. In a similar vein, effective information systems can contribute significantly to cost position, while in some industries top management plays a vital role in dealing with important buyers.[24]

The strong and effective leadership of top executives can also make a significant contribution to an organization's success. As we discussed in Chapter 1, chief executive officers (CEOs) such as Herb Kelleher, Andrew Grove, and Jack Welch have been credited with playing critical roles in the success of Southwest Airlines, Intel, and General Electric. And Carlos Ghosn is considered one of today's top corporate leaders after his turnaround of Nissan, the Japan-based automobile manufacturer—turning losses into a $7 billion profit. He presently has been given the challenge of being CEO of *both* Nissan and its parent, Renault, the French automaker.

Information systems can also play a key role in increasing operating efficiencies and enhancing a firm's performance.[25] Consider Walgreen Co.'s introduction of Intercom Plus, a computer-based prescription management system. Linked by computer to both doctors' offices and third-party payment plans, the system automates telephone refills, store-to-store prescription transfers, and drug reordering. It also provides information on drug interactions and, coupled with revised workflows, frees up pharmacists from administrative tasks to devote more time to patient counseling.

Lawyers often receive a "bad rap," even in the corporate world! However, legal services can be a source of significant competitive advantage. One example is ensuring the protection of a firm's intellectual property through patents, trademarks, and copyrights. Although many companies are not aware of the earnings potential of their patent holdings, Texas Instruments (TI) is one notable exception.[26] In essence, TI began investing the income-generation potential of its patent portfolio in the mid-1980s, when, out of desperation, it faced bankruptcy. Since then, TI has earned an impressive $4 billion in patent royalties; its licensing revenues are estimated to be $800 million per year. Recently, TI signed yet another licensing pact for its semiconductor patents with Hyundai, an agreement that is expected to generate a total of $1 billion in additional royalties over seven years.

Strategy Spotlight 3.6 discusses how Gary Kelly, Southwest Airlines's CEO, added value to the firm when he was its chief financial officer (CFO).

Interrelationships among Value-Chain Activities within and across Organizations

We have defined each of the value-chain activities separately for clarity of presentation, but this approach implicitly understates the importance of relationships among value-chain activities.[27] There are two levels that must be addressed: (1) interrelationships among activities within the firm and (2) relationships among activities within the firm and with other organizations (e.g., customers and suppliers) that are part of the firm's expanded value chain.[28]

With regard to the first level, recall AT&T's innovative Resource Link program wherein employees who have reached their plateau may apply for temporary positions in other parts of the organization. Clearly, this program has the potential to benefit all activities within the firm's value chain because it creates opportunities for top employees to lend their expertise to all of the organization's value-creating activities.

With regard to the second level, Campbell Soup's use of electronic networks enabled it to improve the efficiency of outbound logistics.[29] However, it also helped Campbell manage the ordering of raw materials more effectively, improve its production scheduling, and help its customers better manage their inbound logistics operations.

An example of how a firm's value-creating activity can enhance customer value is provided by Ciba Specialty Chemicals (which merged with Sandoz in 1996 to form Novartis), a Swiss manufacturer of textile dyes.[30] The firm's research and development experts have created dyes that fix more readily to the fabric and therefore require less salt. How does this innovation add value for Ciba's customers? There are three ways. First,

How a Firm's General Administration Can Create Value

A firm's general administration can significantly impact its performance. Southwest Airlines' chief financial officer, Gary Kelly, is a key contributor to the airline's solid financial performance. He drives a red Porsche, which might lead you to believe that the 48-year-old CFO likes speed and recklessness. But he drives the car carefully and conscientiously—the very model of maturity on the road. He takes a similar approach to managing Southwest's finances.

While the rest of the airline industry was laying off workers by the thousands, Southwest did not furlough anyone. Its ability to shine in dire times is a result of its conservative financial culture that values a large cash balance and low debt. Southwest began conserving funds in 2000, when it saw a recession on the horizon. After installing a new computer system and renegotiating contracts with vendors, it managed to boost its cash on hand from $600 million to about $1 billion.

Through the years, Wall Street analysts have criticized Kelly's conservative approach and goaded him to use the extra cash to make acquisitions or buy back stock.

Goldman Sachs's airline analyst actually calls the balance sheet "too strong." Yet it is such fiscal preparedness that has kept the company's debt-to-capital ratio at around 40 percent (compared to the industry average of about 70 percent), which allows for more flexibility during tough times.

Kelly also has come up with some creative measures to get through the recent slumping economy and terrorism threats. For example, he rescheduled the delivery of 19 planes from Boeing by developing an arrangement between Boeing and a collection of banks. This arrangement, whereby the banks formed a group called the Amor Trust, allowed the trust to take delivery from Boeing as scheduled and store the planes in the Mojave Desert until Southwest needed them. The idea was to strike a balance between maintaining the good relationship with Boeing, its only supplier of planes, and holding off spending the cash on the planes it does not yet need. Darryl Jenkins, director of the Aviation Institute at George Washington University, attributes Southwest's success to two things, "Consistency, and the fact that they don't listen to other people."

Note: On July 15, 2004 Gary Kelly became CEO of Southwest Airlines.

Sources: Zellner, W., & Arnadt, M. 2003. Holding steady. *BusinessWeek*, February 3; and Mount, I. 2002. Southwest's Gary Kelly: A tip of the hat to the CFO at the one airline still making money. *Business 2.0*, February 12: 5–7.

it lowers the outlays for salt. Textile companies using the new dyes are able to reduce their costs for salt by up to 2 percent of revenues, a significant drop in an industry with razor-thin profit margins. Second, it reduces manufacturers' costs for water treatment. Used bathwater full of salt and unfixed dye must be treated before it is released into rivers or streams (even in low-income countries where environmental standards are typically lax). Simply put, less salt and less unfixed dye mean lower water-treatment costs. Third, the higher fixation rates of the new dyes make quality control easier, lowering the costs of rework.

We conclude this section with Strategy Spotlight 3.7. It addresses how Cardinal Health expertly integrates several value activities to create value for its suppliers and customers.

Applying the Value Chain to Service Organizations

The value chain is often believed to apply primarily to manufacturing operations. Indeed, the concepts of inbound logistics, operations, and outbound logistics suggest managing the raw materials that might be manufactured into finished products and delivered to customers. But these three steps do not apply only to manufacturing. They correspond to any transformation process in which inputs are converted through a work process into outputs that add value. For example, accounting is a sort of transformation process that converts daily records of individual transactions into monthly financial reports. In this example, the transaction records are the inputs, accounting is the operation that adds value, and financial statements are the outputs.

STRATEGY SPOTLIGHT

Cardinal Health: Creating Value through the Extended Value Chain

Cardinal Health is a wholesale drug distributor that buys sprays, pills, and capsules from pharmaceutical companies and puts them on the shelves in pharmacies or into the hands of emergency-room nurses. Profitability is a problem in this business, because the company is caught between powerful manufacturers and cost-conscious customers. Cardinal, for example, buys pharmaceuticals from the likes of Pfizer (its biggest supplier) and sells them to the likes of CVS (its largest customer).

Cardinal responded to the profitability challenge by trying to add value for both customers and suppliers. It understood how urgent it was for one of its customer groups (hospitals) to control costs, so it began to offer services to hospital pharmacies. Rather than shipping medications to the hospitals' front door, it "followed the pill" into the hospital and right to the patient's room, offering pharmacy-management services and extending those services to customized surgical kits.

As the knowledgeable intermediary, Cardinal realized it could bring significant value to its suppliers (the pharmaceutical manufacturers) by providing services in drug formulation, testing, manufacturing, and packaging, freeing those companies to concentrate on the discovery of the next round of blockbuster medicines. Cardinal even used its position to develop new services for commercial pharmacies. Cardinal's drug-chain customers depend on third-party payments for most of the prescriptions it fills. It worked with a number of leading chains to develop a system called ScriptLINE that automates the reimbursement process for pharmacies and updates rates daily.

The result of this stream of innovations is a wave of growth and profits. Cardinal, with annual sales of $65 billion, has registered compound annual earnings growth of approximately 20 percent or better for the past 15 years.

The Cardinal Health story is a powerful example of extending the value chain and adding value to the many players involved—from the suppliers to the customers. The company found opportunities in an unpromising business landscape by identifying new customer needs related to the activities that surround the products it sells.

Sources: Slywotzky, A., & Wise, R. 2003. Double digit growth in no-growth times. *Fast Company*, April: 66–70; Stewart, T. 2002. Fueling drug growth during an economic drought. *Business 2.0*, May: 17–21; and Lashinsky, A. 2003. Big man in the "middle." *Fortune*, April 14: 161–162.

What are the "operations," or transformation processes, of service organizations? These could be many different things. At times, the difference between manufacturing and service is in providing a customized solution rather than the kind of mass production that is common in manufacturing. For example, a travel agent adds value by creating an itinerary that includes transportation, accommodations, and activities that are customized to your budget and your dates of travel. A law firm renders services that are specific to a client's needs and circumstances. In both cases, the work process (operation) involves the application of specialized knowledge based on the specifics of a situation (inputs) and the outcome that the client seeks to achieve (outputs). In Chapter 8, we will discuss how the Internet is adding value through unique applications of problem-solving capabilities.

The application of the value chain to service organizations suggests that the value-adding process may be configured differently depending on the type of business a firm is engaged in. As the preceding discussion on support activities suggests, activities such as procurement and legal services are critical for adding value. Indeed, the activities that may only provide support to one company may be critical to the primary value-adding activity of another firm.

Exhibit 3.4 provides two models of how the value chain might look in service industries. In the retail industry, there are no manufacturing operations. A firm, such as Circuit City, adds value by developing expertise in the procurement of finished goods and by displaying them in their stores in a way that enhances sales. Thus, the value chain makes procurement activities (i.e., partnering with vendors and purchasing goods) a primary rather than a support activity. Operations refer to the task of operating Circuit City's stores. For an engineering services firm, research and development provides inputs, the transformation

Retail: Primary Value-Chain Activities

Engineering Services: Primary Value-Chain Activities

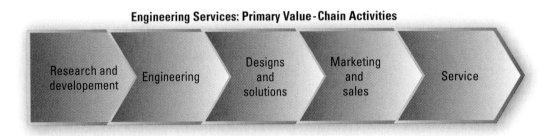

Exhibit 3.4　**Some Examples of Value Chains in Service Industries**

process is the engineering itself, and innovative designs and practical solutions are the outputs. Arthur D. Little, for example, is a large consulting firm with offices in 30 countries. In its technology and innovation management practice, A. D. Little strives to make the best use of the science, technology and knowledge resources available to create value for a wide range of industries and client sectors. This involves activities associated with research and development, engineering, and creating solutions as well as downstream activities such as marketing, sales, and service. These examples suggest that how the primary and support activities of a given firm are configured and deployed will often depend on industry conditions and the extent to which the company is service and/or manufacturing oriented.

>>Resource-Based View of the Firm

The resource-based view (RBV) of the firm combines two perspectives: (1) the internal analysis of phenomena within a company and (2) an external analysis of the industry and its competitive environment.[31] It goes beyond the traditional SWOT (strengths, weaknesses, opportunities, threats) analysis by integrating internal and external perspectives. The ability of a firm's resources to confer competitive advantage(s) cannot be determined without taking into consideration the broader competitive context. That is, a firm's resources must be evaluated in terms of how valuable, rare, and hard they are for competitors to duplicate. Otherwise, at best, the firm would be able to attain only competitive parity. As noted earlier in the chapter (in Strategy Spotlight 3.1), a firm's strengths and capabilities—no matter how unique or impressive—do not necessarily lead to competitive advantages in the marketplace. The criteria for whether advantages are created and whether or not they can be sustained over time will be addressed later in this section. Thus, the RBV is a very useful framework for gaining insights as to why some competitors are more profitable than others. As we will see later in the book, the RBV is also helpful in developing strategies for individual businesses and diversified firms by revealing how core competencies embedded in a firm can help it exploit new product and market opportunities.

In the two sections that follow, we will discuss the three key types of resources that firms possess (summarized in Exhibit 3.5): tangible resources, intangible resources, and

Exhibit 3.5
The Resource-Based
View of the Firm:
Resources and
Capabilities

Tangible Resources

Financial	•	Firm's cash account and cash equivalents.
	•	Firm's capacity to raise equity.
	•	Firm's borrowing capacity.
Physical	•	Modern plant and facilities.
	•	Favorable manufacturing locations.
	•	State-of-the-art machinery and equipment.
Technological	•	Trade secrets.
	•	Innovative production processes.
	•	Patents, copyrights, trademarks.
Organizational	•	Effective strategic planning processes.
	•	Excellent evaluation and control systems.

Intangible Resources

Human	•	Experience and capabilities of employees.
	•	Trust.
	•	Managerial skills.
	•	Firm-specific practices and procedures.
Innovation and creativity	•	Technical and scientific skills.
	•	Innovation capacities.
Reputation	•	Brand name.
	•	Reputation with customers for quality and reliability.
	•	Reputation with suppliers for fairness, non–zero-sum relationships.

Organizational Capabilities

- Firm competencies or skills the firm employs to transfer inputs to outputs.
- Capacity to combine tangible and intangible resources, using organizational processes to attain desired end.

   EXAMPLES:
   - Outstanding customer service.
   - Excellent product development capabilities.
   - Innovativeness of products and services.
   - Ability to hire, motivate, and retain human capital.

Source: Adapted from Barney, J. B. 1991. Firm resources and sustained competitive advantage. *Journal of Management:* 17: 101; Grant, R. M. 1991. *Contemporary Strategy Analysis:* 100–102. Cambridge England: Blackwell Business; Hitt, M. A., Ireland, R. D., & Hoskisson, R. E. 2001. *Strategic management: Competitiveness and globalization* (4th ed.). Cincinnati: South-Western College Publishing.

organizational capabilities. Then we will address the conditions under which such assets and capabilities can enable a firm to attain a sustainable competitive advantage.

It is important to note that resources by themselves typically do not yield a competitive advantage. Even if a basketball team recruited an all-star center, there would be little chance of victory if the other members of the team were continually outplayed by their opponents or if the coach's attitude was so negative that everyone, including the center, became unwilling to put forth their best efforts. And imagine how many World Series titles Joe Torre would have won as manager of the New York Yankees if none of the pitchers on his team could throw fastballs over 70 miles per hour. Although the all-star center and the baseball manager are unquestionably valuable resources, they would *not* enable the organization to attain advantages under these circumstances.

In a business context, Cardinal Health's excellent value-creating activities (e.g., logistics, drug formulation) would not be a source of competitive advantage if those activities were not integrated with other important value-creating activities such as marketing and sales. Thus, a central theme of the resource-based view of the firm is that competitive advantages are created (and sustained) through the bundling of several resources in unique combinations.

Types of Firm Resources

We define firm resources to include all assets, capabilities, organizational processes, information, knowledge, and so forth, controlled by a firm that enable it to develop and implement value-creating strategies.

Tangible Resources   Assets that are relatively easy to identify are called tangible resources. They include the physical and financial assets that an organization uses to create value for its customers. Among them are financial resources (e.g., a firm's cash, accounts receivable, and its ability to borrow funds); physical resources (e.g., the company's plant, equipment, and machinery as well as its proximity to customers and suppliers); organizational resources (e.g., the company's strategic planning process and its employee development, evaluation, and reward systems); and technological resources (e.g., trade secrets, patents, and copyrights).

Many firms are finding that high-tech, computerized training has dual benefits: It develops more effective employees and reduces costs at the same time. Employees at FedEx take computer-based job competency tests every 6 to 12 months.[32] The 90-minute computer-based tests identify areas of individual weakness and provide input to a computer database of employee skills—information the firm uses in promotion decisions.

Intangible Resources   Much more difficult for competitors (and, for that matter, a firm's own managers) to account for or imitate are intangible resources, which are typically embedded in unique routines and practices that have evolved and accumulated over time. These include human resources (e.g., experience and capability of employees, trust, effectiveness of work teams, managerial skills), innovation resources (e.g., technical and scientific expertise, ideas), and reputation resources (e.g., brand name, reputation with suppliers for fairness and with customers for reliability and product quality). A firm's culture may also be a resource that provides competitive advantage.[33]

For example, you might not think that motorcycles, clothes, toys, and restaurants have much in common. Yet Harley-Davidson has entered all of these product and service markets by capitalizing on its strong brand image—a valuable intangible resource.[34] It has used that image to sell accessories, clothing, and toys, and it has licensed the Harley-Davidson Café in New York City to provide further exposure for its brand name and products.

Organizational Capabilities   Organizational capabilities are not specific tangible or intangible assets, but rather the competencies or skills that a firm employs to transform inputs into outputs.[35] In short, they refer to an organization's capacity to deploy tangible and intangible resources over time and generally in combination, and to leverage those capabilities to bring about a desired end.[36] Examples of organizational capabilities are outstanding customer service, excellent product development capabilities, superb innovation processes, and flexibility in manufacturing processes.[37]

Gillette's capability to combine several technologies has been one of the keys to its unparalleled success in the wet-shaving industry. Technologies that are central to its product development efforts include its expertise concerning the physiology of facial hair and skin, the metallurgy of blade strength and sharpness, the dynamics of a cartridge moving across skin, and the physics of a razor blade severing the hair—highly specialized areas for which Gillette has unique capabilities. Combining these technologies has helped the company to develop innovative products such as the Excel, Sensor Excel, and MACH 3 shaving systems.

Dell Inc., with annual revenues of $49 billion and net profits of $3 billion, differentiated itself by pioneering a direct sales approach with user-configurable products to address the diverse needs of the corporate and institutional customer base.[38] Exhibit 3.6 summarizes the Dell recipe for its remarkable success by integrating its tangible resources, intangible resources, and organizational capabilities.

Dell has continued to maintain this competitive advantage by further strengthening its value-chain activities and interrelationships that are critical to satisfying the largest market opportunities. They achieved this by (1) implementing e-commerce direct sales and support processes that accounted for the sophisticated buying habits

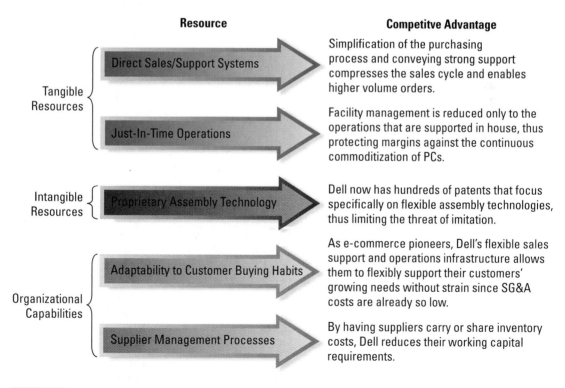

Exhibit 3.6   Dell's Tangible Resources, Intangible Resources, and Organizational Capabilities

of the largest markets, and (2) matching their operations to the purchase options by adopting flexible assembly processes, while leaving inventory management to its extensive supplier network. Dell has sustained these advantages by investing in intangible resources such as proprietary assembly methods and packaging configurations that help to protect against the threat of imitation. Dell recognizes that the PC is a complex product with components sourced from several different technologies and manufacturers. Thus, in working backwards from the customer's purchasing habits, Dell saw that they could build valuable solutions by organizing their resources and capabilities around the build-to-specification tastes, making both the sales and integration processes flexible, and passing on overhead expenses to their suppliers. As the PC industry has become further commoditized, Dell has been one of the few competitors which have retained solid margins. They have accomplished this by adapting their manufacturing and assembly capabilities to match the PC market's trend toward user compatibility.

Firm Resources and Sustainable Competitive Advantages

As we have mentioned, resources alone are not a basis for competitive advantages, nor are advantages sustainable over time. In some cases, a resource or capability helps a firm to increase its revenues or to lower costs but the firm derives only a temporary advantage because competitors quickly imitate or substitute for it. Many e-commerce businesses in the early 2000s have seen their profits seriously eroded because new (or existing) competitors easily duplicated their business model. One noteworthy example is Priceline.com, which expanded its offerings from enabling customers to place bids online for airline tickets and a wide variety of other products. It was simply too easy for competitors (e.g., a consortium of major airlines) to duplicate Priceline's products and services. By the end of 2001, its market capitalization had plummeted roughly 98 percent from its 52-week high.

For a resource to provide a firm with the potential for a sustainable competitive advantage, it must have four attributes.[39] These criteria are summarized in Exhibit 3.7. First, the resource must be valuable in the sense that it exploits opportunities and/or neutralizes threats in the firm's environment. Second, it must be rare among the firm's current and potential competitors. Third, the resource must be difficult for competitors to imitate. Fourth, the resource must have no strategically equivalent substitutes. Let's examine each of these criteria.

Exhibit 3.7
Four Criteria for Assessing Sustainability of Resources and Capabilities

Is the resource or capability . . .	Implications
Valuable	• Neutralize threats and exploit opportunities
Rare	• Not many firms possess
Difficult to imitate	• Physically unique
	• Path dependency (how accumulated over time)
	• Causal ambiguity (difficult to disentangle what it is or how it could be re-created)
	• Social complexity (trust, interpersonal relationships, culture, reputation)
Difficult to substitute	• No equivalent strategic resources or capabilities

Is the Resource Valuable?   Organizational resources can be a source of competitive advantage only when they are valuable. Resources are valuable when they enable a firm to formulate and implement strategies that improve its efficiency or effectiveness. The SWOT framework suggests that firms improve their performance only when they exploit opportunities or neutralize (or minimize) threats.

The fact that firm attributes must be valuable in order to be considered resources (as well as potential sources of competitive advantage) reveals an important complementary relationship among environmental models (e.g., SWOT and five-forces analyses) and the resource-based model. Environmental models isolate those firm attributes that exploit opportunities and/or neutralize threats. Thus, they specify what firm attributes may be considered as resources. The resource-based model then suggests what additional characteristics these resources must possess if they are to develop a sustained competitive advantage.

Is the Resource Rare?   If competitors or potential competitors also possess the same valuable resource, it is not a source of a competitive advantage because all of these firms have the capability to exploit that resource in the same way. Common strategies based on such a resource would give no one firm an advantage. For a resource to provide competitive advantages, it must be uncommon, that is, rare relative to other competitors.

This argument can apply to bundles of valuable firm resources that are used to formulate and develop strategies. Some strategies require a mix of multiple types of resources—tangible assets, intangible assets, and organizational capabilities. If a particular bundle of firm resources is not rare, then relatively large numbers of firms will be able to conceive of and implement the strategies in question. Thus, such strategies will not be a source of competitive advantage, even if the resource in question is valuable.

Can the Resource Be Imitated Easily?   Inimitability (difficulty in imitating) is a key to value creation because it constrains competition.[40] If a resource is inimitable, then any profits generated are more likely to be sustainable. Having a resource that competitors can easily copy generates only temporary value. This has important implications. Since managers often fail to apply this test, they tend to base long-term strategies on resources that are imitable. IBP (Iowa Beef Processors) became the first meatpacking company in the United States to modernize by building a set of assets (automated plants located in cattle-producing states) and capabilities (low-cost "disassembly" of carcasses) that earned returns on assets of 1.3 percent in the 1970s. By the late 1980s, however, ConAgra and Cargill had imitated these resources, and IBP's profitability fell by nearly 70 percent, to 0.4 percent.

Monster.com entered the executive recruiting market by providing, in essence, a substitute for traditional bricks-and-mortar headhunting firms. Although Monster.com's resources are rare and valuable, they are subject to imitation by new rivals—other dot-com firms. Why? There are very low entry barriers for firms wanting to try their hand at recruitment. For example, many job search dot-coms have emerged in recent years, including jobsearch.com, headhunter.com, nationjob.com, and hotjobs.com. In all, there are approximately 30,000 online job boards available to job seekers. Clearly, it would be most difficult for a firm to attain a sustainable advantage in this industry.

Clearly, an advantage based on inimitability won't last forever. Competitors will eventually discover a way to copy most valuable resources. However, managers can forestall them and sustain profits for a while by developing strategies around resources that have at least one of the following four characteristics.[41]

Physical Uniqueness The first source of inimitability is physical uniqueness, which by definition is inherently difficult to copy. A beautiful resort location, mineral rights, or Pfizer's pharmaceutical patents simply cannot be imitated. Many managers believe that several of their resources may fall into this category, but on close inspection, few do.

Path Dependency A greater number of resources cannot be imitated because of what economists refer to as path dependency. This simply means that resources are unique and therefore scarce because of all that has happened along the path followed in their development and/or accumulation. Competitors cannot go out and buy these resources quickly and easily; they must be built up over time in ways that are difficult to accelerate.

The Gerber Products Co. brand name for baby food is an example of a resource that is potentially inimitable. Re-creating Gerber's brand loyalty would be a time-consuming process that competitors could not expedite, even with expensive marketing campaigns. Similarly, the loyalty and trust that Southwest Airlines employees feel toward their firm and its cofounder, Herb Kelleher, are resources that have been built up over a long period of time. Also, a crash R&D program generally cannot replicate a successful technology when research findings cumulate. Clearly, these path-dependent conditions build protection for the original resource. The benefits from experience and learning through trial and error cannot be duplicated overnight.

Causal Ambiguity The third source of inimitability is termed causal ambiguity. This means that would-be competitors may be thwarted because it is impossible to disentangle the causes (or possible explanations) of either what the valuable resource is or how it can be re-created. What is the root of 3M's innovation process? You can study it and draw up a list of possible factors. But it is a complex, unfolding (or folding) process that is hard to understand and would be hard to imitate.

In many cases, causally ambiguous resources are organizational capabilities. They often involve a complex web of social interactions that may even depend on particular individuals. When Continental and United tried to mimic the successful low-cost strategy of Southwest Airlines, the planes, routes, and fast gate turnarounds were not the most difficult aspects for them to copy. Those were all rather easy to observe and, at least in principle, easy to duplicate. However, they could not replicate Southwest's culture of fun, family, frugality, and focus since no one can clearly specify exactly what that culture is or how it came to be.

Social Complexity A final reason that a firm's resources may be imperfectly inimitable is that they may reflect a high level of social complexity. Such phenomena are typically beyond the ability of firms to systematically manage or influence. When competitive advantages are based on social complexity, it is difficult for other firms to imitate them.

A wide variety of firm resources may be considered socially complex. Examples include interpersonal relations with the managers in a firm, its culture, and its reputation with its suppliers and customers. In many of these cases, it is easy to specify how these socially complex resources add value to a firm. Hence, there is little or no causal ambiguity surrounding the link between them and competitive advantage. But an understanding that certain firm attributes, such as quality relations among managers, can improve a firm's efficiency does not necessarily lead to systematic efforts to imitate them. Such social engineering efforts are beyond the capabilities of most firms.

Although complex physical technology is not included in this category of sources of imperfect inimitability, the exploitation of physical technology in a firm typically involves the use of socially complex resources. That is, several firms may possess the same physical technology, but only one of them may have the social relations, culture, group norms, and so on to fully exploit the technology in implementing its strategies. If such complex social resources are not subject to imitation (and assuming they are valuable and rare and no substitutes exist), this firm may obtain a sustained competitive advantage from exploiting its physical technology more effectively than other firms.

Is a resource or capability . . .				
Valuable	**Rare**	**Difficult to Imitate**	**Without Substitutes**	**Implications for Competitiveness**
No	No	No	No	Competitive disadvantage
Yes	No	No	No	Competitive parity
Yes	Yes	No	No	Temporary competitive advantage
Yes	Yes	Yes	Yes	Sustainable competitive advantage

Source: Adapted from Barney, J. B. 1991. Firm resources and sustained competitive advantage. *Journal of Management*, 17: 99–120.

Exhibit 3.8
Criteria for Sustainable Competitive Advantage and Strategic Implications

Are Substitutes Readily Available? The fourth requirement for a firm resource to be a source of sustainable competitive advantage is that there must be no strategically equivalent valuable resources that are themselves not rare or inimitable. Two valuable firm resources (or two bundles of resources) are strategically equivalent when each one can be exploited separately to implement the same strategies.

Substitutability may take at least two forms. First, though it may be impossible for a firm to imitate exactly another firm's resource, it may be able to substitute a similar resource that enables it to develop and implement the same strategy. Clearly, a firm seeking to imitate another firm's high-quality top management team would be unable to copy the team exactly. However, it might be able to develop its own unique management team. Though these two teams would have different ages, functional backgrounds, experience, and so on, they could be strategically equivalent and thus substitutes for one another.

Second, very different firm resources can become strategic substitutes. For example, Internet booksellers such as Amazon.com compete as substitutes for bricks-and-mortar booksellers such as B. Dalton. The result is that resources such as premier retail locations become less valuable. In a similar vein, several pharmaceutical firms have seen the value of patent protection erode in the face of new drugs that are based on different production processes and act in different ways, but can be used in similar treatment regimes. The coming years will likely see even more radical change in the pharmaceutical industry as the substitution of genetic therapies eliminates certain uses of chemotherapy.[42]

To recap this section, recall that resources and capabilities must be rare and valuable as well as difficult to imitate or substitute in order for a firm to attain competitive advantages that are sustainable over time.[43] Exhibit 3.8 illustrates the relationship among the four criteria of sustainability and shows the competitive implications.

In firms represented by the first row of Exhibit 3.8, managers are in a difficult situation. When their resources and capabilities do not meet any of the four criteria, it would be difficult to develop any type of competitive advantage, in the short or long term. The resources and capabilities they possess enable the firm neither to exploit environmental opportunities nor neutralize environmental threats. In the second and third rows, firms have resources and capabilities that are valuable as well as rare, respectively. However, in both cases the resources and capabilities are not difficult for competitors to imitate or substitute. Here, the firms could attain some level of competitive parity. They could perform on par with equally endowed rivals or attain a temporary competitive advantage. But their advantages would be easy for competitors to match. It is only in the fourth row, where all four criteria are satisfied, that competitive advantages can be sustained over time.

The Generation and Distribution of a Firm's Profits: Extending the Resource-Based View of the Firm

Many scholars would agree that the resource-based view of the firm has been useful in determining when firms will create competitive advantages and enjoy high levels of profitability. However, it has not been developed to address how a firm's profits (often referred to as "rents" by economists) will be distributed to a firm's management and employees.[44] This becomes an important issue because firms may be successful in creating competitive advantages that can be sustainable for a period of time but much of the profits can be retained (or "appropriated") by its employees and managers instead of flowing to the owners of the firm (i.e., the stockholders).*

For a simple illustration, let's first consider Viewpoint DataLabs International, a Salt Lake City–based company that makes sophisticated three-dimensional models and textures for film production houses, video games, and car manufacturers. This example will help to show how employees are often able to obtain (or "appropriate") a high proportion of a firm's profits:

> Walter Noot, head of production, was having trouble keeping his highly skilled Generation X employees happy with their compensation. Each time one of them was lured away for more money, everyone would want a raise. "We were having to give out raises every six months— 30 to 40 percent—then six months later they'd expect the same. It was a big struggle to keep people happy."[45]

At Viewpoint DataLabs, it is apparent that much of the profits are being generated by the highly skilled professionals working together on a variety of projects. They are able to exercise their power by successfully demanding more financial compensation. In part, management has responded favorably because they are united in their demands, and their work involves a certain amount of social complexity and causal ambiguity—given the complex, coordinated efforts that their work entails.

Four factors help explain the extent to which employees and managers will be able to obtain a proportionately high level of the profits that they generate.[46] These include:

- **Employee Bargaining Power.** If employees are vital to forming a firm's unique capability, they will earn disproportionately high wages. For example, marketing professionals may have access to valuable information which helps them to understand the intricacies of customer demands and expectations, or engineers may understand unique technical aspects of the products or services. Additionally, in some industries such as consulting, advertising, and tax preparation, clients tend to be very loyal to individual professionals employed by the firm, instead of to the firm itself. This enables them to "take the clients with them" if they leave. This enhances their bargaining power.
- **Employee Replacement Cost.** If employees' skills are idiosyncratic and rare (a source of resource-based advantage), they should have high bargaining power based on the high cost required by the firm to replace them. For example, Raymond Ozzie, the software designer who was critical in the development of Lotus Notes, was able to dictate the terms under which IBM acquired Lotus.
- **Employee Exit Costs.** This factor may tend to reduce an employee's bargaining power. An individual may face high personal costs when leaving the organization. Thus, that individual's threat of leaving may not be credible. In addition,

---

* Economists define rents as profits (or prices) in excess of what is required to provide a normal return.

some of an employee's expertise may be firm-specific. Thus, it would be of limited value to other firms. A related factor is that of causal ambiguity, which would make it difficult for the employee to explain his or her specific contribution to a given project. Thus, a rival firm might be less likely to pay a high wage premium since it would be unsure of the employee's unique contribution to the firm's success.

- *Manager Bargaining Power.* Like other members of the firm, managers' power would be based on how well they create resource-based advantages. They are generally charged with creating value through the process of organizing, coordinating, and leveraging employees as well as other forms of capital such as plant, equipment, and financial capital (issues that we will address in more detail in Chapter 4). Such activities provide managers with sources of information that may not be readily available to others. Thus, although managers may not know as much about the specific nature of customers and technologies, they are in a position to have a more thorough, integrated understanding of the total operation.

We will discuss in Chapter 9 the conditions under which top-level managers (such as CEOs) of large corporations have been, at times, able to obtain levels of total compensation that would appear to be significantly disproportionate to their contributions to wealth generation as well as to top executives in peer organizations. Here, corporate governance becomes a critical control mechanism. For example, William Esrey and Ronald T. LeMay (the former two top executives at Sprint Corporation) were able to earn more than $130 million in stock options primarily because of "cozy" relationships with members of their board of directors, who tended to approve with little debate huge compensation packages.[47] Such diversion of profits from the owners of the business to top management is far less likely when the board does not consist of a high proportion of the firm's management and board members are truly independent outsiders (i.e., they do not have close ties to management). In general, given the external market for top talent, the level of compensation that executives receive is based on factors similar to the ones just discussed that determine the level of their bargaining power.[48]

>>Evaluating Firm Performance: Two Approaches

This section addresses two approaches to use when evaluating a firm's performance. The first is financial ratio analysis, which, generally speaking, identifies how a firm is performing according to its balance sheet and income statement. As we will discuss, when performing a financial ratio analysis, you must take into account the firm's performance from a historical perspective (not just at one point in time) as well as how it compares with both industry norms and key competitors.[49]

The second perspective may be considered a broader stakeholder perspective. Firms must satisfy a broad range of stakeholders, including employees, customers, and owners, to ensure their long-term viability. Central to our discussion will be two well-known approaches—the balanced scorecard and the strategy map—that have been popularized by Robert Kaplan and David Norton.[50]

Financial Ratio Analysis

The beginning point in analyzing the financial position of a firm is to compute and analyze five different types of financial ratios:

- Short-term solvency or liquidity
- Long-term solvency measures

- Asset management (or turnover)
- Profitability
- Market value

The Appendix to this chapter provides detailed definitions for and discussions of each of these types of ratios as well as examples of how each is calculated.

A meaningful ratio analysis must go beyond the calculation and interpretation of financial ratios.[51] It must include an analysis of how ratios change over time as well as how they are interrelated. For example, a firm that takes on too much long-term debt to finance operations will see an immediate impact on its indicators of long-term financial leverage. The additional debt will also have a negative impact on the firm's short-term liquidity ratio (i.e., current and quick ratios) since the firm must pay interest and principal on the additional debt each year until it is retired. Additionally, the interest expenses must be deducted from revenues, reducing the firm's profitability.

A firm's financial position should not be analyzed in isolation. Important reference points are needed. We will address some issues that must be taken into account to make financial analysis more meaningful: historical comparisons, comparisons with industry norms, and comparisons with key competitors.

Historical Comparisons   When you evaluate a firm's financial performance, it is very useful to compare its financial position over time. This provides a means of evaluating trends. For example, Home Depot reported revenues of $73.1 billion and net income of $5.0 billion in 2005. Almost all firms—except a few of the largest and most profitable companies in the world—would be very happy with such success. However, these figures reflect a consistent annual growth in revenue and net income of 11 percent and 18 percent, respectively, for Home Depot for the period from 2002 to 2005. Clearly, had Home Depot reported annual revenues and net income of $40.0 billion and $2.5 billion in 2005, respectively, it would still be a very large and highly profitable enterprise. However, such performance would have probably resulted in significant damage to the stock price as well as to the careers of many executives! Exhibit 3.9 illustrates a 10-year period of return on sales (ROS) for a hypothetical company. As indicated by the dotted trend lines, the rate of growth (or decline) differs substantially over time periods.

Exhibit 3.9
Historical Trends: Return on Sales (ROS) for a Hypothetical Company

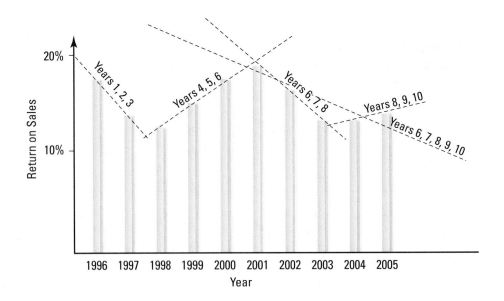

Exhibit 3.10
How Financial
Ratios Differ
across Industries

Financial Ratio	Semiconductors	Grocery Stores	Skilled-Nursing Facilities
Quick ratio (times)	1.9	0.5	1.1
Current ratio (times)	4.0	1.6	1.6
Total liabilities to net worth (%)	30.7	92.0	163.5
Collection period (days)	49.6	2.9	31.2
Assets to sales (%)	187.8	20.2	101.6
Return on sales (%)	5.8	0.8	1.6

Source: Dun & Bradstreet. *Industry Norms and Key Business Ratios, 2003–2004.* One Year Edition, SIC #2000-3999 (Semiconductors); SIC #5200-5499 (Grocery Stores); SIC #6100-8999 (Skilled-Nursing Facilities). New York: Dun & Bradstreet Credit Services.

Comparison with Industry Norms   When you are evaluating a firm's financial performance, remember also to compare it with industry norms. A firm's current ratio or profitability may appear impressive at first glance. However, it may pale when compared with industry standards or norms.

By comparing your firm with all other firms in your industry, you can calculate relative performance. Banks and other lending institutions often use such comparisons when evaluating a firm's creditworthiness. Exhibit 3.10 includes a variety of financial ratios for three industries: semiconductors, grocery stores, and skilled-nursing facilities. Why is there such variation among the financial ratios for these three industries? There are several reasons. With regard to the collection period, grocery stores operate mostly on a cash basis, so they have a very short collection period. Semiconductor manufacturers sell their output to other manufacturers (e.g., computer makers) on terms such as 2/15 net 45, which means they give a 2 percent discount on bills paid within 15 days and start charging interest after 45 days. Skilled-nursing facilities would also have a longer collection period than grocery stores because they typically rely on payments from insurance companies.

The industry norms for return on sales also highlight some differences among these industries. Grocers, with very slim margins, have a lower return on sales than either skilled-nursing facilities or semiconductor manufacturers. But how might we explain the differences between skilled-nursing facilities and semiconductor manufacturers? Health care facilities, in general, are limited in their pricing structures by Medicare/Medicaid regulations and by insurance reimbursement limits, but semiconductor producers have pricing structures determined by the market. If their products have superior performance, semiconductor manufacturers can charge premium prices.

Comparison with Key Competitors   Recall from Chapter 2 that firms with similar strategies are considered members of a strategic group in an industry. Furthermore, competition tends to be more intense among competitors within groups than across groups. Thus, you can gain valuable insights into a firm's financial and competitive position if you make comparisons between a firm and its most direct competitors. Consider Procter & Gamble's ill-fated efforts to enter the highly profitable pharmaceutical industry. Although P&G is a giant in consumer products, its efforts over two decades have produced nominal profits at best. In 1999 P&G spent $380 million on R&D in drugs—22 percent of its total corporate R&D budget. However, its drug unit produced only 2 percent of the company's

Exhibit 3.11

Comparison of Procter & Gamble's and Key Competitors' Drug Revenues and R&D Expenditures

Company (or division)	Sales* ($ billions)	R&D Budget ($ billions)
P&G Drug Division	$ 0.8	$0.38
Bristol-Myers Squibb	20.2	1.80
Pfizer	27.4	4.00
Merck	32.7	2.10

Source: Berner, R. 2000. Procter & Gamble: Just say no to drugs. *BusinessWeek*, October 9: 128; data courtesy of Lehman Brothers and Procter & Gamble.

*Data: Lehman Brothers, Procter & Gamble Co.

$40 billion sales. Why? While $380 million is hardly a trivial amount of capital, its key competitors dwarf P&G. Consider the drug revenues and R&D budgets of P&G compared to its main rivals as shown in Exhibit 3.11. *BusinessWeek*'s take on P&G's chances in an article entitled "Just Say No to Drugs" was this: "Don't bet on it. P&G may be a giant in detergent and toothpaste, but the consumer-products maker is simply outclassed by the competition."[52]

Integrating Financial Analysis and Stakeholder Perspectives: The Balanced Scorecard and the Strategy Map

In the previous section, we focused on what may be considered a good starting point in assessing a firm's performance. Clearly, it is useful to see how a firm is performing over time in terms of the several ratios. However, such traditional approaches to performance assessments can be a double-edged sword.[53] Many important transactions that managers make—investments in research and development, employee training and development, advertising and promotion of key brands, and new product development—may greatly expand a firm's market potential and create significant long-term shareholder value. But such critical investments are not reflected positively in short-term financial reports. Why? Because financial reports typically measure expenses, not the value created. Thus, managers may be penalized for spending money in the short term to improve their firm's long-term competitive viability!

Now consider the other side of the coin. A manager may be destroying the firm's future value by operating in a way that makes customers dissatisfied, depletes the firm's stock of good products coming out of R&D, or damages the morale of valued employees. Such budget cuts, however, may lead to very good short-term financials. The manager may look good in the short run and even receive credit for improving the firm's performance. In essence, such a manager has mastered denominator management, whereby decreasing investments makes the return on investment (ROI) ratio larger, even though the actual return remains constant or shrinks.

The Balanced Scorecard   To provide a meaningful integration of the many issues that come into evaluating a firm's performance, Kaplan and Norton developed a "balanced scorecard."[54] This is a set of measures that provide top managers with a fast but comprehensive view of the business. In a nutshell, it includes financial measures that reflect the results of actions already taken, but it complements these indicators with operational measures of customer satisfaction, internal processes, and the organization's innovation and improvement activities—operational measures that drive future financial performance.

The balanced scorecard enables managers to consider their business from four key perspectives:

- How do customers see us? (customer perspective)
- What must we excel at? (internal perspective)
- Can we continue to improve and create value? (innovation and learning perspective)
- How do we look to shareholders? (financial perspective)

Customer Perspective Clearly, how a company is performing from its customers' perspective is a top priority for management. The balanced scorecard requires that managers translate their general mission statements on customer service into specific measures that reflect the factors that really matter to customers. For the balanced scorecard to work, managers must articulate goals for four key categories of customer concerns: time, quality, performance and service, and cost. For example, lead time may be measured as the time from the company's receipt of an order to the time it actually delivers the product or service to the customer. Also, quality measures may indicate the level of defective incoming products as perceived by the customer, as well as the accuracy of the company's delivery forecasts.

Internal Business Perspective Although customer-based measures are important, they must be translated into indicators of what the firm must do internally to meet customers' expectations. Excellent customer performance results from processes, decisions, and actions that occur throughout organizations in a coordinated fashion, and managers must focus on those critical internal operations that enable them to satisfy customer needs. The internal measures should reflect business processes that have the greatest impact on customer satisfaction. These include factors that affect cycle time, quality, employee skills, and productivity. Firms also must identify and measure the key resources and capabilities they need to ensure continued strategic success.

Innovation and Learning Perspective The customer and internal business process measures on the balanced scorecard identify the parameters that the company considers most critical to success. However, given the rapid rate of markets, technologies, and global competition, the criteria for success are constantly changing. To survive and prosper, managers must make frequent changes to existing products and services as well as introduce entirely new products with expanded capabilities. A firm's ability to improve, innovate, and learn is tied directly to its value. Simply put, only by developing new products and services, creating greater value for customers, and increasing operating efficiencies can a company penetrate new markets, increase revenues and margins, and enhance shareholder value. A firm's ability to do well from an innovation and learning perspective is more dependent on its intangible than tangible assets. Three categories of intangible assets are critically important: human capital (skills, talent, and knowledge), information capital (information systems, networks), and organization capital (culture, leadership). Chapter 4 provides a more detailed analysis of a firm's intangible assets, especially its human capital.

Financial Perspective Measures of financial performance indicate whether the company's strategy, implementation, and execution are indeed contributing to bottom-line improvement. Typical financial goals include profitability, growth, and shareholder value. Periodic financial statements remind managers that improved quality, response time, productivity, and innovative products benefit the firm only when they result in improved sales, increased market share, reduced operating expenses, or higher asset turnover.[55]

Before ending our discussion of the balanced scorecard, we would like to provide an example that illustrates the causal relationships among the multiple perspectives in the model. Sears, the huge retailer, found a strong causal relationship between employee attitudes, customer attitudes, and financial outcomes.[56] Through an ongoing study, Sears developed (and continues to refine) what it calls its total performance indicators, or TPI—a set of indicators that shows how well the company is doing with customers, employees, and investors. Sears's quantitative model has shown that a 5.0 percent improvement in employee attitudes leads to a 1.3 percent improvement in customer satisfaction, which in turn will drive a 0.5 percent improvement in revenue. Thus, if a single store improved its employee attitude by 5.0 percent on a survey scale, Sears could predict with confidence that if the revenue growth in the district as a whole were 5.0 percent, the revenue growth in this particular store would be 5.5 percent. Interestingly, Sears's managers consider such numbers as rigorous as any others that they work with every year. The company's accounting firm audits management as closely as it audits the financial statements.

One final implication of the balanced scorecard is that managers do not need to look at their job as primarily balancing stakeholder demands. They need to avoid the following mind-set: "How many units in employee satisfaction do I have to give up to get some additional units of customer satisfaction or profits?" Instead, when done properly, the balanced scorecard provides a win–win approach—a means of simultaneously increasing satisfaction among a wide variety of organizational stakeholders, including employees (at all levels), customers, and stockholders. And, as we shall see in Chapter 4, indicators of employee satisfaction have become more important in a knowledge economy, where intellectual capital (as opposed to labor and financial capital) is the primary creator of wealth.

Strategy Maps   Building on the concepts that are the foundation of the Balanced Scorecard approach, Kaplan and Norton have recently developed a very useful tool called the strategy map.[57] Strategy maps show the cause and effect links by which specific improvements in different areas lead to a desired outcome. Strategy maps also help employees see how their jobs are related to the overall objectives of the organization. They also help us understand how an organization can convert its assets, both tangible and intangible, into tangible outcomes. We will illustrate how to develop a strategy map using ExxonMobil as an example.

A strategy map starts with the company's vision statement. ExxonMobil's vision is "to be the best integrated refiner-marketer in the United States by efficiently delivering unprecedented value to consumers." They also wanted to increase their return on capital by more than six percentage points within three years. To achieve this, they realized that they have to improve both their revenue growth and productivity (financial perspective). To improve revenue growth, the company decided to expand nongasoline sales (oil, antifreeze, wiper fluid, convenience store products) and ancillary services (car washes, oil changes). Further, within gasoline, they decided to place more emphasis on premium brands. They also decided to improve productivity by slashing operating expenses (for example, by reducing downtime at refineries). The company also decided to focus on premium customers (customers who are not price sensitive) by offering these customers fast and friendly service (customer perspective). These decisions, in turn, led to changes from an internal process perspective. They emphasized processes to create nongasoline products and services, to build best-in-class franchise teams, and to improve inventory management. Finally, from a learning and growth perspective, ExxonMobil identified that their employees needed better understanding of refining and marketing functions. These changes eventually helped the company detect and fill major gaps in its strategies and improve its profit margins.

Exhibit 3.12 presents a simplified version of ExxonMobil's strategy map.

Goal :

Means to achieve goal:

Increase Return on Capital
Increase Revenue Growth
Improve Productivity

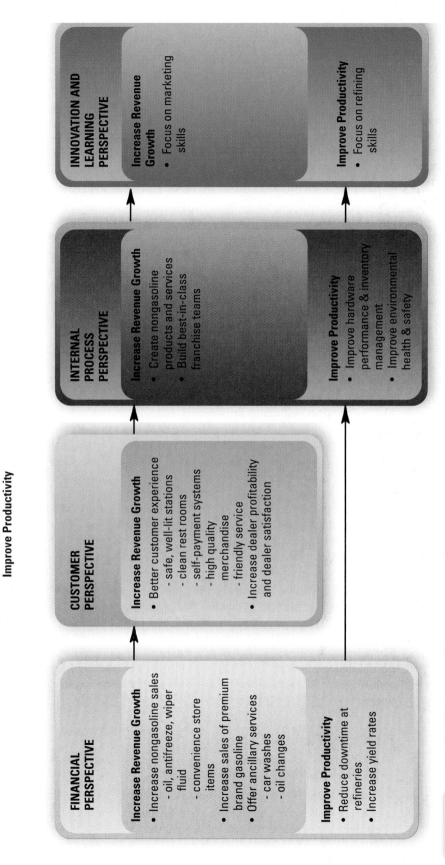

FINANCIAL PERSPECTIVE

Increase Revenue Growth
- Increase nongasoline sales
  - oil, antifreeze, wiper fluid
  - convenience store items
- Increase sales of premium brand gasoline
- Offer ancillary services
  - car washes
  - oil changes

Improve Productivity
- Reduce downtime at refineries
- Increase yield rates

CUSTOMER PERSPECTIVE

Increase Revenue Growth
- Better customer experience
  - safe, well-lit stations
  - clean rest rooms
  - self-payment systems
  - high quality merchandise
  - friendly service
- Increase dealer profitability and dealer satisfaction

INTERNAL PROCESS PERSPECTIVE

Increase Revenue Growth
- Create nongasoline products and services
- Build best-in-class franchise teams

Improve Productivity
- Improve hardware performance & inventory management
- Improve environmental health & safety

INNOVATION AND LEARNING PERSPECTIVE

Increase Revenue Growth
- Focus on marketing skills

Improve Productivity
- Focus on refining skills

Exhibit 3.12 ExxonMobil's Strategy Map

Source: Reprinted by permission of *Harvard Business Review*. Exhibit from "Having Trouble with Your Strategy? Then Map It," by Kaplan, R. S. and Norton, D. P. 2000. Copyright © 2000 by The Harvard Business School Publishing Corporation; all rights reserved.

Summary

In the traditional approaches to assessing a firm's internal environment, the primary goal of managers would be to determine their firm's relative strengths and weaknesses. Such is the role of SWOT analysis, wherein managers analyze their firm's strengths and weaknesses as well as the opportunities and threats in the external environment. In this chapter, we discussed why this may be a good starting point but hardly the best approach to take in performing a sound analysis. There are many limitations to SWOT analysis, including its static perspective, its potential to overemphasize a single dimension of a firm's strategy, and the likelihood that a firm's strengths do not necessarily help the firm create value or competitive advantages.

We identified two frameworks that serve to complement SWOT analysis in assessing a firm's internal environment: value-chain analysis and the resource-based view of the firm. In conducting a value-chain analysis, first divide the firm into a series of value-creating activities. These include primary activities such as inbound logistics, operations, and service as well as support activities such as procurement and human resources management. Then analyze how each activity adds value as well as how *interrelationships* among value activities in the firm and among the firm and its customers and suppliers add value. Thus, instead of merely determining a firm's strengths and weaknesses per se, you analyze them in the overall context of the firm and its relationships with customers and suppliers—the value system.

The resource-based view of the firm considers the firm as a bundle of resources: tangible resources, intangible resources, and organizational capabilities. Competitive advantages that are sustainable over time generally arise from the creation of bundles of resources and capabilities. For advantages to be sustainable, four criteria must be satisfied: value, rarity, difficulty in imitation, and difficulty in substitution. Such an evaluation requires a sound knowledge of the competitive context in which the firm exists. The owners of a business may not capture all of the value created by the firm. The appropriation of value created by a firm between the owners and employees is determined by four factors: employee bargaining power, replacement cost, employee exit costs, and manager bargaining power.

An internal analysis of the firm would not be complete unless you evaluate its performance and make the appropriate comparisons. Determining a firm's performance requires an analysis of its financial situation as well as a review of how well it is satisfying a broad range of stakeholders, including customers, employees, and stockholders. We discussed the concepts of the balanced scorecard and the strategy map, in which four perspectives must be addressed: customer, internal business, innovation and learning, and financial. Central to these concepts is the idea that the interests of various stakeholders can be interrelated. We provide examples of how indicators of employee satisfaction lead to higher levels of customer satisfaction, which in turn lead to higher levels of financial performance. Thus, improving a firm's performance does not need to involve making trade-offs among different stakeholders. Assessing the firm's performance is also more useful if it is evaluated in terms of how it changes over time, compares with industry norms, and compares with key competitors.

Summary Review Questions

1. SWOT analysis is a technique to analyze the internal and external environment of a firm. What are its advantages and disadvantages?

2. Briefly describe the primary and support activities in a firm's value chain.

3. How can managers create value by establishing important relationships among the value-chain activities both within their firm and between the firm and its customers and suppliers?

4. Briefly explain the four criteria for sustainability of competitive advantages.
5. Under what conditions are employees and managers able to appropriate some of the value created by their firm?
6. What are the advantages and disadvantages of conducting a financial ratio analysis of a firm?
7. Summarize the concept of the balanced scorecard. What are its main advantages?

Experiential Exercise

Dell Computer is a leading firm in the personal computer industry, with annual revenues of $49 billion during its 2004 fiscal year. Dell has created a very strong competitive position via its "direct model," whereby it manufactures its personal computers to detailed customer specifications.

Below we address several questions that focus on Dell's value-chain activities and interrelationships among them as well as whether they are able to attain sustainable competitive advantage(s). (We discuss Dell in this chapter on pages 93–94.)

1. Where in Dell's value chain are they creating value for their customer?

Value-Chain Activity	Yes/No	How Does Dell Create Value for the Customer?
Primary:		
Inbound logistics		
Operations		
Outbound logistics		
Marketing and sales		
Service		
Support:		
Procurement		
Technology development		
Human resource management		
General administration		

2. What are the important relationships among Dell's value-chain activities? What are the important interdependencies? For each activity, identify the relationships and interdependencies.

	Inbound logistics	Operations	Outbound logistics	Marketing and sales	Service	Procurement	Technology development	Human resource management	General administration
Inbound logistics									
Operations									
Outbound logistics									
Marketing and sales									
Service									
Procurement									
Technology development									
Human resource management									
General administration									

3. What resources, activities, and relationships enable Dell to achieve a sustainable competitive advantage?

Resource/Activity	Is It Valuable?	Is It Rare?	Are There Few Substitutes?	Is It Difficult to Make?
Inbound logistics				
Operations				
Outbound logistics				
Marketing and sales				
Service				
Procurement				
Technology development				
Human resource management				
General administration				

1. Using published reports, select two CEOs who have recently made public statements regarding a major change in their firm's strategy. Discuss how the successful implementation of such strategies requires changes in the firm's primary and support activities.

2. Select a firm that competes in an industry in which you are interested. Drawing upon published financial reports, complete a financial ratio analysis. Based on changes over time and a comparison with industry norms, evaluate the firm's strengths and weaknesses in terms of its financial position.

3. How might exemplary human resource practices enhance and strengthen a firm's value-chain activities?

4. Using the Internet, look up your university or college. What are some of its key value-creating activities that provide competitive advantages? Why?

1. What are some of the ethical issues that arise when a firm becomes overly zealous in advertising its products?

2. What are some of the ethical issues that may arise from a firm's procurement activities? Are you aware of any of these issues from your personal experience or businesses you are familiar with?

References

1. Halliday, J., & Sanders, L. 2004. Troubled Jaguar searches for marketing panacea. *Automotive News,* November 22: 28; Kerwin, K. 2004. The care and feeding of Jaguar. *BusinessWeek,* October 4: 38; Anonymous. 2005. Jaguar's problems hold back PAG profits. *Birmingham Post,* January 12: np; and, Smith, C. 2004. Don't run down the messenger. *Marketing,* November 10: 28.

2. Our discussion of the value chain will draw on Porter, M. E. 1985. *Competitive advantage:* chap. 2. New York: Free Press.

3. Dyer, J. H. 1996. Specialized supplier networks as a source of competitive advantage: Evidence from the auto industry. *Strategic Management Journal,* 17: 271–291.

4. For an insightful perspective on value-chain analysis, refer to Stabell, C. B., & Fjeldstad, O. D. 1998. Configuring value for competitive advantage: On chains, shops, and networks. *Strategic Management Journal,* 19: 413–437. The authors develop concepts of value chains, value shops, and value networks to extend the value-creation logic across a broad range of industries. Their work builds on the seminal contributions of Porter, 1985, op. cit., and others who have addressed how firms create value through key interrelationships among value-creating activities.

5. Ibid.

6. Maynard, M. 1999. Toyota promises custom order in 5 days. *USA Today,* August 6: B1.

7. Shaw Industries. 1999. Annual report: 14–15.

8. Fisher, M. L. 1997. What is the right supply chain for your product? *Harvard Business Review,* 75(2): 105–116.

9. Jackson. M. 2001. Bringing a dying brand back to life. *Harvard Business Review,* 79(5): 53–61.

10. Anderson, J. C., & Nmarus, J. A. 2003. Selectively pursuing more of your customer's business. *MIT Sloan Management Review,* 44(3): 42–50.

11. An insightful discussion of the role of identity marketing—that is, the myriad labels that people use to express who they are—in successful marketing activities is found in Reed, A., II, & Bolton, L. E. 2005. The complexity of identify. *MIT Sloan Management Review,* 46(3): 18–22.

12. Berggren, E., & Nacher, T. 2000. Why good ideas go bust. *Management Review,* February: 32–36.

13. For an insightful perspective on creating effective brand portfolios, refer to Hill, S., Ettenson, R., & Tyson, D. 2005. Achieving the ideal brand portfolio. *MIT Sloan Management Review,* 46(2): 85–90.

14. Haddad, C., & Grow, B. 2001. Wait a second—I didn't order that! *BusinessWeek,* July 16: 45.

15. Brown, J. 2000. Service, please. *BusinessWeek* E. Biz, October 23: EB 48–50.

16. For a scholarly discussion on the procurement of technology components, read Hoetker, G. 2005. How much you know versus how well I know you: Selecting a supplier for a technically innovative component. *Strategic Management Journal,* 26(1): 75–96.

17. For a discussion on criteria to use when screening suppliers for back-office functions, read Feeny, D., Lacity, M., & Willcocks, L. P. 2005. Taking the measure of outsourcing providers. *MIT Sloan Management Review,* 46(3): 41–48.

18. Imperato, G. 1998. How to give good feedback. *Fast Company,* September: 144–156.

19. Bensaou, B. M., & Earl, M. 1998. The right mindset for managing information technology. *Harvard Business Review,* 96(5): 118–128.

20. Donlon, J. P. 2000. Bonsignore's bid for the big time. *Chief Executive,* March: 28–37.

21. Ulrich, D. 1998. A new mandate for human resources. *Harvard Business Review,* 96(1): 124–134.

22. Wood, J. 2003. Sharing jobs and working from home: The new face of the airline industry. *AviationCareer.net,* February 21.

23. Follow AT&T's lead in this tactic to retain "plateaued" employees. n.d. *Recruitment & Retention:* 1.

24. For a cautionary note on the use of IT, refer to McAfee, A. 2003. When too much IT knowledge is a dangerous thing. *MIT Sloan Management Review,* 44(2): 83–90.

25. Walgreen Co. 1996. *Information technology and Walgreen's: Opportunities for employment,* January; and Dess, G. G., & Picken, J. C. 1997. *Beyond productivity.* New York: AMACOM.

26. Rivette, K. G., & Kline, D. 2000. Discovering new value in intellectual property. *Harvard Business Review,* 78(1): 54–66.

27. For an interesting perspective on some of the potential downsides of close customer and supplier relationships, refer to Anderson, E., & Jap, S. D. 2005. The dark side of close relationships. *MIT Sloan Management Review,* 46(3): 75–82.

28. Day, G. S. 2003. Creating a superior customer-relating capability. *MIT Sloan Management Review,* 44(3): 77–82.

29. To gain insights on the role of electronic technologies in enhancing a firm's connections to outside suppliers and customers, refer to Lawrence, T. B., Morse, E. A., & Fowler, S. W. 2005. Managing your portfolio of connections. *MIT Sloan Management Review,* 46(2): 59–66.

30. Reinhardt, F. L. 1999. Bringing the environment down to earth. *Harvard Business Review,* 77(4): 149–157.

31. Collis, D. J., & Montgomery, C. A. 1995. Competing on resources: Strategy in the 1990's. *Harvard Business Review,* 73(4): 119–128; and Barney, J. 1991. Firm resources and sustained competitive advantage. *Journal of Management,* 17(1): 99–120.

32. Henkoff, R. 1993. Companies that train the best. *Fortune,* March 22: 83; and Dess & Picken, *Beyond productivity,* p. 98.

33. Barney, J. B. 1986. Types of competition and the theory of strategy: Towards an integrative framework. *Academy of Management Review,* 11(4): 791–800.

34. Harley-Davidson. 1993. Annual report.

35. For a rigorous, academic treatment of the origin of capabilities, refer to Ethiraj, S. K., Kale, P., Krishnan, M. S., & Singh, J. V. 2005. Where do capabilities come from and how do they matter? A study of the software services industry. *Strategic Management Journal,* 26(1): 25–46.

36. For an academic discussion on methods associated with organizational capabilities, refer to Dutta, S., Narasimhan, O., & Rajiv, S. 2005. Conceptualizing and measuring capabilities: Methodology and empirical application. *Strategic Management Journal,* 26(3): 277–286.

37. Lorenzoni, G., & Lipparini, A. 1999. The leveraging of interfirm relationships as a distinctive organizational capability: A longitudinal study. *Strategic Management Journal,* 20: 317–338.

38. The following discussion of Dell and Exhibit 3.6 draw on the following sources: Serwer, A. 2005. America's most admired companies. *Fortune,* March 7: 72–82; Weiss, J., & Hughes, J. 2005. Execution without excuses. *Harvard Business Review,* 83(3): 102–111; Brown, E., & Costa, Len A. 1999. America's most admired companies. *Fortune,* March 1: 68–74; Hamel, G., & Sampler, J. 1998. The E-Corporation. *Fortune,* December 7: 80–88; and Rivkin, J. W., & Porter, M. Matching Dell. *Harvard Business School Case* 9-799-158. We would like to thank Ted Khoury, a Ph.D. student at the University of Texas at Dallas, for his assistance in preparing this example.

39. Barney, J. 1991. Firm resources and sustained competitive advantage. *Journal of Management,* 17(1): 99–120.

40. Barney, 1986, op. cit. Our discussion of inimitability and substitution draws upon this source.

41. Deephouse, D. L. 1999. To be different, or to be the same? It's a question (and theory) of strategic balance. *Strategic Management Journal,* 20: 147–166.

42. Yeoh, P. L., & Roth, K. 1999. An empirical analysis of sustained advantage in the U.S. pharmaceutical industry: Impact of firm resources and capabilities. *Strategic Management Journal,* 20: 637–653.

43. Robins, J. A., & Wiersema, M. F. 2000. Strategies for unstructured competitive environments: Using scarce resources to create new markets. In Bresser, R. F., et al., (Eds.), *Winning strategies in a deconstructing world:* 201–220. New York: John Wiley.

44. Amit, R., & Schoemaker, J. H. 1993. Strategic assets and organizational rent. *Strategic Management Journal,* 14(1): 33–46; Collis, D. J., & Montgomery, C. A. 1995. Competing on resources: Strategy in the 1990's. *Harvard Business Review,* 73(4): 118–128; Coff, R. W. 1999. When competitive advantage doesn't lead to performance: The resource-based view and stakeholder bargaining power. *Organization Science,* 10(2): 119–133; and Blyler, M., & Coff, R. W. 2003. Dynamic capabilities, social capital, and rent appropriation: Ties that split pies. *Strategic Management Journal,* 24: 677–686.

45. Munk, N. 1998. The new organization man. *Fortune,* March 16: 62–74.

46. Coff, op. cit.

47. Lavelle, L. 2003. Sprint's board needs a good sweeping, too. *BusinessWeek,* February 24: 40; Anonymous. 2003. Another nail in the coffin. *The Economist,* February 15: 69–70; and Byrnes, N., Dwyer, P., & McNamee, M. 2003. Hacking away at tax shelters, *BusinessWeek,* February 24: 41.

48. We have focused our discussion on how internal stake-holders (e.g., employees, managers, and top executives) may appropriate a firm's profits (or rents). For an interesting discussion of how a firm's innovations may be appropriated by external stakeholders (e.g., customers, suppliers) as well as competitors, refer to Grant, R. M. 2002. *Contemporary strategy analysis* (4th ed.): 335–340. Malden, MA: Blackwell.

49. Luehrman, T. A. 1997. What's it worth? A general manager's guide to valuation. *Harvard Business Review*, 45(3): 132–142.

50. See, for example, Kaplan, R. S., & Norton, D. P. 1992. The balanced scorecard: Measures that drive performance. *Harvard Business Review*, 69(1): 71–79.

51. Hitt, M. A., Ireland, R. D., & Stadter, G. 1982. Functional importance of company performance: Moderating effects of grand strategy and industry type. *Strategic Management Journal*, 3: 315–330.

52. Berner, R. 2000. Procter & Gamble: Just say no to drugs. *BusinessWeek*, October 9: 128.

53. Kaplan & Norton, op. cit.

54. Ibid.

55. For a discussion of the relative value of growth versus increasing margins, read Mass, N. J. 2005. The relative value of growth. *Harvard Business Review*, 83(4): 102–112.

56. Rucci, A. J., Kirn, S. P., & Quinn, R. T. 1998. The employee-customer-profit chain at Sears. *Harvard Business Review*, 76(1): 82–97.

57. Kaplan, R. S., & Norton, D. P. 2000. Having trouble with your strategy? Then map it. *Harvard Business Review*, 78(10): 167–176.

APPENDIX TO CHAPTER 3

Financial Ratio Analysis

Standard Financial Statements

One obvious thing we might want to do with a company's financial statements is to compare them to those of other, similar companies. We would immediately have a problem, however. It's almost impossible to directly compare the financial statements for two companies because of differences in size.

For example, Oracle and IBM are obviously serious rivals in the computer software market, but IBM is much larger (in terms of assets), so it is difficult to compare them directly. For that matter, it's difficult to even compare financial statements from different points in time for the same company if the company's size has changed. The size problem is compounded if we try to compare IBM and, say, SAP (of Germany). If SAP's financial statements are denominated in German marks, then we have a size *and* a currency difference.

To start making comparisons, one obvious thing we might try to do is to somehow standardize the financial statements. One very common and useful way of doing this is to work with percentages instead of total dollars. The resulting financial statements are called *common-size statements*. We consider these next.

Common-Size Balance Sheets

For easy reference, Prufrock Corporation's 2004 and 2005 balance sheets are provided in Exhibit 3A.1. Using these, we construct common-size balance sheets by expressing each item as a percentage of total assets. Prufrock's 2004 and 2005 common-size balance sheets are shown in Exhibit 3A.2.

Notice that some of the totals don't check exactly because of rounding errors. Also notice that the total change has to be zero since the beginning and ending numbers must add up to 100 percent.

In this form, financial statements are relatively easy to read and compare. For example, just looking at the two balance sheets for Prufrock, we see that current assets were 19.7 percent of total assets in 2004, up from 19.1 percent in 2005. Current liabilities declined from 16.0 percent to 15.1 percent of total liabilities and equity over that same time. Similarly, total equity rose from 68.1 percent of total liabilities and equity to 72.2 percent.

Source: Adapted from Rows, S. A., Westerfield, R. W., & Jordan, B. D. 1999. *Essentials of Corporate Finance* (2nd ed.). chap. 3. NewYork: McGraw-Hill. 1999.

Exhibit 3A.1
**Prufrock
Corporation**
Balance Sheets as of
December 31, 2004
and 2005
($ in millions)

	2004	2005
Assets		
Current assets		
Cash	$ 84	$ 98
Accounts receivable	165	188
Inventory	393	422
Total	$ 642	$ 708
Fixed assets		
Net plant and equipment	$2,731	$2,880
Total assets	$3,373	$3,588
Liabilities and Owners' Equity		
Current liabilities		
Accounts payable	$ 312	$ 344
Notes payable	231	196
Total	$ 543	$ 540
Long-term debt	$ 531	$ 457
Owners' equity		
Common stock and paid-in surplus	$ 500	$ 550
Retained earnings	1,799	2,041
Total	$2,299	$2,591
Total liabilities and owners' equity	$3,373	$3,588

Overall, Prufrock's liquidity, as measured by current assets compared to current liabilities, increased over the year. Simultaneously, Prufrock's indebtedness diminished as a percentage of total assets. We might be tempted to conclude that the balance sheet has grown "stronger."

Common-Size Income Statements

A useful way of standardizing the income statement, shown in Exhibit 3A.3, is to express each item as a percentage of total sales, as illustrated for Prufrock in Exhibit 3A.4.

This income statement tells us what happens to each dollar in sales. For Prufrock, interest expense eats up $.061 out of every sales dollar and taxes take another $.081. When all is said and done, $.157 of each dollar flows through to the bottom line (net income), and that amount is split into $.105 retained in the business and $.052 paid out in dividends.

These percentages are very useful in comparisons. For example, a relevant figure is the cost percentage. For Prufrock, $.582 of each $1.00 in sales goes to pay for goods sold. It would be interesting to compute the same percentage for Prufrock's main competitors to see how Prufrock stacks up in terms of cost control.

Ratio Analysis

Another way of avoiding the problems involved in comparing companies of different sizes is to calculate and compare *financial ratios*. Such ratios are ways of comparing and investigating the

	2004	2005	Change
Assets			
Current assets			
Cash	2.5%	2.7%	+ .2%
Accounts receivable	4.9	5.2	+ .3
Inventory	11.7	11.8	+ .1
Total	19.1	19.7	+ .6
Fixed assets			
Net plant and equipment	80.9	80.3	− .6
Total assets	100.0%	100.0%	.0%
Liabilities and Owners' Equity			
Current liabilities			
Accounts payable	9.2%	9.6%	+ .4%
Notes payable	6.8	5.5	− 1.3
Total	16.0	15.1	− .9
Long-term debt	15.7	12.7	− 3.0
Owners' equity			
Common stock and paid-in surplus	14.8	15.3	+ .5
Retained earnings	53.3	56.9	+3.6
Total	68.1	72.2	+4.1
Total liabilities and owners' equities	100.0%	100.0%	.0%

Exhibit 3A.2
Prufrock Corporation
Common-Size Balance Sheets as of December 31, 2004 and 2005 (%)

Note: Numbers may not add up to 100.0% due to rounding.

Sales	$2,311
Cost of goods sold	1,344
Depreciation	276
Earnings before interest and taxes	$ 691
Interest paid	141
Taxable income	$ 550
Taxes (34%)	187
Net income	$ 363
Dividends	$121
Addition to retained earnings	242

Exhibit 3A.3
Prufrock Corporation
2005 Income Statement ($ in millions)

Exhibit 3A.4

**Prufrock
Corporation**

2005 Common-Size
Income Statement (%)

Sales		100.0%
Cost of goods sold		58.2
Depreciation		11.9
Earnings before interest and taxes		29.9
Interest paid		6.1
Taxable income		23.8
Taxes (34%)		8.1
Net income		15.7%
Dividends	5.2%	
Addition to retained earnings	10.5	

relationships between different pieces of financial information. We cover some of the more common ratios next, but there are many others that we don't touch on.

One problem with ratios is that different people and different sources frequently don't compute them in exactly the same way, and this leads to much confusion. The specific definitions we use here may or may not be the same as others you have seen or will see elsewhere. If you ever use ratios as a tool for analysis, you should be careful to document how you calculate each one, and, if you are comparing your numbers to those of another source, be sure you know how its numbers are computed.

For each of the ratios we discuss, several questions come to mind:

1. How is it computed?
2. What is it intended to measure, and why might we be interested?
3. What is the unit of measurement?
4. What might a high or low value be telling us? How might such values be misleading?
5. How could this measure be improved?

Financial ratios are traditionally grouped into the following categories:

1. Short-term solvency, or liquidity, ratios.
2. Long-term solvency, or financial leverage, ratios.
3. Asset management, or turnover, ratios.
4. Profitability ratios.
5. Market value ratios.

We will consider each of these in turn. In calculating these numbers for Prufrock, we will use the ending balance sheet (2005) figures unless we explicitly say otherwise. The numbers for the various ratios come from the income statement and the balance sheet.

Short-Term Solvency, or Liquidity, Measures

As the name suggests, short-term solvency ratios as a group are intended to provide information about a firm's liquidity, and these ratios are sometimes called *liquidity measures.* The primary concern is the firm's ability to pay its bills over the short run without undue stress. Consequently, these ratios focus on current assets and current liabilities.

For obvious reasons, liquidity ratios are particularly interesting to short-term creditors. Since financial managers are constantly working with banks and other short-term lenders, an understanding of these ratios is essential.

One advantage of looking at current assets and liabilities is that their book values and market values are likely to be similar. Often (though not always), these assets and liabilities just don't live long enough for the two to get seriously out of step. On the other hand, like any type of near cash, current assets and liabilities can and do change fairly rapidly, so today's amounts may not be a reliable guide to the future.

Current Ratio   One of the best-known and most widely used ratios is the *current ratio.* As you might guess, the current ratio is defined as:

$$\text{Current ratio} = \frac{\text{Current assets}}{\text{Current liabilities}}$$

For Prufrock, the 2005 current ratio is:

$$\text{Current ratio} = \frac{\$708}{\$540} = 1.31 \text{ times}$$

Because current assets and liabilities are, in principle, converted to cash over the following 12 months, the current ratio is a measure of short-term liquidity. The unit of measurement is either dollars or times. So, we could say Prufrock has $1.31 in current assets for every $1 in current liabilities, or we could say Prufrock has its current liabilities covered 1.31 times over.

To a creditor, particularly a short-term creditor such as a supplier, the higher the current ratio, the better. To the firm, a high current ratio indicates liquidity, but it also may indicate an inefficient use of cash and other short-term assets. Absent some extraordinary circumstances, we would expect to see a current ratio of at least 1, because a current ratio of less than 1 would mean that net working capital (current assets less current liabilities) is negative. This would be unusual in a healthy firm, at least for most types of businesses.

The current ratio, like any ratio, is affected by various types of transactions. For example, suppose the firm borrows over the long term to raise money. The short-run effect would be an increase in cash from the issue proceeds and an increase in long-term debt. Current liabilities would not be affected, so the current ratio would rise.

Finally, note that an apparently low current ratio may not be a bad sign for a company with a large reserve of untapped borrowing power.

Quick (or Acid-Test) Ratio   Inventory is often the least liquid current asset. It's also the one for which the book values are least reliable as measures of market value, since the quality of the inventory isn't considered. Some of the inventory may later turn out to be damaged, obsolete, or lost.

More to the point, relatively large inventories are often a sign of short-term trouble. The firm may have overestimated sales and overbought or overproduced as a result. In this case, the firm may have a substantial portion of its liquidity tied up in slow-moving inventory.

To further evaluate liquidity, the *quick,* or *acid-test, ratio* is computed just like the current ratio, except inventory is omitted:

$$\text{Quick ratio} = \frac{\text{Current assets} - \text{Inventory}}{\text{Current liabilities}}$$

Notice that using cash to buy inventory does not affect the current ratio, but it reduces the quick ratio. Again, the idea is that inventory is relatively illiquid compared to cash.

For Prufrock, this ratio in 2005 was:

$$\text{Quick ratio} = \frac{\$708 - 422}{\$540} = .53 \text{ times}$$

The quick ratio here tells a somewhat different story than the current ratio, because inventory accounts for more than half of Prufrock's current assets. To exaggerate the point, if this inventory consisted of, say, unsold nuclear power plants, then this would be a cause for concern.

Cash Ratio   A very short-term creditor might be interested in the *cash ratio:*

$$\text{Cash ratio} = \frac{\text{Cash}}{\text{Current liabilities}}$$

You can verify that this works out to be .18 times for Prufrock.

Long-Term Solvency Measures

Long-term solvency ratios are intended to address the firm's long-run ability to meet its obligations, or, more generally, its financial leverage. These ratios are sometimes called *financial leverage ratios* or just *leverage ratios*. We consider three commonly used measures and some variations.

Total Debt Ratio   The *total debt ratio* takes into account all debts of all maturities to all creditors. It can be defined in several ways, the easiest of which is:

$$\text{Total debt ratio} = \frac{\text{Total assets} - \text{Total equity}}{\text{Total assets}}$$

$$= \frac{\$3,588 - 2,591}{\$3,588} = .28 \text{ times}$$

In this case, an analyst might say that Prufrock uses 28 percent debt.[1] Whether this is high or low or whether it even makes any difference depends on whether or not capital structure matters.

Prufrock has $.28 in debt for every $1 in assets. Therefore, there is $.72 in equity ($1 − .28) for every $.28 in debt. With this in mind, we can define two useful variations on the total debt ratio, the *debt-equity ratio* and the *equity multiplier:*

$$\text{Debt-equity ratio} = \text{Total debt/Total equity}$$

$$= \$.28/\$.72 = .39 \text{ times}$$

$$\text{Equity multiplier} = \text{Total assets/Total equity}$$

$$= \$1/\$.72 = 1.39 \text{ times}$$

The fact that the equity multiplier is 1 plus the debt-equity ratio is not a coincidence:

$$\text{Equity multiplier} = \text{Total assets/Total equity} = \$1/\$.72 = 1.39$$

$$= (\text{Total equity} + \text{Total debt})/\text{Total equity}$$

$$= 1 + \text{Debt-equity ratio} = 1.39 \text{ times}$$

The thing to notice here is that given any one of these three ratios, you can immediately calculate the other two, so they all say exactly the same thing.

Times Interest Earned   Another common measure of long-term solvency is the *times interest earned* (TIE) *ratio.* Once again, there are several possible (and common) definitions, but we'll stick with the most traditional:

$$\text{Times interest earned ratio} = \frac{\text{EBIT}}{\text{Interest}}$$

$$= \frac{\$691}{\$141} = 4.9 \text{ times}$$

As the name suggests, this ratio measures how well a company has its interest obligations covered, and it is often called the interest coverage ratio. For Prufrock, the interest bill is covered 4.9 times over.

Cash Coverage   A problem with the TIE ratio is that it is based on earnings before interest and taxes (EBIT), which is not really a measure of cash available to pay interest. The reason

---

[1]Total equity here includes preferred stock, if there is any. An equivalent numerator in this ratio would be (Current liabilities + Long-term debt).

is that depreciation, a noncash expense, has been deducted. Since interest is most definitely a cash outflow (to creditors), one way to define the *cash coverage ratio* is:

$$\text{Cash coverage ratio} = \frac{\text{EBIT} + \text{Depreciation}}{\text{Interest}}$$

$$= \frac{\$691 + 276}{\$141} = \frac{\$967}{\$141} = 6.9 \text{ times}$$

The numerator here, EBIT plus depreciation, is often abbreviated EBDIT (earnings before depreciation, interest, and taxes). It is a basic measure of the firm's ability to generate cash from operations, and it is frequently used as a measure of cash flow available to meet financial obligations.

Asset Management, or Turnover, Measures

We next turn our attention to the efficiency with which Prufrock uses its assets. The measures in this section are sometimes called *asset utilization ratios.* The specific ratios we discuss can all be interpreted as measures of turnover. What they are intended to describe is how efficiently, or intensively, a firm uses its assets to generate sales. We first look at two important current assets: inventory and receivables.

Inventory Turnover and Days' Sales in Inventory   During the year, Prufrock had a cost of goods sold of $1,344. Inventory at the end of the year was $422. With these numbers, *inventory turnover* can be calculated as:

$$\text{Inventory turnover} = \frac{\text{Cost of goods sold}}{\text{Inventory}}$$

$$= \frac{\$1,344}{\$422} = 3.2 \text{ times}$$

In a sense, we sold off, or turned over, the entire inventory 3.2 times. As long as we are not running out of stock and thereby forgoing sales, the higher this ratio is, the more efficiently we are managing inventory.

If we know that we turned our inventory over 3.2 times during the year, then we can immediately figure out how long it took us to turn it over on average. The result is the average *days' sales in inventory:*

$$\text{Days' sales in inventory} = \frac{365 \text{ days}}{\text{Inventory turnover}}$$

$$= \frac{365}{3.2} = 114 \text{ days}$$

This tells us that, on average, inventory sits 114 days before it is sold. Alternatively, assuming we used the most recent inventory and cost figures, it will take about 114 days to work off our current inventory.

For example, we frequently hear things like "Majestic Motors has a 60 days' supply of cars." This means that, at current daily sales, it would take 60 days to deplete the available inventory. We could also say that Majestic has 60 days of sales in inventory.

Receivables Turnover and Days' Sales in Receivables   Our inventory measures give some indication of how fast we can sell products. We now look at how fast we collect on those sales. The *receivables turnover* is defined in the same way as inventory turnover:

$$\text{Receivables turnover} = \frac{\text{Sales}}{\text{Accounts receivable}}$$

$$= \frac{\$2,311}{\$188} = 12.3 \text{ times}$$

Loosely speaking, we collected our outstanding credit accounts and reloaned the money 12.3 times during the year.[2]

This ratio makes more sense if we convert it to days, so the *days' sales in receivables* is:

$$\text{Days' sales in receivables} = \frac{365 \text{ days}}{\text{Receivables turnover}}$$

$$= \frac{365}{12.3} = 30 \text{ days}$$

Therefore, on average, we collect on our credit sales in 30 days. For obvious reasons, this ratio is very frequently called the *average collection period* (ACP).

Also note that if we are using the most recent figures, we can also say that we have 30 days' worth of sales currently uncollected.

Total Asset Turnover   Moving away from specific accounts like inventory or receivables, we can consider an important "big picture" ratio, the *total asset turnover ratio*. As the name suggests, total asset turnover is:

$$\text{Total asset turnover} = \frac{\text{Sales}}{\text{Total assets}}$$

$$= \frac{\$2,311}{\$3,588} = .64 \text{ times}$$

In other words, for every dollar in assets, we generated $.64 in sales.

A closely related ratio, the *capital intensity ratio,* is simply the reciprocal of (i.e., 1 divided by) total asset turnover. It can be interpreted as the dollar investment in assets needed to generate $1 in sales. High values correspond to capital intensive industries (e.g., public utilities). For Prufrock, total asset turnover is .64, so, if we flip this over, we get that capital intensity is $1/.64 = $1.56. That is, it takes Prufrock $1.56 in assets to create $1 in sales.

Profitability Measures

The three measures we discuss in this section are probably the best known and most widely used of all financial ratios. In one form or another, they are intended to measure how efficiently the firm uses its assets and how efficiently the firm manages its operations. The focus in this group is on the bottom line, net income.

Profit Margin   Companies pay a great deal of attention to their *profit margin:*

$$\text{Profit margin} = \frac{\text{Net income}}{\text{Sales}}$$

$$= \frac{\$363}{\$2,311} = 15.7\%$$

This tells us that Prufrock, in an accounting sense, generates a little less than 16 cents in profit for every dollar in sales.

All other things being equal, a relatively high profit margin is obviously desirable. This situation corresponds to low expense ratios relative to sales. However, we hasten to add that other things are often not equal.

For example, lowering our sales price will usually increase unit volume, but will normally cause profit margins to shrink. Total profit (or, more importantly, operating cash flow) may go up or down; so the fact that margins are smaller isn't necessarily bad. After all, isn't it possible that,

---

[2]Here we have implicitly assumed that all sales are credit sales. If they were not, then we would simply use total credit sales in these calculations, not total sales.

as the saying goes, "Our prices are so low that we lose money on everything we sell, but we make it up in volume!"[3]

Return on Assets   *Return on assets* (ROA) is a measure of profit per dollar of assets. It can be defined several ways, but the most common is:

$$\text{Return on assets} = \frac{\text{Net income}}{\text{Total equity}}$$

$$= \frac{\$363}{\$3,588} = 10.12\%$$

Return on Equity   *Return on equity* (ROE) is a measure of how the stockholders fared during the year. Since benefiting shareholders is our goal, ROE is, in an accounting sense, the true bottom-line measure of performance. ROE is usually measured as:

$$\text{Return on equity} = \frac{\text{Net income}}{\text{Total assets}}$$

$$= \frac{\$363}{\$2,591} = 14\%$$

For every dollar in equity, therefore, Prufrock generated 14 cents in profit, but, again, this is only correct in accounting terms.

Because ROA and ROE are such commonly cited numbers, we stress that it is important to remember they are accounting rates of return. For this reason, these measures should properly be called *return on book assets* and *return on book equity.* In addition, ROE is sometimes called *return on net worth.* Whatever it's called, it would be inappropriate to compare the results to, for example, an interest rate observed in the financial markets.

The fact that ROE exceeds ROA reflects Prufrock's use of financial leverage. We will examine the relationship between these two measures in more detail below.

Market Value Measures

Our final group of measures is based, in part, on information not necessarily contained in financial statements—the market price per share of the stock. Obviously, these measures can only be calculated directly for publicly traded companies.

We assume that Prufrock has 33 million shares outstanding and the stock sold for $88 per share at the end of the year. If we recall that Prufrock's net income was $363 million, then we can calculate that its earnings per share were:

$$\text{EPS} = \frac{\text{Net income}}{\text{Shares outstanding}} = \frac{\$363}{33} = \$11$$

Price-Earnings Ratio   The first of our market value measures, the *price-earnings,* or PE, *ratio* (or multiple), is defined as:

$$\text{PE ratio} = \frac{\text{Price per share}}{\text{Earnings per share}}$$

$$= \frac{\$85}{\$11} = 8 \text{ times}$$

In the vernacular, we would say that Prufrock shares sell for eight times earnings, or we might say that Prufrock shares have, or "carry," a PE multiple of 8.

Since the PE ratio measures how much investors are willing to pay per dollar of current earnings, higher PEs are often taken to mean that the firm has significant prospects for future growth.

[3]No, it's not; margins can be small, but they do need to be positive!

Of course, if a firm had no or almost no earnings, its PE would probably be quite large; so, as always, be careful when interpreting this ratio.

Market-to-Book Ratio   A second commonly quoted measure is the *market-to-book ratio:*

$$\text{Market-to-book ratio} = \frac{\text{Market value per share}}{\text{Book value per share}}$$

$$= \frac{\$88}{(\$2,591/33)} = \frac{\$88}{\$78.5} = 1.12 \text{ times}$$

Notice that book value per share is total equity (not just common stock) divided by the number of shares outstanding.

Since book value per share is an accounting number, it reflects historical costs. In a loose sense, the market-to-book ratio therefore compares the market value of the firm's investments to their cost. A value less than 1 could mean that the firm has not been successful overall in creating value for its stockholders.

Conclusion

This completes our definition of some common ratios. Exhibit 3A.5 summarizes the ratios we've discussed.

I. Short-term solvency, or liquidity, ratios

$$\text{Current ratio} = \frac{\text{Current assets}}{\text{Current liabilities}}$$

$$\text{Quick ratio} = \frac{\text{Current assets} - \text{Inventory}}{\text{Current liabilities}}$$

$$\text{Cash ratio} = \frac{\text{Cash}}{\text{Current liabilities}}$$

II. Long-term solvency, or financial leverage, ratios

$$\text{Total debt ratio} = \frac{\text{Total assets} - \text{Total equity}}{\text{Total assets}}$$

$$\text{Debt-equity ratio} = \text{Total debt/Total equity}$$

$$\text{Equity multiplier} = \text{Total assets/Total equity}$$

$$\text{Times interest earned ratio} = \frac{\text{EBIT}}{\text{Interest}}$$

$$\text{Cash coverage ratio} = \frac{\text{EBIT} + \text{Depreciation}}{\text{Interest}}$$

III. Asset utilization, or turnover, ratios

$$\text{Inventory turnover} = \frac{\text{Cost of goods sold}}{\text{Inventory}}$$

$$\text{Days' sales in inventory} = \frac{365 \text{ days}}{\text{Inventory turnover}}$$

$$\text{Receivables turnover} = \frac{\text{Sales}}{\text{Accounts receivables}}$$

$$\text{Days' sales in receivables} = \frac{365 \text{ days}}{\text{Receivables turnover}}$$

$$\text{Total asset turnover} = \frac{\text{Sales}}{\text{Total assets}}$$

$$\text{Capital intensity} = \frac{\text{Total assets}}{\text{Sales}}$$

IV. Profitability ratios

$$\text{Profit margin} = \frac{\text{Net income}}{\text{Sales}}$$

$$\text{Return on assets (ROA)} = \frac{\text{Net income}}{\text{Total assets}}$$

$$\text{Return on equity (ROE)} = \frac{\text{Net income}}{\text{Total equity}}$$

$$\text{ROE} = \frac{\text{Net income}}{\text{Sales}} \times \frac{\text{Sales}}{\text{Assets}} \times \frac{\text{Assets}}{\text{Equity}}$$

V. Market value ratios

$$\text{Price-earnings ratio} = \frac{\text{Price per share}}{\text{Earnings per share}}$$

$$\text{Market-to-book ratio} = \frac{\text{Market value per share}}{\text{Book value per share}}$$

Exhibit 3A.5

Recognizing a Firm's Intellectual Assets:

Moving beyond a Firm's Tangible Resources

>chapter objectives

After reading this chapter, you should have a good understanding of:

- Why the management of knowledge professionals and knowledge itself are so critical in today's organizations.

- The importance of recognizing the interdependence of attracting, developing, and retaining human capital.

- The key role of social capital in leveraging human capital within and across the firm.

- Why teams are critical in combining and leveraging knowledge in organizations and how they can be made more effective.

- The vital role of technology in leveraging knowledge and human capital.

- How technology can help to retain knowledge even when employees cannot be retained by the organization.

- How leveraging human capital is critical to strategy formulation at the business, corporate, international, and Internet levels.

One of the most important trends that managers must consider is the significance of the knowledge worker in today's economy. Managers must both recognize the importance of top talent and provide mechanisms to enhance the leveraging of human capital to innovate and, in the end, develop products and services that create value.

The first section addresses the increasing role of knowledge as the primary means of wealth generation in today's economy. A company's value is not derived solely from its physical assets, such as plant, equipment, and machinery. Rather, it is based on knowledge, know-how, and intellectual assets—all embedded in people.

The second section discusses the key resource itself, human capital, which is the foundation of intellectual capital. We explore ways in which the organization can attract, develop, and retain top talent—three important, interdependent activities. With regard to attracting human capital, we address issues such as "hiring for attitude, training for skill." One of the issues regarding developing human capital is encouraging widespread involvement throughout the organization. Our discussion on retaining human capital addresses issues such as the importance of having employees identify with an organization's mission and values. We also address the value of a diverse workforce.

The attraction, development, and retention of human capital are necessary but not sufficient conditions for organizational success. In the third section we address social capital—networks of relationships among a firm's members. This is especially important where collaboration and sharing information are critical. In this section we address why social capital can be particularly important in attracting human capital and making teams effective.

The fourth section addresses the role of technology in leveraging human capital. Examples range from e-mail and the use of networks to facilitate collaboration among individuals to more complex forms of technologies, such as sophisticated knowledge management systems. We discuss how electronic teams can be effectively managed. We also address how technology can help to retain knowledge.

The fifth and final section discusses how leveraging human capital is vital to each of the four levels of strategy formulation—business, corporate, international, and Internet.

Some companies excel in attracting top talent and leveraging such talent. This often leads to positive relationships among individuals within the firm, promoting a social infrastructure that is critical for gaining consensus on major decisions, sharing information, and promoting cooperation. However, at times, hiring top talent or "stars" can have a big downside. Consider the experience of The Wildflower Group, a New York–based licensing and marketing group that represents the trademark owners of such products as home furnishings, giftware, and popular characters, including ALF and Newton's Law (a small bear extremely popular in Great Britain).

To Michael Carlisle, one of Wildflower's partners, it seemed like the coup of a lifetime.[1] Although his firm was just three years old and had only 10 employees, it was able to recruit a highly regarded salesperson from one of the industry's largest and most prestigious companies. She was a bona fide superstar, with a blue-chip resume, a Rolodex brimming with contacts, and a track record for landing top-dollar clients. The excited Carlisle remembers thinking, "She could do a lot for us."

But that was then . . . and things didn't work out as planned. The new employee was accustomed to the comforts and amenities of a large corporation. She became testy and unpleasant when asked to, for example, troubleshoot her own computer problems or alter her travel plans to take advantage of cheaper airfares. And she hardly created warm, positive feelings among her coworkers by trying to fob off administrative chores such as sending faxes. To make matters worse, she was not bringing in new business for Wildflower. Finally, and not too surprisingly, she did not take direction very well. Carlisle would lay out Wildflower's sales plan, and she'd argue about it.

Carlisle and his partner, Fred Paprin, spent many unproductive hours discussing how to best salvage the situation. However, as the complaints mounted, Carlisle began to worry about losing other employees. The final straw came when Carlisle noticed that several younger employees were beginning to emulate the star's poor behavior. The partners agreed it was time for the company to cut its losses. Wildflower's big hiring coup lasted less than 10 months.

Managers are always hunting for stellar employees who can raise the organization to the next level. Unfortunately, as Carlisle discovered, bulletproof credentials are far from a "happily ever after" guarantee. Just the opposite may come true instead.

In this chapter, we will discuss how attracting, developing, and retaining talent is a necessary but not sufficient condition for success. Many firms have experienced problems leveraging talent and technologies into successful products and services. In today's knowledge economy, it doesn't matter too much how big your stock of resources is—whether it be top-level talent, physical resources such as buildings and machinery, or financial capital. Rather, the question becomes: How good is the organization at attracting top talent and leveraging that talent to produce a stream of products and services valued by the marketplace?

>>The Central Role of Knowledge in Today's Economy

Central to our discussion is an enormous change that has accelerated over the past few decades and its implications for the strategic management of organizations.[2] That is, for most of the 20th century, managers were primarily concerned with tangible resources such as land, equipment, and money as well as intangibles such as brands, image, and customer loyalty. Most efforts were directed more toward the efficient allocation of labor and capital—the two traditional factors of production.

How times have changed. Today, more than 50 percent of the gross domestic product (GDP) in developed economies is knowledge-based; that is, it is based on intellectual assets and intangible people skills.[3] In the United States, intellectual and information processes create most of the value for firms in large service industries (e.g., software, medical care, communications, and education), which make up 76 percent of the U.S. GDP. In the manufacturing sector, intellectual activities like R&D, process design, product design, logistics, marketing, or technological innovation produce the preponderance of value added.[4] To drive home the point, consider the perspective of Gary Hamel and C. K. Prahalad, two leading writers in strategic management:

> The machine age was a physical world. It consisted of things. Companies made and distributed things (physical products). Management allocated things (capital budgets); management invested in things (plant and equipment).
>
> In the machine age, people were ancillary, and things were central. In the information age, things are ancillary, knowledge is central. A company's value derives not from things, but from knowledge, know-how, intellectual assets, competencies—all embedded in people.[5]

In a similar vein, Robert Reich, former U. S. Secretary of Labor, provides an example of everyday products:[6]

> The real value of my shirt-and-trouser order lies in the system that translates it into digital instructions along the way, monitors every step to make sure it's done quickly and correctly, and then speeds it back to me. The apparel industry that departed New England in the first half of the twentieth century in pursuit of cheaper labor in the South, and then promptly moved on to Southeast Asia, where labor was even cheaper, is being transformed largely into design, marketing, and software systems located wherever the designers, marketers, and software engineers reside. Only a small fraction of the price of that final garment has anything to do with routine sewing and cutting. I'm mostly buying intangible services.

In the knowledge economy, wealth is increasingly created through the effective management of knowledge workers instead of by the efficient control of physical and financial assets. The growing importance of knowledge, coupled with the move by labor markets to reward knowledge work, tells us that someone who invests in a company is, in essence, buying a set of talents, capabilities, skills, and ideas—intellectual capital—not physical and financial resources.[7]

Let's provide a few examples. People don't buy Microsoft's stock because of its software factories; it doesn't own any. Rather, the value of Microsoft is bid up because of its ability to set standards for personal-computing software, exploit the value of its name, and forge alliances with other companies. Similarly, Merck didn't become the "Most Admired" company, for seven consecutive years in *Fortune*'s annual survey, because it can manufacture pills, but because its scientists can discover medicines. P. Roy Vagelos, who was CEO of Merck, the $23 billion pharmaceutical giant, during its long run atop the "Most Admired" survey, said, "A low-value product can be made by anyone anywhere. When you have knowledge no one else has access to—that's dynamite. We guard our research even more carefully than our financial assets."[8]

To apply some numbers to our arguments, let's ask, What's a company worth?[9] Start with the "big three" financial statements: income statement, balance sheet, and statement of cash flow. If these statements tell a story that investors find useful, then a company's market value* should roughly (but not precisely, because the market looks forward and the books look backward) be the same as the value that accountants ascribe to it—the book value of the firm. However, this is not the case. A study compared the market value with the book value of 3,500 U.S. companies over a period of two decades. In 1978 the

---

* The market value of a firm is equal to the value of a share of its common stock times the number of shares outstanding. The book value of a firm is primarily a measure of the value of its tangible assets. It can be calculated by the formula: total assets − total liabilities.

Exhibit 4.1

Ratio of Market Value to Book Value for Selected Companies

Company	Annual Sales ($ billions)	Market Value ($ billions)	Book Value ($ billions)	Ratio of Market to Book Value
Google	3.2	60.4	2.9	20.8
Genentech	3.9	75.0	6.8	11.0
Yahoo!	3.6	47.9	7.1	6.7
eBay	3.2	42.8	6.7	6.4
Southwest Airlines	6.5	11.7	5.5	2.1
Union Pacific (Railroad)	12.2	16.7	12.7	1.3
Ford Motor Company	171.6	16.7	16.0	1.0

Note: The data on market valuations are as of May 1, 2005. All other financial data is based on the most recently available balance sheets and income statements.

two were pretty well matched: Book value was 95 percent of market value. However, the gap between market values and book values has widened significantly. Twenty years later, book value was just 28 percent of market value. A colorful commentary comes from Robert A. Howell, an expert on the changing role of finance and accounting, "The big three financial statements . . . are about as useful as an 80-year-old Los Angeles road map."

As we might expect based on the above discussion, the gap between a firm's market value and book value is far greater for knowledge-intensive corporations than for firms with strategies based primarily on tangible assets. Exhibit 4.1 shows the ratio of market-to-book value for a selected set of companies. In firms where knowledge and the management of knowledge workers are relatively important contributors to developing products and services—and physical resources are less critical—the ratio of market-to-book value tends to be much higher. Many writers have defined intellectual capital as the difference between a firm's market value and book value—that is, a measure of the value of a firm's intangible assets.[10] This admittedly broad definition includes assets such as reputation, employee loyalty and commitment, customer relationships, company values, brand names, and the experience and skills of employees.[11] Thus, simplifying, we have:

Intellectual capital = Market value of the firm − Book value of the firm

The issue becomes: How do companies create value in the knowledge-intensive economy? As we stated above, the general answer is to attract and leverage human capital effectively through mechanisms that create products and services of value over time. Let's articulate a few of the basic concepts that we will be talking about in this chapter.

First, consider human capital. Human capital is the "*individual* capabilities, knowledge, skills, and experience of the company's employees and managers."[12] This is knowledge that is relevant to the task at hand, as well as the capacity to add to this reservoir of knowledge, skills, and experience through learning.[13]

Second, social capital can be defined as "the network of relationships that individuals have throughout the organization." Such relationships are critical in sharing and leveraging knowledge and in acquiring resources.[14] Social capital also can extend beyond the organizational boundaries to include relationships between the firm and its suppliers, customers, and alliance partners.[15]

Third is the concept of "knowledge," which comes in two different forms. On the one hand, there is explicit knowledge that is codified, documented, easily reproduced, and widely distributed. Examples include engineering drawings, software code, sales collateral, and patents. The other type of knowledge is tacit knowledge.[16] This is knowledge that is, in essence, in the minds of employees and is based on their experiences and backgrounds. Tacit knowledge is shared only with the consent and participation of the individual.

New knowledge is constantly being created in organizations. It involves the continual interaction of explicit and tacit knowledge. Consider, for example, two software engineers working together on a computer code. The computer code itself is the explicit knowledge. However, through their sharing of ideas based on each individual's experience—that is, their tacit knowledge—new knowledge is created when they make modifications to the existing code. Another important issue is the role of "socially complex processes," which include leadership, culture, and trust.[17] These processes play a central role in the creation of knowledge.[18] They represent the "glue" that holds the organization together and helps to create a working environment where individuals are more willing to share their ideas, work in teams, and, in the end, create products and services of value. In a later section, we will address the importance of social capital in the value creation process.

Numerous books have been written on the subject of knowledge management and the central role that it has played in creating wealth in organizations and countries throughout the developed world.[19] Here, we focus on some of the key issues that organizations must address to compete through knowledge.

We will now turn our discussion to the central resource itself—human capital—and some guidelines on how it can be attracted/selected, developed, and retained. Tom Stewart, editor of the *Harvard Business Review,* noted that organizations must also undergo significant efforts to protect their human capital. A firm may "diversify the ownership of vital knowledge by emphasizing teamwork, guard against obsolescence by developing learning programs, and shackle key people with golden handcuffs."[20] In addition, people are less likely to leave an organization if there are effective structures to promote teamwork and information sharing, strong leadership that encourages innovation, and cultures that demand excellence and ethical behavior. Such issues are also central to the topic of this chapter. Although we touch on these issues throughout this chapter, we provide more detail in later chapters. We discuss organizational controls (culture, rewards, and boundaries) in Chapter 9, organization structure and design in Chapter 10, and a variety of leadership and entrepreneurship topics in Chapters 11, 12, and 13.

>>Human Capital: The Foundation of Intellectual Capital

To be successful, organizations must recruit talented people—employees at all levels with the proper sets of skills and capabilities coupled with the right values and attitudes. Such skills and attitudes must be continually developed, strengthened, and reinforced, and each employee must be motivated and his or her efforts focused on the organization's goals and objectives.

The rise to prominence of the knowledge worker as a vital source of competitive advantage is changing the balance of power in today's organization. Knowledge workers place professional development and personal enrichment (financial and otherwise) above company loyalty. Attracting, recruiting, and hiring the "best and the brightest," is a critical first step in the process of building intellectual capital. At a symposium for CEOs, Bill Gates said, "The thing that is holding Microsoft back . . . is simply how [hard] we find it to go out and recruit the kind of people we want to grow our research team."[21]

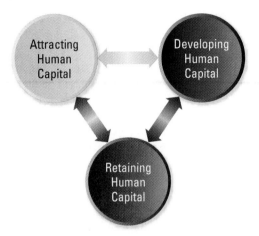

Exhibit 4.2   **Human Capital: Three Interdependent Activities**

But hiring is only the first of three vital processes in which all successful organizations must engage to build and leverage their human capital. Firms must also *develop* employees at all levels and specialties to fulfill their full potential in order to maximize their joint contributions. Finally, the first two processes are for naught if firms can't provide the working environment and intrinsic and extrinsic rewards to *retain* their best and brightest.

These three activities are highly interrelated. We would like to suggest the imagery of a three-legged stool (see Exhibit 4.2).[22] If one leg is weak or broken, the stool collapses.

To illustrate such interdependence, poor hiring impedes the effectiveness of development and retention processes. In a similar vein, ineffective retention efforts place additional burdens on hiring and development. Consider the following anecdote, provided by Jeffrey Pfeffer of the Stanford University Business School:

> Not long ago, I went to a large, fancy San Francisco law firm—where they treat their associates like dog doo and where the turnover is very high. I asked the managing partner about the turnover rate. He said, "A few years ago, it was 25 percent, and now we're up to 30 percent." I asked him how the firm had responded to that trend. He said, "We increased our recruiting." So I asked him, "What kind of doctor would you be if your patient was bleeding faster and faster, and your only response was to increase the speed of the transfusion?"[23]

Clearly, stepped-up recruiting is a poor substitute for weak retention. Although there are no simple, easy-to-apply answers, we can learn from what leading-edge firms are doing to attract, develop, and retain human capital in today's highly competitive and rapidly changing marketplace. Let's begin by discussing hiring and selection practices.

Attracting Human Capital

All we can do is bet on the people we pick. So my whole job is picking the right people.

Jack Welch, former chairman, General Electric Company[24]

As we have noted, the first step in the process of building superior human capital is input control: attracting and selecting the right person. Many human resource professionals still approach employee selection from a "lock and key" mentality—that is, fit a key (a job candidate) into a lock (the job). Such an approach involves a thorough analysis of both the person and the job. Only then can the right decision be made as to how well the two will fit together. How can you fail, the theory goes, if you get a precise match of knowledge, ability, and skill profiles? Frequently, however, the precise matching approach places its primary emphasis on task-specific skills (e.g., motor skills, specific information gathering and processing capabilities, and communication skills) and puts less emphasis on the broad general knowledge and experience, social skills, values, beliefs, and attitudes of employees.

Many have questioned the precise matching approach. Instead, they argue that firms can identify top performers by focusing on key employee mind-sets, attitudes, social skills, and general orientations that lead to success in nearly all jobs. These firms reason that if they get these elements right, the task-specific skills can be learned in relatively short order. (This does not imply, however, that task-specific skills are unimportant; rather, it suggests that the requisite skill sets must be viewed as a necessary but not sufficient condition.) This leads us to a phrase that is popular with many organizations today and serves as the title of the next section.

"Hire for Attitude, Train for Skill"   Organizations are increasingly placing their emphasis on the general knowledge and experience, social skills, values, beliefs, and attitudes of employees. Consider Southwest Airlines's hiring practices, with their strong focus on employee values and attitudes. Given its strong team orientation, Southwest uses an "indirect" approach. For example, the interviewing team asks a group of employees to prepare a five-minute presentation about themselves. During the presentations, the interviewers observe which candidates are enthusiastically supporting their peers and which candidates are focused on polishing their own presentations while the others are presenting.[25] The former are, of course, favored.

Social skills are also important. You need to be both pleasant and collegial to be hired by Rosenbluth International, a travel-management company based in Philadelphia, with annual revenues over $5 billion. Here, job applicants are asked to play a trial game of softball with the company team. Potential executives are frequently flown to the firm's North Dakota ranch to help repair fences or drive cattle. Do athletic ability or ranching skills matter? Not at all. According to Keami Lewis, Rosenbluth's diversity manager, "You can teach a person almost anything. But you can't teach him or her how to be nice."[26] Or, as Tom Stewart has suggested, "You can make a leopard a better leopard, but you can't change its spots."[27]

Alan Cooper, president of Cooper Software, Inc., in Palo Alto, California, goes a few steps further. He cleverly *uses technology* to hone in on the problem-solving ability of his applicants and their attitudes before an interview even takes place. He has devised a "Bozo Filter," a test administered online (see Strategy Spotlight 4.1) that can be applied to any industry. Before you spend time figuring out whether job candidates will work out satisfactorily, find out how their minds work. Cooper advised, "Hiring was a black hole. I don't talk to bozos anymore because 90 percent of them turn away when they see our test. It's a self-administering bozo filter."[28]

The central point is what some have called the Popeye Principle, "I y'am what I y'am," borrowing from the famous cartoon sailor. Many have argued that the most common, and fatal, hiring mistake is to select individuals with the right skills but the wrong mind-set on the theory that "we can change them." According to Alan Davidson, an industrial psychologist in San Diego whose clients include Chevron, Merrill Lynch, and the Internal Revenue Service, "The single best predictor of future behavior is past behavior. Your personality (largely reflecting values, beliefs, attitudes, and social skills) is going to be essentially the same throughout your life."[29]

STRATEGY SPOTLIGHT

Cooper Software's "Bozo Filter"

Hiring is often easier than firing. Even when unemployment rates are low and labor is scarce, it's still easier to find employees than it is to get them out the door if they don't work out. Not only do poor employees affect the morale of better talent, but they also cost the company money in lost productivity.

Cooper Software has found an innovative way to prevent the problem of hiring bad employees. CEO Alan Cooper asks job applicants to visit the company's Web site, where the applicants will find a test that takes between two and five hours to complete. The test asks questions designed to see how prospective employees approach problem-solving tasks. For example, one key question asks software engineer applicants to design a new table-creation software program for Microsoft Word. Candidates provide pencil sketches and a description of

Sources: Cardin, R. 1997. Make your own bozo filter. *Fast Company*, October–November: 56; Coop, A. 1997. Getting design across. Unpublished manuscript, November 23: 1–8; and www.cooper.com.

the new user interface. Another question is used for design communicators. They are asked to develop a marketing strategy for a new touch-tone phone—directed at consumers in the year 1850. Candidates e-mail their answers back to the company, and the answers are circulated around the firm to solicit feedback. Only candidates with the highest marks get interviews.

Jonathan Korman, a design communicator, suggested that the test "told me more about real job duties than any description could." Josh Seiden, a software designer, is even more positive: "It was a fun puzzle—much more engaging than most of what I was doing at my previous job."

That's exactly the kind of attitude Cooper wants. "We get e-mail from some people saying, 'Before I take this test, is the position still open?' I say no, because I don't want anybody who sees it as an effort," claims Cooper. "People who really care take the test and love it. Other people say it's hard. We don't want those people."

Sound Recruiting Approaches and Networking Companies that take hiring seriously must also take recruiting seriously. The number of jobs that successful knowledge-intensive companies must fill is astonishing. Ironically, many companies still have no shortage of applicants. Southwest Airlines typically gets 150,000 résumés a year, yet hires only about 5,000 new employees. And Netscape (now part of Time Warner) reviews 60 résumés for every hire.[30] The challenge becomes having the right job candidates, not the greatest number of them.

Few firms are as thorough as Microsoft when it comes to recruiting. Each year the firm scans the entire pool of 25,000 U.S. computer-science graduates and identifies the 8,000 in which they are interested. After further screening, 2,600 are invited for on-campus interviews at their universities. Out of these, only 800 are invited to the company's Redmond, Washington, headquarters. Of these, 500 receive offers, and usually 400 accept. These massive efforts, however, provide less than 20 percent of the company's hiring needs. To find the other talent, Microsoft maintains a team of 300 recruiting experts whose full-time job is to locate the best and brightest in the industry.[31]

GE Medical Systems, which builds CT scanners and magnetic resonance imaging (MRI) systems, relies extensively on networking. They have found that current employees are the best source for new ones. Recently, Steven Patscot, head of staffing and leadership development, made a few simple changes to double the number of referrals. First, he simplified the process—no complex forms, no bureaucracy, and so on. Second, he increased incentives. Everyone referring a qualified candidate received a gift certificate from Sears. For referrals who were hired, the "bounty" was increased to $2,000 (or $3,000 if the referral was a software engineer). Although this may sound like a lot of money, it is "peanuts" compared to the $15,000 to $20,000 fees that GE typically pays

The "War for Talent": Possible Downsides

Various organizational processes and dynamics arise when organizations adopt a "war for talent" mind-set that can lead to many adverse outcomes. Dr. Jeffrey Pfeffer, a professor at Stanford University's Business School, cautions that not only should a firm *not* try to "win" the war for talent but also that even adopting this imagery to guide recruiting initiatives can be hazardous to an organization's health.

When a firm engages in a war for talent, there is:

- An inevitable emphasis on individual performance (rewarding "stars"). This tends to erode teamwork, increase internal competition, and reduce learning and the spread of best practices within the firm.

- A tendency to become enamored with the talents of those outside the firm and discount the talents and abilities of insiders. This generally leads to decreased motivation in the firm's existing employees and greater turnover, and often causes more

difficulties in future recruiting as the company tries to replace those who left.

- A self-fulfilling prophecy. Those labeled as less capable become less able because they are often asked to do less and are given fewer resources, training, and mentoring. In the process, the organization has far too many people who are in the process of dropping out of the competitive fray.

- A reduced emphasis on repairing the systemic, cultural, and business process issues that are typically much more important for enhanced performance. Why? The company seeks success solely by getting the right people into the company.

- The creation of an elitist, arrogant attitude. After all, once a firm has successfully completed the war for talent, it develops an attitude that makes building a wise organization extremely difficult. In wise organizations, people know what they know and what they don't know. However, companies that believe they have won the war for talent think they are so full of smart people that they know everything!

Source: Pfeffer, J. 2001. Fighting the war for talent is hazardous to your organization's health. *Organizational Dynamics*, 29(4): 248–259.

to headhunters for each person hired.[32] Also, when someone refers a former colleague or friend for a job, his or her credibility is on the line. Thus, employees will tend to be careful in recommending people for employment unless they are reasonably confident that these people are good candidates. This provides a good "screen" for the firm in deciding whom to hire. After all, hiring the right people makes things a lot easier: fewer rules and regulations, less need for monitoring and hierarchy, and greater internalization of organizational norms and objectives.

Before moving on, it is useful to point out an important caveat. While it is important to strive to attract "top talent," managers must avoid a mind-set where they engage in "war for talent." We address this issue in Strategy Spotlight 4.2.

Developing Human Capital

It is not enough to hire top-level talent and expect that the skills and capabilities of those employees remain current throughout the duration of their employment. Rather, training and development must take place at all levels of the organization.[33] For example, Solectron assembles printed circuit boards and other components for its Silicon Valley clients.[34] Its employees receive an average of 95 hours of company-provided training each year. Chairman Winston Chen observed, "Technology changes so fast that we estimate 20 percent of an engineer's knowledge becomes obsolete each year. Training is an obligation we owe to our employees. If you want high growth and high quality, then training is a big part of the equation." Although the financial returns on training may be hard to calculate, most experts believe it is not only real, but also essential. One company that has calculated the benefit from training is Motorola. This high-technology firm has calculated that every dollar spent on training returns $30 in productivity gains over the following three years.

Cinergy, the $12 billion Cincinnati-based gas, electric, and energy services company, is another firm that recognizes that all employees must be the prime investors and beneficiaries of learning.[35] Gone is the focus on executive leadership. In its place is "talent development" which is available to everyone. Elizabeth Lanier, the legal chief of staff, stated, "The premise is that we want to have the smartest people in every layer of the job. If it's the janitor in a power plant, I want him smarter than any other janitor." Lanier is convinced that if you only recruit and train your best talent, you run the risk of having that talent take your investment to the competition.

In addition to the importance of training and developing human capital throughout the organization, let's now discuss three other related topics: encouraging widespread involvement, monitoring and tracking employee development, and evaluating human capital.[36]

Encouraging Widespread Involvement   The development of human capital requires the active involvement of leaders at all levels throughout the organization. It won't be successful if it is viewed only as the responsibility of the human resources department. Each year at General Electric, 200 facilitators, 30 officers, 30 human resource executives, and many young managers actively participate in GE's orientation program at the firm's impressive Crotonville training center outside New York City. Topics include global competition, winning on the global playing field, and personal examination of the new employee's core values vis-à-vis GE's values. As a senior manager once commented, "There is nothing like teaching Sunday school to force you to confront your own values."

The "cascade approach" is another way that managers at multiple levels in an organization become actively involved in developing human capital. For example, Robert Galvin, former chairman of Motorola, requested a workshop for more than 1,000 Motorola senior executives to help them understand the market potential of selected Asian countries. However, rather than bringing in outside experts, participants were asked to analyze the existing competition and to determine how Motorola could compete in these markets. After researching their topics, the executives traveled around the world to directly observe local market developments. Then they taught the concepts of globalization to the next level of 3,000 Motorola managers. By doing so, they not only verified their impressions with firsthand observations, but they also reinforced their learning and shared it by teaching others.

Transferring Knowledge   Often in our lives, we need to either transfer our knowledge to someone else (a child, a junior colleague, a peer) or access accumulated bits of wisdom—someone else's tacit knowledge.[37] A vital aspect of developing human capital is transferring unique and specialized knowledge. However, before we can even begin to plan such a transfer, we need to understand how our brains process incoming information. According to Dorothy Leonard Barton of Harvard University:

> Our existing tacit knowledge determines how we assimilate new experiences. Without receptors—hooks on which to hang new information—we may not be able to perceive and process the information. It is like being sent boxes of documents but having no idea how they could or should be organized.

This cognitive limitation also applies to the organizational level as well. For example, when GE Healthcare sets up or transfers operations from one location to another, it appoints an experienced manager to be the "pitcher" and a team in the receiving plant to be the "catcher." These two teams work together, often over a period of years—first at the pitcher's location and then at the catcher's. In order to ensure a smooth transition, the pitching team needs to be sensitive to the catching team's level of experience and familiarity with GE Healthcare procedures.

How does this work in practice? Here's one example: When a veteran operations manager arrived at a growing GE Healthcare plant in China, the local team was getting ready to move raw materials from the manufacturing facility into a warehouse. Although the operations manager could see numerous potential problems with the chosen site, he knew that simply vetoing it would have transferred little knowledge. Thus, he helped the team to develop a list of critical-to-quality (CTQ) sites. (Although this technique is standard operating procedure at GE, the Chinese plant was not familiar with it.) The list included such factors as proximity to the manufacturing plant, easy access for large trucks, road conditions between facilities, and basic amenities for employees. With the list in hand, the catchers visited the selected site and they could see that it met few of their criteria. Thus, they understood the reasons for using the CTQ model for even apparently simple choices. They now had a framework and some basic experience on which to build future decisions.

Monitoring Progress and Tracking Development   Whether a firm uses on-site formal training, off-site training (e.g., universities), or on-the-job training, tracking individual progress—and sharing this knowledge with both the employee and key managers—becomes essential. At Citibank (part of Citigroup, the large financial services organization), a talent inventory program keeps track of roughly 10,000 employees worldwide—how they're doing, what skills they need to work on, and where else in the company they might thrive. Larry Phillips, head of human resources, considers the program critical to the company's global growth.[38]

Like many leading-edge organizations, GlaxoSmithKline places increasingly greater emphasis on broader experiences over longer periods of time. Dan Phelan, senior vice president and director of human resources, explained, "We ideally follow a two-plus-two-plus-two formula in developing people for top management positions." The formula reflects the belief that SmithKline's best people should gain experience in two business units, two functional units (such as finance and marketing), in two countries. Interestingly, when vacancies occur among the firm's top 300 positions, the company will consider looking outside for talent. According to CEO Jan Leschly, "A little new blood doesn't hurt. If you're not the best person for the job, we'll show no hesitancy to go outside."

Evaluating Human Capital   In today's competitive environment, collaboration and interdependence have become vital to organizational success. Individuals must share their knowledge and work together constructively to achieve collective, not just individual, goals. However, traditional evaluation systems evaluate performance from a single perspective (i.e., "top down") and generally don't address the "softer" dimensions of communications and social skills, values, beliefs, and attitudes.[39]

To address the limitations of the traditional approach, many organizations have begun to use 360-degree evaluation and feedback systems.[40] In these systems, superiors, direct reports, colleagues, and even internal and external customers rate a person's skills. Managers also rate themselves in order to have a personal benchmark. The 360-degree feedback system complements teamwork, employee involvement, and organizational flattening. As organizations continue to push responsibility downward,

Exhibit 4.3

An Excerpt from General Electric's 360-Degree Leadership Assessment Chart

Vision	• Has developed and communicated a clear, simple, customer-focused vision/direction for the organization. • Forward-thinking, stretches horizons, challenges imaginations. • Inspires and energizes others to commit to Vision. Captures minds. Leads by example. • As appropriate, updates Vision to reflect constant and accelerating change affecting the business.

Customer/Quality Focus

Integrity

Accountability/Commitment

Communication/Influence

Shared Ownership/Boundaryless

Team Builder/Empowerment

Knowledge/Expertise/Intellect

Initiative/Speed

Global Mind-Set

Source: Adapted from Slater, R. 1994. *Get better or get beaten:* 152–155. Burr Ridge, IL: Irwin Professional Publishing.

Note: This evaluation system consists of 10 "characteristics"—Vision, Customer/Quality Focus, Integrity, and so on. Each of these characteristics has four "performance criteria." For illustrative purposes, the four performance criteria of "Vision" are included.

traditional top-down appraisal systems become insufficient. For example, a manager who previously managed the performance of 3 supervisors might now be responsible for 10 and might be less likely to have the in-depth knowledge needed to appraise and develop each sufficiently and fairly. Exhibit 4.3 provides a portion of GE's 360-degree evaluation system.

In addition to being more accurate, companies are also adopting multirater feedback systems to shorten the process for developing human capital. "What might have taken four or five years for people to realize about themselves before can happen in much less time," claimed Stella Estevez of Warner-Lambert (now merged into Pfizer), a pharmaceutical firm that uses 360-degree feedback. Similarly, Jerry Wallace of Saturn (a division of General Motors) learned that, although he considered himself flexible, his subordinates did not. Instead they felt that he used excessive control. Wallace claimed, "I got a strong message that I need to delegate more. I thought I'd been doing it. But I need to do it more and sooner."

Finally, evaluation systems must ensure that a manager's success does not come at the cost of compromising the organization's core values. Clearly, such behavior generally leads to only short-term wins for both the manager and the organization. The organization typically suffers long-term losses in terms of morale, turnover, productivity, and so on. Accordingly, Merck's chairman, Ray Gilmartin, told his employees, "If someone is achieving results but not demonstrating the core values of the company, at the expense of our people, that manager does not have much of a career here."

Strategy Spotlight 4.3 summarizes General Electric's "Session C"—an integral part of its leadership evaluation and development process.

General Electric's "Session C" Leadership Evaluation

General Electric, long regarded as one of the top talent producers in the corporate world, has relied on what it calls "Session C" leadership evaluation as an important means of ensuring that its leadership resources are consistent with its business direction. Session C is GE's annual, dialogue-intensive review and one of its most valuable tools for evaluating CEO candidates and for helping its rising stars evaluate themselves.

Every year, GE chooses a different set of 20 to 25 leaders who might eventually become CEOs or top leaders in functional areas. It conducts a three- to four-hour session with each of them along with two human resource executives from outside of the person's own business unit. The HR executives trace these high potential leaders' progression from early childhood (where they grew up, how their parents influenced their style of thinking, what their early values were) through their recent accomplishments. The HR executives then conduct an extensive fact-finding mission both inside and outside the organization, including 360-degree reviews; thorough reference checks; and interviews with their bosses, direct reports, customers, and peers. Rather than relying on psychology, the assessment focuses on observed, measurable performance within the business.

The outcome of this effort is a 15- to 20-page document that summarizes the promising leader's work and development over decades. The report is full of accolades but also includes details on how the leaders can improve their effectiveness. The report is also distributed to the individual's manager, the senior human-resource executive of his or her unit, and to corporate headquarters. There, it is closely reviewed by GE's chairman, the three vice chairmen, and Bill Conaty, senior vice president for corporate human resources. Claims Conaty, "I usually wait until the end of the workday to read one of these because it takes an hour or so. You find out incredibly interesting things about people in the process."

Source: Charan, R. 2005. Ending the CEO succession crisis. *Harvard Business Review,* 83(2): 72–81.

Retaining Human Capital

It has been said that talented employees are like "frogs in a wheelbarrow."[41] They can jump out at any time. By analogy, the organization can either try to force employees to stay in the firm or try to keep them from wanting to jump out by creating incentives. In other words, today's leaders can either provide the work environment and incentives to keep productive employees and management from wanting to bail out, or they can rely on legal means such as employment contracts and noncompete clauses.[42] Clearly, firms must provide mechanisms that prevent the transfer of valuable and sensitive information outside the organization. Failure to do so would be, among other things, the neglect of a leader's fiduciary responsibility to shareholders. However, greater efforts should be directed at the former (e.g., good work environment and incentives), but, as we all know, the latter (e.g., employment contracts and noncompete clauses) have their place.[43]

Let's now discuss the importance of an individual's identification with the organization's mission and values, challenging work and stimulating environment, and financial and nonfinancial rewards and incentives in retaining a firm's human capital.

Identifying with an Organization's Mission and Values People who identify with and are more committed to the core mission and values of the organization are less likely to stray or bolt to the competition. Consider Medtronic, Inc., a $9 billion medical products firm based in Minneapolis.[44] Former CEO Bill George stated, "Shareholder value is a hollow notion as the sole source of employee motivation. If you do business that way, you'll end up like ITT." What motivates its workers to go well beyond Medtronic's 34 percent total return to shareholders? Simply put, it's helping sick people get well. The company's motto is "Restoring patients to full life," and its symbol is an image of a supine human rising toward upright wellness. That sounds good, but how does the "resurrection" imagery come to life?

> Each December, at the company's holiday party, patients, their families, and their doctors are flown in to tell their survival stories. It's for employees—who are moved to tears year after year—and journalists are generally not invited. President Art Collins, a strapping guy with a firm handshake who is not prone to crying fits, said, "I remember my first holiday party and someone asked me if I had brought my Kleenex. I assumed I'd be fine, but these parents got up with their daughter who was alive because of our product. Even surgeons who see this stuff all the time were crying."

So much for the all-consuming emphasis on profits.

Employees can also form strong alliances to organizations that create simple and straightforward missions—"strategic intents"—that channel efforts and generate intense loyalties.[45] Examples include Canon's passion to "beat Xerox" and Honda's early quest to become a second Ford. Likewise, leaders can arouse passions and loyalty by reinforcing the firm's quest to "topple Goliath" or by constantly communicating a history of overcoming adversity and life-threatening challenges.[46] For example, CEO Richard Branson of the Virgin Group constantly uses the "David and Goliath" imagery, pitting his company against such powerful adversaries as British Airways and Coca-Cola. A key part of Southwest Airlines's folklore is its struggle for survival in the Texas courts against such entrenched (and now bankrupt) rivals as Braniff and Texas Air. Southwest does not exist because of regulated or protected markets, but despite them; during its first three years of existence, no planes left the ground!

In addition to identifying with the organization, "tribal loyalty" is another key factor that links people to the organization.[47] A tribe is not the organization as a whole (unless it is very small). Rather, it is teams, communities of practice, and other groups within an organization or occupation.

Brian Hall, CEO of Values Technology in Santa Cruz, California, documented a shift in people's emotional expectations from work. From the 1950s on, a "task first" relationship to the company—"tell me what the job is, and let's get on with it"—dominated employee attitudes. Emotions and personal life were checked at the door. In the past few years, a "relationship-first" set of values has challenged the task orientation. Hall believes that it will become dominant. Employees want to share attitudes and beliefs as well as workspace. They want to establish the relationship (with one another and with the company) before buckling down to the task.

Challenging Work and a Stimulating Environment   Arthur Schawlow, winner of the 1981 Nobel Prize in physics, was once asked what he believed made the difference between highly creative and less creative scientists. His reply: "The labor of love aspect is very important. The most successful scientists often are not the most talented. But they are the ones impelled by curiosity. They've got to know what the answer is."[48]

Such insights highlight the importance of intrinsic motivation: the motivation to work on something because it is interesting, exciting, satisfying, or personally challenging. Consider the perspective of Jorgen Wedel, executive vice president of Gillette's international division, on the relative importance of pay compared with the meaningfulness of work: "I get calls from headhunters who offer bigger salaries, signing bonuses, and such. But the excitement of what I am doing here is equal to a 30 percent pay raise."

To keep competitors from poaching talent, organizations must keep employees excited about the challenges and opportunities available. Scott Cook, chairman of Intuit, understands this reality, "I wake up every morning knowing that if my people don't sense a compelling vision and a big upside, they'll simply leave."[49]

One way successful firms keep highly mobile employees motivated and challenged is through an internal market for opportunities that lower the barriers to an employee's mobility within a company. For example, Shell Oil Company has created an "open sourcing" model for talent. Jobs are listed on Shell's intranet, and, with a two-month notice, employees can go to work on anything that interests them. Monsanto[50] has developed a similar approach. According to one executive:

> Because we don't have a lot of structure, people will flow toward where success and innovation are taking place. We have a free-market system where people can move, so you have an outflow of people in areas where not much progress is being made. Before, the HR function ran processes like management development and performance evaluation. Now it also facilitates this movement of people.

Financial and Nonfinancial Rewards and Incentives   Without a doubt, financial rewards are a vital organizational control mechanism (as we will discuss in Chapter 9). Money—whether in the form of salary, bonus, stock options, and so forth—can mean many different things to people. For some it might mean security, to others recognition, and to still others, a sense of freedom and independence.

An article in *Organizational Dynamics* raised the point that there is little evidence that simply paying people more is the most important factor in attracting and retaining human capital.[51] Most surveys show that money is not the most important reason why people take or leave jobs, and that money, in some surveys, is not even in the top 10. Consistent with these findings, Tandem Computers (now part of Hewlett-Packard) never used to tell people being recruited what their salaries would be. People who asked were told that their salaries were competitive. If they persisted along this line of questioning, they would not be offered a position. Why? Tandem realized a rather simple idea: People who come for money will leave for money. Clearly, money can't be ignored, but it shouldn't be the primary mechanism to attract and retain talent.

Without the proper retention mechanisms (and as we all know, there are no easy answers), organizations can commit time and resources to inadvertently helping the competition develop their human capital.[52] And, given the importance of networking and teams, losses tend to multiply and intensify. The exodus of talent can erode a firm's competitive advantages in the marketplace. Let's now consider what some firms are doing to improve flexibility and amenities.[53]

When discussing firms with an impressive array of amenities to retain (and attract) employees, few compare with USAA, the San Antonio–based insurance and financial services company.

> If you're not keen on driving to work, the company sponsors a van pool. A run in your hose? Pick up a pair at the on-site store. There's also a dry cleaning service, a bank, and several ATMs. Even the cafeteria food is so tasty that several years ago employees began demanding dinner to go. The athletic facilities are striking. The three gyms rival those of many upscale health clubs and one is open 24 hours a day. Outside, employees compete in intramural leagues in basketball and tennis as well as on the softball and tennis courts. Into golf? There's also a driving range.
>
> Many return to campus on weekends with their families. Donna Castillo, a sales manager in consumer finance and auto service, said, "There are playgrounds where they can run around, and it's nice to take pictures when the bluebonnets come out in the spring." USAA also scores high on the emerging trend for on-site child care. The facility can handle 300 children. Raul Navarez, a security officer, said, "My wife and I visited 10 or 12 day care facilities . . . there was no competition."[54]

STRATEGY SPOTLIGHT

4.4

How Dow Chemical Evaluates Its Success in Retaining Top Talent

Dow Chemical is a $40 billion company that develops and sells chemicals, plastic materials, and agricultural and other specialized products and services. In the March 7, 2005, issue of *Fortune* magazine, Dow was ranked second out of 10 companies in the chemical industry, up from ninth place last year. Fortune noted that "Dow Chemical sharply boosted its image among industry peers, jumping a whopping seven places this year. Management finesse and strong ratings for 'community work' lifted its score."

Perhaps an important attribute of Dow Chemical's management system is its ability to fill important positions with internal candidates. Here, the firm has developed explicit benchmarks to evaluate its success in this endeavor.

At Dow Chemical, an internal hire rate of 75 to 80 percent is considered a sign of success. In fact, an outside hire for a role that is considered critical to the firm is viewed as a failure in the internal development process. (The company assumes that some external hires are important in maintaining a fresh perspective and for filling unanticipated roles.)

Dow also measures the attrition rate of its "future leaders," compared to the attrition rate of its entire employee population. "Future leaders" are those individuals who are advanced in their rate of development, perform at a competency level well above that of their colleagues, and are believed to have the potential to fill jobs at senior levels. In 2000, for example, the future leaders' rate of attrition was only 1.5 percent, compared to an overall attrition rate of 5 percent. Dow considers this to be a positive signal that its future leaders are receiving the developmental opportunities that they want and need. It is also useful to note that Dow's top 14 executives have all had cross-functional development opportunities that helped to prepare them for the demands of senior management.

Sources: Useem, J. 2005. America's most admired companies. *Fortune*, March 7: 66–70, 85–97; Cogner, J. A., & Fulmer, R. M. 2003. Developing your leadership pipeline. *Harvard Business Review*, 81(12): 78–85; and, Dychtwald, K., Erickson, T., & Morison, B. 2004. It's time to retire retirement. *Harvard Business Review*, 82(3): 48–56.

Another nonfinancial reward involves accommodating working families with children. Coping with the conflicting demands of family and work is a problem at some point for virtually all employees. After all, women represent 44 percent of today's U.S. workforce, and mothers of children under age six represent the fastest-growing segment. Mothers are often the primary caregivers in a family. It is estimated that 60 percent of working-age women are employed outside the home. And, according to a recent study, 13 percent of women with preschoolers indicated that they would work more hours if additional or better child care were provided.[55]

Strategy Spotlight 4.4 discusses Dow Chemical evaluates how well it retains top talent.

Enhancing Human Capital: The Role of Diversity in the Workforce

Today, a combination of demographic trends and accelerating globalization of business has made the management of cultural differences a critical issue for corporate leaders.[56] Workforces, which reflect demographic changes in the overall population, will be increasingly heterogeneous along dimensions such as gender, race, ethnicity, and nationality. For example, demographic trends in the United States indicate a growth in Hispanic Americans from 6.9 million in 1960 to over 35 million in 2000. This figure also is expected to increase to over 55 million by 2020. Similarly, the Asian-American population should grow to 20 million in 2020 from 12 million in 2000 and only 1.5 million in 1970. And the African-American population is becoming more ethnically heterogeneous. Census estimates project that by 2010 as many as 10 percent of Americans of African descent will be immigrants from Africa or the Caribbean.[57]

Such demographic changes have implications not only for the labor pool but also for customer bases which are also becoming more diverse. This creates important organizational challenges and opportunities. For example:

- Minorities are the majority in six out of the eight largest metropolitan areas in the United States.
- The combined African-American, Hispanic-American and Asian-American buying power is more than $750 billion a year.
- Women are the primary investors in more than half of U. S. households.[58]

Clearly, the effective management of diversity can enhance the social responsibility goals of an organization.[59] However, there are many other benefits as well. Six other areas where sound management of diverse workforces can improve an organization's effectiveness and competitive advantages are: (1) cost, (2) resource acquisition, (3) marketing, (4) creativity, (5) problem-solving, and (6) organizational flexibility. The first two items—cost and resource acquisition—may be considered "inevitability-of-diversity" issues. After all, competitiveness is affected by the need (because of national and cross-national workforce demographic trends) to hire more minorities, women, and foreign nationals. However, the marketing, creativity, problem-solving, and system flexibility arguments are derived from what can be called the "value-in-diversity hypothesis," which states that diversity brings net-added value to organization processes. Here is a summary of the six ways diversity benefits an organization:

- *Cost Argument.* As organizations become more diverse, firms effective in managing diversity will have a cost advantage over those that are not.
- *Resource Acquisition Argument.* Firms with excellent reputations as prospective employers for women and ethnic minorities will have an advantage in the competition for top talent. As labor pools shrink and change in composition, such advantages will become even more important.
- *Marketing Argument.* For multinational organizations, the insight and cultural sensitivity that members with roots in other countries bring to marketing efforts will be very useful. A similar rationale applies to subpopulations within domestic operations.
- *Creativity Argument.* Less emphasis on conformity to norms of the past and a diversity of perspectives will improve the level of creativity.
- *Problem-solving Argument.* Heterogeniety in decision-making and problem-solving groups potentially produces better decisions because of a wider range of perspectives as well as more thorough and critical analysis of issues. To illustrate, Jim Schiro, CEO of PriceWaterhouseCoopers, explains, "When you make a genuine commitment to diversity, you bring a greater diversity of ideas, approaches, and experiences and abilities that can be applied to client problems. After all, six people with different perspectives have a better shot at solving complex problems than sixty people who all think alike."[60]
- *System Flexibility Argument.* With effective programs to enhance workplace diversity, systems become less determinant, less standardized, and therefore more fluid. Such fluidity should lead to greater flexibility to react to environmental changes. Reactions should be faster and less costly.

Many successful companies have been included in *Fortune*'s list of the Best Companies for Minorities for their exemplary diversity programs.[61] One of these firms is Enterprise Rent-a-Car, which is discussed in Strategy Spotlight 4.5.

The Effective Diversity Program at Enterprise Rent-a-Car

Enterprise Rent-a-Car, with locations in 200 countries and territories, is an exemplar of effective diversity programs. It recently sponsored a diversity study with the National Urban League, which surveyed 5,500 American workers, including managers and CEOs. Only 32 percent of U. S. employees think their companies do a good job of hiring and promoting people other than white males. Fewer than half (47 percent) of the executives think that their own diversity efforts are successful, and 59 percent say it's partly their fault for not being more involved. (The complete study "Diversity Practices That Work: The American Worker Speaks," is available at www.nul.org.)

The study singled out eight companies in which diversity is more than a buzzword and described in detail what they are doing. One of these companies was Enterprise Rent-a-Car.

Given the multicultural nature of its customer base, Enterprise Rent-a-Car gets a broad mix in the 6,500 management-track employees that it hires each year. It dispatches diverse teams of recruiters—men, women, African Americans, whites, Asians, and people of widely differing ages. It takes a similar approach in its TV advertisements. The firm also rewards managers for hiring and developing people who reflect local markets. Since its branches are mostly in neighborhoods (only 150 of 5,700 are at airports), staffing in San Francisco, for example, is quite different from that in San Antonio or St. Louis. "We want people who speak the same language, literally and figuratively, as our customers," claims Ed Adams, VP of human resources. "We don't set quotas. We say, 'Reflect your local market.'"

Enterprise has several diversity initiatives. First, from the St. Louis headquarters and working with the company's executive leaders, the Corporate Diversity Manager is responsible for implementing the firm's overall diversity strategy. Second, the National Diversity Team aids the regions in recruiting, developing, and retaining the workforce. Local diversity teams complement the work of the national team by helping individual groups, regions, or business units attain local diversity goals. Third, Enterprise conducts diversity leadership training companywide for its employees. The emphasis is on diversity training that helps create better leaders and managers. Fourth, Enterprise wants its supplier base to bear a reasonable relationship to the communities in which Enterprise does business. Their supplier diversity program identifies and encourages equal opportunities for minority-owned, women-owned and disadvantaged businesses. Enterprise's "deeds" clearly reflect the "words" of its Chairman and CEO, Andrew Taylor: "Enterprise is fully committed to providing every employee with an inclusive workplace that offers respect, training and opportunities to succeed. That's simply who we are as a company, who we are as individuals and how we will continue to build our success in the 21st century."

Such a strategy contributed to Enterprise's recent success—its revenues increased fourfold to $7.4 billion in the past decade, reflecting a compounded growth rate of 15 percent. It is now the industry leader.

Source: Fisher, A. 2004. How you can do better on diversity. *Fortune*, November 15: 60, www.erac.com/recruit/diversity.asp?navID=diversity; and www.nul.org.

>>The Vital Role of Social Capital

Successful firms are well aware that the attraction, development, and retention of talent *is a necessary but not sufficient condition* for creating competitive advantages.[62] In the knowledge economy, it is not the stock of human capital that is important, but the extent to which it is combined and leveraged. In a sense, developing and retaining human capital becomes less important as key players (talented professionals, in particular) take the role of "free agents" and bring with them the requisite skill in many cases. Rather, the development of social capital (that is, the friendships and working relationships among talented individuals) gains importance, because it helps tie knowledge workers to a given firm.[63] Knowledge workers often exhibit greater loyalties to their colleagues and their profession than their employing organization, which may be "an amorphous, distant, and sometimes threatening entity."[64] Thus, a firm must find ways to create "ties" among its knowledge workers.

To illustrate, let's look at a hypothetical example. Two pharmaceutical firms are fortunate enough to hire Nobel Prize–winning scientists to work in their laboratories.[65] In one

How Nucor Shares Knowledge within and between Its Manufacturing Plants

Nucor, with 2003 revenues of $6.3 billion, is the most efficient steel producer in the world. A key aspect of its strategy is to develop strong social relationships and a team-based culture throughout the firm. It is effectively supported by a combination of work-group, plant-level, and corporatewide financial incentives and rewards, wherein knowledge and best practices are eagerly shared by everyone in the organization. How does Nucor do it?

Within Plant Knowledge Transfers. Nucor strives to develop a social community within each plant that promotes trust and open communication. People know each other very well throughout each plant, and they are encouraged to interact. To accomplish this, the firm's policy is to keep the number of employees at each plant between 250 and 300. Such a relatively small number, combined with employees' long tenure, fosters a high degree of interpersonal familiarity. Additionally, each plant's general manager regu-

larly holds dinner meetings for groups of 25 to 30, inviting every employee once a year. The format is free and open and includes a few ground rules: All comments are to remain business-related and are not to be directed to specific individuals. In turn, managers guarantee that they will carefully consider and respond to all suggestions and criticisms.

Between Plant Knowledge Transfers. Nucor uses several mechanisms to transfer knowledge among its plants. First, detailed performance data on each mill are regularly distributed to all of the plant managers. Second, all plant general managers meet as a group three times a year to review each facility's performance and develop formal plans on how to transfer best practices. Third, plant managers, supervisors, and machine operators regularly visit each other's mills. These visits enable operations personnel to go beyond performance data in order to understand firsthand the factors that make particular practices superior or inferior. After all, they possess the true process knowledge. Fourth, given the inherent difficulties in transferring complex knowledge, Nucor selectively assigns people from one plant to another on the basis of their expertise.

Source: Gupta, A. K., & Govindarajan, V. 2000. Knowledge management's social dimension: Lessons from Nucor steel. *Organizational Dynamics*, Fall 2000: 71–80.

case, the scientist is offered a very attractive salary, outstanding facilities and equipment, and told to "go to it!" In the second case, the scientist is offered approximately the same salary, facilities, and equipment plus one additional ingredient. He or she will be working in a laboratory with 10 highly skilled and enthusiastic scientists. Part of the job is to collaborate with these peers and jointly develop promising drug compounds. There is little doubt as to which scenario will lead to a higher probability of retaining the scientist. Clearly, the interaction, sharing, and collaboration will create a situation in which the scientist will develop firm-specific ties and be less likely to "bolt" for a higher salary offer. Such ties are critical because knowledge-based resources tend to be more tacit in nature, as we mentioned early in this chapter. Therefore, they are much more difficult to protect against loss (i.e., the individual quitting the organization) than other types of capital, such as equipment, machinery, and land.

Another way to view this situation is in terms of the resource-based view of the firm that we discussed in Chapter 3. That is, competitive advantages tend to be harder for competitors to copy if they are based on "unique bundles" of resources.[66] So, if employees are working effectively in teams and sharing their knowledge and learning from each other, not only will they be more likely to add value to the firm, but they also will be less likely to leave the organization, because of the loyalties and social ties that they develop over time. Strategy Spotlight 4.6 discusses how Nucor, a highly successful steel manufacturer, develops social capital among its employees and managers. This promotes the sharing of ideas within and across its manufacturing plants.

Next, we'll address a key concept in the New Economy—the Pied Piper Effect. Here, groups of professionals join (or leave) organizations en masse, not one at a time.

How Social Capital Helps Attract and Retain Talent

The importance of social ties among talented professionals is creating a significant challenge (and opportunity) for organizations today. In the *Wall Street Journal,* Bernard Wysocki described the increasing prevalence of a type of "Pied Piper Effect," in which teams or networks of people are leaving one company for another.[67] The trend is to recruit job candidates at the crux of social networks in organizations, particularly if they are seen as having the potential to bring with them a raft of valuable colleagues. This is a process that is referred to as "hiring via personal networks." Let's look at one instance of this practice.

> Gerald Eickhoff, founder of an electronic commerce company called Third Millennium Communications, tried for 15 years to hire Michael Reene. Why? Mr. Eickhoff says that he has "these Pied Piper skills." Mr. Reene was a star at Andersen Consulting in the 1980s and at IBM in the 1990s. He built his businesses and kept turning down overtures from Mr. Eickhoff.
>
> However, in early 2000, he joined Third Millennium as chief executive officer, with a salary of just $120,000 but with a 20 percent stake in the firm. Since then, he has brought in a raft of former IBM colleagues and Andersen subordinates. One protégé from his time at Andersen, Mary Goode, was brought on board as executive vice president. She promptly tapped her own network and brought along a half-dozen friends and former colleagues.
>
> Wysocki considers the Pied Piper effect one of the underappreciated factors in the war for talent today. This is because one of the myths of the New Economy is rampant individualism, wherein individuals find jobs on the Internet career sites and go to work for complete strangers. Perhaps, instead of Me Inc., the truth is closer to We Inc.[68]

Another example of social networks causing human capital mobility is the emigration of talent from an organization to form start-up ventures. Microsoft is perhaps the best-known example of this phenomenon.[69] Professionals have frequently left Microsoft en masse to form venture capital and technology start-ups built around teams of software developers. One example is Ignition Corporation, of Bellevue, Washington, which was formed by Brad Silverberg, a former Microsoft senior vice president. Eight former Microsoft executives, among others, founded the company. Exhibit 4.4 provides a partial listing of other companies that have been formed by groups of former Microsoft employees.

Exhibit 4.4
Microsoft Employees Who Have Left the Company for Other Businesses

Company	What It Does	Defectors from Microsoft
Crossgain	Builds software around XML computer language	23 of 60 employees
ViAir	Makes software for wireless providers	Company declines to specify
CheckSpace	Builds online payment service for small businesses	Company says "a good chunk" of its 30 employees
digiMine	Sells data mining service	About 15% of 62 employees in addition to the 3 founders
Avogadro	Builds wireless notification software	8 of 25 employees
Tellme Networks	Offers information like stock quotes and scores over the phone	About 40 of 250 employees; another 40 from the former Netscape

Source: From Rebecca Buckman, "Tech Defectors from Microsoft Resettle Together," *Wall Street Journal,* Eastern Edition, 2000. Copyright © 2000 by Dow Jones & Company, Inc. Reproduced with permission of Dow Jones & Company, Inc. via Copyright Clearance Center.

STRATEGY SPOTLIGHT

Alumni Programs: A Great Way to Stay in Touch

Michael Jacobson had worked in securities practices at Cooley Godward, a Palo Alto, California law firm, for a dozen years. Nobody was happy when he gave notice in 1998. Everyone felt that it would be difficult to get along without him.

However, a few months later, Cooley Godward's managers couldn't have been happier. Why? Jacobson's new job was as general counsel at a little-known online auction site called eBay! When the site needed outside counsel, Jacobsen tapped his former employer. A few months later, Cooley Godward was lead counsel for eBay's record-breaking $1.3 billion initial public offering. "It's a great relationship," says Mark Pitchford, partner and chief operating officer of the firm.

With such a "lucky break," Cooley Godward no longer leaves such matters to chance. In January 2004, it launched an alumni program to help the firm stay in touch with its former attorneys. Such programs are not particu-

larly new to corporate America. Firms such as McKinsey & Company, Ernst & Young, and Procter & Gamble have had them in place for years. However, as partners at Cooley Godward have found, smaller firms can also benefit from alumni initiatives. "Former employees are a resource," says John Izzo, president of Izzo Consulting, a firm based in Vancouver, Washington. The firm advises small businesses on employee training and retention issues.

Despite the potential benefits of maintaining active contact with former employees, many employers treat them as just another name in the Rolodex—or even worse, as a competitive threat. Izzo warns that this can be a big mistake. Often, he claims, former staffers can act as goodwill ambassadors for their former employers, helping to refer new talent and clients. They may even return at a later point and will requiring little training. And with the job market now showing signs of improvement and many employees more likely to move on, alumni programs could become very important, especially at firms that have a hard time recruiting and retaining qualified professionals.

Source: Rich, L. 2005. Don't be a stranger. *Inc.*, January: 32–33.

The importance of the Pied Piper Effect for today's firms is rather self-evident. Leaders must be aware of social relationships among professionals as important recruiting and retention mechanisms. Some good advice for professionals would be to not invest all their time and effort in enhancing their human capital (skills and competences). Rather, they should be sure to also develop their social networks.[70]

Social networks can provide an important mechanism for obtaining both resources and information from individuals and organizations outside the boundary of a firm.[71] Strategy Spotlight 4.7 touts the benefits of firms' alumni programs. It describes how eBay's general counsel became an excellent source of business for his prior employer.

The Potential Downside of Social Capital

Some companies have been damaged by high social capital that breeds "groupthink"—a tendency not to question shared beliefs.[72] When people identify strongly with a group, they sometimes support ideas that are suboptimal or simply wrong. Too many warm and fuzzy feelings among group members prevent people from challenging one another with tough questions and discourage them from engaging in the "creative abrasion" that Dorothy Leonard of Harvard University described as a key source of innovation.[73] Two firms well known for their collegiality, strong sense of employee membership, and humane treatment—Digital Equipment (now part of Hewlett-Packard Co.) and Polaroid—suffered greatly from market misjudgments and strategic errors. The aforementioned aspects of their culture contributed to their problems.

A recent study of 60 teams in 11 companies representing a variety of industries also provides insight into the drawbacks of too much social capital:[74]

In the most effective teams, about half of the relationships among members were close enough to be considered friendships. However, in teams where that number approached 100 percent, performance dropped dramatically. Such groups suffer lower performance because they are insular, impermeable to outside influences, and unhealthily self-reliant. Sometimes those problems can be avoided by brainstorming or by assigning someone in the group to be a devil's advocate. But where friendships are especially close, even those techniques are unlikely to produce widely different perspectives.

The friendships that benefit teams most were formed outside the group. Business-centered relationships with people in other parts of the company are more important for transmitting simple work flow information. However, even more important are relationships that extended into the social sphere—to lunches and dinners and after-work drinks—because they are especially fertile sources of social capital. Team members who socialize in this way, particularly with top managers and leaders of other teams, bring back to their groups strategic information, task-related advice, and political and social support.

Additionally, some have argued that socialization processes whereby individuals are "socialized in the norms, values, and ways of working inherent to the workgroup and the organization" can be potentially expensive in terms of financial resources and managerial commitment.[75] Such expenses may represent a significant opportunity cost that should be evaluated in terms of the potential costs and benefits. Clearly, if such expenses become excessive, profitability may be eroded.

In general, however, the effects of high social capital are strongly positive. Engagement, collaboration, loyalty, persistence, and dedication are important benefits.[76] Firms such as United Parcel Service, Hewlett-Packard, and SAS Institute have made significant investments in social capital that enable them to attract and retain talent and help them to do their best work. Few of these companies seem to face any imminent danger from an overdose of a good thing.

>>Using Technology to Leverage Human Capital and Knowledge

Sharing knowledge and information throughout the organization can be a means of conserving resources, developing products and services, and creating new opportunities. In this section we will discuss how technology can be used to leverage human capital and knowledge within organizations as well as with customers and suppliers beyond their boundaries. We will start with simple applications, such as the use of e-mail and networks for product development, and then we will discuss how technology can help to enhance the competitive position of knowledge-intensive firms in industries such as consulting, health care, and personal computers. We will close by discussing how technology can help firms to retain employees' knowledge even when they leave, because, even in the most desirable workplaces, people will leave. Technology can help us to make sure they don't take all of the valuable knowledge with them.

Using Networks to Share Information

As we all know, e-mail is an effective means of communicating a wide variety of information. It is quick, easy, and almost costless. Of course, it can become a problem when employees use it extensively for personal reasons and it detracts from productivity. Consider how fast jokes or rumors can spread within and across organizations! For example, at Computer Associates, the $3 billion software giant, e-mail is banned from 10 a.m. to noon and again from 2 p.m. to 4 p.m. because the firm's former chairman, Charles Wang, believes that it detracts from productivity.[77]

Managers and employees must be very careful when using e-mail. Once e-mails are sent, the sender has no control over where they are forwarded or where they are stored. Consider, for example, what can happen when an executive sends out a very negative and threatening mass e-mail.[78]

Neal Patterson, CEO of Cerner Corporation, sent out a rather scathing e-mail to about 400 company managers. He felt that his managers had created "a very unhealthy work environment" and he was troubled by the nearly empty parking lot outside his Kansas City offices at 7:30 a.m. and 6:00 p.m.—a testament, he felt, to a lax work ethic. In his e-mail, he listed punishments that he planned to implement, including having some employees punch a clock as well as possibly laying off some people. In addition, he said that he wanted to see the parking lot "substantially full at 7:30 a.m. and 6:00 p.m. and on Saturday morning." After giving his managers two weeks to turn the situation around, he ended his e-mail with an ominous "Tick, tock."

Unfortunately, after clicking "send," the e-mail took on a life of its own and ended up being posted on Yahoo!, where anybody could read it. This included analysts and investors who took the harsh message as an indication that something was clearly wrong at Cerner. After the leak, the trading volume for Cerner surged, and its stock price dropped 22 percent!

E-mail can, however, be a means for top executives to communicate information efficiently. For example, Martin Sorrell, chairman of WPP Group PLC, a $2.4 billion advertising and public relations firm, is a strong believer in the use of e-mail.[79] He e-mails all of his employees once a month. He discusses how the company is doing, addresses specific issues, and offers his perspectives on hot issues, such as new business models for the Internet. He believes that it is a great way to keep people abreast of what he is working on.

Technology can also enable much more sophisticated forms of communication in addition to knowledge sharing. Consider, for example, Buckman Laboratories, a $300 million specialty chemicals company based in Memphis, Tennessee, with approximately 1,300 employees in over 100 countries. Buckman has successfully used its global knowledge sharing network—known as K'Netix—to enhance its competitive advantages in the marketplace:[80]

Buckman produces more than 1,000 different specialty chemicals in eight factories throughout the world. It competes in a wide variety of industries, including pulp and paper processing and water treatment to leather, agriculture, and personal care. Unlike a typical multinational corporation, it is relatively small, and its competitive advantage is largely due to its ability to apply the power of all of its employees to every customer engagement. Central to this valuable capability is its global knowledge sharing network called K'Netix, which is integral to Buckman's information infrastructure.

Here's an example of how the network can be applied. One of Buckman's paper customers in Michigan realized that the peroxide it was adding to remove ink from old magazines was no longer working. A Buckman sales manager presented this problem to the knowledge network. Within two days, salespeople from Belgium and Finland identified a likely cause: Bacteria in the paper slurry was producing an enzyme that broke down the peroxide. The sales manager recommended a chemical to control the bacteria, and the problem was solved. You can imagine how positive the customer must feel about doing business with Buckman. And with the company and the customer co-creating knowledge, a new level of trust and value can emerge.

As you might expect, the idea of top executives sharing ideas with many or all individuals in their company is hardly new.[81] In the 1800s at British American Tobacco (BAT), the chief executive would write a monthly report to all of BAT's country managers. The executive used a fountain pen, and it generally took about three months for the report to reach India. With e-mail the message gets out in seconds—an enormous difference. Clearly, e-mail can be an effective tool, but it must be used judiciously.

Electronic Teams: Using Technology to Enhance Collaboration

The use of technology has also enabled professionals to work as part of electronic, or virtual, teams to enhance the speed and effectiveness with which products are developed.

For example, Microsoft has concentrated much of its development on electronic teams that are networked together throughout the company.[82] This helps to accelerate design and testing of new software modules that use the Windows-based framework as their central architecture. Microsoft is able to foster specialized technical expertise while sharing knowledge rapidly throughout the organization. This helps the firm learn how its new technologies can be applied rapidly to new business ventures such as cable television, broadcasting, travel services, and financial services.

What are electronic teams (or e-teams)? There are two key differences between e-teams and more traditional teams.[83] First, e-team members either work in geographically separated work places or they may work in the same space but at different times. E-teams may have members working in different spaces and time zones, as is the case with many multinational teams. Second, most of the interactions among members of e-teams occur through electronic communication channels such as fax machines and groupware tools such as e-mail, bulletin boards, chat, and videoconferencing.

The use of e-teams has expanded exponentially in recent years.[84] Organizations face increasingly high levels of complex, dynamic change and environmental uncertainty. E-teams are also effective in helping businesses cope with global challenges. Most e-teams perform very complex tasks and most knowledge-based teams are charged with developing new products, improving organizational processes, and satisfying challenging customer problems. For example, Eastman Kodak's e-teams design new products, Hewlett Packard's e-teams solve clients' computing problems, and Sun Microsystems' e-teams generate new business models.

There are multiple advantages of e-teams.[85] In addition to the rather obvious use of technology to facilitate communications, the potential benefits parallel the other two major sections in this chapter—human capital and social capital. First, e-teams are less restricted by the geographic constraints that are placed on face-to-face teams. Thus, e-teams have the potential to acquire a broader range of "human capital" or the skills and capacities that are necessary to complete complex assignments. So, e-team leaders can draw upon a greater pool of talent to address a wider range of problems since they are not constrained by geographic space. Once formed, e-teams can be more flexible in responding to unanticipated work challenges and opportunities because team members can be rotated out of projects when demands and contingencies alter the team's objectives.

Second, e-teams can be very effective in generating "social capital"—the quality of relationships and networks that leaders and team members form. Such capital is a key lubricant in work transactions and operations. Given the broader boundaries associated with e-teams, members and leaders generally have access to a wider range of social contacts than would be typically available in more traditional face-to-face teams. Such contacts are often connected to a broader scope of clients, customers, constituents, and other key stakeholders.

However, there are challenges associated with making e-teams effective. Successful action by both traditional teams and e-teams requires that:

- Members *identify* who among them can provide the most appropriate knowledge and resources, and,
- E-team leaders and key members know how to *combine* individual contributions in the most effective manner for a coordinated and appropriate response.

Group psychologists have termed such activities "identification and combination" activities and teams that fail to perform them face a "process loss."[86] Process losses prevent teams from reaching high levels of performance because of inefficient interaction dynamics among team members. Such poor dynamics require that some collective energy, time, and effort be devoted to dealing with team inefficiencies, thus diverting the team away from its objectives. For example, if a team member fails to communicate important information at critical phases of a project, other members may waste time and energy. This can lead to conflict and resentment as well as to decreased motivation to work hard to complete tasks. Clearly, team leaders and other members must expend collective energy to repair the breach, resulting in a process loss.

The potential for process losses tends to be more prevalent in e-teams than in traditional teams because the geographical dispersion of members increases the complexity of establishing effective interaction and exchanges. Generally, teams suffer process loss because of low cohesion, low trust among members, a lack of appropriate norms or standard operating procedures, or a lack of shared understanding among team members about their tasks. With e-teams, members are more geographically or temporally dispersed, and the team becomes more susceptible to the risk factors that can create process loss. Such problems can be exacerbated when team members have less than ideal competencies and social skills. This can erode problem-solving capabilities as well as the effective functioning of the group as a social unit.

A recent study explored what made e-teams at Texas-based Sabre computerized reservation system (used by most major airlines) more or less successful in achieving their objectives. Sabre has over 6,000 employees in 45 countries and processes approximately 400 million travel bookings a year. The 65 e-teams in the study were cross-functional, based in the United States and Canada, and averaged about eight members. Sabre's e-teams are highly interdependent and conduct activities such as selling reservation systems, scheduling installation and training appointments, and handling billing and collections. Members communicate via e-mail, telephone, videoconferencing, and Web-based conferencing.

What were the study's key findings? Below, we summarize some of the key challenges that the e-teams faced and how the most successful teams overcame them:

- ***Develop Trust Based on Performance Consistency Rather than Social Bonds.*** Rapid responses by team members fostered trust, and team leaders played a key role in reinforcing timeliness and interaction. Levels of trust based on performance helped to compensate for a lack of social interaction.
- ***Overcome Group Process Losses Associated with Virtual Teams.*** Extensive training in virtual team leadership, conflict management, and meetings management as well as adaptation of decision-making software were used to facilitate problem solving and decision making.
- ***Create an Environment of Inclusiveness and Involvement.*** Individual preferences were taken into account when selecting e-team members. Team members were given a realistic preview of the potential for feeling detached and were provided opportunities for face-to-face contact with clients and other team members.
- ***Identify Team Members with a Proper Balance of Technical and Interpersonal Skills.*** Behavioral interviewing techniques and simulation were used as part of the selection process, and other team members were asked to help recruit and select new team members to ensure a good balance of technical and social skills. Such activities also help to socialize newly appointed team members.
- ***Create Proper Mechanisms for Evaluating Team Members and Providing Coaching and Support.*** A comprehensive evaluation approach that includes both quantitative and qualitative measures was employed to assess idea generation, leadership, and problem-solving skills. Team-member peer reviews were used to assess individual contributions to team effectiveness and online training and development resources were created to enhance members' knowledge, skills, and abilities.

Codifying Knowledge for Competitive Advantage

As we discussed early in this chapter, there are two different kinds of knowledge. Tacit knowledge is embedded in personal experience and shared only with the consent and participation of the individual. Explicit (or codified) knowledge, on the other hand, is knowledge that can be documented, widely distributed, and easily replicated. One of the challenges of knowledge-intensive organizations is to capture and codify the knowledge and experience that, in effect, resides in the heads of its employees. Otherwise, they will have to constantly "reinvent the wheel," which is both expensive and inefficient. Also, the "new wheel" may not necessarily be superior to the "old wheel."[87]

Once a knowledge asset (e.g., a software code or processes, routines for a consulting firm) is developed and paid for, it can be reused many times at very low cost, assuming that it doesn't have to be substantially modified each time. Let's take the case of a consulting company, such as Accenture (formerly Andersen Consulting).[88] Since the knowledge of its consultants has been codified and stored in electronic repositories, it can be employed in many jobs by a huge number of consultants. Additionally, since the work has a high level of standardization (i.e., there are strong similarities across the numerous client engagements), there generally tends to be a rather high ratio of consultants to partners. For example, the ratio of consultants to partners is roughly 30, which is quite high. As one might expect, there must be extensive training of the newly hired consultants for such an approach to work. The recruits are trained at Accenture's Center for Professional Education, a 150-acre campus in St. Charles, Illinois. Using the center's knowledge-management respository, the consultants work through many scenarios designed to improve business processes. In effect, the information technologies enable the consultants to be "implementers, not inventors."

Access Health, a call-in medical center, also uses technology to capture and share knowledge. When someone calls the center, a registered nurse uses the company's "clinical decision architecture" to assess the caller's symptoms, rule out possible conditions, and recommend a home remedy, doctor's visit, or trip to the emergency room. The company's knowledge repository contains algorithms of the symptoms of more than 500 illnesses. According to CEO Joseph Tallman, "We are not inventing a new way to cure disease. We are taking available knowledge and inventing processes to put it to better use." At Access Health, the codified knowledge is in the form of software algorithms. They were very expensive to develop, but the investment has been repaid many times over. The first 300 algorithms that Access Health developed have each been used an average of 8,000 times a year. Further, the company's paying customers—insurance companies and provider groups—save money because many callers would have made expensive trips to the emergency room or the doctor's office had they not been diagnosed over the phone.

The use of information technology in codifying knowledge can also help a firm integrate activities among its internal value-chain activities, customers, and suppliers. Strategy Spotlight 4.8 shows how Dell Computer's sophisticated knowledge-management system is an integral part of its widely admired business model.

Retaining Knowledge When Employees Leave

All organizations—with a few exceptions, such as prisons and the military during periods of conscription—suffer the adverse consequences of voluntary turnover. As we noted in Chapter 3, even SAS Institute, consistently one of *Fortune* magazine's "Most Desirable Places to Work," has a 4 percent turnover (far below the software industry's average of 20 percent). So, turnover—to a high, moderate, or low degree—is simply an organizational

Dell's Knowledge Management System

A company that can successfully assemble and sell 11 million personal computers (PCs) a year, using 40,000 possible configurations (compared with about 100 for competitors), is clearly one that has learned something about knowledge management. Dell Computer Corporation has recruited talented engineers to design these processes, but the company's real strength is found in the way it has codified these processes.

By investing heavily in the ability to determine the necessary configurations up front. Dell is able to reuse this knowledge to its advantage. Although each configuration is used on average only about 275 times each year, Dell has captured the knowledge of its talented engineers in the processes used to custom assemble PCs en masse.

Sources: Hansen, M. T., Nohria, N., & Tierney, T. 1999. What's your strategy for managing knowledge? *Harvard Business Review*, 77 (2): 106–117; Magretta, J. 1998. The power of virtual integration: An interview with Dell Computer's Michael Dell. *Harvard Business Review*, 76(2): 73–84.

Key to Dell's knowledge-management system is a repository that contains a list of available components. Dell uses this system to its competitive advantage through cost containment that is passed on, in part, to consumers. This low-cost advantage provides Dell with a 25 percent share of the U.S. personal computer market.

Dell effectively uses its knowledge-management system to integrate assembly activities from the initial customer order to product delivery. The company's external supply chain is linked to the assembly process by an elaborate inventory-control system that enables the firm to know what parts are currently available, matching these to possible configurations. This enhances Dell's link with customers by giving customers the flexibility to order PCs to their desired specifications. By integrating the entire value chain with its knowledge-management system, Dell has given itself an edge in the intensely competitive PC market.

---

fact of life. However, many leading firms are devising ways to minimize the loss of knowledge when employees leave.

Information technology can often help employers cope with turnover by saving some tacit knowledge that the firm would otherwise lose.[89] Customer relationship software, for example, automates sales and provides salespeople with access to client histories, including prior orders and complaints. This enables salespeople to quickly become familiar with client accounts (about which they might otherwise know nothing). Similarly, groupware applications such as Lotus Notes can standardize interactions and keep records of decisions and crucial contextual information, providing something like an electronic record of employee knowledge. Other programs, such as Open Text's Livelink, enable all employees to track and share documents on their firm's intranet. New simulation software for team-based project management, such as Thinking Tools's Project Challenge, enables new teams to learn how to work together much more rapidly than on-the-job experience alone would permit.

Even a simple technology such as e-mail can help when key employees leave an organization. For example, Pamela Hirshman, a project manager at Young & Rubicam, a large international advertising firm, was asked to take over a project after the entire original project team bolted.[90] Noted Hirshman, "The project file had a record of all the e-mails between the team and the client, and after reviewing about 50 of these, I was up to speed on the problems of the client and where the project was headed."

Motivation is a key issue in such knowledge-management systems. That is, what are the incentives for people to contribute their knowledge? Some organizations have found that such systems work best when they are incorporated into the firm's evaluation and reward system. For example, Bruce Strong, founder and CEO of Context Integration, a Web consulting firm, decided to develop a knowledge-management system to help employees unlock their thoughts and, collectively, help them to be more productive.[91] Six months and a half-million dollars later, he unveiled IAN (Intellectual Assets Network). The objective was to provide a medium for his consultants to share ideas, ask questions, and trace earlier journeys on similar projects. The theory was fine, but Strong was disappointed with the lack of involvement by his employees. This is not surprising. Carla O'Dell, president of the American Productivity and Quality Center, said that of the companies trying knowledge management, fewer than 10 percent succeeded in making it part of their culture.

Why didn't the consultants embrace IAN? There were many reasons:

- Consultants saw depositing notes or project records into the database as one more task in a busy day.
- The task didn't appear to have any urgency.
- Consultants generally did not like to admit they couldn't solve a problem.
- They resented management trying to impose what consultants perceived as a rigid structure on their work.

What was Strong to do? He began to reinforce the many benefits of the system, such as providing better and more consistent service. He also publicly recognized people who stood out as strong IAN contributors, and he made this part of everyone's job description. Perhaps most important, he began paying people to use it. He assigned points when people used the system—for example, one point for posting a résumé on the system, five points for creating a project record, and so on. The results were tallied every three months and the score accounted for 10 percent of a consultant's quarterly bonus. Over a two-month period, overall IAN usage almost doubled. However, more important, many consultants became enthusiastic converts once they had a positive experience with IAN. Not only does IAN continue to help many of them provide excellent service to their clients, but also some of their knowledge remains in the firm when they leave.

We close this section with a series of questions managers should consider in determining (1) how effective their organization is in attracting, developing, and retaining human capital and (2) how effective they are in leveraging human capital through social capital and technology. These questions, included in Exhibit 4.5, summarize some of the key issues addressed in this chapter.

>>The Central Role of Leveraging Human Capital in Strategy Formulation

In this chapter we have emphasized the importance of human capital and how such intangible assets can create the greatest value in today's successful organizations. As we have noted throughout the chapter, attracting top talent is a necessary, but not a sufficient, condition for competitive advantage. It must be not only developed and retained, but also leveraged through effective use of social capital and technology. In this section we will discuss how leveraging human capital is vital to each of the levels of strategy that we will address in the next four chapters (5, 6, 7, and 8) of the book.

Leveraging Human Capital and Business-Level Strategy

At the business level (Chapter 5), firms strive to create advantages that are sustainable over time. To do this, managers must integrate the primary and support activities in their firm's value chain (discussed in Chapter 3). We will discuss how much of Siebel Systems' success can be attributed to its excellent customer relationships, fostered by the firm's insistence on having customer input before the software is written. And FedEx has provided its drivers with handheld computers—a valuable technology—to help them effectively track customer packages. The Siebel Systems and FedEx examples point out how social capital and technology can help a firm enhance business-level strategies by leveraging its human capital.

Human Capital

Recruiting "Top-Notch" Human Capital

- Does the organization assess attitude and "general makeup" instead of focusing primarily on skills and background in selecting employees at all levels?
- How important are creativity and problem solving ability? Are they properly considered in hiring decisions?
- Do people throughout the organization engage in effective networking activities to obtain a broad pool of worthy potential employees? Is the organization creative in such endeavors?

Enhancing Human Capital through Employee Development

- Does the development and training process inculcate an "organizationwide" perspective?
- Is there widespread involvement, including top executives, in the preparation and delivery of training and development programs?
- Is the development of human capital effectively tracked and monitored?
- Are there effective programs for succession at all levels of the organization, especially at the top-most levels?
- Does the firm effectively evaluate its human capital? Is a 360-degree evaluation used? Why? Why not?
- Are mechanisms in place to assure that a manager's success does not come at the cost of compromising the organization's core values?

Retaining the Best Employees

- Are there appropriate financial rewards to motivate employees at all levels?
- Do people throughout the organization strongly identify with the organization's mission?
- Are employees provided with a stimulating and challenging work environment that fosters professional growth?
- Are valued amenities provided (e.g., flex time, child-care facilities, telecommuting) that are appropriate given the organization's mission, strategy, and how work is accomplished?
- Is the organization continually devising strategies and mechanisms to retain top performers?

Social Capital

- Are there positive personal and professional relationships among employees?
- Is the organization benefiting (or being penalized) by hiring (or by voluntary turnover) en masse?
- Does an environment of caring and encouragement rather than competition enhance team performance?
- Does the organization minimize the adverse effects of excessive social capital, such as excessive costs and "groupthink"?

Technology

- Has the organization used technologies such as e-mail and networks to develop products and services?
- Does the organization effectively use technology to transfer best practices across the organization?
- Does the organization use technology to leverage human capital and knowledge both within the boundaries of the organization and among its suppliers and customers?
- Has the organization effectively used technology to codify knowledge for competitive advantage?
- Does the organization try to retain some of the knowledge of employees when they decide to leave the firm?

Source: Adapted from Dess, G. G., & Picken, J. C. 1999. *Beyond Productivity:* 63–64. New York: AMACON.

Exhibit 4.5

Issues to Consider in Creating Value through Human Capital, Social Capital, and Technology

Leveraging Human Capital and Corporate-Level Strategy

In Chapter 6 on corporate-level strategy, we will discuss how firms can create value by managing their business to create synergy; that is, how more value can be created by working together across business units than if they were freestanding units. Managers must determine what important relationships (products, markets, technologies) exist across businesses and how they can be leveraged. We will discuss how Procter & Gamble is able to reapply its customer knowledge and understanding of technologies across many different product markets. For example, P&G's knowledge of oral hygiene and bleaching agents enabled it to develop a special film technology that whitened teeth within 14 days. For such knowledge transfer to occur, managers must be aware of not only their human capital (tacit knowledge), but also their organization's codified knowledge and relationships among key professionals and across business units.

Leveraging Human Capital and International-Level Strategy

In Chapter 7 we will address how companies create value by leveraging resources and knowledge across national boundaries. Here firms are faced with two opposing forces: how to achieve economies of scale and how to adapt to local market needs. We will discuss how some leading-edge firms are able to successfully attain a "transnational strategy" wherein not only do the firms achieve lower costs through economies of scale, but also they are able to adapt successfully to local markets. To do so, firms must facilitate the flow of information and knowledge between business units in different countries. This requires not only attracting, developing, and retaining superior talent, but also leveraging their knowledge and skills through effective working relationships (i.e., social capital) and use of technology.

Leveraging Human Capital and Internet Strategies

Chapter 8 addresses the role of digital and Internet-based technologies in creating competitive advantages. These technologies have enormous strategic implications for managers who use them to lower costs, enhance customer service, and improve performance. We provide the example of BP Amoco, a company that has pursued an aggressive policy of implementing Internet-based capabilities. Managers are able to tap into the company's reservoir of knowledge by using the personalized Web pages that all BP Amoco employees use to report on their areas of expertise. In one example, engineers drilling for oil in the Caribbean saved $600,000 by using a process that had been developed in Norway just a few days earlier. To make such technologies effective, of course, requires both talented professionals to develop and apply knowledge as well as strong, positive working relationships between managers and technology experts.

Summary

Firms throughout the industrial world are recognizing that the knowledge worker is the key to success in the marketplace. However, we also recognize that human capital, although vital, is still only a necessary, but not a sufficient, condition for creating value. We began the first section of the chapter by addressing the importance of human capital and how it can be attracted, developed, and retained. Then we discussed the role of social capital and technology in leveraging human capital for competitive success. We pointed out that intellectual capital—the difference between a firm's market value and its book value—has increased significantly over the past few decades. This is particularly true for firms in knowledge-intensive industries, especially where there are relatively few tangible assets, such as software development.

The second section of the chapter addressed the attraction, development, and retention of human capital. We viewed these three activities as a "three-legged stool"—that is, it is difficult for firms to be successful if they ignore or are unsuccessful in any one of these activities. Among the issues we discussed in *attracting* human capital were "hiring for attitude, training for skill" and the value of using social networks to attract human capital. In particular, it is important to attract employees who can collaborate with others, given the importance of collective efforts such as teams and task forces. With regard to *developing* human capital, we discussed the need to encourage widespread involvement throughout the organization, monitor progress and track the development of human capital, and evaluate human capital. Among the issues that are widely practiced in evaluating human capital is the 360-degree evaluation system. Employees are evaluated by their superiors, peers, direct reports, and even internal and external customers. We also addressed the value of maintaining a diverse workforce. Finally, some mechanisms for retaining human capital are employees' identification with the organization's mission and values, providing challenging work and a stimulating environment, the importance of financial and nonfinancial rewards and incentives, and providing flexibility and amenities. A key issue here is that a firm should not overemphasize financial rewards. After all, if individuals join an organization for money, they also are likely to leave for money. With money as the primary motivator, there is little chance that employees will develop firm-specific ties to keep them with the organization.

The third section of the chapter discussed the importance of social capital in leveraging human capital. Social capital refers to the network of relationships that individuals have throughout the organization as well as with customers and suppliers. Such ties can be critical in obtaining both information and resources. With regard to recruiting, for example, we saw how some firms are able to hire en masse groups of individuals who are part of social networks. Social relationships can also be very important in the effective functioning of groups. Finally, we discussed some of the potential downsides of social capital. These include the expenses that firms may bear when promoting social and working relationships among individuals as well as the potential for "groupthink," wherein individuals are reluctant to express divergent (or opposing) views on an issue because of social pressures to conform.

The fourth section addressed the role of technology in leveraging human capital. We discussed relatively simple means of using technology, such as e-mail and networks where individuals can collaborate by way of personal computers. We provided suggestions and guidelines on how electronic teams can be effectively managed. We also addressed more sophisticated uses of technology, such as sophisticated management systems. Here knowledge can be codified and reused at very low cost, as we saw in the examples of firms in the consulting, health care, and high-technology industries. Also, given that there will still be some turnover—voluntary or involuntary—even in the most desirable places to work, technology can be a valuable means of retaining knowledge when individuals terminate their employment with a firm.

The final section addressed how the leveraging of human capital is critical in strategy formulation at all levels. This includes the business, corporate, international, and Internet levels.

Summary Review Questions

1. Explain the role of knowledge in today's competitive environment.
2. Why is it important for managers to recognize the interdependence in the attraction, development, and retention of talented professionals?
3. What are some of the potential downsides for firms that engage in a "war for talent"?
4. Discuss the need for managers to use social capital in leveraging their human capital both within and across their firm.
5. Discuss the key role of technology in leveraging knowledge and human capital.

Experiential Exercise

Johnson & Johnson, a leading health care firm with $47 billion in 2004 revenues, is often rated as one of *Fortune*'s "Most Admired Firms." It is also considered an excellent place to work and has generated high return to shareholders. Clearly, they value their human capital. Using the Internet and/or library resources, identify some of the actions/strategies Johnson & Johnson has taken to attract, develop, and retain human capital. What are their implications?

Activity	Actions/Strategies	Implications
Attracting human capital		
Developing human capital		
Retaining human capital		

Application Questions Exercises

1. Look up successful firms in a high-technology industry as well as two successful firms in more traditional industries such as automobile manufacturing and retailing. Compare their market values and book values. What are some implications of these differences?

2. Select a firm for which you believe its social capital—both within the firm and among its suppliers and customers—is vital to its competitive advantage. Support your arguments.

3. Choose a company with which you are familiar. What are some of the ways in which it uses technology to leverage its human capital?

4. Using the Internet, look up a company with which you are familiar. What are some of the policies and procedures that it uses to enhance the firm's human and social capital?

Ethics Questions

1. Recall an example of a firm that recently faced an ethical crisis. How do you feel the crisis and management's handling of it affected the firm's human capital and social capital?

2. Based on your experiences or what you have learned in your previous classes, are you familiar with any companies that used unethical practices to attract talented professionals? What do you feel were the short-term and long-term consequences of such practices?

References

1. Wellner, A. S. 2004. The perils of hiring stars. *Inc.,* August: 32–33; Molaro, R. 2005. Bear season. *The Art of Licensing,* Winter: S-11–S13; and personal communication with Michael Carlisle and the authors, February 10, 2005.

2. Parts of this chapter draw upon some of the ideas and examples from Dess, G. G., & Picken, J. C. 1999. *Beyond Productivity.* New York: AMACOM.

3. An acknowledged trend: The world economic survey. 1996. *The Economist,* September 28: 25–28.

4. Quinn, J. B., Anderson, P., & Finkelstein, S. 1996. Leveraging intellect. *Academy of Management Executive,* 10(3): 7–27.

5. Hamel, G., & Prahalad, C. K. 1996. Competing in the new economy: Managing out of bounds. *Strategic Management Journal,* 17: 238.

6. Reich, R. B. 2000. *The future of success:* 21. New York: Random House.

7. Stewart, T. A. 1997. *Intellectual capital: The new wealth of organizations.* New York: Doubleday/Currency.

8. Leif Edvisson and Michael S. Malone have a similar, more detailed definition of *intellectual capital:* "the combined knowledge, skill, innovativeness, and ability to meet the task at hand." They consider intellectual capital to equal human capital plus structural capital. *Structural capital* is defined as "the hardware, software, databases, organization structure, patents, trademarks, and everything else of organizational capability that supports those employees' productivity—in a word, everything left at the office when the employees go home." Edvisson, L., & Malone, M. S. 1997. *Intellectual capital: Realizing your company's true value by finding its hidden brainpower:* 10–14. New York: HarperBusiness.

9. Stewart, T. A. 2001. Accounting gets radical. *Fortune,* April 16: 184–194.

10. Thomas Stewart has suggested this formula in his book *Intellectual Capital.* He provides an insightful discussion on pages 224–225, including some of the limitations of this approach to measuring intellectual capital. We recognize, of course, that during the late 1990s and in early 2000, there were some excessive market valuations of high-technology and Internet firms. For an interesting discussion of the extraordinary market valuation of Yahoo!, an Internet company, refer to Perkins, A. B. 2001. The Internet bubble encapsulated: Yahoo! *Red Herring,* April 15: 17–18.

11. Roberts, P. W., & Dowling, G. R. 2002. Corporate reputation and sustained superior financial performance. *Strategic Management Journal,* 23(12): 1077–1095.

12. For a recent study on the relationships between human capital, learning, and sustainable competitive advantage, read Hatch, N. W., & Dyer, J. H. 2005. Human capital and learning as a source of sustainable competitive advantage. *Strategic Management Journal,* 25: 1155–1178.

13. One of the seminal contributions on knowledge management is Becker, G. S. 1993. *Human capital: A theoretical and empirical analysis with special reference to education* (3rd ed.). Chicago: University of Chicago Press.

14. For an excellent overview of the topic of social capital, read Baron, R. A. 2005. Social capital. In Hitt, M. A., & Ireland, R. D. (Eds.), *The Blackwell encyclopedia of management* (2nd ed.): 224–226. Malden, MA: Blackwell.

15. For an excellent discussion of social capital and its impact on organizational performance, refer to Nahapiet, J., & Ghoshal, S. 1998. Social capital, intellectual capital, and the organizational advantage. *Academy of Management Review,* 23: 242–266.

16. Polanyi, M. 1967. *The tacit dimension.* Garden City, NY: Anchor Publishing.

17. Barney, J. B. 1991. Firm resources and sustained competitive advantage. *Journal of Management,* 17: 99–120.

18. For an interesting perspective of empirical research on how knowledge can adversely affect performance, read Haas, M. R., & Hansen, M. T. 2005. When using knowledge can hurt performance: The value of organizational capabilities in a management consulting company. *Strategic Management Journal,* 26(1): 1–24.

19. Some of the notable books on this topic include Edvisson & Malone, op. cit.; Stewart, op. cit.; and Nonaka, I., & Takeuchi, I. 1995. *The knowledge creating company.* New York: Oxford University Press.

20. Stewart, T. A. 2000. Taking risk to the marketplace. *Fortune,* March 6: 424.

21. Dutton, G. 1997. Are you technologically competent? *Management Review,* November: 54–58.

22. Dess & Picken, op. cit.: 34.

23. Webber, A. M. 1998. Danger: Toxic company. *Fast Company,* November: 152–161.

24. Morris, B. 1997. Key to success: People, people, people. *Fortune,* October 27: 232.

25. Martin, J. 1998. So, you want to work for the best . . . . *Fortune,* January 12: 77.

26. Carbonara, P. 1997. Hire for attitude, train for skill. *Fast Company,* August–September: 66–67.

27. Stewart, T. A. 1996. Why value statements don't work. *Fortune,* June 10: 138.

28. Cardin, R. 1997. Make your own Bozo Filter. *Fast Company,* October–November: 56.

29. Carbonara, op. cit.

30. Martin, op. cit.; Henkoff, R. 1993. Companies that train best. *Fortune,* March 22: 53–60.

31. Bartlett, C. A., & Ghoshal, S. 2002. Building competitive advantage through people. *MIT Sloan Management Review,* 43(2): 34–41.

32. Ibid.

33. An interesting perspective on developing new talent rapidly when they join an organization can be found in Rollag, K., Parise, S., & Cross, R. 2005. Getting new hires up to speed quickly. *MIT Sloan Management Review,* 46(2): 35–41.

34. Stewart, T. A. 1998. Gray flannel suit? moi? *Fortune,* March 18: 80–82.

35. Ibid.

36. An interesting perspective on how Cisco Systems develops its talent can be found in Chatman, J., O'Reilly, C., & Chang, V. 2005. Cisco Systems: Developing a human capital strategy. *California Management Review,* 47(2): 137–166.

37. This section is based on Leonard, D., & Swap, W. 2004. Deep smarts. *Harvard Business Review,* 82(9): 88–97.

38. Morris, B. op. cit.

39. For an innovative perspective on the appropriateness of alternate approaches to evaluation and rewards, refer to Seijts, G. H., & Lathan, G. P. 2005. Learning versus performance goals: When should each be used? *Academy of Management Executive,* 19(1): 124–132.

40. The discussion of the 360-degree feedback system draws on UPS. 1997. 360-degree feedback: Coming from all

sides. *Vision* (a UPS Corporation internal company publication), March: 3; Slater, R. 1994. *Get better or get beaten: Thirty-one leadership secrets from Jack Welch.* Burr Ridge, IL: Irwin; Nexon, M. 1997. General Electric: The secrets of the finest company in the world. *L'Expansion,* July 23: 18–30; and Smith, D. 1996. Bold new directions for human resources. *Merck World* (internal company publication), October: 8.

41. Kets de Vries, M. F. R. 1998. Charisma in action: The transformational abilities of Virgin's Richard Branson and ABB's Percy Barnevik. *Organizational Dynamics,* Winter: 20.

42. We have only to consider the most celebrated case of industrial espionage in recent years, wherein José Ignacio Lopez was indicted in a German court for stealing sensitive product planning documents from his former employer, General Motors, and sharing them with his executive colleagues at Volkswagen. The lawsuit was dismissed by the German courts, but Lopez and his colleagues were investigated by the U.S. Justice Department. Also consider the recent litigation involving noncompete employment contracts and confidentiality clauses of *International Paper v. Louisiana-Pacific, Campbell Soup v. H. J. Heinz Co.,* and *PepsiCo v. Quaker Oats's Gatorade.* In addition to retaining valuable human resources and often their valuable network of customers, firms must also protect proprietary information and knowledge. For interesting insights, refer to Carley, W. M. 1998. CEO gets hard lesson in how not to keep his lieutenants. *Wall Street Journal,* February 11: A1, A10; and Lenzner, R., & Shook, C. 1998. Whose Rolodex is it, anyway? *Forbes,* February 23: 100–103.

43. For an insightful discussion of retention of knowledge workers in today's economy, read Davenport, T. H. 2005. *The care and feeding of the knowledge worker.* Boston, MA: Harvard Business School Press.

44. Lieber, R. B. 1998, Why employees love these companies. *Fortune,* January 12: 72–74.

45. The examples in this section draw upon a variety of sources, including Lubove, S. 1998. New age capitalist. *Forbes,* April 6: 42–43; Kets de Vries, op. cit.; Pfeffer, J. 1995. Producing sustainable competitive advantage through the effective management of people. *Academy of Management Executive,* 9(1): 55–69. The concept of strategic intent is generally credited to Hamel, G., & Prahalad, C. K. 1989. Strategic intent. *Harvard Business Review,* 67: 63–76.

46. Kets de Vries, op. cit.: 73–92.

47. Stewart, T. A. 2001. *The wealth of knowledge.* New York: Currency.

48. Amabile, T. M. 1997. Motivating creativity in organizations: On doing what you love and loving what you do. *California Management Review,* Fall: 39–58.

49. The discussion of internal markets for human capital draws on Hamel, G. 1999. Bringing Silicon Valley inside. *Harvard Business Review,* 77(5): 71–84.

50. Monsanto has been part of Pharmacia since 2002. *Hoover's Handbook of Am. Bus. 2004:* 562.

51. Pfeffer, J. 2001. Fighting the war for talent is hazardous to your organization's health. *Organizational Dynamics,* 29(4): 248–259.

52. For an insightful discussion on strategies for retaining and developing human capital, refer to Coff, R. W. 1997. Human assets and management dilemmas: Coping with hazards on the road to resource-based theory. *Academy of Management Review,* 22(2): 374–402.

53. For an insightful study on the effects of tuition reimbursement on voluntary employee turnover, see Benson, G. S., Finegold, D., & Mohrman, S. A. 2004. You paid for the skills, now keep them: Tuition reimbursement and voluntary turnover. *Academy of Management Journal,* 47(3): 315–331.

54. The examples in this section draw upon the following sources: Stewart, *Intellectual capital;* and Fisher, A. 1998. The 100 best companies to work for in America. *Fortune,* January 12: 69–70.

55. The statistics on child care trends are drawn from Bubbar, S. E., & Aspelin, D. J. 1998. The overtime rebellion: Symptom of a bigger problem? *Academy of Management Executive,* 12: 68–76. The other examples in this section are drawn from various sources, including Munk, N. 1998. The new organization man. *Fortune,* March 16: 68–72; and Hammonds, K. H., Furchgott, R., Hamm, S., & Judge, P. C. 1997. Work and family. *BusinessWeek,* September 15: 96–104.

56. Cox, T. L. 1991. The multinational organization. *Academy of Management Executive,* 5(2): 34–47. Without doubt, a great deal has been written on the topic of creating and maintaining an effective diverse workforce. Some excellent, recent books include: Harvey, C. P., & Allard, M. J. 2005. *Understanding and managing diversity: Readings, cases, and exercises.* (3rd ed.). Upper Saddle River, NJ: Pearson Prentice-Hall; Miller, F. A., & Katz, J. H. 2002. *The inclusion breakthrough: Unleashing the real power of diversity.* San Francisco: Berrett Koehler; and Williams, M. A. 2001. *The 10 lenses: Your guide to living and working in a multicultural world.* Sterling, VA: Capital Books.

57. www.rand.org/publications/RB/RB/5050.

58. www.shrm.org/diversity/businesscase.asp.

59. This section, including the six potential benefits of a diverse workforce, draws on Cox, T. H., & Blake, S. 1991. Managing cultural diversity: Implications for organizational competitiveness. *Academy of Management Executive,* 5(3): 45–56.

60. www.pwcglobal.com/us/eng/careers/diversity/index.html.

61. Refer to www.fortune.com/diversity.

62. This discussion draws on Dess, G. G., & Lumpkin, G. T. 2001. Emerging issues in strategy process research. In Hitt, M. A., Freeman, R. E., & Harrison, J. S. (Eds.). *Handbook of strategic management:* 3–34. Malden, MA: Blackwell.

63. Adler, P. S., & Kwon, S. W. 2002. Social capital: Prospects for a new concept. *Academy of Management Review,* 27(1): 17–40.

64. Capelli, P. 2000. A market-driven approach to retaining talent. *Harvard Business Review,* 78(1): 103–113.

65. This hypothetical example draws on Peteraf, M. 1993. The cornerstones of competitive advantage. *Strategic Management Journal,* 14: 179–191.

66. Wernerfelt, B. 1984. A resource-based view of the firm. *Strategic Management Journal,* 5: 171–180.

67. Wysocki, B., Jr. 2000. Yet another hazard of the new economy: The Pied Piper Effect. *Wall Street Journal,* March 20: A1–A16.

68. Ibid.

69. Buckman, R. C. 2000. Tech defectors from Microsoft resettle together. *Wall Street Journal,* October: B1–B6.

70. For an insightful discussion on the creation of social capital, see Bolino, M. C., Turnley, W. H., & Bloodgood, J. M. 2002. Citizenship behavior and the creation of social capital in organizations. *Academy of Management Review,* 27(4): 505–522.

71. An insightful discussion of the interorganizational aspects of social capital can be found in Dyer, J. H., & Singh, H. 1998. The relational view: Cooperative strategy and sources of interorganizational competitive advantage. *Academy of Management Review,* 23: 66–79.

72. Prusak, L., & Cohen, D. 2001. How to invest in social capital. *Harvard Business Review,* 79(6): 86–93.

73. Leonard, D., & Straus, S. 1997. Putting your company's whole brain to work. *Harvard Business Review,* 75(4): 110–122.

74. Oh, H., Chung, M., & Labianca, G. 2004. Group social capital and group effectiveness: The role of informal socializing ties. *Academy of Management Journal,* 47(6): 860–875; and Labianca, J. 2004. The ties that bind. *Harvard Business Review,* 82(10): 19.

75. Leana, C. R., & Van Buren, H. J., III. 1999. Organizational social capital and employment practices. *Academy of Management Review,* 24: 538–555.

76. Prusak & Cohen, op. cit.: 86–93.

77. Teitelbaum, R. 1997. Tough guys finish first. *Fortune,* July 21: 82–84.

78. Collins, D. 2003. *Communication in a virtual organization.* Mason, OH: Thompson South-Western; and Winston, S. 2004. *Organized for success: Top executives and CEOs reveal the organizing principles that helped them reach the top.* New York: Crown Business.

79. Taylor, W. C. 1999. Whatever happened to globalization? *Fast Company,* December: 228–236.

80. Prahalad, C. K., & Ramaswamy, V. 2004. *The future of competition: Co-creating value with customers.* Boston: Harvard Business School Press.

81. Ibid.

82. Lei, D., Slocum, J., & Pitts, R. A. 1999. Designing organizations for competitive advantage: The power of unlearning and learning. *Organizational Dynamics,* Winter: 24–38.

83. This section draws upon Zaccaro, S. J., & Bader, P. 2002. E-Leadership and the challenges of leading e-teams: Minimizing the bad and maximizing the good. *Organizational Dynamics,* 31(4): 377–387.

84. Kirkman, B. L., Rosen, B., Tesluk, P. E., & Gibson, C. B. 2004. The impact of team empowerment on virtual team performance: The moderating role of face-to-face interaction. *Academy of Management Journal,* 47(2): 175–192.

85. The discussion of the advantages and challenges associated with e-teams draws on Zacarro & Bader, op. cit.

86. For a recent study exploring the relationship between team empowerment, face-to-face interaction, and performance in virtual teams, read Kirkman, Rosen, Tesluk, & Gibson, op. cit.

87. For an innovative study on how firms share knowledge with competitors and the performance implications, read Spencer, J. W. 2003. Firms' knowledge sharing strategies in the global innovation system: Empirical evidence from the flat panel display industry. *Strategic Management Journal,* 24(3): 217–235.

88. The examples of Andersen Consulting and Access Health draw upon Hansen, M. T., Nohria, N., & Tierney, T. 1999. What's your strategy for managing knowledge? *Harvard Business Review,* 77(2): 106–118.

89. Capelli, op. cit.

90. Ibid.

91. Koudsi, S. 2000. Actually, it is brain surgery. *Fortune,* March 20: 233.

Strategic Analysis

Chapter 1
Introduction and Analyzing Goals and Objectives

Chapter 2
Analyzing the External Environment

Chapter 3
Analyzing the Internal Environment

Chapter 4
Assessing Intellectual Capital

Strategic Formulation

Chapter 5
Formulating Business-Level Strategies

Chapter 6
Formulating Corporate-Level Strategies

Chapter 7
Formulating International Strategies

Chapter 8
Digital Business Strategies

Strategic Implementation

Chapter 9
Strategic Control and Corporate Governance

Chapter 10
Creating Effective Organizational Designs

Chapter 11
Strategic Leadership Excellence, Ethics and Change

Chapter 12
Fostering Corporate Entrepreneurship

Chapter 13
Strategic Leadership Creating New Ventures

Case Analysis

Chapter 14
Case Analysis

part two

Strategic Formulation

5

Business-Level Strategy:
Creating and Sustaining Competitive Advantages

After reading this chapter, you should have a good understanding of:

- The central role of competitive advantage in the study of strategic management.

- The three generic strategies: overall cost leadership, differentiation, and focus.

- How the successful attainment of generic strategies can improve a firm's relative power vis-à-vis the five forces that determine an industry's average profitability.

- The pitfalls managers must avoid in striving to attain generic strategies.

- How firms can effectively combine the generic strategies of overall cost leadership and differentiation.

- The importance of considering the industry life cycle to determine a firm's business-level strategy and its relative emphasis on functional area strategies and value-creating activities.

- The need for turnaround strategies and a dynamic perspective on industry change and evolution that enable a firm to reposition its competitive position in an industry.

*h*ow firms compete with each other and how they attain and sustain competitive advantages go to the heart of strategic management. In short, the key issue becomes: Why do some firms outperform others and enjoy such advantages over time? This subject, business-level strategy, is the focus of Chapter 5.

The first part of the chapter draws on Michael Porter's framework of generic strategies. He identifies three strategies—overall cost leadership, differentiation, and focus—that firms may apply to outperform their rivals in an industry. We begin by describing each of these strategies and provide examples of firms that have successfully attained them as a means of outperforming competitors in their industry. Next, we address how these strategies help a firm develop a favorable position vis-à-vis the "five forces" (Chapter 2). We then suggest some of the pitfalls that managers must avoid if they are to successfully pursue these generic strategies. We close this section with a discussion of the conditions under which firms may effectively combine generic strategies to outperform rivals. Firms that fail to consider carefully the potential downsides associated with the generic strategies—separately and in combination—will have the most difficulty either creating or sustaining competitive advantages over time.

The second part of Chapter 5 discusses a vital consideration in the effective use of business-level strategies: industry life cycles. The four stages of the industry life cycle—introduction, growth, maturity, and decline—are indicative of an evolving management process that affects factors such as the market growth rate and the intensity of competition. Accordingly, the stages of an industry's life cycle are an important contingency that managers should take into account when making decisions concerning the optimal overall business-level strategies and the relative emphasis to place on functional capabilities and value-creating activities. At times, firms are faced with performance declines and must find ways to revitalize their competitive positions. The actions followed to do so are referred to as turnaround strategies, which may be needed at any stage of the industry life cycle. However, they occur more frequently during the maturity and decline stages. Finally, managers must recognize the dynamic nature of industry change and evolution. Advantages can be short lived. Managers need to be able to embrace innovations and strive to sustain competitive advantages.

Sharper Image, with revenues of $736 million, was founded in 1987 and established itself with such gadgets as fogless mirrors and water-proof shower radios.[1] In the late 1990s it cashed in on the Razor scooter fad. When that faded, Sharper Image introduced the Ionic Breeze Quadra, which helped it to double annual sales between 1999 and 2003. However, as the firm found out, relying on a single product that rivals can easily imitate can be a very risky strategy.

For several years, the $350 Ionic Breeze Quadra air purifier was Sharper Image's primary money machine, accounting for about 16 percent of its total revenues in a recent year. However, rivals have begun to enter the market and Sharper Image's purifier is facing intense competition. Its most direct rival, Brookstone, is selling its new Pure-Ion UV air purifier for $300. Home Depot and RadioShack are selling their own versions for $200. Sharper Image tried to prop up sales by coming up with an easier-to-clean model. However, the price was too expensive at $400, and it failed to generate significant new sales.

If Sharper Image's product was far superior to its competition, customers might be willing to spend the extra money. However, the firm's product was panned in research conducted by that venerable consumer watchdog *Consumer Reports* (CR). In February 2002, CR published a lengthy article reviewing 16 air purifiers. It placed the Ionic Breeze Quadra dead last in its ranking, saying that the device produced "no measurable reduction in airborne particles." Sharper Image complained because it felt that the tests were unfair since their model needed to run longer in order to be effective. So, according to Steve Williams, an attorney for Consumers Union (the publisher of *Consumer Reports*), they "went back and tested again, this time seeing how much cigarette smoke could be removed over 19 hours. It couldn't even clean the smoke from one-eighth of a cigarette." In addition, CR had its test procedures reviewed by an independent expert who confirmed the validity of their procedure. CR then ran a second article. The result was that the Ionic Breeze Quadra ended up near the bottom of the magazine's rankings.

Sharper Image sued the research group in 2003, alleging product disparagement. Unfortunately, in November 2004, the San Francisco district court ruled that there was "no reasonable probability" that Sharper Image could prove its case. The judge then dismissed the suit under California's so-called anti-SLAPP law, which is designed to deter "strategic litigation against public participation," that is, frivolous suits filed by big companies to silence critics. Sharper Image was also required to reimburse Consumers Union $525,000 for its costs and attorneys' fees. And, to add insult to injury, in the May 2005 issue of *Consumer Reports*, the magazine reported that not only does the Ionic Breeze Quadra fail to significantly clean the air, but it also releases potentially unhealthy levels of ozone.

How much of the product's sales decline is due to CR's negative evaluation and how much is due to intensified competition is, of course, open to question. However, few would argue that the large drop in demand for Sharper Image's major product is a primary reason for the firm's overall recent poor performance. For 2004, the firm's same store sales were down one percent, and its overall profit was down nearly 50 percent from the previous year. And not surprisingly, its stock price has been hit very hard. In early 2005, shares were trading at about $17 a share—down from its all-time high of $40 a year earlier.

Sharper Image's problem was three-fold. First, the Ionic Breeze Quadra did not enjoy any clear differentiation advantage along any product attributes such as quality, styling, or performance. Second, at $350, it did not enjoy a cost advantage either. Third, the Ionic Breeze Quadra was easily imitated by rivals. In addition, when negative product reviews came in, Sharper Image went on a legal offensive instead of addressing the real problem.

Since all firms endeavor to enjoy above-average returns (or profits), the question of how management should go about this is a core issue in strategic management. Organizations that have created sustainable competitive advantages don't rely on a single strength, as Sharper Image has done, but strive for well-rounded strategies. This increases the chances that advantages will be more lasting, or sustainable, instead of temporary.

These avenues of competitive advantage take several forms, known as generic strategies. There are three major types: overall low cost, differentiation, and focus. In the next section, we will discuss how Michael Porter's three generic strategies contribute to a firm's competitive advantage and how firms can successfully combine multiple strategies.

>>Types of Competitive Advantage and Sustainability

Michael Porter presented three generic strategies that a firm can use to overcome the five forces and achieve competitive advantage.[2] Each of Porter's generic strategies has the potential to allow a firm to outperform rivals within the same industry. The first, *overall cost leadership,* is based on creating a low-cost-position relative to a firm's peers. With this strategy, a firm must manage the relationships throughout the entire value chain and be devoted to lowering costs throughout the entire chain. On the other hand, *differentiation* requires a firm (or business unit) to create products and/or services that are unique and valued. Here, the primary emphasis is on "nonprice" attributes for which customers will gladly pay a premium. Finally, a firm following a *focus* strategy must direct its attention (or "focus") toward narrow product lines, buyer segments, or targeted geographic markets. A firm emphasizing a focus strategy must attain advantages either through differentiation or a cost leadership approach. Whereas the overall cost leadership and differentiation strategies strive to attain advantages industrywide, focusers build their strategy with a narrow target market in mind. Exhibit 5.1 illustrates these three strategies on two dimensions: competitive advantage and strategic target.

Before moving on to each generic strategy, it is important to note that both casual observation and research support the notion that firms that identify with one or more of the forms of competitive advantage that Porter identified outperform those that do not.[3] There has been a rich history of strategic management research addressing this topic. One study analyzed 1,789 strategic business units and found that businesses combining multiple forms of competitive advantage (differentiation and overall cost leadership)

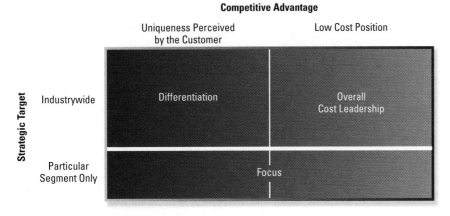

Exhibit 5.1 **Three Generic Strategies**

Competitive Advantage						
	Differentiation and Cost	Differentiation	Cost	Differentiation and Focus	Cost and Focus	Stuck in the Middle
Performance						
Return on investment (%)	35.5	32.9	30.2	17.0	23.7	17.8
Sales growth (%)	15.1	13.5	13.5	16.4	17.5	12.2
Gain in market share (%)	5.3	5.3	5.5	6.1	6.3	4.4
Sample size	123	160	100	141	86	105

Exhibit 5.2   Competitive Advantage and Business Performance

outperformed businesses that used only a single form. The lowest performers were those that did not identify with even a single type of advantage. They were classified as "stuck in the middle." Results of this study are presented in Exhibit 5.2.[4]

Overall Cost Leadership

The first generic strategy is overall cost leadership. Cost leadership requires a tight set of interrelated tactics that include:

- Aggressive construction of efficient-scale facilities.
- Vigorous pursuit of cost reductions from experience.
- Tight cost and overhead control.
- Avoidance of marginal customer accounts.
- Cost minimization in all activities in the firm's value chain, such as R&D, service, sales force, and advertising.

Exhibit 5.3 draws on the value-chain concept (see Chapter 3) to provide examples of how a firm can attain an overall cost leadership strategy in its primary and support activities.

An important concept related to an overall cost leadership strategy is the experience curve, which refers to how business "learns" how to lower costs as it gains experience with production processes. That is, with experience, unit costs of production decline as output increases in most industries. The experience curve concept is discussed in Strategy Spotlight 5.1 and Exhibit 5.4 (page 167).

To generate above-average performance, a firm following an overall cost leadership position must attain parity on the basis of differentiation relative to competitors. In other words, a firm achieving parity is similar to its competitors, or "on par," with respect to differentiated products.[5] Parity on the basis of differentiation permits a cost leader to translate cost advantages directly into higher profits than competitors. Thus, the cost leader earns above-average returns.[6]

The failure to attain parity on the basis of differentiation can be illustrated with an example from the automobile industry—the ill-fated Yugo. Below is an excerpt from a speech by J. W. Marriott, Jr., Chairman of the Marriott Corporation:[7]

> . . . money is a big thing. But it's not the only thing. In the 1980s, a new automobile reached North America from behind the Iron Curtain. It was called the Yugo, and its main attraction was price. About $3,000 each. But the only way they caught on was as the butt of jokes. Remember the guy who told his mechanic, "I want a gas cap for my Yugo." "OK," the mechanic replied, "that sounds like a fair trade."

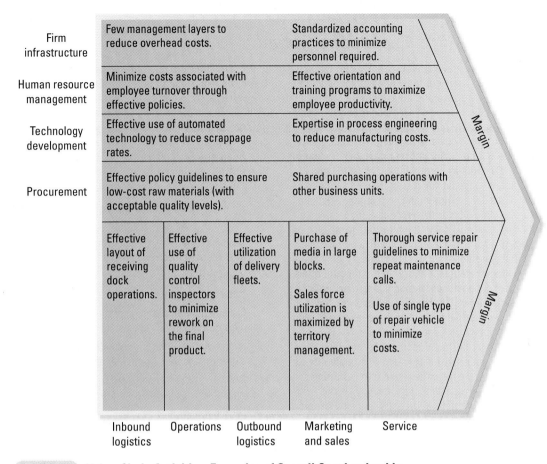

Firm infrastructure
Human resource management
Technology development
Procurement

Exhibit 5.3 Value-Chain Activities: Examples of Overall Cost Leadership

Source: Adapted with the permission of The Free Press, a division of Simon & Schuster Adult Publishing Group, from *Competitive Advantage: Creating and Sustaining Superior Performance* by Michael E. Porter. Copyright © 1985, 1998 by Michael E. Porter. All rights reserved.

Yugo was offering a lousy value proposition. The cars literally fell apart before your eyes. And the lesson was simple. Price is just one component of value. No matter how good the price, the most cost-sensitive consumer won't buy a bad product.

Below, we discuss some examples of how firms enhance cost leadership position in their industries.

While other managed care providers were having a string of weak years, WellPoint, based in Thousand Oaks, California, has had a number of banner years and recently enjoyed a profit growth of 75 percent to approximately $960 million over the past two years.[8] Chairman Leonard Schaeffer credits the company's focus on innovation for both expanding revenues and cutting costs. Recently, for example, WellPoint asked the Food and Drug Administration (FDA) to make the allergy drug Claritin available over the counter. Surprisingly, this may be the first time that an insurer has approached the FDA with this type of request. Schaeffer claimed, "They were kind of stunned," but the FDA agreed to consider it. It was a smart move for WellPoint. If approved as an over-the-counter drug, Claritin would reduce patient visits to the doctor and eliminate the need for prescriptions—two reimbursable expenses for which WellPoint would otherwise be responsible.

Stephen Sanger, CEO of General Mills, recently came up with an idea that helped his firm cut costs.[9] To improve productivity, he sent technicians to watch pit crews during a

STRATEGY SPOTLIGHT

The Experience Curve

The experience curve, developed by the Boston Consulting Group in 1968, is a way of looking at efficiencies developed through a firm's cumulative experience. In its basic form, the experience curve relates production costs to production output. As output doubles, costs decline by 10 percent to 30 percent. For example, if it costs $1 per unit to produce 100 units, the per unit cost will decline to between 70 to 90 cents as output increases to 200 units.

What factors account for this increased efficiency? First, the success of an experience curve strategy depends on the industry life cycle for the product. Early stages of a product's life cycle are typically characterized by rapid gains in technological advances in production efficiency. Most experience curve gains come early in the product life cycle.

Second, the inherent technology of the product offers opportunities for enhancement through gained experience. High-tech products give the best opportunity for gains in production efficiencies. As technology is developed, "value engineering" of innovative production processes is implemented, driving down the per unit costs of production.

Third, a product's sensitivity to price strongly affects a firm's ability to exploit the experience curve. Cutting the price of a product with high demand elasticity—where demand increases when price decreases—rapidly creates consumer purchases of the new product. By cutting prices, a firm can increase demand for its product. The increased demand in turn increases product manufacture, thus increasing the firm's experience in the manufacturing process. So by decreasing price and increasing demand, a firm gains manufacturing experience in that particular product, which drives down per unit production costs.

Fourth, the competitive landscape factors into whether or not a firm might benefit from an experience curve strategy. If other competitors are well positioned in the market, have strong capital resources, and are known to promote their product lines aggressively to gain market share, an experience curve strategy may lead to nothing more than a price war between two or more strong competitors. But if a company is the first to market with the product and has good financial backing, an experience curve strategy may be successful.

In an article in the *Harvard Business Review,* Pankaj Ghemawat recommended answering several questions when considering an experience curve strategy.

- Does my industry exhibit a significant experience curve?
- Have I defined the industry broadly enough to take into account interrelated experience?
- What is the precise source of cost reduction?
- Can my company keep cost reductions proprietary?
- Is demand sufficiently stable to justify using the experience curve?
- Is cumulated output doubling fast enough for the experience curve to provide much strategic leverage?
- Do the returns from an experience curve strategy warrant the risks of technological obsolescence?
- Is demand price-sensitive?
- Are there well-financed competitors who are already following an experience curve strategy or are likely to adopt one if my company does?

Michael Porter suggested, however, that the experience curve is not useful in all situations. Whether or not to base strategy on the experience curve depends on what specifically causes the decline in costs. For example, if costs drop from efficient production facilities and not necessarily from experience, the experience curve is not helpful. But as Sharon Oster pointed out in her book on competitive analysis, the experience curve can help managers analyze costs when efficient learning, rather than efficient machinery, is the source of cost savings.

Sources: Ghemawat, P. 1985. Building strategy on the experience curve. *Harvard Business Review,* March–April: 143–149; Porter, M. E. 1996. *On competition.* Boston: Harvard Business Review Press; Oster, S. M. 1994. *Modern competitive analysis* (2nd ed.). New York: Oxford University Press.

NASCAR race. That experience inspired the techies to figure out how to reduce the time it takes to switch a plant line from five hours to 20 minutes. This provided an important lesson: Many interesting benchmarking examples can take place far outside of an industry. Often, process improvements involve identifying the best practices in other industries and adapting them for implementation in your own firm. After all, when firms benchmark competitors in their own industry, the end result is often copying and playing catch-up.[10]

A business that strives for a low-cost advantage must attain an absolute cost advantage relative to its rivals. This is typically accomplished by offering a no-frills product

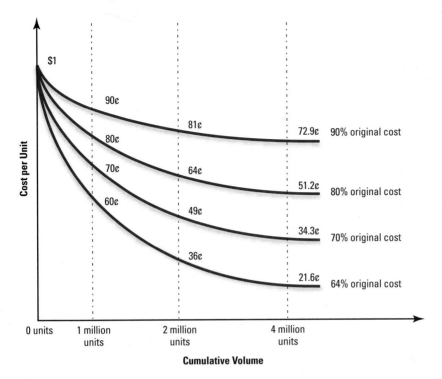

Exhibit 5.4   Comparing Experience Curve Effects

or service to a broad target market using standardization to derive the greatest benefits from economies of scale and experience. However, such a strategy may fail if a firm is unable to attain parity on important dimensions of differentiation such as quick responses to customer requests for services or design changes. Strategy Spotlight 5.2 discusses ING Direct, a financial services company that provides a "no frills" service but very generous rates on savings accounts and other services. In part, it succeeds by providing parity on differentiation through very good account security, ease and speed for customers in opening accounts, and very thorough online and paper account statements."[11]

Overall Cost Leadership: Improving Competitive Position vis-à-vis the Five Forces   An overall low-cost position enables a firm to achieve above-average returns despite strong competition. It protects a firm against rivalry from competitors, because lower costs allow a firm to earn returns even if its competitors eroded their profits through intense rivalry. A low-cost position also protects firms against powerful buyers. Buyers can exert power to drive down prices only to the level of the next most efficient producer. Also, a low-cost position provides more flexibility to cope with demands from powerful suppliers for input cost increases. The factors that lead to a low-cost position also provide substantial entry barriers from economies of scale and cost advantages. Finally, a low-cost position puts the firm in a favorable position with respect to substitute products introduced by new and existing competitors.

A few examples will illustrate these points. ING Direct's close attention to costs helps to protect them from buyer power and intense rivalry from competitors. Thus, they are able to drive down costs and enjoy relatively high power over their customers. By increasing its productivity and lowering unit costs, General Mills (and its competitors in that industry) enjoy greater scale economies and erect higher entry barriers for others

ING Direct: A Highly Successful Low-Cost Strategy

ING Direct, considered the fast-food chain of the financial services industry, may be an extreme example of a low-cost strategy. However, it has been highly successful. For the year 2004, its pretax profit of $250 million was more than twice its profit of $110 million in 2003.

ING Direct has a limited offering of financial services, including savings accounts, CDs, and home equity loans. It is a unit of the Dutch giant ING, which offers banking, insurance, and asset management to over 60 million private, corporate and institutional clients in more than 50 countries. ING employs over 112,000 people in 65 countries, including more than 11,000 in the United States.

ING Direct attracts people who need very little hand-holding—that is, low maintenance customers—with very high interest rates. In fact, its Orange savings account pays 2.6 percent, which is over four times the .56 percent average for a money-market account at a bank. It is able to offer such enticing rates because it does 75 percent of its transactions online and it avoids amenities such as checking.

However, a unique aspect of ING Direct's approach to driving down costs is that it typically "fires" about 3,600 of its 2 million customers each year! It saves about $1 million annually by getting rid of customers who are too time-consuming. ING has driven its cost per account to about one-third of the industry average, even as its total assets have climbed to $30 billion since it entered the U. S. market in 2000.

CEO Arkadi Kuhlmann provides an interesting perspective on how ING Direct gets rid of its overly demanding customers:

> The difference between ING Direct and the rest of the financial industry is like the difference between take-out food and a sit-down restaurant. The business isn't based on relationships; it's based on a commodity product that's high-volume and low-margin. We need to keep expenses down, which doesn't work well when customers want a lot of empathetic contact.
>
> If the average customer phone call costs us $5.25 and the average account revenue is $12 per month, all it takes is 100,000 misbehaving customers for costs to go through the roof. So when a customer calls too many times or wants too many exceptions to the rule, our sales associate can basically say: "Look, this doesn't fit you. You need to go back to your community bank and get the kind of contact you're comfortable with." Of course, we have to use judgment. In some cases, people have legitimate questions. But often it's customers with large balances who are used to special treatment. They like premiums, platinum cards, and special rates. But you don't get that kind of stuff at the take-out window.

Source: Stone, A. 2005. Bare bones, plump profits. *BusinessWeek*, March 14: 88; Esfahani, E. 2004. How to get tough with bad customers. *Business 2.0*, October: 52; and www.home.ingdirect.com.

who want to enter the industry. Finally, as competitors such as WellPoint lower costs through means such as petitioning the FDA to make certain drugs available over the counter, they become less vulnerable to substitutes such as Internet-based competitors.

Potential Pitfalls of Overall Cost Leadership Strategies   There are many benefits from following a strategy of overall cost leadership. However, there are some pitfalls to avoid:

- *Too much focus on one or a few value-chain activities.* Would you consider a person to be astute if he cancelled his newspaper subscription and quit eating out to save money, but then "maxed out" several credit cards, requiring him to pay hundreds of dollars a month in interest charges? Of course not. Similarly, firms need to pay attention to all activities in the value chain to manage their overall costs. Too often managers make big cuts in operating expenses, but don't question year-to-year spending on capital projects. Or managers may decide to cut selling and marketing expenses but leave manufacturing expenses untouched. Managers should explore *all* value-chain activities, including relationships among them, as candidates for cost reductions.

- *All rivals share a common input or raw material.* Firms that compete on overall low-cost strategies are vulnerable to price increases in the factors of production.

Since they're competing on costs, they are less able to pass on price increases, because customers can easily take their business to competitors who have lower prices. Consider the hardship experienced by fertilizer producers in early 2001 when energy prices spiked.[12] The dramatic increase—a quadrupling of prices to $10 per thousand cubic feet of natural gas—forced firms to shut down nearly half of their production capacity. Why? Natural gas accounts for over 70 percent of the fertilizer's cost. According to Betty-Ann Hegge, senior vice president of Potash Corporation of Saskatchewan, Inc., North America's second largest producer, "Many companies are not even covering their cash costs at these prices."

- *The strategy is imitated too easily.* One of the common pitfalls of a cost-leadership strategy is that a firm's strategy may consist of value-creating activities that are easy to imitate.[13] Such was the case with online brokers in recent years.[14] As of early 2001, there were about 140 online brokers, hardly symbolic of an industry where imitation is extremely difficult. But according to Henry McVey, financial services analyst at Morgan Stanley, "We think you need five to ten" online brokers.

    What are some of the dynamics? First, although online brokers were geared up to handle 1.2 million trades a day by early 2001, volume had shrunk to about 834,000—a 30 percent drop. Thus, competition for a smaller pool of business is increasingly intense. Second, when the stock market is down, many investors trust their instincts less and seek professional guidance from brokerages that offer differentiated services. Eric Rajendra of A. T. Kearney, an international consulting company, claimed, "The current (online broker) model is inadequate for the pressures the industry is facing now."

- *A lack of parity on differentiation.* As noted earlier, firms endeavoring to attain cost leadership advantages need to obtain a level of parity on differentiation. An example is organizations providing online degree programs to adults working full-time. Although such firms may offer low prices, they may not be successful unless they can offer instruction that is perceived as comparable to traditional providers. For them, parity can be achieved on differentiation dimensions such as reputation and quality and through signaling mechanisms such as national and regional accreditation agencies.

- *Erosion of cost advantages when the pricing information available to customers increases.* This is becoming a more significant challenge as the Internet dramatically increases both the quantity and volume of information available to consumers about pricing and cost structures. Life insurance firms offering whole life insurance provide an interesting example.[15] One study found that for each 10 percent increase in consumer use of the Internet, there is a corresponding reduction in insurance prices to consumers of 3 to 5 percent. Recently, the nationwide savings (or, alternatively, reduced revenues to providers) was between $115 and $125 million annually.

Differentiation

As the name implies, the strategy of differentiation consists of creating differences in the firm's product or service offering by creating something that is perceived *industrywide* as unique and valued by customers. Differentiation can take many forms:

- Prestige or brand image (Adam's Mark hotels, BMW automobiles).[16]
- Technology (Martin guitars, Marantz stereo components, North Face camping equipment).
- Innovation (Medtronic medical equipment, Nokia cellular phones).

	Inbound logistics	Operations	Outbound logistics	Marketing and sales	Service
Firm infrastructure	Superior MIS—To integrate value-creating activities to improve quality.		Facilities that promote firm image.		Widely respected CEO enhances firm reputation.
Human resource management	Programs to attract talented engineers and scientists.			Provide training and incentives to ensure a strong customer service orientation.	
Technology development	Superior material handling and sorting technology.			Excellent applications engineering support.	
Procurement	Purchase of high-quality components to enhance product image.			Use of most prestigious outlets.	
	Superior material handling operations to minimize damage. Quick transfer of inputs to manufacturing process.	Flexibility and speed in responding to changes in manufacturing specifications. Low defect rates to improve quality.	Accurate and responsive order processing. Effective product replenishment to reduce customer inventory.	Creative and innovative advertising programs. Fostering of personal relationship with key customers.	Rapid response to customer service requests. Complete inventory of replacement parts and supplies.

Margin (upper right), Margin (lower right)

Exhibit 5.5   Value-Chain Activities: Examples of Differentiation

Source: Adapted with the permission of The Free Press, a division of Simon & Schuster Adult Publishing Group, from *Competitive Advantage: Creating and Sustaining Superior Performance* by Michael E. Porter. Copyright © 1985, 1998 by Michael E. Porter. All rights reserved.

- Features (Cannondale mountain bikes, Honda Goldwing motorcycles).
- Customer service (Nordstrom department stores, Sears lawn equipment retailing).
- Dealer network (Lexus automobiles, Caterpillar earth-moving equipment).

Exhibit 5.5 draws on the concept of the value chain as an example of how firms may differentiate themselves in primary and support activities.

Firms may differentiate themselves along several different dimensions at once. For example, BMW is known for its high prestige, superior engineering, and high-quality automobiles. Another example is Harley-Davidson, which differentiates on image and dealer services.[17]

Firms achieve and sustain differentiation advantages and attain above-average performance when their price premiums exceed the extra costs incurred in being unique.[18] For example, both BMW and Harley-Davidson must increase consumer costs to offset added marketing expenses. Thus, a differentiator will always seek out ways of distinguishing itself from similar competitors to justify price premiums greater than the costs incurred by differentiating. Clearly, a differentiator cannot ignore costs. After all, its premium prices would be eroded by a markedly inferior cost position. Therefore, it must attain a level of cost *parity* relative to competitors. Differentiators can do this by reducing costs in all areas that do not affect differentiation. Porsche, for example, invests heavily in engine design—an area in which its customers demand excellence—but it is less concerned and spends fewer resources in the design of the instrument panel or the arrangement of switches on the radio.[19]

Many companies successfully follow a differentiation strategy.[20] For example, some firms have been able to appeal to a very upscale and discriminating segment of the market by offering products with an excellent image and strong brand identification. If you are interested in one of Ferrari's lower-priced models, the 360 Modena, be prepared to pay about $160,000. But it might take more than money; you'll need patience. Recently, there was a 50-person, 18-month waiting list for the all-aluminum, 400-horsepower V8-powered model.[21] And if you want the top-of-the-line Destiny yacht, a 135 footer, be prepared to spend around $13 million. If that is a little steep, a 94-foot model is only $6 million.[22]

Siebel Systems, a leader in software that manages customer relations, is well known for its customer service.[23] No software is written until the customer has significant input. Outside consultants routinely poll clients on satisfaction, and the compensation of managers and technical professionals is heavily based on such reports. How successful is Siebel? In the seven years since its founding, its sales have exceeded $1 billion faster than any other software maker, including Microsoft. CEO Tom Siebel is confident the firm will sustain its growth rate as long as the company, as he expressed it, "shows respect for the customer."

FedEx's CEO and founder, Fred Smith, claims that the key to his firm's success is innovation.[24] He contends his management team didn't understand their real goal when they started the firm in 1971: "We thought that we were selling the transportation of goods; in fact, we were selling peace of mind." To that end, they now provide each driver with a handheld computer and a transmitting device that makes it possible for customers to track their packages right from their desktop PCs.

Lexus, a division of Toyota, provides an example of how a firm can strengthen its differentiation strategy by *achieving integration at multiple points along the value chain.*[25] Although the luxury car line was not introduced until the late 1980s, by the early 1990s the cars had already soared to the top of J. D. Power & Associates's customer satisfaction ratings.

In the spirit of benchmarking, one of Lexus's competitors hired Custom Research Inc. (CRI), a marketing research firm, to find out why Lexus owners were so satisfied. CRI conducted a series of focus groups in which Lexus drivers eagerly offered anecdotes about the special care they experienced from their dealers. It became clear that, although Lexus was manufacturing cars with few mechanical defects, it was the extra care shown by the sales and service staff that resulted in satisfied customers. Such pampering is reflected in the feedback from one customer who claimed she never had a problem with her Lexus. However, upon further probing, she said, "Well, I suppose you could call the four times they had to replace the windshield a 'problem.' But frankly, they took care of it so well and always gave me a loaner car, so I never really considered it a problem until you mentioned it now." An insight gained in CRI's research is that perceptions of product quality (design, engineering, and manufacturing) can be strongly influenced by downstream activities in the value chain (marketing and sales, service).

Let's take a closer look at the Lexus example to reiterate some of the key points of a successful differentiation strategy.[26] The example illustrates how strong relationships among value activities reinforce and strengthen the customer's total perception of value. Value activity integration creates value for the end user. Clearly, Lexus must establish and maintain close ties with its dealers by providing resources such as advertising

VoodooPC: A Successful Differentiation Strategy

When we think of personal computers, commodity products driven by low costs and competitive pricing usually comes to mind. Such is clearly not the case with VoodooPC, a highly successful Canadian company that competes at the high end of the market. As one of its accountants, Jennifer Fraser, notes, "We have an unconventional position in a market saturated by big boring giants."

VoodooPC Ltd. is a world leader in the design and manufacturing of high-performance and stylish personal computer entertainment systems. VoodooPC has won the prestigious Ultimate Gaming Machine Award for the past three years in a row.

Each VoodooPC is unique and custom made for each customer. To buy a Voodoo computer, you order what you think you need through the Voodoo Web site. Then, a Voodoo engineer contacts you to ensure that your Voodoo PC will exactly match your unique requirements. Ninety-five percent of all orders are further refined after customers talked to Voodoo engineers.

In a sense, VoodooPCs are not just PCs. Rather, they are works of art. The cases for VoodooPCs have 11 coats of European automobile paint for maximum gloss and color choice. Their desktops have art cut into the side of the computer tower and they are illuminated from the inside, casting a mysterious glow. Also, the inside of the computer looks different, starting with beautifully folded wires, which they call "origami cabling." Similar to designers of Mercedes Benz cars, the creators of each VoodooPC sign their names on the inside of the case.

Obviously, VoodooPC does not compete on price. While there are some lower-end models, the typical prices are between $4,000 and $5,000. Some of their clientele are willing to pay $19,000 for dual processors, two video chips, and a liquid cooling system. The company even sold a 22-karat-gold-plated desktop for $52,000.

VoodooPC was founded by brothers Rahul and Ravi Sood who branded Voodoo as the PC company for the hard-core game geek. The strategy has worked. During the past four years, Voodoo's sales have soared past $20 million. And while the profit margin on the typical PC is 10 percent, the Soods' gaming machines generally get about 30 percent.

Voodoo prides itself on its custom design capabilities and customer service. It makes sure that the machine fits the buyer like an expensive, custom-made suit. Rahul Sood says, "We sometimes try to undersell you." That approach builds trust and positive buzz in the tight-knit gaming community. Voodoo also claims that it will (literally) go to the ends of the earth to service its machines. In fact, in 2002, it sent a tech support employee all the way to Sydney, Australia, to fix a PC. Rahul claims that the company won enough word-of-mouth sales from that one visit to more than justify the $828 plane ticket.

Sources: Malik, O. 2004. The 22-Karat PC. *Business 2.0,* May: 78; and, Anonymous. 2005. VoodooPC. *Cool Companies,* Calgary and Edmonton Edition: 120–121.

materials, training, parts, supplies, and automobile inventories. Yet you could easily imagine the futility of Lexus's superb marketing, sales, and service efforts if the company could not maintain high production quality, or if procurement were unable to acquire high-quality components. Superb marketing and service alone would be inadequate to support Lexus's strategy. Thus, successful differentiation requires attention to and integration with all parts of a firm's value chain.

Strategy Spotlight 5.3 discusses how VoodooPC has been highly successful with its differentiation strategy in what is generally considered to be a commodity industry—personal computers. Like Lexus, its success can be partially explained by its excellence in downstream activities such as customer service, as well as by its reputation for product excellence.

Differentiation: Improving Competitive Position vis-à-vis the Five Forces Achieving differentiation is a viable strategy for earning above-average returns by creating a defensible position for overcoming Porter's five competitive forces. Differentiation provides protection against rivalry since brand loyalty lowers customer sensitivity to price and raises customer switching costs. By increasing a firm's margins, differentiation also avoids the need for a low-cost position. Higher entry barriers result because of customer loyalty and the firm's ability to provide uniqueness in its products or services. Differentiation also provides higher margins that enable a firm to deal with supplier power. And it reduces buyer power, because buyers lack comparable alternatives and are therefore less price sensitive. Supplier power is also decreased because there is a certain amount of prestige associated with being the supplier to a producer of highly differentiated products and services. Last, a firm that uses differentiation will enjoy high customer loyalty, thus experiencing less threat from substitutes than its competitors.

The examples in this section will be used to illustrate the above points. Lexus has enjoyed enhanced power over buyers because its top J. D. Power ranking makes buyers more willing to pay a premium price. This lessens rivalry, since buyers become less price-sensitive. The prestige associated with these upper-crust brand names such as Destiny yachts and Ferrari automobiles also lowers supplier power since margins are high. Suppliers would probably desire to be associated with prestige brands, thus lessening their incentives to drive up prices. Finally, the loyalty and "peace of mind" associated with a service provider such as FedEx or Siebel Systems make these firms less vulnerable to rivalry or substitute products and services.

Potential Pitfalls of Differentiation Strategies Along with the benefits of differentiation, there are also pitfalls.

- *Uniqueness that is not valuable.* A differentiation strategy must provide unique bundles of products and/or services that customers value highly. It's not enough just to be "different." An example is Gibson's Dobro bass guitar. Gibson came up with a unique idea: Design and build an acoustic bass guitar with sufficient sound volume so that amplification wasn't necessary. The problem with other acoustic bass guitars was that they did not project enough volume because of the low-frequency bass notes. By adding a resonator plate on the body of the traditional acoustic bass, Gibson increased the sound volume. Gibson believed this product would serve a particular niche market—bluegrass and folk artists who played in small group "jams" with other acoustic musicians. Unfortunately, Gibson soon discovered that its targeted market was content with their existing options: an upright bass amplified with a microphone or an acoustic electric guitar. Thus, Gibson developed a unique product, but it was not perceived as valuable by its potential customers.[27]

- *Too much differentiation.* Firms may strive for quality or service that is higher than customers desire. Thus, they are vulnerable to competitors who provide an appropriate level of quality at a lower price. For example, consider the expensive Mercedes-Benz S-Class, which ranges in price between $75,000 and $125,000.[28] *Consumer Reports* recently described it as "sumptuous," "quiet and luxurious," and a "delight to drive." The magazine also considered it to be the least reliable sedan available in the United States. According to David Champion, who runs their testing program, the problems are electronic. "The engineers have gone a little wild," he says. "They've put every bell and whistle that they think of, and sometimes they don't have the attention to detail to make these systems work." Consider some features of these models: a computer-driven suspension that reduces body roll as the vehicle whips around a corner; cruise control that automatically slows the car down if it gets too close to another car; and seats that are adjustable 14 ways and that are ventilated by a system that uses eight fans to whisk away perspiration. Perhaps it is not too surprising that an executive at Mercedes, Sephan Wolfsried, told a symposium in Germany that he eliminated 600 functions from the Mercedes vehicles, "functions nobody needed and nobody knew how to use." And drivers who responded to the *Consumer Reports'* surveys cited "serious" problems with the vehicle's electrical systems, power equipment and accessories. Through the end of October 2004, sales of the S-Class were down 12 percent from the previous year.

- ***Too high a price premium.*** This pitfall is quite similar to too much differentiation. Customers may desire the product, but they are repelled by the price premium compared to that of competitors. For example, Duracell (a division of Gillette) recently charged too high a price for batteries.[29] The firm tried to sell consumers on its superior quality products, but the mass market wasn't convinced. Why? The price differential was simply too high. At a CVS drugstore just one block from Gillette's headquarters, a four-pack of Energizer AA batteries was on sale at $2.99 compared with a Duracell four-pack at $4.59. Not only did Duracell's market share drop 2 percent in a recent two-year period, but its profits declined over 30 percent. Clearly, the price/performance proposition Duracell offered customers was not being accepted.

- ***Differentiation that is easily imitated.*** As we noted in Chapter 3, resources that are easily imitated cannot lead to sustainable advantages. Similarly, firms may strive for, and even attain, a differentiation strategy that is successful for a time. However, the advantages are eroded through imitation. L.A. Gear, a maker of high-end fashion sneakers and shoes, shows what can happen when a firm creates a product that is easy to imitate.[30] At one time, L.A. Gear enjoyed rapid success. Its revenues increased from $36 million in 1986 to $902 million in 1990. But by the early 1990s, intense competition eroded L.A. Gear's competitive position. Sales dropped to $416 million by 1994, but L.A. Gear failed to cut back its investments.

  Several problems plagued L.A. Gear. First, there was increasing price competition. Given low switching costs, rivals were able to attract L.A. Gear's customers with lower prices. Second, L.A. Gear had specialized assets and inventories that locked the company into its position. Thus, as competition intensified, the firm could not exit the industry without walking away from valuable assets.

- ***Dilution of brand identification through product-line extensions.*** Firms may erode their quality brand image by adding products or services with lower prices and less quality. Although this can increase short-term revenues, it may be detrimental in the long run. Profits don't necessarily follow revenues. Consider the case of Gucci.[31] In the 1980s Gucci was determined to capitalize on its prestigious brand name by launching an aggressive strategy of revenue growth. It added a set of lower-priced canvas goods to its product line. It also pushed goods heavily into department stores and duty-free channels and allowed its name to appear on a host of licensed items such as watches, eyeglasses, and perfumes. In the short term, this strategy worked. Sales soared. However, the strategy carried a high price. Gucci's indiscriminate approach to expanding its products and channels tarnished its sterling brand. Sales of its high-end goods (with higher profit margins) fell, causing profits to decline.

- ***Perceptions of differentiation may vary between buyers and sellers.*** The issue here is that "beauty is in the eye of the beholder." Companies must realize that although they may perceive their products and services as differentiated, their customers may view them as commodities. Indeed, in today's marketplace, many products and services have been reduced to commodities.[32] Thus, a firm could overprice its offerings and lose margins altogether if it has to lower prices to reflect market realities.

Focus

The third generic strategy, focus, is based on the choice of a narrow competitive scope within an industry. A firm following this strategy selects a segment or group of segments and tailors its strategy to serve them. The focuser achieves competitive advantages by dedicating itself to these segments exclusively. The essence of focus is the exploitation of a particular market niche that is different from the rest of the industry. As you might expect, narrow focus itself (like merely "being different" as a differentiator) is simply not sufficient for above-average performance. The focus strategy, as indicated in Exhibit 5.1, has two variants. In a cost focus, a firm strives to create a cost advantage in its target segment. In a differentiation focus, a firm seeks to differentiate in its target market. Both variants of the focus strategy rely on providing better service than broad-based competitors who are trying to serve the focuser's target segment. Cost focus exploits differences in cost behavior in some segments, while differentiation focus exploits the special needs of buyers in other segments.

Let's look at examples of two firms that have successfully implemented focus strategies. Network Appliance (NA) has developed a more cost-effective way to store and distribute computer files.[33] Its larger rival, EMC, makes mainframe-style products priced over $1 million that store files and accommodate Internet traffic. NA makes devices that cost under $200,000 for particular storage jobs such as caching (temporary storage) of Internet content. Focusing on such narrow segments has certainly paid off for NA; it has posted a remarkable 20 straight quarters of revenue growth.

The above example was drawn from the high-technology industry. Our next example, Bessemer Trust, competes in the private banking industry.[34] A differentiation focuser, Bessemer targets families with a minimum of $5 million in assets, who desire both capital preservation and wealth accumulation. In other words, these are not people who want to put all their "eggs in a dot-com basket." Bessemer configures its activities for highly personalized service by assigning one account officer for every 14 families. Meetings are more likely to be held at a client's ranch or yacht than in Bessemer's office. Bessemer offers a wide range of customized services, such as investment management, estate administration, oversight of oil and gas investments, and accounting for race horses and aircraft. Despite the industry's most generous compensation of account officers and the highest personnel cost as a percentage of operating expenses, Bessemer's focused differentiation strategy is estimated to yield the highest return on equity in the industry.

Strategy Spotlight 5.4 provides an example of a well-known company that has a successful differentiation focus strategy—Porsche. Here's a firm that thrives by making products nobody needs but everyone seems to want!

Focus: Improving Competitive Position vis-à-vis the Five Forces   As we have seen, firms pursuing a focus strategy can earn above-average returns. Focus requires that a firm either have a low-cost position with its strategic target, high differentiation, or both. As we discussed with regard to cost and differentiation strategies, these positions provide defenses against each competitive force. Focus is also used to select niches that are least vulnerable to substitutes or where competitors are weakest.

Let's look at our examples to illustrate some of these points. First, Bessemer Trust and Porsche experienced less rivalry and lower buyer bargaining power by providing products and services to a targeted market segment that was less price-sensitive. New rivals would have difficulty attracting customers away from these firms based only on lower prices. Similarly, the brand image and quality that these brands evoked heightened the entry barriers for rivals trying to gain market share. Additionally, we could reasonably speculate that these two firms enjoyed some protection against substitute products and services because of their

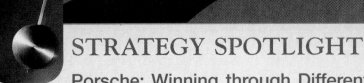

Porsche: Winning through Differentiation Focus

After nearly filing for bankruptcy in the 1990s, Porsche has emerged as a company in a class by itself. It embodies the essence of a differentiation focus strategy. Porsche has one manufacturing plant in Stuttgart, Germany, and the entire company employs only 8,200 employees—fewer than just two or three Detroit automobile factories. And the worst thing (or best?) is that no one *needs* a Porsche.

What's their secret? The answer lies in Porsche's very specific market niche. In fact, their Cayenne, a new sport utility vehicle that was introduced in late 2002, is a "very expensive toy that caters to the person who wants everything," according to Ron Pinelli, an analyst with Autodata Corporation in Woodcliff Lake, New Jersey. Target marketing to a focal segment is Porsche's key to success. Current sales of 40,000 cars a year pales in comparison to the Big Three automakers. To illustrate, General Motors

stopped making the Pontiac Fiero when sales fell below 40,000. By contrast, Porsche's sales of 40,000 units give it enough room to profitably restructure its operations and pull itself out of potential bankruptcy without merging or being acquired by a larger firm. With a break-even point of only 12,000 to 14,000 unit sales, Porsche certainly has a comfortable cushion. Further, with growth in its traditional products and the success of its Cayenne, it will increase annual sales to about 80,000 units.

Their differentiation focus strategy has successfully positioned the company as a producer of highly sought-after luxury sports cars. As noted by CEO Wendelin Wiedekig, "Porsche wants to grow and we want to have exclusive products. That means we will keep following the niche strategy." A recent research report from Deutsche Bank states, "It is the design, the technology, and the brand that make a Porsche stand out." If you can't afford to buy a Porsche, but still want to enjoy the experience, take heart: You can rent a Porsche 996 for a day for *only* $749 at the Driven Image agency in Las Vegas, Nevada.

Sources: Taylor, III, A. "Porsche's Risky Recipe," *Fortune,* February 17, 2003, pp. 90–94; Curry, A. "Dude, Where's My Porsche," *U.S. News & World Report,* November 25, 2002, p. D8; Suhr, J. 2001, "Porsche Has High Hopes for SUV in '02," *Lexington* (KY) *Herald-Leader,* February 2001, p. B10; and Healey, J. "Groomed so as Not to Marry," *USA Today,* August 6, 1999, pp. B1–B2.

relatively high reputation, brand image, and customer loyalty. With regard to the strategy of cost focus, Network Appliances, the successful rival to EMC in the computer storage industry, was better able to absorb pricing increases from suppliers as a result of its lower cost structure. Thus, the effects of supplier power were lessened.

Potential Pitfalls of Focus Strategies   Along with the benefits, managers must be aware of the pitfalls of a focus strategy.

- ***Erosion of cost advantages within the narrow segment.*** The advantages of a cost focus strategy may be fleeting if the cost advantages are eroded over time. For example, Dell's pioneering direct selling model in the personal computer industry, while still the industry standard, is constantly being challenged by competitors as other computer makers gain experience with Dell's distribution method. Similarly, other firms have seen their profit margins drop as competitors enter their product segment.

- ***Even product and service offerings that are highly focused are subject to competition from new entrants and from imitation.*** Some firms adopting a focus strategy may enjoy temporary advantages because they select a small niche with few rivals. However, their advantages may be short-lived as rivals invade their market niche. A notable example is the multitude of dot-com firms that specialize in very narrow segments such as pet supplies, ethnic foods, and vintage automobile accessories. The entry barriers tend to be low, there is little buyer loyalty, and competition becomes intense. And since the marketing strategies and technologies employed by most rivals are largely nonproprietary, imitation is easy. Over time, revenues fall, profits margins are squeezed, and only the strongest players survive the shakeout.

- *Focusers can become too focused to satisfy buyer needs.* Some firms attempting to attain competitive advantages through a focus strategy may have too narrow a product or service. Examples include many retail firms. Hardware chains such as Ace and True Value are losing market share to rivals such as Lowe's and Home Depot who offer a full line of home and garden equipment and accessories. Similarly, many specialty ethnic and gourmet food stores may see their sales and profits shrink as large, national grocers such as Kroger's expand their already broad product lines to include such items. And given the enormous purchasing power of the national chains, it would be difficult for such specialty retailers to attain parity on costs.

Combination Strategies: Integrating Overall Low Cost and Differentiation

There has been ample evidence—in the popular press and in research studies—about the strategic benefits of combining generic strategies. In the beginning of this section, we provided some evidence from nearly 1,800 strategic business units (see Exhibit 5.2) to support this contention. As you will recall, the highest performers were businesses that attained both cost and differentiation advantages, followed by those that had either one or the other. Those strategic business units that had the lowest performance identified with neither generic strategy; that is, they were "stuck in the middle." Results from other studies are consistent with these findings across a wide variety of industries including low-profit industries, the paints and allied products industry, the Korean electronics industry, the apparel industry, and the screw machine products industry.[35]

Perhaps the primary benefit to be enjoyed by firms that successfully integrate low-cost and differentiation strategies is that it is generally harder for competitors to duplicate or imitate. An integrated strategy enables a firm to provide two types of value to customers: differentiated attributes (e.g., high quality, brand identification, reputation) and lower prices (because of the firm's lower costs in value-creating activities). The goal becomes one of providing unique value to customers in an efficient manner.[36] Some firms are able to attain both types of advantages simultaneously. For example, superior quality can lead to lower costs because of less need for rework in manufacturing, fewer warranty claims, a reduced need for customer service personnel to resolve customer complaints, and so forth. Thus, the benefits of combining advantages can be additive, instead of merely involving trade-offs. Next, we consider three approaches to combining overall low-cost and differentiation competitive strategies.

Automated and Flexible Manufacturing Systems   Given the advances in manufacturing technologies such as CAD/CAM (computer aided design and computer aided manufacturing) as well as information technologies, many firms have been able to manufacture unique products in relatively small quantities at lower costs—a concept known as "mass customization."[37]

Let's consider the case of Andersen Windows of Bayport, Minnesota—a $1 billion manufacturer of windows for the building industry.[38] Until about 15 years ago, Andersen was a mass producer, in small batches, of a variety of standard windows. However, to meet changing customer needs, Andersen kept adding to its product line. The result was catalogs of ever-increasing size and a bewildering set of choices for both homeowners and contractors. Over a 6-year period, the number of products tripled, price quotes took several hours, and the error rate increased. This not only damaged the company's reputation, but also added to its manufacturing expenses.

To bring about a major change, Andersen developed an interactive computer version of its paper catalogs that it sold to distributors and retailers. Salespersons can now customize each window to meet the customer's needs, check the design for structural soundness, and provide a price quote. The system is virtually error free, customers get exactly what they want, and the time to develop the design and furnish a quotation has been cut by 75 percent. Each showroom computer is connected to the factory, and customers are assigned a code number that permits them to track the order. The manufacturing system has been developed to use some common finished parts (e.g., mullions, the vertical or horizontal strips separating window panes and sashes), but it also allows considerable variation in the final products. Despite its huge investment in time and money, Andersen has found that the new system has lowered costs, enhanced quality and variety, and improved its response time to customers.

Exploiting the Profit Pool Concept for Competitive Advantage   A profit pool can be defined as the total profits in an industry at all points along the industry's value chain.[39] Although the concept is relatively straightforward, the structure of the profit pool can be complex. The potential pool of profits will be deeper in some segments of the value chain than in others, and the depths will vary within an individual segment. Segment profitability may vary widely by customer group, product category, geographic market, or distribution channel. Additionally, the pattern of profit concentration in an industry is very often different from the pattern of revenue generation.

Consider the automobile industry profit pool in Exhibit 5.6. Here we see little relationship between the generation of revenues and capturing of profits. While manufacturing generates most of the revenue, this value activity is far smaller profitwise than other

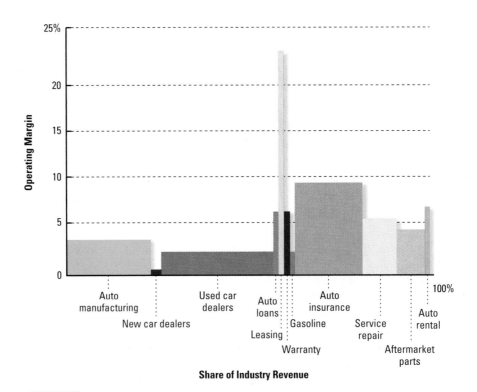

Exhibit 5.6   **The U.S. Automobile Industry's Profit Pool**

Source: Adapted and reprinted by permission of Harvard Business Review, Exhibit from "Profit Pools: A Fresh Look at Strategy," by O. Gadiesh and J. L. Gilbert, May–June 1998. Copyright © 1998 by the Harvard Business School Publishing Corporation; all rights reserved.

value activities such as financing and extended warranty operations. So while a car man-ufacturer may be under tremendous pressure to produce cars efficiently, much of the profit (at least proportionately) can be captured in the aforementioned downstream oper-ations. Thus, a carmaker would be ill-advised to focus solely on manufacturing and leave downstream operations to others through outsourcing.

The profit pool concept helps explain U-Haul's success in the truck rental business. Its 10 percent operating margin is far superior to the industry average of less than 3 per-cent. U-Haul's largest competitor, Ryder, even abandoned the consumer rental business and sold off its fleet in 1996.

What is the key to U-Haul's outstanding performance? Unlike its competitors, U-Haul looked past its core truck rental business and found an untapped source of profit. That source was the accessories business—the sale of boxes and insurance, rentals of trailers and storage space—all the ancillary products and services customers need to complete the moving job that begins when they rent the truck. Profit margins for moving-truck rentals are small; customers shop for the lowest daily rate. But accessories are a different story. With virtually no competition in this part of the value chain, the accessories business enjoys attractive margins. And once a customer signs a rental agreement for a truck, his or her comparison shopping ends. Although the accessory business requires a greater variety of offerings, customers are largely "a captive market" and are, therefore, less price-sensitive. Thus, U-Haul's strategy became one of tightly managing its costs and prices to consumers in the low-profit truck rental part of the business. This enabled them to attract more customers to whom they sold high-margin accessories.

Coordinating the "Extended" Value Chain by Way of Information Technology   Many firms have achieved success by integrating activities throughout the "extended value chain" by using information technology to link their own value chain with the value chains of their customers and suppliers. As noted in Chapter 3, this approach enables a firm to add value not only through its own value-creating activities, but also for its customers and suppliers.

Such a strategy often necessitates redefining the industry's value chain. A number of years ago, Wal-Mart took a close look at its industry's value chain and decided to reframe the competitive challenge.[40] Although its competitors were primarily focused on retailing—merchandising and promotion—Wal-Mart determined that it was not so much in the retailing industry as in the transportation logistics and communications industries. Here, linkages in the extended value chain became central. That became Wal-Mart's chosen battleground. By redefining the rules of competition that played to its strengths, Wal-Mart has attained competitive advantages and dominates its industry.

Strategy Spotlight 5.5 provides some details of how Wal-Mart was able to combine differentiation and overall cost leadership to become the dominant retailer in the world. We also discuss why the company's strategy is highly sustainable; competitors would have a very difficult time imitating it or finding substitutes.

Integrated Overall Low-Cost and Differentiation Strategies: Improving Competitive Position vis-à-vis the Five Forces   Firms that successfully integrate both differentiation and cost advantages create an enviable position relative to industry forces. For example, Wal-Mart's integration of information systems, logistics, and transportation helps it to drive down costs and provide outstanding product selec-tion. This dominant competitive position, along with its excellent reputation, serves to erect high entry barriers to potential competitors that have neither the financial nor phys-ical resources to compete head-to-head. Wal-Mart's size—$288 billion in 2004 sales—provides the chain with enormous bargaining power over suppliers. Its low pricing and

STRATEGY SPOTLIGHT

How Wal-Mart Combines Advantages

One of the most successful retailers of all time, Wal-Mart has trounced its competitors by combining competitive advantages. With net income of $10 billion from total revenues of $288 billion in 2004, Wal-Mart continued to post very impressive performance numbers. During the three-year period from 2001 to 2004, it experienced annual growth rates in revenues and net income of 10 percent and 16 percent, respectively. Wal-Mart has broadened its product offerings in recent years and now offers a diverse product line, including groceries, deli items, pharmaceuticals, and fast food. It has expanded internationally by exporting its data systems and models of efficiency to international markets, including Canada, Mexico, China, Indonesia, the United Kingdom, and Brazil.

Much of Wal-Mart's success can be attributed to its strategic focus, emphasis on key value-chain activities, and combination of competitive advantages. The value chains of merchandise retailers such as Kmart and Target have been much like that of grocery retailers. These value chains focused on cost control, efficiency in distribution and purchasing, and low-overhead facilities. Rivalry in this sector has centered on store location, pricing, and promotion.

Over the past decade, Wal-Mart has left its competitors behind by differentiating itself. In addition to the diverse product lines previously mentioned, Wal-Mart has distinguished itself from competitors by offering optical shops and photofinishing. By moving into such nontraditional areas, Wal-Mart challenges competitors in industries other than traditional discount retailers. Grocery chains, optical shops, fast-food restaurants, photofinishing stores, and pharmacies must now be concerned with the impact on market share each time Wal-Mart opens a new store in their town.

What is Wal-Mart's secret? We'll look at how Wal-Mart competes successfully on multiple forms of competitive advantage. A central feature of Wal-Mart's strategy is the logistics technique of cross-docking. Goods are continuously delivered to the company's warehouses, where they are selected, repacked, and then distributed to stores, often without being placed in inventory. Instead of wasting valuable time in warehouses, merchandise moves across one loading dock to another in 48 hours or less. This lets Wal-Mart achieve economies associated with full-truckload purchasing while avoiding the usual inventory and handling costs. Impressively, this reduces Wal-Mart's cost of sales by 2 to 3 percent compared to its competitors.

The benefits to Wal-Mart and its customers multiply. Lower costs help make possible the retailer's everyday low prices. This, in turn, saves money with less frequent promotions. Stable prices lead to more predictable sales, thus reducing stockouts and excess inventory. Fewer stockouts increase customer loyalty, while inventory control allows quick response to changing customer preferences. Everyday low prices bring in more customer traffic, which translates into more sales.

These economies allow Wal-Mart to staff stores with greeters and additional checkout clerks and to reward employees with stock ownership through a profit-sharing plan. Loyal, dedicated employees and enhanced customer service are elements of differentiation that translate into more customer loyalty and increased sales.

Despite the value of cross-docking, it's not easily copied by competitors. If it were, Wal-Mart's advantage would have long since vanished. The key is that cross-docking is complicated to manage. Wal-Mart made strategic investments in a variety of interlocking support systems that are difficult to imitate. The systems involve:

- Continuous contact between Wal-Mart's distribution centers, suppliers, and every point of sale in each store, so that orders can be executed within hours.

- Fast, responsive transportation, including 19 distribution centers serviced by nearly 2,000 company-owned trucks.

- Fundamental changes in managerial control that allow the stores to pull products when and where they need them rather than having suppliers push products into the system. With less centralized control, a premium is placed on frequent, informed cooperation between stores, distribution centers, and suppliers.

- Information systems that provide store managers with detailed information about customer behavior and a fleet of airplanes that regularly ferry store managers to Wal-Mart's Bentonville, Arkansas, headquarters for training on market trends and merchandising.

- A video link connecting each store.

- Profit sharing for employees, to encourage high customer responsiveness.

The cross-docking logistics strategy and sophisticated information systems reduce costs in a number of ways. By reducing inventories and shortening procurement cycle times, Wal-Mart can increase its flexibility and responsiveness to changing customer preferences. Wal-Mart has understood the business as a process and expanded its boundaries to include customers and *(continued)*

Sources: Kitchen, S. 2005. Wal-Mart's world. *Forbes,* May 9: 40; Useem, J. 2003. One nation under Wal-Mart. *Fortune,* March 3: 65–78; Dess, G. G., & Picken, J. C. 1999. Creating competitive (dis)advantage: Learning from Food Lion's freefall. *Academy of Management Executive,* 13(3): 97–111; Berner, R. 2001. Too many retailers, not enough shoppers. *Business Week,* February 12: 36–42.

wide selection reduce the power of buyers (its customers), because there are relatively few competitors that can provide a comparable cost/value proposition. This reduces the possibility of intense head-to-head rivalry, such as protracted price wars. Finally, Wal-Mart's overall value proposition makes potential substitute products (e.g., Internet competitors) a less viable threat.

Pitfalls of Integrated Overall Cost Leadership and Differentiation Strategies Firms that attain both types of competitive advantage enjoy high returns. However, as with each generic strategy taken individually, there are some pitfalls to avoid.

- *Firms that fail to attain both strategies may end up with neither and become "stuck in the middle."* A key issue in strategic management is the creation of competitive advantages that enable a firm to enjoy above-average returns. Some firms may become "stuck in the middle" if they try to attain both cost and differentiation advantages. J. C. Penney Co., for example, has become, in the words of a *BusinessWeek* writer, "trapped in no-man's land . . . its fashions are tired, its prices unreasonable . . . and [it has] lost . . . cachet with customers."[41] Why? Penney's tried to achieve differentiation and cost control at the same time, but succeeded in neither. It struggled to fend off discounters such as Wal-Mart and Target on one front, and upscale department stores such as Macy's on the other. Not surprisingly, Penney's stock dropped about 80 percent between 1998 and 2000. As you might expect, the key elements of J. C. Penney's CEO Allen Questrom's turnaround plan include elements of both differentiation and cost control:
  - Improve store presentations.
  - Radically rethink merchandise.
  - Market the company brand more effectively.
  - Slash costs, including closing 44 stores and cutting 5,000 jobs.
  - Overhaul management ranks, including more outside recruitment.

- *Underestimating the challenges and expenses associated with coordinating value-creating activities in the extended value chain.* Successfully integrating activities across a firm's value chain with the value chain of suppliers and customers involves a significant investment in financial and human resources. Managers must not underestimate the expenses linked to technology investment, managerial time and commitment, and the involvement and investment required by the firm's customers and suppliers. The firm must be confident that it can generate a sufficient scale of operations and revenues to justify all associated expenses.

- *Miscalculating sources of revenue and profit pools in the firm's industry.* Firms may fail to accurately assess sources of revenue and profits in their value chain. This can occur for several reasons. For example, a manager may be biased due to his or her functional area background, work experiences, and educational background. If the manager's background is in engineering, he or she might perceive that proportionately greater revenue and margins were being created in manufacturing, product, and process design than a person whose background is in a "downstream" value-chain activity such as marketing and sales. Or politics could make managers "fudge" the numbers to put their area of operations in a more favorable light. This would make them responsible for a greater proportion of the firm's profits, thus improving their bargaining position for their share of the firm's internal resources.

A related problem is directing an overwhelming amount of managerial time, attention, and resources to value-creating activities that produce the greatest margins—to the detriment of other important, albeit less profitable, activities. For example, an automobile manufacturer may focus too much on downstream activities, such as warranty fulfillment and financing operations, to the detriment of differentiation and cost of the automobiles themselves. Or, as described earlier in the case of the truck rental industry, management might let the quality of rental trucks deteriorate while directing attention to the more profitable accessory side of the business.

>>Industry Life Cycle Stages: Strategic Implications

The life cycle of an industry refers to the stages of introduction, growth, maturity, and decline that occur over the life of an industry. In considering the industry life cycle, it is useful to think in terms of broad product lines such as personal computers, photocopiers, or long-distance telephone service. Yet the industry life cycle concept can be explored from several levels, from the life cycle of an entire industry to the life cycle of a single variation or model of a specific product or service.

Why is it important to consider industry life cycles?[42] The emphasis on various generic strategies, functional areas, value-creating activities, and overall objectives varies over the course of an industry life cycle. Managers must become even more aware of their firm's strengths and weaknesses in many areas to attain competitive advantages. For example, firms depend on their research and development (R&D) activities in the introductory stage of the life cycle. R&D is the source of new products and features that everyone hopes will appeal to customers. Firms develop products and services to stimulate consumer demand. Later, during the maturity phase, the functions of the product have been defined, more competitors have entered the market, and competition is intense. Managers then place greater emphasis on production efficiencies and process (as opposed to the product) engineering in order to lower manufacturing costs. This helps to protect the firm's market position and to extend the product life cycle because the firm's lower costs can be passed on to consumers in the form of lower prices, and price-sensitive customers will find the product more appealing.

Exhibit 5.7 illustrates the four stages of the industry life cycle and how factors such as generic strategies, market growth rate, intensity of competition, and overall objectives change over time. As we noted earlier, managers must strive to emphasize the key functional areas during each of the four stages and to attain a level of parity in all functional areas and value-creating activities. For example, even though controlling production costs may be a primary concern during the maturity stage, managers should not totally ignore other functions such as marketing and R&D. If they do, they can become so focused on lowering costs that they miss market trends or fail to incorporate important product or process designs. In such cases, the firm may attain low-cost products that have limited market appeal.

It is important to point out a caveat. While the life cycle idea is analogous to a living organism (i.e., birth, growth, maturity, and death), the comparison does have limitations.[43]

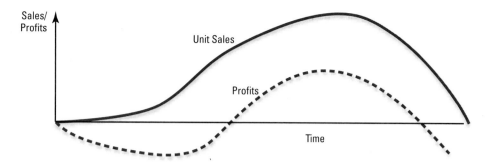

Stage Factor	Introduction	Growth	Maturity	Decline
Generic strategies	Differentiation	Differentiation	Differentiation Overall cost leadership	Overall cost leadership Focus
Market growth rate	Low	Very large	Low to moderate	Negative
Number of segments	Very few	Some	Many	Few
Intensity of competition	Low	Increasing	Very intense	Changing
Emphasis on product design	Very high	High	Low to moderate	Low
Emphasis on process design	Low	Low to moderate	High	Low
Major functional area(s) of concern	Research and development	Sales and marketing	Production	General management and finance
Overall objective	Increase market awareness	Create consumer demand	Defend market share and extend product life cycles	Consolidate, maintain, harvest, or exit

Exhibit 5.7   Stages of the Industry Life Cycle

Products and services go through many cycles of innovation and renewal. For the most part, only fad products have a single life cycle. Maturity stages of an industry can be "transformed" or followed by a stage of rapid growth if consumer tastes change, technological innovations take place, or new developments occur in the general environment. The cereal industry is a good example. When medical research indicated that oat consumption reduced a person's cholesterol, sales of Quaker Oats increased dramatically.[44]

Next we will discuss each stage of the industry life cycle. Then we will summarize how each stage poses important implications for a firm's generic strategies. To do this, we will briefly discuss the evolution of the personal computer industry. Finally, we will discuss turnaround strategies—that is, strategies that are necessary in order to reverse performance erosion and regain competitive position.

Strategies in the Introduction Stage

In the introduction stage, products are unfamiliar to consumers.[45] Market segments are not well defined, and product features are not clearly specified. The early development of an industry typically involves low sales growth, rapid technological change, operating losses, and the need for strong sources of cash to finance operations. Since there are few players and not much growth, competition tends to be limited.

Success in the introduction stage requires an emphasis on research and development and marketing activities to enhance awareness of the product or service. The challenge becomes one of (1) developing the product and finding a way to get users to try it, and (2) generating enough exposure so the product emerges as the "standard" by which all other competitors' products are evaluated.

There's an advantage to being the "first mover" in a market.[46] Consider Coca-Cola's success in becoming the first soft-drink company to build a recognizable global brand. Moving first enabled Caterpillar to get a lock on overseas sales channels and service capabilities. Being a first mover allowed Matsushita to establish Video Home Source (VHS) as the global standard for videocassette recorders.

However, there can also be a benefit to being a "late mover." Target carefully thought out the decision to delay its Internet strategy. Compared to its competitors Wal-Mart and Kmart, Target was definitely the industry laggard. Strategy Spotlight 5.6 explains why its strategy paid off.

Examples of products currently in the introductory stages of the industry life cycle include electric vehicles, digital cameras, and high-definition television (HDTV).

Strategies in the Growth Stage

The second stage of the industry life cycle—growth—is characterized by strong increases in sales. The potential for strong sales (and profits) attracts other competitors who also want to benefit. As products enter the growth stage, the primary key to success is to build consumer preferences for specific brands. This requires strong brand recognition, differentiated products, and the financial resources to support a variety of value-chain activities such as marketing and sales, customer service, and research and development. Whereas marketing and sales initiatives were mainly directed at spurring *aggregate* demand—that is, demand for all such products in the introduction stage—efforts in the growth stage are directed toward stimulating *selective* demand, in which a firm's product offerings are chosen instead of those of its rivals.

Revenues in the growth stage increase at an accelerating rate because (1) new consumers are trying the product and (2) a growing proportion of satisfied consumers are making repeat purchases.[47] In general, as a product moves through its life cycle, the proportion of repeat buyers to new purchasers increases. Conversely, new products and services often fail if there are relatively few repeat purchases. This is especially true with many consumer products that are characterized by relatively low price and frequent purchase. For example, Alberto-Culver introduced Mr. Culver's Sparklers, which were solid air fresheners that looked like stained glass. Although the product quickly went from the introductory to the growth stage, sales then plummeted. Why? Unfortunately, there were few repeat purchasers because buyers treated them as inexpensive window decorations, left them there, and felt little need to purchase new ones. Examples of products currently in the growth stage of the industry life cycle include Internet servers and personal digital assistants (e.g., Palm Pilots).

STRATEGY SPOTLIGHT

Target: An Example of "Late Mover" Advantage

All cutting-edge retailers have Web sites. The first retailer with a Web site gains the largest market share. Only technologically inept stores don't rush to reach customers though the Internet. At least that's the conventional wisdom. Looking back on the success (or lack thereof) gained from these strategies shows that conventional wisdom is sometimes conventional thoughtlessness.

Two of the first movers in Web-based retailing were Kmart and Wal-Mart. While Kmart faltered with Blue-Light.com and Wal-Mart struggled with Walmart.com, Target patiently waited. Electronic retailing, or "e-tailing," was a new area for low-cost retailers. Target's strategy was to learn from the mistakes of the first movers. Target waited until it understood *how* to attract customers with a Web site before it actually tried to attract customers with one. It seems like the conventional wisdom of Kmart and Wal-Mart was just a little too unconventional for Target.

Sources: Stoughton, S. 2000. Target aimed carefully at Web sales, then stepped up and hit the bull's-eye. *Lexington* (KY) *Herald-Leader*, November 20 (Business Monday): 2; Neuborne, E. 2000. E-tailers hit the relaunch key. *Business Week*, October 17: 62.

By waiting, Target gained a "late mover" advantage. The store was able to use competitors' mistakes as its own learning curve. This saved money, and customers didn't seem to mind the wait: When Target finally opened its Web site, it quickly captured market share from both Kmart and Wal-Mart Internet shoppers. Forrester Research Internet analyst Stephen Zrike commented, "There's no question, in our mind, that Target has a far better understanding of how consumers buy online."

"I think the first mover advantage was grossly overrated on the Web," according to Jerry Storch, president of financial services and new business for Target. The conventional wisdom says that the first to market will capture the largest market share. This is often true, but only if the company that is first to market has the ability to do things right. Otherwise, customers become disgruntled; this affects not only the firm's Web store, but also the reputation of its bricks-and-mortar facilities. By waiting until it could do things right, Target now has more Web market share than either of its early mover rivals.

Strategies in the Maturity Stage

In the third stage—maturity—aggregate industry demand begins to slow. Since markets are becoming saturated, there are few opportunities to attract new adopters. It's no longer possible to "grow around" the competition, so direct competition becomes predominant.[48] With few attractive prospects, marginal competitors begin to exit the market. At the same time, rivalry among existing competitors intensifies because there is often fierce price competition at the same time that expenses associated with attracting new buyers are rising. Advantages based on efficient manufacturing operations and process engineering become more important for keeping costs low as customers become more price sensitive. It also becomes more difficult for firms to differentiate their offerings, because users have a greater understanding of products and services.

An article in *Fortune* magazine that addressed the intensity of rivalry in mature markets was aptly titled "A Game of Inches." It stated, "Battling for market share in a slowing industry can be a mighty dirty business. Just ask laundry soap archrivals Unilever and Procter & Gamble."[49] These two firms have been locked in a battle for market share since 1965. Why is the competition so intense? There is not much territory to gain. In 2000, total sales for the industry were flat at $6 billion a year. A Lehman Brothers analyst noted, "People aren't getting any dirtier." Thus, the only way to win is to take market share from the competition. To increase its share, Procter & Gamble (P&G) spends $100 million a year promoting its Tide brand on television, billboards, subways, buses, magazines, and the Internet. But Unilever isn't standing still. Armed with a new $80 million budget, it recently launched a soap tablet product named Wisk Dual Action Tablets. On January 7, 2001, it delivered samples of this product to 24 million U.S. homes in Sunday newspapers, followed by a series of TV ads. P&G launched a counteroffensive with Tide Rapid Action Tablets ads showed in side-by-side comparisons of the two products dropped into beakers of water. In the promotion, P&G claimed that its product is superior because it dissolves faster than Unilever's product. A minor point, but Unilever is challenging P&G in court. And the beat goes on . . . .

Although this is only one example, many product classes and industries, including consumer products such as beer, automobiles, and televisions, are in the maturity stage.

Strategies in the Decline Stage

Although all decisions in the phases of an industry life cycle are important, they become particularly difficult in the decline stage. Hard choices must be made, and firms must face up to the fundamental strategic choices of either exiting or staying and attempting to consolidate their position in the industry.[50]

The decline stage occurs when industry sales and profits begin to fall. Typically, changes in the business environment are at the root of an industry or product group entering this stage.[51] Changes in consumer tastes or a technological innovation can push a product into decline. Typewriters have entered into the decline stage because of the word processing capabilities of personal computers. Compact disks have forced cassette tapes into decline in the prerecorded music industry, and digital video disks (DVDs) may soon replace compact disks. About 20 years earlier, of course, cassette tapes had led to the demise of long-playing records (LPs).

When a product enters the decline stage, it often consumes a large share of management time and financial resources relative to its potential worth. Not only are sales and profits declining, but also competitors may start drastically cutting their prices to raise cash and remain solvent in the short term. The situation is further aggravated by the wholesale liquidation of assets, including inventory, of some of the competitors that have failed. This further intensifies price competition.

In the decline stage, a firm's strategic options become dependent on the actions of rivals. If many competitors decide to leave the market, sales and profit opportunities increase. On the other hand, prospects are limited if all competitors remain.[52] If some competitors merge, their increased market power may erode the opportunities for the remaining players. Managers must carefully monitor the actions and intentions of competitors before deciding on a course of action.

Four basic strategies are available in the decline phase: *maintaining, harvesting, exiting,* or *consolidating.*[53]

- *Maintaining* refers to keeping a product going without significantly reducing marketing support, technological development, or other investments, in the hope that competitors will eventually exit the market. Many offices, for example, still use typewriters for filling out forms and other purposes that cannot be completed on a personal computer. In some rural areas, rotary (or dial) telephones persist because of the older technology used in central switching offices. Thus, if a firm remains in the business and others exit, there may still be the potential for revenues and profits.

- *Harvesting* involves obtaining as much profit as possible and requires that costs in the decline stage be reduced quickly. Managers should consider the firm's value-creating activities and cut associated budgets. Value-chain activities to consider are primary (e.g., operations, sales and marketing) and support (e.g., procurement, information systems, technology development). The objective is to wring out as much profit as possible.

- *Exiting the market* involves dropping the product from a firm's portfolio. Since a residual core of consumers may still use the product, eliminating it should be considered carefully. If the firm's exit involves product markets that affect important relationships with other product markets in the corporation's overall portfolio, an exit could have repercussions for the whole corporation. For example, it may involve the loss of valuable brand names or human capital with a broad variety of expertise in many value-creating activities such as marketing, technology, and operations.

- *Consolidation* involves one firm acquiring at a reasonable price the best of the surviving firms in an industry. This enables firms to enhance market power and acquire valuable assets. One example of a consolidation strategy took place in the defense industry in the early 1990s. As the cliché suggests, "peace broke out" at the end of the Cold War and overall U.S. defense spending levels plummeted.[54] Many companies that make up the defense industry saw more than 50 percent of their market disappear. Only one-quarter of the 120,000 companies that once supplied the Department of Defense still serve in that capacity; the others have shut down their defense business or dissolved altogether. But one key player, Lockheed Martin, became a dominant rival by pursuing an aggressive strategy of consolidation. During the 1990s, it purchased 17 independent entities, including General Dynamics's tactical aircraft and space systems divisions, GE Aerospace, Goodyear Aerospace, and Honeywell ElectroOptics. These combinations enabled Lockheed Martin to emerge as the top provider to three governmental customers: the Department of Defense, the Department of Energy, and NASA. Despite several downsizing initiatives, the firm was ranked for the first time in the Fortune 25 (the largest 25 industrial concerns in the United States). Clearly, the prospects for industry prosperity have increased in the aftermath of the September 11, 2001, terrorist attacks, the wars in Iraq and Afghanistan, and the "War on Terror."

Examples of products currently in the decline stage of the industry life cycle include automotive spark plugs (replaced by electronic fuel ignition), videocassette recorders (replaced by digital video disk recorders), and personal computer zip drives (replaced by compact disk read-write drives). As we mentioned previously, compact disks may soon be replaced by digital video disks (DVDs).

Relating Generic Strategies to Stages of the Industry Life Cycle: The Personal Computer Industry

The personal computer (PC) industry provides an example of how a firm's generic strategies can vary over stages of the industry life cycle. In the introduction and growth stages, there were many players, such as IBM, Compaq, and others, who endeavored to create brand recognition and build loyal followings for their entries. To do so required well-developed and executed differentiation strategies. Apple was further differentiated because it was the only player to have a graphical user interface (GUI). However, well within a decade, the market matured, particularly when the "Wintel" standard (Microsoft's Windows operating system and Intel's microprocessor units) was widely adopted. This, in effect, eroded Apple's unique feature. Price competition then quickly intensified. Why? Consumer awareness and sophistication with personal computers quickly accelerated and the market became saturated with similar products. Here, overall low-cost strategies became the dominant form of competition. However, some firms, such as Dell Computer, were still able to make differentiation a key part of their business-level strategy by offering superior service and rapid fulfillment of customer orders. It now appears that many Web appliances, such as Oracle TalkBack and Intel's Dot.Station (each priced at approximately $200), may become viable substitute products. These products provide many features similar to those of personal computers—Internet access, e-mail delivery, and personal calendars. Thus, demand for these products may drive the personal computer industry into the decline stage by significantly lowering aggregate consumer demand. If, faced with the decline stage, the personal computer companies have to intensify their cost-reduction initiatives and develop focus strategies to seek out niches in the market, that may prove more viable than exiting the industry altogether.

Turnaround Strategies

One problem with the life cycle analogy is that we tend to think that decline is inevitably followed by death. In the case of businesses, however, decline can be reversed by strategies that lead to turnaround and rejuvenation. Such a need for turnaround may occur at any stage in the life cycle. However, it is more likely to occur during the maturity or decline stage.

Most turnarounds require a firm to carefully analyze the external and internal environments. The external analysis leads to identification of market segments or customer groups that may still find the product attractive. Internal analysis results in actions aimed at reduced costs and higher efficiency. Typically, a firm needs to undertake a mix of both internally and externally oriented actions to effect a turnaround.[55]

A study of 260 mature businesses in need of a turnaround identified three strategies used by successful companies.[56]

- **Asset and cost surgery.** Very often, mature firms tend to have assets that do not produce any returns. These include real estate, buildings, etc. Outright sales or sale and leaseback free up considerable cash and improve returns. Investment in new plants and equipment can be deferred. Firms in turnaround situations try to aggressively cut administrative expenses and inventories and speed up collection of receivables. Costs also can be reduced by outsourcing production of various inputs for which market prices may be cheaper than in-house production costs.

- **Selective product and market pruning.** Most mature or declining firms have many product lines that are losing money or are only marginally profitable. One strategy is to discontinue these product lines and focus all resources on a few core profitable areas. For example, in the early 1980s, faced with possible bankruptcy, Chrysler Corporation sold off all their nonautomotive businesses as well as all their production facilities abroad. Focus on the North American market and identification of a profitable niche—namely, minivans—were keys to their eventual successful turnaround.

- **Piecemeal productivity improvements.** There are hundreds of ways in which a firm can eliminate costs and improve productivity. Although individually these are small gains, they cumulate over a period of time to substantial gains. Improving business processes by reengineering them, benchmarking specific activities against industry leaders, encouraging employee input to identify excess costs, reducing R&D and marketing expenses, increasing capacity utilization, and improving employee productivity lead to a significant overall gain.

The turnaround of software maker Intuit is an interesting case of a quick but well-implemented turnaround strategy. After stagnating and stumbling during the dot-com boom, Intuit, which is known for its Quickbook and Turbotax software, hired Stephen M. Bennett, a 22-year GE veteran, in 1999. He immediately discontinued Intuit's online finance, insurance, and bill-paying operations that were losing money. Instead, he focused on software for small businesses that employ less than 250 people. He also instituted a performance-based reward system that greatly improved employee productivity. Within a few years, Intuit was once again making substantial profits and its stock was up 42 percent.[57]

Even when an industry is in overall decline, pockets of profitability remain. These are segments with customers who are relatively price insensitive. For example, the replacement demand for vacuum tubes affords its manufacturers an opportunity to earn above normal returns although the product itself is technologically obsolete. Surprisingly, within

Mitchell Caplan's Successful Turnaround at E*Trade

Mitchell Caplan is an optimist. He was confident that E*Trade Financial Corporation would survive and prosper. However, such optimism seemed to be misplaced given the fact that the shares of the online broker and bank had plunged from $60 at the peak of the Internet frenzy to a low of $3 in 2002. In 2001 and 2002, the firm lost a total of $428 million.

Fortunately for E*Trade (and their shareholders), Mr. Caplan was elevated to the CEO position in 2003, and he initiated what became a very successful turnaround. Let's take a look at how he did it.

First, Caplan had to change the firm's general approach to business. E*Trade had traditionally ignored the red ink as long as the stock price climbed. However, Caplan realized that he had to cut costs and sell off unrelated businesses. This included sharply reducing marketing and advertising expenses. E*Trade no longer splurges on $2 million Super Bowl commercials. In fact, one year, the company spent $500 million on marketing—more than the entire U. S. liquor industry! Now it only spends about $140 million a year. There are also fewer employees— down to about 4,000 now from a peak of 5,000. He also sold off businesses and assets that were unrelated to E*Trade's core. This included a national ATM network, kiosks in Target stores, a palatial New York retail branch that sold E*Trade souvenirs, and a TV business-news service. In addition, new ventures, such as a string of

small storefront offices in major cities, are now rigorously analyzed for profitability. Notes Caplan, "I am adamant— and as a team we are adamant—about financial returns."

Mitch Caplan also felt that he needed to change the organization's culture and instill more discipline. He moved the headquarters from Menlo Park, California, to New York City. In effect, he left behind the propeller beanies, rubber chickens, and geeky props that made the firm's atmosphere rather loose. In its place are jackets and ties.

In addition to cutting costs and changing the culture, Caplan also focused E*Trade on leveraging its core banking operations. Here, it had a clear edge over rivals Charles Schwab Corp. and Ameritrade Inc. By offering banking products such as checking accounts and loans at reduced rates to customers who had brokerage accounts, E*Trade has built the nation's eighth-largest thrift. It also has become a big profit center, accounting for 40 percent of all revenues and 48 percent of profits. Now the company has about 632,000 bank accounts and 2.9 million active brokerage accounts—up from 170,00 bank accounts and 2.4 million brokerage accounts in early 2000.

By focusing on its core business, E*Trade's revenues were only $1.6 billion for the year 2004, which is less than the roughly $2 billion for the years 2003, 2002, 2001. However, profits have soared to $389 million in 2004 compared to an average *loss* of about $75 million for the three previous years. And E*Trade was recently recognized by *Information-Week* as one of the 40 top firms in the financial services industry for delivering IT solutions to solve business problems.

Source: Weber, J. 2005. E*Trade rises from the ashes. *BusinessWeek*, January 17: 58–59; and Schmerken, I. 2004. Innovation in motion. *Wall Street & Technology*, October: 22–26.

declining industries, there may still be segments that are either stable or growing. Cigars and chewing tobacco are examples of profitable segments within the tobacco industry. Although fountain pens ceased to be the writing instrument of choice a long time ago, the fountain pen industry has successfully reconceptualized the product as a high margin luxury item that signals accomplishment, success, and appreciation of the finer things in life. In the final analysis, every business has the potential for rejuvenation. But it takes creativity, persistence, and most of all a clear strategy to translate that potential into reality.

Strategy Spotlight 5.7 summarizes how Mitchell Caplan conducted a successful turnaround at E*Trade. He was able to effectively cut costs and sell off unrelated businesses, change the firm's general approach to business and its culture, and leverage its core banking operations.

Innovation and the Sustainability of Competitive Advantage

Our discussion of competitive advantages and industry life cycle so far has two major limitations. First, it may appear as if once a firm establishes a competitive advantage, all it has to do is to keep investing more resources to sustain that advantage. Second, the industry life cycle seems to suggest that every industry goes through a sequence of gradual and predictable stages. In recent years, at least in some industries, evidence shows that both these assumptions may be far from valid. Rapid technological changes and resulting innovations in products and services have unleashed a "gale of creative destruction"—a concept introduced by famed economist Joseph Schumpeter that has made competitive advantages fleeting and the life cycle of industries far from the predictable sequence of gradual changes that the life cycle analogy suggests.

As we mentioned already, innovation lies at the root of short-lived competitive advantages and abrupt ends to industry life cycles before they have progressed through all the stages. Innovations generally can be divided into two categories: *sustaining innovations* and *disruptive innovations*.[58] Innovations that help incumbents in an industry earn higher margins by selling better products to their best customers are called *sustaining innovations*. Even when incumbents are not the first to innovate, in most cases they end up winning because of their resource advantages and their ties to the existing customers. *Disruptive innovations,* on the other hand, appeal to customers whom the current incumbents are not seeking because they are not considered attractive enough to the existing players in the industry. Unfortunately for incumbents, these customer segments that were once considered unattractive have a way of becoming attractive growth markets subsequently.

Compaq's adoption of Intel's 32-bit 386 microprocessor, Merrill Lynch's introduction of the Cash Management Account (which allowed customers to write checks against their equity holdings), and the recent adoption of online banking by most major banks are examples of sustaining innovations. Each of these innovations enabled the firm to serve an existing customer segment better than before, often realizing better margins in the process as well. On the other hand, Apple's introduction of PCs, Charles Schwab's early entry into discount brokerage services, and the entry of airlines such as EasyJet and RyanAir into the European aviation industry represent disruptive innovations. In each of these cases, the innovation didn't address next-generation needs of leading customers in current markets. Instead, they appealed to a class of customers who were previously out of the market. And better still, the disruptive innovations improved at such a rapid pace that they began to pull in the customers of the mainstream markets by addressing their needs as well.

What determines a company's ability to embrace innovations and sustain their competitive advantages? Three organizational factors play a critical role. First, a firm's *resources,* both tangible and intangible, play a big part in determining what a firm can and cannot do. Access to abundant resources may increase a firm's odds of coping with change, but resources by themselves are seldom enough. Second, the internal *processes* within an organization play an even more important role. Internal processes include patterns of interaction, coordination, communication, and decision making. It is these processes that enable managers to transform resources into products and services and add value to them. Processes developed for a specific task and perfected through countless repetitions over several years can seldom meet the demands of a completely different task. Spotlight 5.8 explains how Digital Equipment Corporation failed to embrace the disruptive innovation of PCs because their internal processes were created to produce minicomputers. Finally, a firm's *values* also determine how successfully it can cope with innovations. Values refer to the standards by which managers set priorities. Values help them prioritize factors such as how to allocate scarce organizational resources, which products to develop, and which customers to sell. Again, in the case of Digital, an organizational value was that products with gross margins of less than 40 percent were not worth making or selling. Similarly, one of Toyota's organizational values has been developing cars with higher and higher margins. Together, resources, processes, and values determine whether a firm is able to successfully embrace an innovation.

5.8 STRATEGY SPOTLIGHT

Failure to Cope with Disruptive Innovation: Digital Equipment Corporation

Digital Equipment Corporation was a phenomenally successful maker of minicomputers during the 1960s, 1970s, and 1980s. It would seem that Digital's success should have continued into the age of personal computers. After all, a maker of minicomputers is closer to the PC market than makers of large mainframes. It looked as if Digital had all the resources to succeed in the PC business. They had a trusted brand, great technology, and plenty of cash. Their engineers routinely built minicomputers which were more sophisticated than PCs. Why did Digital fail to take the obvious road to success in the growing PC industry?

First, Digital designed and built most of the key components of minicomputers internally and then integrated those components into proprietary configurations. This process was time consuming, often taking as many as three years to design a new product platform. PC makers, on the other hand, outsourced most components based on cost, quality, and technological currency, thereby keeping the capital investments low while assembling technologically up-to-date products. This also enabled them to bring

new computer designs into the market in 6 to 12 months. Second, Digital assembled minicomputers in batch mode and sold directly to corporate engineering departments. PCs, in contrast, were manufactured in high volume assembly lines and sold to end users through retail channels. Thus, despite having the technological and financial ability to make and market PCs, Digital was handicapped by processes that were designed and perfected for an industry with an altogether different set of performance characteristics.

Digital was also prevented from entering the PC business by their own resource allocation rules. Digital's financial criteria for new product development were based on gross margins. If a product could generate gross margins of 50 percent or more, it was considered a good business. If gross margins were lower than 40 percent, the product would be abandoned. This was a rule that served them well in the high overhead minicomputer business. PCs are high volume, low margin products and thus did not appeal to Digital! They walked away from a high growth business with few established competitors (at that time) just because it did not meet a decision criterion that was set up for a very different business!

Source: Christensen, C. M., & Overdorf, M. 2000. Meeting the challenge of disruptive change. *Harvard Business Review*, March–April: 66–76.

Summary

How and why firms outperform each other goes to the heart of strategic management. In this chapter, we identified three generic strategies and discussed how firms are able not only to attain advantages over competitors, but also to sustain such advantages over time. Why do some advantages become long-lasting while others are quickly imitated by competitors?

The three generic strategies—overall cost leadership, differentiation, and focus—form the core of this chapter. We began by providing a brief description of each generic strategy (or competitive advantage) and furnished examples of firms that have successfully implemented these strategies. Successful generic strategies invariably enhance a firm's position vis-à-vis the five forces of that industry—a point that we stressed and illustrated with examples. However, as we pointed out, there are pitfalls to each of the generic strategies. Thus, the sustainability of a firm's advantage is always challenged because of imitation or substitution by new or existing rivals. Such competitor moves erode a firm's advantage over time.

We also discussed the viability of combining (or integrating) overall cost leadership and generic differentiation strategies. If successful, such integration can enable a firm to enjoy superior performance and improve its competitive position. However, this is challenging, and managers must be aware of the potential downside risks associated with such an initiative.

The concept of the industry life cycle is a critical contingency that managers must take into account in striving to create and sustain competitive advantages. We identified the four stages of the industry life cycle—introduction, growth, maturity, and decline—and suggested how these stages can play a role in decisions that managers must make at the business level. These include overall strategies as well as the relative emphasis on functional areas and value-creating activities.

When a firm's performance severely erodes, turnaround strategies are needed to reverse its situation and enhance its competitive position. We have discussed three approaches—asset cost surgery, selective product and market pruning, and piecemeal productivity improvements. In addition, managers must be aware of disruptive change that can revolutionize an industry. They need to be able to embrace innovations and strive to sustain competitive advantages.

Summary Review Questions

1. Explain why the concept of competitive advantage is central to the study of strategic management.
2. Briefly describe the three generic strategies—overall cost leadership, differentiation, and focus.
3. Explain the relationship between the three generic strategies and the five forces that determine the average profitability within an industry.
4. What are some of the ways in which a firm can attain a successful turnaround strategy?
5. Describe some of the pitfalls associated with each of the three generic strategies.
6. Can firms combine the generic strategies of overall cost leadership and differentiation? Why or why not?
7. Explain why the industry life cycle concept is an important factor in determining a firm's business-level strategy.

Experiential Exercise

What are some examples of primary and support activities that enable Nucor, an $11 billion steel manufacturer, to achieve a low-cost strategy?

Value Chain Activity	Yes/No	How Does Nucor Create Value for the Customer?
Primary:		
Inbound logistics		
Operations		
Outbound logistics		
Marketing and sales		
Service		
Support:		
Procurement		
Technology development		
Human resource management		
General administration		

1. Go to the Internet and look up www.walmart.com. How has this firm been able to combine overall cost leadership and differentiation strategies?

2. Choose a firm with which you are familiar in your local business community. Is the firm successful in following one (or more) generic strategies? Why or why not? What do you think are some of the challenges it faces in implementing these strategies in an effective manner?

3. Think of a firm that has attained a differentiation focus or cost focus strategy. Are their advantages sustainable? Why? Why not? (*Hint:* Consider its position vis-à-vis Porter's five forces.)

4. Think of a firm that successfully achieved a combination overall cost leadership and differentiation strategy. What can be learned from this example? Are these advantages sustainable? Why? Why not? (*Hint:* Consider its competitive position vis-à-vis Porter's five forces.)

1. Can you think of a company (other than the opening case of Sharper Image) that suffered ethical consequences as a result of an overemphasis on a cost leadership strategy? What do you think were the financial and nonfinancial implications?

2. In the introductory stage of the product life cycle, what are some of the unethical practices that managers could engage in to enhance their firm's market position? What could be some of the long-term implications of such actions?

References

1. Armstrong, D. 2004. A mighty wind. *Forbes,* July 5: 62; Lomax, A. 2004. Sharper Image's dull holidays. *Yahoo finance.com,* December 27; Parloff, R. 2004. The Ionic Breeze is no match for Consumer Reports. *Fortune,* December 13: 57–58; Lee, L. 2004. Sharper Image needs . . . a sharper image. *BusinessWeek,* September 20: 45–46; and, Anonymous. 2005. Magazine taking aim at Sharper Image's air purifier. *Dallas Morning News,* April 5: 5D.

2. For a recent perspective by Porter on competitive strategy, refer to Porter, M. E. 1996. What is strategy? *Harvard Business Review,* 74(6): 61–78.

3. Some useful ideas on maintaining competitive advantages can be found in Ma, H., & Karri, R. 2005. Leaders beward: Some sure ways to lose your competitive advantage. *Organizational Dynamics,* 343(1): 63–76.

4. Miller, A., & Dess, G. G. 1993. Assessing Porter's model in terms of its generalizability, accuracy, and simplicity. *Journal of Management Studies,* 30(4): 553–585.

5. For a scholarly discussion and analysis of the concept of competitive parity, refer to Powell, T. C. 2003. Varieties of competitive parity. *Strategic Management Journal,* 24(1): 61–86.

6. Rao, A. R., Bergen, M. E., & Davis, S. 2000. How to fight a price war. *Harvard Business Review,* 78(2): 107–120.

7. Marriot, J. W. Jr. Our competitive strength: Human capital. A speech given to the Detroit Economic Club on October 2, 2000.

8. Whalen, C. J., Pascual, A. M., Lowery, T., & Muller, J. 2001. The top 25 managers. *BusinessWeek,* January 8: 63.

9. Ibid.

10. For an interesting perspective on the need for creative strategies, refer to Hamel, G., & Prahalad, C. K. 1994. *Competing for the Future.* Boston: Harvard Business School Press.

11. www.epinions.com/content_674557508.

12. Symonds, W. C., Arndt, M., Palmer, A. T., Weintraub, A., & Holmes, S. 2001. Trying to break the choke hold. *BusinessWeek,* January 22: 38–39.

13. For a perspective on the sustainability of competitive advantages, refer to Barney, J. 1995. Looking inside for competitive advantage. *Academy of Management Executive,* 9(4): 49–61.

14. Thornton, E., 2001, Why e-brokers are broker and broker. *BusinessWeek,* January 22: 94.

15. Koretz, G. 2001. E-commerce: The buyer wins. *BusinessWeek,* January 8: 30.

16. For an interesting perspective on the value of corporate brands and how they may be leveraged, refer to Aaker, D. A. 2004, *California Management Review,* 46(3): 6–18.

17. MacMillan, I., & McGrath, R. 1997. Discovering new points of differentiation. *Harvard Business Review,* 75(4): 133–145; Wise, R., & Baumgarter, P. 1999. Beating the clock: Corporate responses to rapid change in the PC industry. *California Management Review,* 42(1): 8–36.

18. For a discussion on quality in terms of a company's software and information systems, refer to Prahalad, C. K., & Krishnan, M. S. 1999. The new meaning of quality in the information age. *Harvard Business Review,* 77(5): 109–118.

19. Taylor, A., III. 2001. Can you believe Porsche is putting its badge on this car? *Fortune,* February 19: 168–172.

20. Ward, S., Light, L., & Goldstine, J. 1999. What high-tech managers need to know about brands. *Harvard Business Review,* 77(4): 85–95.

21. Zesiger, S. 1999. Silicon speed. *Fortune,* September 13: 120.

22. Blank, D. 2001. Down to the sea in mega-yachts. *BusinessWeek,* October 30: 18.

23. Whalen et al., op. cit.

24. Rosenfeld, J. 2000. Unit of one. *Fast Company,* April: 98.

25. Markides, C. 1997. Strategic innovation. *Sloan Management Review,* 38(3): 9–23.

26. Dess, G. G., & Picken, J. C. 1997. *Mission Critical:* 84. Burr Ridge, IL: Irwin.

27. The authors would like to thank Scott Droege, a faculty member at Western Kentucky University, for providing this example.

28. Flint, J. 2004. Stop the nerds. *Forbes,* July 5: 80; and, Fahey, E. 2004. Over-engineering 101. *Forbes,* December 13: 62.

29. Symonds, W. C. 2000. Can Gillette regain its voltage? *BusinessWeek,* October 16: 102–104.

30. McGahan, A. M. 1999. Competition, strategy, and business performance. *California Management Review,* 41(3): 74–102.

31. Gadiesh, O., & Gilbert, J. L. 1998. Profit pools: A fresh look at strategy. *Harvard Business Review,* 76(3): 139–158.

32. Colvin, G. 2000. Beware: You could soon be selling soybeans. *Fortune,* November 13: 80.

33. Whalen et al., op. cit.: 63.

34. Porter, M. E. 1996. What is strategy? *Harvard Business Review,* 74(6): 61–78.

35. Hall, W. K. 1980. Survival strategies in a hostile environment, *Harvard Business Review,* 58: 75–87; on the paint and allied products industry, see Dess, G. G., & Davis, P. S. 1984. Porter's (1980) generic strategies as determinants of strategic group membership and organizational performance. *Academy of Management Journal,* 27: 467–488; for the Korean electronics industry, see Kim, L., & Lim, Y. 1988. Environment, generic strategies, and performance in a rapidly developing country: A taxonomic approach. *Academy of Management Journal,* 31: 802–827; Wright, P., Hotard, D., Kroll, M., Chan, P., & Tanner, J. 1990. Performance and multiple strategies in a firm: Evidence from the apparel industry. In Dean, B. V., & Cassidy, J. C. (Eds.). *Strategic management: Methods and studies:* 93–110. Amsterdam: Elsevier-North Holland; and Wright, P., Kroll, M., Tu, H.,

& Helms, M. 1991. Generic strategies and business performance: An empirical study of the screw machine products industry. *British Journal of Management,* 2: 1–9.

36. Gilmore, J. H., & Pine, B. J., II. 1997. The four faces of customization. *Harvard Business Review,* 75(1): 91–101.

37. Ibid. For interesting insights on mass customization, refer to Cattani, K., Dahan, E., & Schmidt, G. 2005. Offshoring versus "spackling." *MIT Sloan Management Review,* 46(3): 6–7.

38. Goodstein, L. D., & Butz, H. E. 1998. Customer value: The linchpin of organizational change. *Organizational Dynamics,* Summer: 21–34.

39. Gadiesh & Gilbert, op. cit.: 139–158.

40. This example draws on Dess & Picken. 1997. op. cit.

41. Forest, S. A. 2001. Can an outsider fix J. C. Penney? *BusinessWeek,* February 12: 56, 58.

42. For an interesting perspective on the influence of the product life cycle and rate of technological change on competitive strategy, refer to Lei, D., & Slocum, J. W. Jr. 2005. Strategic and organizational requirements for competitive advantage. *Academy of Management Executive,* 19(1): 31–45.

43. Dickson, P. R. 1994. *Marketing Management:* 293. Fort Worth, TX: Dryden Press; Day, G. S. 1981. The product life cycle: Analysis and application. *Journal of Marketing Research,* 45: 60–67.

44. Bearden, W. O., Ingram, T. N., & LaForge, R. W. 1995. *Marketing principles and practices.* Burr Ridge, IL: Irwin.

45. MacMillan, I. C. 1985. Preemptive strategies. In Guth, W. D. (Ed.). *Handbook of Business Strategy:* 9-1–9-22. Boston: Warren, Gorham & Lamont; Pearce, J. A., & Robinson, R. B. 2000. *Strategic management* (7th ed.). New York: McGraw-Hill; Dickson, op. cit.: 295–296.

46. Bartlett, C. A., & Ghoshal, S. 2000. Going global: Lessons for late movers. *Harvard Business Review,* 78(2): 132–142.

47. Berkowitz, E. N., Kerin, R. A., & Hartley, S. W. 2000. *Marketing* (6th ed.). New York: McGraw-Hill.

48. MacMillan, op. cit.

49. Brooker, K. 2001. A game of inches. *Fortune,* February 5: 98–100.

50. MacMillan, op. cit.

51. Berkowitz et al., op. cit.

52. Bearden et al., op. cit.

53. The discussion of these four strategies draws on MacMillan, op. cit.; Berkowitz et al., op. cit.; and Bearden et al., op. cit.

54. Augustine, N. R. 1997. Reshaping an industry: Lockheed Martin's survival story. *Harvard Business Review,* 75(3): 83–94.

55. For some useful ideas on effective turnarounds and handling downsizings, refer to Marks, M. S., & De Meuse, K. P. 2005. Resizing the organization: Maximizing the gain

while minimizing the pain of layoffs, divestitures and closings. *Organizational Dynamics,* 34(1): 19–36.

56. Hambrick, D. C., & Schecter, S. M. 1983. Turnaround strategies for mature industrial product business units. *Academy of Management Journal,* 26(2): 231–248.

57. Mullaney, T. J. 2002. The wizard of Intuit. *BusinessWeek,* October 28: 60–63.

58. This section draws on Christensen, C. M., & Overdorf, M. 2000. Meeting the challenge of disruptive change. *Harvard Business Review,* March-April: 66–76; and Christensen, C. M., Johnson, M. W., & Rigby, D. K. 2002. Foundations for growth: How to identify and build disruptive new businesses. *Sloan Management Review,* Spring: 22–31.

Corporate-Level Strategy:

Creating Value through Diversification

>chapter objectives

After reading this chapter, you should have a good understanding of:

- How managers can create value through diversification initiatives.

- The reasons for the failure of many diversification efforts.

- How corporations can use related diversification to achieve synergistic benefits through economies of scope and market power.

- How corporations can use unrelated diversification to attain synergistic benefits through corporate restructuring, parenting, and portfolio analysis.

- The various means of engaging in diversification—mergers and acquisitions, joint ventures/strategic alliances, and internal development.

- The benefits and potential drawbacks of real options analysis (ROA) in making resource allocation decisions under conditions of high uncertainty.

- Managerial behaviors that can erode the creation of value.

*C*orporate-level strategy addresses two related issues: (1) what businesses should a corporation compete in, and (2) how can these businesses be managed so they create "synergy"—that is, more value by working together than if they were freestanding units? As we will see, these questions present a key challenge for today's managers. Many diversification efforts fail or, in many cases, provide only marginal returns to shareholders. Thus, determining how to create value through entering new markets, introducing new products, or developing new technologies is a vital issue in strategic management.

We begin by discussing why diversification initiatives, in general, have not yielded the anticipated benefits. Then, in the next three sections of the chapter, we explore the two key alternative approaches: related and unrelated diversification. With related diversification, corporations strive to enter product-markets that share some resources and capabilities with their existing business units or increase their market power. Here we suggest four means of creating value: leveraging core competencies, sharing activities, pooled negotiating power, and vertical integration. With unrelated diversification, there are few similarities in the resources and capabilities among the firm's business units, but value can be created in multiple ways. These include restructuring, corporate parenting, and portfolio analysis approaches. Whereas the synergies to be realized with related diversification come from *horizontal relationships* among the business units, the synergies from unrelated diversification are derived from *hierarchical relationships* between the corporate office and the business units.

The last three sections address (1) the various means that corporations can use to achieve diversification, (2) real options analysis, and (3) managerial behaviors (e.g., self-interest) that serve to erode shareholder value. We address merger and acquisitions (M&A), joint ventures/strategic alliances, and internal development. Each of these involves the evaluation of important trade-offs. We also discuss the benefits and potential drawbacks of real options analysis (ROA)—an increasingly popular technique for making resource allocation decisions. Detrimental managerial behaviors, often guided by a manager's self-interest, are "growth for growth's sake," egotism, and antitakeover tactics. Some of these behaviors raise ethical issues because managers, in some cases, are not acting in the best interests of a firm's shareholders.

The pioneering discount broker Charles Schwab and Company became the industry leader through its focus on the customer and the innovative use of information technology. Faced with intense competition from deep-discount Internet brokerages in the late 1990s, Schwab tried to greatly expand its services to wealthy clientele by acquiring U.S. Trust. Below, we discuss why things didn't work out as planned.

"Clicks and mortar" broker Charles Schwab Corp. bought U.S. Trust Corp. in mid-2000 for $3.2 billion, joining a 147-year-old private-client wealth management firm with a leading provider of discount investor services.[1] Schwab paid a premium of 63.5 percent to U.S. Trust shareholders. The steep premium for U.S. Trust reflects the broker's deep pockets as well as its interest in becoming a full-service investment firm. At the time of the acquisition, Schwab was the nation's number one Internet and discount broker and number four financial services company overall.

Several synergies were expected from this acquisition. According to Schwab, the move expanded on its already developed offerings for wealthy clientele, including Schwab's Advisor Source and Signature Services. Schwab saw great potential for growth in the market represented by high-net-worth individuals and hoped its combination of Internet savvy and U.S. Trust's high-touch business lines would be tailor-made for that segment. In all, Schwab expected to leverage on its core competency in investor services to build greater market power.

But the news out of Charles Schwab and Co. has not been good. The bear market took a big bite out of Schwab's trading volume, revenues, and profits. With investment returns eroding, customers were much more sensitive to brokerage and commission fees. The management shake-up at U.S. Trust Corp. in October 2002 also raised serious questions. In its eagerness to tap upscale markets and become more than the people's broker, did the normally savvy Schwab miss serious warning signs at U.S. Trust? What went wrong?

The apparent synergies have not worked out, and deeper incompatibilities surfaced. Former U.S. Trust employees claimed that Schwab was overly enamored by the glossy brand and pedigreed clients of U.S. Trust. The company was too optimistic about Schwab's ability to direct their high-end clients to U.S. Trust, but very few Schwab customers have $2 million in assets, the minimum for U.S. Trust's pricey hand holding. Even those referred were often turned down by the subsidiary. Therefore, the main hope for the acquisition—stopping Schwab's richest customers from defecting to full-service brokerages such as Merrill Lynch—has not panned out. Also, many key managers left when their retention agreements expired in May 2002, taking their clients with them.

By mid-2004, more than 300 wealth advisers had departed. Wealth advisers are the core of U.S. Trust's businesses because they have the direct relationships with the wealthy families that make up its core clientele. When advisers leave, clients often follow them. U.S. Trust has been forced to offer hefty pay packages and bonuses to retain some of its top talent.

Perhaps, the core problem has been a clash between the two cultures. The low-cost discount-broker culture of Schwab discouraged big pay packages and provided only limited services to clients. U.S. Trust, with its plush dining rooms and lavish pay packages, prides itself on its highly personal service to wealthy families. Schwab executives complained about U.S. Trust's arrogance and refusal to adapt to fast-changing financial markets and customer demands. U.S. Trust executives, in contrast, frowned on Schwab's lack of sophistication and obsessive focus on cutting costs. According to one U.S. Trust executive, "It's like the battle between old wealth versus new wealth. U.S. Trust represented the established wealth and complicated needs of wealthy families. Schwab was the upstart that saw the market in more simple terms."

Another major problem has been technology. Despite reports of federal regulators' hinting at system-related problems, Schwab thought it was manageable and was content with its inspection of U.S. Trust's system. However, it eventually discovered the magnitude of the problem when the computer systems failed to detect suspicious patterns of cash transactions. The bank had to pay $10 million in July 2001 to settle charges by the New York State Banking Department and Federal Reserve that it was not complying with anti–money laundering rules. (The bank did not admit or deny fault.) The severity of the technology problem is illustrated by the fact that U.S. Trust did not even use the standard Windows operating system until the late 1990s. Furthermore, its 30 branches are not on a single computer system, hindering back-office operations such as order processing.

Compounding the problems after the compliance fiasco, U.S. Trust started screening clients so closely that it alienated them. This consumed time and money that could otherwise have been spent generating new business. Cost cutting has been another area of concern. U.S. Trust's executives dragged their feet on consolidating their numerous bank charters and cutting costs at offices outside New York, adding to the disappointing performance. Several weak branches will likely be closed.

With problems mounting, Schwab replaced U.S. Trust CEO Jeffrey S. Maurer and the president, Amribeth S. Rahe. They named Alan J. Weber, former head of Citibank's international operations, to be CEO and president. Weber faces the Herculean task of making things work. "The wild card is whether Schwab can transform a high-net-worth business from (one of) steady earnings growth to more dynamic earnings growth," says a Wall Street analyst. It seems that marrying up has not been the ticket to wealth it was supposed to be.

Schwab is not alone in having a disappointing experience with an acquisition. Many large multinational firms and recent big acquirers have failed to effectively integrate their acquisitions, paid too high a premium for the target's common stock, or were unable to understand how the acquired firm's assets would fit with their own lines of business. And, at times, top executives may not have acted in the best interests of shareholders. That is, the motive for the acquisition may have been to enhance the executives' power and prestige rather than improve shareholder returns. At times, the only other people who may have benefited were the shareholders of the *acquired* firms.

Exhibit 6.1 summarizes some of the bottom line results of several studies that were conducted over a variety of time periods. Here are a few examples of the enormous amount of shareholder wealth that has been lost within a few years after some of the more recent well-chronicled acquisitions and mergers.[2]

- Glaxo/SmithKline (2000) $40 billion lost
- Chase/J. P. Morgan (2000) $26 billion lost
- SBC/Ameritech (1999) $68 billion lost
- WorldCom/MCI (1998) $94 billion lost
- Daimler/Chrysler (1998) $36 billion lost

Many acquisitions ultimately result in divestiture—an admission that things didn't work out as planned. In fact, some years ago, a writer for *Fortune* magazine lamented, "Studies show that 33 percent to 50 percent of acquisitions are later divested, giving corporate marriages a divorce rate roughly comparable to that of men and women."[3]

Admittedly, we have been rather pessimistic so far. Clearly, many diversification efforts have worked out very well—whether through mergers and acquisitions, strategic alliances and joint ventures, or internal development. We will discuss many success stories throughout this chapter. Next, we will discuss the primary rationales for diversification.

>>Making Diversification Work: An Overview

Not all diversification moves, including those involving mergers and acquisitions, erode performance. For example, acquisitions in the oil industry, such as British Petroleum PLC's purchases of Amoco and Arco, are performing well, as is the merger of Exxon and Mobil. Similarly, many leading high-tech firms, such as Microsoft and Intel, have

Exhibit 6.1

Diversification and Corporate Performance: A Disappointing History

The summaries of the studies below consistently support the notion that attaining the intended payoffs from diversification efforts is very elusive.

- Michael Porter of Harvard University studied the diversification records of 33 large, prestigious U.S. companies from 1950 to 1986 and found that most of them had divested many more acquisitions than they had kept. The corporate strategies of most companies had dissipated rather than enhanced shareholder value. By taking over companies and breaking them up, corporate raiders had thrived on failed strategies.

- Another study evaluated the stock market reaction to 600 acquisitions over the period between 1975 and 1991. The results indicated that the acquiring firms suffered an average 4 percent drop in market value (after adjusting for market movements) in the three months following the acquisitions announcement.

- A study conducted jointly by *BusinessWeek* and Mercer Management Consulting, Inc., analyzed 150 acquisitions worth more than $500 million that took place between July 1990 and July 1995. Based on total stock returns from three months before the announcement and up to three years after the announcement:
  - 30 percent substantially eroded shareholder returns.
  - 20 percent eroded some returns.
  - 33 percent created only marginal returns.
  - 17 percent created substantial returns.

- In a study by Salomon Smith Barney of U.S. companies acquired since 1997 in deals for $15 billion or more, the stocks of the acquiring firms have, on average, underperformed the S&P stock index by 14 percentage points and underperformed their peer group by 4 percentage points after the deals were announced.

- A study of 12,023 acquisitions from 1980 to 2001 found that acquiring-firm shareholders lost 12 cents per dollar spent on acquisition, for a total loss of $240 billion from 1998 through 2001, whereas they lost only $7 billion in all of the 1980s, or 1.6 cents per dollar spent. The 1998 to 2001 aggregate dollar loss of acquiring-firm shareholders is so large because of a small number of acquisitions with negative synergy gains by firms with extremely high valuations. Without these acquisitions, the wealth of acquiring-firm shareholders would have increased.

Sources: Moeller, S. B., Schlingemann, F. P., & Stulz, R. M. 2005. Wealth destruction on a massive scale? A study of acquiring-firm returns in the recent merger wave. *Journal of Finance* (forthcoming); Lipin, S., & Deogun, N. 2000. Big mergers of the 90s prove disappointing to shareholders. *The Wall Street Journal,* October 30: C1; Dr. G. William Schwert, University of Rochester study cited in Pare, T. P. 1994. The new merger boom. *Fortune,* November 28: 96; and, Porter, M. E. 1987. From competitive advantage to corporate strategy. *Harvard Business Review,* 65(3): 43.

dramatically increased their revenues, profits, and market values through a wide variety of diversification moves, including mergers and acquisitions, strategic alliances and joint ventures, and internal development.

So the question becomes: Why do some diversification efforts pay off and others produce disappointing results? In this chapter we will address this question. Whereas Chapter 5 focused on business-level strategy—that is, how to achieve sustainable advantages in a given business or product market—this chapter addresses two related issues: (1) What businesses should a corporation compete in? and (2) How should these businesses be managed to jointly create more value than if they were freestanding units?

Diversification initiatives—whether through mergers and acquisitions, strategic alliances and joint ventures, or internal development—must be justified by the creation of value for shareholders. But this is not always the case. For example, as noted earlier, acquiring firms typically pay high premiums when they acquire a target firm. However, you and I, as private investors, can diversify our portfolio of stocks very cheaply. With the advent of the intensely competitive online brokerage industry, we can acquire hundreds (or thousands) of shares for a transaction fee of as little as $10.00 or less—a far cry from the 30 to 40 percent (or higher) premiums that corporations typically must pay to acquire companies.

Given the seemingly high inherent downside risks and uncertainties, it might be reasonable to ask why companies should even bother with diversification initiatives. The answer, in a word, is *synergy*, derived from the Greek word *synergos,* which means "working together." This can have two different, but not mutually exclusive, meanings. First, a firm may diversify into *related* businesses. Here, the primary potential benefits to be derived come from *horizontal relationships;* that is, businesses sharing intangible resources (e.g., core competences) and tangible resources (e.g., production facilities, distribution channels). Additionally, firms can enhance their market power through pooled negotiating power and vertical integration. As we will see in this chapter, Procter & Gamble enjoys many synergies from having businesses that share distribution resources.

Second, a corporation may diversify into *unrelated* businesses. In these instances, the primary potential benefits are derived largely from *hierarchical relationships;* that is, value creation derived from the corporate office. Examples of the latter would include leveraging some of the support activities in the value chain that we discussed in Chapter 3, such as information systems or human resource practices. Cooper Industries, another firm we will discuss, has followed a successful strategy of unrelated diversification. There are few similarities in the products it makes or the industries in which it competes. However, the corporate office adds value through such activities as superb human resource practices as well as planning and budgeting systems.

It is important to note that the aforementioned horizontal (derived from related diversification) and hierarchical (derived from related and unrelated diversification) relationships are not mutually exclusive. Many firms that diversify into related areas benefit from information technology expertise in the corporate office, and firms diversifying into unrelated areas often benefit from the "best practices" of sister businesses even though their products, markets, and technologies may differ dramatically.

Exhibit 6.2 provides an overview of how we will address the various means by which firms create value through both related and unrelated diversification and also include a summary of some examples that we will address in this chapter.[4]

>>Related Diversification: Economies of Scope and Revenue Enhancement

As discussed earlier, related diversification enables a firm to benefit from horizontal relationships across different businesses in the diversified corporation by leveraging core competencies and sharing activities (e.g., production facilities and distribution facilities). This enables a corporation to benefit from economies of scope. *Economies of scope* refers to cost savings from leveraging core competencies or sharing related activities among businesses in the corporation. A firm can also enjoy greater revenues if two businesses attain higher levels of sales growth combined than either company could attain independently.

For example, a sporting goods store with one or several locations may acquire other stores. This enables it to leverage, or reuse, many of its key resources—favorable reputation, expert staff and management skills, efficient purchasing operations—the basis

Exhibit 6.2
Creating Value through
Related and Unrelated
Diversification

Related Diversification: Economies of Scope

Leveraging core competences
- 3M leverages its competencies in adhesives technologies to many industries, including automotive, construction, and telecommunications.

Sharing activities
- McKesson, a large distribution company, sells many product lines, such as pharmaceuticals and liquor, through its superwarehouses.

Related Diversification: Market Power

Pooled negotiating power
- The Times Mirror Company increases its power over customers by providing "one-stop shopping" for advertisers to reach customers through multiple media—television and newspapers—in several huge markets such as New York and Chicago.

Vertical integration
- Shaw Industries, a giant carpet manufacturer, increases its control over raw materials by producing much of its own polypropylene fiber, a key input to its manufacturing process.

Unrelated Diversification: Parenting, Restructuring, and Financial Synergies

Corporate restructuring and parenting
- The corporate office of Cooper Industries adds value to its acquired businesses by performing such activities as auditing their manufacturing operations, improving their accounting activities, and centralizing union negotiations.

Portfolio management
- Novartis, formerly Ciba-Geigy, uses portfolio management to improve many key activities, including resource allocation and reward and evaluation systems.

of its competitive advantage(s), over a larger number of stores.[5] Let's next address how to create value by leveraging core competencies.

Leveraging Core Competencies

The concept of core competencies can be illustrated by the imagery of the diversified corporation as a tree.[6] The trunk and major limbs represent core products; the smaller branches are business units; and the leaves, flowers, and fruit are end products. The core competencies are represented by the root system, which provides nourishment, sustenance, and stability. Managers often misread the strength of competitors by looking only at their end products, just as we can fail to appreciate the strength of a tree by looking only at its leaves. Core competencies may also be viewed as the "glue" that binds existing businesses together or as the engine that fuels new business growth.

Core competencies reflect the collective learning in organizations—how to coordinate diverse production skills, integrate multiple streams of technologies, and market and merchandise diverse products and services. The theoretical knowledge necessary to put a radio on a chip does not in itself assure a company of the skill needed to produce a miniature radio approximately the size of a business card. To accomplish this, Casio, a giant electronic products producer, must synthesize know-how in miniaturization, microprocessor design, material science, and ultrathin precision castings. These are the same skills that it applies in its miniature card calculators, pocket TVs, and digital watches.

For a core competence to create value and provide a viable basis for synergy among the businesses in a corporation, it must meet three criteria.[7]

- ***The core competence must enhance competitive advantage(s) by creating superior customer value.*** It must enable the business to develop strengths relative to the competition. Every value-chain activity has the potential to provide a viable basis for building on a core competence.[8] At Gillette, for example, scientists developed the Mach 3 and Sensor Excel after the introduction of the tremendously successful Sensor System because of a thorough understanding of several phenomena that underlie shaving. These include the physiology of facial hair and skin, the metallurgy of blade strength and sharpness, the dynamics of a cartridge moving across skin, and the physics of a razor blade severing hair. Such innovations are possible only with an understanding of such phenomena and the ability to combine such technologies into innovative products. Customers have consistently been willing to pay more for such technologically differentiated products.

- ***Different businesses in the corporation must be similar in at least one important way related to the core competence.*** It is not essential that the products or services themselves be similar. Rather, at least one element in the value chain must require similar skills in creating competitive advantage if the corporation is to capitalize on its core competence. At first glance you might think that motorcycles, clothes, and restaurants have little in common. But at Harley-Davidson, they do.[9] Harley-Davidson has capitalized on its exceptionally strong brand image as well as merchandising and licensing skills to sell accessories, clothing, and toys and has licensed the Harley-Davidson Café in New York City—further evidence of the strength of its brand name and products.

- ***The core competencies must be difficult for competitors to imitate or find substitutes for.*** As we discussed in Chapter 5, competitive advantages will not be sustainable if the competition can easily imitate or substitute them. Similarly, if the skills associated with a firm's core competencies are easily imitated or replicated, they are not a sound basis for sustainable advantages. Consider Sharp Corporation, a $17 billion consumer electronics giant.[10] It has a set of specialized core competencies in optoelectronics technologies that are difficult to replicate and contribute to its competitive advantages in its core businesses. Its most successful technology has been liquid crystal displays (LCDs) that are critical components in nearly all of Sharp's products. Its expertise in this technology enabled Sharp to succeed in videocassette recorders (VCRs) with its innovative LCD viewfinder and led to the creation of its Wizard, a personal electronic organizer.

Strategy Spotlight 6.1 discusses how UPS leverages its core competence in logistics. It ships broken Toshiba laptops to its facility in Louisville, Kentucky, to diagnose and repair them.

Sharing Activities

As we saw above, leveraging core competencies involves transferring accumulated skills and expertise across business units in a corporation. When carried out effectively, this leads to advantages that can become quite sustainable over time. Corporations also can achieve synergy by sharing tangible activities across their business units. These include

STRATEGY SPOTLIGHT 6.1

UPS: Leveraging Its Core Competence in Logistics

Toshiba has recently handed over its entire laptop repair operation to United Parcel Service (UPS) Supply Chain Solutions, the shipper's $2.4 billion logistics outsourcing division. UPS will ship broken Toshiba laptops to its facility in Louisville, Kentucky, where UPS will diagnose and repair defects. The facility consists of a campus that occupies 2 million square feet devoted to more than 70 companies. Consumers will enjoy an immediate benefit. In the past, repairs could take weeks, depending on whether Toshiba needed components from Japan. However, since the UPS repair site is adjacent to its air hub, customers should get their machines back, as good as new, in a matter of days.

Why would Toshiba let a shipping company repair its laptops? Simply put, the challenge of computer repair is more logistical than technical. "Moving a unit around and getting replacement parts consumes most of the time," says Mark Simons, general manager of Toshiba's digital products division. "The actual service only takes about an hour." Plus, UPS already has experience in this area. The company has repaired Lexmark and Hewlett-Packard

printers since 1996 and has performed initial inspections on laptops being returned by Toshiba since 1999.

The expanded relationship with Toshiba is another step in UPS's strategy to broaden its business beyond package delivery into commerce services. Its new marketing mission in 2004 was to market a set of capabilities that go along with its new slogan, "Synchronizing the world of commerce." According to Larry Bloomenkranz, Vice President, Global Brand Management and Advertising, "It's not just the same old UPS. We are a one-brand supplier up and down the supply chain." UPS currently works with clients to manage inventory, ordering, and customs processes, and it has just introduced a service to dispose of unwanted electronics.

If Toshiba's customers are satisfied with the new UPS repair services, other electronics manufacturers will likely also consider UPS as an outsourcing partner. As pointed out by Roger Kay, Vice President for Client Computing at research firm IDC, "A logistics partner who can also do repair is a rare and wonderful thing." Clearly, UPS is able to leverage its core competencies in logistics (e.g., shipping, spare parts supply management) into the seemingly unrelated area of laptop repair to enhance its revenues and profitability.

Sources: James, G. 2004. The next delivery? Computer repairs by UPS. *Business 2.0*, July: 30; Blanchard, D. 2004. It takes a supply chain village. *www.logisticstoday.com*, November: 9; and, Podmolik, M. 2004. UPS promotes commerce, supply-chain capabilities. *B to B*, 89(12): 18.

value-creating activities such as common manufacturing facilities, distribution channels, and sales forces. As we will see, sharing activities can potentially provide two primary payoffs: cost savings and revenue enhancements.

Deriving Cost Savings through Sharing Activities Typically, this is the most common type of synergy and the easiest to estimate. Peter Shaw, head of mergers and acquisitions at the British chemical and pharmaceutical company ICI refers to cost savings as "hard synergies" and contends that the level of certainty of their achievement is quite high. Cost savings come from many sources, including elimination of jobs, facilities, and related expenses that are no longer needed when functions are consolidated, or from economies of scale in purchasing. Cost savings are generally highest when one company acquires another from the same industry in the same country. Shaw Industries, recently acquired by Berkshire Hathaway, is the nation's largest carpet producer. Over the years, it has dominated the competition through a strategy of acquisition which has enabled Shaw, among other things, to consolidate its manufacturing operations in a few, highly efficient plants and to lower costs through higher capacity utilization.

It is important to note that sharing activities inevitably involve costs that the benefits must outweigh. One often overlooked cost is the greater coordination required to manage a shared activity. Even more important is the need to compromise the design or performance of an activity so that it can be shared. For example, a salesperson handling the products of two business units must operate in a way that is usually not what either unit would choose if it were independent. If the compromise erodes the unit's effectiveness, then sharing may reduce rather than enhance competitive advantage.

Enhancing Revenue and Differentiation through Sharing Activities

Often an acquiring firm and its target may achieve a higher level of sales growth together than either company could on its own. Shortly after Gillette acquired Duracell, it confirmed its expectation that selling Duracell batteries through Gillette's existing channels for personal care products would increase sales, particularly internationally. Gillette sold Duracell products in 25 new markets in the first year after the acquisition and substantially increased sales in established international markets. In a similar vein, a target company's distribution channel can be used to escalate the sales of the acquiring company's product. Such was the case when Gillette acquired Parker Pen. Gillette estimated that it could gain an additional $25 million in sales of its own Waterman pens by taking advantage of Parker's distribution channels.

Firms also can enhance the effectiveness of their differentiation strategies by means of sharing activities among business units. A shared order-processing system, for example, may permit new features and services that a buyer will value. Also, sharing can reduce the cost of differentiation. For instance, a shared service network may make more advanced, remote service technology economically feasible. To illustrate the potential for enhanced differentiation though sharing, consider $5.1 billion VF Corporation—producer of such well-known brands as Lee, Wrangler, Vanity Fair, and Jantzen.

> VF's acquisition of Nutmeg Industries and H. H. Cutler provided it with several large customers that it didn't have before, increasing its plant utilization and productivity. But more importantly, Nutmeg designs and makes licensed apparel for sports teams and organizations, while Cutler manufactures licensed brand-name children's apparel, including Walt Disney kids' wear. Such brand labeling enhances the differentiation of VF's apparel products. According to VF President Mackey McDonald, "What we're doing is looking at value-added knitwear, taking our basic fleece from Basset-Walker [one of its divisions], embellishing it through Cutler and Nutmeg, and selling it as a value-added product." Additionally, Cutler's advanced high-speed printing technologies will enable VF to be more proactive in anticipating trends in the fashion-driven fleece market. Claims McDonald, "Rather than printing first and then trying to guess what the customer wants, we can see what's happening in the marketplace and then print it up."[11]

As a cautionary note, managers must keep in mind that sharing activities among businesses in a corporation can have a negative effect on a given business's differentiation. For example, with the merger of Chrysler and Daimler-Benz, many consumers may lower their perceptions of Mercedes's quality and prestige if they feel that common production components and processes are being used across the two divisions. And the Jaguar division of Ford Motor Company may be adversely affected as consumers come to understand that it shares many components with its sister divisions at Ford, including Lincoln.

Strategy Spotlight 6.2 discusses how Freemantle Media leverages its hit television show *American Idol* through its core competences and shared activities to create multiple revenue streams.

>>Related Diversification: Market Power

In the previous section, we explained how leveraging core competencies and sharing activities help firms create economies of scale and scope through related diversification. In this section, we discuss how companies achieve related diversification through market power. We also address the two principal means by which firms achieve synergy through market power: *pooled negotiating power* and *vertical integration*. It is important to recognize that managers have limits on their ability to use market power for diversification,

American Idol: Far More than Just a Television Show

American Idol is one of several of FremantleMedia's (FM) hit television shows. FM is a division of German media giant Bertlesmann, which has approximately $20 billion in revenues. Some of FM's other well-known television shows are *The Apprentice*, *The Swan*, and at a ripe old age of 48—*The Price Is Right*.

First shown in the United States in June 2002, *American Idol* became a tremendous overnight success. Although the show may be crass and occasionally cruel, it is undeniably brilliant. It's become the ultimate testament to a singular business achievement: FM has become extremely successful at creating truly global programming. In part, that is due to the creative minds at Fremantle; it has some of the best professionals in the business who have a talent for developing shows that appeal to huge populations with different backgrounds and circumstances.

Amazingly, FM, which created *Pop Idol* in Britain in 2001, is now rolling out the show in its 30th country. There's *Belgium Idool*, *Portugal Idolos*, *Deutschland Sucht den SuperStar* (Germany), *SuperStar KZ* (Kazakhstan), and of course, the largest and best-known show, *American Idol*, in the United States. *American Idol* is the primary reason that Fremantle's revenue is up 9 percent to more than $1 billion since the show was launched. According to Fremantle's CEO Tony Cohen, "*Idol* has become a national institution in lots of countries." To illustrate, fans cast more than 65 million votes for the *American Idol* finale in May, 2004—that is two-thirds as many people as voted in the 2004 U.S. presidential election.

The real key to Fremantle's success is not just adapting its television hits to other countries, but systematically leveraging its core product—television shows—to create multiple revenue streams. In essence, the "Fremantle Way" holds lessons not just for show business but for all business. It enables a company to use its core competence of making products of mass appeal and then to customize them for places with widely varying languages, cultures, and mores. It then milks the hits for every penny through tie-ins, spinoffs, innovative uses of technology, and marketing masterstrokes.

The *Idol* franchise has created a wide variety of new revenue streams for Fremantle's German parent, Bertelsmann. Here's how much *American Idol* has generated in its first two years since its June 2002 launch:

- *Products ($50 million).* Brand extensions range from videogames and fragrances to a planned microphone-shaped soap-on-a-rope. Fremantle receives a licensing fee from manufacturers.

- *TV Licensing ($75 million).* For its rights fee, Fox gets to broadcast the show and, in turn, sell ads and lucrative sponsorships.

- *Compact Discs (CDs) ($130 million).* The most successful performers on the *Idols* shows have sold millions of CDs; more than one-third of the revenue goes to BMG, which, like Fremantle, is an affiliate of Bertelsmann.

- *Concerts ($35 million).* Although artists and their management get the bulk of the take, concerts sell records and merchandise and promote the next *Idol* show.

In addition, Fremantle Licensing Worldwide signed Warner Brothers Publications to produce and distribute *Idol* audition books with CDs for the United States, Canada, United Kingdom, and Australia. The new books/CDs—*Pop Idol* (UK), *Australian Idol,* and *Canadian Idol*—join the *American Idol* book/CD.

Sources: Sloan, P. 2004. The reality factory. *Business 2.0,* August: 74–82; Cooney, J. 2004. In the news. *License!,* March: 48; and, Anonymous. 2005. Fox on top in Feb; NBC languishing at the bottom. www.indiantelevision.com, March 2.

because government regulations can sometimes restrict the ability of a business to gain very large shares of a particular market.

When General Electric (GE) announced a $41 billion bid for Honeywell, the European Union stepped in. GE's market clout would have expanded significantly as a result of the deal, with GE supplying over one-half the parts needed to build several aircraft engines. The commission's concern, causing them to reject the acquisition, was that GE could use its increased market power to dominate the aircraft engine parts market and crowd out competitors.[12] Thus, while managers need to be aware of the strategic advantages of market power, they must at the same time be aware of regulations and legislation.

Pooled Negotiating Power

Similar businesses working together or the affiliation of a business with a strong parent can strengthen an organization's bargaining position in relation to suppliers and customers and enhance its position vis-à-vis competitors. Compare, for example, the position of an independent food manufacturer with the same business within Nestlé. Being part of Nestlé Corporation provides the business with significant clout—greater bargaining power with suppliers and customers—since it is part of a firm that makes large purchases from suppliers and provides a wide variety of products to its customers. Access to the parent's deep pockets increases the business's strength relative to rivals. Further, the Nestlé unit enjoys greater protection from substitutes and new entrants. Not only would rivals perceive the unit as a more formidable opponent, but the unit's association with Nestlé would also provide greater visibility and improved image.

Consolidating an industry can also increase a firm's market power. This is clearly an emerging trend in the multimedia industry.[13] All of these mergers and acquisitions have a common goal: to control and leverage as many news and entertainment channels as possible. In total, more than $261 billion in mergers and acquisitions in the media industry were announced in 2000—up 12 percent from 1999. For example, consider the Tribune Company's $8 billion purchase of the Times Mirror Company.

> The merger doubled the size of the Tribune and secured its position among the top tier of major media companies. The enhanced scale and scope helped it to compete more effectively and grow more rapidly in two consolidating industries—newspaper and television broadcasting. The combined company would increase its power over customers by providing a "one-stop shop" for advertisers desiring to reach consumers through multiple media in enormous markets such as Chicago, Los Angeles, and New York. The company has estimated its incremental revenue from national and cross-media advertising will grow from $40 to $50 million in 2001 to $200 million by 2005. The combined company should also increase its power relative to its suppliers. The company's enhanced size is expected to lead to increased efficiencies when purchasing newsprint and other commodities.[14]

When acquiring related businesses, a firm's potential for pooled negotiating power vis-à-vis its customers and suppliers can be very enticing. However, managers must carefully evaluate how the combined businesses may affect relationships with actual and potential customers, suppliers, and competitors. For example, when PepsiCo diversified into the fast-food industry with its acquisitions of Kentucky Fried Chicken, Taco Bell, and Pizza Hut (since spun off as Tricon, Inc.), it clearly benefited from its position over these units that served as a captive market for its soft-drink products. However, many competitors such as McDonald's have refused to consider PepsiCo as a supplier of its own soft-drink needs because of competition with Pepsi's divisions in the fast-food industry. Simply put, McDonald's did not want to subsidize the enemy! Thus, although acquiring related businesses can enhance a corporation's bargaining power, it must be aware of the potential for retaliation.

Vertical Integration

Vertical integration represents an expansion or extension of the firm by integrating preceding or successive productive processes.[15] That is, the firm incorporates more processes toward the original source of raw materials (backward integration) or toward the ultimate consumer (forward integration). For example, an automobile manufacturer might supply its own parts or make its own engines to secure sources of supply. Or it might control its own system of dealerships to ensure retail outlets for its products. Similarly, an oil refinery might secure land leases and develop its own drilling capacity to

STRATEGY SPOTLIGHT

Vertical Integration at Shaw Industries

Shaw Industries (now part of Berkshire Hathaway) is an example of a firm that has followed a very successful strategy of vertical integration. By relentlessly pursuing both backward and forward integration, Shaw has become the dominant manufacturer of carpeting products in the United States. According to CEO Robert Shaw, "We want to be involved with as much of the process of making and selling carpets as practical. That way, we're

Sources: White, J. 2003. Shaw to home in on more with Georgia Tufters deal. *HFN: The Weekly Newspaper for the Home Furnishing Network,* May 5: 32; Shaw Industries. 1993, 2000. Annual reports; and Server, A. 1994. How to escape a price war. *Fortune,* June 13: 88.

in charge of costs." For example, Shaw acquired Amoco's polypropylene fiber manufacturing facilities in Alabama and Georgia. These new plants provide carpet fibers for internal use and for sale to other manufacturers. With this backward integration, fully one-quarter of Shaw's carpet fiber needs are now met in-house. In early 1996 Shaw began to integrate forward, acquiring seven floor-covering retailers in a move that suggested a strategy to consolidate the fragmented industry and increase its influence over retail pricing. Exhibit 6.3 provides a simplified depiction of the stages of vertical integration for Shaw Industries.

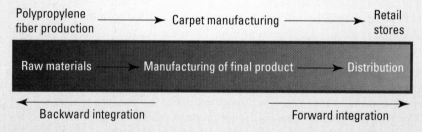

Exhibit 6.3 *Simplified Stages of Vertical Integration: Shaw Industries*

ensure a constant supply of crude oil. Or it could expand into retail operations by owning or licensing gasoline stations to guarantee customers for its petroleum products.

Clearly, vertical integration can be a viable strategy for many firms. Strategy Spotlight 6.3 discusses Shaw Industries, a carpet manufacturer that has attained a dominant position in the industry via a strategy of vertical integration. Shaw has successfully implemented strategies of both forward and backward integration.

Benefits and Risks of Vertical Integration   Although vertical integration is a means for an organization to reduce its dependence on suppliers or its channels of distribution to end users, it represents a major decision that an organization must carefully consider. The benefits associated with vertical integration—backward or forward—must be carefully weighed against the risks.[16]

The *benefits* of vertical integration include (1) a secure supply of raw materials or distribution channels that cannot be "held hostage" to external markets where costs can fluctuate over time, (2) protection and control over assets and services required to produce and deliver valuable products and services, (3) access to new business opportunities and new forms of technologies, and (4) simplified procurement and administrative procedures since key activities are brought inside the firm, eliminating the need to deal with a wide variety of suppliers and distributors.

Winnebago, the leader in the market for drivable recreational vehicles with a 19.3 percent market share, illustrates some of vertical integration's benefits.[17] The word Winnebago means "big RV" to most Americans. And the firm has a sterling reputation for great quality. The firm's huge northern Iowa factories do everything from extruding aluminum for body parts to molding plastics for water and holding tanks and dashboards. Such vertical integration at the factory may appear to be outdated and expensive, but it guarantees excellent quality. The Recreational Vehicle Dealer Association started giving a quality award in 1996, and Winnebago has won it every year.

The *risks* of vertical integration include (1) the costs and expenses associated with increased overhead and capital expenditures to provide facilities, raw material inputs, and distribution channels inside the organization; (2) a loss of flexibility resulting from the inability to respond quickly to changes in the external environment because of the huge investments in vertical integration activities that generally cannot be easily deployed elsewhere; (3) problems associated with unbalanced capacities or unfilled demand along the value chain; and (4) additional administrative costs associated with managing a more complex set of activities. Exhibit 6.4 summarizes the benefits and risks of vertical integration.

In making decisions associated with vertical integration, four issues should be considered.[18]

1. *Is the company satisfied with the quality of the value that its present suppliers and distributors are providing?* If the performance of organizations in the vertical chain—both suppliers and distributors—is satisfactory, it may not, in general, be appropriate for a company to perform these activities themselves. Firms in the athletic footwear industry such as Nike and Reebok have traditionally outsourced the manufacture of their shoes to countries such as China and Indonesia where labor costs are low. Since the strengths of these companies are typically in design and marketing, it would be advisable to continue to outsource production operations and continue to focus on where they can add the most value.

2. *Are there activities in the industry value chain presently being outsourced or performed independently by others that are a viable source of future profits?* Even if a firm is outsourcing value-chain activities to companies that are doing a credible job, it may be missing out on substantial profit opportunities. To illustrate, consider the automobile industry's profit pool. As you may recall from Chapter 5, there is much more potential profit in many downstream activities (e.g., leasing, warranty, insurance, and service) than in the manufacture of automobiles. Not surprising, carmakers such as Ford and General Motors are undertaking forward integration strategies to become bigger players in these high-profit activities.

Exhibit 6.4
Benefits and Risks of Vertical Integration

Benefits

- A secure source of raw materials or distribution channels.
- Protection of and control over valuable assets.
- Access to new business opportunities.
- Simplified procurement and administrative procedures.

Risks

- Costs and expenses associated with increased overhead and capital expenditures.
- Loss of flexibility resulting from large investments.
- Problems associated with unbalanced capacities along the value chain.
- Additional administrative costs associated with managing a more complex set of activities.

3. *Is there a high level of stability in the demand for the organization's products?* High demand or sales volatility would not be conducive to a vertical integration strategy. With the high level of fixed costs in plant and equipment as well as operating costs that accompany endeavors toward vertical integration, widely fluctuating sales demand can either strain resources (in times of high demand) or result in unused capacity (in times of low demand). The cycles of "boom and bust" in the automobile industry are a key reason why the manufacturers have increased the amount of outsourced inputs in recent years.

4. *How high is the proportion of additional production capacity actually absorbed by existing products or by the prospects of new and similar products?* The smaller the proportion of production capacity to be absorbed by existing or future products, the lower is the potential for achieving scale economies associated with the increased capacity—either in terms of backward integration (toward the supply of raw materials) or forward integration (toward the end user). Alternatively, if there is excess capacity in the near term, the strategy of vertical integration may be viable if there is the anticipation of future expansion of products.

Analyzing Vertical Integration: The Transaction Cost Perspective

Another approach that has proved very useful in understanding vertical integration is the *transaction cost perspective.*[19] According to this perspective, every market transaction involves some *transaction costs.* First, a decision to purchase an input from an outside source leads to *search* costs (i.e., the cost to find where it is available, the level of quality, etc.). Second, there are costs associated with *negotiating.* Third, a *contract* needs to be written spelling out future possible contingencies. Fourth, parties in a contract have to *monitor* each other. Finally, if a party does not comply with the terms of the contract, there are *enforcement* costs. Transaction costs are thus the sum of search costs, negotiation costs, contracting costs, monitoring costs, and enforcement costs. These transaction costs can be avoided by internalizing the activity, in other words, by producing the input in-house.

A related problem with purchasing a specialized input from outside is the issue of *transaction-specific investments.* For example, when an automobile company needs an input specifically designed for a particular car model, the supplier may be unwilling to make the investments in plant and machinery necessary to produce that component for two reasons. First, the investment may take many years to recover but there is no guarantee the automobile company will continue to buy from them after the contract expires, typically in one year. Second, once the investment is made, the supplier has no bargaining power. That is, the buyer knows that the supplier has no option but to supply at ever-lower prices because the investments were so specific that they cannot be used to produce alternative products. In such circumstances, again, vertical integration may be the only option.

Vertical integration, however, gives rise to a different set of costs. These costs are referred to as *administrative costs.* Coordinating different stages of the value chain now internalized within the firm causes administrative costs to go up. Decisions about vertical integration are, therefore, based on a comparison of transaction costs and administrative costs. If transaction costs are lower than administrative costs, it is best to resort to market transactions and avoid vertical integration. For example, McDonald's may be the world's biggest buyer of beef, but they do not raise cattle. The market for beef has low transaction costs and requires no transaction-specific investments. On the other hand, if transaction costs are higher than administrative costs, vertical integration becomes an attractive strategy. Most automobile manufacturers produce their own engines because the market for engines involves high transaction costs and transaction-specific investments.

Vertical Integration: Further Considerations   As many companies would attest, successfully executing strategies of vertical integration can be very difficult. For example, Unocal, a major petroleum refiner, which once owned retail gas stations, was slow to capture the potential grocery and merchandise side business that might have resulted from customer traffic to its service stations. Unocal lacked the competencies to develop a separate retail organization and culture. The company eventually sold the assets and brand to Tosco (now part of Phillips Petroleum Co.). Eli Lilly, the pharmaceutical firm, tried to achieve forward integration by acquiring a pharmaceutical mail-order business in 1994, but it was unsuccessful in increasing market share because it failed to integrate its operations. Two years later, Lilly wrote off the venture.

Last, as with our earlier discussion of pooled negotiating power, managers must carefully consider the impact that vertical integration may have on existing and future customers, suppliers, and competitors. After Lockheed Martin, a dominant defense contractor, acquired Loral Corporation, an electronics supplier, for $9.1 billion, it had an unpleasant and unanticipated surprise. Loral, as a captive supplier of Lockheed, is now perceived and treated as a competitor by many of its previous customers. McDonnell Douglas (MD), for example, announced that it would switch its business from Loral to other suppliers of electronic systems such as Litton Industries or Raytheon. Thus, before Lockheed Martin can realize any net synergies from this acquisition, it must make up for the substantial lost business resulting from MD's (now part of Boeing) decision to switch suppliers.

In these two sections we have addressed four means by which firms can achieve synergies through related diversification: leveraging core competences, sharing activities, pooled negotiating power, and vertical integration. In Strategy Spotlight 6.4, we address how Procter & Gamble strengthened its competitive position by combining all four means. We next turn our attention to unrelated diversification.

>>Unrelated Diversification: Financial Synergies and Parenting

With unrelated diversification, unlike related diversification, few benefits are derived from *horizontal relationships*—that is, the leveraging of core competencies or the sharing of activities across business units within a corporation. Instead, potential benefits can be gained from *vertical (or hierarchical) relationships*—the creation of synergies from the interaction of the corporate office with the individual business units. There are two main sources of such synergies. First, the corporate office can contribute to "parenting" and restructuring of (often acquired) businesses. Second, the corporate office can add value by viewing the entire corporation as a family or "portfolio" of businesses and allocating resources to optimize corporate goals of profitability, cash flow, and growth. Additionally, the corporate office enhances value by establishing appropriate human resource practices and financial controls for each of its business units.

Corporate Parenting and Restructuring

So far, we have discussed how corporations can add value through related diversification by exploring sources of synergy *across* business units. In this section, we will discuss how value can be created *within* business units as a result of the expertise and support provided by the corporate office. Thus, we look at these as *hierarchical* sources of synergy.

The positive contributions of the corporate office have been referred to as the "parenting advantage."[20] Many firms have successfully diversified their holdings without

STRATEGY SPOTLIGHT

6.4

Procter & Gamble: Using Multiple Means to Achieve Synergies

To accomplish successful related diversification, a company must combine multiple facets of its business to create synergies across the organization. Procter & Gamble (P&G) is a prime example of such a firm. Using related diversification, it creates synergies by leveraging core competencies, sharing activities, pooling negotiating power, and vertically integrating certain product lines as part of its corporate-level strategy. The following excerpt from a speech by Clayt Daley, Procter & Gamble's chief financial officer, illustrates how the company has done this.

Remarks to Financial Analysts

Today, we already sell 10 brands with sales of one billion dollars or more. Seven of these 10 brands surpassed the billion-dollar sales mark during the '90s. And, in total, these 10 brands accounted for more than half of our sales growth during the decade. Beyond these 10, there are several brands with the potential to achieve a billion dollars in sales by 2005. Olay could surpass a billion dollars in sales in 2001, Iams by 2002.

P&G's unmatched lineup of billion-dollar leadership brands generates consistently strong returns. In virtually every case, P&G's leading brands achieve higher margins and deliver consistently strong shareholder returns. Having a stable of such strong global brands creates significant advantages for P&G—and our total company scale multiplies those advantages.

We can obviously take advantage of our purchasing power for things as varied as raw materials and advertising media. We can leverage the scale of our manufacturing and logistics operations. But we can do far more.

We have the scale of our intellectual property—the knowledge and deep insight that exists throughout our organization. We have scale in our technologies—the enormous breadth of expertise we have across our product categories. There is scale in our go-to-market capabilities and our global customer relationships.

Let me give you three quick examples. First, scale of consumer knowledge. We are able to learn, reapply, and multiply knowledge across many brands with a similar target audience. For example, teens. The teen market is global. Teens in New York, Tokyo, and Caracas wear the same clothes, listen to the same music, and have many of the same attitudes. We have categories they buy and use: cosmetics, hair care, skin care, personal cleansing and body products, feminine protection, snacks and beverages, oral care, and others. Our scale enables us to develop unique insights on teens—like how to identify teen chat leaders—and then reapply that across all our teen-focused businesses.

Another way we can leverage scale is through the transfer of product technologies across categories. We can connect seemingly unrelated technologies to create surprising new products. Our new Crest White Strips are a great example of the innovation that can result. This new product provides a major new tooth-whitening benefit that can be achieved in the home. We have combined our knowledge in oral hygiene, and our knowledge of bleaching agents, with a special film technology to provide a safe and effective product that can whiten teeth within 14 days.

Another important source of scale is our go-to-market capability. No other consumer products company works with retailers the way we do. Our Customer Business Development approach is a fundamentally different way of working with our trade partners. We seek to build businesses across common goals.

We bring a philosophy that encourages a simple, transparent shopping experience—with simple, transparent pricing, efficient assortment, efficient in-store promotion, and efficient replenishment. This approach has helped us build extremely strong relationships with our customers. For example, in the annual Cannondale "Power-Ranking Survey," U.S. retailers consistently ranked P&G at the top on brands, consumer information, supply-chain management, category management, and more.

Source: Daley, C. 2000. Remarks to Financial Analysts. Speech excerpt. Procter & Gamble Company, September 28.

strong evidence of the more traditional sources of synergy (i.e., horizontally across business units). Diversified public corporations such as BTR, Emerson Electric, and Hanson and leveraged buyout firms such as Kohlberg, Kravis, Roberts & Company, and Clayton, Dublilier & Rice are a few examples.[21] These parent companies create value through management expertise. How? They improve plans and budgets and provide especially competent central functions such as legal, financial, human resource management, procurement, and the like. Additionally, they help subsidiaries make wise choices in their own acquisitions, divestitures, and new internal development decisions. Such contributions often help business units to substantially increase their revenues and profits. Consider Texas-based Cooper Industries' acquisition of Champion International, the spark plug company, as an example of corporate parenting.[22]

Cooper applies a distinctive parenting approach designed to help its businesses improve their manufacturing performance. New acquisitions are "Cooperized"—Cooper audits their manufacturing operations; improves their cost accounting systems; makes their planning, budgeting, and human resource systems conform with its systems; and centralizes union negotiations. Excess cash is squeezed out through tighter controls and reinvested in productivity enhancements, which improve overall operating efficiency. As one manager observed, "When you get acquired by Cooper, one of the first things that happens is a truckload of policy manuals arrives at your door." Such active parenting has been effective in enhancing the competitive advantages of many kinds of manufacturing businesses.

Restructuring is another means by which the corporate office can add substantial value to a business.[23] The central idea can be captured in the real estate phrase "buy low and sell high." Here, the corporate office tries to find either poorly performing firms with unrealized potential or firms in industries on the threshold of significant, positive change. The parent intervenes, often selling off parts of the business; changing the management; reducing payroll and unnecessary sources of expenses; changing strategies; and infusing the company with new technologies, processes, reward systems, and so forth. When the restructuring is complete, the firm can either "sell high" and capture the added value or keep the business in the corporate family and enjoy the financial and competitive benefits of the enhanced performance.[24]

For the restructuring strategy to work, the corporate management must have both the insight to detect undervalued companies (otherwise the cost of acquisition would be too high) or businesses competing in industries with a high potential for transformation.[25] Additionally, of course, they must have the requisite skills and resources to turn the businesses around, even if they may be in new and unfamiliar industries.

Restructuring can involve changes in assets, capital structure, or management. _Asset restructuring_ involves the sale of unproductive assets, or even whole lines of businesses, that are peripheral. In some cases, it may even involve acquisitions that strengthen the core business. _Capital restructuring_ involves changing the debt-equity mix, or the mix between different classes of debt or equity. Although the substitution of equity with debt is more common in buyout situations, occasionally the parent may provide additional equity capital. _Management restructuring_ typically involves changes in the composition of the top management team, organizational structure, and reporting relationships. Tight financial control, rewards based strictly on meeting short- to medium-term performance goals, and reduction in the number of middle-level managers are common steps in management restructuring. In some cases, parental intervention may even result in changes in strategy as well as infusion of new technologies and processes.

Hanson, plc, a British conglomerate, made numerous such acquisitions in the United States in the 1980s, often selling these firms at significant profits after a few years of successful restructuring efforts. Hanson's acquisition and subsequent restructuring of the SCM group is a classic example of the restructuring strategy. Hanson acquired SCM, a diversified manufacturer of industrial and consumer products (including Smith-Corona typewriters, Glidden paints, and Durkee Famous Foods), for $930 million in 1986 after a bitter takeover battle. In the next few months, Hanson sold SCM's paper and pulp operations for $160 million, the chemical division for $30 million, Glidden paints for $580 million, and Durkee Famous Foods for $120 million, virtually recovering the entire original investment. In addition, Hanson also sold the SCM headquarters in New York for $36 million and reduced the headquarters staff by 250. They still retained several profitable divisions, including the titanium dioxide operations and managed them with tight financial controls that led to increased returns.[26]

Portfolio Management

During the 1970s and early 1980s, several leading consulting firms developed the concept of portfolio matrices to achieve a better understanding of the competitive position of an overall portfolio (or family) of businesses, to suggest strategic alternatives for each of the businesses, and to identify priorities for the allocation of resources. Several studies have reported widespread use of these techniques among American firms.[27]

The key purpose of portfolio models was to assist a firm in achieving a balanced portfolio of businesses.[28] This consisted of businesses whose profitability, growth, and cash flow characteristics would complement each other and add up to a satisfactory overall corporate performance. Imbalance, for example, could be caused either by excessive cash generation with too few growth opportunities or by insufficient cash generation to fund the growth requirements in the portfolio. Monsanto, for example, used portfolio planning to restructure its portfolio, divesting low-growth commodity chemicals businesses and acquiring businesses in higher-growth industries such as biotechnology.

The Boston Consulting Group's (BCG) growth/share matrix is among the best known of these approaches.[29] In the BCG approach, each of the firm's strategic business units (SBUs) is plotted on a two-dimensional grid in which the axes are relative market share and industry growth rate. The grid is broken into four quadrants. Exhibit 6.5 depicts the BCG matrix. Following are a few clarifications:

1. Each circle represents one of the corporation's business units. The size of the circle represents the relative size of the business unit in terms of revenues.
2. Relative market share, measured by the ratio of the business unit's size to that of its largest competitor, is plotted along the horizontal axis.
3. Market share is central to the BCG matrix. This is because high relative market share leads to unit cost reduction due to experience and learning curve effects and, consequently, superior competitive position.

Each of the four quadrants of the grid has different implications for the SBUs that fall into the category:

- *Stars* are SBUs competing in high-growth industries with relatively high market shares. These firms have long-term growth potential and should continue to receive substantial investment funding.

- *Question marks* are SBUs competing in high-growth industries but having relatively weak market shares. Resources should be invested in them to enhance their competitive positions.

- *Cash cows* are SBUs with high market shares in low-growth industries. These units have limited long-run potential but represent a source of current cash flows to fund investments in "stars" and "question marks."

- *Dogs* are SBUs with weak market shares in low-growth industries. Because they have weak positions and limited potential, most analysts recommend that they be divested.

In using portfolio strategy approaches, a corporation tries to create synergies and shareholder value in a number of ways.[30] Since the businesses are unrelated, synergies

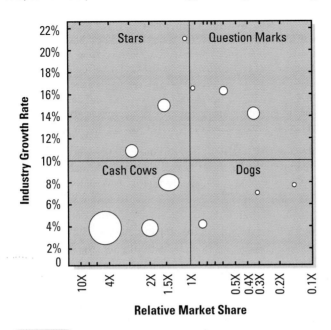

Exhibit 6.5 **The Boston Consulting Group (BCG) Portfolio Matrix**

that develop are those that result from the actions of the corporate office with the individual units (i.e., hierarchical relationships) instead of among business units (i.e., horizontal relationships). First, portfolio analysis provides a snapshot of the businesses in a corporation's portfolio; therefore, the corporation is in a better position to allocate resources among the business units according to prescribed criteria (e.g., use cash flows from the "cash cows" to fund promising "stars"). Second, the expertise and analytical resources in the corporate office provide guidance in determining what firms may be attractive (or unattractive) acquisitions. Third, the corporate office is able to provide financial resources to the business units on favorable terms that reflect the corporation's overall ability to raise funds. Fourth, the corporate office can provide high-quality review and coaching for the individual businesses. Fifth, portfolio analysis provides a basis for developing strategic goals and reward/evaluation systems for business managers. For example, managers of cash cows would have lower targets for revenue growth than managers of stars, but the former would have higher threshold levels of profit targets on proposed projects than the managers of star businesses. Compensation systems would also reflect such realities. Cash cows understandably would be rewarded more on the basis of cash that their businesses generate than would managers of star businesses. Similarly, managers of star businesses would be held to higher standards for revenue growth than managers of cash cow businesses.

To see how companies can benefit from portfolio approaches, consider Ciba-Geigy.

In 1994 Ciba-Geigy adopted portfolio planning approaches to help it manage its business units, which competed in a wide variety of industries, including chemicals, dyes, pharmaceuticals, crop protection, and animal health.[31] It placed each business unit in a category corresponding to the BCG matrix. The business unit's goals, compensation programs, personnel selection, and resource allocation were strongly associated with the category within which the business was placed. For example, business units classified as "cash cows" had much higher hurdles for obtaining financial resources (from the corporate office) for expansion than "question marks" since the latter were businesses for which Ciba-Geigy had high hopes for accelerated future growth and profitability. Additionally, the compensation of a business unit manager in a cash cow would be strongly associated with its success in generating cash to fund other businesses, whereas a manager of a question mark business would be rewarded on his or her ability to increase revenue growth and market share. The portfolio planning approaches appear to be working. In 2004, Ciba-Geigy's (now Novartis) revenues and net income stood at $22 billion and $5.0 billion, respectively. This represents a rather modest 40 percent increase in revenues but a most impressive 150 percent growth in net income over a seven-year period.

Despite the potential benefits of portfolio models, there are also some notable downsides. First, they compare SBUs on only two dimensions, making the implicit but erroneous assumption that (1) those are the only factors that really matter and (2) every unit can be accurately compared on that basis. Second, the approach views each SBU as a stand-alone entity, ignoring common core business practices and value-creating activities that may hold promise for synergies across business units. Third, unless care is exercised, the process becomes largely mechanical, substituting an oversimplified graphical model for the important contributions of the CEO's (and other corporate managers's) experience and judgment. Fourth, the reliance on "strict rules" regarding resource allocation across SBUs can be detrimental to a firm's long-term viability. For example, according to one study, over one-half of all the businesses that should have been cash users (based on the BCG matrix) were instead cash providers.[32] Finally, while colorful and easy to comprehend, the imagery of the BCG matrix can lead to some troublesome and overly simplistic prescriptions. According to one author:

> The dairying analogy is appropriate (for some cash cows), so long as we resist the urge to oversimplify it. On the farm, even the best-producing cows eventually begin to dry up. The farmer's solution to this is euphemistically called "freshening" the cow: The farmer arranges a date for the cow with a bull, she has a calf, the milk begins flowing again. Cloistering the cow—isolating her from everything but the feed trough and the milking machines—assures that she will go dry.[33]

To see what can go wrong, consider Cabot Corporation.

> Cabot Corporation supplies carbon black for the rubber, electronics, and plastics industries. Following the BCG matrix, Cabot moved away from its cash cow, carbon black, and diversified into stars such as ceramics and semiconductors in a seemingly overaggressive effort to create more revenue growth for the corporation. Predictably, Cabot's return on assets declined as the firm shifted away from its core competence to unrelated areas. The portfolio model failed by pointing the company in the wrong direction in an effort to spur growth—away from their core business. Recognizing its mistake, Cabot Corporation returned to its mainstay carbon black manufacturing and divested unrelated businesses. Today the company is a leader in its field with $1.8 billion in 2003 revenues.[34]

Caveat: Is Risk Reduction a Viable Goal of Diversification?

Analysts and academics have suggested that one of the purposes of diversification is to reduce the risk that is inherent in a firm's variability in revenues and profits over time. In essence, the argument is that if a firm enters new products or markets that are affected differently by seasonal or economic cycles, its performance over time will be more stable. For example, a firm manufacturing lawn mowers may diversify into snow blowers to even out its annual sales. Or a firm manufacturing a luxury line of household furniture may introduce a lower-priced line since affluent and lower-income customers are affected differently by economic cycles.

At first glance the above reasoning may make sense, but there are some problems with it. First, a firm's stockholders can diversify their portfolios at a much lower cost than a corporation. As we have noted in this chapter, individuals can purchase their shares with almost no premium (e.g., only a small commission is paid to a discount broker), and they don't have to worry about integrating the acquisition into their portfolio. Second, economic cycles as well as their impact on a given industry (or firm) are difficult to predict with any degree of accuracy.

Notwithstanding the above, some firms have benefited from diversification by lowering the variability (or risk) in their performance over time. Consider Emerson Electronic.

> Emerson Electronic is a $16 billion manufacturer that has enjoyed an incredible run—43 consecutive years of earnings growth![35] It produces a wide variety of products, including measurement devices for heavy industry, temperature controls for heating and ventilation systems, and power tools sold at Home Depot. Recently, many analysts questioned Emerson's purchase of companies that sell power systems to the volatile telecommunications industry. Why? This industry is expected to experience, at best, minimal growth. However, CEO David Farr maintained that such assets could be acquired inexpensively because of the aggregate decline in demand in this industry. Additionally, he argued that the other business units, such as the sales of valves and regulators to the now-booming oil and natural gas companies, were able to pick up the slack. Therefore, while net profits in the electrical equipment sector (Emerson's core business) sharply decreased, Emerson's overall corporate profits increased 1.7 percent.

In summary, risk reduction in and of itself is rarely viable as a means to create shareholder value. It must be undertaken with a view of a firm's overall diversification strategy.

>>The Means to Achieve Diversification

In the prior three sections, we have addressed the types of diversification (e.g., related and unrelated) that a firm may undertake to achieve synergies and create value for its shareholders. In this section, we address the means by which a firm can go about achieving these desired benefits.

We will address three basic means. First, through acquisitions or mergers, corporations can directly acquire the assets and competencies of other firms. Second, corporations may agree to pool the resources of other companies with their resource base. This approach is commonly known as a joint venture or strategic alliance. Although these two forms of partnerships are similar in many ways, there is an important difference. Joint ventures involve the formation of a third-party legal entity where the two (or more) firms each contribute equity, whereas strategic alliances do not. Third, corporations may diversify into new products, markets, and technologies through internal development. This approach, sometimes called corporate entrepreneurship, involves the leveraging and combining of a firm's own resources and competencies to create synergies and enhance shareholder value.

Mergers and Acquisitions

The rate of mergers and acquisitions (M&A) had dropped off beginning in 2001. This trend was largely a result of a recession, corporate scandals, and a declining stock market. However, the situation has changed dramatically. Recently, several large mergers and acquisitions were announced. These include:[36]

- Sprint's merger with Nextel for $39 billion.
- Johnson & Johnson's $25 billion acquisition of medical device maker Guidant.
- Exelon's acquisition of Public Service Enterprise Group for $12 billion.
- SBC's purchase of AT&T for $16 billion.
- Procter & Gamble's purchase of Gillette for $54 billion.
- Kmart Holding Corp.'s acquisition of Sears, Roebuck & Co. for $11 billion.

Let's make some deals
The value of U.S. mergers and acquisitions has been steadily increasing since 2002.

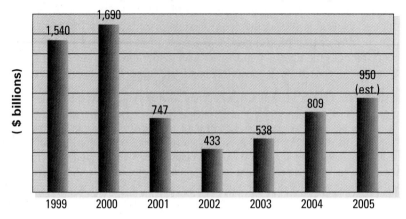

Exhibit 6.6   U.S. Mergers and Acquisitions

Sources: Thomson Financial; and, Coy, P., Thornton, E., Arndt, M. Grow, B. 2005. Shake rattle, and merge. *BusinessWeek,* January 10:34.

Exhibit 6.6 illustrates the dramatic increase in merger and acquisition activity in the United States in the past few years. While the volume is not expected soon to reach the peak level of 1999 and 2000, when the dollar amount totaled over $3 trillion, several factors help to explain the recent rise. First, there is the robust economy and the increasing corporate profits that have boosted stock prices and cash. For example, the Standard & Poor's 500 stock index companies, including financial companies, have a record $2 trillion in cash and other short-term assets, according to S&P Compustat.

Second, the weak U.S. dollar makes U.S. assets more attractive to other countries. That is, from the perspective of a foreign acquirer, compared to any other period in recent memory, U.S. companies are "cheap" today. For example, a Euro which was worth only 80 cents in 1999 was worth $1.25 by early 2005. This makes U.S. companies a relative bargain for a European acquirer. And third, stricter governance standards are requiring poorly performing CEOs and boards of directors to consider unsolicited offers. In essence, top executives and board members are less likely to be protected by anti-takeover mechanisms such as greenmail, poison pills and golden parachutes (which we will discuss at the end of the chapter).

Next, we will address some of the motives and potential benefits of mergers and acquisitions as well as their potential limitations.

Motives and Benefits   Growth through mergers and acquisitions has played a critical role in the success of many corporations in a wide variety of high-technology and knowledge-intensive industries. Here, market and technology changes can occur very quickly and unpredictably.[37] Speed—speed to market, speed to positioning, and speed to becoming a viable company—is critical in such industries. For example, Alex Mandl, then AT&T's president, was responsible for the acquisition of McCaw Cellular. Although many industry experts felt the price was too steep, he believed that cellular technology was a critical asset for the telecommunications business and that it would have been extremely difficult to build that business from the ground up. Mandl claimed, "The plain fact is that acquiring is much faster than building."[38]

As we discussed earlier in the chapter, mergers and acquisitions also can be a means of *obtaining valuable resources that can help an organization expand its product offerings and services.* For example, Cisco Systems, a dominant player in networking equipment, acquired more than 70 companies from 1993 to early 2000.[39] This provides Cisco with access to the latest in networking equipment. Then it uses its excellent sales force to market the new technology to its corporate customers and telephone companies. Cisco also provides strong incentives to the staff of acquired companies to stay on. In order to realize the greatest value from its acquisitions, Cisco also has learned to integrate acquired companies efficiently and effectively.[40]

Mergers and acquisitions also can *provide the opportunity for firms to attain the three bases of synergy that were addressed earlier in the chapter—leveraging core competencies, sharing activities, and building market power.* Consider Procter & Gamble's $54 billion proposed acquisition of Gillette.[41] First, it should help Procter & Gamble to leverage its core competencies in marketing and product positioning in the area of grooming and personal care brands. For example, P&G has experience in repositioning brands such as Old Spice in this market (which recently passed Gillette's Right Guard brand to become No. 1 in the deodorant market). Gillette has very strong brands in razors and blades. Thus, P&G's marketing expertise should help it to enhance its market position. Second, there are opportunities to share value-creating activities. Gillette will benefit from P&G's stronger distribution network in developing countries where the potential growth rate for the industry's products remains higher than in the United States, Europe, or Japan. Consider the insight of A. F. Lafley, P&G's CEO:

> When I was in Asia in the 90s, we had already gone beyond the top 500 cities in China. Today, we're way down into the rural areas. So we add three, four, five Gillette brands, and we don't even have to add a salesperson.

Finally, the addition of Gillette will enhance P&G's market power. In recent years, the growth of powerful global retailers such as Wal-Mart, Carrefour, and Costco has eroded much of the consumer goods industry's pricing power. A central part of P&G's recent strategy has been to focus its resources on enhancing its core brands. Today, 16 of its brands (each with revenues of over $1 billion) account for $30 billion of the firm's $51.4 billion in total revenues. Gillette, with $10.5 billion in total revenues, adds five brands which also have revenues of over $1 billion. P&G anticipates that its growing stable of "superbrands" will help it to weather the industry's tough pricing environment and enhance its power relative to large, powerful retailers.

Merger and acquisition activity also can *lead to consolidation within an industry and can force other players to merge.*[42] In the pharmaceutical industry, the patents for many top-selling drugs are expiring and M&A activity is expected to heat up.[43] For example, SG Cowen Securities predicts that between 2000 and 2005, U.S. patents will expire on pharmaceutical products with annual domestic sales of approximately $34.6 billion. Clearly, this is an example of how the political-legal segment of the general environment (discussed in Chapter 2) can affect a corporation's strategy and performance. Although health care providers and patients are happy about the lower-cost generics that will arrive, drug firms are being pressed to make up for lost revenues. Combining top firms such as Pfizer Inc. and Warner-Lambert Co. as well as Glaxo Wellcome and SmithKline Beecham has many potential long-term benefits. They not only promise significant post-merger cost savings, but also the increased size of the combined companies brings greater research and development possibilities.

Two other industries where consolidation is the primary rationale are telecommunications and software.[44] In 2004, Cingular Wireless became number one in the industry by acquiring AT&T Wireless Communications. Subsequently, Sprint agreed to buy Nextel to form a stronger number three. SBC Communications Inc. desires to have full ownership of Cingular, but BellSouth does not want to sell its 40 percent ownership. Will SBC simply buy all of BellSouth? Says SBC chief operating officer (COO) Randall Stephenson, "I don't want to speculate, but who knows? This industry is going to continue to consolidate." In software, the primary motive for merger is to offer customers a fuller portfolio of products. Many niche players are selling out to serial buyers like Oracle Corp., which recently acquired PeopleSoft Inc. after a long and heated struggle. Symantec Corp. agreed to acquire Veritas Software Corporation for $13.5 billion. Such consolidation raises questions about whether smaller players such as McAfee, BEA Systems, and Siebel Systems are big enough to remain independent. According to Joseph M. Tucci, president and CEO of data-storage giant EMC, "This is going to be a big boys' game. They're going to move very aggressively and quickly."

Strategy Spotlight 6.5 discusses how Ken Hendricks was able to successfully consolidate the highly fragmented, and low-margin industry of roofing supplies. The example shows that industry consolidation can take place in lesser known, and more mundane, industries.

Corporations can also *enter new market segments by way of acquisitions.* Although Charles Schwab & Co. is best known for providing discount trading services for middle America, it clearly is interested in other target markets.[45] In late 2000 Schwab surprised its rivals by paying $2.7 billion to acquire U.S. Trust Corporation, a 147-year-old-financial services institution that is a top estate planner for the wealthy, as noted in the chapter's opening case. However, Schwab is in no way ignoring its core market. The firm also purchased Cybercorp Inc., a Texas brokerage company, for $488 million. That firm offers active online traders sophisticated quotes and stock-screening tools.

Potential Limitations   As noted in the previous section, mergers and acquisitions provide a firm with many potential benefits. However, at the same time, there are many potential drawbacks or limitations to such corporate activity.[46]

First, *the takeover premium that is paid for an acquisition is very high.* Two times out of three, the stock price of the acquiring company falls once the deal is made public. Since the acquiring firm often pays a 30 percent to 40 percent premium for the target company, the acquirer must create synergies and scale economies that result in sales and market gains exceeding the premium price. Firms paying higher premiums set the performance hurdle even higher. For example, Household International paid an 82 percent premium to buy Beneficial, and Conseco paid an 83 percent premium to acquire Green Tree Financial. Historically, paying a high premium over the stock price has been a largely unprofitable strategy.

Second, *competing firms often can imitate any advantages realized or copy synergies that result from the M&A.* Thus, a firm can often see its advantages quickly evaporate if it plans to achieve competitive advantage through M&A activity. Unless the advantages are sustainable and difficult to copy, investors will not be willing to pay a high premium for the stock. Similarly, the time value of money must be factored into the stock price. M&A costs are paid up front. Conversely, firms pay for research and development, ongoing marketing, and capacity expansion over time. This stretches out the payments needed to gain new competencies. The M&A argument is that a large initial investment is worthwhile because it creates long-term advantages. However, stock analysts want to see immediate results from such a large cash outlay. If the acquired firm does not produce results quickly, investors often sell the stock, driving the price down.

Third, *managers' credibility and ego can sometimes get in the way of sound business decisions.* If the M&A does not perform as planned, managers who pushed for the deal find that their reputation may be at stake. Sometimes, this can lead these managers

How Ken Hendricks Consolidated the Roofing Industry

As a child growing up in Janesville, Wisconsin, Ken Hendricks sensed the contempt "the country club set" had for his blue-collar family because of his father's humble job as a roofer. "They looked down their noses at him," Hendricks says. "He went to work every single day of his life. That wasn't good enough? Some kid got to go to a fancy school and that made him different than me? That just sets in your gut."

Whatever has driven Mr. Hendricks, he has become a remarkable success. Last year, his Beloit, Wisconsin–based American Builders & Contractors Supply (ABC) was the largest wholesaler of roofing supplies in the United States and among the largest supplies of vinyl sidings and windows. In 2004, the firm netted $67 million in profits on revenues of $1.8 billion. And as the sole owner of the privately held company, Hendricks joined the Forbes 400 with an estimated net worth of $850 million.

In his early years, Ken worked as an independent roofer, picking up jobs where he could, and subcontracting out some of the work. He had his big break when a major hailstorm hit a small town near where he lived. He met with the insurance company's claims adjuster and he offered to charge his normal pricing in exchange for a contract that combined all of the damaged roofs. (Most of his rivals typically inflated their prices in order to exploit the situation.) Eventually word spread, and before he was 30 years old, he had about 500 roofers working for him around the country.

Several years later—after selling off his business and settling into a leisurely life pursuing a sideline of renovating real estate—he began thinking about the need for a national distribution chain. He recalled that as a contractor he was constantly frustrated by dealing with dozens of suppliers, none of which could sell everything he needed.

And he sensed that there was a tremendous amount of complacency, waste, and room for improvement.

In 1982, Hendricks bought his first three distributors and intensified his acquisition activities over the next 15 years. By 1997, Hendricks had 157 outlets, $789 million in revenues, and a profit of $10 million. In total, he has made over 60 acquisitions, and ABC now has 280 locations in the United States.

He made it work by negotiating volume discounts with manufacturers and exercising very tight cost control. He used to deliver shingles to job sites with used trucks instead of buying new ones. He recycles pallets and sells them back to the manufacturer. ABC's point-of-sales system was built with a $20,000 software package, and it is still the heart of the company's computer system today.

Although Hendricks does not have the latest customer-relationship software, he does have an understanding of customer needs. "I've been up on the roof. I know what those guys are going through. My whole life has been about making that profession respectable."

But how will the competition from the big hardware and home-improvement chains affect ABC? Replies Hendricks, "We've got 256 different shingles by brand, weight, and color. Home Depot's not going to waste the shelf space. It's a low-margin business."

A testimony from a satisfied customer exemplifies ABC's commitment to excellent customer service. Robert Shannon, a contractor in Mineola, New York, has 50 roofers working for him. That makes him a very desirable customer for ABC as well as Home Depot. Some bad customer-service experiences soured him on Home Depot, and he is now loyal to ABC. Says Shannon, "They've delivered shingles overnight from Boston, stuff I needed the next day. No other supplier does that. They understand if you have nine crew members standing around with nothing to do, that costs money."

Sources: Armstrong, D. 2004. Up on the roof. *Forbes,* November 29: 184–188; and Welles, E. O. 2001. Roll your own. *Inc.,* February: 68–72.

to protect their credibility by funneling more money, or escalating their commitment, into an inevitably doomed operation. Further, when a merger fails and a firm tries to unload the acquisition, managers often find that they must sell at a huge discount. These problems further compound the costs and weaken the stock price.

Fourth, *there can be many cultural issues that may doom the intended benefits from M&A endeavors.* Consider, for example, the insights of Joanne Lawrence, who played an important role as vice president and director of communications and investor relations at SmithKline Beecham, in the merger between SmithKline and the Beecham Group, a diversified consumer-oriented group headquartered in the United Kingdom.[47]

The key to a strategic merger is to create a new culture. This was a mammoth challenge during the SmithKline Beecham merger. We were working at so many different cultural levels, it was dizzying. We had two national cultures to blend—American and British—that compounded the challenge of selling the merger in two different markets with two different shareholder bases. There were also two different business cultures: One was very strong, scientific, and academic; the other was much more commercially oriented. And then we had to consider within both companies the individual businesses, each of which has its own little culture.[48]

Strategic Alliances and Joint Ventures

Strategic alliances and joint ventures are assuming an increasingly prominent role in the strategy of leading firms, both large and small.[49] Such cooperative relationships have many potential advantages. Among these are entering new markets, reducing manufacturing (or other) costs in the value chain, and developing and diffusing new technologies.[50]

Entering New Markets   Often a company that has a successful product or service wants to introduce it into a new market. However, it may not have the requisite marketing expertise because it does not understand customer needs, know how to promote the product, or have access to the proper distribution channels.

The partnerships formed between Time-Warner, Inc., and three African American–owned cable companies in New York City are examples of joint ventures created to serve a domestic market. Time-Warner built a 185,000-home cable system in the city and asked the three cable companies to operate it. Time-Warner supplied the product, and the cable companies supplied the knowledge of the community and the know-how to market the cable system. Joining with the local companies enabled Time-Warner to win the acceptance of the cable customers and to benefit from an improved image in the black community.

Reducing Manufacturing (or Other) Costs in the Value Chain   Strategic alliances (or joint ventures) often enable firms to pool capital, value-creating activities, or facilities in order to reduce costs. For example, Molson Companies and Carling O'Keefe Breweries in Canada formed a joint venture to merge their brewing operations. Although Molson had a modern and efficient brewery in Montreal, Carling's was outdated. However, Carling had the better facilities in Toronto. In addition, Molson's Toronto brewery was located on the waterfront and had substantial real estate value. Overall, the synergies gained by using their combined facilities more efficiently added $150 million of pretax earnings during the initial year of the venture. Economies of scale were realized and facilities were better utilized.

Developing and Diffusing New Technologies   Strategic alliances also may be used to build jointly on the technological expertise of two or more companies in order to develop products technologically beyond the capability of the companies acting independently. STMicroelectronics (ST) is a high-tech company based in Geneva, Switzerland, that has thrived—largely due to the success of its strategic alliances.[51] The firm develops and manufactures computer chips for a variety of applications such as mobile phones, set-top boxes, smart cards, and flash memories. In 1995 it teamed up with Hewlett-Packard to develop powerful new processors for various digital applications that are now nearing completion. Another example was its strategic alliance with Nokia to develop a chip that would give Nokia's phones a longer battery life. Here, ST produced a chip that tripled standby time to 60 hours—a breakthough that gave Nokia a huge advantage in the marketplace.

The firm's CEO, Pasquale Pistorio, was among the first in the industry to form R&D alliances with other companies. Now ST's top 12 customers, including HP, Nokia, and Nortel, account for 45 percent of revenues. According to Pistorio, "Alliances are in our DNA." Such relationships help ST keep better-than-average growth rates, even in difficult times. That's because close partners are less likely to defect to other suppliers. ST's financial results are most impressive. During 2000 its revenues grew 55 percent—nearly double the industry average.

Despite their promise, many alliances and joint ventures fail to meet expectations for a variety of reasons. First, without the proper partner, a firm should never consider undertaking an alliance, even for the best of reasons. Each partner should bring the desired complementary strengths to the partnership. Ideally, the strengths contributed by the partners are unique; thus synergies created can be more easily sustained and defended over the longer term. The goal must be to develop synergies between the contributions of the partners, resulting in a win–win situation for both. Moreover, the partners must be compatible and willing to trust each other. Unfortunately, often little attention is given to nurturing the close working relationships and interpersonal connections that bring together the partnering organizations. The human or people factors are not carefully considered or, at worst, they are dismissed as an unimportant consideration.

Internal Development

Firms can also diversify by means of corporate entrepreneurship and new venture development. In today's economy, internal development is such an important means by which companies expand their businesses that we have devoted a whole chapter to it (see Chapter 12). Sony and the Minnesota Mining & Manufacturing Co. (3M), for example, are known for their dedication to innovation, R&D, and cutting-edge technologies. For example, 3M has developed its entire corporate culture to support its ongoing policy of generating at least 25 percent of total sales from products created within the most recent four-year period. During the 1990s, 3M exceeded this goal by achieving about 30 percent of sales per year from new internally developed products.

Many companies use some form of internal development to extend their product lines or add to their service offerings. This approach to internal development is used by many large publicly held corporations as well as small firms. An example of the latter is Rosa Verde, a small but growing business serving the health care needs of San Antonio, Texas.

> This small company began with one person who moved from Mexico to San Antonio, Texas, to serve the health care needs of inner-city residents.[52] Beginning as a sole proprietor, Dr. Lourdes Pizana started Rosa Verde Family Health Care Group in 1995 with only $10,000 obtained from credit card debt. She has used a strategy of internal development to propel the company to where it is today—six clinics, 30 doctors, and a team of other health care professionals.
>
> How was Dr. Pizana able to accomplish this in such a short time? She emphasizes the company's role in the community, forging links with community leaders. In addition, she hires nearly all her professional staff as independent contractors to control costs. These professionals are paid based on the volume of work they do rather than a set salary; Pizana splits her revenue with them, thus motivating them to work efficiently. Her strategy is to grow the company from the inside out through high levels of service, commitment to the community she serves, and savvy leadership. By committing to a solid plan, Pizana has proven that internal growth and development can be a successful strategy.

The luxury hotel chain Ritz-Carlton has long been recognized for its exemplary service. In fact, it is the only service company ever to win two Malcolm Baldrige National Quality Awards. It has built on this capability by developing a highly successful internal venture to offer leadership development programs—both to its employees as well as to outside companies. We address this internal venture in Strategy Spotlight 6.6.

Compared to mergers and acquisitions, firms that engage in internal development are able to capture the value created by their own innovative activities without having to "share the wealth" with alliance partners or face the difficulties associated with combining activities across the value chains of several companies or merging corporate cultures. Another advantage is that firms can often develop new products or services at a relatively lower

STRATEGY SPOTLIGHT

The Ritz-Carlton Leadership Center: A Successful Internal Venture

Companies worldwide often strive to be the "Ritz-Carlton" of their industries. Ritz-Carlton, the large luxury hotel chain, is the only service company to have won the prestigious Malcolm Baldrige National Quality Award twice—in 1992 and 1999 (one year after being acquired by Marriott). It also has placed first in guest satisfaction among luxury hotels in the most recent J.D. Power & Associates hotel survey.

Until a few years ago, being "Ritz-Carlton-like" was just a motivational simile. However, in 2000, the company launched the Ritz-Carlton Leadership Center, where it offers 12 leadership development programs for its employees and seven benchmarking seminars and workshops to outside companies. It also conducts 35 off-site presentations on such topics as "Creating a Dynamic Employee Orientation," and "The Key to Retaining and Selecting Talented Employees." (Incidentally, Ritz-Carlton's annual turnover

rate among nonmanagement employees is 25 percent—roughly half the average rate for U.S. luxury hotels.)

Within its first four years of operation, 800 different companies from such industries as health care, banking and finance, hospitality, and the automotive industries have participated in the Leadership Center's programs. And to date it has generated over $2 million in revenues. Ken Yancey, CEO of the nonprofit small-business consultancy, Score, says the concepts he learned, like "the three steps of service," apply directly to his business. "Hotels are about service to a client," he says. "And we are too."

To give a few specifics on one of the Leadership Center's programs, consider its "Legendary Service I" course. The topics that are covered include empowerment, using customer recognition to boost loyalty, and Ritz-Carlton's approach to quality. The course lasts two days and costs $2,000 per attendee. Well-known companies that have participated include Microsoft, Morgan Stanley, and Starbucks.

Sources: McDonald, D. 2004. Roll out the blue carpet. *Business 2.0*, May: 53; and Johnson, G. 2003. Nine tactics to take your corporate university from good to GREAT. *Training*, July/August: 38–41.

cost and thus rely on their own resources rather than turning to external funding. There are also potential disadvantages. Internal development may be time consuming; thus, firms may forfeit the benefits of speed that growth through mergers or acquisitions can provide. This may be especially important among high-tech or knowledge-based organizations in fast-paced environments where being an early mover is critical. Thus, firms that choose to diversify through internal development must develop capabilities that allow them to move quickly from initial opportunity recognition to market introduction.

>>Real Options Analysis: A Useful Tool

Real options analysis (ROA) is an investment analysis tool from the field of finance. It has been slowly, but increasingly, adopted by consultants and executives to support strategic decision making in firms. What does real options analysis consist of and how can it be appropriately applied to the investments required to initiate strategic decisions? To understand *real* options it is first necessary to have a basic understanding of what *options* are.

Options exist when the owner of the option has the right but not the obligation to engage in certain types of transactions. The most common are stock options. A stock option grants the holder the right to buy (call option) or sell (put option) shares of the stock at a fixed price (strike price) at some time in the future.[53] Another aspect of stock options important to note is that the investment to be made immediately is small, whereas the investment to be made in the future is generally larger. For example, an option to buy a rapidly rising stock currently priced at $50 might cost as little as $.50.[54] An important point to note is that owners of such a stock option have limited their losses to $.50 per share, while the upside potential is unlimited. This aspect of options is attractive because options offer the prospect of high gains with relatively small up-front investments that represent limited losses.

The phrase "real options" applies to situations where options theory and valuation techniques are applied to real assets or physical things as opposed to financial assets. Some of the most common applications of real options are with property and insurance. A real estate option grants the holder the right to buy or sell a piece of property at an established price some time in the future. The actual market price of the property may rise above the established (or strike) price—or the market value may sink below the strike price. If the price of the property goes up, the owner of the option is likely to buy it. If the market value of the property drops below the strike price, the option holder is unlikely to execute the purchase. In the latter circumstance, the option holder has limited his or her loss to the cost of the option, but during the life of the option retains the right to participate in whatever the upside potential might be. Casualty insurance is another variation of real options. With casualty insurance, the owner of the property has limited the loss to the cost of the insurance, while the upside potential is the actual loss, ranging, of course, up to the limit of the insurance.[55]

Applications of Real Options Analysis to Strategic Decisions

The concept of options can also be applied to strategic decisions where management has flexibility; that is, the situation will permit management to decide whether to invest additional funds to grow or accelerate the activity, perhaps delay in order to learn more, shrink the scale of the activity, or even abandon it. Decisions to invest in business activities such as R&D, motion pictures, exploration and production of oil wells, and the opening and closing of copper mines often have this flexibility.[56] Important issues to note are the following:

- Real options analysis is appropriate to use when investments can be staged; in other words, a smaller investment up front can be followed by subsequent investments. In short, real options can be applied to an investment decision that gives the company the right, but not the obligation, to make follow-on investments.

- The strategic decision makers have "tollgates" or key points at which they can decide whether to continue, delay, or abandon the project. In short, the executives have the flexibility. There are opportunities to make other go or no–go decisions associated with each phase.

- It is expected that there will be increased knowledge about outcomes at the time of the next investment and that additional knowledge will help inform the decision makers about whether to make additional investments (i.e., whether the option is in the money or out of the money).

Many strategic decisions have the characteristic of containing a series of options. The phenomenon is called "embedded options," a series of investments in which at each stage of the investment there is a go/no–go decision. For example, pharmaceutical companies have successfully used real options analysis in evaluating decisions about investments in pharmaceutical R&D projects since the early 1990s.[57] Pharmaceuticals have at least four stages of investments: basic research yielding compounds and the three FDA-mandated phases of clinical trials. Generally, each phase is more expensive to undertake than the previous phase. However, as each phase unfolds, management knows more about the underlying drug and the many sources of uncertainty, including the technical difficulties with the drugs themselves as well as external market conditions, such as the results of competitors' research.[58] Management can make the decision to invest more with the intent of speeding up the process, delay the start of the next phase, reduce investment, or even abandon the R&D.[59]

As noted above, the use of real options analysis can provide the firm with many opportunities for learning. In many cases, such learning can extend beyond the specific investment or project at hand. For example, consider Eli Lilly's 1984 investment in a start-up biotechnology firm, Hybritech:[60]

> Within two years of making its investment in Hybritech, Eli Lilly acquired the firm outright, acquiring full access to drugs that Hybritech was pursuing. The first and primary benefit for Eli Lilly was access to a drug before it had been approved by the FDA, allowing them to acquire it at a much lower cost than if they had waited for FDA approval. They also acquired access to Hybritech's management and existing knowledge—another benefit. The benefit easiest to overlook, however, was learning how to partner with a biotechnology start-up with different expertise (i.e., Eli Lilly was engaged in chemical-based science; Hybritech was genetically based). This enabled them to learn how to better work with their biotechnology partners and how to transmit that information inside Eli Lilly more efficiently. They wrote an option to acquire Hybritech and also wrote an option to learn how to partner with other biotechnology firms. Long term, the latter appears to have been the more valuable real option. Lilly has brought more drugs to market from its collaboration with its partners than has nearly anyone else. Lilly's recent FDA-approved drug, Cialis, resulted from a partnership with another biotechnology firm, Icos.

Strategy Spotlight 6.7 provides two examples of companies using ROA to guide their decision-making process.

Potential Pitfalls of Real Options Analysis

Despite the many benefits that can be gained from using real options analysis, managers must be aware of its potential limitations or pitfalls. Below we will address three major issues.[61]

Agency Theory and the Back-Solver Dilemma   Let's assume that companies adopting a real-options perspective invest heavily in training and that their people understand how to effectively estimate variance—that is, the amount of dispersion or range that is estimated for potential outcomes. Such training can help them use ROA. However, it does not solve another inherent problem: managers may have an incentive and the know-how to "game the system." Most electronic spreadsheets permit users to simply back-solve any formula; that is, you can type in the answer you want and ask what values are needed in a formula to get that answer. If managers know that a certain option value must be met in order for the proposal to get approved, they can back-solve the model to find a variance estimate needed to arrive at the answer that upper management desires. What would be the manager's motive to do this?

Agency problems are typically inherent in investment decisions. They may occur when the managers of a firm are separated from its owners—that is, when managers act as "agents" rather than "principals" (owners). Such problems could occur because a manager may have something to gain by not acting in the owner's best interests, or the interests of managers and owners are not co-aligned. Agency theory suggests that as managerial and owner interests diverge, managers will follow the path of their own self-interests. Sometimes this is to secure better compensation. At other times, those interests involve exerting less effort. In terms of securing better compensation, agency problems arise because managers who propose projects may believe that if their projects are approved, they stand a much better chance of getting promoted. So while managers have an incentive to propose projects that *should* be successful, they also have an incentive to propose projects that *might* be successful. And because of the subjectivity involved in formally modeling a real option, managers may have an incentive to choose variance values that increase the likelihood of approval.

Managerial Conceit: Overconfidence and the Illusion of Control
Often, poor decisions are the result of such traps as biases, blind spots, and other human frailties. Much of this literature falls under the concept of *managerial conceit*.[62]

STRATEGY SPOTLIGHT

Applications of Real Options Analysis

The following two examples illustrate how real options analysis (ROA) is enjoying increasing popularity among strategists facing the task of allocating resources in an era of great uncertainty. In the first example, a privately held biotechnology firm is using ROA to analyze an internal development decision. In the second example pharmaceutical giant Merck uses this tool to decide whether to enter into a strategic alliance. In each of these cases, ROA led to a different decision outcome than that of more traditional net present value (NPV) analysis. NPV is the sum of costs and revenues for the life of the project, discounted typically by current interest rates to reflect the time value of money.

- A privately held biotechnology firm had developed a unique technology for introducing the coat protein of a particular virus into animal feedstock. Ingesting the coat protein generated an immune response, thus protecting the animal from the virus. The firm was at the beginning of the preclinical trials stage, the first of a series of tests required by FDA regulation and conducted through the FDA subagency called the Center for Veterinary Medicine. The company expected the stage to take 18 months and cost $2 million. Long-standing experience indicated that 95 percent of new drug investigations are abandoned during this phase. Subsequent stages would decrease somewhat in terms of the possibility of rejection, but costs would rise, with a total outflow from 2002 through anticipated launch in 2007 of at least $18.5 million. The company's best estimate of the market from 2007 through 2017 was about $85 million per year, with the possibility of taking as much as a 50 percent market share. In short, there was huge potential, but in the interim there was tremendous chance of

Sources: Stockley, R. L., Jr., Curtis, S., Jafari, J., and Tibbs, K. 2003. The option value of an early-stage biotechnology investment. *Journal of Applied Finance,* 15(2): 44–55; and Mauboussin, M. H. 1999. Get real: Using real options in security analysis. *Equity Research Series by Credit Suite/First Boston,* 10, June 23: 18.

failure (i.e., high risk), significant early outflows, and delayed inflows. Analysis using a traditional NPV analysis yielded a negative $2 million with an 11 percent risk-adjusted discount rate. Viewing the investment as a multistage option, however, and incorporating management's flexibility to change its decision at a minimum of four points between 2002 and 2007, changes the valuation markedly. A real options analysis approach to the analysis demonstrated a present value of about $22 million. The question was not whether to risk $18.5 million, but whether to invest $2 million today for the opportunity to earn $22 million.

- Merck has applied real options analysis to a number of its strategic decisions. One was the agreement it signed with Biogen, which in the late 1990s had developed an asthma drug. Instead of purchasing Biogen outright, Merck created a real options arrangement. Merck paid Biogen $15 million up front and retained the right to invest up to an additional $130 million at various points as the biotechnology company reached specified milestones. In essence, Merck purchased a stream of options: the right to scale up and scale down, or even abandon, the option. Merck's potential in the deal was unlimited, while its downside risk was limited to the extent of the milestone payments. Analysis suggested that the present value of the deal was about $275 million, considerably more than the present value of the up-front and milestone payments. Using traditional NPV methods would have killed this deal. However, real options analysis encouraged Merck to undertake the arrangement, in part, because Merck was in the process of learning about the underlying technology. Biogen, on the other hand, gained the advantage of committed cash flow to continue development—provided that developments from the various phases continued to be favorable.

Understanding how these traps affect decision makers can help to improve decision making.

First, managerial conceit occurs when managers who have made successful choices in the past may come to believe that they possess superior expertise for managing uncertainty. They believe that their abilities can, therefore, reduce the risks inherent in decision making to a much greater extent than they actually can. Such managers are more likely to shift away from analysis to trusting their own judgment. In the case of real options, they can simply declare that any given decision is a real option and proceed as before. If asked to formally model their decision, they are more likely to employ variance estimates that support their viewpoint.

Second, employing the real-options perspective can encourage decision makers toward a bias for action. Such a bias may lead to carelessness. Managerial conceit is as much a problem (if not more so) for small decisions as for big ones. Why? The cost to write the first stage of an option is much smaller than the cost of full commitment, and managers pay less attention to small decisions than to large ones. Because real options are designed to minimize potential losses while preserving potential gains, any problems that arise are likely to be smaller at first, causing less concern for the manager. Managerial conceit could suggest that managers will assume that those problems are the easiest to solve and control—a concern referred to as the illusion of control. Managers may fail to respond appropriately because they overlook the problem or believe that since it is small, they can easily resolve it. Thus, managers may approach each real-option decision with less care and diligence than if they had made a full commitment to a larger investment.

Managerial Conceit: Irrational Escalation of Commitment   A strength of a real options perspective is also one of its Achilles heels. Both real options and decisions involving escalation of commitment require specific environments with sequential decisions.[63] As the escalation-of-commitment literature indicates, simply separating a decision into multiple parts does not guarantee that decisions made will turn out well. This condition is potentially present whenever the exercise decision retains some uncertainty, which most still do. The decision to abandon also has strong psychological factors associated with it that affect the ability of managers to make correct exercise decisions.[64]

An option to exit requires reversing an initial decision made by someone in the organization. Organizations typically encourage managers to "own their decisions" in order to motivate them. One result is that as managers invest themselves in their decision, it proves harder for them to lose face by reversing course. In effect, for managers making the decision, it feels as if they made the wrong decision in the first place, even if it was initially a good decision. The more specific the manager's human capital becomes, the harder it is to transfer it to other organizations. Hence, there is a greater likelihood that managers will stick around and try to make an existing decision work. They are more likely to continue an existing project even if it should perhaps be ended.[65]

>>How Managerial Motives Can Erode Value Creation

Thus far in the chapter we have implicitly assumed that CEOs and top executives are "rational beings"; that is, they act in the best interests of shareholders to maximize long-term shareholder value. In the real world, however, this is not the case. Frequently, they may act in their own self-interest. Next we address some managerial motives that can serve to erode, rather than enhance, value creation. These include "growth for growth's sake," excessive egotism, and the creation of a wide variety of antitakeover tactics.

Growth for Growth's Sake

There are huge incentives for executives to increase the size of their firm, and many of these are hardly consistent with increasing shareholder wealth. Top managers, including the CEO, of larger firms typically enjoy more prestige, higher rankings for their companies on the Fortune 500 list (which is based on revenues, not profits), greater incomes, more job security, and so on. There is also the excitement and associated recognition of making a major acquisition. As noted by Harvard's Michael Porter, "There's a tremendous allure to mergers and acquisitions. It's the big play, the dramatic gesture. With one stroke of the pen you can add billions to size, get a front-page story, and create excitement in markets."[66]

In recent years many high-tech firms have suffered from the negative impact of their uncontrolled growth. Consider, for example, Priceline.com's ill-fated venture into an online service to offer groceries and gasoline.[67] A myriad of problems—perhaps most importantly, a lack of participation by manufacturers—caused the firm to lose more than $5 million a *week* prior to abandoning these ventures. Similarly, many have questioned the profit potential of Amazon.com's recent ventures into a variety of products such as tools and hardware, cell phones, and service. Such initiatives are often little more than desperate moves by top managers to satisfy investor demands for accelerating revenues. Unfortunately, the increased revenues often fail to materialize into a corresponding hike in earnings.

At times, executives' overemphasis on growth can result in a plethora of ethical lapses, which can have disastrous outcomes for their companies. A good example (of bad practice) is Joseph Bernardino's leadership at Andersen Worldwide. Bernardino had a chance early on to take a hard line on ethics and quality in the wake of earlier scandals at clients such as Waste Management and Sunbeam. Instead, according to former executives, he put too much emphasis on revenue growth. Consequently, the firm's reputation quickly eroded when it audited and signed off on the highly flawed financial statements of such infamous firms as Enron, Global Crossing, and WorldCom. WorldCom, in fact, is recognized as the biggest financial fraud of all time. Bernardino ultimately resigned in disgrace in March 2002, and his firm was dissolved later that year.[68]

Egotism

Most would agree that there is nothing wrong with ego, per se. After all, a healthy ego helps make a leader confident, clearheaded, and able to cope with change. CEOs, by their very nature, are typically fiercely competitive people in the office as well as on the tennis court or golf course. However, sometimes when pride is at stake, individuals will go to great lengths to win—or at least not to back down. Consider the following anecdote:

> When Warner Bros. CEO Robert Daly walked into the first postmerger gathering of senior Time Warner management in the Bahamas, he felt a hand on his shoulder. It was a Time Inc. executive whom he had never met. The magazine man asked the studio executive if he ever considered that General Motors purchased $30 million worth of advertising in Time Inc. publications before Daly acquired *Roger and Me,* a scathing cinematic indictment of the carmaker.
>
> Daly replied, "No. Did you consider that Warner Bros. spent over $50 million on *Batman* before *Time* ran its lousy review of the movie?" The Time executive smiled, patted his new colleague's shoulder and suggested that they continue their jobs in their own way!

Egos can get in the way of a "synergistic" corporate marriage. Few executives (or lower-level managers) are exempt from the potential downside of excessive egos. Consider, for example, the reflections of General Electric's former CEO Jack Welch, considered by many to be the world's most admired executive. He admitted to his regrettable decision for GE to acquire Kidder Peabody.[69] According to Welch, "My hubris got in the way in the Kidder Peabody deal. [He was referring to GE's buyout of the soon-to-be-troubled Wall Street firm.] I got wise advice from Walter Wriston and other directors who said, 'Jack, don't do this.' But I was bully enough and on a run to do it. And I got whacked right in the head." In addition to poor financial results, Kidder Peabody was wracked by a widely publicized trading scandal that tarnished the reputations of both GE and Kidder Peabody. Welch ended up selling Kidder in 1994.

The business press has included many stories of how egotism and greed have infiltrated organizations. Some incidents are considered rather astonishing, such as Tyco's former (and now convicted) CEO Dennis Kozlowski's well-chronicled purchase of a $6,000 shower curtain and vodka-spewing, full-size replica of Michaelangelo's David.[70] Other well-known examples of power grabs and extraordinary consumption of compensation and perks include

STRATEGY SPOTLIGHT

Poison Pills: How Antitakeover Strategies Can Raise Ethical Issues

Poison pills are almost always good for managers but not always so good for shareholders. They present managers with an ethical dilemma: How can they balance their own interests with their fiduciary responsibility to shareholders?

Here's how poison pills work. In the event of a takeover bid, existing shareholders have the option to buy additional shares of stock at a discount to the current market price. This action is typically triggered when a new shareholder rapidly accumulates more than a set percentage of ownership (usually 20 percent) through stock purchases. When this happens, managers fear that the voting rights and increased proportional ownership of the new shareholder might be a ploy to make a takeover play.

To protect existing shareholders, stock is offered at a discount, but only to existing shareholders. As the existing owners buy the discounted stock, the stock is diluted (i.e., there are now more shares, each with a lower value). If there has been a takeover offer at a set price per share, the overall price for the company immediately goes up

since there are now more shares. This assures stockholders of receiving a fair price for the company.

Sounds good, but here's the problem. Executives on the company's board of directors retain the right to allow the stock discount. The discounted stock price for existing shareholders may or may not be activated when a takeover is imminent. This brings in the issue of motive: Why did the board enact the poison pill provision in the first place? At times, it may have been simply to protect the existing shareholders. At other times, it may have been to protect the interests of those on the board of directors. In other words, the board may have enacted the rule not to protect shareholders, but to protect their own jobs.

When the board receives a takeover offer, the offering company will be aware of the poison pill provision. This gives negotiating power to board members of the takeover target. They may include as part of the negotiation that the new company keep them as members of the board. In exchange, the board members would not enact the discounted share price; existing stockholders would lose, but the jobs of the board members would be protected.

When a company offers poison pill provisions to shareholders, the shareholders should keep in mind that things are not always as they seem. The motives may reflect concern for shareholders. But on the other hand . . .

Sources: Vicente, J. P. 2001. Toxic treatment: Poison pills proliferate as Internet firms worry they've become easy marks. *Red Herring,* May 1 and 15: 195; Chakraborty, A., & Baum, C. F. 1998. Poison pills, optimal contracting and the market for corporate control: Evidence from Fortune 500 firms. *International Journal of Finance,* 10(3): 1120–1138; Sundaramurthy, C. 1996. Corporate governance within the context of antitakeover provisions. *Strategic Management Journal,* 17: 377–394.

executives at Enron, the Rigas family who were convicted of defrauding Adelphia of roughly $1 billion, former CEO Bernie Ebbers's $408 million loan from WorldCom, and so on. However, executives in the United States clearly don't have a monopoly on such deeds. Consider, for example, Jean-Marie Messier, former CEO of Vivendi Universal.[71]

> In striving to convert a French utility into a global media conglomerate, Messier seldom passed up a chance for self-promotion. Although most French executives have a preference for discreet personal lives, Messier hung out with rock stars and moved his family into a $17.5 million Park Avenue spread paid for by Vivendi. He pushed the company to the brink of collapse by running up $19 billion in debt from an acquisition spree and confusing investors with inconsistent financial transactions which are now under investigation by authorities in both the United States and France. Not one to accept full responsibility, less than five months after his forced resignation, he published a book, *My True Diary,* that blames a group of French business leaders for plotting against him. And his ego is clearly intact: At a recent Paris press conference, he described his firing as a setback for French capitalism.

Antitakeover Tactics

Unfriendly or hostile takeovers can occur when a company's stock becomes undervalued. A competing organization can buy the outstanding stock of a takeover candidate in sufficient quantity to become a large shareholder. Then it makes a tender offer to gain full control of the company. If the shareholders accept the offer, the hostile firm buys the target company and either fires the target firm's management team or strips them of their power. For this reason, antitakeover tactics are common. Three of these are greenmail, golden parachutes, and poison pills.[72]

The first, *greenmail,* is an effort by the target firm to prevent an impending takeover. When a hostile firm buys a large block of outstanding target company stock and the target firm's management feels that a tender offer is impending, they offer to buy the stock back from the hostile company at a higher price than the unfriendly company paid for it. The positive side is that this often prevents a hostile takeover. On the downside, the same price is not offered to preexisting shareholders. However, it protects the jobs of the target firm's management.

The second strategy is a *golden parachute.* A golden parachute is a prearranged contract with managers specifying that, in the event of a hostile takeover, the target firm's managers will be paid a significant severance package. Although top managers lose their jobs, the golden parachute provisions protect their income.

Strategy Spotlight 6.8 illustrates how poison pills are used to prevent takeovers. *Poison pills* are means by which a company can give shareholders certain rights in the event of a takeover by another firm. In addition to "poison pills," they are also known as shareholder rights plans.

As you can see, antitakeover tactics can often raise some interesting ethical issues.

Summary

A key challenge for today's managers is to create "synergy" when engaging in diversification activities. As we discussed in this chapter, corporate managers do not, in general, have a very good track record in creating value in such endeavors when it comes to mergers and acquisitions. Among the factors that serve to erode shareholder values are paying an excessive premium for the target firm, failing to integrate the activities of the newly acquired businesses into the corporate family, and undertaking diversification initiatives that are too easily imitated by the competition.

We addressed two major types of corporate-level strategy: related and unrelated diversification. With *related diversification* the corporation strives to enter into areas in which key resources and capabilities of the corporation can be shared or leveraged. Synergies come from horizontal relationships between business units. Cost savings and enhanced revenues can be derived from two major sources. First, economies of scope can be achieved from the leveraging of core competencies and the sharing of activities. Second, market power can be attained from greater, or pooled, negotiating power and from vertical integration.

When firms undergo *unrelated diversification* they enter product markets that are dissimilar to their present businesses. Thus, there is generally little opportunity to either leverage core competencies or share activities across business units. Here, synergies are created from vertical relationships between the corporate office and the individual business units. With unrelated diversification, the primary ways to create value are corporate restructuring and parenting, as well as the use of portfolio analysis techniques.

Corporations have three primary means of diversifying their product markets—mergers and acquisitions, joint ventures/strategic alliances, and internal development. There are key trade-offs associated with each of these. For example, mergers and acquisitions are typically the quickest means to enter new markets and provide the corporation with a high level of control over the acquired business. However, with the expensive premiums that often need to be paid to the shareholders of the target firm and the challenges associated with integrating acquisitions, they can also be quite expensive. Strategic alliances between two or more firms, on the other hand, may be a means of reducing risk since they involve the sharing and combining of resources. But such joint initiatives also provide a firm with less control (than it would have with an acquisition) since governance is shared between two independent entities. Also, there is a limit to the potential upside for each partner because returns must be shared as well. Finally, with internal development, a firm is able to capture all of the value from its initiatives (as opposed to sharing it with a merger or alliance partner). However, diversification by means of internal development can be very time-consuming—a disadvantage that becomes even more important in fast-paced competitive environments.

Traditional tools such as net present value (NPV) analysis are not always very helpful in making resource allocation decisions under uncertainty. Real options analysis (ROA) is increasingly used to make better quality decisions in such situations. We also addressed the potential limitations of ROA.

Finally, some managerial behaviors may serve to erode shareholder returns. Among these are "growth for growth's sake," egotism, and antitakeover tactics. As we discussed, some of these issues—particularly antitakeover tactics—raise ethical considerations because the managers of the firm are not acting in the best interests of the shareholders.

Summary Review Questions

1. Discuss how managers can create value for their firm through diversification efforts.
2. What are some of the reasons that many diversification efforts fail to achieve desired outcomes?
3. How can companies benefit from related diversification? Unrelated diversification? What are some of the key concepts that can explain such success?
4. What are some of the important ways in which a firm can restructure a business?
5. Discuss some of the various means that firms can use to diversify. What are the pros and cons associated with each of these?
6. Discuss some of the actions that managers may engage in to erode shareholder value.

Experiential Exercise

Time Warner (formerly AOL Time Warner) is a firm that follows a strategy of related diversification. Evaluate its success (or lack thereof) with regard to how well it has: (1) built on core competencies, (2) shared infrastructures, and (3) increased market power.

Rationale for Related Diversification	Successful/Unsuccessful?	Why?
1. Build on core competencies		
2. Share infrastructures		
3. Increase market power		

1. What were some of the largest mergers and acquisitions over the last two years? What was the rationale for these actions? Do you think they will be successful? Explain.

2. Discuss some examples from business practice in which an executive's actions appear to be in his or her self-interest rather than the corporation's well-being.

3. Discuss some of the challenges that managers must overcome in making strategic alliances successful. What are some strategic alliances with which you are familiar? Were they successful or not? Explain.

4. Use the Internet and select a company that has recently undertaken diversification into new product markets. What do you feel were some of the reasons for this diversification (e.g., leveraging core competencies, sharing infrastructures)?

1. In recent years there has been a rash of corporate downsizing and layoffs. Do you feel that such actions raise ethical considerations? Why or why not?

2. What are some of the ethical issues that arise when managers act in a manner that is counter to their firm's best interests? What are the long-term implications for both the firms and the managers themselves?

References

1. Craig, S., & Brown, K. 2004. Schwab ousts Pottruck as CEO; Founder returns to take the helm. *Wall Street Journal,* July 21: A1; Tabb, L. 2004. Wealth management: Can a leopard change its spots? www.wallstreetand_tech.com, November; Frank, R. 2004. U.S. Trust feels effects of switch; Schwab unit was perceived as ousted CEO's deal; shake-up is likely in offing. *Wall Street Journal,* July 21: A8; Lee, L. 2002, Closed eyes, open wallet. *BusinessWeek,* November 4: 116–117; Shilling, A. G. 2003. Wall Street's fat. *Forbes,* April 14: 242; and Schwab acquires U.S. Trust. 2000. *CNN Money* (online), January 13.

2. Hammonds, K. H. 2002. The numbers don't lie. *Fast Company,* September: 80.

3. Pare, T. P. 1994. The new merger boom. *Fortune,* November 28: 96.

4. Our framework draws upon a variety of sources, including Goold, M., & Campbell, A. 1998. Desperately seeking synergy. *Harvard Business Review,* 76(5): 131–143; Porter, M. E. 1987. From advantage to corporate strategy. *Harvard Business Review,* 65(3): 43–59; and Hitt, M. A., Ireland, R. D., & Hoskisson, R. E. 2001. *Strategic management: competitiveness and globalization* (4th ed.). Cincinnati, OH: South-Western.

5. Collis, D. J., & Montgomery, C. A. 1987. *Corporate strategy: Resources and the scope of the firm.* New York: McGraw-Hill.

6. This imagery of the corporation as a tree and related discussion draws on Prahalad, C. K., & Hamel, G. 1990. The core competence of the corporation. *Harvard Business Review,* 68(3): 79–91. Parts of this section also draw on Picken, J. C., & Dess, G. G. 1997. *Mission critical:* chap. 5. Burr Ridge, IL: Irwin Professional Publishing.

7. This section draws on Prahalad & Hamel, op. cit.; and Porter, op. cit.

8. A recent study that investigates the relationship between a firm's technology resources, diversification, and performance can be found in Miller, D. J. 2004. Firms' technological resources and the performance effects of diversification. A longitudinal study. *Strategic Management Journal,* 25: 1097–1119.

9. Harley-Davidson. 1993. Annual report.

10. Collis & Montgomery, op. cit.

11. Henricks, M. 1994. VF seeks global brand dominance. *Apparel Industry Magazine,* August: 21–40; VF Corporation. 1993. First quarter corporate summary report. *1993 VF Annual Report.*

12. Hill, A., & Hargreaves, D. 2001. Turbulent times for GE-Honeywell deal. *Financial Times,* February 28: 26.

13. Lowry, T. 2001. Media. *BusinessWeek,* January 8: 100–101.

14. The Tribune Company. 1999. *Annual report.*

15. This section draws on Hrebiniak, L. G., & Joyce, W. F. 1984. *Implementing strategy.* New York: MacMillan; and Oster, S. M. 1994. *Modern competitive analysis.* New York: Oxford University Press.

16. The discussion of the benefits and costs of vertical integration draws on Hax, A. C., & Majluf, N. S. 1991. *The strategy concept and process: A pragmatic approach:* 139. Englewood Cliffs, NJ: Prentice Hall.

17. Fahey, J. 2005. Gray winds. *Forbes.* January 10: 143.

18. This discussion draws on Oster, op. cit.; and Harrigan, K. 1986. Matching vertical integration strategies to competitive conditions. *Strategic Management Journal,* 7(6): 535–556.

19. For a scholarly explanation on how transaction costs determine the boundaries of a firm, see Oliver E. Williamson's pioneering books *Markets and Hierarchies: Analysis and Antitrust Implications* (New York: Free Press, 1975) and

The Economic Institutions of Capitalism (New York: Free Press, 1985).

20. Campbell, A., Goold, M., & Alexander, M. 1995. Corporate strategy: The quest for parenting advantage. *Harvard Business Review,* 73(2): 120–132; and Picken & Dess, op. cit.

21. Anslinger, P. A., & Copeland, T. E. 1996. Growth through acquisition: A fresh look. *Harvard Business Review,* 74(1): 126–135.

22. Campbell et al., op. cit.

23. This section draws on Porter, op. cit.; and Hambrick, D. C. 1985. Turnaround strategies. In Guth, W. D. (Ed.). *Handbook of business strategy:* 10-1–10-32. Boston: Warren, Gorham & Lamont.

24. There is an important delineation between companies that are operated for a long-term profit and those that are bought and sold for short-term gains. The latter are sometimes referred to as "holding companies" and are generally more concerned about financial issues than strategic issues.

25. Casico. W. F. 2002. Strategies for responsible restructuring. *Academy of Management Executive,* 16(3): 80–91; and Singh, H. 1993. Challenges in researching corporate restructuring. *Journal of Management Studies,* 30(1): 147–172.

26. Cusack, M. 1987. *Hanson Trust: A review of the company and its prospects.* London: Hoare Govett.

27. Hax & Majluf, op. cit. By 1979, 45 percent of Fortune 500 companies employed some form of portfolio analysis, according to Haspelagh, P. 1982. Portfolio planning: Uses and limits. *Harvard Busines Review,* 60: 58–73. A later study conducted in 1993 found that over 40 percent of the respondents used portfolio analysis techniques, but the level of usage was expected to increase to more than 60 percent in the near future: Rigby, D. K. 1994. Managing the management tools. *Planning Review,* September–October: 20–24.

28. Goold, M., & Luchs, K. 1993. Why diversify? Four decades of management thinking. *Academy of Management Executive,* 7(3): 7–25.

29. Other approaches include the industry attractiveness–business strength matrix developed jointly by General Electric and McKinsey and Company, the life-cycle matrix developed by Arthur D. Little, and the profitability matrix proposed by Marakon. For an extensive review, refer to Hax & Majluf, op. cit.: 182–194.

30. Porter, op. cit.: 49–52.

31. Collis, D. J. 1995. Portfolio planning at Ciba-Geigy and the Newport investment proposal. Harvard Business School Case No. 9-795-040. Novartis AG was created in 1996 by the merger of Ciba-Geigy and Sandoz.

32. Buzzell, R. D., & Gale, B. T. 1987. *The PIMS Principles: Linking Strategy to Performance.* New York: Free Press; and Miller, A., & Dess, G. G. 1996. *Strategic Management,* (2nd ed.). New York: McGraw-Hill.

33. Seeger, J. 1984. Reversing the images of BCG's growth share matrix. *Strategic Management Journal,* 5(1): 93–97.

34. Picken & Dess, op. cit.; Cabot Corporation. 2001. 10-Q filing, Securities and Exchange Commission, May 14.

35. Koudsi, S. 2001. Remedies for an economic hangover. *Fortune,* June 25: 130–139.

36. Coy, P., Thornton, E., Arndt, M., & Grow, B. 2005. Shake, rattle, and merge. *BusinessWeek,* January 10: 32–35; and Anonymous. 2005. Love is in the air. *Economist,* February 5: 9.

37. For an interesting study of the relationship between mergers and a firm's product-market strategies, refer to Krisnan, R. A., Joshi, S., & Krishnan, H. 2004. The influence of mergers on firms' product-mix strategies. *Strategic Management Journal,* 25: 587–611.

38. Carey, D., moderator. 2000. A CEO roundtable on making mergers succeed. *Harvard Business Review,* 78(3): 146.

39. Shinal, J. 2001. Can Mike Volpi make Cisco sizzle again? *BusinessWeek,* February 26: 102–104; Kambil, A. Eselius, E. D., & Monteiro, K. A. 2000. Fast venturing: The quick way to start Web businesses. *Sloan Management Review,* 41(4): 55–67; and Elstrom, P. 2001. Sorry, Cisco: The old answers won't work. *BusinessWeek,* April 30: 39.

40. Like many high-tech firms during the economic slump that began in mid-2000, Cisco Systems has experienced declining performance. On April 16, 2001, it announced that its revenues for the quarter closing April 30 would drop 5 percent from a year earlier—and a stunning 30 percent from the previous three months—to about $4.7 billion. Furthermore, Cisco announced that it would lay off 8,500 employees and take an enormous $2.5 billion charge to write down inventory. By late October 2002, its stock was trading at around $10, down significantly from its 52-week high of $70. Elstrom, op. cit.: 39.

41. Coy, P., Thornton, E., Arndt, M. & Grow, B. 2005, Shake, rattle, and merge. *BusinessWeek,* January 10: 32–35; and, Anonymous. 2005. The rise of the superbrands. *Economist.* February 5: 63–65; and, Sellers, P. 2005. It was a no-brainer. *Fortune,* February 21: 96–102.

42. For a discussion of the trend toward consolidation of the steel industry and how Lakshmi Mittal is becoming a dominant player, read Reed, S., & Arndt, M. 2004. The Raja of steel. *BusinessWeek,* December 20: 50–52.

43. Barrett, A. 2001. Drugs. *BusinessWeek,* January 8: 112–113.

44. Coy, P., et al. 2005, op. cit.

45. Whalen, C. J., Pascual, A. M., Lowery, T., & Muller, J. 2001. The top 25 managers. *BusinessWeek,* January 8: 63.

46. This discussion draws upon Rappaport, A., & Sirower, M. L. 1999. Stock or cash? The trade-offs for buyers and sellers in mergers and acquisitions. *Harvard Business Review,* 77(6): 147–158; and Lipin, S., & Deogun, N. 2000. Big mergers of 90s prove disappointing to shareholders. *Wall Street Journal,* October 30: C1.

47. Mouio, A. (Ed.). 1998. Unit of one. *Fast Company,* September: 82.

48. Ibid.

49. For scholarly perspectives on the role of learning in creating value in strategic alliances, refer to Anard, B. N., & Khanna, T. 2000. Do firms learn to create value? *Strategic*

Management Journal, 12(3): 295–317; and Vermeulen, F., & Barkema, H. P. 2001. Learning through acquisitions. *Academy of Management Journal,* 44(3): 457–476.

50. This section draws on Hutt, M. D., Stafford, E. R., Walker, B. A., & Reingen, P. H. 2000. Case study: Defining the strategic alliance. *Sloan Management Review,* 41(2): 51–62; and Walters, B. A., Peters, S., & Dess, G. G. 1994. Strategic alliances and joint ventures: Making them work. *Business Horizons,* 4: 5–10.

51. Edmondson, G., & Reinhardt, A. 2001. From niche player to Goliath. *BusinessWeek,* March 12: 94–96.

52. Clayton, V. 2000. Lourdes Pizana's passions: Confessions and lessons of an accidental business owner. *E-Merging Business,* Fall–Winter: 73–75.

53. Hoskin, R. E. 1994. *Financial Accounting.* New York: Wiley.

54. We know stock options as derivative assets—that is, "an asset whose value depends on or is derived from the value of another, the underlying asset": Amram, M., & Kulatilaka, N. 1999. *Real options: Managing strategic investment in an uncertain world:* 34. Boston: Harvard Business School Press.

55. Neufville, R. de. 2001. Real options: Dealing with uncertainty in systems planning and design, paper presented to the Fifth International Conference on Technology Policy and Innovation at the Technical University of Delft, Delft, Netherlands, June 29.

56. For an interesting discussion on why it is difficult to "kill options," refer to Royer, I. 2003. Why bad projects are so hard to kill. *Harvard Business Review,* 81(2): 48–57.

57. Triantis, A., et al. 2003. University of Maryland roundtable on real options and corporate practice. *Journal of Applied Corporate Finance,* 15(2): 8–23.

58. Interesting insights on how CEOs use their financial preferences in making decisions is found in Prince, E. T. 2005. The fiscal behavior of CEOs. *MIT Sloan Management Review,* 46(3): 23–26.

59. For a more in-depth discussion of ROA, refer to Copeland, T. E., & Keenan, P. T. 1998. Making real options real. *McKinsey Quarterly,* 3; and Luehrman, T. A. 1998. Strategy as a portfolio of real options. *Harvard Business Review,* September–October.

60. Janney, J. J., & Dess, G. G. 2004. Can real-options analysis improve decision making? Promises and pitfalls. *Academy of Management Executive,* 18(4): 60–75.

61. This section draws on Janney, J. J., & Dess, G. G. 2004. Can real options analysis improve decision-making?

Promises and pitfalls. *Academy of Management Executive,* 18(4): 60–75. For additional insights on pitfalls of real options, consider McGrath, R. G. 1997. A real options logic for initiating technology positioning investment. *Academy of Management Review,* 22(4): 974–994; Coff, R. W., & Laverty, K. J. 2001. Real options on knowledge assets: Panacea or Pandora's box. *Business Horizons,* 73: 79, McGrath, R. G. 1999. Falling forward: Real options reasoning and entrepreneurial failure. *Academy of Management Review,* 24(1): 13–30; and, Zardkoohi, A. 2004.

62. For an understanding of the differences between how managers say they approach decisions and how they actually do, March and Shapira's discussion is perhaps the best. March, J. G., & Shapira, Z. 1987. Managerial perspectives on risk and risk-taking. *Management Science,* 33(11): 1404–1418.

63. A discussion of some factors that may lead to escalation in decision making is included in Choo, C. W. 2005. Information failures and organizational disasters. *MIT Sloan Management Review,* 46(3): 8–10.

64. For an interesting discussion of the use of real options analysis in the application of wireless communications, which helped to lower the potential for escalation, refer to McGrath, R. G., Ferrier, W. J., & Mendelow, A. L. 2004. Real options as engines of choice and heterogeneity. *Academy of Management Review,* 29(1): 86–101.

65. One very useful solution for reducing the effects of managerial conceit is to incorporate an "exit champion" into the decision process. Exit champions provide arguments for killing off the firm's commitment to a decision. For a very insightful discussion on exit champions, refer to Royer, I. 2003. Why bad projects are so hard to kill. *Harvard Business Review,* 81(2): 49–56.

66. Porter, op. cit.: 43–59.

67. Angwin, J. S., & Wingfield, N. 2000. How Jay Walker built WebHouse on a theory that he couldn't prove. *Wall Street Journal,* October 16: A1, A8.

68. *BusinessWeek.* 2003. The fallen. January 13: 80–82.

69. The Jack Welch example draws upon Sellers, P. 2001. Get over yourself. *Fortune,* April 30: 76–88.

70. Polek, D. 2002. The rise and fall of Dennis Kozlowski. *BusinessWeek,* December 23: 64–77.

71. *BusinessWeek.* 2003. op. cit.: 80.

72. This section draws on Weston, J. F., Besley, S., & Brigham, E. F. 1996. *Essentials of Managerial Finance* (11th ed.): 18–20. Fort Worth, TX: Dryden Press, Harcourt Brace.

7

International Strategy:

Creating Value in Global Markets

>chapter objectives

After reading this chapter, you should have a good understanding of:

- The importance of international expansion as a viable diversification strategy.

- The sources of national advantage; that is, why an industry in a given country is more (or less) successful than the same industry in another country.

- The motivations (or benefits) and the risks associated with international expansion, including the emerging trend for greater offshoring and outsourcing activity.

- The two opposing forces—cost reduction and adaptation to local markets—that firms face when entering international markets.

- The advantages and disadvantages associated with each of the four basic strategies: international, global, multidomestic, and transnational.

- The four basic types of entry strategies and the relative benefits and risks associated with each of them.

*t*he global marketplace provides many opportunities for firms to increase their revenue base and their profitability. Furthermore, in today's knowledge-intensive economy, there is the potential to create advantages by leveraging firm knowledge when crossing national boundaries to do business. At the same time, however, there are pitfalls and risks that firms must avoid in order to be successful. In this chapter we will provide insights on how to be successful and create value when diversifying into global markets.

After some introductory comments on the global economy, we address the question: What explains the level of success of a given industry in a given country? To provide a framework for analysis, we draw on Michael Porter's "diamond of national advantage," in which he identified four factors that help to explain performance differences.

In the second section of the chapter, we shift our focus to the level of the firm and discuss some of the major motivations and risks associated with international expansion. Recognizing such potential benefits and risks enables managers to better assess the growth and profit potential in a given country. We also address important issues associated with a topic of growing interest in the international marketplace—offshoring and outsourcing.

Next, in the third section—the largest in this chapter—we address how firms can attain competitive advantages in the global marketplace. We discuss two opposing forces firms face when entering foreign markets: cost reduction and local adaptation. Depending on the intensity of each of these forces, they should select among four basic strategies: international, global, multidomestic, and transnational. We discuss both the strengths and limitations of each of these strategies.

The final section addresses the four categories of entry strategies that firms may choose in entering foreign markets. These strategies vary along a continuum from low investment, low control (exporting) to high investment, high control (wholly owned subsidiaries and greenfield ventures). We discuss the pros and cons associated with each.

Volkswagen has experienced problems with some of the new, high-priced models that it has introduced into the U.S. automobile market. This illustrates that, regardless of a firm's size or resource base, all companies face new opportunities and threats when they venture beyond the boundaries of their home nation.

A number of carmakers worldwide want to get into the luxury vehicle segment. But competition is very tough in this segment, and a high price no longer guarantees a high profit.[1] Volkswagen (VW), the European car manufacturer, also has recently jumped onto this bandwagon, and is currently in the process of transforming itself into a luxury-vehicle company. Ferdinand Piesch, VW's previous chief executive, spent hundreds of millions of dollars to acquire luxury brand names such as Lamborghini, Rolls-Royce/Bentley, and Bugatti. He also started work on VW's own line of luxury models. New production facilities had to be created for manufacturing the luxury models. VW is one of the most successful European car manufacturers in the United States, and it decided to introduce its luxury models in the United States too.

One of these models, the Touareg, launched in January 2003, is a sport utility vehicle (SUV) and costs around $35,000 to $40,000. The Phaeton, launched during the summer in 2003, costs even more—well over $60,000.

However, the results so far have not been encouraging. The Passat W-8 did not generate the excitement that was expected, and VW sold only 2,000 vehicles of this model in the United States by December 2002—much below the expected 5,000. The Phaeton is a question mark because Americans may hesitate to pay such a high price for a Volkswagen, even if the model is a credible competitor to the Mercedes S class. The Touareg's future is also not clear.

Then, there is the problem with the brand name. "The name may sound strange, but we wanted to differentiate the vehicle from everything else," says Jens Neumann, VW's board member responsible for U.S. operations. The name "Touareg" refers to a nomadic tribe in the Sahara who are known for their blue-dyed bodies and their talent for torture. This foreign name is odd and is something that Americans cannot spell or pronounce easily. It is unclear how well this name would be received by U.S. customers. But company officials seem confident. According to Volkswagen spokesman Tony Fouladpour, "Touareg is the name of a resilient, athletic African tribe known for surviving in very hostile environments, including the Sahara desert. So it's a good name for a tough, resilient sport-utility that's athletic on roads and can compete with the best off road." He adds, "Don't forget that Volkswagen is a German company, and the Touareg tribe is well known in Germany, where it's highly regarded. We will sell the Touareg sport-ute internationally and see no reason to give it a different name for America. We knew many Americans wouldn't accept that name at first, but find that many have become accustomed to it now. After all, Volkswagen has used other seemingly obscure names for our cars, such as Passat (the name of a prevailing Atlantic ocean wind), which now are widely accepted."

How have things turned out? Far fewer than the targeted 35,000 units were sold in the United States in 2004. The Touareg was outsold by many comparably equipped competitors, including the Volvo XC90, Nissan's Infiniti FX 35/45, and the Cadillac SRX. In fact, Toyota Motor's $35,000 Lexus RX 330 sold more than three times as many units as Volkswagen's model.

It seems the name "Touareg" itself was the least of Volkswagen's concerns. The major problem was really quite straightforward: price versus perceived value. Despite VW's effort to increase its stature as a luxury brand, it is fighting for the same piece of the market as other already established models by Lexus, BMW, and Mercedes-Benz. Even though the Mercedes ML model is quite dated and does not have the interior feel of the Touareg, it sells almost as well because of that big star (Mercedes' logo) on the hood. And the BMW X5, though fading because it has not been updated, still outsells the VW by several thousand units. Again, it is the "badge thing"—that is, consumers' preoccupation with a car's brand. Overall, VW sales were down 16 percent in 2004.

According to *Forbes* magazine, this is because not only has it failed to find firm footing as a luxury marquee, but also the rest of its lineup is old and uncompetitive with what is really hot in North America—mid-priced near-luxury sedans and crossovers and lower-priced crossovers.

Will Volkswagen eventually succeed in the U.S. luxury car segment? We'll have to wait and see. Some are pessimistic. Stephen Cheetham, an analyst at Sanford C. Bernstein and Co. in London, believes that Volkswagen "is facing the mother of all marketing problems."

>>The Global Economy: A Brief Overview

In this chapter we will discuss how firms can create value and achieve competitive advantage—as well as how to avoid pitfalls—in the global marketplace. We will discuss not only the factors that can influence a nation's success in a particular industry but also how firms can become successful when they diversify by expanding the scope of their business to include international operations. But first, let's talk about some of the broader issues in the global economy.

Today's managers face many opportunities and risks when they diversify abroad.[2] As we know, the trade among nations has increased dramatically in recent years. It is estimated that by 2015, the trade *across* nations will exceed the trade within nations. And in a variety of industries such as semiconductors, automobiles, commercial aircraft, telecommunications, computers, and consumer electronics, it is virtually impossible to survive unless firms scan the world for competitors, customers, human resources, suppliers, and technology.[3]

Fred Hasan, Chairman and CEO of the $8 billion pharmaceutical giant, Schering-Plough, emphasizes the importance of such a perspective:[4]

> We have long lead times—it can take 5 to 15 years for a new product to be born. Individual product bets are into hundreds of millions, if not billions, of dollars. Once you've got an idea that's been turned into a product, you need to pay back the high cost of R&D, so you need to sell it around the world. Good ideas can come from anywhere, and good products can be sold anywhere. The more places you are, the more ideas you will get. And the more ideas you get, the more places you can sell them and the more competitive you will be. Managing in many places requires a willingness to accept good ideas no matter where they come from— which means having a global attitude.

The rise of globalization—meaning the rise of market capitalism around the world— has undeniably contributed to the economic boom in America's New Economy, where knowledge is the key source of competitive advantage and value creation. It is estimated that it has brought phone service to about 300 million households in developing nations and a transfer of nearly $2 trillion from rich countries to poor countries through equity, bond investments, and commercial loans.[5]

Without doubt, there have been extremes in the effect of global capitalism on national economies and poverty levels around the world.[6] Clearly, the economies of East Asia have attained rapid growth, but there has been comparatively little progress in the rest of the world. For example, income in Latin America grew by only 6 percent in the past two decades when the continent was opening up to global capitalism. Average incomes in sub-Saharan Africa and the old Eastern European bloc have actually declined. Indeed, the World Bank estimates that the number of people living on $1 per day has *increased* to 1.3 billion over the past decade.

Such disparities in wealth among nations raise an important question: Why do some countries and their citizens enjoy the fruits of global capitalism while others are mired in poverty? Stated differently, why do some governments make the best use of inflows of foreign investment and know-how and others do not? There are many explanations. Among these are the need of governments to have track records of business-friendly policies to attract multinationals and local entrepreneurs to train workers, invest in modern technology, and nurture local suppliers and managers. Also, it means carefully managing the broader economic factors in an economy, such as interest rates, inflation, and unemployment, as well as a good legal system that protects property rights, strong educational systems, and a society where prosperity is widely shared.

The above policies are the type that East Asia—in locations such as Hong Kong, Taiwan, South Korea, and Singapore—has employed to evolve from the sweatshop economies of the 1960s and 1970s to industrial powers today. On the other hand, many countries have moved in the other direction. For example, in Guatemala, among other unfavorable indicators, only 52.0 percent of males complete fifth grade and an astonishing 39.8 percent of the population subsists on less than $1 per day.[7] (By comparison, the corresponding numbers for South Korea are 98 percent and less than 2 percent, respectively.)

Strategy Spotlight 7.1 provides an interesting perspective on global trade—marketing to the "bottom of the pyramid." This refers to the practice of a multinational firm targeting its goods and services to the nearly 5 billion poor people in the world who inhabit developing countries. Collectively, this represents a very large market with $14 trillion in purchasing power.

In the next section, we will address in more detail the question of why some nations and their industries are more competitive. This discussion establishes an important context or setting for the remainder of the chapter. After we discuss why some *nations and their industries* outperform others, we will be better able to address the various strategies that *firms* can take to create competitive advantage when they expand internationally.

>>Factors Affecting a Nation's Competitiveness

Michael Porter of Harvard University conducted a four-year study in which he and a team of 30 researchers looked at the patterns of competitive success in 10 leading trading nations. He concluded that there are four broad attributes of nations that individually, and as a system, constitute what is termed "the diamond of national advantage." In effect, these attributes jointly determine the playing field that each nation establishes and operates for its industries. These factors are:

- *Factor conditions.* The nation's position in factors of production, such as skilled labor or infrastructure, necessary to compete in a given industry.
- *Demand conditions.* The nature of home-market demand for the industry's product or service.
- *Related and supporting industries.* The presence or absence in the nation of supplier industries and other related industries that are internationally competitive.
- *Firm strategy, structure, and rivalry.* The conditions in the nation governing how companies are created, organized, and managed, as well as the nature of domestic rivalry.

We will now briefly discuss each of these factors.[8] Then we will provide an integrative example—the Indian software industry—to demonstrate how these attributes interact to explain India's high level of competitiveness in this industry.

Marketing to the "Bottom of the Pyramid"

Many executives wrongly believe that profitable opportunities to sell consumer goods exist only in countries where income levels are high. Even when they expand internationally, they often tend to limit their marketing to only the affluent segments within the developing countries. Such narrow conceptualizations of the market cause them to ignore the vast opportunities that exist at "the bottom of the pyramid," according to University of Michigan professor C. K. Prahalad. The *bottom of the pyramid* refers to the nearly 5 billion poor people who inhabit the developing countries. Surprisingly, they represent $14 trillion in purchasing power! And they are looking for products and services that can improve the quality of their lives such as clean energy, personal-care products, lighting, and medicines. Multinationals are missing out on growth opportunities if they ignore this vast segment of the market.

How can the poor buy if they do not have the money? The key is to bring the cost structures of the companies and their product offerings within the reach of the low-income customers. Unilever started marketing single serve sachets of shampoo to the poor in India several years ago. Selling for about a penny, single serve sales account for 60 percent of the total value of shampoo sold in India today! A 20-ounce shampoo bottle may cost more than a farm worker's daily income and thus may be out of her reach. However, the need for shampoo is almost universal. The challenge is to sell it in a way in which the poor can satisfy their need for shampoo.

Other innovative firms have found creative ways to serve the poor and still make a profit. Grameen Bank in Bangladesh is very different from the money center banks of London or New York. Pioneers of the concept of micro-credit, Grameen Bank extends small loans—sometimes as small as $20—to thousands of struggling micro-entrepreneurs who have no collateral to offer. Not only are their loan recovery rates comparable to big banks, but they are also changing the lives of thousands of people while making a profit as well. Casas Bahias, the Brazilian retailer, has built a $2.5 billion-a-year chain selling to the poor who live in the *favelas*, the illegal shanty towns. Another amazing example is Aravind Eye Care, an Indian hospital that specializes in cataract surgeries. Today they are the largest eye care facility in the world, performing more than 200,000 surgeries per year. The secret of their volume: The surgeries cost only about $25! A comparable surgery in the West costs $3,000. And best of all, Aravind has a return on equity of more than 75 percent!

As the above examples demonstrate, in order to sell to the bottom of the pyramid, managers must rethink their costs, quality, scale of operations, and even their use of capital. What prevents managers from selling to this vast market? Often they are victims of their own false assumptions. First, they think that the poor have no purchasing power. But $14 trillion can buy a lot. Second, they assume that poor people have no need for new technologies. We only have to see the demand for cell phones from entrepreneurs who run microbusinesses in villages in India to dispel this myth. Third, they assume that the poor have no use for their products and services. Shampoo, detergents, and banking satisfy universal needs, not just the needs of the rich. Fourth, they assume that managers may not be excited about working in these markets. Recent experience shows that this may be a more exciting environment than dogs fighting for fractions of market shares in the mature markets of the developed countries.

No one is helped by viewing the poor as the wretched of the earth. Instead, they are the latest frontier of opportunity for those who can meet their needs. A vast market that is barely tapped, the bottom of the pyramid offers enormous opportunities.

Sources: Prahalad, C. K. 2004. Why selling to the poor makes for good business. *Fortune,* 150(9): 32–33; Overholt, A. 2005. A new path to profit. *Fast Company,* January: 25–26; and Prahalad, C. K. 2005. *The fortune at the bottom of the pyramid: Eradicating poverty through profits.* Philadelphia: Wharton School Publishing.

Factor Conditions[9]

Classical economics suggests that factors of production such as land, labor, and capital are the building blocks that create usable consumer goods and services.[10] But this tells only part of the story when we consider the global aspects of economic growth. Companies in advanced nations seeking competitive advantage over firms in other nations *create* many of the factors of production. For example, a country or industry dependent on scientific innovation must have a skilled human resource pool to draw upon. This resource pool is not inherited; it is created through investment in industry-specific knowledge and talent. The supporting infrastructure of a country—that is, its transportation and communication systems as well as its banking system—are also critical.

To achieve competitive advantage, factors of production must be developed that are industry and firm specific. In addition, the pool of resources a firm or a country has at its disposal is less important than the speed and efficiency with which these resources are deployed. Thus, firm-specific knowledge and skills created within a country that are rare, valuable, difficult to imitate, and rapidly and efficiently deployed are the factors of production that ultimately lead to a nation's competitive advantage.

For example, the island nation of Japan has little land mass, making the warehouse space needed to store inventory prohibitively expensive. But by pioneering just-in-time inventory management, Japanese companies managed to create a resource from which they gained advantage over companies in other nations that spent large sums to warehouse inventory.

Demand Conditions

Demand conditions refer to the demands that consumers place on an industry for goods and services. Consumers who demand highly specific, sophisticated products and services force firms to create innovative, advanced products and services to meet the demand. This consumer pressure presents challenges to a country's industries. But in response to these challenges, improvements to existing goods and services often result, creating conditions necessary for competitive advantage over firms in other countries.

Demanding consumers push firms to move ahead of companies in other countries where consumers are less demanding and more complacent. Countries with demanding consumers drive firms in that country to meet high standards, upgrade existing products and services, and create innovative products and services. Thus, the conditions of consumer demand influence how firms view a market, with more demanding consumers stimulating advances in products and services. This in turn helps a nation's industries to better anticipate future global demand conditions and proactively respond to product and service requirements before competing nations are even aware of the need for such products and services.

Denmark, for instance, is known for its environmental awareness. Demand from consumers for environmentally safe products has spurred Danish manufacturers to become leaders in water pollution control equipment—products it successfully exports to other nations.

Related and Supporting Industries

Related and supporting industries enable firms to manage inputs more effectively. For example, countries with a strong supplier base benefit by adding efficiency to downstream activities. A competitive supplier base helps a firm obtain inputs using cost-effective, timely methods, thus reducing manufacturing costs. Also, close working relationships with suppliers provide the potential to develop competitive advantages through joint research and development and the ongoing exchange of knowledge, helping both suppliers and manufacturers.

Related industries offer similar opportunities through joint efforts among firms. In addition, related industries create the probability that new entrants will enter the market, increasing competition and forcing existing firms to become more competitive through efforts such as cost control, product innovation, and novel approaches to distribution. Combined, these give the home country's industries a source of competitive advantage over less competitive nations.

In the Italian footwear industry the supporting industries show how they can lead to national competitive advantage. In Italy, shoe manufacturers are geographically located near their suppliers. The manufacturers have ongoing interactions with leather suppliers and learn about new textures, colors, and manufacturing techniques while a shoe is still in the prototype stage. The manufacturers are able to project future demand and gear their factories for new products long before companies in other nations become aware of the new styles. Similarly, geographic proximity of industries related to the pharmaceutical industry (e.g., the dye industry) in Switzerland has given that nation a leadership position in this market, with firms such as Ciba-Geigy, Hoffman LaRoche, and Sandoz using dyes from local manufacturers in many pharmaceutical products.

Firm Strategy, Structure, and Rivalry

Rivalry is particularly intense in nations with conditions of strong consumer demand, strong supplier bases, and high new entrant potential from related industries. This competitive rivalry in turn increases the efficiency with which firms develop, market, and distribute products and services within the home country. Domestic rivalry thus provides a strong impetus for firms to innovate and find new sources of competitive advantage.

Interestingly, this intense rivalry forces firms to look outside their national boundaries for new markets, setting up the conditions necessary for global competitiveness. Among all the points on Porter's diamond of national advantage, domestic rivalry is perhaps the strongest indicator of global competitive success. Firms that have experienced intense domestic competition are more likely to have designed strategies and structures that allow them to successfully compete in world markets.

In the United States, for example, intense rivalry has spurred companies such as Dell Computer to find innovative ways to produce and distribute its products. This is largely a result of competition from IBM and Hewlett-Packard.

Strategy Spotlight 7.2 discusses India's software industry. It provides an integrative example of how Porter's "diamond" can help to explain the relative degree of success of an industry in a given country.

Concluding Comment on Factors Affecting a Nation's Competitiveness

Porter drew his conclusions based on case histories of firms in more than 100 industries. Despite the differences in strategies employed by successful global competitors, a common theme did emerge: Firms that succeeded in global markets had first succeeded in intense competition in their home markets. We can conclude that competitive advantage for global firms typically grows out of relentless, continuing improvement, innovation, and change.

Now that we have talked about the important role that nations play in international strategy, let's turn to the level of the individual firm.[11] In the next section, we will discuss a company's motivations and the risks associated with international expansion.

>>International Expansion: A Company's Motivations and Risks

Motivations for International Expansion

As you would expect, there are many motivations for a company to pursue international expansion. The most obvious one is to *increase the size of potential markets* for a firm's products and services.[12] By the middle of 2005, the world's population approached

STRATEGY SPOTLIGHT

India and the Diamond of National Advantage

Consider the following facts:

- SAP, the German software company, has developed new applications for notebook PCs at its 500-engineer Bangladore facility.

- General Electric plans to invest $100 million and hire 2,600 scientists to create the world's largest research and development lab in Bangalore, India.

- Microsoft plans to invest $400 million in new research partnerships in India.

- Over one-fifth of Fortune 1000 companies outsource their software requirements to firms in India.

Sources: Kripalani, M. 2002. Calling Bangladore: Multinationals are making it a hub for high-tech research *BusinessWeek*, November 25: 52–54; Kapur, D., & Ramamurti, R. 2001. India's emerging competitive advantage in services. 2001. *Academy of Management Executive*, 15(2): 20–33; World Bank. *World development report:* 6. New York: Oxford University Press. Reuters. 2001. Oracle in India push, taps software talent. *Washington Post Online*, July 3.

- McKinsey & Co. projects that the Indian software and services industry will be an $87 billion business by 2008; $50 billion of this will be exported.

- For the past decade, the Indian software industry has grown at a 50 percent annual rate.

- More than 800 firms in India are involved in software services as their primary activity.

- Software and information technology firms in India are projected to employ 2.2 million people by 2008.

What is causing such global interest in India's software services industry? Porter's diamond of national advantage helps clarify this question. See Exhibit 7.1.

First, *factor conditions* are conducive to the rise of India's software industry. Through investment in human resource development with a focus on industry-specific knowledge, India's universities and software firms have literally created this essential factor of production. *(continued)*

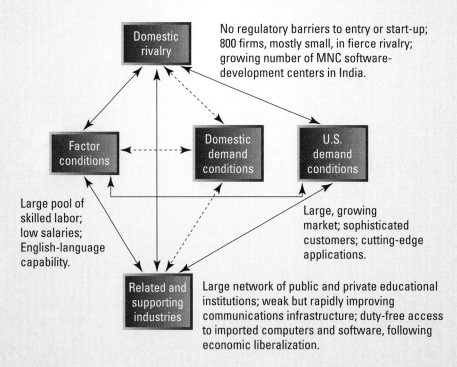

No regulatory barriers to entry or start-up; 800 firms, mostly small, in fierce rivalry; growing number of MNC software-development centers in India.

Large pool of skilled labor; low salaries; English-language capability.

Large, growing market; sophisticated customers; cutting-edge applications.

Large network of public and private educational institutions; weak but rapidly improving communications infrastructure; duty-free access to imported computers and software, following economic liberalization.

Note: Dashed lines represent weaker interactions.

Exhibit 7.1 *India's Diamond in Software*

Source: From Kampur D. and Ramamurti R., "India's Emerging Competition Advantage in Services," *Academy of Management Executive: The Thinking Manager's Source* Copyright © 2001 by Academy of Management. Reproduced with permission of Academy of Management via Copyright Clearance Center.

(continued) For example, India produces the second largest annual output of scientists and engineers in the world, behind only the United States. In a knowledge-intensive industry such as software, development of human resources is fundamental to both domestic and global success.

Second, *demand conditions* require that software firms stay on the cutting edge of technological innovation. India has already moved toward globalization of its software industry; consumer demand conditions in developed nations such as Germany, Denmark, parts of Southeast Asia, and the United States created the consumer demand necessary to propel India's software makers toward sophisticated software solutions.*

Third, India has the *supplier base as well as the related industries* needed to drive competitive rivalry and

* Although India's success cannot be explained in terms of its home market demand (according to Porter's model), the nature of the industry enables software to be transferred among different locations simultaneously by way of communications links. Thus, competitiveness of markets outside India can be enhanced without a physical presence in those markets.

enhance competitiveness. In particular, information technology (IT) hardware prices declined rapidly in the 1990s. Furthermore, rapid technological change in IT hardware meant that latecomers like India were not locked into older-generation technologies. Thus, both the IT hardware and software industries could "leapfrog" older technologies. In addition, relationships among knowledge workers in these IT hardware and software industries offer the social structure for ongoing knowledge exchange, promoting further enhancement of existing products. Further infrastructure improvements are occurring rapidly.

Fourth, with over 800 firms in the software services industry in India, *intense rivalry forces firms to develop competitive strategies and structures.* Although firms like TCS, Infosys, and Wipro have become large, they were quite small only five years ago. And dozens of small and midsized companies are aspiring to catch up. This intense rivalry is one of the primary factors driving Indian software firms to develop overseas distribution channels, as predicted by Porter's diamond of national advantage.

6.5 billion, with the United States representing less than 5 percent. Exhibit 7.2 lists the population of the United States compared to other major markets abroad.

Many multinational firms are intensifying their efforts to market their products and services to countries such as India and China as the ranks of their middle class have increased over the past decade. These include Procter & Gamble's success in achieving a 50 percent share in China's shampoo market as well as PepsiCo's impressive inroads in the Indian soft-drink market.[13] Strategy Spotlight 7.3 discusses the opportunities that are presented by China's emerging middle class.

Expanding a firm's global presence also automatically increases its scale of operations, providing it with a larger revenue and asset base. As we noted in Chapter 5 in discussing overall cost leadership strategies, such an increase in revenues and asset base potentially enables a firm to *attain economies of scale.* This provides multiple benefits. One advantage is the spreading of fixed costs such as research and development over a larger volume of production. Examples would include the sale of Boeing's commercial aircraft and Microsoft's operating systems in many foreign countries.

Country	May 2005 (estimated)
China	1,305,034,000
India	1,077,886,000
United States	295,280,000
Japan	127,418,000
Germany	82,438,000
World Total	6,379,157,000

Source: www.geohive.com/global/pop_data2.php.

Exhibit 7.2
Populations of Selected Nations and the World

STRATEGY SPOTLIGHT

The Opportunities Presented by China's Emerging Middle Class

For many years, Western companies have dreamed of selling to China's 1.3 billion people, only to find out that not enough Chinese can afford their foreign goods. However, China's middle class has finally attained a critical mass—between 35 million and 200 million people, depending on whose definition you prefer. The larger number is preferred by Fan Gong, director of China's National Economic Research Institute, who fixes the lower boundary of "middle" as a family income of $10,000.

Sociologist Bao Degong of China's Northeast University puts the number at about 80 million. He says that the middle class people are primarily found in the coastal areas where the economy rapidly develops. In particular, they tend to be owners of small and medium private enterprises as well as the new and high-tech specialists. The central government's emphasis on science and technologies has boosted the rapid development of higher education, which is the incubator of the middle class, claims Bao.

John Chen, chief executive of American software maker Sybase, whose Chinese revenue has doubled in three years to $40 million, sells to businesses that sell to the new consumers. Chen asserts that "The middle class

Sources: Meredith, R. 2004. Middle kingdom, middle class. *Forbes*, November 15: 188–192; and Anonymous. 2004. Middle class becomes rising power in China. www.Chinadaily.com, November 6.

is really taking off. It is now worth selling one widget to every Chinese who can afford it."

What is happening in China may be viewed as a new example of economies of scale. Many American companies already have factories in China exporting goods. Now that there is a domestic market to go along with the export market, those factories can increase their output with little additional cost. That is one reason why many foreign companies' profits in China have been so strong in recent years.

Consider Kodak. It invested $1.2 billion in China in 1998, planning on a 10- or 12-year payback period. However, Kodak initially overestimated the Chinese market. In the early years domestic demand for cameras and film was well below company forecasts and China operations were in the red, says Ying Yeh, a Chinese-born American and chairman of Kodak's Greater China region. Things have turned around. In recent years, Kodak's sales in China have climbed from very little to a first-place position in the market. In fact, revenues grew 40 percent in the first half of 2004 and the company says it is now ahead of its plan to recoup its investment, with China's profit margins on par with those worldwide. Not surprisingly, China has really helped on the cost side—95 percent of Kodak cameras are made there, some by contract manufacturers but most in its Shanghai factory, which runs three shifts a day.

A second advantage would be *reducing the costs of research and development as well as operating costs.* Recall, for example, the establishment of software development operations by Microsoft and other firms in talent-rich India (see Strategy Spotlight 7.2). A final advantage would be the attainment of greater purchasing power by pooling purchases. For example, as McDonald's increases the number of outlets it has all over the world, it is able to place larger orders for equipment and supplies, thus increasing its bargaining power with suppliers.

International expansion can also *extend the life cycle of a product* that is in its maturity stage in a firm's home country but that has greater demand potential elsewhere. As we noted in Chapter 5, products (and industries) generally go through a four-stage life cycle of introduction, growth, maturity, and decline. In recent decades, U.S. soft-drink producers such as Coca-Cola and PepsiCo have aggressively pursued international markets to attain levels of growth that simply would not be available in the United States. Similarly, personal computer manufacturers such as Dell and Hewlett-Packard have sought out foreign markets to offset the growing saturation in the U.S. market. The worldwide automobile industry is also intensely competitive. Firms such as General Motors and Ford have invested billions of dollars in Latin America in an effort to capture market share in that growing market.

Finally, international expansion can enable a firm to *optimize the physical location for every activity in its value chain.* Recall from our discussions in Chapters 3 and 5 that the value chain represents the various activities in which all firms must engage to produce products and services. They include primary activities, such as inbound logistics, operations, and marketing, as well as support activities, such as procurement, research and development, and human resource management. All firms have to make critical decisions as to where each activity will take place.[14] Optimizing the location for every activity in the value chain can yield one or more of three strategic advantages: performance enhancement, cost reduction, and risk reduction. We will now discuss each of these.

Performance Enhancement Microsoft's decision to establish a corporate research laboratory in Cambridge, England, is an example of a location decision that was guided mainly by the goal of building and sustaining world-class excellence in selected value-creating activities.[15] This strategic decision provided Microsoft with access to outstanding technical and professional talent. Location decisions can affect the quality with which any activity is performed in terms of the availability of needed talent, speed of learning, and the quality of external and internal coordination.

Cost Reduction Two location decisions founded largely on cost-reduction considerations are (1) Nike's decision to source the manufacture of athletic shoes from Asian countries such as China, Vietnam, and Indonesia, and (2) the decision of many multinational companies to set up production operations just south of the United States–Mexico border to access lower-cost labor. These operations are called *maquiladoras*. Such location decisions can affect the cost structure in terms of local manpower and other resources, transportation and logistics, and government incentives and the local tax structure.

Performance enhancement and cost-reduction benefits parallel the business-level strategies (discussed in Chapter 5) of differentiation and overall cost leadership. They can at times be attained simultaneously. Consider our example in the previous section on the Indian software industry. When Oracle set up a development operation in that country, the company benefited both from lower labor costs and operational expenses as well as from performance enhancements realized through the hiring of superbly talented professionals.

Managing across borders can lead to challenging ethical dilemmas. One issue that has received a good deal of attention in the recent business press is the issue of child labor. Strategy Spotlight 7.4 discusses how two multinational companies have taken different approaches to address this issue.

Risk Reduction Given the erratic swings in the exchange ratios between the U.S. dollar and the Japanese yen (in relation to each other as well as other major currencies), an important basis for cost competition between Ford and Toyota has been their relative ingenuity at managing currency risks. One of the ways for such competitors to manage currency risks has been to spread the high-cost elements of their manufacturing operations across a few select and carefully chosen locations around the world. Location decisions such as these can affect the overall risk profile of the firm with respect to currency, economic, and political risks.[16]

Potential Risks of International Expansion

When a company expands its international operations, it does so to increase its profits or revenues. As with any other investment, however, there are potential risks to accompany the anticipated returns.[17] To help companies assess the risk of entering foreign markets, rating systems have been developed to evaluate political, economic, and financial and credit risks.[18] *Euromoney* magazine publishes a semiannual "Country Risk Rating" that evaluates political, economic, and other risks that entrants potentially face. Exhibit 7.3 depicts a sample of country risk ratings, published by the World Bank, from the 178

STRATEGY SPOTLIGHT

Child Labor: How Two Companies Have Addressed This Issue

It is interesting to consider how multinational companies have taken different approaches to address the issue of child labor in their overseas operations. Nike, for example, has revised its code of conduct a few times since 1992, including increasing the minimum age from 14 to 18 years for footwear factory workers and from 14 to 16 for equipment and apparel, which is quite a bit higher than other company codes and the International Labor Organization's (ILO) convention. The company also has started an internal compliance program, supplemented with external monitoring. However, this does not seem to have silenced the staunchest critics. Nike's Web site reflects the way in which the company tries to openly address this critique, providing ample information about the monitoring of facilities and the dilemmas the company faces after the introduction of its latest code.

Chiquita Banana almost completely follows the SA 8000 standard, including all references to international conventions, but with a few modifications, primarily to take account of workplace issues specific to agriculture. (The SA 8000 standard is developed by the Council on Economic Priorities Accreditation Agency and is widely recognized and accepted. It is based on ILO and United Nations conventions.) The company's strict child labor provisions do not apply to family farms or to small-scale holdings in the seasonal, nonbanana business, which do not regularly employ hired workers. This is also meant to allow for employment of a farmer's own children in seasonal activities. In line with its standard, Chiquita Banana tries to address the problem associated with children found to be working in supplying factories by giving "adequate support to enable such children to attend and remain in school until no longer a child."

Source: Kolk, A., & Tulder, R. V. 2004. Ethics in international business: Multinational approaches to child labor. *Journal of World Business*, 39: 49–60.

countries that *Euromoney* evaluates. In the exhibit, note that the lower the score, the higher the country's expected level of risk.

Next we will discuss the four main types of risk: political risk, economic risk, currency risk, and management risk.

Political and Economic Risk Generally speaking, the business climate in the United States is very favorable. However, some countries around the globe may be

Exhibit 7.3

A Sample of International Country Risk Rankings

Rank	Country	Total Risk Assessment	Economic Performance	Political Risk	Total of Debt Indicators	Total of Credit and Access to Finance Indicators
1	Luxembourg	99.51	25.00	24.51	20.00	30.00
2	Switzerland	98.84	23.84	25.00	20.00	30.00
3	United States	98.37	23.96	24.41	20.00	30.00
40	China	71.27	18.93	16.87	19.73	15.74
55	Poland	57.12	18.56	13.97	9.36	15.23
63	Vietnam	52.04	14.80	11.91	18.51	6.82
86	Russia	42.62	11.47	8.33	17.99	4.83
114	Albania	34.23	8.48	5.04	19.62	1.09
161	Mozambique	21.71	3.28	2.75	13.85	1.83
178	Afghanistan	3.92	0.00	3.04	0.00	0.88

Source: Adapted from worldbank.org/html/prddr/trans/so96/art7.htm.

hazardous to the health of corporate initiatives because of political risk.[19] Forces such as social unrest, military turmoil, demonstrations, and even violent conflict and terrorism can pose serious threats.[20] Consider, for example, the ongoing tension and violence in the Middle East between Israelis and Palestinians, and the social and political unrest in Indonesia and Iraq.[21] Because such conditions increase the likelihood of destruction of property and disruption of operations as well as nonpayment for goods and services, countries that are viewed as high risk are less attractive for most types of business. Typical exceptions include providers of munitions and counterintelligence services.

The laws, as well as the enforcement of laws, associated with the protection of intellectual property rights can be a significant potential risk in entering new countries. Microsoft, for example, has lost billions of dollars in potential revenue through piracy of its software products in many countries, including China. Other areas of the globe, such as the former Soviet Union and some eastern European nations, have piracy problems as well. Firms rich in intellectual property have encountered financial losses as imitations of their products have grown due to a lack of law enforcement of intellectual property rights.[22]

Strategy Spotlight 7.5 discusses a problem that presents a severe threat to global trade—piracy. As we will see, estimates are that counterfeiting accounts for between 5 percent and 7 percent of global merchandise trade—the equivalent of as much as $512 billion a year. And the potential corrosive effects include health and safety, not just economic, damage.

Currency Risks   Currency fluctuations can pose substantial risks. A company with operations in several countries must constantly monitor the exchange rate between its own currency and that of the host country. Even a small change in the exchange rate can result in a significant difference in the cost of production or net profit when doing business overseas. When the U.S. dollar appreciates against other currencies, for example, U.S. goods can be more expensive to consumers in foreign countries. At the same time, however, appreciation of the U.S. dollar can have negative implications for American companies that have branch operations overseas. The reason for this is that profits from abroad must be exchanged for dollars at a more expensive rate of exchange, reducing the amount of profit when measured in dollars. For example, consider an American firm doing business in Italy. If this firm had a 20 percent profit in euros at its Italian center of operations, this profit would be totally wiped out when converted into U.S. dollars if the euro had depreciated 20 percent against the U.S. dollar. (U.S. multinationals typically engage in sophisticated "hedging strategies" to minimize currency risk. The discussion of this is beyond the scope of this section.)

It is important to note that even when government intervention is well intended, the macroeconomic effects of such action can be very negative for multinational corporations. Such was the case in 1997 when Thailand suddenly chose to devalue its currency, the baht, after months of trying to support it at an artificially high level. This, in effect, made the baht worthless compared to other currencies. And in 1998 Russia not only devalued its ruble but also elected not to honor its foreign debt obligations.

Management Risks   Management risks may be considered the challenges and risks that managers face when they must respond to the inevitable differences that they encounter in foreign markets (as was the case in our opening example of Volkswagen). These take a variety of forms: culture, customs, language, income levels, customer preferences, distribution systems, and so on.[23] As we will note later in the chapter, even in the case of apparently standard products, some degree of local adaptation will become necessary.

Differences in cultures across countries can also pose unique challenges for managers.[24] Cultural symbols can evoke deep feelings.[25] For example, in a series of advertisements aimed at Italian vacationers, Coca-Cola executives turned the Eiffel Tower, Empire State

Piracy: A Key Threat to World Trade

From the Barbary pirates to the rumrunners of Prohibition to today's e-mail spammers, every period has its unique form of economic criminal: People who flout or break the rules of commerce for their own economic gain. Such problems cannot be eliminated, but a successful society keeps them under control.

By that measure, the era of globalization may be facing one of its greatest challenges. The rapid expansion of manufacturing capability in developed countries, notably China, has raised incomes and boosted trade around the world. But the same production and distribution also have created a threatening phenomenon—an ever-rising flood of counterfeits and fakes coming onto world markets.

What products are involved? Kiwi Shoe Polish, Callaway Golf clubs, Intel computer chips, Bosch power drills, BP oil. We could pick any product from any well-known brand, and the chances are pretty good that there is a counterfeit version of it. Of course, this is not a new phenomenon. Fakes have been around for decades. And only the most naïve person would think that the $20 Rolex watch on Silom Road in Bangkok or the $30 Louis Vuitton bag on New York's Canal Street are genuine.

However, counterfeiting has grown up and has become a major threat to multinational corporations. "We've seen a massive increase in the last five years, and there is a risk that it will spiral out of control," claims Anthony Simon, marketing chief of Unilever Bestfoods. "It is no longer a cottage industry."

The figures are astounding. The World Customs Organization estimates that counterfeiting accounts for about 5 percent to 7 percent of global merchandise trade—equivalent to as much as $512 billion. Seizures of fakes by United States customs jumped 46 percent last year as counterfeiters boosted exports to Western markets. Unilever Groups says that knockoffs of its shampoos, soaps, and teas are growing at a rate of 30 percent annually.

Such counterfeiting can also have health and safety implications as well. The World Health Organization says up to 10 percent of medicines worldwide are counterfeit—a deadly hazard that could be costing the pharmaceutical industry $46 billion a year. "You won't die from purchasing a pair of counterfeit blue jeans or a counterfeit golf club. You can die from taking counterfeit pharmaceutical products. And there's no doubt that people have died in China from bad medicine," says John Theirault, head of global security for American pharmaceutical giant, Pfizer. And,

sadly, cases like the one in China, where fake baby formula recently killed 60 infants, have investigators stepping up enforcement at U.S. ports. Injuries from overheating counterfeit cell phone batteries purchased right on Verizon store shelves sparked a recall. According to Hal Stratton, of the Consumer Product Safety Commission, "We know of at least one apartment fire that's occurred. We know of at least one burn situation of someone's face that's occurred." And bogus car parts are a $12 billion market worldwide. "Counterfeiting has gone from a local nuisance to a global threat," says Hanns Glatz, DaimlerChrysler's point man on intellectual property.

China is the key to any solution. Given the country's economic power, its counterfeiting is turning into quite the problem itself, accounting for nearly two-thirds of all fake and pirated goods worldwide. Dan Chow, a law professor at Ohio State University who specializes in Chinese counterfeiting provides some perspective: "We have never seen a problem of this size and magnitude in world history. There's more counterfeiting going on in China now than we've ever seen anywhere. We know that 15 to 20 percent of all goods in China are counterfeit."

As more Chinese interests have seen profits suffer because of counterfeiting, there may be a tougher response from Beijing. For example, Li-Ning Co., China's number one homegrown athletic footwear and apparel company, has gotten the ultimate compliment from counterfeiters: They're faking its shoes. So today, Li-Ning has three full-time employees who track counterfeiters. The state tobacco monopoly is conducting joint raids with big international tobacco companies, since counterfeiters have started cranking out Double Happiness, Chunghwa, and other Chinese brands. And the government is finally realizing that piracy, which accounts for 92 percent of all software used in the mainland, isn't just setting back the likes of Microsoft Corp. "Piracy is a big problem for the development of the local software industry," says Victor Zhang, senior representative for China of the Business Software Alliance, an industry group. Some fear that Western companies may cut research spending in China if the mainland doesn't crack down.

China, of course, is not alone. Counterfeiting continues to spread. According to *BusinessWeek,* Pakistan and Russia are huge producers of fake pharmaceuticals; while in Italy an estimated 10 percent of all designer clothing is fake, much of it produced locally. Gangs in Paraguay funnel phony cosmetics, designer jeans, and toys from China to the rest of South America. And Bulgarians are masters at bootlegging U.S. liquor brands. This is one fight that will take years to win.

Source: Balfour, F. 2005. Fake! *BusinessWeek,* February 7: 54–64; Anonymous. 2005. Editorial. *BusinessWeek,* February 7: 96; and Simon, B. 2004. The world's greatest fakes. www.cbsnews.com, August 8.

Exhibit 7.4
How Culture Varies
across Nations:
Implications for
Business

Ecuador:

- Dinners at Ecuadorian homes last for many hours. Expect drinks and appetizers around 8:00 p.m., with dinner not served until 11:00 p.m. or midnight. You will dismay your hosts if you leave as early as 1:00 a.m. A party at an Ecuadorian home will begin late and end around 4:00 a.m. or 5:00 a.m. Late guests may sometimes be served breakfast before they leave.

France:

- Most English-speaking French have studied British-style English, which can lead to communication breakdowns with speakers of American-style English. For example, in the United States a presentation that "bombs" has failed, but in England it has succeeded.
- Words in French and English may have the same roots but different meanings or connotations. For example, a French person might "demand" something because *demander* in French means "to ask."

Hong Kong:

- Negotiations occur over cups of tea. Always accept an offer of tea whether you want it or not. When you are served, wait for the host to drink first.
- Chinese negotiators commonly use teacups as visual aids. One cup may be used to represent your company, another cup to represent the Hong Kong company, and the position of the cups will be changed to indicate how far apart the companies are on the terms of an agreement.

Singapore:

- Singaporeans associate all of the following with funerals—do not give them as gifts:
  - (a) Straw sandals
  - (b) Clocks
  - (c) A stork or crane
  - (d) Handkerchiefs (they symbolize sadness or weeping)
  - (e) Gifts or wrapping paper where the predominant color is white, black, or blue.
- Also avoid any gifts of knives, scissors, or cutting tools; to the Chinese they suggest the severing of a friendship. If you're giving flowers, give an even number of flowers—an odd number would be very unlucky.

Source: Morrison, T., Conaway, W., & Borden, G. 1994. *Kiss, bow, or shake hands.* Avon, MA: Adams Media; and www.executiveplanet.com/business-culture/112565157281.html.

Building, and the Tower of Pisa into the familiar Coke bottle. So far, so good. However, when the white marble columns of the Parthenon that crowns the Acropolis in Athens were turned into Coke bottles, the Greeks became outraged. Why? Greeks refer to the Acropolis as the "holy rock," and a government official said the Parthenon is an "international symbol of excellence" and that "whoever insults the Parthenon insults international culture." Coca-Cola apologized for the ad. Exhibit 7.4 demonstrates how cultures

How a Local Custom Can Affect a Manufacturing Plant's Operations

At times, a lack of understanding and awareness of local customs can provide some frustrating and embarrassing situations. Such customs can raise issues that must be taken into account in order to make good decisions.

For example, consider the unique problem that Larry Henderson, plant manager, and John Lichthental, manager of human resources, were faced with when they

Source: Harvey, M., & Buckley, M. R. 2002. Assessing the "conventional wisdoms" of management for the 21st century organization. *Organizational Dynamics,* 30(4): 368–378.

were assigned by Celanese Chemical Corp. to build a new plant in Singapore. The $125 million plant was completed in July, but according to local custom, a plant should only be christened on "lucky" days. Unfortunately, the next "lucky" day was not until September 3.

Henderson and Lichthental had to convince executives at Celanese's Dallas headquarters to delay the plant opening. It wasn't easy. But after many heated telephone conversations and flaming e-mails, the president agreed to open the new plant on the "lucky" day—September 3.

vary across countries and some of the implications for the conduct of business across national boundaries.

Strategy Spotlight 7.6 addresses a rather humorous example of how a local custom can affect operations at a manufacturing plant.

Thus far, we have addressed several of the motivations and risks associated with international expansion. A major trend in recent years has been the dispersion of the value chains of multinational corporations across different countries; that is, the various activities that constitute the value chain of a firm are now spread across several countries and continents. Such dispersion of value occurs mainly through increasing offshoring and outsourcing. Next we address some of the primary benefits and costs associated with this new trend.

Global Dispersion of Value Chains: Outsourcing and Offshoring

A report issued by the World Trade Organization describes the production of a particular U.S. car as follows: "30 percent of the car's value goes to Korea for assembly, 17.5 percent to Japan for components and advanced technology, 7.5 percent to Germany for design, 4 percent to Taiwan and Singapore for minor parts, 2.5 percent to U.K. for advertising and marketing services, and 1.5% to Ireland and Barbados for data processing. This means that only 37 percent of the production value is generated in the U.S."[26] Similarly, in the production of a Barbie doll, Mattel purchases plastic and hair from Taiwan and Japan, the molds from the United States, the doll clothing from China, and paint from the U.S. and assembles the product in Indonesia and Malaysia for sales worldwide. In today's economy these are not isolated examples. Instead, we are increasingly witnessing two interrelated trends: *outsourcing and offshoring. Outsourcing* occurs when a firm decides to utilize other firms to perform value-creating activities that were previously performed in-house.[27] In some cases, it may be a new activity that the firm is perfectly capable of doing, but it still chooses to have someone else perform the function for cost or quality reasons. Outsourcing can be to either a domestic company or a foreign firm.

Offshoring takes place when a firm decides to shift an activity that they were previously performing in a domestic location to a foreign location. For example, both Microsoft and Intel now have R&D facilities in India, employing a large number of

Indian scientists and engineers. In many cases, offshoring and outsourcing go together; that is, a firm may outsource an activity to a foreign supplier, thereby causing the work to be offshored as well.

The recent explosion in the volume of outsourcing and offshoring is due to a variety of factors. Up until the 1960s, for most companies, the entire value chain was in one location. Further, the production took place close to where the customers were in order to keep transportation costs under control. In the case of service industries, it was generally believed that offshoring was not possible because the producer and consumer had to be present at the same place at the same time. After all, a haircut could not be performed if the barber and the client were separated!

In the case of manufacturing industries, the rapid decline in transportation and coordination costs has enabled firms to disperse their value chains over different locations. For example, Nike's R&D takes place in the United States, raw materials are procured from a multitude of countries, actual manufacturing takes place in China or Indonesia, advertising is produced in the United States, and sales and service take place in practically all the countries. Each value-creating activity is performed in the location where the cost is the lowest or the quality is the best. Without finding optimal locations for each activity and the resultant dispersion of the value chain, Nike could not have attained its position as the world's largest shoe company.

The experience of the manufacturing sector was repeated in the service sector as well by the mid-1990s. A trend that began with the outsourcing of low-level programming and data entry work to countries such as India and Ireland suddenly grew manyfold, encompassing a variety of white collar and professional activities ranging from call-centers to R&D. Today, the technical support lines of a large number of U.S. companies are answered from call centers in faraway locations. The cost of a long distance call from the United States to India has come down from about $3 to $0.03 in the last 20 years, thereby making it possible to have call centers located in countries like India where a combination of low labor costs and English proficiency presents an ideal mix of factor conditions. Bangalore, India, in recent years, has emerged as a location where more and more U.S. tax returns are prepared. Sitting in India, U.S.-trained and licensed radiologists interpret chest X-rays and CT scans from U.S. hospitals for half the cost. The advantages from offshoring go beyond mere cost savings today. In many specialized occupations in science and engineering, there is a shortage of qualified professionals in developed countries whereas countries like India, China, and Singapore have what seems like an inexhaustible supply.[28]

For most of the 20th century, domestic companies catered to the needs of local populations. However, with the increasing homogenization of customer needs around the world and the institutionalization of free trade and investment as a global ideology (especially after the creation of the WTO), competition has become truly global. Each company has to keep its costs low in order to survive global competition. They also must find the best suppliers and the most skilled workers. Further, they have to locate each stage of the value chain in places where factor conditions are most conducive. Thus, outsourcing and offshoring are no longer mere options to consider, but an imperative for competitive survival for today's multinationals.

While there is a compelling logic for companies to engage in offshoring, there are many pitfalls associated with it. Strategy Spotlight 7.7 discusses the experience of Misiu Systems, a U.S. alarm systems manufacturer that found out the hard way that offshoring is not for everyone.

Let's now look at how firms can attain competitive advantages when they move beyond the boundaries of their home nation.

Misiu Systems: Outsourcing Is Not for Everyone

When Todd Hodgen, CEO of Misiu Systems, a Bothell, Washington–based manufacturer of alarm systems, learned that he could save 65 percent of his design costs by outsourcing it to a Taiwanese firm, he was really excited. In addition to cost savings, an added bonus was that the Taiwanese engineers would be working after Misiu's engineers had gone home because of the time differences. This meant that the product development cycle could be greatly accelerated. For a start-up financed mostly with loans from friends and family, the twin advantages of cost savings and reduced cycle time were too much to resist.

After several months of discussions with the contractor and a visit to Taiwan, Hodgen signed the outsourcing agreement. However, things did not quite work out as he had expected. His feedback to the design team in Taiwan often went unheeded. The design was eventually delivered eight months late and the quality fell well short of expectations. Why? The Taiwanese engineers who were supposed to be working solely for him were also working for other clients. Business from a small firm like Misiu was not given the same priority that was given to bigger clients. Eventually Hodgen ended up terminating the agreement with the Taiwanese firm and hiring a U.S. firm to finish the project!

Source: Wahlgren, E. 2004. The outsourcing dilemma. *Inc.*, April: 41–43.

>>Achieving Competitive Advantage in Global Markets

We will begin this section by discussing the two opposing forces that firms face when they expand into global markets: cost reduction and adaptation to local markets. Then we will address the four basic types of international strategies that they may pursue: international, global, multidomestic, and transnational. The selection of one of these four types of strategies is largely dependent on a firm's relative pressure to address each of the two forces.

Two Opposing Pressures: Reducing Costs and Adapting to Local Markets

Many years ago, the famed marketing strategist Theodore Levitt advocated strategies that favored global products and brands. That is, he suggested that firms should standardize all of their products and services for all of their worldwide markets. Such an approach would help a firm lower its overall costs by spreading its investments over as large a market as possible. Levitt's approach rested on three key assumptions:

1. Customer needs and interests are becoming increasingly homogeneous worldwide.
2. People around the world are willing to sacrifice preferences in product features, functions, design, and the like for lower prices at high quality.
3. Substantial economies of scale in production and marketing can be achieved through supplying global markets.[29]

However, we can find ample evidence to refute each of these assumptions.[30] With regard to the first assumption—the increasing worldwide homogeneity of customer needs and interests—consider the number of product markets, ranging from watches and handbags to soft drinks and fast foods. Here companies have successfully identified global customer segments and developed global products and brands targeted to those segments. In addition, many other companies adapt lines to idiosyncratic country preferences and develop local brands targeted to local market segments. For example, Nestlé's line of pizzas marketed in the United Kingdom includes cheese with ham and pineapple topping on a French bread crust. Similarly, Coca-Cola in Japan markets Georgia (a tonic drink) as well as Classic Coke and Hi-C.

Consider the second assumption—the sacrifice of product attributes for lower prices. While there is invariably a price-sensitive segment in many product markets, there is no indication that this is on the increase. On the contrary, in many product and service markets—ranging from watches, personal computers, and household appliances, to banking and insurance—there appears to be a growing interest in multiple product features, product quality, and service.

Finally, the third assumption is that significant economies of scale in production and marketing could be achieved for global products and services. Although standardization may lower manufacturing costs, such a perspective does not consider three critical and interrelated points. First, as we discussed in Chapter 5, technological developments in flexible factory automation enable economies of scale to be attained at lower levels of output and do not require production of a single standardized product. Second, the cost of production is only one component, and often not the critical one, in determining the total cost of a product. Third, a firm's strategy should not be product-driven. It should also consider other activities in the firm's value chain, such as marketing, sales, and distribution.

Based on the above, we would have a hard time arguing that it is wise to develop the same product or service for all markets throughout the world. While there are some exceptions, such as Harley-Davidson motorcycles and some of Coca-Cola's soft-drink products, managers must also strive to tailor their products to the culture of the country in which they are attempting to do business. Few would argue that "one size fits all" generally applies. But let's look at what happened when Ford took this approach with the launch of its Escort automobile in Europe in the 1980s. According to the company's then CEO, Jacques Nasser:

> The Escort, which was intended to be our first global product, was engineered on two continents—North America and Europe. Obviously, that made it impossible for us to capitalize on global sourcing for components. And it was launched individually in every country. Not only did every country come up with its own positioning for the car, but each devised its own advertising message and hired its own advertising agency to get that message across. So you had one car and a substantial number of value propositions. One market was saying, "Yeah, this car's a limousine." And another market was saying it was a sports vehicle. That made it impossible for us to get customers' input into the product after it was out there.[31]

What we have briefly discussed so far are two opposing pressures that managers face when they compete in markets beyond their national boundaries. These forces place conflicting demands on firms as they strive to be competitive.[32] On the one hand, competitive pressures require that firms do what they can to lower unit costs so that consumers will not perceive their product and service offerings as too expensive. This may lead them to consider locating manufacturing facilities where labor costs are low and developing products that are highly standardized across multiple countries.

In addition to responding to pressures to lower costs, managers also must strive to be responsive to local pressures in order to tailor their products to the demand of the local market in which they do business. This requires differentiating their offerings and strategies from country to country to reflect consumer tastes and preferences and making changes to reflect differences in distribution channels, human resource practices, and governmental regulations. However, since the strategies and tactics to differentiate products and services to local markets can involve additional expenses, a firm's costs will tend to rise.

The two opposing pressures result in four different basic strategies that companies can use to compete in the global marketplace: international, global, multidomestic, and

Exhibit 7.5
**Opposing Pressures
and Four Strategies**

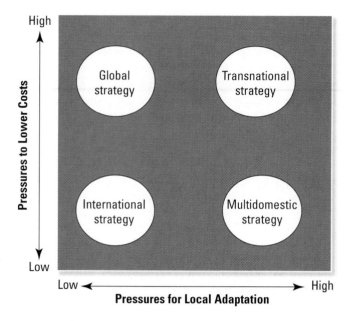

transnational. The strategy that a firm selects depends on the degree of pressure that it is facing for cost reductions and the importance of adapting to local markets. Exhibit 7.5 shows the conditions under which each of these strategies would be most appropriate. As we would expect, there are advantages and disadvantages associated with each of these strategies. In the following sections we will summarize each strategy, discuss where each is most appropriate, and identify relative advantages and disadvantages.

It is important to note that we consider these strategies to be "basic" or "pure"; that is, in practice, all firms will tend to have some elements of international, global, multidomestic, and transnational strategies.

International Strategy

There are a small number of industries in which pressures for both local adaptation and lowering costs are rather low. An extreme example of such an industry is the "orphan" drug industry. These are medicines for diseases that are severe but affect only a small number of people. Diseases such as the Gaucher disease and Fabry disease fit into this category. Companies such as Genzyme and Oxford GlycoSciences are active in this segment of the drug industry. There is virtually no need to adapt their products to the local markets. And the pressures to reduce costs are low; even though only a few thousand patients are affected, the revenues and margins are significant because patients are charged up to $100,000 per year.

An international strategy is based on diffusion and adaptation of the parent company's knowledge and expertise to foreign markets. Country units are allowed to make some minor adaptations to products and ideas coming from the head office, but they have far less independence and autonomy compared to multidomestic companies. The primary goal of the strategy is worldwide exploitation of the parent firm's knowledge and capabilities. All sources of core competencies are centralized.

For most of its history, Ericsson, a Swedish telecommunications firm, has followed this strategy. Because its home market (Sweden) was too small to support the R&D effort necessary in the industry, Ericsson built its strategy on its ability to transfer and adapt its innovative products and process technologies to international markets. This strategy of sequential diffusion of innovation developed at home helped it compete successfully against NEC, which followed a global strategy, and ITT, which followed a multidomestic strategy.[33]

The majority of large U.S. multinationals pursued the international strategy in the decades following World War II. These companies centralized R&D and product development but established manufacturing facilities as well as marketing organizations abroad. Companies such as McDonald's and Kellogg are examples of firms following such a strategy. Although these companies do make some local adaptations, they are of a very limited nature. With increasing pressures to reduce costs due to global competition, especially from low-cost countries, opportunities to successfully employ international strategy are becoming more limited. This strategy is most suitable in situations where a firm has distinctive competencies that local companies in foreign markets lack.

Below, we address some of the risks and challenges associated with an international strategy.

- Different activities in the value chain typically have different optimal locations. That is, R&D may be optimally located in a country with an abundant supply of scientists and engineers, whereas assembly may be better conducted in a low-cost location. Nike, for example, designs its shoes in the United States, but all the manufacturing is done in countries like China or Thailand. The international strategy, with its tendency to concentrate most of its activities in one location, fails to take advantage of the benefits of an optimally distributed value chain.

- The lack of local responsiveness may result in the alienation of local customers. Worse still, the firm's inability to be receptive to new ideas and innovation from its foreign subsidiaries may lead to missed opportunities.

Global Strategy

As indicated in Exhibit 7.5, a firm whose emphasis is on lowering costs tends to follow a global strategy. Competitive strategy is centralized and controlled to a large extent by the corporate office. Since the primary emphasis is on controlling costs, the corporate office strives to achieve a strong level of coordination and integration across the various businesses.[34] Firms following a global strategy strive to offer standardized products and services as well as to locate manufacturing, R&D, and marketing activities in only a few locations.[35]

A global strategy emphasizes economies of scale due to the standardization of products and services, and the centralization of operations in a few locations. As such, one advantage may be that innovations that come about through efforts of either a business unit or the corporate office can be transferred more easily to other locations. Although costs may be lower, the firm following a global strategy may, in general, have to forgo opportunities for revenue growth since it does not invest extensive resources in adapting product offerings from one market to another.

Consistent with Exhibit 7.5, a global strategy is most appropriate when there are strong pressures for reducing costs and comparatively weak pressures for adaptation to local markets. Identifying potential economies of scale becomes an important consideration.[36] Advantages to increased volume may come not only from larger production plants or runs but also from more efficient logistics and distribution networks. Worldwide volume is also especially important in supporting high levels of investment in research and development. As we would expect, many industries requiring high levels of R&D, such as pharmaceuticals, semiconductors, and jet aircraft, follow global strategies.

Another advantage of a global strategy is that it can enable a firm to create a standard level of quality throughout the world. Let's look at what Tom Siebel, chairman of

Siebel Systems, the $2 billion developer of e-business application software, has to say about global standardization.

> Our customers—global companies like IBM, Zurich Financial Services, and Citicorp—expect the same high level of service and quality, and the same licensing policies, no matter where we do business with them around the world. Our human resources and legal departments help us create policies that respect local cultures and requirements worldwide, while at the same time maintaining the highest standards. We have one brand, one image, one set of corporate colors, and one set of messages, across every place on the planet. An organization needs central quality control to avoid surprises.[37]

There are, of course, some risks associated with a global strategy.[38]

- A firm can enjoy scale economies only by concentrating scale-sensitive resources and activities in one or few locations. Such concentration, however, becomes a "double-edged sword." For example, if a firm has only one manufacturing facility, it must export its output (e.g., components, subsystems, or finished products) to other markets, some of which may be a great distance from the operation. Thus, decisions about locating facilities must weigh the potential benefits from concentrating operations in a single location against the higher transportation and tariff costs that result from such concentration.

- The geographic concentration of any activity may also tend to isolate that activity from the targeted markets. Such isolation may be risky since it may hamper the facility's ability to quickly respond to changes in market conditions and needs.

- Concentrating an activity in a single location also makes the rest of the firm dependent on that location. Such dependency on a sole source implies that, unless the location has world-class competencies, the firm's competitive position can be eroded if problems arise. A European executive of Ford Motor Co., reflecting on the firm's concentration of activities during a global integration program in the mid-1990s, lamented, "Now if you misjudge the market, you are wrong in 15 countries rather than only one."

Multidomestic Strategy

According to Exhibit 7.5, a firm whose emphasis is on differentiating its product and service offerings to adapt to local markets follows a multidomestic strategy. In contrast to a global strategy in which decision-making authority tends to be highly centralized in the corporate office, decisions evolving from a multidomestic strategy tend to be more decentralized to permit the firm to tailor its products and respond rapidly to changes in demand. This enables a firm to expand its market and to charge different prices in different markets. For firms following this strategy, differences in language, culture, income levels, customer preferences, and distribution systems are only a few of the many factors that must be considered. Even in the case of relatively standardized products, at least some level of local adaptation is often necessary. Consider, for example, Honda motorcycles.

> Although we could argue that a good product knows no national boundaries, there are subtle differences in ways that a product is used and what customers expect of it. Thus, while Honda uses a common basic technology, it must develop different types of motorcycles for different regions of the world. For example, North Americans primarily use motorcycles for leisure and sports; thus aggressive looks and high horsepower are key. Southeast Asians provide a counterpoint. Here, motorcycles are a basic means of transportation. Thus, they require low cost and ease of maintenance. And, in Australia and New Zealand, shepherds use motorcycles to herd sheep. Therefore, they demand low-speed torque, rather than high speed and maintenance.[39]

7.8 STRATEGY SPOTLIGHT

Dealing with Bribery Abroad

Most multinational firms experience difficult dilemmas when it comes to the question of adapting rules and guidelines, both formal and informal, while operating in foreign countries. A case in point is the Foreign Corrupt Practices Act of 1977, which makes it illegal for U.S. companies to bribe foreign officials to gain business or facilitate approvals and permissions. Unfortunately, in many parts of the world, bribery is a way of life, with large payoffs to government officials and politicians the norm to win government contracts. At a lower level, goods won't clear customs unless routine illegal, but well-accepted, payments, are made to officials. What is an American company to do in such situations?

Intel follows a strict rule-based definition of bribery as "a thing of value given to someone with the intent of obtaining favorable treatment from the recipient." The company strictly prohibits payments to expedite a shipment through customs if the payment did not "follow applicable rules and regulations, and if the agent gives money or payment in kind to a government official for personal benefit." Texas Instruments, on the other hand, follows a middle approach. They require employees to "exercise good judgment" in questionable circumstances "by avoiding activities that could create even the appearance that our decisions could be compromised." And Analog Devices has set up a policy manager as a consultant to overseas operations. The policy manager does not make decisions for country managers. Instead, the policy manager helps country managers think through the issues and provides information on how the corporate office has handled similar situations in the past.

Source: Begley, T. M., & Boyd, D. P. 2003. The need for a corporate global mind-set. *MIT Sloan Management Review*, Winter: 25–32.

In addition to the products themselves, how they are packaged must sometimes be adapted to local market conditions. Some consumers in developing countries are likely to have packaging preferences very different from consumers in the West. For example, single-serve packets, or sachets, are very popular in India.[40] They permit consumers to purchase only what they need, experiment with new products, and conserve cash at the same time. Products as varied as detergents, shampoos, pickles, and cough syrup are sold in sachets in India. It is estimated that they make up 20 percent to 30 percent of the total sold in their categories. In China, sachets are also spreading as a marketing device for such items as shampoos. This reminds us of the importance of considering all activities in a firm's value chain (discussed in Chapters 3 and 5) in determining where local adaptations may be advisable.

Cultural differences may also require a firm to adapt its personnel practices when it expands internationally.[41] For example, some facets of Wal-Mart stores have been easily "exported" to foreign operations, while others have required some modifications.[42] When the retailer entered the German market in 1997, it took along the company "cheer"— Give me a W! Give me an A! Give me an L! Who's Number One? The Customer!— which suited German employees as much as their U.S. counterparts. However, Wal-Mart's 10-Foot Rule, which requires employees to greet any customer within a 10-foot radius, was not so well received in Germany, where employees and shoppers alike weren't comfortable with the custom.

Strategy Spotlight 7.8 describes how U.S. multinationals have adapted to the problem of bribery in various countries while adhering to strict federal laws on corrupt practices abroad.

As you might expect, there are some risks associated with a multidomestic strategy. Among these are the following:

- Typically, local adaptation of products and services will increase a company's cost structure. In many industries, competition is so intense that most firms can ill afford any competitive disadvantages on the dimension of cost. A key challenge of managers is to determine the trade-off between local adaptation and its cost structure. For example, cost considerations led Procter & Gamble to standardize its diaper design across all European markets. This was done despite research data indicating that Italian mothers, unlike those in other countries, preferred diapers that covered the baby's navel. Later, however, P&G recognized that this feature was critical to these mothers, so the company decided to incorporate this feature for the Italian market despite its adverse cost implications.

- At times local adaptations, even when well intentioned, may backfire. When the American restaurant chain TGI Fridays entered the South Korean market, it purposely incorporated many local dishes, such as kimchi (hot, spicy cabbage), in its menu. This responsiveness, however, was not well received. Company analysis of the weak market acceptance indicated that Korean customers anticipated a visit to TGI Fridays as a visit to America. Thus, finding Korean dishes was inconsistent with their expectations.

- Consistent with other aspects of global marketing, the optimal degree of local adaptation evolves over time. In many industry segments, a variety of factors, such as the influence of global media, greater international travel, and declining income disparities across countries, may lead to increasing global standardization. On the other hand, in other industry segments, especially where the product or service can be delivered over the Internet (such as music), the need for even greater customization and local adaptation may increase over time. Firms must recalibrate the need for local adaptation on an ongoing basis; excessive adaptation extracts a price as surely as underadaptation.

Transnational Strategy

Let's briefly review global and multidomestic strategies before we discuss how a transnational strategy can be a vehicle for overcoming the limitations of each of these strategies and, in effect, "getting the best of both worlds."[43]

With a *global strategy,* resources and capabilities are concentrated at the center of the organization. Authority is highly centralized. Thus, a global company achieves efficiency primarily by exploiting potential scale economies in all of its value-chain activities. Since innovation is highly centralized in the corporate office, there is often a lack of understanding of the changing market needs and production requirements outside the local market, and there are few incentives to adapt.

The *multidomestic strategy* can be considered the exact opposite of the global strategy. Resources are dispersed throughout many countries in which a firm does business, and a subsidiary of the multinational company can more effectively respond to local needs. However, such fragmentation inevitably carries efficiency penalties. Learning also suffers because knowledge is not consolidated in a centralized location and does not flow among the various parts of the company.

A multinational firm following a *transnational strategy* strives to optimize the trade-offs associated with efficiency, local adaptation, and learning.[44] It seeks efficiency not for its own sake, but as a means to achieve global competitiveness. It recognizes the importance of local responsiveness but as a tool for flexibility in international operations.[45] Innovations are regarded as an outcome of a larger process of organizational learning that includes the contributions of everyone in the firm.[46] Additionally, a core tenet of the transnational model is that a firm's assets and capabilities are dispersed according to the most beneficial location for a specific activity. Thus, managers avoid the tendency to either concentrate activities in a central location (as with a global strategy) or disperse them across many locations to enhance adaptation (as with a multidomestic strategy). Peter Brabeck, CEO of Nestlé, the giant food company, provides such a perspective.

> We believe strongly that there isn't a so-called global consumer, at least not when it comes to food and beverages. People have local tastes based on their unique cultures and traditions—a good candy bar in Brazil is not the same as a good candy bar in China. Therefore, decision making needs to be pushed down as low as possible in the organization, out close to the markets. Otherwise, how can you make good brand decisions? That said, decentralization has its limits. If you are too decentralized, you can become too complicated—you get too much complexity in your production system. The closer we come to the consumer, in branding, pricing, communication, and product adaptation, the more we decentralize. The more we are dealing with production, logistics, and supply-chain management, the more centralized decision making becomes. After all, we want to leverage Nestlé's size, not be hampered by it.[47]

The Nestlé example illustrates a common approach in determining whether or not to centralize or decentralize a value-chain activity. Typically, primary activities that are "downstream" (e.g., marketing, sales, and service), or closer to the customer, tend to require more decentralization in order to adapt to local market conditions. On the other hand, primary activities that are "upstream" (e.g., logistics and operations), or further away from the customer, tend to be centralized. This is because there is less need for adapting these activities to local markets and the firm can benefit from economies of scale. Additionally, many support activities, such as information systems and procurement, tend to be centralized in order to increase the potential for economies of scale.

A central philosophy of the transnational organization is enhanced adaptation to all competitive situations as well as flexibility by capitalizing on communication and knowledge flows throughout the organization.[48] A principal characteristic is the integration of unique contributions of all units into worldwide operations. Thus, a joint innovation by headquarters and by one of the overseas units can lead potentially to the development of relatively standardized and yet flexible products and services that are suitable for multiple markets.

Asea Brown Boveri (ABB) is a firm that successfully follows a transnational strategy. ABB, with its home bases in Sweden and Switzerland, illustrates the trend toward cross-national mergers that lead firms to consider multiple headquarters in the future. It is managed as a flexible network of units, and one of management's main functions is the facilitation of information and knowledge flows between units. ABB's subsidiaries have complete responsibility for product categories on a worldwide basis. Such a transnational strategy enables ABB to benefit from access to new markets and the opportunity to utilize and develop resources wherever they may be located.

As with the other strategies, there are some unique risks and challenges associated with a transnational strategy.

- The choice of a seemingly optimal location cannot guarantee that the quality and cost of factor inputs (i.e., labor, materials) will be optimal. Managers must ensure that the relative advantage of a location is actually realized, not squandered because of weaknesses in productivity and the quality of internal operations. Ford Motor Co., for example, has benefited from having some of its manufacturing operations in Mexico. While some have argued that the benefits of lower wage rates will be partly offset by lower productivity, this does not always have to be the case. Since unemployment in Mexico is higher than in the United States, Ford can be more selective in its hiring practices for its Mexican operations. And, given the lower turnover among its Mexican employees, Ford can justify a high level of investment in training and development. Thus, the net result can be not only lower wage rates but also higher productivity than in the United States.

Exhibit 7.6
Strengths and
Limitations of Various
Strategies

Strategy	Strengths	Limitations
International	• Leverage and diffusion of parent's knowledge and core competencies. • Lower costs because of less need to tailor products and services. • Greater level of worldwide coordination.	• Limited ability to adapt to local markets. • Inability to take advantage of new ideas and innovations occurring in local markets.
Global	• Strong integration across various businesses. • Standardization leads to higher economies of scale, which lowers costs. • Helps to create uniform standards of quality throughout the world.	• Limited ability to adapt to local markets. • Concentration of activities may increase dependence on a single facility. • Single locations may lead to higher tariffs and transportation costs.
Multidomestic	• Ability to adapt products and services to local market conditions. • Ability to detect potential opportunities for attractive niches in a given market, enhancing revenue.	• Less ability to realize cost savings through scale economies. • Greater difficulty in transferring knowledge across countries. • May lead to "overadaptation" as conditions change.
Transnational	• Ability to attain economies of scale. • Ability to adapt to local markets. • Ability to locate activities in optimal locations. • Ability to increase knowledge flows and learning.	• Unique challenges in determining optimal locations of activities to ensure cost and quality. • Unique managerial challenges in fostering knowledge transfer.

• Although knowledge transfer can be a key source of competitive advantage, it does not take place "automatically." For knowledge transfer to take place from one subsidiary to another, it is important for the source of the knowledge, the target units, and the corporate headquarters to recognize the potential value of such unique know-how. Given that there can be significant geographic, linguistic, and cultural distances that typically separate subsidiaries, the potential for knowledge transfer can become very difficult to realize. Firms must create mechanisms to systematically and routinely uncover the opportunities for knowledge transfer.

Exhibit 7.6 summarizes the relative advantages and disadvantages of international, global, multidomestic, and transnational strategies.

We've discussed the types of strategies that firms pursue in international markets and their relative advantages and disadvantages. Let's now turn to the types of entry modes that companies may use to enter international markets.

>>Entry Modes of International Expansion

A firm has many options available to it when it decides to expand into international markets. Given the challenges associated with such entry, many firms first start on a small scale and then increase their level of investment and risk as they gain greater experience with the overseas market in question.[49]

Exhibit 7.7 illustrates a wide variety of modes of foreign entry, including exporting, licensing, franchising, joint ventures, strategic alliances, and wholly owned subsidiaries.[50] As the exhibit indicates, the various types of entry form a continuum that ranges from exporting (low investment and risk, low control) to a wholly owned subsidiary (high investment and risk, high control).[51]

Admittedly, there can at times be frustrations and setbacks as a firm evolves its international entry strategy from exporting to more expensive types, including wholly owned subsidiaries. For example, according to the CEO of a large U.S. specialty chemical company:

> In the end, we always do a better job with our own subsidiaries; sales improve, and we have greater control over the business. But we still need local distributors for entry, and we are still searching for strategies to get us through the transitions without battles over control and performance.[52]

Let's discuss each of these international entry modes.[53]

Exporting

Exporting consists of producing goods in one country to sell in another. This entry strategy enables a firm to invest the least amount of resources in terms of its product, its organization, and its overall corporate strategy. Not surprisingly, many host countries dislike this entry strategy because it provides less local employment than other modes of entry.[54]

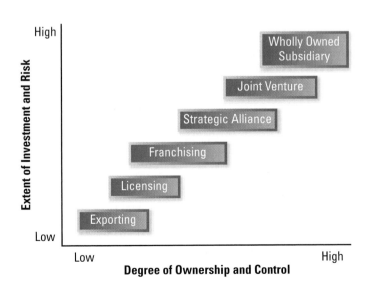

Exhibit 7.7
Entry Modes for International Expansion

Multinationals often stumble onto a stepwise strategy for penetrating markets, beginning with the exporting of products. This often results in a series of unplanned actions to increase sales revenues. As the pattern recurs with entries into subsequent markets, this approach, named a "beachhead strategy," becomes official policy in many organizations.

Such an approach definitely has its advantages. After all, firms start from scratch in sales and distribution when they enter new markets. Because many foreign markets are nationally regulated and dominated by networks of local intermediaries, firms need to partner with local distributors to benefit from their valuable expertise and knowledge of their own markets. Multinationals, after all, recognize that they cannot master local business practices, meet regulatory requirements, hire and manage local personnel, or gain access to potential customers without some form of local partnership.

In addition to the need to partner with local firms, multinationals also want to minimize their own risk. They do this by hiring local distributors and investing very little in the undertaking. In essence, the firm gives up control of strategic marketing decisions to the local partners—much more control than they would be willing to give up in their home market.

As we might expect, exporting is a relatively inexpensive way to enter foreign markets. However, it can still have significant downsides. In a study of 250 instances in which multinational firms used local distributors to implement their exporting entry strategy, the results were dismal. In the vast majority of the cases, the distributors were bought (to increase control) by the multinational firm or fired. In contrast, successful distributors shared two common characteristics:

- They carried product lines that complemented, rather than competed with, the multinational's products.

- They behaved as if they were business partners with the multinationals. They shared market information with the corporations, they initiated projects with distributors in neighboring countries, and they suggested initiatives in their own or nearby markets. Additionally, these distributors took on risk themselves by investing in areas such as training, information systems, and advertising and promotion in order to increase the business of their multinational partners.

The key point is the importance of developing collaborative, win–win relationships.

To ensure more control over operations without incurring significant risks, many firms have used licensing and franchising as a mode of entry. Let's now discuss these and their relative advantages and disadvantages.

Licensing and Franchising

Licensing as an entry mode enables a company to receive a royalty or fee in exchange for the right to use its trademark, patent, trade secret, or other valuable item of intellectual property.[55] In international markets, the advantage is that the firm granting the license incurs little risk, since it does not have to invest any significant resources into the country itself. In turn, the licensee (the firm receiving the license) gains access to the trademark, patent, and so on, and is able to potentially create competitive advantages. In many cases, the country also benefits from the product being manufactured locally. For example, Yoplait yogurt is licensed by General Mills from Sodima, a French cooperative, for sale in the United States. The logos of college and professional athletic teams in the United States are another source of trademarks that generate significant royalty income domestically and internationally.

There are, of course, some important disadvantages with this type of entry. For example, the licensor gives up control of its product and forgoes potential revenues and profits. Furthermore, the licensee may eventually become so familiar with the patent and trade secrets that it may become a competitor; that is, the licensee may make some modifications to the product and manufacture and sell it independently of the licensor without having to pay a royalty fee. This potential situation is aggravated in countries that have relatively weak laws to protect intellectual property. Additionally, if the licensee selected by the multinational firm turns out to be a poor choice, the brand name and reputation of the product may be tarnished.[56]

Although licensing and franchising are both forms of contractual arrangements, franchise contracts generally include a broader range of factors in an operation and have a longer time period during which the agreement is in effect. Franchising has the advantage of limiting the risk exposure that a firm has in overseas markets while expanding the revenue base of the parent company. The other side of the coin is that the multinational firm receives only a portion of the revenues, in the form of franchise fees, instead of the entire revenue, as would be the case if the firm set up the operation itself (e.g., a restaurant) through direct investment.

Franchising remains an overwhelmingly American form of business. According to a recent survey, more than 400 U.S. franchisers have international exposure.[57] This is greater than the combined totals of the next four largest franchiser home countries—France, the United Kingdom, Mexico, and Austria.

Companies often desire a closer collaboration with other firms in order to increase revenue, reduce costs, and enhance their learning—often through the diffusion of technology. To achieve such objectives, they enter into strategic alliances or joint ventures, two entry modes we will discuss next.

Strategic Alliances and Joint Ventures

Joint ventures and strategic alliances have become in recent years an increasingly popular way for firms to enter and succeed in foreign markets. These two forms of partnership differ in that joint ventures entail the creation of a third-party legal entity, whereas strategic alliances do not. In addition, strategic alliances generally focus on initiatives that are smaller in scope than joint ventures.

As we discussed in Chapter 6, these strategies have been effective in helping firms increase revenues and reduce costs as well as enhance learning and diffuse technologies. These partnerships enable firms to share the risks as well as the potential revenues and profits. Also, by gaining exposure to new sources of knowledge and technologies, such partnerships can help firms develop core competencies that can lead to competitive advantages in the marketplace.[58] Finally, entering into partnerships with host country firms can provide very useful information on local market tastes, competitive conditions, legal matters, and cultural nuances.[59] Strategy Spotlight 7.9 discusses how Microsoft has used a variety of partnerships to strengthen its position in East Asia.

Despite the potential benefits, managers must be aware of the risks associated with strategic alliances and joint ventures and how they can be minimized.[60] First, there needs to be a clearly defined strategy that is strongly supported by the organizations that are party to the partnership. Otherwise, the firms may work at cross-purposes and not achieve any of their goals. Second, and closely allied to the first issue, there must be a clear understanding of capabilities and resources that will be central to the partnership. Without such clarification, there will be fewer opportunities

STRATEGY SPOTLIGHT

Microsoft's Partnerships in East Asia

Microsoft is forming strategic alliances and joint ventures with companies in East Asia. Rather than competing with existing firms, Microsoft has entered several countries by cooperating with these firms. It has entered the Japanese and Taiwanese markets by joining efforts with mobile phone operator NTT DoCoMo, which has already established itself as a successful provider of cellular phone service through its Mobimagic service. By teaming with Microsoft, both companies stand to profit by integrating Microsoft's software applications, such as e-mail, into the existing service of cell-phone subscribers. Akio Fujii, head of new product development for Microsoft Japan, envisions adding a Web browser to these cell-phone services.

GigaMedia has 100,000 broadband subscribers offering sports, music, news, video-on-demand, as well as on-line karaoke. By hooking up with Microsoft, GigaMedia is now able to move its services from personal computers (PCs) to televisions, with the television serving as the monitor and a set-top box similar to a cable television box functioning as the PC. In exchange for its contribution,

Microsoft gleans 2 percent of GigaMedia's broadband subscriber fees and significant revenue from GigaMedia's e-commerce sales. In a similar move, the Koos Group, owner of KG Telecom, the second largest cell-phone operator in Taiwan, has joined ranks with Microsoft to integrate Internet capabilities on the televisions and cell phones of subscribers.

Microsoft has taken strategic moves to blunt competition from Palm by joining forces in an alliance with Psion in London, one of Palm's chief rivals. Microsoft has also reduced Palm's competitive threat in the cell-phone market by partnering with Stockholm's Ericsson, a leading manufacturer of mobile phones.

Microsoft has utilized forward-thinking vision to achieve win–win relationships through several joint ventures and strategic alliances throughout the globe. By doing so, it is successfully exporting its influence from an entrenched position in the United States to a global presence. This is good not only for Microsoft and its shareholders; stockholders of other firms around the world stand to prosper from the cooperative agreements Microsoft has forged with their firms. In addition, the added competition from a powerhouse like Microsoft forces other international firms to compete for efficiencies, thus benefiting overall economic prosperity.

Source: Chowdhury, N. 2000. Gates & Co. attack Asia. *Fortune.com*, April 17; Mariano, G. 2001. Palm to groove with liquid audio music. *New York Times Online*, April 11.

for learning and developing competences that could lead to competitive advantages. Third, trust is a vital element. Phasing in the relationship between alliance partners permits them to get to know each other better and develop trust. According to Philip Benton, Jr., former president of Ford Motor Co. (which has been involved in multiple international partnerships over the years), "The first time two companies work together, the chances of succeeding are very slight. But once you find ways to work together, all sorts of opportunities arise." Without trust, one party may take advantage of the other by, for example, withholding its fair share of resources and gaining access to privileged information through unethical (or illegal) means. Fourth, cultural issues that can potentially lead to conflict and dysfunctional behaviors need to be addressed. An organization's culture is the set of values, beliefs, and attitudes that influence the behavior and goals of its employees. Thus, recognizing cultural differences as well as striving to develop elements of a "common culture" for the partnership is vital. Without a unifying culture, it will become difficult to combine and leverage resources that are increasingly important in knowledge-intensive organizations (discussed in Chapter 4).[61]

As we know, not all partnerships are successful, for a variety of reasons. One of the most famous in recent business history was the joint venture formed by General Motors and Daewoo Motor Co.

In the mid-1980s General Motors sought cheap labor in Korea while Daewoo (of Korea) wanted to export automobiles. Thus, the two companies joined forces in 1986 to manufacture the ill-fated Pontiac LeMans. Things did not work out as planned. The LeMans experienced a sales decline of 39 percent from 1988 to 1990 and further declines in 1990 until the partnership was dissolved shortly thereafter.

What went wrong? The first cars had quality problems: GM sent engineers to Korea to correct them. Korea's cheap labor didn't materialize because of economic improvement, devaluation of the dollar, and increasingly strong demands from the newly formed labor unions for higher wages. However, the biggest problem was the differing goals of the two firms. While Daewoo wanted to upgrade the models to gain a larger share of the domestic market, GM wanted to keep costs down.

In effect, the alliance failed from the start, due to minimal understanding of each other's objectives and a lack of effort to reevaluate plans when problems appeared.[62]

Finally, the success of a firm's alliance should not be left to chance.[63] To improve their odds of success, many companies have carefully documented alliance-management knowledge by creating guidelines and manuals to help them manage specific aspects of the entire alliance life cycle (e.g., partner selection and alliance negotiation and contracting). For example, Lotus Corp. (part of IBM) created what it calls its "35 rules of thumb" to manage each phase of an alliance from formation to termination. Hewlett-Packard developed 60 different tools and templates, which it placed in a 300-page manual for guiding decision making in specific alliance situations. The manual included such tools as a template for making the business case for an alliance, a partner evaluation form, a negotiation template outlining the roles and responsibilities of different departments, a list of the ways to measure alliance performance, and an alliance termination checklist.

When a firm desires the highest level of control over its international operations, it develops wholly owned subsidiaries. Although wholly owned subsidiaries can generate the greatest returns, they also come with the highest levels of investment and risk. We will now discuss them.

Wholly Owned Subsidiaries

A wholly owned subsidiary is a business in which a multinational company owns 100 percent of the stock. There are two means by which a firm can establish a wholly owned subsidiary. It can either acquire an existing company in the home country or it can develop a totally new operation. The latter is often referred to as a "greenfield venture." Establishing a wholly owned subsidiary is the most expensive and risky of the various entry modes. However, as expected, it can also yield the highest returns. In addition, it provides the multinational company with the greatest degree of control of all activities, including manufacturing, marketing, distribution, and technology development.[64]

Wholly owned subsidiaries as well as direct investment in greenfield ventures are most appropriate where a firm already has the appropriate knowledge and capabilities that it can leverage rather easily through multiple locations in many countries. Examples range from restaurants to semiconductor manufacturers. To lower costs, for example, Intel Corporation builds semiconductor plants throughout the world—all of which use virtually the same blueprint. In establishing wholly owned subsidiaries, knowledge can be further leveraged by the hiring of managers and professionals from the firm's home country, often through hiring talent from competitors.

As noted, wholly owned subsidiaries are typically the most expensive and risky of the various modes for entering international markets. With franchising, joint ventures, or

STRATEGY SPOTLIGHT

7.10

Häagen-Dazs's Unique Entry Strategy

The ice-cream and frozen yogurt company Häagen-Dazs has taken a unique route for cross-border entry. Rather than follow traditional entry modes, the Bronx, New York–based company has an unconventional way of moving beyond the boundaries of the United States.

The company uses a three-step process. First, it uses high-end retailers to introduce the brand. Next, it finds high-traffic areas to build company-owned stores. The last step is to sell Häagen-Dazs products in convenience stores and supermarkets.

Häagen-Dazs is quick to adapt to local needs. For instance, freezers in some European stores are notorious for their unreliability. Clearly, a freezer malfunction would ruin a store's stock of Häagen-Dazs products. So Häagen-Dazs buys high-quality freezers for stores willing to carry its brand. Small sacrifices such as this have grown the company from a small ice-cream manufacturer in the Bronx to a worldwide franchiser with 650 stores in 55 countries, including Belgium, France, Japan, and the United Kingdom.

Sources: Meremenot, M. 1991. Screaming for Häagen-Dazs. *BusinessWeek*, October 14: 121; Häagen-Dazs. 2001. Information for franchisees. Häagen-Dazs company document: 1–24.

strategic alliances, the risk is shared with the firm's partners. With wholly owned subsidiaries, the entire risk is assumed by the parent company. The risks associated with doing business in a new country (e.g., political, cultural, and legal) can be lessened by hiring local talent.

Wal-Mart's expansion into South Korea points out some of the challenges and risks of creating greenfield ventures.

> Prior to Wal-Mart entering South Korea, local competitors were fearful that the giant retailer would "devour the local fish" with its extensive financial resources and global buying power. However, after its initial foray, many are now talking about what went wrong with Wal-Mart's initial efforts. For one thing, Wal-Mart used a membership approach similar to the one used by its Sam's warehouse stores. According to Song Kye-Hyon, a financial analyst, "It turned out to be a strategic flaw of Wal-Mart when it first adopted the Western policy of the membership where customers were required to pay a membership fee for shopping privileges and no food (only merchandise)." In South Korea, fresh, quality food is a key ingredient of success. It generates half of a store's revenues. To make matters worse, one of Wal-Mart's competitors, E-Mart, has several thousand local food suppliers with which it has nurtured long-term relationships. E-Mart even owns its own farm that supplies its stores.
>
> The local competitors have also developed mechanisms to create greater customer loyalty. They employ green-capped young men who help bring the shopping carts to the customers' cars in the parking lot. And they operate shuttle buses to go through neighborhoods to pick up customers and drop them off at their homes after they have completed their shopping.
>
> Wal-Mart remains undaunted. It has changed course to adopt the supercenter Wal-Mart concept in which it scrapped the memberships and introduced food. Wal-Mart and its competitors have vowed to further expand their operations in an effort to grab a larger piece of the discount retail market which is expected to reach $25 billion by 2004.[65]

In this closing section, we have addressed entry strategies as a progression from exporting through the creation of wholly owned subsidiaries. However, we must point out that many firms do not follow such an evolutionary approach. Instead, such firms follow rather unique entry strategies; see the discussion of Häagen-Dazs in Strategy Spotlight 7.10.

Summary

We live in a highly interconnected global community where many of the best opportunities for growth and profitability lie beyond the boundaries of a company's home country. Along with the opportunities, of course, there are many risks associated with diversification into global markets.

The first section of the chapter addressed the factors that determine a nation's competitiveness in a particular industry. The framework was developed by Professor Michael Porter of Harvard University and was based on a four-year study that explored the competitive success of 10 leading trading nations. The four factors, collectively termed the "diamond of national advantage," were factor conditions, demand characteristics, related and supporting industries, and firm strategy, structure, and rivalry.

The discussion of Porter's "diamond" helped, in essence, to set the broader context for exploring competitive advantage at the firm level. In the second section, we discussed the primary motivations and the potential risks associated with international expansion. The primary motivations included increasing the size of the potential market for the firm's products and services, achieving economies of scale, extending the life cycle of the firm's products, and optimizing the location for every activity in the value chain. On the other hand, the key risks included political and economic risks, currency risks, and management risks. Management risks are the challenges associated with responding to the inevitable differences that exist across countries such as customs, culture, language, customer preferences, and distribution systems. We also addressed some of the managerial challenges and opportunities associated with offshoring and outsourcing.

Next, we addressed how firms can go about attaining competitive advantage in global markets. We began by discussing the two opposing forces—cost reduction and adaptation to local markets—that managers must contend with when entering global markets. The relative importance of these two factors plays a major part in determining which of the four basic types of strategies to select: international, global, multidomestic, or transnational. The chapter covered the benefits and risks associated with each type of strategy.

The final section discussed the four types of entry strategies that managers may undertake when entering international markets. The key trade-off in each of these strategies is the level of investment or risk versus the level of control. In order of their progressively greater investment/risk and control, the strategies range from exporting to licensing and franchising, to strategic alliances and joint ventures, to wholly owned subsidiaries. The relative benefits and risks associated with each of these strategies were addressed.

Summary Review Questions

1. What are some of the advantages and disadvantages associated with a firm's expansion into international markets?

2. What are the four factors described in Porter's diamond of national advantage? How do the four factors explain why some industries in a given country are more successful than others?

3. Explain the two opposing forces—cost reduction and adaptation to local markets—that firms must deal with when they go global.

4. There are four basic strategies—international, global, multidomestic, and transnational. What are the advantages and disadvantages associated with each?

5. Describe the basic entry strategies that firms have available when they enter international markets. What are the relative advantages and disadvantages of each?

Experiential Exercise

The United States is considered a world leader in the motion picture industry. Using Porter's diamond framework for national competitiveness, explain the success of this industry.

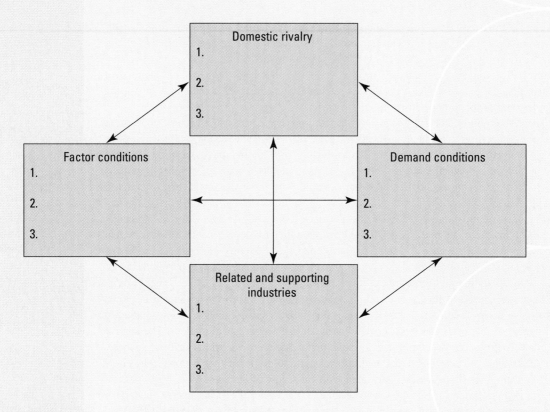

Application Questions Exercises

1. Data on the "competitiveness of nations" can be found at www.imd.ch/wcy/ranking/. This Web site provides a ranking on a variety of criteria for 49 countries. How might Porter's diamond of national advantage help to explain the rankings for some of these countries for certain industries that interest you?

2. The Internet has lowered the entry barriers for smaller firms that wish to diversify into international markets. Why is this so? Provide an example.

3. Many firms fail when they enter into strategic alliances with firms that link up with companies based in other countries. What are some reasons for this failure? Provide an example.

4. Many large U.S.-based management consulting companies such as McKinsey and Company and the BCG Group have been very successful in the international marketplace. How can Porter's diamond explain their success?

Ethics Questions

1. Over the past few decades, many American firms have relocated most or all of their operations from the United States to countries such as Mexico and China that pay lower wages. What are some of the ethical issues that such actions may raise?

2. Business practices and customs vary throughout the world. What are some of the ethical issues concerning payments that must be made in a foreign country to obtain business opportunities?

References

1. Edmondson, G. 2003. Volkswagen needs a jump. *Business-Week,* May 12: 48–49; Flint, J. 2002. Luxury: The cure du jour. *Forbes,* December 9: 88; Snarkhunting.com. 2003. www.snarkhunting.com/2003_01_01_archive.html, January; The name game Touareg? Murano? Where do they get those new car names? 2003. *Chicago Sun-Times,* January 30, www.automobilemag.com/news/news_30_5/; www.vw.com/autoshow/pdf/touareg.pdf; and Frank, M. 2004. Test drives: 2005 Volkswagen Touareg V-10. *Forbes.com,* November 18.

2. For a recent discussion on globalization by one of international business's most respected authors, read Ohmae, K. 2005. *The next global stage: Challenges and opportunities in our borderless world.* Philadelphia: Wharton School Publishing.

3. Our discussion of globalization draws upon Engardio, P., & Belton, C. 2000. Global capitalism: Can it be made to work better? *BusinessWeek,* November 6: 72–98.

4. Green, S., Hasan, F., Immelt, J., Marks, M., & Meiland, D. 2003. In search of global leaders. *Harvard Business Review,* 81(8): 41.

5. Engardio & Belton, op. cit.

6. For insightful perspectives on strategy in emerging economies, refer to the article entitled: Strategy research in emerging economies: Challenging the conventional wisdom in the January 2005 issue of *Journal of Management Studies,* 42(1).

7. The above discussion draws on Clifford, M. L., Engardio, P., Malkin, E., Roberts, D., & Echikson, W. 2000. Up the ladder. *BusinessWeek,* November 6: 78–84.

8. For another interesting discussion on a country perspective, refer to Makino, S. 1999. MITI Minister Kaora Yosano on reviving Japan's competitive advantages. *Academy of Management Executive,* 13(4): 8–28.

9. The following discussion draws heavily upon Porter, M. E. 1990. The competitive advantage of nations. *Harvard Business Review,* March–April: 73–93.

10. Landes, D. S. 1998. *The wealth and poverty of nations.* New York: W. W. Norton.

11. A recent study that investigates the relationship between international diversification and firm performance is Lu, J. W., & Beamish, P. W. 2004. International diversification and firm performance: The s-curve hypothesis. *Academy of Management Journal,* 47(4): 598–609.

12. Part of our discussion of the motivations and risks of international expansion draws upon Gregg, F. M. 1999. International strategy. In Helms, M. M. (Ed.). *Encyclopedia of management:* 434–438. Detroit: Gale Group.

13. These two examples are discussed, respectively, in Dawar, N., & Frost, T. 1999. Competing with giants: Survival strategies for local companies in emerging markets. *Harvard Business Review,* 77(2): 119–129; and Prahalad, C. K., & Lieberthal, K. 1998. The end of corporate imperialism. *Harvard Business Review,* 76(4): 68–79.

14. This discussion draws upon Gupta, A. K., & Govindarajan, V. 2001. Converting global presence into global competitive advantage. *Academy of Management Executive,* 15(2): 45–56.

15. Stross, R. E. 1997. Mr. Gates builds his brain trust. *Fortune,* December 8: 84–98.

16. For a good summary of the benefits and risks of international expansion, refer to Bartlett, C. A., & Ghoshal, S. 1987. Managing across borders: New strategic responses. *Sloan Management Review,* 28(5): 45–53; and Brown, R. H. 1994. *Competing to win in a global economy.* Washington, DC: U.S. Department of Commerce.

17. For an interesting insight into rivalry in global markets, refer to MacMillan, I. C., van Putten, A. B., & McGrath, R. G. 2003. Global gamesmanship. *Harvard Business Review,* 81(5): 62–73.

18. It is important for firms to spread their foreign operations and outsourcing relationships with a broad, well-balanced mix of regions and countries to reduce risk and increase potential reward. For example, refer to Vestring, T., Rouse, T., & Reinert, U. 2005. Hedge your offshoring bets. *MIT Sloan Management Review,* 46(3): 27–29.

19. For a discussion of some of the challenges associated with government corruption regarding entry strategies in foreign markets, read Rodriguez, P., Uhlenbruck, K., & Eden, L. 2005. Government corruption and entry strategies of multinationals. *Academy of Management Review,* 30(2): 383–396.

20. For a discussion of the political risks in China for United States companies, refer to Garten, J. E. 1998. Opening the doors for business in China. *Harvard Business Review,* 76(3): 167–175.

21. Shari, M. 2001. Is a holy war brewing in Indonesia? *BusinessWeek,* October 15: 62.

22. Gikkas, N. S. 1996. International licensing of intellectual property: The promise and the peril. *Journal of Technology Law & Policy,* 1(1): 1–26.

23. For an excellent theoretical discussion of how cultural factors can affect knowledge transfer across national boundaries, refer to Bhagat, R. S., Kedia, B. L., Harveston, P. D., & Triandis, H. C. 2002. Cultural variations in the cross-border transfer of organizational knowledge: An integrative framework. *Academy of Management Review,* 27(2): 204–221.

24. To gain insights on the role of national and regional cultures on knowledge management models and frameworks, read Pauleen, D. J., & Murphy, P. 2005. In praise of cultural bias. *MIT Sloan Management Review,* 46(2): 21–22.

25. Berkowitz, E. N. 2000. *Marketing* (6th ed.). New York: McGraw-Hill.

26. World Trade Organization. *Annual Report 1998.* Geneva: World Trade Organization.

27. Lei, D. 2005. Outsourcing. In Hitt, M. A., & Ireland, R. D. (Eds.). *The Blackwell encyclopedia of management.* Entrepreneurship: 196–199. Malden, MA: Blackwell.

28. The discussion above draws from Colvin, J. 2004. Think your job can't be sent to India? Just watch. *Fortune,* December 13: 80; Schwartz, N. D. 2004. Down and out in white collar America. *Fortune,* June 23: 321–325; Hagel, J. 2004. Outsourcing is not just about cost cutting. *Wall Street Journal,* March 18: A3.

29. Levitt, T. 1983. The globalization of markets. *Harvard Business Review,* 61(3): 92–102.

30. Our discussion of these assumptions draws upon Douglas, S. P., & Wind, Y. 1987. The myth of globalization. *Columbia Journal of World Business,* Winter: 19–29.

31. Wetlaufer, S. 1999. Driving change: An interview with Ford Motor Company's Jacques Nasser. *Harvard Business Review,* 77(2): 76–81.

32. Ghoshal, S. 1987. Global strategy: An organizing framework. *Strategic Management Journal,* 8: 425–440.

33. Bartlett, C. A., & Ghoshal, S. 1989. *Managing across borders: The transnational solution.* Boston: Harvard Business School Press.

34. For insights on global branding, refer to Aaker, D. A., & Joachimsthaler, E. 1999. The lure of global branding. *Harvard Business Review,* 77(6): 137–146.

35. For an interesting perspective on how small firms can compete in their home markets, refer to Dawar & Frost, op. cit.: 119–129.

36. Hout, T., Porter, M. E., & Rudden, E. 1982. How global companies win out. *Harvard Business Review,* 60(5): 98–107.

37. Fryer, B. 2001. Tom Siebel of Siebel Systems: High tech the old-fashioned way. *Harvard Business Review,* 79(3): 118–130.

38. The risks that are discussed for the global, multidomestic, and transnational strategies draw upon Gupta & Govindarajan, op. cit.

39. Sigiura, H. 1990. How Honda localizes its global strategy. *Sloan Management Review,* 31: 77–82.

40. Prahalad & Lieberthal, op. cit.: 68–79. Their article also discusses how firms may have to reconsider their brand management, costs of market building, product design, and approaches to capital efficiency when entering foreign markets.

41. Hofstede, G. 1980. *Culture's consequences: International differences in work-related values.* Beverly Hills, CA: Sage; Hofstede, G. 1993. Cultural constraints in management theories. *Academy of Management Executive,* 7(1): 81–94; Kogut, B., & Singh, H. 1988. The effect of national culture on the choice of entry mode. *Journal of International Business Studies,* 19: 411–432; and Usinier, J. C. 1996. *Marketing across cultures.* London: Prentice Hall.

42. McCune, J. C. 1999. Exporting corporate culture. *Management Review,* December: 53–56.

43. This discussion draws upon Bartlett and Ghoshal, op. cit.; and Raisinghani, M. 2000. Transnational organization. In Helms, M. M. (Ed.). *Encyclopedia of management* (4th ed.): 968–969. Detroit: Gale Group.

44. Prahalad, C. K., & Doz, Y. L. 1987. *The multinational mission: Balancing local demands and global vision.* New York: Free Press.

45. Kidd, J. B., & Teramoto, Y. 1995. The learning organization: The case of Japanese RHQs in Europe. *Management international review,* 35 (Special Issue): 39–56.

46. Gupta, A. K., & Govindarajan, V. 2000. Knowledge flows within multinational corporations. *Strategic Management Journal,* 21(4): 473–496.

47. Wetlaufer, S. 2001. The business case against revolution: An interview with Nestlé's Peter Brabeck. *Harvard Business Review,* 79(2): 112–121.

48. Nobel, R., & Birkinshaw, J. 1998. Innovation in multinational corporations: Control and communication patterns in international R&D operations. *Strategic Management Journal,* 19(5): 461–478.

49. For a rigorous analysis of performance implications of entry strategies, refer to Zahra, S. A., Ireland, R. D., & Hitt, M. A. 2000. International expansion by new venture firms: International diversity, modes of entry, technological learning, and performance. *Academy of Management Journal,* 43(6): 925–950.

50. Li, J. T. 1995. Foreign entry and survival: The effects of strategic choices on performance in international markets. *Strategic Management Journal,* 16: 333–351.

51. For a discussion of how home-country environments can affect diversification strategies, refer to Wan, W. P., & Hoskisson, R. E. 2003. Home country environments, corporate diversification strategies, and firm performance. *Academy of Management Journal,* 46(1): 27–45.

52. Arnold, D. 2000. Seven rules of international distribution. *Harvard Business Review,* 78(6): 131–137.

53. Sharma, A. 1998. Mode of entry and ex-post performance. *Strategic Management Journal,* 19(9): 879–900.

54. This section draws upon Arnold, op. cit.: 131–137; and Berkowitz, op. cit.

55. Kline, D. 2003. Strategic licensing. *MIT Sloan Management Review,* 44(3): 89–93.

56. Arnold, op. cit.; and Berkowitz, op. cit.

57. Martin, J. 1999. Franchising in the Middle East. *Management Review,* June: 38–42.

58. Manufacturer-supplier relationships can be very effective in global industries such as automobile manufacturing. Refer to Kotabe, M., Martin, X., & Domoto, H. 2003. Gaining from vertical partnerships: Knowledge transfer, relationship duration, and supplier performance improvement in the U.S. and Japanese automotive industries. *Strategic Management Journal,* 24(4): 293–316.

59. For a good discussion, refer to Merchant, H., & Schendel, D. 2000. How do international joint ventures create shareholder value? *Strategic Management Journal,* 21(7): 723–738.

60. This discussion draws upon Walters, B. A., Peters, S., & Dess, G. G. 1994. Strategic alliances and joint ventures: Making them work. *Business Horizons,* 37(4): 5–11.

61. For a rigorous discussion of the importance of information access in international joint ventures, refer to Reuer, J. J., & Koza, M. P. 2000. Asymmetric information and joint venture performance: Theory and evidence for domestic and international joint ventures. *Strategic Management Journal,* 21(1): 81–88.

62. Treece, J. 1991. Why Daewoo wound up on the road to nowhere. *BusinessWeek,* September 23: 55.

63. Dyer, J. H., Kale, P., & Singh, H. 2001. How to make strategic alliances work. *MIT Sloan Management Review,* 42(4): 37–43.

64. For a discussion of some of the challenges in managing subsidiaries, refer to O'Donnell, S. W. 2000. Managing foreign subsidiaries: Agents of headquarters, or an independent network? *Strategic Management Journal,* 21(5): 525–548.

65. Mi-Young, A. 2000. Wal-Mart has to adapt to the South Korean consumer. *Deutsche-Presse-agentur,* November 8: 1–3.

Digital Business Strategy:

Leveraging Capabilities in a Disruptive Environment

>chapter objectives

After reading this chapter, you should have a good understanding of:

- How new technologies contribute to competitive disruption and foster economic progress.

- Why use of Internet and digital technologies is more important to achieving competitive advantage than the technologies themselves.

- How the Internet and digitally based capabilities are affecting the five competitive forces and industry profitability.

- How firms are using Internet technologies to add value and achieve unique advantages.

- How Internet-enabled business models are being used to improve strategic positioning.

- How firms can improve their competitive position by effectively deploying digital strategies and avoiding the pitfalls associated with using the Internet and digital technologies.

*t*he technological advances that have swept in the new digital economy and created many Internet- and Web-based business opportunities have enormous strategic implications. Some of the changes require that business be conducted in entirely new ways. Others make it important to pursue traditional business strategies more effectively. This chapter helps sort out the ramifications of the Internet and digitally based capabilities for strategic management practices.

We begin by revisiting Porter's five-forces approach to industry analysis. We outline how industry and competitive practices are being affected by the capabilities provided by Internet technologies. On the one hand, some of the five forces are stronger in a digital economy, thus potentially suppressing profitability in a given industry. On the other hand, new opportunities created by digital technologies are providing firms with new ways to adapt to and overcome the five forces to achieve a competitive advantage. For each of the five forces, we provide examples that illustrate how these technological changes are shifting the nature of competition in several critical ways.

The second section explores how Internet-based businesses and incumbent firms are using digital technologies to add value. We consider four activities—search, evaluation, problem solving, and transaction—as well as three types of content—customer feedback, expertise, and entertainment programming. These technology-enhanced capabilities are providing new means with which firms can achieve competitive advantages.

The third section addresses how competitive strategies should be revised and redeployed in light of the shifts in industry and competitive forces caused by the Internet and digital technologies. Examples show new ways firms are providing low-cost leadership, differentiating, and focusing. For many firms, combination strategies provide the best avenue for building a solid strategy by integrating the new capabilities with sound strategic principles.

Sometimes new technologies are introduced and adopted so rapidly that current practices and business norms are seriously disrupted. Disruptive technologies (see Chapter 5) typically affect whole industries as well as relationships across industries. The innovations that flow from disruptive technologies may have legal ramifications and often pit technically sophisticated entrepreneurial firms against powerful incumbent firms in a struggle for who will control or suppress the use of the new technologies. Such struggles nearly always have enormous strategic implications. Consider the case of Napster.[1]

Created by 19-year-old reformed hacker Shawn Fanning, Napster provided software that enabled digital music files to be shared over the Internet. It was a combination of new technologies that made Napster possible—capabilities that were hardly possible at all just a few years earlier. First, there was MP3 technology, which allows for the kind of digital music typically found on CDs to be compressed into files 10 times smaller without loss of quality. Second, there was a new form of network architecture known as peer-to-peer (P2P) that allowed files to be distributed directly between computers in the network (in contrast to a client/server architecture). Finally, there was the Internet itself, which provided the network through which MP3 files could be shared. The result was that nearly 70 million registered users exchanged billions of high-quality music files simply by going to Napster, finding someone online who had a copy, and downloading it—for free. The technology made Napster the fastest-growing company in history.

To the millions of tech-savvy listeners who were accustomed to paying $10 to $20 to acquire a CD, it was unbelievably good news. But to the music industry giants such as Sony and EMI, who were accustomed to receiving payment every time a CD was sold or even played on the radio, it was nothing less than stealing. In June 2000, the Record Industry Association of America (RIAA), backed by the five major music publishers, filed suit to prohibit Napster from giving away its music. It was David versus Goliath all over again.

Napster claimed that it was not stealing but simply facilitating an exchange. In fact, the company claimed that the Audio Home Recording Act provided for this type of sharing. But RIAA argued that such laws were written when songs were recorded one-at-a-time and could not be applied in an era when new technologies made simultaneous and superfast Internet downloads possible. More importantly, the music industry believed it was losing huge sums of money. And apparently it was. On the weekend before a judge threatened to suddenly close Napster, Massachusetts-based Webnoize Research estimated that 250 million songs were downloaded. This translates into a loss for the music industry of approximately $270 million in a 48-hour period.

On July 1, 2001, after months of court battles, the Napster Web site was shut down and it seemed that Goliath had won. But by then, billions of music files had already been downloaded and competing online music Web sites were waiting to pick up where Napster left off. The online file sharing genie was out of the bottle. And Napster was a household word.

But Napster, the company, would never be the same. It had never been financially strong because it did not charge for its service (which is one reason it could claim in court that it was not profiting from the file-sharing activity). Nor did it make money in other ways, such as by selling online advertising or branded products. When it attempted to save itself by making content licensing agreements with the music publishers, internal squabbling among the founders and conflict with its venture capital firm stymied its efforts to become legitimate. The court action forced Napster to face its strategic and financial shortcomings. During this period, Jupiter Media Metrix senior analyst Aram Sinnreich said of Napster, "It has no clout, no leverage, pending lawsuits, a brand that's fading in the minds of consumers, and nothing that's really proprietary to the company."

This assessment, however, did not stop Bertelsmann AG, the German conglomerate that owned the BMG music label, from pouring $85 million into Napster to keep it from failing during the time it was shut down by the courts. Bertelsmann wanted to buy Napster in bankruptcy. In spite of the support Bertelsmann provided, however, a judge eventually prohibited the sale. Why? Again, it was the other big music labels that objected, claiming the acquisition would give BMG an unfair advantage in the online music business.

Eventually Roxio, a company that made CD-burning software, bought Napster's assets, including its name, for $5 million. Once the sale was complete, Roxio changed its name to Napster, sold its software division and entered the online music market as a legitimate company hoping to capitalize on the Napster name. But the new Napster set sail in a sea of competitors, including market leader Apple iTunes and major players such as Sony, Yahoo, RealNetworks, and even Wal-Mart. By the end of 2004, while Apple was boasting 100 million downloads per quarter at 99 cents per song, Napster was still operating at a loss and could claim just 270,000 subscribers to its Napster To Go subscription service, which allows unlimited downloads for $14.95 per month. And, in the file-sharing universe, unlicensed downloads continued to outpace paid transactions. According to BigChampagne LLC, a company that tracks file sharing activity, 1 billion songs were downloaded in January 2005 alone using P2P networks such as Kazaa, Grokster, and eDonkey. In such an environment, it is unlikely that Napster will ever achieve anything close to its former glory.

What Went Wrong at Napster?   Napster's failure was due, in part, to its extraordinary success. Such failures are rather common among firms that grow faster than their financial resources or ability to manage operations would enable them. From the beginning, Napster was cash-strapped and poorly organized, had a weak management team, and never had a concrete business plan.[2] But it was its greatest asset—the technological innovation that makes Internet-based file sharing possible—that made Napster a threat to the music industry giants. Legal action by these companies may have spurred the company's rapid growth and made Napster a household word, but it also led to the court injunction that shut down the fledgling company and caused it to declare bankruptcy.

Another critical reason for Napster's failure was that it never developed a viable revenue model. In this respect, Napster was like so many firms that grew up too fast during the great Internet expansion of the late 1990s. During that period, Napster was just one of the companies that was caught up in a kind of technological euphoria that was based more on what was technologically possible than on how much money could be earned. However the venture capitalists who sank billions of dollars into Internet businesses did not know that. All they knew was that something big was happening technologically. They, and the millions who invested, knew only that eventually there were great profits to be made and they did not want to be left out when that happened.

For these reasons, Napster in particular, and the Internet bubble in general, are somewhat extreme examples of technological disruption. Both happened so fast and with such profound impact that millions of lives were affected and literally trillions of dollars were involved. Between March 2000 and March 2001, more than $3 trillion of investment wealth was wiped out of the U.S. stock markets, due in large part to the collapse of the dot-com surge.[3] Yet both the Internet and a rather humbled version of Napster are still around. In essence, both have "gone mainstream."

In this chapter we will address the impact of the technological disruptions brought on by the digital revolution and the Internet on business practices and the strategic forces that guide business decisions and actions. The next section describes several dimensions of the digital economy and illustrates the importance of technological innovation to strategic decision making and economic growth. We will also highlight both potential benefits and drawbacks of digitally based capabilities on the future of strategic management.

>>Competitive Disruption, Strategic Management, and the Digital Economy

The Napster case illustrates the important role that technological innovation can have in shaping the strategic forces and competitive pressures affecting business. Schumpeter referred to such impact as one of "creative destruction." This occurs when the creative efforts of a few pioneers who introduce new innovative solutions unravel existing industry relationships and clear the way for a new technological regime with different economic players.[4] The Napster that Shawn Fanning created is no longer viable, but the revolution it brought about has irrevocably changed how the music industry sells music, relates to its customers, and manages its intellectual property.

Another such revolution was brought about in the early 1980s when Apple introduced the first personal computer. Traditional ways of computing, characterized by mainframes and mini-computers were suddenly challenged in unexpected ways. As the desktop PC became the dominant design, not one of the companies that made the previously dominant types of computers became a major player in the personal computer industry.[5] Apple itself has struggled mightily to survive in the face of stiff competition. It made a key strategic error in its early days by refusing to license use of its operating system.[6] As a result MS-DOS, an operating system that is arguably less efficient than Apple's, became dominant and firms such as Microsoft and Dell surged ahead. But Apple's superior technology and its continuous innovation helped it to remain viable. It's ironic that the new Napster's biggest rival today is the once iconoclastic Apple. With its hugely successful iPod MP3 player and its iTunes file-sharing business, Apple has become a dominant incumbent player.

These examples illustrate the importance of technological innovation and competitive disruptions in advancing economic development. In his book *The Free-Market Innovation Machine* economist William J. Baumol argues that the drive to innovate has been more important than price-based competition in explaining the success of free-market economies.[7] Baumol describes a cycle in which breakthrough innovations by entrepreneurial new entrants bring new technologies into mainstream use. Some of these new firms can leverage their early success to become dominant players. Most, however, are acquired by existing large firms that are hungry for fresh ideas to propel them forward. Once disruptive technologies are absorbed, innovation becomes more routine. As more and more firms adopt the technologies, competition intensifies and factors that drive industry competition and sustainable competitive advantage, such as the five forces, the value chain, and cost and differentiation strategies, become increasingly important.

Yet, according to Baumol, for both incumbents and the new firms, it is innovation-driven competition that determines who will succeed or fail. Thus a company like Apple, even though it has faced fierce price competition, has continued to be a viable contender because of its technological leadership and willingness to seize opportunities that are based on disruptive technologies.

Few technologically driven phenomena have been as disruptive, or as brimming with opportunity, as the Internet. Napster, iTunes, and thousands of new technology-driven enterprises would not be possible if it were not for the Internet. According to Jack Welch, former chairman of General Electric, the Internet is "the single most important event in the U.S. economy since the Industrial revolution."[8] Indeed, the Internet has dramatically changed the way business is conducted in every corner of the globe.

The impact of the information technology revolution, however, goes beyond the Internet. At a more basic level, it is the shift from analog to digital technologies that is responsible for so many new IT capabilities. Analog was once the primary technology for conveying information such as music recordings, voice communications, and television signals. It represents a type of physical information that requires large amounts of storage and often works only with hard-wired equipment. By contrast, digital technologies use information in the form of bits, that is, electronic signals expressed as either on or off, one or zero. These bits can be stored in tiny chips, easily reproduced and transferred rapidly and wirelessly.[9] Many technologies have made the switch from analog to digital—phones, photographs, television signals, and even books—and the trend suggests digitization is here to stay. As a result, digital technology capabilities, which, in essence, make the Internet possible, are a major driver in today's economy. Strategy Spotlight 8.1 addresses types of business activity, including the Internet, that have been enabled by digital technology.

These technology-driven initiatives—the Internet, wireless communications, and other digital technologies—are having a significant impact on the economy. They have done so by changing the ways businesses interact with each other and with consumers. These changes, though initially disruptive, create opportunities for firms to address needs more effectively and compete more efficiently.

According to C. K. Prahalad and Venkat Ramaswamy, authors of *The Future of Competition,* the "ubiquitous connectivity" and feedback systems provided the by Internet and digital technologies are contributing to major changes in competitive practices.[10] Because today's consumers are more networked than ever, they can interact with the companies they do business with and thus influence decisions and choices companies make about product design, services features, and so forth.[11] Manufacturing systems are more flexible, databases can be updated instantaneously, and alternative choices can be evaluated in real time. As a result, customers can be involved from the beginning in developing end products.[12] Thus, they are able to personally experience the value creation process.

The authors describe several examples of companies engaged in such co-creation processes:

- Intuit, the maker of Quicken® and other financial software, which has grown by continuously expanding customer's access to financial management capabilities and Internet-based information resources.

- Deere & Company, the farm machinery manufacturer, which is equipping its tractors and combines with global positioning systems (GPS) and biosensor systems that monitor soil conditions, analyze crops, and diagnose equipment problems in advance.

- Sumerset Houseboats, the world's largest houseboat builder, which actively involves customers throughout the houseboat design process.

To excel, these companies are drawing on four building blocks: dialogue, access, risk assessment, and transparency (DART). Exhibit 8.1 illustrates how the Internet is being used to enable the co-creation process.

The Internet has created a new climate for business in which sound principles of strategic management are *more,* not less important.[13] Indeed, the changes caused by the Internet and digital economy have made strategizing more challenging. Rapid improvements in technology, globalization, shifting patterns of demand, and uncertainty about costs and revenues are highlighting the importance of strategy formulation. Successful implementation may be even more difficult in this climate because of the uncertainty surrounding the new technology. Even so, the digital business phenomenon is steadily expanding.

Clearly, the Internet phenomenon has heightened the need for effective strategic management. Digital business success requires a new strategic perspective that builds on the possibilities provided by information technologies and permits Internet connectivity to transform the way business is conducted. Despite the rapid change and competitive disruption, an important lesson about the strategic implications of the Internet and digital technologies remains: It is the actual use of the technologies for profitable transactions,

Building Blocks	Definitions	Role in Co-Creation Process	Internet-based Examples
Dialogue	Sharing and exchanging knowledge to increase levels of understanding among companies, consumers, and communities of interest. • It requires forums in which dialogue can occur.	Generates new knowledge	Using online Internet forums such as newsgroups, weblogs ("blogs") and chat rooms to exchange information. • Used by the "Open Source" software movement (in developing Linux and other programs) to establish guidelines and create standards of quality.
Access	Creating opportunities for experiences at multiple points of interaction. • If users can access capabilities, they don't have to own them to experience them.	Provides experiences	Using computers networked via the Internet to provide resources for on-demand computing. • Companies such as Gateway and IBM are investing in online networks and grid computing systems that make using on-demand computing power just like using electricity.
Risk Assessment	Assessing not just the benefits but the risks associated with using goods and services. • If consumers understand potential dangers, they can make more informed decisions and take action to reduce potential harm.	Promotes shared responsibility	Using the Internet to disclose and disseminate medical information. • Companies such as Iceland's deCODE Genetics are exchanging genetic information and disclosing the latest research findings.
Transparency	Promoting openness, sharing discoveries, and eliminating information asymmetries. • It requires that companies disclose information about prices, costs, and profit margins.	Creates trust	Using the Internet to share scientific knowledge, cumulate findings, and make manufacturing processes and other operations more visible. • Used in the Human Genome Project to promote information sharing and collaboration among scientists.

Sources: Dennis, C. 2003. Draft guidelines ease restrictions on use of genome sequence data. *Nature,* 421: 877–878; Kambil, A., Friesen, G. B., & Sundaram, A. 1999. Co-creation: A new source of value. *Outlook Magazine,* 3(2): 23–29; Nerney, C. 2002. IBM, Grid computing groups to unveil grid services protocols. *Internet News,* www.internetnews.com, February 1; Prahalad, C. K., & Ramaswamy, V. 2004. *The future of competition.* Boston, MA: Harvard Business School Press; and www.decode.com.

Exhibit 8.1
The DART Framework: How the Internet Contributes to the Co-Creation Process

STRATEGY SPOTLIGHT

Beyond the Internet: The Wireless, Digital Economy

The Internet is a leading and highly visible component of a broader technological phenomenon—the emergence of digital technology. The Internet is like a staging area, a platform through which numerous applications of digital technology can be routed. Even technologies that don't require the Internet to function, such as wireless phones and GPS, rely on the Internet for data transfer and communications.

One of the key factors behind the growth of Internet-based applications of digital technologies is the implementation of broadband Internet connections (primarily cable and DSL). At-home broadband use grew 36 percent in 2004; at that rate, over 70 percent of all U.S. homes will have broadband connections by 2006. Worldwide broadband adoptions grew even faster—a one-year increase of about 50 percent in 2004. Since broadband connections are always on, users can get online much faster, and usually do. Broadband users spend 34 percent more time online than users with slower connections. Once there, they also spend more. In a recent period, 69 percent of online purchases were conducted over broadband connections, and broadband users spent 34 percent more than shoppers without broadband. Exhibit 8.2 illustrates worldwide growth trends in Internet use.

Business applications of the Internet are continuing to grow in many sectors of the economy. For example, the banking industry, which was slow to adopt Internet technologies, has experienced such rapid growth that it now has more services available online. Forty-four percent of all Internet users—53 million Americans—were using some form of online banking service by 2005. Small-and medium-sized enterprises (SMEs) are also relying on the Internet more than ever. A recent study found that 87 percent of SMEs are receiving monthly revenue from their Web site, and 42 percent derive more than a quarter of their monthly revenue from their Internet presence. According to Joel Kocher, CEO of Interland, "We are getting to the point in most small-business categories where it will soon be safe to say that if you're not online, you're not really serious about being in business."

This growth is not limited to Internet use. Wireless technologies are increasingly being used by businesses for everything from mission critical communications to attracting singles to a nightclub with text messages that offer free drinks. Mobile devices that connect to the Internet through wireless networks make it possible to conduct business anywhere, anytime. These "always on" technologies, in effect, make the customer the point of sale.

Wireless technologies are being improved in ways that will increase their reach and reliability and threaten existing communication systems. For example, several companies are developing "smart antennas" that concentrate radio signals in a narrow band rather than broadcasting in all directions at once. Using a cluster of 128 pencil size antennas, San Francisco start-up Vivato, Inc has developed a system than can project signals as far as 2.5 miles. This is well beyond the current range of just 300 feet for most Wi-Fi systems.

Wireless and digital technologies still face numerous challenges, however. For example, international standards for wireless communication are still in flux. As a result, cell phones and other devices that work in the U.S. are often useless in many parts of Europe and Asia. And, unlike analog systems, electronic bits of data that are zooming through space can be more easily lost, stolen, or manipulated. However, even with these problems, wireless and digital technologies are undoubtedly the (air) wave of the future. As Alan Greenspan, chairman of the U.S. Federal Reserve System, stated, "the revolution in information technology has altered the structure of the way the American economy works."

Sources: Anonymous. 2005. SMBs believe in the Web. *eMarketer*, www.emarketer.com, May 16. Greenspan, A. U.S. Congressional hearing. Quoted in Lewis, M. 2000. *The new, new thing*. New York: W.W. Norton; McGann, R. 2005. Broadband: High speed, high spend. *ClickZ Network*, www.clickz.com, January 24; McGann, R. 2005. Online banking increased 47 percent since 2002. *ClickZ Network*, www.clickz.com, February 9; Ward, L. 2003. Is M-Commerce dead and buried? *E-Commerce Times*, www.ecommercetimes.com, May 9; Yang, C. 2003. Beyond Wi-Fi: A new wireless age. *BusinessWeek*, December 15: 84–88.

Internet Use Worldwide		
	Internet Users (in millions)	
Geographic Region	**2004**	**2009 (estimated)**
North America	206,000	274,560
Western Europe	195,865	303,072
Eastern Europe/Russia	61,292	124,510
Asia-Pacific	362,388	689,616
South/Central America	65,483	131,821
Middle East/Africa	43,452	110,109
Total Internet Users	934,480	1,633,688

Exhibit 8.2 *Growth in Internet Activity*

Sources: *Computer Industry Almanac.*

not the technology itself, that matters to a company's bottom line. Yet it is the technology that is making it possible to conduct new types of transactions and enhance interactions with nearly every important stakeholder—customers, suppliers, employees, stockholders, competitors, government regulators, and others. Thus, the Internet presents a new strategic challenge: how to make the best use of the new technology without losing sight of important business fundamentals.

As we have seen, strategy can play a key role in the success of Internet-based and digital economy enterprises. Next, we will evaluate Michael Porter's five-forces model in terms of the actual use of the Internet and the new technological capabilities that it makes possible.

>>How the Internet and Digital Technologies Are Affecting the Five Competitive Forces

The Threat of New Entrants

In most industries, the threat of new entrants has increased because digital and Internet-based technologies lower barriers to entry. For example, it is relatively inexpensive for a new firm to create a Web presence that is even more impressive than the Web site of a larger or more established competitor. Unlike the traditional "Main Street" business, where customers could assess the firm's size and quality by walking in the door, businesses that exist in cyberspace can create an appearance that makes them seem like strong competitors, regardless of their actual size or the quality of their operations. Thus, scale economies may be less important in this context and new entrants can go to market with lower capital costs.

Beyond mere appearances, businesses that reach customers primarily through the Internet may enjoy savings on other traditional expenses such as office rent, sales force salaries, printing, and postage. This may encourage more entrants who, because of the lower start-up expenses, see an opportunity to capture market share by offering a product or performing a service more efficiently than existing competitors. Thus, a new cyberentrant can use the savings provided by the Internet to charge lower prices and compete on price despite the incumbent's scale advantages. Alternatively, because digital technologies often make it possible for young firms to provide services that are equivalent or superior to an incumbent, a new entrant may be able to serve a market more effectively, with more personalized services and greater attention to product details. A new firm may be able to build a reputation in its niche and charge premium prices. By so doing, it can capture small pieces of an incumbent's business and erode profitability.

Advances in technology also have created a flood of new entrants in several industries, including software, electronic equipment manufacturing, and online retailing. Strategy Spotlight 8.2 addresses the Internet telephony phenomenon known as VOIP, a digitally based technology that is causing major disruptions in the telecom industry. Not only does this technology change the way phone communications actually take place, but it also is changing how much customers pay for phone service, or if they pay for it at all.

Another potential benefit of Web-based business is access to distribution channels. Manufacturers or distributors that can reach potential outlets for their products more efficiently by means of the Internet may be encouraged to enter markets that were previously closed to them. Such access is not guaranteed, however, because of the strong barriers to entry that may exist in certain industries.[14]

STRATEGY SPOTLIGHT

VOIP: The Telecom Industry's New Threat

"Every week, I see at least one new company pop up and try to sell Internet-based phone service to consumers," writes Om Malik, senior writer for *Business 2.0* magazine. Few digital technologies have inspired a rush of new entrants as intense as Voice over Internet Protocol (VOIP), also known as Internet Voice. Although the technology has been around since the mid-1990s, it is only now being perfected. More importantly, it is finally becoming commercially viable.

Early VOIP users typically sat in front of a computer with a microphone exchanging wavy and halting chunks of conversations over the Internet. But because it was free, it was worth it. Today the technology allows voice information to flow more smoothly and reliably. With some low-cost equipment and a little software, dialers with a broadband connection can make phone calls over the Internet.

The implications are enormous. Federal Communications Commission Chairman Michael Powell claims that VOIP represents the "most significant paradigm shift in the entire history of modern communications since the invention of the telephone." *Fortune* magazine reports:

> VOIP's impact will be more profound than that of either cell phones or the Internet, largely because it encompasses both. Like the wireless and Internet phenomena, VOIP has the potential to buoy a raft of new household brands. Fortunes will rise and fall as traditional phone companies, cable operators, and upstarts fight to sell you more convenient, cheaper and way cooler phone services. And it will increasingly marginalize the century-old traditional phone network, replacing it with a sleek new system of interconnecting data pipelines that will deliver calls, movies, messages, games and whatever else can be digitized.

Such heady predictions have created a frenzy of new entrants. Yet Internet voice systems are far from perfect. Service can be interrupted if Internet connections go down and emergency calls into 911 systems using VOIP are currently unable to inform the dispatcher of the physical location. But using Internet Voice is so much cheaper that many business users are willing to take these risks. For example, Smyth Solutions, a 100-person staffing and recruiting company in New Jersey, has cut its local and long distance phone bill from $100,000 to $80,000 by using

VOIP. Savings on phone bills of 20 to 30 percent are common. "The low cost of Internet voice makes it as disruptive as e-mail," says Frost & Sullivan market analyst Jon Arnold. And, as in the early days of e-mail, there are several online companies offering VOIP for free including Skype, a service started by the group that created the free music-sharing service Kazaa.

Clearly VOIP is a major threat to traditional phone service providers. Analysts predict that by 2008, 16 percent of U.S. homes, or about 17.5 million users, will be "VOIPing," while the revenue of Verizon, SBC, and other regional carriers will slip by 12 percent, or $8 billion. Even so, these large phone companies should be in a strong position to capitalize on VOIP with their market power and brand names. Most users prefer to work with the reliable big phone providers. This raises an interesting question: Who are the new entrants and what are they selling?

Perhaps the biggest threat to traditional phone companies comes from cable operators such as Cox Communications and Comcast, which can use their cable connections to offer Internet voice. By packaging VOIP with its video, voice, and data service, New York-based Cablevision became the second largest VOIP provider in just six months. Upstart Vonage, the largest provider, has a strong following and an aggressive marketing campaign that includes selling do-it-yourself installation kits at Radio Shack and Best Buy.

Hundreds of other new entrants have developed equipment, software, and services that build on VOIP technology. New York–based M5 Networks is using a combination of digital and traditional phone lines to improve sound quality. 8×8, a Santa Clara, California start-up, is offering free videoconferencing and developing a *Hollywood Squares*–style approach that puts multiple people on the video screen at the same time. Because it is digital, VOIP phone systems can be integrated with other digital information such as customer databases. This would allow, for example, law firms to log phone calls into the firm's accounting system automatically, making it easier to account for billable hours.

Eventually there will be a shakeout as weak firms fail and the large incumbents acquire the small companies with good ideas. Industry incumbents will pay handsomely to acquire successful new entrants, and some of those young firms will survive to become major players themselves. Meanwhile, the entire phenomenon is driving prices down, and that will be a threat to the telecom industry for years to come.

Sources: Ferguson, K. 2005. Talk gets cheaper. *BusinessWeek Online*, www.businessweek.com, March 14; Fitzgerald, M. 2004. Can you hear me now? *Inc. Magazine*, November: 63–64; Malik, O. 2005. VOIP madness looks familiar. *Business 2.0*, www.business2.com, January 14; Malik, O. 2004. The technology of the year: Internet Voice. *Business 2.0*, 5(9): 109–110; and, Mehta, S. N. 2004. The future is on the line. *Fortune*, www.fortune.com, July 12.

The Bargaining Power of Buyers

The Internet and wireless technologies may increase buyer power by providing consumers with more information to make buying decisions and by lowering switching costs. But these technologies may also suppress the power of traditional buyer channels that have concentrated buying power in the hands of a few, giving buyers new ways to access sellers. In industries such as book publishing and grocery retailing, where the flow of products to market has traditionally been determined by strong intermediaries such as wholesalers and distributors, buyer power is shifting because of the Internet. To sort out these differences, let's first distinguish between two types of buyers: end users and buyer channel intermediaries.

End users, as the name implies, are the final customers in a distribution channel. They are the consumers who actually buy a product and put it to use. Internet sales activity that is labeled "B2C"—that is, business-to-consumer—is concerned with end users. The Internet is likely to increase the power of these buyers for several reasons. First, a large amount of consumer information is available on the Internet. This gives end users the information they need to shop for quality merchandise and bargain for price concessions. The automobile industry provides an excellent example of this phenomenon. For a small fee, agencies such as Consumers Union (publishers of *Consumer Reports*) will provide customers with detailed information about actual automobile manufacturer costs.[15] This information, available online, can be used to bid down dealers' profits.

Second, an end user's switching costs are also potentially much lower because of the Internet. Setting aside the psychological cost of switching due to an unwillingness by consumers to switch brands, the physical cost of switching may involve only a few clicks of the mouse to find and view a competing product or service online. As a result, according to Web strategist David Siegel, businesses that are serious about selling online will need to become increasingly customer-led. That is, they must be willing to listen to customers more often and respond to them more quickly. "E-customers aren't loyal to a brand," says Siegel. "They may be attracted to a specific business proposition, but their memories are very short. Solve one problem for them, and they have another. Companies must earn their networked customers' loyalty with *every* new deal."[16] In this environment, buyers are likely to have much more bargaining power.[17]

The bargaining power of distribution channel buyers may decrease because of the Internet. *Buyer channel intermediaries* are the wholesalers, distributors, and retailers who serve as intermediaries between manufacturers and end users. In some industries, they are dominated by powerful players that control who gains access to the latest goods or the best merchandise. The Internet and wireless communications, however, make it much easier and less expensive for businesses to reach customers directly. This is especially valuable for specialized companies that can focus their promotional efforts on marketplace segments that are more easily identified via the Internet. Thus, the Internet may increase the power of incumbent firms relative to that of traditional buyer channels.

The book publishing industry illustrates some of the changes brought on by the Internet that have affected the two types of buyers. Prior to the Internet, book publishers worked primarily through large distributors. These intermediaries such as Tennessee-based Ingram, one of the largest and most powerful distributors, exercised strong control over the movement of books from publishers to bookstores. This power was especially strong relative to small, independent publishers who often found it difficult to get their books into bookstores and in front of potential customers. The Internet has changed these relationships. Publishers can now negotiate distribution agreements directly with online retailers such as Amazon and Books-A-Million. And small publishers can use the Internet to sell directly to end users and publicize new titles, without depending on buyer channel intermediaries to handle their books.

Business customers are not the only buyers turning to the Internet to find better deals. State and local governments in the U.S. also have significantly increased their use of online procurement systems to obtain supplies and equipment more efficiently. In a recent period, Minnesota saved 10.6 percent using online procurement to buy commodities such as vehicles, electronic devices, and uniforms; Florida saved $18.3 million (30.4 percent) on purchases of office supplies and paper. To achieve these savings, both states used forms of Internet-based reverse auctions (where multiple sellers bid to do business with one buyer). INPUT, a government marketing intelligence organization, estimates that between 2004 and 2007, government use of reverse auctions for procurement will increase 300 percent.[18]

The Bargaining Power of Suppliers

Use of the Internet and digital technologies to speed up and streamline the process of acquiring supplies is already benefiting many sectors of the economy. But the net effect of the Internet on supplier power will depend on the nature of competition in a given industry. As with buyer power, the extent to which the Internet is a benefit or a detriment may also hinge on the supplier's position along the supply chain.

The role of suppliers typically involves providing products or services to other businesses. Thus, the term "B2B"—that is, business-to-business—is often used to refer to businesses that supply or sell to other businesses. The effect of the Internet on the bargaining power of suppliers is a double-edged sword. On the one hand, Internet technologies make it possible for suppliers to access more of their business customers at a relatively lower cost per customer. On the other hand, suppliers may not be able to hold onto these customers, because buyers can do comparative shopping and price negotiations so much faster on the Internet and can turn to other suppliers with a few clicks of the mouse. This is especially damaging to supply-chain intermediaries, such as product distributors, who may not be able to stop suppliers from directly accessing other potential business customers.

In general, one of the greatest threats to supplier power is that the Internet inhibits the ability of suppliers to offer highly differentiated products or unique services. Most procurement technologies can be imitated by competing suppliers, and the technologies that make it possible to design and customize new products rapidly are being used by all competitors. For example, Moen, the faucet manufacturer, sends digital designs of new faucets by way of e-mail to its suppliers worldwide to review. Suggestions for improvement are consolidated and final adjustments are made simultaneously. In a recent period, these practices cut design time from 24 to 16 months and boosted sales by 17 percent.[19] However, Delta and other competitors have implemented similar techniques to improve their own cycle time and boost sales.

Other factors may also contribute to stronger supplier power. First, the growth of new Web-based business in general may create more downstream outlets for suppliers to sell to. Second, suppliers may be able to create Web-based purchasing arrangements that make purchasing easier and discourage their customers from switching. Online procurement systems, for example, create a direct link between suppliers and customers that reduces transaction costs and paperwork.[20] Third, the use of proprietary software that links buyers to a supplier's Web site may create a rapid, low-cost ordering capability that discourages the buyer from seeking other sources of supply. Amazon.com, for example, created and patented One-Click purchasing technology that speeds up the ordering process for customers who enroll in the service.[21]

Finally, suppliers will have greater power to the extent that they can reach end users directly without intermediaries. Previously, suppliers often had to work through intermediaries who brought their products or services to market for a fee. But a process known as *disintermediation* is removing the organizations or business process layers responsible for intermediary steps in the value chain of many industries.[22] This is a major new business reality that the Internet has made possible, and it has significant strategic implications. As Larry Downes and Chunka Mui state in their book, *Unleashing the Killer App:*

> If buyers and sellers can find each other cheaply over the Internet, who needs agents (for instance, insurance) and distributors (for instance, home computers)? Complex transactions are becoming disaggregated, and middlemen who are not adding sufficient value relative to the open market are being disintermediated.[23]

Just as the Internet is eliminating some business functions, it is creating an opening for new functions. These new activities are entering the value chain by a process known as *reintermediation*—the introduction of new types of intermediaries. Many of these new functions are affecting traditional supply chains. In consumer markets, for example, delivery services are enjoying a boom because of the Internet. Many more consumers are choosing to have products delivered to their door rather than going out to pick them up. Electronic delivery is also becoming common. In business markets, e-commerce has created the need for new types of financial intermediaries that can perform clearing functions for purchases made online. New products (e.g., online credit cards) and new services (e.g., online escrow services) have been introduced as use of the Internet has grown. Consider the following examples of reintermediation:

- ***Extremetix, Inc.***—Developed ClicknPrint Tickets®, an online ticketing system that allows tickets to be printed at home using any standard ink-jet or laser printer. The tickets, which contain a two-dimensional bar-code, can be e-mailed to others for printing. If lost or damaged, a new one with a new number can be printed, canceling the previous ticket. In 2004, Extremetix became the largest provider of eTicketing to independent amusement parks, waterparks, and attractions.[24]

- ***Pitney Bowes***—Used its knowledge of electronic billing, encryption, and document management to turn around its 84-year-old postal meter business. By acquiring several market-leading digital communication companies and leveraging its relationship with the U.S. Postal Service, its profit growth jumped to 13 percent a year. Recently, eBay chose it to be its online postage provider.[25]

- ***E-Trade***—Developed Club eTrade, an online service designed to provide personal attention to high net worth customers. The system has improved customer service and significantly boosted performance. In the first four months of operation, it generated $460 million in new assets by directing 2,200 existing customers to new financial products.[26]

Exhibit 8.3 demonstrates how the processes of disintermediation and reintermediation are altering the traditional channels by which manufacturers reach consumers.

The Threat of Substitutes

Along with traditional marketplaces, the Internet has created a new marketplace; along with traditional channels, it has become a new channel. In general, therefore, the threat of substitutes is heightened because the Internet introduces new ways to accomplish the same tasks.

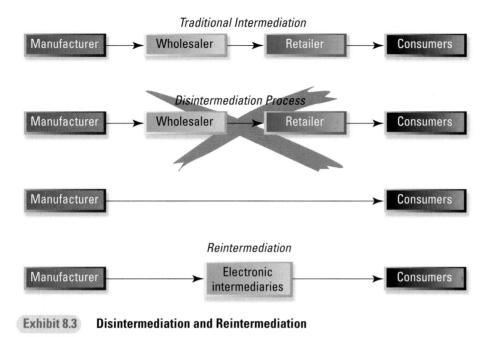

Exhibit 8.3   **Disintermediation and Reintermediation**

The primary factor that leads to substitution is economic. Consumers will generally choose to use a product or service until a substitute that meets the same need becomes available at a lower cost. The economies created by Internet technologies have led to the development of numerous substitutes for traditional ways of doing business. For example, a company called Conferenza is offering an alternative way to participate in conferences for people who don't want to spend the time and money to attend. The Web site provides summaries of many conference events, quality ratings using an "event intelligence" score, and schedules of upcoming events.[27]

Another example of substitution is in the realm of electronic storage. With expanded use of desktop computing capabilities during the last 20 years, the need to store information electronically has increased dramatically. Until recently, the trend has been to create increasingly larger desktop storage capabilities and techniques for compressing information that create storage efficiencies. But a viable substitute has recently emerged: storing information on the Internet. Companies such as My Docs Online Inc. are providing Web-based storage that firms can access simply by going online. Rather than purchasing more megabytes of storage space, firms can now lease cyberspace. Since these storage places are virtual, they can be accessed anywhere the Web can be accessed. This makes it possible for a traveler to access important documents and files without transporting them physically from place to place. Cyberstorage is not free, but it is still cheaper and more convenient than purchasing and carrying additional disk storage.[28]

Another substitute is in market research, which was traditionally conducted through mailed questionnaires and test marketing. These can be expensive to plan and administer. Questionnaires must be designed, printed, and mailed—all activities that have a hard cost. New products were often rolled out one city at a time to test the responses of a typical group of a few shoppers before a major launch. But Web technologies have reduced the time and cost of marketing. Insight Express is an online market research firm that can survey 300 people for around $1,000. Initially launched to conduct test marketing for mom-and-pop operations, the company is now test-marketing new names,

Adware and Spyware: Bad News *and* Good News?

Internet technologies have created new and far-reaching ways to invade consumer privacy. The way Internet service is provided creates many of these problems. For example, whenever you visit a Web site, a record of that visit is stored as a data packet on your own hard drive. These data packets are known as cookies and are used to speed up processing by remembering information such as products left in a shopping cart. But they can also be used to gather name and address information as well as a Web user's browsing habits.

Another example relates to the increased use of broadband for Internet access. Everyone knows the advantage of broadband is speed. But to provide speed, the Internet connection is typically always on (unless you turn off your computer or manually terminate the connection). This always-on feature increases the chance that unwelcome visitors are peering in on your Internet activity or leaving a "bug" that enables them to spy on you in the future.

Such bugs, appropriately labeled "spyware," are actually software applications that secretly track your behavior by monitoring system activity. Some spyware can even capture login data, including passwords, and transmit them to a remote computer. Spyware applications may be bundled with other legitimate software that an individual or business willingly downloads. Most users have no idea how spyware ever got on their computers.

Adware uses spyware technology but with a twist: They have your permission. Have you ever downloaded a free program, such as the file-sharing software Kazaa,

without actually reading the user agreement? If so, at least in the case of Kazaa, you would have also downloaded and agreed to the terms of Claria's GAIN, the leading source of adware. Claria then tracks your online activity and uses that information to plaster your screen with targeted ads. Such advertising antics are not just part of some Internet underground; Claria's customers include American Express and Sprint.

A Dell executive who recently testified to the FTC about invasive software reported that adware and spyware had become the number one reason that customers call Dell's tech support. But even though it may be a nuisance, is it unethical? Would you feel invaded if your personal buying habits were linked to your Internet surfing history, and this information was sold to businesses that wanted to send you targeted advertising? Or is this simply a case of "let the buyer beware"? That is, is using such software just a form of clever marketing, and is it ultimately the responsibility of consumers to know it and protect themselves?

Whatever the ethics of the situation may be, it can be said that this phenomenon has been good for business in two ways. First, adware seems to improve advertising effectiveness. Surfers click on adware-informed pop-ups 20 percent of the time according to WhenU, Claria's biggest adware rival. This is far better than the click rate for traditional, untargeted pop-ups. Second, the market for products that combat spyware—such as Spy Sweeper and PestPatrol, which was recently acquired by Computer Associates—will exceed $100 million in 2005. It seems certain that spyware fighters will profit from the battle to protect your privacy.

Source: Desmond, M. 2004. Threat assessment. *PCWorld*, www.pcworld.com, August 26; Deutschman, A. 2004. The ad agency on your hard drive. *Fast Company*, 88: 46; and Myser, M. 2005. Invasion of the corporate spyware. *Business 2.0*, 6(2): 30.

logos, product ideas, and even business concepts for major online players such as E-Trade and Yahoo![29]

Products can be tested more quickly in cyberspace. This is driven in part by the Internet's ability to capture detailed information about a person's Web-surfing habits, including information such as how long a visitor views a Web page, whether he or she clicks through a banner ad, and whether a purchase is made.[30] Such detailed information is invaluable to marketers trying to determine how to target their advertising. However, it can also be used maliciously to steal personal information or invade consumer privacy. Strategy Spotlight 8.3 describes some of the ethical issues surrounding this powerful new Internet capability.

The Intensity of Competitive Rivalry

Because the Internet creates more tools and means for competing, rivalry among competitors is likely to be more intense. Only those competitors that can use digital technologies and the Web to give themselves a distinct image, create unique product offerings, or provide "faster, smarter, cheaper" services are likely to capture greater profitability with the new technology. Such gains are hard to sustain, however, because in most cases the new technology can be imitated quickly. Thus, the Internet tends to increase rivalry by making it difficult for firms to differentiate themselves and by shifting customer attention to issues of price.

As we saw in Chapter 2, rivalry is more intense when switching costs are low and product or service differentiation is minimized. Because the Internet makes it possible to shop around with a few clicks of the mouse, it has "commoditized" products that might previously have been regarded as rare or unique. Since the Internet eliminates the importance of location, products that previously had to be sought out in geographically distant outlets are now readily available online. This makes competitors in cyberspace seem more equally balanced, thus intensifying rivalry.

The problem is made worse for marketers by the presence of shopping robots ("bots") and infomediaries that search the Web for the best possible prices. Consumer Web sites like mySimon and PriceSCAN seek out all the Web locations that sell similar products and provide price comparisons.[31] Obviously, this hinders a firm's ability to establish unique characteristics and focuses the consumer exclusively on price. Some shopping infomediaries, such as BizRate and CNET, not only search for the lowest prices on many different products but also rank the customer service quality of different sites that sell similarly priced items.[32] This is important because research indicates that customer service is three times more important than price to repeat online sales.[33] Such infomediary services are good for consumers because they give them the chance to compare services as well as price. For businesses, however, they increase rivalry by consolidating the marketing message that consumers use to make a purchase decision to a few key pieces of information over which the selling company has little control.

Recognizing that this phenomenon is part of the new Internet reality, many companies willingly participate in such services.[34] For example, BestBookBuys.com is a site that searches for the best prices among the Web sites of 24 different booksellers, including major ones such as Amazon and Barnes & Noble.[35] The booksellers featured on the site are member participants. They have agreed to have their prices included because it provides another kind of access to consumers. If they refused to be included, book buyers might never consider doing business with them. At least this way, there is a possibility that a new buyer will be attracted to a bookseller's site and make a return visit.

The online music business, discussed earlier in the chapter, provides a good example of how Internet and digital technologies have increased competitive rivalry. In addition to Napster and Apple iTunes, dozens of online music providers are vying for business. The competition is heating up around issues of price and capacity, i.e., the number of available titles. Competitors such as RealNetworks have offered songs for as little as $0.49 each (compared to about $0.99 on Apple iTunes).[36] The Internet amplifies this price-based rivalry in several ways. Switching costs are very low for Internet-based businesses. Compared to physically visiting another store to purchase music, alternative Web sites can be visited quickly and easily. The end products themselves are almost completely undifferentiated—one digital version of a song is virtually the same as another. The fact that the deliverable is digital also makes distribution very simple. All a consumer needs is access to a computer and the software (which is generally provided free) with which to download. These Internet-enabled factors make rivalry in the music selling industry more competitive than ever.

Exhibit 8.4 summarizes many of the ways the Internet is affecting industry structure. These influences will also change how companies develop and deploy strategies to generate above-average profits and sustainable competitive advantage. We turn to these topics next.

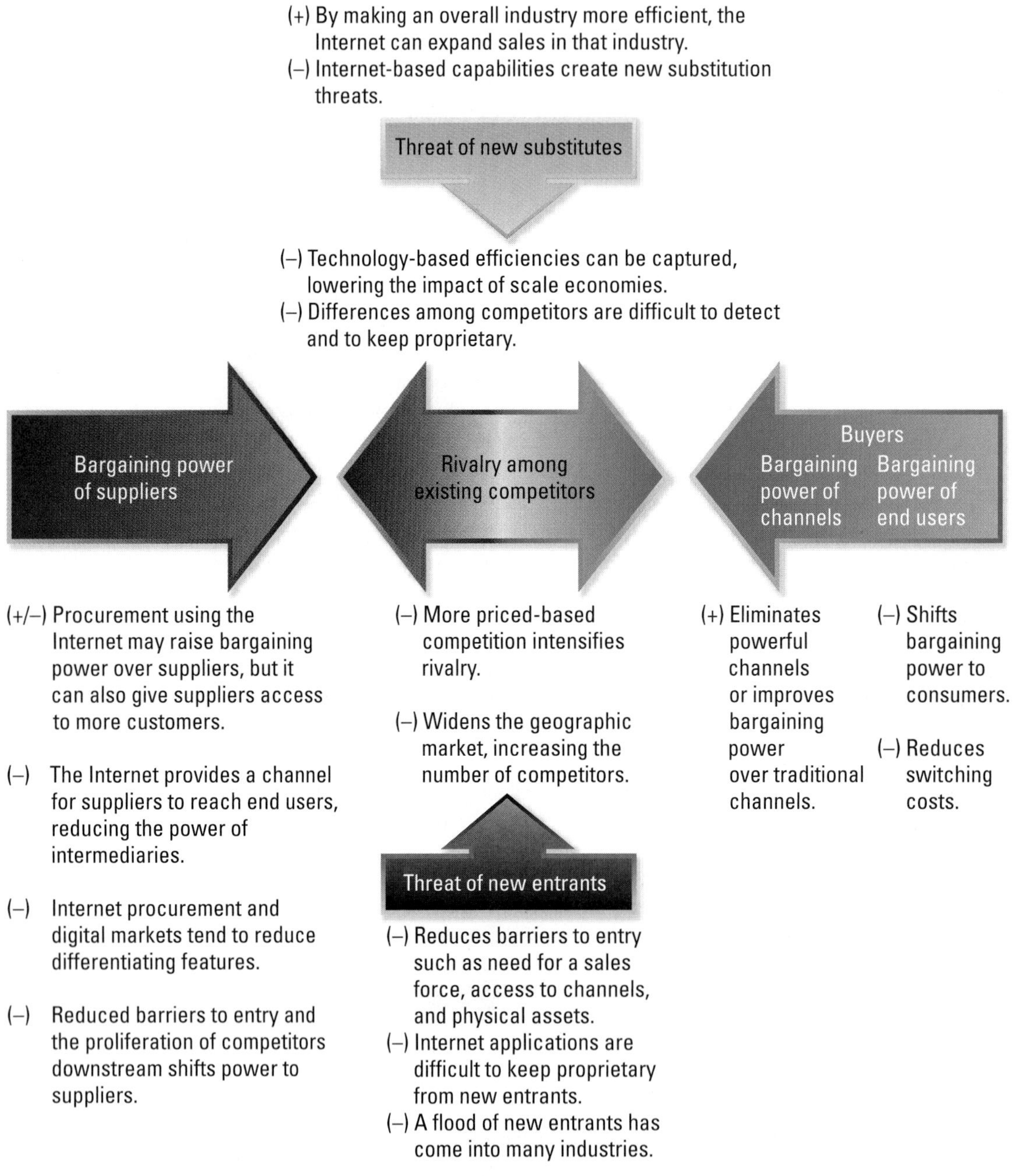

(+) By making an overall industry more efficient, the Internet can expand sales in that industry.
(−) Internet-based capabilities create new substitution threats.

Threat of new substitutes

(−) Technology-based efficiencies can be captured, lowering the impact of scale economies.
(−) Differences among competitors are difficult to detect and to keep proprietary.

Bargaining power of suppliers

Rivalry among existing competitors

Buyers
Bargaining power of channels   **Bargaining power of end users**

(+/−) Procurement using the Internet may raise bargaining power over suppliers, but it can also give suppliers access to more customers.

(−)   The Internet provides a channel for suppliers to reach end users, reducing the power of intermediaries.

(−)   Internet procurement and digital markets tend to reduce differentiating features.

(−)   Reduced barriers to entry and the proliferation of competitors downstream shifts power to suppliers.

(−) More priced-based competition intensifies rivalry.

(−) Widens the geographic market, increasing the number of competitors.

Threat of new entrants

(−) Reduces barriers to entry such as need for a sales force, access to channels, and physical assets.
(−) Internet applications are difficult to keep proprietary from new entrants.
(−) A flood of new entrants has come into many industries.

(+) Eliminates powerful channels or improves bargaining power over traditional channels.

(−) Shifts bargaining power to consumers.

(−) Reduces switching costs.

Exhibit 8.4   How the Internet Influences Industry Structure

Source: Adapted and reprinted by permission of *Harvard Business Review.* Exhibit from "Strategy and the Internet," by M. E. Porter, March 2001. Copyright © 2001 by the Harvard Business School Publishing Corporation; all rights reserved.

>>How the Internet and Digital Technologies Add Value

Using a five-forces framework, we have identified how the Internet and other digital technologies are influencing the competitive landscape. Next we turn to how companies can use these technologies to add value and create competitive advantages. As we noted earlier, the technology itself, whether it is digital or Internet, becomes strategically significant only when its practical application creates new value.

Clearly, the Internet has changed the way business is conducted. By conducting business online and using digital technologies to streamline operations, the Internet is helping companies create new value propositions. Let's take a look at several ways these changes have added new value. Exhibit 8.5 illustrates four related activities that are being revolutionized by the Internet—search, evaluation, problem solving, and transaction.[37]

Search Activities

Search refers to the process of gathering information and identifying purchase options. The Internet has enhanced both the speed of information gathering and the breadth of information that can be accessed. This enhanced search capability is one of the key reasons the Internet has lowered switching costs—by decreasing the cost of search. These efficiency gains have greatly benefited buyers. Suppliers also have benefited. Small suppliers that had difficulty getting noticed can more easily be found, and large suppliers can publish thousands of pages of information for a fraction of the cost that hard-copy catalogs once required. Additionally, online search engines have accelerated the search process to incredible speeds. Consider the example of Google:

> Google, a search engine developed as a project by two graduate students, became the number one search service in just four years. Why? Because it is capable of incredible things: Using 10,000 networked computers, it searches 3 billion Web pages in an average of 500 milliseconds. To do the same search manually, by thumbing through 3 billion pages at the rate of one minute per page, would take 5,707 years. This ability has made Google an essential tool for many businesses. As a result, Google has built a powerful advertising business. Mark Kini, who runs a small limousine service in Boston, spends 80 percent of his advertising budget on Google and other search engines. "It's how we survive," says Kini.[38]

Evaluation Activities

Evaluation refers to the process of considering alternatives and comparing the costs and benefits of various options. Online services that facilitate comparative shopping, provide

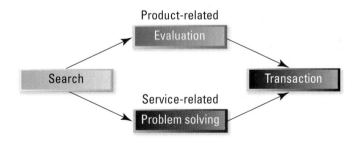

Exhibit 8.5 **Internet Activities That Add Value**

Sources: Adapted from Zeng, M., & Reinartz, W. 2003. Beyond online search: The road to profitability. *California Management Review,* Winter: 107–130; and Stabell, C. B., & Fjeldstad, O. D. 1998. Configuring value for competitive advantage: On chains, shops, and networks. *Strategic Management Journal,* 19: 413–437.

product reviews, and catalog customer evaluations of performance have made the Internet a valuable resource.[39] For example, BizRate.com offers extensive product ratings that can help evaluate products. Sites such as CNET that provide comparative pricing have helped lower prices even for quality products that have traditionally maintained premium prices. Opinion-based sites such as ePinions.com and PlanetFeedback.com provide reports of consumer experiences with various vendors.

Many Internet businesses, according to digital business experts Ming Zeng and Werner Reinartz, could improve their performance by making a stronger effort to help buyers evaluate purchases.[40] Even so, only certain types of products can be evaluated online. Products such as CDs that appeal primarily to the sense of sound sell well on the Internet. But products that appeal to multiple senses are harder to evaluate online. This explains why products such as furniture and fashion have never been strong online sellers. It's one thing to look at a leather sofa, but to be able to sit in it, touch, and smell the leather online are impossible.

Problem-Solving Activities

Problem solving refers to the process of identifying problems or needs and generating ideas and action plans to address those needs. Whereas evaluation is primarily product-related, problem solving is typically used in the context of services. Customers usually have unique problems and therefore are handled one at a time. For example, online travel services such as Travelocity help customers select from many options to form a unique travel package. Furthermore, problem solving often involves providing answers immediately (compared to the creation of a new product). Firms in industries such as medicine, law, and engineering are using the Internet and digital technologies to deliver many new solutions.

Many products involve both a service and a product component; therefore, both problem solving and evaluation may be needed. Dell Computer's Web site is an example of a site that has combined the benefits of both. By creating a Web site that allows for customization of individual computers, they address the unique concerns of customers "one computer at a time." But the site also features a strong evaluative component because it allows users to compare the costs and features of various options. Shoppers can even compare their customized selection to refurbished Dell computers that are available at a substantially lower cost.

Transaction Activities

Transaction refers to the process of completing the sale, including negotiating and agreeing contractually, making payments, and taking delivery. Numerous types of Internet-enabled activities have contributed to lowering this aspect of overall transaction costs. Auctions of various sorts, from raw materials used in manufacturing to collectibles sold on eBay, facilitate the process of arriving at mutually agreed-on prices. Services such as PayPal provide a third-party intermediary that facilitates transactions between parties who never have (and probably never will!) meet. Amazon.com's One-Click technology allows for very rapid purchases, and Amazon's overall superiority in managing order fulfillment has made its transactions process rapid and reliable. Amazon's success today can be attributed to a large extent to its having sold this transaction capability to other companies such as Target, Toys "R" Us and even Borders (another bookstore!).[41]

These four factors are primary ways that organizations go about adding value. Strategy Spotlight 8.4 describes several examples of how the automobile industry and car buyers have used each of these activities to benefit their own value-adding efforts.

Adding Value in the Auto Industry

The auto industry jumped on the Internet bandwagon in a big way. One of the early successes was Autobytel, and many online auto sales Web sites quickly followed. Today, the automakers—and the auto-buying public—have found ways to use the Internet profitably. Here are a few examples:

Search EBay, the online auction giant that makes searching for products of all sorts fast and simple, has become a serious player in the used car business. Beginning with a few private individuals, the auto auction business took off unexpectedly, so the company formed eBay Motors, which contributed about $100 million to eBay's total revenue of $1.2 billion in a recent year. EBay's technology speeds the process of online search, and buyers who may have been reluctant to shop for cars online are comforted by eBay's reputation. EBay and other online auto sales sites make searching for insurance and auto financing easier as well.

Problem Solving To help its dealers manage inventories more effectively, General Motors developed SmartAuction. For vehicles that are coming off lease, SmartAuction notifies customers to bring in cars for an inspection before the lease expires. The condition of the car is logged into the system and sent to GM dealers, who use it to purchase cars electronically for their used car lots. The system helps dealers find cars that fit their target audience, manages the auto titling process, and shortens the time cars are carried in inventory.

Evaluation In the early days of the Internet, most thought that cars would never sell online, because customers like to kick the tires and take a test drive. This is often still true. But customers who go for a test drive and also have already researched the car online usually save money when they buy. Economists researching this phenomenon have labeled it the "information effect"—auto shoppers who first gather information online are better able to evaluate their purchase.

Transaction Auto referral services such as CarsDirect have streamlined the transaction process by brokering purchases between dealers and consumers. Through these companies, both new and used cars can be purchased online, sight unseen. One shopper, who bought a used car online, flew to Fort Worth, Texas, to pick it up, and drove it 18 hours back home to Ohio, said, "In retrospect, I had more information about this vehicle than if I had gone onto a dealer's lot and started haggling over price." Online auto shoppers typically save money due to the "contract effect," which occurs because third-party auto referral services monitor the information provided by dealers and facilitate the transaction.

Sources: Postrell, V. 2003. How much is that Civic online? *New York Times,* April 24, www.nytimes.com; Stepanek, M. 2003. New routes in the Internet car business. *CIO Insight,* January 23, www.cioinsight.com; and, Wingfield, N., & Lundegaard, K. 2003. EBay is emerging as unlikely giant in used-car sales. *Wall Street Journal,* February 7.

Other Sources of Competitive Advantage

There are other factors that can be important sources of competitive advantage. One of the most important of these is content. The Internet makes it possible to capture vast amounts of content at a very low cost. REI.com, for example, a provider of recreational equipment and apparel, has over 78,000 items described on its 45,000-page Web site.[42] But firms have not always managed content in ways that add value. Garden.com, a site that started strongly in 1999 and raised enormous venture capital, spent millions on creating detailed and attractive content. But the expense did not generate sales. Content adds value only if it contributes to the overall value proposition. As a result, Garden.com failed in early 2001 (but the name is still being used by the Burpee Company, a 125-year-old supplier of garden products, who bought rights to the name).[43]

Three types of content can improve the value proposition of a Web site—customer feedback, expertise, and entertainment programming.

- *Customer feedback.* Buyers often trust what other buyers say more than a company's promises. One type of content that can enhance a Web site is customer testimonials. Remember the leather sofa in the example above? Even though individuals can't feel and smell a sofa online, the testimonials of other buyers can build confidence and add to the chances that the purchaser will buy online sight unseen. This is one way that content can be a source of competitive advantage. Being able to interact with like-minded customers by reading their experiences or hearing how they have responded to a new product offering builds a sense of belonging that is otherwise hard to create.

- **Expertise.** The Internet has emerged as a tremendously important learning tool. Fifty-one percent of users compare the Internet to a library.[44] The prime reason many users go to the Web is to gain expertise. Web sites that provide new knowledge or unbiased information are highly valuable. Additionally the problem-solving function often involves educating consumers regarding options and implications of various choices. For example, LendingTree.com, the online loan company, provides a help center that includes extensive information and resources about obtaining loans, maintaining good credit, and so forth. Further, the expertise function is not limited to consumer sites. In the case of B2B businesses, Web sites that facilitate sharing expert knowledge help build a sense of community in industry or professional groups.

- **Entertainment programming.** The Internet is being used by more and more people as an entertainment medium. With technologies such as streaming media, which allows the Internet to send televisionlike images and sound, computers can provide everything from breaking news to video games to online movies. A study by the Pew Internet and American Life Project indicates that among people using high-speed broadband service, TV viewing is down and online activity has increased. One reason is that the technology is interactive, which means that viewers don't just passively watch, but they use the Web to create art or play online games. Businesses have noticed this trend, of course, and are creating Web content that is not just informative but entertaining. Strategy Spotlight 8.5 tells how online game developer Skyworks Technologies is using games to increase product sales.

These three types of content—customer feedback, expertise, and entertainment programming—are potential sources of competitive advantage. That is, they create advantages by making the value creation process even stronger. Or, if they are handled poorly, they diminish performance.

Next we turn to the topic of Internet business models. How the Internet creates value depends to a great extent on how a value proposition is enacted. Business models provide a guide to the effectiveness of the value-adding process.

Business Models

The Internet provides a unique platform or staging area for business activity, which has become, in some ways, like a new marketplace. How do firms conduct business in this new arena? One way of addressing this question is by describing various Internet business models. A business model is a method and a set of assumptions that explain how a business creates value and earns profits in a competitive environment. Some of these models are quite simple and traditional even when applied in an Internet context. Others have features that are unique to the digitally networked, online environment. In this section, we discuss seven Internet business models that account for the vast majority of business conducted online.[45]

- **Commission-based** models are used by businesses that provide services for a fee. The business is usually a third-party intermediary, and the commission charged is

STRATEGY SPOTLIGHT

"Advergaming": Making Advertisements Interactive and Fun

Video games were popular well before the Web came along. But new digital technologies have made it possible to feature some of the best games online. Combine this with advertisers' need to use the Net's interactivity to make online ads more interesting and what do you get? Advergaming—online games that weave advertisements into the experience. Here are some examples:

- A game designed for Pepsi involves an auto race in which the goal is to recover a stolen shipment of Mountain Dew Code Red. The top 100 gamers received a free case of the soft drink.

- Some games make you buy something to play. To play the Pebbles Big Barney Chase game, players must answer a question; to learn the answer, you have to purchase a box of Post Cereal.

- Candystand.com, a Web site developed by Skyworks Technologies to promote Life Savers for Kraft Foods, features dozens of card, racing, and arcade games and ranks as the sixth most popular gaming destination on the Web.

Sources: Athitakis, M. 2003. The entertainer. *Business 2.0*, May: 88; Suciu, P. 2003. Mobility takes the forum. *GameSpy*, May 2, www.gamespy.com; www.candystand.com; www.skyworkstech.com; Keighley, G. 2004. Quick-change ads for the joystick generation. *Business 2.0*, 5(8): 31–32; and www.ssx3.com.

- SSX 3, an extreme sports games that pits gamers against the thrills and perils of a massive mountain, lets players snowboard through the open door of a Honda Element SUV.

Spending on advergaming is expected to more than double from $21 million in 2004 to $44 million in 2007. This kind of growth was enough to prompt Nielsen Interactive Entertainment (compiler of the all-important Nielsen Ratings) to develop a "people meter" to gauge how long people play games, which ads they see while playing, and how long they see them. "Measured media is going to lend credibility to the videogame space," says Sam Bloom of Camelot Communications, a media marketing firm whose clients include Blockbuster and Southwest Airlines.

According to Skyworks founder Garry Kitchen, advergaming can leave a deeper and more positive impression than television commercials. The idea is catching on. In a recent year, Skyworks made $4.3 million in revenues, and industry analyst Kent Allen of the Aberdeen Group expects the trend to continue, especially among consumer packaged-goods marketers. "The consumer guys are starting to understand advergaming," says Allen. "They're realizing it's a great way to connect with people."

often based on the size of the transaction. The most common type is a brokerage service, such as a stockbroker (e.g., Schwab.com), real estate broker (e.g., Remax.com), or transaction broker (e.g., Paypal.com). This category also includes auction companies such as eBay. In exchange for putting buyers and sellers together, eBay earns a commission.

- *Advertising-based* models are used by companies that provide content and/or services to visitors and sell advertising to businesses that want to reach those visitors. It is similar to the broadcast television model, in which viewers watch shows produced with advertising dollars. A key difference is that online visitors can interact with both the ads and the content. Large portals such as Yahoo.com are in this category as well as specialty portals such as iNest.com, which provides services for buyers of newly constructed homes. EPinions.com, a recommender system, is just one example of the many types of content that are often available.

- *Markup-based* models are used by businesses that add value in marketing and sales (rather than production) by acquiring products, marking up the price, and reselling them at a profit. Also known as the merchant model, it applies to both wholesalers and retailers. Amazon.com is the best-known example in this category.

It also includes bricks-and-mortar companies such as Wal-Mart, which has a very successful online operation, and vendors whose products are purely digital such as Fonts.com, which sells downloadable fonts and photographs.

- **Production-based** models are used by companies that add value in the production process by converting raw materials into value-added products. Thus, it is also referred to as the manufacturing model. The Internet adds value to this model in two key ways. First, it lowers marketing costs by enabling direct contact with end users. Second, such direct contact facilitates customization and problem solving. Dell's online ordering system is supported by a state-of-the-art customized manufacturing process. Travelocity uses its rich database of travel options and customer profiles to identify, produce, and deliver unique solutions.

- **Referral-based** models are used by firms that steer customers to another company for a fee. One type is the affiliate model, in which a vendor pays an affiliate a fee each time a visitor clicks through the affiliate's Web site and makes a purchase from the vendor. Many name-brand companies use affiliate programs. For example, WeddingChannel.com, which provides a bridal registry where wedding guests can buy gifts from companies such as Tiffany's, Macy's, or Crate & Barrel, receives a fee each time a sale is made through its Web site. Another referral-based example is Yesmail.com, which generates leads using e-mail marketing.

- **Subscription-based** models are used by businesses that charge a flat fee for providing either a service or proprietary content. Internet service providers are one example of this model. Companies such as America Online and Earthlink supply Internet connections for fees that are charged whether buyers use the service or not. Subscription-based models are also used by content creators such as the *Economist* or the *New York Times.* Although these recognizable brands often provide free content, only a small portion is available free. The *Economist,* for example, advertises that 70 percent of its content is available only to subscribers.

- **Fee-for-service-based** models are used by companies that provide ongoing services similar to a utility company. Unlike the commission-based model, the fee-for-service model involves a pay-as-you-go system. That is, activities are metered and companies pay only for the amount of service used. Application service providers fall in this category. For example, eProject.com provides virtual work space where people in different physical locations can collaborate online. Users essentially rent Internet space, and a host of tools that make it easy to interact, for a fee based on their usage.

Exhibit 8.6 summarizes the key feature of each Internet business model, suggests what role content may play in the model, and addresses how the four value-adding activities—search, evaluation, problem solving, and transaction—can be sources of competitive advantage.

It's important to keep in mind that many companies combine these models to achieve competitive advantages. For example, a company such as LendingTree not only sells advertising but also earns a commission as a third-party intermediary and earns fees by referring viewers to other sites through its affiliate programs.

Next, we turn to the topic of how the Internet and digital technologies are influencing the three competitive strategies—overall low cost, differentiation, and focus—and

Exhibit 8.6
Internet Business
Models

Type	Features and Content	Sources of Competitive Advantage
Commission-based	Charges commissions for brokerage or intermediary services. Adds value by providing expertise and/or access to a wide network of alternatives.	Search Evaluation Problem solving Transaction
Advertising-based	Web content paid for by advertisers. Adds value by providing free or low-cost content—including customer feedback, expertise, and entertainment programming—to audiences that range from very broad (general content) to highly targeted (specialized content).	Search Evaluation
Markup-based	Resells marked-up merchandise. Adds value through selection, through distribution efficiencies, and by leveraging brand image and reputation. May use entertainment programming to enhance sales.	Search Transaction
Production-based	Sells manufactured goods and custom services. Adds value by increasing production efficiencies, capturing customer preferences, and improving customer service.	Search Problem solving
Referral-based	Charges fees for referring customers. Adds value by enhancing a company's product or service offering, tracking referrals electronically, and generating demographic data. Expertise and customer feedback often included with referral information.	Search Problem solving Transaction
Subscription-based	Charges fees for unlimited use of service or content. Adds value by leveraging strong brand name, providing high-quality information to specialized markets, or providing access to essential services. May consist entirely of entertainment programming.	Evaluation Problem solving
Fee-for-service-based	Charges fees for metered services. Adds value by providing service efficiencies, expertise, and practical outsourcing solutions.	Problem solving Transaction

Sources: Afuah, A., & Tucci, C. L. 2003. *Internet business models and strategies* (2nd ed.). New York: McGraw-Hill; Rappa, M. 2005. Business models on the Web, digitalenterprise.org/models/models.html; and Timmers, P. 1999. *Electronic commerce.* New York: Wiley.

discuss further the role of combination strategies in creating competitive advantages for Internet companies.

>>How the Internet and Digital Technologies Are Affecting the Competitive Strategies

As we have seen, the Internet and digital technologies are sweeping across the economy and affecting in many ways how business is conducted. The Internet is a resource that companies around the world can access. Thus, to stay competitive, firms must update their strategies to reflect the new possibilities and constraints that these phenomena represent. In this section we will revisit the three competitive strategies introduced in Chapter 5—overall cost leadership, differentiation, and focus—and address how the Internet and digital technologies can be used to enhance firm performance. We will also consider two major impacts that the Internet is having on business: lowering transaction costs and enabling mass customization. Finally, we will briefly discuss the pitfalls associated with using the new technologies and will address the role of combination strategies in achieving competitive advantages.

Overall Cost Leadership

An overall low-cost leadership strategy involves managing costs in every activity of a firm's value chain and offering no-frills products that are an exceptional value at the best possible price. We have seen how companies such as Wal-Mart and Southwest Airlines achieved this position through vigilant attention to cost control. Internet and digital technologies now provide even more opportunities to manage costs and achieve greater efficiencies. But these capabilities are available to many competing firms, and even specialized capabilities (i.e., those that firms might realize by using proprietary software) often provide only a short-lived advantage.

Nevertheless, managing costs, and even changing the cost structures of certain industries, is a key feature of the new digital economy. Most analysts agree that the Internet's ability to lower transaction costs will transform business. Broadly speaking, *transaction costs* refer to all the various expenses associated with conducting business. It applies not just to buy/sell transactions but to the costs of interacting with every part of a firm's value chain, within and outside the firm. Think about it. Hiring new employees, meeting with customers, ordering supplies, addressing government regulations—all of these exchanges have some costs associated with them. Because business can be conducted differently on the Internet, new ways of saving money are changing the competitive landscape.

Consider how one company, British Petroleum (BP), has used the Internet and digital technologies to lower procurement costs and create efficient methods to communicate:[46]

> British Petroleum has achieved a number of strategic advantages with its Internet initiatives, including a $300 million savings in a recent year. Led by John Leggate, BP's group vice president for digital business, the company has pursued an aggressive policy of implementing Internet-based cost savings. For example:
>
> - Instead of sending teams to far-off exploration targets, BP scientists now gather in any of 15 data centers around the globe to view digital 3-D images of drilling sites sent over the Internet. *Payoff:* Up to $250 million in annual savings.
> - All BP employees have personalized Web pages listing their areas of expertise. This helps managers tap into BP's reservoir of knowledge. *Payoff:* In one case, engineers in the Caribbean saved $600,000 by adopting a drilling process developed in Norway just a few days earlier.

Such practices are strengthening the role of the Internet and digital technologies in cutting expenses and managing transaction costs throughout the value chain.

Other factors also help to lower transaction costs. The process of disintermediation, described earlier in this chapter, has a similar effect. Each time intermediaries are used in a transaction, additional costs are added. Removing those intermediaries lowers transaction costs. The Internet reduces the costs of traveling to a location to search for a product or service, whether it is a retail outlet (as in the case of consumers) or a trade show (as in the case of business-to-business shoppers). Not only is the need for travel eliminated, but so is the need to maintain a physical address, whether it's a permanent retail location or a temporary presence at a trade show.

In terms of strategizing, therefore, the Internet and digital technologies are creating new opportunities for firms to achieve low-cost advantages.[47] Of course, the same potential benefits are available to all companies relatively equally, but some companies have adopted these capabilities more rapidly or implemented them more efficiently. These cost savings are available throughout a firm's value chain, in both primary and support activities:

- Direct access to progress reports and the ability for customers to periodically check work in progress is minimizing rework.
- Online bidding and order processing are eliminating the need for sales calls and are minimizing sales force expenses.
- Online purchase orders are making many transactions paperless, thus reducing the costs of procurement and paper.
- Collaborative design efforts using Internet technologies that link designers, materials suppliers, and manufacturers are reducing the costs and speeding the process of new-product development.
- Human resources departments are using online testing and evaluation techniques in the hiring process and in online training after they hire.

Potential Internet-Related Pitfalls for Low-Cost Leaders As Internet and digital technologies become more widespread, the cost advantages that early users of these technologies enjoyed may be available to many firms. One of the biggest threats to low-cost leaders is imitation. This problem is intensified for business done on the Internet. Most of the advantages associated with contacting customers directly, and even capabilities that are software driven (e.g., customized ordering systems or real-time access to the status of work in progress that lowers the cost of rework), can be duplicated quickly and without threat of infringement on proprietary information.

Another major pitfall for low-cost providers is the availability of information online that allows consumers to comparison shop much more easily. Also, companies that become overly enamored with the Internet and its ability to cut costs may suffer if they place too much attention on one business activity and ignore others. They may jeopardize customer relations or neglect other cost centers, such as providing services or controlling turnover and recruiting expenses, which then dig into their cost advantages.

Differentiation

A differentiation strategy involves providing unique, high-quality products and services that promote a favorable reputation and strong brand identity and usually command a premium price. Throughout this text we have seen examples of strong differentiators—Disney, Nokia, BMW, and others. The Internet and digital technologies have created new ways for firms to achieve a competitive advantage. Some of these capabilities are being used to threaten the position of companies that have traditionally maintained the best reputations or strong leadership positions. Other technologies are being employed by industry leaders to make their position even stronger.

Consider the example of emachineShop.com, which provides computer-aided design (CAD) software for free to companies seeking to custom-design machine-made parts.[48] The downloadable software not only allows users to create three-dimensional designs, but also analyzes the shape, materials, and finished appearance and automatically informs the user of any limitations of the design. Once the design is finalized, the software prices the finished product and orders the parts over the Internet. Then, eMachineShop.com actually manufactures the part. The process is far faster than previous methods and the easy-to-use software allows for direct customer involvement in the end product.

Among the most striking trends that the new technologies foster are new ways to interact with consumers. In particular, the Internet is creating new ways of differentiating by enabling *mass customization,* which improves the response of companies to customer wishes. Mass customization is not a new phenomenon; it has been growing for years as flexible manufacturing systems have made manufacturing more adaptable and electronic data interchange has made communications more direct. But the Internet has generated a giant leap forward in the amount of control customers can have in influencing the process. Such capabilities are changing the way companies develop unique product and service offerings, make their reputation, and preserve their brand image. The new technology may affect the structure of entire industries. In the old days, manufacturers built products and waited for customers to respond. Now they are taking directions from customers before manufacturing any products. Consider the following examples.

- Dell Computer has strengthened its leadership position by creating an online ordering system that allows customers to configure their own computers before they are built.[49]

- 7 Eleven, a convenience store operator, has created a finely tuned feedback system that monitors subtle shifts in customer demand and recommends revisions to its product offerings on a daily basis.[50]

- Footwear giant Nike lets customers choose the color of their shoes and add a personal name or nickname through its NIKEiD program. Customers can view their selection at the Nike.com Web site before finalizing the order.[51]

Methods like mass customization, which are changing the way companies go to market, are challenging some of the tried-and-true techniques of differentiation. Traditionally, companies reached customers in various ways—the high-end catalog, the showroom floor, the personal sales call—and used numerous means to make products more inviting—prestige packaging, celebrity endorsements, charity sponsorships. All of these avenues are still available and may still be effective, depending on a firm's competitive environment. But many consumers now judge the quality and uniqueness of a product or service by their ability to be involved in planning and design, combined with speed of delivery and reliability of results. Internet and digitally based capabilities are thus changing the way differentiators make exceptional products and achieve superior service. And these improvements are being made at a reasonable cost, allowing firms to achieve parity on the basis of overall cost leadership relative to competitors (see Chapter 5).

Here again, opportunities to differentiate using Internet and digital technologies are available in all parts of a company's value chain. Some of the techniques firms are using to achieve competitive advantage are fast becoming industry norms; successful differentiators will need to remain attentive to the evolving capabilities of the new technologies. These capabilities are evident in both primary and support activities.

- Internet-based knowledge management systems that link all parts of the organization are shortening response times and accelerating organization learning.

- Personalized online access provides customers with their own "site within a site" in which their prior orders, status of current orders, and requests for future orders are processed directly on the supplier's Web site.

- Quick online responses to service requests and rapid feedback to customer surveys and product promotions are enhancing marketing efforts.

- Online access to real-time sales and service information is being used to empower the sales force and continually update R&D and technology development efforts.

- Automated procurement and payment systems provide both suppliers and customers with access to detailed status reports and purchasing histories.

Potential Internet-Related Pitfalls for Differentiators   As applications of these technologies become part of the mainstream, it will become harder to use the Web to differentiate. The sustainability of Internet-based gains from differentiation will deteriorate if companies offer differentiating features that customers don't want or create a sense of uniqueness that customers don't value. This has been the case with some of the personalization and customization software that early dot-com companies added to their sites at great expense. Users did not care about these features and that led to a failed value proposition—the value companies thought they were offering did not translate into sales. Other problems can result from overpricing products and services or developing brand extensions that dilute a company's image or reputation.

Now consider the efforts of one firm that has drawn on the Internet's technological capabilities to attempt a new approach to strategizing. Strategy Spotlight 8.6 profiles Buy.com, an Internet company with an unusual approach. Is it a differentiator or an overall cost leader? Whether the answer is "neither" or "both," Buy.com appears so far to have defied traditional strategic thinking.

Focus

A focus strategy involves targeting a narrow market segment with customized products and/or specialized services. For companies that pursue focus strategies, the Internet offers new avenues in which to compete because they can access markets less expensively (low cost) and provide more services and features (differentiation). Some claim that the Internet has opened up a new world of opportunities for niche players who seek to access small markets in a highly specialized fashion.[52] Niche businesses are among the most active users of digital technologies and e-business solutions. According to the ClickZ.com division of Jupitermedia Corporation, 77 percent of small businesses agree that a Web site is essential for small business success. Small businesses also report that the Internet has helped them grow (58 percent), made them more profitable (51 percent), and helped reduce business costs (49 percent).[53] Clearly, niche players and small businesses are using the Internet and digital technologies to create more viable focus strategies.

Nevertheless, even though the Internet and digital technologies present some exciting new possibilities, the same problems that low-cost leaders and differentiators face in

STRATEGY SPOTLIGHT

Buy.Com's Risky Strategy

In terms of Michael Porter's competitive strategies, Buy.com tried something very risky. It tried to build brand with an overall cost leadership strategy. Developing a brand image that customers will turn to and rely on is traditionally associated with a differentiation strategy. Heavy investments in advertising to create brand recognition are generally considered ineffective for low-cost providers because customers seeking the lowest price tend to be less loyal. They follow the low price, not the brand.

This didn't stop Buy.com, an online retailer of electronics, books, video games, and more. From the beginning it sought to build a reputation as the lowest-cost provider with the advertising slogan "lowest prices on earth." It purchased hundreds of domain names that started with the term "buy": BuyNokia.com, BuySony.com, and so forth. Then it offered incredibly low prices, well below market value. In the case of hot, new high-demand products, it sold loss leaders at negative gross margins to attract buyers. It hoped to make up the difference in advertising revenues. As a self-proclaimed "superstore" offering 30,000 different products, Buy.com sought to build a reputation as the best place to shop for low prices and thus an ideal venue for the ads of other vendors.

Has this strategy worked? It's still too early to tell. Buy.com did achieve $100 million in sales faster than any other company in history, but it also chalked up significant losses. In addition to negative profitability, Buy.com has had numerous problems with order fulfillment and has developed a reputation for advertising products that were back-ordered for weeks. Its hopes for advertising revenue were not fulfilled either, as the luster of banner ads faded and the dot-com downturn caused everyone to have second thoughts about online advertising.

In late 2001, Buy.com founder Scott Blum reacquired the company for $23.6 million and took it private. This purchase price was equivalent to 17 cents per share even though at one time the company's stock sold for $35 per share. Blum, who earlier in 2001 had provided Buy.com with $9 million in interim financing, said he would return the company to its "Internet Superstore" roots and relaunch its "Lowest Prices on Earth" marketing campaign. More recently, Buy.com has launched a glossy magazine and boasted it will outperform Amazon.com by offering free shipping on everything.

Such features are costly and make Buy.com appear to be differentiating. However, it continues to position itself as an overall low-cost leader in terms of pricing. "I do not believe that Buy.com's pricing assault on Amazon.com is sustainable," said Ken Cassar, senior analyst at Jupiter Media Metrix. "It is very likely . . . that Buy.com will steal market share from Amazon in the short term. Whether that is sustainable will depend upon whether customers will come back to Buy.com when there is no promotion."

Clearly the firm's long-term prospects are still uncertain. But that hasn't kept Blum, who owns 98 percent of the stock, from pursuing another unorthodox strategy. In 2005, he filed papers with the SEC to take Buy.com public—again. Will investors bite? "Buy.com has lot of a baggage," according to Tom Taulli, co-founder of CurrentOfferings.com. "Seven years ago Buy.com had sizzle. But this doesn't have a lot of sizzle to it." Indeed, in its eight years of existence, the company has never had a profitable year. And at the end of 2004, it had about $22 million in debt. Repaying that debt will be a top priority with the proceeds from the initial public offering (IPO).

Others see it more positively. Pattie Freeman Evans, a retail analyst for Jupiter Research says, "They've expanded in ways that make sense—like moving into books through books about computers." Buy.com's 2004 sales were $290.8 million. Still, that's way down from the $787.6 million in revenues for 2000. During the same period Overtock.com, one of its closest competitors, grew revenues from $25.5 million in 2000 to $494.6 million in 2004.

Buy.com continues to invest in its potentially risky strategy. Now it is asking investors to buy in as well.

Sources: *Economist.* 1999. Playing i-ball. November 6: 65; Porter, M. E. 2001. Strategy and the Internet. *Harvard Business Review,* March: 63–78; Cox, B. 2002. E-commerce price war escalates, Amazon expands. *InternetNews,* June 25, www.internetnews.com; Cox, B. 2002. And now, Buy.com the magazine. *InternetNews,* February 27; Singer, M. 2001. Scott Blum re-acquires. Buy.com. *InternetNews,* November 28; B. Cox. 2001. Buy.com returns to its roots. *InternetNews,* September 25. Lacy, S. 2005. Back to the future at Buy.com. *BusinessWeek Online,* www.businessweek.com, January 26; Hellweg, E. 2005. BuyersBeware.com. *Business 2.0,* www.business2.com, January 31; and www.hoovers.com.

a digital economy will affect focusers as well. Achieving competitive advantage will depend on how effectively firms use Internet technologies and deploy focus strategies. Let's look at SalvageSale, Inc., an online broker of salvage goods.

SalvageSale, Inc., has become the top choice of insurance and transportation companies that need to quickly liquidate commercial salvage goods. The Houston-based company has been

opportunities. Traditional companies are also using the Internet and digital capabilities to create new strategic ventures. Consider InnoCentive, the Internet-based initiative launched by pharmaceutical giant Eli Lilly:

> InnoCentive, as the name implies, provides incentives for innovation. It does so by providing a platform for scientists from around the world to work in virtual communities to solve complex problems. The effort not only benefits Lilly but provides a virtual, open source R&D organization that any member company can use. Here's how it works: Drug companies, called "Seekers," put up "Wanted" posters describing problems that need addressing. Bounty-hunting scientists, labeled "Solvers," sign confidentiality agreements that gain them admission to a secure project room where they can access data and product specifications related to the problem. If they solve the problem, they get a reward—around $25,000 to $30,000 depending on the problem. According to InnoCentive president and CEO Darren J. Carroll, what Lilly has done is revolutionary. By creating a global community of scientists, "We're punching a hole in the side of the laboratory and exposing mission-critical problems to the outside world," says Carroll. "It's using the Net to communicate, collaborate, and innovate."[55]

On the other hand, the cycle of dot-com failures that burst the Internet bubble suggests that applications of Internet and digital technologies may be only temporary if they are built on an unsustainable base. Most observers agree that the downturn resulted, to a great extent, from overestimating the importance of the technology itself, ignoring business fundamentals, or overlooking basic economic requirements. Another major reason why so many start-ups failed was that the service or capability that they offered could be imitated easily. This was especially damaging for the young start-ups and "pure plays" (i.e., firms that exist only in cyberspace and have no other physical outlets). The reason? Larger firms with greater resources could observe what was working over time and bring more resources and talent to bear on an effective imitation strategy.

Thus, Internet technologies can benefit firms that use them effectively in ways that genuinely set them apart from rivals. But the extent to which the Internet can create advantages that are rare and difficult to imitate is highly questionable. Perhaps combination strategies (see Chapter 5) hold the key to successful digital business.

Are Combination Strategies the Key to E-Business Success?

Because of the changing dynamics presented by digital- and Internet-based technologies, new strategic combinations that make the best use of the competitive strategies just described may hold the greatest promise for future success.[56] Several things are clear in this regard. First, the Internet in general is eroding opportunities for sustainable advantage. Many experts agree that the net effect of the digital economy is fewer rather than more opportunities for sustainable advantages.[57] This means strategic thinking is even more important in the Internet age.

More specifically, the Internet has provided all companies with greater tools for managing costs. So it may be that cost management and control will increase in importance as a management tool. In general, this may be good if it leads to an economy that makes more efficient use of its scarce resources. However, for individual companies, it may shave critical percentage points off profit margins and create a climate that makes it impossible to survive, much less achieve sustainable above-average profits.

Many differentiation advantages are also diminished by the Internet. The ability to comparison shop—to check product reviews and inspect different choices with a few clicks of the mouse—is depriving some companies, such as auto dealers, of the unique

Liberty Mutual's Electronic Invoice System: Combining Low Cost and Differentiation Advantages

Boston-based Liberty Mutual Group is a leading global insurer and the sixth largest property and casualty insurer in the United States. Its largest line of business is personal automobile insurance. Liberty Mutual has $64.4 billion in assets and $16.6 billion in annual revenues—ranking the firm 116th on the Fortune 500 list of the largest corporations.

In 2000, Liberty Mutual became one of the first companies to experiment with electronic invoices. It set up a pilot program with a few law firms to submit its bills through a secured Web site. These firms, for the most part, handle claims litigation for Liberty, defending its policyholders in lawsuits. Its success with this program convinced Liberty that it could achieve significant cost savings and also pass along differentiating features to its customers and strategic partners. Liberty now processes nearly 400,000 electronic legal-services invoices a year—70 percent of the total invoices that the firm receives.

As expected, the initial transition was quite expensive. The company invested nearly $1 million in the first four years. However, Liberty estimates that the electronic invoice program saves the company $750,000 a year in direct costs by streamlining the distribution, payment, storage, and retrieval of invoices. E-invoices enable Liberty to move from intake to payment with half the staff that it had taken to process paper invoices. The firm has also created new efficiencies by cutting costs resulting from data entry errors, late payments, and overpayments. As a relatively minor issue, Liberty saves more than $20,000 per year on postage, photocopying, archiving, and retrieval costs.

The legal invoices are organized by litigation phase or task—for example, taking a deposition or reporting a witness statement. Work is diced into tiny increments of six minutes or less. A single invoice that covers a month of complex litigation, for example, can include well over 1,000 lines. However, by building and mining a database of law firm billing practices, Liberty is able to generate a highly granular report card about law firm activities and performance. The new knowledge generated by this system not only increases internal effectiveness but also allows Liberty to provide detailed feedback to clients and other external stakeholders.

Online invoicing has also helped speed up both processing and response time. Liberty can instantaneously see how firms deploy and bill for partners, paralegals, and other staff; how they compare with each other on rates, hours, and case outcomes; and whether, how, and how often they send duplicate invoices or charge for inappropriate services. The system also allows Liberty to instantly review all of the time billed for a particular attorney across many cases, enabling the firm to reconstruct the total time billed to Liberty during a single day. More than once they have found that attorneys have billed more than 24 hours in a day. Liberty is also able to easily expose prohibited formula billing patterns (wherein, for example, they are billed a set amount for a service instead of actual time spent). In two cases in which formula billing was used, Liberty found that there were more than $28,000 in suspected overcharges.

Liberty Mutual is in the process of developing a large database of law firms' billing practices on different types of cases. The database should eventually enable Liberty to evaluate a law firm's billing activities and compare them to the norms of all of its partner firms. With such intelligence, it will be a rather straightforward matter to rate each firm's cost effectiveness in handling certain types of cases and match firms with cases accordingly.

Liberty's decision to use electronic invoices was initially based on the potential for cost savings. But the differentiating advantages it has achieved—in terms of rapid feedback, decreased response time, and a knowledge trove in databases that can be electronically mined—has provided the company with a fruitful combination of Internet-based strategic advantages.

Sources: Coyle, M., & Cusolito, J. 2005. Liberty Mutual Group (LMG) to release 2004 financial results on March 2, 2005. www.libertymutual.com; and Smunt, T. L., & Sutcliffe, C. L. 2004. There's gold in them bills. *Harvard Business Review*, 82(9): 24–25.

advantages that were the hallmark of their success in a previous time. Differentiating is still an important strategy, of course. But how firms achieve it may change, and the best approach may be to combine a differentiation strategy with other competitive strategies. Strategy Spotlight 8.8 describes the efforts of Liberty Mutual, a traditional firm that has used digital technology to achieve both differentiation and cost advantages.

Perhaps the greatest beneficiaries are the focusers, who can use the Internet to capture a niche that previously may have been inaccessible. Even this is not assured, however, because the same factors that make it possible for a small niche player to be a contender may make that same niche attractive to a big company. That is, an incumbent firm that previously thought a niche market was not worth the effort may use Internet technologies to enter that segment for a lower cost than in the past. The larger firm can then bring its market power and resources to bear in a way that a smaller competitor cannot match.

Firms using combination strategies may also fall short if they underestimate the demands of combining strategic approaches and get "stuck in the middle." This can lead to inaccurately assessing the costs and benefits of a strategy that combines differentiating and low-cost features. Firms may believe they can keep prices and costs low but still offer high-end services that are expensive to provide.

Another potential pitfall for companies using combination strategies relates to the difficulty of managing complex strategies. Managers tend to develop a bias in favor of the functional areas with which they are most familiar. Furthermore, companies in general tend to fall into the trap of believing that there is "one best way" to accomplish organizational goals. A combination strategy, by definition, challenges a company to carefully blend alternative strategic approaches and remain mindful of the impact of different decisions on the firm's value-creating processes and its extended value-chain activities. Strong leadership is needed to maintain a bird's-eye perspective on a company's overall approach and to coordinate the multiple dimensions of a combination strategy.

Indeed, the key to effectively implementing any digital- or Internet-based strategy is for the leaders of today's firms to recognize that the digital economy has forever changed the way business is conducted and to adopt practices that use the advantages that new technologies have to offer without ignoring business fundamentals. Companies will increasingly need to adapt to the Internet and implement the capabilities that make digitally based business possible because, as Intel's former Chairman Andy Grove expressed it, "The world now runs on Internet time."[58]

>>Leveraging Internet Capabilities

In this chapter we have emphasized the importance of the Internet and digital technologies in creating new business capabilities and new strategic initiatives. We have addressed how the Internet is affecting the five competitive forces and how it contributes to a firm's efforts to add value and create competitive advantages. We conclude by discussing how digital technologies and Internet-based capabilities can affect business-level strategy (Chapter 5), corporate-level strategy (Chapter 6), and international-level strategy (Chapter 7).

Leveraging Internet Capabilities and Business-Level Strategy   Chapter 5 addressed attributes and potential pitfalls of business-level strategies. Earlier in this chapter, we presented a rather detailed section on how the Internet and digital technologies are affecting overall low-cost, differentiation, and focus strategies and how combination strategies may be effective in the context of e-business. By providing new ways to add value and shifting the power of the five competitive forces, the Internet and digital technologies have altered the competitive climate in numerous industries. These changes often require modifications in generic strategies, sometimes leading to new strategic combinations. While many strategic imperatives remain the same, in some cases, such as Buy.com, this has led to a complete rethinking of how firms use resources and position themselves in a competitive environment.

Leveraging Internet Capabilities and Corporate-Level Strategy

Chapter 6 addressed how firms strategically diversify and manage portfolios of businesses at the corporate level. In the case of related diversification, the Internet has created new means of generating synergies and enhancing revenue among elements of a diverse firm. For example, by linking sources of supply more efficiently and streamlining distribution, digital technologies can enhance profitability. In the case of unrelated diversification, corporate offices that manage portfolios of businesses can use the Internet to deal with suppliers more efficiently and can increase negotiating power. In both cases, when the Internet becomes integrated into a corporation's infrastructure and procurement system, it supports activities that contribute to the bottom line. In terms of internal development and acquisition as avenues of corporate growth, e-business models that have proven successful can be a welcome addition to a firm's portfolio. Internet-related business initiatives, such as the online postage capability developed by Pitney-Bowes, are creating new strategic advantages for many corporations.

Leveraging Internet Capabilities and International-Level Strategies

Chapter 7 addressed how and why businesses grow beyond their national boundaries. Expanding into international markets involves special challenges that may be mitigated by using Internet and digital technologies. In terms of controlling costs, the Internet has enhanced the ability to conduct business without the time and expense of physically traveling to various locations. In terms of adapting to local markets, the ability to conduct research and communicate online has increased the level of access to local cultures and market conditions. This combination of capabilities has, in some cases, enhanced the ability of firms to pursue a transnational strategy by addressing both cost reduction and local adaptation issues. The Internet also has allowed firms to leapfrog the usual path of international development with technologies that reach customers and facilitate transactions around the globe. Whereas prior to the Internet, local distributors or licensees were essential international partners for firms expanding into new regions, now an online presence can accomplish the same thing. Additionally, new types of international commerce are possible, as suggested by Eli Lilly's InnoCentive venture, which enables scientists from around the world to address difficult problems. Collaboration at such a scale was virtually impossible prior to the Internet.

Summary

New technologies often unleash forces in the economy that are highly disruptive. The innovations that flow from such technologies often radically change the competitive landscape. Under such conditions innovation-driven competition creates new strategic capabilities that alter the rules of competition. Few technologically driven phenomena have been as disruptive—or as rich with opportunity—as the Internet, wireless communications, and other digital technologies. As Internet-based capabilities and related information technologies become more widespread in all parts of the globe, strategic managers need to increasingly integrate the Internet and digital capabilities into their strategic plans.

In terms of the competitive environment, most of the changes brought about by the digital economy can be understood in the context of Porter's five-forces model of industry analysis. The threat of new entrants is expected to increase as digital and Internet technologies reduce many barriers to entry. The process of disintermediation has enhanced the power of some suppliers by simplifying supply chains, but it may also shift bargaining power to customers. Buyer power has increased for many end users due to lower switching costs. The threat of substitutes will generally be higher, because Internet and digital technologies are providing new methods for achieving old tasks. Finally, intensity of rivalry among similar competitors is heightened in the digital economy as competition tends to be more price-oriented and technology-based advantages are easily imitated.

The Internet and digital technologies have created new opportunities for firms to add value. Four value-adding activities that have been enhanced by Internet capabilities are search, evaluation, problem solving, and transaction. Search activities include processes for gathering information and identifying purchase options. Evaluation activities refers to the process of considering alternatives and comparing the costs and benefits of various options. Problem-solving activities include identifying problems or needs and generating ideas and action plans to address those needs. Transaction activities involve the process of completing a sale, including negotiating and agreeing contractually, making payments, and taking delivery. These four activities are supported by three different types of content that Internet businesses often use—customer feedback, expertise, and entertainment programming. Strategic use of these attributes can help build competitive advantages and contribute to profitability. Seven business models have been identified that are proving successful for use by Internet firms. These include commission, advertising, markup, production, referral, subscription, and fee-for-service based models. Firms also have found that combinations of these business models can contribute to greater success.

The way companies formulate and deploy strategies is also changing because of the impact of the Internet and digital technologies on many industries. Overall low-cost strategies may be more important as some firms use Internet technologies to lower transaction costs and increase the efficiency of their operations. Differentiation strategies may be harder to achieve for many firms, because the Internet is eroding some of their most unique features. Further, Internet technologies are enabling the mass customization capabilities of greater numbers of competitors. Focus strategies are likely to increase in importance because the Internet provides highly targeted and lower-cost access to narrow or specialized markets. These strategies are not without their pitfalls, however, and firms need to understand the dangers as well as the potential benefits of Internet-based approaches.

Thus, the digital economy, while promising to provide new opportunities for creating value and fostering growth, may make the competitive landscape more challenging for many firms. In this chapter we have addressed both the potential and the pitfalls of the Internet and digital technology in today's economy.

Summary Review Questions

1. How do Porter's five competitive forces affect companies that compete primarily on the Internet? Provide an example.

2. What effects do digital capabilities and the Internet have on the three competitive strategies—overall low-cost, differentiation, and focus? How does this relate to a firm's competitive advantage?

3. What effect do digital technologies and the Internet have on the profitability an industry is able to achieve? How can companies use these technologies to enhance their own profitability?

4. Explain the difference between the effective use of technology and the technology *itself* in terms of achieving and sustaining competitive advantages.

5. Describe how the three competitive strategies can be combined to create competitive advantages among firms that compete primarily by leveraging digital capabilities.

Experiential Exercise

Using the Internet, identify two firms—one an Internet "pure play" and the second a traditional bricks-and-mortar company—that have a strong Internet presence. Consider how each of these firms is adding value by using the Internet and digital technologies.

1. Bricks-and-mortar firm: _____

Which of the following Internet-based activities is the company using to add value?

Value-Adding Activity	Examples of How the Company Uses the Activity	Is It Creating Value? (Yes/No)
Type:		
Search		
Evaluation		
Problem solving		
Transaction		
Content:		
Customer feedback		
Expertise		
Entertainment programming		

2. Internet pure-play firm: _____

Which of the following Internet-based activities is the company using to add value?

Value-Adding Activity	Examples of How the Company Uses the Activity	Is It Creating Value? (Yes/No)
Type:		
Search		
Evaluation		
Problem solving		
Transaction		
Content:		
Customer feedback		
Expertise		
Entertainment programming		

3. How do the two firms compare? Is one adding more value than the other? What is the pure play doing that might help the bricks-and-mortar firm? What is the bricks-and-mortar firm doing that could benefit the pure play?

1. Select a company that has used digital technologies to change or enhance its competitive strategy. Look up the company on the Internet and discuss how it has increased (or decreased) its competitive advantage vis-à-vis Porter's five forces.

2. Choose an Internet pure play that is competing with a bricks-and-mortar company. What are the relative advantages and disadvantages of the Internet pure play? Do you think it will be successful in the long term?

3. Select a small firm that has used the Internet to its advantage in entering international markets. Do you believe such advantages will be sustainable over time? Explain.

4. How can a firm use the Internet and/or digital technologies to enhance its overall cost leadership or differentiation competitive advantages? Provide examples.

1. Discuss the ethical implications of the use of adware or spyware by companies to track customer Internet surfing and shopping activities.

2. Discuss the ethical implications of online music file sharing. Can Internet companies that provide free access to other users' computers to download copyrighted material (e.g., Kazaa) guard against infringing on the rights of the artists who develop the material?

References

1. Banerjee, S., & Garrity, B. 2004. Roxio bets future on Napster brand. *Billboard,* 116(34): 8, 62; Garrity, B. 2002. Embattled Napster rumored for sale. *Billboard,* 114(17): 10; McGuire, D. 2005. Downloading: The next generation. *BizReport,* www.bizreport.com, February 28; Menn, J. 2003. *All the rave: The rise and fall of Shawn Fanning's Napster.* New York: Crown Business; Taylor, K. 2005. Napster: Can iTunes do this? *The Motley Fool,* www.fool.com, March 11; and Wood, C. 2001. The heirs of Napster. *Maclean's,* 114(9): 52–53.

2. Menn, op. cit.

3. Coy, P., & Vickers, M. 2001. How bad will it get? *BusinessWeek,* March 12: 36–42.

4. Schumpeter, J. A. 1934. *The theory of economic development.* Cambridge, MA: Harvard University Press.

5. Christensen, C. M. 1997. *The innovator's dilemma.* Boston: Harvard University Press.

6. Linzmayer, O. W. 2004. *Apple Confidential 2.0: The definitive history of the world's most colorful company* (2nd ed.). San Francisco, CA: No Starch Press.

7. Baumol, W. J. 2002. *The free-market innovation machine.* Princeton, NJ: Princeton University Press.

8. Quoted in Mandel, M. J., & Hof, R. D. 2001. Rethinking the Internet. *BusinessWeek,* March 26: 117–122.

9. Evans, P., & Wurster, T. S. 2000. *Blown to bits.* Cambridge, MA: Harvard Business School Press; Negroponte, N. 1995. *Being digital.* New York: Alfred A. Knopf.

10. Prahalad, C. K., & Ramaswamy, V. 2004. *The future of competition.* Boston: Harvard Business School Press.

11. For an interesting discussion of the role of interactivity on the performance of Internet-based businesses, see Auger, P. 2005. The impact of interactivity and design sophistication on the performance of commercial websites for small businesses. *Journal of Small Business Management,* 43(2): 119–137.

12. For interesting insights on the role of customers in co-creating value see Groth, M. 2005. Customers as good soldiers: Examining citizenship behaviors in Internet service deliveries. *Journal of Management,* 31(1): 7–27; Sawhney, M., Prandelli, E., & Verona, G. 2003. The power of innomediation. *Sloan Management Review,* 44(2): 77–82; and Xue, M., & Harker, P. T. 2002 Customer efficiency: Concepts and its impact on e-business management. *Journal of Service Research,* 4: 253–267.

13. Porter, M. E. 2001. Strategy and the Internet. *Harvard Business Review*, 79: 63–78.

14. For an interesting perspective on changing features of firm boundaries, refer to Afuah, A. 2003. Redefining firm boundaries in the face of Internet: Are firms really shrinking? *Academy of Management Review*, 28(1): 34–53.

15. www.consumerreports.org.

16. Siegel, D. 1999. *Futurize your enterprises:* New York: Wiley.

17. For an alternative perspective on the role of customers in an Internet environment, refer to Nambisan, S. 2002. Designing virtual customer environments for new product development: Toward a theory. *Academy of Management Review*, 27(3): 392–413.

18. Brynda, T. 2004. Reverse auction use by states to increase 300 percent, but low impact on IT. *INPUT/Output*, December: 1–7.

19. Keenan, F. 2001. Opening the spigot. *BusinessWeek e.biz*, June 4: EB17–EB20.

20. Time to rebuild. 2001. *Economist*, May 19: 55–56.

21. www.amazon.com.

22. For more on the role of the Internet as an electronic intermediary, refer to Carr, N. G. 2000. Hypermediation: Commerce as clickstream. *Harvard Business Review*, 78(1): 46–48.

23. Downes, L., & Mui, C. 1998. *Unleashing the killer app:* 45–46. Boston: Harvard Business School Press.

24. Dawson, J. D. 2002. Company turns computers into box offices with click of a ticket. *Houston Business Journal*, www.bizjournals.com/houston, September 27; and www.tickettrends.com.

25. McDonald, D. 2004. Meet eBay's new postman. *Business 2.0*, 5(8): 52–54.

26. Collins, A. 2001. Personal touch pays off. *Business 2.0*, www.business2.com, March.

27. Olofson, C. 2001. The next best thing to being there. *Fast Company*, April: 175; and www.conferenza.com.

28. Lelii, S. R. 2001. Free online storage a thing of the past? *eWEEK*, April 22.

29. McKay, N. 2000. Ballpark figures. *Red Herring*, May: 360; www.insightexpress.com.

30. www.privacy.net; and www.epic.org.

31. www.mysimon.com; and www.pricescan.com.

32. www.cnet.com; and www.bizrate.com.

33. Hanrahan, T. 1999. Price isn't everything. *Wall Street Journal*, July 12: R20.

34. For a discussion of strategic implications of partnering and competing, refer to Gulati, R., Nohria, N., and Zaheer, A.

2000. Strategic networks. *Strategic Management Journal*, 21: 203–215.

35. www.bestbookbuys.com.

36. McGuire, op. cit.

37. The ideas in this section draw on several sources, including Zeng, M., & Reinartz, W. 2003. Beyond online search: The road to profitability. *California Management Review*, Winter: 107–130; and Stabell, C. B., & Fjeldstad, O. D. 1998. Configuring value for competitive advantage: On chains, shops, and networks. *Strategic Management Journal*, 19: 413–437.

38. Hardy, Q. 2003. All eyes on Google. *Forbes*, May 26, www.forbes.com.

39. For an interesting discussion of how successful Internet-based companies are using evaluation to add value see Weiss, L. M., Capozzi, M. M., & Prusak, L. 2004. Learning from the Internet giants. *Sloan Management Review*, 45(4): 79–84.

40. Zeng & Reinartz, op. cit.

41. Bayers, C. 2002. The last laugh. *Business 2.0*, September: 86–93.

42. Yamada, K. 2001. Web trails. *Forbes*, December 3; and www.rei.com.

43. Weintraub, A. 2001. E-assets for sale—dirt cheap. *BusinessWeek e.biz*, May 14: EB20–EB22.

44. Greenspan, R. 2003. Internet not for everyone. *CyberAtlas*, April 16, www.cyberatlas.com.

45. Afuah, A., & Tucci, C. L. 2003. *Internet business models and strategies* (2nd ed.). New York: McGraw-Hill; Timmers, P. 1999. *Electronic commerce.* New York: Wiley.

46. Echikson, W. 2001. When oil gets connected. *BusinessWeek*, www.businessweek.com, December 3: EB28–EB30.

47. For an interesting discussion of the cost and pricing implications of Internet technology, refer to Sinha, I. 2000. Cost transparency: The net's real threat to prices and brands. *Harvard Business Review*, 78(2): 43–51.

48. Wailgum, T. 2004. Machine shop dreams. *CIO Magazine*, www.cio.com, November 15; www.emachineshop.com.

49. Evans, P., & Wurster, T. S. 2000. *Blown to bits:* 82–83. Boston: Harvard Business School Press.

50. Over the counter e-commerce. 2001. *Economist*, May 26: 77–78.

51. Collett, S. 1999. Nike offers mass customization online. *ComputerWorld*, November 23.

52. Seybold, P. 2000. Niches bring riches. *Business 2.0*, June 13: 135.

53. Greenspan, R. 2004. Net drives profits to small biz. *ClickZ.com*, March 25, www.clickz.com; Greenspan, R. 2002. Small biz benefits from Internet tools. *ClickZ.com*, March 28, www.clickz.com.

54. Lii, J. 2001. Salvagesale.com gets the goods where they're needed. *Lexington* (KY) *Herald-Leader,* February 25: H2.

55. Breen, B. 2002. Lilly's R&D prescription. *Fast Company,* 57: 44. Sawhney, M. 2002. What lies ahead: Rethinking the global corporation, *Digital Frontier Conference 2002,* www. mohansawhney.com; and www. innocentive.com.

56. Empirical support for the use of combination strategies in an e-business context can be found in Kim, E., Nam, D., & Stimpert, J. L. 2004. The applicability of Porter's generic strategies in the Digital Age: Assumptions, conjectures, and suggestions. *Journal of Management,* 30(5): 569–589.

57. Porter, op. cit.: 63–78.

58. Downes & Mui, op. cit.: 13.

Strategic Analysis

Chapter 1
Introduction
and Analyzing
Goals and
Objectives

Chapter 2
Analyzing
the External
Environment

Chapter 3
Analyzing
the Internal
Environment

Chapter 4
Assessing
Intellectual
Capital

Strategic Formulation

Chapter 5
Formulating
Business-
Level
Strategies

Chapter 6
Formulating
Corporate-
Level
Strategies

Chapter 7
Formulating
International
Strategies

Chapter 8
Digital
Business
Strategies

Strategic Implementation

Chapter 9
Strategic
Control and
Corporate
Governance

Chapter 10
Creating
Effective
Organizational
Designs

Chapter 11
Strategic Lead-
ership Excel-
lence, Ethics
and Change

Chapter 12
Fostering
Corporate
Entrepreneur-
ship

Chapter 13
Strategic
Leadership
Creating New
Ventures

Case Analysis

Chapter 14
Case
Analysis

Strategic Implementation

Strategic Control and Corporate Governance

>chapter objectives

After reading this chapter, you should have a good understanding of:

- The value of effective strategic control systems in strategy implementation.

- The key difference between "traditional" and "contemporary" control systems.

- The imperative for "contemporary" control systems in today's complex and rapidly changing competitive and general environments.

- The benefits of having the proper balance among the three levers of behavioral control: culture, rewards and incentives, and boundaries.

- The three key participants in corporate governance: shareholders, management (led by the CEO), and the board of directors.

- The role of corporate governance mechanisms in ensuring that the interests of managers are aligned with those of shareholders from both the United States and international perspectives.

*O*rganizations must have effective strategic controls if they are to successfully implement their strategies. This includes systems that exercise both informational control and behavioral control. In addition, a firm must promote sound corporate governance as well as have controls that are consistent with the strategy that the firm is following.

In the first section, we address the need to have effective informational control, contrasting two approaches to informational control. The first approach, which we call "traditional," is highly sequential. Goals and objectives are set, then implemented, and after a set period of time, performance is compared to the desired standards. In contrast, the second approach, termed "contemporary," is much more interactive. Here, the internal and external environments are continually monitored, and managers determine whether the strategy itself needs to be modified. Today the contemporary approach is required, given the rapidly changing conditions in virtually all industries.

Next, we discuss behavioral control. Here the firm must strive to maintain a proper balance between culture, rewards, and boundaries. We also argue that organizations that have strong, positive cultures and reward systems can rely less on boundaries, such as rules, regulations, and procedures. When individuals in the firm internalize goals and strategies, there is less need for monitoring behavior, and efforts are focused more on important organizational goals and objectives.

The third section addresses the role of corporate governance in ensuring that managerial and shareholder interests are aligned. We provide examples of both effective and ineffective corporate governance practices. We discuss three governance mechanisms for aligning managerial and shareholder interests: a committed and involved board of directors, shareholder activism, and effective managerial rewards and incentives. Public companies are also subject to external control. We discuss several external control mechanisms, such as the market for corporate control, auditors, banks and analysts, the media, and public activists. We close with a discussion of corporate governance from an international perspective.

Incentives are designed to boost productivity and help a company achieve its goals.[1] This works as long as the incentives are designed with organizational goals in mind. Problems can arise quickly when incentives are not designed in a way that aligns the goals of employees with those of the firm.

Consider the case of Lantech, a $100 million company headquartered in Louisville, Kentucky, that had to face this problem. The firm has a dominant position in a market that it pioneered—stretch wrapping equipment that encases pallet loads of products (such as Kellogg's Corn Flakes) in clear plastic film for shipment to customers.

Lantech wanted to increase the productivity of its workers, and the obvious way seemed to be to reward high-performing divisions with productivity incentives. Each of the firm's manufacturing divisions was offered a productivity bonus that could increase the pay of each employee in the division by 10 percent.

Unfortunately, the results weren't exactly what Lantech's managers had in mind. The bonus was based on each division's productivity, and because one measure of productivity is the ratio of costs to revenues, employees began to devise ways to decrease costs in their division. But rather than *cutting* costs, employees focused their efforts on *shifting* costs.

Production at Lantech required mutual cooperation between divisions; each division relied on the others for parts and engineering expertise. However, the incentive plan inadvertently encouraged workers to assign costs to other divisions while claiming revenue for themselves. Workers argued over who was responsible for shared costs, with no division wanting to accept its fair share. But, needless to say, they were all willing to claim responsibility for revenues. It got to the point that one division wanted to assign a greater percentage of toilet paper costs to another division with a higher number of employees of a certain gender, arguing that one gender used more toilet paper than the other!

Chairman Pat Lancaster claimed that he spent 95 percent of his time resolving arguments after he had initiated this new incentive plan. He claimed that, "The bonuses moved managers in the direction of favoring short-term profit over long-term customer satisfaction. They were so busy fighting over who was going to pay for what that they couldn't make decisions that were good for the customers as a whole." And CEO Jim Lancaster, his son, said that the new system caused "so much secrecy, politicking, and sucking noise that you wouldn't believe it."

It should come as no surprise that the plan was eliminated after just a short period. In its place, Lantech offered a profit-sharing plan where employees benefited only if the entire firm performed well. The bottom line is that incentive plans must align the employees' desire for extra income with the firm's need for profits.

In this chapter, we will focus on how organizations can develop and use effective strategic control.[2] We first explore two central aspects of strategic control: (1) *informational control,* which is the ability to respond effectively to environmental change, and (2) *behavioral control,* which is the appropriate balance and alignment among a firm's culture, rewards, and boundaries. In the final section of this chapter, we focus on strategic control from a much broader perspective—what is referred to as *corporate governance.* Here, we direct our attention to the need for a firm's shareholders (the owners) and their elected representatives (the board of directors) to ensure that the firm's executives (the management team) strive to fulfill their fiduciary duty of maximizing long-term shareholder value.

>>Ensuring Informational Control: Responding Effectively to Environmental Change

In this section we will discuss two broad types of control systems. The first one, which we label "traditional," is based largely on a feedback approach; that is, there is little or no action taken to revise strategies, goals, and objectives until the end of the time period in question, usually a quarter or a month. The second one, which we call "contemporary,"

Exhibit 9.1   **Traditional Approach to Strategic Control**

emphasizes the importance of continually monitoring the environment (both internal and external) for trends and events that signal the need to make modifications to a firm's strategies, goals, and objectives. As both general and competitive environments become more unpredictable and complex, the need for contemporary systems increases.

A Traditional Approach to Strategic Control

The traditional approach to strategic control is sequential: (1) strategies are formulated and top management sets goals, (2) strategies are implemented, and (3) performance is measured against the predetermined goal set, as illustrated in Exhibit 9.1.

Control is based on a feedback loop from performance measurement to strategy formulation. This process typically involves lengthy time lags, often tied to a firm's annual planning cycle. Such traditional control systems, termed "single-loop" learning by Chris Argyris of Harvard University, simply compare actual performance to a predetermined goal.[3] They are most appropriate when the environment is stable and relatively simple, goals and objectives can be measured with a high level of certainty, and there is little need for complex measures of performance. Sales quotas, operating budgets, production schedules, and similar quantitative control mechanisms are typical. The appropriateness of the business strategy or standards of performance is seldom questioned.[4]

The idea that well-managed companies should move forward in accordance with detailed and precise plans has come under attack from several directions.[5] James Brian Quinn of Dartmouth College has argued that grand designs with precise and carefully integrated plans seldom work. Rather, most strategic change proceeds incrementally— one step at a time. Leaders can best serve their organizations by introducing some sense of direction, some logic in incremental steps.[6]

Similarly, McGill University's Henry Mintzberg has written about leaders "crafting" a strategy.[7] Drawing on the parallel between the potter at her wheel and the strategist, Mintzberg pointed out that the potter begins work with some general idea of the artifact she wishes to create, but the details of design—even possibilities for a different design— emerge as the work progresses. For businesses facing complex and turbulent business environments, the craftsperson's method seems more appropriate than that provided by the traditional, more rational, planner. The former helps us deal with the uncertainty about how a design will work out in practice and allows for a creative element.

Mintzberg's argument, like Quinn's, casts doubt on the value of rigid planning and goal-setting processes. Fixed strategic goals also become dysfunctional for firms competing in highly unpredictable competitive environments where strategies need to change frequently and opportunistically. An inflexible commitment to predetermined goals and milestones can prevent the very adaptability that is often required of a good strategy.

Even organizations that have been extremely successful in the past can become complacent or fail to adapt their goals and strategies to the new conditions. An example of such a firm is Cisco Systems, whose market value at one time approached an astonishing $600 billion, but as of late 2005 was about $110 billion. Cisco has minimized the potential for such problems in the future by improving its informational control systems. Other firms

STRATEGY SPOTLIGHT 9.1

When the Tech Bubble Burst

We can learn some lessons from fallen stars. Cisco Systems, Inc., once the invincible momentum stock adored by Wall Street, came crashing down just as we were beginning the 21st century. What went wrong?

Problems started when Cisco announced a $2.2 billion inventory write-off; Wall Street severely punished the stock as a result. With all of its experience, why didn't Cisco see the problems coming? Cisco made a common mistake: It projected the past into the future.

Past demand had been vigorous, but customers were requiring less and less of the firm's products. And financing was cheap—it was no problem for a company like Cisco to find capital to finance ongoing operations even when things didn't look so bright on the horizon. Overtaken by its own success, Cisco failed to see the slowdown in

Sources: Weber, J. 2001. Management lessons from the bust. *BusinessWeek*, August 27: 104–112; Morrison, S. 2001. Positive sales news takes the sting out of Cisco revamp. *Financial Times Online*, August 26; Reuters. 2001. Siebel sees economic rebound late 2002: August 20.

customer demand. John Sterman at MIT sums up the situation: "If you were in the pasta business, you want to know how much pasta people are cooking and eating, not how much they're buying, and certainly not how much supermarkets and distributors are ordering from the factory." Consumers ultimately determine demand; Cisco missed this important point and inaccurately forecast new sales orders. When the orders didn't materialize, a stockpile of inventory sat on the shelves while Wall Street annulled the short-lived marriage between investors and their beloved Cisco.

In contrast, Siebel Systems, Inc., kept its eye on the future. The company rewarded its sales force for providing accurate information concerning future demand. Salespeople receive commissions not only for sales, but also for forecast information. Haim Mendelson at Stanford University remarked that this provides the company "with a deep understanding of what customers are going to do."

such as Siebel Systems have been more successful in anticipating change and have made proper corrections to their strategies. We discuss these firms in Strategy Spotlight 9.1.

Without doubt, the traditional "feedback" approach to strategic control has some important limitations. Is there another, better, way?

A Contemporary Approach to Strategic Control

Adapting to and anticipating both internal and external environmental change is an integral part of strategic control. The relationships between strategy formulation, implementation, and control are highly interactive, as suggested by Exhibit 9.2. It also illustrates two different types of strategic control: informational control and behavioral control. Informational control is primarily concerned with whether or not the organization is "doing the right things." Behavioral control, on the other hand, asks if the organization is "doing things right" in the implementation of its strategy. Both the informational and behavioral components of strategic control are necessary, but not sufficient, conditions for success. That is, what good is a well-conceived strategy that cannot be implemented? Or, alternatively, what use is an energetic and committed workforce if it is focused on the wrong strategic target?

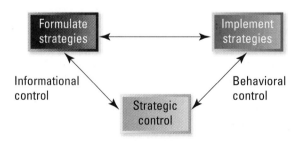

Exhibit 9.2 Contemporary Approach to Strategic Control

John Weston is the former CEO of ADP Corporation, the largest payroll and tax-filing processor in the world. He captures the essence of contemporary control systems.

> At ADP, 39 plus 1 adds up to more than 40 plus 0. The 40-plus-0 employee is the harried worker who at 40 hours a week just tries to keep up with what's in the "in" basket. He tries to do whatever he thinks he's supposed to do. Because he works with his head down, he takes zero hours to think about what he's doing, why he's doing it, and how he's doing it. Does he need to do it in the first place? On the other hand, the 39-plus-1 employee takes at least 1 of those 40 hours to think about what he's doing and why he's doing it. That's why the other 39 hours are far more productive.[8]

Informational control deals with the internal environment as well as the external strategic context. It addresses the assumptions and premises that provide the foundation for an organization's strategy. The key question addressed by information control is: Do the organization's goals and strategies still "fit" within the context of the current strategic environment?

This involves two key issues. First, managers must scan and monitor the external environment, as we discussed in Chapter 2. Recall, for example, the failure of Interstate Bakeries Corporation (IBC) to change their strategies to reflect changes in consumer tastes, such as the trend toward healthier foods and low-carb diets. Also, conditions can change in the internal environment of the firm, as we discussed in Chapter 3, requiring changes in the strategic direction of the firm. These may include, for example, the resignation of key executives or delays in the completion of major production facilities.

In the contemporary approach, information control is part of an ongoing process of organizational learning that continuously updates and challenges the assumptions that underlie the organization's strategy. In such "double-loop" learning, the organization's assumptions, premises, goals, and strategies are continuously monitored, tested, and reviewed. The benefits of continuous monitoring are evident—time lags are dramatically shortened, changes in the competitive environment are detected earlier, and the organization's ability to respond with speed and flexibility is enhanced.

A key question becomes: OK, but how is this done? Contemporary control systems must have four characteristics to be effective.[9]

1. They must focus on constantly changing information that top managers identify as having potential strategic importance.
2. The information is important enough to demand frequent and regular attention from operating managers at all levels of the organization.
3. The data and information generated by the control system are best interpreted and discussed in face-to-face meetings of superiors, subordinates, and peers.
4. The contemporary control system is a key catalyst for an ongoing debate about underlying data, assumptions, and action plans.

Contemporary control systems track the strategic uncertainties that may keep senior managers awake at night. Depending on the type of business, such uncertainties may relate to changes in technology, customer tastes, government regulation, and industry competition. Since control systems must be designed to gather information that might challenge the strategic visions of the future, they are, by definition, hot buttons for senior managers.

An executive's decision to use the control system interactively—in other words, to invest the time and attention to review and evaluate new information—sends a clear signal to the organization about what is important. The dialogue and debate that emerge from such an interactive process can often lead to new strategies and innovations.

STRATEGY SPOTLIGHT

USA Today's Interactive Control System

Top managers at Gannett-owned *USA Today* meet each Friday to discuss ongoing strategy. Every week, they review information ranging from day-to-day operations to year-to-date data. This information enables top management to check the pulse of the industry on a frequent basis and minimizes the surprises that frequently beset other companies that don't keep close tabs on available information. Senior managers frequently meet with operations-level managers for intensive discussion to analyze the weekly information. The results of these high-level meetings on information control allow managers from the operating core of the newspaper to respond to industry trends and events on nearly a real-time basis.

By controlling information, *USA Today* managers:

- Compare projected advertising volume with actual volume.

Sources: Simons, R. 1995. Control in an age of empowerment. *Harvard Business Review*, 73(2): 80–88; Caney, D. 2001. Gannett, Knight Ridder walloped by ad slump. Reuters, July 17.

- Assess new advertising revenues by client type to better target client markets.

- Quickly discover revenue shortfalls before major problems arise.

- Become aware of unexpected successes that have often led to innovations.

These weekly meetings have returned significant rewards for *USA Today*. Innovations that have been implemented as a result of high information control include:

- A new market survey service targeted at the automobile industry (a potential source of high-volume advertising).

- The addition of fractional page color advertising (increasing the number of advertisers that use color, thereby increasing advertising revenue).

- Expanding the job function of circulation employees to include regional sales of advertising space.

- Developing a program of advertising inserts targeted toward specific customers and products.

Strategy Spotlight 9.2 discusses how executives at *USA Today,* Gannett Co.'s daily newspaper, review information delivered each Friday.

Let's now turn our attention to behavioral control.

>> Attaining Behavioral Control: Balancing Culture, Rewards, and Boundaries

Behavioral control is focused on implementation—doing things right. Effectively implementing strategy requires manipulating three key control "levers": culture, rewards, and boundaries. These three levers are illustrated in Exhibit 9.3. Furthermore, there are two compelling reasons for an increased emphasis on culture and rewards in implementing a system of behavioral controls.

First, the competitive environment is increasingly complex and unpredictable, demanding both flexibility and quick response to its challenges. As firms simultaneously downsize and face the need for increased coordination across organizational boundaries, a control system based primarily on rigid strategies and rules and regulations is dysfunctional. Thus, the use of rewards and culture to align individual and organizational goals becomes increasingly important.

Second, the implicit long-term contract between the organization and its key employees has been eroded.[10] Today's younger managers have been conditioned to see themselves as "free agents" and view a career as a series of opportunistic challenges. As managers are advised to "specialize, market yourself, and have work, if not a job," the importance of culture and rewards in building organizational loyalty claims greater importance. (We addressed this issue at length in Chapter 4.)

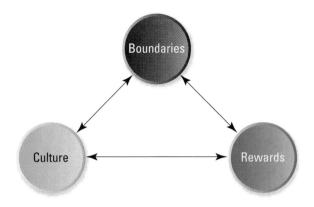

Exhibit 9.3   **Essential Elements of Behavioral Control**

Each of the three levers—culture, rewards, and boundaries—must work in a balanced and consistent manner. Let's consider the role of each.

Building a Strong and Effective Culture

What is culture? Consistent with our discussion in Chapter 4, organizational culture is a system of shared values (what is important) and beliefs (how things work) that shape a company's people, organizational structures, and control systems to produce behavioral norms (the way we do things around here). How important is culture? Very. Over the years, numerous best sellers, such as *Theory Z, Corporate Cultures, In Search of Excellence,* and *Good to Great,*[11] have emphasized the powerful influence of culture on what goes on within organizations and how they perform.

Collins and Porras argued in *Built to Last* that the key factor in sustained exceptional performance is a cultlike culture.[12] You can't touch it, you can't write it down, but it's there, in every organization, and its influence is pervasive. It can work for you or against you.[13] Effective leaders understand its importance and strive to shape and use it as one of their important levers of strategic control.[14]

The Role of Culture   Culture wears many different hats, each woven from the fabric of those values that sustain the organization's primary source of competitive advantage. Some examples are:

- Federal Express and Southwest Airlines focus on customer service.
- Lexus (a division of Toyota) and Hewlett-Packard emphasize product quality.
- Newell Rubbermaid and 3M place a high value on innovation.
- Nucor (steel) and Emerson Electric are concerned, above all, with operational efficiency.

Culture sets implicit boundaries—that is, unwritten standards of acceptable behavior—in dress, ethical matters, and the way an organization conducts its business.[15] By creating a framework of shared values, culture encourages individual identification with the organization and its objectives. Thus, culture acts as a means of reducing monitoring costs.[16]

Sustaining an Effective Culture   Powerful organizational cultures just don't happen overnight, and they don't remain in place without a strong commitment—both in terms of words and deeds—by leaders throughout the organization. A viable and productive organizational culture can be strengthened and sustained. However, it cannot be "built" or "assembled"; instead, it must be cultivated, encouraged, and "fertilized."

Storytelling is one way effective cultures are maintained. Many are familiar with the story of how Art Fry's failure to develop a strong adhesive led to 3M's enormously successful Post-it Notes. Perhaps less familiar is the story of Francis G. Okie.[17] In 1922 Okie came up with the idea of selling sandpaper to men as a replacement for razor blades. The idea obviously didn't pan out, but Okie was allowed to remain at 3M. Interestingly, the technology developed by Okie led 3M to develop its first blockbuster product: a waterproof sandpaper that became a staple of the automobile industry. Such stories foster the importance of risk taking, experimentation, freedom to fail, and of course innovation—all vital elements of 3M's culture.

Rallies or "pep talks" by top executives also serve to reinforce a firm's culture. The late Sam Walton was well known for his pep rallies at local Wal-Mart stores. Four times a year, the founders of Home Depot—CEO Bernard Marcus and Arthur Blank—used to don orange aprons and stage Breakfast with Bernie and Arthur, a 6:30 a.m. pep rally, broadcast live over the firm's closed-circuit TV network to most of its 45,000 employees.[18]

Southwest Airlines' "Culture Committee" is a unique vehicle designed to perpetuate the company's highly successful culture. The following excerpt from an internal company publication describes its objectives:

> The goal of the Committee is simple—to ensure that our unique Corporate Culture stays alive. . . . Culture Committee members represent all regions and departments across our system and they are selected based upon their exemplary display of the "Positively Outrageous Service" that won us the first-ever Triple Crown; their continual exhibition of the "Southwest Spirit" to our Customers and to their fellow workers; and their high energy level, boundless enthusiasm, unique creativity, and constant demonstration of teamwork and love for their fellow workers.[19]

Motivating with Rewards and Incentives

Reward and incentive systems represent a powerful means of influencing an organization's culture, focusing efforts on high-priority tasks, and motivating individual and collective task performance.[20] Just as culture deals with influencing beliefs, behaviors, and attitudes of people within an organization, the reward system—by specifying who gets rewarded and why—is an effective motivator and control mechanism.[21] Strategy Spotlight 9.3 discusses how the China-based Legend Group varies its incentives based upon the different hierarchical levels in its organization.

The Potential Downside   Generally speaking, people in organizations act rationally, each motivated by his or her personal best interest.[22] However, the collective sum of individual behaviors of an organization's employees does not always necessarily result in what is best for the organization; that is, individual rationality does not always guarantee organizational rationality.

As corporations grow and evolve, they often develop different business units with multiple reward systems. They may differ based on industry contexts, business situations, stage of product life cycles, and so on. Thus, subcultures within organizations may reflect differences among an organization's functional areas, products, services, and divisions. To the extent that reward systems reinforce such behavioral norms, attitudes, and belief systems, organizational cohesiveness is reduced; important information is hoarded rather than shared, individuals begin working at cross-purposes, and they lose sight of overarching goals and objectives.

Such conflicts are commonplace in many organizations. For example, sales and marketing personnel promise unrealistically quick delivery times to bring in business, much to the dismay of operations and logistics; overengineering by R&D creates headaches for manufacturing; and so on. Conflicts also arise across divisions when divisional profits

STRATEGY SPOTLIGHT

Legend Group: Providing Incentives at All Levels

One of the key tasks of management is to keep the employees motivated. Designing the right kind of incentives that meet the expectations of employee groups at different levels in the hierarchy is a big challenge. Here is how Liu Chuanzhi, chairman of Legend Group, dealt with this issue. Legend is a global personal computer manufacturer based in Beijing, China.

> Our executive team needs a sense of ownership in the company. Many state-owned enterprises in China face a special challenge: They cannot give their senior executives stock. But we took an untraditional approach; we reformed our ownership structure to make Legend a joint stock company, enabling us to give all our executive team members stock. In addition, senior executives need recognition, so we provide them with opportunities to speak to the media. To date, we've lost no senior executives to other companies.
>
> Midlevel managers want to become senior managers, so they respond best to challenges—to opportunities to display and hone their talents. We set very high performance standards for our middle managers, and we let them participate in strategic processes, in designing their own work, and in making and executing their own decisions. If they get good results, they are handsomely rewarded.
>
> Line employees need a sense of stability. If they take responsibility and are conscientious, they earn a predictable bonus. We also tie team performance to company or unit performance, and individual performance to team performance. For example, we might let the team decide how to allocate a percentage of their team bonus to individuals, with some general guidelines from the corporate level.

Source: Chuanzhi, L. 2003. Set different incentive levels. *Harvard Business Review*, 81(1): 47.

become a key compensation criterion. As ill will and anger escalate, personal relationships and performance may suffer.

Creating Effective Reward and Incentive Programs   To be effective, incentive and reward systems need to reinforce basic core values and enhance cohesion and commitment to goals and objectives. They also must not be at odds with the organization's overall mission and purpose.[23]

Consider how incentives are used at General Mills. To ensure a manager's interest in the overall performance of his or her unit, half of a manager's annual bonus is linked to business-unit results and half to individual performance.[24] For example, if a manager simply matches a rival manufacturer's performance, his or her salary is roughly 5 percent lower. However, if a manager's product ranks in the industry's top 10 percent in earnings growth and return on capital, the manager's total compensation can rise to nearly 30 percent beyond the industry norm.

Effective reward and incentive systems share a number of common characteristics.

- Objectives are clear, well understood, and broadly accepted.
- Rewards are clearly linked to performance and desired behaviors.
- Performance measures are clear and highly visible.
- Feedback is prompt, clear, and unambiguous.
- The compensation "system" is perceived as fair and equitable.
- The structure is flexible; it can adapt to changing circumstances.[25]

The perception that a plan is "fair and equitable" is critically important. Similarly, the firm must have the flexibility to respond to changing requirements as its direction and objectives change. In recent years many companies have begun to place more emphasis on growth. Emerson Electric is one company that has shifted its emphasis from cost cutting to growth. To ensure that changes take hold, the management compensation formula has been changed from a largely bottom-line focus to one that emphasizes growth, new products, acquisitions, and international expansion. Discussions about profits are handled separately, and a culture of risk taking is encouraged.[26]

Setting Boundaries and Constraints

In an ideal world, a strong culture and effective rewards should be sufficient to ensure that all individuals and subunits work toward the common goals and objectives of the whole organization.[27] In the real world, however, this is not usually the case. Counterproductive behavior can arise because of motivated self-interest, lack of a clear understanding of goals and objectives, or outright malfeasance. Boundaries and constraints, when used properly, can serve many useful purposes for organizations, including:

- Focusing individual efforts on strategic priorities.
- Providing short-term objectives and action plans to channel efforts.
- Improving efficiency and effectiveness.
- Minimizing improper and unethical conduct.

Focusing Efforts on Strategic Priorities   Boundaries and constraints play a valuable role in focusing a company's strategic priorities. A well-known strategic boundary in U.S. industry is Jack Welch's (former CEO of General Electric) demand that any business in the corporate portfolio be ranked first or second in its industry. In a similar vein, Eli Lilly has reduced its research efforts to five broad areas of disease, down from eight or nine a decade ago.[28] This concentration of effort and resources provides the firm with greater strategic focus and the potential for stronger competitive advantages in the remaining areas.

Norman Augustine, Lockheed Martin's former chairman, provided four criteria for selecting candidates for diversification into "closely related" businesses.[29] They must (1) be high tech, (2) be systems-oriented, (3) deal with large customers (either corporations or government) as opposed to consumers, and (4) be in growth businesses. Augustine said, "We have found that if we can meet most of those standards, then we can move into adjacent markets and grow."

Boundaries also have a place in the nonprofit sector. For example, a British relief organization uses a system to monitor strategic boundaries by maintaining a list of companies whose contributions it will neither solicit nor accept. Such boundaries clearly go beyond simply taking the moral high road. Rather, they are essential for maintaining legitimacy with existing and potential benefactors.

Providing Short-Term Objectives and Action Plans   In Chapter 1 we discussed the importance of a firm having a vision, mission, and strategic objectives that are internally consistent and that provide strategic direction. In addition, short-term objectives and action plans provide similar benefits. That is, they represent boundaries that help to allocate resources in an optimal manner and to channel the efforts of employees at all levels throughout the organization.[30] To be effective, short-term objectives must have several attributes. They should:

- Be specific and measurable.
- Include a specific time horizon for their attainment.
- Be achievable, yet challenging enough to motivate managers who must strive to accomplish them.

Research has found that performance is enhanced when individuals are encouraged to attain specific, difficult, yet achievable, goals (as opposed to vague "do your best" goals).[31]

Short-term objectives must provide proper direction and at the same time provide enough flexibility for the firm to keep pace with and anticipate changes in the external environment. Such changes might include new government regulations, a competitor introducing a substitute product, or changes in consumer taste. Additionally, unexpected events within a firm may require a firm to make important adjustments in both strategic and short-term objectives. For example, the emergence of new industries can have a drastic effect on the demand for products and services in more traditional industries.

Along with short-term objectives, action plans are critical to the implementation of chosen strategies. Unless action plans are specific, there may be little assurance that managers have thought through all of the resource requirements for implementing their strategies. In addition, unless plans are specific, managers may not understand what needs to be implemented or have a clear time frame for completion. This is essential for the scheduling of key activities that must be implemented. Finally, individual managers must be held accountable for the implementation of action plans. This helps to provide the necessary motivation and "sense of ownership" to implement action plans on a timely basis. Strategy Spotlight 9.4 illustrates how action plans fit into the mission statement and objectives of a small manufacturer of aircraft interior components.

Improving Operational Efficiency and Effectiveness   Rule-based controls are most appropriate in organizations with the following characteristics:

- Environments are stable and predictable.
- Employees are largely unskilled and interchangeable.
- Consistency in product and service is critical.
- The risk of malfeasance is extremely high (e.g., in banking or casino operations), and controls must be implemented to guard against improper conduct.[32]

For example, McDonald's Corp. has extensive rules and regulations that regulate the operation of its franchises.[33] Its policy manual states, "Cooks must turn, never flip, hamburgers. If they haven't been purchased, Big Macs must be discarded in 10 minutes after being cooked and French fries in 7 minutes. Cashiers must make eye contact with and smile at every customer."

Guidelines can also be effective in setting spending limits and the range of discretion for employees and managers, such as the $2,500 limit that hotelier Ritz-Carlton uses to empower employees to placate dissatisfied customers. Regulations also can be initiated to improve the use of an employee's time at work.[34] Computer Associates restricts the use of e-mail during the hours of 10 a.m. to noon and 2 p.m. to 4 p.m. each day.[35]

Minimizing Improper and Unethical Conduct   Guidelines can be useful in specifying proper relationships with a company's customers and suppliers.[36] For example, many companies have explicit rules regarding commercial practices, including the prohibition of any form of payment, bribe, or kickback. Cadbury Schweppes has followed a rather simple but effective step in controlling the use of bribes by specifying that all payments, no matter how unusual, are recorded on the company's books. Its chairman, Sir Adrian Cadbury, contended that such a practice causes managers to pause and consider whether a payment is simply a bribe or a necessary and standard cost of doing business.[37] Consulting companies, too, typically have strong rules and regulations directed at protecting client confidentiality and conflicts of interest.

Regulations backed up with strong sanctions can also help an organization avoid conducting business in an unethical manner. In the wake of the corporate scandals of the early 21st century and the passing of the Sarbanes-Oxley Act (which, among other things, provides for stiffer penalties for financial reporting misdeeds), many chief financial officers (CFOs) have taken steps to ensure ethical behavior in the preparation of financial statements. For example, Home Depot's CFO, Carol B. Tome, strengthened the firm's code of ethics and developed stricter guidelines. Now all 25 of her subordinates must sign

Developing Meaningful Action Plans: Aircraft Interior Products, Inc.

MSA Aircraft Interior Products, Inc., is a manufacturing firm based in San Antonio, Texas, that was founded in 1983 by Mike Spraggins and Robert Plenge. The firm fulfills a small but highly profitable niche in the aviation industry with two key products. The Accordia line consists of patented, light-weight, self-contained window-shade assemblies. MSA's interior cabin shells are state-of-the-art assemblies that include window panels, side panels, headliners, and suspension system structures. MSA's products have been installed on a variety of aircraft, such as the Gulfstream series; the Cessna Citation; and Boeing's 727, 737, 757, and 707.

Much of MSA's success can be attributed to carefully articulated action plans consistent with the firm's mission and objectives. During the past five years, MSA has increased its sales at an annual rate of 15 to 18 percent. It has also succeeded in adding many prestigious companies to its customer base. Below are excerpts from MSA's mission statement and objectives as well as the action plans to achieve a 20 percent annual increase in sales.

Mission Statement

- Be recognized as an innovative and reliable supplier of quality interior products for the high-end, personalized transportation segments of the aviation, marine, and automotive industries.

- Design, develop, and manufacture interior fixtures and components that provide exceptional value to the customer through the development of innovative designs in a manner that permits decorative design flexibility while retaining the superior functionality, reliability, and maintainability of well-engineered, factory-produced products.

- Grow, be profitable, and provide a fair return, commensurate with the degree of risk, for owners and stockholders.

Objectives

1. Achieve sustained and profitable growth over the next three years:
   - 20 percent annual growth in revenues
   - 12 percent pretax profit margins
   - 18 percent return on shareholder's equity

2. Expand the company's revenues through the development and introduction of two or more new products capable of generating revenues in excess of $8 million a year by 2008.

3. Continue to aggressively expand market opportunities and applications for the Accordia line of window-shade assemblies, with the objective of sustaining or exceeding a 20 percent annual growth rate for at least the next three years.

Exhibit 9.4 details an "Action Plan" for Objective 3.

Description	Primary Responsibility	Target Date
1. Develop and implement 2006 marketing plan, including specific plans for addressing Falcon 20 retrofit programs and expanded sales of cabin shells.	R. H. Plenge (V.P. Marketing)	December 15, 2005
2. Negotiate new supplier agreement with Gulfstream Aerospace.	M. Spraggins (President)	March 1, 2006
3. Continue and complete the development of the UltraSlim window and have a fully tested and documented design ready for production at a manufacturing cost of less than $900 per unit.	D. R. Pearson (V.P. Operations)	June 15, 2006
4. Develop a window design suitable for L-1011 and similar wide-body aircraft and have a fully tested and documented design ready for production at a manufacturing cost comparable to the current Boeing window.	D. R. Pearson (V.P. Operations)	September 15, 2006

Exhibit 9.4 *Action Plan for Objective 3*

(continued)

(continued)

MSA's action plans are supported by detailed month-by-month budgets and strong financial incentives for its

executives. Budgets are prepared by each individual department and include all revenue and cost items. Managers are motivated by their participation in a profit-sharing program, and the firm's two founders each receive a bonus equal to 3 percent of total sales.

Source: For purposes of confidentiality, some of the information presented in this spotlight has been disguised. We would like to thank company management and Joseph Picken, consultant, for providing us with the information used in this application.

personal statements that all of their financial statements are correct—just as she and her boss, CEO Robert Nardelli, have to do now according to the congressional legislation.[38]

Behavioral Control in Organizations: Situational Factors

We have discussed the behavioral dimension of control. Here, the focus is on ensuring that the behavior of individuals at all levels of an organization is directed toward achieving organizational goals and objectives. The three fundamental types of control are culture, rewards and incentives, and boundaries and constraints. An organization may pursue one or a combination of them on the basis of a variety of internal and external factors.

Not all organizations place the same emphasis on each type of control.[39] For example, in professional organizations, such as high-technology firms engaged in basic research, members may work under high levels of autonomy. Here, an individual's performance is generally quite difficult to measure accurately because of the long lead times involved in research and development activities. Thus, internalized norms and values become very important.

In organizations where the measurement of an individual's output or performance is quite straightforward, control depends primarily on granting or withholding rewards. Frequently, a sales manager's compensation is in the form of a commission and bonus tied directly to his or her sales volume, which is relatively easy to determine. Here, behavior is influenced more strongly by the attractiveness of the compensation than by the norms and values implicit in the organization's culture. Furthermore, the measurability of output precludes the need for an elaborate system of rules to control behavior.

Control in bureaucratic organizations has long been recognized as dependent on members following a highly formalized set of rules and regulations. In such situations, most activities are routine and the desired behavior can be specified in a detailed manner because there is generally little need for innovative or creative activity. In business organizations, for example, managing an assembly plant requires strict adherence to many rules as well as exacting sequences of assembly operations. In the public sector, the Department of Motor Vehicles in most states must follow clearly prescribed procedures when issuing or renewing driver licenses.

Exhibit 9.5 provides alternate approaches to behavioral control and some of the situational factors associated with them.

Evolving from Boundaries to Rewards and Culture

In most environments, organizations should strive to provide a system of rewards and incentives, coupled with a culture strong enough that boundaries become internalized. This reduces the need for external controls such as rules and regulations. We suggest several ways to move in this direction.

Approach	Some Situational Factors
Culture: A system of unwritten rules that forms an internalized influence over behavior.	• Often found in professional organizations. • Associated with high autonomy. • Norms are the basis for behavior.
Rules: Written and explicit guidelines that provide external constraints on behavior.	• Associated with standardized output. • Tasks are generally repetitive and routine. • Little need for innovation or creative activity.
Rewards: The use of performance-based incentive systems to motivate.	• Measurement of output and performance is rather straightforward. • Most appropriate in organizations pursuing unrelated diversification strategies. • Rewards may be used to reinforce other means of control.

First, hire the right people—individuals who already identify with the organization's dominant values and have attributes consistent with them. We addressed this issue in detail in Chapter 4; recall the "Bozo Filter" that was developed by Cooper Software of Palo Alto, California. Microsoft's David Pritchard is well aware of the consequences of failing to hire properly.

> If I hire a bunch of bozos, it will hurt us, because it takes time to get rid of them. They start infiltrating the organization and then they themselves start hiring people of lower quality. At Microsoft, we are always looking for people who are better than we are.

Second, training plays a key role. For example, in elite military units such as the Green Berets and Navy SEALs, the training regimen so thoroughly internalizes the culture that individuals, in effect, lose their identity. The group becomes the overriding concern and focal point of their energies. At firms such as FedEx, training not only builds skills, but also plays a significant role in building a strong culture on the foundation of each organization's dominant values.

Third, managerial role models are vital. Andy Grove at Intel doesn't need (or want) a large number of bureaucratic rules to determine who is responsible for what, who is supposed to talk to whom, and who gets to fly first class (no one does). He encourages openness by not having many of the trappings of success—he works in a cubicle like all the other professionals. Can you imagine any new manager asking whether or not he can fly first class? Grove's personal example eliminates such a need.

Fourth, reward systems must be clearly aligned with the organizational goals and objectives. Where do you think rules and regulations are more important in controlling behavior—Home Depot, with its generous bonus and stock option plan, or Kmart, which does not provide the same level of rewards and incentives?

>>The Role of Corporate Governance

In the first two sections of this chapter we addressed how management can exercise strategic control over the firm's overall operations through the use of informational and behavioral controls. Now we address the issue of strategic control in a broader perspective, typically referred to as "corporate governance." Here we focus on the need for both shareholders (the owners of the corporation) and their elected representatives, the board of directors, to actively ensure that management fulfills its overriding purpose of increasing long-term shareholder value.

Robert Monks and Nell Minow, two leading scholars in corporate governance, define it as "the relationship among various participants in determining the direction and performance of corporations. The primary participants are (1) the shareholders, (2) the management (led by the chief executive officer), and (3) the board of directors."* Consistent with Monks and Minow's definition, our discussion will center on how corporations can succeed (or fail) in aligning managerial motives with the interests of the shareholders and their elected representatives, the board of directors. As you will recall from Chapter 1, we discussed the important role of boards of directors and provided some examples of effective and ineffective boards.[40]

There is little doubt that effective corporate governance can affect a firm's bottom line. Good corporate governance plays an important role in the investment decisions of major institutions, and a premium is often reflected in the price of securities of companies that practice it. The corporate governance premium is larger for firms in countries with sound corporate governance practices compared to countries with weaker corporate governance standards.[41] In addition, there is a strong correlation between strong corporate governance and superior financial performance. Strategy Spotlight 9.5 briefly summarizes three studies that provide support for this contention.

As indicated in our discussion above and in Strategy Spotlight 9.5, there is solid evidence linking good corporate governance with higher performance. At the same time, few topics in the business press are generating as much interest (and disdain!) as corporate governance.

Some recent notable examples of flawed corporate governance include:[42]

- Board members of Nortel Networks meet with governance-minded investors to discuss possible changes to the board. This is after 10 executives and accounting officials are fired for artificially boosting the company's 2003 financial results. (September 30, 2004)
- The Chairman of Boeing Company, Philip M. Condit, presides over a series of manipulations in accounting, acquisitions, and strategy. He conceals a $2.6 billion cost overrun from shareholders for months while his merger with McDonnell Douglas Corporation is completed, and as a result, he is forced to resign by the board. (December 15, 2003)
- Royal Ahoud NV (owner of Stop and Shop), the world's third largest supermarket operator, fires its CEO and CFO for inappropriate accounting for discounts from suppliers. The company also reduces earnings for the prior two years by $500 million. (February 25, 2003)
- AOL buys Time Warner in a deal worth $183 billion—which later results in a $54 billion write-off, the largest ever. (April 25, 2002)
- The New York State Attorney General charges that Merrill Lynch analysts were privately referring to certain stocks as "crap" and "junk" while publicly recommending them to investors. (April 8, 2002)

---

* Management, of course, cannot ignore the demands of other important firm stakeholders such as creditors, suppliers, customers, employees, and government regulators. At times of financial duress, powerful creditors can exert strong and legitimate pressures on managerial decisions. In general, however, the attention to stakeholders other than the owners of the corporation must be addressed in a manner that is still consistent with maximizing long-term shareholder returns. For a seminal discussion on stakeholder management, refer to Freeman, R. E. 1984. *Strategic management: A stakeholder approach.* Boston: Pitman.

STRATEGY SPOTLIGHT

Good Corporate Governance and Performance: Research Evidence

Three studies found a positive relationship between the extent to which a firm practices good corporate governance and its performance outcomes. The results of these studies are summarized below.

1. *A strong correlation between corporate governance and price performance of large companies.* Over a recent three-year period, the average return of large capitalized firms with the best governance practices was more than five times higher than the performance of firms in the bottom corporate governance quartile.

2. *Across emerging markets.* In 10 of the 11 Asian and Latin American markets, companies in the top corporate governance quartile for their respective regions had a significantly higher (averaging 10 percentage points) return on capital employed (ROCE) than their market sample. In 12 of the emerging markets analyzed, companies in the lowest corporate governance quartile had a lower ROCE than the market average.

Sources: McKinsey & Company. 2000. *Investor opinion survey on corporate governance,* June; Gill, Amar, Credit Lyonnais Securities (Asia). 2001. *Corporate governance in emerging markets: Saints and sinners,* April; and Low, C. K. 2002. *Corporate governance: An Asia-Pacific critique.* Hong Kong: Sweet & Maxwell Asia.

3. *Attitudes toward investing.* McKinsey & Company conducted three surveys from September 1999 to April 2000 that studied attitudes toward investing in Asia, Europe, the United States, and Latin America. Over three-quarters of the more than 200 investors surveyed agreed that "board practices were at least as important as financial performance." Over 80 percent of investors agreed that they "would pay a premium for the shares of a better-governed company than for those of a poorly governed company with comparable financial performance." Interestingly, the study demonstrated that the value of good corporate governance—that is, the premium that investors are willing to pay—varied across regions. Good corporate governance in the United States and the United Kingdom brought the lowest premium at 18 percent. However, for investments in Asian and Latin American countries, the premium rose to between 20 and 28 percent. The difference in the premium reflected the lack of good corporate governance standards in Asia and Latin America compared to the standards of companies in the United States and the United Kingdom.

- Tyco International discloses that it paid a director $10 million in cash and gave an additional $10 million to his favorite charity in exchange for his help in closing an acquisition deal. (January 29, 2002)
- Global Crossing, once a high-flying telecom service provider, files for Chapter 11. In the preceding three years, the company's insiders had cashed in $1.3 billion in stock. (January 28, 2002)
- Former company CEO Al Dunlap agrees to pay $15 million to settle a lawsuit from Sunbeam shareholders and bondholders alleging that he cooked the books of the small appliances maker. (January 11, 2002)
- Arthur Andersen, the accounting firm, agrees to pay $110 million to settle a shareholders suit for alleged fraud in its audit of Sunbeam. (May, 2001)
- Oracle CEO Larry Ellison exercises 23 million stock options for a record gain of more than $706 million—weeks before lowering earnings forecasts. (January, 2001)

Clearly, because of the many lapses in corporate governance, we can see the benefits associated with effective practices. However, corporate managers may behave in their own self-interest, often to the detriment of shareholders. Next we address the implications of the separation of ownership and management in the modern corporation, and some mechanisms that can be used to ensure consistency (or alignment) between the interests of shareholders and those of the managers to minimize potential conflicts.

The Modern Corporation: The Separation of Owners (Shareholders) and Management

Some of the proposed definitions for a *corporation* include:

- "The business corporation is an instrument through which capital is assembled for the activities of producing and distributing goods and services and making investments. Accordingly, a basic premise of corporation law is that a business corporation should have as its objective the conduct of such activities with a view to enhancing the corporation's profit and the gains of the corporation's owners, that is, the shareholders." (Melvin Aron Eisenberg, *The Structure of Corporation Law*)
- "A body of persons granted a charter legally recognizing them as a separate entity having its own rights, privileges, and liabilities distinct from those of its members." (*American Heritage Dictionary*)
- An ingenious device for obtaining individual profit without individual responsibility." (Ambrose Bierce, *The Devil's Dictionary*)[43]

All of these definitions have some validity and each one (including that from *The Devil's Dictionary!*) reflects a key feature of the corporate form of business organization—its ability to draw resources from a variety of groups and establish and maintain its own persona that is separate from all of them. As Henry Ford once said, "A great business is really too big to be human."

Simply put, a corporation is a mechanism created to allow different parties to contribute capital, expertise, and labor for the maximum benefit of each party. The shareholders (investors) are able to participate in the profits of the enterprise without taking direct responsibility for the operations. The management can run the company without the responsibility of personally providing the funds. And, in order to make both of these possible, the shareholders have limited liability as well as rather limited involvement in the company's affairs. However, they reserve the right to elect directors who have the fiduciary obligation to protect their interests.

Over 70 years ago, Columbia University professors Adolf Berle and Gardiner C. Means addressed the divergence of the interests of the owners of the corporation from the professional managers who are hired to run it. They warned that widely dispersed ownership "released management from the overriding requirement that it serve stockholders." The separation of ownership from management has given rise to a set of ideas called "agency theory." Central to agency theory is the relationship between two primary players—the *principals* who are the owners of the firm (stockholders) and the *agents*, who are the people paid by principals to perform a job on their behalf (management). The stockholders elect and are represented by a board of directors that has a fiduciary responsibility to ensure that management acts in the best interests of stockholders to ensure long-term financial returns for the firm.

Agency theory is concerned with resolving two problems that can occur in agency relationships.[44] The first is the agency problem that arises (1) when the goals of the principals and agents conflict, and (2) when it is difficult or expensive for the principal to verify what the agent is actually doing. In a corporation, this means that the board of directors would be unable to confirm that the managers were actually acting in the shareholders' interests because, in most cases, managers are "insiders" with regard to the businesses they operate and thus are better informed than the principals. Thus, managers may act "opportunistically" in pursuing their own interests—to the detriment of the corporation.[45] Managers may, for example, spend corporate funds on expensive perquisites (e.g., company jets and expensive art), devote time and resources to pet projects (initiatives in which they have a personal interest but that have limited market potential), engage in power struggles (where they may fight

STRATEGY SPOTLIGHT

9.6

Crony Capitalism: Several Examples

When President George W. Bush signed the Sarbanes-Oxley Act into law on July 30, 2002, one of its goals was to prevent the kind of self-dealing and other conflicts of interest that had brought down Enron, WorldCom, Adelphia, and other corporate giants. Among other things, the Sarbanes-Oxley Act bans company loans to executives and prohibits extending the terms of existing loans.

Many companies, however, acted quickly *before* the bill was signed. For example, *one day* before the bill was signed, Crescent Real Estate Equities of Fort Worth, Texas, extended the payback deadline by 10 years on a loan of $26 million to its chief executive, John Goff. And Electronic Arts gave a $4 million loan to Warren Johnson, its chief financial officer, admitting in a filing that it was doing so a month prior to the "prohibition on loans to executive officers."

Despite legislation such as Sarbanes-Oxley and pressures from shareholders, related-party deals are quite common. According to the Corporate Library, a research group in Portland, Maine, 75 percent of 2,000 companies that were studied still engage in them. In essence, that means that companies must make embarrassing disclosures in their proxy statements about nepotism, property leased from top managers, corporate-owned apartments, and other forms of "insiderism."

Consider some examples:

- Two hundred companies have leased or bought airplanes from insiders. For example, Pilgrim's Pride of

Pittsburgh, Texas, a chicken processor with $2.6 billion in annual sales has leased an airplane from its chief executive and founder Lonnie Pilgrim since 1985. Mr. Pilgrim made $656,000 in fiscal 2003 from this deal to go along with his $1.7 million in compensation. The company defends the pact as cost-efficient since its headquarters is located in a small town. Pilgrim also provides some bookkeeping services for his personal businesses, but he won't provide details.

- Micky M. Arison is chief executive of Carnival, the big cruise line. He is also chief executive and owner of the Miami Heat of the National Basketball Association. Carnival paid the Heat $675,000 in fiscal 2002 and 2003 for sponsorship and advertising as well as season tickets. Although that may be a rather small sum, given Carnival's $2.2 billion in net income for the period, we could still ask if the money would have been spent on something else if Arison didn't own the team.

- Alliance Semiconductor CEO N. Damodar Reddy has committed $20 million to Solar Ventures, a venture capital company run by his brother C. N. Reddy. Other unnamed insiders purchased undisclosed stakes in Solar. However, Alliance won't disclose whether its CEO is one of them. To date it has invested $12.5 million in Solar. Beth Young, senior research associate of the Corporate Library poses an interesting question: "Is Reddy using shareholder capital just to keep afloat his brother's fund and the insiders' investment?"

Source: MacDonald, E. 2004. Crony capitalism. *Forbes*, June 21: 140–146.

over resources for their own betterment and to the detriment of the firm), and negate (or sabotage) attractive merger offers because they may result in increased employment risk.[46]

The second issue is the problem of risk sharing. This arises when the principal and the agent have different attitudes and preferences toward risk. For example, the executives in a firm may favor additional diversification initiatives because, by their very nature, they increase the size of the firm and thus the level of executive compensation. At the same time, such diversification initiatives may erode shareholder value because they fail to achieve some of the synergies that we discussed in Chapter 6 (e.g., building on core competencies, sharing activities, or enhancing market power). In effect, agents (executives) may have a stronger preference toward diversification than shareholders because it reduces their personal level of risk from potential loss of employment. In contrast, research has shown that executives who have large holdings of stock in their firms were more likely to have diversification strategies that were more consistent with shareholder interests—that is, increasing long-term returns.[47]

At times, top-level managers engage in actions that reflect their self-interest rather than the interests of shareholders. Some examples of such conflicts of interest are addressed in Strategy Spotlight 9.6.

Governance Mechanisms: Aligning the Interests of Owners and Managers

As noted above, a key characteristic of the modern corporation is the separation of ownership from control. To minimize the potential for managers to act in their own self-interest, or "opportunistically," the owners can implement some governance mechanisms.[48] We address three of these in the next sections. First, there are two primary means of monitoring the behavior of managers. These include (1) a committed and involved *board of directors* that acts in the best interests of the shareholders to create long-term value for shareholders and (2) *shareholder activism,* wherein the owners of the corporation view themselves as share*owners* instead of share*holders* and become actively engaged in the governance of the corporation. As we will see later in this section, shareholder activism has increased dramatically in recent years. Finally, there are managerial incentives, sometimes called "contract-based outcomes," which consist of *reward and compensation agreements*. Here the goal is to carefully craft managerial incentive packages to align the interests of management with those of the stockholders.

A Committed and Involved Board of Directors   The board of directors acts as a fulcrum between the owners and controllers of a corporation. In effect, they are the intermediaries who provide a balance between a small group of key managers in the firm based at the corporate headquarters and a sometimes vast group of shareholders typically spread out over the world. In the United States, the law imposes on the board a strict and absolute fiduciary duty to ensure that a company is run consistent with the long-term interests of the owners—the shareholders. The reality, as we have seen, is somewhat more ambiguous.[49]

The Business Roundtable, representing the largest U.S. corporations, describes the duties of the board as follows:

1. Select, regularly evaluate, and, if necessary, replace the chief executive officer. Determine management compensation. Review succession planning.
2. Review and, where appropriate, approve the financial objectives, major strategies, and plans of the corporation.
3. Provide advice and counsel to top management.
4. Select and recommend to shareholders for election an appropriate slate of candidates for the board of directors; evaluate board processes and performance.
5. Review the adequacy of the systems to comply with all applicable laws/regulations.[50]

Given these principles, what makes for a good board of directors? According to the Business Roundtable, the most important quality is a board of directors who are active, critical participants in determining a company's strategies.[51] That does not mean board members should micromanage or circumvent the CEO. Rather, they should provide strong oversight that goes beyond simply approving the chief executive's plans. Today, a board's primary responsibilities are to ensure that strategic plans undergo rigorous scrutiny, evaluate managers against high performance standards, and take control of the succession process.

Although boards in the past were often dismissed as CEO's rubber stamps, increasingly they are playing a more active role by forcing out CEOs who cannot deliver on performance. According to a recent study by the consulting firm Booz Allen Hamilton, the rate of CEO departures for performance reasons has more than tripled, from 1.3 percent to 4.2 percent, between 1995 and 2002.[52] Well-known CEOs like Gerald M. Levin of AOL Time Warner and Jack M. Greenberg of McDonald's paid the price for poor financial performance by being forced to leave. Others, such as Bernard Ebbers of WorldCom, Inc., and Dennis Kozlowski of Tyco International, lost their jobs due to scandals. "Deliver or depart" is clearly the new message from the boards.

Another key component of top-ranked boards is director independence. Governance experts believe that a majority of directors should be free of all ties to either the CEO or the company. That means a minimum of "insiders" (past or present members of the management team) should serve on the board, and that directors and their firms should be barred from doing consulting, legal, or other work for the company.[53] Interlocking directorships—in which CEOs and other top managers serve on each other's boards—are not desirable. But perhaps the best guarantee that directors act in the best interests of shareholders is the simplest: Most good companies now insist that directors own significant stock in the company they oversee.[54]

Such guidelines are not always followed. At times, it would appear that the practices of the boards of directors of some companies are the antithesis of such guidelines. Consider the Walt Disney Co. Over a recent five-year period, Michael Eisner pocketed an astonishing $531 million. Although, over a 10-year period, Eisner had led Disney to provide shareholder returns of over 20 percent, he likely had very little resistance from his board of directors.

> Many investors view the Disney board as an anachronism. Among Disney's 16 directors is Eisner's personal attorney—who for several years was chairman of the company's compensation committee! There was also the architect who designed Eisner's Aspen home and his parents' apartment. Joining them are the principal of an elementary school once attended by his children and the president of a university to which Eisner donated $1 million. The board also includes the actor Sidney Poitier, seven current and former Disney executives, and an attorney who does business with Disney. Moreover, most of the outside directors own little or no Disney stock. "It is an egregiously bad board—a train wreck waiting to happen," warns Michael L. Useem, a management professor at the University of Pennsylvania's Wharton School.[55]

This example also demonstrates that "outside directors" are only beneficial to strong corporate governance if they are engaged and vigilant in carrying out their responsibilities.[56] As humorously suggested by Warren Buffett, founder and chairman of Berkshire Hathaway: "The ratcheting up of compensation has been obscene. . . . There is a tendency to put cocker spaniels on compensation committees, not Doberman pinschers."[57]

Many firms do have exemplary board practices. Below, for example, we list some of the excellent practices at Intel Corp., the world's largest semiconductor chip manufacturer, with $34 billion in revenues:[58]

- *Mix of inside and outside directors.* The board believes that there should be a majority of independent directors on the board. However, the board is willing to have members of management, in addition to the chief executive officer, as directors.

- *Board presentations and access to employees.* The board encourages management to schedule managers to be present at meetings who: (a) can provide additional insight into the items being discussed because of personal involvement in these areas, or (b) have future potential that management believes should be given exposure to the board.

9.7   STRATEGY SPOTLIGHT

Continental Airlines:Selecting Competent Directors for its Board

Continental Airlines took explicit action to select directors who could face the challenges of its industry. The board thoroughly analyzed Continental's business issues in order to assess what skills and experience it needed and zeroed in on the knowledge of the airline and travel industries, an understanding of marketing and consumer behavior, access to key business and political contacts, and experience with industry reconfiguration.

The board then defined the capabilities and qualities that were required of all directors, such as independence,

business credibility, confidence, and teamwork. To be as representative as possible, it determined the directors' knowledge of geographic markets, especially their knowledge of key Continental hubs, CEO experience, leadership in business sectors, and gender and ethnic diversity.

After this analysis, the board evaluated all of its directors and mapped their skills, experience, and backgrounds against the new criteria. The gaps became critical information for targeting new directors. Ultimately, several board members voluntarily resigned to make way for new directors who had the capabilities and background that Continental needed to compete more successfully.

Source: Nadler, D. A. 2004. Building better boards. *Harvard Business Review*, 82(5): 102–111.

- **Formal evaluation of officers.** The Compensation Committee conducts, and reviews with the outside directors, an annual evaluation to help determine the salary and executive bonus of all officers, including the chief executive officer.

To be effective, boards of directors also have to be composed of members who have the requisite competencies and backgrounds. Strategy Spotlight 9.7 discusses the intricate process that Continental Airlines has undertaken to improve the quality of the members of its board of directors.

Shareholder Activism   As a practical matter, there are so many owners of the largest American corporations that it makes little sense to refer to them as "owners" in the sense of individuals becoming informed and involved in corporate affairs. However, even an individual shareholder has several rights, including (1) the right to sell the stock, (2) the right to vote the proxy (which includes the election of board members), (3) the right to bring suit for damages if the corporation's directors or managers fail to meet their obligations, (4) the right to certain information from the company, and (5) certain residual rights following the company's liquidation (or its filing for reorganization under bankruptcy laws), once creditors and other claimants are paid off.[59]

Collectively, shareholders have the power to direct the course of corporations.[60] This may involve acts such as being party to shareholder action suits and demanding that key issues be brought up for proxy votes at annual board meetings. In addition, the power of shareholders has intensified in recent years because of the increasing influence of large institutional investors such as mutual funds (e.g., T. Rowe Price and Fidelity Investments) and retirement systems such as TIAA-CREF (for university faculty members and school administrative staff).[61] Institutional investors hold approximately 50 percent of all listed corporate stock in the United States.

Many institutional investors are aggressive in protecting and enhancing their investments. In effect, they are shifting from traders to owners. They are assuming the role of permanent shareholders and rigorously analyzing issues of corporate governance. In the process they are reinventing systems of corporate monitoring and accountability.[62]

Consider the proactive behavior of CalPERS, the California Public Employees' Retirement System, which manages approximately $150 billion in assets and is the third largest pension fund in the world. Every year CalPERS reviews the performance of U.S. companies in its stock portfolio and identifies those that are among the lowest long-term relative performers and have governance structures that do not ensure full accountability to company owners. This generates a long list of companies, each of which may potentially be publicly identified as a CalPERS "Focus Company"—corporations to which CalPERS directs specific suggested governance reforms. CalPERS meets with the directors of each of these companies to discuss performance and governance issues. The CalPERS Focus List contains those companies that continue to merit public and market attention at the end of the process.

Emerson Electric, based in St. Louis, Missouri, has $5 billion in revenues and is one of the four firms on the CalPERS 2004 Focus List. CalPERS holds 2.19 million shares (0.52 percent of the total outstanding shares). Following is list of the governance changes that CalPERS wants Emerson to make:[63]

- Formalize director evaluations.
- Commit to independent board members and reduce the employee representation on the board.
- Provide an analysis of retaining former CEO Charles Knight as Chairman of the Board member and commit to renegotiating the excessive terms of Mr. Knight's contract and perquisites.
- Seek shareholder approval of the company's poison pill.
- Seek shareholder approval to eliminate the supermajority requirements and declassify the board by the 2005 annual meeting.
- Tie a significant portion of the company's long-term compensation to performance-based measures.
- Improve communication and transparency of good governance initiatives.

While appearing punitive to company management, such aggressive activism has paid significant returns for CalPERS (and other stockholders of the "Focused" companies). For example, a Wilshire Associates study of the "CalPERS Effect" of corporate governance examined the performance of 62 targets over a five-year period. The results indicated that, while the stock of these companies trailed the Standard & Poors Index by 89 percent in the five-year period before CalPERS acted, the same stocks outperformed the index by 23 percent in the following five years, adding approximately $150 million annually in additional returns to the fund.

Managerial Rewards and Incentives   As we discussed earlier in the chapter, incentive systems must be designed to help a company achieve its goals. Similarly, from the perspective of governance, one of the most critical roles of the board of directors is to create incentives that align the interests of the CEO and top executives with the interests of owners of the corporation—long-term shareholder returns.[64] After all, shareholders rely on CEOs to adopt policies and strategies that maximize the value of their shares.[65] A combination of three basic policies may create the right monetary incentives for CEOs to maximize the value of their companies:

1. Boards can require that the CEOs become substantial owners of company stock.
2. Salaries, bonuses, and stock options can be structured so as to provide rewards for superior performance and penalties for poor performance.
3. Threat of dismissal for poor performance can be a realistic outcome.

In recent years the granting of stock options has enabled top executives of publicly held corporations to earn enormous levels of compensation. In 2001 the CEOs of large corporations in the United States averaged $11 million, or 411 times as much as the average factory worker. Over the past decade, the wages of rank-and-file workers increased only 36 percent while the pay of CEOs climbed 340 percent. Many boards have awarded huge option grants despite poor executive performance, and others have made performance goals easier to reach. In 2002 nearly 200 companies swapped or repriced options—all to enrich wealthy executives who are already among the country's richest people. However, stock options can be a valuable governance mechanism to align the CEO's interests with those of the shareholders. The extraordinarily high level of compensation can often be grounded in sound governance principles.[66] For example, Howard Solomon, CEO of Forest Laboratories, received a total compensation of $148.5 million in 2001.[67] This represented $823,000 in salary, $400,000 in bonus, and $147.3 million in stock options that were exercised. However, shareholders also did well, receiving gains of 40 percent. The firm has enjoyed spectacular growth over the past five years and Solomon has been CEO since 1977. Thus, huge income is attributed largely to gains that have built up over many years. As stated by compensation committee member Dan Goldwasser, "If a CEO is delivering substantial increases in shareholder value . . . it's only appropriate that he be rewarded for it."

However, the "pay for performance" principle doesn't always hold. Consider Oracle, for example.

> By 2001, with the tech bubble bursting, Oracle stock was in a free fall. Rather than sit tight in a show of confidence, CEO Laurence Ellison sold 29 million shares in a single week in January, flooding the market when investors already were jittery. He exercised 23 million options the same week for a gain of more than $706 million. Within a month, Oracle stock had lost a third of its value and the company was announcing that it would miss third-quarter forecasts. That triggered further price declines and a rash of shareholder lawsuits alleging that Ellison engaged in "what appears to be the largest insider trading in the history of the U.S. financial market," according to one suit. Ellison's stock sales were a factor in the sell-off that followed, says Henry Asher, president of Northstar Group, Inc., which owns 48,000 Oracle shares. "Was that a ringing endorsement for the company's short-term prospects?" asks Asher. "I don't think so."[68]

In addition to the granting of stock options, boards of directors are often failing to fulfill their fiduciary responsibilities to shareholders when they lower the performance targets that executives need to meet in order to receive millions of dollars. At General Motors, for example, CEO G. Richard Wagoner, Jr., and other top executives were entitled to a special performance bonus if the company's net profit margin reached 5 percent by the end of 2003. However, the 5 percent target was later lowered.

TIAA-CREF has provided several principles of corporate governance with regard to executive compensation.[69] These include the importance of aligning the rewards of all employees—rank and file as well as executives—to the long-term performance of the corporation; general guidelines on the role of cash compensation, stock, and "fringe benefits"; and the mission of a corporation's compensation committee. Exhibit 9.6 addresses TIAA-CREF's principles on the role of stock in managerial compensation.

External Governance Control Mechanisms

Our discussion so far has been on internal governance mechanisms. Internal controls, however, are not always enough to ensure good governance. The separation of ownership and control that we discussed earlier requires multiple control mechanisms, some internal and some external, to ensure that managerial actions lead to shareholder value maximization. Further, society-at-large wants some assurance that this goal is met without harming other stakeholder groups. In this section, we discuss several external control mechanisms that have developed in most modern economies. These include the market for corporate control, auditors, governmental regulatory bodies, banks and analysts, media, and public activists.

Exhibit 9.6

TIAA-CREF's
Principles on the Role
of Stock in Executive
Compensation

Stock-based compensation plans are a critical element of most compensation programs and can provide opportunities for managers whose efforts contribute to the creation of shareholder wealth. In evaluating the suitability of these plans, considerations of reasonableness, scale, linkage to performance, and fairness to shareholders and all employees also apply. TIAA-CREF, the largest pension system in the world, has set forth the following guidelines for stock-based compensation. Proper stock-based plans should:

- Allow for creation of executive wealth that is reasonable in view of the creation of shareholder wealth. Management should not prosper through stock while shareholders suffer.
- Have measurable and predictable outcomes that are directly linked to the company's performance.
- Be market oriented, within levels of comparability for similar positions in companies of similar size and business focus.
- Be straightforward and clearly described so that investors and employees can understand them.
- Be fully disclosed to the investing public and be approved by shareholders.

Source: www.tiaa-cref.org/pubs.

The Market for Corporate Control   Let us assume for a moment that internal control mechanisms in a company are failing. This means that the board is ineffective in monitoring managers and is not exercising the oversight required of them and that shareholders are passive and are not taking any actions to monitor or discipline managers. Theoretically, under these circumstances managers may behave opportunistically.[70] Opportunistic behavior can take many forms. First, they can *shirk* their responsibilities. Shirking means that managers fail to exert themselves fully, as is required of them. Second, they can engage in *on the job consumption.* Examples of on the job consumption include private jets, club memberships, expensive artwork in the offices, and so on. Each of these represents consumption by managers that does not in any way increase shareholder value. Instead, they actually diminish shareholder value. Third, managers may engage in *excessive product-market diversification.*[71] As we discussed in Chapter 6, such diversification serves to reduce only the employment risk of the managers rather than the financial risk of the shareholders, who can more cheaply diversify their risk by owning a portfolio of investments. Is there any external mechanism to stop managers from shirking, consumption on the job, and excessive diversification?

The market for corporate control is one such external mechanism that provides at least some partial solution to the problems described. If internal control mechanisms fail and the management is behaving opportunistically, the likely response of most shareholders will be to sell their stock rather than engage in activism.[72] As more and more stockholders vote with their feet, the value of the stock begins to decline. As the decline continues, at some point the market value of the firm becomes less than the book value. That is, a corporate raider can take over the company for a price less than the book value of the assets of the company. The first thing that the raider may do on assuming control over the company will be to fire the underperforming management. The risk of being acquired by a hostile raider is often referred to as the *takeover constraint.* The takeover constraint deters management from engaging in opportunistic behavior.[73]

Although in theory the takeover constraint is supposed to limit managerial opportunism, in recent years its effectiveness has become diluted as a result of a number of defense tactics adopted by incumbent management (see Chapter 6). Foremost among them are poison pills, greenmail, and golden parachutes. Poison pills are provisions adopted by the company to reduce its worth to the acquirer. An example would be payment of a huge one-time dividend, typically financed by debt. Greenmail involves buying back the stock from the acquirer, usually at an attractive premium. Golden parachutes are employment contracts that cause the company to pay lucrative severance packages to top managers fired as a result of a takeover, often running to several million dollars.

Auditors   Even when there are stringent disclosure requirements, there is no guarantee that the information disclosed will be accurate. Managers may deliberately disclose false information or withhold negative financial information. It is also possible that they may use accounting methods that distort results based on highly subjective interpretations. Therefore, all accounting statements are required to be audited and certified to be accurate by external auditors. These auditing firms are independent organizations staffed by certified professionals who verify the books of accounts of the company. Audits can unearth financial irregularities and ensure that financial reporting by the firm conforms to standard accounting practices.

Recent developments leading to the bankruptcy of firms such as Enron and World-Com and a spate of earnings restatements raise questions about the failure of the auditing firms to act as effective external control mechanisms. Why did an auditing firm like Arthur Andersen, with decades of reputation in the auditing profession at stake, fail to raise red flags about accounting irregularities? First, auditors are appointed by the firm being audited. The desire to continue that business relationship sometimes makes them overlook financial irregularities. Second, most auditing firms also do consulting work and often have lucrative consulting contracts with the firms that they audit. Understandably, some of them tend not to ask too many difficult questions, because they fear jeopardizing the consulting business, which is often more profitable than the auditing work.

The recent restatement of earnings by Xerox is an example of the lack of independence of auditing firms. The Securities and Exchange Commission filed a lawsuit against KPMG, the world's third largest accounting firm, in January 2003 for allowing Xerox to inflate its revenues by $3 billion between 1997 and 2000. Of the $82 million that Xerox paid KPMG during these four years, only $26 million was for auditing. The rest was for consulting services. When one of the auditors objected to Xerox's practice of booking revenues for equipment leases earlier than it should have, Xerox asked KPMG to replace him, which it did.[74]

Banks and Analysts   Two external groups that monitor publicly held firms are financial institutions and stock analysts. Commercial and investment banks do so because they have lent money to corporations and therefore have to ensure that the borrowing firm's finances are in order and that the loan covenants are being followed. Stock analysts conduct ongoing in-depth studies of the firms that they follow and make recommendations to their clients to buy, hold, or sell. Their rewards and reputation depend on the quality of these recommendations. Their access to information, knowledge of the industry and the firm, and the insights they gain from interactions with the management of the company enable them to alert the investing community of both positive and negative developments relating to a company.

In reality, it is generally observed that analyst recommendations are often more optimistic than warranted by facts. "Sell" recommendations tend to be exceptions rather than the norm. Many analysts seem to have failed to grasp the gravity of the problems surrounding failed companies such as Enron and Global Crossing till the very end. Part of the explanation may lie in the fact that most analysts work for firms that also have investment banking relationships with the companies they follow. Negative recommendations by analysts can displease the management, who may decide to take their investment banking business to a rival firm. Thus, otherwise independent and competent analysts may be pressured to overlook negative information or tone down their criticism. A recent settlement between the Securities and Exchange Commission and the New York State Attorney General with 10 banks requires them to pay $1.4 billion in penalties and to fund independent research for investors.[75]

Regulatory Bodies   All corporations are subject to some regulation by the government. The extent of regulation is often a function of the type of industry. Banks, utilities, and pharmaceuticals, for example, are subject to more regulatory oversight because of their importance to society. Public corporations are subject to more regulatory requirements than private corporations. All public corporations are required to disclose a substantial amount of financial information by bodies such as the Securities and Exchange Commission. These include quarterly and annual filings of financial performance, stock trading by insiders, and details of executive compensation packages. There are two primary reasons behind such requirements. First, markets can operate efficiently only when the investing public has faith in the market system. In the absence of disclosure requirements, the average investor suffers from a lack of reliable information and therefore may completely stay away from the capital market. This will negatively impact an economy's ability to grow. Second, disclosure of information such as insider trading protects the small investor to some extent from the negative consequences of information asymmetry. That is, the insiders and large investors typically have more information than the small investor and can therefore use that information to buy or sell before the information becomes public knowledge.

The failure of a variety of external control mechanisms led the U.S. Congress to pass the Sarbanes-Oxley Act in 2002. This act calls for many stringent measures that would ensure better governance of U.S. corporations. Some of these measures include:[76]

- *Auditors* are barred from certain types of nonaudit work. They are not allowed to destroy records for five years. Lead partners auditing a client should be changed at least every five years.
- *CEOs* and *CFOs* must fully reveal off-balance-sheet finances and vouch for the accuracy of the information revealed.
- *Executives* must promptly reveal the sale of shares in firms they manage and are not allowed to sell when other employees cannot.
- *Corporate lawyers* must report to senior managers any violations of securities law lower down.

Strategy Spotlight 9.8 discusses some of the expenses that companies have incurred in complying with the Sarbanes-Oxley Act. You may wonder whether the costs outweigh some of the benefits.

Media and Public Activists   The press is not usually recognized as an external control mechanism in the literature on corporate governance. There is, however, no denying that in all developed capitalist economies, the financial press and media play an important indirect role in monitoring the management of public corporations. In the United States, business magazines such as *BusinessWeek* and *Fortune,* financial newspapers such as *The Wall Street Journal* and *Investors Business Daily,* as well as television networks like Financial News Network and CNBC are constantly reporting on companies. Public perceptions about

Governance Reform: The Costs Add Up

In the aftermath of Enron and Worldcom and a spate of corporate scandals early in the decade, the U.S. Congress passed the Sarbanes-Oxley Act in 2002. It was an effort to restore investor confidence in the governance of corporations in general and financial reporting in particular. Three years later, a backlash seems to be developing among executives about the high compliance costs and some of the more draconian requirements.

The major source of resentment is the issue of cost. It is estimated that large corporations with revenues over $4 billion have to spend an average of $35 million a year to implement Sarbanes-Oxley. Medium-sized companies spend $3.1 million a year on average. Smaller companies find the cost of compliance particularly burdensome because they have a smaller revenue base. Some critics go to the extent of arguing that this amounts to a form of regressive taxation against small businesses. Many are even considering delisting to avoid compliance costs.

Costs are not the only problem that companies face. Meeting the requirements of Sarbanes-Oxley is very time consuming as well. For example, the law requires that financial numbers such as value of inventory and receivables are cross-checked. But it requires an army of additional people and significant additional costs to ensure this. Yellow Roadway Corporation, the nation's largest trucking firm, had to use 200 employees and $9 million to accomplish this in 2004. This was 3% of their total profits. And just think of the lost productivity!

How much has Sarbanes-Oxley succeeded in improving governance and ensuring the accuracy and reliability of financial reporting? While it is too early to assess the impact, there is at least some anecdotal evidence that it is having some impact. Visteon Corp., an auto-parts supplier, reported that they uncovered problems with their accounts receivable while complying with the requirements of the act. Similarly, SunTrust Banks Inc. fired three officers after discovering errors in the calculation of loan allowances in their portfolios. Tough but fair regulations can improve governance, but the costs of compliance cannot be ignored.

Source: Henry, D. 2005. Death, taxes & Sarbanes-Oxley? *BusinessWeek*, January 17: 28–31.

a company's financial prospects and the quality of its management are greatly influenced by the media. For example, Food Lion's reputation was sullied when ABC's *Prime Time Live* in 1992 charged the company with employee exploitation, false package dating, and unsanitary meat handling practices. Bethany McLean of *Fortune* magazine is often credited as the first to raise questions about Enron's long-term financial viability.[77]

Similarly, consumer groups and activist individuals often take a crusading role in exposing corporate malfeasance. Well-known examples include Ralph Nader and Erin Brockovich, who played important roles in bringing to light the safety issues related to GM's Corvair and environmental pollution issues concerning Pacific Gas and Electric Company, respectively. Exhibit 9.7 summarizes the many watchdog groups founded by Ralph Nader to monitor and change the behavior and strategies of major corporations.

Corporate Governance: An International Perspective

As we have noted in this chapter (and in Chapter 1), the topic of corporate governance has long been dominated by agency theory and based on the explicit assumption of the separation of ownership and control.[78] The central conflicts are principal–agent conflicts between shareholders and management. However, such an underlying assumption seldom applies outside of the United States and the United Kingdom. This is particularly true in emerging economies and continental Europe. Here, there is often concentrated ownership, along with extensive family ownership and control, business group structures, and weak legal protection for minority shareholders. Thus, serious conflicts tend to exist between two classes of principals: controlling shareholders and minority shareholders. Such conflicts can be called

Ralph Nader, an activist politician in the United States, established more than 30 public interest groups to act as "watchdogs" for corporate America. Together, the loose federation of independent groups constitutes, in effect, an anticorporate conglomerate. Here are a few examples.

- **Aviation Consumer Action Project:** Works to propose new rules to prevent flight delays, impose penalties for deceiving passengers about problems, and push for higher compensation for lost luggage.
- **Center for Auto Safety:** Helps consumers find plaintiff lawyers and agitates for vehicle recalls, increased highway safety standards, and lemon laws.
- **Center for Study of Responsive Law:** This is Nader's headquarters. Home of a consumer project on technology, this group sponsored seminars on Microsoft remedies and pushed for tougher Internet privacy rules. It also took on the drug industry over costs.
- **Commercial Alert:** This group fights excessive commercialism. Its targets include Primedia for delivering ads in educational programming and Coke and Pepsi for aggressive sales tactics in schools.
- **Pension Rights Center:** This center helped employees of IBM, General Electric, and other companies to organize themselves against cash-balance pension plans.
- **Public Citizen:** This is the umbrella organization that sponsors Global Trade Watch, Congress Watch, the Critical Mass Energy & Environment program, Health Research Group, and Public Citizen Litigation Group. Issues taken up include tort reform, oil mergers, and reform of campaign finance.

Source: From Bernstein, A., "Too Much Corporate Power?" *BusinessWeek,* Sept. 2000. Reprinted with permission.

Exhibit 9.7
Watchdogs for Corporate America

principal–principal (PP) conflicts as opposed to *principal–agent* conflicts. Exhibits 9.8 and 9.9 address how principal–principal conflicts and principal–agent conflicts differ.

Strong family control is one of the leading indicators of concentrated ownership. For example, in East Asia (excluding China), approximately 57 percent of the corporations have board chairmen and CEOs from the controlling families. In continental Europe, this number is 68 percent. A very common practice is the appointment of family members as board chairman, CEOs, and other top executives. This happens because the families are controlling (not necessarily majority) shareholders. For example, in 2003, 30-year-old James Murdoch was appointed CEO of British Sky Broadcasting (BSkyB), Europe's largest satellite broadcaster. There was very vocal resistance by minority shareholders. Why was he appointed in the first place? James's father just happened to be Rupert Murdoch, who controlled 35 percent of BSkyB and chaired the board. Clearly, this is a case of a principal–principal conflict.

In general, three conditions must be met for PP conflicts to occur. First, there must be a dominant owner or group of owners who have interests that are distinct from minority shareholders. Second, there must be motivation for the controlling shareholders to exercise their dominant positions to their advantage. And third, there must be few formal (such as legislation or regulatory bodies) or informal constraints that would discourage or prevent the controlling shareholders from exploiting their advantageous positions.

The result is often that family managers, who represent (or actually are) the controlling shareholders, engage in *expropriation* of minority shareholders, which is defined as activities that enrich the controlling shareholders at the expense of minority shareholders. What is their motive? After all, controlling shareholders have incentives to maintain firm value. But controlling shareholders may take actions that decrease aggregate firm

	Principal–Agent Conflicts	Principal–Principal Conflicts
Goal Incongruence	Between shareholders and professional managers who own a relatively small portion of the firm's equity.	Between controlling shareholders and minority shareholders.
Ownership Pattern	Dispersed—5%–20% is considered "concentrated ownership."	Concentrated—Often greater than 50% of equity is controlled by controlling shareholders.
Manifestations	Strategies that benefit entrenched managers at the expense of shareholders in general (e.g., shirking, pet projects, excessive compensation, and empire building).	Strategies that benefit controlling shareholders at the expense of minority shareholders (e.g., minority shareholder expropriation, nepotism, and cronyism).
Institutional Protection of Minority Shareholders	Formal constraints (e.g., judicial reviews and courts) set an upper boundary on potential expropriation by majority shareholders. Informal norms generally adhere to shareholder wealth maximization.	Formal institutional protection is often lacking, corrupted, or un-enforced. Informal norms are typically in favor of the interests of controlling shareholders ahead of those of minority investors.

Source: Adapted from Young, M., Peng, M. W., Ahlstrom, D., & Bruton, G. 2002. Governing the corporation in emerging economies: A principal–principal perspective. *Academy of Management Best Papers Proceedings,* Denver.

Exhibit 9.8

Traditional Principal–Agent Conflicts versus Principal–Principal Conflicts: How they Differ Along Dimensions

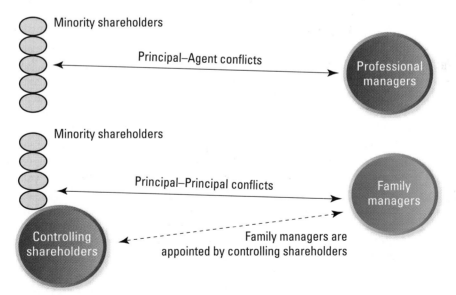

Exhibit 9.9   **Principal–Agent Conflicts and Principal–Principal Conflicts: A Diagram**

Source: Young, M. N., Peng, M. W., Ahlstrom, D., Bruton, G. D., Jiang, Y. 2005. Principal–principal conflicts in corporate governance (unpublished manuscript); and Peng, M. V. 2006. *Global strategy.* Cincinnati: Thomson South-Western. We are very appreciative of the helpful comments of Mike Young of the Chinese University of Hong Kong and Mike Peng of the Ohio State University.

STRATEGY SPOTLIGHT

Effective and Ineffective Corporate Governance in Hong Kong

Finding examples of exemplary corporate governance in Hong Kong isn't easy due to the high incidence of family-controlled corporations and the lack of laws to protect minority shareholders. An exception is CLP, one of the largest electric utilities in Asia, which is 35 percent controlled by Chairman Michael Kadoorie and his family. Admirers say it is an example of how even a family-controlled company can move toward more transparency. The company's board has several independent directors, and its Web site gives comprehensive information on its corporate governance policy. Kadoorie says family shareholders are treated the same as others.

At the other end of the continuum is Henderson Land Development. The company is controlled by Lee Shau Kee, one of Hong Kong's wealthiest tycoons. In its latest corporate-governance snafu, Henderson attempted to buy 73 percent of its publicly listed subsidiary, Henderson Investment, for 30 percent below its reported net asset

value. However, the related transaction was thwarted by minority shareholders, including the powerful Templeton Asset Management. At the time, Henderson Land Vice-Chairman Colin Lam insisted the dissenting investors had placed "a very, very high valuation on Henderson Investment," implying that this placed too high a value on its shares. Needless to say, the minority shareholders would hardly agree. However, it was perfectly legal in Hong Kong, and had it gone through, the minority shareholders would have been left holding the bag.

Had the Henderson Investment deal occurred in the United States, a shareholder lawsuit would have been launched. In Hong Kong, however, class-action lawsuits are not allowed. Consider the sentiment of Andrew Sheng, head of the Hong Kong Securities & Futures Commission, in the face of an action by another company taking advantage of minority shareholders: if the investors didn't like what was happening, they could simply sell their shares. Such a "buyer beware" attitude, even by regulatory bodies in one of the most developed emerging economies, causes firms to trade at a discount compared to firms in more mature economies.

Sources: Balfour, F., & Tashiro, H. 2004. A change in attitude. *BusinessWeek*, May 17: 48–50; Clifford, M. 2002. China Journal: Hong Kong's cautionary Christmas carol. *BusinessWeek* Online, August; and Young, M. N., Peng, M. W., Ahlstrom, D., Bruton, G. D., & Jiang, Y. 2005. Principal–principal conflicts in corporate governance Unpublished manuscript.

performance if their personal gains from expropriation exceed their personal losses from their firm's lowered performance.

Another ubiquitous feature of corporate life outside of the United States and Great Britain are *business groups* such as the keiretsus of Japan and the chaebols of South Korea. This is particularly dominant in emerging economies. A business group is "a set of firms which, though legally independent, are bound together by a constellation of formal and informal ties and are accustomed to taking coordinated action."[79] Business groups are especially common in emerging economies, and they are different from other organizational forms in that the groups are communities of firms without clear boundaries. Business groups have many advantages that can enhance the value of a firm. For example, they often facilitate technology transfer or intergroup capital allocation that otherwise might be impossible because of inadequate institutional infrastructure such as excellent financial services firms. On the other hand, informal ties—such as cross-holdings, board interlocks, and coordinated actions—can often result in intragroup activities and transactions, often at very favorable terms to member firms. For example, expropriation can be legally done through *related transactions,* which can occur when controlling owners sell firm assets to another firm they own at below market prices or spin off the most profitable part of a public firm and merge it with another of their private firms. Strategy Spotlight 9.9 provides examples from Hong Kong of effective corporate governance as well as how a firm attempted a related transaction that would have benefited controlling shareholders at the expense of minority shareholders.

For firms to be successful, they must practice effective strategic control and corporate governance. Without such controls, the firm will not be able to achieve competitive advantages and outperform rivals in the marketplace.

Summary

We began the chapter with the key role of informational control. We contrasted two types of control systems: what we termed "traditional" and "contemporary" information control systems. Whereas traditional control systems may have their place in placid, simple competitive environments, there are fewer of those in today's economy. Instead, we advocated the contemporary approach wherein the internal and external environment are constantly monitored so that when surprises emerge, the firm can modify its strategies, goals, and objectives.

Behavioral controls are also a vital part of effective control systems. We argued that firms must develop the proper balance between culture, rewards and incentives, and boundaries and constraints. Where there are strong and positive cultures and rewards, employees tend to internalize the organization's strategies and objectives. This permits a firm to spend fewer resources on monitoring behavior, and assures the firm that the efforts and initiatives of employees are more consistent with the overall objectives of the organization.

In the final section of this chapter, we addressed corporate governance, which can be defined as the relationship between various participants in determining the direction and performance of the corporation. The primary participants include shareholders, management (led by the chief executive officer), and the board of directors. We reviewed studies that indicated a consistent relationship between effective corporate governance and financial performance. There are also several internal and external control mechanisms that can serve to align managerial interests and shareholder interests. The internal mechanisms include a committed and involved board of directors, shareholder activism, and effective managerial incentives and rewards. The external mechanisms include the market for corporate control, banks and analysts, regulators, the media, and public activists. We also addressed corporate governance from both a United States and an international perspective.

Summary Review Questions

1. Why are effective strategic control systems so important in today's economy?

2. What are the main advantages of "contemporary" control systems over "traditional" control systems? What are the main differences between these two systems?

3. Why is it important to have a balance between the three elements of behavioral control—culture, rewards and incentives, and boundaries?

4. Discuss the relationship between types of organizations and their primary means of behavioral control.

5. Boundaries become less important as a firm develops a strong culture and reward system. Explain.

6. Why is it important to avoid a "one best way" mentality concerning control systems? What are the consequences of applying the same type of control system to all types of environments?

7. What is the role of effective corporate governance in improving a firm's performance? What are some of the key governance mechanisms that are used to ensure that managerial and shareholder interests are aligned?

8. Define principal–principal (PP) conflicts. What are the implications for corporate governance?

Experiential Exercise

McDonald's Corporation, the world's largest fast-food restaurant chain, with revenues of $19 billion, has encountered declining shareholder value in the early 2000s. Using the Internet or library sources, evaluate the quality of the corporation in terms of management, the board of directors, and shareholder activism. Are the issues you list favorable or unfavorable for sound corporate governance?

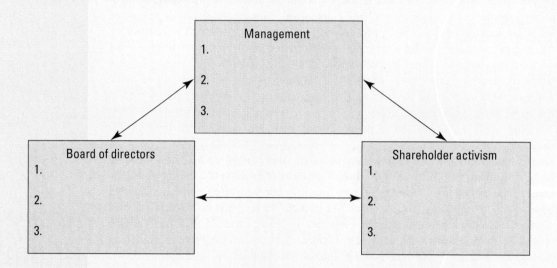

Application Questions Exercises

1. The problems of many firms may be attributed to a "traditional" control system that failed to continuously monitor the environment and make necessary changes in their strategy and objectives. What companies are you familiar with that responded appropriately (or inappropriately) to environmental change?

2. How can a strong, positive culture enhance a firm's competitive advantage? How can a weak, negative culture erode competitive advantages? Explain and provide examples.

3. Use the Internet to research a firm that has an excellent culture and/or reward and incentive system. What are this firm's main financial and nonfinancial benefits?

4. Using the Internet, go to the Web site of a large, publicly held corporation in which you are interested. What evidence do you see of effective (or ineffective) corporate governance?

Ethics Questions

1. Strong cultures can have powerful effects on employee behavior. How does this create inadvertent control mechanisms? That is, are strong cultures an ethical way to control behavior?

2. Rules and regulations can help reduce unethical behavior in organizations. To be effective, however, what other systems, mechanisms, and processes are necessary?

References

1. Limperis, J. 2004. Frame of mind. *The Manufacturer.com,* October 31; Cavanaugh, M. 2001. When the wheels start turning. *Business First,* March 9: B3; Nulty, P. 1995. Incentive plans can be crippling. *Fortune,* November 13: 235; and Lancaster, P. R. 1994. Incentive pay isn't good for your company. *Inc.,* September: 23–24.

2. This chapter draws upon Picken, J. C., & Dess, G. G. 1997. *Mission critical.* Burr Ridge, IL: Irwin Professional Publishing.

3. Argyris, C. 1977. Double-loop learning in organizations. *Harvard Business Review,* 55: 115–125.

4. Simons, R. 1995. Control in an age of empowerment. *Harvard Business Review,* 73: 80–88. This chapter draws on this source in the discussion of informational control.

5. Goold, M., & Quinn, J. B. 1990. The paradox of strategic controls. *Strategic Management Journal,* 11: 43–57.

6. Quinn, J. B. 1980. *Strategies for change.* Homewood, IL: Richard D. Irwin.

7. Mintzberg, H. 1987. Crafting strategy. *Harvard Business Review,* 65: 66–75.

8. Weston, J. S. 1992. Soft stuff matters. *Financial Executive,* July–August: 52–53.

9. This discussion of control systems draws upon Simons, op. cit.

10. For an interesting perspective on this issue and how a downturn in the economy can reduce the tendency toward "free agency" by managers and professionals, refer to Morris, B. 2001. White collar blues. *Fortune,* July 23: 98–110.

11. Ouchi, W. 1981. *Theory Z.* Reading, MA: Addison-Wesley; Deal, T. E., & Kennedy, A. A. 1982. *Corporate cultures.* Reading, MA: Addison-Wesley; Peters, T. J., & Waterman, R. H. 1982. *In search of excellence.* New York: Random House; Collins, J. 2001. *Good to great.* New York: HarperCollins.

12. Collins, J. C., & Porras, J. I. 1994. *Built to last: Successful habits of visionary companies.* New York: HarperBusiness.

13. Lee, J., & Miller, D. 1999. People matter: Commitment to employees, strategy, and performance in Korean firms. *Strategic Management Journal,* 6: 579–594.

14. For an insightful discussion of IKEA's unique culture, see Kling, K., & Goteman, I. 2003. IKEA CEO Anders Dahlvig on international growth and IKEA's unique corporate culture and brand identity. *Academy of Management Executive,* 17(1): 31–37.

15. For a discussion of how professionals inculcate values, refer to Uhl-Bien, M., & Graen, G. B. 1998. Individual self-management: Analysis of professionals' self-managing activities in functional and cross-functional work teams. *Academy of Management Journal,* 41(3): 340–350.

16. A perspective on how antisocial behavior can erode a firm's culture can be found in Robinson, S. L., & O'Leary-Kelly, A. M. 1998. Monkey see, monkey do: The influence of work groups on the antisocial behavior of employees. *Academy of Management Journal,* 41(6): 658–672.

17. Mitchell, R. 1989. Masters of innovation. *BusinessWeek,* April 10: 58–63.

18. Sellers, P. 1993. Companies that serve you best. *Fortune,* May 31: 88.

19. Southwest Airlines Culture Committee. 1993. *Luv Lines* (company publication), March–April: 17–18; for an interesting perspective on the "downside" of strong "cultlike" organizational cultures, refer to Arnott, D. A. 2000. *Corporate cults.* New York: AMACOM.

20. Kerr, J., & Slocum, J. W., Jr. 1987. Managing corporate culture through reward systems. *Academy of Management Executive,* 1(2): 99–107.

21. For a unique perspective on leader challenges in managing wealthy professionals, refer to Wetlaufer, S. 2000. Who wants to manage a millionaire? *Harvard Business Review,* 78(4): 53–60.

22. These next two subsections draw upon Dess, G. G., & Picken, J. C. 1997. *Beyond Productivity.* New York: AMACOM.

23. For a discussion of the benefits of stock options as executive compensation, refer to Hall, B. J. 2000. What you need to know about stock options. *Harvard Business Review,* 78(2): 121–129.

24. Tully, S. 1993. Your paycheck gets exciting. *Fortune,* November 13: 89.

25. For a recent discussion linking pay to performance, refer to Rappaport, A. 1999. New thinking on how to link pay to performance. *Harvard Business Review,* 77(2): 91–105.

26. Zellner, W., Hof, R. D., Brandt, R., Baker, S., & Greising, D. 1995. Go-go goliaths. *BusinessWeek,* February 13: 64–70.

27. This section draws on Dess & Picken, op. cit.: chap. 5.

28. Simons, op. cit.

29. Davis, E. 1997. Interview: Norman Augustine. *Management Review,* November: 11.

30. This section draws upon Dess, G. G., & Miller, A. 1993. *Strategic management.* New York: McGraw-Hill.

31. For a good review of the goal-setting literature, refer to Locke, E. A., & Latham, G. P. 1990. *A theory of goal setting and task performance.* Englewood Cliffs, NJ: Prentice Hall.

32. For an interesting perspective on the use of rules and regulations that is counter to this industry's (software) norms, refer to Fryer, B. 2001. Tom Siebel of Siebel Systems: High tech the old fashioned way. *Harvard Business Review,* 79(3): 118–130.

33. Thompson, A. A., Jr., & Strickland, A. J., III. 1998. *Strategic management: Concepts and cases* (10th ed.): 313. New York: McGraw-Hill.

34. Ibid.

35. Teitelbaum, R. 1997. Tough guys finish first. *Fortune,* July 21: 82–84.

36. Weaver, G. R., Trevino, L. K., & Cochran, P. L. 1999. Corporate ethics programs as control systems: Influences of executive commitment and environmental factors. *Academy of Management Journal*, 42(1): 41–57.

37. Cadbury, S. A. 1987. Ethical managers make their own rules. *Harvard Business Review*, 65: 3, 69–73.

38. Weber, J. 2003. CFOs on the hot seat. *BusinessWeek*, March 17: 66–70.

39. William Ouchi has written extensively about the use of clan control (which is viewed as an alternate to bureaucratic or market control). Here, a powerful culture results in people aligning their individual interests with those of the firm. Refer to Ouchi, op. cit. This section also draws on Hall, R. H. 2002. *Organizations: Structures, processes, and outcomes* (8th ed.). Upper Saddle River, NJ: Prentice Hall.

40. Monks, R., & Minow, N. 2001. *Corporate governance* (2nd ed.). Malden, MA: Blackwell.

41. Pound, J. 1995. The promise of the governed corporation. *Harvard Business Review*, 73(2): 89–98.

42. Heinzl, M. 2004. Nortel's directors and investors discuss changes to the board. *Wall Street Journal*, September 30: B4; Editorial. 2003. Pulling Boeing out of a tailspin. *BusinessWeek*, December 15: 136; and Zimmerman, A., Ball, D., & Veen, M. 2003. A global journal report: Supermarket giant Ahoud ousts CEO in big accounting scandal. *Wall Street Journal*, February 25: A1; Ibid.

43. This discussion draws upon Monks & Minow, op. cit.

44. Eisenhardt, K. M. 1989. Agency theory: An assessment and review. *Academy of Management Review*, 14(1): 57–74. Some of the seminal contributions to agency theory include Jensen, M., & Meckling, W. 1976. Theory of the firm: Managerial behavior, agency costs, and ownership structure. *Journal of Financial Economics*, 3: 305–360; Fama, E., & Jensen, M. 1983. Separation of ownership and control. *Journal of Law and Economics*, 26: 301, 325; and Fama, E. 1980. Agency problems and the theory of the firm. *Journal of Political Economy*, 88: 288–307.

45. Managers may also engage in "shirking"—that is, reducing or withholding their efforts. See, for example, Kidwell, R. E., Jr., & Bennett, N. 1993. Employee propensity to withhold effort: A conceptual model to intersect three avenues of research. *Academy of Management Review*, 18(3): 429–456.

46. For an interesting perspective on agency and clarification of many related concepts and terms, visit the following Web site: www.encycogov.com.

47. Argawal, A., & Mandelker, G. 1987. Managerial incentives and corporate investment and financing decisions. *Journal of Finance*, 42: 823–837.

48. For an insightful, recent discussion of the academic research on corporate governance, and in particular the role of boards of directors, refer to Chatterjee, S., & Harrison, J. S. 2001. Corporate governance. In Hitt, M. A., Freeman, R. E., & Harrison, J. S. (Eds.). *Handbook of strategic management*: 543–563. Malden, MA: Blackwell.

49. This opening discussion draws on Monks & Minow, op. cit. 164, 169; see also Pound, op. cit.

50. Business Roundtable. 1990. *Corporate governance and American competitiveness*, March: 7.

51. Byrne, J. A., Grover, R., & Melcher, R. A. 1997. The best and worst boards. *BusinessWeek*, November 26: 35–47. The three key roles of boards of directors are monitoring the actions of executives, providing advice, and providing links to the external environment to provide resources. See Johnson, J. L., Daily, C. M., & Ellstrand, A. E. 1996. Boards of directors: A review and research agenda. *Academy of Management Review*, 37: 409–438.

52. McGeehan, P. 2003. More chief executives shown the door, study says. *New York Times*, May 12: C2.

53. There are benefits, of course, to having some insiders on the board of directors. Inside directors would be more aware of the firm's strategies. Additionally, outsiders may rely too often on financial performance indicators because of information asymmetries. For an interesting discussion, see Baysinger, B. D., & Hoskisson, R. E. 1990. The composition of boards of directors and strategic control: Effects on corporate strategy. *Academy of Management Review*, 15: 72–87.

54. Hambrick, D. C., & Jackson, E. M. 2000. Outside directors with a stake: The linchpin in improving governance. *California Management Review*, 42(4): 108–127.

55. Ibid.

56. Disney has begun to make many changes to improve its corporate governance, such as assigning only independent directors to important board committees, restricting directors from serving on more than three boards, and appointing a lead director who can convene the board without approval by the CEO. In recent years, the Disney Co. has shown up on some "best" board lists. In addition Eisner has recently relinquished the chairman position.

57. Talk show. 2002. *BusinessWeek*, September 30: 14.

58. Ward, R. D. 2000. *Improving corporate boards*. New York: Wiley.

59. Monks and Minow, op. cit.: 93.

60. A discussion of the factors that lead to shareholder activism is found in Ryan, L. V., & Schneider, M. 2002. The antecedents of institutional investor activism. *Academy of Management Review*, 27(4): 554–573.

61. There is strong research support for the idea that the presence of large block shareholders is associated with value-maximizing decisions. For example, refer to Johnson, R. A., Hoskisson, R. E., & Hitt, M. A. 1993. Board of director involvement in restructuring: The effects of board versus managerial controls and characteristics. *Strategic Management Journal*, 14:33–50.

62. For an interesting perspective on the impact of institutional ownership on a firm's innovation strategies, see Hoskisson, R. E., Hitt, M. A., Johnson, R. A., & Grossman, W. 2002. *Academy of Management Journal*, 45(4): 697–716.

63. www.calpers.ca/gov/index.

64. Jensen, M. C., & Murphy, K. J. 1990. CEO incentives—It's not how much you pay, but how. *Harvard Business Review,* 68(3): 138–149.

65. For a perspective on the relative advantages and disadvantages of "duality"—that is, one individual serving as both Chief Executive Office and Chairman of the Board, see Lorsch, J. W., & Zelleke, A. 2005. Should the CEO be the chairman. *MIT Sloan Management Review,* 46(2): 71–74.

66. Research has found that executive compensation is more closely aligned with firm performance in companies with compensation committees and boards dominated by outside directors. See, for example, Conyon, M. J., & Peck, S. I. 1998. Board control, remuneration committees, and top management compensation. *Academy of Management Journal,* 41: 146–157.

67. Lavelle, L., Jespersen, F. F., & Arndt, M. 2002. Executive pay. *BusinessWeek,* April 15: 66–72.

68. Ibid.

69. www.tiaa-cref.org/pubs.

70. Such opportunistic behavior is common in all principal-agent relationships. For a description of agency problems, especially in the context of the relationship between shareholders and managers, see Jensen, M. C., & Meckling, W. H. 1976. Theory of the firm: Managerial behavior, agency costs, and ownership structure. *Journal of Financial Economics,* 3: 305–360.

71. Hoskisson, R. E., & Turk, T. A. 1990. Corporate restructuring: Governance and control limits of the internal market. *Academy of Management Review,* 15: 459–477.

72. For an insightful perspective on the market for corporate control and how it is influenced by knowledge intensity, see Coff, R. 2003. Bidding wars over R&D-intensive firms: Knowledge, opportunism, and the market for corporate control. *Academy of Management Journal,* 46(1): 74–85.

73. Walsh, J. P., & Kosnik, R. D. 1993. Corporate raiders and their disciplinary role in the market for corporate control. *Academy of Management Journal,* 36: 671–700.

74. Gunning for KPMG. 2003. *Economist,* February 1: 63.

75. Timmons, H. 2003. Investment banks: Who will foot their bill? *BusinessWeek,* March 3: 116.

76. Wishy-washy: The SEC pulls its punches on corporate-governance rules. 2003. *Economist,* February 1: 60.

77. McLean, B. 2001. Is Enron overpriced? *Fortune,* March 5: 122–125.

78. This section draws upon Young, M. N., Peng, M. W., Ahlstrom, D., Bruton, G. D., Jiang, Y. 2005. Principal-principal conflicts in corporate governance (unpublished manuscript); and, Peng, M. W. 2006. *Global strategy.* Cincinnati: Thomson South-Western. We are very appreciative of the helpful comments of Mike Young of the Chinese University of Hong Kong and Mike Peng of the Ohio State University.

79. Khanna, T., & Rivkin, J. 2001. Estimating the performance effects of business groups in emerging markets. *Strategic Management Journal,* 22: 45–74.

10

Creating Effective Organizational Designs

>chapter objectives

After reading this chapter, you should have a good understanding of:

- The importance of organizational structure and the concept of the "boundaryless" organization in implementing strategies.

- The growth patterns of major corporations and the relationship between a firm's strategy and its structure.

- Each of the traditional types of organizational structure: simple, functional, divisional, and matrix.

- The relative advantages and disadvantages of traditional organizational structures.

- The implications of a firm's international operations for organizational structure.

- Why there is no "one best way" to design strategic reward and evaluation systems, and the important contingent roles of business- and corporate-level strategies.

- The different types of boundaryless organizations—barrier-free, modular, and virtual—and their relative advantages and disadvantages.

- The need for creating ambidextrous organizational designs that enable firms to explore new opportunities and effectively integrate existing operations.

*t*o implement strategies successfully, firms must have appropriate organizational structures. These include the processes and integrating mechanisms necessary to ensure that boundaries among internal activities and external parties, such as suppliers, customers, and alliance partners, are flexible and permeable. A firm's performance will suffer if its managers don't carefully consider both of these organizational design attributes.

In the first section, we begin by discussing the growth patterns of large corporations to address the important relationships between the strategy that a firm follows and its corresponding structure. For example, as firms diversify into related product-market areas, they change their structure from functional to divisional. We then address the different types of traditional structures—simple, functional, divisional, and matrix—and their relative advantages and disadvantages. We close with a discussion of the implications of a firm's international operations for the structure of its organization. The primary factors that are taken into account are (1) the type of international strategy (e.g., global or multidomestic), (2) the level of product diversity, and (3) the extent to which a firm depends on foreign sales.

The second section takes the perspective that there is no "one best way" to design an organization's strategic reward and evaluation system. Here we address two important contingencies: business- and corporate-level strategy. For example, when strategies require a great deal of collaboration, as well as resource and information sharing, there must be incentives and cultures that encourage and reward such initiatives.

The third section discusses the concept of the "boundaryless" organization. We do *not* argue that organizations should have no internal and external boundaries. Instead, we suggest that in rapidly changing and unpredictable environments, organizations must strive to make their internal and external boundaries both flexible and permeable. We suggest three different types of boundaryless organizations: barrier-free, modular, and virtual. Whereas the barrier-free type focuses on creating flexible and permeable internal and external boundaries, the modular type addresses the strategic role of outsourcing, and the virtual type centers on the viability of strategic alliances and network organizations in today's global economy.

The fourth section focuses on the need for managers to recognize that they typically face two opposing challenges: (1) being proactive in taking advantage of new opportunities and (2) ensuring the effective coordination and integration of existing operations. This suggests the need for ambidextrous organizations, that is, firms that can both be efficient in how they manage existing assets and competencies and take advantage of opportunities in rapidly changing and unpredictable environments—conditions that are becoming more pronounced in today's global markets.

The National Health Service (NHS) was created in July 1948 to provide health care for all British citizens, based on need, not on the ability to pay.[1] The NHS, whose 2005 budget was 63 billion British pounds (about $110 billion), was originally split into three parts:

- Hospital services
- Family doctors, dentists, opticians, and pharmacists
- Local authority health services, including community nursing

As you would imagine, since 1948, there have been huge increases in the overall budget as well as major changes to both the organizational structure and the way that patient services are provided. And, in 2001, the NHS Modernization Agency was established to bring together individuals and teams from the NHS with reputations for modernizing services and developing leadership within the NHS. A few of the eight teams that make up the agency are the Leadership Center, the Redesign, and the New Ways of Working Team. However, as we note below, even with the Modernization Agency, the NHS does not seem to be a paragon of efficiency.

> One of the examples of waste was played out in a hospital where catering staff provided dozens of meals a day for nonexistent patients in wards that had been closed to save money. Management confirmed that this occurred and that it went on for days. The explanation was that there had been a breakdown in communications between staff. One of the NHS hospitals explained that the extra meals were cooked because of a failure to notify the catering staff of the unit closures. "We advise our wards to give as much notice to the catering departments as possible," a spokeswoman said. "As is often the case, it's a matter of improving communication and reminding staff of procedures and letting other people know what's happening." However, the hospital was also wasting money by routinely sending patient referral letters for surgeries to doctors by first-class mail, even though an internal delivery system had been set up specifically to deal with such correspondence.
>
> The details of such waste had been disclosed by David James, a doctor who is leading the Conservative Party's investigation of public sector waste. He contends that it may be typical of "a whole culture of management which is deficient" and which, across the entire NHS, will see millions of pounds of taxpayers' money, in effect, thrown away.
>
> In 2001, an investigation revealed that the NHS was wasting more than 18 million British pounds (about $30 million) every year in its catering operations. The study attributed the waste to bad practice and poor standards. The whistle-blower who contacted Dr. James felt that little had been done to correct things since that inquiry was conducted.
>
> The meals were repeatedly delivered when it was clear they were not being eaten. Perhaps, this is evidence of staff having learned to follow procedures rather than to think for themselves. Or could it be an indication of a culture of sticking to the job description and not worrying about costs that may be incurred in the process?

One of the central concepts in this chapter is the importance of boundaryless organizations. That is, successful organizations create permeable boundaries among the internal activities as well as between the organization and its external customers, suppliers, and alliance partners. We introduced this idea in Chapter 3 in our discussion of the value-chain concept, which consisted of several primary (e.g., inbound logistics, marketing and sales) and support activities (e.g., procurement, human resource management). Clearly, the underlying cause of NHS's problem was its inability to establish close and effective working relationships between its internal departments.

The most important implication of this chapter is that today's managers are faced with two ongoing and vital activities in structuring and designing their organizations. First, they must decide on the most appropriate type of organizational structure. Second, they need to assess what mechanisms, processes, and techniques are most helpful in enhancing the permeability of the internal and external boundaries of their organization.

>>Traditional Forms of Organizational Structure

Organizational structure refers to the formalized patterns of interactions that link the tasks, technologies, and people of a firm.[2] Structures are designed to ensure that resources are used most effectively toward accomplishing an organization's mission. Structure provides managers with a means of balancing two conflicting forces: a need for the division of tasks into meaningful groupings and the need to integrate such groupings in order to ensure organizational efficiency and effectiveness. Structure identifies the executive, managerial, and administrative organization of a firm and indicates responsibilities and hierarchical relationships. It also influences the flow of information as well as the context and nature of human interactions.

Most organizations begin very small and either die or remain small. Those few that survive and prosper embark on strategies designed to increase the overall scope of operations and enable them to enter new product-market domains. Such growth places additional pressure on executives to control and coordinate the firm's increasing size and diversity. The most appropriate type of structure depends on the nature and magnitude of growth in a firm. In this section, we address various types of structural forms, their advantages and disadvantages, and their relationships to the strategies that organizations undertake.

Patterns of Growth of Large Corporations

A firm's strategy and structure change as it increases in size, diversifies into new product markets, and expands its geographic scope.[3] Exhibit 10.1 illustrates some of the common growth patterns that firms may follow.

A new firm with a *simple structure* typically increases its sales revenue and volume of outputs over time. It may also engage in some vertical integration to secure sources of supply (backward integration) as well as channels of distribution (forward integration). After a time, the simple-structure firm implements a *functional structure* to concentrate efforts on both increasing efficiency and enhancing its operations and products. This structure enables the firm to group its operations into either functions, departments, or geographic areas. As its initial markets mature, a firm looks beyond its present products and markets for possible expansion. Such a strategy of related diversification requires a need to reorganize around product lines or geographic markets. This leads to a *divisional structure*. As the business expands in terms of sales revenues, and domestic growth opportunities become somewhat limited, a firm may seek opportunities in international markets. At this time, a firm has a wide variety of structures to choose from. These include *international division, geographic area, worldwide product division, worldwide functional,* and *worldwide matrix.* As we will see later in this section, deciding upon the most appropriate structure when a firm has international operations depends on three primary factors: the extent of international expansion, type of strategy (global, multidomestic, or transnational), and the degree of product diversity.[4]

There are some other common growth patterns. For example, some firms may find it advantageous to diversify into several product lines rather than focus their efforts on strengthening distributor and supplier relationships through vertical integration. Thus, they would organize themselves according to product lines by implementing a divisional structure. Also, some firms may choose to move into unrelated product areas, typically by acquiring existing businesses. Frequently, their rationale is that acquiring assets and competencies is more economical or expedient than developing them internally. Such an unrelated, or conglomerate, strategy requires relatively little integration across businesses

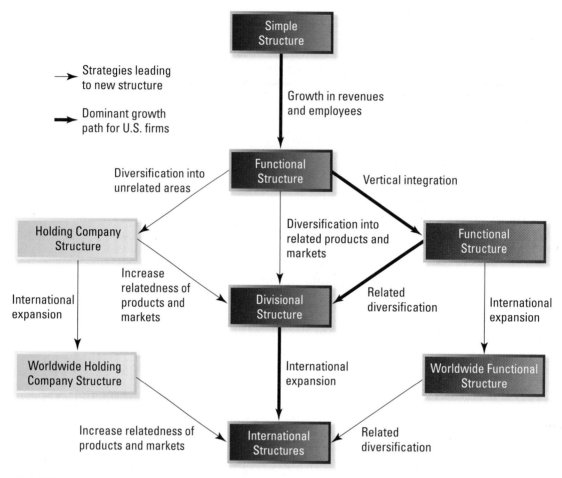

Exhibit 10.1   **Dominant Growth Patterns of Large Corporations**

Source: From *Strategy Implementation: The Role of Structure and Process,* 2nd edition by J. R. Galbraith and R. K. Kazanjian. Copyright © 1986. Reprinted with permission of South-Western, a division of Thomson Learning: www.thomsonrights.com. Fax: 800-730-2215.

and sharing of resources. Thus, a *holding company structure* becomes appropriate. As we would expect, there are many other growth patterns, but these are the most common.*

Now we will discuss some of the most common types of organizational structures—simple, functional, divisional (including two variants: *strategic business unit* and *holding company*), and matrix and their advantages and disadvantages. We will close the section with a discussion of the structural implications when a firm expands its operations into international markets.

---

* The lowering of transaction costs and globalization have led to some changes in the common historical patterns that we have discussed. Some firms are, in effect, bypassing the vertical integration stage. Instead, they focus on core competencies and outsource other value-creation activities. Also, even relatively young firms are going global early in their history because of lower communication and transportation costs. For an interesting perspective on global start-ups, see McDougall, P. P., & Oviatt, B. M. 1996. New venture internationalization, strategic change and performance: A follow-up study. *Journal of Business Venturing,* 11: 23–40; and McDougall, P. P., & Oviatt, B. M. (Eds.). 2000. The special research forum on international entrepreneurship. *Academy of Management Journal,* October: 902–1003.

Simple Structure

As we might expect, the simple structure is the oldest, and most common, organizational form. After all, most organizations are very small and have a single or very narrow product line in which the owner-manager (or top executive) makes almost all of the decisions. In effect, the owner-manager controls all activities, and the staff serves as an extension of the top executive's personality.

The simple structure is highly informal and the coordination of tasks is accomplished by direct supervision. Decision making is highly centralized, there is little specialization of tasks, few rules and regulations, and an informal evaluation and reward system. Although the owner-manager is intimately involved in almost all phases of the business, a manager is often employed to oversee day-to-day operations.

A small firm with a simple structure may often foster creativity and individualism since there are generally few rules and regulations. However, such "informality" may lead to problems. Employees may not clearly understand their responsibilities, which can lead to conflict and confusion. Employees also may take advantage of the lack of regulations and act in their own self-interest. Such actions can erode motivation and satisfaction as well as lead to the possible misuse of organizational resources. Further, small organizations have flat structures (i.e., few vertical, hierarchical levels) that limit opportunities for upward mobility. Without the potential for future advancement, recruiting and retaining talent may become very difficult.

Functional Structure

When an organization is small (15 employees or less), it is not necessary to have a variety of formal arrangements and groupings of activities. However, as firms grow, excessive demands may be placed on the owner-manager in order to obtain and process all of the information necessary to run the business. Chances are the owner will not be skilled in all specialties (e.g., accounting, engineering, production, marketing) at a level necessary to run a growing business. Thus, he or she will need to hire specialists in the various functional areas. Such growth in the overall scope and complexity of the business necessitates a functional structure wherein the major functions of the firm are grouped internally and led by a specialist. The coordination and integration of the functional areas becomes one of the most important responsibilities of the chief executive of the firm. Exhibit 10.2 presents a diagram of a functional structure.

Functional structures are generally found in organizations in which there is a single or closely related product or service, high production volume, and some vertical integration. Initially, firms tend to expand the overall scope of their operations by penetrating existing markets, introducing similar products in additional markets, or increasing

Exhibit 10.2   **Functional Organizational Structure**

STRATEGY SPOTLIGHT

Two Examples of Successful Functional Organization Structures

Sharp Corporation is a top performer in the consumer electronics industry, with $21 billion in annual sales. The firm is organized into functional units, allowing coordination of tasks involving research and development, production, marketing, and management. Key components such as LCDs (liquid crystal displays) are developed and produced in single functional units using the talents of these specialties. By using a centralized, functional structure, Sharp is able to achieve economies of scale with its applied research and manufacturing skills. It would be much more expensive if such skills and resources were distributed over many different, relatively autonomous business units. To make sure that these units are not completely sealed off from the other business units in the firm, product managers have the responsibility of coordinating similar products in multiple functional areas throughout the organization.

Sources: Stewart, C. 2003. The perfect yarn. *The Manufacturer.com*, July 31; www.parkdalemills.com; Berman, P. 1987. The fast track isn't always the best track. *Forbes*, November 2: 60–64; personal communication with Duke Kimbrell, March 11, 2005; and Collins, D. J., & Montgomery, C. A. 1998. Creating corporate advantage. *Harvard Business Review*, 76(3): 70–83.

For more than 80 years, Parkdale Mills, with approximately $1 billion in revenues, has been the industry leader in the production of cotton and cotton blend yarns. Their expertise comes by concentrating on a single product line, perfecting processes, and welcoming innovation. According to CEO Andy Warlick, "I think we've probably spent more than any two competitors combined on new equipment and robotics. We do this because we have to compete in a global market where a lot of the competition has a lower wage structure and gets subsidies that we don't receive, so we really have to focus on consistency and cost control." Yarn making is generally considered to be a commodity business, and Parkdale is the industry's low-cost producer.

Tasks are highly standardized and authority is centralized with Duke Kimbrell, founder and chairman, and CEO Andy Warlick. The firm operates a bare-bones staff with a small staff of top executives. Kimbrell and Warlick are considered shrewd about the cotton market, technology, customer loyalty, and incentive pay.

the level of vertical integration. Such expansion activities clearly increase the scope and complexity of the operations. Fortunately, the functional structure provides for a high level of centralization that helps to ensure integration and control over the related product-market activities or multiple primary activities (from inbound logistics to operations to marketing, sales, and service) in the value chain (addressed in Chapters 3 and 4).

Strategy Spotlight 10.1 provides two examples of effective functional organization structures—Sharp Corporation and Parkdale Mills.

As with any type of organizational structure, there are some relative advantages and disadvantages associated with the functional structure. By bringing together specialists into functional departments, a firm is able to enhance its coordination and control within each of the functional areas. The structure also ensures that decision making in the firm will be centralized at the top of the organization. This enhances the organizational-level (as opposed to functional area) perspective across the various functions in the organization. In addition, the functional structure provides for a more efficient use of managerial and technical talent since functional area expertise is pooled in a single department (e.g., marketing) instead of being spread across a variety of product-market areas. Finally, career paths and professional development in specialized areas are facilitated.

There also are some significant disadvantages associated with the functional structure. First, the differences in values and orientations among functional areas may impede communication and coordination. Edgar Schein of MIT has argued that shared assumptions, often based on similar backgrounds and experiences of members, form around functional units in an organization. This leads to what are often called "stove pipes" or "silos," in which departments view themselves as isolated, self-contained units with little need for interaction and coordination with other departments. This erodes communication because functional groups may have not only different goals but also differing meanings of words and concepts. According to Schein:

> The word "marketing" will mean product development to the engineer, studying customers through market research to the product manager, merchandising to the salesperson, and constant change in design to the manufacturing manager. When they try to work together, they will often attribute disagreements to personalities and fail to notice the deeper, shared assumptions that color how each function thinks.[5]

Such narrow functional orientations also may lead to short-term thinking based largely upon what is best for the functional area, not the organization as a whole. For example, in a manufacturing firm, sales may want to offer a wide range of customized products to appeal to the firm's customers; research and development may overdesign products and components to achieve technical elegance; and manufacturing may favor no-frills products that can be produced at low cost by means of long production runs. In addition, functional structures may overburden the top executives in the firm because conflicts have a tendency to be "pushed up" to the top of the organization since there are no managers who are responsible for the specific product lines. Finally, functional structures make it difficult to establish uniform performance standards across the whole organization. Whereas it may be relatively easy to evaluate production managers on the basis of production volume and cost control, establishing performance measures for engineering, research and development, and accounting become more problematic.

Divisional Structure

The divisional structure (sometimes called the multidivisional structure or M-Form) is organized around products, projects, or markets. Each of the divisions, in turn, includes its own functional specialists who are typically organized into departments. A divisional structure encompasses a set of relatively autonomous units governed by a central corporate office. The operating divisions are relatively independent and consist of products and services that are different from those of the other divisions. Operational decision making in a large business places excessive demands on the firm's top management. In order to attend to broader, longer-term organizational issues, top-level managers must delegate decision making to lower-level managers. Thus, divisional executives play a key role. In conjunction with corporate-level executives, they help to determine the product-market and financial objectives for the division as well as their division's contribution to overall corporate performance.[6] The rewards are based largely on measures of financial performance such as net income and revenue. Exhibit 10.3 illustrates a divisional structure.

General Motors was among the earliest firms to adopt the divisional organizational structure.[7] In the 1920s the company formed five major product divisions (Cadillac, Buick, Oldsmobile, Pontiac, and Chevrolet) as well as several industrial divisions. Since then, many firms have discovered that as they diversified into new product-market activities, functional structures—with their emphasis on single functional departments—were unable to manage the increased complexity of the entire business.

There are many advantages associated with the divisional structure. By creating separate divisions to manage individual product markets, there is a separation of strategic and operating control. That is, divisional managers can focus their efforts on improving operations in the product markets for which they are responsible, and corporate officers can devote their time to overall strategic issues for the entire corporation. The focus on a division's products and markets—by the divisional executives—provides the corporation with an enhanced ability to respond quickly to important changes in the external

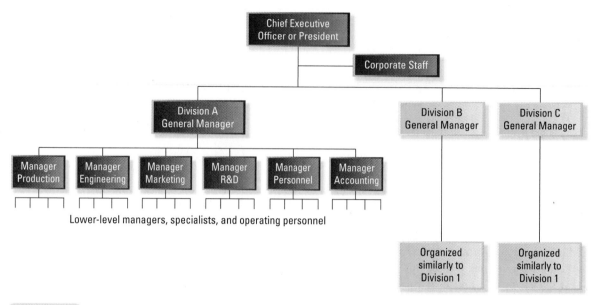

Exhibit 10.3   Divisional Organizational Structure

environment. Since there are functional departments within each division of the corporation, the problems associated with sharing resources across functional departments are minimized. Finally, because there are multiple levels of general managers (that is, executives responsible for integrating and coordinating all functional areas), the development of general management talent is enhanced. Strategy Spotlight 10.2 discusses the rationale behind Brinker Corporation's change in structure from functional to divisional.

As you would expect, a divisional structure also has potential disadvantages. First, it can be very expensive; that is, there can be increased costs due to the duplication of personnel, operations, and investment since each division must staff multiple functional departments. There also can be dysfunctional competition among divisions since each division tends to become concerned solely about its own operations. Furthermore, divisional managers are often evaluated on common measures such as return on assets and sales growth. Thus, if goals are conflicting, there can be a sense of a "zero-sum" game that would discourage sharing ideas and resources among the divisions for the common good of the corporation. As noted by Ghoshal and Bartlett, two leading scholars in strategic management:

> As their label clearly warns, divisions divide. The divisional model fragmented companies' resources; it created vertical communication channels that insulated business units and prevented them from sharing their strengths with one another. Consequently, the whole of the corporation was often less than the sum of its parts.[8]

Another potential disadvantage is that with many divisions providing different products and services, there is the chance that differences in image and quality may occur across divisions. For example, one division may offer no-frills products of lower quality that may erode the brand reputation of another division that has top quality, highly differentiated offerings. Finally, since each division is evaluated in terms of financial measures such as return on investment and revenue growth, there is often an urge to focus on short-term performance. For example, if corporate management uses quarterly profits as

Brinker International's Change in Organizational Structure

Although Brinker International had a traditional functional structure, changes in its competitive outlook forced management to take a closer look at the organizational design of the firm. The firm controls a variety of restaurant chains and bakeries, including Wildfire, Big Bowl, and Chili's.

With all these interests under one corporate roof, management of these disparate entities became difficult. The fragmented $330 billion restaurant and bakery industry caters to highly focused market niches. The original functional design of the Brinker chain had some disadvan-

tages as the company grew. With areas separated by function, it became hard to focus efforts on a single restaurant chain. The diverse markets served by the bakeries and restaurants began to lose their focus.

As a result, Brinker International changed to a divisional structure. This allowed the company to consolidate individuals who worked with a single restaurant or bakery chain into a separate division. Brinker referred to these as concept teams, with each concept team responsible for the operation of a single line of business. This focused effort streamlined the company's ability to concentrate on the market niche served by each of its restaurants and bakeries.

Source: CEO interview: Ronald A. McDougall, Brinker International. 1999. *Wall Street Transcript*, January 20: 1–4.

---

the key performance indicator, divisional management may tend to put significant emphasis on "making the numbers" and minimizing activities, such as advertising, maintenance, and capital investments, which would detract from short-term performance measures.

Before moving on, we'll discuss two variations of the divisional form of organizational structure: the strategic business unit (SBU) and holding company structures.

Strategic Business Unit (SBU) Structure Corporations that are highly diversified such as ConAgra, a $15 billion food producer, may consist of dozens of different divisions.[9] If ConAgra were to use a purely divisional structure, it would be nearly impossible for the corporate office to plan and coordinate activities because the span of control would be too large. Instead, to attain synergies, ConAgra has put its diverse businesses into three primary SBUs: food service (restaurants), retail (grocery stores), and agricultural products.

With an SBU structure, divisions with similar products, markets, and/or technologies are grouped into homogenous groups in order to achieve some synergies. These include those discussed in Chapter 6 for related diversification, such as leveraging core competencies, sharing infrastructures, and market power. Generally speaking, the more related businesses are within a corporation, the fewer SBUs will be required. Each of the SBUs in the corporation operates as a profit center.

The major advantage of the SBU structure is that it makes the task of planning and control by the corporate office more manageable. Also, since the structure provides greater decentralization of authority, individual businesses can react more quickly to important changes in the environment than if all divisions had to report directly to the corporate office.

There are also some disadvantages to the SBU structure. Since the divisions are grouped into SBUs, it may become difficult to achieve synergies across SBUs. That is, if divisions that are included in different SBUs have potential sources of synergy, it may become difficult for them to be realized. The additional level of management increases the number of personnel and overhead expenses, while the additional hierarchical level removes the corporate office further from the individual divisions. Thus, the corporate office may become unaware of key developments that could have a major impact on the corporation.

Holding Company Structure   The holding company structure (sometimes referred to as a *conglomerate*) is also a variation of the divisional structure. Whereas the SBU structure is often used when similarities exist between the individual businesses (or divisions), the holding company structure is appropriate when the businesses in a corporation's portfolio do not have much in common. Thus, the potential for synergies is limited.

Holding company structures are most appropriate for firms that follow a strategy of unrelated diversification. Companies such as Hanson Trust, ITT, and the CP group of Thailand have relied on the holding company structure to implement their unrelated diversification strategies. Since there are few similarities across the businesses, the corporate offices in these companies provide a great deal of autonomy to operating divisions and rely on financial controls and incentive programs to obtain high levels of performance from the individual businesses. As you would expect, corporate staffs at these firms tend to be small because their involvement in the overall operation of their various businesses is limited.[10]

An important advantage of the holding company structure is the cost savings associated with fewer personnel and the lower overhead resulting from a small corporate office and fewer levels in the corporate hierarchy. In addition, the autonomy of the holding company structure increases the motivational level of divisional executives and enables them to respond quickly to market opportunities and threats.

The primary disadvantage of the holding company structure is the inherent lack of control and dependence that corporate-level executives have on divisional executives. Major problems could arise if key divisional executives leave the firm, because the corporate office has very little "bench strength"—that is, additional managerial talent ready to fill key positions on short notice. And, if problems arise in a division, it may become very difficult to turn around individual businesses because of limited staff support in the corporate office.

Matrix Structure

At times, managers may find that none of the structures that we have described above fully meet their needs. One approach that tries to overcome the inadequacies inherent in the other structures is the matrix structure. It is, in effect, a combination of the functional and divisional structures. Most commonly, functional departments are combined with product groups on a project basis. For example, a product group may want to develop a new addition to its line; for this project, it obtains personnel from functional departments such as marketing, production, and engineering. These personnel work under the manager of the product group for the duration of the project, which can vary from a few weeks to an open-ended period of time. The individuals who work in a matrix organization become responsible to two managers: the project manager and the manager of their functional area. Exhibit 10.4 illustrates a matrix structure.

In addition to the product-function matrix, other bases may be related in a matrix. Some large multinational corporations rely on a matrix structure to combine product groups and geographical units. Product managers have global responsibility for the development, manufacturing, and distribution of their own line, while managers of geographical regions have responsibility for the profitability of the businesses in their regions. In the mid-1990s, Caterpillar, Inc., implemented this type of structure.

Michael Eisner, CEO of Disney, relies on the matrix concept—with its dual-reporting responsibility—to enhance synergy. Consider the perspective that he shared in an interview.[11]

> We're also trying to increase the amount of synergy in our global operations country by country. We've just reorganized our international organization into a hybrid type of structure, so the person running movies in Italy, for instance, not only reports to an executive in the movie

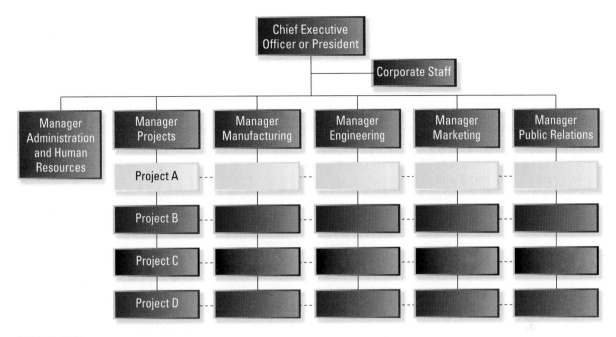

Exhibit 10.4   **Matrix Organizational Structure**

division, as he or she did before, but also reports to a country head. That country head is responsible for synergy. Hopefully, this will duplicate what we do in Burbank [Disney's head-quarters] every week.

A primary advantage of the matrix structure is that it facilitates the use of special-ized personnel, equipment, and facilities. Rather than duplicating functions, as would be the case in a divisional structure based on products, the resources are shared as needed. Individuals with high expertise can divide their time among multiple projects at one time. Such resource sharing and collaboration enable a firm to use resources more efficiently and to respond more quickly and effectively to changes in the competitive environment. In addition, the flexibility inherent in a matrix structure provides professionals with a broader range of responsibility. Such experience enables them to develop their skills and competencies.

There are also many potential disadvantages associated with matrix structures. The dual-reporting structures can result in uncertainty and lead to intense power struggles and conflict over the allocation of professional personnel and other resources. Additional-ly, working relationships become more complicated. This may result in excessive reliance on group processes and teamwork, along with a diffusion of responsibility, which in turn may erode timely decision making. Exhibit 10.5 briefly summarizes the advantages and disadvantages of the functional, divisional, and matrix organizational structures.

International Operations: Implications for Organizational Structure

Today's managers must maintain an international outlook on their firm's businesses and competitive strategies. To be successful in the global marketplace, managers must ensure consistency between their strategies (at the business, corporate, and international levels)

Functional Structure

Advantages	Disadvantages
• Pooling of specialists enhances coordination and control.	• Differences in functional area orientation impede communication and coordination.
• Centralized decision making enhances an organizational perspective across functions.	• Tendency for specialists to develop short-term perspective and narrow functional orientation.
• Efficient use of managerial and technical talent.	• Functional area conflicts may overburden top-level decision makers.
• Facilitates career paths and professional development in specialized areas.	• Difficult to establish uniform performance standards.

Divisional Structure

Advantages	Disadvantages
• Increases strategic and operational control, permitting corporate-level executives to address strategic issues.	• Increased costs incurred through duplication of personnel, operations, and investment.
• Quick response to environmental changes.	• Dysfunctional competition among divisions may detract from overall corporate performance.
• Increases focus on products and markets.	• Difficult to maintain uniform corporate image.
• Minimizes problems associated with sharing resources across functional areas.	• Overemphasis on short-term performance.
• Facilitates development of general managers.	

Matrix Structure

Advantages	Disadvantages
• Increases market responsiveness through collaboration and synergies among professional colleagues.	• Dual-reporting relationships can result in uncertainty regarding accountability.
• Allows more efficient utilization of resources.	• Intense power struggles may lead to increased levels of conflict.
• Improves flexibility, coordination, and communication.	• Working relationships may be more complicated and human resources duplicated.
• Increases professional development through a broader range of responsibility.	• Excessive reliance on group processes and teamwork may impede timely decision making.

Exhibit 10.5

Functional, Divisional, and Matrix Organizational Structures: Advantages and Disadvantages

and the structure of their organization. As firms expand into foreign markets, they generally follow a pattern of change in structure that parallels the changes in their strategies. Three major contingencies that seem to influence the structure adopted by firms with international operations are (1) the type of strategy that is driving a firm's foreign operations, (2) product diversity, and (3) the extent to which a firm is dependent on foreign sales.[12]

As international operations become an important part of a firm's overall operations, managers must make changes that are consistent with their firm's structure. The primary types of structures used to manage a firm's international operations are:[13]

- International division
- Geographic-area division
- Worldwide functional
- Worldwide product division
- Worldwide matrix

As we discussed in Chapter 7, multidomestic strategies are driven by political and cultural imperatives that require managers within each country to respond to local conditions. The structures that would be consistent with such a strategic orientation are the *international division* and *geographic-area division* structures. Here local managers are provided with a high level of autonomy to manage their operations within the constraints and demands of their geographic market. As a firm's foreign sales increase as a percentage of its total sales, it will likely change from an international division structure to a geographic-area division structure. And, as a firm's product and/or market diversity becomes large, it is more likely to benefit from a *worldwide matrix structure.*

Global strategies, on the other hand, are driven by economic pressures that require managers to view operations in different geographic areas as only a component of an overall operation that must be managed for overall efficiency. The structures consistent with the efficiency perspective are the *worldwide functional* and *worldwide product division* structures. Here, division managers view the marketplace as homogeneous and devote relatively little attention to local market, political, and economic factors. The choice between these two types of structures is guided largely by the extent of product diversity. Firms with relatively low levels of product diversity may opt for a worldwide product division structure. However, when a firm has significant product-market diversity resulting from a series of highly unrelated international acquisitions, a worldwide holding company structure is likely to be implemented. Such firms are characterized by very little commonality among products, markets, or technologies, and have little need for integration.

Global Start-Ups: A New Phenomenon

Our discussion of dominant patterns of growth earlier in the section suggested that international expansion occurs rather late in the history of most corporations, typically after possibilities of domestic growth are exhausted. Increasingly, we are seeing two interrelated phenomena. First, many firms now decide to expand internationally relatively early in their history. Second, some firms are "born global"—that is, from the very beginning, many start-ups are global in their activities. For example, Logitech Inc., the leading producer of the "mouse" that helps you use the personal computer, was global in its operations from day one. Founded in 1982 by a Swiss national and two Italians, the company was headquartered both in California and Switzerland. R&D and manufacturing were also conducted in both locations and, subsequently, in Taiwan and Ireland as well.[14]

The success of companies such as Logitech challenges the conventional wisdom that a company must first build up assets, internal processes, and experience before venturing into faraway lands. It also raises a number of questions: What exactly is a global start-up? Under what conditions should a company start out as a global start-up? What does it take to succeed as a global start-up?

A global start-up has been defined as a business organization that, from inception, seeks to derive significant competitive advantage from the use of resources and the sale of outputs in multiple countries. That is, right from the beginning, it uses inputs from around the world and sells its products and services to customers around the world. Geographical boundaries of nation-states are, by and large, irrelevant for a global start-up.

There is no reason for every start-up to be global. Being global necessarily involves higher communication, coordination, and transportation costs. Therefore, it is important to identify the circumstances under which going global from the beginning is advantageous.[15] First, if the required human resources are globally dispersed, going global may be the best way to access those resources. For example, Italians are masters in fine leather and Europeans in ergonomics. Second, in many cases foreign financing may be easier to obtain and more suitable for the project. Traditionally, U.S. venture capitalists have shown greater willingness to bear risk, but have shorter time horizons in their expectations for return. If a U.S. start-up is looking for patient capital, it may be better off looking overseas. Third, the target customers in many specialized industries are located in other parts of the world. Fourth, in many industries a gradual move from domestic markets to foreign markets is no longer possible because, if a product is successful, foreign competitors may immediately imitate it. Therefore, preemptive entry into foreign markets may be the only option. Finally, because of high up-front development costs, a global market is necessary to recover the costs in many industries. This is particularly true for start-ups from smaller nations that do not have access to large domestic markets.

Successful management of a global start-up presents many challenges. As already mentioned, communication and coordination across time zones and cultures are always problematic. Given that most global start-ups have far less resources than well-established corporations, one key for success is to internalize a minimal proportion of activities and outsource the rest. It is absolutely important that managers of such firms have considerable prior international experience so that they can successfully handle the communication problems and cultural conflicts that are inevitable. Another key for success is to keep the communication and coordination costs low. The only way to achieve this is by creating less costly administrative mechanisms. The boundaryless organizational designs that we discuss in the next section are particularly suitable for global start-ups because of their flexibility and low cost.

Strategy Spotlight 10.3 discusses two global start-ups that are based in Israel.

How an Organization's Structure Can Influence Strategy Formulation

Generally speaking, discussions of the relationship between strategy and structure strongly imply that structure follows strategy. That is, the strategy that a firm chooses (e.g., related diversification) dictates such structural elements as the division of tasks, the appropriate patterns of information flow, the need for integration of activities, and authority relationships within the organization. However, we must also recognize the role that an existing structure can play in strategy formulation. For example, once a firm's structure is in place, it is very difficult and expensive to change.[16] Executives may not be able to modify their duties and responsibilities greatly, or may not welcome the disruption associated with a transfer to a new location. Further, there may be costs associated with hiring, training, and replacing executive, managerial, and operating personnel. Thus, strategy cannot be formulated without considering structural elements.

The type of organizational structure can also strongly influence a firm's strategy, day-to-day operations and performance.[17] For example, as we discussed earlier, the functional structure of Sharp Corp., the consumer electronics giant, enables the company to achieve economies of scale with its applied research and manufacturing skills. Also,

Israel: Home of Global Start-Ups

Israel may be a minor player in the world of international commerce, but surprisingly, the country has been the home base for a disproportionately large number of global start-ups. Blue chip venture capital firms and private equity firms from the United States funded as many as 111 start-ups in Israel in the fourth quarter of 2003. Here are some examples:

- Cash-U, founded by Gal Nachum and Amir Peleg, initially thought of developing games for cell phones but soon realized that it was difficult to come up with games that have universal appeal. Instead, they now supply a software platform that helps others develop games for cell phones. Once they created the product in their labs outside Tel Aviv, they opened sales offices in London and Singapore. Today, their customers include firms such as Vodafone and Telefonica and their revenue growth is around 75 percent annually.

- Baradok Pridor, 38, and Yonatan Aumann, 42, founders of ClearForest, developed an innovative software product—a program that can analyze unstructured electronic data, such as a Web page or a video clip, as if it were already in a spreadsheet or database. Instead of waiting for customers to show up, right from the beginning, they started sending their engineers to make presentations to potential

clients around the world. Today the company's customers include Dow Chemical, Thomson Financial, and the FBI itself! They have raised $33 million so far in three rounds of venture financing. Interestingly, the headquarters of the 83-person company is in Boston!

- HyperRoll, a company that makes software for analyzing massive databases, has raised $28 million in venture funding. Referring to their hiring practices, Yossi Matias, founder of HyperRoll, says, "We build the strongest team possible, unconstrained by locality, affinity, or culture. It requires every employee to accept and support a multicultural environment." Although essentially an Israeli start-up, he even banned the use of Hebrew in the office to facilitate greater integration between the American and Israeli employees!

Why is Israel home to so many global start-ups? First, being a small country of 6 million people, the home market is too small to support the growth of domestic companies. Second, the political uncertainties of the region encourage entrepreneurs to diversify their risk by establishing an international presence. Third, many younger generation Israelis have international networks of contacts either due to education or travel. More importantly, the country has an educated workforce with a work ethic second to none. No wonder, many international start-ups are blooming in this desert country!

Sources: Copeland, M. V. 2004. The start-up oasis. *Business 2.0,* August 46–48; and Brown, E. 2004. Global start-up. *Forbes,* November 29: 150–161.

managers have the responsibility to coordinate similar products in multiple functional areas throughout the organization. Such structural arrangements should help increase operating performance because of lower costs and should enable Sharp to enter new product markets through its applied research. These opportunities would likely not be realized if Sharp had extensive redundant manufacturing resources throughout its divisions and did not effectively coordinate functional area operations across its divisions. Sharp's successful history of functional structure also suggests that the company is unlikely to consider diversification—a strategy that would require them to move away from the functional structure. Similarly, we discussed Brinker International's move to a divisional structure in order to organize its restaurant groups into different units to focus on market niches. This new structure should enable the firm to adapt to change more rapidly and innovate more effectively with the various restaurant brands. Brinker's management did not feel that they were as effective with their previous functional organizational structure.

Today, most organizations compete in environments that may be characterized as rapidly changing and unpredictable. To succeed, they must make their boundaries more flexible and permeable. Later in the chapter, we will discuss three types of what we term "boundaryless" organizations: barrier-free, modular, and virtual.

>>Linking Strategic Reward and Evaluation Systems to Business-Level and Corporate-Level Strategies

The effective use of reward and evaluation systems can play a critical role in motivating managers to conform to organizational strategies, achieve performance targets, and reduce the gap between organizational and individual goals. In contrast, reward systems, if improperly designed, can lead to behaviors that either are detrimental to organizational performance or can lower morale and cause employee dissatisfaction.

As we will see in this section, there is no "one best way" to design reward and evaluation systems for an organization. Instead, it is contingent on many factors. Two of the most important factors are a firm's business-level strategy (see Chapter 5) and its corporate-level strategy (see Chapter 6).

Business-Level Strategy: Reward and Evaluation Systems

In Chapter 5 we discussed two different approaches that firms may take to secure competitive advantages in the marketplace: overall cost leadership and differentiation.[18] As we might expect, implementing these strategies requires fundamentally different organizational arrangements, approaches to control, and reward and incentive systems.

Overall Cost Leadership   This strategy requires that product lines remain rather stable and that innovations deal mostly with production processes. Given the emphasis on efficiency, costly changes even in production processes tend to be rare. Since products are quite standardized and change rather infrequently, procedures can be developed to divide work into its basic components—those that are routine, standardized, and ideal for semiskilled and unskilled employees. As such, firms competing on the basis of cost must implement tight cost controls, frequent and comprehensive reports to monitor the costs associated with outputs, and highly structured tasks and responsibilities. As we might expect, incentives tend to be based on explicit financial targets since innovation and creativity are expensive and might tend to erode competitive advantages. Let's look at Nucor, a highly successful steel producer with $11 billion in revenues.

Nucor competes primarily on the basis of cost and, has a reward and incentive system that is largely based on financial outputs and financial measures.[19] Nucor uses four incentive compensation systems that correspond to the levels of management.

1. *Production incentive program.* Groups of 20 to 40 people are paid a weekly bonus based on either anticipated product time or tonnage produced. Each shift and production line is in a separate bonus group.
2. *Department managers.* Bonuses are based on divisional performance, primarily measured by return on assets.
3. *Employees not directly involved in production.* These include engineers, accountants, secretaries, receptionists, and others. Bonuses are based on two factors: divisional and corporate return on assets.
4. *Senior incentive programs.* Salaries are lower than comparable companies, but a significant portion of total compensation is based on return on stockholder equity. A portion of pretax earnings is placed in a pool and divided among officers as bonuses that are part cash and part stock.

As we might expect, the culture at Nucor reflects its reward and incentive system. Since incentive compensation can account for more than half of their paychecks, employees become nearly obsessed with productivity and apply a lot of pressure on each other. Ken Iverson, a former CEO, recalled an instance in which one employee arrived at work in sunglasses instead of safety glasses, preventing the team from doing any work. Furious, the other workers chased him around the plant with a piece of angle iron!

Differentiation   This strategy typically involves the development of innovative products and services that require using experts who can identify the crucial elements of intricate, creative designs and marketing decisions. Highly trained professionals such as scientists and engineers are essential for devising, assessing, implementing and continually changing complex product designs. New product design also requires extensive collaboration and cooperation among specialists and functional managers from different areas within a firm. Such individuals must, for example, evaluate and implement a new design, constantly bearing in mind marketing, financial, production, and engineering considerations.

Given the need for cooperation and coordination among professionals in many functional areas, it becomes quite difficult to evaluate individuals using set quantitative criteria. It also is difficult to measure specific outcomes of such efforts and attribute outcomes to specific individuals. Thus, more behavioral measures (such as how effectively employees collaborate and share information) and intangible incentives and rewards become necessary to support a strong culture and to motivate employees. Consider 3M, a highly innovative company whose core value is innovation.

> At 3M, rewards are tied closely to risk-taking and innovation-oriented behavior. Managers are not penalized for product failures; instead, those same people are encouraged to work on another project that borrows from their shared experience and insight. A culture of creativity and "thinking out of the box" is reinforced by their well-known "15 percent rule," which permits employees to set aside 15 percent of their work time to pursue personal research interests. And a familiar 3M homily, "Thou shall not kill new ideas for products," is known as the 11th commandment. It is the source of countless stories, including one that tells how L. D. DeSimone (3M's former CEO) tried five times (and failed) to kill the project that yielded the 3M blockbuster product, Thinsulate.[20]

Corporate-Level Strategy: Strategic Reward and Evaluation Systems

In Chapter 6 we discussed two broad types of diversification strategies: related and unrelated. The type of diversification strategy that a firm follows has important implications for the type of reward and evaluation systems that it should use.

Sharp Corporation, a $21 billion Japanese consumer electronics giant, that we discussed earlier in this chapter, follows a strategy of *related* diversification.[21] Its most successful technology has been liquid crystal displays (LCDs) that are critical components in nearly all of the firm's products. With their expertise in this area, they are moving into high-end displays for cellular telephones, hand-held computers, and digital computers.[22]

Given the need to leverage such technologies across multiple product lines, Sharp must have reward and evaluation systems that foster coordination and sharing. It must focus more on individuals' behavior rather than on short-term financial outcomes. For example, promotion is the most powerful incentive, and it is generally based on seniority and subtle skills exhibited over time, such as teamwork and communication. It is critical to ensure that the company's reward system will not reward short-term self-interested orientations.

Like many Japanese companies, Sharp's culture reinforces the view that the firm is a family or community whose members should cooperate for the greater good. In accordance with the policy of lifetime employment, turnover is low. This encourages employees to pursue what is best for the entire company. Such an outlook lessens the inevitable conflict over sharing important resources such as R&D knowledge.

In contrast to Sharp, firms such as Hanson PLC (a British conglomerate) followed a strategy of unrelated diversification for most of its history. At one time it owned as many as 150 operating companies in areas such as tobacco, footwear, building products, brewing, and food. There were limited product similarities across businesses and therefore little need for sharing of resources and knowledge across divisional boundaries. James Hanson and Gordon White, founders of the company, actually did not permit any sharing of resources between operating companies even if it was feasible!

Their reward and evaluation system placed such heavy emphasis on individual accountability that they viewed resource sharing, with its potential for mutual blaming, unacceptable. The operating managers had more than 60 percent of their compensation tied to annual financial performance of their subsidiaries. All decision making was decentralized so that subsidiary managers could be held responsible for the return on capital they employed. However, there was one area in which they had to obtain approval from the corporate office. No subsidiary manager was allowed to incur a capital expenditure greater than $3,000 without permission from the corporate office. Hanson managed to be successful with a very small corporate office because of its decentralized structure, tight financial controls, and an incentive system that motivated managers to meet financial goals. Gordon White was proud of claiming that he had never visited any of the operating companies that were part of the Hanson empire.[23]

To summarize our discussion of the contingent relationship between levels of strategy and evaluation and reward systems, the key issue becomes the need for *inde*pendence versus *inter*dependence. In the cases of cost leadership strategies and unrelated diversification, there tends to be less need for interdependence. Thus, the reward and evaluation systems focus more on the use of financial indicators because unit costs, profits, and revenues can be rather easily attributed to a given business unit or division.

In contrast, firms that follow differentiation or related diversification strategies have intense needs for tight interdependencies among the functional areas and business units within the corporation. In these firms, sharing of resources, including raw materials, R&D knowledge, marketing information, and so on, is critical to organizational success. That is, it is more important to achieve synergies with value-creating activities and business units than with cost leadership or unrelated strategies. To facilitate sharing and collaboration, reward and evaluation systems tend to incorporate more behavioral indicators. Exhibit 10.6 summarizes our discussion of the relationship between strategies and control systems.

Exhibit 10.6

Summary of Relationships between Reward and Evaluation Systems and Business-Level and Corporate-Level Strategies

Level of Strategy	Types of Strategy	Need for Interdependence	Primary Type of Reward and Evaluation System
Business-level	Overall cost leadership	Low	Financial
Business-level	Differentiation	High	Behavioral
Corporate-level	Related diversification	High	Behavioral
Corporate-level	Unrelated diversification	Low	Financial

Boundary Types

There are primarily four types of boundaries that place limits on organizations. In today's dynamic business environment, different types of boundaries are needed to foster high degrees of interaction with outside influences and varying levels of permeability.

1. *Vertical boundaries between levels in the organization's hierarchy.* SmithKline Beecham asks employees at different hierarchical levels to brainstorm ideas for managing clinical trial data. The ideas are incorporated into action plans that significantly cut the new product approval time of its breakthrough pharmaceuticals. This would not have been possible if the barriers between levels of individuals in the organization had been too high.

2. *Horizontal boundaries between functional areas.* Fidelity Investments makes the functional barriers more porous and flexible among divisions, such as marketing, operations, and customer service, in order to offer customers a more integrated experience when conducting business with the company. Customers can take their questions to one person, reducing the chance that customers will "get the runaround" from employees who feel customer service is not their responsibility. At Fidelity, customer service is everyone's business, regardless of functional area.

3. *External boundaries between the firm and its customers, suppliers, and regulators.* GE Lighting, by working closely with retailers, functions throughout the value chain as a single operation. This allows GE to track point-of-sale purchases, giving it better control over inventory management.

4. *Geographic boundaries between locations, cultures, and markets.* The global nature of today's business environment spurred PricewaterhouseCoopers to use a global groupware system. This allows the company to instantly connect to its 26 worldwide offices.

Source: Ashkenas, R. 1997. The organization's new clothes. In Hesselbein, F., Goldsmith, M., and Beckhard, R. (Eds.). *The organization of the future:* 104–106. San Francisco: Jossey Bass.

Finally, we must apply an important caveat. Exhibit 10.6 suggests guidelines on how an organization should match its strategies to its evaluation and reward systems. In actual practice, there is clearly a need for all organizations to have combinations of both financial and behavioral rewards. Both overall cost leadership and unrelated diversification strategies require a need for collaboration and the sharing of best practices across both value-creating activities and business units. General Electric, for example, has developed many integrating mechanisms to enhance sharing "best practices" across what would appear to be rather unrelated businesses such as jet engines, appliances, and network television. And for both differentiation and related diversification strategies, financial indicators such as revenue growth and profitability should not be overlooked at both the business-unit and corporate levels.

>>Boundaryless Organizational Designs

The term *boundaryless* may bring to mind a chaotic organizational reality in which "anything goes." This is not the case. As Jack Welch, GE's former CEO, has suggested, boundaryless does not imply that all internal and external boundaries vanish completely. Although boundaries may continue to exist in some form, they become more open and permeable.[24] Strategy Spotlight 10.4 discusses four types of boundaries and provides examples of how organizations have made them more permeable.

We are not suggesting that boundaryless structures replace the traditional forms of organizational structure, but rather that they should complement them. For example, Sharp Corp. has implemented a functional structure to attain economies of scale with its applied research and manufacturing skills. However, to bring about this key objective,

Sharp has relied on several integrating mechanisms and processes that are key attributes of the boundaryless concept.

> To prevent functional groups from becoming vertical chimneys that obstruct product development, Sharp's product managers have responsibility—but not authority—for coordinating the entire set of value-chain activities. And the company convenes enormous numbers of cross-unit and corporate committees to ensure that shared activities, including the corporate R&D unit and sales forces, are optimally configured and allocated among the different product lines. Sharp invests in such time-intensive coordination to minimize the inevitable conflicts that arise when units share important activities.[25]

We will discuss three approaches to making boundaries more permeable. In the process, these approaches help to facilitate the widespread sharing of knowledge and information across both the internal and external boundaries of the organization. We'll begin with the *barrier-free* type, which involves making all organizational boundaries—internal and external—more permeable. We'll place particular emphasis on team concepts, because we view teams as a central building block for implementing the boundaryless organization. In the next two sections, we will address the *modular* and *virtual* types of organizations. These forms focus on the need to create seamless relationships with external organizations such as customers or suppliers. While the modular type emphasizes the outsourcing of noncore activities, the virtual (or network) organization focuses on alliances among independent entities formed to exploit specific market opportunities.

The Barrier-Free Organization

The "boundary" mind-set is ingrained deeply into bureaucracies. It is evidenced by such clichés as "That's not my job," "I'm here from corporate to help," or endless battles over transfer pricing. In the traditional company, boundaries are clearly delineated in the design of an organization's structure. These boundaries are rigid. Their basic advantage is that the roles of managers and employees are simple, clear, well-defined, and long-lived. A major shortcoming was pointed out to the authors during an interview with a high-tech executive: "Structure tends to be divisive; it leads to territorial fights."

Today such structures are being replaced by fluid, ambiguous, and deliberately ill-defined tasks and roles. Just because work roles are no longer defined by traditional structures, however, does not mean that differences in skills, authority, and talent disappear.

A barrier-free organization enables a firm to bridge real differences in culture, function, and goals to find common ground that facilitates information sharing and other forms of cooperative behavior. Eliminating the multiple boundaries that stifle productivity and innovation can enhance the potential of the entire organization.

Strategy Spotlight 10.5 describes how GE has used the boundaryless concept to develop its wind energy business. This business unit draws on GE's expertise in transportation and jet engines.

Creating Permeable Internal Boundaries   For barrier-free organizations to work effectively, the level of trust and shared interests among all parts of the organization must be raised. Similarly, the organization needs to develop among its employees the skill level needed to work in a more democratic organization. Barrier-free organizations also require a shift in the organization's philosophy from executive development to organizational development, and from investments in high-potential individuals to investments in leveraging the talents of all individuals.

STRATEGY SPOTLIGHT

Boundarylessness: A Key to GE's Success in Wind Energy

Among GE's most promising businesses is a business unit that sells wind-power turbines. GE Wind Energy's revenues are more than $1 billion annually, and the company has become the world's number 2 maker of wind-power systems.

GE Wind Energy primarily designs and builds turbines at plants in California, Florida, Germany, Spain, and the Netherlands. Sometimes the company provides services to wind farms. Other times, it plans major projects, installs the turbines, and operates the plants, as seen in the Clear Sky project in Texas. Thanks to heavy government support in some U.S. states and overseas, GE has won many major projects recently from Colorado to California and from Britain to Belgium.

The key to GE's success comes from a combination of buying into the business and bringing to bear technologies and expertise from all across the giant company. GE acquired Enron's wind assets in 2002 for $285 million and immediately faced a big problem: The erratic nature of the power source—wind gusts—is taxing on turbine components, especially the gearbox, which is vital for transforming the spinning of the blades into electricity. GE has extensive expertise in gearboxes. Its transportation division makes huge, highly efficient ones, including those used in 300-ton mining trucks. Such expertise helped GE develop more reliable wind-turbine gearboxes.

GE jet-engine scientists began working on fiber composites to lighten the giant blades—each about the size of a Boeing 747's wingspan. They plan to cut the blades' weight by 25 percent. GE also has teams of PhDs in India and China working on computer simulations to test components for new wind turbine models (there are 23 now, each designed for specific wind conditions). "We really understand the physics of the machine," says Steve Zwolinski, GE Wind's CEO.

Such efforts are paying off. The wind turbines are much more durable and efficient than when GE acquired the business. Manufacturing costs have also come down 30 percent. Wind power is expected to become an increasingly important part of the global energy picture.

Industry experts predict wind energy—the world's fastest-growing energy source—to expand at least 20 percent annually between 2003 and 2008. Although pragmatic about the chances of wind dominating the world's energy portfolio, John Rice, GE Power Systems CEO and president, asserts that return on sales could be 10 percent in five years. "Is it a $2 billion to $3 billion business or a $5 to $6 billion business over the next five or ten years?" Rice asks. "Either way, I think it's going to be substantial."

Sources: Carey, J. 2005. Tax credits put wind in the sails of renewables. *BusinessWeek*, January 10: 94; Schonfeld, E. 2004. GE sees the light. *Business 2.0*, July: 80–86; and, Rubner, J. 2003. GE Power rides wind energy. *Atlanta Business Chronicle*, November 7: 10–12.

Teams can be an important aspect of barrier-free structures.[26] Jeffrey Pfeffer, author of several insightful books, including *The Human Equation,* suggests that teams have three primary advantages.[27] First, teams substitute peer-based control for hierarchical control of work activities. In essence, employees control themselves, reducing the time and energy management needs to devote to control.

Second, teams frequently develop more creative solutions to problems because they encourage the sharing of the tacit knowledge held by individual team members.[28] Brainstorming, or group problem solving, involves the pooling of ideas and expertise to enhance the chances that at least one group member will think of a way to solve the problems at hand.

Third, by substituting peer control for hierarchical control, teams permit the removal of layers of hierarchy and absorption of administrative tasks previously performed by specialists. This avoids the cumbersome costs of having people whose sole job is to watch the people who watch other people do the work. To carry the argument one step further, Norman Augustine humorously pointed out in *Augustine's Laws* that "If a sufficient number of management layers are superimposed on top of each other, it can be assured that disaster is not left to chance!"[29]

Effective barrier-free organizations must go beyond achieving close integration and coordination within divisions in a corporation. Past research on the multidivisional type of organization has pointed to the importance of interdivisional coordination and resource sharing.[30] Means to this end include interdivisional task forces and committees, reward and incentive systems that emphasize interdivisional cooperation, and common training programs.

A study of professional service firms provides some additional insights.[31] The most important assets of these firms were not the individual technical expertise of their members. That was merely a precondition at these firms. Rather, the collective wisdom of multidisciplinary teams was what set them apart. Further, the researchers found that the average performers excel at using the combined knowledge of boundary-crossing teams to solve especially complex problems with the speed and efficiency that competitors could not match. The competitor of a top-performing investment bank lamented:

> They are the team to beat. Why? They don't slow themselves down with the clutter of bureaucracy. They overwhelm the problem. That *could* yield inefficiency, but it doesn't. They are smart and quick and work seamlessly together.

Given the importance of collaboration and collective efforts, what makes a good team becomes of critical importance. Frank Carruba (former head of Hewlett-Packard's labs) provides some interesting insights.[32] He discovered over time that the difference between mediocre teams and good teams was generally varying levels of motivation and talent. But what explained the difference between good teams and truly superior teams? Carruba found that the key difference—and this explained a 40 percent overall difference in performance—was the way members treated each other; that is, the degree to which they believed in one another and created an atmosphere of encouragement rather than competition. In other words, vision, talent, and motivation could carry a team only so far. What clearly stood out in the "super" teams were higher levels of authenticity and caring, which allowed the full synergy of their individual talents, motivation, and vision to be expressed without barriers.

Developing Effective Relationships with External Constituencies   In barrier-free organizations, managers must also create flexible, porous organizational boundaries and establish communication flows and mutually beneficial relationships with internal (e.g., employees) and external (e.g., customers) constituencies. Michael Dell, founder and CEO of Dell Computer, is a strong believer in fostering close relationships with his customers. In an interview, he explained:

> We're not going to be just your PC vendor anymore. We're going to be your IT department for PCs. Boeing, for example, has 100,000 Dell PCs, and we have 30 people that live at Boeing, and if you look at the things we're doing for them or for other customers, we don't look like a supplier, we look more like Boeing's PC department. We become intimately involved in planning their PC needs and the configuration of their network.
>
> It's not that we make these decisions by ourselves. They're certainly using their own people to get the best answer for the company. But the people working on PCs together, from both Dell and Boeing, understand the needs in a very intimate way. They're right there living it and breathing it, as opposed to the typical vendor who says, "Here are your computers. See you later."[33]

Thus far, we have argued that barrier-free organizations create successful relationships between both internal and external constituencies. However, there is one additional constituency—competitors—with whom some organizations have benefited as they developed cooperative relationships.

For example, after years of seeing its empty trucks return from warehouses back to production facilities after deliveries, General Mills teamed up with 16 of its competitors to form an e-commerce business that allows the companies to find carriers with empty cargo trailers to piggyback freight loads to distributors near the production facilities.[34] This increases revenue for all network members and reduces wasted carrier miles.

Risks, Challenges, and Potential Downsides   In spite of its potential benefits, many firms are discovering that creating and managing a barrier-free organization can be frustrating.[35] For example, Puritan-Bennett Corporation, a Lenexa, Kansas, manufacturer of respiratory equipment, found that its product development time more than doubled after it adopted team management. Roger J. Dolida, director of R&D, attributed this failure to a lack of top management commitment, high turnover among team members, and infrequent meetings. Very often, managers trained in rigid hierarchies find it difficult to make the transition to the more democratic, participative style that teamwork requires.

Christopher Barnes, now a consultant with PricewaterhouseCoopers in Atlanta, previously worked as an industrial engineer for Challenger Electrical Distribution (a subsidiary of Westinghouse, now part of CBS) at a plant in Jackson, Mississippi, which produced circuit-breaker boxes. His assignment was to lead a team of workers from the plant's troubled final-assembly operation with the mission: "Make things better." Not surprisingly, that vague notion set the team up for failure.

After a year of futility, the team was disbanded. In retrospect, and after several successes with teams, Barnes identified several reasons for the debacle in Jackson: (1) limited personal credibility—he was viewed as an "outsider"; (2) a lack of commitment to the team—everyone involved was forced to be on the team; (3) poor communications—nobody was told why the team was important; (4) limited autonomy—line managers refused to give up control over team members; and (5) misaligned incentives—the culture rewarded individual performance over team performance. Barnes's experience has important implications for all types of teams, whether they are composed of managerial, professional, clerical, or production personnel.[36] The pros and cons of barrier-free structures are summarized in Exhibit 10.7.

Pros	Cons
• Leverages the talents of all employees. • Enhances cooperation, coordination, and information sharing among functions, divisions, SBUs, and external constituencies. • Enables a quicker response to market changes through a single-goal focus. • Can lead to coordinated win–win initiatives with key suppliers, customers, and alliance partners.	• Difficult to overcome political and authority boundaries inside and outside the organization. • Lacks strong leadership and common vision, which can lead to coordination problems. • Time-consuming and difficult-to-manage democratic processes. • Lacks high levels of trust, which can impede performance.

Exhibit 10.7

Pros and Cons of Barrier-Free Structures

The Modular Organization

As Charles Handy, author of *The Age of Unreason,* has noted:

> Organizations have realized that, while it may be convenient to have everyone around all the time, having all of your workforce's time at your command is an extravagant way of marshaling the necessary resources. It is cheaper to keep them outside the organization, employed by themselves or by specialist contractors, and to buy their services when you need them.[37]

To capture Handy's vision, the modular organization type outsources nonvital functions, tapping into the knowledge and expertise of "best in class" suppliers of goods and services, but retains strategic control. Outsiders may be used to manufacture parts, handle logistics, or perform accounting activities. As we discussed in Chapters 3 and 5, the value chain can be used as a framework to identify the key primary and support activities performed by a firm to create value. The key question becomes: Which activities do we keep "in-house" and which activities do we outsource to suppliers?[38] In effect, the organization becomes a central hub surrounded by networks of outside suppliers and specialists and, much like Lego blocks, parts can be added or taken away. Both manufacturing and service units may be modular.[39]

In the personal computer industry, the shift to the modular structure has been pioneered by relative newcomers like Dell and Gateway, as well as by workstation innovators like Sun Microsystems. These companies either buy their products ready-made or purchase all the parts from suppliers and perform only the final assembly. Their larger, more established competitors—IBM and Hewlett-Packard—produce most of their parts in-house. As a result, the smaller modular companies are often ahead of their older rivals in profitability.[40]

Apparel is another industry in which the modular type has been widely adopted. Nike and Reebok, for example, have succeeded by concentrating on their strengths: designing and marketing high-tech, fashionable footwear. Nike has very limited production facilities and Reebok owns no plants. These two companies contract virtually all their footwear production to suppliers in Taiwan, South Korea, and other countries with low-cost labor. Avoiding large investments in fixed assets helps them derive large profits on minor sales increases. By being modular, Nike and Reebok can keep pace with changing tastes in the marketplace because their suppliers have become expert at rapidly retooling for the manufacture of new products.

In a modular company, outsourcing the noncore functions offers three advantages.

1. A firm can decrease overall costs, stimulate new product development by hiring suppliers whose talent may be superior to that of in-house personnel, avoid idle capacity, realize inventory savings, and avoid becoming locked into a particular technology.
2. Outsourcing enables a company to focus scarce resources on the areas where it holds a competitive advantage. These benefits can translate into more funding for research and development, hiring the best engineers, and providing continuous training for sales and service staff.
3. By enabling an organization to tap into the knowledge and expertise of its specialized supply-chain partners, it adds critical skills and accelerates organizational learning.[41]

The modular type enables a company to leverage relatively small amounts of capital and a small management team to achieve seemingly unattainable strategic objectives.[42] Freed from the need to make big investments in fixed assets, the modular company can achieve rapid growth. Certain preconditions must exist or be created, however, before the modular approach can be successful. First, the company must work closely with suppliers to ensure that the interests of each party are being fulfilled. Companies need to find loyal, reliable vendors who can be trusted with trade secrets. They also need assurances that suppliers will dedicate their financial, physical, and human resources to satisfy strategic objectives such as lowering costs or being first to market. Second, the modular company must make sure that it selects the proper competencies to keep in-house. For Nike and Reebok, the core competencies are design and marketing, not shoe manufacturing; for Honda, the core competence is engine technology. These firms are unlikely to outsource any activity that involves their core competence. An organization must be wary of outsourcing components of its business that may compromise long-term competitive advantages.

Strategic Risks of Outsourcing   While adopting the modular form clearly has some advantages, managers must also weigh associated risks. The main strategic concerns are (1) loss of critical skills or developing the wrong skills, (2) loss of cross-functional skills, and (3) loss of control over a supplier.[43]

Too much outsourcing can result in a firm "giving away" too much skill and control. Outsourcing relieves companies of the requirement to maintain skill levels needed to manufacture essential components. Over time, these skills that were once part of the knowledge base of the company disappear. At one time, semiconductor chips seemed like a simple technology to outsource. But now, they have become a critical component of a wide variety of products. Companies that have outsourced the manufacture of these chips run the risk of losing the ability to manufacture them as the technology has rapidly escalated. Thus, they may become increasingly dependent upon their suppliers.

Cross-functional skills refer to the skills acquired through the interaction of individuals in various departments within a company. Often, such interaction assists a department in solving problems as employees interface with others across functional units. However, if a firm outsources key functional responsibilities, such as manufacturing, communication across departments can become more difficult. This is because a firm and its employees must now integrate their activities with a new, outside supplier. This typically brings about new challenges in the coordination of joint efforts.

Another serious drawback can occur when the outsourced products give suppliers too much power over the manufacturer. This can happen when the manufacturer is dependent on a single supplier, or just a few suppliers, for critical components. Suppliers that are key to a manufacturer's success can, in essence, hold the manufacturer "hostage." Nike manages this potential problem by sending full-time "product expatriates" to work at the plants of its suppliers. Also, the company often brings top members of supplier management and technical teams to Nike headquarters. This way, Nike keeps close tabs on the pulse of new developments, builds rapport and trust with suppliers, and develops long-term relationships with suppliers to prevent hostage situations.

Strategy Spotlight 10.6 discusses how Sony outsources for talent to develop games for its highly successful video game business. Exhibit 10.8 summarizes the pros and cons of modular structures.[44]

The Virtual Organization

In contrast to the "self-reliant" thinking that guided traditional organizational designs, the strategic challenge today has become doing more with less and looking outside the firm for opportunities and solutions to problems. The virtual type of organization provides a new means of leveraging resources and exploiting opportunities.[45]

STRATEGY SPOTLIGHT

Outsourcing for Talent: How Sony Develops Video Games

The convergence of Hollywood and Silicon Valley has led to the explosive growth of the worldwide video game industry, with revenues of $24.5 billion in 2004. Recently, it has overtaken the movie industry's box office receipts. The industry's sales are expected to soar to $55 billion by 2008, according to PricewaterhouseCoopers.

While broadcast TV audiences dwindle and moviegoing stagnates, gaming is emerging as the newest and perhaps strongest pillar in the media world. So it's no surprise that film studios, media giants, gamemakers, and Japanese electronics companies are all battling to win the "Games Wars." "This is a huge shift we're seeing, and nobody wants to be left behind," says Sony Entertainment Chairman, Michael Lynton.

In this sprawling market where controlling a broad portfolio of businesses is crucial, nobody is better positioned than Sony. Unlike other rivals, it has already assembled all of the pieces of a true video game empire. It sells hardware with its PlayStation consoles, and it has developed its handheld PlayStation Portable product. It also develops games such as the popular *Gran Turismo* racing and *EverQuest* online. And it owns Sony Pictures and MGM movie studios, whose Spider-Man and James Bond franchises have been mega hit games for Activision and EA. This combination has enabled

Sony to sell 80 million Play Station 2 (PS2) consoles worldwide.

The real payoff for Sony comes in game software sales. While Sony and other console makers sell their hardware for a loss, they typically make $5 to $10 in royalties for every game sold on their platform. PS2 has more than 2,000 software titles, with more than 775 million total game copies sold.

Central to Sony's strategy is how it has used outside developers to produce most of its games. It has even reached out to gamers themselves. "We didn't want outside developers to be peripheral to our business model," says Andrew House, an early PlayStation team member and executive vice president of Sony Computer Entertainment America. "We knew that the widest variety of content possible was the best way to build the largest consumer base possible."

Sony has searched high and low for talent. In 1997, it launched a developer kit aimed at hobbyists. "We sent it to budding college developers who wanted to try their hands," House says. Ideas from those amateurs made their way into commercial games in Japan. Meanwhile, externally developed titles like *Final Fantasy* and *Madden NFL Football* helped put Sony's second generation console, the PS2, at the top of the heap in 2001. Sony also launched a Linux developer kit for just $199 in 2002. "It's our way of feeding the market for the future. Some of the first great games were developed by people at home in their garages," say House. "If we're not getting people involved and looking for opportunities very early on, we really are missing out."

Sources: House, A. 2004. Sony. *Fast Company,* April: 65; and Grover, R. Edwards, C., Rowley, I., & Moon, I. 2005. Game wars. *BusinessWeek,* February 28: 35–40.

Exhibit 10.8

Pros and Cons of Modular Structures

Pros	Cons
• Directs a firm's managerial and technical talent to the most critical activities.	• Inhibits common vision through reliance on outsiders.
• Maintains full strategic control over most critical activities—core competencies.	• Diminishes future competitive advantages if critical technologies or other competences are outsourced.
• Achieves "best in class" performance at each link in the value chain.	• Increases the difficulty of bringing back into the firm activities that now add value due to market shifts.
• Leverages core competencies by outsourcing with smaller capital commitment.	• Leads to an erosion of cross-functional skills.
• Encourages information sharing and accelerates organizational learning.	• Decreases operational control and potential loss of control over a supplier.

The virtual type can be viewed as a continually evolving network of independent companies—suppliers, customers, even competitors—linked together to share skills, costs, and access to one another's markets.[46] The members of a virtual organization, by pooling and sharing the knowledge and expertise of each of the component organizations, simultaneously "know" more and can "do" more than any one member of the group could do alone. By working closely together in a cooperative effort, each gains in the long run from the resulting individual and organizational learning that takes place.[47] The term *virtual,* meaning "being in effect but not actually so," is commonly used in the computer industry. A computer's ability to appear to have more storage capacity than it really possesses is called virtual memory. Similarly, by assembling resources from a variety of entities, a virtual organization may seem to have more capabilities than it really possesses.[48]

The virtual organization consists of a grouping of units of different organizations that have joined in an alliance to exploit complementary skills in pursuing common strategic objectives. A case in point is Lockheed Martin's use of specialized coalitions between and among three entities—the company, academia, and government—to enhance competitiveness. According to former CEO Norman Augustine:

> The underlying beauty of this approach is that it forces us to reach outward. No matter what your size, you have to look broadly for new ideas, new approaches, new products. Lockheed Martin used this approach in a surprising manner when it set out during the height of the Cold War to make stealth aircraft and missiles. The technical idea came from research done at the Institute of Radio Engineering in Moscow in the 1960s that was published, and publicized, quite openly in the academic media.
>
> Despite the great contrasts among government, academia and private business, we have found ways to work together that have produced very positive results, not the least of which is our ability to compete on a global scale.[49]

Virtual organizations need not be permanent. Participating firms may be involved in multiple alliances at any one time. Virtual organizations may involve different firms performing complementary value activities, or different firms involved jointly in the same value activities, such as production, R&D, advertising, and distribution. The percentage of activities that are jointly performed with alliance partners may vary significantly from alliance to alliance.[50]

How does the virtual type of structure differ from the modular type? Unlike the modular type, in which the focal firm maintains full strategic control, the virtual organization is characterized by participating firms that give up part of their control and accept interdependent destinies. Participating firms pursue a collective strategy that enables them to cope with uncertainty in the environment through cooperative efforts. The benefit is that, just as virtual memory increases storage capacity, the virtual organizations enhance the capacity or competitive advantage of participating firms. Strategy Spotlight 10.7 addresses the variety of collaborative relationships in the biotechnology industry.

Each company (as Strategy Spotlight 10.7 illustrates) that links up with others to create a virtual organization contributes only what it considers its core competencies. It will mix and match what it does best with the best of other firms by identifying its critical capabilities and the necessary links to other capabilities.[51]

Challenges and Risks Despite their many advantages, such alliances often fail to meet expectations. For example, the alliance between IBM and Microsoft soured in early 1991 when Microsoft began shipping Windows in direct competition to OS/2, which was jointly developed by the two firms. The runaway success of Windows frustrated IBM's

Collaborative Relationships in Biotechnology

Collaboration in biotechnology has benefited a variety of firms. Amgen collaborates with a number of smaller firms including ARRIS, Environgen, Glycomex, and Interneuron, among others. The companies work on joint marketing projects and bring R&D scientists together to explore opportunities for new pharmaceutical product development. In exchange for the expertise of the scientists and marketers at the smaller companies, Amgen provides financial clout and technical assistance when new-product opportunities are identified.

Source: Powell, W. W. 1998. Learning from collaboration: Knowledge and networks in the biotechnology and pharmaceutical industries. *California Management Review,* 40 (3): 228–240; Williams, E., & Langreth, R. 2001. "A biotech wonder grows up. *Forbes,* September 3: 118.

Another biotech company that utilizes collaborative relationships with competitors is Biogen. This large pharmaceutical firm once outsourced clinical testing of its new drugs. But now, the company brings experts from other firms to Biogen laboratories to work with their scientists.

Chiron, one of the largest pharmaceutical firms, with over 7,500 employees, makes extensive use of collaborative efforts with its competitors. The company currently collaborates with over 1,400 companies, tapping into the knowledge base of R&D experts with a wide variety of skill and expertise in the field. Chiron considers this network one of its core competencies.

ability to set an industry standard. In retaliation, IBM entered into an alliance with Microsoft's archrival, Novell, to develop network software to compete with Microsoft's LAN Manager.

The virtual organization demands a unique set of managerial skills. Managers must build relationships with other companies, negotiate win–win deals for all parties involved, find the right partners with compatible goals and values, and provide the temporary organization with the right balance of freedom and control. In addition, information systems must be designed and integrated to facilitate communication with current and potential partners.

An ever-changing pattern of alliances that is constantly being formed and dissolved does not necessarily imply mutually exploitative arrangements or lack of long-term relationships. The key is for managers to be clear about the strategic objectives while forming alliances. Some objectives are time bound, and those alliances need to be dissolved once the objective is fulfilled. Some alliances may have relatively long-term objectives and will need to be clearly monitored and nurtured to produce mutual commitment and avoid bitter fights for control. The highly dynamic personal computer industry, for example, is characterized by multiple temporary alliances among hardware, operating systems, and software producers.[52] But alliances in the more stable automobile industry, such as those involving Nissan and Volkswagen as well as Mazda and Ford, have long-term objectives and tend to be relatively stable.

The virtual organization is a logical culmination of joint-venture strategies of the past. Shared risks, shared costs, and shared rewards are the facts of life in a virtual organization.[53] When virtual organizations are formed, they involve tremendous challenges for strategic planning. As with the modular corporation, it is essential to identify core competencies. However, for virtual structures to be successful, a strategic plan is also needed to determine the effectiveness of combining core competencies.

The strategic plan must address the diminished operational control and overwhelming need for trust and common vision between the partners. This new structure may be appropriate for firms whose strategies require merging technologies (e.g., computing and communication) or for firms exploiting shrinking product life cycles that require simultaneous entry into multiple geographical markets. Further, it may be effective for firms

Pros	Cons
• Enables the sharing of costs and skills.	• Harder to determine where one company ends and another begins, due to close interdependencies among players.
• Enhances access to global markets.	
• Increases market responsiveness.	• Leads to potential loss of operational control among partners.
• Creates a "best of everything" organization since each partner brings core competencies to the alliance.	• Results in loss of strategic control over emerging technology.
• Encourages both individual and organizational knowledge sharing and accelerates organizational learning.	• Requires new and difficult-to-acquire managerial skills.

Exhibit 10.9
Pros and Cons of Virtual Structures

Source: Miles, R. E., & Snow, C. C. 1986. Organizations: New concepts for new forms. *California Management Review,* Spring: 62–73; Miles & Snow. 1999. Causes of failure in network organizations. *California Management Review,* Summer: 53–72; and Bahrami, H. 1991. The emerging flexible organization: Perspectives from Silicon Valley. *California Management Review,* Summer: 33–52.

that desire to be quick to the market with a new product or service; an example is the recent profusion of alliances among airlines, primarily motivated by the need to provide seamless travel demanded by the full-fare paying business traveler. Exhibit 10.9 summarizes the advantages and disadvantages of the virtual form.

Boundaryless Organizations: Making Them Work

Designing an organization that simultaneously supports the requirements of an organization's strategy, is consistent with the demands of the environment, and can be effectively implemented by the people around the manager is a tall order for any manager.[54] Many times, the most effective solution is a combination of organizational types. That is, a firm may outsource many parts of its value chain to reduce costs and increase quality, engage simultaneously in multiple alliances to take advantage of technological developments or penetrate new markets, and break down barriers within the organization to enhance flexibility. In Strategy Spotlight 10.8, we look at how an innovative firm, Technical Computer Graphics, effectively combines both barrier-free and virtual forms of an organization.

When an organization faces external pressures, resource scarcity, and declining performance, it tends to become more internally focused, rather than directing its efforts toward managing and enhancing relationships with existing and potential external stakeholders. We believe that this may be the most opportune time for managers to carefully analyze their value-chain activities and evaluate the potential for adopting elements of modular, virtual, and barrier-free organizational types.

Regardless of the form of organization ultimately chosen, achieving the coordination and integration necessary to maximize the potential of an organization's human capital involves much more than just creating a new structure. Techniques and processes designed and implemented to ensure the necessary coordination and integration of an organization's key value-chain activities are critical. Teams are key building blocks of the new organizational forms, and teamwork requires new and flexible approaches to coordination and integration.

STRATEGY SPOTLIGHT

Technical Computer Graphics' Boundaryless Organization

The Technical Computer Graphics (TCG) group manufactures items such as handheld bar code readers and scanning software. The company uses 13 "alliances," or small project teams, employing a total of 200 employees. Each team is responsible for either specific customers or specific products. Alliance teams share a common infrastructure, but they can develop new business opportunities without approval from upper management. Projects often emerge from listening to what customers need.

TCG uses a "triangulation approach"—alliances that include customers, suppliers, and other alliances. Suppliers and customers who provide funding are involved at the outset of the project. The alliances recognize that attaining the initial customer funding is crucial; it stimulates them to focus on what customers have to say. With an emphasis on speed, new products come to market quickly, providing the firm and its partners with tangible benefits.

Source: Snow, C. 1997. Twenty-first century organizations: Implications for a new marketing paradigm. *Journal of the Academy of Marketing Science,* Winter: 72–74; Allred, B. Snow, C. & Miles, R. 1996. Characteristics of managerial careers of the 21st century. *Academy of Management Executive,* November: 17–27; Herzog, V. L. 2001. Trust building on corporate collaborative teams. *Project Management Journal,* March: 28–41.

Sometimes another alliance acts as either the customer or the supplier and provides funding.

While each alliance is independent, it shares financial concern for other alliance teams. When a new business opportunity is discovered, an alliance draws on technical expertise from the other alliances. The purpose is not only to acquire additional knowledge, but also to share accumulated learning. There's no benefit to hoarding information: Learning gained from one software project might prove especially valuable to one under way in another alliance. This technological diffusion of information produces products that quickly reach the market.

TCG's formal structure is designed to ensure that such knowledge diffusion occurs. The company's culture is structured to encourage this as well. The TCG culture attracts both the entrepreneur and the team-oriented person at the same time. Working with multiple stakeholders through TCG's triangulation model forces employees to listen to the customers and respond quickly. Because the customer matters more than the functional title, teams lend expertise to each other in return for sharing the gains realized from supplying value to the customer.

Often managers trained in rigid hierarchies find it difficult to make the transition to the more democratic, participative style that teamwork requires. As Douglas K. Smith, coauthor of *The Wisdom of Teams,* pointed out, "A completely diverse group must agree on a goal, put the notion of individual accountability aside and figure out how to work with each other. Most of all, they must learn that if the team fails, it's everyone's fault."[55] Within the framework of an appropriate organizational design, managers must select a mix and balance of tools and techniques to facilitate the effective coordination and integration of key activities. Some of the factors that must be considered include:

- Common culture and shared values.
- Horizontal organizational structures.
- Horizontal systems and processes.
- Communications and information technologies.
- Human resource practices.

Common Culture and Shared Values Shared goals, mutual objectives, and a high degree of trust are essential to the success of boundaryless organizations. It is neither feasible nor desirable to attempt to "control" suppliers, customers, or alliance partners in the traditional sense. In the fluid and flexible environments of the new organizational architectures, common cultures, shared values, and carefully aligned incentives are often less expensive to implement and are often a more effective means of strategic control than rules, boundaries, and formal procedures.

Horizontal Organizational Structures   Horizontal organizational structures, which group similar or related business units under common management control, facilitate sharing resources and infrastructures to exploit synergies among operating units and help to create a sense of common purpose. Consistency in training and the development of similar structures across business units facilitates job rotation and cross training and enhances understanding of common problems and opportunities. Cross-functional teams and interdivisional committees and task groups represent important opportunities to improve understanding and foster cooperation among operating units.

Horizontal Systems and Processes   Organizational systems, policies, and procedures are the traditional mechanisms for achieving integration among functional units. Too often, however, existing policies and procedures do little more than institutionalize the barriers that exist from years of managing within the framework of the traditional model. The concept of business reengineering focuses primarily on these internal processes and procedures. Beginning with an understanding of basic business processes in the context of "a collection of activities that takes one or more kinds of input and creates an output that is of value to the customer," Michael Hammer and James Champy's 1993 best-selling *Reengineering the Corporation* outlined a methodology for redesigning internal systems and procedures that has been embraced, in its various forms, by many organizations.[56] Proponents claim that successful reengineering lowers costs, reduces inventories and cycle times, improves quality, speeds response times, and enhances organizational flexibility. Others advocate similar benefits through the reduction of cycle times, total quality management, and the like.

Communications and Information Technologies   Improved communications through the effective use of information technologies can play an important role in bridging gaps and breaking down barriers between organizations. Electronic mail and videoconferencing can improve lateral communications across long distances and multiple time zones and, by short-circuiting vertical structures, tend to circumvent many of the barriers of the traditional model. Information technology can be a powerful ally in the redesign and streamlining of internal business processes and in improving coordination and integration between suppliers and customers. Internet technologies have eliminated the paperwork of purchase order and invoice documentation in many buyer–supplier relationships, enabling cooperating organizations to reduce inventories, shorten delivery cycles, and reduce operating costs. Today information technology must be viewed more as a prime component of an organization's overall strategy than simply in terms of its more traditional role as administrative support. The close relationships that must exist between technology and other value-creating activities were addressed in Chapters 3, 4, and 8.

Human Resource Practices   Change, whether in structure, process, or procedure, always involves and impacts the human dimension of organizations. As we noted in Chapter 4, the attraction, development, and retention of human capital are vital to value creation. As boundaryless structures are implemented, processes are reengineered, and organizations become increasingly dependent on sophisticated information technologies, the skills of workers and managers alike must be upgraded to realize the full benefits.

>>Creating Ambidextrous Organizations

In rapidly changing and complex competitive environments, organizations face two opposing challenges.[57] First, firms must explore new opportunities and adjust to volatile markets in order to avoid complacency. They must ensure that they maintain *adaptability* and remain proactive in expanding and/or modifying their product-market scope to anticipate and satisfy market conditions. Such competences are especially challenging when change is rapid and unpredictable—conditions that are becoming more pronounced in global markets.

Second, organizations must also effectively exploit the value of their existing assets and competencies. They need to have *alignment,* which is a clear sense of how value is being created in the short term and how activities are integrated and properly coordinated. Firms that achieve both adaptability and alignment are considered *ambidextrous organizations*—aligned and efficient in how they manage today's business but flexible enough to changes in the environment so that they will prosper tomorrow.

As we would expect, handling such opposing demands is difficult because there will always be some degree of conflict. Such trade-offs can never really be entirely eliminated, and firms often suffer when they place too strong a priority on either adaptability or alignment. If it places too much focus on adaptability, the firm will suffer low profitability in the short term. On the other hand, if managers direct their efforts primarily at alignment, they will likely miss out on promising business opportunities.

The Challenge of Achieving Ambidexterity: Some Examples from Business Practice

Clearly, it is hard to become an ambidextrous organization and get the balance of adaptability and alignment just right. Let's look at a couple of brief cases in which firms went too far in one direction.

- Lloyds TSB Bank Plc, based in the United Kingdom, became highly successful in providing stellar shareholder returns throughout the 1980s and 1990s by focusing on a single performance indicator—return on equity. Under the direction of CEO Brian Pittman, little attention was paid to monitoring and understanding either the changing needs of their customer base or the morale of the workforce—two factors that ultimately eroded the bank's performance. Too much emphasis was placed on maintaining efficient operations. The result was that between 1998 and 2003, Lloyds TSB lost 60 percent of its market value. Clearly, this was a situation of too much alignment and a lack of adaptability.

- Sweden's Ericsson made the opposite mistake—too much adaptability at the expense of short-term performance. The firm led in the development of the telephony industry and developed one of the first analog mobile systems. In addition, it was a leader in designing the global system of mobile communication and pioneered third-generation mobile technology standards. Unfortunately, the impressive growth in sales came at a very high cost and a bloated organization structure. There was a great deal of duplication of effort, largely because of an R&D organization that had grown to 30,000 people in approximately 100 technology centers. When the crash in the telecom industry hit in 2000, Ericsson suffered much more than its rivals. The firm eventually cut 60,000 employees and closed most of its technology centers in its effort to become profitable again.

Fortunately, some firms do seem to make the right trade-offs and, in essence, get the "best of both worlds." For example, Finland's Nokia Corp. is experimenting with a wide array of mobile technologies. At the same time, it continues to invest in its dominant handset franchise. And GlaxoSmithKline PLC is experimenting with alternative organization models, alliance partners, and technologies in its search for new blockbuster drugs. At the same time, the pharmaceutical firm is striving to maximize the return from the existing drug portfolio.

Ambidextrous Organizations: Key Design Attributes

A recent study by Charles O'Reilly and Michael Tushman[58] provides some insights into how some firms were able to create successful ambidextrous organizations. These researchers and their colleagues investigated companies that attempted to simultaneously pursue modest, incremental innovations as well as more dramatic, breakthrough innovations. In all, the team investigated 35 attempts to launch breakthrough innovations undertaken by 15 business units in nine different industries. They studied the organizational designs and the processes, systems, and cultures associated with the breakthrough projects as well as their impact on the operations and performance of the traditional businesses.

Companies tended to structure their breakthrough projects in one of four primary ways:

- Seven were carried out within existing *functional organizational structures*. The projects were completely integrated into the regular organizational and management structure.

- Nine were organized as *cross-functional teams*. The groups operated within the established organization but outside of the existing management structure.

- Four were organized as *unsupported teams*. Here, they became independent units set up outside the established organization and management hierarchy.

- Fifteen were conducted within *ambidextrous organizations*. Here, the breakthrough efforts were organized within structurally independent units, each having its own processes, structures, and cultures. However, they were integrated into the existing senior management structure.

Exhibit 10.10 depicts each of these four organization structures. The performance results of the 35 initiatives were tracked along two dimensions:

- Their success in creating desired innovations was measured by either the actual commercial results of the new product or the application of practical market or technical learning.

- The performance of the existing business was evaluated.

The study found that the organizational structure and management practices employed had a direct and significant impact on the performance of both the breakthrough initiative and the traditional business. The ambidextrous organizational designs were more effective than the other three designs on both dimensions: launching breakthrough products or services (i.e., adaptation) and improving the performance of the existing business (i.e., alignment).

Why was the ambidextrous organization the most effective structure? The study found that there were many factors. A clear and compelling vision, consistently communicated by the company's senior management team was critical in building the ambidextrous designs. The structure enabled cross-fertilization among business units while avoiding cross-contamination. The tight coordination and integration at the managerial levels enabled the newer units to share important resources from the traditional units such as cash, talent, expertise, and so on. Such sharing was encouraged and facilitated by effective reward systems that emphasized overall company goals. At the same time, the organizational separation ensured that the new units' distinctive processes, structures, and cultures were not overwhelmed by the forces of "business as usual." Furthermore, the established units were shielded from the distractions of launching new businesses, and they continued to focus

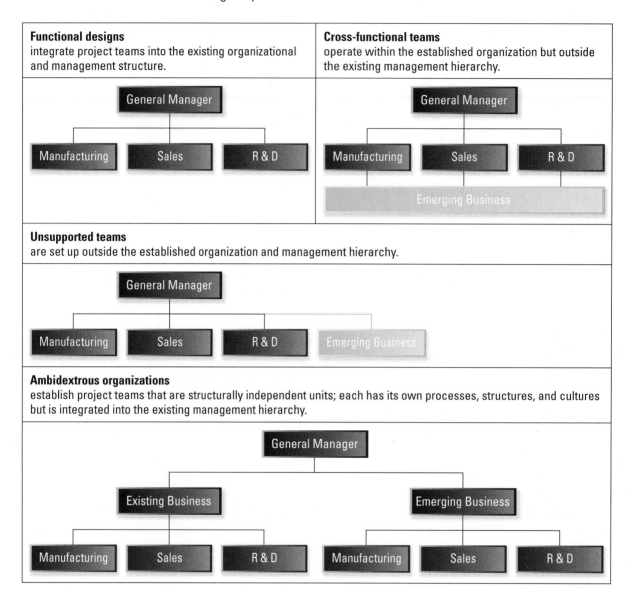

Functional designs
integrate project teams into the existing organizational and management structure.

Cross-functional teams
operate within the established organization but outside the existing management hierarchy.

Unsupported teams
are set up outside the established organization and management hierarchy.

Ambidextrous organizations
establish project teams that are structurally independent units; each has its own processes, structures, and cultures but is integrated into the existing management hierarchy.

Exhibit 10.10   **Organizational Designs for Adaptation and Alignment**

In an examination of 35 different attempts at breakthrough innovation, businesses tended to apply one of four organizational designs to develop and deliver their innovations. More than 90 percent of businesses using the ambidextrous structure succeeded in their attempts, while none of the cross-functional or unsupported teams and only 25 percent of those using functional designs reached their goals.

Source: Reprinted by permission of *Harvard Business Review.* Exhibit from "The Ambidextrous organization," by O' Reilly, C. A. and Tushman, M. L. 2004. Copyright © 2004 by the Harvard Business School Publishing Corporation; all rights reserved.

all of their attention and energy on refining their operations, enhancing their products, and serving their customers.

Let's look at one of these organizations in more detail. Strategy Spotlight 10.9 discusses *USA Today*'s success and helps us identify some of the key managerial and organizational characteristics that underpin the ambidextrous organization and how it attains both adaptability and alignment.

USA Today: Success through an Ambidextrous Organization

USA Today was not an overnight success. Launched in 1982 as a division of the Gannett Corporation, its colorful brand of journalism was widely ridiculed by critics. However, during the 1990s it turned around an initial decade of losses and posted some impressive profits. It became the most widely read daily newspaper in the United States. Well-heeled business travelers made up a good chunk of its subscriber base and, not surprisingly, *USA Today* became an attractive platform for national advertisers.

By the end of the 1990s, however, some unfavorable external trends were emerging. Newspaper readership was steadily decreasing, especially among young people. Competition was intensifying, as more customers were looking toward television and Internet media outlets for their news. Furthermore, newsprint costs were escalating.

Tom Curley, *USA Today*'s president and publisher, knew that he could not keep operating "business as usual." He recognized that he would have to move the company beyond its traditional print media in order to maintain strong growth and profits. Such expansion, he realized, would require dramatic innovations and the company would need to discover ways to apply the existing news-gathering and editing capabilities to entirely new media.

In 1999, Curley decided that *USA Today* should adopt a "network strategy," in which it would share news content across three platforms: the newspaper, USATODAY.com (an online news service), and Gannett's 21 local television stations. Curley explained his vision: "We're no longer in the newspaper business—we're in the news information space, and we'd better learn to deliver content regardless of forms."

Sounds like a great vision, but how did Curley make it work? To execute the strategy, Curley knew he needed to create an ambidextrous organization by sustaining the print business and also pursuing innovations in broadcasting and online news. To launch the bold initiative, Curley appeared at a company meeting dressed as a cyberpunk, complete with blue hair. The message, he recalled, was "It's a new world, and we need to be ready to move into it." In addition to the theatrics, he appointed a new leader in 2000 for USATODAY.com who was a strong supporter of the network strategy, and he brought in an outsider to create a television operation, *USAToday* Direct. Both the online and television organizations remained separate and distinct from the newspaper, maintaining unique processes, structures and cultures. However, Curley demanded that the senior leadership of all three businesses be tightly integrated and coordinated.

Karen Jurgenson, the editor of *USA Today*, and the leaders of the online and television units instituted daily editorial meetings to review stories and assignments, share ideas, and identify other potential synergies. They quickly saw, for example, that eliciting the cooperation of *USA Today*'s reporters would be vital to the success of the strategy (print journalists are notorious for hoarding stories), and they jointly decided to train the print reporters in television and Web broadcasting and equip them with video cameras so that they could file stories simultaneously in the different media. These moves quickly paid off; reporters soon realized that they would have the chance to appear on TV. And a new position of "network editor" was also created in the newsroom to help reporters sharpen their stories for the broadcast media.

All along, Curley knew that he had to make some broader changes to the organization in terms of its culture, processes, structures, and personnel. He fired several senior executives who clearly did not "buy in" to his network strategy. Such firm action was required to ensure that his team would present a united front and deliver consistent messages to all employees. He also changed the incentive program for executives by replacing an emphasis on unit-specific goals with a common bonus program tied to growth targets across all three media. Human resource policies were changed to encourage transfers of talent across the three units, and promotion and compensation decisions began to include people's willingness to share stories and other content. As part of the overall effort, a "Friends of the Network" recognition was established to explicitly reward cross-unit accomplishments.

Yet while all of the sharing and synergy was being emphasized, the organizational integrity of the three units was carefully maintained. The three units were physically separate, and they each followed different staffing models. For example, the employees at USATODAY.com were, on average, much younger than the newspaper's reporters, and they remained far more collaborative and fast paced. Reporters continued to be fiercely independent and focused more on in-depth coverage of stories than the television staff.

USA Today, with its ambidextrous organization, has been able to compete aggressively in the mature business of daily print news, develop a strong Internet franchise, and provide Gannett television stations with coverage of breaking news. And, during the Internet collapse several years ago, *USA Today* made $60 million. This success was largely due to the company's ability to continue to attract national advertisers and revenues from its profitable USAToday.com operation.

Source: O'Reilly, C. A. III., & Tushman, M. L. 2004. The ambidextrous organization. *Harvard Business Review*, 82(4): 74–81.

Summary

Successful organizations must ensure that they have the proper type of organizational structure. Furthermore, they must ensure that their firms incorporate the necessary integration and processes so that the internal and external boundaries of their firms are flexible and permeable. Such a need is increasingly important as the environments of firms become more complex, rapidly changing, and unpredictable.

In the first section of the chapter, we discussed the growth patterns of large corporations. Although most organizations remain small or die, some firms continue to grow in terms of revenues, vertical integration, and diversity of products and services. In addition, their geographical scope may increase to include international operations. We traced the dominant pattern of growth, which evolves from a simple structure to a functional structure as a firm grows in terms of size and increases its level of vertical integration. After a firm expands into related products and services, its structure changes from a functional to a divisional form of organization. Finally, when the firm enters international markets, its structure again changes to accommodate the change in strategy.

We also addressed the different types of organizational structure—simple, functional, divisional (including two variations—strategic business unit and holding company), and matrix as well as their relative advantages and disadvantages. We closed the section with a discussion of the implications for structure when a firm enters international markets. The three primary factors to take into account when determining the appropriate structure are type of international strategy, product diversity, and the extent to which a firm is dependent on foreign sales.

In the second section, we took a contingency approach to the design of reward and evaluation systems. That is, we argued that there is no one best way to design such systems; rather, it is dependent on a variety of factors. The two that we discussed are business- and corporate-level strategies. With an overall cost leadership strategy and unrelated diversification, it is appropriate to rely primarily on cultures and reward systems that emphasize the production outcomes of the organization, because it is rather easy to quantify such indicators. In contrast, differentiation strategies and related diversification require cultures and incentive systems that encourage and reward creativity initiatives as well as the cooperation among professionals in many different functional areas. Here it becomes more difficult to measure accurately each individual's contribution, and more subjective indicators become essential.

The third section of the chapter introduced the concept of the boundaryless organization. We did not suggest that the concept of the boundaryless organization replaces the traditional forms of organizational structure. Rather, it should complement them. This is necessary to cope with the increasing complexity and change in the competitive environment. We addressed three types of boundaryless organizations. The barrier-free type focuses on the need for the internal and external boundaries of a firm to be more flexible and permeable. The modular type emphasizes the strategic outsourcing of noncore activities. The virtual type centers on the strategic benefits of alliances and the forming of network organizations. We discussed both the advantages and disadvantages of each type of boundaryless organization as well as suggested some techniques and processes that are necessary to successfully implement them. These are common culture and values, horizontal organizational structures, horizontal systems and processes, communications and information technologies, and human resource practices.

The final section addresses the need for managers to develop ambidextrous organizations. In today's rapidly changing global environment, managers must be responsive and proactive in order to take advantage of new opportunities. At the same time, they must effectively integrate and coordinate existing operations. Such requirements call for organizational designs that establish project teams that are structurally independent units, with each having its own processes, structures, and cultures. But, at the same time, each unit needs to be effectively integrated into the existing management hierarchy.

Summary Review Questions

1. Why is it important for managers to carefully consider the type of organizational structure that they use to implement their strategies?

2. Briefly trace the dominant growth pattern of major corporations from simple structure to functional structure to divisional structure. Discuss the relationship between a firm's strategy and its structure.

3. What are the relative advantages and disadvantages of the types of organizational structure—simple, functional, divisional, matrix—discussed in the chapter?

4. When a firm expands its operations into foreign markets, what are the three most important factors to take into account in deciding what type of structure is most appropriate? What are the types of international structures discussed in the text and what are the relationships between strategy and structure?

5. Briefly describe the three different types of boundaryless organizations: barrier-free, modular, and virtual.

6. What are some of the key attributes of effective groups? Ineffective groups?

7. What are the advantages and disadvantages of the three types of boundaryless organizations: barrier-free, modular, and virtual?

8. When are ambidextrous organizational designs necessary? What are some of their key attributes?

Many firms have recently moved toward a modular structure. For example, they have increasingly outsourced many of their information technology (IT) activities. Identify three such organizations. Using secondary sources, evaluate (1) the firm's rationale for IT outsourcing and (2) the implications for performance.

Experiential Exercise

Firm	Rationale	Implication(s) for Performance
1.		
2.		
3.		

Application Questions Exercises

1. Select an organization that competes in an industry in which you are particularly interested. Go on the Internet and determine what type of organizational structure this organization has. In your view, is it consistent with the strategy that it has chosen to implement? Why? Why not?

2. Choose an article from *BusinessWeek, Fortune, Forbes, Fast Company,* or any other well-known publication that deals with a corporation that has undergone a significant change in its strategic direction. What are the implications for the structure of this organization?

3. Go on the Internet and look up some of the public statements or speeches of an executive in a major corporation about a significant initiative such as entering into a joint venture or launching a new product line. What do you feel are the implications for making the internal and external barriers of the firm more flexible and permeable? Does the executive discuss processes, procedures, integrating mechanisms, or cultural issues that should serve this purpose? Or are other issues discussed that enable a firm to become more boundaryless?

4. Look up a recent article in the publications listed in question 2 above that addresses a firm's involvement in outsourcing (modular organization) or in strategic alliance or network organizations (virtual organization). Was the firm successful or unsuccessful in this endeavor? Why? Why not?

Ethics Questions

1. If a firm has a divisional structure and places extreme pressures on its divisional executives to meet short-term profitability goals (e.g., quarterly income), could this raise some ethical considerations? Why? Why not?

2. If a firm enters into a strategic alliance but does not exercise appropriate behavioral control of its employees (in terms of culture, rewards and incentives, and boundaries—as discussed in Chapter 9) that are involved in the alliance, what ethical issues could arise? What could be the potential long-term and short-term downside for the firm?

References

1. Wheatcroft, P. 2004. An expensive farce has been played out in NHS. *The Times,* April 24: 58; and www.nhs.uk.

2. This introductory discussion draws upon Hall, R. H. 2002. *Organizations: Structures, processes, and outcomes* (8th ed.). Upper Saddle River, NJ: Prentice Hall; and Duncan, R. E. 1979. What is the right organization structure? Decision-tree analysis provides the right answer. *Organizational Dynamics,* 7(3): 59–80. For an insightful discussion of strategy-structure relationships in the organization theory and strategic management literatures, refer to Keats, B., & O'Neill, H. M. 2001. Organization structure: Looking through a strategy lens. In Hitt, M. A., Freeman, R. E., & Harrison, J. S. 2001. *The Blackwell handbook of strategic management:* 520–542. Malden, MA: Blackwell.

3. This discussion draws upon Chandler, A. D. 1962. *Strategy and structure.* Cambridge, MA: MIT Press; Galbraith J. R., & Kazanjian, R. K. 1986. *Strategy implementation: The role of structure and process.* St. Paul, MN: West Publishing;

and Scott, B. R. 1971. Stages of corporate development. Intercollegiate Case Clearing house, 9-371-294, BP 998. Harvard Business School.

4. Our discussion of the different types of organizational structures draws on a variety of sources, including Galbraith & Kazanjian, op. cit.; Hrebiniak, L. G., & Joyce, W. F. 1984. *Implementing strategy.* New York: Macmillan; Distelzweig, H. 2000. Organizational structure. In Helms, M. M. (Ed.). *Encyclopedia of management:* 692–699. Farmington Hills, MI: Gale; and Dess, G. G., & Miller, A. 1993. *Strategic management.* New York: McGraw-Hill.

5. Schein, E. H. 1996. Three cultures of management: The key to organizational learning. *Sloan Management Review,* 38(1): 9–20.

6. For a discussion of performance implications, refer to Hoskisson, R. E. 1987. Multidivisional structure and performance: The contingency of diversification strategy. *Academy of Management Journal,* 29: 625–644.

7. For a thorough and seminal discussion of the evolution toward the divisional form of organizational structure in the United States, refer to Chandler, op. cit. A rigorous empirical study of the strategy and structure relationship is found in Rumelt, R. P. 1974. *Strategy, structure, and economic performance.* Cambridge, MA: Harvard Business School Press.

8. Ghoshal, S., & Bartlett, C. A. 1995. Changing the role of management: Beyond structure to processes. *Harvard Business Review,* 73(1): 88.

9. Koppel, B. 2000. Synergy in ketchup? *Forbes,* February 7: 68–69; and Hitt, M. A., Ireland, R. D., & Hoskisson, R. E. 2001. *Strategic management: Competitiveness and globalization* (4th ed.). Cincinnati, OH: Southwestern Publishing.

10. Pitts, R. A. 1977. Strategies and structures for diversification. *Academy of Management Journal,* 20(2): 197–208.

11. Wetlaufer, S. 2000. Common sense and conflict: An interview with Disney's Michael Eisner. *Harvard Business Review,* 78(1): 121.

12. Daniels, J. D., Pitts, R. A., & Tretter, M. J. 1984. Strategy and structure of U.S. multinationals: An exploratory study. *Academy of Management Journal,* 27(2): 292–307.

13. Habib, M. M., & Victor, B. 1991. Strategy, structure, and performance of U.S. manufacturing and service MNCs: A comparative analysis. *Strategic Management Journal,* 12(8): 589–606.

14. Our discussion of global start-ups draws from Oviatt, B. M., & McDougall, P. P. 2005. The internationalization of entrepreneurship. *Journal of International Business Studies,* 36(1): 2–8; Oviatt, B. M., & McDougall, P. P. 1994. Toward a theory of international new ventures. *Journal of International Business Studies,* 25(1): 45–64; and Oviatt, B. M., & McDougall, P. P. 1995. Global start-ups: Entrepreneurs on a worldwide stage. *Academy of Management Executive,* 9(2): 30–43.

15. Some useful guidelines for global start-ups are provided in Kuemmerle, W. 2005. The entrepreneur's path for global expansion. *MIT Sloan Management Review,* 46(2): 42–50.

16. See, for example, Miller, D., & Friesen, P. H. 1980. Momentum and revolution in organizational structure. *Administrative Science Quarterly,* 13: 65–91.

17. Many authors have argued that a firm's structure can influence a firm's strategy and performance. These include Amburgey, T. L., & Dacin, T. 1995. As the left foot follows the right? The dynamics of strategic and structural change. *Academy of Management Journal,* 37: 1427–1452; Dawn, K., & Amburgey, T. L. 1991. Organizational inertia and momentum: A dynamic model of strategic change. *Academy of Management Journal,* 34: 591–612; Fredrickson, J. W. 1986. The strategic decision process and organization structure. *Academy of Management Review,* 11: 280–297; Hall, D. J., & Saias, M. A.

1980. Strategy follows structure! *Strategic Management Journal,* 1: 149–164; and Burgelman, R. A. 1983. A model of the interaction of strategic behavior, corporate context, and the concept of strategy. *Academy of Management Review,* 8: 61–70.

18. This discussion of generic strategies and their relationship to organizational control draws upon Porter, M. E. 1980. *Competitive strategy.* New York: Free Press; and Miller, D. 1988. Relating Porter's business strategies to environment and structure: Analysis and performance implications. *Academy of Management Journal,* 31(2): 280–308.

19. Rodengen, J. L. 1997. *The legend of Nucor Corporation.* Fort Lauderdale, FL: Write Stuff Enterprises.

20. The 3M example draws upon *Blueprints for service quality.* 1994. New York: American Management Association; personal communication with Katerine Hagmeier, program manager, external communications, 3M Corporation, March 26, 1998; Lei, D., Slocum, J. W., & Pitts, R. A. 1999. Designing organizations for competitive advantage: The power of unlearning and learning. *Organizational Dynamics,* 27(3): 24–38; and Graham, A. B., & Pizzo, V. G. 1996. A question of balance: Case studies in strategic knowledge management. *European Management Journal,* 14(4): 338–346.

21. The Sharp Corporation and Hanson plc examples are based on Collis, D. J., & Montgomery, C. A. 1998. Creating corporate advantage. *Harvard Business Review,* 76(3): 70–83.

22. Kunii, I. 2002. Japanese companies' survival skills. *BusinessWeek,* November 18: 18.

23. White, G. 1988. How I turned $3,000 into $10 billion. *Fortune,* November 7: 80–89. After the death of the founders, the Hanson plc conglomerate was found to be too unwieldy and was broken up into several separate, publicly traded corporations. For more on its more limited current scope of operations, see www.hansonplc.com.

24. An interesting discussion on how the Internet has affected the boundaries of firms can be found in Afuah, A. 2003. Redefining firm boundaries in the face of the Internet: Are firms really shrinking? *Academy of Management Review,* 28(1): 34–53.

25. Collis & Montgomery, op. cit.

26. For a discussion of the role of coaching on developing high performance teams, refer to Kets de Vries, M. F. R. 2005. Leadership group coaching in action: The zen of creating high performance teams. *Academy of Management Executive,* 19(1): 77–89.

27. Pfeffer, J. 1998. *The human equation: Building profits by putting people first.* Cambridge, MA: Harvard Business School Press.

28. For a discussion on how functional area diversity affects performance, see Bunderson, J. S., & Sutcliffe, K. M. 2002. *Academy of Management Journal,* 45(5): 875–893.

29. Augustine, N. R. 1983. *Augustine's laws.* New York: Viking Press.

30. See, for example, Hoskisson, R. E., Hill, C. W. L., & Kim, H. 1993. The multidivisional structure: Organizational fossil or source of value? *Journal of Management,* 19(2): 269–298.

31. Kuedtjam, H., Haskins, M. E., Rosenblum, J. W., & Weber, J. 1997. The generative cycle: Linking knowledge and relationships. *Sloan Management Review,* 39(1): 47–58.

32. Pottruck, D. A. 1997. Speech delivered by the co-CEO of Charles Schwab Co., Inc., to the Retail Leadership Meeting, San Francisco, CA, January 30; and Miller, W. 1999. Building the ultimate resource. *Management Review,* January: 42–45.

33. Magretta, J. 1998. The power of virtual integration: An interview with Dell Computer's Michael Dell. *Harvard Business Review,* 76(2): 75.

34. Forster, J. 2001. Networking for cash. *BusinessWeek,* January 8: 129.

35. Dess, G. G., Rasheed, A. M. A., McLaughlin, K. J., & Priem, R. 1995. The new corporate architecture. *Academy of Management Executive,* 9(3): 7–20.

36. Barnes, C. 1998. A fatal case. *Fast Company,* February–March: 173.

37. Handy, C. 1989. *The age of unreason.* Boston: Harvard Business School Press; Ramstead, E. 1997. APC maker's low-tech formula: Start with the box. *Wall Street Journal,* December 29: B1; Mussberg, W. 1997. Thin screen PCs are looking good but still fall flat. *Wall Street Journal,* January 2: 9; Brown, E. 1997. Monorail: Low cost PCs. *Fortune,* July 7: 106–108; and Young, M. 1996. Ex-Compaq executives start new company. *Computer Reseller News,* November 11: 181.

38. For a discussion of some of the downsides of outsourcing, refer to Rossetti, C., & Choi, T. Y. 2005. On the dark side of strategic sourcing: Experiences from the aerospace industry. *Academy of Management Executive,* 19(1): 46–60.

39. Tully, S. 1993. The modular corporation. *Fortune,* February 8: 196.

40. For a recent review of the relationship between outsourcing and firm performance, see Gilley, K. M., & Rasheed, A. 2000. Making more by doing less: An analysis of outsourcing and its effects on firm performance. *Journal of Management,* 26(4): 763–790.

41. Quinn, J. B. 1992. *Intelligent enterprise: A knowledge and service based paradigm for industry.* New York: Free Press.

42. For an insightful perspective on outsourcing and its role in developing capabilities, read Gottfredson, M., Puryear, R., & Phillips, C. 2005. Strategic sourcing: From periphery to the core. *Harvard Business Review,* 83(4): 132–139.

43. This discussion draws upon Quinn, J. B., & Hilmer, F. C. 1994. Strategic outsourcing. *Sloan Management Review,* 35(4): 43–55.

44. See also Stuckey, J., & White, D. 1993. When and when not to vertically integrate. *Sloan Management Review,* Spring: 71–81; Harrar, G. 1993. Outsource tales. *Forbes ASAP,* June 7: 37–39, 42; and Davis, E. W. 1992. Global outsourcing: Have U.S. managers thrown the baby out with the bath water? *Business Horizons,* July–August: 58–64.

45. For a discussion of knowledge creation through alliances, refer to Inkpen, A. C. 1996. Creating knowledge through collaboration. *California Management Review,* 39(1): 123–140; and Mowery, D. C., Oxley, J. E., & Silverman, B. S. 1996. Strategic alliances and interfirm knowledge transfer. *Strategic Management Journal,* 17 (Special Issue, Winter): 77–92.

46. Doz, Y., & Hamel, G. 1998. *Alliance advantage: The art of creating value through partnering.* Boston: Harvard Business School Press.

47. DeSanctis, G., Glass, J. T., & Ensing, I. M. 2002. Organizational designs for R&D. *Academy of Management Executive,* 16(3): 55–66.

48. Barringer, B. R., & Harrison, J. S. 2000. Walking a tightrope: Creating value through interorganizational alliances. *Journal of Management,* 26: 367–403.

49. Davis, E. 1997. Interview: Norman Augustine. *Management Review,* November: 14.

50. One contemporary example of virtual organizations is R&D consortia. For an insightful discussion, refer to Sakaibara, M. 2002. Formation of R&D consortia: Industry and company effects. *Strategic Management Journal,* 23(11): 1033–1050.

51. Bartness, A., & Cerny, K. 1993. Building competitive advantage through a global network of capabilities. *California Management Review,* Winter: 78–103. For an insightful historical discussion of the usefulness of alliances in the computer industry, see Moore, J. F. 1993. Predators and prey: A new ecology of competition. *Harvard Business Review,* 71(3): 75–86.

52. See Lorange, P., & Roos, J. 1991. Why some strategic alliances succeed and others fail. *Journal of Business Strategy,* January–February: 25–30; and Slowinski, G. 1992. The human touch in strategic alliances. *Mergers and Acquisitions,* July–August: 44–47. A compelling argument for strategic alliances is provided by Ohmae, K. 1989. The global logic of strategic alliances. *Harvard Business Review,* 67(2): 143–154.

53. Some of the downsides of alliances are discussed in Das, T. K., & Teng, B. S. 2000. Instabilities of strategic alliances: An internal tensions perspective. *Organization Science,* 11: 77–106.

54. This section draws upon Dess, G. G., & Picken, J. C. 1997. *Mission critical.* Burr Ridge, IL: Irwin Professional Publishing.

55. Katzenbach, J. R., & Smith, D. K. 1994. *The wisdom of teams: Creating the high performance organization.* New York: HarperBusiness.

56. Hammer, M., & Champy, J. 1993. *Reengineering the corporation: A manifesto for business revolution.* New York: HarperCollins.

57. This section draws on Birkinshaw, J., & Gibson, C. 2004. Building ambidexterity into an organization. *MIT Sloan Management Review,* 45(4): 47–55; and Gibson, C. B., & Birkinshaw, J. 2004. The antecedents, consequences, and mediating role of organizational ambidexterity. *Academy of Management Journal,* 47(2): 209–226. Robert Duncan is generally credited with being the first to coin the term "ambidextrous organizations" in his article entitled: Designing dual structures for innovation. In Kilmann, R. H., Pondy, L. R., & Slevin, D. (Eds.). 1976. *The management of organizations,* vol. 1: 167–188. For a seminal academic discussion of the concept of exploration and exploitation, which parallels adaptation and alignment, refer to: March, J. G. 1991. Exploration and exploitation in organizational learning. *Organization Science,* 2: 71–86.

58. This section is based on O'Reilly, C. A., & Tushman, M. L. 2004. The ambidextrous organization. *Harvard Business Review,* 82(4): 74–81.

11

Strategic Leadership:

Creating a Learning Organization and an Ethical Organization

After reading this chapter, you should have a good understanding of:

- The three key activities in which all successful leaders must be continually engaged.

- The importance of recognizing the interdependence of the three key leadership activities and the salience of power in overcoming resistance to change.

- The crucial role of emotional intelligence (EI) in successful leadership as well as its potential drawbacks.

- The value of creating and maintaining a "learning organization" in today's global marketplace.

- The five central elements of a "learning organization."

- The leader's role in establishing an ethical organization.

- The benefits of developing an ethical organization.

- The high financial and nonfinancial costs associated with ethical crises.

*t*o compete in the global marketplace, organizations need to have strong and effective leadership. This involves the active process of both creating and implementing proper strategies. In this chapter we address key activities in which leaders throughout the organization must be involved to be successful in creating competitive advantages.

In the first section we provide a brief overview of the three key leadership activities. These are (1) setting a direction, (2) designing the organization, and (3) nurturing a culture committed to excellence and ethical behavior. Each of these activities is "necessary but not sufficient"; that is, to be effective, leaders must give proper attention to each of them. We also address the importance of a leader's effective use of power to overcome resistance to change.

The second section discusses the vital role of emotional intelligence (EI) in effective strategic leadership. EI refers to an individual's capacity for recognizing his or her emotions and those of others. It consists of five components: self-awareness, self-regulation, motivation, empathy, and social skills. We also address potential downsides or drawbacks that may result from the ineffective use of EI.

Next we address the important role of a leader in creating a "learning organization." Here leaders must strive to harness the individual and collective talents of individuals throughout the entire organization. Creating a learning organization becomes particularly important in today's competitive environment, which is increasingly unpredictable, dynamic, and interdependent. Clearly, everyone must be involved in learning. It can't be only a few people at the top of the organization. The key elements of a learning organization are inspiring and motivating people with a mission or purpose, empowering employees at all levels, accumulating and sharing internal and external information, and challenging the status quo to enable creativity.

The final section discusses a leader's challenge in creating and maintaining an ethical organization. There are many benefits of having an ethical organization. In addition to financial benefits, it can enhance human capital and help to ensure positive relationships with suppliers, customers, society at large, and governmental agencies. On the other hand, the costs of ethical crises can be very expensive for many reasons. We address four key elements of an ethical organization: role models, corporate credos and codes of conduct, reward and evaluation systems, and policies and procedures.

Scott A. Livengood was fired as Chief Executive Officer (CEO) of Krispy Kreme on January 19, 2005.[1] He hasn't received very much good news lately. The firm's stock went up 10 percent the day of that announcement. And he received the rather dubious honor of being recognized as one of *BusinessWeek*'s seven "Worst Managers" of 2004.

What brought about the demise of Livengood, a 28-year veteran of the doughnut maker who had been CEO since 1998? Let's look at two of the central issues.

First, under his direction Krispy Kreme expanded far too rapidly. After its initial public offering in 2001, it continued to open stores at breakneck speed. Hoping to cash in on the nation's sweet tooth, the chain created media events in places like New York, San Francisco, and Boston. At times, cars would line up for blocks just to bring a box of the tasty confections to work. Unfortunately, while the craze faded, the costs of operating the franchises did not. By 2003, same-store sales had declined 16 percent, while the company's overhead continued to rise. In short, the brand quickly lost its novelty. Soon Krispy Kreme realized that many of its franchises would fail.

Recent financial results reflect the poor strategy. The once high-flying company posted a $3 million third-quarter loss in November 2004—its second losing quarter of the year. And in February 2005, the firm stated that it would restate earnings for the previous year, lowering previously reported income by as much as 8.6 percent.

Second, there are what *Fortune* has called "shady deals" surrounding how the firm conducted buybacks of some franchises owned by corporate insiders. For example, Krispy Kreme didn't disclose that a California franchise it repurchased in 2004 was partly owned by Livengood's ex-wife, whose stake was valued at $1.5 million. While executives aren't required to disclose transactions with former spouses, Livengood could be in trouble if the deal was made as part of a settlement or in lieu of alimony.

An even more troubling transaction is the 2003 deal in which the chain repurchased six stores in Dallas and Shreveport, Louisiana, that were partly owned by Krispy Kreme's former chairman and current director, Joseph McAleer. McAleer got a pretty good deal—$67 million (or $11 million per store). This comes to more than three times what the firm paid for many other shops! According to David Gourevitch, a former Securities and Exchange Commission (SEC) enforcement attorney, "At some point a transaction is not remotely reasonable, and it approximates a gift or payoff." Worst case scenario: The SEC could impose fines and require some officials to step down.

The SEC continues to investigate the firm and it upgraded its informal inquiry to a formal probe. Although customers may continue to enjoy Krispy Kreme's products, the investors have hardly had a pleasant experience. Krispy Kreme's stock price has continued to sink. By late 2005 it was at $7—less than one-sixth of the $45 peak that it reached in July 2003. This fall reflects a loss of market capitalization of over $2 billion.

Clearly, many of the decisions and actions of Scott A. Livengood were not in the best interests of the firm and its shareholders. In contrast, effective leaders play an important and often pivotal role in the development and implementation of strategies.

This chapter provides insights into how organizations can more effectively manage, change, and cope with increased environmental complexity and uncertainty. Below we will define leadership and introduce what are considered to be the three most important leadership activities as well as the important role of power. The second section focuses on a key trait—emotional intelligence—that has become increasingly recognized as critical to successful leadership. Then, the third major section, "Developing a Learning Organization," provides a useful framework for how leaders can help their firms learn and proactively adapt in the face of accelerating change. Central to this contemporary idea is the concept of empowerment, wherein employees and managers throughout the organization truly come to have a sense of self-determination, meaning, competence, and impact. The fourth section addresses the leader's role in building an ethical organization. Here, we address both the value of an ethical culture for a firm as well as the key elements that it encompasses.

>>Leadership: Three Interdependent Activities

In today's chaotic world, few would argue against the need for leadership, but how do we go about encouraging it? Let's focus on business organizations. Is it enough to merely keep the organization afloat, or is it essential to make steady progress toward some well-defined objective? We believe custodial management is not leadership. Rather, leadership is proactive, goal-oriented, and focused on the creation and implementation of a creative vision. *Leadership is the process of transforming organizations from what they are to what the leader would have them become.* This definition implies a lot: *dissatisfaction* with the status quo, a *vision* of what should be, and a *process* for bringing about change. An insurance company executive recently shared the following insight on leadership, "I lead by the Noah Principle: It's all right to know when it's going to rain, but, by God, you had better build the ark."

Doing the right thing is becoming increasingly important in today's competitive environment. After all, many industries are declining; the global village is becoming increasingly complex, interconnected, and unpredictable; and product and market life cycles are becoming increasingly compressed. Recently, when asked to describe the life cycle of his company's products, the CEO of a supplier of computer components replied, "Seven months from cradle to grave—and that includes three months to design the product and get it into production!" Richard D'Aveni, author of *Hypercompetition,* went even further. He argued that in a world where all dimensions of competition appear to be compressed in time and heightened in complexity, *sustainable* competitive advantages are no longer possible.

Despite the importance of doing the "right thing," leaders must also be concerned about doing "things right." Charan and Colvin argued strongly that implementation (or execution) is also essential to success.

> Any way that you look at it, mastering execution turns out to be the odds-on best way for a CEO to keep his job. So what's the right way to think about that sexier obsession, strategy? It's vitally important—obviously. The problem is that our age's fascination feeds the mistaken belief that developing exactly the right strategy will enable a company to rocket past competitors. In reality, that's less than half the battle.[2]

Thus, leaders are change agents whose success is measured by how effectively they implement a strategic vision and mission.

Accordingly, many authors contend that successful leaders must recognize three interdependent activities that must be continually reassessed for organizations to succeed. As shown in Exhibit 11.1, these are: (1) determining a direction, (2) designing the organization, and (3) nurturing a culture dedicated to excellence and ethical behavior.[3]

The interdependent nature of these three activities is self-evident. Consider an organization with a great mission and a superb organizational structure and design, but a culture that implicitly encourages shirking and unethical behavior. Or a strong culture and organizational design but little direction and vision—in caricature, a highly ethical and efficient buggy whip manufacturer. Or one with a sound direction and strong culture, but counterproductive teams and a "zero-sum" reward system that leads to the dysfunctional situation in which one party's gain is viewed as another party's loss, and collaboration and sharing are severely hampered. Obviously, the examples could go on and on. We contend that much of the failure of today's organizations can be attributed to a lack of equal consideration of these three activities. The imagery of a three-legged stool is instructive: It will collapse if one leg is missing or broken. Let's briefly look at each of these activities. We'll also address the important role of a leader's power in overcoming resistance to change.

Exhibit 11.1   **Three Interdependent Activities of Leadership**

Setting a Direction

Leaders need a holistic understanding of an organization's stakeholders. This requires an ability to scan the environment to develop a knowledge of all of the company's stakeholders (e.g., customers, suppliers, shareholders) and other salient environmental trends and events and integrate this knowledge into a vision of what the organization could become. It necessitates the capacity to solve increasingly complex problems, become proactive in approach, and develop viable strategic options. Developing a strategic vision provides many benefits: a clear future direction; a framework for the organization's mission and goals; and enhanced employee communication, participation, and commitment. Strategy Spotlight 11.1 discusses how Chairman Howard Schultz's vision of Starbucks as a "third place" has spurred the firm's remarkable growth.

At times the creative process involves what the CEO of Yokogawa, GE's Japanese partner in the Medical Systems business, called "bullet train" thinking.[4] That is, if you want to increase the speed by 10 miles per hour, you look for incremental advances. However, if you want to double the speed, you've got to think "out of the box" (e.g., widen the track, change the overall suspension system). In today's challenging times, leaders typically need more than just keeping the same train with a few minor tweaks. Instead, they must come up with more revolutionary visions.

Consider how Robert Tillman, CEO of Lowe's, dramatically revitalized his firm by setting a clear and compelling direction. He made it into a formidable competitor to Home Depot, Inc., the Goliath of the home-improvement and hardware retailing industry.[5] In his six years as CEO, Tillman has transformed the $36.5 billion chain, based in Wilkesboro, North Carolina. Its shares have more than doubled over the past four years, while Home Depot's have fallen about 20 percent.

Tillman has redirected Lowe's strategy by responding effectively to research showing that women initiate 80 percent of home projects. While Home Depot has focused on the professionals and male customers, Tillman has redesigned Lowe's stores to give them a brighter appearance, stocked them with more appliances, and focused on higher-margin goods (including everything from Laura Ashley paints to high-end bathroom fixtures). And, like Wal-Mart, Lowe's has one of the best inventory systems in retailing. As a result, Lowe's profits are expected to continue to rise faster than Home Depot's.

Howard Schultz's Vision of Starbucks as a "Third Place"

Most people think of Starbucks as an expensive place to get a cup of coffee. However, Chairman Howard Schultz sees the 8,000-store chain as a "third place" for people to hang out besides home and work. That is why the seemingly unrelated service of offering wireless Net access in its stores that started in 2002 turned out to be so successful. Although Starbucks Corp. will not quantify the revenue impact, people using the service typically stay nine times longer than the usual five minutes—almost certainly enough time to consume more lattes. Further, 90 percent of customers who log on are doing so after peak morning hours, which helps to fill the stores during previously slow

Source: Burrows, P., Hamm, S., Brady, D. & Rowley, I. 2004. Managing for innovation. *BusinessWeek*, October 11: 192–200; and Gray, S. 2005. Starbucks brews broader menu; coffee chain's cup runneth over with breakfast, lunch, music. *Wall Street Journal*, February 9: B9.

periods. According to Anne Saunders, Starbucks' senior vice-president of marketing, "If we'd only thought of ourselves as a coffee company, we wouldn't have done this."

The wireless network also inspired a new initiative that could again remake the Seattle-based company. Its recently introduced Hear Music Coffeehouses features dozens of listening stations where people can make custom CDs, at about a dollar a tune, from hundreds of thousands of songs. Eventually, Starbucks plans to have a Hear Music media bar in about half of its stores. In addition to offering this new service, Schultz has said he thinks Starbucks could transform the music business. Although that might be debatable, he's transforming Starbucks once again. And who would have ever thought that Apple and Starbucks might become competitors?

Let's now turn to another key leadership activity: the design of the organization's structure, processes, and evaluation and control systems.

Designing the Organization

At times, almost all leaders have difficulty implementing their vision and strategies. Such problems—many of which we discussed in Chapter 10—may stem from a variety of sources, including:

- Lack of understanding of responsibility and accountability among managers.
- Reward systems that do not motivate individuals (or collectives such as groups and divisions) toward desired organizational goals.
- Inadequate or inappropriate budgeting and control systems.
- Insufficient mechanisms to coordinate and integrate activities across the organization.

Successful leaders are actively involved in building structures, teams, systems, and organizational processes that facilitate the implementation of their vision and strategies. For example, we discussed the necessity for consistency between business-level and corporate-level strategies and organizational control in Chapter 9. Clearly, a firm would generally be unable to attain an overall low-cost advantage without closely monitoring its costs through detailed and formalized cost and financial control procedures. In a similar vein, achieving a differentiation advantage would necessitate encouraging innovation, creativity, and sensitivity to market conditions. Such efforts would be typically impeded by the use of a huge set of cumbersome rules and regulations, as well as highly centralized decision making. With regard to corporate-level strategy, in Chapter 9 we addressed how a related diversification strategy would necessitate reward systems that emphasize behavioral measures to promote sharing across divisions within a firm, whereas an unrelated strategy should rely more on financial (or objective) indicators of

STRATEGY SPOTLIGHT   11.2

Marshall Industries: Problems with Incentives

Marshall Industries is a large Los Angeles distributor of 170,000 different electronic components. The company has 30,000 customers and receives supplies from more than 150 suppliers. CEO Rod Rodin became concerned about some irregularities in the company. He saw that an average of 20 percent of monthly sales were being shipped in the last three days of the month. He discovered that divisions within the company were hiding customer returns and opening bad credit accounts to beef up monthly numbers. Employees in divisions with scarce supplies were hiding the supplies from other divisions. Sales representatives, working on commission, were constantly fighting with one another over how commissions should be split on joint sales efforts.

Rodin came to the conclusion that his employees were doing exactly what they were being paid to do. The commission structure encouraged employees to hide re-

turns, put in nonexistent orders the last few days of a month to make their monthly sales goals, and hide resources from one another. The key objective, of course, was sales, but the compensation structure failed to motivate employees in that direction. "Creative accounting" could easily make sure representatives made their sales goals each month whether or not the sales actually occurred. Until Rodin noticed the irregularities, there were few control mechanisms in place to integrate sales activities between divisions.

Rodin's solution? Scrap the commission system. From now on, all salespeople would receive a salary plus a bonus based on company profitability. *Electronic Buyers News* published an editorial criticizing the decision. Most people thought it was a crazy idea. But sometimes crazy ideas work pretty well. Four years after the change, sales had grown from $582 million to $1.2 billion, and the stock price of Marshall Industries had nearly quadrupled. Aligning the goals of employees with the objectives of the company seemed to be just the thing needed to bring control, integration, and coordination out of chaos.

Sources: Dess, G. G., & Picken, J. C. 1999. *Beyond productivity.* New York: AMACOM: Muoio, A. 1998. The truth is, the truth hurts. *Fast Company,* April–May: 93–102; Wilson, T. 1998. Marshall Industries: Wholesale shift to the Web. *InternetWeek,* July 20: 14–15.

performance, such as revenue gains and profitability, since there is less need for collaboration across business units because they would have little in common.

Strategy Spotlight 11.2 focuses on how the reward and evaluation system at Marshall Industries had unintended consequences, making budgeting and control very difficult. However, Rod Rodin, Marshall's CEO, recognized the problem and took decisive and bold action. This example shows how leaders must, at times, make decisions that appear to be counter to "conventional wisdom."

Nurturing a Culture Dedicated to Excellence and Ethical Behavior

In Chapter 9 we discussed how organizational culture can be an effective and positive means of organizational control. Leaders play a key role in developing and sustaining—as well as changing, when necessary—an organization's culture. Strategy Spotlight 11.3 discusses how the leadership at the Container Store has created such an exemplary culture.

Leaders actions can, of course, also have a very detrimental effect on a firm's culture and ethics. Consider Kenneth Lay, the infamous former CEO of Enron. He, along with other top executives, led Enron into a megascandal that resulted in bankruptcy and an investor loss of $67 billion. He will stand trial in Houston, Texas, in early 2006 on criminal conspiracy charges.[6] Sherron Watkins, a former vice president at Enron, provides an interesting example of and perspective on how Lay's actions served to erode Enron's culture and ethical standards:[7]

> Ken Lay, although well known for his charitable giving and his verbal commitment to Enron's four core values (Respect, Integrity, Communication, and Excellence), was not quite walking

The Container Store: The Best Place to Work in America

The Container Store, a Dallas-based chain of 20 specialty retail stores that sell everything you need to organize your home, office, car, or even your life, has been consistently ranked as one of the "Best Companies to Work For" by *Fortune* magazine. In the five years from 2000 to 2004, they were always ranked in the top three, and they were number one in 2000 and 2001. This is truly surprising considering that the retail industry typically has a very high employee turnover, poorly trained workers on minimum wages, and low skill levels. The Container Store is also one of the 14 companies that Dr. Leonard Berry identified as providing exemplary service through values-driven marketing. What makes the Container Store so special?

First of all, they pay very well. The average salary for salespersons is $36,000—one of the highest salaries in the industry. The benefits are substantial too. But the financial benefits are only a small part of the story. The employees consider the Container Store a happy place to work. It is a community that they belong to. Nearly 40 percent of the company's new hires are referrals from existing employees. The company invests heavily in employee training. Stores welcome new employees with Foundation Week, a week-long orientation to the company, its products, and philosophy along with a welcome box that contains $150 worth of company products as gifts. During the first year, an employee receives 235 hours of training! At the headquarters, the Fun Committee builds a sense of community among employees through lunch-time activities such as silent auctions. At birthday celebrations, teams gather for lunch and cake. It is the birthday person's responsibility to bring cake for the next birthday honoree. The company offers employees yoga classes, chair massages, and an online exercise and nutrition diary personalized to every employee! More importantly, the company's books are open to every employee every day. This helps them make better business decisions.

The company has no thick policy manuals. Instead, they are guided by six Foundational Principles that are easy to remember:

1. "Fill the other guy's basket to the brim." Each employee is trained to work with the customer in creative and imaginative ways to help them choose the best products for organizing.

2. "Man-in-the-desert." A thirsty man reaching an oasis needs more than just water. Similarly, each employee is expected to "astonish" the customer by exceeding his expectations.

3. "1 average person = 3 lousy people. 1 good person = 3 average people. 1 great person = 3 good people." The Container Store seeks only great people. Others may be happy with 9 lousy people!

4. "Intuition does not come to the unprepared mind." The heavy emphasis on training helps to prepare the employees to create unique solutions for customers.

5. "The best selection of products anywhere + the best service anywhere + the best pricing in our markets."

6. "Air of excitement." Three steps into the door and customers realize that they are in a different place.

Kip Tindal, CEO of the Container Store, explains:

TCS's Foundational Principles empower employees to serve the customer in the true sense of the word. Employees are trusted to make whatever decision necessary to help a customer. TCS is said to provide exemplary service through values-driven marketing practices. Its employees delight in helping customers solve problems—and they possess the freedom and confidence to do so. The quest for excellence pays off in human terms, as well as financial terms.

Sources: Gavin, J. H., & Mason, R. O. 2004. The virtuous organization: The value of happiness in the workplace. *Organizational Dynamics*, 33(4): 379–392; and Berry, L. 1999. *Discovering the soul of service: Nine drivers of sustainable business success.* New York: Free Press.

the walk. For example, he always had Enron employees use his sister's travel agency. And not just us; the local Andersen office and Enron's outside attorneys, Vinson and Elkins, were pressured into using her agency as well. Trouble was that it provided neither low cost nor good service. Domestically, you could manage, but when it came to international travel—that agency sucked. I was stuck in Third World countries, where I didn't speak the language, without a hotel room or with an insufficient airline ticket home, despite paperwork that indicated otherwise. The incompetence was hard to understand. I would try using a different agency, but after one or two expense reports, I'd get a finger-wagging voice mail or e-mail reminding me that I needed to use Enron's preferred agency, Travel Agency in the Park. We called it Travel Agency in the Dark.

   In some perverse way, Andy Fastow (Enron's Chief Financial Officer) might have justified his behavior by saying to himself, "Well, my LJM partnership is helping Enron meet its financial statement goals. Why can't I just take a little for myself, just like Lay has been taking a little Enron money and transferring it to his sister for all these years?"[8]

Clearly, a leader's ethical behavior can make a strong impact on an organization—for good or for bad. Given the importance of this topic, we address it in detail in the last major section of this chapter.

Managers and top executives must also accept personal responsibility for developing and strengthening ethical behavior throughout the organization. They must consistently demonstrate that such behavior is central to the vision and mission of the organization. Several elements must be present and reinforced for a firm to become a highly ethical organization: role models, corporate credos and codes of conduct, reward and evaluation systems, and policies and procedures.

Overcoming Barriers to Change and the Effective Use of Power

Now that we have discussed the three interdependent activities that leaders perform, we must address a key question: What are the barriers to change that leaders often encounter, and how can they use power to bring about meaningful change in their organizations? After all, people generally have some level of choice about how strongly they support or resist a leader's change initiatives. Why is there often so much resistance? There are many reasons why organizations and managers at all levels are prone to inertia and are slow to learn, adapt, and change.

1. Many people have *vested interests in the status quo.* There is a broad stream of organizational literature on the subject of "escalation," wherein certain individuals (in both controlled laboratory settings and actual management practice) continue to throw "good money at bad decisions" despite negative performance feedback.[9]

2. There are *systemic barriers.* Here, the design of the organization's structure, information processing, reporting relationships, and so forth impede the proper flow and evaluation of information. A bureaucratic structure with multiple layers, onerous requirements for documentation, and rigid rules and procedures will often "inoculate" the organization against change.

3. *Behavioral barriers* are associated with the tendency of managers to look at issues from a biased or limited perspective. This can be attributed to their education, training, work experiences, and so forth. For example, consider an incident shared by David Lieberman, marketing director at GVO, an innovation consulting firm based in Palo Alto, California.

   A company's creative type had come up with a great idea for a new product. Nearly everybody loved it. However, it was shot down by a high-ranking manufacturing representative who exploded: "A new color? Do you have any idea of the spare-parts problem that it will create?" This was not a dimwit exasperated at having to build a few storage racks at the warehouse. He'd been hearing for years about cost cutting, lean inventories, and "focus." Lieberman's comment: "Good concepts, but not always good for innovation."

4. *Political barriers* refer to conflicts arising from power relationships. This can be the outcome of a myriad of symptoms such as vested interests (e.g., the aforementioned escalation problems), refusal to share information, conflicts over resources, conflicts between departments and divisions, and petty interpersonal differences.

5. *Personal time constraints* bring to mind the old saying about "not having enough time to drain the swamp when you are up to your neck in alligators." In effect, Gresham's law of planning states that operational decisions will drive out the time necessary for strategic thinking and reflection. This tendency is accentuated in organizations experiencing severe price competition or retrenchment wherein managers and employees are spread rather thin.

Successful leadership requires effective use of power in overcoming barriers to change.[10] Power refers to a leader's ability to get things done in a way he or she wants them to be done. It is the ability to influence other people's behavior, to persuade them to do things that they otherwise would not do, and to overcome resistance and opposition to changing direction. Effective exercise of power is essential for successful leadership.[11]

A leader derives his or her power from several sources or bases. Numerous classifications of such sources or bases abound in the literature on power. However, the simplest way to understand the bases of power is by classifying them as organizational and personal, as shown in Exhibit 11.2.

Organizational bases of power refer to the power that a person wields because of holding a formal management position. These include legitimate power, reward power, coercive power, and information power. *Legitimate power* is derived from organizationally conferred decision-making authority and is exercised by virtue of a manager's position in the organization. *Reward power* depends on the ability of the leader or manager to confer rewards for positive behaviors or outcomes. *Coercive power* is the power a manager exercises over employees using fear of punishment for errors of omission or commission. *Information power* arises from a manager's access, control, and distribution of information that is not freely available to everyone in an organization.

Apart from the organizationally derived power, a leader might be able to influence subordinates because of his or her personality characteristics and behavior. These would be considered the "personal" bases of power. The personal bases of power are referent power and expert power. The source of *referent power* is a subordinate's identification with the leader. A leader's personal attributes or charisma might influence subordinates and make them devoted to that leader. On the other hand, the source of *expert power* is the leader's

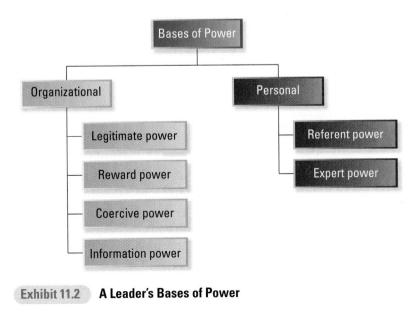

Exhibit 11.2   A Leader's Bases of Power

STRATEGY SPOTLIGHT

William Bratton: Using Multiple Bases of Power

William Bratton, Chief of the Los Angeles Police Department has an enviable track record in turning around police departments in crime-ridden cities. First, while running the police division of Massachusetts Bay Transit Authority (MBTA) in Boston, then as police commissioner of New York in the mid-1990s, and now in Los Angeles since 2002, Chief Bratton is credited with reducing crime and improving police morale in record time. An analysis of his success at each of these organizations reveals very similar patterns both in terms of the problems he faced and the many ways in which he used the different bases of power to engineer a rapid turnaround.

In Boston, New York, and Los Angeles, Chief Bratton faced similar hurdles: organizations wedded to the status quo, limited resources, demotivated staffs, and opposition from powerful vested interests. But he does not give up in the face of these seemingly insurmountable problems. He is persuasive in calls for change, capable of mobilizing the commitment of key players, silencing vocal naysayers, and building rapport with superiors and subordinates while building bridges with external constituencies.

Chief Bratton's persuasion tactics are unconventional, yet effective. When he was running the MBTA police, the Transit Authority decided to buy small squad cars, which are cheaper to buy and to run, but very inadequate for the police officer's task. Instead of arguing, Bratton invited the general manager for a tour of the city. He rode with the general manager in exactly the same type of car that was ordered for ordinary officers, and drove over every pothole on the road. He moved the seats forward so that the general manager could feel how little leg room was there. And he put on his belt, cuffs, and gun so that the general manager could understand how limited the space was. After two hours in the cramped car, the general manager was ready to change the order and get more suitable cars for the officers!

Another tactic Bratton used effectively was insisting on community meetings between police officers and citizens. This went against the long-standing practice of detachment between police and community to decrease the chances of corruption. The result was that his department had a better understanding of public concerns and rearranged their priorities, which in turn led to better community relations. For internal communications, he relied mainly on professionally produced videos instead of long, boring memos.

Chief Bratton also shows a remarkable talent for building political bridges and silencing naysayers. As he was introducing his zero-tolerance policing approach that aggressively targets "quality of life" crimes such as panhandling, drunkenness, and prostitution, opposition came from the city's courts which feared being inundated by a large number of small-crimes cases. Bratton enlisted the support of Rudolph Giuliani, the mayor of New York, who had considerable influence over the district attorneys, the courts, and the city jail. He also took the case to the *New York Times,* and managed to get the issue of zero-tolerance on the front pages of the newspaper. The courts were left with no alternative but to cooperate.

To a great extent, Bratton's success can be attributed to his understanding of the subtleties of power, including persuasion, motivation, coalition building, empathy for subordinates, and a focus on goals.

Sources: Chan Kim, W., & Renee Mauborgne, R. 2003. Tipping point leadership. *Harvard Business Review,* 81(4): 60–69; and McCarthy, T. 2004. The gang buster. *Time,* January 19: 56–58.

expertise and knowledge in a particular field. The leader is the expert on whom subordinates depend for information that they need to do their jobs successfully.

Successful leaders use the different bases of power, and often a combination of them, as appropriate to meet the demands of a situation, such as the nature of the task, the personality characteristics of the subordinates, the urgency of the issue, and other factors. Leaders must recognize that persuasion and developing consensus are often essential, but so is pressing for action. Clearly, at some point stragglers must be prodded into line.[12] Peter Georgescu, who recently retired as CEO of Young & Rubicam (an advertising and media giant acquired by the UK-based WPP Group in 2000), summarized a leader's dilemma brilliantly (and humorously), "I have knee pads and a .45. I get down and beg a lot, but I shoot people too."[13]

Strategy Spotlight 11.4 addresses some of the subtleties of power. It focuses on William Bratton, Chief of the Los Angeles Police Department, who has enjoyed a very successful career in law enforcement.

>>Emotional Intelligence: A Key Leadership Trait

In the previous section, we discussed three of the salient activities of strategic leadership. In a sense, the focus was on "what leaders *do.*" In this section, the issue becomes "who leaders *are,*" that is, what are the most important traits (or capabilities) of leaders. Clearly, these two issues are related, because successful leaders possess the valuable traits that enable them to perform effectively in order to create value for their organization.

There has been, as we would expect, a vast amount of literature on the successful traits of leaders, including business leaders at the highest level.[14] These traits include integrity, maturity, energy, judgment, motivation, intelligence, expertise, and so on. However, for simplicity, these traits may be grouped into three broad sets of capabilities:

- Purely technical skills (like accounting or operations research).
- Cognitive abilities (like analytical reasoning or quantitative analysis).
- Emotional intelligence (such as the ability to work with others and a passion for work).

One attribute of successful leaders that has become popular in both the literature and management practice in recent years is "emotional intelligence."[15] Some evidence of this popularity is that *Harvard Business Review* articles published in 1998 and 2000 by psychologist/journalist Daniel Goleman, who is most closely associated with the concept, have become this widely read management journal's most highly requested reprint articles. And two of Goleman's recent books, *Emotional Intelligence* and *Working with Emotional Intelligence,* were both on the *New York Times*'s best-seller lists. Goleman defines emotional intelligence (EI) as the capacity for recognizing one's own emotions and those of others.[16]

Recent studies of successful managers have found that effective leaders consistently have a high level of emotional intelligence.[17] Findings indicate, for example, that EI is a better predictor of life success (economic well-being, satisfaction with life, friendship, family life), including occupational attainments, than IQ. Such evidence has been extrapolated to the catchy phrase: "IQ gets you hired, but EQ (Emotional Quotient) gets you promoted." And surveys show that human resource managers believe this statement to be true, and perhaps even for highly technical jobs such as those of scientists and engineers.

This is not to say that IQ and technical skills are irrelevant. Obviously, they do matter, but they should be viewed as "threshold capabilities." That is, they are the necessary requirements for attaining higher-level managerial positions. EI, on the other hand, is essential for leadership success. Without it, Goleman has argued, a manager can have excellent training, an incisive analytical mind, and many smart ideas but will still not be a great leader.

There are five components of EI: self-awareness, self-regulation, motivation, empathy, and social skill. They are included in Exhibit 11.3. Next, we will briefly discuss each of them.

Self-Awareness

Self-awareness is the first component of EI and brings to mind that Delphic oracle who gave the advice "know thyself" thousands of years ago. Self-awareness involves a person having a deep understanding of his or her emotions, strengths, weaknesses, and drives. People with strong self-awareness are neither overly critical nor unrealistically optimistic. Instead, they are honest with themselves and others.

	Definition	Hallmarks
Self-management skills:		
Self-awareness	• The ability to recognize and understand your moods, emotions, and drives, as well as their effect on others.	• Self-confidence • Realistic self-assessment • Self-deprecating sense of humor
Self-regulation	• The ability to control or redirect disruptive impulses and moods. • The propensity to suspend judgment—to think before acting.	• Trustworthiness and integrity • Comfort with ambiguity • Openness to change
Motivation	• A passion to work for reasons that go beyond money or status. • A propensity to pursue goals with energy and persistence.	• Strong drive to achieve • Optimism, even in the face of failure • Organizational commitment
Managing relationships:		
Empathy	• The ability to understand the emotional makeup of other people. • Skill in treating people according to their emotional reactions.	• Expertise in building and retaining talent • Cross-cultural sensitivity • Service to clients and customers
Social skill	• Proficiency in managing relationships and building networks. • An ability to find common ground and build rapport.	• Effectiveness in leading change • Persuasiveness • Expertise in building and leading teams

Source: Adapted and reprinted by permission of *Harvard Business Review.* Exhibit from "What Makes a Leader," by D. Goleman, January 2004. Copyright © 2004 by the Harvard Business School Publishing Corporation; all rights reserved.

Exhibit 11.3

The Five Components of Emotional Intelligence at Work

People generally admire and respect candor. Further, leaders are constantly required to make judgment calls that require a candid assessment of capabilities—their own and those of others. People who assess themselves honestly (i.e., self-aware people) are well suited to do the same for the organizations they run.

Self-Regulation

Biological impulses drive our emotions. Although we cannot do away with them, we can strive to manage them. Self-regulation, which is akin to an ongoing inner conversation, frees us from being prisoners of our feelings. People engaged in such conversation feel bad moods and emotional impulses just as everyone else does. However, they find ways to control them and even channel them in useful ways.

People who are in control of their feelings and impulses are able to create an environment of trust and fairness. In such an environment, political behavior and infighting are sharply reduced and productivity tends to be high. Further, people who have mastered their emotions are better able to bring about and implement change in an organization. When a new initiative is announced, they are less likely to panic; rather, they are able to suspend judgment, seek out information, and listen to executives explain the new program.

Motivation

Successful executives are driven to achieve beyond expectations—their own and everyone else's. They are driven to achieve. Although many people are driven by external factors, such as money and prestige, those with leadership potential are driven by a deeply embedded desire to achieve for the sake of achievement.

How can a person tell if he or she is motivated by a drive for achievement instead of external rewards? Look for a sign of passion for the work itself, such as seeking out creative challenges, a love of learning, and taking pride in a job well done. Also, motivated people have a high level of energy to do things better as well as a restlessness with the status quo. They are eager to explore new approaches to their work.

Empathy

Empathy is probably the most easily recognized component of EI. In a business setting, empathy means thoughtfully considering an employee's feelings, along with other factors, in the process of making intelligent decisions. Empathy is particularly important in today's business environment for at least three reasons: the increasing use of teams, the rapid pace of globalization, and the growing need to retain talent.[18]

When leading a team, a manager is often charged with arriving at a consensus—often in the face of a high level of emotions. Empathy enables a manager to sense and understand the viewpoints of everyone around the table.

Globalization typically involves cross-cultural dialogue that can easily lead to miscues. Empathetic people are attuned to the subtleties of body language; they can hear the message beneath the words being spoken. In a more general sense, they have a deep understanding of the existence and importance of cultural and ethnic differences.

Empathy also plays a key role in retaining talent. As we discussed in Chapter 4, human capital is particularly important to a firm in the knowledge economy when it comes to creating advantages that are sustainable. Leaders need empathy to develop and keep top talent. Today, that's even more important, because when high performers leave, they take their tacit knowledge with them.

Social Skill

While the first three components of emotional intelligence are all self-management skills, the last two—empathy and social skill—concern a person's ability to manage relationships with others. Social skill may be viewed as friendliness with a purpose: moving people in the direction you desire, whether that's agreement on a new marketing strategy or enthusiasm about a new product.

Socially skilled people tend to have a wide circle of acquaintances as well as a knack for finding common ground and building rapport. They recognize that nothing gets done alone, and they have a network in place when the time for action comes.

Social skill can be viewed as the culmination of the other dimensions of EI. People will be effective at managing relationships when they can understand and control their own emotions and can empathize with the feelings of others. Motivation also contributes to social skill. People who are driven to achieve tend to be optimistic, even when confronted with setbacks or failure. And when people are upbeat, their "glow" is cast upon conversations and other social encounters. They are popular, and for good reason.

STRATEGY SPOTLIGHT

Emotional Intelligence: Pat Croce

Every businessperson knows the story of a highly qualified, well-trained executive who was promoted to a leadership position, only to fail at the job. This is not because the executive didn't have a high IQ or sound technical fundamentals. It is about the presence or lack of *emotional intelligence*. When Pat Croce took over as the new president of the Philadelphia 76ers in May 1996, people were skeptical of his cornball style and unabashed attitude. At his national debut as the president of the 76ers, he erupted with glee as the team wound up with the number one pick at the nationally televised broadcast of the NBA's draft lottery. He leaped to his feet, pumped his fists and slapped the palms of the other team representatives. But that was not all. He then hugged David Stern, the gray-haired, tight-laced NBA commissioner, kissing him on the cheek and patting him on the sleeve of his suit jacket.

People who meet Croce on the street or at work salute him with either a high-five or a "Hey dude." Those who know him say his high energy and red-bloodedness are infectious and his vivacious style is how he exhibits the virtues of a can-do attitude and never-say-die perseverance. A self-made man, Croce founded a fitness center called the Sports Physical Therapists (SPT), successfully turned it into an 11-state chain, and eventually sold it off for $40 million in 1993.

His record as the basketball baron is no less impressive. His team was the Cinderella story of the NBA. Before he took over, the team's dismal business management and apathetic player attitudes had led to a very unimpressive record. Croce is widely credited with reinvigorating the business with his hurricane-force personality and leading the born-again team to its first chance to compete in the NBA finals in more than a decade. And for all this, Croce has but his emotional intelligence to thank. His self-awareness, motivation, and social skills make him detail-oriented and competitive—the stereotypical qualities of a successful entrepreneur.

Sources: Rosenbloom, J. 2002. Why it's Pat Croce's world. *Inc.*, April: 77–83; www.patcroce.com/NonMember/pages/index.html; and Brokaw, L. 2002. Pat Croce's bottom line. *Fast Company*, January 1: 45–47.

Strategy Spotlight 11.5 discusses Pat Croce's approach to leadership and illustrates some of the components of emotional intelligence. Croce is president of the National Basketball Association's Philadelphia 76ers.

Consider some comments from Dan Goleman, who has made many important contributions to our understanding of EI.

> It would be foolish to assert that good old-fashioned IQ and technical ability are not important ingredients to strong leadership. But the recipe would not be complete without emotional intelligence. It was once thought that the components of emotional intelligence were "nice to have" in business leaders. But now we know that, for the sake of performance, these are ingredients that leaders "need to have."
>
> It is fortunate, then, that emotional intelligence can be learned. The process is not easy. It takes time and, most of all, commitment. But the benefits that come from having a well-developed emotional intelligence, both for the individual and for the organization, make it worth the effort.[19]

Emotional Intelligence: Some Potential Drawbacks and Cautionary Notes

Many great leaders have been found to have great reserves of empathy, interpersonal astuteness, awareness of their own feelings, and an awareness of their impact on others.[20] And, more importantly, they apply these capabilities judiciously as best benefits the situation. In essence, the key to this is self-regulation; having some minimum level of these emotional intelligences will help a person be effective as a leader as long as they are channeled appropriately. However, if a person has a high level of these capabilities it may become "too much of a good thing" if they are allowed to drive inappropriate behaviors. Let's consider two insights from experts that appeared in a 2004 *Harvard Business Review* article:[21]

> . . . there is always a danger in being preoccupied with, or overusing, one aspect of EI. For example, if you overemphasize the emotional intelligence competencies of initiative or achievement, you'll always be changing things at your company. Nobody would know what you are going to do next, which would be quite destabilizing for the organization. If you overuse empathy, you might never fire anybody. If you overuse teamwork, you might never build diversity or listen to a lone voice. Balance is essential.

> If you're extremely self-aware but short on empathy, you might come off as self-obsessed. If you're excessively empathetic, you risk being too hard to read. If you're great at self-management but not very transparent, you might seem inauthentic. Finally, at times, leaders have to deliberately avoid getting too close to the troops in order to ensure that they're seeing the bigger picture. Emotionally intelligent leaders know when to rein it in.

Some additional potential drawbacks of EI can be gleaned from the flip side of the benefits from some of its essential components.

Effective Leaders Have Empathy for Others However, they also must be able to make the "tough decisions." Leaders must be able to appeal to logic and reason and acknowledge others' feelings so that people feel the decisions are correct. However, it is easy to overidentify with others or confuse empathy with sympathy. This will make it more difficult to make the tough decisions.

Effective Leaders Are Astute Judges of People A danger is that leaders may become judgmental and overly critical about the shortcomings they perceive in others. They are likely to dismiss other people's insights, making them feel disrespected and undervalued.

Effective Leaders Are Passionate about What They Do, and They Show It This doesn't necessarily mean that they are always cheerleaders. Rather, they may express their passion as persistence in pursuing an objective or a relentless focus on a valued principle. However, there is a fine line between being excited about something and letting your passion close your mind to other possibilities or cause you to ignore realities that others see.

Effective Leaders Create Personal Connections with Their People Most effective leaders take time to engage employees individually and in groups, listening to their ideas, suggestions and concerns, and responding in ways that make people feel that their ideas are respected and appreciated. However, the downside of such visibility is that if the leader makes too many unannounced visits, it may create a culture of fear and micromanagement. Clearly, striking a correct balance is essential.

Finally, from a moral standpoint, emotional leadership is neither good nor bad. Emotional leaders can be altruistic, focused on the general welfare of the company and its employees, and highly principled. On the other hand, they can be manipulative, selfish, and dishonest. For example, if a person is using leadership solely to gain formal or informal power, that is not leadership at all.[22] Rather, they are using their EI to grasp what people want and pander to those desires in order to gain authority and influence. After all, easy answers sell.

Many people with high emotional intelligence and charisma aren't interested in asking the deeper questions, because they get so much emotional gain from the adoring crowd.[23] For them, that is the end in itself. They are satisfying their own hungers and vulnerabilities—their need to be liked, their need for power and control, or their need to be needed and to feel important—which renders them vulnerable to grandiosity. But that's not leadership. It's hunger for authority.[24]

In the next section, we will discuss some guidelines for developing a "learning organization." In today's competitive environment, the old saying about "a chain is only as strong as the weakest link" applies more than ever before. People throughout organizations must become involved in leadership processes and play greater roles in the formulation and implementation of an organization's strategies and tactics. Put another way, to learn and adapt proactively, firms need "eyes, ears, and brains" throughout all parts of the organization. One person, or a small group of individuals, can no longer think and learn for the entire entity.

>>Developing a Learning Organization

Charles Handy, author of *The Age of Unreason* and *The Age of Paradox* and one of today's most respected business visionaries, shared an amusing story:

> The other day, a courier could not find my family's remote cottage. He called his base on his radio, and the base called us to ask directions. He was just around the corner, but his base managed to omit a vital part of the directions. So he called them again, and they called us again. Then the courier repeated the cycle a third time to ask whether we had a dangerous dog. When he eventually arrived, we asked whether it would not have been simpler and less aggravating to everyone if he had called us directly from the roadside telephone booth where he had been parked. "I can't do that," he said, "because they won't refund any money I spend." "But it's only pennies!" I exclaimed. "I know," he said, "but that only shows how little they trust us!"[25]

At first glance, it would appear that the story simply epitomizes the lack of empowerment and trust granted to the hapless courier: Don't ask questions, Do as you're told![26] However, implicit in this scenario is also the message that learning, information sharing, adaptation, decision making, and so on are *not* shared throughout the organization. In contrast to this admittedly rather extreme case, leading-edge organizations recognize the importance of having everyone involved in the process of actively learning and adapting. As noted by today's leading expert on learning organizations, MIT's Peter Senge, the days when Henry Ford, Alfred Sloan, and Tom Watson *"learned **for** the organization"* are gone.

> In an increasingly dynamic, interdependent, and unpredictable world, it is simply no longer possible for anyone to "figure it all out at the top." The old model, "the top thinks and the local acts," must now give way to integrating thinking and acting at all levels. While the challenge is great, so is the potential payoff. "The person who figures out how to harness the collective genius of the people in his or her organization," according to former Citibank CEO Walter Wriston, "is going to blow the competition away."[27]

Learning and change typically involve the ongoing questioning of an organization's status quo or method of procedure. This means that all individuals throughout the organization—not just those at the top—must reflect. Although this seems simple enough, it is easy to ignore. After all, organizations, especially successful ones, are so caught up in carrying out their day-to-day work that they rarely, if ever, stop to think objectively about themselves and their businesses. They often fail to ask the probing questions that might lead them to call into question their basic assumptions, to refresh their strategies, or to reengineer their work processes. According to Michael

Hammer and Steven Stanton, the pioneer consultants who touched off the reengineering movement:

> Reflection entails awareness of self, of competitors, of customers. It means thinking without preconception. It means questioning cherished assumptions and replacing them with new approaches. It is the only way in which a winning company can maintain its leadership position, by which a company with great assets can ensure that they continue to be well deployed.[28]

Successful learning organizations create a proactive, creative approach to the unknown, actively solicit the involvement of employees at all levels, and enable all employees to use their intelligence and apply their imagination. Higher-level skills are required of everyone, not just those at the top. A learning environment involves organizationwide commitment to change, an action orientation, and applicable tools and methods.[29] It must be viewed by everyone as a guiding philosophy and not simply as another change program that is often derisively labeled the new "flavor of the month."

A critical requirement of all learning organizations is that everyone feels and supports a compelling purpose. In the words of William O'Brien, CEO of Hanover Insurance, "Before there can be meaningful participation, people must share certain values and pictures about where we are trying to go. We discovered that people have a real need to feel that they're part of an enabling mission."[30]

Inspiring and motivating people with a mission or purpose is a necessary but not sufficient condition for developing an organization that can learn and adapt to a rapidly changing, complex, and interconnected environment. In the next four sections, we'll address four other critical ongoing processes of learning organizations:

- Empowering employees at all levels.
- Accumulating and sharing internal knowledge.
- Gathering and integrating external information.
- Challenging the status quo and enabling creativity.

Empowering Employees at All Levels

"The great leader is a great servant," asserted Ken Melrose, CEO of Toro Company and author of *Making the Grass Greener on Your Side*.[31] A manager's role becomes one of creating an environment where employees can achieve their potential as they help move the organization toward its goals. Instead of viewing themselves as resource controllers and power brokers, leaders must truly envision themselves as flexible resources willing to assume numerous (and perhaps unaccustomed) roles as coaches, information providers, teachers, decision makers, facilitators, supporters, or listeners, depending on the needs of their employees.

The central key to empowerment is effective leadership. Empowerment can't occur in a leadership vacuum. According to Melrose, "I came to understand that you best lead by serving the needs of your people. You don't do their jobs for them; you enable them to learn and progress on the job." In their article in *Organizational Dynamics*, Robert Quinn and Gretchen Spreitzer made an interesting point regarding what may be viewed as two diametrically opposite perspectives on empowerment.[32] In the top-down perspective, empowerment is about delegation and accountability—senior management has developed a clear vision and has communicated specific plans to the rest of the organization. This strategy for empowerment encompasses the following:

- Start at the top.
- Clarify the organization's mission, vision, and values.

- Clearly specify the tasks, roles, and rewards for employees.
- Delegate responsibility.
- Hold people accountable for results.

By contrast, the bottom-up view looks at empowerment as concerned with risk taking, growth, and change. It involves trusting people to "do the right thing" and having a tolerance for failure. It encourages employees to act with a sense of ownership and typically "ask for forgiveness rather than permission." Here the salient elements of empowerment are:

- Start at the bottom by understanding the needs of employees.
- Teach employees self-management skills and model desired behavior.
- Build teams to encourage cooperative behavior.
- Encourage intelligent risk taking.
- Trust people to perform.

Clearly, these two perspectives draw a sharp contrast in assumptions that people make about trust and control. Interestingly, Quinn and Spreitzer recently shared these contrasting views of empowerment with a senior management team. After an initial heavy silence, someone from the first group voiced a concern about the second group's perspective, "We can't afford loose cannons around here." A person in the second group retorted, "When was the last time you saw a cannon of any kind around here?"

Many leading-edge organizations are moving in the direction of the second perspective—recognizing the need for trust, cultural control, and expertise (at all levels) instead of the extensive and cumbersome rules and regulations inherent in hierarchical control.[33] Some have argued that too often organizations fall prey to the "heroes-and-drones syndrome," wherein the value of those in powerful positions is exalted and the value of those who fail to achieve top rank is diminished. Such an attitude is implicit in phrases such as "Lead, follow, or get out of the way" or, even less appealing, "Unless you're the lead horse, the view never changes." Of course, few will ever reach the top hierarchical positions in organizations, but in the information economy, the strongest organizations are those that effectively use the talents of all the players on the team. Strategy Spotlight 11.6 illustrates how one company, Chaparral Steel, empowers its employees.

Accumulating and Sharing Internal Knowledge

Effective organizations must also *redistribute information, knowledge* (i.e., skills to act on the information), and *rewards.*[34] For example, a company might give frontline employees the power to act as "customer advocates," doing whatever is necessary to please the customers. Employees, however, also need to have the appropriate training to act as businesspeople. The company needs to disseminate information by sharing customer expectations and feedback as well as financial information. The employees need to know about the goals and objectives of the business as well as how key value-creating activities in the organization are related to each other. Finally, organizations should allocate rewards on the basis of how effectively employees use information, knowledge, and power to improve customer service quality and the company's financial performance.

Jack Stack is the president and CEO of Springfield ReManufacturing Corporation (SRC) in Springfield, Missouri, and author of *The Great Game of Business.* He is generally considered the pioneer of "open book" management—an innovative way to gather and disseminate internal information. Implementing this system involves three core activities.[35] First, numbers are generated daily for each of the company's employees, reflecting his or her work performance and production costs. Second, this information is aggregated once

Employee Empowerment at Chaparral Steel

Managers at Chaparral Steel, a steel minimill in Midlothian, Texas, are convinced that employee ownership empowers workers to act in the best interests of the company. They believe that ownership is not composed solely of the firm's equity but also of its knowledge. By sharing financial and knowledge resources with employees, Chaparral Steel is a model of employee empowerment—90 percent of its employees own company stock and everyone is salaried, wears the same white hard hats, drinks the same free coffee, and has access to the knowledge that goes into the innovative processes at the firm's manufacturing plants.

Rather than using managers as buffers between customers and line workers, Chaparral directly involves employees with customers. Customer concerns are routed directly to the line workers responsible for manufacturing a customer's specific products. "Everyone here is part of the sales department," president and CEO Gordon Forward said. "They carry their own business cards. If they visit a customer, we want them to come back and look at their own process differently. This helps employees from all levels to view operations from the customer's perspective." Forward believes that "if a melt shop crew understands why a customer needs a particular grade of steel, it will make sure the customer gets that exact grade."

This encourages employees to think beyond traditional functional boundaries and find ways to improve the organization's processes. By integrating the customer's perspective into their efforts, employees at Chaparral Steel become more than just salaried workers; they feel responsible to the firm as if each production process was their own creation and responsibility.

Sources: Johnson, D. 1998. Catching the third wave: How to succeed in business when it's changing at the speed of light. *Futurist*, March: 32–38; Petry, C. 1997. Chaparral poised on the brink of breakthrough: Chaparral Steel developing integrated automobile shredder-separation facility. *American Metal Market*, September 10: 18; Leonard-Barton, D. 1992. The factory as a learning laboratory. *Sloan Management Review*, 34: 23–38; and TXI Chaparral Steel Midlothian registered to ISO 2002. Chaparral Steel press release, July 8, 2001.

a week and shared with all of the company's people from secretaries to top management. Third, employees receive extensive training in how to use and interpret the numbers—how to understand balance sheets as well as cash flows and income statements.

In explaining why SRC embraces open book management, Stack provided an insightful counterperspective to the old adage "Information is power."

> We are building a company in which everyone tells the truth every day—not because everyone is honest but because everyone has access to the same information: operating metrics, financial data, valuation estimates. The more people understand what's really going on in their company, the more eager they are to help solve its problems. Information isn't power. It's a burden. Share information, and you share the burdens of leadership as well.

These perspectives help to point out both the motivational and utilitarian uses of sharing company information. It can apply to organizations of all sizes. Let's look at a very small company—Leonhardt Plating Company, a $1.5 million company that makes steel plating.

> Its CEO, Daniel Leonhardt, became an accidental progressive, so to speak. Recently, instead of trying to replace his polishing foreman, he resorted to a desperate, if cutting-edge, strategy. He decided to let the polishing department rule itself by committee.
>
> The results? Revenues have risen 25 percent in the past year. After employees had access to company information such as material prices, their decisions began paying off for the whole firm. Says Leonhardt: "The workers are showing more interest in the company as a whole." Not surprisingly, he plans to introduce committee rule to other departments.[36]

Additional benefits of management sharing company information can be gleaned from a look at Whole Foods Market, Inc., the largest natural foods grocer in the United States.[37] An important benefit of the sharing of internal information at Whole Foods becomes the active process of *internal benchmarking*. Competition is intense at Whole Foods. Teams compete against their own goals for sales, growth, and productivity; they compete against different teams in their stores; and they compete against similar teams at different stores and regions. Similarly, there is an elaborate system of peer reviews through which teams benchmark each other. The "Store Tour" is the most intense. On a periodic schedule, each Whole Foods store is toured by a group of as many as 40 visitors from another region. The tour is a mix of social interaction, reviews, performance audits, and structured feedback sessions. Lateral learning—discovering what your colleagues are doing right and carrying those practices into your organization—has become a driving force at Whole Foods.

In addition to enhancing the sharing of company information both up and down as well as across the organization, leaders also have to develop means to tap into some of the more informal sources of internal information. In a recent survey of presidents, CEOs, board members, and top executives in a variety of nonprofit organizations, respondents were asked what differentiated the successful candidates for promotion. The consensus: The executive was seen as a person who listens. According to Peter Meyer, the author of the study, "The value of listening is clear: You cannot succeed in running a company if you do not hear what your people, customers, and suppliers are telling you. Poor listeners do not survive. Listening and understanding well are key to making good decisions."[38]

John Chambers, president and CEO of Cisco Systems, the networking giant, also uses an effective vehicle for getting candid feedback from employees and for discovering potential problems.[39] Every year during their birthday month, employees at Cisco's corporate headquarters in San Jose, California, receive an e-mail invitation to a "birthday breakfast" with Chambers. Each month, several dozen of the employees fire some pretty tough questions, including bruising queries about partnering strategy and stark assessments of perceived management failings. Any question is fair game, and directors and vice presidents are strongly discouraged from attending.

Although not always pleasant, Chambers believes it is an indispensable hour of unmediated interaction. At times, he finds there is inconsistency between what his executives say they are doing and what is actually happening. For example, at one quarterly meeting with 500 managers, Chambers asked how many managers required potential hires to have five interviews. When all raised their hands, he retorted, "I have a problem, because at the past three birthday breakfasts, I asked the new hires how many had interviewed that way, and only half raised their hands. You've got to fix it." His take on the birthday breakfasts: "I'm not there for the cake."

Strategy Spotlight 11.7 discusses how Intel Corporation effectively shares information through a unique mentoring program.

Gathering and Integrating External Information

Recognizing opportunities, as well as threats, in the external environment is vital to a firm's success. Focusing exclusively on the efficiency of internal operations may result in a firm becoming, in effect, the world's most efficient producer of manual typewriters or leisure suits—hardly an enviable position! As organizations *and* environments become more complex and evolve rapidly, it is far more critical for employees and managers to become more aware of environmental trends and events—both general and industry-specific—and more knowledgeable about their firm's competitors and customers. Next, we will discuss some ideas on how to do it.

First, the Internet has dramatically accelerated the speed with which anyone can track down useful information or locate people who might have useful information. Prior to the Net, locating someone who used to work at a company—always a good source of

Information Sharing through Mentoring Relationships at Intel

Intel veteran Ann Otero seems to be an unlikely mentor. She is neither a star engineer nor a fast-track sales executive. She has, however, been with the company for the past 12 years and is currently a senior administrative assistant. Ann is part of Intel's new wedge—an innovative new mentoring movement that matches people not by job title or years of service but by specific skills that are in demand. The program uses an intranet-based questionnaire to match partners with the right mentor, creating relationships that stretch across state lines and national boundaries. The system works by having potential mentors list their top skills at Circuit, Intel's internal employee site. Partners click on topics they want to master, then an algorithm computes all of the variables and the database

hashes out a list of possible matches. Once a match is made, an automatic e-mail goes to the mentor asking her to set up a time to meet and talk. The mentor and partner learn and follow some simple guidelines:

1. The partner controls the relationship.

2. A mentoring contract is drawn up about what needs to be accomplished by the end of the mentoring.

3. Both the partner and the mentor decide what to talk about.

Unlike many corporations, Intel does not use its mentoring for career advancement. Its style is all about learning and sharing the knowledge pool of someone whom you have probably never met.

Sources: www.intel.com/jobs/news/news.htm; Warner, F. 2002. Inside Intel's mentoring movement. *Fast Company*, April: 67–69.

---

information—was quite a challenge. However, today people post their résumés on the Web; they participate in discussion groups and talk openly about where they work. It is pretty straightforward.

An example of the effective use of the Internet is provided by Marc Friedman, manager of market research at Andrew Corporation, a fast-growing manufacturer of wireless communications products with annual revenues of nearly $1 billion.[40] One of Friedman's preferred sites to visit is Corptech's Web site, which provides information on 45,000 high-tech companies and more than 170,000 executives. One of his firm's product lines consisted of antennae for air-traffic control systems. He got a request to provide a country-by-country breakdown of upgrade plans for various airports. Although he knew nothing about air-traffic control at the time, he found a site on the Internet for the International Civil Aviation Organization. Fortunately, it had a great deal of useful data, including several research companies working in his area of interest.

Second, in addition to the Internet, company employees at all levels can use "garden variety" traditional sources to acquire external information. Much can be gleaned by reading trade and professional journals, books, and popular business magazines such as *BusinessWeek, Forbes, Fortune,* and *Fast Company.* (Some professional journals might have an extremely narrow focus and, while they could prove to be very useful, they are not fireside reading for the general public.) Other venues for gathering external information include membership in professional or trade organizations and attendance at meetings and conventions. Networking among colleagues inside and outside of your industry is also very useful. Intel's Andy Grove, for example, gathers information from people like DreamWorks SKG's Steven Spielberg and Tele-Communications Inc.'s John Malone.[41] He believes that such interaction provides insights into how to make personal computers more entertaining and better at communicating. Internally, Grove spends time with the young "propeller-heads" who run Intel Architecture labs, an Oregon-based facility that Grove hopes will become the de facto R&D lab for the entire PC industry.

Third, benchmarking can be a useful means of employing external information. Here managers seek out the best examples of a particular practice as part of an ongoing effort to improve the corresponding practice in their own organization.[42] There are two primary types of benchmarking. *Competitive benchmarking* restricts the search for best practices to competitors, while *functional benchmarking* endeavors to determine best practices regardless of industry. Industry-specific standards (e.g., response times required to repair power outages in the electric utility industry) are typically best handled through competitive benchmarking, whereas more generic processes (e.g., answering 1-800 calls) lend themselves to functional benchmarking because the function is essentially the same in any industry.

Ford Motor Company benefited from benchmarking by studying Mazda's accounts payable operations.[43] Its initial goal of a 20 percent cut in its 500-employee accounts payable staff was ratcheted up to 75 percent—and met. Ford's benchmarkers found that staff spent most of their time trying to match often conflicting data in a mass of paper, including purchase orders, invoices, and receipts. Following Mazda's example, Ford created an "invoiceless system" in which invoices no longer trigger payments to suppliers. The receipt does the job.

Fourth, focus directly on customers for information. For example, William McKnight, head of 3M's Chicago sales office, required that salesmen of abrasives products talk directly to the workers in the shop to find out what they needed, instead of calling on only front-office executives.[44] This was very innovative at the time—1909! But it illustrates the need to get to the end user of a product or service. (McKnight went on to become 3M's president from 1929 to 1949 and chairman from 1949 to 1969.) More recently, James Taylor, senior vice president for global marketing at Gateway 2000, discussed the value of customer input in reducing response time, a critical success factor in the PC industry.

> We talk to 100,000 people a day—people calling to order a computer, shopping around, looking for tech support. Our Web site gets 1.1 million hits per day. The time it takes for an idea to enter this organization, get processed, and then go to customers for feedback is down to minutes. We've designed the company around speed and feedback.[45]

Challenging the Status Quo and Enabling Creativity

Earlier in this chapter we discussed some of the barriers that leaders face when trying to bring about change in an organization. These included vested interests in the status quo, systemic barriers, behavioral barriers, political barriers, and personal time constraints. For a firm to become a "learning organization," it must overcome such barriers in order to foster creativity and enable it to permeate the firm. This becomes quite a challenge, of course, if the firm is entrenched in a status quo mentality.

Perhaps the primary means to directly challenge the status quo is for the leader to forcefully create a sense of urgency. For example, Tom Kasten, vice president of Levi Strauss, has a direct approach to initiating change. He is charged with leading the campaign to transform the company for the 21st century.

> You create a compelling picture of the risks of *not* changing. We let our people hear directly from customers. We videotaped interviews with customers and played excerpts. One big customer said, "We trust many of your competitors implicitly. We sample their deliveries. We open *all* Levi's deliveries." Another said, "Your lead times are the worst. If you weren't Levi's, you'd be gone." It was powerful. I wish we had done more of it.[46]

Such initiative—if sincere and credible—establishes a shared mission and the need for major transformations. If effective, it can channel energies to bring about both change and creative endeavors.

Establishing a "culture of dissent" can be another effective means of questioning the status quo and serving as a spur toward creativity. Here norms are established whereby dissenters can openly question a superior's perspective without fear of retaliation or retribution. Consider the perspective of Steven Balmer, Microsoft's CEO.

> Bill [Gates] brings to the company the idea that conflict can be a good thing. . . . Bill knows it's important to avoid that gentle civility that keeps you from getting to the heart of an issue quickly. He likes it when anyone, even a junior employee, challenges him, and you know he respects you when he starts shouting back.[47]

Motorola has, in effect, gone a step further and institutionalized its culture of dissent.[48] By filing a "minority report," an employee can go above his or her immediate supervisor's head and officially lodge a different point of view on a business decision. According to former CEO George Fisher, "I'd call it a healthy spirit of discontent and a freedom by and large to express your discontent around here or to disagree with whoever it is in the company, me or anybody else."

Closely related to the culture of dissent is the fostering of a culture that encourages risk taking. "If you're not making mistakes, you're not taking risks, and that means you're not going anywhere," claimed John Holt, coauthor of *Celebrate Your Mistakes.*[49] "The key is to make errors faster than the competition, so you have more chances to learn and win."

Companies that cultivate cultures of experimentation and curiosity make sure that *failure* is not, in essence, an obscene word. People who stretch the envelope and ruffle feathers are protected. More importantly, they encourage mistakes as a key part of their competitive advantage. Wood Dickinson, CEO of the Kansas City–based Dickinson movie theater chain, told his property managers that he wanted to see them committing "intelligent failures in the pursuit of service excellence."[50] This philosophy was shared by Stan Shih, CEO of Acer, a Taiwan-based computer company. If a manager at Acer took an intelligent risk and made a mistake—even a costly one—Shih wrote off the loss as tuition payment for the manager's education. Such a culture must permeate the entire organization. As a high-tech executive told us during an interview: "Every person has a freedom to fail."

Strategy Spotlight 11.8 provides examples of how failures led to highly successful innovations.

>>Creating an Ethical Organization

What is ethics?[51] Ethics may be defined as a system of right and wrong. Ethics assists individuals in deciding when an act is moral or immoral, socially desirable or not. There are many sources for an individual's ethics. These include religious beliefs, national and ethnic heritage, family practices, community standards and expectations, educational experiences, and friends and neighbors. Business ethics is the application of ethical standards to commercial enterprise.

Individual Ethics versus Organizational Ethics

Many leaders may think of ethics as a question of personal scruples, a confidential matter between employees and their consciences. Such leaders are quick to describe any wrongdoing as an isolated incident, the work of a rogue employee. They assume the company should not bear any responsibility for an individual's misdeeds—it may not ever even enter their minds. After all, in their view, ethics has nothing to do with leadership.

In fact, ethics has everything to do with leadership. Seldom does the character flaw of a lone actor completely explain corporate misconduct. Instead, unethical business practices typically involve the tacit, if not explicit, cooperation of others and reflect the values,

STRATEGY SPOTLIGHT

Failures That Led to Later Successes

Experimentation can often fail. At times, such failures can be the seeds that lead to very successful products. As the famous writer James Joyce once said, "Mistakes are the portals for discovery." Below, we summarize three failures that evolved into remarkable innovations.

W. L. Gore & Associates is the well-known company that produces such innovative products as Gore-Tex, the material that is used in many outdoor clothing products to help keep out moisture, and Glide, a dental floss. It also has become the second-leading manufacturer in the $100 million stringed-instrument business—largely as the result of a failed product.

In 1997, a team at Gore was testing a material for the cables that control puppets at Disney's theme parks. The prototype failed. But it was the beginning of a successful product. "We gave it to guitar players to try out, and they were amazed that it didn't go dead," explains Steve Young, who now heads Gore's Elixir business.

It turned out that Gore's strings lasted up to five times longer than most others then available. However, they cost twice as much. How did they market the new product? Gore went straight to the musicians. It bought magazine subscriber lists and showed up at festivals, giving out samples and building some buzz. It hired musically trained sales reps to develop relationships with retailers and got Taylor Guitars, a leading acoustical manufacturer, to install Elixir on all of its guitars. Today, Elixir Strings are sold by more than half the music stores in the United States.

Rubber shortages during World War II prompted the U.S. government to try to develop a synthetic rubber. It seemed to make sense to make this substitute out of something that was very plentiful. Silicone seemed to be the logical solution. An inventor at General Electric added a little boric acid to silicone oil and developed a gooey, bouncy substance.

Although the substance failed as a substitute for rubber, after the war it became a very popular toy—Silly Putty. Apollo 8 astronauts later used it to stabilize their tools in zero gravity. (The astronauts carried their Silly Putty in sterling silver eggs.) Today Binney & Smith produces about 20,000 eggs' worth of Silly Putty a day.

Wilson Greatbatch, a medical researcher, was working on a device to record irregular heartbeats. He accidentally inserted a resistor of the wrong size and he noticed that the circuit pulsed, stopped, and pulsed again—just like a human heart. After two years of tinkering, Greatbatch developed the first implantable pacemaker. He later invented a corrosion-free lithium battery to power it. Millions have benefited from his efforts.

Sources: Sacks, D. 2003. The Gore-Tex of guitar strings. *Fast Company*, December: 46; Jones, C. 1994. *Mistakes that worked*. New York: Random House; and Brokenbrough, M. 2005. *The greatest mistakes of all time*. encarta. msn.com, January 8: np.

attitudes, and behavior patterns that define an organization's operating culture. Clearly, ethics is as much an organizational as a personal issue. Leaders who fail to provide proper leadership to institute proper systems and controls that facilitate ethical conduct share responsibility with those who conceive, execute, and knowingly benefit from corporate misdeeds.

The ethical orientation of a leader is generally considered to be a key factor in promoting ethical behavior among employees. Ethical leaders must take personal, ethical responsibility for their actions and decision making. Leaders who exhibit high ethical standards become role models for others in the organization and raise its overall level of ethical behavior. In essence, ethical behavior must start with the leader before the employees can be expected to perform accordingly.

Over the last few decades, there has been a growing interest in corporate ethical performance. Perhaps some reasons for this trend may be the increasing lack of confidence regarding corporate activities, the growing emphasis on quality of life issues, and a spate of recent corporate scandals at such firms as Enron and Tyco. Clearly, concerns about protecting the environment, fair employment practices, and the distribution of unsafe products have served to create powerful regulatory agencies such as the Environmental Protection Agency, the Equal Opportunity Commission, and the Federal Drug Administration. Recently, however, other concerns are becoming salient, such as problems associated with fetal tissue for research, disproportionate executive pay levels, corporate crises such as the Firestone/Ford Explorer tire fiasco, race debacles at Texaco and at Denny's Restaurants, the *Exxon Valdez* oil spill, and the practices of major financial services institutions in the wake of the dot-com crash. Merely adhering to the minimum regulatory standards may not be enough to remain competitive in a world that is becoming more socially conscious.

Without a strong ethical culture, the chance of ethical crises occurring is enhanced. Ethical crises can be very expensive—both in terms of financial costs and in the erosion of human capital and overall firm reputation. Consider, for example, Texaco's class-action discrimination lawsuit.

> In 1994 a senior financial analyst, Bari-Ellen Roberts, and one of her co-workers, Sil Chambers, filed a class-action discrimination suit against Texaco after enduring racial slurs and being passed over for promotion on several occasions. The discrimination suit charged Texaco with using an "old boys network" to systematically discriminate against African Americans.
>
> Roberts remembers, "The hardest part of the suit was deciding to do it. I'd worked so hard to get where I was, and I had to risk all of that. Then I had to deal with loneliness and isolation. Even some of the other African Americans viewed me as a troublemaker. When you're standing up and calling for change, it makes people fear for their own security."
>
> Two years later, in 1996, Texaco settled the suit, paying $141 million to its African-American workers. This was followed with an additional $35 million to remove discriminatory practices.[52]

Please note that the financial cost alone of $176 million was certainly not the proverbial "drop in the bucket." This amount represented nearly 10 percent of Texaco Inc.'s entire net income for 1996.

As we are all aware, the past several years have been characterized by numerous examples of unethical and illegal behavior by many top-level corporate executives. These include executives of firms such as Enron, Tyco, Worldcom, Inc., Adelphia, and Healthsouth Corp., who were all forced to resign and are facing (or have been convicted of) criminal charges. Exhibit 11.4 briefly summarizes the unethical and/or illegal activities of other well-known corporate leaders.

The ethical organization is characterized by a conception of ethical values and integrity as a driving force of the enterprise.[53] Ethical values shape the search for opportunities, the design of organizational systems, and the decision-making process used by individuals and groups. They provide a common frame of reference that serves as a unifying force across different functions, lines of business, and employee groups. Organizational ethics helps to define what a company is and what it stands for.

There are many potential benefits of an ethical organization, but they are often indirect. The research literature in organizational behavior has found somewhat inconsistent results concerning the overall relationship between ethical performance and measures of financial performance.[54] However, positive relationships have generally been found between ethical performance and strong organizational culture, increased employee efforts, lower turnover, higher organizational commitment, and enhanced social responsibility.

Clearly, the advantages of a strong ethical orientation can have a positive effect on employee commitment and motivation to excel. This is particularly important in today's knowledge-intensive organizations, where human capital is critical in creating value and competitive advantages. As we discussed in Chapter 4, positive, constructive relationships among individuals (i.e., social capital) are vital in leveraging human capital and other resources in an organization. However, there are many other potential benefits as well. Drawing on the concept of stakeholder management that we discussed in Chapter 1, an ethically sound organization can also strengthen its bonds among its suppliers,

Exhibit 11.4
Unethical and Illegal Behavior by Top-Level Corporate Executives

Martha Stewart, CEO Martha Stewart Living Omnimedia	In December 2001, Stewart sold over one-quarter million dollars' worth of ImClone Systems stock prior to the stock's subsequent plunge. Her defense claimed that she had discussed selling the large sum of stock since the stock had dropped below $60 per share. However, it was later revealed that she and her broker were guilty of insider trading based on inside information from ImClone Systems' CEO Sam Waksal (who also was found guilty of the same felony and is now serving six years in a Pennsylvania prison camp). On July 16, 2004, Stewart was sentenced to five months in federal prison and five months house arrest and was fined $30,000.
Harry C. Stonecipher, CEO Boeing Co.	There are ethical dilemmas, of course, that fall outside the more recent focus on corrupt financial behavior. Boeing's Stonecipher engaged in an extramarital affair with fellow executive, Deborah Peabody. This raised a particularly difficult decision for Boeing's board of directors. In only 15 months on the job, Stonecipher had helped the company recover from ethical credibility problems created by a Pentagon scandal that landed two of its executives in prison. During Stonecipher's brief time at the top, the company's market valuation had climbed 50 percent. On February 28, 2005, Boeing's board requested that he cease his relationship with Peabody. The 68-year-old Stonecipher, ignoring the shareholder consequences of his questionable image, declined this request. The board responded with a demand for his resignation.
Maurice Greenberg, CEO American Insurance Group (AIG)	The Greenberg family may show that unethical behavior can be hereditary. In September 2004, New York Attorney General Eliot Spitzer insisted that the son of AIG's CEO Maurice "Hank" Greenberg, Jeffrey Greenberg, CEO of the world's largest insurance broker, Marsh & McLennan, resign due to account fixing and bid rigging charges. In Marsh's case, the defense attempted to plead that Jeffrey Greenberg "did not understand how the insurance business operated." In November 2004, AIG paid an $80 million fine to the U.S. Department of Justice to settle complaints concerning the crooked sale of insurance products. In April 2005, AIG's board requested that Maurice Greenberg, 79, step down from his position in the face of similar scandals associated with rigging bids of nontraditional insurance products that were pitched to the heads of other companies.

Sources: Kahn, J. 2004. Why CEOs should hope Martha walks. *Fortune,* February 9: 24–25; Sellers, P. 2004. Why Martha may choose jail now. *Fortune,* August 9: 36; Revell, J. 2004. Martha gets 5 to 20; Investors get life. *Fortune,* March 22: 40; Holmes, S. 2005. Why Boeing's culture breeds turmoil. *BusinessWeek,* March 21: 34–36; Henry, D., France, M., & Lavelle, Louis. 2005. The boss on the sidelines. April 25: 86–96; Elkind, P., & Devin, L. 2005. More bad news for AIG's Greenberg? *Fortune,* March 7: 28; Condon, B., & Coolidge, C. 2005. When gray becomes black-and-white. *Forbes,* May 9: 90–92; and http://www.insurancejournal.com/news/national/2004/10/15/46937.htm.

STRATEGY SPOTLIGHT

Procter & Gamble: Using Ethics to "Build the Spirit of the Place"

John Pepper, former CEO and chairman of Procter & Gamble Company, shares his perspective on ethics.

Let me start by saying that while ethics may seem like a soft concept—not as hard, say, as strategy or budgeting or operations—it is, in fact, a very hard concept. It is tangible. It is crucial . . . it is good for business.

There are several reasons for this. First, a company's values have a tremendous impact on who is attracted to your company and who will stay with it. We only have one life to live. All of us want to live it as part of an institution committed to high goals and high-sighted means of reaching these goals. This is true everywhere I've been. In our most mature countries and our newest.

Strong corporate values greatly simplify decision making. It is important to know the things you won't even think about doing. Diluting a product. Paying a bribe. Not being fair to a customer or an employee.

Strong values earn the respect of customers and suppliers and governments and other companies, too. This is absolutely crucial over the long term.

A company which pays bribes in a foreign market becomes an open target for more bribes when the word gets out. It never stops.

A company which is seen to be offering different trade terms to different customers based on how big they are or how hard they push will forever be beset by requests for special terms.

A company which is seen by a government as having weak or varying standards will not be respected by that government.

And more positively, governments and other companies really do want to deal with companies they feel are pursuing sound values because in many, if not most, cases, they believe it will be good for them.

One final but very fundamental reason for operating ethically is that strong values create trust and pride among employees. Simply put, they build the spirit of the place.

Source: Pepper, J. E. 1997. The boa principle: Operating ethically in today's business environment. Speech presented at Florida A&M University, Tallahassee, January 30.

customers, and governmental agencies. John E. Pepper, former chairman of Procter & Gamble, addresses such a perspective in Strategy Spotlight 11.9.

Integrity-Based versus Compliance-Based Approaches to Organizational Ethics

Before discussing the key elements for building an ethical organization, it is important to understand the essential links between organizational integrity and the personal integrity of an organization's members.[55] There cannot be high-integrity organizations without high-integrity individuals. At the same time, individual integrity is rarely self-sustaining. Even good people can lose their bearings when faced with pressures, temptations, and heightened performance expectations in the absence of organizational support systems and ethical boundaries. Organizational integrity, on the other hand, is beyond personal integrity. It rests on a concept of purpose, responsibility, and ideals for an organization as a whole. An important responsibility of leadership in building organizational integrity is to create this ethical framework and develop the organizational capabilities to make it operational.

It is also important to know the approaches or strategies organizations take in dealing with ethics. Lynn Paine, a researcher at Harvard, identifies two such approaches: the compliance-based approach and the integrity-based approach. (See Exhibit 11.5 for a comparison of compliance-based and integrity-based strategies.) Faced with the prospect of litigation, several organizations reactively implement compliance-based ethics programs. Such programs are typically designed by a corporate counsel with the goal of preventing, detecting, and punishing legal violations. But being ethical is much more

Characteristics	Compliance-Based Approach	Integrity-Based Approach
Ethos	Conformity with externally imposed standards	Self-governance according to chosen standards
Objective	Prevent criminal misconduct	Enable responsible conduct
Leadership	Lawyer-driven	Management-driven with aid of lawyers, HR, and others
Methods	Education, reduced discretion, auditing and controls, penalties	Education, leadership, accountability, organizational systems and decision processes, auditing and controls, penalties
Behavioral Assumptions	Autonomous beings guided by material self-interest	Social beings guided by material self-interest, values, ideals, peers

Source: Paine, L. S. 1994. Managing for organizational integrity. *Harvard Business Review,* 72(2): 113 (with permission).

Exhibit 11.5

Approaches to Ethics Management

than being legal, and an integrity-based approach addresses the issue of ethics in a more comprehensive manner.

An integrity-based approach to ethics management combines a concern for law with an emphasis on managerial responsibility for ethical behavior. This approach is broader, deeper, and more demanding than a legal compliance initiative. It is broader in that it seeks to enable responsible conduct. It is deeper in that it cuts to the ethos and operating systems of an organization and its members, their core guiding values, thoughts, and actions. And it is more demanding because it requires an active effort to define the responsibilities and aspirations that constitute an organization's ethical compass. Most importantly, in this approach, organizational ethics is seen as the work of management. A corporate counsel may play a role in designing and implementing integrity strategies, but it is managers at all levels and across all functions that are involved in the process. Once integrated into the day-to-day operations of an organization, such strategies can help prevent damaging ethical lapses, while tapping into powerful human impulses for moral thought and action. Ethics then become the governing ethos of an organization and not burdensome constraints to be adhered to. Here is an example of an organization that goes beyond mere compliance to laws in building an ethical organization:

> In teaching ethics to its employees, Texas Instruments, the $8 billion chip and electronics manufacturer, asks them to run an issue through the following steps: Is it legal? Is it consistent with the company's stated values? Will the employee feel bad doing it? What will the public think if the action is reported in the press? Does the employee think it is wrong? Further, if the employees are not sure of the ethicality of the issue, they are encouraged to ask someone until they are clear about it. In the process, employees can approach high-level personnel and even the company's lawyers. As can be clearly noted, at Texas Instruments, the question of ethics goes much beyond merely being legal. It is no surprise, therefore, that this company is a benchmark for corporate ethics and has been a recipient of three ethics awards: the David C. Lincoln Award for Ethics and Excellence in Business, American Business Ethics Award, and Bentley College Center for Business Ethics Award.[56]

To sum up, compliance-based approaches are externally motivated—that is, based on the fear of punishment for doing something unlawful. On the other hand, integrity-based approaches are driven by a personal and organizational commitment to ethical behavior.

A firm must have several key elements before it can become a highly ethical organization. These elements must be both present and constantly reinforced in order for the firm to be successful:

- Role models.
- Corporate credos and codes of conduct.
- Reward and evaluation systems.
- Policies and procedures.

These elements are highly interrelated. For example, reward structures and policies will be useless if leaders throughout the organization are not sound role models. That is, leaders who implicitly say, "Do as I say, not as I do," will quickly have their credibility eroded and such actions will, in effect, sabotage other elements that are essential to building an ethical organization.

Role Models

For good or for bad, leaders are role models in their organizations. As we noted in Chapter 9, leaders must "walk the talk"; that is, they must be consistent in their words and deeds. The values as well as the character of leaders become transparent to an organization's employees through their behaviors. In addition, when leaders do not believe in the ethical standards that they are trying to inspire, they will not be effective as good role models. Being an effective leader often includes taking responsibility for ethical lapses within the organization—even though the executives themselves are not directly involved. Consider, for example, the perspective of Dennis Bakke, CEO of AES, the $8 billion global electricity company based in Arlington, Virginia.

> There was a major breach (in 1992) of the AES values. Nine members of the water treatment team in Oklahoma lied to the EPA about water quality at the plant. There was no environmental damage, but they lied about the test results. A new, young chemist at the plant discovered it, and she told a team leader, and, of course, we then were notified. Now, you could argue that the people who lied were responsible and were accountable, but the senior management team also took responsibility by taking pay cuts. My reduction was about 30 percent.[57]

Such action enhances the loyalty and commitment of employees throughout the organization. Many would believe that it would have been much easier (and personally less expensive!) for Bakke and his management team to merely take strong punitive action against the nine individuals who were acting contrary to the behavior expected in AES's ethical culture. However, by taking responsibility for the misdeeds, the top executives—through their highly visible action—made it very clear that responsibility and penalties for ethical lapses go well beyond the "guilty" parties. Such courageous behavior by leaders helps to strengthen an organization's ethical environment.

Corporate Credos and Codes of Conduct

Corporate credos or codes of conduct are another important element of an ethical organization. Such mechanisms provide a statement and guidelines for norms and beliefs as well as guidelines for decision making. They provide employees with a clear understanding of the organization's position regarding employee behavior. Such guidelines also provide the basis for employees to refuse to commit unethical acts and help to make them aware of issues before they are faced with the situation. For such codes to be truly effective, organization members must be aware of them and what behavioral guidelines they contain.[58]

Large corporations are not the only ones to develop and use codes of conduct. Consider the example of Wetherill Associates (WAI), a small, privately held supplier of electrical parts to the automotive market.

> Rather than a conventional code of conduct, WAI has a Quality Assurance Manual—a combination of philosophy text, conduct guide, technical manual, and company profile—that describes the company's commitment to honesty, ethical action, and integrity.
>
> Interestingly, WAI doesn't have a corporate ethics officer, because the company's corporate ethics officer is top management. Marie Bothe, WAI's chief executive officer, sees her main function as keeping the 350-employee company on the path of ethical behavior and looking for opportunities to help the community. She delegates the "technical" aspects of the business—marketing, finance, personnel, and operations—to other members of the organization.[59]

Perhaps the best-known credo, a statement describing a firm's commitment to certain standards, is that of Johnson & Johnson (J&J). It is reprinted in Exhibit 11.6. The credo stresses honesty, integrity, superior products, and putting people before profits. What

Exhibit 11.6

Johnson & Johnson's Credo

We believe our first responsibility is to the doctors, nurses and patients, to mothers and fathers and all others who use our products and services. In meeting their needs everything we do must be of high quality. We must constantly strive to reduce our costs in order to maintain reasonable prices. Customers' orders must be serviced promptly and accurately. Our suppliers and distributors must have an opportunity to make a fair profit.

We are responsible to our employees, the men and women who work with us throughout the world. Everyone must be considered as an individual. We must respect their dignity and recognize their merit. They must have a sense of security in their jobs. Compensation must be fair and adequate, and working conditions clean, orderly, and safe. We must be mindful of ways to help our employees fulfill their family responsibilities. Employees must feel free to make suggestions and complaints. There must be equal opportunity for employment, development, and advancement for those qualified. We must provide competent management, and their actions must be just and ethical.

We are responsible to the communities in which we live and work and to the world community as well. We must be good citizens—support good works and charities and bear our fair share of taxes. We must encourage civic improvements and better health and education. We must maintain in good order the property we are privileged to use, protecting the environment and natural resources.

Our final responsibility is to our stockholders. Business must make a sound profit. We must experiment with new ideas. Research must be carried on, innovative programs developed, and mistakes paid for. New equipment must be purchased, new facilities provided, and new products launched. Reserves must be created to provide for adverse times. When we operate according to these principles, the stockholders should realize a fair return.

Source: Reprinted with permission of Johnson & Johnson Co.

distinguishes the J&J credo from those of other firms is the amount of energy the company's top managers devote to ensuring that employees live by its precepts.

Over a three-year period, Johnson & Johnson undertook a massive effort to assure that its original credo, already decades old, was still valid. More than 1,200 managers attended two-day seminars in groups of 25, with explicit instructions to challenge the credo. The president or CEO of the firm personally presided over each session. In the end, the company came out of the process believing that its original document was still valid. However, the questioning process continues. Such "challenge meetings" are still replicated every other year for all new managers. These efforts force J&J to question, internalize, and then implement its credo. Such investments have paid off handsomely many times—most notably in 1982, when eight people died from swallowing capsules of Tylenol, one of its flagship products, that someone had laced with cyanide. Leaders such as James Burke, who without hesitation made an across-the-board recall of the product even though it affected only a limited number of untraceable units, send a strong message throughout their organization.

Reward and Evaluation Systems

It is entirely possible for a highly ethical leader to preside over an organization that commits several unethical acts. How? It may reflect a flaw in the organization's reward structure. A reward and evaluation system may inadvertently cause individuals to act in an inappropriate manner if rewards are seen as being distributed on the basis of outcomes instead of the means by which goals and objectives are achieved.[60]

Consider the example of Sears, Roebuck & Co.'s automotive operations. Here, unethical behavior, rooted in a faulty reward system, took place primarily at the operations level: its automobile repair facilities.[61]

> In 1992 Sears was flooded with complaints about its automotive service business. Consumers and attorneys general in more than 40 states accused the firm of misleading customers and selling them unnecessary parts and services, from brake jobs to front-end alignments. What were the causes?
>
> In the face of declining revenues and eroding market share, Sears's management attempted to spur the performance of its auto centers by introducing new goals and incentives for mechanics. Automotive service advisers were given product-specific quotas for a variety of parts and repairs. Failure to meet the quotas could lead to transfers and reduced hours. Many employees spoke of "pressure, pressure, pressure" to bring in sales.
>
> Not too surprisingly, the judgment of many employees suffered. In essence, employees were left to chart their own course, given the lack of management guidance and customer ignorance. The bottom line: In settling the spate of lawsuits, Sears offered coupons to customers who had purchased certain auto services over the most recent two-year period. The total cost of the settlement, including potential customer refunds, was estimated to be $60 million. The cost in terms of damaged reputation? Difficult to assess, but certainly not trivial.

The Sears automotive example makes two important points. First, inappropriate reward systems may cause individuals at all levels throughout an organization to commit unethical acts that they might not otherwise commit. Second, the penalties in terms of damage to reputations, human capital erosion, and financial loss—in the short run and long run—are typically much higher than any gains that could be obtained through such unethical behavior.

Policies and Procedures

Many situations that a firm faces have regular, identifiable patterns. Typically, leaders tend to handle such routine by establishing a policy or procedure to be followed that can

STRATEGY SPOTLIGHT

No More Whistleblowing Woes!

The landmark Sarbanes-Oxley Act of 2002 gives those who expose corporate misconduct strong legal protection. Henceforth, an executive who retaliates against the corporate whistleblower can be held criminally liable and imprisoned for up to 10 years. That's the same sentence a mafia don gets for threatening a witness. The Labor Department can order a company to rehire an employee without going to court. If the fired workers feel their case is moving too slowly, they can request a federal jury after six months.

Companies need to revisit their current policies, including nondisclosure pacts. They may no longer be able to enforce rules requiring employees to get permission to speak to the media or lawyers. Even layoffs should be planned in advance, lest they seem retaliatory.

Sources: www.sarbanes-oxley.com/pcaob.php/level=2&pub_id=Sarbanes-Oxley&chap_id=PCAOB11; Dwyer, P., Carney, D., Borrus, A., Woellert, L., & Palmeri, C. 2002. Year of the WhistleBlower. *BusinessWeek*, December 16: 107–109; and www.buchalter.com/FSL5CS/articles/articles204.asp.

Employees of publicly traded companies are now the most protected whistleblowers. Provisions coauthored by Senator Grassley in the Sarbanes-Oxley corporate-reform law:

- Make it unlawful to "discharge, demote, suspend or threaten, harass, or in any manner discriminate against" a whistleblower.

- Establish criminal penalties of up to 10 years in jail for executives who retaliate against whistleblowers.

- Require board audit committees to establish procedures for hearing whistleblower complaints.

- Allow the secretary of labor to order a company to rehire a terminated whistleblower with no court hearings whatsoever.

- Give a whistleblower a right to jury trial, bypassing months or years of cumbersome administrative hearings.

be applied rather uniformly to each occurrence. As we noted in Chapter 9, such guidelines can be useful in specifying the proper relationships with a firm's customers and suppliers. For example, Levi Strauss has developed stringent global sourcing guidelines and Chemical Bank (now part of J. P. Morgan Chase Bank) has a policy of forbidding any review that would determine whether or not suppliers are Chemical customers when the bank awards contracts.

Clearly, it is important to carefully develop policies and procedures to guide behavior so that all employees will be encouraged to behave in an ethical manner. However, it is not enough merely to have policies and procedures "on the books." Rather, they must be reinforced with effective communication, enforcement, and monitoring, as well as sound corporate governance practices. Strategy Spotlight 11.10 describes how the recently enacted Sarbanes-Oxley Act provides considerable legal protection to employees of publicly traded companies who report unethical or illegal practices.

Summary

Strategic leadership is vital in ensuring that strategies are formulated and implemented in an effective manner. Leaders must play a central role in performing three critical and interdependent activities: setting the direction, designing the organization, and nurturing a culture committed to excellence and ethical behavior. In the chapter we provided the imagery of these three activities as a "three-legged stool." If leaders ignore or are ineffective at performing any one of the three, the organization will not be very successful. Leaders must also use power effectively to overcome barriers to change.

For leaders to effectively fulfill their activities, emotional intelligence (EI) is very important. Five elements that contribute to EI are self-awareness, self-regulation, motivation, empathy, and social skill. The first three elements pertain to self-management skills, whereas the last two are associated with a person's ability to manage relationships with others. We also addressed some of the potential drawbacks from the ineffective use of EI. These include the dysfunctional use of power as well as a tendency to become overly empathetic, which may result in unreasonably lowered performance expectations.

Leaders must also play a central role in creating a learning organization. Gone are the days when the top-level managers "think" and everyone else in the organization "does." With the rapidly changing, unpredictable, and complex competitive environments that characterize most industries, leaders must engage everyone in the ideas and energies of people throughout the organization. Great ideas can come from anywhere in the organization—from the executive suite to the factory floor. The five elements that we discussed as central to a learning organization are inspiring and motivating people with a mission or purpose, empowering people at all levels throughout the organization, accumulating and sharing internal knowledge, gathering external information, and challenging the status quo to stimulate creativity.

In the final section of the chapter, we addressed a leader's central role in instilling ethical behavior in the organization. We discussed the enormous costs that firms face when ethical crises arise—costs in terms of financial and reputational loss as well as the erosion of human capital and relationships with suppliers, customers, society at large, and governmental agencies. And, as we would expect, the benefits of having a strong ethical organization are also numerous. We contrasted compliance-based and integrity-based approaches to organizational ethics. Compliance-based approaches are largely externally motivated; that is, they are motivated by the fear of punishment for doing something that is unlawful. Integrity-based approaches, on the other hand, are driven by a personal and organizational commitment to ethical behavior. We also addressed the four key elements of an ethical organization: role models, corporate credos and codes of conduct, reward and evaluation systems, and policies and procedures.

Summary Review Questions

1. Three key activities—setting a direction, designing the organization, and nurturing a culture and ethics—are all part of what effective leaders do on a regular basis. Explain how these three activities are interrelated.

2. Define emotional intelligence (EI). What are the key elements of EI? Why is EI so important to successful strategic leadership?

3. The knowledge a firm possesses can be a source of competitive advantage. Describe ways that a firm can continuously learn to maintain its competitive position.

4. How can the five central elements of "learning organizations" be incorporated into global companies?

5. What are the benefits to firms and their shareholders of conducting business in an ethical manner?

6. Firms that fail to behave in an ethical manner can incur high costs. What are these costs and what is their source?

7. What are the most important differences between an "integrity organization" and a "compliance organization" in a firm's approach to organizational ethics?

8. What are some of the important mechanisms for promoting ethics in a firm?

Experiential Exercise

Select two well-known business leaders—one you admire and one you do not. Evaluate each of them on the five characteristics of emotional intelligence.

Emotional Intelligence Characteristics	Admired Leader	Leader Not Admired
Self-awareness		
Self-regulation		
Motivation		
Empathy		
Social skills		

Application Questions Exercises

1. Identify two CEOs whose leadership you admire. What is it about their skills, attributes, and effective use of power that causes you to admire them?
2. Founders have an important role in developing their organization's culture and values. At times, their influence persists for many years. Identify and describe two organizations in which the cultures and values established by the founder(s) continue to flourish. You may find research on the Internet helpful in answering these questions.
3. Some leaders place a great emphasis on developing superior human capital. In what ways does this help a firm to develop and sustain competitive advantages?
4. In this chapter we discussed the five elements of a "learning organization." Select a firm with which you are familiar and discuss whether or not it epitomizes some (or all) of these elements.

Ethics Questions

1. Sometimes organizations must go outside the firm to hire talent, thus bypassing employees already working for the firm. Are there conditions under which this might raise ethical considerations?
2. Ethical crises can occur in virtually any organization. Describe some of the systems, procedures, and processes that can help to prevent such crises.

References

1. Gagnier, M. 2005. Kremed again. *BusinessWeek,* January 17:40; Anonymous. 2005. Worst managers. *BusinessWeek,* January 10: 74–77; Stires, D. 2004. Krispy Kreme is in the hole—again. *Fortune,* November 11: 42–43; and, McGowan, W. P. 2005. Krispy Kreme: A recipe for business failure. *Canyon News,* 19: 23.

2. Charan, R., & Colvin, G. 1999. Why CEOs fail. *Fortune,* June 21: 68–78.

3. These three activities and our discussion draw from Kotter, J. P. 1990. What leaders really do. *Harvard Business Review,* 68(3): 103–111; Pearson, A. E. 1990. Six basics for general managers. *Harvard Business Review,* 67(4): 94–101; and Covey, S. R. 1996. Three roles of the leader in the new paradigm. In *The leader of the future:* 149–160. Hesselbein, F., Goldsmith, M., & Beckhard, R. (Eds.). San Francisco: Jossey-Bass. Some of the discussion of each of the three leadership activity concepts draws on Dess, G. G., & Miller, A. 1993. *Strategic management:* 320–325. New York: McGraw-Hill.

4. Day, C., Jr., & LaBarre, P. 1994. GE: Just your average everyday $60 billion family grocery store. *Industry Week,* May 2: 13–18.

5. The best (& worst) managers of the year. 2003. *Business-Week,* January 13: 63.

6. Johnson, C. 2005. Lay, Skilling go on trial in January. *Washington Post,* February 25: E3.

7. Watkins, S. 2003. Former Enron vice president Sherron Watkins on the Enron collapse. *Academy of Management Executive,* 17(4): 119–125. Ms. Watkins has been widely recognized as a "whistleblower" and for her courage in bringing the Enron scandal to light. For example, she was one of three individuals to be recognized as *Time* magazine's Persons of the Year in 2002. She also received the Scales of Justice Award, Everyday Hero's Award, Women Mean Business Award, and the Academy of Management's 2003 Distinguished Executive Speaker.

8. In January 2004, Fastow agreed to serve a 10-year sentence, pay a $23 million fine, and cooperate with the U.S. government's continuing investigation. He had been charged with 78 counts of fraud, money laundering, and conspiracy.

9. For insightful perspectives on escalation, refer to Brockner, J. 1992. The escalation of commitment to a failing course of action. *Academy of Management Review,* 17(1): 39–61; and Staw, B. M. 1976. Knee-deep in the big muddy: A study of commitment to a chosen course of action. *Organizational Behavior and Human Decision Processes,* 16: 27–44. The discussion of systemic, behavioral, and political barriers draws on Lorange, P., & Murphy, D. 1984. Considerations in implementing strategic control. *Journal of Business Strategy,* 5: 27–35. In a similar vein, Noel M. Tichy has addressed three types of resistance to change in the context of General Electric: technical resistance, political resistance, and cultural resistance. See Tichy, N. M. 1993. Revolutionalize your company. *Fortune,* December 13: 114–118. Examples draw from O'Reilly, B. 1997. The secrets of America's most admired corporations: New ideas and new products. *Fortune,* March 3: 60–64.

10. This section draws on Champoux, J. E. 2000. *Organizational behavior: Essential tenets for a new millennium.* London: South-Western; and The mature use of power in organizations. 2003. *RHR International-Executive Insights,* May 29, 12.19.168.197/execinsights/8-3.htm.

11. An insightful perspective on the role of power and politics in organizations is provided in Ciampa, K. 2005. Almost ready: How leaders move up. *Harvard Business Review,* 83(1): 46–53.

12. A discussion of the importance of persuasion in bringing about change can be found in Garvin, D. A., & Roberto, M. A. 2005. Change through persuasion. *Harvard Business Review,* 83(4): 104–113.

13. Lorsch, J. W., & Tierney, T. J. 2002. *Aligning the stars: How to succeed when professionals drive results.* Boston: Harvard Business School Press.

14. For a review of this literature, see Daft, R. 1999. *Leadership: Theory and practice.* Fort Worth, TX: Dryden Press.

15. This section draws on Luthans, F. 2002. Positive organizational behavior: Developing and managing psychological strengths. *Academy of Management Executive,* 16(1): 57–72; and Goleman, D. 1998. What makes a leader? *Harvard Business Review,* 76(6): 92–105.

16. EI has its roots in the concept of "social intelligence" that was first identified by E. L. Thorndike in 1920 (Intelligence and its uses. *Harper's Magazine,* 140: 227–235). Psychologists have been uncovering other intelligences for some time now and have grouped them into such clusters as abstract intelligence (the ability to understand and manipulate verbal and mathematical symbols), concrete intelligence (the ability to understand and manipulate objects), and social intelligence (the ability to understand and relate to people). See Ruisel, I. 1992. Social intelligence: Conception and methodological problems. *Studia Psychologica,* 34(4–5): 281–296. Refer to trochim.human.cornell.edu/gallery.

17. See, for example, Luthans, op. cit.; Mayer, J. D., Salvoney, P., & Caruso, D. 2000. Models of emotional intelligence. In Sternberg, R. J. (Ed.). *Handbook of intelligence.* Cambridge, UK: Cambridge University Press; and Cameron, K. 1999. Developing emotional intelligence at the Weatherhead School of Management. *Strategy: The Magazine of the Weatherhead School of Management,* Winter: 2–3.

18. An insightful perspective on leadership, which involves discovering, developing and celebrating what is unique about each individual, is found in Buckingham, M. 2005. What great managers do. *Harvard Business Review*, 83(3): 70–79.

19. Goleman, op. cit.: 102.

20. This section draws upon Klemp. G. 2005. *Emotional intelligence and leadership: What really matters*. Cambria Consulting, Inc., www.cambriaconsulting.com.

21. Mayer, J. D. et al. 2004. Leading by feel. *Harvard Business Review*, 82(1): 27–37.

22. Heifetz, R. 2004. Question authority. *Harvard Business Review*, 82(1): 37.

23. Ibid.

24. For another insightful perspective, refer to Goleman, D., Boyztzis, R., & McKee, A. 2002. *Primal leadership: Realizing the power of emotional Intelligence*. Boston: Harvard Business School. In particular, this book addresses the advantages and drawbacks of six leadership styles that draw upon the EI concept.

25. Handy, C. 1995. Trust and the virtual organization. *Harvard Business Review*, 73(3): 40–50.

26. This section draws upon Dess, G. G., & Picken, J. C. 1999. *Beyond productivity*. New York: AMACOM. The elements of the learning organization in this section are consistent with the work of Dorothy Leonard-Barton. See, for example, Leonard-Barton, D. 1992. The factory as a learning laboratory. *Sloan Management Review*, 11: 23–38.

27. Senge, P. M. 1990. The leader's new work: Building learning organizations. *Sloan Management Review*, 32(1): 7–23.

28. Hammer, M., & Stanton, S. A. 1997. The power of reflection. *Fortune*, November 24: 291–296.

29. For some guidance on how to effectively bring about change in organizations, refer to Wall, S. J. 2005. The protean organization: Learning to love change. *Organizational Dynamics*, 34(1): 37–46.

30. Covey, S. R. 1989. *The seven habits of highly effective people: Powerful lessons in personal change*. New York: Simon & Schuster.

31. Melrose, K. 1995. *Making the grass greener on your side: A CEO's journey to leading by servicing*. San Francisco: Barrett-Koehler.

32. Quinn, R. C., & Spreitzer, G. M. 1997. The road to empowerment: Seven questions every leader should consider. *Organizational Dynamics*, 25: 37–49.

33. Helgesen, S. 1996. Leading from the grass roots. In *Leader of the future:* 19–24 Hesselbein et al.

34. Bowen, D. E., & Lawler, E. E., III. 1995. Empowering service employees. *Sloan Management Review*, 37: 73–84.

35. Stack, J. 1992. *The great game of business*. New York: Doubleday/Currency.

36. Lubove, S. 1998. New age capitalist. *Forbes*, April 6: 42–43.

37. Schafer, S. 1997. Battling a labor shortage? It's all in your imagination. *Inc.*, August: 24.

38. Meyer, P. 1998. So you want the president's job . . . . *Business Horizons*, January–February: 2–8.

39. Goldberg, M. 1998. Cisco's most important meal of the day. *Fast Company*, February–March: 56.

40. Imperato, G. 1998. Competitive intelligence: Get smart! *Fast Company*, May: 268–279.

41. Novicki, C. 1998. The best brains in business. *Fast Company*, April: 125.

42. The introductory discussion of benchmarking draws on Miller, A. 1998. *Strategic management:* 142–143. New York: McGraw-Hill.

43. Port, O., & Smith, G. 1992. Beg, borrow—and benchmark. *BusinessWeek*, November 30: 74–75.

44. Main, J. 1992. How to steal the best ideas around. *Fortune*, October 19: 102–106.

45. Taylor, J. T. 1997. What happens after what comes next? *Fast Company*, December–January: 84–85.

46. Sheff, D. 1996. Levi's changes everything. *Fast Company*, June–July: 65–74.

47. Isaacson, W. 1997. In search of the real Bill Gates. *Time*, January 13: 44–57.

48. Baatz, E. B. 1993. Motorola's secret weapon. *Electronic Business*, April: 51–53.

49. Holt, J. W. 1996. *Celebrate your mistakes*. New York: McGraw-Hill.

50. Harari, O. 1997. Flood your organization with knowledge. *Management Review*, November: 33–37.

51. This opening discussion draws upon Conley, J. H. 2000. Ethics in business. In Helms, M. M. (Ed.). *Encyclopedia of management* (4th ed.): 281–285; Farmington Hills, MI: Gale Group; Paine, L. S. 1994. Managing for organizational integrity. *Harvard Business Review*, 72(2): 106–117; and Carlson, D. S., & Perrewe, P. L. 1995. Institutionalization of organizational ethics through transformational leadership. *Journal of Business Ethics*, 14: 829–838.

52. Kiger, P. J. 2001. Truth and consequences. *Working Woman*, May: 57–61.

53. Soule, E. 2002. Managerial moral strategies—in search of a few good principles. *Academy of Management Review*, 27(1): 114–124.

54. Carlson & Perrewe, op. cit.

55. This discussion is based upon Paine. Managing for organizational integrity; Paine, L. S. 1997. *Cases in leadership, ethics, and organizational integrity: A Strategic approach*. Burr Ridge, IL: Irwin; and Fontrodona, J. 2002. Business ethics across the Atlantic. Business Ethics Direct, www.ethicsa.org/BED_art_fontrodone.html.

56. www.ti.com/corp/docs/company/citizen/ethics/benchmark. shtml; and www.ti.com/corp/docs/company/citizen/ethics/ quicktest.shtml.

57. Wetlaufer, S. 1999. Organizing for empowerment: An interview with AES's Roger Sant and Dennis Bakke. *Harvard Business Review,* 77(1): 110–126.

58. For an insightful, academic perspective on the impact of ethics codes on executive decision making, refer to Stevens, J. M., Steensma, H. K., Harrison, D. A., & Cochran, P. S. 2005. Symbolic or substantive document? The influence of ethics code on financial executives' decisions. *Strategic Management Journal,* 26(2): 181–195.

59. Paine. Managing for organizational integrity.

60. For a recent study on the effects of goal setting on unethical behavior, read Schweitzer, M. E., Ordonez, L., & Douma, B. 2004. Goal setting as a motivator of unethical behavior. *Academy of Management Journal,* 47(3): 422–432.

61. Paine. Managing for organizational integrity.

12

Managing Innovation and Fostering Corporate Entrepreneurship

After reading this chapter, you should have a good understanding of:

- The importance of implementing strategies and practices that foster innovation.

- The challenges and pitfalls of managing corporate innovation processes.

- The role of product champions and exit champions in internal corporate venturing.

- How independent venture teams and business incubators are used to develop corporate ventures.

- How corporations create an internal environment and culture that promote entrepreneurial development.

- How an entrepreneurial orientation can enhance a firm's efforts to develop promising corporate venture initiatives.

*t*o remain competitive, established firms must continually seek out opportunities for growth and new methods for strategically renewing their performance. Changes in customer needs, new technologies, and shifts in the competitive landscape require that companies continually innovate and initiate corporate ventures in order to compete effectively. This chapter addresses how entrepreneurial activities can be an avenue for achieving competitive advantages.

In the first section, we address the importance of innovation in identifying venture opportunities and strategic renewal. Innovations can take many forms, including radical breakthrough innovations as well as incremental innovative improvements, and be used either to update products or renew organizational processes. We discuss how firms can successfully manage the innovation process. Impediments and challenges to effective innovation are discussed and examples of good innovation practices are presented.

We discuss the unique role of corporate entrepreneurship in the strategic management process in the second section. Here we highlight two types of activities corporations use to remain competitive—focused and dispersed. New venture groups and business incubators are often used to focus a firm's entrepreneurial activities. In other corporations, the entrepreneurial spirit is dispersed throughout the organization and gives rise to product champions and other autonomous strategic behaviors that organizational members engage in to foster internal corporate venturing.

In the final section we describe how a firm's entrepreneurial orientation can contribute to its growth and renewal as well as enhance the methods and processes strategic managers use to recognize opportunities and develop initiatives for internal growth and development. The chapter also evaluates the pitfalls that firms may encounter when implementing entrepreneurial strategies.

Companies often grow by commercializing new technologies. This is one of the most important paths to corporate entrepreneurship. But technologies change and yesterday's exciting innovation eventually becomes today's old news. Consider the case of Polaroid, a company that captivated the marketplace with its instant photography technology and grew to become a multibillion dollar enterprise on the strength of that innovation.[1]

Polaroid Corporation's founder, Edward Land, was a Harvard dropout. He was also a genius in optics, chemistry, and engineering who started his Cambridge, Massachusetts, company in 1937 to focus on sunglasses and other technologies that polarize light. During World War II, the company built infrared filters for gunsights and dark-adaptation goggles. It was after the war, however, that one of Land's innovations struck gold. In 1947 he introduced a single-step photographic process that would develop film in 60 seconds and launched the Land Camera. Over the next 30 years, the camera and its film evolved into the Polaroid One-Step, and sales surged to $1.4 billion by 1978.

In the process, Polaroid became one of the most admired companies and a best bet among stock pickers. It was a member of the "Nifty Fifty," a group of companies known for their innovative ideas whose stocks regularly traded at 40 or more times earnings. In 1991 it won a huge patent infringement lawsuit against rival Eastman Kodak, which had to pay Polaroid $925 million. The company also continued to launch new products using its instant film technology in a variety of different cameras with updated features.

On the surface, Polaroid seemed to be the picture of success. Land had been hailed as a new breed of corporate leader—both technically savvy and entrepreneurial. But by 1991, the year Land died, the company he built was unraveling. Instead of using the cash from the Kodak lawsuit to pay down its heavy debt, Polaroid spent the money to develop a new camera—the Captiva—which flopped in the marketplace. A few years later the I-Zone Pocket Camera, a product targeted at adolescents, had weak sales because the image quality was inconsistent and replacement film was considered too expensive for teens. Meanwhile, internally, Polaroid was spending 37 percent of its sales on administrative costs, compared to Kodak's 21 percent. Even though the company continued to sell millions of cameras each year—a record 13.1 million in 2000—its strength was deteriorating.

Polaroid's most serious problems began when it failed to get on the digital photography bandwagon. Rather than make the move into digital, Polaroid decided to stick with its proprietary technology. Once Polaroid realized the extent of the digital photography trend, it was too late. It eventually introduced digital cameras but they were often ranked low in consumer ratings. Polaroid even developed digital printing technologies, called Opal and Onyx, designed to deliver high resolution digital images. But because of its weakened financial state, it could not get the funding from investors to advertise and develop them. By 2001, it was in real trouble. Its debt was $950 million, it laid off 2,950 employees—35 percent of its workforce—and began missing interest payments to bondholders. In October 2001, it filed for Chapter 11 bankruptcy protection. Sale of its stock, which had traded as high as $60 in July 1997, was halted at 28 cents per share on the New York Stock Exchange.

The final blow to its reputation came in 2005 when it was announced, as part of a deal to sell Polaroid to a Minnesota-based conglomerate, that thousands of former Polaroid employees would have their pensions wiped out. Retirees and ex-employees, who also lost their health coverage and life insurance, received a total of just $47 for their years of service, while four former Polaroid executives split a $30 million dollar settlement among them![2]

What Went Wrong at Polaroid?   Considered by many to be one of the first great research-based companies, Polaroid failed largely because it lost its ability to effectively innovate and launch new products. Many factors contributed to its downfall. Clearly, its failure to respond quickly to the digital photography phenomenon caused a serious setback. But the roots of the problem were deeper. As one writer put it, "They overestimated the value of their core business." That is, Polaroid's overconfidence in its early success prevented it from envisioning a purpose beyond its instant imaging capability. This phenomenon is sometimes referred to as "the innovator's dilemma"—firms become so preoccupied with meeting current needs that they fail to take steps to meet future needs.[3] This dilemma inhibited Polaroid's ability to change and affected every aspect of its business:

- Even though sales of its core products were strong, it lost touch with its customers. As a result, several of its innovations failed in the marketplace.

- It did not have a long-term strategy for financing growth. Because it relied heavily on investors to finance new product initiatives, when one failed, it created cash flow problems. To regain profitability, Polaroid would offer more shares and bonds to investors, which, in turn, devalued the stock and created even more indebtedness. Eventually, investors turned away.

- Buoyed by revenues that grew annually for over 30 years, it failed to control personnel costs and was weighed down by too many employees. Eventually these expenses overtook its sales.

In short, Polaroid stopped thinking and acting like an entrepreneurial firm. The Polaroid brand is still loved by many, and its products can still be found in the marketplace. (In 2002, Polaroid's assets were purchased by OEP Imaging Operating Corporation and, as part of the agreement, OEPI changed its name to Polaroid Corporation.) But the company that had once changed the world of photography was itself unable to make the changes necessary to remain viable. As a result of its lack of vision and failure to change, what had once been a leading innovator and top financial performer slowly fizzled out.[4]

Managing change, as we suggested in Chapter 11, is one of the most important functions performed by strategic leaders. The transformative activity of bringing organizations "from what they are to what the leader would have them become" requires fresh ideas and a vision of the future. Most organizations want to grow. To do so, they must expand their product offering, reach into new markets, and obtain new customers. Sometimes profitability can be increased by streamlining processes and operating more efficiently. These activities inevitably involve change, and a firm's leaders must be effective change agents.

What options are available to organizations that want to change and grow? This chapter addresses two major avenues through which companies can expand or improve their business—innovation and corporate entrepreneurship. These two activities go hand-in-hand because they both have similar aims. The first is strategic renewal. Innovations help an organization stay fresh and reinvent itself as conditions in the business environment change. This is why managing innovation is such an important strategic implementation issue. The second is the pursuit of venture opportunities. Innovative breakthroughs, as well as new product concepts, evolving technologies, and shifting demand, create opportunities for corporate venturing. In this chapter we will explore these topics—how change and innovation can stimulate strategic renewal and foster corporate entrepreneurship. First we turn to the challenge of managing innovation.

>>Managing Innovation

One of the most important sources of growth opportunities is innovation. Innovation involves using new knowledge to transform organizational processes or create commercially viable products and services. The sources of new knowledge may include the latest technology, the results of experiments, creative insights, or competitive information. However it comes about, innovation occurs when new combinations of ideas and information bring about positive change.

STRATEGY SPOTLIGHT

12.1

Rubbermaid: Building Advantages through Marketing Innovations

Rubbermaid is a consistent winner of innovation kudos, including the *Chicago Sun-Times* Innovation Awards and *Retail Merchandiser*'s 2002 Marketing Innovation award winner in two categories. Yet Rubbermaid's innovations would rarely be considered "high-tech." Although the company (which consolidated in 1999 to form Newell Rubbermaid, Inc.) is known for its synthetic rubber materials, it is the application of those materials to develop innovative products that is responsible for its winning strategies. Here are some examples:

Tool Tower—Consumers have been crying out for help in organizing their garages, according to Adrian Fernandez, director of product management for Rubbermaid's Home Products unit. In fact, storing tools efficiently is the number one complaint by homeowners about garages. The Tool Tower, a simple and efficient plastic rack designed to hold long- and short-handle tools in one place, was a welcome solution. It is easily assembled, takes up little space, and is much safer than hanging tools on nails or racks.

Sources: Kuczmarski, T. D. 2005. Award winners find innovation is profitable. *Chicago Sun-Times*, June 16; www.suntimes.com; Schmitt, W. 1997. Rubbermaid Inc. In Kanter, R. M., Kao, J., & Wiersma, F. (Eds.), *Innovation: Breakthrough thinking at 3M, DuPont, GE, Pfizer, and Rubbermaid:* 168–170. New York: HarperCollins; www.retail-merchandiser.com; and www.rubbermaid.com.

High-Heat Scraper—While on site at one of its restaurant customers, a Rubbermaid business team noticed that chefs preferred synthetic rubber scrapers instead of metal spatulas when using nonstick cookware. But the scrapers quickly warped from the heat and lost their shape. Based on this experience, a new scraper of pliable synthetic rubber was developed with chefs in mind. It still did not scratch but could sustain temperatures as high as 500 degrees Fahrenheit.

Hardware Blue—Many products are tested in the company's "Everything Rubbermaid" experimental lab stores. Rubbermaid noticed that more and more women were buying tool boxes and workshop organizers. They wondered how women shoppers liked their traditional colors—yellow, black, and gray. Through focus groups, they identified a new color, "Hardware Blue," that outsold all other colors and appealed to both men and women.

Clearly, the high-heat scraper required technological know-how to develop. But the impetus for it came from proactive customer contact, and the product itself was simple. As can be seen from these examples, Rubbermaid is concerned not only with technologically based innovations but also with marketing innovations.

The emphasis on newness is a key point. For example, for a patent application to have any chance of success, one of the most important attributes it must possess is novelty. You can't patent an idea that has been copied. This is a central idea. In fact, the root of the word *innovation* is the Latin *novus,* which means new. Innovation involves introducing or changing to something new.[5]

Among the most important sources of new ideas is new technology. Technology creates new possibilities. Technology provides the raw material that firms use to make innovative new products and services. But technology is the only source of innovations. There can be innovations in human resources, firm infrastructure, marketing, service, or in many other value-adding areas that have little to do with anything "high-tech." Strategy Spotlight 12.1 highlights three innovations by the Rubbermaid Corporation that met customer needs and generated sales but were relatively low-tech.

As the Rubbermaid example suggests, innovation can take many forms. Next we will consider two frameworks that are often used to distinguish types of innovation.

Types of Innovation

Although innovations are not always high-tech, changes in technology can be an important source of change and growth. When an innovation is based on a sweeping new technology, it often has a more far-reaching impact. However, sometimes even a small innovation can add value and create competitive advantages. Innovation can and should occur throughout an organization—in every department and all aspects of the value chain.

One way to view the impact of an innovation is in terms of its degree of innovativeness, which falls somewhere on a continuum that extends from incremental to radical.[6]

- **Radical innovations** produce fundamental changes by evoking major departures from existing practices. These breakthrough innovations usually occur because of technological change. They tend to be highly disruptive and can transform a company or even revolutionize a whole industry. They may lead to products or processes that can be patented, giving a firm a strong competitive advantage. Examples include electricity, the telephone, the transistor, desktop computers, fiber optics, artificial intelligence, and genetically engineered drugs.

- **Incremental innovations** enhance existing practices or make small improvements in products and processes. They may represent evolutionary applications within existing paradigms of earlier, more radical innovations. Because they often sustain a company by extending or expanding its product line or manufacturing skills, incremental innovations can be a source of competitive advantage. They increase revenues by creating a new marketplace offering or reduce costs by providing new capabilities that minimize expenses or speed productivity. Examples include frozen food, sports drinks, steel-belted radial tires, electronic bookkeeping, shatterproof glass, and digital telephones.

Some innovations are highly radical; others are only slightly incremental. But most innovations fall somewhere between these two extremes. Exhibit 12.1 shows where several innovations fall along the radical–incremental continuum.

Another distinction that is often used when discussing innovation is between process innovation and product innovation.[7] *Product innovation* refers to efforts to create product designs and applications of technology to develop new products for end users. Recall from Chapter 5 how generic strategies were typically different depending on the stage of the industry life cycle. Product innovations tend to be more radical and are more common during the earlier stages of an industry's life cycle. As an industry matures, there

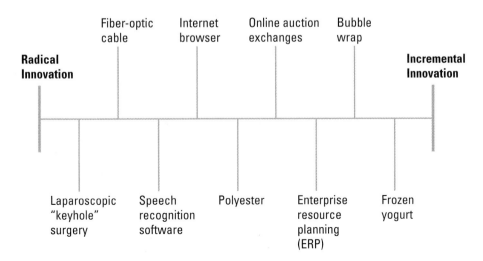

Exhibit 12.1   Continuum of Radical and Incremental Innovations

are fewer opportunities for newness, so the innovations tend to be more incremental. Product innovations are also commonly associated with a differentiation strategy. Firms that differentiate by providing customers with new products or services that offer unique features or quality enhancements often engage in product innovation.

Process innovation, by contrast, is typically associated with improving the efficiency of an organizational process, especially manufacturing systems and operations. By drawing on new technologies and an organization's accumulated experience (Chapter 5), firms can often improve materials utilization, shorten cycle time, and increase quality. Process innovations are more likely to occur in the later stages of an industry's life cycle as companies seek ways to remain viable in markets where demand has flattened out and competition is more intense. As a result, process innovations are often associated with overall cost leader strategies, because the aim of many process improvements is to lower the costs of operations.

As you can see from this discussion of different types of innovation, the innovation process itself has numerous strategic implications. Innovation is a force in both the external environment (technology, competition) and also a factor affecting a firm's internal choices (generic strategy, value-adding activities). Nevertheless, innovation can be quite difficult for some firms to manage, especially those that have become comfortable with the status quo. Next, we turn to the challenges associated with successful innovation.

Challenges of Innovation

Innovation is essential to sustaining competitive advantages. Recall from Chapter 3 that one of the four elements of the Balanced Scorecard is the innovation and learning perspective. The extent and success of a company's innovation efforts are indicators of its overall performance. As management guru Peter Drucker warned, "An established company which, in an age demanding innovation, is not capable of innovation is doomed to decline and extinction."[8] To put it simply, in today's competitive environment, most firms have only one choice: "Innovate or die."

As with change, however, firms are often resistant to innovation. Only those companies that actively pursue innovation, even though it is often difficult and uncertain, will get a payoff from their innovation efforts. But managing innovation is challenging. As former Pfizer chairman and CEO William Steere puts it: "In some ways, managing innovation is analogous to breaking in a spirited horse. You are never sure of success until you achieve your goal. In the meantime, everyone takes a few lumps."[9]

What is it that makes innovation so difficult? Clearly the uncertainty about outcomes is one factor. Companies that keep an eye on their bottom line (and most of them do!) are often reluctant to invest time and resources into activities with an unknown future. Another factor is that the innovation process involves so many choices. These choices present five dilemmas that companies must wrestle with when pursuing innovation.[10]

- **Seeds versus Weeds.** Most companies have an abundance of innovative ideas. They must decide which of these is most likely to bear fruit—the "Seeds"—and which should be cast aside—the "Weeds." This is an ongoing dilemma that is often complicated by the fact that some innovation projects require a considerable level of investment before a firm can fully evaluate whether they are worth pursuing. As a result, firms need a mechanism with which they can choose among various innovation projects.

- **Experience versus Initiative.** Companies must decide who will lead an innovation project. Senior managers may have experience and credibility but tend to be more risk averse. Midlevel employees, who may be the innovators themselves, may have more enthusiasm because they can see firsthand how an innovation would address specific problems. As a result, firms need to support and reward organizational members who bring new ideas to light.

- *Internal versus External Staffing.* Innovation projects need competent staffs to succeed. People drawn from inside the company may have greater social capital and know the organization's culture and routines. But this knowledge may actually inhibit them from thinking outside the box. Staffing innovation projects with external personnel requires that project managers justify the hiring and spend time recruiting, training, and relationship building. As a result, firms need to streamline and support the process of staffing innovation efforts.

- *Building Capabilities versus Collaborating.* Innovation projects often require new sets of skills. Firms can seek help from other departments and/or partner with other companies that bring resources and experience as well as share costs of development. However, such arrangements can create dependencies and inhibit internal skills development. Further, struggles over who contributed the most or how the benefits of the project are to be allocated may arise. As a result, firms need a mechanism for forging links with outside parties to the innovation process.

- *Incremental versus Preemptive Launch.* Companies must manage the timing and scale of new innovation projects. An incremental launch is less risky because it requires fewer resources and serves as a market test. But a launch that is too tentative can undermine the project's credibility. It also opens the door for a competitive response. A large-scale launch requires more resources, but it can effectively preempt a competitive response. As a result, firms need to make funding and management arrangements that allow for projects to hit the ground running and be responsive to market feedback.

These dilemmas highlight why the innovation process can be daunting even for highly successful firms. Strategy Spotlight 12.2 addresses the challenges and pitfalls that Microsoft faces in its efforts to be a strong innovator. How can companies successfully address these innovation challenges? Next, we consider three steps that firms can take to manage the innovation process.[11]

Defining the Scope of Innovation

Firms must have a means to focus their innovation efforts. By defining the "strategic envelope"—that is, the scope of a firm's innovation efforts—firms ensure that their innovation efforts are not wasted on projects that are highly uncertain or outside the firm's domain of interest. Strategic enveloping defines the range of acceptable projects. As Alistair Corbett, an innovation expert who directs the Toronto office of the global consulting firm Bain & Company, recently said, "One man's radical innovation is another man's incremental innovation."[12] Thus, a strategic envelope creates a firm-specific view of innovation that defines how a firm can create new knowledge and learn from an innovation initiative even if the project fails. Although such limitations might seem overly constraining, they also give direction to a firm's innovation efforts, which helps separate seeds from weeds and build internal capabilities.

One way to determine which projects to work on is to focus on a common technology. Then, innovation efforts across the firm can aim at developing skills and expertise in a given technical area. Another potential focus is on a market theme.

STRATEGY SPOTLIGHT

Microsoft's Innovation Challenges

You would think that Microsoft, the dominant software seller in the world with a $6.8 billion annual research and development budget, would be a major innovator. Instead, innovation seems to be Microsoft's Achilles' heel. From its earliest days, Microsoft has had far more success as an imitator than an innovator. Despite having well-funded research labs at its Redmond, Washington, headquarters, Microsoft has little to show for years of efforts to come up with the next big breakthrough innovation. Why is Microsoft is so innovation-challenged?

- **Innovation is hard.** There is no doubt that Microsoft is working hard at it. From 2000 to 2005, Microsoft acquired 2,188 patents to protect its researchers' work. But creating a commercially viable breakthrough innovation such as the Web browser (created by Netscape), the streaming media player (by RealNetworks) or interactive television (TiVo) is not easy. In many cases, it is more about luck and timing than money, dedication, and brilliance.

- **Bigger isn't better.** Large companies simply find it more difficult than smaller ones to sustain rapid growth through innovation. Good ideas are scarce everywhere and most new innovations take a few years to get off the ground. Because of Microsoft's sheer size, the contribution that a new product can make is relatively small. For example, if Microsoft had matched Google's recent growth record, that business activity would have added only 4 percent to Microsoft's top line.

- **Defense is easier.** Most of Microsoft's research efforts go to helping it sustain its strong leadership in software products such as MS Office. Of every dollar it spends on research and development (R&D), "probably something on the order of 90 percent is directly in line, or in service of, the existing business groups," according to Craig Mundie, Microsoft's co-chief technology officer. In this respect, Microsoft is a victim of "the innovator's dilemma"—spending so much more time protecting its established lines of business and satisfying existing customers that it misses opportunities to make breakthroughs.

Microsoft continues to support innovation and its breakthrough product may come any day. But even its new project, the second generation videogame console known as XBox 360, lags far behind Sony's PlayStation2 in sales and market penetration. Microsoft may not be producing the next big thing, but as a fast follower of technology breakthroughs, it has been highly successful.

Sources: Grossman, L. 2005. Out of the Xbox. *Time,* May 23: 44–53; and Hawn, C. 2004. What money can't buy. *Fast Company,* 89: 68–73.

Consider how DuPont responded to a growing concern for environmentally sensitive products:

> In the early 1990s, DuPont sought to use its knowledge of plastics to identify products to meet a growing market demand for biodegradable products. Over the next decade, it conducted numerous experiments with a biodegradable polyester resin it named Biomax. By trying different applications and formulations demanded by potential customers, the company was finally able to create a product that could be produced economically and had market appeal. Recently, Biomax was certified biodegradable and compostable by the Biodegradable Products Institute, an endorsement that should further boost sales.[13]

In defining a strategic envelope, companies must be clear not only about the kinds of innovation they are looking for but also the expected results. Therefore, each company needs to develop a set of questions to ask itself about its innovation efforts:

- How much will the innovation initiative cost?
- How likely is it to actually become commercially viable?
- How much value will it add; that is, what will it be worth if it works?
- What will be learned if it does not pan out?

In other words, however a firm envisions its innovation goals, it needs to develop a systematic approach to evaluating its results and learning from its innovation initiatives. Viewing innovation from this perspective helps firms manage the process.[14]

Managing the Pace of Innovation

Along with clarifying the scope of an innovation by defining a strategic envelope, firms also need to regulate the pace of innovation. An advantage of assessing the extent to which an innovation is radical or incremental is that it helps determine how long it will take for an innovation initiative to realistically come to fruition. The project time line of an incremental innovation may be six months to 2 years, whereas a more radical innovation is typically long term—10 years or more.[15] Thus, radical innovations often begin with a long period of exploration in which experimentation makes strict timelines unrealistic. In contrast, firms that are innovating incrementally in order to exploit a window of opportunity may use a milestone approach that is more stringently driven by goals and deadlines. As suggested in Chapter 9, this kind of sensitivity to realistic time frames helps companies separate dilemmas temporally so they are easier to manage.

The idea of time pacing can also be a source of competitive advantage, because it helps a company manage transitions and develop an internal rhythm.[16] In their book *Competing on the Edge,* Shona Brown and Kathleen Eisenhardt contrasted time pacing with event pacing. They argue that, by controlling the pace of the innovation process (time pacing), a company can more effectively learn from it and grow internally. In contrast, when outside events, such as shifts in technology or the actions of competitors, determine the pace of innovation (event pacing), then firms lose their ability to manage the change process. Time pacing does not mean the company ignores the demands of market timing. Instead, it means that companies have a sense of their own internal clock in a way that allows them to thwart competitors by controlling the innovation process.

Not all innovation lends itself to speedy development, however. Radical innovation often involves open-ended experimentation and time-consuming mistakes. Further, the creative aspects of innovation are often difficult to time. When software maker Intuit's new CEO, Steve Bennett, began to turn around that troubled business, he required every department to implement Six Sigma, a quality control management technique that focuses on being responsive to customer needs. Everybody, that is, but the techies.

> "We're not GE, we're not a company where Jack says 'Do it,' and everyone salutes," says Bill Hensler, Intuit's vice president for process excellence. That's because software development, according to many, is more of an art than a science. At the Six Sigma Academy, president of operations Phil Samuel says even companies that have embraced Six Sigma across every other aspect of their organization usually maintain a hands-off policy when it comes to software developers. Techies, it turns out, like to go at their own pace.[17]

The example of software developers makes an important point about strategic pacing: some projects can't be rushed. Companies that hurry up their research efforts or go to market before they are ready can damage their ability to innovate—and their reputation. Thus, managing the pace of innovation can be an important factor in long-term success.

Collaborating with Innovation Partners

Innovation involves gathering new knowledge and learning from your mistakes. It is rare for any one work group or department to have all the information it needs to carry an innovation from concept to commercialization. Even a company that is highly competent with its current operations usually needs new capabilities to achieve new results. Innovation partners can provide the skills and insights that are often needed to make innovation projects succeed.

Partners can come from several sources:

- Other personnel within the department.
- Personnel within the firm but from another department.
- Partners outside the firm.

Innovation partners may also come from nonbusiness sources, including research universities and the federal government. Each year the federal government issues requests for proposals (RFPs) asking private companies for assistance in improving services or finding solutions to public problems. Universities are another type of innovation partner. Chip-maker Intel, for example, has benefited from underwriting substantial amounts of university research. Rather than hand universities a blank check, Intel bargains for rights to patents that emerge from Intel-sponsored research. The university retains ownership of the patent, but Intel gets royalty-free use of it.[18]

Strategic partnering has other benefits as well. It requires firms to identify their strengths and weaknesses and make choices about which capabilities to leverage, which need further development, and which are outside the firm's current or projected scope of operations. Such knowledge can bring a level of realism to the process. It also helps managers get clear about what they need partners to do.

Consider the example of Nextel in its decision to partner with RadioFrame Networks, a Seattle-based start-up.

> RadioFrame had developed an innovative radio transmitter that could be used inside buildings to make cell-phone signals clearer. Nextel, which did not have as much network capacity as some of its larger competitors, saw this as a way to increase bandwidth and add value to its existing set of services. Not only did the two firms form a partnership, but Nextel also became involved in the development process by providing senior engineers and funding to help build the system. "We really worked hand-in-hand with Nextel," says RadioFrame CEO Jeff Brown, "from user requirements to how to physically get the finished product into their distribution systems."[19]

Firms need a mechanism to help decide whom to partner with. Several factors will enter into the decision, including the issues mentioned above regarding the pace and scope of innovation initiatives. To choose partners, firms need to ask what competencies they are looking for and what the innovation partner will contribute. These contributions might include knowledge of markets, technology expertise, or contacts with key players in an industry. Innovation partnerships also typically need to specify how the rewards of the innovation will be shared and who will own the intellectual property that is developed.[20]

Innovation efforts that involve multiple partners and the speed and ease with which partners can network and collaborate are changing the way innovation is conducted. These changes have prompted one Harvard University professor to claim that the innovation process itself has experienced a paradigm shift. Strategy Spotlight 12.3 emphasizes the role of collaboration and partnerships in a new approach to innovation labeled "open innovation."

As this section indicates, managing innovation is an important and challenging organizational activity. For it to be successful, the innovation process has to stay focused on its ultimate purpose—to introduce new products and/or deploy new processes that build competitive advantages and make the company profitable. Innovation involves a companywide commitment because the results of innovation affect every part of the organization. Innovation also requires an entrepreneurial spirit and skill set to be effective. One of the most important ways that companies improve and grow is when innovation is put to the task of creating new corporate ventures. We will look at that topic next.

Open Innovation: A Better Way to Build Value?

Recall from Chapter 8 the example of InnoCentive, the Internet-based collaboration platform launched by Eli Lilly to provide an open source, virtual R&D community to solve complex scientific problems. Not only is InnoCentive a savvy application of digital technology, it is also an example of what Harvard business professor Henry Chesbrough calls "open innovation." The concept of open innovation builds on two other concepts seen in previous chapters— the importance of intellectual assets in today's economy (Chapter 4) and the use of boundaryless organizational arrangements to achieve strategic ends (Chapter 10).

Chesbrough claims that the open innovation model will become increasingly important in the future. His argument is as follows: Innovation teams and R&D departments have acted with a fairly traditional mind-set for years about how to profit from innovation initiatives. The old mind-set, however, has created a paradox—in an era when ideas and knowledge abound, innovation and industrial research seem less effective. The old way of innovating no longer seems to be bearing fruit, because new technologies and the speed of innovation are creating new demands on companies to look beyond their traditional boundaries and share their intellectual property (IP). The innovation process itself, according to Chesbrough, needs innovating.

The old approach to innovation, labeled "closed innovation," operates on several key assumptions:

1. The smart people in our field work for us.

2. We should control the IP developed by our smart people so that competitors don't profit from our ideas.

3. To profit from R&D and innovation, we have to discover it, develop it, and ship it ourselves.

Source: Chesbrough, H. 2003. The era of open innovation. *MIT Sloan Management Review*, 44(3): 35–41; Chesbrough, H. 2003. *Open innovation: The new imperative for creating and profiting from technology.* Boston: Harvard Business School Press.

4. If we discover it first, we will get it to market first.

5. If we get it to market first, we win.

In contrast, Chesbrough argues, the open way to successfully innovate involves collaborating and drawing on the knowledge and resources of competitors and other strategic partners. In other words, disclose your intellectual property, cross organizational boundaries to achieve innovation goals, and let others share in the wealth. Here are the contrasting assumptions that are central to open innovation:

1. Not all the smart people work for us. Some of the smart people that we need to work with work somewhere else.

2. We should profit when others use our IP and be willing to buy their IP if it advances our innovation business model.

3. Internal R&D is not the only way to add value; external R&D can also benefit us.

4. We don't have to originate the research to profit from it.

5. Building a smarter innovation business model is better than getting to market first.

In his book, Chesbrough describes how innovation leader IBM, once an exemplar of the closed innovation approach, has transformed itself by being willing to cross boundaries and share its IP with others. He also describes how companies such as Cisco and Intel have succeeded by using an open approach while their rivals Lucent and Xerox have struggled. It remains to be seen whether other companies will adopt open innovation, but Chesbrough is convinced that the ones that are willing to seize this new approach will be the long-term winners.

>>Corporate Entrepreneurship

Corporate entrepreneurship (CE) has two primary aims: the pursuit of new venture opportunities and strategic renewal.[21] The innovation process keeps firms alert by exposing them to new technologies, making them aware of marketplace trends, and helping them evaluate new possibilities. Corporate entrepreneurship uses the fruits of the innovation process to help firms build new sources of competitive advantage and renew their value propositions. Just as the innovation process helps firms to make positive improvements, corporate entrepreneurship helps firms identify opportunities and launch new ventures. In Chapter 6 we addressed corporate growth through mergers and acquisitions as well as through joint ventures and strategic alliances. Here the focus is on internal venture development and growth.

Corporate new venture creation was labeled "intrapreneuring" by Gifford Pinchot because it refers to building entrepreneurial businesses within existing corporations.[22] However, to engage in corporate entrepreneurship that yields above-average returns and contributes to sustainable advantages, it must be done effectively. In this section we will examine the sources of entrepreneurial activity within established firms and the methods large corporations use to stimulate entrepreneurial behavior.

In a typical corporation, what determines how entrepreneurial projects will be pursued? That depends on many factors, including:

- Corporate culture.
- Leadership.
- Structural features that guide and constrain action.
- Organizational systems that foster learning and manage rewards.

In other words, all of the factors that influence the strategy implementation process will also shape how corporations engage in internal venturing.

Other factors will also affect how entrepreneurial ventures will be pursued.

- The use of teams in strategic decision making.
- Whether the company is product or service oriented.
- Whether its innovation efforts are aimed at product or process improvements.
- The extent to which it is high-tech or low-tech.

Because these factors are different in every organization, some companies may be more involved than others in identifying and developing new venture opportunities. These factors will also influence the nature of the CE process. In this section, we will address several avenues by which companies pursue growth and profit opportunities through entrepreneurial activities.

Successful corporate entrepreneurship typically requires firms to reach beyond their current operations and markets in the pursuit of new opportunities. In fact, it is often the breakthrough opportunities that provide the greatest returns. A recent study found that 86 percent of firms expand by making incremental improvements such as extending an existing product line. Only 14 percent ventured into arenas that were new to the world or new to the firm. Although line extensions provided 62 percent of the total revenues, they accounted for only 39 percent of total profits. By contrast, the companies that entered new markets and industries enjoyed total profits of 61 percent from 38 percent of total revenues.[23]

These findings led W. Chan Kim and Renee Mauborgne in their new book *Blue Ocean Strategy* to conclude that companies that are willing to venture into market spaces where there is little or no competition—labeled "blue oceans"—will outperform those firms that limit growth to incremental improvements in competitively crowded industries—labeled "red oceans." Companies that identify and pursue blue ocean strategies follow somewhat different rules than those that are "bloodied" by the competitive practices in red oceans. Consider the following elements of a blue ocean strategy:

- ***Create uncontested market space.*** By seeking opportunities where they are not threatened by existing competitors, blue ocean firms can focus on customers rather than on competition.

- ***Make the competition irrelevant.*** Rather than using the competition as a benchmark, blue ocean firms cross industry boundaries to offer new and different products and services.

STRATEGY SPOTLIGHT

Cirque du Soleil's Blue Ocean Strategy

The blue ocean strategy of Cirque du Soleil is a prime example of creating new market space within a declining industry. The promotional tagline that the Canadian-based circus company sometimes uses explains how they did it: "We reinvent the circus." By altering the industry boundaries that had traditionally defined the circus concept, Cirque has created a new type of circus experience that audiences have enthusiastically embraced. Since 1984, when it was founded by a group of street performers, Cirque du Soleil has staged a variety of different productions that have been seen by over 40 million people in some 90 cities around the world.

How did they do it? One of the keys to redefining the circus business was to challenge conventional thinking and create a new vision of circus entertainment. Since the days of Ringling Bros. and Barnum & Bailey, the circus had consisted of animal acts, star performers, and Bozo-like clowns. Cirque questioned this formula and sought to understand what its audiences really wanted. It found that interest in animal acts was declining in part because of public concerns over the treatment of circus animals. Since managing animals—and the celebrity trainers who performed with them—created a heavy economic burden, Cirque eliminated them.

Instead Cirque has focused on three elements of the classic circus tent event that still captivated audiences: acrobatic acts, clowns, and the tent itself. Elegant acrobatics became a central feature of its performances, and clown humor became more sophisticated and less slapstick. Cirque also preserved the image of the tent by creating exotic facades that captured the symbolic elements of the traditional tent.

For Cirque to sail into a blue ocean, however, it had to make even bigger changes. It did so by introducing theatrical elements into its circus acts. Each production provides a range of features more commonly found in theatres than in circus tents—from using theatrical story lines to replacing hard benches with comfortable seating. Rather than displaying three different acts simultaneously, as in the classic three-ring circus, Cirque offers multiple productions giving audiences a reason to go to the circus more often. Each production has a different theme and its own original musical score.

As it has rolled out all of these changes, Cirque has kept its eye on the bottom line. In fact, a key motivator for many of its changes was to find ways to lower costs and increase revenues in the declining circus industry. Cutting the cost of animal acts and star performers as well as boosting revenues by offering a variety of productions has allowed it to achieve both low cost and differentiation advantages. Such a strategy creates value for both the company and its customers. The essence of its success, however, lies not in the extent to which it has outperformed competitors, but in how it has surpassed them by redefining the circus concept and becoming a prime mover in the market space it created.

Sources: Kim, W. C., & Mauborgne, R. 2004. Blue ocean strategy. *Harvard Business Review*, 82(10): 76–84; and Tischler, L. 2005. Join the circus. *Fast Company*, 96: 52–58.

- *Create and capture new demand.* Rather than fighting over existing demand, blue ocean companies seek opportunities in uncharted territory.

- *Break the value/cost trade-off.* Blues ocean firms reject the idea that a trade-off between value and cost is inevitable and instead seek opportunities in areas that benefit both their cost structure and their value proposition to customers.

- *Pursue differentiation and low cost simultaneously.* By integrating the range of a firm's utility, price, and cost activities, blue ocean companies align their whole system to create sustainable strategies.

As the above imperatives suggest, the essence of blue ocean strategy is not just to find an uncontested market, but to create one. Some blue oceans arise because new technologies create new possibilities, such as eBay's online auction business. Yet technological innovation is not a defining feature of a blue ocean strategy. Most blue oceans are created from within red oceans by companies that push beyond the existing industry boundaries. Strategy Spotlight 12.4 describes how Cirque du Soleil created a new market for circus entertainment by making traditional circus acts more like theatrical productions.

Once created, a blue ocean strategy is difficult to imitate. If customers flock to blue ocean creators, firms rapidly achieve economies of scale, learning advantages, and synergies across their organizational systems. Wal-Mart, for example, was able to integrate its operations and functions so efficiently that would-be imitators were effectively discouraged. Another example is Body Shop, which chartered new territory by refusing to focus solely on beauty products. Traditional competitors such as Estee Lauder and L'Oreal, whose brands are based on promises of eternal youth and beauty, found it difficult to imitate this approach without repudiating their current images.

These factors suggest that blue ocean strategies provide an avenue by which firms can pursue corporate entrepreneurship. Such strategies are not without risks, however. In the sections that follow, we will address some of the strategic choice and implementation issues that influence the success or failure of CE activities. How various companies approach corporate venturing is a key factor. Two distinct approaches to corporate venturing are found among firms that pursue entrepreneurial aims. The first is *focused* corporate venturing, in which CE activities are isolated from a firm's existing operations and worked on by independent work units. The second approach to CE is *dispersed*, in which all parts of the organization and every organization member are engaged in intrapreneurial activities. In the next two sections, we will address these approaches and provide examples of each.

Focused Approaches to Corporate Entrepreneurship

Firms using a focused approach typically separate the corporate venturing activity from the other ongoing operations of the firm. That is, corporate entrepreneurship is usually the domain of autonomous work groups that pursue entrepreneurial aims independent of the rest of the firm. The advantage of this approach is that it frees entrepreneurial team members to think and act without the constraints imposed by existing organizational norms and routines. This independence is often necessary for the kind of open-minded creativity that leads to strategic breakthroughs. The disadvantage is that, because of their isolation from the corporate mainstream, the work groups that concentrate on internal ventures may fail to obtain the resources or support needed to carry an entrepreneurial project through to completion. Two forms—new venture groups (NVGs) and business incubators—are among the most common types of focused approaches.

New Venture Groups (NVGs)   Corporations often form new venture groups whose goal is to identify, evaluate, and cultivate venture opportunities. These groups typically function as semi-autonomous units with little formal structure. The new venture group may simply be a committee that reports to the president on potential new ventures. Or it may be organized as a corporate division with its own staff and budget. The aims of the new venture group may be open-ended in terms of what ventures it may consider. Alternatively, some corporations use them to promote concentrated effort on a specific problem. In both cases, they usually have a substantial amount of freedom to take risks and a supply of resources to do it with.[24]

New venture groups usually have a larger mandate than a typical R&D department. That is, their involvement extends beyond innovation and experimentation to coordinating with other corporate divisions, identifying potential venture partners, gathering resources, and, in some cases, actually launching the venture.

Nortel Networks, a global producer of telecom equipment, provides an example of how the NVG of a major corporation successfully launches new ventures.[25] Responsibility for its venturing activities lies with a senior vice president who oversees corporate strategy, alliances, and venturing, including the company's NVG. Company employees

Corporate Venture Capital

What does a company do when it wants to enjoy the benefits of an entrepreneurial start-up but does not want to acquire a venture or take time to develop one internally? It finances one by providing venture capital.

Since the 1970s, major U.S. corporations such as Exxon Mobil have invested in externally generated business ideas in order to strengthen their innovation profile. Some firms invest in technologies that are similar to their core business or provide potential future synergies. Intel, for example, has invested in several e-business start-ups that are in a position to increase demand for Intel processors. With the high growth potential of industries such as information technology and biotechnology, the level of corporate venture capital is increasing. During the booming dot-com era, corporate venture unit investments jumped by a factor of five, from $1.4 billion to $7.8 billion. In 2000 alone, corporations worldwide invested nearly $17 billion in venture capital.

Several major corporations have launched venture financing efforts. In Germany alone there are over 20 corporate venture funds, including global players Siemens, Bertelsmann, and Deutsche Telekom. Even utilities are investing in emerging companies. AEP, a major U.S. electric power company, recently invested in PHPK, a cryogenics firm based in Columbus, Ohio. PHPK is poised to provide support of superconductivity applications, a rapidly growing energy niche that is seeking innovations. AEP

Sources: Stein, T. 2002. Rip cord. *Red Herring,* November 28, www.redherring.com; Franzke, E. 2001. Four keys to corporate venturing success. *European Venture Capital Journal,* June 1: 36–37; Letzelter, J. 2000. The new venture capitalists: Utilities go shopping for deals. *Public Utilities Fortnightly,* December: 34–38; Rabinovitz, J. 2000. Venture capital, Inc. *Industry Standard,* April 17: 88–90; and, Worrell, D. 2003. The big guns. *Entrepreneur,* November, www.entrepreneur.com.

prefers expansion-stage firms that need capital and guidance rather than earlier-stage firms. And AEP invests only in energy-related companies. PHPK has nearly doubled its business since AEP made its investment, which served as an immediate endorsement of PHPK's technology and capabilities.

The result? Intel, for one, has enjoyed tremendous returns. It has a portfolio of businesses worth $8 billion. But Intel's goal is not just to make money—it is looking for ways to cement ties early with promising start-ups. "Companies have discovered that it's a good way to do market development," according to Les Vadasz, head of Intel's venture program. "I do see it as a competitive weapon."

Louis Rajczi, managing partner at Siemens Venture Capital, agrees. Unlike traditional VCs which invest in businesses strictly for the financial returns, corporations invest in new ventures to advance their strategic vision and beat the competition. "If we get in on more good deals at an earlier stage than our competitors, we'll end up getting ahead," says Rajczi. "That will increase the value of the company and increase our returns."

Even so, corporate funding for external ventures dried up rapidly after the technology bubble burst in the early 2000s. In the first half of 2002, only $1.1 billion was invested, compared to $17 billion in 2000. Not only have new investments by corporations dropped dramatically, but also corporations such as Hewlett-Packard and Accenture have sold off large portions of their portfolios. Nevertheless, as a long-term strategy, corporate venture funding can benefit both new ventures and corporations and remains a viable alternative to internal corporate venturing.

---

submit ideas through a company intranet. Once the NVG decides to pursue an opportunity, two teams are set up—an opportunity team, which investigates the marketability of the venture concept, and a commercialization team, which manages venture investments and value development. Nortel's NVG is only interested in ventures that are likely to become stand-alone businesses, not extensions of current product lines. As a result, governance of new ventures usually includes outside board members and external investors who can be involved in managing the venture once it is spun off. Recently, Nortel used this process to create a spin-off called NetActive, which offers digital rights management (DRM) technology used to protect Internet-based content.

Firms that want to expand by way of new venture start-ups usually acquire existing ventures, as discussed in Chapter 6, or develop ventures internally. Strategy Spotlight 12.5 describes a third alternative for firms that want to be entrepreneurial but still maintain their autonomy: corporate venture funding.

Business Incubators   The term *incubator* was originally used to describe a device in which eggs are hatched. Business incubators are designed to "hatch" new businesses. They are a type of corporate new venture group with a somewhat more specialized purpose—to support and nurture fledgling entrepreneurial ventures until they can thrive on their own as stand-alone businesses. Corporations often use incubators as a way to grow businesses identified by the new venture group. Although they often receive support from many parts of the corporation, they still operate independently until they are strong enough to go it alone. Then, depending on the type of business, they are either integrated into an existing corporate division or continue to operate as a subsidiary of the parent firm. Additionally, the type of corporate venturing support reported in Strategy Spotlight 12.5 that external new ventures receive may also include allowing a young venture into the corporation's incubator.

Incubators are sometimes found outside the domain of corporate entrepreneurship (see Chapter 13). However, a company-sponsored incubator often has advantages because of the experience and resources that the parent corporation can provide. Incubators typically provide some or all of the following five functions.[26]

- *Funding.* Usually includes capital investments but may also include in-kind investments and loans.

- *Physical space.* A common problem for new ventures; incubators in which several start-ups share space often provide fertile ground for new ideas and collaboration.

- *Business services.* Along with office space, young ventures need basic services and infrastructure; may include anything from phone systems and computer networks to public relations and personnel management.

- *Mentoring.* Senior executives and skilled technical personnel often provide coaching and experience-based advice.

- *Networking.* Contact with other parts of the firm and external resources such as suppliers, industry experts, and potential customers facilitates problem solving and knowledge sharing.

As the above list suggests, business incubators provide a safe and supportive environment for corporate ventures. Nevertheless, the risk associated with launching ventures should not be overlooked. Companies have at times spent millions incubating new ideas with very little to show for it. Major corporations such as Lucent, British Airways, and Hewlett-Packard inactivated their incubators and scaled back new venture portfolios after experiencing major declines in value since the early 2000s.[27]

Thus, to encourage entrepreneurship, corporations sometimes need to do more than create independent work groups or venture incubators to generate new enterprises. In some firms, the entrepreneurial spirit is spread throughout the organization. It is this dispersed approach to corporate entrepreneurship that we turn to next.

Dispersed Approaches to Corporate Entrepreneurship

The second type of corporate entrepreneurship is dispersed. For some companies, a dedication to the principles and practices of entrepreneurship is spread throughout the organization. One advantage of this approach is that organizational members don't have to be reminded to think entrepreneurially or be willing to change. The ability to change is considered to be a core capability. Such corporations often have a reputation for being entrepreneurial. This leads to a second advantage: Because of this entrepreneurial reputation, stakeholders such as vendors, customers, or alliance partners can bring new ideas or venture opportunities to anyone in the organization and expect them to be well-received. Such opportunities make it possible for the firm to stay ahead of the competition.

However, there are disadvantages as well. Firms that are overzealous about corporate entrepreneurship sometimes feel they must change for the sake of change, causing them to lose vital competencies or spend heavily on R&D and innovation to the detriment of the bottom line. Two related aspects of dispersed entrepreneurship include entrepreneurial cultures that have an overarching commitment to CE activities and the use of product champions in promoting entrepreneurial behaviors.

Entrepreneurial Culture   In some large corporations, the corporate culture embodies the spirit of entrepreneurship. A culture of entrepreneurship is one in which the search for venture opportunities permeates every part of the organization. Recall from Chapter 3 that the key to creating value successfully is viewing every value-chain activity as a source of competitive advantage. In a similar way, the effect of corporate entrepreneurship on a firm's strategic success is strongest when it animates all parts of an organization. It is found in companies where the strategic leaders and the culture together generate a strong impetus to innovate, take risks, and seek out new venture opportunities.

In companies with an entrepreneurial culture, everyone in the organization is attuned to opportunities to leverage the assets and capabilities of the corporation to help create new businesses. Many such firms use a top-down approach to stimulate entrepreneurial activity. That is, the top leaders of the organization support programs and incentives that foster a climate of entrepreneurship. Many of the best ideas for new corporate ventures, however, come from the bottom up. Here's what Martin Sorrell, CEO of the WPP Group, a London-based global communication services group, says about drawing on the talents of lower-level employees:

> The people at the so-called bottom of an organization know more about what's going on than the people at the top. The people in the trenches are the ones in the best position to make critical decisions. It's up to the leaders to give those people the freedom and the resources they need.[28]

Thus, an entrepreneurial culture is one in which change and renewal are on everybody's mind. Sony, 3M, Intel, and Cisco are among the corporations best known for their corporate venturing activities. Many fast-growing young corporations also attribute much of their success to an entrepreneurial culture. Virgin Group, the British conglomerate that began as Virgin Airlines under the leadership of Richard Branson, has spawned nearly 200 new businesses in its short history. Strategy Spotlight 12.6 describes a few of Virgin's start-up successes as well as some ambitious future plans.

Product Champions   CE does not always involve making large investments in start-ups or establishing incubators to spawn new divisions. Often, innovative ideas emerge in the normal course of business and are brought forth and become part of the way of doing business. In many firms, especially small, informally run ones, this may happen organically through the energetic efforts of individuals with good ideas. Larger firms often have more formal efforts to encourage innovation among their employees. In both cases, it is often product champions who are needed to take charge of internally generated ventures. Product (or project) champions are those individuals working within a corporation who bring entrepreneurial ideas forward, identify what kind of market exists for the product or service, find resources to support the venture, and promote the venture concept to upper management.[29]

When lower-level employees identify a product idea or novel solution, they will take it to their supervisor or someone in authority. Similarly, a new idea that is generated in a technology lab may be introduced to others by its inventor. If the idea has merit, it gains support and builds momentum across the organization.[30] Thus, even though the corporation may not be looking for new ideas or have a program for cultivating internal ventures, the independent behaviors of a few organizational members can have important strategic consequences.

STRATEGY SPOTLIGHT

Growing New Ventures at Virgin Group

While most large companies have to work hard to stoke the fires of entrepreneurship, they burn with ferocious intensity at the Virgin Group. As a $4.25 billion U.S. company that has created nearly 200 businesses, it stands as clear evidence that ideas, capital, and talent can flow as freely in big, far-flung organizations as they can among the start-ups of Silicon Valley.

The mix of businesses that Virgin has spawned is indicative of the fun-loving, eclectic culture that its chairman, Richard Branson, has developed. Branson and his deputies have worked hard to create a culture where employees speak up and share their ideas. There are no gleaming corporate headquarters or executive privileges, just a large house in London where meetings are held in a small room. "Rules and regulations are not our forte," Branson said. "Analyzing things to death is not our kind of thing."

There aren't even any job descriptions at Virgin, because they are thought to place too many limits on what people can do. Instead, senior executives work shoulder to shoulder with first-line employees. Branson believes that employees should be given top priority, and he has created a friendly, nonhierarchical, familylike environment in which people have fun and enjoy themselves. His advice to his employees reflects his personal philosophy: "Do things that you like. If your work and your hobby are the same, you will work long hours because you are motivated."

The result is that Virgin's businesses include entertainment megastores, cinemas, a fun-to-fly airline, an all-in-one consumer banking system, a hip radio station, and a passenger train service. Smaller ventures have also been launched by persistent employees with good ideas. "We've got people all over the world who are coming up with great new ideas, and trying them doesn't actually cost us a lot relative to the overall size of the group," says Branson.

Some of those good ideas are now integral parts of the Virgin legend:

- A woman who believed the company's airline should offer passengers onboard massages camped on Branson's doorstep until she was allowed to give him a neck and shoulder rub. Now an in-flight massage is a valued perk in Virgin Atlantic's Upper Class.

- A soon-to-be-married flight attendant came up with the idea of offering an integrated bridal planning service, everything from wedding apparel and catering to limousines and honeymoon reservations. She became the first CEO of Virgin Bride.

Virgin's latest ambitions are out of this world—literally. Branson recently teamed-up with Burt Rutan, winner of the X-Prize competition which awarded $10 million to the first nongovernment-funded flight to reach an altitude of 62 miles twice with the same vehicle. With Rutan's help, Virgin wasted no time in forming a new spin-off: Virgin Galactic. The enterprise will use a "stretch" version of SpaceShipOne, the name of the winning vehicle, to ferry ordinary citizens to outer space. Tickets on these flights are already selling for about $210,000 each, and the flights are expected to begin in 2008. According to Rutan, "Space tourism will be a multibillion-dollar industry." It's just that kind of vision—and risk taking—that has made the 54-year-old Branson's Virgin Group one of the most exciting and profitable examples of corporate entrepreneurship.

Sources: Hamel, G. 1999. Bringing Silicon Valley inside. *Harvard Business Review*, 77(5): 71–84; Kets de Vries, M. F. R. 1998. The transformational abilities of Virgin's Richard Branson and ABB's Percy Barnevik. *Organizational Dynamics*, 26(3): 7–21; Freedman, D. H. 2005. Burt Rutan, entrepreneur of the year. *Inc. Magazine*, January: 58–66; Hopkins, M. J. 2005. Richard Branson. *Inc. Magazine*, April: 100–102; and Port, O. 2004. SpaceShipOne's heady flight path. *BusinessWeek Online*, October 1, www.businessweek.com.

No matter how an entrepreneurial idea comes to light, however, a new venture concept must pass through two critical stages or it may never get off the ground: project definition and project impetus:

1. ***Project definition.*** A promising opportunity has to be justified in terms of its attractiveness in the marketplace and how well it fits with the corporation's other strategic objectives.

2. ***Project impetus.*** For a project to gain impetus, its strategic and economic impact must be supported by senior managers who have experience with similar projects. The project then becomes an embryonic business with its own organization and budget.

For a project to advance through these stages of definition and impetus, a product champion is often needed to generate support and encouragement. Champions are especially important during the time after a new project has been defined but before it gains momentum. They form a link between the definition and impetus stages of internal development, which they do by procuring resources and stimulating interest for the product among potential customers.[31] Often, they must work quietly and alone. Consider the example of Ken Kutaragi, the Sony engineer who championed the PlayStation.

> Even though Sony had made the processor that powered the first Nintendo video games, no one at Sony in the mid-1980s saw any future in such products. "It was a kind of snobbery," Kutaragi recalled. "For Sony people, the Nintendo product would have been very embarrassing to make because it was only a toy." But Kutaragi was convinced he could make a better product. He began working secretly on a video game. Kutaragi said, "I realized that if it was visible, it would be killed." He quietly began enlisting the support of senior executives, such as the head of R&D. He made a case that Sony could use his project to develop capabilities in digital technologies that would be important in the future. It was not until 1994, after years of "underground" development and quiet building of support, that Sony introduced the PlayStation. By the year 2000, Sony had sold 55 million of them, and Kutaragi became CEO of Sony Computer Entertainment. By 2005, Kutagari was Sony's Chief Operating Officer, and plans to launch the third generation version of the market-leading PlayStation (PS3) were well under way.[32]

Thus, product champions play an important entrepreneurial role in a corporate setting by encouraging others to take a chance on promising new ideas.[33]

Measuring the Success of Corporate Entrepreneurship Activities

At this point in the discussion, it is reasonable to ask whether corporate entrepreneurship is successful. Corporate venturing, like the innovation process, usually requires a tremendous effort. Is it worth it? In this section we consider factors that corporations need to take into consideration when evaluating the success of CE programs. We also examine techniques that companies can use to limit the expense of venturing or to cut their losses when CE initiatives appear doomed.

Comparing Strategic and Financial CE Goals   Not all corporate venturing efforts are financially rewarding. Recall the example of NetActive, the Nortel Networks venture. The company was greeted with great enthusiasm once Nortel spun it off, and it attracted over $20 million in capital investment from the venture community. It also provided a technology that was highly demanded. But NetActive became . . . inactive. The company's Web site went dark, and it was put up for sale, a victim of the dot-com crash.[34] By most accounts, Nortel Networks did all the right things in developing NetActive in terms of establishing it as a stand-alone business and endowing it with assets and funding. But the business was a flop financially.

In terms of financial performance, slightly more than 50 percent of corporate venturing efforts reach profitability (measured by ROI) within six years of their launch.[35] If this were the only criterion for measuring success, it would seem to be a rather poor return. On the one hand, these results should be expected, because CE is riskier than other investments such as expanding ongoing operations. On the other hand, corporations expect a higher return from corporate venturing projects than from normal operations. Thus, in terms of the risk-return trade-off, it seems that CE often falls short of expectations.[36]

There are several other important criteria, however, for judging the success of a corporate venture initiative. In addition to financial goals, most CE programs have strategic goals. The strategic reasons for undertaking a corporate venture include strengthening competitive position, entering into new markets, expanding capabilities by learning and acquiring new knowledge, and building the corporation's base of resources and experience. Different corporations may emphasize some of these goals more than others, but in general three questions should be used to assess the effectiveness of a corporation's venturing initiatives:[37]

1. *Are the products or services offered by the venture accepted in the marketplace?* That is, is the venture considered to be a market success? If so, the financial returns are likely to be satisfactory. In addition, the venture may open doors into other markets and suggest avenues for other venture projects.
2. *Are the contributions of the venture to the corporation's internal competencies and experience valuable?* That is, does the venture add to the worth of the firm internally? If so, strategic goals such as leveraging existing assets, building new knowledge, and enhancing firm capabilities are likely to be met.
3. *Is the venture able to sustain its basis of competitive advantage?* That is, does the value proposition offered by the venture insulate it from competitive attack? If so, it is likely to place the corporation in a stronger position relative to competitors and provide a base from which to build other advantages.

As you can see, these criteria include both strategic and financial goals of CE. Another way to evaluate a corporate venture is in terms of the four criteria from the Balanced Scorecard (Chapter 3). In a successful venture, not only are financial and market acceptance (customer) goals met but so are the internal business and innovation and learning goals. Thus, when assessing the success of corporate venturing, it is important to look beyond simple financial returns and consider a well-rounded set of criteria.[38]

Next, we revisit the concept of real options as a way to evaluate the progress of a venture development program and consider the role of "exit champions" in helping corporations limit their exposure to venture projects that are unlikely to succeed.

Exit Champions   Although a culture of championing venture projects is advantageous for stimulating an ongoing stream of entrepreneurial initiatives, many—in fact, most—of the ideas will not work out. At some point in the process, a majority of initiatives will be abandoned. Sometimes, however, companies wait too long to terminate a new venture and do so only after large sums of resources are used up or, worse, result in a marketplace failure. Motorola's costly global satellite telecom project known as Iridium provides a useful illustration. Even though problems with the project existed during the lengthy development process, Motorola refused to pull the plug. Only after investing $5 billion and years of effort was the project abandoned.[39]

How can companies avoid these costly and discouraging defeats? One way is to support a key role in the CE process: "exit champions." In contrast to product champions and other entrepreneurial enthusiasts within the corporation, exit champions are willing to question the viability of a venture project.[40] By demanding hard evidence and challenging the belief system that is carrying an idea forward, exit champions hold the line on ventures that appear shaky.

Both product champions and exit champions must be willing to energetically stand up for what they believe. Both put their reputations on the line. But they also differ in important ways. Product champions deal in uncertainty and ambiguity. Exit champions reduce ambiguity by gathering hard data and developing a strong case for why a project should be killed. Product champions are often thought to be willing to violate procedures and operate outside normal channels. Exit champions, by contrast, often have to reinstate procedures and reassert the decision-making criteria that are supposed to guide venture decisions. Whereas product champions often emerge as heroes, exit champions run the risk of losing status by opposing popular projects.

Thus, the role of exit champion may seem unappealing. But it is one that could save a corporation both financially and in terms of its reputation in the marketplace. It is especially important because one measure of the success of a firm's CE efforts is the extent to which it knows when to cut its losses and move on.

Real Options   Another way firms can minimize failure and avoid losses from pursuing faulty ideas is to apply the logic of real options (Chapter 6). Applied to entrepreneurship, real options suggest a path that corporations can use to manage the uncertainty associated with launching new ventures.

Options are created whenever a company begins to explore a new venture concept. That is, initial investments, such as conducting market tests, building prototypes, and forming venture teams, bestow an option to invest further. Retail giant Wal-Mart provides an interesting example of this limited approach. It's safe to say Wal-Mart could enter just about any market it wanted to in a big way. But its recent decision to enter the used-car business began with an experiment. Four dealerships were set up in the Houston, Texas, area under a brand called Price 1 Auto Stores. According to Ira Kalish, chief economist for Retail Forward, Inc., a consulting group that specializes in retailing, "Wal-Mart will seek to test the outer boundaries of what consumers are willing to let Wal-Mart be."[41]

With its four-store experiment, Wal-Mart is obtaining an option to invest more at a later date. The results of Wal-Mart's market test will be factored into the next round of decisions. This is consistent with the logic of real options—based on feedback at each stage of development, firms decide whether to exercise their options by making further investments. Alternatively, they may decide that the idea is not worth further consideration. In so doing—that is, by making smaller and more incremental investments—firms keep their total investment low and minimize downside risk. Often it's the job of an exit champion or some other practically minded organization member to decide that a project does not warrant further investment.

Consider the real options logic that Johnson Controls, a maker of car seats, instrument panels, and interior control systems uses to advance or eliminate entrepreneurial ideas.[42] Johnson options each new innovative idea by making a small investment in it. To decide whether to exercise an option, the idea must continue to prove itself at each stage of development. Here's how Jim Geschke, vice president and general manager of electronics integration at Johnson, describes the process:

> Think of Johnson as an innovation machine. The front end has a robust series of gates that each idea must pass through. Early on, we'll have many ideas and spend a little money on each of them. As they get more fleshed out, the ideas go through a gate where a go or no-go decision is made. A lot if ideas get filtered out, so there are far fewer items, and the spending on each goes up. . . . Several months later each idea will face another gate. If it passes, that means it's a serious idea that we are going to develop. Then the spending goes way up, and the number of ideas goes way down. By the time you reach the final gate, you need to have a credible business case in order to be accepted. At a certain point in the development process, we take our idea to customers and ask them what they think. Sometimes they say, "That's a terrible idea. Forget it." Other times they say, "That's fabulous. I want a million of them."

This process of evaluating ideas by separating winning ideas from losing ones in a way that keeps investments low has helped Johnson Controls grow its revenues at a double-digit rate to over $28 billion a year. Thus, using real options logic to advance the development process is a key way that firms reduce uncertainty and minimize innovation-related failures.[43]

The types of venture projects and entrepreneurial initiatives that corporations pursue are more likely to succeed if their organizational members behave entrepreneurially. In the next section, we look at the practices and characteristics that are associated with an entrepreneurial orientation.

>>Entrepreneurial Orientation

Firms that want to engage in successful corporate entrepreneurship need to have an entrepreneurial orientation (EO). EO refers to the strategy-making practices that businesses use in identifying and launching corporate ventures. It represents a frame of mind and a perspective toward entrepreneurship that is reflected in a firm's ongoing processes and corporate culture.[44]

An entrepreneurial orientation has five dimensions that permeate the decision-making styles and practices of the firm's members. These are autonomy, innovativeness, proactiveness, competitive aggressiveness, and risk taking. These factors can work together to enhance a firm's entrepreneurial performance. But even those firms that are strong in only a few aspects of EO can be very successful.[45] Exhibit 12.2 summarizes the dimensions of an entrepreneurial orientation. Below we discuss the five dimensions of entrepreneurial orientation and how they have been used to enhance internal venture development.

Autonomy

Autonomy refers to a willingness to act independently in order to carry forward an entrepreneurial vision or opportunity. It applies to both individuals and teams that operate outside an organization's existing norms and strategies. In the context of corporate entrepreneurship, autonomous work units are often used to leverage existing strengths in new arenas, identify opportunities that are beyond the organization's current capabilities, and encourage development of new ventures or improved business practices.[46]

Exhibit 12.2

Dimensions of Entrepreneurial Orientation

Dimension	Definition
Autonomy	Independent action by an individual or team aimed at bringing forth a business concept or vision and carrying it through to completion.
Innovativeness	A willingness to introduce novelty through experimentation and creative processes aimed at developing new products and services as well as new processes.
Proactiveness	A forward-looking perspective characteristic of a marketplace leader that has the foresight to seize opportunities in anticipation of future demand.
Competitive aggressiveness	An intense effort to outperform industry rivals characterized by a combative posture or an aggressive response aimed at improving position or overcoming a threat in a competitive marketplace.
Risk taking	Making decisions and taking action without certain knowledge of probable outcomes; some undertakings may also involve making substantial resource commitments in the process of venturing forward.

Source: Dess, G. G., & Lumpkin, G. T. 2005. The role of entrepreneurial orientation in stimulating effective corporate entrepreneurship. *Academy of Management Executive,* 19(1): 147–156; Covin, J. G., & Slevin, D. P. 1991. A conceptual model of entrepreneurship as firm behavior. *Entrepreneurship Theory & Practice,* Fall: 7–25; Lumpkin, G. T., and Dess, G. G. 1996. Clarifying the entrepreneurial orientation construct and linking it to performance. *Academy of Management Review,* 21: 135–172; Miller, D. 1983. The correlates of entrepreneurship in three types of firms. *Management Science,* 29: 770–791.

The need for autonomy may apply to either dispersed or focused entrepreneurial efforts. Clearly, because of the emphasis on venture projects that are being developed outside of the normal flow of business, a focused approach suggests a working environment that is relatively autonomous. But autonomy may also be important in an organization where entrepreneurship is part of the corporate culture. Everything from the methods of group interaction to the firm's reward system must make organizational members feel as if they can think freely about venture opportunities, take time to investigate them, and act without fear of condemnation. This implies a respect for the autonomy of each individual and an openness to the independent thinking that goes into championing a corporate venture idea. Thus, autonomy represents a type of empowerment (see Chapter 11) that is directed at identifying and leveraging entrepreneurial opportunities.

Two techniques that organizations often use to promote autonomy include:

1. *Using skunkworks to foster entrepreneurial thinking.* To help managers and other employees set aside their usual routines and practices, companies often develop independent work units called "skunkworks" to encourage creative thinking and brainstorming about new venture ideas. The term is used to represent a work environment that is often physically separate from corporate headquarters and free of the normal job requirements and pressures. Nearly every major corporation that grows by means of entrepreneurship uses some form of skunkworks.[47] That's what Overstock.com, the successful online retailer, did when it decided to explore creating an auction service that would compete with eBay. Led by 29-year-old Holly MacDonald-Korth, a group of Overstock staffers set up shop in a corner of one of its company warehouses. The group started by reselling merchandise that had been returned to Overstock on eBay. "We started this business on eBay just like someone would probably start it in their garage," says MacDonald-Korth. "I really wanted to understand all the problems a small business would face." Within four months, their e-selling experiment was bringing in about $30,000 per week. Soon after, they used their newly gained knowledge of selling online to create a new division called Overstock Auctions. The Overstock approach aims to improve on eBay's service in a few key ways, including offering listing fees that are 30 percent lower and extending auctions to prevent last minute bidders from scooping up items during the last few seconds of an auction.[48]

2. *Designing organization structures that support independent action.* Sometimes corporations need to do more than create independent think tanks to help stimulate new ideas. Changes in organizational structure may also be necessary. Established firms with traditional structures often have to break out of such molds in order to remain competitive. This was the conclusion of Deloitte Consulting, a division of Deloitte Touche Tohmatsu, one of the world's largest accounting consultancies. After losing millions in consulting jobs to young Internet-based consultancies, Deloitte decided to reorganize. The first step was to break the firm into small, autonomous groups called "chip-aways" that could operate with the speed and flexibility of a start-up. "This allows them to react more like a Navy SEAL team rather than an Army division," according to Tom Rodenhauser, author of *Inside Consulting*. One of Deloitte's first chip-aways was Roundarch, a Web technology and marketing venture that projected first-year revenues of $40 million and beat its own projections by 10 percent.[49] Other organization structures may also help promote autonomy, such as virtual organizations that allow people to work independently and communicate via the Web.

Creating autonomous work units and encouraging independent action may have pitfalls that can jeopardize their effectiveness. Autonomous teams, for example, often lack coordination. Excessive decentralization has a strong potential to create inefficiencies, such as duplication of effort and wasting resources on projects with questionable feasibility. For example, Chris Galvin, former CEO of Motorola, scrapped the skunkworks approach the company had been using to develop new wireless phones. Fifteen teams had created 128 different phones, which led to spiraling costs and overly complex operations.[50]

Thus, for autonomous work units and independent projects to be effective, such efforts have to be measured and monitored. This requires a delicate balance for corporations. They must have the patience and budget to tolerate the explorations of autonomous groups and have the strength to cut back efforts that are not bearing fruit. It must be undertaken with a clear sense of purpose—namely, to generate new sources of competitive advantage.

Innovativeness

Innovativeness refers to a firm's efforts to find new opportunities and novel solutions. In the beginning of this chapter we discussed innovation; here the focus is on innovativeness—that is, a firm's attitude toward innovation and willingness to innovate. It involves creativity and experimentation that result in new products, new services, or improved technological processes. Innovativeness is one of the major components of an entrepreneurial strategy. As indicated at the beginning of the chapter, however, the job of managing innovativeness can be very challenging.

Innovativeness requires that firms depart from existing technologies and practices and venture beyond the current state of the art. Inventions and new ideas need to be nurtured even when their benefits are unclear. However, in today's climate of rapid change, effectively producing, assimilating, and exploiting innovations can be an important avenue for achieving competitive advantages.

As our earlier discussion of CE indicated, many corporations owe their success to an active program of innovation-based corporate venturing.[51] Few, however, have a more exemplary reputation for effective entrepreneurship than W. L. Gore. Exhibit 12.3 describes the policies that create a climate of innovativeness at W. L. Gore.

Two of the methods companies can use to enhance their competitive position through innovativeness are:

1. ***Fostering creativity and experimentation.*** To innovate successfully, firms must break out of the molds that have shaped their thinking. They also must create avenues for employees to express themselves. Tim Warren, director of research and technical services at the oil giant Royal Dutch/Shell, was sure that Shell's employees had vast reserves of innovative talent that had not been tapped. He also felt that more radical innovations were needed for Shell to achieve its performance goals. So Warren allocated $20 million to be used for breakthrough ideas that would change the playing field. He also asked his people to devote up to 10 percent of their time to nonlinear thinking. The initiative became known as the "GameChanger." With the help of Strategos Consulting, the GameChanger review panel developed an Innovation Lab to help employees develop game-changing ideas. The first lab attracted 72 would-be entrepreneurs who learned how to uncover new opportunities and challenge industry conventions. By the end of the three-day lab, a portfolio of 240 ideas had been generated. The GameChanger process, which now provides funding of $100,000 to $600,000 within 10 days after approval, has now found a permanent home within Shell and has become a critical part of its internal entrepreneurial process.[52]

2. ***Investing in new technology, R&D, and continuous improvement.*** For successful innovation, companies must seek advantages from the latest technologies. This

Rule	Implications
The power of small teams	Gore believes that small teams promote familiarity and autonomy. Even its manufacturing plants are capped at just 200 people. That way everyone can get to know one another on a first-name basis and work together with minimal rules. This also helps to cultivate "an environment where creativity can flourish," according to CEO Chuck Carroll.
No ranks, no titles, no bosses	Because Gore believes in maximizing individual potential, employees, dubbed "associates," decide for themselves what new commitments to take on. Associates have "sponsors," rather than bosses, and there are no standardized job descriptions or categories. Everyone is supposed to take on a unique role. Committees of co-workers evaluate each team member's contribution and decide on compensation.
Take the long view	Although impatient about the status quo, Gore exhibits great patience with the time—often years, sometimes decades—it takes to nurture and develop breakthrough products and bring them to market.
Make time for face time	Gore avoids the traditional hierarchical chain of command, opting instead for a team-based environment that fosters personal initiative. Gore also discourages memos and e-mail and promotes direct, person-to-person communication among all associates—anyone in the company can talk to anyone else.
Lead by leading	Associates are encouraged to spend about 10 percent of their time pursuing speculative new ideas. Anyone is free to champion products, as long as they have the passion and ideas to attract followers. Many of Gore's breakthroughs started with one person acting on his or her own initiative and developed as colleagues helped in their spare time.
Celebrate failure	When a project doesn't work out and the team decides to kill it, they celebrate just as they would if it had been a success—with some beer and maybe a glass of champagne. Rather than condemning failure, Gore figures that celebrating it encourages experimentation and risk taking.

Source: Deutschman, A. 2004. The fabric of creativity. *Fast Company*, 89: 54–62; Levering, R., & Moskowitz, M. 2005. The 100 best companies to work for. *Fortune*, 151(2): 61–72; and www.gore.com.

Exhibit 12.3
W. L. Gore's New Rules for Fostering Innovativeness

often requires a substantial investment. Consider, for example, Dell Computer Corp.'s new production capability. With its new OptiPlex manufacturing system, Dell is attempting to revolutionize the way computers are made. Of course, it is still necessary to connect part A to part B—that is, to conduct the basic assembly process. But how those parts are received, handled, and turned into finished product is changing radically because of Dell's state-of-the-art automation techniques. The OptiPlex factory is managed by a network of computers that takes in orders, communicates with suppliers, draws in components, organizes the assembly process, and arranges shipping. The result: Hundreds of computers can be custom-built in an eight-hour shift, productivity per person increased 160 percent, and most parts are kept on hand for a mere two hours. Dell was already leading other major PC manufacturers by maintaining product inventories for only 5 or 6 days compared with the industry average of 50 to 90 days. With its latest innovation, Dell now expects to cut inventory turnover down to $2\frac{1}{2}$ days.[53]

Innovativeness can be a source of great progress and strong corporate growth, but there are also major pitfalls for firms that invest in innovation. Expenditures on R&D aimed at identifying new products or processes can be a waste of resources if the effort does not yield results. Another danger is related to the competitive climate. Even if a company innovates a new capability or successfully applies a technological breakthrough, another company may develop a similar innovation or find a use for it that is more profitable. Finally, in many firms, R&D and other innovation efforts are among the first to be cut back during an economic downturn.

Therefore, even though innovativeness is an important means of internal corporate venturing, it also involves major risks because investments in innovations may not pay off. For strategic managers of entrepreneurial firms, however, successfully developing and adopting innovations can generate competitive advantages and provide a major source of growth for the firm.

Proactiveness

Proactiveness refers to a firm's efforts to seize new opportunities. Proactive organizations monitor trends, identify the future needs of existing customers, and anticipate changes in demand or emerging problems that can lead to new venture opportunities. Proactiveness involves not only recognizing changes but also being willing to act on those insights ahead of the competition. Strategic managers who practice proactiveness have their eye on the future in a search for new possibilities for growth and development.

Such a forward-looking perspective is important for companies that seek to be industry leaders. Many proactive firms seek out ways not only to be future oriented but also to change the very nature of competition in their industry. From its beginning, Dell sold personal computers directly to consumers, diminishing the role of retail stores as a way to reach customers. Its success changed the way PCs were sold.[54]

Proactiveness is especially effective at creating competitive advantages, because it puts competitors in the position of having to respond to successful initiatives. The benefit gained by firms that are the first to enter new markets, establish brand identity, implement administrative techniques, or adopt new operating technologies in an industry is called first mover advantage.[55]

First movers usually have several advantages. First, industry pioneers, especially in new industries, often capture unusually high profits because there are no competitors to drive prices down. Second, first movers that establish brand recognition are usually able to retain their image and hold on to the market share gains they earned by being first. Sometimes these benefits also accrue to other early movers in an industry, but, generally speaking, first movers have an advantage that can be sustained until firms enter the maturity phase of an industry's life cycle.[56]

First movers are not always successful. For one thing, the customers of companies that introduce novel products or embrace breakthrough technologies may be reluctant to commit to a new way of doing things. In his book *Crossing the Chasm,* Geoffrey A. Moore noted that most firms seek evolution, not revolution, in their operations. This makes it difficult for a first mover to sell promising new technologies.[57] Second, some companies try to be a first mover before they are ready. Consider Apple Computer's Newton.

Newton, the first personal digital assistant (PDA), was released in 1993. Because it was revolutionary, it generated a great deal of media attention and initial sales success. But the Newton was troubled from the beginning because it was launched before it was ready. For too many customers, it could not do what it claimed: recognize handwriting. But Apple was desperate to launch ahead of Microsoft. "We cut corners and ignored problems . . . to gain an edge in a reckless public relations battle," said Larry Tesler, who headed the Newton group until a few months before its release. In 1998, after five years of trying to recover from its initial failure, the Newton project was killed.[58]

Even with these caveats, however, companies that are first movers can enhance their competitive position. Firms can use two other methods to act proactively.

1. ***Introducing new products or technological capabilities ahead of the competition.*** Maintaining a high level of proactiveness is central to the corporate culture of some major corporations. Sony's mission statement asserts, for example, "We should always be the pioneers with our products—out front leading the market. We believe in leading the public with new products rather than asking them what kind of products they want."[59] Sony has launched numerous new products that not only have succeeded financially but have changed the competitive landscape. Walkman, PlayStation, Betacam, and Vaio laptop computers are just a few of the many leading products that Sony has introduced.

2. ***Continuously seeking out new product or service offerings.*** Firms that provide new resources or sources of supply can benefit from a proactive stance. Aerie Networks is a Denver company that aspires to expand the U.S. fiber-optic network extensively. Two factors make its efforts especially proactive. First, it is laying cable that contains 432 fibers (compared with the 96 strands that established companies like AT&T typically install). This approach fits Aerie's goal of being the low-cost wholesaler of bandwidth to long-distance carriers and other fiber users. Second, it worked for over a year to form an alliance with gas pipeline rivals that made it possible to use up to 25,000 miles of pipeline rights-of-way across 26 states. The partnering was more difficult than the technology—Aerie had to give a 30 percent stake to the gas pipeline companies—but the potential payoff is enormous.[60]

Being an industry leader does not always lead to competitive advantages. Some firms that have launched pioneering new products or staked their reputation on new brands have failed to get the hoped-for payoff. Two major beverage companies—Coca-Cola and PepsiCo—invested $75 million to launch sodas that would capitalize on the low-carb diet trend. But with half the carbohydrates taken out, neither *C2,* Coke's entry, nor *Pepsi Edge* tasted very good. The two new brands combined never achieved more than one percent market share. PepsiCo announced in would halt production in 2006 and Coca-Cola was expected to follow suit.[61] Such missteps are indicative of the dangers of trying to proactively anticipate demand. Strategy Spotlight 12.7, in contrast, describes another type of proactiveness—how some organizations are using entrepreneurial thinking and practices to effectively promote corporate social responsibility.

Thus, careful monitoring and scanning of the environment, as well as extensive feasibility research, are needed for a proactive strategy to lead to competitive advantages. Firms that do it well usually have substantial growth and internal development to show for it. Many of them have been able to sustain the advantages of proactiveness for years.

Competitive Aggressiveness

Competitive aggressiveness refers to a firm's efforts to outperform its industry rivals. Companies with an aggressive orientation are willing to "do battle" with competitors.

Socially Responsible Corporate Entrepreneurship

One of the most important trends in U.S. business today is corporate social responsibility (CSR). Proactively oriented firms are seizing opportunities to take a leading role in issues such as the environment, product safety, and fair trade. Among the most interesting examples of this, as suggested in the Chapter 1 section on social innovation, are those firms that are taking an entrepreneurial approach to CSR. That is, they are using new technologies, environmentally friendly ventures, and entrepreneurial practices to advance their social responsibility goals. Following is a sample of three corporations that are taking a very entrepreneurial approach to corporate social responsibility.

Whirlpool Corporation—From efficiency to advocacy

Whirlpool is perhaps best known for its "white boxes"—the refrigerators, freezers, and laundry appliances that account for over 60 percent of its $13 billion in annual sales. To explore what creates customer loyalty, Whirlpool conducted a global survey of its customers. "We discovered there is a strong correlation between a company's performance in appliance markets and their social response to issues such as energy efficiency and pollution," said Steve Willis, director of Whirlpool's global environment, health, and safety programs. One result has been its innovative Duet Series of washers and dryers that significantly reduces energy consumption. Recently, Whirlpool decided to take its environmental efforts a step farther: It joined The Natural Step, an entrepreneurial organization that is advancing the movement toward environmental sustainability by advocating the development of innovative products that meet high standards of ecological sustainability.

Interface, Inc.—Doing more with less

In Chapter 1, we saw how some companies have changed their corporate missions to include socially responsible goals like protecting the environment. Carpet maker Interface Inc. has found a way not only to become more environmentally friendly but also to achieve a universal entrepreneurial objective: Do more with less. By leasing rather than selling carpets, Georgia-based Interface is able to take back worn carpets and "remanufacture" them. As a

result, it has cut its raw materials input costs by nearly 100 percent and its business customers get to deduct the cost of leasing. "Our costs are down, not up," according to CEO Ray Anderson. "Sustainability doesn't cost more, it saves." Recently, Interface instituted a program known as EcoSense to educate its employees about sustainability and reward them for making environmental improvements. These savings helped Interface survive the 40 percent decline in sales of office furnishings that followed the dot-com collapse and the September 11th terrorist attack. "We might not have made it if it were not for our EcoSense programs," says Anderson.

Green Mountain Coffee Roasters—Empowering local entrepreneurs

As the name suggests, this NASDAQ-listed corporation (GMCR) is located in the Green Mountains of Vermont. But its reach is global. As a roaster and distributor of specialty coffees, GMCR has become a leading advocate for fair trade practices and providing financial support for local coffee growers. "Our president and CEO Robert Stiller visited places where coffee is grown and was struck by the levels of poverty. He wanted to do something about it," said Rick Peyser, director of public relations. As a result, GMCR now purchases coffee beans from small farm cooperatives in Peru, Mexico, and Sumatra. It also provides micro-loans to underwrite family businesses that are trying to create more diverse agricultural economies. Back home in its Waterbury, Vermont, roasting facility, GMCR uses a 95-kilowatt cogeneration system that captures waste heat from its propane-fired generator and recycles it for both coffee roasting and space heating.

Each of these companies has recently been named one of the 100 Best Corporate Citizens by *Business Ethics* magazine. However, major corporations still have their critics. In fact, companies that claim to be making progress in advancing CSR are often the most loudly criticized. For example, British Petroleum, which has endeavored to be an oil industry leader in supporting environmentally sensitive energy development, is often attacked by environmental groups despite initiatives such as investing $48 million to develop the world's largest solar energy project. Despite such criticism, it is encouraging to note that entrepreneurial activities can help companies achieve their social responsibility goals as well as their innovation and growth goals.

Sources: Asmus, P. 2005. 100 best corporate citizens for 2005. *Business Ethics*, www.business-ethics.com; Asmus, P. 2003. 100 best corporate citizens for 2003. *Business Ethics*, www.business-ethics.com; Baker, M. 2001. BP announces world's largest solar project. *Business Respect*, 1: April 6; Hawken, P., Lovins, A., & Lovins, H. 2000. *Natural capitalism*. Boston: Back Bay Books; see also www.bp.com; www.domini.com; www.hoovers.com; and www.ifsia.com.

They might slash prices and sacrifice profitability to gain market share or spend aggressively to obtain manufacturing capacity. As an avenue of firm development and growth, competitive aggressiveness may involve being very assertive in leveraging the results of other entrepreneurial activities such as innovativeness or proactiveness.

Unlike innovativeness and proactiveness, however, which tend to focus on market opportunities, competitive aggressiveness is directed toward competitors. The SWOT (strengths, weaknesses, opportunities, threats) analysis discussed in Chapters 2 and 3 provides a useful way to distinguish between these different approaches to corporate entrepreneurship. Proactiveness, as we saw in the last section, is a response to opportunities—the O in SWOT. Competitive aggressiveness, by contrast, is a response to threats—the T in SWOT. A competitively aggressive posture is important for firms that seek to enter new markets in the face of intense rivalry.

Strategic managers can use competitive aggressiveness to combat industry trends that threaten their survival or market position. Sometimes firms need to be forceful in defending the competitive position that has made them an industry leader. Firms often need to be aggressive to ensure their advantage by capitalizing on new technologies or serving new market needs.

Two of the ways competitively aggressive firms enhance their entrepreneurial position are:

1. ***Entering markets with drastically lower prices.*** Smaller firms often fear the entry of resource-rich large firms into their marketplace. Because the larger firms usually have deep pockets, they can afford to cut prices without being seriously damaged by an extended period of narrow margins. In the mid-1990s, the retail record store business was nearly wiped out when larger new entrants launched a price war. It started when Best Buy, a "big box" electronics retailer with hundreds of stores, was looking for a way to increase traffic in its large suburban stores. It decided to sell compact disks (CDs). Most record stores were paying about $10 at wholesale for CDs and selling them for $14 or more. Best Buy priced new releases at $9.98. Soon, archrival Circuit City also started retailing CDs and a major price war followed. Within two years, seven record stores declared bankruptcy. The Best Buy executive who championed the CD policy said, "The whole goal of getting into business is taking market share and building your business. That's what it's about."[62]

2. ***Copying the business practices or techniques of successful competitors.*** We've all heard that imitation is the highest form of flattery. But imitation may also be used to take business from competitors; as long as the idea or practice is not protected by intellectual property laws, it's not illegal. This was the conclusion of Chris Bogan, CEO of Best Practices, LLC, a North Carolina consulting group with $8 million in revenues. Best Practices seeks out best practices in order to repackage and resell them or use them internally. Its mission is to find superstar performers in the business world and then sell their secrets to others. Best Practices's revenues come from one-time consulting projects and products like databases and benchmarking reports on subjects such as managing call centers and launching new products. Bogan's philosophy is that companies don't have to invent solutions to their problems; they can "steal" them from successful companies.[63]

Another practice companies use to overcome the competition is to make preannouncements of new products or technologies. This type of signaling is aimed not only at potential customers but also at competitors to see how they will react or to discourage them from launching similar initiatives. Sometimes the preannouncements are made just to scare off competitors, an action that has potential ethical implications.

Competitive aggressiveness may not always lead to competitive advantages. Some companies (or their CEOs) have severely damaged their reputations by being overly aggressive. Microsoft is a good example. Although it continues to be a dominant player, its highly aggressive profile makes it the subject of scorn by some businesses and individuals. Microsoft's image also contributed to the huge antitrust suit brought against it by the U.S. government and several states. Efforts to find viable replacements for the Microsoft products upon which users have become overly dependent may eventually erode Microsoft's leading role as a software provider.

Therefore, competitive aggressiveness is a strategy that is best used in moderation. Companies that aggressively establish their competitive position and vigorously exploit opportunities to achieve profitability may, over the long run, be better able to sustain their competitive advantages if their goal is to defeat, rather than decimate, their competitors.

Risk Taking

Risk taking refers to a firm's willingness to seize a venture opportunity even though it does not know whether the venture will be successful—to act boldly without knowing the consequences. To be successful through corporate entrepreneurship, firms usually have to take on riskier alternatives, even if it means forgoing the methods or products that have worked in the past. To obtain high financial returns, firms take such risks as assuming high levels of debt, committing large amounts of firm resources, introducing new products into new markets, and investing in unexplored technologies.

In some ways, all of the approaches to internal development that we have discussed are potentially risky. Whether they are being aggressive, proactive, or innovative, firms on the path of corporate entrepreneurship must act without knowing how their actions will turn out. Before launching their strategies, corporate entrepreneurs must know their firm's appetite for risk. How far is it willing to go without knowing what the outcome will be?

Three types of risk that organizations and their executives face are business risk, financial risk, and personal risk:

- *Business risk taking* involves venturing into the unknown without knowing the probability of success. This is the risk associated with entering untested markets or committing to unproven technologies.

- *Financial risk taking* requires that a company borrow heavily or commit a large portion of its resources in order to grow. In this context, risk is used to refer to the risk/return trade-off that is familiar in financial analysis.

- *Personal risk taking* refers to the risks that an executive assumes in taking a stand in favor of a strategic course of action. Executives who take such risks stand to influence the course of their whole company, and their decisions also can have significant implications for their careers.

In many business situations, all three types of risk taking are present. Taking bold new actions rarely affects just one part of the organization. Consider the example of David D'Alessandro of John Hancock Financial Services, Inc.

David D'Alessandro joined insurance giant John Hancock in 1984 as its vice president of corporate communications. At the time, Hancock's image was weak due in part to a series of forgettable TV ads that failed to distinguish it from other insurance carriers. D'Alessandro championed a new advertising campaign that featured "real life" images, such as a husband and wife arguing, and a lesbian couple adopting a Vietnamese baby. Although it was costly to produce and risky for the image of the traditional insurance carrier, sales surged 17 percent in the first year of the ad campaign. The risk also paid off for D'Alessandro personally: In

May 2000 he was named the youngest chairman and CEO in John Hancock's history. (In 2004, John Hancock was acquired by Toronto-based Manulife Financial Corporation.)[64]

Even though risk taking involves taking chances, it is not gambling. The best-run companies investigate the consequences of various opportunities and create scenarios of likely outcomes. Their goal is to reduce the riskiness of business decision making. As we saw in the section on product champions, a key to managing entrepreneurial risks is to evaluate new venture opportunities thoroughly enough to reduce the uncertainty surrounding them.

Companies can use the following two methods to strengthen their competitive position through risk taking.

1. *Researching and assessing risk factors to minimize uncertainty.* Although all new business endeavors are inherently risky, firms that do their homework can usually reduce their risk. For example, Graybar Electric Co., a privately held 136-year-old provider of data and telecom equipment, had to revamp its warehouse and distribution system. The Internet was creating booming demand. But with 231 local distribution centers, each run independently, Graybar could not get its products to customers fast enough. After careful analysis, the company hatched a plan that consolidated 16 supply warehouses without displacing any local managers, thus preserving the quality of service for both customers and employees. The changeover was expensive—$144 million over four years. But the plan called for a payback after five years, and even with telecom sector sales slipping, Graybar's prudent risk taking led to a 21 percent surge in sales in 2000. By 2004, its annual revenues exceeded $4 billion.[65]

2. *Using techniques that have worked in other domains.* Risky methods that other companies have applied successfully may be used to advance corporate ventures. Consider the actions of Autobytel.com, one of the first companies to sell cars online. Although it had enjoyed early success by being a first mover, it wanted to jump-start its sales. It decided to make a risky move. In a year when Autobytel.com earned only $6 million in revenues, it committed $1.2 million to a 30-second TV advertisement. But that ad was run during the Super Bowl and Autobytel was the first dot-com ever to use that venue. The free publicity and favorable business press it received extended far beyond the 30 seconds that Autobytel's $1.2 million had bought it.[66]

Risk taking, by its nature, involves potential dangers and pitfalls. Only carefully managed risk is likely to lead to competitive advantages. Actions that are taken without sufficient forethought, research, and planning may prove to be very costly. The era of dot-com start-ups and subsequent failures proved that businesses are often launched—at great expense—without a clear sense of the long-term or even, in some cases, short-term consequences. When the Internet bubble burst, more than $3 trillion of investment wealth was wiped out of the U.S. stock markets, due in large part to the collapse of the dot-com surge.[67] Along with the financial losses, the business and personal losses were enormous.

Strategic managers must always remain mindful of potential risks. In his book *Innovation and Entrepreneurship,* Peter Drucker argued that successful entrepreneurs are typically not risk takers. Instead, they take steps to minimize risks by carefully understanding them. That is how they avoid focusing on risk and remain focused on opportunity.[68] Thus, risk taking is a good place to close this chapter on corporate entrepreneurship. Companies that choose to grow through internal corporate venturing must remember that entrepreneurship always involves embracing what is new and uncertain.

Summary

To remain competitive in today's economy, established firms must find new avenues for development and growth. This chapter has addressed how innovation and corporate entrepreneurship can be a means of internal venture creation and strategic renewal, and how an entrepreneurial orientation can help corporations enhance their competitive position.

Innovation is one of the primary means by which corporations grow and strengthen their strategic position. Innovations can take several forms, ranging from radical breakthrough innovations to incremental improvement innovations. Innovations are often used to update products and services or for improving organizational processes. Managing the innovation process is often challenging, because it involves a great deal of uncertainty and there are many choices to be made about the extent and type of innovations to pursue. By defining the scope of innovation, managing the pace of innovation, and collaborating with innovation partners, firms can more effectively manage the innovation process.

We also discussed the role of corporate entrepreneurship in venture development and strategic renewal. Entrepreneurial firms that pursue a blue ocean strategy find success by breaking down traditional industry barriers and creating new arenas in which to achieve market dominance. Other corporations usually take either a focused or dispersed approach to corporate venturing. Firms with a focused approach usually separate the corporate venturing activity from the ongoing operations of the firm in order to foster independent thinking and encourage entrepreneurial team members to think and act without the constraints imposed by the corporation. In corporations where venturing activities are dispersed, a culture of entrepreneurship permeates all parts of the company in order to induce strategic behaviors by all organizational members. In measuring the success of corporate venturing activities, both financial and strategic objectives should be considered.

Most entrepreneurial firms need to have an entrepreneurial orientation: the methods, practices, and decision-making styles that strategic managers use to act entrepreneurially. Five dimensions of entrepreneurial orientation are found in firms that pursue corporate venture strategies. Autonomy, innovativeness, proactiveness, competitive aggressiveness, and risk taking each make a unique contribution to the pursuit of new opportunities. When deployed effectively, the methods and practices of an entrepreneurial orientation can be used to engage successfully in corporate entrepreneurship and new venture creation. However, strategic managers must remain mindful of the pitfalls associated with each of these approaches.

Summary Review Questions

1. What is meant by the concept of a continuum of radical and incremental innovations?
2. What are the dilemmas that organizations face when deciding what innovation projects to pursue? What steps can organizations take to effectively manage the innovation process?
3. What is the difference between focused and dispersed approaches to corporate entrepreneurship?
4. How are business incubators used to foster internal corporate venturing?
5. What is the role of the product champion in bringing a new product or service into existence in a corporation? How can companies use product champions to enhance their venture development efforts?
6. Explain the difference between proactiveness and competitive aggressiveness in terms of achieving and sustaining competitive advantage.
7. Describe how the entrepreneurial orientation (EO) dimensions of innovativeness, proactiveness, and risk taking can be combined to create competitive advantages for entrepreneurial firms.

Select two different major corporations from two different industries (you might use Fortune 500 companies to make your selection). Compare and contrast these organizations in terms of their entrepreneurial orientation.

Entrepreneurial Orientation	Company A	Company B
Autonomy		
Innovativeness		
Proactiveness		
Competitive Aggressiveness		
Risk Taking		

Based on Your Comparison:

1. How is the corporation's entrepreneurial orientation reflected in its strategy?
2. Which corporation would you say has the stronger entrepreneurial orientation?
3. Is the corporation with the stronger entrepreneurial orientation also stronger in terms of financial performance?

1. Select a firm known for its corporate entrepreneurship activities. Research the company and discuss how it has positioned itself relative to its close competitors. Does it have a unique strategic advantage? Disadvantage? Explain.
2. Explain the difference between product innovations and process innovations. Provide examples of firms that have recently introduced each type of innovation. What are the types of innovations related to the strategies of each firm?
3. Using the Internet, select a company that is listed on the NASDAQ or New York Stock Exchange. Research the extent to which the company has an entrepreneurial culture. Does the company use product champions? Does it have a corporate venture capital fund? Do you believe its entrepreneurial efforts are sufficient to generate sustainable advantages?
4. How can an established firm use an entrepreneurial orientation to enhance its overall strategic position? Provide examples.

1. Innovation activities are often aimed at making a discovery or commercializing a technology ahead of the competition. What are some of the unethical practices that companies could engage in during the innovation process? What are the potential long-term consequences of such actions?
2. Discuss the ethical implications of using entrepreneurial policies and practices to pursue corporate social responsibility goals. Are these efforts authentic and genuine or just an attempt to attract more customers?

References

1. Sources for the Polaroid example include Charan, R., & Useem, J. 2002. Why companies fail. *Fortune,* May 15; Knox, N. 2001. Rivals push Polaroid toward Chapter 11. *USA Today,* October 11; McLaughlin, T. 2001. Harvard dropout made Polaroid an icon. *Toronto Star,* October 15; Pope, J. 2001. Polaroid's fortunes rose with Land, but fell under the burden of debt. *Daily Kent Stater* (OH), October 15; and www.polaroid.com.

2. Eagan, M. 2005. How did Polaroid's faithful ever land in this predicament? *Boston Herald,* April 28: 20; and St. Anthony, N. 2005. Petters wraps up Polaroid. *Star Tribune,* April 28: 1D.

3. Christensen, C. M. 1997. *The innovator's dilemma: When new technologies cause great firms to fail.* Cambridge, MA: Harvard Business School Press.

4. For a discussion about Polaroid, see Gavetti, G., & Levinthal, D. 2000. Looking forward and looking backward: Cognitive and experiential search. *Administrative Science Quarterly,* 45: 113–137.

5. For an interesting discussion, see Johannessen, J. A., Olsen, B., & Lumpkin, G. T. 2001. Innovation as newness: What is new, how new, and new to whom? *European Journal of Innovation Management,* 4(1): 20–31.

6. The discussion of radical and incremental innovations draws from Leifer, R., McDermott, C. M., Colarelli, G., O'Connor, G. C., Peters, L. S., Rice, M. P., & Veryzer, R. W. 2000. *Radical innovation: How mature companies can outsmart upstarts.* Boston: Harvard Business School Press; Damanpour, F. 1996. Organizational complexity and innovation: Developing and testing multiple contingency models. *Management Science,* 42(5): 693–716; and Hage, J. 1980. *Theories of organizations.* New York: Wiley.

7. The discussion of product and process innovation is based on Roberts, E. B. (Ed.). 2002. *Innovation: Driving product, process, and market change.* San Francisco: Jossey-Bass; Hayes, R., & Wheelwright, S. 1985. Competing through manufacturing. *Harvard Business Review,* 63(1): 99–109; and Hayes, R., & Wheelwright, S. 1979. Dynamics of product-process life cycles. *Harvard Business Review,* 57(2): 127–136.

8. Drucker, P. F. 1985. *Innovation and entrepreneurship:* 2000 New York: Harper & Row.

9. Steere, W. C., Jr., & Niblack, J. 1997. Pfizer, Inc. In Kanter, R. M., Kao, J., & Wiersema, F. (Eds.), *Innovation: Breakthrough thinking at 3M, DuPont, GE, Pfizer, and Rubbermaid:* 123–145. New York: HarperCollins.

10. Morrissey, C. A. 2000. Managing innovation through corporate venturing. *Graziadio Business Report,* Spring, gbr.pepperdine.edu; and Sharma, A. 1999. Central dilemmas of managing innovation in large firms. *California Management Review,* 41(3): 147–164.

11. Sharma, op. cit.

12. Canabou, C. 2003. Fast ideas for slow times. *Fast Company,* May: 52.

13. Biodegradable Products Institute. 2003. "Compostable Logo" of the Biodegradable Products Institute gains momentum with approval of DuPont™ Biomax® resin, www.bpiworld.org, June 12; Leifer et al., op. cit.

14. For more on defining the scope of innovation, see Valikangas, L., & Gibbert, M. 2005. Boundary-setting strategies for escaping innovation traps. *MIT Sloan Management Review,* 46(3): 58–65.

15. Leifer et al., op. cit.

16. Bhide, A. V. 2000. *The origin and evolution of new businesses.* New York: Oxford University Press; Brown, S. L., & Eisenhardt, K. M. 1998. *Competing on the edge: Strategy as structured chaos.* Cambridge, MA: Harvard Business School Press.

17. Caulfield, B. 2003. Why techies don't get Six Sigma. *Business 2.0,* June: 90.

18. Chesbrough, H. 2003. *Open innovation: The new imperative for creating and profiting from technology.* Boston: Harvard Business School Press.

19. Bick, J. 2003. Gold bond. *Entrepreneur,* March: 54–57.

20. For an interesting perspective on the role of collaboration among multinational corporations see Hansen, M. T., & Nohria, N. 2004. How to build collaborative advantage. *MIT Sloan Management Review,* 46(1): 22–30.

21. Guth, W. D., & Ginsberg, A. 1990. Guest editor's introduction: Corporate entrepreneurship. *Strategic Management Journal,* 11: 5–15.

22. Pinchot, G. 1985. *Intrapreneuring.* New York: Harper & Row.

23. Kim, W. C., & Mauborgne, R. 2005. *Blue ocean strategy.* Boston, MA: Harvard Business School Press; and Kim, W. C., & Mauborgne, R. 2005. Blue ocean strategy: From theory to practice. *California Management Review,* 47(3): 105–121.

24. Birkinshaw, J. 1997. Entrepreneurship in multinational corporations: The characteristics of subsidiary initiatives. *Strategic Management Journal,* 18(3): 207–229; and Kanter, R. M. 1985. *The change masters.* New York: Simon & Schuster.

25. The information in this example is from Leifer et al., op. cit.; Vance, A. 2000. NetActive looks to role as download police. *IDG News Service,* November 14, www.idg.net; and www.hoovers.com.

26. Hansen, M. T., Chesbrough, H. W., Nohria, N., & Sull, D. 2000. Networked incubators: Hothouses of the new economy. *Harvard Business Review,* 78(5): 74–84.

27. Stein, T. 2002. Corporate venture investors are bailing out. *Red Herring,* December: 74–75.

28. Is your company up to speed? 2003. *Fast Company,* June: 86.

29. For an interesting discussion, see Davenport, T. H., Prusak, L., & Wilson, H. J. 2003. Who's bringing you hot ideas and how are you responding? *Harvard Business Review,* 80(1): 58–64.

30. Howell, J. M. 2005. The right stuff. Identifying and developing effective champions of innovation. *Academy of Management Executive,* 19(2): 108–119. See also Greene, P., Brush, C., & Hart, M. 1999. The corporate venture champion: A resource-based approach to role and process. *Entrepreneurship theory & practice,* 23(3): 103–122; and Markham, S. K., & Aiman-Smith, L. 2001. Product champions: Truths, myths and management. *Research Technology Management,* May–June: 44–50.

31. Burgelman, R. A. 1983. A process model of internal corporate venturing in the diversified major firm. *Administrative Science Quarterly,* 28: 223–244.

32. Hamel, G. 2000. *Leading the revolution.* Boston: Harvard Business School Press.

33. Greene, Brush, & Hart, op. cit.; and Shane, S. 1994. Are champions different from non-champions? *Journal of Business Venturing,* 9(5): 397–421.

34. Vance, op. cit.; and www.info-mech.com/netactive.html.

35. Block, Z., & MacMillan, I. C. 1993. *Corporate venturing—Creating new businesses with the firm.* Cambridge, MA: Harvard Business School Press.

36. For an interesting discussion of these trade-offs, see Stringer, R. 2000. How to manage radical innovation. *California Management Review,* 42(4): 70–88; and Gompers, P. A., & Lerner, J. 1999. *The venture capital cycle.* Cambridge, MA: MIT Press.

37. Albrinck, J., Hornery, J., Kletter, D., & Neilson, G. 2001. Adventures in corporate venturing. *Strategy + Business,* 22: 119–129; and McGrath, R. G., & MacMillan, I. C. 2000. *The entrepreneurial mind set.* Cambridge, MA: Harvard Business School Press.

38. For an interesting discussion of how different outcome goals affect organizational learning and employee motivation, see Seijts, G. H., & Latham, G. P. 2005. Learning versus performance goals: When should each be used? *Academy of Management Executive,* 19(1): 124–131.

39. Crockett, R. O. 2001. Motorola. *BusinessWeek,* July 15: 72–78.

40. The ideas in this section are drawn from Royer, I. 2003. Why bad projects are so hard to kill. *Harvard Business Review,* 80(1): 48–56.

41. Breen, B. 2003. How does a 900-pound gorilla get to be an 1,800-pound gorilla? *Fast Company,* January: 87–89.

42. Slywotzky, A., & Wise, R. 2003. Double-digit growth in no-growth times. *Fast Company,* April: 66–72; www.hoovers.com; and www.johnsoncontrols.com.

43. For more on the role of real options in entrepreneurial decision making, see Folta, T. B., & O'Brien, J. P. 2004. Entry in the presence of dueling options. *Strategic Management Journal,* 25: 121–138.

44. Covin, J. G., & Slevin, D. P. 1991. A conceptual model of entrepreneurship as firm behavior. *Entrepreneurship Theory and Practice,* 16(1): 7–24; Lumpkin, G. T., & Dess, G. G. 1996. Clarifying the entrepreneurial orientation construct and linking it to performance. *Academy of Management Review,* 21(1): 135–172; and McGrath, R. G., & MacMillan, I. C. 2000. *The entrepreneurial mind set.* Cambridge, MA: Harvard Business School Press.

45. Lumpkin, G. T., & Dess, G. G. 2001. Linking two dimensions of entrepreneurial orientation to firm performance: The moderating role of environment and life cycle. *Journal of Business Venturing,* 16: 429–451.

46. For an interesting discussion, see Day, J. D., Mang, P. Y., Richter, A., & Roberts, J. 2001. The innovative organization: Why new ventures need more than a room of their own, *McKinsey Quarterly,* 2: 21–31.

47. Quinn, J. B. 1992. *Intelligent enterprise.* New York: Free Press.

48. Wagner, M. 2005. Out of the skunkworks. *Internet Retailer,* January, www.internetretailer.com.

49. Cross, K. 2001. Bang the drum quickly. *Business 2.0,* May 1: 28–30.

50. Crockett, R. O. 2001. Chris Galvin shakes things up—again. *BusinessWeek,* May 28: 38–39.

51. For an interesting discussion of the impact of innovativeness on organizational outcomes see Cho, H. J., & Pucik, V. 2005. Relationship between innovativeness, quality, growth, profitability, and market value. *Strategic Management Journal,* 26(6): 555–575.

52. Hamel, G. 1999. Bringing Silicon Valley inside. *Harvard Business Review,* 77(5): 71–84.

53. Perman, S. 2001. Automate or die. www.business2.com, July; and Dell, M. 1999. *Direct from Dell.* New York: HarperBusiness.

54. Evans, P., & Wurster, T. S. 2000. *Blown to bits.* Boston: Harvard Business School Press.

55. Lieberman, M. B., & Montgomery, D. B. 1988. First mover advantages. *Strategic Management Journal,* 9 (Special Issue): 41–58.

56. The discussion of first mover advantages is based on several articles, including Lambkin, M. 1988. Order of entry and performance in new markets. *Strategic Management Journal,* 9: 127–140; Lieberman & Montgomery, op. cit.: 41–58; and Miller, A., & Camp, B. 1985. Exploring determinants of success in corporate ventures. *Journal of Business Venturing,* 1(2): 87–105.

57. Moore, G. A. 1999. *Crossing the chasm* (2nd ed.). New York: HarperBusiness.

58. Tesler, L. 2001. Why the Apple Newton failed, www.techtv.com/print/story/0,23102,3013675,00.html; Veitch, M. 1998. Apple kills off Newton PDA, news.zdnet.co.uk/story/printer/0,,s2067739,00.html.

59. Collins, J. C. & Porras, J. I. 1997. *Built to last.* New York: HarperBusiness; see also www.sony.com.

60. Hardy, Q., & Godwin, J. 2000. Other people's money. *Forbes,* August 7: 116–118.

61. Mallas, S. 2005. PepsiCo loses its Edge. *The Motley Fool,* June 1, www.fool.com.

62. Carvell, T., 1997, The crazy record business: These prices are really insane. *Fortune,* August 4: 109–16.

63. Bogan, C. E., & English, M. J. 1994. *Benchmarking for best practices.* New York: McGraw-Hill; Mochari, I. 2001. Steal this strategy. *Inc.,* July: 62–67.

64. Helman, C. 2001. Stand-up brand. *Forbes,* July 9: 27; and www.hoovers.com.

65. Keenan, F., & Mullaney, T. J. 2001. Clicking at Graybar. *BusinessWeek,* June 18: 132–134; and www.graybar.com.

66. Weintraub, A. 2001. Make or break for Autobytel. *BusinessWeek e.biz,* July 9: EB30–EB32; see also www.autobytel.com.

67. Coy, P., & Vickers, M. 2001. How bad will it get? *BusinessWeek,* March 12: 36–42.

68. Drucker, op. cit., pp. 109–110.

13

Recognizing Opportunities and Creating New Ventures

>chapter objectives

After reading this chapter, you should have a good understanding of:

- The role of new ventures and small businesses in the U.S. economy.

- The importance of opportunity recognition, as well as the role of opportunities, resources, and entrepreneurs, in successfully pursuing new ventures.

- The role of vision, dedication, and commitment to excellence in determining the quality of entrepreneurial leadership.

- The different types of financing that are available to new ventures depending on their stage of development.

- The importance of human capital and social capital as well as government resources in supporting new ventures and small businesses.

- The three types of entry strategies—pioneering, imitative, and adaptive—that are commonly used to launch a new venture.

- How the generic strategies of overall cost leadership, differentiation, and focus are used by new ventures and small businesses.

*n*ew technologies, shifting social and demographic trends, and sudden changes in the business environment create opportunities for entrepreneurship. New ventures, which often emerge under such conditions, face unique strategic challenges if they are going to survive and grow. Small businesses, which are a major engine of growth in the U.S. economy because of their role in job creation and innovation, must rely on sound strategic principles to be successful.

This chapter addresses how new ventures and small businesses can achieve competitive advantages. In the first section we review various perspectives of entrepreneurship and how the size, age, and growth goals of a firm affect small businesses and entrepreneurial firms. We also examine the contribution of small businesses to the U.S economy.

In the second section we address the role of opportunity recognition in the process of new venture creation. We highlight the importance of three factors in determining whether a potential venture opportunity should be pursued—the nature of the opportunity itself, the resources available to undertake it, and the characteristics of the entrepreneur(s) pursuing it.

In section three we expand on the topic of entrepreneurial resources. We discuss various types of financing that may be available during early and later stages of the new venture creation process. We also address how other factors, including human capital, social capital, and government programs aimed at supporting entrepreneurial firms, provide important resources for the small business owner.

In the fourth section we focus on the qualities of entrepreneurial leadership. Business founders need vision in order to conceive realities that do not yet exist. Dedication and drive are essential to maintain the level of motivation and persistence needed to succeed. A commitment to excellence as seen in the quality of products and services, the talent and skill level of employees, and superior customer service are other elements of effective entrepreneurial leadership.

In section five we show how many of the strategic concepts discussed in this text apply to new ventures and small businesses. Three different types of new entry strategies are discussed—pioneering, imitative, and adaptive. Then, the generic strategies (discussed in Chapter 5) as well as combination strategies are addressed in terms of how they apply to new ventures and entrepreneurial firms. Additionally, some of the pitfalls associated with each of these strategic approaches are presented.

The success of an entrepreneurial venture—whether it is undertaken by a major corporation or a small start-up—depends on many factors. The right combination of resources, know-how, and strategic action can lead to above-average profitability and new advantages. However, many things can go wrong. To see how a firm's entrepreneurial efforts can turn to failure, consider the example of Great Plains Airlines.

The airlines industry is both competitive and volatile. For many years it was regulated in an effort to make sure all markets were served and to prevent any one airline from becoming overly dominant. After the industry was deregulated, however, some of the major airlines abandoned unprofitable markets and consolidated their efforts around hub cities such as Dallas, Atlanta, Los Angeles, and New York. A notable exception was Southwest Airlines, which became highly successful by avoiding expensive hub operations in favor of point-to-point flights into smaller airports. Start-up airlines, which began to flourish after deregulation, tended to imitate the Southwest model. One such start-up was Great Plains Airlines, Inc., a regional airline launched in Tulsa, Oklahoma.[1]

> The goal of founders James Swartz and John Knight was to fly 50-seater airplanes nonstop between Tulsa and the U.S. coasts. Not only did the entrepreneurs aim to focus on unserved markets, but they also sought a competitive advantage by avoiding big hubs and flying into underutilized airports. From the start, the entrepreneurs pledged not to compete head-on with the major airlines and pinned their hopes on the belief that the big airlines would return the favor.
>
> The early going for Great Plains seemed very promising. Key members of the Tulsa Chamber of Commerce along with support from the Tulsa City Council and local airport and industrial officials helped Great Plains amass $30 million in start-up capital. *The Wall Street Journal* named Great Plains one of four start-ups to watch in 2001 in their series labeled "The Challengers," which highlighted young new entrant firms that were challenging existing big players.
>
> From the start, however, it seemed that Great Plains was in for a rocky ride. Even with $30 million under its belt, the company was plagued by insufficient resources. "The one big problem is, they are undercapitalized," said Darryl Jenkins, an airline consultant and director of the aviation-studies program at George Washington University. The lack of resources dogged the founders as they shopped for airplanes. Although they were able to obtain two 32-seaters by purchasing nearly defunct Ozark Air, the planes did not hold enough fuel to make trips to the coast. With the two planes, service was started to Nashville and Albuquerque instead.
>
> Another problem came from the incumbent airlines, which took steps to squash the fledgling airlines. Soon after Great Plains announced it would offer service to the west coast, American Airlines announced it would inaugurate nonstop service between Tulsa and Los Angeles. "We tried for years to get them to fly that route," said Brent Kitchen, director of the Tulsa airport authority. "I think American figured, 'We're going to try it before Great Plains gets there.'"
>
> Finally, the funding Great Plains received was apparently obtained illegally through a convoluted loan agreement that violated a federal ban against local airports subsidizing airlines. By March 2004, when the loan came due, Great Plains defaulted. The airline had already filed for Chapter 11 bankruptcy protection and suspended service. After an investigation by the FBI and U.S. Department of Transportation, Great Plains filed a Chapter 7 bankruptcy in January 2005 and closed down for good.

What Went Wrong with Great Plains Airlines?   Great Plains failed because it could not get off the ground fast enough to prevent major airlines from entering the same markets and preempting its planned services. It also made a classic entrepreneurial mistake by starting with insufficient resources. Great Plains' problems were compounded by their lack of strategic planning. Its business plan called for leasing planes since, at $20 million each, purchasing a fleet would be very costly. But airplane leasing is highly complicated and time consuming. The founders, who had successfully launched Jet Arizona, an air ambulance service, seemed unprepared for the delays a leasing agreement would create. The 50-seat planes were also in short supply, something that better research would likely have revealed. Finally, even though it recognized the need to form strong alliances and a network of support, Great Plains got mixed up in a shady and very public financing debacle.

The Great Plains case illustrates the importance of thinking and acting strategically in the entrepreneurial process. Even though Great Plains aimed to fill a market need and obtained $30 million of financial support, it was not able to convert its investment into a profitable business. Even when market conditions are creating new opportunities, poor planning and industry and competitive forces may prevent a new entrant from reaching the marketplace. Thus, to be successful, new ventures need to apply the lessons of strategic management to evaluate business conditions, assess their internal capabilities, formulate effective strategies, and implement sound business practices. New ventures and small businesses are often vulnerable because they lack experience and/or resources, and because established firms may be relatively more powerful. In this chapter we address how new ventures and small businesses, by applying the principles and practices of strategic management, can improve their chances of success. To begin our discussion, we address some of the differences and similarities found among the many types of entrepreneurial firms and address the importance of entrepreneurship to the economy.

>>New Ventures and Small Businesses

The majority of new business creation is the result of entrepreneurial efforts by new ventures and small businesses. The strategic concepts introduced in this text can be applied to the effective management of entrepreneurial firms. Because there are several types of entrepreneurial firms, the application of these principles may differ somewhat depending on factors such as the size, age, or growth goals of the firm. Generally speaking, however, entrepreneurial activities will be more successful if strategic thinking guides decision making.

In this section we will investigate several types of entrepreneurial ventures and how the unique circumstances surrounding each type affect the strategies they pursue. First, let's consider the important role that small business and entrepreneurship play in the U.S. economy. Strategy Spotlight 13.1 addresses some of the reasons why small business and entrepreneurship are viewed favorably in the United States.

Categories of Entrepreneurial Ventures

There are many ways to categorize entrepreneurial ventures. The term *entrepreneurship* itself has come to represent a wide array of meanings.[2] For example:

- Working for oneself rather than for someone else for a salary.
- Entering into a new or established market with new or existing products or services.
- Operating a firm in which there is no separation between ownership and management.
- Discovering, evaluating, and exploiting opportunities.
- Creating new organizations.

All of these definitions have been used to characterize entrepreneurial firms and/or small businesses. For purposes of strategic analysis, it is useful to note three differences among entrepreneurial firms, because these distinctions have strategic implications. The first of these is size. Small businesses, of course, are small. However, some ventures are small because they are new. This leads to the second criterion—age. Start-ups and new ventures are often considered to be entrepreneurial simply because they are young. That is, size is often correlated with age. New ventures usually begin small and grow over time as their business activity increases. Thus, as the age of a firm increases, so does its size. There is a third factor, however, that may limit an entrepreneurial firm's size—its growth goals.

Firms that do not aspire to grow large usually don't. Therefore, a young firm's growth goals often determine whether it will remain small as it ages or grow large. In

The Contribution of Small Business and Entrepreneurship to the U.S. Economy

In the late 1970s, MIT professor David Birch launched a study to explore the sources of business growth. "I wasn't really looking for anything in particular," says Birch. But the findings surprised him: Small businesses create the most jobs. Since then, Birch and others have shown that it's not just big companies that power the economy. The actual number of businesses, as measured by tax returns, has been growing faster than the civilian labor force for the past three decades. There is no sign of a reversal in that trend. Small business and entrepreneurship have become a major component of the economy.

Here are the facts:

- In the United States, there are approximately 5.7 million companies with fewer than 100 employees.

Another 100,000 companies have 100 to 500 employees. In addition, 17.0 million individuals are nonemployer sole proprietors.

- Small businesses create the majority of new jobs. According to recent data, small business created three-quarters of U.S. net new jobs in a recent period (2.5 million of the 3.4 million total). A small percentage of the fastest growing entrepreneurial firms (5 to 15 percent) account for a majority of the new jobs created.

- Small businesses (fewer than 500 employees) employ more than half of the private sector workforce (54 million in 2001) and account for more *(continued)*

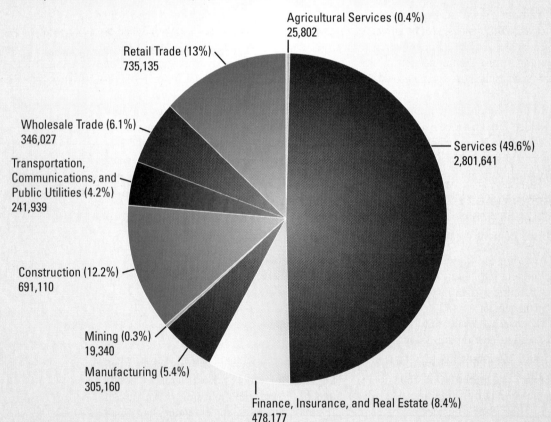

Exhibit 13.1 *All U.S. Small Companies by Industry**

* Businesses with 500 or fewer employees in 2001.

Source: Small Business Administration's Office of Advocacy, based on data provided by the U.S. Census Bureau, statistics of U.S. businesses. (Percentages don't add to 100% because of rounding.)

(continued) than 50 percent of nonfarm private gross domestic product (GDP).

- Small firms produce 13 to 14 times more patents per employee than large patenting firms and employ 39 percent of high-tech workers (such as scientists, engineers, and computer workers). In addition, smaller entrepreneurial firms account for 55 percent of all innovations.

- Small businesses make up 97 percent of all U.S. exporters and accounted for 29 percent of known U.S. export value in 2001.

Sources: Small Business Administration. 2004. *The small business economy.* Washington, DC: U.S. Government Printing Office; Small Business Administration. 2005. Small business by the numbers. *SBA Office of Advocacy,* June, www.sba.gov/advo/; *Inc.* 2001. Small business 2001: Where we are now. May 29: 18–19; Dennis, Jr., W. J. 1999. *Business starts and stops.* Washington, DC: National Federation of Independent Business; Mioniti, M., & Bygrave, W. D. 2004. *Global entrepreneurship monitor—National entrepreneurship assessment: United States of America 2004, executive report.* Kansas City, MO: Kauffman Center for Entrepreneurial Leadership; and *Fortune.* 2001. The heroes: A portfolio. October 4: 74.

Exhibit 13.1 shows the number of small businesses in the United States and how they are distributed through different sectors of the economy.

Even though thousands of small businesses are formed each year, thousands also close. In a recent year, between 600,000 and 800,000 businesses with employees were formed. This translates into an annual birth rate of 14 to 16 percent. But in the same year, 12 to 14 percent of existing businesses were terminated, resulting in a net annual increase of about 2 percent. Among those that close each year, about one-fourth are sold or transferred (e.g., through inheritance). Another half simply "fade away," (i.e., the owners allow them to become inactive). Some of the deactivated firms are terminated not because they were unprofitable, but because the owner found a better business opportunity elsewhere. Thus, even though some businesses fail or turn out to be less lucrative than expected, the overall trend is positive. Small business and entrepreneurship will continue to be a major force in the economy for years to come.

fact, growth goals are one of the key factors used to distinguish between entrepreneurial firms and small businesses. Small businesses are generally thought to have low or modest growth goals. Because small business owners prefer to maintain control of their business, they are often unwilling to take steps that are necessary to grow, even though they may have growth potential. These steps include, most notably, borrowing heavily or going public to obtain the funding needed to finance growth. As a result, they remain small businesses.

By contrast, entrepreneurial firms generally favor growth. Because growth is a priority, founders with high growth goals will often sell a share of the business (thus giving up some control) in order to finance growth. As a result, successful businesses founded by high-growth entrepreneurs develop a life of their own. In contrast, small businesses are often associated so closely with their founders that when the founder is gone, the business ceases to operate. Of course, there may be intervening factors that affect growth outcomes unexpectedly. For example, some entrepreneurs may want to grow large businesses but cannot, and others may become bigger than they ever expected because market forces propel them onto a growth curve they did not anticipate. But in general, the difference between entrepreneurial firms and small businesses is related to their path of growth.

These three factors—size, age, and growth goals—are captured in a model of entrepreneurial firms that was developed by David Birch, the famed small-business researcher whose findings are presented in Spotlight 13.1 Birch identified three categories of firms—elephants, mice, and gazelles. Let's look briefly at each of these.

Elephants   As the name suggests, these are large firms. They also tend to be older and are the types of firms that appear in the Fortune 500. They have some disadvantages relative to entrepreneurial firms. For one thing, they cannot change direction quickly, and it is sometimes difficult to get them to move forward at all. As a group, these large firms have laid off more people than they have hired in the last 25 years.[3] On the other hand, they have obvious advantages. They can be hard chargers and move quite rapidly because of their overall power in the marketplace. Like elephants, these large firms usually command respect and can influence marketplace conditions (competition, technology) as well as business conditions (political/legal) in their industry.

As you might imagine from the image of the lumbering elephant, it is often difficult for such firms to be entrepreneurial. That's why some of the large firms introduced in Chapter 12 that have been strong innovators and generated an entrepreneurial spirit—3M, Sony, W. L. Gore, Virgin Group—have been so highly successful.

Mice   This term refers to the many small firms that power the U.S. economy. Over 80 percent of all firms in the United States have fewer than 20 employees.[4] The mice represent the many types of locally run businesses, including small retailers, small manufacturers, and all kinds of local service firms from auto repair shops and heating and air conditioning contractors to restaurants and banks. Mice typically do not have as much market power as large firms, but they can change direction more quickly in response to changes in business conditions.

As suggested earlier, many of these firms do not aspire to grow large as long as they remain profitable and competitive. Even so, since 1980, small businesses have added more jobs than large firms.[5] Even small firms that are committed to remaining small often add jobs or become the target of corporate takeovers. Consider the example of Timbuk2, a small manufacturer that decided to remain small rather than pursue rapid growth when a major buyer came calling:

> When CompUSA agreed to carry its urban shoulder bag products, California-based Timbuk2 thought it had it made. But after just four months, CEO Mark Dwight cancelled the deal. CompUSA's high-volume, low-margin requirements were eating too far into Timbuk2's profits. Going mainstream also threatened Timbuk2's quirky messenger bag image. "We're a specialty brand," says Dwight. By refocusing on specialty retailers such as REI and the Apple Stores, Timbuk2 has increased its margins, strengthened its specialty image, and helped double sales to over $10 million in just two years.[6]

Small businesses represent a bedrock of economic strength in the U.S. economy. Although many have chosen to remain small, many others aspire to grow into major corporations. It is these growth-oriented firms that we turn to next.

Gazelles   An important third category identified by Birch is known as gazelles. These are firms that seek rapid growth and above average profitability. They are likely to be listed in the *Inc.* 500 or the *Entrepreneur* Hot 100, both of which highlight the fastest-growing small companies. To be a gazelle, a firm must grow at least 20 percent a year for four years, from a base of at least $100,000 in revenues.[7] A firm that meets these criteria doubles in size during the four-year period.

Gazelles are important to the economy for several reasons. For one thing, their value proposition often includes a radical innovation or the implementation of a new technology. Thus, they are an important engine for innovation in the U.S. economy. For example, SurModics, Inc. is a Minnesota-based manufacturer of coatings for medical devices such as stents—metal coils that help hold blood vessels open after heart surgery. SurModics's coatings help make stents more slippery, which reduces the risk of stroke and makes them less likely to carry infections, thus improving their effectiveness. By partnering with companies such as Johnson & Johnson, which pays SurModics to conduct innovative research and then pays again to license the technology, SurModics has created a winning business model that recently earned it a place on the Fortune FSB 100 list of fast-growing small businesses. In a recent year, with fewer than 200 employees, it had revenues of $43.2 million and posted sales growth of 31 percent and net income growth of 47 percent.[8]

Ariat International: Riding High on the Heels of Success

For the twenty million horseback riders around the world, Ariat International is the Reebok of riding boots. Founded by Beth Cross, who, as a Bain & Company consultant, once helped Reebok market innovative materials such as gel padding and air pockets, Ariat has become a leading manufacturer of performance footwear for equestrians. Ariat's ergonomically designed boots have caught the attention of both cowboys and city slickers. Between 2000 and 2004, the company grew more than 25 percent per year and now owns about 17 percent of the U.S. market for western wear. Not bad, considering that Ariat's two leading competitors—Justin Boots and Tony Lama—have been around since the days of Wyatt Earp and are now owned by Warren Buffet.

Cross founded the company in her Union City, California home in 1991. At first it was slow going. With $250,000 from family and friends, initially she was able to produce only a few styles. But with some patents under her belt and an infusion of venture funding in 1996, the company began to take off. Recent growth has been propelled by a string of awards including the prestigious Innovation Award from the British Equestrian Trade Association (BETA) and Manufacturer of the Year Award from The National Foundation Quarter Horse Association (NFQHA). According to Sam Summers, NFQHA's Editor in Chief, "While attending horse shows, we sometimes gather around the horse trailer camps after the day's events and inevitably the subject of boots comes up. Ariat is always leading the discussion for its comfort and craftsmanship."

Here are some of the factors that helped Ariat succeed:

- ***Find the Market's Blind Spot***—Having grown up on a horse farm, Cross knew about boots. While working on the Reebok account, Cross recognized that leather-soled riding boots was a niche that could probably benefit from an upgrade. Market research helped convince her there was room for another brand.

- ***Make Friends in High Places***—In the early days of Ariat, Cross was able to attract a key supporter—Angel Martinez, Reebok's head of business development, whose daughter rode horses. With Martinez on board, Cross was able to recruit other high-profile board members with expertise in footwear, retailing, and finance. These industry bigwigs, in turn, helped Ariat secure an estimated $9 million in venture funding.

- ***Pay Less, Charge More***—Ariat has only 100 employees; most of them are in sales and customer service. China-based manufacturers who were already making boots for Timberland and Wolverine produce the boots using leather sourced from Europe and various components patented by Ariat. Compared to Justin, which manufactures its boots in Texas and Missouri, Ariat is able to charge more but has significantly lower costs.

- ***Create Your Own Demand***—In the early days, Ariat had a very small marketing budget, but it did have boots. So Cross traveled to rodeos and horse shows and actually gave the boots away to young hotshots and promising amateurs. Once others saw these rising stars wearing Ariats, they began asking western stores and tack shops to carry them. "There's no better way to get a retailer to stock your product than to have people start calling for it," says Cross.

Ariat's rapid growth has created new opportunities. It now offers several new product lines including riding pants, shirts, and clogs. And the boots have become a fashion item. In 2004, Ariat was featured in *Vogue* magazine and was chosen to participate in New York City's famed "Fashion Week" event. With its 25 percent growth rate and sales over $80 million in a recent year, the privately held company is leaving other boot makers in the dust.

Sources: Copeland, M. V. 2004. These boots really were made for walking. *Business 2.0*, 5(9): 72–74; Grant, K. 2004. Ariat International featured on runway of New York's famed "Fashion Week." *Ariat International*, www.ariat .com, February 12; Grant, K. 2004. NFQHA names Ariat International "Manufacturer of the Year." *Ariat International*, www.ariat.com, May 4; and www .elle.com.

Although technology is often a hot growth area, the majority of gazelles are not in high-tech fields. Some are using existing technologies in new arenas. Strategy Spotlight 13.2 describes Ariat International, a fast growing boot maker that has adapted athletic footwear technology to the making of riding and cowboy boots. Approximately 30 percent are in retail and wholesale trades (primarily low-tech) and another 30 percent are in services (including both high- and low-tech). Gazelles are not necessarily young either. Although some young firms take off rapidly from birth, many firms have growth spurts only after a long period of gradual development. Around one-fifth of gazelles have been in operation 30 years or more.[9]

Perhaps the most important contribution gazelles make is in job growth. Because gazelles are highly entrepreneurial, they seek growth rather than control. As they grow, their need for additional employees also increases rapidly.[10] As a result, the Small Business Administration (SBA) has estimated that gazelles, of which there were approximately 386,000 in 2002, have created as many jobs during the last 25 years as have the mice, which numbered around 17 million in 2002.[11] Thus, it is no surprise that local and state governments often seek out gazelles because of their role in boosting economic development in a region.

There are many other ways to categorize new ventures and small businesses. For example, according to the IRS, over 20 million self employment tax returns (Schedule C) were filed in a recent year, indicating that a large proportion of the adult population is engaged in money-making enterprises. Exhibit 13.2 identifies three other major business categories that are generally considered to be entrepreneurial in nature—franchises, family businesses, and home-based businesses.

All entrepreneurial firms that wish to launch a new venture must first identify a strong business opportunity. Thus, next we address the strategic issues and techniques that firms use to recognize and develop new venture opportunities.

>>Opportunity Recognition: Identifying and Developing Market Opportunities

The starting point for any new venture is the presence of an entrepreneurial opportunity. Where do opportunities come from? For new business start-ups, opportunities come from many sources—current or past work experiences, hobbies that grow into businesses or lead to inventions, suggestions by friends or family, or a chance event that makes an entrepreneur aware of an unmet need. For established firms, new business opportunities come from the needs of existing customers, suggestions by suppliers, or technological developments that lead to new advances.[12] For all types of firms, there is a major, overarching factor that is behind all viable opportunities that emerge in the business landscape: change. Change creates opportunities. Entrepreneurial firms make the most of changes brought about by new technology, sociocultural trends, and shifts in consumer demand. Even tragedy stimulates business development. Since September 11, 2001, initiatives related to strengthening homeland security and building military capabilities have stimulated billions of dollars of demand for new products and services such as night vision systems and unmanned aerial vehicles.[13]

The Opportunity Recognition Process

How do changes in the external environment lead to new business creation? They spark creative new ideas and innovation. Businesspeople often have ideas for entrepreneurial ventures. However, not all such ideas are good ideas—that is, viable business opportunities. To determine which ideas are strong enough to become new ventures, entrepreneurs must go through a process of identifying, selecting, and developing potential opportunities. This is the process of opportunity recognition.

Opportunity recognition refers to more than just the "Eureka!" feeling that people sometimes experience at the moment they identify a new idea. Although such insights

Type	Characteristics
Family businesses	• *Definition:* A family business, broadly defined, is a privately held firm in which family members have some degree of effective control over the strategic direction of the firm and intend for the business to remain within the family.
	• *Scope:* According to the Family Firm Institute (FFI), family-owned businesses that meet the broad definition above comprise 80 to 90 percent of all business enterprises in North America, 30 to 35 percent of the Fortune 500 companies, and the majority of enterprises internationally. Further, 50 percent of the U.S. Gross Domestic Product (GDP), over $3.3 trillion, is generated by family-owned businesses.
Franchises	• *Definition:* A franchise exists when a firm that already has a successful product or service (franchisor) contracts with another business to be a dealer (franchisee) by using the franchisor's name, trademark, and business system in exchange for a fee. There are several types, but the most common is the business format franchise, in which the franchisor provides a complete plan, or format, for managing the business.
	• *Scope:* According to the International Franchise Association (IFA), franchising accounted for $1 trillion in annual retail sales in the United States since 2000. There are about 320,000 franchise businesses employing more than 8 million people in 75 different industries.
Home-based businesses	• *Definition:* A home-based business, also commonly referred to as SOHO (small office/home office), consists of a company with 20 or fewer employees, including the self-employed, free agents, e-lancers, telecommuters, or other independent professionals working from a home-based setting.
	• *Scope:* According to the National Association of Home-Based Businesses (NAHBB), approximately 20 million businesses are home-based. The U.S. Commerce Department estimates that more than half of all small businesses are home-based.

Exhibit 13.2
Types of Entrepreneurial Ventures

are often very important, the opportunity recognition process involves two phases of activity—discovery and formation—that lead to viable new venture opportunities.[14]

The discovery phase refers to the process of becoming aware of a new business concept.[15] Many entrepreneurs report that their idea for a new venture occurred to them in an instant, as a sort of "Aha!" experience—that is, they had some insight or epiphany, often based on their prior knowledge, that gave them an idea for a new business. This may occur unintentionally, because the discovery of new opportunities is often spontaneous and unexpected. For example, Howard Schultz, CEO of Starbucks, was in Milan, Italy, when he suddenly realized that the coffee-and-conversation café model that was common in Europe would work in the United States as well. According

STRATEGY SPOTLIGHT

Opportunity Recognition: Great Businesses that Started with a Simple Idea

In the founding of a business, there is always a moment when the opportunity is first recognized. The recognition may unfold in tiny steps over time or appear suddenly as an Aha! experience. When founding entrepreneurs act on such realizations, the rest, as they say, is history. And speaking of history, here are a few examples of the initial sparks that eventually resulted in some very big businesses.

Carl Westcott, founder of 1-800-Flowers

While visiting Los Angeles in 1979, Carl Westcott decided to send flowers back home to his wife. It was late but he finally found a florist that was open. The only problem was, it wouldn't take his credit card over the phone. "Bottom line," recalls Westcott, "I didn't send the flowers." While trying to get the florist to take his order, however, he noticed that the word "flowers" had seven digits. The next day he dialed 1-800-356-9377. The backhaul trucker that answered wasn't too surprised—he had already heard from FTD. But Westcott persisted and offered the man $15,000 and 3 percent of the 1-800-FLOWERS business. Both the trucker and Westcott made out pretty well when he sold the business for $4 million just 18 months later.

David Cook, founder of TollTags

When David Cook heard that the Los Alamos National Laboratories in New Mexico was going to implant miniaturized radio frequency chips under the skin of cattle to track their location, he laughed and thought, "That's just insane—and tough to market." Soon after, while driving

Sources: Hall, C. 2004. The big ideas that started here. *Dallas Morning News*, December 26: 1D–6D. www.eds.com; www.hoovers.com; and, www.ntta.org.

on a toll road, he realized the same technology could be used to enable drivers to pay tolls automatically. To prove that TollTags would work, he raised $6 million from investors to build an electronic payment system on a toll road in Dallas, Texas, with the agreement that the tollway authority could scrap the system with just 24 hours notice. "It was by far the riskiest thing I've ever done in my life," recalls Cook. But it paid off. Today the North Texas Tollway Authority sells nearly 1 million TollTags annually. As for opportunity recognition, Cook says, "You have to believe in your idea and your ability to take your accumulated knowledge and intuition and apply that as you build your business."

Ross Perot, founder of Electronic Data Systems (EDS)

Ross Perot was a salesman at IBM when he had his epiphany: Computer customers don't especially care about computer hardware. What they really need is computing *power*. "It was obvious to me . . . that people wanted a system that worked, which included the computer, the software, the whole package," recalls Perot. He took the idea to his bosses who weren't interested. At the time, 80 cents of every dollar spent on computing was for hardware and IBM dominated the market. But Perot knew he was onto something. "I was sitting in a barbershop reading an old *Reader's Digest* that had a quote from Thoreau that said, 'The mass of men lead lives of quiet desperation.' That's when I made the decision that I had to try it." With $1,000 of his wife's money, he launched EDS in 1962. Today, this provider of information technology and business process outsourcing services enjoys annual revenues of about $20 billion.

---

to Schultz, he didn't need to do research to find out if Americans would pay $3 for a cup of coffee—he just *knew*. Starbucks was just a small business at the time but Schultz began literally shaking with excitement about growing it into a bigger business.[16] Strategy Spotlight 13.3 tells how three other highly successful entrepreneurs identified their business opportunities.

Opportunity discovery also may occur as the result of a deliberate search for new venture opportunities or creative solutions to business problems. New venture ideas often emerge only after a concerted effort to identify good opportunities or realistic solutions. It is very similar to a creative process, which may be unstructured and "chaotic" at first but eventually leads to a practical solution or business innovation. To stimulate the discovery of new opportunities, companies often encourage creativity, out-of-the-box thinking, and brainstorming. Consider the example of Oakshire Mushroom Farm, Inc.

While trying to figure out how to recover from its 40 percent decline in market share for shii-take mushrooms, Oakshire came up with an idea that at first seemed ridiculous—selling a product to competitors. "We kicked around a lot of ideas—franchising, expanding geograph-ically to be more local" to supermarkets and restaurants, explained Gary Schroeder, CEO of the Kennett Square, Pennsylvania, grower. "But these other competitors were already there." Finally, they decided to sell rival farms their most unique innovation: a sawdust log for grow-ing shiitakes that reduces the harvest time from four years to four months. The solution worked, and sales increased 45 percent to $5 million in the first year and nearly doubled the next. Now the logs account for about 10 percent of its revenues, and Oakshire has become a vendor within other segments of its industry.[17]

New ventures are often launched because founding entrepreneurs find innovative ways to apply new technologies. This is supported by the statistics in Strategy Spotlight 13.1, which indicates that a majority of patents and innovations come from small firms. Why is this so? Research indicates that entrepreneurial firms are often more successful at discovering radically different technology-based venture opportunities than large firms. Strategy Spotlight 13.4 explains why young firms often have a competitive edge when it comes to technological innovation.

Opportunity formation, which occurs after an opportunity has been identified, involves evaluating an opportunity to determine whether it is viable and strong enough to be developed into a full-fledged new venture. Ideas that have been developed by new-product groups or in brainstorming sessions are tested by various methods, includ-ing talking to potential target customers and discussing operational requirements with production or logistics managers. A technique known as feasibility analysis is used to evaluate these and other critical success factors. This type of analysis often leads to the decision that a new venture project should be discontinued. If the venture concept continues to seem viable, a more formal business plan may be developed.

Among the most important factors to evaluate is the market potential for the prod-uct or service. Established firms tend to operate in established markets. They have to adjust to market trends and to shifts in consumer demand, of course, but they usually have a customer base for which they are already filling a marketplace need. New ventures, in contrast, must first determine whether a market exists for the product or service they are contemplating. Thus, a critical element of opportunity recognition is assessing to what extent the opportunity is viable *in the marketplace.* Most definitions of entrepreneurial opportunity suggest that, for it to be an opportunity, it must be viable in terms of its potential to earn a profit.

Several of the techniques suggested in Chapters 2 and 3 can be used to assess the market potential of a business concept. Questions that might emerge in a test of the mar-ket for a new product or service include:

- Do market forces support the product's introduction? For example, is market demand growing because of shifting demographics or sociocultural trends?
- How is the need that it addresses currently being met?
- What firms would be the closest competitors?
- How are competitive products priced?
- What is its value proposition—that is, in what ways does it add value relative to products or services already being sold?
- Can its value be enhanced by combining it with other value-adding activities?

For a more complete assessment of how well a new business concept would be received, marketing techniques such as product concept testing, focus groups, and/or extended trial runs with end users are often necessary. In some respects, assessing

STRATEGY SPOTLIGHT

Technological Innovation: Why Entrepreneurial Firms Have a Competitive Advantage

Young firms have a knack for seeing things differently. As a result, they tend to be net winners in the game of technological innovation. This was also the finding of Harvard Professor Clayton M. Christensen, author of *The Innovator's Dilemma.* In his study of disruptive technologies (technologies that change the rules of an industry, similar to radical innovations) in the computer disk drive industry, Christensen found that new entrants outperformed incumbent firms—"from the simplest to the most radical, the firms that led the industry in every instance of developing and adopting disruptive technologies were entrants to the industry, not its incumbent leaders."

What makes entrepreneurial firms better innovators? For one thing, they are able to recognize possibilities and approach problems with a fresh perspective. They are not burdened by old ways of thinking or beliefs about how things have always been. Here are three examples of what entrepreneurial firms do to excel at innovation:

1. ***Painting pictures, not assembling puzzles.*** Innovative thinking requires a broad perspective, just as a painter needs to draw on a full palette of colors when creating an image that is wholly new. Entrepreneurial firms often have the freedom to see the big picture as well as its component parts. Large companies, because of the constraints under which they operate, are often required to approach innovation as they would assembling a puzzle—piecing together a set number of predetermined shapes (in the form of personnel, budgets, existing technologies, and so forth) that someone else has devised.

   Consider the example of Carol Latham, a staff chemist at British Petroleum (BP), who discovered how plastic parts could be used to keep computers cool. When she approached the top brass with her idea at BP's Ohio research lab where she worked, they weren't interested. It turns out that BP, generally considered to be entrepreneurially minded, was having a bad year—oil stock values were down—and the company did not want to fund any initiatives that detracted from its core business. Perhaps more importantly, most of Latham's colleagues were researching ceramics, and her plastics idea seemed threatening to their efforts. BP just couldn't see what she could see. But Latham was sure she was on to something. She quit her job, labored for months in her basement with mixing bowls and a blender, and formed Thermagon, Inc.

Once she had an actual product—superthin polymer sheets cut to fit between computer components, they sold themselves. After being named to the *Inc.* 500 list of fastest growing companies three years in a row and reaching annual revenues of $19 million, Thermagon was acquired by Laird Technologies of St. Louis, Missouri, in April 2004.

2. ***Solving the big guy's little problems.*** Small firms often succeed by forming alliances with larger firms. And quite often, the big firms need the help. As an incumbent firm grows, the task of management becomes more complicated. Some large firms find it difficult to manage internal processes because their problem-solving capability does not match the complexity of their problems. The innovation process is loaded with choices and uncertainties, making it one of the areas where large firms often lose their edge. One of the ways large firms deal with such problems is by turning to small firms for help.

   Foster-Miller is an engineering and technology development firm that specializes in innovative solutions. With its staff of 200 engineers and scientists, Foster-Miller tackles problems the big firms can't seem to solve. For example, Nabisco, the largest cookie maker in the world, was having trouble making a low-fat version of its Fig Newton because the fat-free batter kept sticking to the cutting equipment. Unable to solve the problem, Nabisco called in Foster-Miller, which designed a noncontact cookie cutter that solved the problem.

3. ***Setting up a big tent.*** Recall from Strategy Spotlight 12.3 the closed model of innovation. According to that perspective, many large firms believe they should "go it alone and do it ourselves" when it comes to innovation. The problem with that approach, according to *Open Innovation* author Henry Chesbrough, is that firms miss out on talent and resources that could make the innovation process more efficient and cost effective. Additionally, other firms that might benefit from an innovation are left out or left to discover it on their own.

   MicroUnity, Inc., a designer of microprocessor software for communications, approaches innovation differently. For one thing, it accepts the fact that it is small. As a result, the private ***(continued)***

marketability is as much an art as it is a science. Nevertheless, it is essential to create a model of how the product or service will perform in the marketplace in order to develop a plan for launching it. Thus, the aim of the opportunity recognition process is to explore and test a new venture concept in order to determine whether it is a viable opportunity.

Characteristics of Good Opportunities

The opportunity recognition process involves discovering and forming business concepts into realistic business opportunities. For an opportunity to be viable, it needs to have four qualities.[18]

- *Attractive.* The opportunity must be attractive in the marketplace; that is, there must be market demand for the new product or service.

- *Achievable.* The opportunity must be practical and physically possible.

- *Durable.* The opportunity must be attractive long enough for the development and deployment to be successful; that is, the window of opportunity must be open long enough for it to be worthwhile.

- *Value creating.* The opportunity must be potentially profitable; that is, the benefits must surpass the cost of development by a significant margin.

If a new business concept meets these criteria, two other factors must be considered before the opportunity is launched as a business. First, the readiness and skills of the entrepreneurial founder or team must be evaluated. Do the founders have the necessary knowledge and experience to make the venture successful? Second, the availability and access to resources needed for the launch must be considered. Given an analysis of the start-up costs and operational expenses, can the venture obtain the necessary funding? These three factors—the nature of the opportunity itself, the resources available to undertake it, and the characteristics of the entrepreneur(s) pursuing it—are essential for the successful launch of a new venture.[19] Exhibit 13.3 identifies the three factors that are needed to successfully proceed—opportunity, resources, and entrepreneur(s). In the next section, we address the issue of entrepreneurial resources; following that, we address the importance of entrepreneurial leadership.

Exhibit 13.3   Opportunity Analysis Framework

Sources: Based on Timmons, J. A., & Spinelli, S. 2004.
New venture creation (6th ed.). New York: McGraw-Hill/
Irwin; and Bygrave, W. D. 1997. The entrepreneurial
process. In W. D. Bygrave (Ed.), *The portable MBA in
entrepreneurship* (2nd ed.). New York: Wiley.

>>Entrepreneurial Resources

As Exhibit 13.3 indicates, resources are an essential component of a successful entrepreneurial launch. One of the major challenges that entrepreneurial firms face is a lack
of resources. For start-ups, the most important resource is usually money. A new firm
typically has to expend substantial sums just to start up the business. However, financial resources are not the only kind of resource a young firm needs. Human capital and
social capital are also important during the early days of a new venture and throughout
the life of a small business. Some small firms also rely on government resources to
help them thrive.

Young and small firms have many of the same needs as larger firms—financial
resources, skilled and experienced workers, and the ability to operate in a network of
beneficial relationships. But they also have unique needs that stem from being young or
small. Nearly all young firms face the liability of newness.[20] This phrase refers to the
vulnerability that most new firms feel because they lack experience, are unknown in their
industry, and are unfamiliar to customers. Until they have proven themselves, young
firms lack credibility: Banks often will not lend them money, and suppliers may not
extend them credit.

To overcome the liability of newness and build credibility, therefore, founders must
find practical ways to obtain resources. These include financial as well as other resources.
In this section we will address some of the resource requirements of entrepreneurial firms
and how they can meet their needs.

New-Venture Financing

Hand-in-hand with the importance of markets (and marketing) to new-venture creation,
start-up firms must also have financing. In fact, the level of available financing is often
a strong determinant of how the business is launched and its eventual success. Cash
finances are, of course, highly important. But access to capital, such as a line of credit
or favorable payment terms with a supplier, can also help a start-up to succeed.

A new firm's financing requirements and sources of funds typically change as it grows. In the next two sections, we address sources of financing in the earlier and later stages of launching a new venture.

Early-Stage Financing   The vast majority of new firms are low-budget start-ups launched with personal savings and the contributions of family and friends.[21] Even among firms included in the *Entrepreneur* list of the 100 fastest-growing new businesses in a recent year, 61 percent reported that their start-up funds came from personal savings.[22] Although bank financing, public financing, and venture capital are important sources of small business finance, these types of financial support are typically available only after a company has started to conduct business and generate sales. Therefore, the founders usually carry the initial burden of financing most new firms.

The burdens are many: renting space, buying inventory, installing phones and equipment, obtaining insurance, and paying salaries. How does a cash-strapped entrepreneur make ends meet? One way is by *bootstrapping.* The term is used to describe persons who rely on their personal resources and resourcefulness to succeed. Applied to entrepreneurs, it refers to techniques used to minimize borrowing and avoid selling parts of a business to investors or venture capitalists. For the young start-up, this involves getting the most out of every dollar and doing without anything but the bare necessities. It may mean buying used equipment, operating out of a basement, or forgoing a new car purchase in order to reinvest in the business.

The typical new business owner has just $4,000 invested the day the business opens.[23] Therefore, bootstrapping to make ends meet is a common practice among start-up entrepreneurs. For example, Brad and Gia Boyle of Moab, Utah, got their start running Walkabout Travel Gear out of a 37-foot recreational vehicle. Using a motor home as an office not only helped them save money on rent, it also kept them in touch with their industry—travel. Their bootstrapping philosophy is expressed by a quote on their Web site: "A tight budget is the mother of adventure." In a recent year, the business brought in about $250,000.[23]

Bootstrapping may shift a start-up's priorities. To successfully bootstrap, a new firm may have to get cash-generating products or services to market quickly in order to jump-start cash flow. As a result, the new firm may postpone development activities or investments in technology. Consider the example of Stacy's Pita Chip Co.:

> In 1996 founders Mark and Stacy Andrus were operating a successful pita-wrap sandwich business that was ready to grow. But customers kept asking for the baked chips they made every night from leftover pita bread and handed out free to customers waiting in line. "We thought we could get bigger faster with the chips," said Stacy. The couple, who were still paying off six-figure student loans, decided to take their chips nationwide. The business they created is a model of bootstrapping efficiency. The paper sign on the door, folding tables, and used dining room chairs are the first signs of their spartan approach to business. They also saved over $250,000 buying used equipment. "Everything goes into the business," said Stacy, who takes home a scavenger-level salary. But it has paid off. Their baked pita chips' annual revenues recently hit $1.3 million, with sales in 37 states.[24]

If personal savings and bootstrapping efforts are insufficient to finance the business, entrepreneurs must turn to other sources of funds. One of the most common mistakes business founders make, as suggested by the Great Plains Airline opening incident, is trying to launch a business with insufficient capital. Thus, seeking external sources of financing is often essential for start-up success.

Funding that comes from others, unless it is a gift, will take one of two forms—debt or equity. There are important differences between the two types of financing:

- **Debt.** This refers to borrowed funds, such as an interest-bearing loan, that must be repaid regardless of firm performance. To obtain it usually requires that some business or personal assets be used as collateral.

- **Equity.** This refers to invested funds, such as in shares of stock, that increase or decrease in value depending on the performance of the business. To obtain it usually requires that business founders give up some ownership and control of the business.

There are many possible sources of external funding. One of the most important sources is family and friends. This can be an especially helpful resource during the very early stages of a new venture. Among the *Entrepreneur* 100 fastest-growing firms, 18 percent received start-up financing from family and friends.[25] This type of financing may be in the form of either debt or equity.

To preserve cash, another technique start-up businesses use involves relying on unconventional or creative financing sources. For example, credit card financing is one of the fastest growing techniques for financing a start-up. About half of all small businesses finance their launch or expansion with credit cards.[26] Another example is supplier financing in which suppliers give buyers as long as 60 or 90 days to pay for purchases. This arrangement, which may also help suppliers increase sales, is an alternative that can help a cash-strapped start-up.[27]

Later-Stage Financing   Once an entrepreneur has a going concern, certain types of financing become more readily available. Young firms that have contracted with a first customer or can demonstrate several months of sales are considered a better risk by investors and creditors. Even "angel" investors—private individuals who provide seed capital during the early stages of a new venture—favor companies that already have a winning business model and dominance in a market niche.[28] According to Cal Simmons, coauthor of *Every Business Needs an Angel,* "I would much rather talk to an entrepreneur who has already put his money and his effort into proving the concept. And I think most angels I know feel the same way right now."[29]

Angel investors are an important source of equity investment for many entrepreneurial firms. They often invest modest amounts—under $1 million—and help firms that are trying to grow beyond their initial start-up success. Angels also provide mentoring and contacts for young firms that are trying to become established.

Start-ups that involve large capital investments or extensive development costs—such as manufacturing or engineering firms that are trying to commercialize an innovative product—may have high cash requirements soon after they are founded. Others need financing only when they are on the brink of rapid growth. To obtain such funding, entrepreneurial firms often seek venture capital. Venture capital is a form of private equity financing through which entrepreneurs raise money by selling shares in the new venture. In contrast to angel investors, who are actively engaged in investing their own money, venture capital companies are organized to place the funds of private investors into lucrative business opportunities. Equity financing, however, often comes with strings attached. On the one hand, venture capitalists often have high performance expectations and demand a regular accounting. On the other hand, sometimes these "strings" can enhance a firm's chances for success. Venture capital groups often provide important managerial advice, links to key contacts in an industry, and the peace of mind of knowing that financial backers support your project. But founders who use venture capital forfeit part of the payoff if the venture succeeds. Further, they must agree to let the venture capitalists influence management decisions.

Venture capital is an important source of funding for certain types of entrepreneurial firms.[30] Entrepreneurs who seek large infusions of capital usually turn to some form of private capital financing. Venture capital was a primary driver of the rapid growth in Internet start-ups. Although loans by venture capitalists have declined sharply since their rapid expansion during the Internet boom of 1999 to 2000, annual venture capital investing remains over $21 billion.[31] Despite the importance of venture capital to many fast-growing firms, the vast majority of funding for young and small firms comes from informal sources such as family and friends. Exhibit 13.4, based on the *Global Entrepreneurship Monitor* survey of entrepreneurial firms, demonstrates this dramatic difference. A closer look, however, reveals an interesting fact: Firms that obtain venture capital receive funding of about $2.6 million each. In contrast, companies that obtain funding from informal sources typically receive only about $10,000 each. Although relatively few companies receive venture funding, they are attractive to venture capitalists because their profit potential and impact on innovation, job growth, and wealth creation tends to be much greater.

Venture capital groups also help start-ups by sponsoring independent business incubators. Recall from Chapter 12 the use of in-house incubators by large corporations to

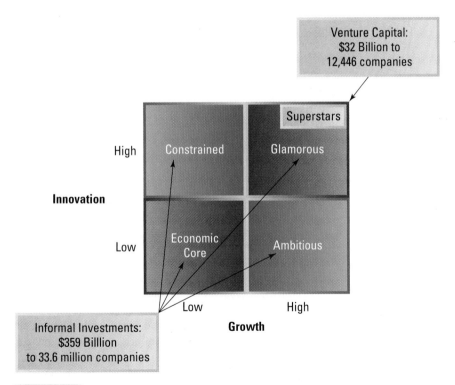

Exhibit 13.4   How Different Types of Young Firms Are Financed: Informal Investment versus Venture Capital

Source: Reynolds, P. D., Bygrave, W. D., & Autio, E. 2004. *Global Entrepreneurship Monitor: 2003 executive report.* Babson College, London Business School, and the Kauffman Foundation. The classification of companies system used by GEM is based on Kirchhoff, B. 1994. *Entrepreneurship and dynamic capitalism.* London: Praeger.

launch new ventures. Incubators are also used by or in conjunction with venture capital groups to help facilitate the growth of both start-up and later-stage companies. The venture capital groups provide management assistance; the incubators provide office space, technology infrastructure, and business support services. An example is TechSpace, an international network of incubators with offices in New York, California, and several other global locations. Besides providing the usual incubator services, TechSpace and its venture capital partners often invest in the young firms that reside in its office communities.[32]

Angels and venture capitalists provide equity investments for entrepreneurial firms. Another important source of funding is from debt. The primary provider of debt financing for new ventures is commercial banks. Although credit cards often provide an important source of funding for very young firms (see Exhibit 13.4), banks provide an important source of ongoing funding. Because banks make their money by receiving interest on the loans as well as a return of principal, they are keenly interested in the firm's ability to repay the loan. That is why businesses with a track record of generating revenues are more likely to get bank loans. Besides cash flow, banks are also interested in collateral—assets that an entrepreneurial firm could sell to repay its loan in the event of a default. As a result, one of the ways that young firms often get start-up capital is through a home equity loan. Why? Because the house provides collateral which, in the event that the entrepreneur fails to make payments, the bank could force the homeowner to sell to satisfy its debt.

Clearly, financial resources are essential for new ventures and small businesses.[33] But other types of resources are also vitally important. In the next section, we will address the role of human capital, social capital, and government resources in the entrepreneurial start-up process.

Other Entrepreneurial Resources

Whether an entrepreneur starts by bootstrapping or brings a large sum of assets to a new venture, founders often turn to three other types of resources that were discussed in Chapter 4: human capital, social capital, and government resources. Young and small firms have many of the same needs as larger firms—skilled and experienced workers and the ability to operate in a network of beneficial relationships. But they also have unique needs that stem from being young or small. By relying on the talents of other people, their network of contacts, and support services provided by government programs, entrepreneurial firms can often strengthen their ability to survive and succeed.

Human Capital   The most important human capital may be in the founding team. Bankers, venture capitalists, and angel investors who invest in start-up firms and small businesses agree that the most important asset an entrepreneurial firm can have is strong and skilled management. According to Stephen Gaal, founding member of Walnut Venture Associates, venture investors do not invest in businesses; instead "We invest in people . . . very smart people with very high integrity." Managers need to have a strong base of experience and extensive domain knowledge, as well as an ability to make rapid decisions and change direction as shifting circumstances may require. Additionally, among start-ups, more is better. New ventures that are started by teams of three, four, or five entrepreneurs are more likely to succeed in the long run than are ventures launched by "lone wolf" entrepreneurs.[34]

Social Capital   New ventures founded by entrepreneurs who have extensive social contacts are more likely to succeed than are ventures started without the support of a social network.[35] This is one of the major avenues for overcoming the liability problem of newness. Even though a firm may be new, if the founders have contacts who will vouch for them, they gain exposure and build legitimacy faster.[36] This support can come from several sources: prior jobs, industry organizations, and local business groups such as the chamber of commerce. These contacts can all contribute to a growing network that provides support for the young or small firm. Janina Pawlowski, cofounder of the online lending company E-Loan, attributes part of her success to the strong advisors she persuaded to serve on her board of directors, including Tim Koogle, CEO of Yahoo![37]

Strategic alliances represent a type of social capital that can be especially important to young and small firms. Strategy Spotlight 13.5 presents a few examples of alliances and some potential pitfalls of using alliances.

Government Resources   In the United States, the federal government is an important resource for many young and small businesses. It provides support for entrepreneurial firms in two key arenas—financing and government contracting. The Small Business Administration (SBA) has several loan guarantee programs designed to support the growth and development of entrepreneurial firms. The government itself does not lend money but underwrites loans made by banks to small businesses, thus reducing the risk associated with lending to firms that have unproven records. The SBA also offers training, counseling, and support services through its local offices and Small Business Development Centers.[38]

Another key area of support is in government contracting. Programs sponsored by the SBA and other government agencies ensure that small businesses have the opportunity to bid on contracts to provide goods and services to the government. Strategy Spotlight 13.6 on page 490 describes how several small firms have benefited from government contracts.

State and local governments also have hundreds of programs to provide funding, contracts, and other support for new ventures and small businesses. Local economic development initiatives such as the Southwest Minnesota Initiative Fund (SWMIF) are often designed specifically to stimulate small business activity. State-sponsored microenterprise funds such as the Utah Microenterprise Loan Fund (UMLF) provide funding as well as training for companies with fewer than five employees that are seeking less than $25,000.[39] Consider the example of Lissa D'Aquanni, who launched a gourmet chocolate business in her basement in 1998. As the business grew, she needed more space. To get it, she combined creative financing with government support.

D'Aquanni had her eye on an abandoned building close to her home, but it cost $95,000 and needed $260,000 of renovation—more than her business could afford. So she turned to the local community. First, she asked for the support of local residents who were attracted to her plans to revitalize an empty building in the neighborhood and helped raised $25,000. Then the Albany Local Development Corporation, an economic development group, loaned her $95,000 to buy the building. A local credit union provided her with a government guaranteed loan to begin the renovations. A community development group helped her apply to a state program that funds energy-efficient upgrades such as windows, siding, and light fixtures. A matching grant program to encourage commercial development provided funds to upgrade the buildings facade. Eventually, she got the whole job done. "There are pockets of money out there, whether it be municipalities, counties, chambers of commerce," says Bill Brigham, director of the Albany Small Business Development Center. "Those are the loan programs that no one seems to have information about. A lot of these programs will not require the collateral and cash that is typical of traditional [loans]."[40]

As you can see from the example above, the government provides numerous funding opportunities for small business and new ventures. Although working with the government sometimes has its drawbacks in terms of issues of regulation and time-consuming decision

STRATEGY SPOTLIGHT

Strategic Alliances: A Key Entrepreneurial Resource

Strategic alliances provide a key avenue for growth by entrepreneurial firms. By partnering with other companies, young or small firms can expand or give the appearance of entering numerous markets and/or handling a range of operations. Here are several examples of alliances that have been used to extend or strengthen entrepreneurial firms:

Technology Alliances

Often large firms seek out tech-savvy entrepreneurial firms that have mastered a new technology. The alliance allows the large firm to enhance its capabilities and expands the revenue and reach of the smaller firm. Such was the case when Intel announced in 2005 that it was forming an alliance with ArrayComm, LLC, a start-up formed to develop "smart" antenna technology. These antennas can be used to provide wireless Internet access for whole cities using a technology known as WiMax, an extended version of WiFi technology. Intel is a strong proponent of WiMax and sought the alliance to help it develop new chips that meet the standards needed for communicating with ArrayComm's smart antenna technology.

Manufacturing Alliances

Outsourcing with foreign manufacturers was once considered something that only big firms could manage. But enhanced global communications and a worldwide spirit of entrepreneurship is changing all that. Not only are some firms "born global" as discussed in Chapter 7, but also there are new ventures that can profitably launch only because their products are manufactured overseas. This is how Philip McCaleb was able to introduce the Stella scooter, a Vespa knock-off manufactured in India. McCaleb had run a scooter parts business for nine years when he learned that Vespa was going to end its production alliance with scooter maker LML. McCaleb and a staff of three partnered with LML and in just three years rolled out 2,500 Stellas. McCaleb expects to double that number by 2006. The scooters sell for just $2,699—37 percent less than a comparable Vespa.

Sources: Clark, D. 2005. Intel deal could link start-up to nascent WiMax technology. *The Wall Street Journal*, June 22: B5; Copeland, M. V., & Tilin, A. 2005. Get someone to build it. *Business 2.0*, 6(5): 88–90; Monahan, J. 2005. All systems grow. *Entrepreneur*, March: 78–82; Prince, C. J. 2005. Foreign affairs. *Entrepreneur*, March: 56; Torres, N. L. 2005. Love thine enemy. *Entrepreneur*, March: 102; and Weaver, K. M., & Dickson, P. 2004. Strategic alliances. In W. J. Dennis, Jr. (Ed.), *NFIB national small business poll*. Washington, DC: National Federation of Independent Business.

Retail Alliances

One of the best ways for small businesses to extend their sales is through licensing. Although the company gives up some profits with a license agreement, it also shifts some of the financial burden and expands its market. This helped Taggies, Inc., a maker of blankets and toys with satiny tags, expand its sales from $2 million to $3 million in one year when children's book publisher Scholastica, Inc., licensed its products for use in book promotions.

Licensing can also be used to go global. Specialty products—the types sometimes made by entrepreneurial firms—often seem more exotic when sold in another country. This was the view of a Japanese vendor that approached Meliorra, an Idaho-based beauty supply manufacturer, about selling its products in Japan. The young company was skeptical at first because it required a shift in priorities. But once it crunched the numbers, Meliorra realized it was an opportunity not to be missed. The deal is estimated to account for 30 percent of its 2005 sales—about $4.5 million.

Alliances with Competitors

Lee Labrada, founder of a line of low-carb food products name CarbWatchers, was surprised one day when he was surfing the Internet and found a company using the very same name for a low-carb weight loss center in New York City. Because he trademarked the name, Labrada figured he could solve the problem by sending a cease and desist letter. But then he had a better idea. When the owner of the New York company called to resolve the problem, he suggested she carry his products in her store. Both would profit from the partnership as well as build their brand awareness. "We came to a meeting of the minds," says Labrada, one that helped his company grow to $20 million in yearly sales.

According to the National Federation of Independent Business (NFIB), nearly two-thirds of small businesses currently hold or have held some type of alliance. Strategic alliances among entrepreneurial firms can take many different forms. Exhibit 13.5 shows the different types of partnering that small businesses and small manufacturers in the NFIB study often use.

Although such alliances often sound good, there are also potential pitfalls. Lack of oversight and control is one danger of partnering with foreign firms. Problems with product quality, timely delivery, and receiving payments can also sour an alliance relationship *(continued)*

(continued) if it is not carefully managed. With technology alliances, there is a risk that big firms may take advantage of the technological know-how of their entrepreneurial partners. However, even with these potential problems, strategic alliances provide a good means for young and small firms to develop and grow.

Type of Alliance and/or Long-Term Agreement*	Small Manufacturers	Small Businesses
Licensing	20.0%	32.5%
Export/Import	14.4%	7.3%
Franchise	5.0%	5.3%
Marketing	18.0%	25.2%
Distribution	20.1%	20.5%
Production	26.5%	11.3%
Product/Services R&D	12.2%	12.6%
Process R&D	6.7%	5.3%
Purchaser/Supplier	23.5%	13.9%
Outside Contracting	23.2%	28.5%

*Columns add to over 100 percent because firms may use multiple alliances.

Exhibit 13.5 *Use of Strategic Alliances by Small Businesses and Small Manufacturers*

Source: From Weaver, K. M., & Dickson, P. 2004. Strategic Alliances. In W. J. Dennis, Jr. (Ed.), *NFIB National Small Business Poll.* Washington, DC: National Federation of Independent Business. Reprinted with permission.

making, programs to support young and small firms constitute an important resource for firms to use during the start-up and growth process.

Clearly, the resource needs of new ventures are enormous. Unlike established firms, which often have a stockpile of resources—both human and physical—to draw upon, entrepreneurial firms are usually starting from scratch. Meeting the resource requirements of a new venture can be critically important to its success in the short run and over the long term. In the next section we will consider another type of capability that is especially important for the success of small or young firms: entrepreneurial leadership.

>>Entrepreneurial Leadership

Whether a venture is launched by an individual entrepreneur or an entrepreneurial team, effective leadership is needed. Launching a new venture requires a special kind of leadership. It involves courage, belief in your convictions, and the energy to work hard even in difficult circumstances. Entrepreneurs and small business owners work for themselves. They don't have bosses to inspire them or tell them what to do. Their next paycheck will arrive only as a result of their own efforts. They must oversee all aspects of a company's operations as well as monitor quality and performance. Yet these are the very challenges that motivate most business owners. Entrepreneurs put themselves to the test and get their satisfaction from acting independently, overcoming obstacles, and thriving financially. To

Government Work: It's Good Enough for Many Small Businesses

Homeland security, the war in Afghanistan, the rebuilding of Iraq—these projects and more have been keeping the U.S. government busy since the September 11 tragedies. To meet the needs created by these initiatives, more and more private companies are being called on to serve as contractors. Federal spending on information technology (IT) alone increased 18 percent from 2002 to 2003 to $59 billion, and it is expected to grow. This has allowed companies such as Cyveillance, a northern Virginia start-up that specializes in Internet espionage software, to grow its business by providing online monitoring services for the government.

To encourage businesses to bid on contracts, government agencies are proactively seeking bidders. This has created numerous opportunities for small businesses, because federal law requires that prime contracts use subcontractors on any job that is larger than $500,000. Although the big contracts go to major contractors like Boeing, Unisys, and Lockheed Martin, there are many sub-contracting opportunities. This is how Gryphon Technologies, an IT logistics company, got its start. Its first contract was a small job for Northrop Grumman. Although at the time it seemed to founder Pam Braden like a low-level opportunity, she did not hesitate to take it. This led to bigger contracts, and now Gryphon is a prime contractor for the Department of Defense. "If you want to be a large business, which I want to be," says Braden, "you need to network the big companies and the government itself."

Not all of the government work is IT related. Thousands of projects, ranging from high-end engineering to maintenance and supply projects, are available to small business subcontractors. There are many peacetime opportunities available as well. The Small Business Administration (SBA) in cooperation with the National Science Foundation (NSF) runs a program known as Small Business Innovation Research (SBIR). The program recently funded nearly $2 billion in research, including $1 billion for the Department of Defense in 2005. Here is a description of SBIR's goals from its Web site:

> SBIR targets the entrepreneurial sector because that is where most innovation and innovators thrive. However, the risk and expense of conducting serious R&D efforts are often beyond the means of many small businesses. By reserving a specific percentage of federal R&D funds for small business, SBIR protects the small business and enables it to compete on the same level as larger businesses. SBIR funds the critical start-up and development stages, and it encourages the commercialization of the technology, product, or service, which, in turn, stimulates the U.S. economy.

As these various programs suggest, the federal government is potentially a rich resource for small firms, which supports innovation and the successful commercialization of new venture opportunities. Dealing with the government, however, can be time consuming and involve lots of "red tape"—that is, reporting requirements and regulations that are quite demanding. Even so, many small companies owe their success to the support they have gotten from government-sponsored programs.

Sources: Chen, C. Y. 2003. Getting a piece of the D.C. pie. *Fortune*, May 12:34; Kurtz, R. 2003. What your country can do for you. *Inc.*, July: 33–34; www.cyveillance.com; and www.sba.gov/sbir/.

do so, they must embody three characteristics of leadership—vision, dedication and drive, and commitment to excellence—and pass these on to all those who work with them.

Vision

Vision may be an entrepreneur's most important asset. The entrepreneur has to envision realities that do not yet exist. This may consist of a new product or a unique service. It may include a competitive goal, such as besting a close competitor. For many entrepreneurs, the vision may be personal—building something from scratch, being your own boss, making a difference, achieving financial security. In every case, entrepreneurs must exercise a kind of transformational leadership that aims to create something new and, in some way, change their world. Not all founders of new ventures succeed. Indeed, the majority fail. But without a vision, most entrepreneurs would never even get a new business off the ground.

The idea of creating something new is captured in the vision of Paul Robbins, founder of Caribbean Shipping & Cold Storage.

> In a run-down part of Jacksonville, Florida, Paul Robbins envisioned opportunity. Where others saw a stretch of ramshackle houses, a lot strewn with rubble, and an abandoned warehouse, Robbins saw promise and profits. Caribbean Shipping & Cold Storage handles food products that need cold storage on their way to Puerto Rico and other Caribbean islands. In the past, shipments from far-flung U.S. locations might be transferred from truck to train to ship as many as six times. Instead of making arrangements with all those carriers, customers such as Outback Steakhouse and the Ritz-Carlton have Robbins handle the entire shipment. So why the run-down lot in Jacksonville? Because it's one block from Interstate 95 and only half a mile from Interstate 10. CSX train lines are so close that train whistles interrupt meetings. And the lot is adjacent to Jacksonville's shipping port. In other words, it's a crossroads—one that has paid off. Caribbean Shipping's revenues rose from $3.5 million to $20 million in just four years.[41]

By itself, however, just having a vision is not enough. The new venture idea must be effectively articulated as well. To develop support, get financial backing, and attract employees, entrepreneurial leaders must share their vision with others. The following leadership skills are needed to enact an entrepreneurial vision:[42]

- *Be able to communicate with a wide audience.* Entrepreneurial founders must reach a diverse collection of stakeholders. Understanding how these constituencies differ and fitting the vision message to their concerns is an important element of good leadership.
- *Be willing to make unpopular decisions.* As the new venture concept is developed, tough decisions will have to be made that define and shape the boundaries of the vision. Good leaders realize their decisions will not please everyone, but they still have to make them and move on.
- *Be determined to make sure your message gets through.* Employees of a venture start-up must have a clear sense of the leader's vision. But it's not enough to just make a vision statement. Good leaders must demonstrate how it is defining the direction of the company so the employees internalize it.
- *Create and implement quality systems and methods that will survive.* For a vision to be meaningful on a daily basis, leaders need to think of it as a tool. As such, it can be used to identify benchmarks that are needed to maintain quality, control outcomes, and measure success.

Creating and articulating a vision provide an essential starting point for an entrepreneurial venture. Without enthusiasm and perseverance, however, many ventures never get off the ground. Next, we turn to the important qualities of dedication and drive.

Dedication and Drive

Dedication and drive are key success factors for the start-up entrepreneur. Dedication and drive are reflected in hard work. They require patience, stamina, and a willingness to work long hours. One of the key reasons that start-up businesses fail is that the founders lack commitment and neglect the business. Thus, drive involves internal motivation, while dedication calls for an intellectual commitment to the enterprise that keeps the entrepreneur going even in the face of bad news or poor luck. Entrepreneurs typically have a strong enthusiasm, not just for their venture but for life in general. As a result, their dedication and drive are like a magnet that draws people to the business and builds confidence in what the entrepreneurs are doing. Consider the example of Bill Nguyen.

Bill Nguyen is the founder and CEO of Seven Networks, a wireless software development start-up. Nguyen, who is only 30 years old and sleeps just three hours a night, has already been a part of six high-tech start-ups. One month after selling his previous start-up, Onebox.com, to Openwave Systems for $850 million, Nguyen launched Seven Networks and started raising venture capital. Initially, the venture capital firm Ignition and Greylock told him, "Bill, we love you, but it's not going to work." This didn't stop Nguyen. He went home and worked on the technical problems for three days straight with no sleep. When he showed up at Ignition's offices with a revised plan, he had solved the problem. Soon thereafter, the venture capitalists pledged $34 million to Nguyen's Seven Networks venture. According to Brad Silverberg, CEO at Ignition, "He's a rocket; you just strap in and try to hold on."[43]

Clearly, Nguyen is an example of a driven entrepreneur who has used his personal experience and sheer stamina to make his businesses succeed. Such dedication may be more important for some entrepreneurial firms. However, a business built on the heroic efforts of one person may suffer in the long run, especially if something happens to that person. Dedication and drive are important to success. But even hard-charging entrepreneurs can fail if they don't make an effort to do quality work or lack the competencies to achieve their aims. It is this commitment to excellence that we turn to next.

Commitment to Excellence

Successfully managing the many elements of an entrepreneurial start-up requires a commitment to excellence. As we learned previously, new firms are often vulnerable because they lack credibility and experience. To improve the chances of survival, entrepreneurial founders must devote themselves to surpassing the performance of other competitors. To do so, they need to develop a sensitivity to how the elements of their value chain fit together and contribute to overall success. To achieve excellence, therefore, venture founders and small business owners must:

- Understand the customer.
- Provide quality products and services.
- Manage the business knowledgeably and expertly.
- Pay attention to details.
- Learn continuously.

Having this type of "whole organization" perspective can help a venture founder manage the synergies that might exist between different value-adding functions in a firm's value chain. For the firm to survive and become successful, the entrepreneurial leader must manage a firm's value proposition and set high standards for quality and customer service. Consider the example of Sue Bhatia and Rose International:

Rose International is a fast-growing information technology firm located in St. Louis, Missouri. Its CEO is Sue Bhatia, whose commitment to excellence helped her firm grow to 250 employees in just seven years despite its being a minority, female-owned firm in a male-dominated industry. Bhatia said, "I think it's important to remember that the customer is looking for good service. They don't care what your gender or race is. They want to see you deliver your service better than anyone, every time. If you can do that, you have a chance." According to Joe Hartmann, president of Digital Dimensions, Inc., who hired Bhatia's company to provide database architecture and network management solutions, Rose is a model of excellence. "Rose International has delivered more than promised since day one," Hartmann said. "They listen, and have an ability to draw upon their nationwide resources to provide the best solution possible."[44]

Another indicator of an entrepreneur's commitment to excellence is what kind of people they surround themselves with. Founders who think they can "do it all" and fail to recognize the importance of drawing on the talents and experience of others often fail.

Successful entrepreneurs often report that they owe their success to hiring people smarter than themselves to make things happen.

In his book *Good to Great,* Jim Collins makes an important point: Great companies are typically not led by lone-wolf leaders. Building a start-up on the vision or charisma of a single person can hinder a young firm, because when that person leaves, it creates a vacuum that may be hard to fill. In fact, the reason some companies never go from good to great is because they never fill the void left by the founder. Instead, business leaders with a commitment to excellence recognize that skilled and experienced people are needed to make the business successful. Such people are themselves leaders who attract other top-quality people to the organization.[45]

Another important practice is to let people go who don't fit with the company's culture. Even skilled persons can create problems for a firm if they do not embrace the company's goals and work ethic. Success requires focused and disciplined action. In the case of employees, that means leaders must have a willingness to get rid of people who are not working out. In an excellent company, says Collins, "Those people who do not share the company's core values find themselves surrounded by corporate antibodies and ejected like a virus."[46]

Although entrepreneurs must also exhibit other qualities of strong leadership, as we have suggested in earlier chapters, the combined elements of vision, dedication, drive, and commitment to excellence are especially important to the start-up entrepreneur. Next, we will turn to the elements of entrepreneurial strategy that are commonly associated with successful new venture creation.

>>Entrepreneurial Strategy

Successfully creating new ventures requires several ingredients. As indicated in Exhibit 13.3, three factors are necessary—a viable opportunity, sufficient resources, and a skilled and dedicated entrepreneur or entrepreneurial team. The previous three sections have addressed these requirements. Once these elements are in place, the new venture needs a strategy. For any given venture, the best strategy for the enterprise will be determined to some extent by the unique features of the opportunity, resources, and entrepreneur(s) in combination with other conditions in the business environment. But there are still numerous strategic choices to be made. The tools and techniques introduced in this text, such as five-forces and value-chain analyses, can also be used to guide decision making among new ventures and small businesses. In this section, we consider several different strategic factors that are unique to new ventures and also how the generic strategies introduced in Chapter 5 can be applied to entrepreneurial firms. We also indicate how combination strategies might benefit young and small firms and address the potential pitfalls associated with launching new venture strategies.

To be successful, small and new ventures must evaluate industry conditions, the competitive environment, and market opportunities in order to position themselves strategically. However, a traditional strategic analysis may have to be altered somewhat to fit the entrepreneurial situation. For example, five-forces analysis (as discussed in Chapter 2) is typically used by established firms. It can also be applied to the analysis of new ventures to assess the impact of industry and competitive forces. But you may ask, How does a new entrant evaluate the threat of new entrants?

First, the new entrant needs to examine barriers to entry. If the barriers are too high, the potential entrant may decide not to enter or to gather more resources before attempting to do so. Compared to an older firm with an established reputation and available resources, the barriers to entry may be insurmountable for an entrepreneurial start-up. Therefore, understanding the force of these barriers is critical in making a decision to launch.

A second factor that may be especially important to a young or small firm is the threat of retaliation by incumbents. In many cases, entrepreneurial ventures *are* the new entrants that pose a threat to incumbent firms. Therefore, in applying the five-forces model to young firms, the threat of retaliation by established firms needs to be considered. This threat can be deadly for a young start-up.

New ventures often face challenges that threaten their survival. They tend to have less power than large firms, which can put them at a disadvantage. To overcome this problem, small firms and start-ups must look for a strategic opportunity to offer a unique value proposition to potential customers. Part of any decision about what opportunity to pursue is a consideration of how a new entrant will actually enter a new market. The concept of entry strategies provides a useful means of addressing the types of choices that new ventures have, and that is the subject we turn to next.

Entry Strategies

As suggested earlier, one of the most challenging aspects of launching a new venture is finding a way to begin doing business that generates cash flow, builds credibility, attracts good employees, and overcomes the liability of newness. One aspect of that effort is the initial decision about how to get a foothold in the market. The idea of an entry strategy or "entry wedge" describes several approaches that firms may take.[47] Several factors discussed earlier will affect this decision.

- Does the entrepreneur prefer control or growth?
- Is the product/service high-tech or low-tech?
- What resources are available for the initial launch?
- What are the industry and competitive conditions?
- What is the overall market potential?

In some respects, any type of entry into a market for the first time may be considered entrepreneurial. But the entry strategy will vary depending on how risky and innovative the new business concept is. New-entry strategies typically fall into one of three categories—pioneering new entry, imitative new entry, or adaptive new entry.

Pioneering New Entry   A young firm with a radical new product or highly innovative service may change the way business is conducted in an industry. This kind of pioneering—creating new ways to solve old problems or meeting customer's needs in a unique new way—is referred to as a pioneering new entry. If the product or service is unique enough, a pioneering new entrant may actually have little direct competition. The first personal computer was a pioneering product; there had never been anything quite like it and it revolutionized computing. The first Internet browser provided a type of pioneering service. These breakthroughs created whole new industries and changed the competitive landscape. But breakthrough innovations continue to inspire pioneering entrepreneurial efforts. Consider the example of SkyTower Telecommunications, a year 2000 start-up that is hoping to take wireless communications to new heights:

> Wireless communications systems have only three ways to get to your cell phone or computer— radio towers that are often not tall enough, satellites that cost $50 million to $400 million to launch, and short-range Wi-Fi transmitters (see Chapter 8). SkyTower proposes a fourth alternative: unmanned, solar-powered airplanes that look like flying wings and send out Internet, mobile phone, and high-definition TV signals. The planes have already been successfully tested over Hawaii. They are able to fly at an altitude of 12 miles in a tight 2,000-foot-wide circle for six months at a time without landing. Designed as private communication systems for both businesses and consumers, they are able to deliver Internet service for about a third of the cost

of DSL or cable. SkyTower has already received the backing of NASA and $80 million in investment capital. Its target customers are major Internet Service Providers (ISPs). The plan is not without problems, however. For one thing, the Federal Aviation Administration (FAA) currently prohibits the launch of unpiloted planes. Even so, SkyTower's flying wing satellite is a breakthrough technology that addresses the increasing demand for cost-effective wireless communications.[48]

The pitfalls associated with a pioneering new entry are numerous. For one thing, there is a strong risk that the product or service will not be accepted by consumers. The history of entrepreneurship is littered with new ideas that never got off the launching pad. Take, for example, Smell-O-Vision, an invention designed to pump odors into movie theatres from the projection room at preestablished moments in a film. It was tried only once (for the film *Scent of a Mystery*) before it was declared a major flop. Innovative? Sure. But hardly a good idea at the time.[49]

A pioneering new entry is disruptive to the status quo of an industry. It is likely based on a technological breakthrough such as the one proposed by SkyTower. If it is successful, other competitors will rush in to copy it. This can create issues of sustainability for an entrepreneurial firm, especially if a larger company with greater resources introduces a similar product. For a new entrant to sustain its pioneering advantage, therefore, it may be necessary to protect its intellectual property, advertise heavily to build brand recognition, form alliances with businesses that will adopt its products or services, and offer exceptional customer service.

Imitative New Entry   In many respects, an imitative new-entry strategy is the opposite of entering by way of pioneering. Whereas pioneers are often inventors or tinkerers with new technology, imitators usually have a strong marketing orientation. They look for opportunities to capitalize on proven market successes. An imitation strategy is used by entrepreneurs who see products or business concepts that have been successful in one market niche or physical locale and introduce the same basic product or service in another segment of the market.

Sometimes the key to success with an imitative strategy is to fill a market space where the need had previously been filled inadequately. This was the approach used by Fixx Services, Inc., a restaurant and retail store maintenance service.

> Maintenance and repairs is hardly a new business concept. But Mark Bucher found that restaurants and retail stores were poorly served. He provides a facility management service designed to alleviate the headaches associated with keeping everything running. "Customers want one number to call if their oven breaks or if someone throws a brick through their front window," says Bucher. Founded in 1999, home-based and self-funded for the first three years, Fixx Services now has 12 employees and annual sales of nearly $10 million.[50]

Entrepreneurs are also prompted to be imitators when they realize that they have the resources or skills to do a job better than an existing competitor. This can actually be a serious problem for entrepreneurial start-ups if the imitator is an established company. Consider the example of Hugger Mugger Yoga Products, a Salt Lake City producer of yoga apparel and equipment such as yoga mats for practitioners of the ancient exercise art, with sales of $7.5 million annually.

> When founder Sara Chambers started the business in the mid-1980s, there was little competition. But once yoga went mainstream and became the subject of celebrity cover stories, other competitors saw an opportunity to imitate. Then Nike and Reebok jumped into the business with their own mats, clothes, and props. Hugger Mugger was a leading provider and had enjoyed 50 percent annual growth. But even after introducing a mass market line for stores such as Linens 'n' Things and hiring 50 independent sales reps, its growth rate has leveled off.[51]

STRATEGY SPOTLIGHT 13.7

Franchising: A Tried-and-True Imitative Strategy

Franchising, by any measure, is a success story. One of every 12 retail businesses is a franchise—just over 8 percent of all retailers. Yet these businesses account for 40 percent of all retail sales in the United States. Franchising as an opportunity to own a business and work independently continues to expand. Industry experts estimate that a new franchise outlet opens somewhere in the United States every eight minutes, and franchising is rapidly becoming a global phenomenon.

Many people are familiar with major franchises. The first names that come to mind when most people think of franchises are the fast-food chains—McDonald's, Wendy's, Subway. But there are hundreds of other franchise businesses in industries such as accounting, printing and copying, advertising services, home repair and remodeling, environmental services, education services, and automotive repairs, to name a few. These businesses provide entrepreneurial opportunities for business owners and employment for hundreds of thousands of workers.

The most common type of franchise is known as the business format franchise, in which the franchisor provides the franchisee with a step-by-step guide for managing all major aspects of the business. With this approach, everything from the operational systems to the name, logo, and color scheme are prescribed by the franchisor. Regulations have been introduced during the last 10 years to provide franchisees with the essential information they need to choose a franchisor. This has taken away some of the mystery in the deals being offered by franchisors and made franchisees more confident about buying in. At the same time, the procedures for operating the business

systems have also improved. "It's easier for a new franchisee to enter the system now," says Paul Sweeney, a McDonald's franchisee in Cranberry Township, Pennsylvania. "They give you handbooks that tell you how to run your business so you don't have to come up with the context for construction and development on your own."

Clearly, franchising is built on the idea of imitating what another business has already done. If a business format is so easy to imitate, can it possibly have any competitive advantages? In the minds of many consumers of franchise products and services, the advantage is *because of* imitation. That is, consumers have confidence in franchises because they are familiar with them. "As time has gone by, the public has come to embrace franchising because they're familiar with the successful franchises and brand," claims Tony DeSio, founder of Mail Boxes Etc. "They know that, from one location to another, they can rely on product consistency." Thus, imitation is one of the central reasons why franchises are successful.

Even though consistency and sameness are highly valued in a franchise system, most franchisors are also open to suggestions for how to improve. Franchisees who think of a better way to market a service or showcase products are usually welcome to do so. For example, Navin Bhatia, owner of nine Valvoline Instant Oil Changes in San Antonio, Texas, masterminded the "good, better, best" marketing strategy for differentiating between the type of oil and level of service that is recommended to customers. Thus, through the efforts of independent franchisees, many franchises are able to continually improve their systems and hone their product and service offerings. Of course, when that happens, what do most of the other franchisees in the system do? They imitate it.

Sources: Williams, G. 2002. Keep thinking. *Entrepreneur*, September: 100–103; Smith, D. 2002. Want franchises with that? *Entrepreneur*, May: 102–106; and www.franchise.org.

Recall from Chapter 3 that the quality "difficult to imitate" was viewed as one of the keys to building sustainable advantages. A strategy that can be imitated, therefore, seems like a poor way to build a business. In essence, this is true. But then consider the example of a franchise. Strategy Spotlight 13.7 addresses the question of how and why the franchise approach to imitation has worked well for many entrepreneurs.

Adaptive New Entry   Most new entrants use a strategy somewhere between "pure" imitation and "pure" pioneering. That is, they offer a product or service that is somewhat new and sufficiently different to create new value for customers and capture market share. Such firms are adaptive in the sense that they are aware of marketplace conditions and conceive entry strategies to capitalize on current trends.

According to business creativity coach Tom Monahan, "Every new idea is merely a spin of an old idea. [Knowing that] takes the pressure off from thinking [you] have to

AltiTunes: Success through Adaptation

"Darwin said it is not the strongest or fastest that survive but those that can adapt quickly," says Thomas Barry, chief investment officer at Bjurman, Barry & Associates. That's what Amy Nye Wolf learned when she launched her AltiTunes Partners LP business. She had been listening to the same music over and over during a six-week backpacking trip through Europe. At the end of the trip, she was elated to find a store selling music at London's Heathrow Airport. "I was so sick of the music I had, and I was just happy to see it."

About five years later, after finishing college and working as an investment banker, Wolf remembered her experience in the airport. She realized that selling CDs

was not an original idea but she thought there might be a need anyway. "I stole the idea," says Wolf, "and then did some serious adapting." Airports, she figured, constituted a unique market niche. She estimated that if she could sell just 30 CDs per day, she could keep the business afloat. Naming her business AltiTunes, Wolf took the plunge.

Today, AltiTunes sells 3,000 to 4,000 CDs per day at 27 stores in 20 airports and one train station. Sales of CDs and products such as portable stereos and computer games now exceed $15 million annually. And Wolf is still adapting. Her latest innovation is a gadget that lets shoppers roam around the store and sample any CD on the racks. It's a PDA-sized device developed by a company name MusiKube, LLC, that shoppers use by scanning a CD bar code to hear selections of music. It's just the latest improvement in Wolf's plan to stay cutting edge by continually adapting what she calls her "small format, extraordinary-location," music retailing business.

Sources: Barrett, A., & Foust, D. 2003. Hot growth companies. *BusinessWeek*, June 9: 74–77; Goldsmith, G. 2003. Retailers try new devices to make CD purchasing more enjoyable. *Wall Street Journal*, June 12, www.wsj.com; Williams, G. 2002. Looks like rain. *Entrepreneur*, September: 104–111; and www.altitunes.com.

be totally creative. You don't. Sometimes it's one slight twist to an old idea that makes all the difference."[52] Thus, an adaptive approach does not involve "reinventing the wheel," nor is it merely imitative either. It involves taking an existing idea and adapting it to a particular situation. Let's look at the example of Citipost:

> Richard Trayford was working temporarily while he waited for his new job in music promotion to begin. But he noticed that the bicycle-messenger company he was working for charged just one dollar for overnight delivery as a gimmick to get customers to use its more expensive same-day delivery service. Trayford realized that some customers would pay much more as long as it was less expensive than UPS and FedEx. So he borrowed $19,500 and launched Citipost. His strategy was to adapt an overnight delivery service to high-volume customers in New York's central business district. Citipost's first customer was Random House, a publisher that sends hundreds of overnight packages to agents, reviewers, and others within Manhattan every day. The service saved Random House 50 percent on delivery costs, and within four months Citipost was handling all of its deliveries. Twice named to the *Inc.* 500 list of the fastest-growing companies, Citipost now operates low-cost central city overnight delivery services in a dozen cities around the globe and earns revenues of $30 million annually.[53]

There are several pitfalls that might limit the success of an adaptive new entrant. First, the value proposition set forth by the new entrant firm must be perceived as unique. Unless potential customers believe a new product or service does a superior job of meeting their needs, they will have little motivation to try them out. Second, there is nothing to prevent a close competitor from mimicking the new firm's adaptation as a way to hold on to its customers. Third, once an adaptive entrant achieves initial success, the challenge is to keep the idea fresh. If the attractive features of the new business wear off or are copied, the entrepreneurial firm must find ways to adapt and improve the product or service offering. Strategy Spotlight 13.8 describes how adaptive new entrant Amy Nye Wolf has continually improved her entrepreneurial venture in order to hold her customers' interest and grow her business.

A new entrant must decide not only the best way to enter into business for the first time, but also what type of strategic positioning will work best as the business goes forward. Those strategic choices can be informed by the guidelines suggested for the generic strategies. We turn to that subject next.

Generic Strategies

Typically, an entrepreneurial firm begins with a single business model that is equivalent in scope to a business-level strategy (Chapter 5). Thus, most small businesses and new ventures can benefit from applying the generic strategies. There is rarely any reason for a new venture to consider a corporate-level strategy (Chapter 6) except in a case when an entrepreneur decides to diversify into related or unrelated businesses or to purchase an existing business. Then, some of the guidelines that make the acquisition process more successful may be helpful to new entrants. In general, however, new ventures are single-business firms using business-level strategies. In this section we address how overall low cost, differentiation, and focus strategies can be used by new ventures to achieve competitive advantages.

Overall Cost Leadership   One of the ways entrepreneurial firms achieve success is by doing more with less. That is, by holding down costs or making more efficient use of resources than larger competitors, new ventures are often able to offer lower prices and still be profitable. Thus, under the right circumstances, a low-cost leader strategy is a viable alternative for some new ventures. The way new ventures achieve low-cost leadership, however, is typically different for young or small firms. Let's look first at why a cost-leadership strategy might be difficult for a new venture.

Recall from Chapter 5 that three of the features of a low-cost approach included operating at a large enough scale to spread costs over many units of production (i.e., economies of scale), making substantial capital investments in order to increase scale economies, and using knowledge gained from experience to make cost-saving improvements. These elements of a cost-leadership strategy may be unavailable to new ventures. Because new ventures are typically small, they usually don't have high economies of scale relative to competitors. Because they are usually cash strapped, they can't make large capital investments to increase their scale advantages. And because they are young, they often don't have a wealth of accumulated experience to draw on to achieve cost reductions.

Given these constraints, how can new ventures successfully deploy cost-leader strategies? Compared to large firms, new ventures often have simple organizational structures that make decision making both easier and faster. The smaller size also helps young firms change more quickly when upgrades in technology or feedback from the marketplace indicate that improvements are needed. New ventures are also able to make decisions at the time they are founded that help them deal with the issue of controlling costs. For example, they may source materials from a supplier that provides them more cheaply or set up manufacturing facilities in another country where labor costs are especially low. Thus, new firms have several avenues for achieving low cost leadership.

Consider the example of UTStarcom, a fast-growing wireless phone service being marketed in mainland China:

> Taiwan-born founder Hong Liang Lu was an executive at Japan's Kyocera Corp. when he made his first visit to China in 1990. He found a population that badly needed decent phone service. "Before that trip, I hadn't really thought about doing business in China. Afterward, I felt it made no sense to do business anywhere else." Using Personal Access System (PAS), a technology that had never caught on in Japan, he created a low-cost service that uses existing copper networks as its backbone. The service costs only $100 per subscriber to deploy, about half the price of cellular-based systems. Customers pay nothing for incoming calls and outgoing ones are 25 percent of the cellular rate. Competing against the big telecom providers was difficult at first, but once they marketed the "Little Smart" as a low cost alternative to cellular, sales took off. Average

annual revenues have grown 73 percent since 1999, and 2003 sales reached $1.96 billion. Says CEO Lu, "Our biggest problem is keeping up with demand."[54]

Whatever methods young firms use to achieve a low-cost advantage, this has always been a way that entrepreneurial firms take business away from incumbents—by offering a comparable product or service at a lower price.

Differentiation   Both pioneering and adaptive entry strategies involve some degree of differentiation. That is, the new entry is based on being able to offer a differentiated value proposition. Clearly, in the case of pioneers, the new venture is attempting to do something strikingly different, either by using a new technology or deploying resources in a way that radically alters the way business is conducted. Often, entrepreneurs do both.

Jeff Bezos set out to use Internet technology to revolutionize the way books are sold. He garnered the ire of other booksellers and the attention of the public by making bold claims about being the world's largest bookseller. As a bookseller, Bezos was not doing anything that had not been done before. But two key differentiating features—doing it on the Internet and offering extraordinary customer service—have made Amazon a differentiated success.

Even though the Internet and new technologies have provided many opportunities for entrepreneurs, differentiators don't have to be highly sophisticated to succeed. Consider the example of Spry Learning Co., a Portland, Oregon, start-up begun in 2000.

> Founders Sarah Chapman and Devin Williams believed that older people would benefit from using computers and surfing the Internet—if they only knew how. Working with gerontologists and instructional designers, they designed a computer-skills curriculum aimed at seniors. After piloting the program at two retirement communities, they successfully launched the differentiated service and, after just a few years, projected annual revenues over $4 million.[55]

There are several factors that make it more difficult for young firms to be successful as differentiators. For one thing, the strategy is generally thought to be expensive to enact. For example, differentiation is often associated with strong brand identity, and establishing a brand is usually considered to be expensive because of the cost of advertising and promotion, paid endorsements, exceptional customer service, aggressive warranties and return guarantees, as well as other expenses typically associated with building brand. Differentiation successes are sometimes built on superior innovation or use of technology. These are also factors where it may be challenging for young firms to excel relative to established competitors.

On the other hand, all of these areas—innovation, technology, customer service, distinctive branding—are also arenas where new ventures have sometimes made a name for themselves even though they must operate with limited resources and experience. To be successful, according to Garry Ridge, CEO of the WD-40 Company, "You need to have a great product, make the end user aware of it, and make it easy to buy."[56] It sounds simple, but it is a difficult challenge for entrepreneurs with differentiation strategies.

Focus   Because of the competitive environment facing most ventures, focus or "niche" strategies provide one of the most effective strategies for any new firm. A niche represents a small segment within a market. A young or small firm can play an important role in such a market space if there is an opportunity to thrive in that environment. Typically, a focus strategy is used to pursue a niche. Focus strategies are associated with small businesses because there is a natural fit between the narrow scope of the strategy and the small size of the firm. As we learned earlier, a focus strategy may include elements of differentiation and overall cost leadership, as well as combinations of these approaches. But to be successful within a market niche, the key strategic requirement is to stay focused. Here's why:

Despite all the attention given to fast-growing new industries, most start-ups enter industries that are mature.[57] In mature industries, growth in demand tends to be slow and there are often many competitors. Therefore, if a start-up wants to get a piece of the action, it often has to take business away from an existing competitor. If a start-up enters a market with a broad or aggressive strategy, it is likely to evoke retaliation from a more powerful competitor. Therefore, young firms can often succeed best by finding a market niche where they can get a foothold and make small advances that erode the position of existing competitors.[58] From this position, they can build a name for themselves and grow. Consider the example of Corporate Interns, Inc.:

> When Jason Engen was an undergraduate student at the University of St. Thomas in St. Paul, Minnesota, he learned the value of internships in which students worked for local companies. He wrote a business plan for one of his classes about forming an internship placement service in which he would screen students and match them with local companies. It's a "win–win situation," said Engen. "The student gets the experience, and the company gets eager talent." The interest in his idea was high, and a week after graduation he started Corporate Interns, Inc. It was difficult at first, however, because companies handle internships differently than other placement activities. But as Engen learned more, he realized this difference was an advantage: By positioning himself only in the college intern market, he avoided competing directly with large staffing companies. "Specialization is important," says Engen. "You have to stay focused on that niche." For Engen, that niche now generates $2 million in annual revenues.[59]

As the Corporate Interns example indicates, many small businesses are very successful even though their share of the market is quite small. Giant companies such as Procter & Gamble, Johnson & Johnson, and Ford are often described in terms of their market share—that is, their share of sales in a whole market. But many of the industries that small firms participate in have thousands of participants that are not direct competitors. For example, small restaurants and auto repair shops in California don't compete with those in Michigan or Georgia. These industries are considered "fragmented" because no single company is strong enough to have power over other competitors. Therefore, small firms need to focus on the market share only in their trade area. This may be defined as a geographical area or a small segment of a larger product group.

Consider, for example, the "Miniature Editions" line of books launched by Running Press, a small Philadelphia publisher. The books are palm-sized minibooks positioned at bookstore cash registers as point-of-sale impulse items costing about $4.95. Beginning with just 10 titles in 1993, Running Press grew rapidly and within 10 years had sold over 20 million copies. Even though these books represent just a tiny fraction of total sales in the $23 billion publishing industry, they have been a mainstay for Running Press, which eventually had to sue other publishers to protect its two-and-a-half by three-inch "trade dress" format.[60]

Although each of the three strategies holds promise, and pitfalls, for new ventures and small businesses, firms that can make unique combinations of the generic approaches may have the greatest chances of success. It is that subject we turn to next.

Combination Strategies

Strategic positioning has different implications for small firms and entrepreneurial start-ups. For small firms, the issues they face in terms of their marketplace are often confined to a geographical locale or a small class of products. For start-ups, a key issue is the scope of their strategic efforts relative to those of their competitors. In determining a strategic position, both types of firms must address fundamental issues of how to achieve a distinct competitive advantage that will earn above-average profits as well as how to create value for their customers in the marketplace.

STRATEGY SPOTLIGHT

Combining Strategies at AllDorm.com

"There are two ways to be successful in e-commerce," according to Jim Crawford, vice president at the research firm Retail Forward. "Operate on a large scale, or find an audience that isn't served by brick-and-mortar stores." It was the second of those two ways that motivated All-Dorm.com co-founder Ryan Garman. Standing in line at 5:00 a.m. with 2,400 other students after a grueling 13-hour drive pulling a U-Haul packed with his stuff, the entering freshman figured there had to be a better way. With that bleary-eyed epiphany, he found his unserved niche: college students moving into dorm rooms. A year and a half later, Garman and three college sophomore buddies founded AllDorm.com . . . in a dorm room.

Alldorm.com is an online retailer that specializes in the furnishings and accessories that students need to live in the shared and usually cramped space of a dorm room. According to the National Retail Federation, students and parents spend $2.6 billion annually furnishing dorm rooms and student apartments.

Beyond focusing on a lucrative niche, AllDorm has other strategic advantages as well. Its product selection—over 6,000 items—gives AllDorm differentiation advantages. For one thing, the products it offers are not just

Source: Torres, N. L. 2005. Inside job. *Entrepreneur*, March: 132; Myser, M. 2004. Giving college kids a smoother move. *Business 2.0*, June: 82; and www.alldorm.com.

the usual bean bag chair and mini-fridge. AllDorm goes for the latest in dorm design trends. "Students know what they want," says Gina LaGuardia of *The College Bound Network*, a magazine that targets the precollege market. "Practical items that have that funky element to them will really sell." Beside furnishings, it also sells hard-to-find products, such as extra long bedsheets, and products useful for group living, such as shower kits with sandals for trips to the communal bathroom. The company also coordinates deliveries with universities to make sure that shipments do not arrive too early.

Alldorm also concentrates on controlling costs. To help select products and keep in touch with trends in the student market, current college students are hired as interns to test new items. It also carefully controls back-end costs; rather than maintaining large inventories, AllDorm uses proprietary e-commerce software to coordinate direct shipments from suppliers.

Garman and his partners reflected recently on their success: "When you're in college, you have time to do things well. You can study, you can party, or you can start a company. We chose to start a company." Theirs was a good decision, apparently. Just four years after it was founded, AllDorm's revenues jumped to over $25 million per year and it's still growing.

One of the best ways for new ventures and small businesses to achieve success is by pursuing combination strategies. By combining the best features of low-cost, differentiation, and focus strategies, young and small firms can often achieve something that is truly distinctive.

Entrepreneurial firms are often in a strong position to offer a combination strategy, because they have the flexibility to approach situations uniquely. For example, holding down expenses can be difficult for big firms because each layer of bureaucracy adds to the cost of communicating and doing business. To get a part made, for example, or to outsource it, may be complicated and expensive for many large firms. By contrast, the Nartron Corporation, a small engineering firm whose innovations include the first keyless automobile entry system, solves that problem by building everything itself. By engineering its own products from its own designs, it not only saves money but also creates better parts. "Our parts look different from other people's because we keep adding functionality," says Nartron CEO Norman Rautiola. According to Rautiola, this capability allows the company to "run rings" around its competitors, which include Texas Instruments and Motorola.[61]

A similar argument could be made about entrepreneurial firms that differentiate. Large firms often find it difficult to offer highly specialized products or superior customer services. Entrepreneurial firms, by contrast, can often create high-value products and services through their unique differentiating efforts. Strategy Spotlight 13.9 examines AllDorm, a start-up founded by college students who made good use of a combination strategy.

For nearly all small firms, one of the major dangers is that a large firm with more resources will copy what they are doing. That is, well-established larger competitors that observe the success of a new entrant's product or service will copy it and use their market power to overwhelm the smaller firm. Although this happens often, the threat may be lessened for firms that use combination strategies. Because of the flexibility and quick decision-making ability of entrepreneurial firms, they can often enact their combination strategies in ways that the large firms cannot copy. This makes the strategies much more sustainable.

Perhaps more threatening than large competitors for many entrepreneurial firms are other small firms that are close competitors. Because they have similar structural features that help them adjust quickly and be flexible in decision making, close competitors are often a danger to young and small firms. Here again, a carefully crafted and executed combination strategy may be the best way for an entrepreneurial firm to thrive in a competitive environment.

Summary

New ventures and small businesses that capitalize on marketplace opportunities make an important contribution to the U.S. economy. They are leaders in terms of implementing new technologies and introducing innovative products and services. Entrepreneurial firms face unique challenges if they are going to survive and grow. The size, age, and growth goals of small firms affect how they achieve competitive advantages.

To successfully launch new ventures or implement new technologies, firms must develop a strong ability to recognize viable opportunities. Opportunity recognition is a process of determining which venture ideas are, in fact, promising business opportunities. It consists of two phases. First is the discovery phase, in which new ideas are identified by alert individuals or generated by means of deliberate search processes. Second is the formation phase, in which the feasibility of opportunities is evaluated and plans are made to support and fund the new venture. In addition to strong opportunities, entrepreneurial firms need sufficient resources and entrepreneurial leadership to thrive.

The resources that start-ups need include financial resources as well as human capital and social capital. Strategic alliances are another resource that often benefits young and small firms. Many small firms also benefit from government programs that support their development and growth. Various avenues for obtaining resources are available to start-ups, depending on whether the new venture is in early or later stages of development. In early stages, personal savings and financial support from family and friends are the most common types of initial funding. Most start-ups can also benefit from bootstrapping, that is, operating economically and relying on as few outside resources as possible. Bank financing and venture capital are often used by entrepreneurial firms in later stages of development.

Young and small firms thrive best when they are led by founders or owners who have vision, drive and dedication, and a commitment to excellence. Vision provides entrepreneurial leaders with an ability to conceive of realities that do not yet exist. Dedication and drive are needed in order to persist in the face of difficulties and keep up the level of motivation necessary to succeed. Commitment to excellence is reflected in an entrepreneurial leader's focus on quality and customer service as well as a desire to be surrounded by talented and skilled employees.

New ventures and small businesses face numerous strategic challenges. However, many of the tools of strategic management can be applied to these firms. Decisions about the strategic positioning of young and small firms can benefit from applying five-forces analysis and evaluating the requirements of niche markets. Entry strategies used by new ventures take several forms, including pioneering new entry, imitative new entry, and adaptive new entry. Entrepreneurial firms can benefit from using overall low-cost, differentiation, and focus strategies, although each of these approaches has pitfalls that are unique to young and small firms. Entrepreneurial firms are also in a strong position to benefit from combination strategies.

Summary Review Questions

1. Explain how an entrepreneurial firm's size, age, and growth goals help determine its character and strategic direction.

2. What is the difference between discovery and formation in the process of opportunity recognition? Give an example of each.

3. What types of financing are typically available to entrepreneurs in early stages and later stages of a new venture start-up?

4. How can bootstrapping help a young start-up or small business minimize its resource requirements? How might bootstrapping efforts affect decisions about strategic positioning?

5. Describe the three characteristics of entrepreneurial leadership: vision, dedication and drive, and commitment to excellence.

6. Briefly describe the three types of entrepreneurial entry strategies: pioneering, imitative, and adaptive.

7. Explain why entrepreneurial firms are often in a strong position to use combination strategies.

E-Loan is a young firm that offers lending services over the Internet. Evaluate the qualities of the opportunity E-Loan identified in terms of the four characteristics of an opportunity. In each category:

Experiential Exercise

1. Evaluate the extent to which they met the criteria (using high, medium, or low).

2. Explain your rationale. That is, what features of the opportunity account for the score you gave them?

Characteristics	High/Medium/Low	Rationale
1. Attractive		
2. Achievable		
3. Durable		
4. Value Creating		

Application Questions Exercises

1. Using the Internet, research the Web site of the Small Business Administration (www.sba.gov). What different types of financing are available to small firms? Besides financing, what other programs are available to support the growth and development of small businesses?

2. Think of an entrepreneurial firm that has been successfully launched in the last 10 years. What are the characteristics of the entrepreneur(s) who launched the firm?

3. Select a small business that you are familiar with in your local community. Research the company and discuss how it has positioned itself relative to its close competitors. Does it have a unique strategic advantage? Disadvantage? Explain.

4. Using the Internet, find an example of a young entrepreneurial firm (founded within the last five years). What kind of entry strategy did it use—pioneering, imitative, or adaptive? Since the firm's initial entry, how has it used or combined overall low-cost, differentiation, and/or focus strategies?

Ethics Questions

1. Imitation strategies are based on the idea of copying another firm's idea and using it for your own purposes. Is this unethical or simply a smart business practice? Discuss the ethical implications of this practice (if any).

2. The prices of some foreign products that enter the United States are regulated to keep prices high, and "dumping" laws have been established to prevent some foreign companies from selling below wholesale prices. Should price wars that drive small businesses or new entrants out of business be illegal? What ethical considerations are raised (if any)?

References

1. Lassek, P. J. 2004. No criminal activity found in city probe. *Tulsa World,* November 11, www.tulsaworld.com; Wysocki, B. 2001. Airline faces turbulence enroute to takeoff. *WSJ.com Startup Journal,* April 16, www.startupjournal.com; Wysocki, B. 2001. Airline's plan flies away as big carriers take root. *WSJ.com Startup Journal,* August 21, www.startupjournal .com; and www.tulsatoday.com.

2. Shane, S., & Venkataraman, S. 2000. The promise of entrepreneurship as a field of research. *Academy of Management Review,* 25(1): 217–226; Lumpkin, G. T., & Dess, G. G. 1996. Clarifying the entrepreneurial orientation construct and linking it to performance. *Academy of Management Review,* 21(1): 135–172; and Gartner, W. B. 1988. Who is an entrepreneur? is the wrong question. *American Journal of Small Business,* 12(4): 11–32.

3. Martin, J., & Birch, D. 2002. Slump? What slump? *Fortune,* December 1, www.fortune.com.

4. Dennis, W. J., Jr. 2000. *NFIB small business policy guide.* Washington, DC: National Federation of Independent Business; and www.nfib.com.

5. Small Business Administration. 2002. A report from Advocacy's 25th anniversary symposium. *SBA Office of Advocacy,* February 22, www.sba.gov/advo/.

6. Tilin, A. 2005. Bagging the right customers. *Business 2.0,* 6(4): 56–57.

7. Case, J. 2001. The gazelle theory. *Inc.,* May 15, www.inc .com; and Birch, D. 1979. *The job generation process.* MIT Program on Neighborhood and Regional Change. Cambridge, MA: MIT Press.

8. Sloane, J. 2003. Hearts and minds. *Fortune,* July 11, www .fortune.com; www.surmodics.com; and www.hoovers.com.

9. Case, J., op. cit.

10. Maintaining high levels of both wealth creation and employment growth is very challenging for most small firms. For an interesting perspective on how small ad medium-sized enterprises can manage fluctuations in growth, see Nicholls-Nixon, C. L. 2005. Rapid growth and high performance: The entrepreneur's "impossible dream"? *Academy of Management Executive,* 19(1): 77–89.

11. Small Business Administration, op. cit.

12. Fromartz, S. 1998. How to get your first great idea. *Inc.,* April 1: 91–94; and Vesper, K. H. 1990. *New venture strategies* (2nd ed.). Englewood Cliffs, NJ: Prentice Hall.

13. Carey, J., & Yang, C. 2001. From smart to brilliant weapons. *BusinessWeek,* October 8: 62–63.

14. Gaglio, C. M. 1997. Opportunity identification: Review, critique and suggested research directions. In J. A. Katz (Ed.), *Advances in entrepreneurship, firm emergence and growth,* vol. 3: 139–202. Greenwich, CT: JAI Press; Hills, G. E., Shrader, R. C., & Lumpkin, G. T. 1999. Opportunity recognition as a creative process. In *Frontiers of entrepreneurship research:* 216–227. Wellesley, MA: Babson College; and Long, W., & McMullan, W. E. 1984. Mapping the new venture opportunity identification process. In *Frontiers of entrepreneurship research:* 567–590. Wellesley, MA: Babson College.

15. For an interesting discussion of different aspects of opportunity discovery, see Shepherd, D. A., & DeTienne, D. R. 2005. Prior knowledge, potential financial reward, and opportunity identification. *Entrepreneurship Theory & Practice,* 29(1): 91–112; and Gaglio, C. M. 2004. The role of mental simulations and counterfactual thinking in the

opportunity identification process. *Entrepreneurship Theory & Practice,* 28(6): 533–552.

16. Stewart, T. A. 2002. How to think with your gut. *Business 2.0,* November: 99–104.
17. Bennet, E. 2000. Fungus fanatic. *Philadelphia Business Journal,* February 18, www.bizjournals.com/philadelphia/; and Greco, S. 1998. Where great ideas come from. *Inc.,* April: 76–86.
18. Timmons, J. A. 1997. Opportunity recognition. In Bygrave, W. D. (Ed.). *The portable MBA in entrepreneurship* (2nd ed.): 26–54. New York: Wiley.
19. Timmons, J. A., & Spinelli, S. 2004. *New venture creation* (6th ed.). New York: McGraw-Hill/Irwin; and Bygrave, W. D. 1997. The entrepreneurial process. In W. D. Bygrave (Ed.), *The portable MBA:* 1–26.
20. Stinchcombe, A. L. 1965. Social structure in organizations. In March, J. G. (Ed.), *Handbook of organizations:* 142–193. Chicago: Rand McNally.
21. *Inc.* 2001. Small business 2001: Where are we now? May 29: 18–19; and Zacharakis, A. L., Bygrave, W. D., & Shepherd, D. A. 2000. *Global entrepreneurship monitor—National entrepreneurship assessment: United States of America 2000 executive report.* Kansas City, MO: Kauffman Center for Entrepreneurial Leadership.
22. Cooper, S. 2003. Cash cows. *Entrepreneur,* June: 36.
23. Small business 2001: Where are we now? op. cit.; and Dennis, W. J., Jr. 1997. *Business starts and stops.* Washington, DC: National Federation of Independent Business.
23. www.keepwalking.com; and www.walkabouttravelgear.com.
24. Stuart, A. 2001. The pita principle. *Inc.,* August: 58–64.
25. Cooper, op. cit.
26. Gossage, B. 2004. Charging ahead. *Inc.,* January: 42–44.
27. Fraser, J. A. 2001. Plans for growth. *Inc.,* March: 56–57; and Fraser, J. A. 1998. A hitchhiker's guide to capital resources. *Inc.,* February: 74–82.
28. Seglin, J. L. 1998. What angels want. *Inc.,* May: 43–44.
29. Torres, N. L. 2002. Playing an angel. *Entrepreneur,* May: 130–138.
30. Fraser, J. A. 2001. The money hunt. *Inc.,* March: 49–63.
31. Lefteroff, T. T. 2003. The thrill of the chase. *Entrepreneur,* July: 56.
32. *Economist.* 2000. Hatching a new plan, August 12: 53–54; www.techspace.com; and www.nbia.org.
33. For more on how different forms of organizing entrepreneurial firms as well as different stages of new firm growth and development affect financing, see Cassar, G. 2004. The financing of business start-ups. *Journal of Business Venturing,* 19(2): 261–283.
34. Eisenhardt, K. M., & Schoonhoven, C. B. 1990. Organizational growth: Linking founding team, strategy, environment, and growth among U.S. semiconductor ventures, 1978–1988. *Administrative Science Quarterly* 35: 504–529.
35. Dubini, P., & Aldrich, H. 1991. Personal and extended networks are central to the entrepreneurship process. *Journal of Business Venturing,* 6(5): 305–333.
36. For more on the role of social contacts in helping young firms build legitimacy, see Chrisman, J. J., & McMullan, W. E. 2004. Outside assistance as a knowledge resource for new venture survival. *Journal of Small Business Management,* 42(3): 229–244.
37. Vogel, C. 2000. Janina Pawlowski. *Working Woman,* June: 70.
38. For more information, go to the Small Business Administration Web site at www.sba.gov.
39. Torres, N. L. 2002. Under the microscope. *Entrepreneur,* August: 106–109.
40. Detamore-Rodman, C. 2003. Out on a limb. *Entrepreneur,* March: 78–83.
41. Tanner, J. 2000. Meals on wheels (and rails and water). *Inc.,* May: 124–126.
42. Based on Kurlantzick, J. 2003. Got what it takes? *Entrepreneur,* March: 52.
43. Briody, D. 2001. Top ten entrepreneurs: Bill Nguyen. *Red Herring,* August 1: 58–60.
44. Himanshu "Sue" Bhatia. 2000. *Working Woman,* June: 91; see also roseint.com.
45. Collins, J. 2001. *Good to great.* New York: HarperBusiness.
46. Ibid.; and Collins. J. 2003. Bigger, better, faster. *Fast Company,* June: 74–78.
47. The idea of entry wedges was discussed by Vesper, K. 1990. *New venture strategies* (2nd ed.). Englewood Cliffs, NJ: Prentice Hall; and Drucker, P. F. 1985. *Innovation and entrepreneurship.* New York: HarperBusiness.
48. Frauenfelder, M. 2002. Look! Up in the sky! It's a flying cell phone tower! *Business 2.0,* November: 108–112.
49. Maiello, M. 2002. They almost changed the world. *Forbes,* December 22: 217–220.
50. Pedroza, G. M. 2003. Blanket statement. *Entrepreneur,* March: 92.
51. Gull, N. 2003. Just say om. *Inc.,* July: 42–44.
52. Williams, G. 2002. Looks like rain. *Entrepreneur,* September: 104–111.
53. Fromartz, op. cit.; and Grossman, J. 1999. Courier's foreign niche. *Inc.,* October 15: 57.
54. Burrows, P. 2003. Ringing off the hook in China. *BusinessWeek,* June 9: 80–82; www.hoovers.com.
55. Pedroza, G. M. 2002. Tech tutors. *Entrepreneur,* September: 120.
56. Barrett, A. 2003. Hot growth companies. *BusinessWeek,* June 9: 74–77.
57. Dennis, W. J., Jr. 1992. *The state of small business: A report of the president, 1992:* 65–90. Washington, DC: U.S. Government Printing Office.
58. Romanelli, E. 1989. Environments and strategies of organization start-up: Effects on early survival. *Administrative Science Quarterly,* 34(3): 369–387.
59. Torres, N. L. 2003. A perfect match. *Entrepreneur,* July: 112–114.
60. Wallace, B. 2000. Brothers. *Philadelphia Magazine,* April: 66–75.
61. Buchanan, L. 2003. The innovation factor: A field guide to innovation. *Forbes,* April 21, www.forbes.com.

Strategic Analysis

Chapter 1
Introduction and Analyzing Goals and Objectives

Chapter 2
Analyzing the External Environment

Chapter 3
Analyzing the Internal Environment

Chapter 4
Assessing Intellectual Capital

Strategic Formulation

Strategic Implementation

Chapter 5
Formulating Business-Level Strategies

Chapter 9
Strategic Control and Corporate Governance

Chapter 6
Formulating Corporate-Level Strategies

Chapter 7
Formulating International Strategies

Chapter 10
Creating Effective Organizational Designs

Chapter 11
Strategic Leadership Excellence, Ethics and Change

Chapter 8
Digital Business Strategies

Chapter 12
Fostering Corporate Entrepreneurship

Chapter 13
Strategic Leadership Creating New Ventures

Case Analysis

Chapter 14
Case Analysis

Case Analysis

14 Analyzing Strategic Management Cases

Cases

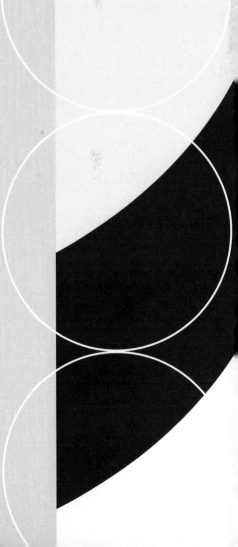

Analyzing Strategic Management Cases

>chapter objectives

After reading this chapter, you should have a good understanding of:

- How strategic case analysis is used to simulate real-world experiences.

- How analyzing strategic management cases can help develop the ability to differentiate, speculate, and integrate when evaluating complex business problems.

- The steps involved in conducting a strategic management case analysis.

- How conflict-inducing discussion techniques can lead to better decisions.

- How to get the most out of case analysis.

- How to use the strategic insights and material from each of the 13 previous chapters in the text to analyze issues posed by strategic management cases.

*C*ase analysis is one of the most effective ways to learn strategic management. It provides a complement to other methods of instruction by asking you to use the tools and techniques of strategic management to deal with an actual business situation. Strategy cases include detailed descriptions of management challenges faced by executives and business owners. By studying the background and analyzing the strategic predicaments posed by a case, you first see that the circumstances businesses confront are often difficult and complex. Then you are asked what decisions you would make to address the situation in the case and how the actions you recommend will affect the company. Thus, the processes of analysis, formulation, and implementation that have been addressed by this textbook can be applied in a real-life situation.

In this chapter we will discuss the role of case analysis as a learning tool in both the classroom and the real world. One of the benefits of strategic case analysis is to develop the ability to differentiate, speculate, and integrate. We will also describe how to conduct a case analysis and address techniques for deriving the greatest benefit from the process, including the effective use of conflict-inducing decision techniques. Finally, we will discuss how case analysis in a classroom setting can enhance the process of analyzing, making decisions, and taking action in real-world strategic situations.

>>Why Analyze Strategic Management Cases?

It is often said that the key to finding good answers is to ask good questions. Strategic managers and business leaders are required to evaluate options, make choices, and find solutions to the challenges they face every day. To do so, they must learn to ask the right questions. The study of strategic management poses the same challenge. The process of analyzing, decision making, and implementing strategic actions raises many good questions.

- Why do some firms succeed and others fail?
- Why are some companies higher performers than others?
- What information is needed in the strategic planning process?
- How do competing values and beliefs affect strategic decision making?
- What skills and capabilities are needed to implement a strategy effectively?

How does a student of strategic management answer these questions? By strategic case analysis. Case analysis simulates the real-world experience that strategic managers and company leaders face as they try to determine how best to run their companies. It places students in the middle of an actual situation and challenges them to figure out what to do.[1]

Asking the right questions is just the beginning of case analysis. In the previous chapters we have discussed issues and challenges that managers face and provided analytical frameworks for understanding the situation. But once the analysis is complete, decisions have to be made. Case analysis forces you to choose among different options and set forth a plan of action based on your choices. But even then the job is not done. Strategic case analysis also requires that you address how you will implement the plan and the implications of choosing one course of action over another.

A strategic management case is a detailed description of a challenging situation faced by an organization.[2] It usually includes a chronology of events and extensive support materials, such as financial statements, product lists, and transcripts of interviews with employees. Although names or locations are sometimes changed to provide anonymity, cases usually report the facts of a situation as authentically as possible.

One of the main reasons to analyze strategic management cases is to develop an ability to evaluate business situations critically. In case analysis, memorizing key terms and conceptual frameworks is not enough. To analyze a case, it is important that you go beyond textbook prescriptions and quick answers. It requires you to look deeply into the information that is provided and root out the essential issues and causes of a company's problems.

The types of skills that are required to prepare an effective strategic case analysis can benefit you in actual business situations. Case analysis adds to the overall learning experience by helping you acquire or improve skills that may not be taught in a typical lecture course. Three capabilities that can be learned by conducting case analysis are especially useful to strategic managers—the ability to differentiate, speculate, and integrate.[3] Here's how case analysis can enhance those skills.

1. ***Differentiate.*** Effective strategic management requires that many different elements of a situation be evaluated at once. This is also true in case analysis. When analyzing cases, it is important to isolate critical facts, evaluate whether assumptions are useful or faulty, and distinguish between good and bad information. Differentiating between the factors that are influencing the situation presented by a case is necessary for making a good analysis. Strategic management also involves understanding that problems are often complex and multilayered. This applies to case analysis as well. Ask whether the case deals with operational, business-level, or corporate issues. Do the problems stem from weaknesses in the internal value chain or threats

in the external environment? Dig deep. Being too quick to accept the easiest or least controversial answer will usually fail to get to the heart of the problem.

2. **Speculate.** Strategic managers need to be able to use their imagination to envision an explanation or solution that might not readily be apparent. The same is true with case analysis. Being able to imagine different scenarios or contemplate the outcome of a decision can aid the analysis. Managers also have to deal with uncertainty since most decisions are made without complete knowledge of the circumstances. This is also true in case analysis. Case materials often seem to be missing data or the information provided is contradictory. The ability to speculate about details that are unknown or the consequences of an action can be helpful.

3. **Integrate.** Strategy involves looking at the big picture and having an organization-wide perspective. Strategic case analysis is no different. Even though the chapters in this textbook divide the material into various topics that may apply to different parts of an organization, all of this information must be integrated into one set of recommendations that will affect the whole company. A strategic manager needs to comprehend how all the factors that influence the organization will interact. This also applies to case analysis. Changes made in one part of the organization affect other parts. Thus, a holistic perspective that integrates the impact of various decisions and environmental influences on all parts of the organization is needed.

In business, these three activities sometimes "compete" with each other for your attention. For example, some decision makers may have a natural ability to differentiate among elements of a problem but are not able to integrate them very well. Others have enough innate creativity to imagine solutions or fill in the blanks when information is missing. But they may have a difficult time when faced with hard numbers or cold facts. Even so, each of these skills is important. The mark of a good strategic manager is the ability to simultaneously make distinctions and envision the whole, and to imagine a future scenario while staying focused on the present. Thus, another reason to conduct case analysis is to help you develop and exercise your ability to differentiate, speculate, and integrate.

Case analysis takes the student through the whole cycle of activity that a manager would face. Beyond the textbook descriptions of concepts and examples, case analysis asks you to "walk a mile in the shoes" of the strategic decision maker and learn to evaluate situations critically. Executives and owners must make decisions every day with limited information and a swirl of business activity going on around them. Consider the example of Sapient Health Networks, an Internet start-up that had to undergo some analysis and problem solving just to survive. Strategy Spotlight 14.1 describes how this company transformed itself after a serious self-examination during a time of crisis.

As you can see from the experience of Sapient Health Networks, businesses are often faced with immediate challenges that threaten their lives. The Sapient case illustrates how the strategic management process helped it survive. First, the company realistically assessed the environment, evaluated the marketplace, and analyzed its resources. Then it made tough decisions, which included shifting its market focus, hiring and firing, and redeploying its assets. Finally, it took action. The result was not only firm survival, but also a quick turnaround leading to rapid success.

>>How to Conduct a Case Analysis

The process of analyzing strategic management cases involves several steps. In this section we will review the mechanics of preparing a case analysis. Before beginning, there are two things to keep in mind that will clarify your understanding of the process and make the results of the process more meaningful.

STRATEGY SPOTLIGHT

14.1

Analysis, Decision Making, and Change at Sapient Health Network

Sapient Health Network (SHN) had gotten off to a good start. CEO Jim Kean and his two cofounders had raised $5 million in investor capital to launch their vision: an Internet-based health care information subscription service. The idea was to create an Internet community for people suffering from chronic diseases. It would provide members with expert information, resources, a message board, and chat rooms so that people suffering from the same ailments could provide each other with information and support. "Who would be more voracious consumers of information than people who are faced with life-changing, life-threatening illnesses?" thought Bill Kelly, one of SHN's cofounders. Initial market research and beta tests had supported that view.

During the beta tests, however, the service had been offered for free. The troubles began when SHN tried to convert its trial subscribers into paying ones. Fewer than 5 percent signed on, far less than the 15 percent the company had projected. Sapient hired a vice president of marketing who launched an aggressive promotion, but after three months of campaigning SHN still had only 500 members. SHN was now burning through $400,000 per month, with little revenue to show for it.

At that point, according to SHN board member Susan Clymer, "there was a lot of scrambling around trying to figure out how we could wring value out of what we'd already accomplished." One thing SHN had created was an expert software system which had two components: an "intelligent profile engine" (IPE) and an "intelligent query

engine" (IQE). SHN used this system to collect detailed information from its subscribers.

SHN was sure that the expert system was its biggest selling point. But how could they use it? Then the founders remembered that the original business plan had suggested there might be a market for aggregate data about patient populations gathered from the Web site. Could they turn the business around by selling patient data? To analyze the possibility, Kean tried out the idea on the market research arm of a huge East Coast health care conglomerate. The officials were intrigued. SHN realized that its expert system could become a market research tool.

Once the analysis was completed, the founders made the decision: They would still create Internet communities for chronically ill patients, but the service would be free. And they would transform SHN from a company that processed subscriptions to one that sold market research.

Finally, they enacted the changes. Some of it was painful, including laying off 18 employees. Instead, SHN needed more health care industry expertise. It even hired an interim CEO, Craig Davenport, a 25-year veteran of the industry, to steer the company in its new direction. Finally, SHN had to communicate a new message to its members. It began by reimbursing the $10,000 of subscription fees they had paid.

All of this paid off dramatically in a matter of just two years. Revenues jumped to $1.9 million in 1998. Early in 1999 SHN was purchased by WebMD and less than a year later, WebMD merged with Healtheon. The combined company still operates a thriving office out of SHN's original location in Portland, Oregon.

Sources: Brenneman, K. 2000. Healtheon/WebMD's local office is thriving. *Business Journal of Portland,* June 2; Raths, D. 1998. Reversal of fortune. *Inc. Technology,* 2: 52–62.

First, unless you prepare for a case discussion, there is little you can gain from the discussion and even less that you can offer. Effective strategic managers don't enter into problem-solving situations without doing some homework—investigating the situation, analyzing and researching possible solutions, and sometimes gathering the advice of others. Good problem solving often requires that decision makers be immersed in the facts, options, and implications surrounding the problem. In case analysis, this means reading and thoroughly comprehending the case materials before trying to make an analysis.

The second point is related to the first. To get the most out of a case analysis you must place yourself "inside" the case—that is, think like an actual participant in the case situation. However, there are several positions you can take. These are discussed in the following paragraphs:

- **Strategic decision maker.** This is the position of the senior executive responsible for resolving the situation described in the case. It may be the CEO, the business owner, or a strategic manager in a key executive position.

- **Board of directors.** Since the board of directors represents the owners of a corporation, it has a responsibility to step in when a management crisis threatens the company. As a board member, you may be in a unique position to solve problems.

- **Outside consultant.** Either the board or top management may decide to bring in outsiders. Consultants often have an advantage because they can look at a situation objectively. But they also may be at a disadvantage since they have no power to enforce changes.

Before beginning the analysis, it may be helpful to envision yourself assuming one of these roles. Then, as you study and analyze the case materials, you can make a diagnosis and recommend solutions in a way that is consistent with your position. Try different perspectives. You may find that your view of the situation changes depending on the role you play. As an outside consultant, for example, it may be easy for you to conclude that certain individuals should be replaced in order to solve a problem presented in the case. However, if you take the role of the CEO who knows the individuals and the challenges they have been facing, you may be reluctant to fire them and will seek another solution instead.

The idea of assuming a particular role is similar to the real world in various ways. In your career, you may work in an organization where outside accountants, bankers, lawyers, or other professionals are advising you about how to resolve business situations or improve your practices. Their perspective will be different from yours but it is useful to understand things from their point of view. Conversely, you may work as a member of the audit team of an accounting firm or the loan committee of a bank. In those situations, it would be helpful if you understood the situation from the perspective of the business leader who must weigh your views against all the other advice that he or she receives. Case analysis can help develop an ability to appreciate such multiple perspectives.

One of the most challenging roles to play in business is as a business founder or owner. For small businesses or entrepreneurial start-ups, the founder may wear all hats at once—key decision maker, primary stockholder, and CEO. Hiring an outside consultant may not be an option. However, the issues faced by young firms and established firms are often not that different, especially when it comes to formulating a plan of action. Business plans that entrepreneurial firms use to raise money or propose a business expansion typically revolve around a few key issues that must be addressed no matter what the size or age of the business. Strategy Spotlight 14.2 reviews business planning issues that are most important to consider when evaluating any case, especially from the perspective of the business founder or owner.

Next we will review five steps to follow when conducting a strategic management case analysis: becoming familiar with the material, identifying the problems, analyzing the strategic issues using the tools and insights of strategic management, proposing alternative solutions, and making recommendations.[4]

Become Familiar with the Material

Written cases often include a lot of material. They may be complex and include detailed financials or long passages. Even so, to understand a case and its implications, you must become familiar with its content. Sometimes key information is not immediately apparent. It may be contained in the footnotes to an exhibit or an interview with a lower-level employee. In other cases the important points may be difficult to grasp because the subject matter is so unfamiliar. When you approach a strategic case try the following technique to enhance comprehension:

- Read quickly through the case one time to get an overall sense of the material.
- Use the initial read-through to assess possible links to strategic concepts.
- Read through the case again, in depth. Make written notes as you read.

STRATEGY SPOTLIGHT

Using a Business Plan Framework to Analyze Strategic Cases

Established businesses often have to change what they are doing in order to improve their competitive position or sometimes simply to survive. To make the changes effectively, businesses usually need a plan. Business plans are no longer just for entrepreneurs. The kind of market analysis, decision making, and action planning that is considered standard practice among new ventures can also benefit going concerns that want to make changes, seize an opportunity, or head in a new direction.

The best business plans, however, are not those loaded with decades of month-by-month financial projections or that depend on rigid adherence to a schedule of events that is impossible to predict. The good ones are focused on four factors that are critical to new-venture success. These same factors are important in case analysis as well because they get to the heart of many of the problems found in strategic cases.

1. *The People.* "When I receive a business plan, I always read the résumé section first," says Harvard Professor William Sahlman. The people questions that are critically important to investors include: What are their skills? How much experience do they have? What is their reputation? Have they worked together as a team? These same questions also may be used in case analysis to evaluate the role of individuals in the strategic case.

2. *The Opportunity.* Business opportunities come in many forms. They are not limited to new ventures. The chance to enter new markets, introduce new products, or merge with a competitor provide many of the challenges that are found in strategic management cases. What are the consequences of such actions? Will the proposed changes affect the firm's business concept? What factors might stand in the way of success? The same issues are also present in most strategic cases.

3. *The Context.* Things happen in contexts that cannot be controlled by a firm's managers. This is particularly true of the general environment where social trends, economic changes, or events such as the September 11, 2001, terrorist attacks can change business overnight. When evaluating strategic cases, ask: Is the company aware of the impact of context on the business? What will it do if the context changes? Can it influence the context in a way that favors the company?

4. *Risk and Reward.* With a new venture, the entrepreneurs and investors take the risks and get the rewards. In strategic cases, the risks and rewards often extend to many other stakeholders, such as employees, customers, and suppliers. When analyzing a case, ask: Are the managers making choices that will pay off in the future? Are the rewards evenly distributed? Will some stakeholders be put at risk if the situation in the case changes? What if the situation remains the same? Could that be even riskier?

Whether a business is growing or shrinking, large or small, industrial or service oriented, the issues of people, opportunities, context, and risks and rewards will have a large impact on its performance. Therefore, you should always consider these four factors when evaluating strategic management cases.

Sources: Wasserman, E. 2003. A simple plan. *MBA Jungle,* February: 50–55; DeKluyver, C. A. 2000. *Strategic thinking: An executive perspective.* Upper Saddle River, NJ: Prentice Hall; Sahlman, W. A. 1997. How to write a great business plan. *Harvard Business Review,* 75(4): 98–108.

- Evaluate how strategic concepts might inform key decisions or suggest alternative solutions.
- After formulating an initial recommendation, thumb through the case again quickly to help assess the consequences of the actions you propose.

Identify Problems

When conducting case analysis, one of your most important tasks is to identify the problem. Earlier we noted that one of the main reasons to conduct case analysis was to find solutions. But you cannot find a solution unless you know the problem. Another saying you may have heard is, "A good diagnosis is half the cure." In other words, once you have determined what the problem is, you are well on your way to identifying a reasonable solution.

Some cases have more than one problem. But the problems are usually related. For a hypothetical example, consider the following: Company A was losing customers to a new competitor. Upon analysis, it was determined that the competitor had a 50 percent faster delivery time even though its product was of lower quality. The managers of company A could not understand why customers would settle for an inferior product. It turns out that no one was marketing to company A's customers that its product was superior. A second problem was that falling sales resulted in cuts in company A's sales force. Thus, there were two related problems: inferior delivery technology and insufficient sales effort.

When trying to determine the problem, avoid getting hung up on symptoms. Zero in on the problem. For example, in the company A example above, the symptom was losing customers. But the problems were an underfunded, understaffed sales force combined with an outdated delivery technology. Try to see beyond the immediate symptoms to the more fundamental problems.

Another tip when preparing a case analysis is to articulate the problem.[5] Writing down a problem statement gives you a reference point to turn to as you proceed through the case analysis. This is important because the process of formulating strategies or evaluating implementation methods may lead you away from the initial problem. Make sure your recommendation actually addresses the problems you have identified.

One more thing about identifying problems: Sometimes problems are not apparent until *after* you do the analysis. In some cases the problem will be presented plainly, perhaps in the opening paragraph or on the last page of the case. But in other cases the problem does not emerge until after the issues in the case have been analyzed. We turn next to the subject of strategic case analysis.

Conduct Strategic Analyses

This textbook has presented numerous analytical tools (e.g., five-forces analysis and value-chain analysis), contingency frameworks (e.g., when to use related rather than unrelated diversification strategies), and other techniques that can be used to evaluate strategic situations. The previous 13 chapters have addressed practices that are common in strategic management, but only so much can be learned by studying the practices and concepts. The best way to understand these methods is to apply them by conducting analyses of specific cases.

The first step is to determine which strategic issues are involved. Is there a problem in the company's competitive environment? Or is it an internal problem? If it is internal, does it have to do with organizational structure? Strategic controls? Uses of technology? Or perhaps the company has overworked its employees or underutilized its intellectual capital. Has the company mishandled a merger? Chosen the wrong diversification strategy? Botched a new product introduction? Each of these issues is linked to one or more of the concepts discussed earlier in the text. Determine what strategic issues are associated with the problems you have identified. Remember also that most real-life case situations involve issues that are highly interrelated. Even in cases where there is only one major problem, the strategic processes required to solve it may involve several parts of the organization.

Once you have identified the issues that apply to the case, conduct the analysis. For example, you may need to conduct a five-forces analysis or dissect the company's competitive strategy. Perhaps you need to evaluate whether its resources are rare, valuable, difficult to imitate, or difficult to substitute. Financial analysis may be needed to assess the company's economic prospects. Perhaps the international entry mode needs to be reevaluated because of changing conditions in the host country. Employee empowerment techniques may need to be improved to enhance organizational learning. Whatever the case, all the strategic concepts introduced in the text include insights for assessing their effectiveness. Determining how well a company is doing these things is central to the case analysis process.

Ratio	What It Measures
Short-term solvency, or liquidity, ratios:	
Current ratio	Ability to use assets to pay off liabilities.
Quick ratio	Ability to use liquid assets to pay off liabilities quickly.
Cash ratio	Ability to pay off liabilities with cash on hand.
Long-term solvency, or financial leverage, ratios:	
Total debt ratio	How much of a company's total assets are financed by debt.
Debt-equity ratio	Compares how much a company is financed by debt with how much it is financed by equity.
Equity multiplier	How much debt is being used to finance assets.
Times interest earned ratio	How well a company has its interest obligations covered.
Cash coverage ratio	A company's ability to generate cash from operations.
Asset utilization, or turnover, ratios:	
Inventory turnover	How many times each year a company sells its entire inventory.
Days' sales in inventory	How many days on average inventory is on hand before it is sold.
Receivables turnover	How frequently each year a company collects on its credit sales.
Days' sales in receivables	How many days on average it takes to collect on credit sales (average collection period).
Total asset turnover	How much of sales is generated for every dollar in assets.
Capital intensity	The dollar investment in assets needed to generate $1 in sales.
Profitability ratios:	
Profit margin	How much profit is generated by every dollar of sales.
Return on assets (ROA)	How effectively assets are being used to generate a return.
Return on equity (ROE)	How effectively amounts invested in the business by its owners are being used to generate a return.
Market value ratios:	
Price-earnings ratio	How much investors are willing to pay per dollar of current earnings.
Market-to-book ratio	Compares market value of the company's investments to the cost of those investments.

Exhibit 14.1

Summary of Financial Ratio Analysis Techniques

Financial analysis is one of the primary tools used to conduct case analysis. The Appendix to Chapter 3 includes a discussion and examples of the financial ratios that are often used to evaluate a company's performance and financial well-being. Exhibit 14.1 provides a summary of the financial ratios presented in the Appendix to Chapter 3.

In this part of the overall strategic analysis process, it is also important to test your own assumptions about the case.[6] First, what assumptions are you making about the case materials? It may be that you have interpreted the case content differently than your team members or classmates. Being clear about these assumptions will be important in determining how to analyze the case. Second, what assumptions have you made about the best way to resolve the problems? Ask yourself why you have chosen one type of analysis over another. This process of assumption checking can also help determine if you have gotten to the heart of the problem or are still just dealing with symptoms.

As mentioned earlier, sometimes the critical diagnosis in a case can only be made after the analysis is conducted. However, by the end of this stage in the process, you should know the problems and have completed a thorough analysis of them. You can now move to the next step: finding solutions.

Propose Alternative Solutions

It is important to remember that in strategic management case analysis, there is rarely one right answer or one best way. Even when members of a class or a team agree on what the problem is, they may not agree upon how to solve the problem. Therefore, it is helpful to consider several different solutions.

After conducting strategic analysis and identifying the problem, develop a list of options. What are the possible solutions? What are the alternatives? First, generate a list of all the options you can think of without prejudging any one of them. Remember that not all cases call for dramatic decisions or sweeping changes. Some companies just need to make small adjustments. In fact, "Do nothing" may be a reasonable alternative in some cases. Although that is rare, it might be useful to consider what will happen if the company does nothing. This point illustrates the purpose of developing alternatives: to evaluate what will happen if a company chooses one solution over another.

Thus, during this step of a case analysis, you will evaluate choices and the implications of those choices. One aspect of any business that is likely to be highlighted in this part of the analysis is strategy implementation. Ask how the choices made will be implemented. It may be that what seems like an obvious choice for solving a problem creates an even bigger problem when implemented. But remember also that no strategy or strategic "fix" is going to work if it cannot be implemented. Once a list of alternatives is generated, ask:

- Can the company afford it? How will it affect the bottom line?
- Is the solution likely to evoke a competitive response?
- Will employees throughout the company accept the changes? What impact will the solution have on morale?
- How will the decision affect other stakeholders? Will customers, suppliers, and others buy into it?
- How does this solution fit with the company's vison, mission, and objectives?
- Will the culture or values of the company be changed by the solution? Is it a positive change?

The point of this step in the case analysis process is to find a solution that both solves the problem and is realistic. A consideration of the implications of various alternative solutions will generally lead you to a final recommendation that is more thoughtful and complete.

Make Recommendations

The basic aim of case analysis is to find solutions. Your analysis is not complete until you have recommended a course of action. In this step the task is to make a set of recommendations that your analysis supports. Describe exactly what needs to be done. Explain why this course of action will solve the problem. The recommendation should also include suggestions for how best to implement the proposed solution because the recommended actions and their implications for the performance and future of the firm are interrelated.

Recall that the solution you propose must solve the problem you identified. This point cannot be overemphasized; too often students make recommendations that treat only symptoms or fail to tackle the central problems in the case. Make a logical argument that shows how the problem led to the analysis and the analysis led to the recommendations you are proposing. Remember, an analysis is not an end in itself; it is useful only if it leads to a solution.

The actions you propose should describe the very next steps that the company needs to take. Don't say, for example, "If the company does more market research, then I would recommend the following course of action. . . ." Instead, make conducting the research part of your recommendation. Taking the example a step further, if you also want to suggest subsequent actions that may be different *depending* on the outcome of the market research, that's OK. But don't make your initial recommendation conditional on actions the company may or may not take.

In summary, case analysis can be a very rewarding process but, as you might imagine, it can also be frustrating and challenging. If you will follow the steps described above, you will address the different elements of a thorough analysis. This approach can give your analysis a solid footing. Then, even if there are differences of opinion about how to interpret the facts, analyze the situation, or solve the problems, you can feel confident that you have not missed any important steps in finding the best course of action.

Students are often asked to prepare oral presentations of the information in a case and their analysis of the best remedies. This is frequently assigned as a group project. Or you may be called upon in class to present your ideas about the circumstances or solutions for a case the class is discussing. Exhibit 14.2 provides some tips for preparing an oral case presentation.

>>How to Get the Most from Case Analysis

One of the reasons case analysis is so enriching as a learning tool is that it draws on many resources and skills besides just what is in the textbook. This is especially true in the study of strategy. Why? Because strategic management itself is a highly integrative task that draws on many areas of specialization at several levels, from the individual to the whole of society. Therefore, to get the most out of case analysis, expand your horizons beyond the concepts in this text and seek insights from your own reservoir of knowledge. Here are some tips for how to do that.[7]

- *Keep an open mind.* Like any good discussion, a case analysis discussion often evokes strong opinions and high emotions. But it's the variety of perspectives that makes case analysis so valuable: Many viewpoints usually lead to a more complete analysis. Therefore, avoid letting an emotional response to another person's style or opinion keep you from hearing what he or she has to say. Once you evaluate what is said, you may disagree with it or dismiss it as faulty. But unless you keep an open mind in the first place, you may miss the importance of the other person's contribution. Also, people often place a higher value on the opinions of those they consider to be good listeners.

- *Take a stand for what you believe.* Although it is vital to keep an open mind, it is also important to state your views proactively. Don't try to figure out what your friends or the instructor wants to hear. Analyze the case from the perspective of your own background and belief system. For example, perhaps you feel that a

Rule	Description
Organize your thoughts.	Begin by becoming familiar with the material. If you are working with a team, compare notes about the key points of the case and share insights that other team members may have gleaned from tables and exhibits. Then make an outline. This is one of the best ways to organize the flow and content of the presentation.
Emphasize strategic analysis.	The purpose of case analysis is to diagnose problems and find solutions. In the process, you may need to unravel the case material as presented and reconfigure it in a fashion that can be more effectively analyzed. Present the material in a way that lends itself to analysis—don't simply restate what is in the case. This involves three major categories with the following emphasis:
	Background/Problem Statement 10–20%
	Strategic Analysis/Options 60–75%
	Recommendations/Action Plan 10–20%
	As you can see, the emphasis of your presentation should be on analysis. This will probably require you to reorganize the material so that the tools of strategic analysis can be applied.
Be logical and consistent.	A presentation that is rambling and hard to follow may confuse the listener and fail to evoke a good discussion. Present your arguments and explanations in a logical sequence. Support your claims with facts. Include financial analysis where appropriate. Be sure that the solutions you recommend address the problems you have identified.
Defend your position.	Usually an oral presentation is followed by a class discussion. Anticipate what others might disagree with and be prepared to defend your views. This means being aware of the choices you made and the implications of your recommendations. Be clear about your assumptions. Be able to expand on your analysis.
Share presentation responsibilities.	Strategic management case analyses are often conducted by teams. Each member of the team should have a clear role in the oral presentation, preferably a speaking role. It's also important to coordinate the different parts of the presentation into a logical, smooth-flowing whole. How well a team works together is usually very apparent during an oral presentation.

Exhibit 14.2

Preparing an Oral Case Presentation

decision is unethical or that the managers in a case have misinterpreted the facts. Don't be afraid to assert that in the discussion. For one thing, when a person takes a strong stand, it often encourages others to evaluate the issues more closely. This can lead to a more thorough investigation and a more meaningful class discussion.

- *Draw on your personal experience.* You may have experiences from work or as a customer that shed light on some of the issues in a case. Even though one of the purposes of case analysis is to apply the analytical tools from this text, you may be able to add to the discussion by drawing on your outside experiences and background. Of course, you need to guard against carrying that to extremes. In other words, don't think that your perspective is the only viewpoint that matters! Simply recognize that firsthand experience usually represents a welcome contribution to the overall quality of case discussions.

- *Participate and persuade.* Have you heard the phrase, "Vote early . . . and often"? Among loyal members of certain political parties, it has become rather a joke. Why? Because a democratic system is built on the concept of one person, one vote. Even though some voters may want to vote often enough to get their candidate elected, it is against the law. Not so in a case discussion. People who are persuasive and speak their mind can often influence the views of others. But to do so, you have to be prepared and convincing. Being persuasive is more than being loud or long-winded. It involves understanding all sides of an argument and being able to overcome objections to your own point of view. These efforts can make a case discussion more lively. And they parallel what happens in the real world; in business, people frequently share their opinions and attempt to persuade others to see things their way.

- *Be concise and to the point.* In the previous point, we encouraged you to speak up and "sell" your ideas to others in a case discussion. But you must be clear about what you are selling. Make your arguments in a way that is explicit and direct. Zero in on the most important points. Be brief. Don't try to make a lot of points at once by jumping around between topics. Avoid trying to explain the whole case situation at once. Remember, other students usually resent classmates who go on and on, take up a lot of "airtime," or repeat themselves unnecessarily. The best way to avoid this is to stay focused and be specific.

- *Think out of the box.* It's OK to be a little provocative; sometimes that is the consequence of taking a stand on issues. But it may be equally important to be imaginative and creative when making a recommendation or determining how to implement a solution. Albert Einstein once stated, "Imagination is more important than knowledge." The reason is that managing strategically requires more than memorizing concepts. Strategic management insights must be applied to each case differently—just knowing the principles is not enough. Imagination and out-of-the-box thinking help to apply strategic knowledge in novel and unique ways.

- *Learn from the insights of others.* Before you make up your mind about a case, hear what other students have to say. Get a second opinion, and a third, and so forth. Of course, in a situation where you have to put your analysis in writing, you may not be able to learn from others ahead of time. But in a case discussion, observe how various students attack the issues and engage in problem solving. Such observation skills also may be a key to finding answers within the case. For example, people tend to believe authority figures, so they would place a higher value on what a company president says. In some cases, however, the statements of middle managers may represent a point of view that is even more helpful for finding a solution to the problems presented by the case.

- *Apply insights from other case analyses.* Throughout the text, we have used examples of actual businesses to illustrate strategy concepts. The aim has been to show you how firms think about and deal with business problems. During the course, you may be asked to conduct several case analyses as part of the learning experience. Once you have performed a few case analyses, you will see how the concepts from the text apply in real-life business situations. Incorporate the insights learned from the text examples and your own previous case discussions into each new case that you analyze.

- *Critically analyze your own performance.* Performance appraisals are a standard part of many workplace situations. They are used to determine promotions, raises, and work assignments. In some organizations, everyone from the top executive down is subject to such reviews. Even in situations where the owner or CEO is not evaluated by others, they often find it useful to ask themselves regularly, Am I being effective? The same can be applied to your performance in a case analysis situation. Ask yourself, Were my comments insightful? Did I make a good contribution? How might I improve next time? Use the same criteria on yourself that you use to evaluate others. What grade would you give yourself? This technique will not only make you more fair in your assessment of others but also will indicate how your own performance can improve.

- *Conduct outside research.* Many times, you can enhance your understanding of a case situation by investigating sources outside the case materials. For example, you may want to study an industry more closely or research a company's close competitors. Recent moves such as mergers and acquisitions or product introductions may be reported in the business press. The company itself may provide useful information on its Web site or in its annual reports. Such information can usually spur additional discussion and enrich the case analysis. (*Caution:* It is best to check with your instructor in advance to be sure this kind of additional research is encouraged. Bringing in outside research may conflict with the instructor's learning objectives.)

Several of the points suggested above for how to get the most out of case analysis apply only to an open discussion of a case, like that in a classroom setting. Exhibit 14.3 provides some additional guidelines for preparing a written case analysis.

>>Using Conflict-Inducing Decision-Making Techniques in Case Analysis

Next we address some techniques often used to improve case analyses that involve the constructive use of conflict. In the classroom—as well as in the business world—you will frequently be analyzing cases or solving problems in groups. While the word *conflict* often has a negative connotation (e.g., rude behavior, personal affronts), it can be very helpful in arriving at better solutions to cases. It can provide an effective means for new insights as well as for rigorously questioning and analyzing assumptions and strategic alternatives. In fact, if you don't have constructive conflict, you may only get consensus. When this happens, decisions tend to be based on compromise rather than collaboration.

In your organizational behavior classes, you probably learned the concept of "groupthink."[8] Groupthink, a term coined by Irving Janis after he conducted numerous studies on executive decision making, is a condition in which group members strive to reach agreement or consensus without realistically considering other viable alternatives. In effect, group norms bolster morale at the expense of critical thinking and decision making is impaired.[9]

Many of us have probably been "victims" of groupthink at one time or another in our life. We may be confronted with situations when social pressure, politics, or "not wanting to stand out" may prevent us from voicing our concerns about a chosen course of action. Nevertheless, decision making in groups is a common practice in the management of many businesses. Most companies, especially large ones, rely on input from various top managers to provide valuable information and experience from their specialty area as well as their unique perspectives. Chapter 11 emphasized the importance of empowering individuals at all levels to participate in decision-making processes. In terms of this course, case analysis

Rule	Description
Be thorough.	Many of the ideas presented in Exhibit 14.2 about oral presentations also apply to written case analysis. However, a written analysis typically has to be more complete. This means writing out the problem statement and articulating assumptions. It is also important to provide support for your arguments and reference case materials or other facts more specifically.
Coordinate team efforts.	Written cases are often prepared by small groups. Within a group, just as in a class discussion, you may disagree about the diagnosis or the recommended plan of action. This can be healthy if it leads to a richer understanding of the case material. But before committing your ideas to writing, make sure you have coordinated your responses. Don't prepare a written analysis that appears contradictory or looks like a patchwork of disconnected thoughts.
Avoid restating the obvious.	There is no reason to restate material that everyone is familiar with already, namely, the case content. It is too easy for students to use up space in a written analysis with a recapitulation of the details of the case—this accomplishes very little. Stay focused on the key points. Only restate the information that is most central to your analysis.
Present information graphically.	Tables, graphs, and other exhibits are usually one of the best ways to present factual material that supports your arguments. For example, financial calculations such as break-even analysis, sensitivity analysis, or return on investment are best presented graphically. Even qualitative information such as product lists or rosters of employees can be summarized effectively and viewed quickly by using a table or graph.
Exercise quality control.	When presenting a case analysis in writing, it is especially important to use good grammar, avoid misspelling words, and eliminate typos and other visual distractions. Mistakes that can be glossed over in an oral presentation or class discussion are often highlighted when they appear in writing. Make your written presentation appear as professional as possible. Don't let the appearance of your written case keep the reader from recognizing the importance and quality of your analysis.

Exhibit 14.3

Preparing a Written Case Analysis

involves a type of decision making that is often conducted in groups. Strategy Spotlight 14.3 provides guidelines for making team-based approaches to case analysis more effective.

Clearly, understanding how to work in groups and the potential problems associated with group decision processes can benefit the case analysis process. Therefore, let's first look at some of the symptoms of groupthink and suggest ways of preventing it. Then, we will suggest some conflict-inducing decision-making techniques—devil's advocacy and dialectical inquiry—that can help to prevent groupthink and lead to better decisions.

Symptoms of Groupthink and How to Prevent It

Irving Janis identified several symptoms of groupthink, including:

- *An illusion of invulnerability.* This reassures people about possible dangers and leads to overoptimism and failure to heed warnings of danger.

- *A belief in the inherent morality of the group.* Because individuals think that what they are doing is right, they tend to ignore ethical or moral consequences of their decisions.

STRATEGY SPOTLIGHT

Making Case Analysis Teams More Effective

Working in teams can be very challenging. Not all team members have the same skills, interests, or motivations. Some team members just want to get the work done. Others see teams as an opportunity to socialize. Occasionally, there are team members who think they should be in charge and make all the decisions; other teams have freeloaders—team members who don't want to do anything except get credit for the team's work.

One consequence of these various styles is that team meetings can become time wasters. Disagreements about how to proceed, how to share the work, or what to do at the next meeting tend to slow down teams and impede progress toward the goal. While the dynamics of case analysis teams are likely to always be challenging depending on the personalities involved, one thing nearly all members realize is that, ultimately, the team's work must be completed. Most team members also aim to do the highest quality work possible. The following guidelines provide some useful insights about how to get the work of a team done more effectively.

Spend More Time Together

One of the factors that prevents teams from doing a good job with case analysis is their failure to put in the necessary time. Unless teams really tackle the issues surrounding case analysis—both the issues in the case itself and organizing how the work is to be conducted—the end result will probably be lacking because decisions that are made too quickly are unlikely to get to the heart of the problem(s) in the case. "Meetings should be a precious resource, but they're treated like a necessary evil," says Kenneth Sole, a consultant who specializes in organizational behavior. As a result, teams that care more about finishing the analysis than getting the analysis right often make poor decisions.

Therefore, expect to have a few meetings that run long, especially at the beginning of the project when the work is being organized and the issues in the case are being sorted out, and again at the end when the team must coordinate the components of the case analysis that will be presented. Without spending this kind of time together, it is doubtful that the analysis will be comprehensive and the presentation is likely to be choppy and incomplete.

Make a Focused and Disciplined Agenda

To complete tasks and avoid wasting time, meetings need to have a clear purpose. To accomplish this at Roche, the Swiss drug and diagnostic product maker, CEO Franz Humer implemented a "decision agenda." The agenda focuses only on Roche's highest value issues and discussions are limited to these major topics. In terms of case analysis, the major topics include sorting out the issues of the case, linking elements of the case to the strategic issues presented in class or the text, and assigning roles to various team members. Such objectives help keep team members on track.

Agendas also can be used to address issues such as the time line for accomplishing work. Otherwise the purpose of meetings may only be to manage the "crisis" of getting the case analysis finished on time. One solution is to assign a team member to manage the agenda. That person could make sure the team stays focused on the tasks at hand and remains mindful of time constraints. Another role could be to link the team's efforts to the steps presented in Exhibits 14.2 and 14.3 on how to prepare a case analysis.

Pay More Attention to Strategy

Teams often waste time by focusing on unimportant aspects of a case. These may include details that are interesting but irrelevant or operational issues rather than strategic issues. It is true that useful clues to the issues in the case are sometimes embedded in the conversations of key managers or the trends evident in a financial statement. But once such insights are discovered, teams need to focus on the underlying strategic problems in the case. To solve such problems, major corporations such as Cadbury Schweppes and Boeing hold meetings just to generate strategic alternatives for solving their problems. This gives managers time to consider the implications of various courses of action. Separate meetings are held to evaluate alternatives, make strategic decisions, and approve an action plan.

Once the strategic solutions or "course corrections" are identified—as is common in most cases assigned—the operational implications and details of implementation will flow from the strategic decisions that companies make. Therefore, focusing primarily on strategic issues will provide teams with insights for making recommendations that are based on a deeper understanding of the issues in the case.

Produce Real Decisions

Too often, meetings are about discussing rather than deciding. Teams often spend a lot of time talking without reaching any conclusions. As Raymond Sanchez, CEO of Florida-based Security Mortgage Group, says, meetings are often used to "rehash the hash that's already been hashed." To be efficient and productive, team meetings need to be about more than just information sharing and group input. For example, an initial meeting may result in the team realizing that it needs to study the case in greater depth and examine links to strategic issues more carefully. Once more analysis is conducted, the team needs to reach a *(continued)*

Sources: Mankins, M. C. 2004. Stop wasting valuable time. *Harvard Business Review*, September: 58–65; and Sauer, P. J. 2004. Escape from meeting hell. *Inc. Magazine*, May, www.inc.com.

- *Stereotyped views of members of opposing groups.* Members of other groups are viewed as weak or not intelligent.

- *The application of pressure to members who express doubts about the group's shared illusions or question the validity of arguments proposed.*

- *The practice of self-censorship.* Members keep silent about their opposing views and downplay to themselves the value of their perspectives.

- *An illusion of unanimity.* People assume that judgments expressed by members are shared by all.

- *The appointment of mindguards.* People sometimes appoint themselves as mindguards to protect the group from adverse information that might break the climate of consensus (or agreement).

Clearly, groupthink is an undesirable and negative phenomenon that can lead to poor decisions. Irving Janis considers it to be a key contributor to such faulty decisions as the failure to prepare for the attack on Pearl Harbor, the escalation of the Vietnam conflict, and the failure to prepare for the consequences of the Iraqi invasion. Many of the same sorts of flawed decision making occur in business organizations—as we discussed above with the EDS example. Janis has provided several suggestions for preventing groupthink that can be used as valuable guides in decision making and problem solving:

- Leaders must encourage group members to address their concerns and objectives.
- When higher-level managers assign a problem for a group to solve, they should adopt an impartial stance and not mention their preferences.
- Before a group reaches its final decision, the leader should encourage members to discuss their deliberations with trusted associates and then report the perspectives back to the group.
- The group should invite outside experts and encourage them to challenge the group's viewpoints and positions.
- The group should divide into subgroups, meet at various times under different chairpersons, and then get together to resolve differences.
- After reaching a preliminary agreement, the group should hold a "second chance" meeting which provides members a forum to express any remaining concerns and rethink the issue prior to making a final decision.

Using Conflict to Improve Decision Making

In addition to the above suggestions, the effective use of conflict can be a means of improving decision making. Although conflict can have negative outcomes, such as ill will, anger, tension, and lowered motivation, both leaders and group members must strive to assure that it is managed properly and used in a constructive manner.

Two conflict-inducing decision-making approaches that have become quite popular are *devil's advocacy* and *dialectical inquiry.* Both approaches incorporate conflict into the decision-making process through formalized debate. A group charged with making a decision or solving a problem is divided into two subgroups and each will be involved in the analysis and solution.

Devil's Advocacy   With the devil's advocate approach, one of the groups (or individuals) acts as a critic to the plan. The devil's advocate tries to come up with problems with the proposed alternative and suggest reasons why it should not be adopted. The role of the devil's advocate is to create dissonance. This ensures that the group will take a hard look at its original proposal or alternative. By having a group (or individual) assigned the role of devil's advocate, it becomes clear that such an adversarial stance is legitimized. It brings out criticisms that might otherwise not be made.

Some authors have suggested that the use of a devil's advocate can be very helpful in helping boards of directors to ensure that decisions are addressed comprehensively and to avoid groupthink.[10] And Charles Elson, a director of Sunbeam Corporation, has argued that:

> Devil's advocates are terrific in any situation because they help you to figure a decision's numerous implications. . . . The better you think out the implications prior to making the decision, the better the decision ultimately turns out to be. That's why a devil's advocate is always a great person, irritating sometimes, but a great person.

As one might expect, there can be some potential problems with using the devil's advocate approach. If one's views are constantly criticized, one may become demoralized. Thus, that person may come up with "safe solutions" in order to minimize embarrassment or personal risk and become less subject to criticism. Additionally, even if the devil's advocate is successful with finding problems with the proposed course of action, there may be no new ideas or counterproposals to take its place. Thus, the approach sometimes may simply focus on what is wrong without suggesting other ideas.

Dialectical Inquiry   Dialectical inquiry attempts to accomplish the goals of the devil's advocate in a more constructive manner. It is a technique whereby a problem is approached from two alternative points of view. The idea is that out of a critique of the opposing perspectives—a thesis and an antithesis—a creative synthesis will occur. Dialectical inquiry involves the following steps:

1. Identify a proposal and the information that was used to derive it.
2. State the underlying assumptions of the proposal.
3. Identify a counterplan (antithesis) that is believed to be feasible, politically viable, and generally credible. However, it rests on assumptions that are opposite to the original proposal.
4. Engage in a debate in which individuals favoring each plan provide their arguments and support.
5. Identify a synthesis which, hopefully, includes the best components of each alternative.

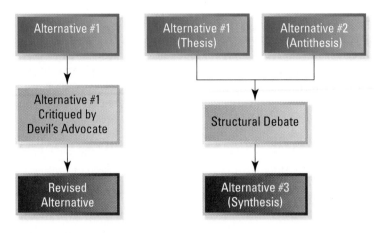

Exhibit 14.4   **Two Conflict-Inducing Decision-Making Processes**

There are some potential downsides associated with dialectical inquiry. It can be quite time consuming and involve a good deal of training. Further, it may result in a series of compromises between the initial proposal and the counterplan. In cases where the original proposal was the best approach, this would be unfortunate.

Despite some possible limitations associated with these conflict-inducing decision-making techniques, they have many benefits. Both techniques force debate about underlying assumptions, data, and recommendations between subgroups. Such debate tends to prevent the uncritical acceptance of a plan that may seem to be satisfactory after a cursory analysis. The approach serves to tap the knowledge and perspectives of group members and continues until group members agree on both assumptions and recommended actions. Given that both approaches serve to use, rather than minimize or suppress, conflict, higher quality decisions should result. Exhibit 14.4 briefly summarizes these techniques.

>>Following the Analysis-Decision-Action Cycle in Case Analysis

In Chapter 1 we defined strategic management as the analysis, decisions, and actions that organizations undertake to create and sustain competitive advantages. It is no accident that we chose that sequence of words because it corresponds to the sequence of events that typically occurs in the strategic management process. In case analysis, as in the real world, this cycle of events can provide a useful framework. First, an analysis of the case in terms of the business environment and current events is needed. To make such an analysis, the case background must be considered. Next, based on that analysis, decisions must be made. This may involve formulating a strategy, choosing between difficult options, moving forward aggressively, or retreating from a bad situation. There are many possible decisions, depending on the case situation. Finally, action is required. Once decisions are made and plans are set, the action begins. The recommended action steps and the consequences of implementing these actions are the final stage.

Each of the previous 13 chapters of this book includes techniques and information that may be useful in a case analysis. However, not all of the issues presented will be important in every case. As noted earlier, one of the challenges of case analysis is to identify the most critical points and sort through material that may be ambiguous or unimportant.

In this section we draw on the material presented in each of the 13 chapters to show how it informs the case analysis process. The ideas are linked sequentially and in terms of an overarching strategic perspective. One of your jobs when conducting case analysis is to see how the parts of a case fit together and how the insights from the study of strategy can help you understand the case situation.

1. *Analyzing organizational goals and objectives.* A company's vision, mission, and objectives keep organization members focused on a common purpose. They also influence how an organization deploys its resources, relates to its stakeholders, and matches its short-term objectives with its long-term goals. The goals may even impact how a company formulates and implements strategies. When exploring issues of goals and objectives, you might ask:

   - Has the company developed short-term objectives that are inconsistent with its long-term mission? If so, how can management realign its vision, mission, and objectives?
   - Has the company considered all of its stakeholders equally in making critical decisions? If not, should the views of all stakeholders be treated the same or are some stakeholders more important than others?
   - Is the company being faced with an issue that conflicts with one of its long-standing policies? If so, how should it compare its existing policies to the potential new situation?

2. *Analyzing the external environment.* The business environment has two components. The general environment consists of demographic, sociocultural, political/legal, technological, economic, and global conditions. The competitive environment includes rivals, suppliers, customers, and other factors that may directly affect a company's success. Strategic managers must monitor the environment to identify opportunities and threats that may have an impact on performance. When investigating a firm's external environment, you might ask:

   - Does the company follow trends and events in the general environment? If not, how can these influences be made part of the company's strategic analysis process?
   - Is the company effectively scanning and monitoring the competitive environment? If so, how is it using the competitive intelligence it is gathering to enhance its competitive advantage?
   - Has the company correctly analyzed the impact of the competitive forces in its industry on profitability? If so, how can it improve its competitive position relative to these forces?

3. *Analyzing the internal environment.* A firm's internal environment consists of its resources and other value-adding capabilities. Value-chain analysis and a resource-based approach to analysis can be used to identify a company's strengths and weaknesses and determine how they are contributing to its competitive advantages. Evaluating firm performance can also help make meaningful comparisons with competitors. When researching a company's internal analysis, you might ask:

   - Does the company know how the various components of its value chain are adding value to the firm? If not, what internal analysis is needed to determine its strengths and weakness?
   - Has the company accurately analyzed the source and vitality of its resources? If so, is it deploying its resources in a way that contributes to competitive advantages?
   - Is the company's financial performance as good as or better than that of its close competitors? If so, has it balanced its financial success with the performance criteria of other stakeholders such as customers and employees?

4. ***Assessing a firm's intellectual assets.*** Human capital is a major resource in today's knowledge economy. As a result, attracting, developing, and retaining talented workers is a key strategic challenge. Other assets such as patents and trademarks are also critical. How companies leverage their intellectual assets through social networks and strategic alliances, and how technology is used to manage knowledge may be a major influence on a firm's competitive advantage. When analyzing a firm's intellectual assets, you might ask:

- Does the company have underutilized human capital? If so, what steps are needed to develop and leverage its intellectual assets?
- Is the company missing opportunities to forge strategic alliances? If so, how can it use its social capital to network more effectively?
- Has the company developed knowledge-management systems that capture what it learns? If not, what technologies can it employ to retain new knowledge?

5. ***Formulating business-level strategies.*** Firms use the competitive strategies of differentiation, focus, and overall cost leadership as a basis for overcoming the five competitive forces and developing sustainable competitive advantages. Combinations of these strategies may work best in some competitive environments. Additionally, an industry's life cycle is an important contingency that may affect a company's choice of business-level strategies. When assessing business-level strategies, you might ask:

- Has the company chosen the correct competitive strategy given its industry environment and competitive situation? If not, how should it use its strengths and resources to improve its performance?
- Does the company use combination strategies effectively? If so, what capabilities can it cultivate to further enhance profitability?
- Is the company using a strategy that is appropriate for the industry life cycle in which it is competing? If not, how can it realign itself to match its efforts to the current stage of industry growth?

6. ***Formulating corporate-level strategies.*** Large firms often own and manage portfolios of businesses. Corporate strategies address methods for achieving synergies among these businesses. Related and unrelated diversification techniques are alternative approaches to deciding which business should be added to or removed from a portfolio. Companies can diversify by means of mergers, acquisitions, joint ventures, strategic alliances, and internal development. When analyzing corporate-level strategies, you might ask:

- Is the company competing in the right businesses given the opportunities and threats that are present in the environment? If not, how can it realign its diversification strategy to achieve competitive advantages?
- Is the corporation managing its portfolio of businesses in a way that creates synergies among the businesses? If so, what additional business should it consider adding to its portfolio?
- Are the motives of the top corporate executives who are pushing diversification strategies appropriate? If not, what action can be taken to curb their activities or align them with the best interests of all stakeholders?

7. ***Formulating international-level strategies.*** Foreign markets provide both opportunities and potential dangers for companies that want to expand globally. To decide which entry strategy is most appropriate, companies have to evaluate the trade-offs between two factors that firms face when entering foreign markets: cost reduction and local adaptation. To achieve competitive advantages, firms will typically

choose one of three strategies: global, multidomestic, or transnational. When evaluating international-level strategies, you might ask:

- Is the company's entry into an international marketplace threatened by the
  actions of local competitors? If so, how can cultural differences be minimized
  to give the firm a better chance of succeeding?

- Has the company made the appropriate choices between cost reduction and
  local adaptation to foreign markets? If not, how can it adjust its strategy to
  achieve competitive advantages?

- Can the company improve its effectiveness by embracing one international
  strategy over another? If so, how should it choose between a global, multidomestic, or transnational strategy?

8. *Formulating Internet strategies.* The Internet and digital technologies have created
   a new arena for strategic analysis, decisions, and action. The technologies and
   applications that the Internet makes possible are having an impact on competitive
   forces in many industries. Internet business models and value-adding strategies
   that combine elements of low cost, differentiation, and focus are creating new
   wealth in this new economy. When conducting an analysis that involves Internet
   strategies, you might ask:

- Has the company correctly assessed shifts in the five competitive forces that
  have been brought about by the Internet? If so, what new strategies should it
  formulate to take advantage of—or defend itself—in the new Internet economy?

- Does the company have an opportunity to lower its transaction costs by using
  digital technologies or doing business over the Internet? If so, what supply-
  chain or distribution channel relationships might be disrupted?

- Is the company using the right mix of competitive strategies to make the most
  of Internet-based technologies? If not, how might it deploy its resources and
  capabilities differently?

9. *Achieving effective strategic control.* Strategic controls enable a firm to implement
   strategies effectively. Informational controls involve comparing performance to
   stated goals and scanning, monitoring, and being responsive to the environment.
   Behavioral controls emerge from a company's culture, reward systems, and organizational boundaries. When assessing the impact of strategic controls on implementation, you might ask:

- Is the company employing the appropriate informational control systems? If
  not, how can it implement a more interactive approach to enhance learning
  and minimize response times?

- Does the company have a strong and effective culture? If not, what steps can
  it take to align its values and rewards system with its goals and objectives?

- Has the company implemented control systems that match its strategies? If so,
  what additional steps can be taken to improve performance?

10. *Creating effective organizational designs.* Organizational designs that align with
    competitive strategies can enhance performance. As companies grow and change,
    their structures must also evolve to meet new demands. In today's economy, firm
    boundaries must be flexible and permeable to facilitate smoother interactions with
    external parties such as customers, suppliers, and alliance partners. New forms of
    organizing are becoming more common. When evaluating the role of organiza-
    tional structure on strategy implementation, you might ask:

- Has the company implemented organizational structures that are suited to the
  type of business it is in? If not, how can it alter the design in ways that
  enhance its competitiveness?

- Is the company employing boundaryless organizational designs where appropriate? If so, how are senior managers maintaining control of lower-level employees?
- Does the company use outsourcing to achieve the best possible results? If not, what criteria should it use to decide which functions can be outsourced?

11. ***Creating a learning organization and an ethical organization.*** Strong leadership is essential for achieving competitive advantages. Two leadership roles are especially important. The first is creating a learning organization by harnessing talent and encouraging the development of new knowledge. Second, leaders play a vital role in motivating employees to excellence and inspiring ethical behavior. When exploring the impact of effective strategic leadership, you might ask:

- Do company leaders promote excellence as part of the overall culture? If so, how has this influenced the performance of the firm and the individuals in it?
- Is the company committed to being a learning organization? If not, what can it do to capitalize on the individual and collective talents of organizational members?
- Have company leaders exhibited an ethical attitude in their own behavior? If not, how has their behavior influenced the actions of other employees?

12. ***Fostering corporate entrepreneurship.*** Many firms continually seek new growth opportunities and avenues for strategic renewal. In some corporations, autonomous work units such as business incubators and new-venture groups are used to focus corporate venturing activities. In other corporate settings, product champions and other firm members provide companies with the impetus to expand into new areas. When investigating the impact of entrepreneurship on strategic effectiveness, you might ask:

- Has the company resolved the dilemmas associated with managing innovation? If so, is it effectively defining and pacing its innovation efforts?
- Has the company developed autonomous work units that have the freedom to bring forth new product ideas? If so, has it used product champions to implement new venture initiatives?
- Does the company have an entrepreneurial orientation? If not, what can it do to encourage entrepreneurial attitudes in the strategic behavior of its organizational members?

13. ***Creating new ventures.*** Young and small firms launch ventures that add jobs and create new wealth. In order to do so, they must identify opportunities that will be viable in the marketplace. The strategic management concepts introduced in this text can guide new ventures and small businesses in their efforts to identify markets, obtain resources, and create effective strategies. When examining the role of strategic thinking on the success of small business management and new venture creation, you might ask:

- Is the company engaged in an ongoing process of opportunity recognition? If not, how can it enhance its ability to recognize opportunities?
- Do the entrepreneurs who are launching new ventures have vision, dedication and drive, and a commitment to excellence? If so, how have these affected the performance and dedication of other employees involved in the venture?
- Have strategic principles been used in the process of obtaining valuable resources and crafting effective entrepreneurial strategies? If not, how can the venture apply the tools of five-forces and value-chain analyses to improve its strategy making and performance?

Strategic management case analysis provides an effective method of learning how companies analyze problems, make decisions, and resolve challenges. Strategic cases include detailed accounts of actual business situations. The purpose of analyzing such cases is to gain exposure to a wide variety of organizational and managerial situations. By putting yourself in the place of a strategic decision maker, you can gain an appreciation of the difficulty and complexity of many strategic situations. In the process you can learn how to ask good strategic questions and enhance your analytical skills. Presenting case analyses can also help develop oral and written communication skills.

In this chapter we have discussed the importance of strategic case analysis and described the five steps involved in conducting a case analysis: becoming familiar with the material, identifying problems, analyzing strategic issues, proposing alternative solutions, and making recommendations. We have also discussed how to get the most from case analysis. Finally, we have described how the case analysis process follows the analysis-decision-action cycle of strategic management and outlined issues and questions that are associated with each of the previous 13 chapters of the text.

Summary

Ford

References

1. The material in this chapter is based on several sources, including Barnes, L. A., Nelson, A. J., & Christensen, C. R. 1994. *Teaching and the case method: Text, cases and readings.* Boston: Harvard Business School Press: Guth, W. D. 1985. Central concepts of business unit and corporate strategy. In W. D. Guth (Ed.). *Handbook of business strategy:* 1–9. Boston: Warren, Gorham & Lamont; Lundberg, C. C., & Enz, C. 1993. A framework for student case preparation. *Case Research Journal,* 13 (Summer): 129–140; and Ronstadt, R. 1980. *The art of case analysis: A guide to the diagnosis of business situations.* Dover, MA: Lord Publishing.

2. Edge, A. G., & Coleman, D. R. 1986. *The guide to case analysis and reporting* (3rd ed.). Honolulu, HI: System Logistics.

3. Morris, E. 1987. Vision and strategy: A focus for the future. *Journal of Business Strategy* 8: 51–58.

4. This section is based on Lundberg & Enz, op. cit., and Ronstadt, op. cit.

5. The importance of problem definition was emphasized in Mintzberg, H., Raisinghani, D., & Theoret, A. 1976. The structure of "unstructured" decision processes. *Administrative Science Quarterly,* 21(2): 246–275.

6. Drucker, P. F. 1994. The theory of the business. *Harvard Business Review,* 72(5): 95–104.

7. This section draws on Edge & Coleman, op. cit.

8. Irving Janis is credited with coining the term *groupthink,* and he applied it primarily to fiascos in government (such as the Bay of Pigs incident in 1961). Refer to Janis, I. L. 1982. *Victims of groupthink* (2nd ed.). Boston: Houghton Mifflin.

9. Much of our discussion is based upon Finkelstein, S., & Mooney, A. C. 2003. Not the usual suspects: How to use board process to make boards better. *Academy of Management Executive,* 17(2): 101–113; Schweiger, D. M., Sandberg, W. R., & Rechner, P. L. 1989. Experiential effects of dialectical inquiry, devil's advocacy, and consensus approaches to strategic decision making. *Academy of Management Journal,* 32(4): 745–772; and Aldag, R. J., & Stearns, T. M. 1987. *Management.* Cincinnati: South-Western Publishing.

10. Finkelstein and Mooney, op. cit.

APPENDIX TO CHAPTER 14: *Sources of Company and Industry Information**

In order for business executives to make the best decisions when developing corporate strategy, it is critical for them to be knowledgeable about their competitors and about the industries in which they compete. The process used by corporations to learn as much as possible about competitors is often called "competitive intelligence." This appendix provides an overview of important and widely available sources of information that may be useful in conducting basic competitive

*This information was compiled by Ruthie Brock and Carol Byrne, Business Librarians at the University of Texas at Arlington. We greatly appreciate their valuable contribution.

intelligence. Much information of this nature is available in libraries in article databases, business reference books, and on Web sites. This list will recommend a variety of them. Ask a librarian for assistance because library collections and resources vary.

The information sources are organized into 10 categories: Competitive Intelligence; Public or Private, Subsidiary or Division, U.S. or Foreign?; Annual Report Collections—Public Companies; Guides and Tutorials; SEC Filings/EDGAR—Company Disclosure Reports; Company Rankings; Business Metasites and Portals; Strategic and Competitive Analysis—Information Sources; Sources for Industry Research and Analysis; and Search Engines.

Competitive Intelligence

Students and other researchers who want to learn more about the value and process of competitive intelligence should see five recent books on this subject.

David L. Blenkhorn and Craig S. Fleisher, eds. *Competitive Intelligence and Global Business*. Westport, CT: Praeger Publishers, 2005.

Helen N. Rothberg and G. Scott Erickson. *From Knowledge to Intelligence: Creating Competitive Advantage in the Next Economy*. Burlington, MA: Elsevier Butterworth-Heinemann, 2005.

Murugan Anandarajan, Asokan Anandarajan, and Cadambi A. Srinivasan, eds. *Business Intelligence Techniques: A Perspective from Accounting and Finance*. New York: Springer-Verlag, 2004.

Benjamin Gilad. *Early Warning: Using Competitive Intelligence to Anticipate Market Shifts, Control Risk, and Create Powerful Strategies*. New York: American Management Association, 2004.

Conor Vibert, ed. *An Introduction to Online Competitive Intelligence Research: Search Strategies, Research Case Study, Research Problems, and Data Source Evaluations and Reviews*. Mason, OH: Thomson Texere, 2004.

Public or Private, Subsidiary or Division, U.S. or Foreign?

Companies traded on stock exchanges in the United States are required to file a variety of reports that disclose information about the company. This begins the process that produces a wealth of data on public companies and at the same time distinguishes them from private companies, which often lack available data. Similarly, financial data of subsidiaries and divisions are typically filed in a consolidated financial statement by the parent company, rather than treated independently, thus limiting the kind of data available on them. On the other hand, foreign companies that trade on U.S. stock exchanges are required to file 20F reports, similar to the 10-K for U.S. companies, the most comprehensive of the required reports, although the number of foreign companies doing so is relatively small.

Corporate Directory of U.S. Public Companies. San Mateo, CA: Walker's Research, LLC, 2005.
The *Corporate Directory* provides company profiles of more than 9,000 publicly traded companies in the United States, including foreign companies trading on the U.S. exchanges (American depository receipts, or ADRs).

Corporate Affiliations. New Providence, NJ: A LexisNexis Group, 2005.
This directory features brief profiles of major U.S. and foreign corporations, both public and private, as well as their subsidiaries, divisions, and affiliates. The directory also indicates hierarchy of corporate relationships. An online version of the directory allows retrieval of a list of companies that meet specific criteria. Results can be downloaded to a spreadsheet. The online version requires a subscription.

Ward's Business Directory of U.S. Private and Public Companies. Detroit, MI: Thomson Gale, 2005. 8 vols.

Ward's Business Directory lists brief profiles on more than 110,000 public and private companies and indicates whether they are public or private, a subsidiary or division. Two volumes of the set are arranged using the Standard Industrial Classifications (SIC) and the North American Industry Classification System (NAICS) and feature company rankings within industries.

Annual Report Collections—Public Companies

A growing number of companies have their Annual Report to Shareholders and other financial reports available on their corporate Web site. A few "aggregators" have cumulated links to many of these Web sites for both U.S. and international corporations.

AnnualReports.com. IR Solutions. Weston, FL.
This Web site contains annual reports in HTML or PDF format. Reports can be retrieved by company name, ticker symbol, exchange, industry, or sector.
www.annualreports.com

Company Annual Reports Online (CAROL). Carol Ltd. London, UK.
This Web site is based in the United Kingdom; therefore, many reports are European. Links are also provided for companies in Asia and the United States. A pull-down menu allows selection of companies within an industry. Access is free, but registration is required.
www.carol.co.uk/

Public Register's Online Annual Report Service. Baytact Corp. Woodstock Valley, CT.
Visitors to this Web site may choose from more than 4,500 company annual reports and 10-K filings to view online or order a paper copy. Access is free, but registration is required.
www.annualreportservice.com/

Mergent Online. Mergent, Inc. New York, NY.
Mergent Online provides company financial data for public companies headquartered in the United States as well as those headquartered in other countries, including a large collection of corporate annual reports in PDF format. For industry analysis, *Mergent Online* offers an advanced search option. Library subscriptions to *Mergent Online* may vary.

Guides and Tutorials

Guide to Corporate Filings and Forms. U.S. Securities and Exchange Commission. Washington, DC.
This part of the Securities Exchange Commission (SEC) Web site explains and defines a 10-K and other SEC required reports that corporations must file.
www.sec.gov/edaux/forms.htm

Guide to Financials. IBM. Armonk, NY.
This guide gives basic information on how to read the financial statements in a company's annual report.
www.ibm.com/investor/financialguide/

Researching Companies Online. Debbie Flanagan. Fort Lauderdale, FL.
This Web site provides a step-by-step process for finding free company and industry information on the Web.
www.learnwebskills.com/company/

SEC Filings/EDGAR—Company Disclosure Reports

SEC Filings are the various reports that publicly traded companies must file with the Securities Exchange Commission to disclose information about themselves. These are often referred to as "EDGAR" filings, an acronym for the Electronic Data Gathering Analysis and Retrieval System.

Some Web sites and commercial databases improve access to these reports by offering additional retrieval features not available on the official (www.sec.gov) Web site.

EDGAR Database. U.S. Securities and Exchange Commission. Washington, DC.
The 10-K reports, and other corporate documents, are made available in the EDGAR database within 24 hours after being filed. Annual reports, on the other hand, are typically sent directly to shareholders and are not required by the SEC as part of EDGAR, although some companies voluntarily include them. Both 10-Ks and shareholders' annual reports are considered basic sources of company research.
http://www.sec.gov/edgar/searchedgar/webusers.htm

EdgarScan—An Interface to the SEC EDGAR Database. PricewaterhouseCoopers. New York, NY.
Using filings from the SEC's servers, EdgarScan's intelligent interface parses the data automatically to a common format that is comparable across companies. A small Java applet called the "Benchmarking Assistant" performs graphical financial benchmarking interactively. Extracted financial data from the 10-K includes ratios with links to indicate where the data were derived and how it was computed. Tables showing company comparisons can be downloaded as Excel charts.
http://edgarscan.pwcglobal.com/servlets/edgarscan

LexisNexis Academic—SEC Filings & Reports. LexisNexis. Bethesda, MD.
EDGAR filings and reports are available through the "Business" option of LexisNexis Academic. These reports and filings can be retrieved by company name, industry code (SIC) or ticker symbol for a particular time period or by a specific report. Proxy, prospectus, and registration filings are also available.

Mergent Online—EDGAR. Mergent, Inc. New York, NY.
From the "EDGAR Search" tab within Mergent Online, EDGAR SEC filings and reports can be searched by company name or ticker symbol, filing date range, and file type (10-K, 8-K, ARS). The reports are available in HTML or MS Word format. Using the "Find in Page" option from the browser allows users to jump to specific sections of an SEC report.

Company Rankings

Fortune 500. Time Inc. New York, NY.
The Fortune 500 list and other company rankings are published in the printed edition of *Fortune* magazine, but are available on *Fortune*'s Web site for subscribers only.
www.fortune.com/fortune/fortune500

Hoover's Handbook of American Business. Austin, TX: Hoovers, Inc., 2005
This two-volume set gives a company overview, a list of competitors, and basic financial information for large American companies. A special feature is a section called "The List Lovers' Companion," which includes a variety of lists with company rankings, some that include companies listed in *Hoover's Handbooks* and others reprinted from *Fortune, Forbes,* and other publications. In addition to the American edition, *Hoover's Handbooks* are available for private companies, emerging companies, and companies headquartered outside of the United States.

Ward's Business Directory of U.S. Private and Public Companies. Detroit, MI: Thomson Gale, 2004. 8 vols.
Ward's Business Directory is one of the few directories to rank both public and private companies together by sales within an industry, using both the Standard Industrial Classification system (in Volume 5 only) and the North American Industry Classification System (in Volume 8 only). With this information, it is easy to spot who the big "players" are in a particular product or industry category. Market share within an industry group can be calculated by determining what percentage a company's sales figure is of the total given by Ward's for that industry group.

Business Metasites and Portals

@Brint.com, The Biz Tech Network. Brint Institute. Syracuse, NY.
Brint's business metasite has a concentration of Web links related to e-business, knowledge management, and technology.
www.brint.com/

CI CorporateInformation. Winthrop Corporation. Milford, CT.
CorporateInformation's Web site includes information on both U.S. and global public and private companies. It also provides access to company profiles and research reports alphabetically, geographically by specific countries or U.S. states, and by industry sector. Each interactive research report analyzes sales, dividends, earnings, profit ratios, research and development, and inventory and allows up to three companies to be compared to the company selected. Full access requires a paid subscription. Limited access is allowed free with registration.
www.corporateinformation.com/

Hoover's Online. Hoover's Inc., Dun & Bradstreet Corporation. Short Hills, NJ.
Hoover's Online includes brief company fact sheets, links to corporate Web sites, current company news, and "CEOs on Camera" video clips. The site also provides data on Initial Public Offerings (IPOs) via "IPO Central." Additional information is available to member subscribers only (indicated by the "lock" symbol).
www.hoovers.com/free/

Strategic and Competitive Analysis—
Information Sources

Analyzing a company can take the form of examining its internal and external environment. In the process, it is useful to identify the company's strengths, weaknesses, opportunities, and threats (SWOT). Sources for this kind of analysis are varied, but perhaps the best would be articles from *The Wall Street Journal,* business magazines, and industry trade publications. Publications such as these can be found in the following databases available at many public and academic libraries. When using a database that is structured to allow it, try searching the company name combined with one or more key words, such as "IBM and competition" or "Microsoft and lawsuits" or "AMR and fuel costs" to retrieve articles relating to the external environment.

ABI/Inform. Ann Arbor, MI: ProQuest Information & Learning.
ABI/Inform provides abstracts and full text articles covering management, law, taxation, human resources, and company and industry information from more than 1,000 business and management journals. *ABI/Inform* includes market condition reports, corporate strategies, case studies, and executive profiles.

Business & Company Resource Center. Detroit, MI. Thomson Gale.
Business & Company Resource Center provides company and industry intelligence for a selection of public and private companies. Company profiles include parent-subsidiary relationships, industry rankings, products and brands, current investment ratings, and financial ratios. Use the geographic search to locate company contact information. A selection of full-text investment reports from Investext Plus are also available.

Business Source Premier. Ispswich, MA. EBSCO Publishing.
Business Source Premier is a full text database with over 3,800 scholarly business journals covering management, economics, finance, accounting, international business, and more. The database also includes detailed company profiles for the world's 5,000 largest companies as well as selected country economic reports provided by the Economist Intelligence Unit (EIU). *Business Source Premier* contains over 1,100 peer-reviewed business journals.

Investext Plus. Detroit, MI: Thomson Gale.
Investext Plus offers full-text analytical reports on more than 11,000 public and private companies and 53 industries. Developed by a global roster of brokerage, investment

banking, and research firms, it is notable that these full-text investment reports include hard-to-find private company data and historical reports useful for evaluating companies over time.

International Directory of Company Histories. Detroit, MI: St. James Press, 1988 to present. 68 volumes to date.

This directory covers more than 4,500 multinational companies and the series is still adding volumes. Each company history is approximately three to four pages in length and provides a summary of the company's mission, goals, and ideals, followed by company milestones, principal subsidiaries, and competitors. Strategic decisions made during the company's period of existence are usually noted. This series covers public and private companies and nonprofit entities. Entry information includes a company's legal name, headquarters information, URL, incorporation date, ticker symbol, stock exchange, sales figures, and the primary North American Industry Classification System (NAICS) code. Further reading selections complete the entry information.

LexisNexis Academic. Bethesda, MD: LexisNexis.

The "Business" category in *LexisNexis Academic* provides access to a wide range of business information. Timely business articles can be retrieved from newspapers, magazines, journals, wires, and broadcast transcripts. Other information available in this section includes detailed company financials, company comparisons, and industry and market information for over 25 industries.

LexisNexis Statistical. Bethesda, MD: LexisNexis.

LexisNexis Statistical provides access to a variety of statistical publications indexed in the American Statistics Index (ASI), Statistical Reference Index (SRI), and the Index to International Statistics (IIS). Use the PowerTables search to locate historical trends, future projections, industry or demographic information. *LexisNexis Statistical* provides links to originating government Web sites when available.

Notable Corporate Chronologies. Julie A. Mitchell, ed. Detroit, MI: Thomson Gale. 2001.

This two-volume set provides dates of significant changes for over 1,800 corporations that operate in the United States and abroad. Each company entry includes a timeline and a further reading selection. The timeline explains the major events that affected the company's history. Dates of mergers and acquisitions, product introductions, financial milestones, and major stock offerings are also included in the chronologies. The Chronology Highlights in volume 2 provide a historical snapshot of major events for the companies listed.

CorpTech Database. Concord, MA: Corporate Technology Information Services, Inc.

The CorpTech CD-ROM database covers over 50,000 technology-related companies, both public and private, headquartered in the United States or affiliated with a foreign parent company. Narrative descriptions of each company, along with sales, number of employees, and other details are provided by the database. CorpTech can be searched by industry, product, geographic location, sales category, employee size, and so forth to create lists of companies that meet certain criteria. Percentage of employment growth compared to prior year is stated. Web site addresses, 800 numbers, or fax numbers are frequently provided. CorpTech is one of the best sources for information on technology-related private companies.

The Wall Street Journal. New York: Dow Jones and Reuters Business Interactive.

This respected business newspaper is available in searchable full-text from 1984 to present in the *Factiva* database. The "News Pages" link provides access to current articles and issues of *The Wall Street Journal.* Dow Jones, publisher of the print version of *The Wall Street Journal,* also has an online subscription available at wsj.com.

Sources for Industry Research and Analysis

Factiva. New York: Dow Jones Reuters Business Interactive.

The *Factiva* database has several options for researching an industry. One would be to search the database for articles in the business magazines and industry trade publications.

A second option in *Factiva* would be to search in the Companies/Markets category for company/industry comparison reports.

Mergent Online. New York: Mergent Inc.
Mergent's enhanced Basic Search option features searching by primary industry codes (either SIC or NAICS). Once the search is executed, a list of companies in that industry should be shown. A comparison or standard peer group analysis can be created to analyze companies in the same industry on various criteria. The improved Advanced Search allows the user to search a wider range of financial and textual information. Results, including ratios for a company and its competitors, can be downloaded to a spreadsheet.

Industry Norms and Key Business Ratios. New York: Dun & Bradstreet, 2004.
Industry Norms and Key Business Ratios provides key financial measures and business ratios, based on efficiency, profitability, and solvency, that are used as a benchmark to compare the performance of a company against the industry's average. Industries are presented by the four-digit Standard Industrial Classification (SIC) code and cover agriculture, mining, construction, transportation, communication, utilities, manufacturing, wholesaling, retailing, financial, real estate, and services.

Standard & Poor's Industry Surveys. New York: Standard & Poor's, 2005. 3 vols.
Standard & Poor's Industry Surveys provide an overview of 52 U.S. industries. Each industry report includes a table of contents, narrative description, history, trends, financial and company information, glossary of terms, and a section on how to perform an analysis of the company. Industry References (associations, periodicals, and Web sites), Composite Industry Data (industry norms and ratios), and Comparative Company Analysis (comparison of 50 major companies, their operating ratios, P/E, revenue, and so forth) complete the industry report section. All charts and graphs cite the information source. NetAdvantage is Standard and Poor's online product that offers online access to industry surveys, stock reports, corporation records, and several other S&P products.

Search Engines

Google. Mountain View, CA: Google, Inc.
Recognized for its advanced technology, quality of results, and simplicity, the Google search engine is highly recommended by librarians and other expert Web "surfers."
www.google.com

Vivisimo. Pittsburgh, PA: Vivisimo, Inc.
This search engine not only finds relevant results, but organizes them in logical subcategories.
www.vivisimo.com

Yahoo Finance. Sunnyvale, CA: Yahoo! Inc.
This metasite links to information on U.S. markets, world markets, data sources, finance references, investment editorials, financial news, and other helpful Web sites.
http://finance.yahoo.com

Case 1   JetBlue Airways*

Is "High Touch Service" the Key Driver for JetBlue's Future Success?

On December 4, 2003, JetBlue withdrew its services from Atlanta in the wake of a huge retaliation from the airline majors, Delta Air Lines and United Airlines. Following JetBlue's May 2003 entry into Atlanta, both Delta and United (ranking number 2 and number 3, respectively, in the U.S. airline industry) slashed their prices by more than half and boosted their flight schedules. JetBlue's withdrawal raised questions in the minds of both airline travelers and investors alike about the growth and profitability of low-cost carriers. The low-cost carriers grew from carrying less than 10 percent of domestic air traffic in 1990 to carrying about 25 percent in 2003. However, rapid growth and increased entries also meant that the market was getting crowded and further growth was becoming constrained.[1] Could JetBlue continue its spectacular growth? Were its competitive advantages sustainable?

During the five years since its inception, JetBlue had become the 11th largest airline in the United States (based on revenue passenger miles).[2] The firm posted a profit for its 12th consecutive quarter on January 29, 2004. Exhibit 1 provides a comparative statement of JetBlue's operating performance (see the Appendix on page 547 for a description of key terms) on a few key indicators.

Several analysts downgraded the stock because they were skeptical about the costs of expansion as well as the increased competition in the discount segment by major carriers.[3] Even business travelers, an important segment for the company, were becoming more price-sensitive. However, David Neeleman, the CEO and chairman of JetBlue, was optimistic. He said, "In light of the difficult competitive environment we faced in the fourth quarter, we're pleased to report a double-digit operating margin. We begin 2004 from a strong position characterized by excellent cost control diligence, a healthy balance sheet, and a top-rated product offering delivered by dedicated Crewmembers. These key advantages give us tremendous confidence in our continued growth through what is expected to be a very competitive year."[4]

The United States Airline Industry[5]

Deregulation of the U.S. airline industry in 1978 ushered in competition in the previously protected industry. Several low-cost, low-fare operators entered the competitive

landscape that Southwest pioneered. In 1971 Southwest initiated service as a regional carrier, but by 1990 it became a major airline when its revenues crossed the $1 billion mark.[6] The Southwest model was based on operating a single-type aircraft fleet with high utilization, a simplified fare structure with single-class seating, and high productivity from its human and physical assets. On the other hand, the "hub-and-spoke" system, increased labor costs, and increases in multitype aircraft fleets bloated the cost structure of the major airlines.

There are three primary segments in the airline industry: major airlines, regional airlines, and low-fare airlines. Major U.S. airlines, as defined by the Department of Transportation, are those with annual revenues of over $1 billion. Eleven passenger airlines belong to this category, the largest of which include American Airlines, Continental Airlines, Delta Air Lines, Northwest Airlines, and United Airlines. These airlines offer scheduled flights to most large cities within the United States and abroad and also serve numerous smaller cities. Most major airlines adopted the hub-and-spoke route system. In this system, the operations are concentrated in a limited number of hub cities while other destinations are served by providing one-stop or connecting service through the hub.

Regional airlines typically operate smaller aircraft on lower-volume routes than major airlines. Unlike the low-fare airlines, the regional airlines do not have an independent route system. They typically enter into relationships with major airlines and carry their passengers on the "spoke"—that is, between a hub or larger city and a smaller city.

The low-fare airlines, on the other hand, operate from "point to point" and have their own route system. The target segment of low-fare airlines is fare-conscious leisure and business travelers who might otherwise have used alternative forms of transportation or not traveled at all. Low-fare airlines stimulated demand in this segment and also have been successful in weaning business travelers from the major airlines. The main bases of competition in the airline industry are fare pricing, customer service, routes served, flight schedules, types of aircraft, safety record and reputation, code-sharing relationships, in-flight entertainment systems, and frequent flyer programs.

The economic downturn in the late 1990s and the terrorist attacks on the World Trade Center and the Pentagon on September 11, 2001, severely affected the airline industry. The demand for air travel dropped significantly and led to a reduction in traffic and revenue. Security concerns, security costs, and liquidity concerns increased. The major U.S. airlines reported operating losses of $10 billion for two consecutive years, 2001 and 2002. Several

*This case study was prepared by Naga Lakshmi Damaraju of the University of Texas at Dallas, John R. Gaetz, former graduate student of the University of Texas at Dallas, Marilyn L. Taylor of the University of Missouri at Kansas City, and Gregory G. Dess of the University of Texas at Dallas. All rights reserved to the authors. This case study has been developed purely from secondary sources. The purpose of the case is to stimulate class discussion rather than to illustrate effective or ineffective handling of a business situation. The authors thank Dr. Michael Oliff, the University of Texas at Dallas, and Dr. Alan Eisner for their comments on an earlier version of this case.

Exhibit 1   JetBlue's Operating Statistics (unaudited)

	Year Ended December			
	2003	**2002**	**2001**	**2000**
Revenue passengers	9,011,552	5,752,105	3,116,817	1,144,421
Revenue passenger miles (000)	11,526,945	6,835,828	3,281,835	1,004,496
Available seat miles (000)	13,639,488	8,239,938	4,208,267	1,371,836
Load factor	84.5%	83.0%	78.0%	73.2%
Breakeven load factor	72.5%	71.5%	73.7%	90.6%
Aircraft utilization (hours per day)	13	12.9	12.6	12
Average fare	$107.09	$106.95	$99.62	$88.84
Yield per passenger mile	$ .0837	$ .0900	$ .0946	$ .1012
Passenger revenue per available seat mile	$ .0708	$ .0747	$ .0738	$ .0741
Operating revenue per available seat mile	$ .0732	$ .0771	$ .0761	$ .0763
Operating expense per available seat mile	$ .0608	$ .0643	$ .0698	$ .0917
Airline operating expense per available seat mile	$ .0607	$ .0643	$ .0698	$ .0917
Departures	66,920	44,144	26,334	10,265
Average stage length (miles)	1,272	1,152	986	825
Average number of operating aircraft during period	44	27	14.7	5.8
Full-time equivalent employees at period end	4,892	3,572	1,983	1,028
Average fuel cost per gallon	$ .8508	$ .7228	$ .7563	$ .9615
Fuel gallons consumed (000)	173,157	105,515	55,095	18,340
Percent of sales through jetblue.com during period	73.0%	63.0%	44.1%	28.7%

Source: JetBlue annual reports.

major airlines filed for bankruptcy under Chapter 11 during 2001 and 2002. Many airlines significantly decreased their capacity, reduced their routes, and postponed purchases of new aircraft. More than 1,000 planes were grounded in the six months following September 11, 2001, and some airlines reported a 50 percent reduction in routes and flight frequency. For example, on the East Coast, US Airways eliminated its MetroJet operation, which was designed to compete with low-cost, low-fare airlines such as Southwest and JetBlue. Delta Air Lines significantly reduced the capacity of Delta Express service, its low-fare, leisure-oriented service provider in the Northeast and Midwest to Florida. In November 2002 National Airlines ceased operations, which opened up the New York–Las Vegas market to other discounters much earlier than originally anticipated. All these events provided opportunities for the low-cost carriers not only to increase the number of flights but also to introduce services on new routes.

The economy started rebounding by the end of 2003, which boosted demand for business and leisure travel. Industrywide capacity was expected to grow by 7 percent after three years of flight reductions and fewer routes. Low-cost operators such as Southwest and JetBlue were expected to benefit from this trend. On the other hand, the major airlines saw their revenues stabilize after the three-year retreat, made deep cost reductions in their operations, and renewed their confidence to fight back. The majors and their regional partners were expected to boost their domestic capacity by 5 percent in 2004. Much of this expansion was aimed at markets with low-cost competition. And much of this expansion was to come at lower costs, that is, by increasing the utilization of existing aircraft in terms of the number of flights per aircraft, not by purchasing new aircraft.

David Neeleman and JetBlue Airways[7]

Born in São Paulo, Brazil, and brought up in Salt Lake City, David Neeleman dropped out of the University of Utah after his freshman year to move back to Brazil and become a missionary. After two years of missionary work, he made his modest beginning in establishing his own business by renting out condominiums in Hawaii. He then established his own travel agency and began chartering flights from Salt Lake City to the islands to bring in prospective clients for his rental services.

Neeleman's sales prowess caught the attention of June Morris, who owned one of Utah's largest corporate travel agencies. Soon after, in 1984, Neeleman and Morris launched the Utah-based "Morris Air," a charter operation. Morris Air was closely modeled after Southwest Airlines, the legendary discount airlines in the United States. Neeleman considered Herb Kelleher, Southwest's founder, his idol. He studied everything Kelleher accomplished and tried to do it better, which meant keeping costs low and turning planes around quickly among a host of other operational and strategic activities/choices. While following the Southwest model, Neeleman brought his own innovations into the business. He pioneered the use of "at-home reservation agents"—routing calls to agents' homes to save money on office rent and infrastructure expense. He also developed the first electronic ticketing system in the airline industry. By 1992 Morris Air had grown into a regularly scheduled airline and was ready for an initial public offering (IPO) when Southwest, impressed by Morris's low costs and high revenue, bought the company for $129 million. Neeleman became the executive vice president of Southwest. However, Neeleman could not adjust to Southwest's pace of doing things. By 1994, he was at odds with the top executives and left after signing a five-year noncompete agreement.

In the interim between leaving Southwest and establishing JetBlue, Neeleman developed the electronic ticketing system he initiated at Morris Air into one of the world's simplest airline reservation systems: Open Skies. He sold Open Skies to Hewlett-Packard in 1999. During the same period, he was also a consultant to a low-fare Canadian start-up airline, WestJet Airlines.[8] After the completion of the noncompete agreement with Southwest Airlines in 1999, Neeleman launched his own airline. He raised about $130 million of capital in a span of two weeks, an unprecedented amount for a start-up airline.[9] Weston Presidio Capital and Chase Capital, venture capital firms that backed Neeleman's prior ventures, were return investors, and financier George Soros was also brought into the deal. "David's a winner; I knew anything David touched would turn to gold," said Michael Lazarus of Weston Presidio Capital that had earlier funded Morris Air. "We were intrigued with his ideas about a low-cost airline."[10] With such strong support from venture capitalists, JetBlue began as the highest funded start-up airline in U.S. aviation history.

In "JetBlue" Skies

Incorporated in Delaware in August 1998, JetBlue commenced operations in August 2000, with John F. Kennedy International Airport (JFK) as its primary base of operations. In 2001 JetBlue extended its operations to the West Coast from its base at Long Beach Municipal Airport, which served the Los Angeles area. In 2002 the company went public with its IPO and was listed on the Nasdaq as JBLU. JetBlue had expected to sell 5.5 million shares at about $24–$26 in its initial public offering. Instead, it sold 5.87 million shares at $27 per share through its lead underwriters Morgan Stanley and Merrill Lynch. The shares closed at $47, up by $18, on the first day of trading. JetBlue's stock offering was one of the hottest IPOs of the year.[11]

JetBlue was established with the goal of being a leading low-fare passenger airline that offered customers a differentiated product and high-quality customer service. It was positioned as a low-cost, low-fare airline providing quality customer service on point-to-point routes. JetBlue had a geographically diversified flight schedule that included both short-haul and long-haul routes.

The mission of the company, according to David Neeleman, was "to bring humanity back to air travel." The airline focused on underserved markets and large metropolitan areas that had high average fares in order to stimulate demand. The "JetBlue effect" aspired to create fares going down, traffic going up, and JetBlue ending up with a big chunk of business. Exhibit 2 shows the JetBlue effect in the markets it served.

JetBlue was committed to keeping its costs low. To achieve this objective, the company operated a single-type aircraft fleet comprising Airbus A320 planes as opposed to the more popular but costly Boeing 737. The A320s had 162 seats compared to 132 seats in the Boeing 737. According to JetBlue, the A320 was thus cheaper to maintain and also was more fuel-efficient. Since all of JetBlue's planes were new, the costs of maintenance were also lower. In addition, the single type of aircraft kept training costs low and increased manpower utilization. JetBlue was the first to introduce the "paperless cockpit" in which pilots, equipped with laptops, had ready access to flight manuals that were constantly updated at headquarters. As a result, pilots could quickly calculate the weight and balance and take-off performance of the aircraft instead of having to download and print the manuals for making the calculations. The paperless cockpit thus ensured faster take-offs by reducing paperwork and helped in achieving quicker turnarounds and higher aircraft utilization.[12] There were no meals served on the planes, and pilots even had to be ready, if need be, to do the cleanup work on the plane to keep the time the aircraft was on the ground as short as possible. Innovation was everywhere; for example, there were no paper tickets to lose and no mileage statements to mail to frequent fliers.

Exhibit 2   The JetBlue Effect

Route	Increase in Daily Passengers %	Decrease in Average Fare %	JetBlue's Share of Local Traffic %
New York to Miami/Ft. Lauderdale	14%	17% (to $121.50)	23.1%
New York to Los Angeles basin	2	26 (to $219.31)	18.0
New York to Buffalo	94	40 (to $86.09)	61.2

Figures as of second quarter, 2003.

Source: Data from Back Aviation Solutions: adapted from Zellner, W. 2004. Is JetBlue's flight plan flawed? *BusinessWeek*, February 16.

JetBlue also deliberately chose underutilized airports for its operations. In large metropolitan areas with multiple airports, there typically was an airport, or even two, that received little attention in terms of domestic air traffic. JetBlue chose to operate in such airports. The reason, according to Neeleman, was that, with less congestion, it was far easier to get planes in and out of such airports more quickly. Also, when runways were too close, even with a bit of adverse weather, the flights at major airports might be delayed for a couple of hours. However, JetBlue could minimize all such problems by simply not choosing to go to the most popular airports.[13]

Differentiation was another key part of JetBlue's strategy. The airline offered its passengers a unique flying experience by providing new aircraft, leather seats, simple and low fares, free live satellite television with up to 24 channels of DIRECTV programming free of charge at every seat, preassigned seating, and reliable performance.[14] Unlike Southwest, which ferried business travelers on short hauls, JetBlue flew larger planes on typically longer routes. This enabled JetBlue to set its fares even lower than Southwest on a per mile basis.[15] JetBlue also offered more legroom than any other airline, even though it meant having fewer seats per plane. In each of its A320s, the company removed one row of seats, bringing down the number of seats from 162 to 156. That created greater legroom by extending seat pitch—the space from the back of one seat to the back of the seat behind it—to 34 inches on 65 percent of its seats, with the exception of nine rows in the front that remained at 32 inches. Customers could check online at the airline's Web site for more information and assistance in selecting their preferred seat location. "We've always offered an award-winning and very comfort-able product but now we've figured out a way to give more customers even more room without changing our fare structure," said David Neeleman.[16] To reward its loyal customers, JetBlue started the "True Blue" program that gave its customers points rather than miles. Points were earned depending on whether the trip was a short (2 points if booked by phone; 4 points if booked online), medium (4 points) or long (6 points) haul. Customers earned double points if they booked their tickets through the company's Web site. For every 100 points earned, customers earned a free round-trip flight to any destination that JetBlue served.

Another important feature is that JetBlue never overbooked its flights. Other airlines routinely overbooked their flights to ensure that they would not fly empty, even if it meant significant inconvenience to customers who were bumped. At JetBlue, a customer would never be left behind, except in a rare circumstance such as the need to get to a family member in distress. Even in such situations, it would be the voluntary choice of another customer to opt out of the particular flight. Despite this policy, JetBlue had a smaller percentage of empty seats than its competitors— only 20 percent in September 2003, which was about 13 percent lower than all its larger competitors. JetBlue, in essence, made overbooking redundant by better inventory management. What it gave customers was peace of mind that they would not be bumped when they were expecting to fly. For those who valued their time and appointments, this was a key feature of JetBlue's service.[17]

Passengers were encouraged to book directly through the company's Web site instead of through agents. All tickets were nonrefundable. Passengers were required to call the airline in advance if they were to miss a flight and could rebook another flight at a charge of $25.[18] According to JetBlue officials, passengers holding nonrefundable tickets were more likely to show up for a flight. With these simple methods, JetBlue achieved near total control of its seat sales.

The core of JetBlue's culture was safety, caring, integrity, fun, and passion. Service was top priority at JetBlue and Neeleman referred to JetBlue as "a service company . . . *not* just another airline." For example, even Neeleman sometimes hauled luggage alongside his crews to help meet schedules. On one occasion, he and his crew made phone calls at 3:00 a.m. to alert passengers that their 6:00 a.m. flight was delayed and they need not reach the airport early. JetBlue's policy was to communicate openly and honestly with customers in case of delays. On one Ontario, California, to New York flight, there was a slight skid during the landing at JFK; JetBlue gave out free round-trip tickets to all onboard, even though no one was injured.[19] Neeleman himself flew at least once a week on JetBlue flights and served snacks to get firsthand information and feedback from customers. He expected this service formula to percolate down to all levels of the organization. In his words, "We don't want jaded people working here. If you don't like people or can't deal with customers, you'll be fired."

Neeleman understood the importance of employees in delivering service excellence. JetBlue invested in selecting, training, and maintaining a productive workforce of caring, passionate, fun, and friendly people who wanted to provide customers with the best flying experience possible. Employees were called "Crewmembers" and were offered flexible work hours, initial paid training, free uniforms (unheard of in the industry), and benefits that began the day they started work. Training that emphasized the importance of safety was provided for pilots, flight attendants, technicians, customer service agents, dispatchers, and reservation agents. JetBlue shared its success with employees by providing compensation packages that included competitive salaries, benefits, profit sharing, and a discounted Crewmember stock purchase plan. In addition, a significant number of Crewmembers also participated in the stock option plan. Compensation packages were reviewed regularly to make them competitive so that JetBlue hired and retained the best people possible. JetBlue salary expenses were still less than those of its competitors. Other aspects such as job security, overtime pay, and opportunities for advancement helped offset the purely monetary component of rewards. In Neeleman's opinion, "great People drive solid operating Performance which yields continued Prosperity."[20] He strongly believed that his people were the foundation upon which the company's success was built.[21] To support him in running the company, Neeleman handpicked some noted industry veterans:

- David Barger, president and CEO, who was earlier the vice president in charge of Continental Airlines' Newark hub from 1994 to 1998 and had extensive experience in airline operations in the New York area.

- John Owen, the chief financial officer, who earlier served as treasurer of Southwest Airlines from 1984 to 1998 and had expertise in aircraft purchase, leasing, and finance transactions.
- Thomas Kelly, executive vice president and secretary who had worked with Neeleman for more than 18 years as executive vice president and general counsel at Morris Air, Open Skies.

JetBlue's initiatives translated into superior operational performance. Compared to its competitors, the company enjoyed a better completion factor (i.e., the number of flights scheduled versus the number of flights operated), on-time performance, fewer mishandled bags, fewer customer complaints, and virtually no customers denied boarding. In terms of operational efficiency, JetBlue's planes flew 12 hours a day compared with 11 hours at Southwest and 9 at United, US Airways, and American.[22] In its own internal customer surveys, 94 percent ranked their JetBlue experience as "much better" than other airlines and 99 percent said they "definitely would" recommend the airline to others.[23] In 2002 JetBlue was one of only two airlines that made money when all others experienced losses.[24] JetBlue has won numerous awards since it commenced operations in 2000. The company was voted the number one domestic airline in both *Conde Nast Traveler* for 2003 and Readers' Choice Awards in 2002, and it received the highest score of any airline in the 2003 *Conde Nast Traveler* Business Traveler Awards "coach-only" category. During 2003 JetBlue was also named the number two domestic airline in *Travel and Leisure*'s 2003 World's Best Awards and the "best value for cost." The airline enjoyed an increasing customer base of about 18 million and became the 11th largest passenger carrier in the United States by December 2003.[25] (See Exhibit 3 for a comparison of JetBlue with its competitors, Exhibit 4 for a comparison of JetBlue's stock price with the S&P 500, and Exhibits 5 and 6 for JetBlue's income statements and balance sheets, 1999 to 2003.)

Competitive Reaction

The success of low-cost players in general and JetBlue in particular invoked strong competitive responses. The big players reacted. In April 2003 Delta launched its discount spin-off "Song" airlines to compete directly on JetBlue's routes, with daily flights to West Palm Beach from all three major New York airports. Like JetBlue, Song had all-leather seats, more legroom, and a high-tech in-flight entertainment system. The airline promised to add many more features, including MP3 music and Internet access by early 2004.[26] In addition, Song developed a frequent-flier program that it planned to share with Delta and its partners. Delta Air Lines also strongly retaliated when JetBlue launched its service from Atlanta in May 2003. Delta slashed fares and increased its capacity to Los Angeles

Exhibit 3   Direct Competitor Comparison

	JetBlue	American Airlines	Southwest Airlines	United Airlines	Delta Air Lines	Industry
Market capitalization ($ billions)	$2.53	$2.45	$11.43	$.166	$1.13	$.931
Employees	4,704	96,400	32,847	63,000	75,100	10,770
Revenue growth (%)	57.20%	(8.80)%	7.50%	(11.50)%	(4.10)%	3.30%
Revenue ($ millions)	$998	$17,440	$5,940	$13,720	$13,300	$1,520
Gross margin (%)	41.31%	17.26%	29.97%	7.72%	8.18%	19.74%
EBITDA ($ millions)	$219.23	$533.00	$867.00	$(392.00)	$336.00	$140.93
Operating margins (%)	16.91%	(4.84)%	8.14%	(9.91)%	(6.40)%	2.73%
Net income ($ millions)	$103.90	(1,230.00)	$443.00	$(2,820.00)	$785.00	$7.30
Earnings per share	$0.969	$(7.855)	$0.538	$(28.213)	$(6.46)	$0.21
Price/earnings ratio	25.59		26.91			17.28

Sources: Company annual reports.

airports by nearly 50 percent. United, the number three airline in the United States, also reacted similarly. As a result, JetBlue had to withdraw from Atlanta in December 2003.[27] In early 2004, retaliation by other big players appeared imminent. "We're not running from these carriers anymore," vowed the CEO of American Airlines, Gerard J. Arpey, in November 2003. In the same month, United Airlines, the number three player, unveiled plans to launch its low-cost carrier "Ted" (as in UniTED), mainly from Denver.[28] Virgin Airlines' chief executive Richard Branson, who tried to establish a joint venture with Neeleman as early as 1998, was again becoming more interested in entering the U.S. market and had plans to launch Virgin there by early 2005.[29]

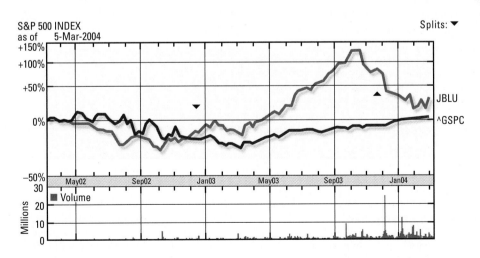

Exhibit 4   Stock Performance of JetBlue versus S&P 500 (March 2002–March 2004)

Source: http://finance.yahoo.com/.

Exhibit 5   Income Statements of JetBlue, 1999–2003

	Year Ended December 31				
	2003	2002	2001	2000	1999
	(in $ thousands, except per share data)				
Statements of Income Data					
Operating revenues	$998,351	$635,191	$320,414	$104,618	$ —
Operating expenses:					
Salaries, wages, and benefits	267,334	162,191	84,762	32,912	6,000
Aircraft fuel	147,316	76,271	41,666	17,634	4
Landing fees and other rents	68,691	43,881	27,342	11,112	447
Aircraft rent	59,963	40,845	32,927	13,027	324
Sales and marketing	53,587	44,345	28,305	16,978	887
Depreciation and amortization	50,397	26,922	10,417	3,995	111
Maintenance materials and repairs	23,114	8,926	4,705	1,052	38
Other operating expenses	159,116	126,823	63,483	29,096	6,405
Total Operating Expenses	**829,518**	**530,204**	**293,607**	**125,806**	**14,216**
Operating income (loss)	168,833	104,987	26,807	(21,188)	(14,216)
Government compensation[a]	22,761	407	18,706	—	—
Other income (expense)	(16,155)	(10,370)	(3,598)	(381)	685
Income (loss) before income taxes	175,439	95,024	41,915	(21,569)	(13,531)
Income tax expense (benefit)[b]	71,541	40,116	3,378	(239)	233
Net Income (Loss)	**103,898**	**54,908**	**38,537**	**(21,330)**	**(13,764)**
Earnings (loss) per common share:					
Basic	1.07	0.73	4.39	(11.85)	(16.36)
Diluted	0.97	0.56	0.51	(11.85)	(16.36)
Other Financial Data:					
Operating margin	16.90%	16.50%	8.40%	(20.30)%	—
Ratio of earnings to fixed charges[c]	3.2x	2.7x	1.9x	—	—
Net cash provided by (used in) operating activities	286,337	216,477	111,279	2,824	(6,556)
Net cash used in investing activities	(751,530)	(744,461)	(289,855)	(241,130)	(67,452)
Net cash provided by financing activities	789,136	657,214	261,695	254,463	80,740

[a]Note 14 to the consolidated financial statements on Form 10-K provides a detailed discussion.

[b]In 2001 JetBlue's income tax expense was reduced due to the full reversal of its deferred tax asset valuation allowance. JetBlue does not expect any similar reductions in the future. Note 9 to JetBlue's consolidated financial statements provides details.

[c]According to Form 10-K, earnings were inadequate to cover fixed charges by $26.0 million and $14.2 million for the years ended December 31, 2000 and 1999, respectively.

Source: JetBlue 10-K reports.

Southwest had a clear lead over upstart JetBlue and had been profitable for over 30 straight years. However, Southwest's executives took Neeleman very seriously. "We've got to be prepared for intense competition," said Southwest's CFO, Gary Kelly. Southwest started automating its baggage-handling and boarding pass processes in 2003, aspects that Neeleman had originally pushed for while he worked there. It was also reported that in 2003, Southwest's Kelly sent model JetBlue planes to his executives with a note reading "Know Your Enemy," even though the two airlines did not compete directly at many of the same airports.[30]

According to some analysts, the low-cost carriers seemed to have pretty clear geographic niches. However,

Exhibit 6   JetBlue's Balance Sheet Information, 1999–2003

| | Year Ended December 31 | | | | |
	2003	2002	2001	2000	1999
			(in $ thousands)		
Cash and cash equivalents	$ 570,695	$ 246,752	$117,522	$ 34,403	$ 18,246
Total assets	2,185,757	1,378,923	673,773	344,128	138,182
Total debt	1,108,595	711,931	374,431	177,048	14,577
Convertible redeemable preferred stock	—	—	210,441	163,552	133,478
Common stockholders' equity (deficit)	671,136	414,673	(32,167)	(54,153)	(18,893)

Source: JetBlue 10-K reports.

further growth initiatives such as expanding into newer routes were likely to bring them into head-on competition.[31] For JetBlue, growth into any of the other "fortress hubs"—for example, Chicago (United and American), Dallas (American), and Detroit (Northwest)—could provoke strong retaliation from other large players.[32] JetBlue had already experienced such retaliation from Delta in Atlanta and with American in New York. In January 2004 American Airlines initiated an aggressive offer of one trip free for every two trips made on a route in which American competed against JetBlue. The offer was primarily aimed at keeping its customers in New York and Boston from switching to JetBlue.[33] Also, the domestic airline segment was becoming crowded. However, officials of low-cost airlines had a different opinion. According to Southwest's Kelly, "You say, 'Is it getting crowded?' but this is a big country. There's bound to be some competition in the future, but right now there's relatively little overlap." He said that even without adding new cities, the carriers could still grow by adding flights between the existing airports they served.[34]

JetBlue believed that its continued growth would be accomplished by adding additional frequencies on existing routes, connecting new city pairs among the destinations it already served, and entering new markets.[35] JetBlue announced its intention to extend its route network overseas to Caribbean destinations.[36]

Although JetBlue continued looking ambitious, its bases of competitive advantage would not be unchallenged. Competition and imitation followed on the heels of this advantage and eroded differentiation. On the other hand, JetBlue's cost advantages were not fully developed either. Low labor costs were unlikely to last long given the possibility of unionization of the workforce as the company grew. The aging of its aircraft made the increase in maintenance costs inevitable. The growth in the size of the company and consequently the increase in the number of employees posed challenges to maintaining JetBlue's core culture. Amidst these challenges, in June 2003 JetBlue placed an order for 100 new Embraer 190 jet aircraft (from Embraer, the Brazilian jetmaker) with options for another 100. These planes were smaller than the Airbus A320s. They had 100 seats compared to the 156-seat configuration of the A320s and could be used to penetrate midsized markets that the low-cost carriers had largely ignored.[37] JetBlue CFO John Owen said that the planes could be used to connect midsized cities such as Columbus, Ohio, in the midwest with the eastern markets that JetBlue served.[38] Cities such as Austin, Texas, would also be attractive targets because passengers who disliked making connections at Dallas/Fort Worth International Airport for American Airlines or other carriers would like a nonstop flight to New York. Passengers would be willing to pay more on average for such nonstop service, according to Dave Barger, JetBlue's president and chief operating officer.[39] However, the move meant a change in JetBlue's one-type aircraft operations model that was at the heart of its low-cost strategy. The change imminently meant added complexities and costs to maintenance, pilot training, and scheduling. It could also complicate labor relations since pilots on smaller planes would be paid less. Also, the smaller Embraer aircraft would have higher expenses per each seat mile, the standard way of measuring expenses in the industry.[40] Even without the Embraer, strains to JetBlue's business model were evident in the decrease in operating margins with increased haul distances. Are JetBlue's competitive advantages sustainable? Can it sustain its growth momentum?

Appendix   Key Terms Used

Aircraft utilization. The average number of block hours operated per day per aircraft for the total fleet of aircraft.

Available seat miles. The number of seats available for passengers multiplied by the number of miles the seats are flown.

Average fare. The average one-way fare paid per flight segment by a revenue passenger.

Average stage length. Average number of miles flown per flight.

Breakeven load factor. The passenger load factor that will result in operating revenues being equal to operating expenses, assuming constant revenue per passenger mile and expenses.

Load factor. The percentage of aircraft seating capacity that is actually utilized (revenue passenger miles divided by available seat miles).

Operating expense per available seat mile. Operating expenses divided by available seat miles.

Operating revenue per available seat mile. Operating revenues divided by available seat miles.

Passenger revenue per available seat mile. Passenger revenue divided by available seat miles.

Revenue passenger miles. The number of miles flown by revenue passengers.

Revenue passengers. The total number of paying passengers flown on all flight segments.

Yield per passenger mile. The average amount one passenger pays to fly one mile.

Source: JetBlue. SEC filings for 2003.

Endnotes

1. Isidore, C. 2003. Too much of a cheap thing? *CNN Money,* December 4; http://money.cnn.com/2003/12/04/news/companies/discount_airlines/.
2. JetBlue, 10-K reports.
3. Spitz, J. 2004. Downgrades hit Delta and JetBlue, www.marketwatch.com; Barker, R. 2004. Some of my pans should have been picks. *BusinessWeek,* January 19: 90.
4. JetBlue, 2004, company press release, January 29; www.jetblue.com/learnmore/pressDetail.asp?newsId=230.
5. This section draws heavily from the SEC filings of JetBlue for the year 2002. Other sources include: Zellner, W. 2003. Look who's buzzing the discounters. *BusinessWeek,* November 24; Zellner, W. 2004. Folks are finally packing their bags. *BusinessWeek,* January 12; and a joint study by Kearney, A.T., & the Society of British Aerospace Companies, The emerging airline industry, www.atkearney.com/shared_res/pdf/Emerging_Airline_Industry_S.pdf.
6. www.southwest.com/about_swa/airborne.html.
7. This section draws from Gajilan, A. T. 2004. The Amazing JetBlue. *Fortune Small Business,* www.fortune.com/.
8. Brazilian-Amercian Chamber of Commerce of Florida. 2004. Chamber News, 2004 Excellence Award; www.brazilchamber.org/news/chambernews/ExcellenceAward2004.htm.
9. JetBlue Airways Corporation, *International Directory of Company Histories;* http://galenet.galegroup.com.
10. Gajilan. 2004. Amazing JetBlue; DiCarlo, L. 2001. Management and trends, Jet Blue skies. *Forbes.com,* January 31; www.forbes.com/2001/01/31/0131jetblue.html.
11. JetBlue IPO soars. 2002. *CNNmoney,* April 12; http://money.cnn.com/2002/04/12/markets/ipo/jetblue/.
12. WEBSMART50. 2003. *BusinessWeek,* November 24: 92.
13. Interview with David Neeleman by Willow Bay of CNN Business Unusual. 2002. Aired June 23; www. cnn.com/TRANSCRIPTS/0206/23/bun.00.html.
14. JetBlue, 10-K Reports.
15. Wells, M. 2002. Lord of the skies. *Forbes.com,* November 14.
16. JetBlue. 2003. Company press release. November 13; www.jetblue.com/learnmore/pressDetail.asp?newsId=213.
17. Woodyard, C. 2003. Unlike rivals, JetBlue won't do the bump. *USA Today,* October 24; www.upgradebuddy.com/docs/jetblue.html.
18. Ibid.
19. DiCarlo. 2001. Management and trends, Jet Blue Skies.
20. Neeleman, David. 2002. Letter to shareholders, JetBlue annual report; www.jetblue.com/onlineannualreport/letter.html.
21. JetBlue, www.jetblue.com/onlineannualreport/our-people.html.
22. Wells. 2002. Lord of the skies.
23. The Motley Fool (fool.com). 2003. June 20.
24. Wells. 2002. Lord of the skies.
25. JetBlue, www.jetblue.com/learnmore/index.html; 10-K report, 2003.
26. Delta Air Lines Song—News and Information, www.upgradebuddy.com/docs/song.html; Song Web site www.flysong.com/song_and_you/experience/index.jsp.
27. Isidore. 2003. Too much of a cheap thing?
28. Zellner. 2003. Look who's buzzing the discounters.
29. Capell, K., & and Zellner, W. 2004. Richard Branson's next big adventure. *BusinessWeek,* March 8.
30. Gajilan, 2004, The amazing JetBlue.
31. Ibid.
32. Donnelly, S. B. 2003. Blue skies: Is JetBlue the next great airline—or just a little too good to be true? *Time Online edition,* May 2; www.time.com.

33. McGinnis, C. 2004. Wherever JetBlue goes goodies follow. CNN.com, January 27; www.cnn.com. Gillin, E. 2004. AMR takes aim at JetBlue, *The Street.com.* January 7; www.thestreet.com/_yahoo/markets/ericgillin/10135607.html.

34. Isidore. 2003. Too much of a cheap thing?

35. JetBlue. 2003. 10-K report.

36. JetBlue continuing expansion plan, looking overseas. 2004. *USAToday,* March 3; www.usatoday.com/travel/news/2004-03-03-jetblue-growth_x.htm.

37. Zellner, W. 2003. Strafing the big boys—again. *BusinessWeek,* June 23.

38. Souder, E. 2004. JetBlue plans Carribean services expansion. *DowJones Business News,* March 2; http://biz.yahoo.com/djus/040302/1232000698_2.html.

39. Torbenson, E. 2004. Breaking from formation. *Dallas Morning News,* February 22: 1-D.

40. Zellner. 2003. Strafing the big boys.

Case 2 — Ford Motor Company in 2004

Entering Second Century of Existence*

In its centennial year, 2003, Ford Motor Company, the company that revolutionized car production in the world, was facing doubts about its existence. There were rumors about the possibility of Ford filing for Chapter 11. From a company sitting on an overwhelming $23 billion cash reserve in 1998[1] and optimistic about ousting General Motors (GM) from its leadership position, Ford in 2003 was in deep red with its bonds poised on junk status. William Clay Ford Jr., 45 (the great-grandson of Henry Ford who founded Ford Motor Company), appointed chief executive of Ford Motor Company after the ousting of Jacques Nasser in October 2001, was faced with the monumental task of reviving the world famous automaker from the brink of death. William Clay Ford Jr., also called Bill Ford, believed that the company had lost focus in several areas, and launched the "back to basics" campaign throughout the company. He wanted to make the "blue oval" shine again. He was optimistic about the company's turnaround and said, "When people look back on 2003, I want them to remember it as a turning point."[2]

However, reality indicated that the optimism might have been a bit premature. The automaker was losing money on almost every car sale. There was mounting pressure in terms of increased competition, declining market share, a poor cash situation, large unfunded pension and retiree medical liabilities, and, above all, a top management team that was not working together. Quality improvement programs had stalled and product introductions were being delayed. To nail it all, Toyota Motor Company, the Japanese carmaker, unseated Ford from the world's number two automaker position in January 2004.[3] The company slipped from the zenith to a nadir in a span of just four years.

Bill Ford and Ford Motor Company[4]

Bill Ford replaced Nasser as the chief executive officer of Ford Motor Company in October 2001. Bill Ford brought with him a new management team: Nick Scheele, the group vice president of North America, became the chief operating officer; James Padilla, group vice president for manufacturing and quality, succeeded Nick Scheele as group vice president North America; and Carl Reichardt, a longtime board member of Ford and retired CEO and chairman of Wells Fargo & Co., became the vice chairman of the board and was to take an active role overseeing financial operations, including that of

Ford Credit. Several other seniors who left Ford on early retirement during Nasser's term were brought back.

In terms of experience in managing a company of Ford's size and complexity, Bill Ford and his team (Scheele and Padilla) did not compare very well with the top management teams of other big automobile companies. Of course Bill Ford had some promising attributes. Ford was known to have a "nontraditional personality" for a CEO. He was also known for his strong views regarding environment protection which gave him a "tree hugger" label. According to many sources, he had a relatively "pro-employee, even pro-union reputation." He was very popular among the company's blue-collar and white-collar employees who distrusted Nasser. Workers gave him an enthusiastic response on October 30, 2001, when he became the CEO. Bill Ford viewed building relationships as his key job going forward. "You can't build the business if you don't have strong partnerships," Ford said. "Dealers, United Autoworkers Union, white-collar employees, suppliers, Wall Street—we have a lot of relationships that are important to us. A lot of those are broken and not healthy," he said.

According to some sources, Bill Ford was the right person to lead the Ford company at that juncture. The Ford name gave him the credibility and employee support so crucial for the success of any efforts for change. He considered bringing back a focus on operations as crucial for success. "We won't hesitate to pull the trigger if something isn't fitting in well," said Ford. "I think we have lost the focus in a couple of areas." Consistent with his beliefs, Ford and his team outlined a back-to-basics approach for the company in which the company's focus was to be on "designing, building, and selling the industry's best cars and trucks—and restoring the company's profitability." He wanted a "product-led renaissance." As part of this strategy, a sweeping restructuring plan that included closure of three assembly plants in North America, closure of two plants making auto parts, employee layoffs, and sale of noncore assets including the Kwik-Fit retail chain was announced in January 2002. The company also planned to reduce production by more than 1 million cars, keeping in view the chronic overcapacity in the industry. Additionally, he unveiled plans to cut off every bit of wasteful expenditure.

Another area that received attention was Ford Credit. The expansion of Ford Credit, which generated more profit margins than the core auto business, was of questionable benefit in the changing times. With a shrinking market share, expansion of Ford Credit meant lending not only for Ford's own vehicles but also for other brands and sometimes for customers with less than a strong credit history. Even risky borrowers were charged highly competitive interest rates in its ambition to become "global auto-finance superpower." The strategy might not have been wise in a

*This case study was prepared by Ms. Naga Lakshmi Damaraju of the University of Texas at Dallas, and Professors John C. Byrne and Alan B. Eisner at Pace University. All rights reserved to the authors. The purpose of the case is to stimulate class discussion rather than to illustrate effective or ineffective handling of a business situation. The authors thank Dr. Michael Oliff and Mr. Charles Hazzard at the University of Texas at Dallas for their valuable comments on an earlier version of this case. A special thanks is expressed to Charles Hazzard for the extensive research support he extended.

soft economy where default rates increased. The company abandoned this ambition in January 2002 and decided to concentrate on lending for its own vehicles.

In the meantime, in January 2002, Ford shocked Wall Street by writing off $1 billion on its palladium stockpile. Palladium, a precious metal, was used in catalytic converters to make the emissions from automobiles cleaner. Due to the erratic nature of the metal's availability, Ford's purchasing department was building up its palladium inventory while there were concurrent research efforts to reduce the amount of palladium required in its products. With a change in the demand–supply situation, and also because of technological breakthroughs, the massive stockpile had to be written off. While General Motors and other companies successfully hedged their risks on purchases of precious metals, the lack of communication between the purchasing and treasury departments (which routinely engaged in "hedging") led to the huge write-off.[5] The communication failure between purchasing, research, and the treasury departments reflected the deep-rooted problems at Ford Motor Company. The problem of internal fights for power that led to the palladium stockpile episode continued. Even the new management team assembled by Bill Ford was mired with problems to the extent that the top executives needed coaching by etiquette trainers to learn how to deal with each other.[6]

As a result of the transformation efforts of Bill Ford, the company announced in January 2004 net earnings of $495 million compared to a net loss of $980 million in 2002 (refer to Exhibit 1 for financial information).[7] The company had cut its cost per vehicle by $240 and trimmed expenses by $3.2 billion and raised $1 billion from the sale of assets.[8] The company was still credited with having 3 or 4 of the top 10 selling vehicles in America in the previous 10 years (see Exhibit 2 for top selling cars in February 2004), and it had a history of great resilience in coming out of crisis situations. However, Wall Street might not yet have been convinced. While stocks traded at $14.10 a share in March 2004 compared to an all-time low of $6.54 in March 2003, its bonds continued to be just above "junk" status.[9] See Exhibit 3 for Ford's stock performance compared to the Standard & Poor (S&P) 500.

Automobile Industry in the United States

The automotive industry in the United States was a highly competitive cyclical business. The number of cars and trucks sold to retail buyers or "industry demand" varied substantially from year to year depending on "general economic conditions, the cost of purchasing and operating cars and trucks, the availability of credit and fuel."[10] Because cars and trucks were durable items, consumers could wait to replace them; industry demand reflected this factor. The U.S. automobile industry was characterized by a capability to overproduce as many as 20 million cars a year.[11] Also, competition in the United States had intensified in the last few decades with Japanese carmakers (e.g., Toyota

and Honda) gaining a foothold in the market. To counter the "foreign" problem, Japanese companies had set up production facilities in the United States and gained acceptance from American consumers. Product quality and lean production were judged to be the major weapons that Japanese carmakers used to gain an advantage over American carmakers. In addition, increasing concern for the environment led companies to explore newer hybrid technologies to produce more environmentally friendly cars.

Cost pressures, cutthroat pricing, and overcapacity heralded a phase of consolidation in the industry. The 1998 merger between Daimler Benz of Germany and the Chrysler Corporation in the United States sparked the phenomenon. According to industry experts, the 40 players in the automobile industry were expected to shrink to 6 in the span of a decade during which each company needed a sales volume of more than 5 million vehicles just to remain profitable.[12] Yet in 1999, only two companies—General Motors and Ford—qualified for that mark while other companies worked feverishly to reach that level. Faced with increased competition and fast-changing customer preferences, innovative product designs became more critical then ever in the industry. Highly competitive consumer financing offers, in an attempt to retain or gain market share, squeezed the profit margins of even the major players and American companies faced growth without profitability. However, Japanese carmakers, with their better product designs and quality, were capturing better value than American carmakers.[13] The troubles in the automotive industry were accentuated by the attacks on the World Trade Center and Pentagon on September 11, 2001, and the recession in the economy pushed the already stressed automakers to the edge.

While there was a glut in the U.S. market for automobiles, the markets of Asia, Central and South America, and central and eastern Europe all showed increasing promise for automobiles, and the automobile industry entered into an era of "global motorization."[14] To address this opportunity for expansion, companies had to gear up to meet the tastes and preferences of customers around the world if they wished to secure market leadership.

Ford Motor Company—The Background

Ford Motor Company was started by Henry Ford in 1903 to produce and sell the automobiles he designed and engineered. The company was incorporated in Delaware in 1919 and went public in 1956, but the Ford family still retained 40 percent of the voting shares.[15] The company founded the first modern auto assembly line, which allowed its Model T to be produced at a cost within the reach of the masses.[16] However, Ford lost its leadership position to General Motors soon after it produced the Model T because the company was not able to address the market need for vehicles that were other than "black."

The two core businesses of Ford were automotive and financial services. The automotive sector encompassed the

	Years Ended				
	2003	2002	2001	2000	1999
Total Company					
Sales and revenues	$ 164,196	$ 162,256	$ 160,504	$ 168,930	$ 160,053
Income/(loss) before income taxes	1,370	951	(7,419)	8,311	9,856
Provision/(credit) for income taxes	135	301	(2,096)	2,722	3,247
Minority interests in net income of subsidiaries	314	367	24	127	112
Income/(loss) from continuing operations	921	283	(5,347)	5,462	6,497
Income/(loss) from discontinued/held-for-sale operations	(8)	(62)	(106)	257	740
Loss on disposal of discontinued/held-for-sale operations	(154)	(199)	—	(2,252)	—
Cumulative effects of change in accounting principle	(264)	(1,002)	—	—	—
Net income/(loss)	$ 495	$ (980)	$ (5,453)	$ 3,467	$ 7,237
Automotive Sector					
Sales	$ 138,442	$ 134,273	$ 130,736	$ 140,765	$ 135,022
Operating income/(loss)	(1,531)	(528)	(7,390)	5,298	7,190
Income/(loss) before income taxes	(1,957)	(1,153)	(8,857)	5,333	7,296
Financial Services Sector					
Revenues	$ 25,754	$ 27,983	$ 29,768	$ 28,165	$ 25,031
Income/(loss) before income taxes	3,327	2,104	1,438	2,978	2,560
Total Company Data per Share of Common and Class B Stock[a]					
Basic:					
Income/(loss) from continuing operations	1	0.15	(2.96)	3.69	5.38
Income/(loss) from discontinued/held-for-sale operations	—	(0.04)	(0.06)	0.18	0.61
Loss on disposal of discontinued/held-for-sale operations	(0)	(0.11)	—	(1.53)	—
Cumulative effects of change in accounting principle	(0)	(0.55)	—	—	—
Net income/(loss)	$ 0	$ (0.55)	$ (3.02)	$ 2.34	$ 5.99
Diluted:					
Income/(loss) from continuing operations	1	0.15	(2.96)	3.62	5.26
Income/(loss) from discontinued/held-for-sale operations	—	(0.03)	(0.06)	0.17	0.60
Loss on disposal of discontinued/held-for-sale operations	(0)	(0.11)	—	(1.49)	—
Cumulative effects of change in accounting principle	(0)	(0.55)	—	—	—
Net income/(loss)	$ 0	$ (0.54)	$ (3.02)	$ 2.30	$ 5.86
Cash dividends[b]	0	0.4	1.05	1.8	1.88
Common stock price range (NYSE Composite)					
High	17	18.23	31.42	31.46	37.3
Low	7	6.9	14.7	21.69	25.42
Average number of shares of Common and Class B stock outstanding (in millions)	1,832	1,819	1,820	1,483	1,210
Total Company Balance Sheet Data at Year-End					
Assets					
Automotive sector	$ 120,641	$ 107,790	$ 88,319	$ 94,312	$ 99,201
Financial services sector	195,279	187,432	188,224	189,078	171,048
Total assets	$ 315,920	$ 295,222	$ 276,543	$ 283,390	$ 270,249
Long-term Debt					
Automotive	$ 18,987	$ 13,607	$ 13,467	$ 11,769	$ 10,398
Financial Services	100,764	106,525	107,024	86,865	67,170
Total long-term debt	$ 119,751	$ 120,132	$ 120,491	$ 98,634	$ 77,568
Stockholders' Equity	$ 11,651	$ 5,590	$ 7,786	$ 18,610	$ 27,604

[a]Share data have been adjusted to reflect stock dividends and stock splits. Common stock price range (NYSE Composite) has been adjusted to reflect the spin-offs of Visteon and The Associates and a recapitalization known as the Value Enhancement Plan.

[b]Adjusted for the Value Enhancement Plan effected in August 2000; cash dividends were $1.16 per share in 2000.

Source: SEC filings for 2003; www.sec.gov.

Exhibit 2   Top Selling Vehicles in February 2004

No.	Vehicle Name	No.	Vehicle Name
1	Ford F-Series pickup	11	Chevrolet TrailBlazer
2	Chevy Silverado-C/K pickup	12	Nissan Altima
3	Toyota Camry	13	Dodge Caravan
4	Dodge Ram pickup	14	Chevrolet Cavalier
5	Ford Explorer	15	Jeep Grand Cherokee
6	Honda Accord	16	Ford Focus
7	Toyota Corolla/Matrix	17	Jeep Liberty
8	Honda Civic	18	Chevrolet Tahoe
9	Chevrolet Impala	19	Toyota Sienna
10	Ford Taurus	20	GMC Sierra pickup

Source: Reports of Detroit carmakers; http://biz.yahoo.com/rf/040302/ autos_top20_table_1.html.

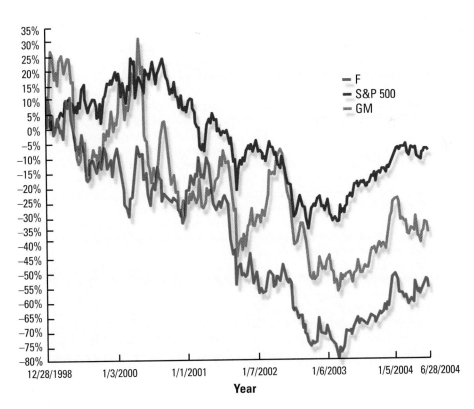

Exhibit 3   Price History—Ford Motor Company (12/28/1998–7/2/2004)
Source: MSN Money, CSI

design, development, manufacture, sale, and services of cars and trucks. The financial services sector operations were comprised of the Ford Motor Credit Company, a wholly owned subsidiary of Ford, and the Hertz Corporation, an indirect wholly owned subsidiary. Ford Credit provided leasing, insurance, and vehicle-related financing while Hertz rented cars, light trucks, and industrial and construction equipment.[17] Ford was the world's largest producer of trucks and second to GM as the largest producer of cars and trucks in the United States.[18]

Ford had production facilities on six continents and sold its products worldwide. The majority of its sales, like that of other major carmakers, came from the U.S. market. Ford had an extremely strong brand recognition and a strong financial and marketing network and was known for its innovative products. Several of its products were particularly well known and enjoyed great demand. About one million of the Mustang models were built in the two years following their introduction. The Ford Escort set a record as the "fastest first million units for a new car" and the original Model T was named as the car of the century in 1999.[19] Ford had nearly $5.9 billion in net income from continuing operations in 1998, making it the world's most profitable automaker. Ford's Taurus, Explorer, and other brands were extremely popular, and Ford also managed to gain a stronghold in the markets for sport utility vehicles (SUVs) and pickup trucks, the profitability of which then attracted many other automakers to vie for the segment. Ford had been named among the best-managed companies in Detroit, if not the world.[20] Ford's stock price rose by 130 percent since 1996, and by 1999 it was far ahead of the 71 percent gain of the S&P 500 stock price index and its global auto rivals.[21] With nearly $23 billion in cash reserves, Ford was eager to oust GM from its leadership position in the auto industry, and some predicted it soon would.

Jacques Nasser, who became the chief executive officer of Ford Motor Company in January 1999, pursued an ambitious diversification strategy. It was understood as the cradle-to-grave strategy in which Ford was to deal with all aspects of the car business (e.g., retailing and junkyard recycling, among others), not just making cars. To implement part of this strategy, Ford paid about $1.6 billion to acquire Kwik-Fit, a chain of nearly 20,000 auto service centers in Great Britain.[22] These were high-margin businesses that were expected to "add value" to Ford's operations. Ford also bought dealerships in selected U.S. markets and sold back a majority stake to the dealers who formerly owned them. The move was expected to protect Ford's distribution network base by not allowing a concentration of dealerships with a few big retail chains such as Auto Nation Inc.[23] Lower-margin operations, such as Visteon automotive systems which made automotive parts, were spun off.

The luxury car business division was substantially increased with the acquisition of the Swedish automaker Volvo for $6.47 billion in 1999 and Land Rover from BMW in 2000. Additional resources were spent on Mazda and Lincoln to restore the ailing units to good health, and the Jaguar line was expanded. Ford created the Premier Automotive Group (PAG) to manage these luxury brands; the luxury brand business was expected to contribute one-third of global profits by 2005.[24] On the personnel front, a new performance review ranking system was introduced to promote internal competition. Under this system, the managers were to be ranked against each other. Those who received poor grades (the bottom 5 percent) for two consecutive evaluation periods were to be fired.[25] Many of these initiatives ended up alienating various stakeholder groups in the organization. The diversification strategy did not pay off as well as expected because of aggressive competition during that period. General Motors' Silverado and Sierra pickups, for instance, overtook the Ford Division's top-selling F-series in 2001. New pickups launched by Toyota and Dodge also cut into F-series sales and profits.[26]

Added to this was the issue with Firestone over the Wilderness AT tires. These Firestone tires installed on SUVs were believed to cause the vehicles to roll over and crash for reasons other than tread separation. The problem was claimed to be more prevalent with Ford Explorer than other vehicles. A formal investigation by the National Highway Traffic and Safety Administration (NHTSA) was launched in May 2000. Both companies blamed each other, leading to bad publicity and loss of customer trust.[27] Firestone issued a massive recall of 6.5 million tires in August 2000. Ford followed in 2001 by issuing a recall of all its vehicles that had these Firestone tires on them. The move cost the company over $3 billion, one of the biggest recalls ever in the automobile industry, and also ended the century-old relationship between Firestone and Ford.[28]

Further, there was the growing divide between Bill Ford and Jacques Nasser. Ford felt that Nasser was cutting off his communication with top executives. With the downturn in the industry after the September 11, 2001, terrorist attacks and with his loss of corporate support, Nasser was replaced by Bill Ford as chief executive in October 2001. From being the world's most profitable automaker in 1999 with $7.2 billion in net income,[29] Ford posted a $500 million loss in October 2001 for the preceding quarter, the first time that the company was in the red for two successive quarters since the 1992 recession.[30] Overall, the company incurred a loss of $5.5 billion by 2001.[31] Ford's market share and quality ratings dropped, as did its S&P credit rating.[32]

The Challenges for Bill Ford

Despite Bill Ford's efforts, the situation did not change much by March 2004. Ford's problems persisted. Its car market share fell from 20.3 percent in 2002 to 19.5 percent in 2003, according to Autodata Corp, a New Jersey–based research firm.[33] Ford's combined car and truck market share in the United States fell from 21.1 percent in 2002 to 20.5 percent in 2003 (see Exhibit 4).[34] By March 2004

Exhibit 4 Market Share Data in the U.S. Market

U.S. Car Market Shares*
%

	Years Ended December 31				
	2003	2002	2001	2000	1999
Company Name					
Ford**	6.9%	7.7%	8.6%	9.5%	9.9%
General Motors	11.5	12.1	13.0	14.2	14.9
DaimlerChrysler	3.8	4.1	4.1	4.5	5.1
Toyota	5.9	5.8	5.5	5.5	5.1
Honda	4.8	4.9	5.1	5.0	4.9
All Other***	12.0	12.7	11.9	11.0	10.0
Total U.S. Car Retail Deliveries	44.9%	47.3%	48.2%	49.7%	49.9%

U.S. Truck Market Shares*
%

	Years Ended December 31				
	2003	2002	2001	2000	1999
Company Name					
Ford**	13.6%	13.4%	14.2%	14.2%	14.3%
General Motors	16.4	16.2	15.0	13.6	13.9
DaimlerChrysler	10.0	10.0	10.1	10.8	11.1
Toyota	5.1	4.5	4.5	3.6	3.4
Honda	3.1	2.4	1.8	1.6	1.3
All Other***	6.9	6.2	6.2	6.5	6.1
Total U.S. Truck Retail Deliveries	55.1%	52.7%	51.8%	50.3%	50.1%

U.S. Combined Car and Truck Market Shares*
%

	Years Ended December 31				
	2003	2002	2001	2000	1999
Company Name					
Ford**	20.5%	21.1%	22.8%	23.7%	24.2%
General Motors	27.9	28.3	28.0	27.8	28.8
DaimlerChrysler	13.8	14.1	14.2	15.3	16.2
Toyota	11.0	10.3	10.0	9.1	8.5
Honda	7.9	7.3	6.9	6.6	6.2
All Other***	18.9	18.9	18.1	17.5	16.1
Total U.S. Car and Truck Retail Deliveries	100.0%	100.0%	100.0%	100.0%	100.0%

*All U.S. retail sales data are based on publicly available information from the media and trade publications.

**Ford purchased Volvo Car on March 31, 1999 and Land Rover on June 30, 2000. The figures shown here include Volvo Car and Land Rover on a pro forma basis for the periods prior to their acquisition by Ford. In 1999 Land Rover represented less than 0.2 of total market share.

***"All Other" includes primarily companies based in various European countries, Korea, and other Japanese manufacturers; the U.S. Truck Market Shares table and U.S. Combined Car and Truck Market Shares table include heavy truck manufacturers.

Exhibit 5   J. D. Power's Long-Term Quality Survey: Problems per 100 Vehicles

Manufacturer	Score*	Manufacturer	Score*
Porsche	193	Ford	287
Toyota	196	DaimlerChrysler	311
Honda	215	Mitsubishi	339
Nissan	258	Hyundai	342
BMW	262	Isuzu	368
General Motors	264	Volkswagen	378
Subaru	266	Suzuki	403
Average	273	Kia	509

*A lower score means fewer problems per 100 vehicles.

Source: J. D. Power and Associates. 2003. Car quality: Japanese dominate. *CNNMoney,* July 8; http://money.cnn.com.

weak sales and rising inventories forced Ford to slash second-quarter production by 5 percent compared with the previous year.[35] Ford was struggling to retain its market share.[36]

The Premier Automotive Group had engineering facilities in Sweden, England, and Michigan though marketing was headquartered in its California offices. While grand plans were being made for each brand, the businesses were shrinking. Lincoln lost $1 billion in 2001, Jaguar lost $500 million in 2002, and Land Rover turned profitable only in 2003. Lincoln's expansion plans have been scaled down.[37] PAG posted a slim operating profit of $164 million for 2003 compared to a loss of $897 million in 2002 largely attributable to the introduction of hot new products: Jaguar's new flagship XJ sedans and Volvo's XC90 SUV.[38] PAG shifted its focus away from mass markets where its rivals took the lead. Ford continued to bet on its redesigned F-150 pickup truck to make it big again.

According to industry analysts, Ford's survival depended on concentrating in the major areas of product development, manufacturing systems, and finance.[39] Vehicle development at Ford was hampered by virtually no sharing of designs and technologies among similar vehicles. It was estimated that it took Ford at least 25 percent more time to produce a vehicle design than its competitors; the result was an "overly engineered," costly vehicle for the hypercompetitive U.S. car market. As recently as April 2003, Ford's engineering operations were built around five teams organized by vehicle types, each with its own budget and technologies. The teams often created their own unique body frames, suspension, brakes, engines, and transmis-

sions and seldom made any effort to share the technologies.[40] Indicative of this creative approach were at least 126 different types of fuel caps used in Ford vehicles in Europe alone.[41] There were many concerns that the better companies thrived on commonality—the sharing of designs and the use of common platforms of basic architecture—to roll out similar models faster and more efficiently. Ford just embarked on the process.[42]

On the manufacturing front, Ford's Japanese rivals, and even GM, progressed well with their flexible manufacturing systems. Flexible manufacturing systems allowed the production of two or three different sizes and shapes of cars in one plant without major production halts.[43] It would take Ford at least a decade to catch up. Quality problems persisted. *Consumer Reports* of April 2003 ranked Ford low among the big auto companies in terms of quality and reliability.[44] Ford's older factories were a possible reason because even the new models had defects. According to J. D. Power's 2003 Vehicle Dependability Study, which measured the durability of vehicles three years after their purchase, Toyota was in the number two position while Ford was eighth and below the industry average in terms of long-term quality (see Exhibit 5).[45] Even as late as March 2004, quality issues forced Ford to recall more than 1.3 million 2000 to 2003 models Taurus and Sable cars.[46] The Ford Focus model (after a lot of reworking) was the only Ford vehicle that made it as the top pick in 2 out of 10 categories, according to *Consumer Reports Annual 2004;* all other eight slots were taken up by the Japanese manufacturers Toyota and Honda.[47]

Ford's key focus was more on financing options for its customers than on competing with better models and

Exhibit 6   The Percentage Increase in Automaker Incentives, 2003–2004

Company Name	Consumer/Dealer Incentives (Jan. 2004)	Increase %
General Motors	$4,431	12%
Ford	4,296	23
Toyota	2,891	33
Honda	1,593	65
Nissan	1,631	10

Source: Tierney, C. 2004. Foreign automakers turn up volume on incentives. *Detroit News,* March 6; CNW Marketing Research Inc.

quality. Even its newest models were being sold only with the help of incentives and discounts.[48] To add to the company's woes, in 2004 Japanese rivals started launching incentive schemes more aggressively, thereby intensifying the price-based competition. While the American automakers aimed at attracting consumers with discounts, the foreign automakers were effective in luring the dealers to close the sale (see Exhibit 6).[49] To compete at this level, Ford became concerned that it could run into dangerously low levels of cash, jeopardizing new product launches and factory modernization. Already the balance sheet, with huge retiree obligations and massive debt from Ford Credit, was a serious concern. With credit ratings declining, the cost of its debt was on the rise. Also, the models already in the pipeline and those due in the years to come would cost Ford more than the vehicles they replaced, forcing the company into further cost cutting.[50] While Ford was making gains with respect to cost cutting, its market share and new product launches were still falling behind target. Even the slim profit that Ford posted for 2003 came primarily from its lending to car and truck buyers and other financial operations rather than its core automotive manufacturing business.[51]

Will Bill Ford's optimism prove realistic? Will Ford be able to make a turnaround?

Endnotes

1. Muller, J., Kerwin, K., Welch, D., Moore, P. L., & Brady, D. 2001. Ford: Why it's worse than you think. *BusinessWeek Online,* June 25; www.businessweek.com.
2. Kerwin, K. 2003. Can Ford pull out of its skid? *BusinessWeek Online,* March 31; www.businessweek.com.
3. Toyota surpasses Ford as no. 2 carmaker, January 25, 2004; http://biz.yahoo.com/ap/040125/japan_toyota_4.html.
4. This discussion draws heavily from the following sources: Isidore, C. 2001. Nasser out as Ford CEO. *CNNmoney,* October 30; http://money.cnn.com/2001/10/30/ceos/ford/; Taylor, A., III. 2003. Getting Ford in gear. *Fortune,* April 28; www.fortune.com; Teather, D. 2002. Ford's losses climb to $5.5 bn for year. *Guardian,* January 18; www.guardian .co.uk; Kerwin, K. 2002. Where are Ford's hot cars? *BusinessWeek Online,* June 24; www.businessweek.com; Shirouzu, N., White, G. L., & White, J. B. 2002. Ford's retrenchment seeks to cut costs and make its factories more flexible. *Wall Street Journal,* January 14:1; http://interactive.wsj.com.
5. White, G. L. 2002. A mismanaged palladium stockpile was catalyst for Ford's write-off. *Wall Street Journal,* February 6.
6. Taylor. 2003. Getting Ford in gear.
7. Hakim, D. 2004. Ford reports 2003 profit but posts loss in 4th quarter. *New York Times,* January 23.
8. Associated Press. 2004. Ford's 4Q loss widens to $793 million. *New York Times,* January 23.
9. *New York Times.* 2004, March 6; http://marketwatch.nytimes.com.
10. SEC filings, www.sec.gov.
11. Naughton, K., Miller, K. L., Muller, J., Thornton, E., & Edmondson, G. 1999. Autos: The global six. *BusinessWeek Online,* January 25; www.businessweek.com.
12. Ibid.
13. Muller, J., Kerwin, K., Welch, D., Moore, P. L., & Brady D. 2001. Ford: Why it's worse than you think. *BusinessWeek Online,* June 25; www.businessweek.com; Hakim, D. 2002. All that easy credit haunts Detroit now. *New York Times,* January 6; Hakim, D. 2003. Long road ahead for Ford. *New York Times,* March 14.
14. Okuda, H. 2002. Chairman's messages. August; www.toyota.co.jp.
15. Ford Motor Company. 2002. SEC filings; www.sec.gov.
16. www.ford.com/en/heritage/history/default.htm.
17. Ford Motor Co., company profile, yahoo finance, http://biz.yahoo.com/p/f/f.html.
18. General Motors, 2000, press release, November 16; http://media.gm.com/news/releases/corp_infrastructure_111600.html.
19. Ford Motor Company, www.fordmotorcompany.co.za/corporate/history/ford.asp.
20. Ford worries overshadow auto show. 2002. Fox Channel News, January 7; www.foxnews.com.
21. Kerwin, K., & Naughton, K. 1999. Remaking Ford. *BusinessWeek,* October 11: 132–136; www.businessweek.com.
22. Kerwin & Naughton. 1999. Remaking Ford; www.businessweek.com.
23. Box, T. 2002. Ford sells last of retail network. *Dallas Morning News,* April 5; www.dallasnews.com.
24. Kerwin & Naughton. 1999. Remaking Ford.
25. Labor and Employment Law Update. 2002. The lessons of Ford's forced ranking performance review system. June; www.shpclaw.com/updates/lessonsford.html.
26. Kerwin. 2002. Where are Ford's hot cars?
27. Ackman, D. 2001. Ford, Firestone on the hill. *Forbes,* June 19; www.forbes.com.
28. Recalled Tire—Firestone and Ford, www.recalledproduct.com/recalledtire/.

29. Muller, Kerwin et al. 2001. Ford: Why it's worse than you think.; Jackson, M. 2002. The leaders who run toward crises. *New York Times,* December 22; www.nytimes.com.

30. Treanor, J., & Gow, D. 2001. Ford ploughs deeper into red. *Guardian,* October 18; www.guardian.co.uk; Glover, M. 2001. Analysis: Nasser lost clan's confidence as PR disasters kept growing. October 31; http://classic.sacbee.com/ib/news/old/ib_news03_20011031.html.

31. Teather. 2002. Ford's losses climb to $5.5 bn.

32. Treanor & Gow. 2001. Ford ploughs deeper into red.

33. Associated Press. 2004. Ford's 4Q loss widens to $793 million.

34. Ford Motor Company. 2003. SEC filings.

35. Bloomberg news. 2004. Ford sales fall, but GM and Chrysler gain. *International Herald Tribune Online,* March 3.

36. Kerwin, K. 2003. Can Ford pull out of its skid? *BusinessWeek Online,* March 31; www.businessweek.com.

37. Taylor. 2003. Getting Ford in gear.

38. Kerwin, K. 2004. Ford learns the lessons of luxury. *BusinessWeek,* March 1: 116–117.

39. Shirouzu, White, & White. 2002. Ford's retrenchment seeks to cut costs.

40. Shirouzu, N. 2003. Ford's new development plan: Stop reinventing its wheels. *Wall Street Journal,* April 16.

41. Morris, B. 2002. Can Ford save Ford? *Fortune,* November 18; www.fortune.com.

42. Shirouzu, White, & White. 2002. Ford's retrenchment seeks to cut costs.

43. Ibid.

44. Kerwin. 2003. Can Ford pull out of its skid?; Smith, B. C. 2003. Back to basics. *Automotive Design and Production,* www.autofieldguide.com/columns/smith/1201ob.html.

45. Car Quality: Japanese dominate; http://money.cnn.com/2003/07/08/pf/autos/bc.autos.durability/?cnn=yes.

46. Ford recalls Taurus and Sable sedans. 2004. *Automotive News,* March 10; www.autonews.com/news.cms?newsId=8079.

47. Consumer Reports: U.S. cars beat Europeans, still trail Asians in reliability. 2004. *Automotive News,* March 9; www.autonews.com/news.cms?newsId=8057.

48. Shirouzu, White, & White. 2002. Ford's retrenchment seeks to cut costs.

49. Tierney, C. 2004. Foreign automakers turn up volume on incentives. *Detroit News,* March 6; www.detnews.com/2004/autosinsider/0403/02/a01e79606.htm.

50. Kim, C. R., & Hyde, J. 2004. Toyota overtakes Ford as world's no. 2 auto maker. Reuters news dispatch, January 25.

51. Hakim. 2004. Ford reports 2003 profit.

Case 3   Starbucks Corporation: Competing in a Global Market*

Starbucks Corporation is a coffee company based in Seattle, Washington. It buys, roasts, and sells whole bean specialty coffees and coffee drinks through an international chain of retail outlets. From its beginnings as a seller of packaged, premium specialty coffees, Starbucks has evolved into a firm known for its coffeehouses, where people can purchase beverages and food items as well as packaged whole bean and ground coffee. Starbucks is credited with changing the way Americans—and people around the world—view and consume coffee, and its success has attracted global attention.

Starbucks has consistently been one of the fastest-growing companies in the United States. Over a 10-year period starting in 1992, the company's net revenues increased at a compounded annual growth rate of 20 percent, to $3.3 billion in fiscal 2002. Net earnings have grown at an annual compounded growth rate of 30 percent to $218 million in fiscal 2002, which is the highest reported net earnings figure in the company's history (see Exhibit 1). As *BusinessWeek* tells it:

> On Wall Street, Starbucks is the last great growth story. Its stock, including four splits, has soared more than 2,200 percent over the past decade, surpassing Wal-Mart, General Electric, PepsiCo, Coca-Cola, Microsoft, and IBM in total return. Now at $21 [September 2002], it is hovering near its all-time high of $23 in July [2002], before the overall market drop.[1]

To continue this rapid pace of growth, the firm's senior executives are looking to expand internationally. Specifically, they are interested in further expansion in Europe (including the Middle East), Asia-Pacific (including Australia and New Zealand), and Latin America. Expanding in these three continents represents both a challenge and an opportunity to Starbucks. While the opportunity of increased revenues from further expansion is readily apparent to the company's top management, what is not clear is how to deal with growing "antiglobalization" sentiment around the world.

This case looks at issues that are arising as Starbucks seeks to dominate specialty coffee markets around the world and explores what changes in strategy might be required.

Background

In 1971, three Seattle entrepreneurs—Jerry Baldwin, Zev Siegl, and Gordon Bowker—started selling whole bean coffee in Seattle's Pike Place Market. They named their store Starbucks, after the first mate in *Moby Dick*.[2] By 1982 the business had grown to five stores, a small roasting facility, and a wholesale business selling coffee to local restaurants. At the same time, Howard Schultz had been working as vice president of U.S. operations for Hammarplast, a Swedish housewares company in New York, marketing coffeemakers to a number of retailers, including Starbucks. Through selling to Starbucks, Schultz was introduced to the three founders, who then recruited him to bring marketing savvy to their company. Schultz, 29 and recently married, was eager to leave New York. He joined Starbucks as manager of retail sales and marketing.

A year later, Schultz visited Italy for the first time on a buying trip. He noticed that coffee is an integral part of the culture in Italy; Italians start their day at an espresso bar and later in the day return with their friends. There are 200,000 coffee bars in Italy, and about 1,500 in Milan alone. Schultz believed that, given the chance, Americans would pay good money for a premium cup of coffee and a stylish place to enjoy it. Enthusiastic about his idea, Schultz returned to tell Starbucks' owners of his plan for a national chain of cafes styled on the Italian coffee bar. The owners, however, did not want to be in the restaurant business. Undaunted, Schultz wrote a business plan and began looking for investors. By April 1985 he had opened his first coffee bar, Il Giornale (named after the Italian newspaper), where he served Starbucks coffee. Following Il Giornale's immediate success, he expanded to three stores. In 1987 the owners of Starbucks agreed to sell the firm to Schultz for $4 million. The Il Giornale coffee bars took on the name of Starbucks.

Convinced that Starbucks would one day be in every neighborhood in America, Schultz focused on growth. At first, the company's losses almost doubled (to $1.2 million in fiscal 1990), as overhead and operating expenses ballooned with the expansion. Starbucks lost money for three years running, and the stress was hard on Schultz, but he stuck to his conviction not to "sacrifice long-term integrity and values for short-term profit."[3] In 1991 sales shot up 84 percent, and the company turned profitable. In 1992 Schultz took the firm public at $17 a share.

Believing that market share and name recognition were critical to the company's success, Schultz continued to expand the business aggressively. Schultz observed, "There is no secret sauce here. Anyone can do it." From the beginning, Schultz has professed a strict growth policy. Although many other coffeehouses or espresso bars are franchised, Starbucks owns all of its North American stores outright, with the exception of license agreements in airports. Further, rather than trying to capture all the potential markets as soon as possible, Starbucks goes into a geographic market and tries to dominate it completely before setting its sights on further expansion. Using this strategy,

*Suresh Kotha and Debra Glassman, both from the University of Washington, prepared this case for the basis of class discussion rather than to illustrate either effective or ineffective handling of an administrative situation. The case was originally developed for the 2003 Global Business Challenge case competition at the University of Washington Business School. The authors thank the Global Business Center, the University of Washington, and the Starbucks Corporation for their generous support in preparing the case. All rights reserved to the authors. Copyright © 2003 Kotha & Glassman.

Exhibit 1   Starbucks Selected Financial and Store Data
(In thousands, except earnings per share and store operating data)

	As of and for the Fiscal Year Ended[1]				
	Sept. 29, 2002 (52 Wks)	Sept. 30, 2001 (52 Wks)	Oct. 1, 2000 (52 Wks)	Oct. 3, 1999 (53 Wks)	Sept. 27, 1998 (52 Wks)
Results of Operations Data					
Net revenues:					
Retail	$2,792,904	$2,229,594	$1,823,607	$1,423,389	$1,102,574
Specialty	496,004	419,386	354,007	263,439	206,128
Total net revenues	3,288,908	2,648,980	2,177,614	1,686,828	1,308,702
Merger expenses[2]	—	—	—	—	8,930
Operating income	318,725	281,094	212,252	156,711	109,216
Internet-related investment losses	—	2,940	58,792	—	—
Gain on sale of investment	13,361	—	—	—	—
Net earnings	$ 215,073	$ 181,210	$ 94,564	$ 101,693	$ 68,372
Net earnings per common share—diluted	$ 0.54	$ 0.46	$ 0.24	$ 0.27	$ 0.19
Balance Sheet Data					
Working capital	$ 310,048	$ 148,661	$ 146,568	$ 135,303	$ 157,805
Total assets	2,292,736	1,846,519	1,491,546	1,252,514	992,755
Long-term debt (including current portion)	5,786	6,483	7,168	7,691	1,803
Shareholders' equity	1,726,638	1,375,927	1,148,399	961,013	794,297
Store Operating Data					
Percentage change in comparable store sales[3]					
North America	7%	5%	9%	6%	5%
International	(3)%	2%	23%	20%	28%
Consolidated	6%	5%	9%	6%	5%
Systemwide retail store sales[4]	$3,796,000	$2,950,000	$2,250,000	$1,633,000	$1,190,000
Systemwide stores opened during the year:[5]	1,177	1,208	1,003	612	474
Systemwide stores open at year end:					
Continental North America					
Company-operated stores	3,496	2,971	2,446	2,038	1,622
Licensed stores	1,078	809	530	179	133
International					
Company-operated stores	384	295	173	97	66
Licensed stores	928	634	352	184	65
Total	5,886	4,709	3,501	2,498	1,886

[1]The company's fiscal year ends on the Sunday closest to September 30. All fiscal years presented include 52 weeks, except fiscal 1999, which includes 53 weeks.

[2]Merger expenses relate to the business combination with Seattle Coffee Holdings Limited.

[3]Includes only company-operated stores open 13 months or longer.

[4]Systemwide retail store sales include sales at company-operated and licensed stores and are believed by management to measure global penetration of Starbucks retail stores.

[5]Systemwide store openings are reported net of closures.

Source: Starbucks Corporation.

Starbucks has grown from 17 coffee shops in 1987 to 5,688 outlets in 28 countries by the end of fiscal 2002 (see Exhibit 2). It also employed over 60,000 individuals, including approximately 50,000 in retail stores, at the end of 2002.

Starbucks Corporation is organized into two business units that correspond to the company's operating segments: North American and International. In 1995 Starbucks Coffee International, a wholly owned subsidiary of Starbucks Coffee Company, was set up to build Starbucks' businesses outside North America, including opening company-owned, licensed, and joint-venture-based retail stores worldwide.

A recent article in *BusinessWeek* noted:

> Starbucks also has a well-seasoned management team. Schultz, 49, stepped down as chief executive in 2000 to become chairman and chief global strategist. Orin Smith, 60, the company's numbers-cruncher, is now CEO and in charge of day-to-day operations. The head of North American operations is Howard Behar, 57, a retailing expert who returned last September, two years after retiring. The management trio is known as H$_2$O, for Howard, Howard, and Orin."[4]

Exhibit 3 provides a partial list of Starbucks' top management, and the Appendix on page 572 provides a timeline and history of Starbucks.

The Starbucks Model

Howard Schultz's goal was to: "Establish Starbucks as the premier purveyor of the finest coffee in the world while maintaining uncompromising principles as we grow." The company's 25-year goal is to "become an enduring, great company with the most recognized and respected brand in the world, known for inspiring and nurturing the human spirit." The company's mission statement articulates several guiding principles to measure the appropriateness of the firm's decisions (see Exhibit 4). In describing Starbucks' unique approach to competition, *Fortune* noted:

> The strategy is simple: Blanket an area completely, even if the stores cannibalize one another's business. A new store will often capture about 30% of the sales of a nearby Starbucks, but the company considers that a good thing: The Starbucks-everywhere approach cuts down on delivery and management costs, shortens customer lines at individual stores, and increases foot traffic for all the stores in an area. Last week 20 million people bought a cup of coffee at a Starbucks. A typical customer stops by 18 times a month; no American retailer has a higher frequency of customer visits. Sales have climbed an average of 20% a year since the company went public. Even in a down economy, when other retailers have taken a beating, Starbucks store traffic has risen between

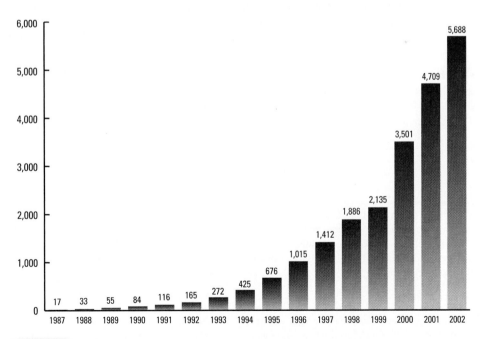

Exhibit 2   Number of Starbucks Store Locations (As of November 2002)

Source: Starbucks Corporation.

Exhibit 3   Starbucks Top Management Team

Howard Schultz is the founder of the company and has been chairman of the board since its inception in 1985. Mr. Schultz served as chief executive officer from 1985 until June 2000, when he transitioned into the role of chief global strategist. From 1985 to June 1994, Mr. Schultz was also the company's president. From September 1982 to December 1985, Mr. Schultz was the director of Retail Operations and Marketing for Starbucks Coffee Company, a predecessor to the company; and from January 1986 to July 1987, he was the chairman of the board, chief executive officer, and president of Il Giornale Coffee Company, a predecessor to the company.

Orin C. Smith joined Starbucks Corporation in 1990 and has served as president and chief executive officer of the company since June 2000. From June 1994 to June 2000, Mr. Smith served as the company's president and chief operating officer. Prior to June 1994, Mr. Smith served as the company's vice president and chief financial officer and later, as its executive vice president and chief financial officer.

Peter Maslen joined Starbucks in August 1999 as president, Starbucks Coffee International, Inc. Prior to joining Starbucks, Mr. Maslen served in various executive positions within Asia-Pacific and Europe with Mars Inc., PepsiCo, Inc., and Tricon Global Restaurants. From 1992 to 1999, as senior vice president with Tricon, he served as president of its German, Swiss, Austrian, and Central Europe divisions.

Jim Donald joined Starbucks in November 2002 as president, Starbucks North America. He is responsible for managing Starbucks North America company-owned and licensed stores, business alliances (food service, grocery, club channels of distribution, joint venture partnerships with Pepsi-Cola Company and Dreyer's Grand Ice Cream, Inc.) in the United States and Canada, store development, retail systems, administration, and retail partner resources. Mr. Donald brings 32 years of experience in the retail and food industry. Prior to joining Starbucks, he was chairman, president, and chief executive officer at Pathmark Stores, Inc., since 1996. In addition, he has held several senior leadership positions at top-tier retail companies including Safeway, Wal-Mart, and Albertson's.

Michael Casey joined Starbucks in August 1995 as senior vice president and chief financial officer and was promoted to executive vice president, chief financial officer, and chief administrative officer in September 1997. Prior to joining Starbucks, Mr. Casey served as executive vice president and chief financial officer of Family Restaurants, Inc., from its inception in 1986. During his tenure there, he also served as a director from 1986 to 1993, and as president and chief executive officer of its El Torito Restaurants, Inc., subsidiary from 1988 to 1993.

Eduardo R. (Ted) Garcia joined Starbucks in April 1995 as senior vice president, Supply Chain Operations, and was promoted to executive vice president, Supply Chain and Coffee Operations, in September 1997. From May 1993 to April 1995, Mr. Garcia was an executive for Gemini Consulting. From January 1990 until May 1993, he was the vice president of Operations Strategy for Grand Metropolitan PLC, Food Sector.

Source: Starbucks Corporation, November 2002.

6% and 8% a year. Perhaps even more notable is the fact that Starbucks has managed to generate those kinds of numbers with virtually no marketing, spending just 1% of its annual revenues on advertising. (Retailers usually spend 10% or so of revenues on ads.)[5]

BusinessWeek added:

Clustering stores increases total revenue and market share, [CEO] Orin Smith argues, even when individual stores poach on each other's sales. The strategy works, he says, because of Starbucks' size. It is large enough to absorb losses at existing stores as new ones open up, and soon overall sales grow beyond what they would have with just one store. Meanwhile, it's cheaper to deliver to and manage stores located close together. And by clustering, Starbucks can quickly dominate a local market.[6]

And Schultz pointed out:

The market is much larger than we originally thought. . . . In most cases local competitors benefit from our arrival because of the expansion of the marketplace. Our strategy is never to eliminate or hurt the competition.

Exhibit 4   Starbucks Mission Statements and Guiding Principles

---

Mission Statement

Establish Starbucks as the premier purveyor of the finest coffee in the world while maintaining our uncompromising principles while we grow.

The following six guiding principles will help us measure the appropriateness of our decisions:

- Provide a great work environment and treat each other with respect and dignity.
- Embrace diversity as an essential component in the way we do business.
- Apply the highest standards of excellence to the purchasing, roasting, and fresh delivery of our coffee.
- Develop enthusiastically satisfied customers all of the time.
- Contribute positively to our communities and our environment.
- Recognize that profitability is essential to our future success.

Environmental Mission Statement

Starbucks is committed to a role of environmental leadership in all facets of our business.

We fulfill this mission by a commitment to:

- Understanding environmental issues and sharing information with our partners.
- Developing innovative and flexible solutions to bring about change.
- Striving to buy, sell, and use environmentally friendly products.
- Recognizing that fiscal responsibility is essential to our environmental future.
- Instilling environmental responsibility as a corporate value.
- Measuring and monitoring our progress for each project.
- Encouraging all partners to share in our mission.

Source: Starbucks Corporation.

We never underprice our coffee and it's clear that we position ourselves so as not to undercut the pricing structure in the marketplace.

Schultz observed that the company is still in its early days of growth worldwide. "We are opening three or four stores every day," he noted. "We feel strongly that the driver of the equity of the brand is directly linked to the retail experience we create in our stores. Our commitment to the growth of the company is significant and will continue to be based on the long-term growth potential of our retail format."

Securing the Finest Raw Materials   Starbucks' coffee quality begins with the purchase of high-quality *arabica* coffee beans. Although many Americans were raised on a commodity-like coffee made from lower-quality *robusta* beans (or arabica beans mixed with less-expensive filler beans), Starbucks coffee is strictly arabica, and the company ensures that only the highest-quality beans are used. Dave Olsen, the company's then senior

vice president and chief coffee procurer, scoured mountain trails in Indonesia, Kenya, Guatemala, and elsewhere in search of Starbucks' premium bean. His standards were demanding, and he conducted exacting experiments in order to get the proper balance of flavor, body, and acidity.

From the company's inception, it has worked on developing relationships with the countries from which it buys coffee beans. Traditionally, Europeans and Japanese bought most of the premium coffee beans. Olsen sometimes had to convince coffee growers to sell to Starbucks—especially since American coffee buyers are notorious purchasers of the "dregs" of the coffee beans. In 1992 Starbucks set a new precedent by outbidding European buyers for the exclusive Narino Supremo bean crop.[7] Starbucks collaborated with a mill in the tiny town of Pasto, located on the side of the Volcano Galero. There they set up a special operation to single out the particular Narino Supremo bean, and Starbucks guaranteed to purchase the entire yield. This enabled Starbucks to be the exclusive purveyor of Narino Supremo, purportedly one of the best coffees in the world.[8]

Roasting   Roasting the coffee bean is close to an art form at Starbucks. Starbucks currently operates multiple roasting and distribution facilities. Roasters are promoted from within the company and trained for over a year, and it is considered quite an honor to be chosen. The coffee is roasted in a powerful gas-fired drum roaster for 12 to 15 minutes while roasters use sight, smell, hearing, and computers to judge when beans are perfectly done. The color of the beans is even tested in an Agtron blood-cell analyzer, with the whole batch being discarded if the sample is not deemed perfect.

The Starbucks Experience   According to Schultz, "We're not just selling a cup of coffee, we are providing an experience." In order to create American coffee enthusiasts with the dedication of their Italian counterparts, Starbucks provides a seductive atmosphere in which to imbibe. Its stores are distinctive and sleek, yet comfortable. Though the sizes of the stores and their formats vary, most are modeled after the Italian coffee bars where regulars sit and drink espresso with their friends.

Starbucks stores tend to be located in high-traffic locations such as malls, busy street corners, and even grocery stores. They are well lighted and feature plenty of light cherry wood and artwork. The people who prepare the coffee are referred to as "baristas," Italian for bartender. Jazz or opera music plays softly in the background. The stores range from 200 to 4,000 square feet, with new units tending to range from 1,500 to 1,700 square feet. In 2003 the average cost of opening a new store (including equipment, inventory, and leasehold improvements) is in the neighborhood of $350,000; a "flagship" store costs much more.

Building a Unique Culture   While Starbucks enforces almost fanatical standards about coffee quality and service, the policy at Starbucks toward employees is laid-back and supportive. They are encouraged to think of themselves as partners in the business. Schultz believes that happy employees are the key to competitiveness and growth.

> We can't achieve our strategic objectives without a workforce of people who are immersed in the same commitment as management. Our only sustainable advantage is the quality of our workforce. We're building a national retail company by creating pride in—and stake in—the outcome of our labor.[9]

On a practical level, Starbucks promotes an empowered employee culture through generous benefits programs, an employee stock ownership plan, and thorough employee training, Each employee must have at least 24 hours of training. Classes cover everything from coffee history to a seven-hour workshop called "Brewing the Perfect Cup at Home." This workshop is one of five classes that all employees must complete during their first six weeks with the company. Reports *Fortune:*

It's silly, soft-headed stuff, though basically, of course, it's true. Maybe some of it sinks in. Starbucks is a smashing success, thanks in large part to the people who come out of these therapy-like training programs. Annual barista turnover at the company is 60 percent compared with 140 percent for hourly workers in the fast-food business.[10]

Starbucks offers its benefits package to both part-time and full-time employees. The package includes medical, dental, vision, and short-term disability insurance, as well as paid vacation, paid holidays, mental health/chemical dependency benefits, an employee assistance program, a 401(k) savings plan, and a stock option plan. It also offers dependent coverage that includes same-sex partners.[11] Schultz believes that without these benefits, people do not feel financially or spiritually tied to their jobs. He argued that stock options and the complete benefits package increase employee loyalty and encourage attentive service to the customer.[12]

Employee turnover is also discouraged by Starbucks' stock option plan known as the Bean Stock Plan. Implemented in August 1991, the plan made Starbucks the only private company to offer stock options unilaterally to all employees.

Starbucks' concern for employee welfare extends beyond its retail outlets to coffee producers. The company's guidelines call for overseas suppliers to pay wages and benefits that "address the basic needs of workers and their families" and to allow child labor only when it does not interrupt required education.[13] This move has set a precedent for other importers of agricultural commodities.

Leveraging the Brand   *Multiple Channels of Distribution*   Besides its stand-alone stores, Starbucks has set up cafes and carts in hospitals, banks, office buildings, supermarkets, and shopping centers. Other distribution agreements have included office coffee suppliers, hotels, and airlines. Office coffee is a large segment of the coffee market. Associated Services (an office coffee supplier) provides Starbucks coffee exclusively to thousands of businesses around the United States. Starbucks has deals with airlines, such as an agreement with United Airlines to provide Starbucks coffee to United's nearly 75 million passengers a year. Starbucks, through a licensing agreement with Kraft Foods Inc., offers its coffee in grocery stores across the United States.

Brand Extensions   In 1995 Starbucks launched a line of packaged and prepared teas in response to growing demand for teahouses and packaged tea. Tea is a highly profitable beverage for restaurants to sell, costing only 2 cents to 4 cents a cup to produce.[14] As its tea line became increasingly popular, the company in January 1999 acquired Tazo, a tea company based in Portland, Oregon.

Starbucks coffee is also making its way onto grocery shelves by way of a carefully planned series of joint ventures.[15] An agreement with PepsiCo Inc. brought a bottled version of Starbucks Frappuccino (a cold, sweetened coffee drink) to store shelves in August 1996. In another 50–50 partnership, Dreyer's Grand Ice Cream Inc. distributes seven quart-product and two bar-product varieties of Starbucks coffee ice cream.

Other partnerships by the company are designed to form new product associations with coffee. For instance, the company's music subsidiary, Hear Music, regularly releases CDs, some in collaboration with major record labels, that are then sold through Starbucks retail stores.

While Starbucks is the largest and best known of the coffeehouse chains and its presence is very apparent in metropolitan areas, the firm's estimates indicate that only a small percentage (about 7 percent) of the U.S. population has tried its products. Through distribution agreements and the new product partnerships, Starbucks hopes to capture more of the U.S. market.

International Expansion

For many years analysts have observed that the U.S. coffee bar market may be reaching saturation. They have pointed to market consolidation, as bigger players snapped up some of the smaller coffee bar competitors.[16] Further, they have noted that Starbucks' store base is also maturing, leading to a slowdown in the growth of unit volume and firm profitability. In response, some have argued, Starbucks has turned its attention to foreign markets for continued growth. For instance, *BusinessWeek* noted:

> To duplicate the staggering returns of its first decade, Starbucks has no choice but to export its concept aggressively. Indeed, some analysts give Starbucks only two years at most before it saturates the U.S. market. The chain now [in August 2002] operates 1,200 international outlets, from Beijing to Bristol. That leaves plenty of room to grow. Indeed, about 400 of its planned 1,200 new stores this year will be built overseas, representing a 35 percent increase in its foreign base. Starbucks expects to double the number of its stores worldwide, to 10,000 in three years.[17]

However, of the predicted three or four stores that will open each day, the majority will continue to be in the United States.

Early Expansion   In 1995 the firm established a subsidiary called Starbucks Coffee International, Inc. At that time, the subsidiary consisted of 12 managers located in Seattle. Today this subsidiary is led by Australian expatriate Peter Maslen and is staffed with about 180 experienced multinational and multilingual managers located in Seattle and three regional offices around the world. This group is responsible for all of Starbucks' business development outside North America, including developing new businesses, financing and planning stores, managing operations and logistics, merchandising, and training and developing Starbucks' international managers.

Starbucks' first non-North American store was opened in 1996 in Tokyo. In reflecting on this early step in internationalizing the chain, Schultz noted:

> Two years prior to opening up in Japan, we hired this blue-chip consulting firm to guide us to succeed here. Basically, they said we would not succeed in Japan. There were a number of things they told us to change. [They said] we had to have smoking, but that was a nonstarter for us. They also said no Japanese would ever lose face by drinking from a cup in the street. And third, they said that given the [high] rent, stores couldn't be larger than 500 square feet. . . . Well, our no-smoking policy made us an oasis in Japan. As for our to-go business, you can't walk down a street in Tokyo today and not see someone holding a cup of Starbucks coffee. And our store size in Japan is identical to our store size in the United States, about 1,200 to 1,500 square feet. It just shows the power of believing in what you do. And also that Starbucks is as relevant in Tokyo, Madrid, or Berlin as it is in Seattle.[18]

The Starbucks Way   According to *US News and World Report*:

> When venturing overseas, there is a Starbucks way. The company finds local business partners in most foreign markets. . . . It tests each country with a handful of stores in trendy districts, using experienced Starbucks managers. It sends local baristas to Seattle for 13 weeks of training. Then it starts opening stores by the dozen. Its coffee lineup doesn't vary, but Starbucks does adapt its food to local tastes. In Britain, it won an award for its mince pie. In Asia, Starbucks offers curry puffs and meat buns. The company also fits its interior decor to the local architecture, especially in historic buildings. "We don't stamp these things out cookie-cutter style," says Peter Maslen, president of Starbucks Coffee International.[19]

Although Starbucks is committed to owning its North American stores, it has sought partners for much of its overseas expansion. As Kathy Lindemann, senior vice president of Operations for Starbucks International, describes it:

> Our approach to international expansion is to focus on the *partnership first, country second*. We rely on the local connection to get everything up and working. The key is finding the right local partners to negotiate local regulations and other issues. We look for partners who share our values, culture, and goals about community development. We are primarily interested in partners who can guide us through the process of starting up in a foreign location. We look for firms with: (1) a similar philosophy to ours in terms of shared values, corporate

citizenship, and commitment to be in the business for the long haul, (2) multiunit restaurant experience, (3) financial resources to expand the Starbucks concept rapidly to prevent imitators, (4) strong real-estate experience with knowledge about how to pick prime real estate locations, (5) knowledge of the retail market, and (6) the availability of the people to commit to our project.

In an international joint venture, it is the partner that chooses store sites. These are submitted for approval to Starbucks, but the partner does all the preparatory and selection work. Cydnie Horwat, vice president for International Assets Development Systems & Infrastructure, explains how a Starbucks market entry plan starts with brand building, which then facilitates rapid further expansion in a country:

> When first entering a market, we're looking for different things in the first one to three years than later on. During these early years, we're building our brand. Our stores are the biggest source of advertising, since we do not do a lot of separate advertising. So we have a higher investment in stores in the first three years. About 60–70 percent of stores opened in these first three years are our high brand-builders.

Horwat added:

> First, we look for extremely visible sites in well-trafficked areas and focus on three major factors: demographics, branding potential, and financials. Second, we categorize sites on an A to D scale. "A" sites are "signature" sites that are qualitatively superior to all other sites within the trade area [an area within which Starbucks chooses to locate one store]. We rarely take a "C" or "D" store.[20] Third, we ask our international Market Business Unit[21] (MBU) to send in the "site" submittal package with quantitative and qualitative measures, such as how the site meets Starbucks' established criteria and the partner's agreed-upon criteria. This package is reviewed by a number of functional units—operations, finance, and real estate—within the International Group. Fourth, we move into the design phase, which is done in Seattle using information provided by the partner. Next we negotiate the lease with the landlord and initiate the construction when the appropriate permits are obtained. Finally, we turn over the store to operations. The whole process takes about 13–16 weeks from start to finish.

Establishing Starbucks as a Global Brand   Based on the success in Japan and other locations, Schultz's goal is for Starbucks to have a ubiquitous image as one of the most respected brands in the world. He noted:

> Whenever we see the reception we're getting in markets in places such as China, the Philippines, Malaysia, the U.K., and most recently Spain and Germany, we recognize that the growth potential for the company [overseas]

is very significant. We want to accelerate that growth, maintain our leadership position, and, ultimately, become one of the most respected brands in the world.[22]

Since its early foray into the Japanese market, the pace of international expansion has picked up significantly. In 1998 Starbucks acquired Seattle Coffee Company in the United Kingdom, a chain with more than 38 retail locations. That same year, it opened stores in Taiwan, Thailand, New Zealand, and Malaysia. In 1999 Starbucks opened in China (Beijing), Kuwait, South Korea, and Lebanon. In 2000 it entered another seven markets (China—Hong Kong and Shanghai, Dubai, Australia, Qatar, Saudi Arabia, and Bahrain). It added three markets in 2001 (Switzerland, Israel, and Austria). Last year, another nine markets were opened (Oman, Spain, Indonesia, Germany, Southern China—Macau and Shenzhen, Mexico, Puerto Rico, and Greece). Exhibit 5 highlights the growth of international stores, and Exhibit 6 provides the list of countries where Starbucks has a presence.

Schultz says that this expansion is only beginning and confidently predicts more to come:

> Ten years ago, we had 125 stores and 2,000 employees. Today we have 62,000 people working in 30 countries outside of North America, serving approximately 22 million customers a week. Our core customer is coming in about 18 times a month. With the majority of adults around the world drinking two cups of coffee a day and with Starbucks having less than a 7 percent share of total coffee consumption in the United States and less than 1 percent worldwide, these are the early days for the growth and development of the company. We've got a model that has been well tested from market to market.

Starbucks is well on its way to becoming a global brand. According to *BusinessWeek:*

> [T]he Starbucks name and image connect with millions of consumers around the globe. It was one of the fastest-growing brands in a *BusinessWeek* survey of the top 100 global brands published August 5 [2002]. At a time when one corporate star after another has crashed to earth, brought down by revelations of earnings misstatements, executive greed, or worse, Starbucks hasn't faltered.[23]

But becoming a global company is not without risks. As *BusinessWeek* pointed out,

> Global expansion poses huge risks for Starbucks. For one thing, it makes less money on each overseas store because most of them are operated with local partners. While that makes it easier to start up on foreign turf, it reduces the company's share of the profits to only 20 percent to 50 percent."[24]

In addition, the firm is becoming a target for antiglobalization activists around the world.

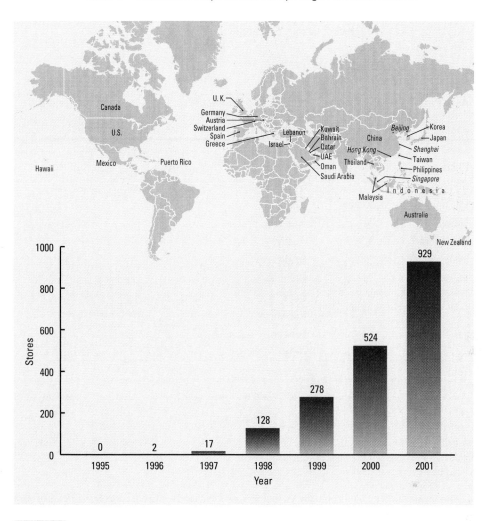

Exhibit 5   Growth of International Stores, 1995–2001

Source: Starbucks International Group.

Perils of Globalization

As Starbucks establishes a global presence, its growing ubiquity has not gone unnoticed by antiglobalization activists. A clear manifestation of this came in November 1999, as tens of thousands of protesters took to the streets of downtown Seattle when the World Trade Organization (WTO) held its third ministerial conference there. Although nongovernmental organizations (NGOs) and activists had gathered to oppose the WTO, some activists deliberately targeted multinationals like Starbucks, Nike, and McDonald's.[25] A small, but vocal, percentage of these protestors garnered international press coverage by committing acts of vandalism against carefully chosen targets.

Protesters flooded Seattle's streets, and among their targets was Starbucks, a symbol, to them, of free-market capitalism run amok, another multinational out to blanket the earth. Amid the crowds of protesters and riot police were black-masked anarchists who trashed the store, leaving its windows smashed and its tasteful green-and-white decor smelling of tear gas instead of espresso.[26]

Recalling this incident against his firm, Schultz said: "It's hurtful. I think people are ill-informed. It's very difficult to protest against a can of Coke, a bottle of Pepsi, or a can of Folgers. Starbucks is both a ubiquitous brand and a place where you can go and break a window. You can't break a can of Coke."

Antiglobalization protesters target recognizable global brands because they are convenient symbols. The following excerpt from "The Ruckus Society's Action Planning Manual" illustrates the close ties between global brands and the principles of direct action against them:[27]

First, [we] use direct action to reduce the issues to symbols. These symbols must be carefully chosen for their

Exhibit 6   Licensed Starbucks International Stores
(as of September 2002)

Asia-Pacific		Europe/Middle East/Africa		Latin America/International	
Japan	397	United Arab Emirates	23	Hawaii	30
Taiwan	99	Saudi Arabia	22	Mexico	1
China	88	Kuwait	16	Puerto Rico	1
South Korea	53	Switzerland	12		
Philippines	49	Lebanon	11		
New Zealand	34	Israel	6		
Singapore	32	Austria	5		
Malaysia	26	Spain	5		
Indonesia	5	Germany	4		
		Qatar	3		
		Bahrain	2		
		Greece	2		
		Oman	2		
Total	783		113		32

Product sales to, and royalty and license fee revenues from, licensed international retail stores accounted for approximately 17% of specialty revenues in fiscal 2002.

These figures do not include company-operated stores.

Source: Starbucks 10-K report.

utility in illustrating a conflict: an oil company vs. an indigenous community, a government policy vs. the public interest. Then we work to place these symbols in the public eye, in order to identify the evildoer, detail the wrongdoing and, if possible, point to a more responsible option.

The message that activists want to communicate focuses on the overseas activities of corporations. They accuse multinationals of paying less than a living wage to workers in the Third World, of engaging in labor and environmental practices that would be outlawed in their home countries, of driving local competitors out of business, and of furthering "cultural imperialism." As one Global Trade Watch field organizer described it:

The rules by which trade is governed need to have more to do with the interests of citizens than with the back pockets and cash wads of a couple of corporate CEOs. And we want to make sure that there is a balance consideration. Obviously people are always going to be concerned with their profits—it's business, we understand that, we accept that. But we think that needs to be

balanced with concern for the rights of workers, basic human rights, [and] protecting the environment.[28]

Critics further accuse international organizations like the WTO, World Bank, and the International Monetary Fund (IMF) of promoting corporate globalization by supporting trade liberalization, by promoting export-based economic development, and by facilitating foreign direct investment. According to an organization that bills itself as Mobilization for Global Justice:

Most of the world's most impoverished countries have suffered under IMF/World Bank programs for two decades: They've seen debt levels rise, unemployment skyrocket, poverty increase, and environments devastated. Urged to export, they focus on cash crops like coffee instead of food for their own people, and allow foreign governments to build sweatshops—which also puts pressure on jobs in the U.S.[29]

When Starbucks opened its first store in Mexico in September 2002, it chose a site in the Sheraton Hotel on the Paseo de la Reforma (Boulevard of the Reform) in

Mexico City. This was Starbucks' first store in Latin America and its first in an "origin country," that is, a coffee-producing country. An article on the Organic Consumers Association Web site described Starbucks' Mexican flagship store:

> The new Starbucks on Reforma features soft lighting and an aromatic ambiance. . . . Behind the counter, well-groomed employees whip out the signature Frappuccinos and lattes. Indeed, the only jarring note is the 36 pesos ($3.60) the young woman at the register wants for a double latte, 10 times the price Indian farmers are getting for a pound of their product in Chiapas, Oaxaca, and other coffee-rich states of southern Mexico. . . . There is no starker contrast in the economics of coffee these days than between the cushy comforts and gourmet blends of the Starbucks "Experiencia" and the grim, daily existence of 360,000 mostly Indian coffee farmers who work small plots carved from the jungle mountains of southern Mexico.[30]

Multinational corporations and their supporters responded that the effects of—and solutions for—globalization are more complicated than the critics contend. They noted that multinationals create jobs, pay better prices and wages than domestic firms, and conform to *local* labor and environmental regulations.

> The skeptics are right to be disturbed by sweatshops, child labor, bonded labor and the other gross abuses that go on in many poor countries (and in the darkest corners of rich ones, too). But what makes people vulnerable to these practices is poverty. . . . The more thoroughly these companies [multinationals] penetrate the markets of the Third World, the faster they introduce their capital and working practices, the sooner poverty will retreat and the harder it will be for such abuses to persist.[31]

Moreover, multinationals argued, they have responded to the criticism of profit-driven behavior by developing corporate codes of conduct, corporate social responsibility programs, and partnerships with nongovernmental organizations.[32] They pointed out, however, that they are in a no-win situation vis-à-vis their critics, because they can always be criticized for not doing enough.

Starbucks has found that global concerns often get mixed up with and intertwined with local issues. Even the mere act of opening a Starbucks retail store in a neighborhood can result in local activism and community "push-back" against the Starbucks brand. For example, when Starbucks opened a store in Cambridge, Massachusetts, in 1998, it was greeted by picketers carrying signs that read, "Don't Let Corporate Greed Destroy Our Neighborhood." A lawyer who helps communities keep national chains out, said: "It's part of the growing tension in the world between the mass-market economy and people's desire to retain self-control and some local culture. . . . If you've got a beef with Starbucks, you've got a beef with capitalism."[33]

Starbucks has faced a variety of "community push-back" situations around the world. Soon Beng Yeap, one of Starbucks International brand reputation managers, noted: "This [community push-back] is a live issue and Starbucks manages each push-back incident case by case. In some markets [we] have gone in and in some [we] have pulled out." He cited two recent examples, one in London, where Starbucks decided to withdraw its efforts to open a store after local activists actively campaigned against the firm, and the other in Beijing, where the firm opened a store in a historic district and, following subsequent and significant adverse comment reported in local and international media, decided to stay put.

Primrose Hill and Starbucks' Decision to Withdraw
In 2002 Starbucks made plans to open a store in Primrose Hill, a London suburb. Located in North West London, Primrose Hill is a well-known historical and picturesque area comprised of a public park, a shopping "village" area, and attractive Victorian residential housing. Residents of Primrose Hill—many of whom are writers, photographers, actors, and musicians—take great pride in the area and are protective of their local environment, acting to ensure that no chain stores operate in the area.[34]

In early 2002 Starbucks selected Primrose Hill as a potential site for a store and submitted an application to the local council. When this information was published in the local papers, it received considerable negative feedback from the residents, in particular from the Primrose Hill Conservation Area Advisory Committee. This committee claimed that litter, noise, and disruption from deliveries to the Starbucks store in Primrose Hill would ruin the village ambience and contribute to the "homogenization of the high street." The opposition surprised Starbucks because Primrose Hill residents, associations (including the Primrose Hill Conservation Area Advisory Committee), and businesses had been contacted as part of the consultation period for the potential site. Although the objections to Starbucks' entry focused on local planning issues, there was an antiglobalization element as well. One critic was quoted saying that Starbucks was "renowned for not paying proper money to coffee growers."[35]

In response to the critics, Starbucks offered to arrange meetings between the planning committee, local councillors, and its representatives to discuss the issue and hear their concerns. Despite Starbucks' efforts, no meeting offers were accepted and minimal responses were received.

In the meantime, the Primrose Hill Conservation Area Advisory Committee began to campaign strongly against Starbucks. It collected more than 1,300 letters of objection, which it then presented to the local council. Many celebrities, such as the actor Jude Law, National Theatre director Nicholas Hytner, broadcaster Joan Bakewell, singer Neneh Cherry, author Jeanette Winterson, and artist Patrick Caufield, lent their support by opposing the Starbucks application. Media coverage that was initially local became national when celebrities became involved. According to Horwat, the vice president for International Assets Development Systems for Starbucks:

> Primrose Hill was an "A" site. A very affluent neighborhood, little or no competition and we knew it would be a winner. Everyone [at Starbucks Coffee International] loved it. The real estate people, the finance people, and others signed off on the deal. Opposition came only when city council was about to approve [our application]. The opposition claimed that our entry would raise rents in the community. So we went back to city council to argue our case. But activists brought in movie stars and got local and national media attention.

In early June 2002, when it was apparent that Starbucks was not welcome in Primrose Hill, the company decided against opening the store. Reflecting on the decision to withdraw, Horwat explained:

> We care about the views of the communities of which we are a part. We try to have our stores be part of a community. We had hoped to make a positive contribution for people to get together in Primrose Hill. If the community does not welcome us, it's not someplace we want to be.

Soon Beng Yeap added:

> You have to understand the bigger picture in the U.K. to appreciate what was going on locally at that time—Starbucks was seen as an American chain coming into the British market and the British media tend to be very cynical. The specialty coffee market was becoming crowded and extremely competitive with several other chains such as Café Nero, Coffee Republic, and Costa Coffee making a strong push for market share. The Starbucks team reviewed all the factors involved as well as listened carefully to the community concerns. At the end of the day, we decided to withdraw our application.

Beijing and Starbucks' Decision to Stay   Starbucks opened its first outlet in Beijing in January 1999 and has over 100 stores in China today. However, Starbucks touched a nationalist nerve in 2000 when it opened a small coffee shop in Beijing's Forbidden City.[36] In highlighting this particular store, the *New York Times* noted:

> If ever there was an emblem of the extremes to which globalization has reached, this is it: mass-market American coffee culture in China's most hallowed historic place. Even a McDonald's in the Kremlin would not come as close. Starbucks opened its Forbidden City shop a month ago [September 2000] with a signature menu board advertising the usual Americano and decaf latte coffee and a glass display case filled with fresh glazed donuts, cinnamon rings, and banana walnut muffins.[37]

Starbucks, for its part, had taken extraordinary care to ensure that its presence was unobtrusive. To avoid ruining the atmosphere of the Forbidden City, the signs and brand images were placed inside for this store. This small store (barely a closet according to some reports) had only two small tables and few chairs. It was located on the edge of the Forbidden City, among 50 other retailers, including some selling souvenirs and trinkets. Despite such a low-key presence, this store ignited controversy. Dozens of Chinese newspapers reported on reactions to the shop. According to one report in the *People's Daily*:

> The reason for the uproar is due to the cafe's location: the Forbidden City, the world's largest imperial palace. . . . First constructed in 1406, the Forbidden City is China's best-preserved ancient architecture encircled by a rampart of three kilometers. The cafe, named Starbucks, is situated in the southeastern corner of the Hall of Preserving Harmony (Baohedian), one of the three most impressive buildings on the palace ground. The hall used to be the venue to hold feasts by emperors and nobles of ethnic groups on New Year's Eve of China's lunar calendar. . . . Debates over the mini-cafe took place first on the Web. A survey by Sina.com showed that over 70 percent of nearly 60,000 people surveyed were opposed to the cafe's entry into the Forbidden City, the main reason being the damaging effects to the Chinese cultural heritage and its atmosphere.[38]

The administrators of the Forbidden Palace and other government officials took note of the controversy but were supportive of Starbucks. Chen Junqi, a spokesperson for the Forbidden City Museum, maintained that allowing Starbucks into the Forbidden City was part of their efforts to improve services in the area. Moreover, Chen added: "The reaction has been very intense. Some people say this is a gem of Chinese culture and that foreign brands should not be allowed in. . . . We can't give up eating for the fear of choking."[39]

According to Horwat:

> The Forbidden City location was a "C" site at best. But definitely not a "D" site, because there was still the benefit of brand presence. But the government said, "We think you should come in," and it was difficult to say no. There was no local community, only tourists.

Following the flurry of articles in the Chinese media, CNN began to run news clips of this story in the United States. Watching this unfold in the U.S. media, some senior managers at Starbucks became alarmed at the negative publicity. According to Soon Beng Yeap:

> The immediate reaction was to "close the store!" due to the relentless negative coverage generated by the international media. After serious discussion among the senior executives, we felt as guests in a foreign country, we should be respectful of our hosts—the Forbidden City officials—who invited us to be there in the first place. We decided to not pull out because it was the international media that stirred up the whole controversy. Unlike the

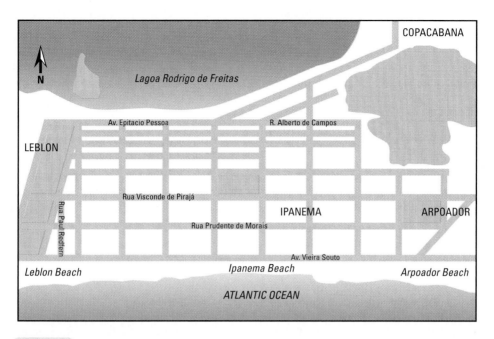

Exhibit 7 Map of the Ipanema Area, Rio de Janeiro, Brazil

Source: www.ipanema.com

Primrose Hill case, there was no real local community "push-back." It was all media-driven. A few reporters got hold of the story and ran with it, all citing the same survey by Sina.com. We were very disappointed by the negative media coverage, which created a false sense of "cultural imperialism" about our intentions in opening the store, especially when we worked very hard to be culturally sensitive and listen to the local community.

The controversy has since died down, as a recent report (February 2003) in the *Straits Times* of Singapore indicated:

> [Today] if anything, the tourists were more upset than the Beijing residents about the presence of Starbucks in the Forbidden City, complaining that it was out of place in a historical site. . . . Asked what were the hottest issues of the day for ordinary citizens, taxi driver Liu Zhiming said: "Cars, apartments, and making money. What else?"[40]

Entering Rio De Janeiro, Brazil

Peter Maslen, president of Starbucks Coffee International, hurriedly convened a meeting of his key executives in Starbucks International, including Julio Gutierrez, his president for Latin America. Starbucks' entry into Brazil was in jeopardy, because certain activists opposing Starbucks' presence in the country were gaining momentum.

Brazil is the largest coffee-producing country in the world, and this was Starbucks' second foray into Latin America (after Mexico). The company chose not to seek a joint venture partner to enter Brazil. Since many copycat chains had sprung up in Rio de Janeiro, some imitating

Starbucks to the last detail, Maslen felt that his team had to move quickly before any particular group established itself as the premier chain. After several years of work by Gutierrez's Latin America team, no suitable joint venture partner had been identified, and Maslen was considering establishing a 100 percent Starbucks owned MBU (as it had already done in the U.K., Australia, and Thailand).

The business development group, with Gutierrez's team, had picked a site in the Ipanema area of Rio de Janeiro. They proposed that a flagship store be opened on this neighborhood's main commercial street—Rua Visconde de Pirajá (see Exhibit 7). Many of Rio's most traditional boutiques started in Ipanema, later to be exported to the malls and other parts of town. Many world-renowned brands such as Cartier, Louis Vuitton, and Polo Ralph Lauren had stores on the Rua Visconde de Pirajá. It is often said that news in Ipanema makes headlines all over Brazil.

Starbucks had also chosen other sites, four to be specific, where the company could open stores immediately following the opening of the flagship Ipanema store. One of these stores was to be located in the posh neighborhood of Barra de Tijuca; another was slated for Leblon, and two others for shopping malls located in affluent residential neighborhoods in the city. The Real Estate group was ready to sign the lease with the agents of the Ipanema property owner, but was awaiting a formal response from the city council members.

The business development group, led by Troy Alstead, senior vice president of finance and business development at Starbucks International, was confident that the Ipanema location was an "A" category site. "The demographics of this area are just right for a flagship store. They are affluent, young, and love American brands." The business development group's financial projections indicated that the Ipanema Starbucks store would be profitable in a short time, and Alstead believed that this was a conservative figure. Further, he pointed out:

> Based on the company's experiences of opening flagship stores in similar, high traffic posh neighborhoods in other cites around the world—our store in Ginza, Japan comes to mind—we believe the Ipanema store would be viable for Starbucks. We estimate meeting store level ROI targets in aggregate for the first five stores within two years.

Exhibit 8 provides the finance group's forecast for the Ipanema and the other four stores in Brazil for the first five years of operations.

But Maslen had some concerns. He was troubled by reports of rising levels of violence and street crime in Rio de Janeiro and São Paulo. In response to this growing violence, some of the most fashionable retailers were relocating themselves in shopping malls. He also questioned whether the timing for Starbucks was off. Current world events had generated anti-American feeling in many countries.

Following the standard practice, Starbucks had been working with the local chamber of commerce since January 2003, and with the local city council for the required permits. The members of the city council and local chamber of commerce were positive about granting Starbucks permission to begin construction. While the formal voting had yet to be undertaken, it looked certain that, barring anything unusual, permission would be granted.

But nongovernmental organizations like the Organic Consumers Association and Global Exchange were mobilizing faster than expected to oppose Starbucks' entry into Brazil. They found out about Starbucks' intent to enter Brazil when the Ipanema district chamber of commerce newsletter proudly announced that, "We are extremely pleased to welcome Starbucks into the fashionable district of Ipanema. By opening a store in our neighborhood, they will join other global brands and help enhance further our district's image as *the* place to be in Rio."

The NGOs were recruiting local activists and had informed Starbucks that they would oppose its entry into Brazil by petitioning the local council to reject its application. They also threatened to start picketing in front of the store once construction was initiated. The "brand" group at Starbucks was concerned about the turn of events. Soon Beng Yeap elaborated:

> People in Latin America know the brand because of their proximity to the U.S. Potential partners are always contacting us about coming in. Before we go into a place like Brazil, what is the due diligence we have to do? It's an origin country for us [i.e., coffee-producing country]. It's

a very vocal place, and there is a love-hate relationship with the United States. Finance people always want to say yes to a store when the numbers look good. Today some in Starbucks, at least in our group, say that maintaining and protecting our strong "brand" reputation is equally important. Others counter: If our brand is strong then why worry about it? This is a discussion we have here every day in the company. While the "push-back" is not totally unexpected, it is hard to gauge the severity of the situation and its likely impact on our brand.

Maslen asked Alstead's business development group to work with Gutierrez's Latin American team to estimate how the picketing in front of the store might impact the financial projections his group had prepared. Their answer:

> Our financial estimates for the Ipanema store are based on comparables from other flagship stores in locations similar to Rio in other parts of the world. Our financial models are sensitive to the demographics of the area. We project that demand could fall from 5 to 25 percent, because of people picketing in front of the store. We acknowledge it is much harder to guess what the impact on our entire system in Brazil might be as we open new stores. It all depends upon the type of media coverage the activists are able to muster and the issues the media choose to highlight.

Soon Beng Yeap volunteered:

> The tide of public opinion is unpredictable. We review each "push-back" incident the best we can, and we have a reasonable track record of predicting outcomes. But, every time we walk into a potential site somewhere in the world, we potentially face this [push-back]. It would be great to have a foolproof tool or system to help us evaluate these sorts of issues and make the appropriate decisions.

Maslen had to leave Seattle to attend an important meeting in Europe the following day. He called together his key managers and said,

> Look, we've experienced a variety of "push-backs" and protests before. What lessons have we learned? We've been deciding whether to go into sites or pull out on a case-by-case basis. If we're going to grow to 25,000 stores, we cannot keep taking an ad hoc approach. We need a systematic method to respond to push-back—to decide whether we stay with a site or pull out. I want you to come up with a way to help me decide whether to go into Rio at all. And it's got to be a system or decision process that would work equally well in London or Beijing or anyplace else that we want to open. Let's meet again when I get back to town in a couple days.

The managers of Starbucks Coffee International had their work cut out for them. But they looked forward to tackling the issues raised by Peter Maslen.

Exhibit 8   Financial Analysis for the First Five Brazilian Stores

Projected Profits and Losses for Ipanema Store (US$)					
	Year 1	Year 2	Year 3	Year 4	Year 5
Net sales[1]	$1,000,000	$1,100,000	$1,210,000	$1,270,500	$1,334,025
Cost of goods sold[2]	350,000	330,000	326,700	343,035	360,187
Gross profit	$ 650,000	$ 770,000	$ 883,300	$ 927,465	$ 973,838
Staff costs	200,000	225,000	250,000	250,000	250,000
Marketing[3]	75,000	50,000	50,000	50,000	50,000
Other costs	75,000	100,000	125,000	125,000	125,000
Occupancy costs	175,000	175,000	175,000	175,000	175,000
Total costs	$ 525,000	$ 550,000	$ 600,000	$ 600,000	$ 600,000
Operating cash flow	$ 125,000	$ 220,000	$ 283,300	$ 327,465	$ 373,838
Depreciation[4]	54,200	54,200	54,200	54,200	54,200
Store pretax profit	$ 70,800	$ 165,800	$ 229,100	$ 273,265	$ 319,638
Construction costs[5]	$ 400,000				
Key money[6]	$1,000,000				

Projected Profits and Losses for a "Typical" Store in Locations outside the Ipanema Area (US$)*					
	Year 1	Year 2	Year 3	Year 4	Year 5
Net sales[1]	$ 625,000	$ 650,000	$ 700,000	$ 735,000	$ 771,750
Cost of goods sold[2]	218,750	195,000	189,000	198,450	208,373
Gross profit	$ 406,250	$ 455,000	$ 511,000	$ 536,550	$ 563,378
Staff costs	100,000	115,000	135,000	135,000	135,000
Marketing[3]	45,000	30,000	30,000	30,000	30,000
Other costs	60,000	75,000	75,000	75,000	75,000
Occupancy costs	70,000	70,000	70,000	70,000	70,000
Operating cash flow	$ 131,250	$ 165,000	$ 201,000	$ 226,550	$ 253,378
Depreciation[4]	25,000	25,000	25,000	25,000	25,000
Store pretax profit	$ 106,250	$ 140,000	$ 176,000	$ 201,550	$ 228,378
Construction costs[5]	$ 215,000				
Key money[6]	$ 400,000				

*Starbucks intends to open four such stores in Rio, in addition to the one in Ipanema.

[1]Net sales are projected to grow at 10% for years 1 and 2, and at 5% thereafter.

[2]Due to increases in efficiency, the cost of goods sold are estimated at 35% for year 1, 30% for year 2, and 27% thereafter.

[3]Marketing costs are higher for year 1.

[4]Straight-line 10-year depreciation for construction and equipment costs.

[5]These represent initial design and construction costs.

[6]Monies paid to the landlord to secure the site.

1971 Starbucks opens its first location in Seattle's Pike Place Market.

1982 Howard Schultz joins Starbucks as director of retail operations and marketing. Starbucks begins providing coffee to fine restaurants and espresso bars.

1983 Schultz travels to Italy where, impressed with the popularity of espresso bars in Milan, he sees the potential to develop a similar coffee bar culture in Seattle.

1984 Schultz convinces the founders of Starbucks to test the coffee bar concept in a new location in downtown Seattle. This successful experiment is the genesis for a company that Schultz founds in 1985.

1985 Schultz founds Il Giornale, offering brewed coffee and espresso beverages made from Starbucks coffee beans.

1987 With the backing of local investors, Il Giornale acquires Starbucks assets and changes its name to Starbucks Corporation.
Opens in Chicago and Vancouver, B.C. Starbucks location total = 17

1988 Starbucks introduces mail order catalog with service to all 50 states. Starbucks location total = 33

1989 Opens in Portland, Oregon. Starbucks location total = 55

1990 Starbucks expands headquarters in Seattle and builds a new roasting plant. Starbucks location total = 84

1991 Establishes a relationship with CARE, the international relief and development organization, and introduces the CARE coffee sampler.
Becomes the first U.S. privately owned company to offer a stock option program that includes part-time employees.
Opens first licensed airport location with HMS Host at Sea-Tac International Airport.
Opens in Los Angeles. Starbucks location total = 116

1992 Completes initial public offering with common stock traded on the Nasdaq National Market under the trading symbol "SBUX."
Opens in San Francisco; San Diego; Orange County, California; and Denver. Starbucks location total = 165

1993 Begins Barnes & Noble, Inc., relationship.
Opens in Washington, D.C. Starbucks location total = 272

1994 Awarded ITT/Sheraton (now Starwood Hotels) account.
Opens in Minneapolis, Boston, New York, Atlanta, Dallas, and Houston. Starbucks location total = 425

1995 Based on an extremely popular in-house music program, Starbucks begins selling compact disks.
Awarded United Airlines account.
Begins serving Frappuccino blended beverages, a line of low-fat, creamy, iced coffee beverages.
Forms alliance with Canadian bookstore Chapters Inc.
Starbucks Coffee International forms joint venture with SAZABY, Inc., to develop Starbucks coffeehouses in Japan.
Opens in Philadelphia, Pittsburgh, Las Vegas, Cincinnati, Baltimore, San Antonio, and Austin, Texas. Starbucks location total = 676

1996 Starbucks Coffee International opens locations in Japan, Hawaii, and Singapore.
Awarded Westin (now Starwood Hotels) account.
Starbucks and Dreyer's Grand Ice Cream, Inc., introduce Starbucks Ice Cream and Starbucks Ice Cream bars. Starbucks Ice Cream quickly becomes the number one brand of coffee ice cream in the United States.
North American Coffee Partnership (Starbucks and Pepsi-Cola Company business venture) begins selling a bottled version of Starbucks Frappuccino blended beverage.
Opens in Rhode Island, Idaho, North Carolina, Arizona, Utah, and Ontario, Canada.
Starbucks location total = 1,015

1997 Starbucks Coffee International opens locations in the Philippines.

Awarded Canadian Airlines account.

Forms alliance with eight companies to enable the gift of more than 320,000 new books for children through the All Books for Children first annual book drive.

Establishes The Starbucks Foundation, benefiting local literacy programs in communities where Starbucks has coffeehouses.

Opens in Florida, Michigan, and Wisconsin. Starbucks location total = 1,412

1998 Starbucks Coffee International opens locations in Taiwan, Thailand, New Zealand, and Malaysia.

Introduces Tiazzi blended juice tea, a refreshing mixture of tea, fruit juice, and ice.

Acquires Seattle Coffee Company in the United Kingdom with more than 60 retail locations.

Acquires Pasqua Inc., a San Francisco–based coffee retailer.

Forms Urban Coffee Opportunities, a joint venture with Earvin "Magic" Johnson's Johnson Development Corp., to develop Starbucks Coffee locations in underserved, urban neighborhoods throughout the United States.

Signs a licensing agreement with Kraft Foods Inc. to extend the Starbucks brand into grocery channels across the United States.

Launches Starbucks.com.

Opens two new coffeehouse concepts: Cafe Starbucks in Seattle and Circadia Coffee House in San Francisco.

Opens in New Orleans; St. Louis; Kansas City, Missouri; and Portland, Maine. Starbucks location total = 1,886

1999 Starbucks Coffee International opens locations in China, Kuwait, Korea, and Lebanon.

Acquires Tazo, a Portland, Oregon–based tea company.

Partners with Conservation International to promote environmentally sound methods of growing coffee.

Introduces Shade Grown Mexico Coffee.

Acquires Hear Music, a San Francisco–based music company.

Enters agreement with Albertson's, Inc., to open more than 100 Starbucks locations in their supermarkets in the year 2000.

Opens in Memphis and Nashville, Tennessee; and Saskatchewan, Canada. Starbucks location total = 2,135

2000 Enters into licensing agreement with TransFair USA to market and sell Fair Trade Certified coffee.

Introduces a Commitment to Origins coffee category that includes shade-grown, organic, and Fair Trade Certified selections.

Expands contribution to Conservation International to establish conservation efforts in five new sites.

Enters agreement with Host Marriott International to open locations in select properties. Starbucks Coffee International opens in Dubai, Hong Kong, Shanghai, Qatar, Bahrain, Saudi Arabia, and Australia. Starbucks location total = 3,501

2001 Introduces coffee sourcing guidelines developed in partnership with The Center for Environmental Leadership in Business, a division of Conservation International.

Commits to the purchase of one million pounds of Fair Trade Certified coffee.

Offers $1 million in financial support to coffee farmers through Calvert Community Investments.

Begins to offer high-speed wireless Internet access in stores.

The Starbucks Foundation awards more than 450 grants totaling $4.2 million to literacy, schools, and community-based organizations across North America.

Begins offering the Starbucks Card, a stored value card for customers to use and reload.

Enters agreement with Hyatt Hotels Corp.

Starbucks Coffee Japan introduces a stock option program for eligible full and part-time partners and successfully implements IPO.

Starbucks and international business partners seed Starbucks Cares Fund with $1.2 million contribution to benefit September 11th Fund. Customers and partners contribute more than $1.4 million to Starbucks Cares.

Starbucks opens 300th location in Japan and celebrates fifth year of business in Japan.

Starbucks Coffee International opens in Switzerland, Israel, and Austria. Starbucks location total = 4,709

2002 Signs memorandum of understanding with Fairtrade Labelling Organizations International (FLO) that enables the company to enter into licensing agreements with national FairTrade organizations to sell Fair Trade Certified coffee in the countries where Starbucks does business.
Publishes its first Corporate Social Responsibility Annual Report.
Celebrates 10-year anniversary of Starbucks IPO.
Introduces Starbucks DoubleShot to the ready-to-drink coffee category.
Signs licensing agreement with TransFair Canada to bring Fair Trade Certified coffee to more than 270 retail locations in Canada.
Starbucks Coffee International opens in Oman, Indonesia, Germany, and Spain. Starbucks location total = 5,688

Endnotes

1. *BusinessWeek.* 2002. Planet Starbucks. September 9: 100–110.
2. "The name came about when the original owners looked to Seattle history for inspiration and chose the moniker of an old mining camp: Starbo. Further refinement led to Starbucks, after the first mate in *Moby Dick,* which they felt evoked the seafaring romance of the early coffee traders (hence the mermaid logo)." Planet Starbucks, 2002, 103.
3. *Success,* 1993, April.
4. Planet Starbucks, 100–110.
5. *Fortune.* 2003. Mr. Coffee. March 30.
6. Planet Starbucks, 2002, 103.
7. This Colombian coffee bean crop is very small and grows only in the high regions of the Cordillera mountain range. For years, the Narino beans were guarded zealously by western Europeans, who prized their colorful and complex flavor. It was usually used for upgrading blends. Starbucks was determined to make them available for the first time as a pure varietal. This required breaking western Europe's monopoly over the beans by convincing the Colombian growers that it intended to use "the best beans for a higher purpose."
8. *Canada Newswire.* 1993. March 1.
9. *Inc.* 1993. January.
10. *Fortune.* 1996. December 9.
11. The decision to offer benefits even to part-time employees (who represent roughly two-thirds of Starbucks' 10,000 employees) has gained a great deal of attention in the press. According to a Hewitt Associates LLC survey of more than 500 employers, only 25 percent of employers offer medical coverage to employees working less than 20 hours a week. It was difficult to get insurers to sign Starbucks up since they did not understand why Starbucks would want to cover part-timers.
12. *Inc.* 1993. January.
13. *Wall Street Journal.* 1995. October 23.
14. *Nations Restaurant News.* 1995. July 10.
15. The Specialty Coffee Association of America notes that supermarkets account for over 60 percent of all coffee sold in America, followed by gourmet stores (14 percent), mass market (11 percent), mail order (8 percent) and other.
16. *Washington Post.* 1995. August 1.
17. Schultz, however, firmly believes that Starbucks' growth is far from saturation both in the United States and overseas: "We have less than 7 percent of the coffee-consuming opportunities in North America. People are still drinking bad coffee." Planet Starbucks, 2002, 102.
18. *BusinessWeek.* 2002. Online Extra: Q&A with Starbucks' Howard Schultz. September 9.
19. *US News and World Report.* 2001. February 19.
20. The difference between an "A" store and a "D" store can be substantial. A "D" store is expected to have about 50 to 60 percent lower sales. Starbucks classifies a store as "A" if the store location is the focal point of the area, with great visibility, readily available parking, and excellent access to and from the site; cannot be outpositioned by competitors; and fits with Starbucks' desire to build a distinctive image.
21. Starbucks' international businesses are typically joint ventures in which Starbucks holds various levels of equity (ranging from 5 percent to 100 percent). These ventures are referred to as Market Business Units (MBUs). Regardless of the level of equity Starbucks holds, it supports all of its MBUs in an "ownership blind" manner by providing all MBUs with the same level of support.
22. *BusinessWeek.* Online Extra: Q&A with Starbucks' Howard Schultz, 2002.
23. Planet Starbucks, 2002, 102.
24. Ibid.
25. The protesters claimed that international organizations like the WTO and International Monetary Fund (IMF) are tools of multinational corporations. Since Seattle, violent protests have been the norm at events such as the annual meetings of the IMF and World Bank, G8 summits, and the World Economic Forum.
26. Planet Starbucks, 2002.
27. Ruckus Society Web site, http://ruckus.org/man/action_planning.html, accessed March 14, 2003.
28. Interview with Alesha Daughtrey, Global Trade Watch field organizer, August 17, 2000; archived in the WTO History Project, University of Washington Center for Labor Studies, http://depts.washington.edu/wtohist/Interviews/Interviews.htm.

29. Mobilization for Global Justice, http://sept.globalizethis.org, accessed March 14, 2003.

30. Ross, John. The unloving cup. Organic Consumers Association, December 12; www.organicconsumers.org/starbucks.

31. *The Economist.* 1997. Grinding the poor. November 6.

32. For example, Starbucks' *Commitment to Origins* is a four-part Corporate Social Responsibility program that includes offering Fair Trade certified coffee, organic certified coffee, Farm Direct (single-origin coffees purchased directly from the farmer), and Conservation coffees (emphasizing shade-grown in partnership with the NGO Conservation International). See www.starbucks.com/aboutus/cto_coffees.asp.

33. *Christian Science Monitor.* 1998. Brewing a tempest in a coffee cup. Quoting Edward McMahon. February 25.

34. This desire for protection dates back to 1841 when the residents actively campaigned against the area being opened up to the general public. Such actions discouraged further building developments, thus enabling the residents to retain the look and feel of their neighborhood.

35. *Independent on Sunday* (London). 2002. Stars v. Starbucks: Not a bean for the coffee shop giant. June 2.

36. *The Economist.* 2001. Coffee with your tea? 2001. October 4.

37. *The New York Times,* 2000. Globalization puts a Starbucks into the Forbidden City in Beijing. November 25.

38. *People's Daily* (Shanghi). 2002. Starbucks cafe in Forbidden City under fire. November 24.

39. *The New York Times.* 2000. Globalization puts a Starbucks into the Forbidden City in Beijing. November 25.

40. *Straits Times.* 2003. Capitalism runs amok. February 16.

Case 4   The Skeleton in the Corporate Closet*

"David," Donna Cooper exclaimed. "You won't believe it, but these look like love letters! And look, they're from when he was in the service!"

David Fisher, the corporate archivist for GPC Incorporated, hastened toward the young woman sprawled on his dusty floor but cheerily holding aloft a packet of yellowed envelopes. Unaccustomed to so much commotion in this room, he was still trying to process what had just happened. A moment ago, he'd been giving Miss Cooper, the writer hired to pen GPC's 75th anniversary book, a tour of his admittedly cluttered storeroom. Following at some distance, she'd chosen another path through the debris, only to reach an impasse. He'd glanced back just in time to see her give a shove to—of all things—the founder's writing desk. The brittle wooden legs, now in their 100th year at least, could hardly have been expected to scoot across the rough cement swirls of the basement floor. One had snapped immediately, the desk had toppled, and Miss Cooper had followed the whole wreck down.

Which was when, even through the air of the old storeroom, semiopaque with suspended dust, and even despite the early-stage cataract in his left eye, David spotted something that made his historian's heart leap. The back of the desk, now splintered, had mysteriously yielded a drawer, one he had never discovered in his years of puttering around it. Visible inside were some papers. Following his wondering gaze, the infuriating, wonderful Miss Cooper had spied, and snatched out, the treasure.

A Bittersweet Discovery

She was right, of course. They were letters composed to a sweetheart by Hudson Parker after he'd shipped out with Company K, the 137th U.S. Infantry unit made up of recruits from Kansas and Missouri. The first was dated August 6, 1917—a full decade before he'd founded General Parkelite Company. David took quick note of the addressee: Mary Beatrice White. Not a name he'd heard before. Clearly this romance preceded Virginia, the woman Hud had married. David was faintly scandalized to realize that old Hud had squirreled away these letters, no doubt unbeknownst to his wife. At the same time, he was touched at the thought of an unforgotten first love. And although his first instinct would usually have been to don cotton gloves and carry the letters into better light, he instead cleared a bit of floor space near Miss Cooper and sat. There was an undeniable charm in having this young woman eagerly extract letters from envelopes and read them aloud.

Harvard Business Review's cases, which are fictional, present common managerial dilemmas and offer concrete solutions from experts.

Reprinted by permission of *Harvard Business Review*. "The Skeleton in the Corporate Closet" by Julia Kirby, June 2002. Copyright © 2002 by the Harvard Business School Publishing Corporation; all rights reserved.

"My dearest Mary," she recited. "It began raining here this morning, and it is still at it. No drill today, so I will have time to write a letter or two." Impatient to find something juicier, she scanned the rest of the letter before handing it over. "Oh, look, David, how he signs it: 'With best of love to my own little girl.'" David accepted the letter and pushed his glasses down on his nose to peer over them. As always, he took a moment to appreciate the superior penmanship of an earlier age. Then his trained eye went to work on the page, drilling for facts that could be cataloged and cross-referenced with other accounts of the founder's war years. Donna, meanwhile, merrily called out other quaint snippets.

A half-hour passed in this way before David's joints, chilled by the bare floor, started to protest, and he suggested a change of venue. "Yeah," said Donna. "It's pretty musty in here, isn't it?" But as David took a moment to prop up the damaged desk and replace its drawer, Donna pulled another paper from an envelope. "Oh, this is the kind of thing you'll like," she noted, unfolding what looked, curiously, like drafting paper. She thrust it toward him and promptly launched into the accompanying letter. "You will recall from my last letter that we expect to see action this week, Mary darling. Enclosed is a document I hardly expect you to find interesting but entreat you to keep safe till my return." Indeed, it didn't interest Donna, so she rose to her feet and briskly dusted her skirt. "Honestly, David, I don't know how you work in here. My eyes are beginning to burn." But when she turned toward him, she was dismayed to see him staring at the paper he was clutching, his own eyes filling with tears.

Our Founder, a Thief?

A day passed before David appeared at the door of Jill Pierce, the communications VP who was his boss, and asked for a meeting at her convenience. Masking her surprise (in her seven years as his superior, she couldn't recall his ever initiating contact), she invited him in on the spot. Soon she was holding the letter herself and listening to David explain its import. Shockingly, it proved that the formula for Parkelite—the miracle plastic that was the company's first patent and its bread and butter for two full decades—had been someone else's innovation, not Hud Parker's. Not to put too fine a point on it, GPC's revered founder was a thief.

David filled in the parts of the story she didn't know. Of course, she needed no reminder of what Parkelite was. Although it had long since been superseded by better materials, it had been a huge technological advance in its day. A dense synthetic polymer, it could be molded or extruded and had the advantage of not changing shape after being mixed and heated. Most important, it wasn't flammable like earlier celluloid plastics. Manufacturers had used it to make things like engine parts, radio boxes, switches—even costume jewelry and inexpensive dinnerware. At the height of its popularity, General Parkelite was producing some 200,000 tons of the stuff per year.

What Jill had never heard was that in 1938, a lawsuit had been brought against Hud Parker and General Parkelite by the father of Karl Gintz, claiming that his son had been the true, sole inventor of Parkelite. Hud and Karl had studied chemistry together at Princeton, David explained, and had been star pupils who had egged each other on. But as well as being competitors, they were close friends, even to the extent that when war broke out in Europe, they enlisted together. Both dreamed of becoming pilots in the Army's Signal Corps, and both easily made the grade. They were transferred to the 94th Pursuit Group and posted to France. But in August 1918—just a week, Jill noted with a shiver, prior to the postmark on the envelope she held—Karl had been killed in maneuvers when the wing of his French-built trainer had collapsed. David pointed out that the formulas and diagrams neatly lettered on the graph paper were clearly the genesis of Parkelite, which Hud Parker had patented in 1920. Just as clearly, they were the work of Karl Gintz. "This is the document," David concluded, "that would have allowed the Gintz family to win its case."

Unprepared for the Worst

Jill had kept her composure while David was in her office, but as soon as he left, she opened her desk drawer, fished out a bottle of liquid antacid, and took a slug. David's chief concern seemed to be who would tell Hap—that is, Hudson Parker III, GPC's longtime CEO and the grandson of the founder. But that was the least of her worries. Clearly, this was a potential PR disaster, and her mind raced through the various ways it might play out. In honor of GPC's 75th anniversary, she'd introduced a heavy dose of nostalgia into this year's advertising. Hud Parker's image was splashed everywhere, along with the tag line, "He started it all." More like he *stole* it all, Jill thought bitterly, then felt guilty that such a remark would even occur to her. What a contrast to the pride she'd felt last summer when some focus groups she'd observed had come up with words like "trusted," "straight shooting," and "dependable" to describe the GPC brand. This was a catastrophe. And with all the extra planning that the special anniversary promotions required, she was already working flat out.

On her way to the CEO's office that afternoon, she lost her nerve at least three times. The fourth time, she even had Hap's doorway in sight, only to detour to the elevator lobby instead. She had a sudden determination to go down to the archives and urge David to destroy the incriminating paper and forget about it. But the fantasy died quickly as she recalled his haggard look in her office that morning. He'd already struggled with whether he could do that, she now realized, and decided he couldn't. She stopped short of hitting the down button and turned back toward the corner office.

History in the Remaking

Three days later, it was Hap Parker who was deciding what to do with the unwelcome news and 80-year-old graph paper now in his possession.

He'd been shocked, of course, and indeed had lost an entire weekend working through the implications on a purely personal level. On Saturday morning, he'd driven the two hours to the lakeside cottage where he'd spent summer days with his grandfather half a century before. He sat cross-legged on the dock, looked across the glittering water, then put his face in his hands and wept. First for his grandfather, who regardless of this incident didn't deserve to be impugned. The Parkelite patent, after all, was only a formula. It still took a great man to build a great company—and he had. And he had hardly coasted on that initial success. Instead, he'd infused the whole organization with the importance and excitement of constant innovation. It was his continuing attention to R&D that had led to General Parkelite's next generation of products, which, along with those of competitors, had made Parkelite obsolete. He'd won the respect of business leaders—indeed, of his country. He was a World War I ace, for God's sake! And a fair-dealing businessman, philanthropist, and community leader. A compassionate employer, certainly. And a dear grandfather, revered no less by his grandchildren for his tendency to dote on them.

This line of thought led Hap directly to self-pity. For neither did he, who had always held himself to the highest standard—with his grandfather's example as his North Star—deserve to have his name smeared. What was that line from Exodus about the sins of the fathers? He struggled to retrieve a long-forgotten catechism. Something about being visited on even the third and fourth generations. And now a fresh horror occurred to him: How much would Chip suffer, and even little Teddy, if this became known?

If. Had he really allowed himself to think "if"? He meant "when."

Reputation—or Reparation?

By Monday, Hap's thoughts were back with GPC and its employees, shareholders, and customers. He was listening to Newland Lowell, GPC's legal counsel, weigh in on the matter. No doubt about it, Newland was sharp. He'd come up with angles on this thing Hap hadn't anticipated.

As soon as he'd pressed the door shut behind him, in fact, Newland had broken into an improbable grin. "I know you're upset, Hap, so I'm going to get to the bottom line first," he said. "We haven't been able to turn up an heir to Karl Gintz." When he got no reaction, he hastened to pull out his other notes. "So. Let's take this from the top."

Newland first outlined a carefully reasoned argument that the letter, had it been introduced at trial long ago, would not necessarily have changed the verdict. The jury, he managed to persuade Hap, was fundamentally sympathetic to Hud Parker and not a little suspicious of Gintz's family. "If there's one thing I've learned," Newland said, "it's that jurors vote with their hearts and then find the legal hook to hang their emotions on." Besides, there would have been no proof that Karl hadn't meant to give the intellectual property to his friend and fellow soldier. "After all, no one else in his family was a chemist. They wouldn't have been able to make heads or tails of his notes. How do we know it wasn't his intent to let your grandfather take it forward? Maybe they were collaborating on it."

"But, Newland," Hap interjected. "If that had been the case, why wouldn't Hud have simply said so?"

"We're talking about a court case," Lowell reminded him. "His legal counsel would never have let him say that."

Hap fell silent again and let Newland continue to lay out his next argument: that there was no way of knowing when the letters Hud had sent to Mary Beatrice White had come back into his possession. It could have been years after the court case. "Not to mention," Newland added, "that if he needed this paper to fudge his own documentation for the patent, then why was it still in that envelope? Isn't it conceivable that the innovation was essentially your grandfather's but that Karl had taken careful notes on it to study and perhaps improve upon?"

Believing his arguments were carrying the day, Newland finally plunged into his last set of notes. These were legal strategies for "containing the discovery"—in essence placing a gag order on the few people in the organization who knew the truth. But Hap had already begun to chafe at what were sounding increasingly like elaborate rationalizations, and this was a bridge too far. He stood up from his desk and nodded to Newland. "Thank you, that's as much as I care to hear this afternoon."

Newland Lowell had known Hap Parker long enough not to mistake his tone, courteous though it might have seemed to others. He sighed as he swept his files back into his briefcase and rose from his chair. "Look, Hap. I'll be straight with you. I know you have a strong sense of what's ethical here. But you also have an organization to take care of. Your employees will be better off, not to mention your shareholders—hell, the *world* is better off if Hud Parker remains a hero. Don't be overly fastidious about this."

Doing the Right Thing

Packing up for the day, Hap had made up his mind. It was absurd that a company whose culture was all about honesty and integrity would tolerate a lie at its core. Maybe there was no one deserving of reparations out there, but surely the company deserved to pay some. He'd find some heir, somewhere.

He wasn't 20 yards down the hall, though, before he encountered a group of three GPC managers, two of them quite new to the company and the other a veteran. As he approached, he overheard the veteran, whose back was to Hap, saying patiently to one of the others, "Well, but, of course, Kevin, that just wouldn't be right." Then, catching sight of Hap, he fell into step with him, hoping to sound out the boss on some other matter.

Just out of earshot, Hap tilted his head back toward where the three had been standing and asked, "What was that about?" The manager explained that Kevin had proposed a marketing idea that seemed a little, well, not exactly underhanded, but. . . . The kid had come to GPC from a competitor with a certain industry reputation. "You know, people there learn to work all the angles and do a lot of things with a wink," he shrugged. "Don't worry, though. He wasn't comfortable there—that's why we got him."

"So you think he's got the potential to be a GPC'er?" Hap pressed.

"Well, that's the great thing about a strong culture, isn't it, Hap? It rubs off. He'll soon pick up on how things are done around here."

The unintended irony of those words made Hap queasy. Suddenly, he couldn't imagine damaging the strong belief in GPC held by this decent man and his 8,000 coworkers. Maybe Newland was right, he thought, and he was being too narrow in his ethics—even self-indulgent.

Was it possible for the right thing to be a lie?

Case 5   Green Mountain Coffee Roasters*

In comparing the growing strength of Starbucks, Bob Britt, Green Mountain Coffee's former vice president and CFO, questioned whether Green Mountain Coffee Roasters (GMCR) was missing the window of opportunity by not moving faster to expand. Growth was imminent for Green Mountain but competition was growing increasingly fierce. As Britt sipped his cup of Rain Forest Nut coffee, his thoughts turned to distribution.

To accelerate distribution of its coffee brand in the grocery channel, Starbucks had selected a long-term licensing agreement with Kraft. In contrast, GMCR relied on its own distribution and sales force to expand the Green Mountain brand in the grocery channel. According to Britt, the Starbucks-Kraft venture was believed to generate, on average, sales of 20–40 pounds of coffee per store per week. In comparison, GMCR averaged 100 pounds of coffee per store per week in the grocery channel. Primarily generated through the retail and office channels, consumer demand pulled specialty coffee through the grocery channel.

Background

In 1981 Green Mountain Coffee Roasters hung its shingle on the front of a small cafe in Waitsfield, Vermont. The company roasted and served premium coffee on the premises. The demand for high-quality, freshly roasted coffee soon grew beyond the cafe's walls. Restaurants and inns in the area asked for coffee and equipment. Green Mountain Coffee Roasters was soon in the wholesale business. Before long, skiers asked if the cafe could send Green Mountain Coffee to their homes in New York, Connecticut, Pennsylvania, and Florida. This demand was filled by the birth of the company's mail-order business. Today, Green Mountain is one of the leading specialty coffee companies in its established markets. See Exhibit 1 for established markets.

Green Mountain Coffee roasts over 25 high-quality Arabica beans to produce over 100 varieties of finished coffee products, which it sells through a coordinated multichannel distribution network in its wholesale and direct mail operations.

The majority of Green Mountain's revenue is derived from more than 7,000 wholesale customer accounts located primarily in the northeastern United States. The wholesale operation serves supermarkets, specialty food stores, convenience stores, food service, hotels, restaurants, universities, and travel and office coffee services. Wholesale customers resell the coffee in whole bean or ground form for home consumption and/or brew and sell

*This case was prepared by graduate student Keith F. Moody and Professor Alan B. Eisner of Pace University as a basis for class discussion rather than to illustrate either effective or ineffective handling of an administrative situation. Copyright © 2004 Keith F. Moody and Alan B. Eisner.

coffee beverages at their places of business. Green Mountain offers single-origin, estate, certified organic, Fair Trade, flavored, and proprietary blends of coffee. The company roasts its coffee in small batches to ensure consistency. Green Mountain utilizes state-of-the-art roasting software that enables it to duplicate specific roasts more exactly, ensuring Green Mountain's ability to offer consistent taste profiles.

Green Mountain uses convection air roasters, offering a higher degree of flexibility than other commercially available roasters. In addition, the company has developed specific roasting programs for each bean type to establish a Green Mountain "signature" for that type, which the company calls its "appropriate roast." Green Mountain believes that this process distinguishes it from other specialty coffee companies and has resulted in strong customer brand loyalty.

Green Mountain flushes nitrogen into its packaged coffee and employs one-way valve bag packaging technology that provides a minimum shelf life of six months for the company's coffees. This technology enables Green Mountain to expand its distribution while maintaining its high standards for quality and freshness. For 2003 *Forbes* magazine ranked Green Mountain Coffee 70 overall, 20 by five-year average return on equity, and 10 by five-year earnings per share growth. The criterion used to screen the *Forbes* list of the "200 Best Small Companies in America" was rigorous. Companies had to have sales of between $5 million and $600 million for the latest 12-month period, a five-year average return on equity of 5 percent or more, a stock price of $5 or more, and a net profit margin of 5 percent or more, excluding extraordinary and nonrecurring items.

Retail Operations

In fiscal 1997 Green Mountain Coffee Roasters was operating 12 company-owned stores in Vermont, Connecticut, Illinois, Maine, Massachusetts, New Hampshire, and New York, which made up approximately 10 percent of total revenues. However, by April 1998, sales had fallen to 6 percent of total net sales. Reasons for the decrease included the elimination of the Plattsburgh, New York, store (for which the lease had expired), the temporary closing of two stores due to relocation, and overall flat sales in other company-owned retail stores. Furthermore, the stores did not generate positive cash flows, nor did they contribute positively to the company's net income. Management at Green Mountain Coffee Roasters made the strategic decision to close the company-owned and -operated retail stores. Since 1981 the company-owned stores had been an important part of Green Mountain's strategy of getting consumers to sample its own brand of coffee by the cup (see Exhibit 2 for financial data).

Exhibit 1   Wholesale Coffee Pounds by Geographic Region
(As a % of total wholesale coffee lbs. sold)

	52 Weeks Ended		Full Year to Year Increase	
Region	September 27, 2003 (%)	September 28, 2002 (%)	(lbs.)	(%)
Northern New England (ME, NH, VT)	29.7%	31.6%	358,000	8.4%
Southern New England (MA, CT, RI)	19.3	21.0	162,000	5.7
Mid-Atlantic (NY, NJ, PA)	28.4	27.9	652,000	17.3
South Atlantic	9.3	8.6	283,000	24.3
South Central	4.0	3.7	124,000	24.6
Midwest	3.5	3.4	95,000	20.9
West	5.0	3.1	370,000	89.4
International	0.8	0.6	22,000	25.3
Pounds sold	**15,569,000**	**13,503,000**	**2,066,000**	**15.3%**

Source: Green Mountain Coffee Roasters, Inc., 2003 Annual Report.

Socially Responsible Business Practices

Green Mountain is committed to conducting its business in a socially responsible manner. The company believes that doing well financially can go hand in hand with giving back to the community and protecting the environment. In fiscal 2003 the company contributed over 5 percent of its pretax income to various coffee farms, cooperatives, and nonprofit organizations in the United States and in coffee-producing countries. Domestic organizations benefiting from cash or coffee product donations in 2003 included Heifer International, Grounds for Health, Coffee Kids, and the National Wildlife Federation.

The company is committed to improving the quality of life in coffee-producing countries, and therefore supports projects that foster self-sufficiency which, it believes, yield the best results. In fiscal year 2003, GMCR donated over

Exhibit 2   Green Mountain Financial Data

Fiscal Year Ended	Sept. 27, 2003	Sept. 28, 2002	Sept. 29, 2001	Sept. 30, 2000	Sept. 25, 1999
		(In thousands, except per share data)			
Coffee pounds sold	15,570	13,504	12,408	10,871	9,004
Net sales from continuing operations[1]	$116,727	$100,000	$95,576	$84,001	$64,881
Income from continuing operations[1]	$ 6,266	$ 5,970	$ 5,782	$ 4,153	$ 2,247
Income per share from continuing operations—diluted	$ .86	$ 0.82	$ 0.80	$ 0.59	$ 0.32
Total assets	$ 59,990	$ 54,687	$34,496	$27,244	$23,878

Source: Green Mountain Coffee Roasters, Inc., 2003 Annual Report.

[1]Excludes results from the company's discontinued company-owned retail store operations.

$180,000 to social and environmental partners in Mexico, Guatemala, Peru, Indonesia, and other coffee-growing countries. Examples of projects include environmental improvements on farms in Mexico and Guatemala with the Rainforest Alliance, improvements in coffee-milling operations in the war-torn Indonesian region of Aceh, and a new customer-based initiative with Wild Oats Markets, Inc. to construct organic vegetable gardens for coffee-growers in rural Mexico. In an effort to enhance its impact in coffee-growing countries, GMCR partnered with the U.S. Agency for International Development (USAID) and Ecological Enterprise Ventures, Inc. (EEV), a nonprofit organization, to develop a new preharvest financing mechanism for sustainable coffee producers. The $1 million award from USAID to EEV will help coffee producers address cash flow needs throughout the year. GMCR also expanded partnerships with Heifer International, Inc., and Newman's Own Organics, and started a new effort with the National Wildlife Federation to use proceeds from the sale of Green Mountain coffee to support social and environmental causes. GMCR was ranked number eight on *Business Ethics*' list of "100 Best Corporate Citizens" and *Global Finance* included Green Mountain Coffee Roasters on its list of "The World's Most Socially Responsible Companies" in October 2003.

The Coffee Industry

Today the U.S. coffee market is flat, even with the success of the specialty sector. The dynamism it once displayed has moved on to Europe and Asia, particularly Japan. The United States, responsible for up to 80 percent of world coffee consumption during World War II, now accounts for only 20 percent. While part of this decline results from a stagnant U.S. market, much of it has been due to growth in coffee drinking elsewhere. Consumption has grown in traditional and new coffee-drinking countries in Europe and Asia, and also in coffee-producing countries to the extent that Brazil is now the second-largest consumer after the United States. According to the National Coffee Association, more than 108 million people in the United States are daily coffee drinkers, and more than 166 million have consumed coffee in the past. Americans consumed more than 6.2 billion gallons of coffee in 2002, a 1.8 percent increase over consumption in 2001.[1] The annual U.S. per capita consumption of coffee is estimated to be 424 servings, which includes in-home and out-of-home roast and ground, instant, and ready-to-drink (bottled or canned) coffee.[2] The total coffee market in 2003 is estimated to be 1.8 billion pounds, or $19.3 billion.[3] According to the National Coffee Association's 2003 Trend Report, the average American coffee drinker now consumes over three cups a day. More daily coffee drinkers consume regular coffee (41 percent) than any other type; 12 percent drink specialty coffee, 8 percent drink decaf, and 7 percent drink instant coffee.[4]

According to marketing consultants Adrian Slywotzky and Kevin Mundt:

> What occurred was value migration. . . . The majors' business designs—their customer selection, resource allocation, and growth strategies—were marred by an overly categorical definition of products and benefits, a limited field of competitive vision, and an obsolete view of the customer. New innovators implemented business designs that anticipated shifts in customer priorities ahead of the established three.

Value migration occurred rapidly. The three majors held nearly 90 percent of the multibillion-dollar retail market in 1987. Within six years, the gourmet, whole bean roasters, Starbucks, and other regional cafes had collectively created nearly $1 billion in shareholder value, and together obtained 22 percent of the coffee market share. By the end of 1993, the approximate market value of the majors was $4 billion, down $1 billion from 1988. The majors failed to create a new design for their coffee business to respond to the trend. Instead, they reverted to price-cutting and coupons.[5]

During the 1980s and 1990s, the large corporations paid scant attention to the new specialty roasters. Industry executives spent millions on advertising to maintain their firms' share in the shrinking market. Discounting and millions of coupons did nothing to raise brand prestige. Despite constant price promotion, coffee was a supermarket loss leader.

The Big Three—Procter & Gamble (P&G), Altria Group (formerly Philip Morris/Kraft), Nestlé—did not feel threatened by the growing host of regional whole bean roasters who were marketing their premium brands in supermarkets and specialty stores (see Exhibit 3). Although these start-ups were experiencing double-digit growth rates, their total sales seemed minuscule to the majors. It was difficult for the majors to measure or even imagine the momentum of such tiny numbers relative to a $5 billion industry. Having made several failed attempts at marketing gourmet coffee, the brand leaders falsely assumed that gourmet coffee was a fad.[6]

In the United States, and increasingly abroad, the specialty coffee industry continues to grow. By the year 2005, sales of specialty coffee at Starbucks alone will exceed $5.0 billion, up from total specialty coffee sales of $1.5 billion in 1990. According to the Specialty Coffee Association of America (SCAA), sales of brewed, whole bean, and ground specialty coffee totaled approximately $8.4 billion in the United States alone. This new U.S. industry now consumes 5 percent of the world's coffee output—diverting some fine coffees from European markets that were accustomed to high-quality beans.

An important aspect of the specialty coffee industry is that it does not consider coffee purely as a commodity. Where the conglomerates had been concerned only with coffee's price and consistency, the new industry considers

Exhibit 3   Market Share, Revenues, and Brands of Major Coffee Companies

Company	Share of U.S. Coffee Market %	Revenue from U.S. Coffee Sales		Brands
		%	1996 $ billions	
Procter & Gamble	35%	4%	$1.5	Folgers High Point Millstone
Altria Group (formerly Philip Morris/Kraft)	30	2	1.2	Maxim Maxwell House Brim Gevalia Sanka General Foods International Coffee Chase & Sanborn
Nestlé SA	10	0.9	0.4	Hills Bros. MJB Nescafé Taster's Choice

origin, quality, processing, and cultivation methods as relevant qualities of the bean. It also extends the option of choosing roasts, grinds, and so on to the consumer, thus creating a much richer, personal coffee landscape.

The next step in this industry's development is now taking place. As specialty coffee continues to grow and develop a major presence, it has begun to consolidate into a few major corporate brands. Many regional companies are planning to expand. The market is looking to see what firm will become number two to Starbucks.[7]

The traditional coffee sector has finally taken notice of this boom. The majors have launched their own specialty coffee brands, such as Philip Morris's Gevalia, the world's largest mail-order coffee business, with annual revenues of more than $100 million; Procter & Gamble's Millstone brand, a gourmet whole bean supermarket entry; and Chock Full O'Nuts' short-lived cafes and their Quickava drive-throughs. The majors brought on the poor coffee image prior to the development of the specialty coffee industry. The idea of a Maxwell House or Nescafé gourmet coffee is contradictory—their French and espresso roasts are undermined by their being vacuum packed in cans or instant.

Developed during a time of uncertain affluence, specialty coffee has been part of a larger trend that includes developments such as microbrewed beer, single malt scotch whiskey, and organic vegetables. In each case, a consumer product has been recast as something more authentic, traditional, diverse, flavorful, and healthful than the mass-produced product it supplants. In each case, the new "specialty" product is hyped as the original item that had been debased by mass production and corporatism.

The Specialty Coffee Industry

Specialty coffee is coffee roasted using mainly high-quality Arabica beans. The Arabica bean is widely considered superior to its counterpart, the Robusta, which is used mainly in nonspecialty coffee. Arabica beans usually grow at high elevations, absorb little moisture, and mature slowly. These factors result in beans with a mild aroma and a bright, pleasing flavor that is suitable for specialty coffee.

The specialty coffee industry consists of two distinct business segments: *whole bean,* including ground, coffee sales (for home, office, and restaurant consumption) and *coffee beverage sales.* One major thrust behind the specialty coffee growth is the increase in the number of specialty coffeehouses, which grew from 500 units in 1991 to over 12,000 in 2000. The Specialty Coffee Association of America (SCAA) predicts that approximately 5,000 new coffee bars will open every year in the United States and that this industry will not peak until the year 2015.[8] The National Coffee Drinking Trends survey of 2000 discovered that 79 percent of adults 18 years or older consumed coffee over the past year, compared to 78 percent in 1999 and 75 percent in 1997.[9] Daily consumption in 2000 was 54 percent, an increase of one million new daily drinkers over 1999. Factors contributing to this increase include the development of new quality beverages, an expanding coffee menu, and a new public place for coffee's social consumption: the gourmet coffeehouse. Daily consumption in the gourmet coffee sector has grown from less than 3 percent of the adult population in 1995 to 9 percent in 2000. Occasional consumption in the gourmet coffee sector has increased from 35 percent of the population in 1997 to 53 percent in 2000, while 52 percent of the American adult population (age 18 and over) drink some type of coffee beverage on a daily basis.

In its diversity and focus on quality and distinctiveness, the specialty coffee industry is singularly profitable. Specialty beans that retail for $12 a pound are purchased wholesale before roasting (green) for about $2 per pound. The sale of whole bean coffee has grown in popularity because the increasingly sophisticated consumer grinds the beans at home and brews freshly ground coffee which is palatable even to coffee connoisseurs. According to the 1999 Gallup Survey on Coffee Consumption, nearly 36 percent of all coffee drinkers purchased specialty whole bean coffee for home consumption. In the same survey, consumers stated that 33 percent of those whole bean purchases were made at a retail price of more than $7.00 a pound, reflecting the interest in high-quality, premium-priced coffee.

Consumers favor the supermarket or grocery store for the purchase of whole bean specialty coffee. The 1999 Gallup Survey reported that 61 percent of those consumers did so most frequently in a supermarket or grocery store. Other important purchase locations included specialty coffee stores (14 percent), mail-order catalogs or clubs (4 percent), and gourmet food stores (2 percent).

The whole bean specialty coffee category is highly fragmented and competitive. Green Mountain competes against all sellers; its primary competitors include Gevalia, Illy Café, Millstone, Peet's Coffee & Tea, Seattle's Best, and Starbucks. An estimated 500 smaller and regional brands also compete in this category. In addition, Green Mountain competes indirectly against all other coffee brands on the market.

In the office coffee service (OCS), convenience store, and food service areas, Sara Lee, Kraft, Procter & Gamble, and New England Coffee are specialty coffee competitors, as are retailers such as Starbucks and Dunkin' Donuts (a subsidiary of Allied Domecq). In fiscal 2002 GMCR acquired a 42 percent ownership in Keurig to focus on the Keurig single-cup Brewer as a way to reach consumers in the office. The Keurig K-Cup allows the office coffee drinker to brew just one cup of coffee from a wide variety of coffee selections. Additionally, Green Mountain competes with "commercial" coffee roasters, to the extent that it is also trying to "upsell" consumers to the specialty coffee segment.

Green Mountain Coffee Roasters expects intense competition, both within its primary geographic territory, the eastern United States, and in other regions of the United States, as it expands its current territories.

Green Mountain Coffee's Growth Strategy

Green Mountain Coffee is focused on building the brand with profitability growing the business. Management believes it can continue to increase sales over the next few years at a rate similar to its historical five-year growth rate (13–18 percent) by increasing market share in existing markets and expanding into new geographic markets.

In recent years, the primary growth in the coffee industry has come from the specialty coffee category, driven by the wider availability of high-quality coffee, the emergence of upscale coffee shops throughout the country, and the general level of consumer education.

Green Mountain coffee is available in various distribution channels and customer categories in its primary geographic area. This multichannel strategy provides widespread exposure to the brand in a variety of settings, ease of access to the products, and many tasting opportunities for consumer trial. Green Mountain coffee is widely available throughout the day: at home in the morning, in hotels, on airplanes and trains, at convenience stores on the way to work, at the office, in restaurants, in supermarkets, and at the movie theater. See Exhibit 4 for sales distribution by channel.

The company believes that the availability of its coffee for consumer trial through convenience stores, office coffee services, and food service establishments is a significant advantage and a key component of its growth strategy. It has been the company's experience that consumer trial of Green Mountain coffee at one level of distribution often leads to a subsequent purchase at another.

As brand awareness increases through trial by consumers of the company's coffee by the cup, demand for whole bean sales of Green Mountain coffee for home consumption also increases. The National Coffee Association's study of coffee drinking trends stated that "over 75 percent of coffee drinkers drink coffee at home." As brand equity is built, wholesale expansion typically continues through customers such as supermarkets and specialty food stores, which in turn sell the company's whole bean coffee to consumers. This expansion process capitalizes upon this cup/whole bean interrelationship. The strategy is designed to further increase Green Mountain's market share in the geographic areas where it already operates in order to increase sales density and drive operational and brand-equity efficiencies. Flagship customers such as Amtrak, Exxon-Mobil, JetBlue Airways, and American Skiing Company

Exhibit 4   Coffee Pounds Sold (Whole Bean and Ground) by Sales Channel, 2002–2003

Sales Channel	52 Weeks Ended		Full Year to Year Increase	
	September 27 2003 (%)	September 28 2002 (%)	(lbs.)	(%)
Supermarkets	30.3%	28.0%	930,000	24.6%
Convenience stores	29.1	29.4	559,000	14.1
Other retail	1.9	2.3	(16,000)	−5.2
Restaurants	7.3	8.6	(18,000)	−1.6
Office coffee service	21.4	21.7	394,000	13.4
Other food service	7.4	7.3	171,000	17.3
Consumer direct	2.7	2.7	46,000	12.4
Totals (lbs. sold)	15,569,000	13,503,000	2,066,000	15.3%

Source: Green Mountain Coffee Roasters, Inc., Form 10-K for the fiscal year ended September 27, 2003.

are key to the company's geographic expansion strategy, as they provide great visibility and sampling opportunities. See Exhibit 5 for notable wholesale accounts including flagship customers.

Competitor Analysis: Starbucks

Starbucks has a significant presence in supermarkets nationwide. It has a distribution agreement with Kraft Foods, Inc. ("Kraft"), to place Starbucks coffee in supermarkets along with Kraft's Maxwell House brand. Starbucks posted net revenues of $2.5 billion for the 26 weeks ended March 28, 2004, an increase of 28.8 percent from $2.0 billion for the corresponding period of fiscal 2003. During the 26-week period, Starbucks derived approximately 84.5 percent of total net revenues from its company-operated retail stores. Revenues from these stores increased 28.5 percent to $2.1 billion for the 26 weeks ended March 28, 2004, from $1.7 billion for the same period in 2003. The increase was primarily attributable to the opening of 671 new company-operated retail stores in the last 12 months and comparable store sales growth of 11 percent. The increase in comparable store sales was due to a 10 percent increase in the number of customer transactions and a 1 percent increase in the average dollar value per transaction. Management at Starbucks believes increased traffic in company-operated retail stores continues to be driven by new product innovation, continued popularity of core products, a high level of customer satisfaction, and improved speed of service through enhanced technology, training, and execution at retail stores. All Starbucks stores are located in leased premises. Starbucks derived the remaining 15.5

percent of total net revenues from its specialty operations. Specialty revenues, which include licensing revenues and food service and other revenue, increased 30.9 percent to $391.3 million for the 26 weeks ended March 28, 2004. Licensing revenues, which are derived from retail store licensing arrangements, grocery and warehouse club licensing, and certain other branded-product operations, increased 33.9 percent to $256.0 million for the 26 weeks ended March 28, 2004. The increase was primarily attributable to the opening of 705 new licensed retail stores in the last 12 months, increased grocery revenues as a result of the acquisition of Seattle Coffee Company in the fourth quarter of fiscal 2003, and increased warehouse club revenue due to growth in existing accounts. Food service and other revenue increased 25.5 percent to $135.3 million for the 26 weeks ended March 28, 2004. The increase was primarily attributable to the growth of the food service business as a result of the acquisition of Seattle Coffee Company and the growth in new and existing Starbucks food service accounts.

Starbucks' strategy for expanding its specialty operations is to reach customers where they work, travel, shop, and dine by establishing relationships with prominent third parties who share the company's values. These relationships take various forms, including retail store licensing agreements, wholesale accounts, grocery channel licensing agreements, and joint ventures. Starbucks sells whole bean and ground coffee to several types of wholesale accounts, including office coffee distributors, hotels, airlines, retailers, and restaurants as well as institutional food service companies that handle business, industry, education, and

Exhibit 5 Green Mountain: Notable Wholesale Accounts

Convenience Stores	Restaurants	Supermarkets	Office Coffee Services	Other Food Services
ExxonMobil convenience stores	Trapp Family Lodge	Fred Meyer—131 stores	Allied Office Products	Amtrak—Northeast corridor
Mirabito Fuel Group doing business as Quickway	Culinary Institute of America	Hannaford Bros.—142 stores	ARAMARK Refreshment Services	American Skiing Company
RL Vallee, Inc., doing business as Maplefields	New England Culinary Institute	Kash n' Karry Food Stores—141 stores	Bostonbean Coffee Company	Columbia University
TETCO	The Harvard Club, New York City	Kings Super Markets—27 stores	Corporate Coffee Systems	JetBlue Airways
Uni-Marts		Price Chopper—105 stores	Crystal Rock/Vermont Pure Springs	Sodexho
		Roche Bros.—14 stores	Dispenser Services Inc.	Stowe Mountain Resort
		Stop & Shop—322 stores (primarily coffee by the cup)	Nestlé Waters of North America	
		Shaw's/Star Market—152 stores		
		Wild Oats Markets—73 stores		

Source: Green Mountain Coffee Roasters, Inc., Form 10-K, 2000–2003.

585

health care accounts. In 1995 Starbucks became the coffee supplier to the 20 million passengers who fly United Airlines each year, and its mail-order sales division accounted for roughly 2 percent of total revenue. Management believes that its direct-response marketing effort helped pave the way for retail expansion into new markets and reinforced brand recognition in existing markets.

In 1998 Starbucks entered into a long-term licensing agreement with Kraft Foods to accelerate growth of the Starbucks brand into the grocery channel in the United States. Pursuant to this agreement, Kraft manages all distribution, marketing, advertising, and promotion for Starbucks coffee in grocery, warehouse club, and mass merchandise stores. By the end of 2003 Starbucks coffee was available in 18,000 supermarkets throughout the United States. It featured distinctive, elegant packaging; prominent positions in grocery aisles; and the same premium quality as that sold in its stores.

Starbucks has spent limited funds on advertising, preferring instead to build the brand cup by cup with customers and depending on word of mouth and the appeal of storefronts. Nevertheless, the company is engaged in a growing effort to extend the Starbucks brand and penetrate new markets, including joint ventures with Dreyer's for a branded ice cream and with Pepsi to distribute bottled Frappuccino; licensee partners; mail-order and specialty sales; and international expansion.

Industry analysts see Starbucks becoming the Nike or Coca-Cola of the specialty coffee segment. It is the only specialty coffee company with a national market coverage. Starbucks' vision is to become the most recognized and respected brand of coffee in the world. The company's efforts to increase its sphere of strategic interest by means of its joint ventures with Pepsi and Dreyer's and its move to sell coffee in supermarkets represent an ongoing drive on CEO Howard Schultz's part to continually reinvent the way Starbucks does business. To sustain the company's growth and make Starbucks a strong global brand, Schultz believes the company must challenge the status quo, be innovative, take risks, and alter its vision of who it is, what it does, and where it is headed.

The Future of Green Mountain Coffee

In fiscal 2002 Green Mountain acquired a 42 percent ownership in Keurig, Incorporated ("Keurig"), by acquiring shares from early investors in Keurig for approximately $15 million. Keurig manufactures brewing equipment that allows users to brew high-quality coffee one cup at a time. As an early investor, Green Mountain has been involved with Keurig since 1994, supporting the development of the brewing system. The appeal of the Keurig K-Cup—perfectly brewing just one cup of coffee from a variety of coffee selections—has contributed to GMCR's success in the office coffee service, or OCS, channel. In fiscal 2003 GMCR introduced Celestial Seasonings tea in K-Cups,

contributing further to sales growth. Both Keurig and Green Mountain are undertaking similar endeavors to sell K-Cups to the home consumer. Bob Stiller, president and CEO of Green Mountain Coffee Roasters, stated:

> I believe that the launch of the "Keurig at home" brewer, tied into a Green Mountain K-Cup continuity program, can be a real growth engine for us over the next few years. In fact, over time, we believe the opportunity for Keurig in the home is even bigger than for Keurig in the office. . . . I would like to acknowledge that there is uncertainty concerning the magnitude of Keurig's spending in connection with its own launch of the Keurig Single-Cup Brewer for the home, as well as the time frame for Keurig's return to profitability. [But] when I weigh the risks and the longer-term potential rewards, I am as excited as ever about our compelling prospects both as a roaster selling our coffee in K-Cups and as an equity investor in Keurig.

GMCR was the first roaster to sell its coffee in Keurig's innovative single-cup brewing system and has established a dominant position in the sale of single-cup Keurig portions. GMCR does, however, compete for Keurig sales with three other North American roasters: Diedrich Coffee, Timothy's, and Van Houtte, a vertically integrated roaster and office coffee service distributor in Canada and the United States.

During fiscal 2003, 2002, and 2001, approximately 94 percent, 95 percent, and 96 percent, respectively, of Green Mountain's sales were derived from its wholesale operations located primarily in the eastern United States. Unlike most of its competitors, Green Mountain's wholesale operation services a large variety of establishments, from individual upscale restaurants to major supermarket chains. This strategy enables a deeper penetration in a geographic market, exposing consumers to the brand throughout the day in a variety of locations. The diversity of end users limits the risks of Green Mountain's dependence on any single distribution channel. In the convenience store channel, GMCR's pounds shipped increased by over 14 percent. While the total number of locations serving Green Mountain Coffee increased by about 5 percent over the prior year (to 3,300 at the close of fiscal 2003), the majority of the growth in this channel was driven by improved business with current customers. GMCR's relationship with Exxon Mobil Corporation continues to be a strong driver for growth in this convenience store channel. The supermarket channel experienced growth of more than 24 percent in coffee pounds shipped in fiscal year 2003 versus 2002, a growth driven largely by new distribution. Since the beginning of fiscal 2003, GMCR has added two large customers: Wild Oats Markets, Inc., a leading chain in the rapidly growing natural food category, and Costco Wholesale Corp., a leading buyers' club retailer. GMCR is the exclusive supplier of bulk certified Fair Trade and organic coffee for all Wild Oats locations. Growth in the supermarket channel continued throughout 2003, with the addition of several other chains, including D'Agostino Supermarkets, Harris Teeter, and Wegmans Food Markets. In November 2003 GMCR also began selling to Publix Super Markets.

An important task in global marketing is learning to recognize the extent to which marketing plans and programs can be extended worldwide, as well as the extent to which they must be adapted. Green Mountain cannot afford to replicate Nestlé's marketing blunder. Nestlé sought to transfer its great success with a four-coffee line from Europe to the United States. Nestlé's U.S. competitors were delighted because the transfer led to a decline of 1 percent in Nestlé's U.S. market share.[10]

Green Mountain is focused on the wholesale channel in the gourmet coffee niche. Green Mountain has made trade-offs, divesting its retail store operations to focus on wholesale. GMCR expects intense competition, both within its primary geographic territory and other U.S. regions, as it expands from its current territory. The specialty coffee market is expected to become even more competitive as regional companies expand and attempt to build brand awareness in new markets. Green Mountain competes primarily by providing high-quality coffee, easy access to its products, and superior customer service. GMCR believes that its ability to provide a convenient network of outlets from which to purchase coffee is an important factor in its ability to compete. Through its multichannel distribution network of wholesale and consumer direct operations and its "by the cup" / "by the pound" strategy, GMCR believes it differentiates itself from many of its competitors. Green Mountain also believes that one of the distinctive features of its business is that it is one of the few companies that roasts its coffee individually prior to blending, varying both the degree and timing of the roast to maximize a coffee's particular taste characteristic. GMCR also seeks to differentiate itself by being socially and environmentally responsible. Finally, GMCR believes that being an independent roaster allows it to be better focused and in tune with its wholesale customers' needs than its larger, multiproduct competitors. While the company believes it currently competes favorably with respect to these factors, there can be no assurance that GMCR will be able to compete successfully in the future.

The question for Bob Stiller and Daniel Martin, vice president of sales and marketing at Green Mountain Coffee Roasters, remains: What strategic paths should GMCR pursue to achieve its objective of becoming the most recognized and respected brand of coffee in the world? Brand awareness could provide a host of competitive advantages for Green Mountain Coffee.

Endnotes

1. Beverage Marketing Group.
2. Nestlé SA.
3. Datamonitor.
4. *Quarterly Grind.* 2003. October.
5. Slwotzky, Adrian J., & Mundt, Kevin. 1996. Hold the sugar; Starbucks Corp.'s business success. *Across the Board,* 33(8): 39.
6. Ibid., 39.
7. Peel, Carl. 1997. Los Angeles, a microcosm of the country. *Tea and Coffee Trade Journal,* 169(4): 16–28.
8. Specialty Coffee Association of America.
9. National Coffee Association.
10. Keegan, Warren J. Interview with Raymond Viault, vice chairman of General Mills, Inc. *Global Marketing Management,* 7.

Case 6   Pixar Animation Studios*

Basking in the success of its latest release, *Finding Nemo,* Pixar Animation Studios announced in late January 2004 that it had decided to end its talks with Walt Disney on continuing its 12-year-old partnership. The current agreement is set to expire after Pixar has delivered its next two films by the end of 2005. "After 10 months of trying to strike a deal with Disney, we're moving on," stated Steve Jobs, the Apple Computer chief executive who also heads the animation firm. "We've had a great run together—one of the most successful in Hollywood history—and it's a shame that Disney won't be participating in Pixar's future success."[1]

Since Pixar signed its first distribution pact with Disney, it has delivered a string of five straight hits: *Toy Story, A Bug's Life, Toy Story 2, Monsters Inc.* and *Finding Nemo.* Including estimates for the revenues from its latest hit, Pixar films will have earned well over $2.75 billion at the box office worldwide and sold more than 200 million DVDs and videos, making it one of the world's most successful animation companies. (See Exhibit 1 for the top 10 animated films.) "They're the ultimate pure-play media company," said Merrill Lynch analyst Andrew Slabin.[2]

But Jobs has been trying to negotiate with Michael Eisner, Disney's chief executive, about the share of profits that Pixar would get and the amount of control that it would maintain over its films. Under their current agreement, Disney gives Pixar half of the profits that are generated by each of its films from ticket sales, video sales, and merchandising royalties. But Disney also charges Pixar a fee of 12.5 percent of total revenues for distributing its movies, which is deducted before any profits are assessed. Furthermore, although Pixar shares the cost of producing and marketing its films with Disney, Disney retains the rights to the use of all of the characters and the rights to any sequels that would be developed.

Jobs made it clear that he wants Pixar to finance and market its own movies and to retain all of the profits that they generate. He was willing to give Disney a distribution fee that would run between 7 percent and 10 percent of a film's revenues. Clearly, Pixar has the funds to produce and market its own films because its successes have provided it with a strong balance sheet, with over $500 million in cash and no debt. Eisner felt that Disney would not stand to gain much from making such a deal with Pixar. See Exhibits 2 and 3 for Pixar's income statement and balance sheet.

However, many analysts do believe that Jobs should be able to get one of the Hollywood studios to agree to his terms. The prospect of a new deal has raised expectations for the firm's future. Pixar posted profits of $90 million in 2002 on sales of $202 million. Prudential Securities expects that, with a contract for 100 percent of profits after distribution fees, Pixar's net income would surge to $163 million in 2007 on sales of $361 million. Such hopes have lifted the firm's stock to just over $70, a rise of just over 50 percent from the start of 2002.

Pushing for Computer-Animated Films

The roots of Pixar stretch back to 1975 with the founding of a vocational school in Old Westbury, New York, called the New York Institute of Technology. It was there that Edwin E. Catmull, a straitlaced Mormon from Salt Lake City who loved animation but couldn't draw, teamed up with the people who would later form the core of Pixar. "It was artists and technologists from the very start," recalled Alvy Ray Smith, who worked with Catmull during those years. "It was like a fairy tale."[3]

By 1979, Catmull and his team decided to join forces with famous Hollywood director George W. Lucas, Jr. They were hopeful that this would allow them to pursue their dream of making animated films. As part of Lucas's filmmaking facility in San Rafael, California, Catmull's group of aspiring animators was able to make substantial progress in the art of computer animation. But the unit was not able to generate any profits, and Lucas was not willing to let it grow beyond using computer animation for special effects.

Catmull finally turned to Jobs, in 1985 who had just been ousted from Apple. Jobs was reluctant to invest in a firm that wanted to make full-length feature films using computer animation. But a year later, Jobs did decide to buy Catmull's unit for just $10 million, which represented a third of Lucas's asking price. While the newly named Pixar Animation Studios tried to push the boundaries of computer animation over the next five years, Jobs ended up having to invest an additional $50 million—more than 25 percent of his total wealth at the time. "There were times that we all despaired, but fortunately not all at the same time," said Jobs.[4]

Still, Catmull's team did continue to make substantial breakthroughs in the development of computer generated full-length feature films. In 1991, Disney ended up giving Pixar a three-film contract that started with *Toy Story.* When the movie was finally released in 1995, its success surprised everyone in the film industry. Rather than the nice little film Disney had expected, *Toy Story* became the sensation of 1995. It rose to the rank of the third-highest-grossing animated film of all time, earning $362 million in worldwide box office revenues.

Within days, Jobs decided to take Pixar public. When the shares, priced at $22, shot past $33, Jobs called his best friend, Oracle CEO Lawrence J. Ellison, to tell him he had company in the billionaire's club. With Pixar's sudden

*This case was prepared by Professor Jamal Shamsie of Michigan State University. This case was developed from published sources as a basis for class discussion rather than to illustrate either effective or ineffective handling of an administrative situation. Copyright © 2004 Jamal Shamsie.

Exhibit 1   Leading Animated Films

All five of Pixar's films released to date have ended up among the top 10 animated films of all time based on worldwide box office revenues.

	Title	Year Released	Box Office Gross (in $ millions)	Studio
1	*The Lion King*	1994	$768	Disney
2	*Finding Nemo*	2003	$740	Pixar
3	*Monsters, Inc.*	2001	$523	Pixar
4	*Aladdin*	1992	$502	Disney
5	*Toy Story 2*	1999	$485	Pixar
6	*Shrek*	2001	$477	Dreamworks
7	*Tarzan*	1999	$435	Disney
8	*Toy Story*	1995	$362	Pixar
9	*A Bug's Life*	1998	$361	Pixar
10	*Beauty and the Beast*	1991	$352	Disney

Source: Adapted from *Variety*.

success, Jobs returned to strike a new deal with Disney. Early in 1996, at a lunch with Walt Disney chief Michael D. Eisner, Jobs made his demands: an equal share of the profits, equal billing on merchandise and on-screen credits, and guarantees that Disney would market Pixar films as they did their own.

Boosting the Creative Component

With the success of *Toy Story*, Jobs realized that he had hit something big. He had obviously tapped into his Silicon Valley roots and turned to computers to forge a unique style of creative moviemaking. In each of its subsequent films, Pixar has continued to develop computer animation that has allowed for more lifelike backgrounds, texture, and movement than ever before. For example, since real leaves are translucent, Pixar's engineers developed special software algorithms that both reflect and absorb light, creating luminous scenes among jungles of clover.

In spite of the significance of these advancements in computer animation, Jobs was well aware that successful feature films would require a strong creative spark. He understood that it would be the marriage of technology with creativity that would allow Pixar to rise above most of its competition. To get that, Jobs fostered a campuslike environment within the newly formed outfit similar to the freewheeling, charged atmosphere in the early days of his beloved Apple, where he also returned as acting CEO. "It's not simply the technology that makes Pixar," said Dick Cook, President of Walt Disney studios.[5]

Even though Jobs has played a crucial supportive role, it is Catmull, now elevated to the position of Pixar's president, who has been mainly responsible for ensuring that the firm's technological achievements help to pump up the firm's creative efforts. He has been the keeper of the company's unique innovative culture, which has blended Silicon Valley techies, Hollywood production honchos, and artsy animation experts. In the pursuit of Catmull's vision, this eclectic group has transformed their office cubicles into tiki huts, circus tents, and cardboard castles with bookshelves that are stuffed with toys and desks that are adorned with colorful iMac computers.

Catmull has also been working hard to build upon this pursuit of creative innovation by creating programs to develop the employees. Each new hire is expected to spend 10 weeks at Pixar University, an in-house training program that includes courses in live improvisation, drawing, and cinematography. The school's dean is Randall E. Nelson, a former juggler who has been known to perform his act using chain saws so students in animation classes have something compelling to draw.

It is such an emphasis on the creative use of technology that has kept Pixar on the cutting edge. The firm has turned out ever more lifelike short films, including 1998's Oscar-winning *Geri's Game*, which used a technology called subdivision surfaces. This makes realistic simulation of human skin and clothing possible. "They're absolute geniuses," gushed Jules Roman, cofounder and CEO of rival

Exhibit 2   Pixar's Income Statement

	Period Ending		
	January 3, 2004	December 28, 2002	December 29, 2001
		(All numbers in thousands)	
Total of Revenue	262,498	201,724	70,223
Cost of revenue	38,058	41,534	12,318
Gross Profit	224,440	160,190	57,905
Operating expenses			
Research & development	15,311	8,497	6,341
Selling, general, and administrative	15,205	11,011	10,048
Nonrecurring	—	—	—
Others	—	—	—
Total operating expenses	—	—	—
Operating Income or Loss	193,924	140,682	41,516
Income from continuing operations			
Total other income/expenses, net	10,517	10,342	14,355
Earnings before interest and taxes	204,441	151,024	55,871
Interest expense	—	—	—
Income before tax	204,441	151,024	55,871
Income tax expense	79,673	61,074	19,865
Minority interest	—	—	—
Net income from continuing operations	124,768	89,950	36,006
Nonrecurring events			
Discontinued operations	—	—	211
Extraordinary items	—	—	—
Effect of accounting changes	—	—	—
Other items	—	—	—
Net Income	124,768	89,950	36,217
Preferred stock and other adjustments	—	—	—
Net Income Applicable to Common Shares	$124,768	$89,950	$36,217

Source: Pixar annual reports.

Tippett Studio. "They're the people who created computer animation really."[6]

Becoming Accomplished Storytellers

A considerable part of the creative energy goes into story development. Jobs understands that a film works only if its story can move the hearts and minds of families round the world. His goal is to develop Pixar into an animated movie studio that becomes known for the quality of its story-telling above everything else. "We want to create some great stories and characters that endure with each generation," Jobs recently stated.[7]

Exhibit 3   Pixar's Balance Sheet

	Period Ending		
	January 3, 2004	December 28, 2002	December 29, 2001
		(All numbers in thousands)	
Assets			
Current assets			
Cash and cash equivalents	48,320	44,431	56,289
Short term investments	—	294,652	222,310
Net receivables	203,794	136,911	20,660
Inventory	107,667	—	—
Other current assets	—	13,826	—
Total Current Assets	**359,781**	**489,820**	**299,259**
Long term investments	473,603	—	—
Property plant and equipment	115,026	117,423	111,995
Goodwill	—	—	—
Intangible assets	—	92,104	86,839
Accumulated amortization	—	—	—
Other assets	1,047	—	3,528
Deferred long term asset charges	51,496	32,719	21,673
Total Assets	**1,000,953**	**732,066**	**523,294**
Liabilities			
Current liabilities			
Accounts payable	52,405	11,663	15,495
Short/current long term debt	—	—	—
Other current liabilities	—	7,341	2,113
Total Current Liabilities	**52,405**	**19,004**	**17,608**
Long term debt	—	—	—
Other liabilities	8,038	—	—
Deferred long term liability charges	—	—	—
Minority interest	—	—	—
Negative goodwill	—	—	—
Total Liabilities	**60,443**	**19,004**	**17,608**
Stockholders' Equity			
Misc. stock options warrants	—	—	—
Redeemable preferred stock	—	—	—
Preferred stock	—	—	—
Common stock	546,999	442,477	325,362
Retained earnings	393,197	268,429	178,479
Treasury stock	—	—	—
Capital surplus	—	—	—
Other stockholder equity	314	2,156	1,845
Total Stockholder Equity	**940,510**	**713,062**	**505,686**
Net Tangible Assets	**$940,510**	**$620,958**	**$418,847**

Source: Pixar

For story development, Pixar relies heavily on 41-year-old John Lasseter, who goes by the title of vice president of the creative. Known for his Hawaiian shirts and irrepressible playfulness, Lasseter has been the key to the appeal of all of Pixar's films. Lasseter gets very passionate about developing great stories and then harnessing computers to tell these stories. Most of Pixar's employees believe it is this passion that has allowed the studio to ensure that each of its films has been a commercial hit. In fact, Lasseter is being regarded as the Walt Disney of the 21st century.

When it's time to start a project, Lasseter isolates a group of eight or so writers and directs them to forget about the constraints of technology. While many studios try to rush from script to production, Lasseter takes up to two years just to develop the story. Once the script has been developed, artists create storyboards and copy them onto videotapes called reels. Even computer-animated films must begin with pencil sketches that are viewed on tape. "You can't really shortchange the story development," Lasseter emphasized.[8]

Only after the basic story has been set does Lasseter begin to think about what he'll need from Pixar's technologists. And it's always more than the computer animators expect. Lasseter, for example, demanded that the crowds of ants in A Bug's Life not be a single mass of look-alike faces. To solve the problem, computer expert William T. Reeves developed software that randomly applied physical and emotional characteristics to each ant. In another instance, writers brought a model of a butterfly named Gypsy to researchers, asking them to write code so that when she rubs her antennas, you can see the hairs press down and pop back up.

At any stage during the process, Lasseter may go back to potential problems that he may see with the story. In A Bug's Life, for example, the story was totally revamped after more than a year of work had been completed. Originally, it was about a troupe of circus bugs run by P. T. Flea that tries to rescue a colony of ants from marauding grasshoppers. But because of a flaw in the story—why would the circus bugs risk their lives to save stranger ants?—codirector Andrew Stanton recast the story to be about Flik, the heroic ant who recruits Flea's troupe to fight the grasshoppers. "You have to rework and rework it," explained Lasseter. It is not rare for a scene to be rewritten as many as 30 times.[9]

Pumping Out the Hits

In spite of its formidable string of hits, Pixar has had difficulty stepping up its pace of production. Although they may cost 30 percent less, computer-generated animated films do still take considerable time to develop. Furthermore, because of the emphasis on every single detail, Pixar used to complete most of the work on a film before moving on to the next one. Catmull and Lasseter have since decided to work on several projects at the same time, but it still took 18 months for the studio to follow up Monsters Inc. with Finding Nemo. Jobs stated he would like Pixar to release a movie each year.

To push for this ambitious goal, Pixar has nearly doubled in size since 1998, to 750 employees. It is also turning to a stable of directors to oversee its movies. Lasseter, who directed Pixar's first three films, is supervising other directors who are taking helm of various films that the studio chooses to develop. Monsters Inc. and Finding Nemo were directed by some of this new talent. But there are concerns about the number of directors that Pixar can rely upon to turn out high-quality animated films. Michael Savner of Bank of America Securities commented: "You can't simply double production. There is a finite amount of talent."[10]

To meet the faster production pace, Catmull also has added new divisions, including one to help with the development of new movies and one to oversee movie development shot by shot. The eight-person development team has helped to generate more ideas for new films. "Once more ideas are percolating, we have more options to choose from so no one artist is feeling the weight of the world on their shoulders," said Sarah McArthur, Pixar's vice president of production.[11]

Finally, Catmull is turning to new technology to help ramp up production. His goal is to reduce the number of animators to no more than 100 per film. Towards this end, Catmull has been overseeing the development of new animation software, called Luxo, which will allow fewer people to do more work. While the firm's old system did allow animators to easily make a change to a specific character, Luxo adjusts the environment as well. For example, if an animator adds a new head to a monster, the system automatically casts the proper shadow.

Above all, Catmull has been working hard to retain Pixar's commitment to quality even as it grows. He has been using Pixar University to encourage collaboration among all employees so that they can develop and retain the key values that are tied to their success. And he has helped devise ways to avoid collective burnout. A masseuse and a doctor now come by Pixar's campus each week, and animators must get permission from their supervisors if they want to work more than 50 hours a week.

Jobs is well aware of the dangers of growth for a studio whose successes came out of a lean structure that wagered everything on each film. It remains to be seen whether Pixar may be able to draw on its talent to increase production without compromising the high standards that have been set by Catmull and Lasseter. The question is whether the company can keep making hits if it's doubling the number of films it makes. "You wonder, are they at risk

Exhibit 4   Pixar's Proprietary Software

Marionette
An animation software system used for modeling, animating, and lighting.

Ringmaster
A production management software system for scheduling, coordinating, and tracking a computer animation project.

Renderman
A rendering software system for high-quality, photo-realistic image synthesis.

Source: Pixar.

of becoming formulaic?" asked Merrill Lynch analyst Andrew Slabin.[12]

To Infinity and Beyond?

Jobs' decision to break off talks with Disney took industry observers by surprise. It is clear that Disney has been relying heavily on Pixar since its own animated films have not performed well. But there are questions about Pixar's ability to continue its success without any support from Disney. Pixar may no longer need Disney's assistance with the financing and production of its films. But Disney has provided much more critical support for the marketing and distribution of these films and any associated merchandise such as toys and videos.

Pixar may not have sufficient experience to handle these marketing and distribution functions. It has managed to release just five films so far, even though these films have risen to the top of the list of box office leaders among animated films. Most observers believe that Pixar relied heavily upon Disney's capabilities to achieve its early success. It was Disney that had the marketing might that helped to transform characters such as Woody and Nemo from mere images on the big screen into household names.

Furthermore, Pixar stands to lose some revenue over the next couple years by not maintaining its relationship with Disney. Under its present contract, Disney will still distribute the next two Pixar films: *The Incredibles,* due later in 2004, and *Cars,* due sometime in 2005. Disney had been willing to adjust the profit split on these two films if Pixar chose to continue with the present arrangement. By deciding to make a deal with another Hollywood studio, Pixar will have to wait until 2006 before it can keep more of the profits from its own films.

Even if Pixar is able to get a greater share of the profits from its films, it will still have to keep generating hits. But Catmull and Lasseter are confident that they have the talent to keep pushing out great animated films. "We're not jumping on the bandwagon, we're making it," claimed Catmull.[13] Sarah McArthur, Pixar's executive vice president of production echoes this feeling: "There's an atmosphere of building something. There's energy, camaraderie, creativity. We're trying to make this work."[14]

Furthermore, Pixar's talent does not have Hollywood style costs attached to them. Employees are happy to receive stock options, and no one in the firm has long-term contracts. Even under these conditions, the firm has little turnover. "We have the lowest turnover rate in Hollywood history," said Lasseter. "We created the studio we want to work in. We have an environment that's wacky. It's a creative brain trust: It's not a place where I make my movies—it's a place where a group of people make movies."[15]

Pixar certainly comes as close to a sure thing as exists in the unpredictable movie business, but no one expects it to have an endless winning streak. "It's hard to put a string of 10 mega blockbusters together," said Michael Savner of Bank of America Securites.[16] The risk of a failure is likely to rise as Pixar tries to ramp up production. "Things like creativity don't necessarily scale up," said Sasa Zorovic, an analyst at Robert Stephens in San Francisco.[17]

Endnotes

1. Holson, Laura M. 2004. Pixar, creator of *Finding Nemo,* sees end to its Disney partnership. *New York Times,* January 30: A1.
2. Burrows, Peter. 2003. Pixar's unsung hero. *BusinessWeek,* June 30: 68.
3. Burrows, Peter, & Grover, Ronald. 1998. Steve Jobs: Movie mogul. *BusinessWeek,* November 23: 150.
4. *BusinessWeek.* 1998. November 23: 150.
5. *BusinessWeek.* 1998. November 23: 146.
6. *BusinessWeek.* 1998. November 23: 146.
7. Graser, Marc. 1999. Pixar run by focused group. *Variety,* December 20: 74.
8. *Variety.* 1999. December 20: 74.
9. *BusinessWeek.* 1998. November 23: 146.
10. Bary, Andrew. 2003. Coy story. *Barron's,* October 13: 21.
11. Tam, Pui-Wing. Will quantity hurt Pixar's quality? *Wall Street Journal,* February 15: B4.
12. *BusinessWeek.* 2003. June 30: 69.
13. *BusinessWeek.* 1998. November 23: 146.
14. *Variety.* 1999. December 20: 74.
15. *Variety.* 1999. December 20: 74.
16. *Barron's.* 2003. October 13: 21.
17. *Wall Street Journal.* 2001. February 15: B1.

Case 7   eBay: King of the Online Auction Industry*

As Pierre Omidyar (pronounced oh-*mid*-ee-ar), chairman and founder of eBay, set his morning copy of the *Wall Street Journal* down on the desk, he nervously wondered how long eBay's amazing run of success would continue. He had just read an article detailing the explosion in sales of Amazon.com to $650 million during the fourth quarter of 1999, a number that exceeded the company's entire sales for the year of 1998. Even more disconcerting to Pierre was that online auctions were the fastest-growing part of Amazon's business in 1999. Competition from Amazon.com, Yahoo!, and several other enterprising dot-com companies that had started holding auctions at their Web sites had reduced eBay's dominant market share from 80 percent to 60 percent during 1999. Other outsiders, including Microsoft and Dell, had announced plans to fund new ventures to enter the online auction business.

When Pierre formed eBay in 1995, he had never imagined the company would become so successful. He had continued to work at his old job even after forming eBay. Soon, however, he realized that the online auction industry represented a tremendous market opportunity—eBay gave hobbyists and collectors a convenient way to locate items of interest, a way for sellers to generate income, and a means for bargain hunters to pick up a wanted item at less than they might have paid in a retail store. Still, the rapid growth of eBay had surprised almost everyone (see Exhibit 1).

By 1999, when people thought about online auctions, the first name that popped into their heads was eBay. Going into 2000, eBay had created the world's largest Web-based community of consumer-to-consumer auctions using an entertaining format that allowed people to buy and sell collectibles, automobiles, jewelry, high-end and premium art items, antiques, coins and stamps, dolls and figures, pottery and glass, sports memorabilia, toys, consumer electronics products, and a host of other practical and miscellaneous items. At year-end 1999, eBay had listed over 3 million items in over 3,000 categories; browsers and buyers could search listings by item, category, key word, seller name, or auction dates. The company Web site had approximately 10 million registered users and, on average, attracted 1.8 million unique visitors daily. eBay members listed more than 375,000 items on the site every day.

However, Pierre Omidyar, Margaret Whitman (eBay's president and CEO), and other eBay executives were well aware that eBay needed to address a myriad of emerging market challenges. The complexion of the online auction industry was changing almost daily. While eBay's management team had met past challenges successfully, it wasn't going to be easy to hurdle the competitive and market challenges ahead.

*Case written by Louis Marino, The University of Alabama, and Patrick Kreiser, The University of Alabama. Copyright © 2000 by Lou Marino; all rights reserved.

The Growth of e-Commerce and Online Auctions

Although the ideas behind the Internet were first conceived in the 1960s, it wasn't until the 1990s that the Internet garnered widespread use and became a part of everyday life. The real beginning of the Internet economy took place in 1991, when the National Science Foundation (NSF) lifted a restriction on commercial use of the Internet, making electronic commerce, or business conducted over the Internet, a possibility for the first time. By 1996, there were Internet users in almost 150 countries worldwide, and the number of computer hosts was close to 10 million. International Data Corporation (IDC) estimated there would be 320 million Internet users worldwide by 2002 and 500 million by year-end 2003.

The GartnerGroup forecast that business-to-business e-commerce would grow from $145 billion in 1999 to $7.29 trillion in 2004, while business-to-consumer revenues would climb from $31.2 billion in 1999 to over $380 billion in 2003. Within the business-to-consumer segment, where eBay operated, U.S. e-commerce accounted for over 65 percent of all Internet transactions in 1999 but was expected to account for only about 38 percent in 2003, due to rapid expansion in other parts of the world.

Business-to-consumer e-commerce in Europe was projected to grow from $5.4 billion in 1999 (17.3 percent of the world total) to over $115 billion (more than 30 percent of the world total) by 2003. As can be seen from Exhibit 2, online auction sales of collectibles and personal merchandise was expected to represent an $18.7 billion market in 2002.

Key Success Factors in Online Retailing   While it was relatively easy to create a Web site that functioned like a retail store, the big challenge was for an online retailer to generate traffic to the site in the form of both new and returning customers. Most online retailers strived to provide extensive product information, include pictures of the merchandise, make the site easily navigable, and have enough new things happening at the site to keep customers coming back. (A site's ability to generate repeat visitors was known as "stickiness.") Retailers also had to overcome users' nervousness about using the Internet itself to shop for items they generally bought at stores and their wariness about entering their credit card numbers over the Internet. Online retailing had severe limitations in the case of those goods and services people wanted to see in person to verify their quality. From the retailer's perspective, there was the issue of collecting payment from buyers who wanted to use checks or money orders instead of a credit card.

History of Auctions

An auction is a method of buying and selling goods to the highest bidder. A seller offers a particular product or service for sale, and the buyer who makes the highest offer for it is considered the auction winner. As the demand for a

Exhibit 1   Selected Indicators of eBay's Growth, 1996–99

	1996	1997	1998	1999
Number of registered users	41,000	341,000	2,181,000	10,006,000
Gross merchandise sales	$7 million	$95 million	$745 million	$2.8 billion
Number of auctions listed	289,000	4,394,000	33,668,000	129,560,000

Exhibit 2   Estimated Growth in Global e-Commerce and Online Auction Sales, 1999–2004

	1999	2000	2001	2002	2003	2004
Estimated business-to business sales	$145 billion	$403 billion	$953 billion	$2.18 trillion	$3.95 trillion	$7.29 trillion

Source: GartnerGroup.

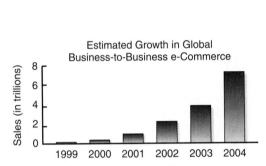

Estimated Growth in Global Business-to-Business e-Commerce

Source: Keenan Vision Inc. *Mercury News.*

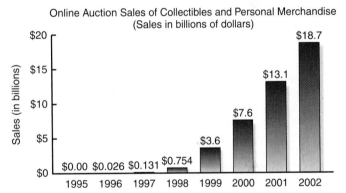

Online Auction Sales of Collectibles and Personal Merchandise (Sales in billions of dollars)

particular good rises among the buyers (typically due to its scarcity or desirability), the price also rises. Competition among bidders for a desirable good drives up the price. Sometimes the highest bid will exceed the generally accepted market value of the good, a phenomenon known as the "winner's curse." In this situation, the buyer becomes so emotionally attached to the good or to placing the highest bid that he or she ends up bidding more than the good would cost in a nonauction setting.

The first known auctions were held in Babylon around 500 BC. In these auctions, women were sold to the highest bidder on the condition that they marry the auction winner. In ancient Rome, soldiers would auction the spoils of their victories and wealthy citizens would auction their expensive belongings and prized possessions. In 193 AD, the entire Roman Empire was put up for auction after the emperor Pertinax was executed. Didius Julianus bid 6,250

drachmas per royal guard and was immediately named emperor of Rome. However, Julianus was executed only two months later, indicating that he may have been the first-ever victim of the winner's curse.

Since that time, auctions have been conducted in every corner of the globe. The possessions of deceased Buddhist monks were auctioned off as early as the seventh century. In the late 16th century, auctions began to be held in taverns and alehouses in Great Britain. Sotheby's was founded in 1744, and Christie's was established in 1766; both have now become world-renowned auction houses for rare and valuable items. Auctions for tobacco, horses, and other domestic animals were commonplace in colonial America.

Auctions have endured throughout history for several reasons. First, they give sellers a convenient way to find a buyer for something they would like to dispose of. Second, auctions are an excellent way for people to collect difficult-to-find items, such as Beanie Babies or historical memorabilia, that have a high value to them personally. Finally, auctions are one of the "purest" markets that exist for goods, in that they bring buyers and sellers into contact to arrive at a mutually agreeable price. Experts estimated that the national market for auctions, garage sales, flea markets, and classified purchases was greater than $100 billion in 1999.

Online Auctions

Online auctions worked in essentially the same way as traditional auctions, the difference being that the auction process occurred over the Internet rather than at a specific geographic location with buyers and sellers physically present. In 2000, there were three categories of online auctions:

1. Business-to-business auctions, which accounted for $2.5 billion in sales in 1998 and involved such items as computers, used equipment, and surplus merchandise.
2. Business-to-consumer auctions, in which businesses sold goods and services to consumers via the Internet. Many such auctions involved companies interested in selling used or discontinued goods, or liquidating unwanted inventory.
3. Person-to-person auctions, which gave interested sellers and buyers the opportunity to engage in competitive bidding.

Since eBay's pioneering of the person-to-person online auction process in 1995, the number of online auction sites on the Internet had grown to well over 1,600 by the end of 1999. Forrester Research predicted that 6.5 million customers would use online auctions in 2002. In 1999 an estimated 8.2 percent of Internet users had registered at an auction site; the percentage was expected to be 14.5 percent by 2002.

Online auction operators could generate revenue in four principal ways:

1. Charging sellers for listing their good or service.
2. Charging a commission on all sales.
3. Selling advertising on their Web sites.
4. Selling their own new or used merchandise via the online auction format.

Most sites charged sellers either a fee or a commission and sold advertising to companies interested in promoting their goods or services to users of the auction site.

Auction Software Packages
In 1996, OpenSite Technologies began to offer packaged software applications to firms interested in creating their own online auction Web sites. Moai Technologies and Ariba, Inc., were other sources for auction software. The ready availability of commercial software packages made it easy for firms to create and operate online auction sites. OpenSite had marketed over 600 auction packages to such companies as The Sharper Image, CNET, and John Deere. OpenSite claimed that its purpose was to bring together "buyers and sellers, helping businesses dynamically manage inventory, create sales

channels, attract customers, and test-market new products, to create efficient markets for goods and services."

Providers of Site Hosting and Online Auction Services

Auction firms could, if they wished, outsource all the hosting functions associated with online auctions to independent site-hosting enterprises and could even turn the entire auction process over to an independent online auction specialist. FairMarket, the leader in auction outsourcing in 1999, provided companies such as ZDNet, MicroWarehouse, and CollegeBytes.com with a means of selling their goods at online auction at Fair-Market's Web site. The use of site hosts and independent online auction services was a particularly appealing option for companies that wanted to use online auctions as a distribution channel but preferred to devote only minimal time and energy to site construction and upkeep. By paying FairMarket an annual hosting fee between $2,000 and $10,000, as well as a percentage fee on all transactions, firms were able to have an auction site without having to worry about the hassle of site upkeep.

Online Auction Users
Participants in online auctions could be grouped into three categories: (1) bargain hunters, (2) hobbyists/collectors, and (3) sellers.

Bargain Hunters   Bargain hunters viewed online auctions primarily as a form of entertainment; their objective usually was to find a great deal. One bargain hunter described the eBay experience as follows:

> A friend and I would spend one day a week going flea marketing and auctioning. Since school has started again, time has become a hot commodity. We've found that we can use eBay to fill that flea marketing, auctioning need. We'll call each other, then get on eBay and hunt and find things together even though we can't be together. EBay has definitely been a great way to spend quality time together!

Bargain hunters were thought to make up only 8 percent of active online users but 52 percent of eBay visitors. To attract repeat visits from bargain hunters, industry observers said, sites must appeal to them on both rational and emotional levels, satisfying their need for competitive pricing, the excitement of the search, and the desire for community.[1]

Hobbyists and Collectors   Hobbyists and collectors used auctions to search for specific goods that had a high value to them personally. They were very concerned with both price and quality. Collectors prized eBay for its wide variety of product offerings. One user commented:

> My sister collects Princess House hand-blown ornaments. She needed the first three to complete her series. I posted to the Wanted Board several times, and also put a note on my About Me page. Well, we have now successfully completed her series. We could never have done this without eBay because the first one is so hard to find. Thanks eBay!

Sellers   Those in the sellers category could be further differentiated into at least three types: casual sellers, hobbyists/collectors, and power sellers. Casual sellers included individuals who used eBay as a substitute for a classified ad listing or a garage sale to dispose of items they no longer wanted. While many casual sellers listed only a few items, some used eBay to raise money for some new project. One such seller stated:

> Thank you! After just starting to use your site less than a month ago, I have increased my earnings by over $1,000. I have not yet received all the cash, but so far the response has been fantastic. This all started with a Kool-Aid container and four cups I had that were collecting dust in a box in the attic. I was "browsing for bargains" and saw someone else had made $29.00 from those plastic things! I was AMAZED! Needless to say, I listed them. I only made $8.00, but I received my first positive feedback. Since then I am listing daily.
>
> My wife and I are scrimping to save for an adoption of a baby. The fees are much more than our modest income can afford, and this extra cash will come in handy. My wife and I sincerely thank you and your company for the opportunity to be a part of eBay.

Sellers who were hobbyists or collectors typically dealt in a limited category of goods and looked to eBay as a way to sell selected items in their collections to others who might want them. Power sellers were typically small- to medium-sized businesses that favored eBay as a primary distribution channel for their goods and often sold tens of thousands of dollars' worth of goods every month on the site. One estimate suggested that while these power sellers accounted for only 4 percent of eBay's population, they were responsible for 80 percent of eBay's total business.[2]

Concerns about Buyer Addiction to Online Auctions

Some members of the online auction community reportedly found the experience so intriguing that they became addicted. According to the Center for Online Addiction, symptoms of online auction addiction ranged from "using online auctions as a way of escaping from problems or relieving feelings of helplessness, guilt, anxiety, or depression" to "needing to bid with increasing amounts of money in order to achieve the desired excitement."[3] The center predicted that "online auction houses will be the next frenzy leading to shopping addiction" and had treated online auction addicts who had to take out a second mortgage or file bankruptcy as a result of their excessive online purchases.[4] One online auction addict told of his experience as follows:

> It became critical when my boss confronted me. [My employer] had monitored my Internet use, and it was even more than I was aware of. My boss told me he had no choice but to terminate me. I've been at this job almost five years, have achieved recognition at the national level for the program, and have previously been a very capable employee. How can I [justify] throwing all that away? There is no doubt, though, that my productivity had really begun to suffer.
>
> I was truthful with my boss about how this had become a compulsion I just could not control. I attributed it to some real stresses in my personal life, and kept telling myself that when things settled down, I would get a handle on it. He has put me on [administrative] leave while he thinks things over.[5]

Pierre Omidyar and the Founding of eBay

Pierre Omidyar was born in Paris, France, to parents who had left Iran decades earlier. The family emigrated to the United States when Pierre's father began a residency at Johns Hopkins University Medical Center. Pierre grew up in modest circumstances; his parents divorced when he was two but remained near each other so he could be with both of them. Pierre's passion for computers began at an early age; he would sneak out of gym class in high school to play with computers. While still in high school, at age 14 he took his first computer-related job in the school's library, where he was hired for $6.00 an hour to write a program to print catalog cards.[6] After high school Pierre attended Tufts University, where he met his future wife, Pamela Wesley, who came to Tufts from Hawaii to get a degree in biology. Upon graduating in 1988, the couple moved to California, where Pierre, who had earned a BS in computer science, joined Claris, an Apple Computer subsidiary in Silicon Valley, and wrote a widely used graphics application, MacDraw. In 1991, Omidyar left Claris and cofounded Ink Development (later renamed eShop), which became a pioneer in online shopping and was eventually sold to Microsoft in 1996. In 1994 Omidyar joined General Magic as a developer services engineer and remained there until mid-1996, when he left to pursue full-time development of eBay.

Internet folklore has it that eBay was founded solely to allow Pamela to trade Pez dispensers with other collectors. While Pamela was certainly a driving force in launching the initial Web site, Pierre had long been interested in how one could establish a marketplace to bring together a fragmented market. Pierre saw eBay as a way to create a person-to-person trading community based on a democratized, efficient market where everyone could have equal access through the same medium, the Internet. Pierre set out to develop his marketplace and to meet both his and Pamela's goals. In 1995 he launched the first online auction under the name of Auctionwatch at the domain name of www.eBay.com. The name eBay stood for "electronic Bay area," coined because Pierre's initial concept was to attract neighbors and other interested San Francisco Bay area residents to the site to buy and sell items of mutual interest. The first auctions charged no fees to either buyers or sellers and contained mostly

Exhibit 3   eBay's Income Statements, 1996–99 ($000, Except Per Share Figures)

	1996	1997	1998	1999
Net revenues	$32,051	$41,370	$86,129	$224,724
Cost of net revenues	6,803	8,404	16,094	57,588
Gross profit	25,248	32,966	70,035	167,136
Operating expenses				
Sales and marketing	13,139	15,618	35,976	95,956
Product development	28	831	4,640	23,785
General and administrative	5,661	6,534	15,849	43,055
Amortization of acquired intangibles	—	—	805	1,145
Merger related costs	—	—	—	4,359
Total operating expenses	18,828	22,983	57,270	168,300
Income (loss) from operations	6,420	9,983	12,765	(1,164)
Interest and other income (expense), net	(2,607)	(1,951)	(703)	21,377
Income before income taxes	3,813	8,032	12,062	20,213
Provision for income taxes	(475)	(971)	(4,789)	(9,385)
Net income	$ 3,338	$ 7,061	$ 7,273	$ 10,828
Net income per share				
Basic	$0.39	$0.29	$0.14	$0.10
Diluted	.07	0.08	0.06	0.08
Weighted average shares				
Basic	8,490	24,428	52,064	108,235
Diluted	45,060	84,775	116,759	135,910

Source: Company financial documents.

computer equipment (and no Pez dispensers). Pierre's fledgling venture generated $1,000 in revenue the first month and an additional $2,000 the second. Traffic grew rapidly, however, as word about the site spread in the Bay area; a community of collectors emerged, using the site to trade and chat—some marriages resulted from exchanges in eBay chat rooms.[7]

By February 1996, the traffic at Pierre Omidyar's site had grown so much that his Internet service provider informed him that he would have to upgrade his service. When Pierre compensated for this by charging a listing fee for the auction, and saw no decrease in the number of items listed, he knew he was on to something. Although he was still working out of his home, Pierre began looking for a partner and in May asked his friend Jeffrey Skoll to join him in the venture. While Jeff had never cared much about money, his Stanford MBA degree provided the firm with the business background that Pierre lacked.[8] With Pierre as the visionary and Jeff as the strategist, the company

embarked on a mission to "help people trade practically anything on earth." Their concept for eBay was to "create a place where people could do business just like in the old days—when everyone got to know each other personally, and we all felt we were dealing on a one-to-one basis with individuals we could trust."

In eBay's early days, Pierre and Jeff ran the operation alone, using a single computer to serve all of the pages. Pierre served as CEO, chief financial officer, and president, while Jeff functioned as co-president and director. It was not long until Pierre and Jeff grew the company to a size that forced them to move out of Pierre's living room, due to the objections of Pamela, and into Jeff's living room. Shortly thereafter, the operations moved into the facilities of a Silicon Valley business incubator for a time until the company settled in its current facilities in San Jose, California.

Exhibits 3 and 4 present eBay's recent financial statements.

Exhibit 4   eBay's Consolidated Balance Sheets, 1997–99 ($000)

	December 31, 1997	December 31, 1998	December 31, 1999
Assets			
Current assets			
Cash and cash equivalents	$3,723	$ 37,285	$219,679
Short-term investments	—	40,401	181,086
Accounts receivable, net	1,024	12,425	36,538
Other current assets	220	7,479	22,531
Total current assets	4,967	97,590	459,834
Property and equipment, net	652	44,062	111,806
Investments	—	—	373,988
Deferred tax asset	—	—	5,639
Intangible and other assets, net	—	7,884	12,675
Total assets	$5,619	$149,536	$963,942
Liabilities and Stockholders' Equity			
Current liabilities			
Accounts payable	$252	$ 9,997	$ 31,538
Accrued expenses and other current liabilities	—	6,577	32,550
Deferred revenue and customer advances	128	973	5,997
Debt and leases, current portion	258	4,047	12,285
Income taxes payable	169	1,380	6,455
Deferred tax liabilities	—	1,682	—
Other current liabilities	128	5,981	7,632
Total current liabilities	1,124	24,656	88,825
Debt and leases, long-term portion	305	18,361	15,018
Other liabilities	157		
Total liabilities	1,586	48,998	111,475
Series B mandatorily redeemable convertible preferred stock and Series B warrants	3,018	—	—
Total stockholders' equity	1,015	100,538	852,467
Total liabilities and stockholders' equity	$5,619	$149,536	$963,942

Source: Company financial documents.

eBay's Transition to Professional Management

From the beginning Pierre Omidyar intended to hire a professional manager to serve as the president of eBay: "[I would] let him or her run the company so . . . [I could] go play."[9] In 1997 both Omidyar and Skoll agreed that it was time to locate an experienced professional to function as CEO and president. In late 1997 eBay's headhunters came up with a candidate for the job: Margaret Whitman, then general manager for Hasbro Inc.'s preschool division.

Whitman had received her BA in economics from Princeton and her MBA from the Harvard Business School; her first job was in brand management at Procter & Gamble. Her experience also included serving as the president and CEO of FTD, the president of Stride Rite Corporation's Stride Rite Division, and as the senior vice president of marketing for the Walt Disney Company's consumer product division.[10]

When first approached by eBay, Whitman was not especially interested in joining a company that had fewer than 40 employees and less than $6 million in revenues the previous year. It was only after repeated pleas that Whitman agreed to meet with Omidyar in Silicon Valley. After a second meeting, Whitman realized the company's enormous growth potential and agreed to give eBay a try. According to Omidyar, Meg Whitman's experience in global marketing with Hasbro's Teletubbies, Playskool, and Mr. Potato Head brands made her "the ideal choice to build upon eBay's leadership position in the one-to-one online trading market without sacrificing the quality and personal touch our users have grown to expect."[11] In addition to convincing Margaret Whitman to head eBay's operations, Omidyar had been instrumental in helping bring in other talented senior executives and in assembling a capable board of directors. Notable members of eBay's board of directors included Scott Cook, the founder of Intuit, a highly successful financial software company, and Howard Schultz, the founder and CEO of Starbucks. (For a profile of eBay's senior management team, check out the Company Overview section at www.ebay.com.)

Whitman ran the operation from the time she came on board. Omidyar, who owned 27.9 percent of eBay's stock (worth approximately $6 billion as of March 2000), spent considerable time in Paris. He and Pamela, still in their mid-30s and concerned about the vast wealth they had accumulated in such a short period of time, were devoting a substantial amount of their energy to exploring philanthropic causes.[12] They had decided to give most of their fortune to charity and were scrutinizing alternative ways to maximize the impact of their philanthropic contributions on the overall well-being of society. Jeffrey Skoll owned 16.7 percent of eBay's shares (worth about $3.6 billion), and Margaret Whitman owned 5.2 percent (worth about $1 billion).

How an eBay Auction Worked

eBay endeavored to make it very simple to buy and sell goods. In order to sell or bid on goods, users first had to register at the site. Once they registered, users selected both a user name and a password. Nonregistered users were able to browse the Web site but were not permitted to bid on any goods or list any items for auction. On the Web site, search engines helped customers determine what goods were currently available. When registered users found an item they desired, they could choose to enter a single bid or to use automatic bidding. In automatic bidding the customer entered an initial bid sufficient to make him or her the high bidder and then the bid would be automatically increased as others bid for the same object until the auction ended and either the bidder won or another bidder surpassed the original customer's maximum specified bid. Regardless of which bidding method they chose, users could check bids at any time and either bid again, if they had been outbid, or increase their maximum amount in the automatic bid. Users could choose to receive e-mail notification if they were outbid. Once the auction had ended, the buyer and seller were each notified of the winning bid and were given each other's e-mail address. The parties to the auction would then privately arrange for payment and delivery of the good.

Fees and Procedures for Sellers   eBayers were not charged a fee for bidding on items on the site, but sellers were charged an insertion fee and a "final value" fee; they could also elect to pay additional fees to promote their listing. Listing, or insertion, fees ranged from 25 cents for auctions with opening bids between $0.01 and $9.99, to $2.00 for auctions with opening bids of $50.00 and up. Final value fees ranged from 1.25 to 5 percent of the final sale price and were computed based on a graduated fee schedule in which the percentage fell as the final sales price rose. As an example, in a basic auction with no promotion, if the item had brought an opening bid of $100 and eventually sold for $1,500, the total fee paid by the seller would be $33.88—the $2.00 insertion fee plus $31.88. The $31.88 is based on a fee structure of 5 percent of the first $25.00 (or $1.25), 2.5 percent of the additional amount between $25.01 and $1,000.00 (or $24.38), and 1.25 percent of the additional amount between $1,000.01 and $1,500.00 (or $6.25).

A seller who wished to promote an item could choose a bold heading for an additional fee of $2.00. A seller with a favorable feedback rating (discussed below) could have his or her auction listed either as a "Featured Auction" for $99.95, which allowed the seller's item to be rotated on the eBay home page, or as a "Category Featured Auction" for $14.95, which allowed the item to be featured within a particular eBay category. For $1.00, a seller could choose to place a seasonal icon (such as a shamrock in connection with St. Patrick's Day) next to his or her listing. A seller could also include a description of the product with links to the seller's Web site. In addition, a seller could indicate a photograph in the item's description if the seller posted the photograph on a Web site and provided eBay with the appropriate Web address. Items could be showcased in the Gallery section with a catalog of pictures rather than text. A seller who used a photograph in his or her listing could have this photograph included in the Gallery section for 25 cents or featured there for $19.95. A Gallery section was available in all categories of eBay. Certain categories of items—such as real estate, automobiles, and "Great Collections"—had special promotion rates.

New sellers were required to file a credit card number with eBay for automatic monthly billing, while sellers who had opened accounts prior to October 22, 1999, could alternatively choose a pay-as-you-go method. The latter option, however, was relatively unattractive since it allowed eBay to block any account whose balance due reached $25.00. The block was removed once the fee was paid, or once the seller had registered a credit card with eBay.

How Transactions Are Completed   When an auction ended, the eBay system validated that the bid fell within the acceptable price range. If the sale was successful, eBay automatically notified the buyer and seller via e-mail; the buyer and seller could then work out the transaction details independent of eBay. At no point during the process did eBay take possession of either the item being sold or the buyer's payment. Rather, the buyer and seller had to independently arrange for the shipment of and payment for the item; buyers typically paid for shipping. A seller could view a buyer's feedback rating (discussed below) and then determine the manner of payment, such as personal check, cashier's check, or credit card, and also whether to ship the item before or after receiving payment. Under the terms of eBay's user agreement, if a seller received one or more bids above the stated minimum, or reserve, price, the seller was obligated to complete the transaction, although eBay had no enforcement power beyond suspending a noncompliant buyer or seller from using eBay's service. In the event the buyer and seller were unable to complete the transaction, the seller notified eBay, which then credited the seller the amount of the final value fee. When items carrying a reserve price sold, sellers were credited the $1.00 reserve fee. Invoices for placement fees, additional listing fees, and final value fees were sent via e-mail to sellers on a monthly basis.

Feedback Forum   In early 1996 eBay pioneered a feature called Feedback Forum to build trust among buyers and sellers and to facilitate the establishment of reputations within its community. Feedback Forum encouraged individuals to record comments about their trading partners. At the completion of each auction, both the buyer and seller were allowed to leave positive, negative, or neutral comments about each other. Individuals could dispute feedback left about them by annotating comments in question. By assigning values of +1 for a positive comment, 0 for a neutral comment, and –1 for a negative comment, each trader earned a ranking that was attached to his or her user name. A user who had developed a positive reputation over time had a color-coded star symbol displayed next to his or her user name to indicate the amount of positive feedback. The highest ranking a trader could receive was "over 10,000," indicated by a shooting star. Well-respected high-volume traders could have rankings well into the thousands. Users who received a sufficiently negative net feedback rating (typically a –4) had their registrations suspended and were thus unable to bid on or list items for sale. eBay users could review a person's feedback profile before deciding to bid on an item listed by that person or before choosing payment and delivery methods.

The terms of eBay's user agreement prohibited actions that would undermine the integrity of the Feedback Forum, such as leaving positive feedback about oneself through other accounts or leaving multiple negative comments about someone else through other accounts. eBay's Feedback Forum system had several automated features designed to detect and prevent some forms of abuse. For example, feedback posted from the same account, positive or negative, could not affect a user's net feedback rating by more than one point, no matter how many comments an individual made. Furthermore, a user could only make comments about his or her trading partners in completed transactions. The company believed its Feedback Forum was extremely useful in overcoming users' initial hesitancy about trading over the Internet, since it reduced the uncertainty of dealing with an unknown trading partner.

eBay's Strategy to Sustain Its Market Dominance

Meg Whitman assumed the helm of eBay in February 1998 and began acting as the public face of the company. Pierre Omidyar stepped back to become chairman of eBay's board of directors and focused his time and energy on overseeing eBay's strategic direction and growth, business model and site development, and community advocacy. Jeff Skoll, who became the vice president of strategic planning and analysis, concentrated on competitive analysis, new business planning and incubation, the development of the organization's overall strategic direction, and supervision of customer support operations.

The Move to Go Public   Within months of assuming the presidency of eBay, Whitman took on the challenge of preparing the company to raise capital for expansion through an initial public offering (IPO) of common stock. Through a series of road shows designed to convince investors of the potential of eBay's business model, Whitman and her team generated significant interest in eBay's IPO. When the shares opened for trading on September 24, 1998, eBay's executives had high hopes for the offering, but none of them dreamed that it would close the day at $47, or 160 percent over the initial offering of $18 per share. The IPO generated $66 million in new capital for the company and was so successful that *Bloomberg Personal* magazine designated eBay as the "Hot IPO of 1998"; *Euromoney* magazine named eBay as the best IPO in the U.S. market in January 1999. The success of the September 1998 offering led eBay to issue a follow-up offering in April 1999 that raised an additional $600 million. As a qualification to the IPOs, eBay's board of directors retained the right to issue as many as 5 million additional shares of preferred stock with no further input from the current shareholders in case of a hostile takeover attempt.

With the funds received from the IPOs, eBay launched strategic initiatives aimed at six specific objectives:[13]

1. Growing the eBay community and strengthening our brand, both to attract new members and to maintain the vitality of the eBay community;
2. Broadening the company's trading platform by growing existing product categories, promoting new product categories, and offering services for specific regions;

3. Fostering eBay community affinity and increasing community trust and safety through services such as user verification and insurance;

4. Enhancing Web site features and functionality through the introduction of personalization features such as About Me, which permits users to create their own home page free of charge, and the Gallery, an opportunity for sellers to showcase their items as pictures in a photo catalog;

5. Expanding pre- and post-trade value-added services, such as assistance with scanning and uploading photographs of listed items, third-party escrow services, and arrangements to make shipping of purchased items easier;

6. Developing international markets by actively marketing and promoting our Web site in selected countries.

To pursue these objectives, eBay employed three main competitive tactics. First, it sought to build strategic partnerships in all stages of its value chain, creating an impressive portfolio of over 250 strategic alliances with companies such as America Online (AOL), Yahoo!, Lycos, Compaq, and Warner Brothers. Second, it actively sought customer feedback and made improvements based on this information. Third, it actively monitored the external environment for developing opportunities.

eBay's Business Model   eBay's business model was based on creating and maintaining a person-to-person trading community where buyers and sellers could readily and conveniently exchange information and goods. eBay's role was to function as a value-added facilitator of online buyer-seller transactions by providing a supportive infrastructure that enabled buyers and sellers to come together in an efficient and effective manner. Success depended not only on the quality of eBay's infrastructure but also on the quality and quantity of buyers and sellers attracted to the site. In management's view, this entailed maintaining a compelling trading environment, a number of trust and safety programs, a cost-effective and convenient trading experience, and strong community affinity. By developing the eBay brand name and increasing the customer base, eBay endeavored to attract a sufficient number of high-quality buyers and sellers necessary to meet the organization's goals. The online auction format meant that eBay carried zero inventory and could operate a marketplace without the need for a traditional sales force.

Growing the eBay Community and Strengthening the Brand   In developing the eBay brand name and attracting new users, the company initially relied largely on word-of-mouth advertising, supplemented by public relations initiatives such as executive interviews and speaking engagements, special online events, and astute management of the public press. Then, with funds from the public offerings of common stock, eBay expanded its marketing activities to include advertising online as well as in traditional media, such as national magazines like *Parade, People, Entertainment Weekly, Newsweek,* and *Sports Illustrated.* A cornerstone of the strategy to increase eBay's exposure was the formation of alliances with a variety of partners, including Kinko's, First Auction, and Z Auction as well as Internet portals AOL, Netscape, and GO.com.

The Alliance with First Auction   In January 1998, eBay entered into a marketing agreement with First Auction, the auction division of the Internet Shopping Network. The terms of this agreement allowed both companies to advertise their services on each other's sites. While both organizations offered online auctions, eBay featured person-to-person trading, and First Auction engaged in business-to-consumer transactions, which eBay did not consider direct competition. A similar agreement was formed in February 1998 with Z Auction, another vendor-based auction site.

The Alliance with America Online   eBay's initial alliance with AOL, announced in February 1998, was limited to eBay's providing a person-to-person online auction service in AOL's classifieds section. However, in September 1998 this agreement was expanded. In return for $12 million in payments over three years, AOL made eBay the preferred provider of personal trading services to AOL's 13 million members and the 2 million members of AOL's affiliate CompuServe. In 1998 eBay also became a "distinguished partner" of Netscape's Netcenter. In February 1999 eBay's relationship with Netscape was broadened to include banner ads and bookmarks. In March 1999 eBay's arrangement with AOL was expanded to feature eBay as the preferred provider of personal trading services on all of AOL's proprietary services, including Digital Cities, ICQ, CompuServe (both international and domestic), Netscape, and AOL.com. In return for this four-year arrangement, eBay agreed to pay CompuServe $75 million and to develop a co-branded version of its services for each of AOL's properties involved in the agreement, with AOL receiving all of the advertising revenues from these co-branded sites.[14]

The Alliance with Kinko's   In February 2000 eBay formed strategic marketing agreements with Kinko's, a global retail provider of document copying and business services, and GO.com, the Internet arm of Walt Disney Company. eBay's alliance with Kinko's allowed eBay to place signage in Kinko's stores across the country, and to offer its users 15 minutes of free computing rental at Kinko's locations. In return, eBay featured Web links to Kinko's Web pages in eBay's Computer, Business/Office, and Big Ticket categories, and encouraged users to go to Kinko's for photo scanning, e-mail, document faxing, and teleconferencing services.

The Alliance with GO.com   The long-term intention for the cooperative agreement with GO.com was for eBay to eventually become the exclusive online trading service across all of Disney's Internet properties. In the initial stages of the agreement, however, eBay was only to market and develop co-branded person-to-person and merchant-to-person sites on behalf of the Walt Disney Company.[15]

Broadening the Trading Platform   Efforts intended to broaden the eBay trading platform concentrated on growing the content within current categories, on broadening the range of products offered according to user preferences, and on developing regionally targeted offerings. Growth in existing product categories was facilitated by deepening the content within the categories through the use of content-specific chat rooms and bulletin boards as well as targeted advertising at trade shows and in industry-specific publications. Further, in April 1998, custom home pages were created for each category so collectors could search for their next treasured acquisition without having to sort through the entirety of eBay's offerings.

In June 1999 eBay formed a collaborative relationship with the Collecting Channel, a portal owned by Channel-Space Entertainment, Inc. The Collecting Channel was a premier Internet information source for virtually every conceivable category of collectibles. It delivered content in media ranging from original audio/video programming to live chats to live videoconferencing. eBay's agreement called for The Collecting Channel to provide in-depth content to eBay collectors and for eBay, in return, to provide links to The Collecting Channel's Web site.

Part of eBay's strategy to broaden its user base was to establish regional auctions. In 1999 eBay launched 53 regional auction sites focused on the 50 largest metropolitan areas in the United States. Management believed that having regional auction sites would encourage the sale of items that were prohibitively expensive to ship, items that tended to have only a local appeal, and items that people preferred to view before purchasing. eBay had also done several promotional or feature auctions, partnering with Guernsey to sell home-run balls hit by baseball stars Mark McGwire and Sammy Sosa in their 1998 home-run race and partnering with BMW in 1999 to auction and deliver the first BMW X5 sports activity vehicle, with the proceeds going to the Susan G. Komen Breast Cancer Foundation.

Additional efforts to broaden the trading platform involved the development of new product categories. Over 2,000 new categories were added between 1998 and 2000, bringing the total to 3,000 categories (greatly expanded from the original 10 categories in 1995). One of the most significant new categories was eBay Great Collections, a showcasing of rare collectibles such as coins, stamps, jewelry, and timepieces as well as fine art and antiques from leading auction houses around the world. This category came from eBay's April 1999 acquisition of Butterfield and Butterfield, one of the world's largest and most prestigious auction houses.

The growing popularity of automobile trading on the eBay Web site prompted the creation of a special automotive category supported by Kruse International, one of the world's most respected organizations for automobile collectors. The automotive category was further expanded in March 2000 through a partnership with AutoTrader.com, the world's largest used-car marketplace, that established a co-branded auction site for consumers and dealers to buy and sell used cars.

Fostering eBay Community Affinity and Building Trust   Since its founding in 1995, eBay had considered developing a loyal, vivacious trading community to be a cornerstone of its business model. To foster a sense of community among eBay users, the company employed tools and tactics designed to promote both business and personal interactions between consumers, to foster trust between bidders and sellers, and to instill a sense of security among traders.

Interactions between community members were facilitated through the creation of chat rooms based on personal interests. These chat rooms allowed individuals to learn about their chosen collectibles and to exchange information about items they collected. To manage the flow of information in the chat rooms, eBay employees went to trade shows and conventions to seek out individuals who had both knowledge about and a passion for either a specific collectible or a category of goods. These enthusiasts would act as community leaders or ambassadors; they were never referred to as employees but were compensated $1,000 a month to host online discussions with experts.

Although personal communication between members fostered a sense of community, as eBay's community grew from "the size of a small village to a large city"[16] additional measures were necessary to ensure a continued sense of trust and honesty among users. One of eBay's earliest trust-building efforts was the 1996 creation of the Feedback Forum, described earlier.

Unfortunately, the Feedback Forum was not always sufficient to ensure honesty and integrity among traders. While eBay estimated that far less than 1 percent of the millions of auctions completed on the site involved some sort of fraud or illegal activity, some users would agree with Clay Monroe, a Seattle-area trader of computer equipment, who estimated that while "ninety percent of the time everybody is on the up and up . . . ten percent of the time you get some jerk who wants to cheat you."[17] Fraudulent or illegal acts perpetrated by sellers included misrepresentation of goods; trading in counterfeit goods or pirated goods that infringed on others' intellectual property rights; failure to deliver goods paid for by buyers; and shill bidding, whereby sellers would use a false bidder to artificially drive up the price of a good. Buyers could manipulate bids by placing an unrealistically high bid on a good to discourage other bidders and then withdraw their bid at the last moment to allow an ally to win the auction at a bargain price. Buyers could also fail to deliver payment on a completed auction.

Recognizing that fraudulent activities represented a significant danger to eBay's future, management took the Feedback Forum a step further in 1998 by launching the SafeHarbor program to provide guidelines for trade, provide information to help resolve user disputes, and respond to reports of misuse of the eBay service.[18] The SafeHarbor initiative was expanded in 1999 to provide additional safeguards and to actively work with law enforcement agencies and members of the trading community to make eBay more secure. New elements of SafeHarbor included free insurance, with a $25.00 deductible, through Lloyd's of London for transactions under $200.00; enhancements to the Feedback Forum; a new class of verified eBay users with an accompanying icon; easy access to escrow services; tougher policies relating to nonpaying bidders and shill bidders; clarification of which items were not permissible to list for sale; and a strengthened anti-piracy and anti-infringement program. The use of verified buyer and seller accounts was viewed as especially significant because it allowed eBay to ensure that suspended users did not open new eBay accounts under different names. User information was verified through Atlanta-based Equifax Inc.

To implement these new initiatives between 1999 and 2000, eBay increased the number of positions in its Safe-Harbor department from 24 to 182, including full-time employees and independent contractors. It also organized the department around the functions of investigations, community watch, and fraud prevention. The investigations group was responsible for examining reported trading violations and possible misuses of eBay. The fraud-prevention group mediated customer disputes over such things as the quality of the goods sold. If a written complaint of fraud was filed against a user, eBay generally suspended the alleged offender's account, pending an investigation. The community watch group worked with over 100 industry-leading companies, ranging from software publishers to toy manufactures to apparel makers, to protect intellectual property rights. To ensure that illegal items were not being sold and sale items listed did not violate intellectual property rights, this SafeHarbor group automated daily keyword searches on auction content. Offending auctions were closed and the seller was notified of the violation. Repeated violations resulted in suspension of the seller's account.

As eBay expanded its categories to include Great Collections and the new automobile categories, new safeguards were introduced to meet the unique needs of these areas. In the eBay Great Collections category, the company partnered with Collector's Universe to offer authentication and grading services for specific products such as trading cards, coins, and autographs. In the automobile area, eBay partnered with carclub.com to provide users with access to carclub.com's inspection and warranty service.

Enhancing Web Site Features and Functionality

In designing its Web site, eBay went to great lengths to make it intuitive, easy to use by both buyers and sellers, and reliable. Efforts to ensure ease of use ranged from narrowly defining categories (to allow users to quickly locate desired products) to introducing services designed to personalize a user's eBay experience. Two specific services developed by eBay to increase personalization were "My eBay" and "About Me."

My eBay was launched in May 1998 to give users centralized access to confidential, current information regarding their trading activities. From his or her My eBay page a user could view information pertaining to his or her current account balances with eBay; feedback rating; the status of any auctions in which he or she was participating, as either a buyer or a seller; and auctions in favorite categories. In October of the same year, eBay introduced the About Me service, which allowed users to create customized home pages that could be viewed by all other eBay members. These pages could include elements from the My eBay page such as user ratings or items the user had listed for auction, as well as personal information and pictures. This service not only increased customer ease of use but also contributed to the sense of community among the traders; one seller stated that the About Me service "made it easier and more rewarding for me to do business with others."[19]

When eBay first initiated service, the only computer resource it had was a single Sun Microsystems setup with no backup capabilities. By 1999 eBay's explosive growth required 200 Windows NT servers and a Sun Microsystems server to manage the flow of users on the site, process new members, accept bids, and manage the huge database containing the list of all items sold on the site. On June 10, 1999, the strain of managing these processes while attempting to integrate new product and service offerings proved too much for the system and the eBay site crashed. It stayed down for 22 hours. The outage not only seriously shook user confidence in eBay's reliability but also cost the company some $4 million in fees; the company's stock price reacted to the outage by falling from $180 to $136.[20]

Unfortunately, the June 10 site crash proved to be the first in a string of outages. While none of them was as significant as the first (most lasted only one to four hours), confidence in eBay continued to decline in both the online community and on Wall Street as eBay's stock fell to $87^{11}/_{16}$ in August 1999. To counter these problems, eBay sought out Maynard Webb, a premier software engineer and troubleshooter who was working at Gateway Computer.

Webb put a moratorium on new features until system stability was restored. Webb believed that it was virtually impossible to completely eliminate outages, so he set a goal of reducing system downtime and limiting outages to one hour.[21] To achieve this goal Webb believed he would need a backup for the 200 Windows NT servers, another for the Sun Microsystems unit, and a better system for managing communications between the Windows NT and Sun systems. In attacking these challenges, eBay acquired seven new Sun servers, each valued at $1 million, and outsourced its technology and Web site operations to Exodus Communications and Abovenet. These outsourcing agreements were intended to allow Exodus and Abovenet to "manage network capacity and provide a more robust backbone" while eBay focused on its core business.[22] While eBay still experienced minor outages when it changed or expanded services (for example, a system crash coincided with the introduction of the 22 regional Web sites), system downtime decreased. However, the stability of the system under eBay's explosive growth and continuous introduction of new features and services was a major and continuing management concern.

Expanding Value-Added Services   To make it easier for eBay's sellers and buyers to transact business, in 1998 the company announced that it would offer an "'end-to-end' person-to-person trading service . . . [by providing] a variety of pre- and post-trade services to enhance the user experience."[23] Pre-trade services that eBay planned to offer included authentication and appraisal services, while planned post-trade services included third-party escrow services as well as shipping and payment services.

In preparation for Christmas 1998, eBay formed alliances with Parcel Plus, a leading shipping service, and with Tradesafe and I-Escrow, both of which guaranteed that buyers would get what they paid for. According to eBay's agreement with I-Escrow, monies paid to the seller were held in an escrow account until the buyer received and approved the merchandise. eBay's arrangement with Tradesafe called for the seller to register a credit card with Tradesafe to guarantee funds up to $1,200; proceeds of a sale were deposited directly into the seller's bank account. If the buyer was not satisfied with the transaction, all or part of the money was refunded. Both I-Escrow and Tradesafe charged a small percentage of the purchase price for their services.

In April 1999, eBay entered into a five-year partnership with Mail Boxes, Etc. (the world's largest franchiser of retail business, communications, and postal service centers), and iShip.com (the leader in multicarrier Web-based shipping services for e-commerce) to offer person-to-person e-commerce shipping solutions.[24] eBay's agreement with iShip gave eBay users access to accurate zip-code-to-zip-code shipping rates with various shipping services and allowed users to track packages. The agreement with Mail Boxes, Etc. (MBE), required eBay to promote MBE's retail locations as a place where sellers could pack and ship their

goods; eBay and MBE were contemplating expanding their agreement to allow buyers to open and inspect their newly purchased goods at MBE retail stores prior to accepting the shipment.

To facilitate person-to-person credit card payments, eBay acquired Billpoint, a company that specialized in transferring money from one cardholder to another. Using the newly acquired capabilities of Billpoint, eBay was able to offer sellers the option of accepting credit card payments from other eBay users; for this service, eBay charged sellers a small percentage of the transaction. eBay's objective was to make credit card payment a "seamless and integrated part of the trading experience."[25] In March 2000 eBay and Wells Fargo, the owner-operator of the largest Internet bank, entered into an arrangement whereby Wells Fargo would purchase a minority stake in Billpoint and Billpoint would use Wells Fargo's extensive customer care and payment processing infrastructure to process credit card payments from eBay buyers to eBay sellers.

In January 2000, eBay entered into an exclusive agreement with E-Stamp that allowed E-Stamp to become the exclusive provider of Internet postage from the U.S. Postal Service on eBay's Web site. In return for being prominently featured on eBay's Web site, E-Stamp gave eBay users easy access to its Web site, offered them reduced fees for its service, and gave them a significant discount on the E-Stamp Internet postage starter kit. According to sources close to the deal, E-Stamp paid eBay close to $10 million a year for gaining such access to eBay's customers.[26]

Developing International Markets   As competition increased in the online auction industry, eBay began to seek growth opportunities in international markets in an effort to create a global trading community. While international buyers and sellers had been trading on eBay for some time, there were no facilities designed especially for the needs of these community members. In entering international markets, eBay considered three options. It could build a new user community from the ground up, acquire a local organization, or form a partnership with a strong local company. In realizing its goals of international growth, eBay employed all three strategies.

In late 1998 eBay's initial efforts at international expansion into Canada and the United Kingdom relied on building new user communities. The first step in establishing these communities was creating customized home pages for users in those countries. These home pages were designed to provide content and categories locally customized to the needs of users in specific countries, while providing them with access to a global trading community. Local customization in the United Kingdom was facilitated through the use of local management, grassroots and online marketing, and participation in local events.[27]

In February 1999 eBay partnered with PBL Online, a leading Internet company in Australia, to offer a customized Australian and New Zealand eBay home page. When the site went live in October 1999, transactions were denominated in Australian dollars and, while buyers could bid on auctions anywhere in the world, they could also search for items located exclusively in Australia. Further, local chat boards were designed to facilitate interaction between Australian users; country-specific categories, such as Australian coins and stamps as well as cricket and rugby memorabilia, were offered.

To further expand its global reach, eBay acquired Germany's largest online person-to-person trading site, alando.de AG, in June 1999. eBay's management handled the transition of service in a manner calculated to be smooth and painless for alando.de AG's users. While users would have to comply with eBay rules and regulations, the only significant change for alando.de AG's 50,000 registered users was that they would have to go to a new URL to transact their business.

To establish an Asian presence, in February 2000 eBay formed a joint venture with NEC to launch eBay Japan. According to the new CEO of eBay Japan, Merle Okawara, an internationally renowned executive, NEC was pleased to help eBay in leveraging the tried-and-trusted eBay business model to provide Japanese consumers with access to a global community of active online buyers and sellers. In customizing the site to the needs of Japanese users, eBay wrote the content exclusively in Japanese and allowed users to bid in yen. The site had over 800 categories ranging from internationally popular categories (such as computers, electronics, and Asian antiques) to categories with a local flavor (such as Hello Kitty, Pokémon, and pottery). The eBay Japan site also debuted a new merchant-to-person concept known as Supershops, which allowed consumers to bid on items listed by companies.

Honors and Awards   As a result of the relentless implementation of its business model, eBay had met with significant success. Not only was the company financially profitable from its first days (see again Exhibits 3 and 4), but it had won many prestigious honors and awards in 1998 and 1999. Among the most significant were Best Internet Auction Site (*San Francisco Bay Guardian,* July 1998); Electronic Commerce Excellence (CommerceNet, October 1998); Top e-Commerce Program/Service (Computer Currents Readers' Choice Awards, February 1999); Editor's Choice Award (*PC* magazine, March 1999), and Top 50 CEOs (*Worth* magazine, May 1999).

How eBay's Auction Site Compared with That of Rivals

Auction sites varied in a number of respects: site design and ease of use, the range of items up for auction, number of simultaneous auctions, duration of the bidding process, and fees. Gomez Advisors, a company designed to help Internet users select which online enterprises to do business with, had developed rankings for the leading online auction sites as a basis for recommending which sites were best for bargain hunters, hobbyists/collectors, and sellers. To be considered in the Gomez ratings, an auction site had to (1) have more than 500 lots of original content; (2) conduct auctions for items in at least three of the following six categories: collectibles, computers/electronics, jewelry, sports, stamps/coins, and toys; (3) have more than five lots in each qualifying category; and (4) have sustained bidding activity in each category. Exhibit 5 shows the winter 1999 Gomez ratings of online auction competitors—the latest ratings can be viewed at www.gomez.com.

eBay's Main Competitors

In the broadest sense, eBay competed with classified advertisements in newspapers, garage sales, flea markets, collectibles shows, and other venues such as local auction houses and liquidators. As eBay's product mix broadened beyond collectibles to include practical household items, office equipment, toys, and so on, the company's competitors broadened to include brick-and-mortar retailers, import/export companies, and catalog and mail order companies. Management saw these traditional competitors as inefficient because their fragmented local and regional nature made it expensive and time-consuming for buyers and sellers to meet, exchange information, and complete transactions. Moreover, they suffered from three other deficiencies: (1) they tended to offer limited variety and breadth of selection as compared to the millions of items available on eBay, (2) they often had high transactions costs, and (3) they were "information inefficient" in the sense that buyers and sellers lacked a reliable and convenient means of setting prices for sales or purchases. Thus, eBay's management saw its online auction format as competitively superior to these rivals because it (1) facilitated buyers and sellers meeting, exchanging information, and conducting transactions; (2) allowed buyers and sellers to bypass traditional intermediaries and trade directly, thus lowering costs; (3) provided global reach, greater selection, and a broader base of participants; (4) permitted trading at all hours and provided continuously updated information; and (5) fostered a sense of community among individuals with mutual interests.

From an e-commerce perspective, Amazon.com and Yahoo! Auctions had emerged as eBay's main competitors going into 2000, but FairMarket, AuctionWatch, GO Network Auctions, and Auctions.com were beginning to make market inroads and contribute to erosion of eBay's share of the online auction business. Moreover, the prospects of attractive profitability and low barriers to entry were stimulating more firms to enter the online

Exhibit 5   Comparative Gomez Advisors' Ratings of Leading Online Auction Sites

A. Ratings Based on Site Characteristics (Rating scale: 0 = lowest; 10 = highest)

Auction Site	Ease of Use[a]	Customer Confidence[b]	On-Site Resources[c]	Relationship Services[d]	Overall Score
1. eBay	9.07	6.99	8.40	8.40	7.97
2. Amazon.com	9.05	8.49	7.03	6.17	7.67
3. Yahoo! Auctions	8.69	6.91	4.18	8.62	7.11
4. GO Network Auctions	9.14	7.44	6.49	5.89	7.00
5. FairMarket Network	7.97	6.89	6.73	5.17	6.42
6. Auctions.com	8.22	6.78	5.50	5.10	6.41
7. utrade	8.87	4.60	2.43	6.57	5.65
8. Boxlot	7.20	7.83	3.19	4.09	5.63
9. Haggle Online	7.62	4.65	4.80	4.72	5.29
10. edeal	8.05	4.04	2.35	5.83	5.17
11. ehammer	7.59	5.35	4.21	3.15	5.09

[a]Based on such factors as screen layout, tightly integrated content, functionality, useful demos, and the extensiveness of online help.

[b]Includes the reliability and security of the online auction site, knowledgeable and accessible customer service, and quality guarantees.

[c]Based on the range of products, services, and information offered, information look-up tools, and transactions data.

[d]Based on personalization options, programs, and perks that build a sense of community and customer loyalty to the site.

B. Ratings Based on Type of Auction Site User (Rating scale: 0 = lowest; 10 = highest)*

Auction Site	Bargain Hunters	Hobbyists/Collectors	Sellers
1. eBay	8.43	7.98	7.94
2. Amazon.com	7.46	7.71	6.87
3. Yahoo! Auctions	7.37	6.67	6.96
4. GO Network Auctions	6.84	6.72	6.54
5. FairMarket Network	6.16	6.44	6.10
6. Auctions.com	5.94	6.31	5.47
7. utrade	5.65	5.01	5.34
8. edeal	5.61	4.83	4.89
9. ehammer	5.05	5.27	4.60
10. Haggle Online	5.00	4.88	5.07
11. Boxlot	4.79	5.57	4.57

*Each of the four criteria in part A above were weighted according to their perceived importance to bargain hunters, hobbyists/collectors, and sellers. These criteria were then averaged together to develop a score for each of the three types of on-line auction site users.

Source: Gomez Advisors, www.gomez.com, March 2, 2000.

auction industry and imitate eBay's business model. eBay management saw competition in the online auction industry as revolving around 9 factors: the volume and selection of goods, the population of buyers and sellers, community interaction, customer service, reliability of delivery and payment by users, brand image, Web site construction, fees and prices, and quality of search tools.

Exhibit 6 provides selected statistics for the leading competitors in the online auction market. Exhibit 7 provides comparative financial data, and Exhibit 8 provides comparative Web site traffic.

Exhibit 6   Selected Auction Statistics for eBay, Amazon, and Yahoo!, December 1999

	eBay	Yahoo! Auctions	Amazon.com
Number of items listed for auction	3.8 million	1.3 million	415,000
Percentage of listed auctions closing with a sale	65%	14%	11%
Average number of bids per item	3.03	0.59	0.33
Average selling price for completed auctions	$65.19	$31.09	$25.77

Source: Taken from "Internet: eBay: Crushing the Competition," *Individual Investor,* January 21, 2000.

Exhibit 7   Comparative 1999 Financial Statistics for eBay, Amazon, and Yahoo!*

	eBay	Amazon.com	Yahoo.com
Net revenues	$224,724,000	$1,639,839,000	$588,608,000
Cost of goods sold	57,588,000	1,349,194,000	92,334,000
Net income	10,828,000	(719,968,000)	61,133,000
Net income per share	$0.04	$(2.20)	$0.20

*Includes all business areas for Amazon.com and Yahoo!, not just online auctions.

Source: 1999 company financial statements.

Exhibit 8   Number of Unique Visitors during December 1999

Web Site	Total Number of Unique Visitors
Yahoo! sites	42,361,000
GO Network	21,348,000
Amazon.com	16,631,000
eBay.com	10,388,000

Source: www.mediametrix.com.

Exhibit 9   Amazon.com's Losses

Year	Net Loss
1996	$ 6.2 million
1997	31.0 million
1998	124.5 million
1999	720.0 million

Amazon.com   At the end of 1999, Gomez.com ranked Amazon.com as the second best online auction Web site. Amazon.com, created in July 1995 as an online bookseller, had rapidly turned into a full-line, one-stop-shopping retailer with a product offering that included books, music, toys, electronics, tools and hardware, lawn and patio products, video games, software, and a mall of boutiques (called z-shops)—some 18 million items at last count. Amazon.com was the Internet's number one music, video, and book retailer. The company's 1999 revenues of $1.64 billion were up 169 percent over 1998,

but despite the company's rapid revenue growth it was incurring huge losses due to the expenses of (1) establishing an infrastructure to support its sales (the company expanded its worldwide distribution capacity from 300,000 square feet to over 5 million square feet in 1999) and (2) attracting customers via advertising and online (see Exhibit 9).

While Amazon's management was under mounting pressure to control expenses and prove to investors that its business model and strategy were capable of generating good bottom-line profitability, it was clear that management's decisions and strategy were focused on the long term and on solidifying Amazon's current position as a market leader. Management believed that its business model was inherently capital efficient, citing the fact that going into 2000 the company had achieved annualized sales of $2 billion with just $220 million in inventory and $318 million in fixed assets. The company's customer base rose from 6.2 million to 16.9 million during 1999. The company invested more than $300 million in infrastructure in 1999 and opened two international sites: Amazon.co.uk and Amazon.de. These two sites, along with Amazon.com, were the three most popular online retail domains in Europe. Amazon also entered into a number of strategic alliances. During the fourth quarter of 1999 and the first month of 2000, the company announced partnerships with NextCard, Ashford.com, Greenlight.com, Audible, and living.com, as well as an expanded partnership with drugstore.com. It already had e-commerce partnerships with Gear.com; Homegrocer.com; Della.com (an online service for gift registry, gift advice, and personalized gift suggestions); Pets.com; and Sotheby's (a leading auction house for art, antiques, and collectibles).

With its customer base of almost 17 million users in over 150 countries and a very well-known brand name, Amazon.com was considered an imposing competitive threat to eBay. Amazon.com launched its online auction site in March 1999. The site charged sellers for listing their products and also charged a commission on sales. Although Amazon's selection of auctions did not match the one offered by eBay, the company reported that online auctions were the fastest-growing part of its business. The number of auctions on Amazon grew from 140,000 to 415,000 during the second half of 1999. Amazon.com offered three major marketplaces for its users: auctions, zShops, and sothebys.amazon.com. Its auction site formed partnerships with DreamWorks to promote that company's films *Stuart Little* and *American Beauty* (72 auctions, averaging 27 bids per auction, total gross merchandise sales of over $25,000, yielding an average of over $400 per item) and with television celebrity Oprah Winfrey (25 auctions, averaging 38 bids per auction, total gross merchandise sales of over $130,000, yielding an average of over $6,000 per item).[28]

Yahoo! Auctions Yahoo.com, the first online navigational guide to the Web, launched Yahoo! Auctions in 1997. Yahoo.com offered services to nearly 120 million users every month and the Yahoo! Network operated in North America, Europe, Asia, and Latin America. Yahoo! reported net revenues of $588 million in 1999 (up 140 percent from 1998) and net income of $142 million. Yahoo's user base grew from 60 million to 120 million during 1999, and 40 million of these users were outside the United States. In December 1999, Yahoo's traffic increased to an average of 465 million page views per day. Yahoo! had entered into numerous alliances and marketing agreements to generate additional site traffic and was investing in new technology to improve the site's performance and attractiveness.

Its auction services were provided to users free of charge, and the number of auctions listed on Yahoo! increased from 670,000 to 1.3 million during the second half of 1999. Yahoo! Auctions was expanded to include Hong Kong, Taiwan, Korea, Mexico, Brazil, and Denmark at the end of 1999. Localized Yahoo! auctions outside the United States were being conducted in 16 countries in 11 different languages. Yahoo! Japan Auctions was the largest localized online auction service in Japan. At the end of 1999, Yahoo! launched Yahoo! Merchant Auctions and Featured Auctions in order to allow retailers and sellers to promote their auctions. Yahoo! Auctions also offered many extra services to its users. Gomez.com rated Yahoo! Auctions as the number one online auction site in the Relationship Services category.

FairMarket FairMarket, a new online auction provider that went online in September 1999, had quickly emerged as one of the leading providers of private-label, outsourced, networked auction services for business clients. It offered a number of formats: hosted auctions, fixed-price auctions, declining-price or markdown auctions for merchants wishing to dispose of overstocked merchandise, and shopping-by-request services. The company was formed through an alliance of Microsoft, Dell Computer, Lycos, Excite, CBS Sportsline, CompUSA, and several others. The FairMarket network of auctions included Alta Vista Auctions, CityAuction, Excite Auctions, GO Auction, Lycos Auctions, and MSN Auctions. The company went public in early 2000, raising approximately $75 million to support expansion.

FairMarket managed and maintained online auctions for such customers as JCPenney (which had auctions that allowed customers to purchase new, quality merchandise and auctions that incorporated an automatic markdown format for overstocked merchandise from JCPenney retail store and catalog operations); the Times Digital Company (which conducted local auctions in New York City and other locations); Dell Computer (which held auctions for customers wishing to sell their used computers and for equipment coming off lease); Ritz Camera (which used auctions to sell end-of-life camera equipment); Outpost.com (which auctioned a mix of new and refurbished computer and computer accessory items); and SportingAuction (which used FairMarket's network systems to auction an extensive selection of high-quality sporting goods). FairMarket received a percentage fee of all the items sold on auctions it conducted for its customer-sellers.

AuctionWatch   AuctionWatch.com was formed in July 1998 and incorporated in January 1999 as a privately held company backed by several venture capital firms and private investors. The company, a very small online auction site originally, had raised $10 million in capital in August 1999 to expand both its site and its available features. The AuctionWatch site was designed to model eBay and had many of the same types of offerings. By the end of 1999, AuctionWatch.com was conducting over 25,000 auctions daily, had served over 2 million auction images per day, and received over 20,000 posts each month in its visitor center. AuctionWatch catered to businesses looking to use online auctions as a new distribution channel and to attract new customers. One of the unique features at Auction-Watch was a content service that allowed users to compare and contrast the fee structures of the top consumer-to-consumer, business-to-consumer, and business-to-business auction sites; the information was updated monthly.

As of April 2000, AuctionWatch had over 250,000 registered users and was conducting about 1 million auctions monthly. AuctionWatch attracted 1.7 million unique visitors in March 2000, an increase of over 100 percent from February and over 500 percent from December 1999. In the first quarter of 2000, businesses and auction enthusiasts used AuctionWatch to sell over $120 million worth of merchandise.

GO Network Auctions   GO.com was the result of a November 1999 merger between Walt Disney's online unit, the Buena Vista Internet Group (BVIG), and Infoseek Corporation. The company oversaw ABC.com, ESPN.com, and Disney.com, as well as several other popular Web sites; its chief activity was serving as the Internet business arm of the Walt Disney Company. The GO.com portal focused on entertainment, leisure, and recreation activities. The online auction section of the GO Network, auction.go.com, was experiencing rapid growth. GO Network Auctions offered over 100 product categories and provided users with a guarantee against fraudulent listings; one of its main features was auctioning Disney products, including movie sets, props, and memorabilia from movies produced by Walt Disney Studios and from ABC-produced shows. The Web site was also considered extremely easy to navigate. Gomez.com ranked GO Network Auctions number one in the Ease of Use category among online auctions.

In February 2000 GO.com and eBay announced a four-year agreement to develop and market online trading and auction experiences in a co-branded person-to-person site and new merchant-to-person sites. According to terms of the agreement, eBay would ultimately become the online trading and auction service for all of Disney's Internet properties, including the GO Network portal, and would collaborate on merchant-to-person auctions for authenticated products, props, and memorabilia from throughout the Walt Disney Company.

Auctions.com   Auctions.com was originally launched as Auction Universe in November 1997. After being acquired by Classified Ventures in 1998, the site was relaunched as Auctions.com on December 13, 1999. The company claimed to be "the world's fastest growing online auction network" at the beginning of 2000.[29] Auctions.com had hundreds of categories and several thousand product listings available for users. Not only did the company's Web site offer 24-hour customer service support, but it also had the premier online transaction security program (Bid$afe). The Federal Trade Commission claimed that Bid$afe was one of the "best fraud protection programs on the Web."[30]

Formed in 1997 and headquartered in London, QXL.com was moving rapidly to try to dominate the online auction market in Europe. Rather than create one Web site for Europe, QXL's strategy was to methodically enter one European country after another, launching its own new sites in some countries and acquiring already established players in others. While QXL was thinking globally, it was acting locally, operating in 12 different languages, accommodating 12 different currencies (until use of the euro), and tailoring its merchandise features to the preferences of users in each country. QXL's market reach included Great Britain, Germany, France, Italy, Spain, the Netherlands, Denmark, Finland, Poland, Norway, and Sweden. QXL was developing technology so that it could quickly and economically customize its sites for each country. Currently, however, its sites were slow and antiquated compared to eBay.

In 2000, the online aution market in Europe was much less developed than in the United States; there were not as many Internet users and many European Web surfers were leery of entering bids to purchase an item online. To combat the wariness of online auctions exhibited by actual and prospective visitors to its online auction site, QXL was conducting a number of auctions for goods put up for sale by retail merchants. QXL management reasoned that site visitors who were reluctant to buy items from a stranger would feel comfortable enough to enter bids to buy merchandise from an established retailer.

Niche Auctions

Many new competitors had also begun offering auctions targeted at smaller segments of the online auction industry. These auctions primarily specialized in one product or service type, such as computers/electronics, fine art, industrial products, music-related goods, international auctions, and just about any other product or service imaginable. There were sites offering laptop computers (AuctionLaptops.com), guitars (Guitarauction.com), German wines (Koppe and Partner Wine Auctions), and even a site that auctioned nothing but racing pigeons (ipigeon. com). There were several significant companies conducting niche auctions:

- **Outpost.com**—Outpost.com was founded in 1995 to service primarily the small-office/home-office market. By the end of 1999, the company offered over 170,000 products online, primarily in the computer/electronics area. Bizrate.com rated Outpost.com the number one consumer shopping experience on the Web, and Forrester Research awarded the company the 1999 number one PowerRanking for Computing. The company had a half million customers and 4 million monthly visitors. In 2000, the company announced separate partnerships with Golf Galaxy and Computer.com. Outpost claimed to differentiate itself from other online auction sites "by focusing on the needs of the customer and delivering its services with reliability, fully encrypted secure servers, depth of product selection, and building a team of dedicated and knowledgeable professionals that support all efforts of the business."[31]

- **eWanted.com**—eWanted.com pioneered the idea of the "backward auction" in October 1998. A backward auction was the exact opposite of a traditional online auction. Buyers would place ads specifying the item they wanted, as well as the product's primary characteristics. Then sellers would browse these ads and submit offers to the buyers. The theory was that sellers would compete with each other for a particular buyer, thus driving the auction price down. In return, sellers entered a marketplace where they knew that buyers existed for their particular product or service.

- **eRock.com**—eRock.com specialized in offering rock-and-roll memorabilia to "serious die-hard fans, collectors, and dealers."[32] The site had 12 different categories of music auctions available, and also offered a chat room for users to talk about their musical interests and links to the Web pages of several popular rock groups.

The Future

As eBay headed into the second quarter of 2000, it was looking for new avenues to expand its services. According to Brian Swette, eBay's chief operating officer, the company was "at the five yard line with its core business."[33] The next driver of the company's growth was expected to be international expansion, followed by business-to-business and automobile and regional sites.[34] Swette predicted that each of these areas could wind up "as large as the core eBay."[35]

In response to the increasing opportunities in the business-to-business auction segment, and the number of small companies trading on eBay, the company developed the eBay Business Exchange in March 2000. To avoid head-on competition with other auction sites in this market segment, eBay was focusing on businesses with fewer than 100 employees. Swette saw Business Exchange as a natural evolution of eBay's business model and expected that larger companies would eventually participate. Specific categories offered in the new eBay Business Exchange included computer hardware, software, electronics, industrial equipment, office equipment, and professional tools.

eBay had recently announced plans to enter France, Europe's third largest online commerce market. eBay management viewed France as critical in capturing the European market. However, well-established competition existed in the French market in the form of QXL.com, the leading British online auctioneer, and the I-Bazar Group, a French-based corporation that had anticipated eBay's arrival in 1998 and purchased the domain name eBay.fr.

While the number of concurrently active eBay auctions soared from approximately 1 million to 4.5 million between 1998 and year-end 1999, from January 2000 to March 2000 the number of auctions was holding at a relatively constant 4.2 to 4.4 million. eBay spokesperson Kevin Pursglove dismissed the flat trend, stating, "Listings are an interesting thing to look at, but sellers are more interested in selling their merchandise."[36] Wall Street analysts, however, saw the lack of growth in the number of auctions as signaling a coming slowdown in eBay's revenue and profit growth and an indication of market share erosion.

Pierre Omidyar folded his newspaper to prepare for a meeting with Meg Whitman and Jeff Skoll to discuss two developing situations. The first topic on the list was to review the possibility of a cross-marketing strategic alliance with competitor Yahoo! to gain broader exposure to Yahoo's broad customer base. Partnering with a competitor that also offered auction services seemed to have pluses and minuses. The second item on the agenda involved the potential of launching storefront operations where eBayers could purchase goods at a fixed price, much like Amazon. As he headed down the hall to the meeting, Pierre recalled a statement that Meg Whitman had made in a recent interview: "I have this philosophy that you really need to do things 100 percent. Better to do 5 things at 100 percent than 10 things at 80 percent. Because the devil in so much of this is in the detail and while we have to move very, very fast, I think you are not well served by moving incredibly rapidly and not doing things that well."[37] Given recent developments, Pierre was forced to wonder if they were operating at 100 percent. Also, if Forrester Research was correct in their recent prediction that the majority of online retailers would be out of business by the end of 2000, would 100 percent be enough?[38] The recent drop in the company's stock price had been troubling (see Exhibit 10), and the company needed to launch strategic initiatives that would sustain rapid growth and get it back on the road to market dominance.

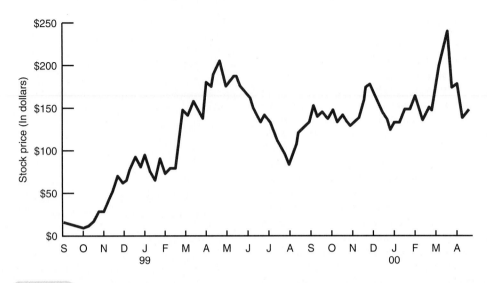

Exhibit 10   eBay's Stock Price Performance, September 1998–April 2000

Endnotes

1. PR Newswire. 2000. Internet consumer segments identified for first time. April 17.
2. Tristram, Claire. 1990. "Amazoning" Amazon. www.contextmag.com, November.
3. www.netaddiction.com, April 16, 2000.
4. Ibid.
5. www.auctionwatch.com, April 16, 2000.
6. tbwt.com/interaction/1pomid/1pomid.htm.
7. Hardy, Quentin. 2000. The radical philanthropist. *Forbes,* May 1: 118.
8. Cohen, Adam. The eBay revolution, www.time.com.
9. Business 2.0. 1999. Billionaires of the Web. *The Candyman,* June.
10. www.ebay.com. Company Overview page.
11. eBay press release, May 7, 1998.
12. Hardy, The radical philanthropist.
13. eBay company S-1 filing with the Securities and Exchange Commission. 1999. March 25: 4.
14. eBay's 1999 10-K report.
15. eBay press release, www.ebay.com, February 8, 2000.
16. Tristram. "Amazoning" Amazon.
17. Buel, Stephen. 1998. eBay Inc. feeling growing pains. *San Jose Mercury News,* December 26.
18. eBay 10-K, filed July 15, 1998.
19. Pearson, Ann. eBay press release, October 15, 1998.
20. Pita, Julia. 1999. Webb master. *Forbes,* December 13.
21. Ibid.
22. eBay press release, October 8, 1999.
23. eBay S-1 report filed July 15, 1998, p. 46.
24. eBay press release, April 8, 1999.
25. eBay press release, May 18, 1999.
26. Weaver, Jane. 2000. eBay: Can it keep customers loyal? www.zdnet.com, May 13.
27. eBay 10-K report filed March 30, 2000.
28. Amazon.com press release, February 2, 2000.
29. Auctions.com, www.auctions.com/backgrounder.asp, April 20, 2000.
30. Ibid.
31. www.outpost.com, Investor Relations, April 20, 2000.
32. www.erock.com, April 20, 2000.
33. The one thing not for sale on eBay, www.thestandard.com, April 20, 2000.
34. Ibid.
35. Ibid.
36. *Barron's Online.* 2000. Auction growth slows at eBay, Can earnings growth be far behind? April 17.
37. *BusinessWeek Online.* 1999. What's behind the boom at eBay? May 21.
38. Forrester.com press release, April 11, 2000.

Case 8   The Best-Laid Incentive Plans*

Hiram Phillips finished tying his bow tie and glanced in the mirror. Frowning, he tugged on the left side, then caught sight of his watch in the mirror. Time to get going. Moments later, he was down the stairs, whistling cheerfully and heading toward the coffeemaker.

"You're in a good mood," his wife said, looking up from the newspaper and smiling. "What's that tune? 'Accentuate the Positive'?"

"Well done!" Hiram called out. "You know, I do believe you're picking up some pop culture in spite of yourself." It was a running joke with them. She was a classically trained cellist and on the board of the local symphony. He was the one with the Sinatra and Bing Crosby albums and the taste for standards. "You're getting better at naming that tune."

"Or else you're getting better at whistling." She looked over her reading glasses and met his eye. They let a beat pass before they said in unison: "Naaah." Then, with a wink, Hiram shrugged on his trench coat, grabbed his travel mug, and went out the door.

Fat and Happy

It was true. Hiram Phillips, CFO and chief administrative officer of Rainbarrel Products, a diversified consumer-durables manufacturer, was in a particularly good mood. He was heading into a breakfast meeting that would bring nothing but good news. Sally Hamilton and Frank Ormondy from Felding & Company would no doubt already be at the office when he arrived and would have with them the all-important numbers—the statistics that would demonstrate the positive results of the performance management system he'd put in place a year ago. Hiram had already seen many of the figures in bits and pieces. He'd retained the consultants to establish baselines on the metrics he wanted to watch and had seen various interim reports from them since. But today's meeting would be the impressive summation capping off a year's worth of effort. Merging into the congestion of Route 45, he thought about the upbeat presentation he would spend the rest of the morning preparing for tomorrow's meeting of the corporate executive council.

It was obvious enough what his introduction should be. He would start at the beginning—or, anyway, his own beginning at Rainbarrel Products a year ago. At the time, the company had just come off a couple of awful quarters.

Harvard Business Review's cases, which are fictional, present common managerial dilemmas and offer concrete solutions from experts.

*Steve Kerr is the chief learning officer at Goldman Sachs in New York. Prior to joining Goldman Sachs in 2001, he spent seven years as the chief learning officer and head of leadership development at General Electric. He was responsible for GE's leadership development center at Crotonville.

It wasn't alone. The sudden slowdown in consumer spending, after a decade-long boom, had taken the whole industry by surprise. But what had quickly become clear was that Rainbarrel was adjusting to the new reality far less rapidly than its biggest competitors.

Keith Randall, CEO of Rainbarrel, was known for being an inspiring leader who focused on innovation. Even outside the industry, he had a name as a marketing visionary. But over the course of the ten-year economic boom, he had allowed his organization to become a little lax.

Take corporate budgeting. Hiram still smiled when he recalled his first day of interviews with Rainbarrel's executives. It immediately became obvious that the place had no budget integrity whatsoever. One unit head had said outright, "Look, none of us fights very hard at budget time, because after three or four months, nobody looks at the budget anyway." Barely concealing his shock, Hiram asked how that could be; what did they look at, then? The answer was that they operated according to one simple rule: "If it's a good idea, we say yes to it. If it's a bad idea, we say no."

"And what happens," Hiram had pressed, "when you run out of money halfway through the year?" The fellow rubbed his chin and took a moment to think before answering. "I guess we've always run out of good ideas before we've run out of money." Unbelievable!

"Fat and happy" was how Hiram characterized Rainbarrel in a conversation with the headhunter who had recruited him. Of course, he wouldn't use those words in the CEC meeting. That would sound too disparaging. In fact, he'd quickly fallen in love with Rainbarrel and the opportunities it presented. Here was a company that had the potential for greatness but that was held back by a lack of discipline. It was like a racehorse that had the potential to be a Secretariat but lacked a structured training regimen. Or a Ferrari engine that needed the touch of an expert mechanic to get it back in trim. In other words, the only thing Rainbarrel was missing was what someone like Hiram Phillips could bring to the table. The allure was irresistible; this was the assignment that would define his career. And now, a year later, he was ready to declare a turnaround.

Lean and Mean

Sure enough, as Hiram steered toward the entrance to the parking garage, he saw Sally and Frank in a visitor parking space, pulling their bulky file bags out of the trunk of Sally's sedan. He caught up to them at the security checkpoint in the lobby and took a heavy satchel from Sally's hand.

Moments later, they were at a conference table, each of them poring over a copy of the consultants' spiral-bound report. "This is great," Hiram said. "I can hand this out just as it is. But what I want to do while you're here is to really

613

nail down what the highlights are. I have the floor for 40 minutes, but I guess I'd better leave ten for questions. There's no way I can plow through all of this."

"If I were you," Sally advised, "I would lead off with the best numbers. I mean, none of them are bad. You hit practically every target. But some of these, where you even exceeded the stretch goal. . . ."

Hiram glanced at the line Sally was underscoring with her fingernail. It was an impressive achievement: a reduction in labor costs. This had been one of the first moves he'd made, and he'd tried to do it gently. He'd come up with the idea of identifying the bottom quartile of performers throughout the company and offering them fairly generous buyout packages. But when that hadn't attracted enough takers, he'd gone the surer route. He'd imposed an across-the-board headcount reduction of 10% on all the units. In that round, the affected people were given no financial assistance beyond the normal severance.

"It made a big difference," he nodded. "But it wasn't exactly the world's most popular move." Hiram was well aware that a certain segment of the Rainbarrel workforce currently referred to him as "Fire 'em." He pointed to another number on the spreadsheet. "Now, that one tells a happier story: lower costs as a result of higher productivity."

"And better customer service to boot," Frank chimed in. They were talking about the transformation of Rainbarrel's call center—where phone representatives took orders and handled questions and complaints from both trade and retail customers. The spreadsheet indicated a dramatic uptick in productivity: The number of calls each service rep was handling per day had gone up 50%. A year earlier, reps were spending up to six minutes per call, whereas now the average was less than four minutes. "I guess you decided to go for that new automated switching system?" Frank asked.

"No!" Hiram answered. "That's the beauty of it. We got that improvement without any capital investment. You know what we did? We just announced the new targets, let everyone know we were going to monitor them, and put the names of the worst offenders on a great big 'wall of shame' right outside the cafeteria. Never underestimate the power of peer pressure!"

Sally, meanwhile, was already circling another banner achievement: an increase in on-time shipments. "You should talk about this, given that it's something that wasn't even being watched before you came."

It was true. As much as Rainbarrel liked to emphasize customer service in its values and mission statement, no reliable metric had been in place to track it. And getting a metric in place hadn't been as straightforward as it might've seemed—people had haggled about what constituted "on time" and even what constituted "shipped." Finally, Hiram had put his foot down and insisted on the most objective of measures. On time meant when the

goods were promised to ship. And nothing was counted as shipped till it left company property. Period. "And once again," Hiram announced, "not a dollar of capital expenditure. I simply let people know that, from now on, if they made commitments and didn't keep them, we'd have their number."

"Seems to have done the trick," Sally observed. "The percentage of goods shipped by promise date has gone up steadily for the last six months. It's now at 92%."

Scanning the report, Hiram noticed another huge percentage gain, but he couldn't recall what the acronym stood for. "What's this? Looks like a good one: a 50% cost reduction?"

Sally studied the item. "Oh, that. It's a pretty small change, actually. Remember we separated out the commissions on sales to employees?" It came back to Hiram immediately. Rainbarrel had a policy that allowed current and retired employees to buy products at a substantial discount. But the salespeople who served them earned commissions based on the full retail value, not the actual price paid. So, in effect, employee purchases were jacking up the commission expenses. Hiram had created a new policy in which the commission reflected the actual purchase price. On its own, the change didn't amount to a lot, but it reminded Hiram of a larger point he wanted to make in his presentation: the importance of straightforward rules—and rewards—in driving superior performance.

"I know you guys don't have impact data for me, but I'm definitely going to talk about the changes to the commission structure and sales incentives. There's no question they must be making a difference."

"Right," Sally nodded. "A classic case of 'keep it simple,' isn't it?" She turned to Frank to explain. "The old way they calculated commissions was by using this really complicated formula that factored in, I can't remember, at least five different things."

"Including sales, I hope?" Frank smirked.

"I'm still not sure!" Hiram answered. "No, seriously, sales were the most important single variable, but they also mixed in all kinds of targets around mentoring, prospecting new clients, even keeping the account information current. It was all way too subjective, and salespeople were getting very mixed signals. I just clarified the message so they don't have to wonder what they're getting paid for. Same with the sales contests. It's simple now: If you sell the most product in a given quarter, you win."

With Sally and Frank nodding enthusiastically, Hiram again looked down at the report. Row after row of numbers attested to Rainbarrel's improved performance. It wouldn't be easy to choose the rest of the highlights, but what a problem to have! He invited the consultants to weigh in again and leaned back to bask in the superlatives. And his smile grew wider.

Cause for Concern

The next morning, a well-rested Hiram Phillips strode into the building, flashed his ID badge at Charlie, the guard, and joined the throng in the lobby. In the crowd waiting for the elevator, he recognized two young women from Rainbarrel, lattes in hand and headphones around their necks. One was grimacing melodramatically as she turned to her friend. "I'm so dreading getting to my desk," she said. "Right when I was leaving last night, an e-mail showed up from the buyer at Sullivan. I just know it's going to be some big, hairy problem to sort out. I couldn't bring myself to open it, with the day I'd had. But I'm going to be sweating it today trying to respond by five o'clock. I can't rack up any more late responses, or my bonus is seriously history."

Her friend had slung her backpack onto the floor and was rooting through it, barely listening. But she glanced up to set her friend straight in the most casual way. "No, see, all they check is whether you responded to an e-mail within 24 hours of opening it. So that's the key. Just don't open it. You know, till you've got time to deal with it."

Then a belltone announced the arrival of the elevator, and they were gone.

More Cause for Concern

An hour later, Keith Randall was calling to order the quarterly meeting of the corporate executive council. First, he said, the group would hear the results of the annual employee survey, courtesy of human resources VP Lew Hart. Next would come a demonstration by the chief marketing officer of a practice the CEO hoped to incorporate into all future meetings. It was a "quick market intelligence," or QMI, scan, engaging a few of Rainbarrel's valued customers in a prearranged—but not predigested—conference call, to collect raw data on customer service concerns and ideas. "And finally," Keith concluded, "Hiram's going to give us some very good news about cost reductions and operating efficiencies, all due to the changes he's designed and implemented this past year."

Hiram nodded to acknowledge the compliment. He heard little of the next ten minutes' proceedings, thinking instead about how he should phrase certain points for maximum effect. Lew Hart had lost him in the first moments of his presentation on the "people survey" by beginning with an overview of "purpose, methodology, and historical trends." Deadly.

It was the phrase "mindlessly counting patents" that finally turned Hiram's attention back to his colleague. Lew, it seemed, was now into the "findings" section of his remarks. Hiram pieced together that he was reporting on an unprecedented level of negativity in the responses from Rainbarrel's R&D department and was quoting the complaints people had scribbled on their surveys. "Another one put it this way," Lew said. "We're now highly focused on who's getting the most patents, who's getting the most copyrights, who's submitting the most grant proposals, etc. But are we more creative? It's not that simple."

"You know," Rainbarrel's chief counsel noted, "I have thought lately that we're filing for a lot of patents for products that will never be commercially viable."

"But the thing that's really got these guys frustrated seems to be their 'Innovation X' project," Lew continued. "They're all saying it's the best thing since sliced bread, a generational leap on the product line, but they're getting no uptake."

Eyes in the room turned to the products division president, who promptly threw up his hands. "What can I say, gang? We never expected that breakthrough to happen in this fiscal year. It's not in the budget to bring it to market."

Lew Hart silenced the rising voices, reminding the group he had more findings to share. Unfortunately, it didn't get much better. Both current and retired employees were complaining about being treated poorly by sales personnel when they sought to place orders or obtain information about company products. There was a lot of residual unhappiness about the layoffs, and not simply because those who remained had more work to do. Some people had noted that, because the reduction was based on headcount, not costs, managers had tended to fire low-level people, crippling the company without saving much money. And because the reduction was across the board, the highest performing departments had been forced to lay off some of the company's best employees. Others had heard about inequities in the severance deals: "As far as I can tell, we gave our lowest performers a better package than our good ones," he quoted one employee as saying.

And then there was a chorus of complaints from the sales organization. "No role models." "No mentoring." "No chance to pick the veterans' brains." "No knowledge sharing about accounts." More than ever, salespeople were dissatisfied with their territories and clamoring for the more affluent, high-volume districts. "It didn't help that all the sales-contest winners this year were from places like Scarsdale, Shaker Heights, and Beverly Hills," a salesperson was quoted as saying. Lew concluded with a promise to look further into the apparent decline in morale to determine whether it was an aberration.

The Ugly Truth

But if the group thought the mood would improve in the meeting's next segment—the QMI chat with the folks at longtime customer Brenton Brothers—they soon found out otherwise. Booming out of the speakerphone in the middle of the table came the Southern-tinged voices of Billy Brenton and three of his employees representing various parts of his organization.

"What's up with your shipping department?" Billy called out. "My people are telling me it's taking forever to get the stock replenished."

Hiram sat up straight, then leaned toward the speakerphone. "Excuse me, Mr. Brenton. This is Hiram Phillips—I don't believe we've met. But are you saying we are not shipping by our promise date?"

A cough—or was it a guffaw?—came back across the wire. "Well, son. Let me tell you about that. First of all, what y'all promise is not always what we are saying we require—and what we believe we deserve. Annie, isn't that right?"

"Yes, Mr. Brenton," said the buyer. "In some cases, I've been told to take a late date or otherwise forgo the purchase. That becomes the promise date, I guess, but it's not the date I asked for."

"And second," Billy continued, "I can't figure out how you fellas define 'shipped.' We were told last Tuesday an order had been shipped, and come to find out, the stuff was sitting on a railroad siding across the street from your plant."

"That's an important order for us," another Brenton voice piped up. "I sent an e-mail to try to sort it out, but I haven't heard back about it." Hiram winced, recalling the conversation in the lobby that morning. The voice persisted: "I thought that might be the better way to contact your service people these days? They always seem in such an all-fired hurry to get off the phone when I call. Sometimes it takes two or three calls to get something squared away."

The call didn't end there—a few more shortcomings were discussed. Then Keith Randall, to his credit, pulled the conversation onto more positive ground by reaffirming the great regard Rainbarrel had for Brenton Brothers and the mutual value of that enduring relationship. Promises were made and hearty thanks extended for the frank feedback. Meanwhile, Hiram felt the eyes of his colleagues on him. Finally, the call ended and the CEO announced that he, for one, needed a break before the last agenda item.

Dazed and Confused

Hiram considered following his boss out of the room and asking him to table the whole discussion of the new metrics and incentives. The climate was suddenly bad for the news he had looked forward to sharing. But he knew that delaying the discussion would be weak and wrong. After all, he had plenty of evidence to show he was on the right track. The problems the group had just been hearing about were side effects, but surely they didn't outweigh the cure.

He moved to the side table and poured a glass of ice water, then leaned against the wall to collect his thoughts. Perhaps he should reframe his opening comments in light of the employee and customer feedback. As he considered how he might do so, Keith Randall appeared at his side.

"Looks like we have our work cut out for us, eh, Hiram?" he said quietly—and charitably enough. "Some of those metrics taking hold, um, a little too strongly?" Hiram started to object but saw the seriousness in his boss's eyes.

He lifted the stack of reports Felding & Company had prepared for him and turned to the conference table. "Well, I guess that's something for the group to talk about."

Should Rainbarrel revisit its approach to performance management?

Case 9   American Red Cross in 2002*

As Marsha "Marty" Johnson Evans took the helm of the American Red Cross on August 5, 2002, she was faced with the challenge of restoring the public's faith in the organization. During the past 24 months, there had been a barrage of negative publicity regarding the American Red Cross. In June 2000 Red Cross workers went on strike. The organization was hit by a lawsuit filed by HemaCare Corporation and Coral Blood Services in January 2001. The plaintiffs alleged that the American Red Cross engaged in unfair trade practices in the pricing of blood. The Better Business Bureau made false public statements about the ability of the American Red Cross to meet their standards for charitable solicitations. Then on September 11, 2001, Americans watched in horror as terrorists flew two planes into the World Trade Center buildings and a third into the Pentagon in Washington. In the aftermath of this tragedy, donations poured into the American Red Cross, and a special fund—the Liberty Disaster Relief Fund—was established by the then-president of the Red Cross, Dr. Bernadine Healy. When it was announced that not all donations would be used for victims of the 9/11 disaster, there was a huge public outcry from donors. Healy was forced to retire, and interim president and CEO Harold Decker announced that all donations to the Liberty Disaster Relief Fund would be used in the organization's 9/11 relief efforts. Finally, on March 10, 2002, *60 Minutes,* a CBS news show, ran a misleading and inaccurate story about the American Red Cross.

On June 27, 2002, Marsha Johnson Evans was named the new CEO and president of the American Red Cross. At the time of this announcement, Evans stated:

> This is a time of great challenge for many charitable organizations including the American Red Cross. On the one hand, we need to motivate Americans to donate their time and their treasure, which is never easy, but always comes down to whether they trust an organization and believe in their work. On the other hand, we face a host of challenges including the need to better prepare this nation for disasters both natural and man-made; as well as the rigors of furnishing a safe and available blood supply with all the costs and complexity this involves.[1]

History and Operations of the American Red Cross

Henry Dunant set forth the idea of the Red Cross in 1859 when he saw wounded and dying soldiers on the battlefield in Solferino, Italy. He organized local people to bind the

*This case was prepared by Professors Debora J. Gilliard and Rajendra Khandekar of Metropolitan State College–Denver as a basis for class discussion rather than to illustrate either effective or ineffective handling of an administrative situation. Copyright © 2004 Deborah J. Gilliard and Rajendra Khandekar. All rights reserved.

soldiers' wounds and to feed and care for them. Henry Dunant called for the creation of a national relief society and this pointed the way to the future Geneva Convention. Four years later, in 1863, the International Red Cross was created in Geneva, Switzerland, with the purpose of providing nonpartisan care in time of war. The Red Cross emblem was adopted as a symbol of neutrality although today the Red Crescent is also a recognized symbol. Today the Red Cross incorporates the International Committee of the Red Cross and the International Federation of Red Cross and Red Crescent Societies as well as national societies in 175 countries. The fundamental principles of the International Red Cross are listed in Exhibit 1. Clara Barton successfully organized the first lasting Red Cross Society in America in Washington, D.C., on May 21, 1881. The American Red Cross provided services beyond those of the International Red Cross by providing disaster relief in addition to battlefield assistance. Clara Barton served as the organization's president through 1904.[2]

As stated in its 2000–2001 Annual Report, "the American Red Cross is a humanitarian organization, led by volunteers, whose mission is to provide relief to victims of disasters and help people prevent, prepare for, and respond to emergencies." The vision of the American Red Cross is "the American Red Cross . . . always there . . . touching more lives, in new ways . . . under the same trusted symbol." Since its founding, the American Red Cross has symbolized the nobility of the human spirit by representing service and goodwill across America. Its purpose, or intent, is to "prevent and relieve human suffering." Each year March is proclaimed as American Red Cross month. To support the fundamental principles of the International Red Cross, the American Red Cross has adopted a set of values (see Exhibit 2).

The American Red Cross is governed by a Board of Governors that formulates policy and delegates authority to the volunteer boards of its 1,000 local chapters. Decentralization allows the Red Cross to provide immediate, effective, and efficient assistance to those in need.[3] Annually, the American Red Cross helps victims of more than 63,000 natural and man-made disasters. The worst disaster ever dealt with by the American Red Cross was the hurricane that killed an estimated 6,000 people in Galveston, Texas, in 1900.

The American Red Cross helps victims through a wide range of services:[4]

- Armed Forces Emergency Services. Provides military families with emergency communication services, financial assistance, counseling, and so forth.
- Biomedical Services. Blood, tissue, and plasma services; research; and national testing labs. In fiscal year 2001 more than 3.8 million volunteers donated

Exhibit 1 Principles of International Red Cross

- **Humanity:** The International Red Cross and Red Crescent Movement, born of a desire to bring assistance without discrimination to the wounded on the battlefield, endeavors, in its international and national capacity, to prevent and alleviate human suffering where it may be found. Its purpose is to protect life and health and to ensure respect for the human being. It promotes mutual understanding, friendship, cooperation, and lasting peace amongst all peoples.
- **Impartiality:** It makes no discrimination as to nationality, race, religious beliefs, class, or political opinions. It endeavors to relieve the suffering of individuals, being guided solely by their needs, and to give priority to the most urgent cases of distress.
- **Neutrality:** In order to continue to enjoy the confidence of all, the Movement may not take sides in hostilities or engage at any time in controversies of a political, racial, religious, or ideological nature.
- **Independence:** The Movement is independent. The National Societies, while auxiliaries in the humanitarian services of their governments and subject to the laws of their respective countries, must always maintain their autonomy so that they may be able at all times to act in accordance with the principles of the Movement.
- **Voluntary Service:** It is a voluntary relief movement not prompted in any manner by desire for gain.
- **Unity:** There can be only one Red Cross or one Red Crescent Society in any one country. It must be open to all. It must carry on its humanitarian work throughout its territory.
- **Universality:** The International Red Cross and Red Crescent Movement, in which all Societies have equal status and share equal responsibilities and duties in helping each other, is worldwide.

Source: American Red Cross, www.redcross.org.

Exhibit 2 Values of the American Red Cross

- **Humanitarianism:** We exist to serve others in need, independently, and without discrimination, providing relief for victims of disasters and helping people prevent, prepare for, and respond to emergencies.
- **Stewardship:** We act responsibly, effectively, and efficiently with resources entrusted to us, always seeking to improve.
- **Helping Others:** We are attentive and responsive to those we serve, always listening to their needs and looking for ways to serve through existing or new initiatives.
- **Respect:** We acknowledge, respect, and support the rights and diversity of each person in our organization and in the communities we serve.
- **Voluntary Spirit:** As a family of donors, volunteers, and staff we search for ways to provide hope to those we serve while demonstrating compassion, generosity, and appreciation.
- **Continuous Learning:** We seek, collectively and individually, to identify, obtain, and maintain competencies and the awareness required for exceptional service.
- **Integrity:** We act with honesty, demonstrate courage and accountability under pressure, and openly share ideas and information with each other.

Source: www.redcross.org.

in excess of 6 million pints of blood. The American Red Cross supplies 3,000 hospitals with about half of the blood used in the United States.

- Community Services. Help for the homeless, seniors, and youth; food and nutrition information; transportation; and so forth.

- Disaster Services. Educational services to prepare for disasters. Each year 83,000 volunteers help disaster victims by providing food, shelter, financial assistance, mental health counseling, and so on.
- Health and Safety Services. Swimming and lifeguard classes, HIV/AIDS education, living well programs, and so forth. Each year more than 12 million Americans take advantage of lifesaving courses offered by the Red Cross.
- International Services. Emergency disaster response, feeding programs, primary health care programs, Geneva Conventions, and so on. The Red Cross is able to provide long-term aid and education to those in need. Also, Red Cross delegates help local citizens rebuild infrastructure, strengthen public health, and improve response time to local disasters.
- Nursing. Student nurses, Jane Delano Society, and so forth.
- Youth Involvement. Helping kids, teens, and young adults.
- Volunteering. Recruiting and organizing volunteers.

Financial Overview

In fiscal year 2001–2002 the American Red Cross had operating revenues of $4.117 billion. Total operating revenues for fiscal year 2000–2001 were $2.743 billion. Three main funding sources for the American Red Cross were:[5]

- Contributions: Fund-raising efforts by the United Way & Combined Federal Campaign, legacies, grants, other monetary and in-kind contributions.
- Products and services: Fees for products, materials, and courses; fees from collecting, testing, and distributing blood and tissue.
- Investment income and other income: Investment income from endowments and reserve funds and income from contracts to provide various programs.

Total operating expenses for the 2000–2001 fiscal year were $2.712 billion, and major expenses included:[6]

- Disaster costs: Assistance to victims.
- Funding disaster services: Expenses to solicit donations, administer funds; staff expenses at disaster sites; and so on.
- Biomedical services: Facility maintenance; expenses in blood, plasma, and tissue services.

Total operating expenses for the fiscal year 2001–2002 were $3.570 billion (see Exhibits 3, 4, and 5).[7]

Technology and Operations

Technology has helped the American Red Cross better coordinate its efforts among its 1,400 chapters and to expand its reach across America. In 2000 it launched "iGiveLife," a service that enables blood drive sponsors to use their intranets to recruit donors and allows hospital customers to order blood products online.[8]

The Internet provides information about nonprofit organizations and can provide "click-to-donate" sites for those individuals who are willing to help out with contributions while they are online. These "click" sites appeal to a newer and often younger audience for the nonprofits. For Cindee Archer, online media manager for the American Red Cross in Washington, D.C., the Internet serves as a vital source of information to the American public and as a new way to collect donations. Archer stated, "The Internet has definitely changed how the whole organization thinks. You feel this sense of urgency whenever there's a disaster—you want that information up as quickly as you can get it."[9] Archer worked on developing a Web site where visitors could enter a zip code and quickly find information. The Web site helps visitors locate local Red Cross shelters, find relatives in a disaster area, keep up with breaking news, and obtain information about donating and volunteering. Cindy Archer also believed that "more and more people are coming online—this isn't going to go away, it's only going to get more pervasive."[10] However, there were costs associated with a Web site that many nonprofit groups did not realize. Russ Finkelstein, director of outreach at Action Without Borders has stated, "Some of them think this is going to be a kind of panacea for doing fund-raising, and it's not necessarily that."[11]

About 12 million Americans enroll in Red Cross courses each year. It is now possible to make these courses available online. The Red Cross has routinely published the latest public health information, and the use of new technology will make this information available online. Wireless communication allows the American Red Cross to make faster damage assessment at the scene. The communication network allows it to locate family members during crises more efficiently. In the near future, it may be possible for the American Red Cross to offer an online shopping network to generate additional resources.[12]

Strategic Alliances

The American Red Cross has established a number of alliances with other organizations. It works with the World Health Organization to alleviate malnutrition, lack of pure water, and diarrhea in poor countries and to support primary health care. A donation to the World Hemophilia Foundation of plasma product is used to treat hemophilia. In 1999 the American Red Cross joined the Federal Emergency Management Agency for "TOPOFF," a nationwide disaster simulation to help prepare for acts of terrorism. As a result of recent research and development, Massachusetts General Hospital and the American Red Cross jointly own a patent for a protein associated with the underlying cause of Alzheimer's disease. In addition, the American Red Cross supplies over 3,000 hospitals with blood donations.[13]

In February 2001 the American Red Cross teamed up with Coinstar, Inc., to collect Red Cross donations for

Exhibit 3   Consolidated Statement of Financial Position, June 30, 2002 (with summarized information as of June 30, 2001) (in thousands)

				Totals	
Assets	Unrestricted	Temporarily Restricted	Permanently Restricted	2002	2001
Current assets:					
Cash and cash equivalents	$ 146,247	$439,569	$ 1,386	$ 587,202	$ 177,492
Investments	309,913	11,050	12,514	333,477	355,090
Receivables, net of allowance for doubtful accounts of $19,604 in 2002 and $19,301 in 2001:					
Trade	304,543	15,258	—	319,801	317,767
Contributions, current portion	16,411	110,103	56	126,570	133,183
Other	—	—	15,825	15,825	9,302
Inventories, net of allowance for obsolescence of $7,750 in 2002 and $6,784 in 2001	197,252	6,402	—	203,654	190,272
Other assets	12,547	3,162	183	15,892	23,289
Total current assets	986,913	585,544	29,964	1,602,421	1,206,395
Investments	548,633	155,674	325,238	1,029,545	1,120,773
Contributions receivable	4,209	28,374	2,243	34,826	39,339
Prepaid pension costs	—	—	—	—	11,858
Land, buildings, and other property, net	823,541	—	—	823,541	733,177
Other assets	11,089	1,500	22,704	35,293	26,171
Total assets	2,374,385	771,092	380,149	3,525,626	3,137,713
Liabilities and Net Assets					
Current liabilities:					
Accounts payable and accrued expenses	287,209	9,453	—	296,662	293,476
Current portion of debt and capital leases	39,894	—	—	39,894	89,372
Postretirement benefits	18,924	—	—	18,924	16,807
Other current liabilities	20,653	2,840	63	23,556	18,068
Total current liabilities	366,680	12,293	63	379,036	417,723
Debt and capital leases	357,453	—	—	357,453	360,870
Pension and postretirement benefits	120,042	—	—	120,042	108,339
Other liabilities	92,623	1,180	20	93,823	86,644
Total liabilities	936,798	13,473	83	950,354	973,576
Net assets	1,437,587	757,619	380,066	2,575,272	2,164,137
Commitments and contingencies					
Total liabilities and net assets	$2,374,385	$771,092	$380,149	$3,525,626	$3,137,713

Source: American Red Cross. 2002. Annual Report.

Exhibit 4 Consolidated Statement of Activities, Year ended June 30, 2002 (with summarized information for the year ended June 30, 2001) (in thousands)

	Unrestricted	Temporarily Restricted	Permanently Restricted	Totals 2002	Totals 2001
Operating revenues and gains					
Public Support:					
United Way and other federated	$ 65,616	$ 122,452	$ —	$ 188,068	$ 205,549
Disaster relief	—	133,376	—	133,376	84,601
Liberty disaster relief—Sept. 11 response	—	989,060	—	989,060	—
Legacies and bequests	67,118	6,745	22,022	95,885	115,594
Services and materials	22,034	96,222	—	118,256	49,728
Grants	21,236	67,175	—	88,411	76,351
Other contributions	213,289	36,915	705	250,909	230,845
Products and services:					
Biomedical	1,924,077	—	—	1,924,077	1,686,090
Program materials	136,582	906	—	137,488	121,724
Contracts	58,171	—	—	58,171	50,175
Investment income	81,394	1,069	—	82,463	81,405
Other revenues	49,089	2,008	—	51,097	40,844
Net assets released from restrictions	1,035,410	(1,035,410)	—	—	—
Total operating revenues and gains	3,674,016	420,518	22,727	4,117,261	2,742,906
Operating expenses					
Program services:					
Armed Forces Emergency Services	61,513	—	—	61,513	65,756
Disaster services	308,156	—	—	308,156	284,822
Liberty disaster relief—Sept. 11 response	617,960	—	—	617,960	—
Biomedical services	1,872,967	—	—	1,872,967	1,699,978
Health and safety services	213,614	—	—	213,614	203,058
Community services	152,902	—	—	152,902	150,108
International services	32,736	—	—	32,736	45,238
Total program services	3,259,848	—	—	3,259,848	2,448,960
Supporting services:					
Fund raising	136,901	—	—	136,901	108,616
Management and general	174,182	—	—	174,182	154,726
Total supporting services	311,083	—	—	311,083	263,342
Total operating expenses	3,570,931	—	—	3,570,931	2,712,302
Change in net assets from operations	103,085	420,518	22,727	546,330	30,604
Nonoperating gains (losses)	(131,900)	(548)	(2,747)	(135,195)	(63,876)
Cumulative effect of accounting change	—	—	—	—	2,201
Change in net assets	(28,815)	419,970	19,980	411,135	(31,071)
Net assets, beginning of year	1,466,402	337,649	360,086	2,164,137	2,195,208
Net assets, end of year	$1,437,587	$ 757,619	$380,066	$2,575,272	$2,164,137

Source: American Red Cross. 2002. Annual Report.

Exhibit 5 Consolidated Statement of Functional Expenses, Year ended June 30, 2002 (with summarized information for the year ended June 30, 2001) (in thousands)

	Armed Forces Emergency Services	Disaster Services	Liberty Disaster Relief—Sept. 11 Response	Program Services Biomedical Services	Health and Safety Services	Community Services	International Services	Total Program Services
Salaries and wages	$35,329	$ 76,450	$ 4,966	$ 749,046	$100,866	$ 66,654	$ 8,340	$1,041,651
Employee benefits	6,701	16,758	773	165,697	19,894	13,698	1,706	225,227
Subtotal	42,030	93,208	5,739	914,743	120,760	80,352	10,046	1,266,878
Travel and maintenance	1,673	20,479	32,601	35,515	5,068	4,111	1,826	101,273
Equipment maintenance and rental	1,173	11,105	11,387	62,322	5,005	5,950	515	97,457
Supplies and materials	3,394	25,095	10,416	417,349	44,001	21,937	849	523,041
Contractual services	8,252	42,887	61,479	379,081	27,643	20,859	1,788	541,989
Financial and material assistance	2,803	106,406	496,338	14,132	3,528	13,811	17,236	654,254
Depreciation and amortization	2,188	8,976	—	49,825	7,609	5,882	476	74,956
Total expenses	$61,513	$308,156	$617,960	$1,872,967	$213,614	$152,902	$32,736	$3,259,848

	Supporting Services			Total Operating Expenses	
	Fund Raising	Management and General	Total Supporting Services	2002	2001
Salaries and wages	$ 42,260	$ 81,174	$123,434	$1,165,085	$1,046,171
Employee benefits	8,436	16,145	24,581	249,808	199,204
Subtotal	50,696	97,319	148,015	1,414,893	1,245,375
Travel and maintenance	3,708	6,466	10,174	111,447	78,208
Equipment maintenance and rental	1,902	5,260	7,162	104,619	84,227
Supplies and materials	35,167	6,494	41,661	564,702	477,547
Contractual services	41,147	44,991	86,138	628,127	563,436
Financial and material assistance	1,713	4,285	5,998	660,252	175,994
Depreciation and amortization	2,568	9,367	11,935	86,891	87,515
Total expenses	$136,901	$174,182	$311,083	$3,570,931	$2,712,302

Source: American Red Cross. 2002. Annual Report.

disaster relief efforts. Consumers could drop loose change into the Coinstar machines located in local supermarkets. Coinstar machines were located within two miles of 130 million Americans. John Clizbe, vice president of Disaster Services at the American Red Cross, indicated that "If every American near a Coinstar machine would donate a handful of change on their next supermarket visit, the Red Cross would be that much better prepared to respond to disaster immediately." Rich Stillman, COO of Coinstar, said, "You no longer need a credit card or checkbook to provide financial support to those in need. If all Americans donate the change in their wallet or pocket, those handfuls will make a huge difference in our capacity to help others this year."[14]

Masterfoods USA, a Mars Incorporated Company, created a special package of red, white, and blue M&Ms specifically to benefit the Red Cross. The national campaign theme used for this promotion was "Taking Care of America Everyday." "Through appearances on television, radio and newspapers, and creative displays in stores across the country, the new 'M&Ms' captured the heart of America," stated Skip Seitz, senior vice president, American Red Cross Growth and Integrated Development.[15] One hundred percent of all profits from the sales of these M&Ms were donated to the American Red Cross Disaster Relief Fund. In January 2002 Masterfoods USA presented a check to the Red Cross in the amount of $3.5 million.

In August 2001 the American Red Cross and the American Society of Association Executives (ASAE) signed an agreement under which the two organizations will share data regarding disasters, declarations, and changes in legislation, and will explore efforts in joint training exercises. The ASAE provides the Red Cross with demographic information about associations and assistance with identifying organizations they wish to contact during times of need.[16]

Recent Problems

Events between 2000 and 2002 provided the American Red Cross with a number of challenges.

Worker Strike   In June 2000 Red Cross workers who collected blood donations and delivered them to hospitals went on strike after rejecting a contract offer by the American Red Cross. The workers were unhappy about long hours, frequent schedule changes, and increasing health benefit costs.[17]

Unfair Trade Practices Lawsuit   The Red Cross derived 60 percent of its revenues from the sale of blood. In providing more than half the nation's blood, the Red Cross had annual sales of more than $1.3 billion.[18] In January 2001 a California blood supplier filed an antitrust suit against the American Red Cross claiming the organization used its clout to eliminate competitors. HemaCare Corp. and Coral Blood

Services alleged the Red Cross had cost them more than $25 million in lost business. They further alleged that the American Red Cross priced some blood products (e.g., platelets) below production costs to drive out competitors while it charged higher prices for the same products in markets where there is no competition. In the lawsuit, the plaintiffs alleged the Red Cross violated Section 2 of the Sherman Antitrust Act, which prohibits monopolization. The lawsuit also charged tortuous interference, unfair trade practices, and unfair competition under the California Business and Professional Code. William Nicely, HemaCare's chief executive officer, stated, "We believe that's unfair and illegal. The Red Cross is a fine organization. We just want them to play by the rules that are reasonable and fair and compete on a level playing field."[19] Blythe Kubina, a Red Cross spokeswoman, said in a written statement, "We believe the American Red Cross has done nothing inappropriate regarding HemaCare's claims to unfair business practices and we were surprised by this lawsuit. We have been in full compliance with the law, and we will vigorously defend this lawsuit."[20]

Liberty Disaster Relief Fund   After the terrorist attacks on September 11, the American Red Cross rose to the challenge of providing the most extensive relief operation in its 120-year history. In response to the tragedy, the Red Cross set up family assistance centers to provide counseling, child care, food, financial assistance, and other services to victims' families and others affected. Respite centers were set up in New York City, Somerset County, Pennsylvania, and at the Pentagon to provide meals, sleeping quarters, and other items to relief workers and volunteers. Funds were used for travel, lodging, and meals for volunteers and staff working on-site. Financial assistance, counseling, and transportation were provided to families of missing foreign nationals.

Millions of dollars, thousands of blood donations, and help from a myriad of volunteers contributed to Red Cross efforts to provide aid to survivors, victims' families, and relief workers. Because of the large dollar amount of donations from the American people, the Red Cross created the Liberty Disaster Relief Fund to be used exclusively to meet the needs of people directly affected by the September 11 tragedy.

Within 15 days of the September 11, 2001, attack, the Red Cross had collected $202 million in donations. Deborah Goldburg, a Red Cross spokesperson, stated, "Everything is happening at such a fast pace. Right now we are just trying to keep up with responses."[21] Goldburg stated that the entire amount raised by the Red Cross since the disaster would go into the newly created Liberty Fund. She indicated that organization officials earmarked $100 million from the fund to provide short-term financial assistance to families of victims. Bernadine Healy, MD, the president and chief executive officer of the Red Cross, said in a written statement, "What has taken place is extraordinary, and we must respond in an extraordinary way. The American

Red Cross has a heavy burden—to live up to the inspiration and memory of those lost. It is with great humility and pride that we carry out this noble obligation."[22]

On October 12, 2001, the American Red Cross released a spending plan for the first $300 million in the Liberty Fund. Less than 50 percent of the money raised was targeted for victims, their families, or rescue workers. The remainder was earmarked to help the Red Cross improve its own organization and expand into new aid programs that might be needed in the event of future terrorist attacks.[23] This planned distribution of funds, based on Healy's policy of using donations for a "long period of uncertainty and recovery," caused a huge uproar.[24] The donors blasted Healy because they expected their donations to be helping September 11 disaster victims now. The attorney general of New York State threatened legal action.[25] Healy finally responded with her announcement of retirement. "I had no choice," she said, claiming that the organization's board had pushed her out.[26]

On November 14, 2001, interim CEO and president of the Red Cross, Harold Decker, announced changes adopted by the American Red Cross Board of Governors to meet the immediate and long-term needs of people affected by the September 11 terrorist attacks. The Red Cross would provide increased financial support to families, participate in a database to be shared among relief agencies, hire an additional 200 caseworkers, and extend the use of toll-free telephone lines. David T. McLaughlin, chairman of the American Red Cross Board of Governors, stated, "The people of this country have given the Red Cross their hard-earned dollars, their trust, and very clear direction for our September 11 relief effort. Regrettably, it took us too long to hear their message."[27] In an article in *U.S. News & World Report*, David McLaughlin stated, "If we don't subject ourselves to public scrutiny, we will never have public trust."[28]

In addition to donating money, the American public donated blood for the disaster victims. These donations were given in response to Healy's "Together, we can save a life" public service announcement. Experts questioned the wisdom of calling for blood donations when there were very few blood recipients. By November 2001 about 10 percent of the red blood cells collected on September 11 and 12 had expired.[29] In a congressional hearing, Healy was confronted with allegations of "panicking the public into wasteful donations of blood." *The Lancet* reported, "Donors charged the organization with abuse of their good intentions."[30]

On March 7, 2002, the American Red Cross saluted the staff and volunteers who provided assistance to the more than 54,500 families affected by the attacks. David McLaughlin stated, "Today we are recognizing the work of our staff, volunteers, and donors who responded to September 11th." Harold Decker, interim president, announced that the American Red Cross received $930

million in contributions and this money was used to provide the following:[31]

	$ millions
Direct assistance to 3,266 families of deceased and seriously injured	$169
Assistance to 51,000 families of displaced workers and disaster workers	270
Provision for 14 million meals, mental health services for 232,000 people, and health services for 129,000 people	94

BBB Wise Giving Alliance   On February 16, 2002, the Better Business Bureau Wise Giving Alliance removed the American Red Cross from its "give.org" Web site, allegedly because the American Red Cross did not provide a timely report to the alliance. In addition, H. Art Taylor, president of the alliance, made some unsupported public statements regarding the Red Cross that were reported in the *Philadelphia Inquirer.* A letter from Harold Decker to the Wise Giving Alliance explained that a request by the alliance for an updated report from the Red Cross was received in January 2002. Given the recent activities of the American Red Cross, it was determined that such a report could not be provided by the due date. Jack Campbell, CFO of the Red Cross, and Bennett Weiner, COO of the alliance, agreed to a March 30 deadline for the updated report. In his letter Decker requested a public retraction of Taylor's statements and that the Better Business Bureau's current report on the Red Cross be restored to the give.org Web site.[32]

60 Minutes Program   Another onslaught of negative publicity for the American Red Cross occurred March 10, 2002, on the CBS news show *60 Minutes*. It appears to have contained some inaccuracies concerning floods, fires, and the financial accountability of Red Cross chapters. Deborah Daley, a spokesperson for the Red Cross, sent a letter to CBS News indicating the errors and an explanation:[33]

1.   In a comment about advertising practices, Mike Wallace reported, "They also decided to put a disclaimer in their ads saying that donations will be used for this and other disasters. The trouble is, it's in small print."

In response, Deborah Daley reported, "In the West Virginia flood ad, the "this and other disasters" language appears in the same font and size as the rest of the body copy appealing for support.

2.   Wallace reported, "Outside audits of local Red Cross chapters are rare. In fact, there is so little accountability that local chapters—and there are more than

one thousand of them—aren't even required to submit financial reports to Red Cross headquarters in Washington."

Deborah Daley responded that chapters are accountable in a number of ways. All chapters must have an independent annual review. Chapters that have over $100,000 in annual expenses must have an external audit conducted by an independent CPA. The largest 126 chapters must send quarterly financial reports to the national Red Cross. The Red Cross does regular audits of chapters. Chapters must meet specific national guidelines to maintain their charters. She stated that Wallace's claim that chapters "are not even required to submit financial reports" is completely false.

3. As for the Alpine fire in Southern California, Wallace reported, "As of last week, 14 months after the fire, San Diego was still waiting for a full accounting of how the money donated for the fire victims has been and will be spent."

Deborah Daley responded that the chapter has provided up-to-date financial information on its response to the Alpine fire three times since November.

Looking to the Future

After a five-month search, Marsha Johnson Evans was named president and CEO of the American Red Cross on June 27, 2002. Evans has served as national executive director of the Girl Scouts of the USA for the past four years, prior to which she had a 29-year career in the U.S. Navy, where she earned the rank of rear admiral. In his announcement, David McLaughlin, chairman of the Board of Governors of the American Red Cross, said, "Marty's unique style of leadership along with her experience as established administrator will bring new vigor to the American Red Cross. With great insight into our mission, she is well poised to guide our organization as we continue to provide vital services in a world faced by new challenges."[34] Evans remarked that:

> In the midst of responding to the extraordinary demands of 9/11 and a lot of criticism about these efforts, my observation is that the Red Cross never lost sight of its responsibility to every community and every victim of the other disasters that occurred, some 45,000 in the months since last September. The timely and capable response day-in and day-out to these disasters speaks volumes about the character of the volunteers and staff, their talent, and most especially their dedication.[35]

As she begins to guide the organization, Marsha Johnson Evans must confront the many issues faced by the American Red Cross. How should she proceed?

Endnotes

1. American Red Cross. 2002. Press release, June 27.
2. American Red Cross. www.redcross.org.
3. American Red Cross. 2002. Press release, February 1.
4. American Red Cross. 2000–2001. Annual Reports.
5. American Red Cross. 2001–2002. Annual Reports.
6. Ibid.
7. Ibid.
8. American Red Cross. 2000. Annual Report.
9. Sanborn, Stephanie. 2000. Nonprofits reap rewards of the Web—Internet proves to be a great fund-raising tool for charities, but there are costs. *Infoworld,* 22(25): 37.
10. Ibid.
11. Ibid.
12. American Red Cross. 2000. Annual Report.
13. Ibid.
14. *US Newswire.* 2001. American Red Cross and Coinstar to launch new fundraising technology to prepare for disasters. February 12.
15. American Red Cross. 2002. Press release, February 1.
16. *Association Management.* 2001. ASAE and American Red Cross formalize partnership agreement. 53(8): 12.
17. *Fund Raising Management.* 2000. Red Cross workers on strike. 31(4): 33.
18. Greenberg, Daniel S. 2001. Blood, politics, and the American Red Cross. *Lancet,* November 24: 1789; Taylor, Mark. 2001. Red Cross faces antitrust lawsuit. *Modern Healthcare* 31, January 1: 20.
19. Taylor, Red Cross faces antitrust lawsuit.
20. Ibid.
21. Becker, Cinda. 2001. A torrent of donations; charities wrestle with how best to spend money pouring in since attacks. *Modern Healthcare* 31, October 1: 8.
22. Ibid.
23. Tyrangiel, Josh. 2001. The charity olympics: After weeks of record giving, Americans want to know: Is that money helping? *Time,* November 5: 75.
24. *PR Newswire.* 2001. Newsweek: Former Red Cross head says her fundraising message was clear. . . . December 9.
25. Greenberg, Blood, politics, and the American Red Cross.
26. Tyrangiel, Charity olympics.
27. *US Newswire.* 2001. Red Cross announces major changes in Liberty Fund: Fund solely used for people affected by September 11 tragedy. November 14.
28. Levine, Samantha. 2001. Red Crossroads. *U.S. News & World Report,* November 19.
29. Tyrangiel, Charity olympics.
30. Greenberg, Blood, politics, and the American Red Cross.
31. American Red Cross. 2002. Press release, March 7.
32. *PR Newswire.* 2002. American Red Cross letter to Better Business Bureau's Wise Giving Alliance. February 16.
33. Red Cross announces major changes in Liberty Fund.
34. American Red Cross. 2002. Press release, June 27.
35. Ibid.

Case 10   Yum! Brands, Pizza Hut, and KFC*

Yum! Brands, Inc., was the world's largest fast-food company in 2004. It operated more than 33,000 KFC, Pizza Hut, Taco Bell, Long John Silver's, and A&W restaurants worldwide. It was the market leader in the chicken, pizza, Mexican, and seafood segments of the U.S. fast-food industry. Yum! Brands also operated more than 12,000 restaurants outside the United States. KFC and Pizza Hut accounted for more than 96 percent of the company's international restaurant base and managed restaurants in 116 countries. Among the first fast-food chains to go international in the late 1950s and 1960s, KFC and Pizza Hut were two of the world's most recognizable brands. Both KFC and Pizza Hut expanded through the 1990s by growing their restaurants into as many countries as possible. However, Yum! Brands realized that different countries offered different opportunities to contribute to the company's worldwide operating profits.

By 2004 Yum! Brands began to focus more attention on portfolio management in individual countries. It increasingly focused its international strategy on developing strong market share positions in a small number of high-growth markets such as Japan, Canada, the United Kingdom, China, Australia, Korea, and Mexico. It also hoped to build strong positions in continental Europe, Brazil, and India. Consumer awareness in these markets, however, was still low and neither KFC nor Pizza Hut had strong operating capabilities there. China and India were appealing markets because of their large populations. From a regional point-of-view, Latin America was appealing because of its close proximity to the United States, language and cultural similarities, and the potential for a future World Free Trade Area of the Americas, which would eliminate tariffs on trade within North and South America. The most important long-term challenge for Yum! Brands was to strengthen its position in a set of core international markets while also developing new markets where consumer awareness and operating capabilities were weak.

Company History

Kentucky Fried Chicken Corporation

Fast-food franchising was still in its infancy in 1952 when Harland Sanders began his travels across the United States to speak with prospective franchisees about his "Colonel Sanders Recipe Kentucky Fried Chicken." By 1960, "Colonel" Sanders had granted Kentucky Fried Chicken (KFC) franchises to more than 200 take-home retail outlets and restaurants across the United States. Four years later, at the age of 74, he sold KFC to two Louisville businessmen for $2 million. In 1966 KFC went public and was listed on the

New York Stock Exchange. In 1971 Heublein, Inc., a distributor of wine and alcoholic beverages, successfully approached KFC with an offer and merged KFC into a subsidiary. Eleven years later, R.J. Reynolds Industries, Inc. (RJR) acquired Heublein and merged it into a wholly owned subsidiary. The acquisition of Heublein was part of RJR's corporate strategy of diversifying into unrelated businesses such as energy, transportation, food, and restaurants to reduce its dependence on the tobacco industry. In 1985 RJR acquired Nabisco Corporation in an attempt to redefine RJR as a world leader in the consumer foods industry. As RJR refocused its strategy on processed foods, it decided to exit the restaurant industry. It sold KFC to PepsiCo, Inc., one year later.

Pizza Hut

In 1958 two students at Wichita State University—Frank and Dan Carney—decided to open a pizza restaurant in an old building at a busy intersection in downtown Wichita. To finance their new business, they borrowed $500 from their mother. They called the restaurant the "Pizza Hut," a reference to the old tavern beside the market that they renovated to open the new business. They opened four more restaurants during the next two years. The Pizza Hut concept was so well received by consumers that they were soon licensing the concept to franchises. By 1972 the Carneys had opened 1,000 restaurants and listed the firm on the New York Stock Exchange. In less than 15 years, Pizza Hut had become the number one pizza restaurant chain in the world in terms of sales and number of units. Internationally, they opened their first restaurant in Canada in 1968 and soon established franchises in Mexico, Germany, Australia, Costa Rica, Japan, and the United Kingdom. In 1977 they sold the business to PepsiCo, Inc. Pizza Hut's headquarters remained in Wichita and Frank Carney served as Pizza Hut's president until 1980. (It is interesting to note that Frank opened a Papa John's Pizza franchise in 1994. Today he is one of Papa John's largest franchisees.)

PepsiCo, Inc.

PepsiCo believed the restaurant business complemented its consumer product orientation. The marketing of fast food followed many of the same patterns as soft drinks and snack foods. Pepsi-Cola and Pizza Hut pizza, for example, could be marketed in the same television and radio segments, which provided higher returns for each advertising dollar. Restaurant chains also provided an additional outlet for the sale of Pepsi soft drinks. In 1978 PepsiCo acquired Taco Bell. After acquiring KFC in 1986, PepsiCo controlled the leading brands in the pizza, Mexican, and chicken segments of the fast-food industry. PepsiCo's strategy of diversifying into three distinct but related markets created one of the world's largest food companies.

In the early 1990s, PepsiCo's sales grew at an annual rate of more than 10 percent. Its rapid growth, however,

627

masked troubles in its fast-food businesses. Operating margins at Pepsi-Cola and PepsiCo's Frito-Lay division averaged 12 and 17 percent, respectively. Margins at KFC, Pizza Hut, and Taco Bell, however, fell from an average of 8 percent in 1990 to 4 percent in 1996. Declining margins reflected increasing maturity in the U.S. fast-food industry, intense competition, and the aging of KFC and Pizza Hut restaurants. PepsiCo's restaurant chains absorbed nearly one-half of PepsiCo's annual capital spending but generated less than one-third of its cash flows. Cash had to be diverted from PepsiCo's soft drink and snack food businesses to its restaurant businesses. This reduced PepsiCo's corporate return on assets, made it more difficult to compete effectively with Coca-Cola, and hurt its stock price. In 1997 PepsiCo decided to spin off its restaurant businesses into a new company called Tricon Global Restaurants, Inc.

Yum! Brands, Inc.   The spin-off created a new, independent, publicly traded company that managed the KFC, Pizza Hut, and Taco Bell franchises. David Novak became Tricon's new CEO. He moved quickly to create a new culture within the company. One of his primary objectives was to reverse the long-standing friction between management and franchisees that was created under PepsiCo ownership. Novak announced that PepsiCo's top-down management system would be replaced by a new management emphasis on providing support to the firm's franchise base. Franchises would have greater independence, resources, and technical support. Novak symbolically changed the name on the corporate headquarters building in Louisville to "KFC Support Center" to drive home his new philosophy.

The firm's new emphasis on franchise support had an immediate effect on morale. In 1997, the year of the divestiture, the company recorded a loss of $111 million in net income. In 2003 it recorded net income of $617 million on sales of $7.4 billion, a return on sales of 8.3 percent. In 2002 Tricon acquired Long John Silver's and A&W All-American Food Restaurants. The acquisitions increased Tricon's worldwide system to almost 33,000 units. One week later, shareholders approved a corporate name change to Yum! Brands, Inc. (Exhibit 1). The acquisitions signaled a shift in the company's strategy from a focus on individual to multibranded units. Multibranding combined two brands in a single restaurant such as KFC and Taco Bell, KFC and A&W, Pizza Hut and Taco Bell, and Pizza Hut and Long John Silver's. Multibranded units attracted a larger consumer base by offering them a broader menu selection in one location. By 2004 the company was operating more than 2,400 multibrand restaurants in the United States.

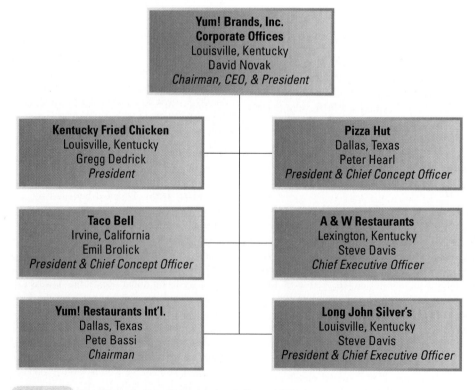

Exhibit 1   Yum! Brands, Inc.: Organizational Chart, 2004

Fast-Food Industry

The National Restaurant Association (NRA) estimated that U.S. food service sales increased by 3.3 percent to $422 billion in 2003. More than 858,000 restaurants made up the U.S. restaurant industry and employed 12 million people. Sales were highest in the full-service, sit-down sector, which grew 3.3 percent to $151 billion. Fast-food sales rose at a slower rate, 2.7 percent to $119 billion. The fast-food sector was increasingly viewed as a mature market. As U.S. incomes rose during the late 1990s and early 2000s, more consumers frequented sit-down restaurants that offered better service and a more comfortable dining experience. Together, the full-service and fast-food segments made up about 64 percent of all U.S. food service sales.

Major Fast-Food Segments

Eight major segments made up the fast-food segment of the restaurant industry: sandwich chains, pizza chains, family restaurants, grill buffet chains, dinner houses, chicken chains, non-dinner concepts, and other chains. Sales data for the leading chains in each segment are shown in Exhibit 2. Most striking is the dominance of McDonald's, which had sales of more than $22 billion in 2003. McDonald's accounted for 14 percent of the sales of the top 100 chains. To put McDonald's dominance in perspective, the second largest chain—Burger King—held less than a 5 percent share of the market.

Sandwich chains made up the largest segment of the fast-food market. McDonald's controlled 35 percent of this segment, while Burger King ran a distant second with a 12 percent share. Sandwich chains struggled through early 2003 as the U.S. recession lowered demand and the war in Iraq increased consumer uncertainty. U.S. consumers were also trending away from the traditional hamburger, fries, and soft drink combinations and demanding more healthy food items and better service. Many chains attempted to attract new customers through price discounting. Instead of drawing in new customers, however, discounting merely lowered profit margins. By mid-2003 most chains had abandoned price discounting and began to focus on improved service and product quality. McDonald's, Taco Bell, and Hardee's were particularly successful. They slowed new restaurant development, improved drive-through service, and introduced a variety of new menu items. McDonald's and Hardee's, for example, introduced larger, higher-priced hamburgers to increase value perceptions and ticket prices. The shift from price discounting to new product introductions increased average ticket sales and helped sandwich chains improve profitability in 2004.

Dinner houses made up the second-largest and fastest-growing fast-food segment. Segment sales increased by almost 9.0 percent in 2003, surpassing the average increase of 5.5 percent in the other segments. Much of the growth in dinner houses came from new unit construction in suburban areas and small towns. Applebee's, Chili's, Outback Steakhouse, Red Lobster, and Olive Garden dominated the segment. Each chain generated sales of more than $2 billion in 2003. The fastest-growing dinner houses, however, were newer chains generating less than $700 million in sales, such as P. F. Chang's China Bistro, the Cheesecake Factory, Carrabba's Italian Grill, and LongHorn Steakhouse. Each chain was increasing sales at a 20 percent annual rate. Dinner houses continued to benefit from rising household incomes in the United States. As incomes rose, families were able to move up from quick-service restaurants to more upscale, higher-priced dinner houses. In addition, higher incomes enabled many professionals to purchase more expensive homes in new suburban developments, thereby providing additional opportunities for dinner houses to build new restaurants in unsaturated areas.

Increased growth among dinner houses came at the expense of sandwich chains, pizza and chicken chains, grill buffet chains, and family restaurants. "Too many restaurants chasing the same customers" was responsible for much of the slower growth in these other fast-food categories. Sales growth within each segment, however, differed from one chain to another. In the family segment, for example, Denny's (the segment leader in sales), Shoney's, Perkins, and Big Boy shut down poorly performing restaurants. At the same time, IHOP, Bob Evans, and Cracker Barrel expanded their bases. The hardest-hit segment was grill buffet chains. Declining sales caused both Sizzlin' and Western Sizzlin' to drop out of the list of Top 100 chains, leaving only three chains in the Top 100 (Golden Corral, Ryan's, and Ponderosa). Each of these three chains shut down restaurants in 2003. Dinner houses, because of their more upscale atmosphere and higher-ticket items, were better positioned to take advantage of the aging and wealthier U.S. population.

Yum! Brands: Brand Leadership

Exhibit 3 shows sales and restaurant data for the pizza, chicken, and sandwich segments. Yum! Brands generated U.S. sales of $16.3 billion across its five brands. It operated close to 21,000 U.S. and 12,000 non-U.S. restaurants, or more than 33,000 restaurants worldwide. Four of its brands—Pizza Hut (pizza), KFC (chicken), Taco Bell (Mexican), and Long John Silver's (seafood)—were the market leaders in their segments. Taco Bell was the third most profitable restaurant concept behind McDonald's and Starbucks. Profitability at McDonald's was primarily driven by volume; each McDonald's restaurant generated an annual average of $1.6 million in sales compared to an industrywide average of $1.0 million. Starbucks, in contrast, generated less revenue per store—about $660 million each year—but premium pricing for its specialty coffee drinks drove high profit margins. Taco Bell was able to generate greater overall profits because of its lower operating costs. Products

Exhibit 2   Top U.S. Fast-Food Restaurants (Ranked by 2003 Sales, $ millions)

Sandwich Chains	Sales	Change		Dinner Houses	Sales	Change
McDonald's	$22,121	8.9%		Applebee's	$ 3,520	10.6%
Burger King	7,680	−2.8		Chili's	2,505	11.8
Wendy's	7,315	5.2		Outback Steakhouse	2,456	7.1
Subway	5,690	8.8		Red Lobster	2,315	−1.9
Taco Bell	5,346	2.8		Olive Garden	2,165	11.6
Arby's	2,710	0.6		TGI Friday's	1,791	2.6
Jack in the Box	2,360	5.4		Ruby Tuesday	1,450	14.8
Sonic Drive-In	2,359	7.0		Romano's	699	9.4
Dairy Queen	2,165	−1.1		Cheesecake Factory	689	20.6
Hardee's	1,662	−2.3		Hooter's	670	6.5
Other Chains	3,934	9.4		Other Chains	5,277	10.7
Total Segment	$63,342	5.2%		Total Segment	$23,537	8.8%
Pizza Chains				**Chicken Chains**		
Pizza Hut	$ 5,033	−1.3%		KFC	$ 4,936	2.8%
Domino's	3,003	2.6		Chick-fil-A	1,534	11.8
Papa John's	1,719	−2.4		Popeyes	1,274	1.6
Little Caesars	1,200	4.3		Church's	700	−2.5
Chuck E. Cheese's	476	3.5		Boston Market	646	0.8
CiCi's Pizza	380	13.9		El Pollo Loco	396	8.7
Round Table Pizza	378	1.1		Bojangles'	375	8.0
Total Segment	$12,189	0.7%		Total Segment	$ 9,861	3.8%
Family Restaurants				**Other Dinner Chains**		
Denny's	$ 2,132	0.6%		Panera Bread	$ 908	32.0%
IHOP	1,676	14.7		Long John Silver's	777	2.8
Cracker Barrel	1,480	5.3		Disney Theme Parks	707	0.4
Bob Evans	954	9.0		Old Country Buffet	548	−4.5
Waffle House	789	2.7		Captain D's Seafood	506	1.7
Perkins	787	−1.3		Total Segment	$ 3,446	7.0%
Other Chains	2,162	1.2		**Non-Dinner Concepts**		
Total Segment	$ 9,980	4.3%		Starbucks	$ 3,118	25.8%
Grill Buffet Chains				Dunkin' Donuts	2,975	10.2
Golden Corral	$ 1,247	7.8%		7-Eleven	1,410	5.6
Ryan's	814	0.2		Krispy Kreme	957	24.0
Ponderosa	537	−2.1		Baskin-Robbins	510	−2.5
Total Segment	$ 2,598	3.2%		Total Segment	$ 8,970	14.9%

Source: *Nation's Restaurant News*. Sales rankings for contract and hotel chains not included.

Exhibit 3   Leading Pizza, Chicken, and Sandwich Chains, 2003

Pizza Chains	Sales ($ millions)	Growth Rate (%)	Units	Growth Rate (%)	Sales per Unit ($000s)
Pizza Hut	$ 5,033.0	(1.3)%	7,523	(1.0)%	$ 665.7
Domino's Pizza	3,003.4	2.6	4,904	1.2	616.0
Papa John's Pizza	1,718.5	(2.4)	3,035	(0.4)	661.5
Little Caesars Pizza	1,200.0	4.4	2,593	(0.2)	395.1
Chuck E. Cheese's	476.2	3.5	485	5.1	1,070.1
CiCi's Pizza	380.4	13.9	465	11.5	862.6
Round Table Pizza	378.4	1.1	456	(5.6)	757.6
Total	$12,189.9	3.1%	19,461	1.5%	$ 718.3
Chicken Chains					
KFC	$ 4,936.0	2.8%	5,524	1.0%	$ 897.8
Chick-fil-A	1,534.4	11.8	1,235	4.9	1,394.3
Popeyes Chicken	1,274.0	1.6	1,447	3.8	896.9
Church's Chicken	700.0	(2.5)	1,235	(1.0)	564.1
Boston Market	646.0	0.8	630	(3.1)	1,009.4
El Pollo Loco	395.7	8.7	314	2.6	1,276.5
Bojangles'	374.8	8.0	320	9.6	1,224.8
Total	$ 9,860.9	4.5%	10,705	2.6%	$1,037.7
Sandwich Chains					
McDonald's	$22,121.4	8.9%	13,609	0.9%	$1,632.6
Burger King	7,680.0	(2.8)	7,656	(3.1)	987.1
Wendy's	7,315.0	5.2	5,761	3.8	1,293.5
Subway	5,690.0	8.8	16,499	13.6	366.8
Taco Bell	5,346.0	2.8	5,989	(2.9)	879.7
Arby's	2,710.0	0.6	3,303	1.6	827.1
Jack in the Box	2,360.0	5.4	1,947	4.6	1,239.2
Total	$53,222.4	4.1%	54,764	2.6%	$1,032.3
Long John Silver's	777.0	2.8	1,204	(1.4)	640.8
A&W Restaurants	200.0	NA	576	(13.4)	NA
Yum! Brands Total	16,292.0	NA	20,822	(1.4)	NA

Source: *Nation's Restaurant News.*

Note: Sales per unit are calculated based on a mathematical equation of annual systemwide sales growth and changes in the number of operating units.

such as tacos, burritos, gorditas, and chalupas used similar ingredients. In addition, cooking machinery was simpler, less costly, and required less space than pizza ovens or chicken broilers.

Pizza Hut controlled the pizza segment with a 41 percent share, followed by Domino's (25 percent) and Papa John's (14 percent). As the pizza segment became increasingly mature, the traditional pizza chains were forced to close old or underperforming restaurants. Only relatively new pizza chain concepts such as CiCi's Pizza, which offered an inexpensive all-you-can-eat salad and pizza buffet, and Chuck E. Cheese's, which focused on family entertainment, were able to significantly grow their restaurant bases during 2003. Most chains could no longer rely on new restaurant construction to drive sales. Another problem was the proliferation of new diets. Many Americans were eating pizza less often as they pursued the Atkins Diet (low carbohydrates), "The Zone" (balanced meals containing equal parts of carbohydrates, protein, and unsaturated fat), or a traditional low-fat diet. Each diet discouraged users from eating pizza, which was high in both fat and carbohydrates.

Operating costs were also rising because of higher cheese and gasoline prices. Pizza chains were forced to develop unique strategies that attracted more customers but protected profit margins. Some chains raised pizza prices to offset higher-priced ingredients or raised home delivery charges to offset higher gasoline costs. Most chains, however, responded with new product introductions. Pizza Hut introduced a low-fat "Fit 'n Delicious" pizza that used one-half the cheese of normal pizzas and toppings with lower fat content. It also introduced a "4forAll" pizza that contained four individually topped six-inch square pizzas in the same box. Domino's introduced a Philly cheese steak pizza, its first new product introduction since 2000. Papa John's introduced a new barbeque chicken and bacon pizza. In addition, it began a campaign that allowed customers to choose one of three free DVDs with the purchase of a large pizza. By matching pizza and movies, Papa John's hoped to encourage customers to eat pizza more often. Pizza Hut quickly responded with its own offer for a free DVD with the purchase of any pizza at the regular price.

KFC continued to dominate the chicken segment with sales of $4.9 billion in 2003, more than 50 percent of sales in the chicken segment. Its nearest competitor, Chick-fil-A, ran a distant second with sales of $1.5 billion. KFC's leadership in the U.S. market was so extensive that it had fewer opportunities to expand its U.S. restaurant base. Despite its dominance, KFC was slowly losing market share as other chicken chains increased sales at a faster rate. Sales data indicated that KFC's share of the chicken segment fell from a high of 64 percent in 1993, a 10-year drop of 14 percent. During the same period, Chick-fil-A and Boston Market increased their combined share by 11 percent. On the surface, it appeared that these market share gains came by taking customers away from KFC. The growth in sales at KFC restaurants, however, had generally remained steady during the last two decades. In reality, the three chains competed for different market groups. Boston Market, for example, appealed to professionals with higher incomes and health-conscious consumers who didn't regularly frequent KFC. It expanded the chicken segment by

offering healthy, "home-style" alternatives to nonfried chicken in a setting resembling an upscale deli. Chick-fil-A concentrated on chicken sandwiches rather than fried chicken and most of its restaurants were still located in shopping mall food courts.

The maturity of the U.S. fast-food industry intensified competition within the chicken segment. As in the pizza segment, chicken chains could not rely on new restaurant construction to build new sales. In addition, chicken costs, which represented about one-half of total food costs, increased dramatically in 2004. A boneless chicken breast, which cost $1.20 per pound in early 2001, cost $2.50 per pound in 2004, an increase of more than 100 percent. Profit margins were being squeezed from both the revenue and cost sides. All chains focused on very different strategies. KFC added new menu boards and introduced new products such as oven roasted strips and roasted twister sandwich wraps. Boston Market experimented with home delivery and began to sell through supermarkets. Chick-fil-A continued to build freestanding restaurants to expand beyond shopping malls. Church's focused on adding drive-through service. The intensity of competition led chicken chains to implement very different strategies for differentiating their product and brand.

Trends in the Restaurant Industry

A number of demographic and societal trends influenced the demand for food eaten outside the home. Rising income, greater affluence among a larger percentage of American households, higher divorce rates, and the marriage of people later in life contributed to the rising number of single households and the demand for fast-food. More than 50 percent of women worked outside the home, a dramatic increase since 1970. This number was expected to rise to 65 percent by 2010. Double-income households contributed to rising household incomes and increased the number of times families ate out. Less time to prepare meals inside the home added to this trend. Countering these trends, however, was the slower growth rate of the U.S. population and a proliferation of fast-food chains that increased consumer alternatives and intensified competition.

Baby boomers (ages 35 to 50) constituted the largest consumer group for fast-food restaurants. Generation Xers (ages 25 to 34) and the "mature" category (ages 51 to 64) made up the second and third largest groups, respectively. As consumers aged, they became less enamored of fast-food and were more likely to trade up to more expensive restaurants such as dinner houses and full-service restaurants. Sales for many Mexican restaurants, which were extremely popular during the 1980s, began to slow as Japanese, Indian, and Vietnamese restaurants became more fashionable. Ethnic foods were rising in popularity as U.S. immigrants, who constituted 13 percent of the U.S.

population in 2004, looked for establishments that sold their native foods.

Labor was the top operational challenge of U.S. restaurant chains. Restaurants relied heavily on teenagers and college-age workers. Twenty percent of all employed teenagers worked in food service, compared to only 4 percent of all employed men over the age of 18 and 6 percent of all employed women over age 18. As the U.S. population aged, fewer young workers were available to fill food service jobs. The short supply of high school and college students meant they had greater work opportunities outside food service. Turnover rates were notoriously high. The National Restaurant Association estimated that about 96 percent of all fast-food workers quit within a year, compared to about 84 percent of employees in full-service restaurants.

Labor costs made up about 30 percent of a fast-food chain's total costs, second only to food and beverage costs. To deal with the decreased supply of employees in the age 16 to 24 category, many restaurants were forced to hire less reliable workers. This affected service and restaurant cleanliness. To improve quality and service, restaurants hired elderly employees who wanted to return to the workforce. To attract more workers, especially the elderly, restaurants offered health insurance, noncontributory pension plans, and profit-sharing benefits. To combat high turnover rates, restaurants turned to training programs and mentoring systems that paired new employees with experienced ones. Mentoring systems were particularly helpful in increasing the learning curve of new workers and providing better camaraderie among employees.

The Global Fast-Food Industry

As the U.S. market matured, more restaurants turned to international markets to expand sales. Foreign markets were attractive because of their large customer bases and comparatively little competition. McDonald's, for example, operated 48 restaurants for every one million U.S. residents. Outside the United States, it operated only one restaurant for every five million residents. McDonald's, Pizza Hut, KFC, and Burger King were the earliest and most aggressive chains to expand abroad beginning in the 1960s. This made them formidable competitors for chains investing abroad for the first time. Subway, TCBY, and Domino's were more recent global competitors. By 2004 each was operating in more than 65 countries. Exhibit 4 lists the world's 35 largest restaurant chains.

The global fast-food industry had a distinctly American flavor. Twenty-eight chains (80 percent of the total) were headquartered in the United States. U.S. chains had the advantage of a large domestic market and ready acceptance by the American consumer. European firms had less success developing the fast-food concept because Europeans were more inclined to frequent midscale restaurants where they spent several hours enjoying multicourse meals in a formal setting. KFC had trouble breaking into the German market during the 1970s and 1980s because Germans were not accustomed to buying takeout or ordering food over the counter. McDonald's had greater success in Germany because it made changes to its menu and operating procedures to appeal to German tastes. German beer, for example, was served in all of McDonald's restaurants in Germany. In France, McDonald's used a different sauce that appealed to the French palate on its Big Mac sandwich. KFC had more success in Asia and Latin America where chicken was a traditional dish.

Yum! Brands operated more than 12,000 restaurants outside the United States (see Exhibit 5). The early international experience of KFC and Pizza Hut put them in a strong position to exploit the globalization trend in the industry. A separate subsidiary in Dallas—Yum! Brands International—managed the international activities of all five brands. As a result, the firm had significant international experience concentrated in one location and a well-established worldwide distribution network. KFC and Pizza Hut accounted for almost all of the firm's international restaurants. Yum! Brands planned to open 1,000 new KFC and Pizza Hut restaurants outside the United States each year, well into the future. This came at a time when both KFC and Pizza Hut were closing units in the mature U.S. market.

Of the KFC and Pizza Hut restaurants located outside the United States, 77 percent were owned by local franchisees or joint venture partners who had a deep understanding of local language, culture, customs, law, financial markets, and marketing characteristics. Franchising allowed firms to expand more quickly, minimize capital expenditures, and maximize return on invested capital. It was also a good strategy for establishing a presence in smaller markets like Grenada, Bermuda, and Suriname where the small number of consumers only allowed for a single restaurant. The costs of operating company-owned restaurants were prohibitively high in these markets. In larger markets such as China, Canada, Australia, and Mexico, there was a stronger emphasis on building company-owned restaurants. Fixed costs could be spread over a larger number of units and the company could coordinate purchasing, recruiting, training, financing, and advertising. This reduced per unit costs. Company-owned restaurants also allowed the company to maintain tighter control over product quality and customer service.

Country Evaluation and Risk Assessment

International Business Risk   Worldwide demand for fast food was expected to grow rapidly during the next two decades as rising per capita income made eating out more affordable for greater numbers of consumers.

Exhibit 4 The World's 35 Largest Fast-Food Chains in 2004

Franchise	Corporate Headquarters	Home Country	Number of Countries with Operations
1. McDonald's	Oak Brook, Illinois	U.S.	121
2. KFC	Louisville, Kentucky	U.S.	99
3. Pizza Hut	Dallas, Texas	U.S.	92
4. Subway Sandwiches	Milford, Connecticut	U.S.	74
5. TCBY	Little Rock, Arkansas	U.S.	67
6. Domino's Pizza	Ann Arbor, Michigan	U.S.	65
7. Burger King	Miami, Florida	U.S.	58
8. TGI Friday's	Dallas, Texas	U.S.	53
9. Baskin-Robbins	Glendale, California	U.S.	52
10. Dunkin' Donuts	Randolph, Massachusetts	U.S.	40
11. Wendy's	Dublin, Ohio	U.S.	34
12. Chili's Grill & Bar	Dallas, Texas	U.S.	22
13. Dairy Queen	Edina, Minnesota	U.S.	22
14. Little Caesars Pizza	Detroit, Michigan	U.S.	22
15. Popeyes	Atlanta, Georgia	U.S.	22
16. Outback Steakhouse	Tampa, Florida	U.S.	20
17. A&W Restaurants	Lexington, Kentucky	U.S.	17
18. PizzaExpress	London	U.K.	16
19. Carl's Jr.	Anaheim, California	U.S.	14
20. Church's Chicken	Atlanta, Georgia	U.S.	12
21. Taco Bell	Irvine, California	U.S.	12
22. Hardee's	Rocky Mount, North Carolina	U.S.	11
23. Applebee's	Overland Park, Kansas	U.S.	9
24. Sizzler	Los Angeles, California	U.S.	9
25. Arby's	Ft. Lauderdale, Florida	U.S.	7
26. Denny's	Spartanburg, South Carolina	U.S.	7
27. Skylark	Tokyo	Japan	7
28. Lotteria	Seoul	Korea	5
29. Taco Time	Eugene, Oregon	U.S.	5
30. Mos Burger	Tokyo	Japan	4
31. Orange Julius	Edina, Minnesota	U.S.	4
32. Yoshinoya	Tokyo	Japan	4
33. IHOP	Glendale, California	U.S.	3
34. Quick Restaurants	Brussels	Belgium	3
35. Red Lobster	Orlando, Florida	U.S.	3

Source: Case author's research.

Exhibit 5 Yum! Brands, Inc.—Largest International Markets, 2004

	KFC	Pizza Hut	Taco Bell	Long John Silver's	A&W	Yum! Brands
			Number of Restaurants			
United States	5,524	7,523	5,989	1,207	579	20,822
International	7,354	4,560	249	31	183	12,377
Worldwide	12,878	12,083	6,238	1,238	762	33,199
International Total (%)	57.1%	37.7%	4.0%	2.5%	24.0%	37.3%
Top Foreign Markets						
1. Japan	1,167	327	24			1,518
2. Canada	733	353	84			1,170
3. U.K.	591	556				1,147
4. China	979	127	1			1,107
5. Australia	516	319	7			842
6. Korea	209	299				508
7. Malaysia	329	106	32	6	26	499
8. Mexico	309	180	1		1	491
9. Thailand	299	77	28		28	432
10. Indonesia	198	85	69		74	426
11. South Africa	360	3				363
12. Philippines	128	113	6		6	253
Other Latin America						
Puerto Rico	95	60	32			187
Ecuador	45	20	4			69
Costa Rica	15	41	11			67
Brazil	3	63				66
Chile	30	28				58
Other Asia						
Taiwan	132	111				242
Singapore	73	34	24	24		155
Other Selected Markets						
France	24	126				150
Germany	45	77				122
Saudi Arabia	50	92	9		9	160
India	2	65				67

Source: Yum! Brands, Inc.

International business, however, carried a variety of risks not present in the domestic market. Long distances between headquarters and foreign franchises made it more difficult to control the quality of individual restaurants. Large distances also caused servicing and support problems, and transportation and other resource costs were higher. In addition, time, cultural, and language differences increased communication problems and made it more difficult to get timely and accurate information.

During the 1970s and 1980s, KFC and Pizza Hut attempted to expand their restaurant bases into as many countries as possible—the greater the number of countries, the greater the indicator of success. By the early years of the 21st century, however, it became apparent that serving a large number of markets with a small number of restaurants was a costly business. If a large number of restaurants could be established in a single market or region, then significant economies of scale could be achieved by spreading fixed costs of purchasing, advertising, and distribution across a larger restaurant base. Higher market share, as a result, was typically associated with greater cash flow and higher profitability.

Country analysis was an important part of the strategic decision-making process. Few companies had sufficient resources to invest everywhere simultaneously. Choices had to be made about when and where to invest scarce capital. Country selection models typically assessed countries on the basis of market size, growth rates, the number and type of competitors, government regulations, and economic and political stability. In an industry such as fast food, however, an analysis of economic and political variables was insufficient. As mentioned earlier, KFC had trouble establishing a presence in Germany because many consumers there didn't accept the fast-food concept. An analysis of Germany's large, stable economy would otherwise have indicated a potentially profitable market.

An important challenge for multinational firms was to accurately assess the risks of doing business in different countries and regions in order to make good choices about where to invest. A useful framework for analyzing international business risk was to separate risk into factors of country, industry, and firm. Country factors, for example, included risks associated with changes in a country's political and economic environment. These included political risk (e.g., war, revolution, changes in government, price controls, tariffs, and government regulations), economic risk (e.g., inflation, high interest rates, foreign exchange rate volatility, balance of trade movements, social unrest, riots, and terrorism), and natural risk (e.g., rainfall, hurricanes, earthquakes, and volcanic activity).

Industry factors addressed changes in industry structure that inhibited a firm's ability to compete successfully in its industry. These included supplier risk (e.g., changes in supplier quality and supplier power), product market risk (e.g., consumer tastes and the availability of substitute products), and competitive risk (e.g., rivalry among competitors, new market entrants, and new product innovations).

Last, firm factors examined a firm's ability to control its internal operations. They included labor risk (e.g., labor unrest, absenteeism, employee turnover, and labor strikes), supplier risk (e.g., raw material shortages and unpredictable price changes), trade secret risk (e.g., protection of trade secrets and intangible assets), credit risk (e.g., problems in collecting receivables), and behavioral risk (e.g., control over franchise operations, product quality and consistency, service quality, and restaurant cleanliness). Each of these factors—country, industry, and firm—had to be analyzed simultaneously to fully understand the costs and benefits of international investment.[1]

Country Risk Assessment in Latin America

Latin America is comprised of some 50 countries, island nations, and principalities that were settled by the Spanish, Portuguese, French, Dutch, and British during the 1500s and 1600s. Spanish is spoken in most countries, the most notable exception being Brazil where the official language is Portuguese. Despite commonalities in language, religion, and history, however, political and economic policies differ significantly from one country to another.

Mexico   Many U.S. companies considered Mexico to be one of the most attractive investment locations in Latin America in the 1990s. Its population of 105 million was more than one-third as large as the United States, and three times larger than Canada's population of 32 million. Prior to 1994, Mexico levied high tariffs on many goods imported from the United States. As a result, many U.S. consumers purchased less expensive products from Asia or Europe. In 1994 the North American Free Trade Agreement (NAFTA) was signed. NAFTA eliminated tariffs on goods traded between the United States, Canada, and Mexico. It created a trading bloc with a larger population and gross domestic product than the European Union. The elimination of tariffs led to an immediate increase in trade between Mexico and the United States. By 2004, 85 percent of Mexico's exports were purchased by U.S. consumers. In turn, 68 percent of Mexico's total imports came from the United States.

Most Mexicans (70 percent) lived in urban areas such as Mexico City, Guadalajara, and Monterrey. Mexico City's population of 18 million made it one of the most populated areas in Latin America. Many U.S. firms had operations in or around Mexico City. The fast-food industry was well developed in Mexico's cities. The leading U.S. fast-food chains already had significant restaurant bases in Mexico, most importantly KFC (274 restaurants), McDonald's (261), Pizza Hut (174), Burger King (154), and Subway (71). Mexican consumers readily accepted the fast-food concept. Chicken was also a staple product in Mexico and helped explain KFC's wide popularity. Mexico's large population and ready acceptance of fast-food represented a significant opportunity for fast-food chains. Competition, however, was intense.

Brazil   Brazil, with a population of 182 million, was the largest country in Latin America and the fifth largest country in the world. Its land base was almost as large as the United States and bordered 10 countries. It was the world's largest coffee producer and largest exporter of sugar and tobacco. In addition to its abundant natural resources and strong export position in agriculture, Brazil was a strong industrial power. Its major exports were airplanes, automobiles, and chemicals. Its gross domestic product of $1.3 trillion was larger than Mexico's and the largest in Latin America (see Exhibit 6). Some firms viewed Brazil as one of the most important emerging markets, along with China and India.

Exhibit 6 Latin America: Selected Economic and Demographic Data

	United States	Canada	Mexico	Colombia	Venezuela	Peru	Brazil	Argentina	Chile
Population (millions)	290.3	32.2	104.9	41.7	24.7	28.4	182.0	38.7	15.7
Growth rate (%)	0.9%	0.9%	1.4%	1.6%	1.5%	1.6%	1.5%	1.1%	1.1%
Population Data: Origin									
European (non-French origin)	65.1%	43.0%	9.0%	20.0%	21.0%	15.0%	55.0%	97.0%	95.0%
European (French origin)		23.0%							
African	12.9%			4.0%	10.0%		6.0%		
Mixed African and European				14.0%		37.0%	38.0%		
Latin American (Hispanic)	12.0%								
Asian	4.2%	6.0%							
Amerindian or Alaskan native	1.5%	2.0%	30.0%	1.0%	2.0%	45.0%			3.0%
Mixed Amerindian and Spanish			60.0%	58.0%	67.0%				
Mixed African and Amerindian				3.0%					
Other	4.3%	26.0%	1.0%			3.0%	1.0%	3.0%	2.0%
Total	100.0%	100.0%	100.0%	100.0%	100.0%	100.0%	100.0%	100.0%	100.0%
GDP ($ billions)	$10,400	$ 923	$ 900	$ 268	$ 133	$ 132	$1,340	$ 391	$ 151
Per capita income (US $)	$37,600	$29,400	$9,000	$6,500	$5,500	$4,800	$7,600	$10,200	$10,000
Real GDP growth rate	2.5%	3.4%	1.0%	2.0%	−8.9%	4.8%	1.0%	−14.7%	1.8%
Inflation rate	1.6%	2.2%	6.4%	6.2%	31.2%	0.2%	8.3%	41.0%	2.5%
Unemployment rate	5.8%	7.6%	3.0%	17.4%	17.0%	9.4%	6.4%	21.5%	9.2%
Literacy rate	97.0%	97.0%	92.2%	92.5%	93.4%	90.9%	86.4%	97.0%	96.2%

Source: U.S. Central Intelligence Agency. 2002. *The World Factbook.* Demographic data is 2003 estimate; economic data as of year-end 2002.

The fast-food industry in Brazil was less developed than in Mexico or the Caribbean. This was partly the result of the structure of the fast-food industry that was dominated by U.S. restaurant chains. U.S. chains expanded further away from their home base as they gained experience operating in Latin America. As firms gained a foothold in Mexico and Central America, it was a natural progression to move into South America. McDonald's understood the importance of Brazil. It opened its first restaurant in 1979 and by 2004 was operating 1,200 restaurants, ice-cream kiosks, and McCafés there. Many restaurant chains such as Burger King, Pizza Hut, and KFC built restaurants in Brazil in the early- to mid-1990s but eventually closed them because of poor sales. Like Germany, many Brazilians were not quick to accept the fast-food concept.

One problem facing U.S. fast-food chains was eating customs. Brazilians ate their big meal in the early afternoon. In the evening, it was customary to have a light meal such as soup or a small plate of pasta. Brazilians rarely ate food with their hands, preferring to eat with a knife and fork. This included food like pizza, which Americans typically ate with their hands. They also were not accustomed to eating sandwiches; if they did eat sandwiches, they wrapped the sandwich in a napkin. U.S. fast-food chains catered to a different kind of customer who wanted more than soup but less than a full sit-down meal. U.S. fast-food chains were more popular in larger cities such as São Paulo and Rio de Janeiro where business people were in a hurry. Food courts were well developed in Brazil's shopping malls but included sit-down as well as fast-food restaurants. U.S. restaurant chains were, therefore, faced with the challenge of changing the eating habits of Brazilians or convincing Brazilians of the attractiveness of fast-food, American style.

Risks and Opportunities

Yum! Brands faced difficult decisions surrounding the design and implementation of an effective international strategy over the next 20 years. Its top seven markets generated more than 70 percent of its international profits. As a result, it planned to continue its aggressive investments in its primary markets. It was also important, however, to improve brand equity in other regions of the world such as continental Europe, Brazil, and India where consumer acceptance of fast food was still weak and the company had limited operational capabilities. Latin America as a region was of particular interest because of its geographic proximity to the United States, cultural similarities, and NAFTA. The company needed to sustain its leadership position in Mexico and the Caribbean but also looked to strengthen its position in countries such as Brazil, Venezuela, and Argentina. Limited resources and cash flow limited KFC's ability to aggressively expand in all countries simultaneously. Country evaluation and risk assessment would be an important tool for developing and implementing an effective international strategy.

Endnote

1. For an in-depth discussion of international business risk, see Miller, Kent D. 1992. A framework for integrated risk management in international business. *Journal of International Business Studies,* 21(2): 311–331.

Case 11   Crown Cork & Seal in 1989*

John F. Connelly, Crown Cork & Seal's ailing octogenarian chairman, stepped down and appointed his long-time disciple, William J. Avery, chief executive officer of the Philadelphia can manufacturer in May 1989. Avery had been president of Crown Cork & Seal since 1981, but had spent the duration of his career in Connelly's shadow. As Crown's new CEO, Avery planned to review Connelly's long-followed strategy in light of the changing industry outlook.

The metal container industry had changed considerably since Connelly took over Crown's reins in 1957. American National had just been acquired by France's state-owned Pechiney International, making it the world's largest beverage can producer. Continental Can, another long-standing rival, was now owned by Peter Kiewit Sons, a privately held construction firm. In 1989, all or part of Continental's can-making operations appeared to be for sale. Reynolds Metals, a traditional supplier of aluminum to can makers, was now also a formidable competitor in cans. The moves by both suppliers and customers of can makers to integrate into can manufacturing themselves had profoundly redefined the metal can industry since John Connelly's arrival.

Reflecting on these dramatic changes, Avery wondered whether Crown, with $1.8 billion in sales, should consider bidding for all or part of Continental Can. Avery also wondered whether Crown should break with tradition and expand its product line beyond the manufacture of metal cans and closures. For 30 years Crown had stuck to its core business, metal can making, but analysts saw little growth potential for metal cans in the 1990s. Industry observers forecast plastics as the growth segment for containers. As Avery mulled over his options, he asked: Was it finally time for a change?

The Metal Container Industry

The metal container industry, representing 61% of all packaged products in the United States in 1989, produced metal cans, crowns (bottle caps), and closures (screw caps, bottle lids) to hold or seal an almost endless variety of consumer and industrial goods. Glass and plastic containers split the balance of the container market with shares of 21% and 18%, respectively. Metal cans served the beverage, food, and general packaging industries.

*Professor Stephen P. Bradley and Research Associate Sheila M. Cavanaugh prepared this case. Harvard Business School cases are developed solely as the basis for class discussion. Cases are not intended to serve as endorsements, sources of primary data, or illustrations of effective or ineffective management.

Harvard Business School Case No. 9-793-035. Reprinted by permission of Harvard Business School Publishing. Copyright © 2003 by the President and Fellows of Harvard College. All rights reserved. To order copies or request permission to reproduce materials, call 1-800-545-7685, write Harvard Business School Publishing, Boston, MA 02163, or go to http://www.hbsp.harvard.edu. No part of this publication may be reproduced, stored in a retrieval system, used in a spreadsheet, or transmitted in any form or by any means—electronic, mechanical, photocopying, recording, or otherwise—without the permission of Harvard Business School.

Metal cans were made of aluminum, steel, or a combination of both. Three-piece cans were formed by rolling a sheet of metal, soldering it, cutting it to size, and attaching two ends, thereby creating a three-piece, seamed can. Steel was the primary raw material of three-piece cans, which were most popular in the food and general packaging industries. Two-piece cans, developed in the 1960s, were formed by pushing a flat blank of metal into a deep cup, eliminating a separate bottom, a molding process termed "drawn and ironed." While aluminum companies developed the original technology for the two-piece can, steel companies ultimately followed suit with a thin-walled steel version. By 1983, two-piece cans dominated the beverage industry where they were the can of choice for beer and soft drink makers. Of the 120 billion cans produced in 1989, 80% were two-piece cans.

Throughout the decade of the 1980s, the number of metal cans shipped grew by an annual average of 3.7%. Aluminum can growth averaged 8% annually, while steel can shipments fell by an average of 3.1% per year. The number of aluminum cans produced increased by almost 200% during the period 1980–1989, reaching a high of 85 billion, while steel can production dropped by 22% to 35 billion for the same period (see Exhibit 1).

Industry Structure   Five firms dominated the $12.2 billion U.S. metal can industry in 1989, with an aggregate 61% market share. The country's largest manufacturer—American National Can—held a 25% market share. The four firms trailing American National in sales were Continental Can (18% market share), Reynolds Metals (7%), Crown Cork & Seal (7%), and Ball Corporation (4%). Approximately 100 firms served the balance of the market.

Pricing   Pricing in the can industry was very competitive. To lower costs, managers sought long runs of standard items, which increased capacity utilization and reduced the need for costly changeovers. As a result, most companies offered volume discounts to encourage large orders. Despite persistent metal can demand, industry operating margins fell approximately 7% to roughly 4% between 1986 and 1989. Industry analysts attributed the drop in operating margins to (1) a 15% increase in aluminum can sheet prices at a time when most can makers had guaranteed volume prices that did not incorporate substantial cost increases; (2) a 7% increase in beverage can production capacity between 1987 and 1989; (3) an increasing number of the nation's major brewers producing containers in house; and (4) the consolidation of soft drink bottlers throughout the decade. Forced to economize following costly battles for market share, soft drink bottlers used their leverage to obtain packaging price discounts.[1] Overcapacity and a shrinking customer base contributed to an unprecedented squeeze on manufacturers' margins, and the can manufacturers themselves contributed to the margin

Exhibit 1   Metal Can Shipments by Market and Product, 1981–1989 (millions of cans)

	1981	%	1983	%	1985	%	1987	%	(Est.) 1989	%
Total Metal Cans Shipped	88,810		92,394		101,899		109,214		120,795	
By Market										
For sale:	59,433	67	61,907	67	69,810	69	81,204	74	91,305	76
Beverage	42,192		45,167		52,017		62,002		69,218	
Food	13,094		12,914		13,974		15,214		18,162	
General packaging	4,147		3,826		3,819		3,988		3,925	
For own use:	29,377	33	31,039	33	32,089	31	28,010	26	29,490	24
Beverage	14,134		16,289		18,160		14,771		17,477	
Food	15,054		14,579		13,870		13,167		11,944	
General packaging	189		171		59		72		69	
By Product										
Beverage:	56,326	63	61,456	67	70,177	69	76,773	70	86,695	72
Beer	30,901		33,135		35,614		36,480		37,276	
Soft drinks	25,425		28,321		34,563		40,293		49,419	
Food:	28,148	32	26,941	29	27,844	27	28,381	26	30,106	25
Dairy products	854		927		1,246		1,188		1,304	
Juices	13,494		11,954		11,385		11,565		12,557	
Meat, poultry, seafood	2,804		3,019		3,373		3,530		3,456	
Pet food	3,663		3,571		4,069		4,543		5,130	
Other	7,333		7,470		7,771		7,555		7,659	
General packaging:	4,336	5	3,997	4	3,878	4	4,060	4	3,994	3
Aerosol	2,059		2,144		2,277		2,508		2,716	
Paint: varnish	813		817		830		842		710	
Automotive products	601		229		168		128		65	
Other nonfoods	863		807		603		582		503	
By Materials Used										
Steel	45,386	52	40,116	45	34,316	37	34,559	34	35,318	29
Aluminum	42,561	48	48,694	55	58,078	63	67,340	66	85,477	71

Source: Can Shipment Report, Can Manufacturers Institute, 1981–1989.

deterioration by aggressively discounting to protect market share. As one manufacturer confessed, "When you look at the beverage can industry, it's no secret that we are selling at a lower price today than we were 10 years ago."

Customers   Among the industry's largest users were the Coca-Cola Company, Anheuser-Busch Companies, Inc., Pepsico Inc., and Coca-Cola Enterprises Inc. (see Exhibit 2). Consolidation within the soft drink segment of the bottling industry reduced the number of bottlers from approximately 8,000 in 1980 to about 800 in 1989 and placed a significant amount of beverage volume in the hands of a few large companies.[2] Since the can constituted about 45% of the total cost of a packaged beverage, soft drink bottlers and brewers usually maintained relationships with more

than one can supplier. Poor service and uncompetitive prices could be punished by cuts in order size.

Distribution   Due to the bulky nature of cans, manufacturers located their plants close to customers to minimize transportation costs. The primary cost components of the metal can included (1) raw materials at 65%; (2) direct labor at 12%; and (3) transportation at roughly 7.5%. Various estimates placed the radius of economical distribution for a plant at between 150 and 300 miles. Beverage can producers preferred aluminum to steel because of aluminum's lighter weight and lower shipping costs. In 1988, steel cans weighed more than twice as much as aluminum.[3] The costs incurred in transporting cans to overseas markets made international trade uneconomical. Foreign markets were

Exhibit 2   Top U.S. Users of Containers, 1989

Rank	Company	Soft Drink/ Beverage Sales ($000)	Principal Product Categories
1	The Coca-Cola Company[a] (Atlanta, GA)	$8,965,800	Soft drinks, citrus juices, fruit drinks
2	Anheuser-Busch Companies, Inc.[b] (St. Louis, MO)	7,550,000	Beer, beer imports
3	PepsiCo Inc. (Purchase, NY)	5,777,000	Soft drinks, bottled water
4	The Seagram Company, Ltd. (Montreal, Quebec, Canada)	5,581,779	Distilled spirits, wine coolers, mixers, juices
5	Coca-Cola Enterprises, Inc.[a] (Atlanta, GA)	3,881,947	Soft drinks
6	Philip Morris Companies, Inc. (New York, NY)	3,435,000	Beer
7	The Molson Companies, Ltd. (Toronto, Ontario, Canada)	1,871,394	Beer, coolers, beer imports
8	John Labatt, Ltd. (London, Ontario, Canada)	1,818,100	Beer, wine
9	The Stroh Brewery Company[c] (Detroit, MI)	1,500,000	Beer, coolers, soft drinks
10	Adolph Coors Company[d] (Golden, CO)	1,366,108	Beer, bottled water

Source: Beverage World, 1990–1991 Databank.

[a]The Coca-Cola Company and Coca-Cola Enterprises purchased (versus in-house manufacture) all of its cans in 1989. Coca-Cola owned 49% of Coca-Cola Enterprises—the largest Coca-Cola bottler in the United States.

[b]In addition to in-house manufacturing at its wholly owned subsidiary (Metal Container Corporation), Anheuser-Busch Companies purchased its cans from four manufacturers. The percentage of cans manufactured by Anheuser-Busch was not publicly disclosed.

[c]Of the 4 to 5 billion cans used by The Stroh Brewery in 1989, 39% were purchased and 61% were manufactured in-house.

[d]Adolph Coors Company manufactured all of its cans, producing approximately 10 to 12 million cans per day, five days per week.

served by joint ventures, foreign subsidiaries, affiliates of U.S. can manufacturers, and local overseas firms.

Manufacturing   Two-piece can lines cost approximately $16 million, and the investment in peripheral equipment raised the per-line cost to $20–$25 million. The minimum efficient plant size was one line and installations ranged from one to five lines. While two-piece can lines achieved quick and persistent popularity, they did not completely replace their antecedents—the three-piece can lines. The food and general packaging segment—representing 28% of the metal container industry in 1989—continued using three-piece cans throughout the 1980s. The beverage segment, however,

had made a complete switch from three-piece to two-piece cans by 1983.

A typical three-piece can production line cost between $1.5 and $2 million and required expensive seaming, end-making, and finishing equipment. Since each finishing line could handle the output of three or four can-forming lines, the minimum efficient plant required at least $7 million in basic equipment. Most plants had 12 to 15 lines for the increased flexibility of handling more than one type of can at once. However, any more than 15 lines became unwieldy because of the need for duplication of set-up crews, maintenance, and supervision. The beverage industry's switch from three- to two-piece lines prompted many manufacturers

Exhibit 3   Comparative Performance of Major Aluminum Suppliers, 1988 (dollars in millions)

	Sales	Net Income	Net Profit Margin %	Long-Term Debt	Net Worth	Earnings Per Share
Alcan Aluminum						
1988	$8,529.0	$931.0	10.9%	$1,199.0	$4,320.0	$3.85
1987	6,797.0	445.0	6.5	1,336.0	3,970.0	1.73
1986	5,956.0	177.0	3.0	1,366.0	3,116.0	.79
1985	5,718.0	25.8	0.5	1,600.0	2,746.0	.12
1984	5,467.0	221.0	4.0	1,350.0	2,916.0	1.00
Alcoa						
1988	9,795.3	861.4	8.8	1,524.7	4,635.5	9.74
1987	7,767.0	365.8	4.7	2,457.6	3,910.7	4.14
1986	4,667.2	125.0	2.7	1,325.6	3,721.6	1.45
1985	5,162.7	107.4	2.1	1,553.5	3,307.9	1.32
1984	5,750.8	278.7	4.8	1,586.5	3,343.6	3.41
Reynolds Metals[a]						
1988	5,567.1	482.0	8.7	1,280.0	2,040.1	9.01
1987	4,283.8	200.7	4.7	1,567.7	1,599.6	3.95
1986	3,638.9	50.3	1.4	1,190.8	1,342.0	.86
1985	3,415.6	24.5	0.7	1,215.0	1,151.7	.46
1984	3,728.3	133.3	3.6	1,146.1	1,341.1	3.09

Source: *Value Line.*

[a]Reynolds Metals Company was the second-largest aluminum producer in the United States. The company was also the third-largest manufacturer of metal cans with a 7% market share.

to sell complete, fully operational three-piece lines "as is" for $175,000 to $200,000. Some firms shipped their old lines overseas to their foreign operations where growth potential was great, there were few entrenched firms, and canning technology was not well understood.

Suppliers   Since the invention of the aluminum can in 1958, steel had fought a losing battle against aluminum. In 1970, steel accounted for 88% of metal cans, but by 1989 had dropped to 29%. In addition to being lighter, of higher, more consistent quality, and more economical to recycle, aluminum was also friendlier to the taste and offered superior lithography qualities. By 1989, aluminum accounted for 99% of the beer and 94% of the soft drink metal container businesses, respectively.

The country's three largest aluminum producers supplied the metal can industry. Alcoa, the world's largest aluminum producer with 1988 sales of $9.8 billion, and

Alcan, the world's largest marketer of primary aluminum, with 1988 sales of $8.5 billion, supplied over 65% of the domestic can sheet requirements. Reynolds Metals, the second-largest aluminum producer in the United States, with 1988 sales of $5.6 billion, supplied aluminum sheet to the industry and also produced about 11 billion cans itself.[4] Reynolds Metals was the only aluminum company in the United States that produced cans (see Exhibit 3).

Steel's consistent advantage over aluminum was price. According to The American Iron and Steel Institute in 1988, steel represented a savings of from $5 to $7 for every thousand cans produced, or an estimated savings of $500 million a year for can manufacturers. In 1988, aluminum prices increased an estimated 15%, while the lower steel prices increased by only 5% to 7%. According to a representative of Alcoa, the decision on behalf of the firm to limit aluminum price increases was attributed to the threat of possible inroads by steel.[5]

Industry Trends   The major trends characterizing the metal container industry during the 1980s included (1) the continuing threat of in-house manufacture; (2) the emergence of plastics as a viable packaging material; (3) the steady competition from glass as a substitute for aluminum in the beer market; (4) the emergence of the soft drink industry as the largest end-user of packaging, with aluminum as the primary beneficiary; and (5) the diversification of, and consolidation among, packaging producers.

In-House Manufacture   Production of cans at "captive" plants—those producing cans for their own company use—accounted for approximately 25% of the total can output in 1989. Much of the expansion in in-house manufactured cans, which persisted throughout the 1980s, occurred at plants owned by the nation's major food producers and brewers. Many large brewers moved to hold can costs down by developing their own manufacturing capability. Brewers found it advantageous to invest in captive manufacture because of high-volume, single-label production runs. Adolph Coors took this to the extreme by producing all their cans in-house and supplying almost all of their own aluminum requirements from their 130-million-pound sheet rolling mill in San Antonio, Texas.[6] By the end of the 1980s, the beer industry had the capacity to supply about 55% of its beverage can needs.[7]

Captive manufacturing was not widespread in the soft drink industry, where many small bottlers and franchise operations were generally more dispersed geographically compared with the brewing industry. Soft drink bottlers were also geared to low-volume, multilabel output, which was not as economically suitable for the in-house can manufacturing process.

Plastics   Throughout the 1980s, plastics was the growth leader in the container industry with its share growing from 9% in 1980 to 18% in 1989. Plastic bottle sales in the United States were estimated to reach $3.5 billion in 1989, with food and beverage—buoyed by soft drinks sales—accounting for 50% of the total. Plastic bottles accounted for 11% of domestic soft drink sales, with most of its penetration coming at the expense of glass. Plastic's light weight and convenient handling contributed to widespread consumer acceptance. The greatest challenge facing plastics, however, was the need to produce a material that simultaneously retained carbonation and prevented infiltration of oxygen. The plastic bottle often allowed carbonation to escape in less than 4 months, while aluminum cans held carbonation for more than 16 months. Anheuser-Busch claimed that U.S. brewers expected beer containers to have at least a 90-day shelf-life, a requirement that had not been met by any plastic can or bottle.[8] Additionally, standard production lines that filled 2,400 beer cans per minute required containers with perfectly flat bottoms, a feature difficult to achieve using plastic.[9] Since 1987, the growth of plastics had slowed somewhat apparently due to the impact on the environment of

plastic packaging. Unlike glass and aluminum, plastics recycling was not a "closed loop" system.[10]

There were many small players producing plastic containers in 1988, often specializing by end-use or geographic region. However, only seven companies had sales of over $100 million. Owens-Illinois, the largest producer of plastic containers, specialized in custom-made bottles and closures for food, health and beauty, and pharmaceutical products. It was the leading supplier of prescription containers, sold primarily to drug wholesalers, major drug chains, and the government. Constar, the second-largest domestic producer of plastic containers, acquired its plastic bottle operation from Owens-Illinois, and relied on plastic soft drink bottles for about two-thirds of its sales. Johnson Controls produced bottles for the soft drink industry from 17 U.S. plants and six non-U.S. plants, and was the largest producer of plastic bottles for water and liquor. American National and Continental Can both produced plastic bottles for food, beverages, and other products such as tennis balls (see Exhibit 4 for information on competitors).

Glass   Glass bottles accounted for only 14% of domestic soft drink sales, trailing metal cans at 75%. The cost advantage that glass once had relative to plastic in the popular 16-ounce bottle size disappeared by the mid-1980s because of consistently declining resin prices. Moreover, soft drink bottlers preferred the metal can to glass because of a variety of logistical and economic benefits: faster filling speeds, lighter weight, compactness for inventory, and transportation efficiency. In 1989, the delivered cost (including closure and label) of a 12-ounce can (the most popular size) was about 15% less than that of glass or plastic 16-ounce bottles (the most popular size).[11] The area in which glass continued to outperform metal, however, was the beer category where consumers seemed to have a love affair with the "long neck" bottle that would work to its advantage in the coming years.[12]

Soft Drinks and Aluminum Cans   Throughout the 1980s, the soft drink industry emerged as the largest end-user of packaging. In 1989, soft drinks captured more than 50% of the total beverage market. The soft drink industry accounted for 42% of metal cans shipped in 1989—up from 29% in 1980. The major beneficiary of this trend was the aluminum can. In addition to the industry's continued commitment to advanced technology and innovation, aluminum's penetration could be traced to several factors: (1) aluminum's weight advantage over glass and steel; (2) aluminum's ease of handling; (3) a wider variety of graphics options provided by multipack can containers; and (4) consumer preference.[13] Aluminum's growth was also supported by the vending machine market, which was built around cans and dispensed approximately 20% of all soft drinks in 1989. An estimated 60% of Coca Cola's and 50% of Pepsi's beverages were packaged in metal cans. Coca Cola Enterprises and Pepsi Cola Bottling Group

Exhibit 4   Major U.S. Producers of Blow-Molded Plastic Bottles, 1989 (dollars in millions)

Company	Total Sales	Net Income	Plastic Sales	Product Code	Major Market
Owens-Illinois	$3,280	$ (57)	$754	1,3,4,6	Food, health and beauty, pharmaceutical
American National	4,336	52	566	1,2,3,6	Beverage, household, personal care, pharmaceutical
Constar	544	12	544	1,2,3,4,6	Soft drink, milk, food
Johnson Controls	3,100	104	465	2	Soft drink, beverages
Continental Can	3,332	18	353	1,2,3,4,5,6	Food, beverage, household, industrial
Silgan Plastics	415	96	100	1,2,3,4,6	Food, beverage, household, pharmaceutical, personal care
Sonoco Products Co.	1,600	96	N/A	1,3,4,6	Motor oil, industrial

Source: *The Rauch Guide to the U.S. Plastics Industry.* 1991; company annual reports.

Product code: (1) HDPE; (2) PET; (3) PP; (4) PVC; (5) PC; (6) multilayer.

together accounted for 22% of all soft drink cans shipped in 1989.[14] In 1980, the industry shipped 15.9 billion aluminum soft drink cans. By 1989, that figure had increased to 49.2 billion cans. This increase, representing a 12% average annual growth rate, was achieved during a decade that experienced a 3.6% average annual increase in total gallons of soft drinks consumed.

Diversification and Consolidation   Low profit margins, excess capacity, and rising material and labor costs prompted a number of corporate diversifications and subsequent consolidations throughout the 1970s and 1980s. While many can manufacturers diversified across the spectrum of rigid containers to supply all major end-use markets (food, beverages, and general packaging), others diversified into nonpackaging businesses such as energy (oil and gas) and financial services.

Over a 20-year period, for example, American Can reduced its dependence on domestic can manufacturing, moving into totally unrelated fields, such as insurance. Between 1981 and 1986 the company invested $940 million to acquire all or part of six insurance companies. Ultimately, the packaging businesses of American Can were acquired by Triangle Industries in 1986, while the financial services businesses re-emerged as Primerica. Similarly, Continental Can broadly diversified its holdings, changing its name to Continental Group in 1976 when can sales dropped to 38% of total sales. In the 1980s, Continental Group invested heavily in energy exploration, research, and transportation, but profits were weak and they were ultimately taken over by Peter Kiewit Sons in 1984.

While National Can stuck broadly to containers, it diversified through acquisition into glass containers, food canning, pet foods, bottle closures, and plastic containers. However, instead of generating future growth opportunities, the expansion into food products proved a drag on company earnings.

Under the leadership of John W. Fisher, Ball Corporation, a leading glass bottle and can maker, expanded into the high-technology market and by 1987 had procured $180 million in defense contracts. Fisher directed Ball into such fields as petroleum engineering equipment, and photo-engraving and plastics, and established the company as a leading manufacturer of computer components.

Major Competitors in 1989   For over 30 years, three of the current five top competitors in can manufacturing dominated the metal can industry. Since the early 1950s, American Can, Continental Can, Crown Cork & Seal, and National Can held the top four rankings in can manufacturing. A series of dramatic mergers and acquisitions among several of the country's leading manufacturers throughout the 1980s served to shift as well as consolidate power at the top. Management at fourth-ranked Crown Cork & Seal viewed the following four firms as constituting its primary competition in 1989: American National Can, Continental Can, Reynolds Metals, and Ball Corporation. Two smaller companies—Van Dorn Company and Heekin Can—were strong competitors regionally (see Exhibit 5).

American National Can   Representing the merger of two former, long-established competitors, American National—a wholly-owned subsidiary of the Pechiney International Group—generated sales revenues of $4.4 billion in

Exhibit 5   Comparative Performance of Major Metal Can Manufacturers (dollars in millions)

Company[a]	Net Sales	SG&A as a % of Sales	Gross Margin	Operating Income	Net Profit	Return on Sales	Return on Average Assets	Return on Average Equity
Ball Corporation								
1988	$1,073.0	8.1%	$161.7	$113.0	$47.7	4.4%	5.7%	11.6%
1987	1,054.1	8.5	195.4	147.6	59.8	5.7	7.8	15.7
1986	1,060.1	8.2	168.0	150.5	52.8	5.0	7.6	15.2
1985	1,106.2	7.5	140.7	140.5	51.2	4.6	8.1	16.4
1984	1,050.7	7.9	174.1	123.9	46.3	4.4	7.8	16.6
1983	909.5	8.2	158.2	114.6	39.0	4.3	7.3	15.6
1982	889.1	8.4	147.4	100.5	34.5	3.9	6.9	15.8
Crown Cork & Seal								
1988	1,834.1	2.8	264.6	212.7	93.4	5.1	8.6	14.5
1987	1,717.9	2.9	261.3	223.3	88.3	5.1	8.7	14.5
1986	1,618.9	2.9	235.3	202.4	79.4	4.9	8.8	14.3
1985	1,487.1	2.9	216.4	184.4	71.7	4.8	8.6	13.9
1984	1,370.0	3.1	186.6	154.8	59.5	4.4	7.3	11.4
1983	1,298.0	3.3	182.0	138.9	51.5	4.0	6.2	9.3
1982	1,351.8	3.3	176.2	132.5	44.7	3.3	5.2	7.9
Heekin Can, Inc.								
1988	275.8	3.7	38.9	36.4	9.6	3.5	4.8	22.6
1987	230.4	4.0	33.6	30.2	8.8	3.8	5.8	26.3
1986	207.6	4.1	31.1	28.0	7.0	3.4	5.4	27.5
1985	221.8	3.2	31.8	29.0	6.8	3.1	5.2	42.5
1984	215.4	2.7	28.4	26.5	5.5	2.6	4.3	79.7
1983	181.6	3.2	24.4	22.8	3.8	2.1	3.3	102.7
1982[b]	—							
Van Dorn Company								
1988	333.5	16.5	75.3	26.7	11.7	3.5	6.6	12.2
1987	330.0	15.7	73.6	28.4	12.3	3.7	7.7	12.7
1986	305.1	16.3	70.4	26.5	11.7	3.8	7.7	12.9
1985	314.3	15.1	75.6	33.6	15.4	4.9	10.6	19.0
1984	296.4	14.7	74.9	36.5	16.8	5.7	12.9	24.9
1983	225.9	14.8	48.5	20.1	7.4	3.3	6.8	12.8
1982	184.3	16.1	37.7	12.7	3.6	2.0	3.5	6.6
American Can Company[c]								
1985	2,854.9	22.6	813.4	1670.0	149.1	5.2	5.2	10.9
1984	3,177.9	18.0	740.8	168.3	132.4	4.2	4.9	11.2
1983	3,346.4	15.0	625.4	123.6	94.9	2.8	3.5	9.7
1982	4,063.4	16.1	766.3	113.4	23.0	0.6	0.8	2.4
1981	4,836.4	15.0	949.6	223.0	76.7	1.2	2.7	7.2
1980	4,812.2	15.8	919.5	128.1	85.7	1.8	3.1	8.0

(*continued*)

Exhibit 5   (*Continued*)

Company[a]	Net Sales	SG&A as a % of Sales	Gross Margin	Operating Income	Net Profit	Return on Sales	Return on Average Assets	Return on Average Equity
National Can Company[d]								
1983	1,647.5	5.1	215.3	93.5	22.1	1.3	2.7	6.3
1982	1,541.5	4.6	206.3	100.7	34.1	2.2	4.4	10.0
1981	1,533.9	4.6	191.7	86.3	24.7	1.6	3.1	7.5
1980	1,550.9	5.4	233.7	55.0	50.6	3.3	6.4	16.7
The Continental Group, Inc.[e]								
1983	4,942.0	6.3	568.0	157.0	173.5	3.5	4.4	9.4
1982	5,089.0	6.4	662.0	217.0	180.2	3.5	4.3	9.6
1981	5,291.0	7.2	747.0	261.0	242.2	4.6	5.9	13.6
1980	5,171.0	7.2	700.0	201.0	224.8	4.3	5.5	13.7
1979	4,544.0	6.5	573.0	171.0	189.2	4.2	5.3	13.1

Source: *Value Line* and company annual reports (for SGA, COGS, and Asset figures).

[a]Refer to Exhibit 3 for Reynolds Metals Company. [b]Figures not disclosed for 1982. [c]In 1985, packaging made up 60% of total sales at American Can, with the remainder in specialty retailing. In 1986 Triangle Industries purchased the U.S. packaging business of American Can. In 1987, American National Can was formed through the merger of American Can Packaging and National Can Corporation. In 1989, Triangle sold American National Can to Pechiney, SA. [d]In 1985, Triangle Industries bought National Can. [e]In 1984, Peter Kiewit Sons purchased The Continental Group. SG&A as a percentage of sales for Continental Can hovered around 6.5% through the late 1980s.

1988. In 1985, Triangle Industries, a New Jersey–based maker of video games, vending machines, and jukeboxes, bought National Can for $421 million. In 1986, Triangle bought the U.S. packaging businesses of American Can for $550 million. In 1988, Triangle sold American National Can (ANC) to Pechiney, SA, the French state-owned industrial concern, for $3.5 billion. Pechiney was the world's third-largest producer of aluminum and, through its Cebal Group, a major European manufacturer of packaging. A member of the Pechiney International Group, ANC was the largest beverage can maker in the world—producing more than 30 billion cans annually. With more than 100 facilities in 12 countries, ANC's product line of aluminum and steel cans, glass containers, and caps and closures served the major beverage, food, pharmaceuticals, and cosmetics markets.

Continental Can   Continental Can had long been a financially stable container company; its revenues increased every year without interruption from 1923 through the mid-1980s. By the 1970s, Continental had surpassed American Can as the largest container company in the United States. The year 1984, however, represented a turning point in Continental's history when the company became an attractive takeover target. Peter Kiewit Sons Inc., a private construction firm in Omaha, Nebraska, purchased Continental Group for $2.75 billion in 1984. Under the direction of Vice Chairman Donald Strum, Kiewit dismantled Continental Group in an effort to make the operation more profitable. Within a year, Strum had sold $1.6 billion worth of insurance, gas pipelines, and oil and gas reserves. Staff at Continental's Connecticut headquarters was reduced from 500 to 40. Continental Can generated sales revenues of $3.3 billion in 1988, ranking it second behind American National. By the late 1980s, management at Kiewit considered divesting—in whole or in part—Continental Can's packaging operations, which included Continental Can USA, Europe, and Canada, as well as metal packaging operations in Latin America, Asia, and the Middle East.

Reynolds Metals   Based in Richmond, Virginia, Reynolds Metals was the only domestic company integrated from aluminum ingot through aluminum cans. With 1988 sales revenues of $5.6 billion and net income of $482 million, Reynolds served the following principal markets: packaging and containers; distributors and fabricators; building and construction; aircraft and automotive; and electrical. Reynolds' packaging and container revenue amounted to $2.4 billion in 1988. As one of the industry's leading can makers, Reynolds was instrumental in establishing new uses for the aluminum can and was a world leader in can-making technology. Reynolds' developments included high-speed can-forming machinery with capabilities in excess of 400 cans per minute, faster inspection equipment (operating at speeds of up to 2,000 cans per minute), and spun aluminum tops which contained less material. The company's next generation of can end-making technology was scheduled for installation in the early 1990s.

Ball Corporation   Founded in 1880 in Muncie, Indiana, Ball Corporation generated operating income of $113 million on sales revenues of $1 billion in 1988. Considered one of the industry's low-cost producers, Ball was the fifth-largest manufacturer of metal containers as well as the third-largest glass container manufacturer in the United States. Ball's packaging businesses accounted for 82.5% of total sales and 77.6% of consolidated operating earnings in 1988. Ball's can-making technology and manufacturing flexibility allowed the company to make shorter runs in the production of customized, higher-margin products designed to meet customers' specifications and needs. In 1988, beverage can sales accounted for 62% of total sales. Anheuser-Busch, Ball's largest customer, accounted for 14% of sales that year. In 1989, Ball was rumored to be planning to purchase the balance of its 50%-owned joint venture, Ball Packaging Products Canada, Inc. The acquisition would make Ball the number two producer of metal beverage and food containers in the Canadian market.

Van Dorn Company   The industry's next two largest competitors, with a combined market share of 3%, were Van Dorn Company and Heekin Can, Inc. Founded in 1872 in Cleveland, Ohio, Van Dorn manufactured two product lines: containers and plastic injection molding equipment. Van Dorn was one of the world's largest producers of drawn aluminum containers for processed foods, and a major manufacturer of metal, plastic, and composite containers for the paint, petroleum, chemical, automotive, food, and pharmaceutical industries. Van Dorn was also a leading manufacturer of injection molding equipment for the plastics industry. The company's Davies Can Division, founded in 1922, was a regional manufacturer of metal and plastic containers. In 1988, Davies planned to build two new can manufacturing plants at a cost of about $20 million each. These facilities would each produce about 40 million cans annually. Van Dorn's consolidated can sales of $334 million in 1988 ranked it sixth overall among the country's leading can manufacturers.

Heekin Can   James Heekin, a Cincinnati coffee merchant, founded Heekin Can in 1901 as a way to package his own products. The company experienced rapid growth and soon contained one of the country's largest metal lithography plants under one roof. Three generations of the Heekin family built Heekin into a strong regional force in the packaging industry. The family sold the business to Diamond International Corporation, a large, diversified publicly held company, in 1965. Diamond operated Heekin as a subsidiary until 1982 when it was sold to its operating

management and a group of private investors. Heekin went public in 1985. With 1988 sales revenues of $275.8 million, seventh-ranked Heekin primarily manufactured steel cans for processors, packagers, and distributors of food and pet food. Heekin represented the country's largest regional can maker.

Crown Cork & Seal Company

Company History   In August 1891, a foreman in a Baltimore machine shop hit upon an idea for a better bottle cap—a piece of tin-coated steel with a flanged edge and an insert of natural cork. Soon this crown-cork cap became the hit product of a new venture, Crown Cork & Seal Company. When the patents ran out, however, competition became severe and nearly bankrupted the company in the 1920s. The faltering Crown was bought in 1927 by a competitor, Charles McManus.[15]

Under the paternalistic leadership of McManus, Crown prospered in the 1930s, selling more than half of the United States and world supply of bottle caps. He then correctly anticipated the success of the beer can and diversified into can making, building one of the world's largest plants in Philadelphia. However, at one million square feet and containing as many as 52 lines, it was a nightmare of inefficiency and experienced substantial losses. Although McManus was an energetic leader, he engaged in nepotism and never developed an organization that could run without him. Following his death in 1946, the company ran on momentum, maintaining dividends at the expense of investment in new plants. Following a disastrous attempt to expand into plastics and a ludicrous diversification into metal bird cages, Crown reorganized along the lines of the much larger Continental Can, incurring additional personnel and expense that again brought the company near to bankruptcy.

At the time, John Connelly was just a fellow on the outside, looking to Crown as a prospective customer and getting nowhere. The son of a Philadelphia blacksmith, Connelly had begun in a paperbox factory at 15 and worked his way up to become eastern sales manager of the Container Corporation of America. When he founded his own company, Connelly Containers, Inc., in 1946, Crown promised him some business. That promise was forgotten by the post-McManus regime, which loftily refused to "take a chance" on a small supplier like Connelly. By 1955, when Crown's distress became evident, Connelly began buying stock and in November 1956 was asked to be an outside director—a desperate move by the ailing company.[16]

In April 1957, Crown Cork & Seal teetered on the verge of bankruptcy. Bankers Trust Company withdrew Crown's line of credit; it seemed that all that was left was to write the company's obituary when John Connelly took over the presidency. His rescue plan was simple—as he called it, "just common sense." Connelly's first move was to pare down the organization. Paternalism ended in a blizzard of pink slips. Connelly moved quickly to cut headquarters staff by half to reach a lean force of 80. The company returned to a simple functional organization. In 20 months Crown had eliminated 1,647 jobs or 24% of the payroll. As part of the company's reorganization, Connelly discarded divisional accounting practices; at the same time he eliminated the divisional line and staff concept. Except for one accountant maintained at each plant location, all accounting and cost control was performed at the corporate level; the corporate accounting staff occupied one-half the space used by the headquarters group. In addition, Connelly disbanded Crown's central research and development facility.

The second step was to institute the concept of accountability. Connelly aimed to instill a deep-rooted pride of workmanship throughout the company by establishing Crown managers as "owner-operators" of their individual businesses. Connelly gave each plant manager responsibility for plant profitability, including any allocated costs. (All company overhead, estimated at 5% of sales, was allocated to the plant level.) Previously, plant managers had been responsible only for controllable expenses at the plant level. Although the plant managers' compensation was not tied to profit performance, one senior executive pointed out that the managers were "certainly rewarded on the basis of that figure." Connelly also held plant managers responsible for quality and customer service.

The next step was to slow production to a halt and liquidate $7 million in inventory. By mid-July Crown paid off the banks. Connelly introduced sales forecasting dovetailed with new production and inventory controls. This move put pressure on the plant managers, who were no longer able to avoid layoffs by dumping excess products into inventory.

By the end of 1957, Crown had, in one observer's words, "climbed out of the coffin and was sprinting." Between 1956 and 1961, sales increased from $115 million to $176 million and profits soared. Throughout the 1960s, the company averaged an annual 15.5% increase in sales and 14% in profits. Connelly, not satisfied simply with short-term reorganizations of the existing company, developed a strategy that would become its hallmark for the next three decades.

Connelly's Strategy

According to William Avery, "From his first day on the job, Mr. Connelly structured the company to be successful. He took control of costs and did a wonderful job taking us in the direction of becoming owner-operators." But what truly separated Connelly from his counterparts, Avery explained, was that while he was continually looking for new ways of controlling costs, he was equally hell-bent on improving quality. Connelly, described by *Forbes* as an individual with a "scrooge-like aversion to fanfare and overhead," emphasized cost efficiency, quality, and customer service as the essential ingredients for Crown's strategy in the decades ahead.

Products and Markets   Recognizing Crown's position as a small producer in an industry dominated by American Can and Continental Can, Connelly sought to develop a product line built around Crown's traditional strengths in metal forming and fabrication. He chose to emphasize the areas Crown knew best—tin-plated cans and crowns—and to concentrate on specialized uses and international markets.

A dramatic illustration of Connelly's commitment to this strategy occurred in the early 1960s. In 1960, Crown held over 50% of the market for motor oil cans. In 1962, R. C. Can and Anaconda Aluminum jointly developed fiber-foil cans for motor oil, which were approximately 20% lighter and 15% cheaper than the metal cans then in use. Despite the loss of sales, management decided that it had other more profitable opportunities and that new materials, such as fiber-foil, provided too great a threat in the motor oil can business. Crown's management decided to exit from the oil can market.

In the early 1960s Connelly singled out two specific applications in the domestic market: beverage cans and the growing aerosol market. These applications were called "hard to hold" because cans required special characteristics to either contain the product under pressure or to avoid affecting taste. Connelly led Crown directly from a soldered can into the manufacture of two-piece steel cans in the 1960s. Recognizing the enormous potential of the soft drink business, Crown began designing its equipment specifically to meet the needs of soft drink producers, with innovations such as two printers in one line and conversion printers that allowed for rapid design changeover to accommodate just-in-time delivery.[17] After producing exclusively steel cans through the late 1970s, Connelly spearheaded Crown's conversion from steel to aluminum cans in the early 1980s.

In addition to the specialized product line, Connelly's strategy was based on two geographic thrusts: expand to national distribution in the United States and invest heavily abroad. Connelly linked domestic expansion to Crown's manufacturing reorganization; plants were spread out across the country to reduce transportation costs and to be nearer customers. Crown was unusual in that it did not set up plants to service a single customer. Instead, Crown concentrated on providing products for a number of customers near their plants. In international markets, Crown invested heavily in developing nations, first with crowns and then with cans as packaged foods became more widely accepted. Metal containers generated 65% of Crown's $1.8 billion 1988 sales, while closures generated 30% and packaging equipment 5%.

Manufacturing   When Connelly took over in 1957, Crown had perhaps the most outmoded and inefficient production facilities in the industry. Dividends had taken precedence over new investment, and old machinery combined with the cumbersome Philadelphia plant had generated very high production and transportation costs. Soon after he gained control, Connelly took drastic action, closing down the Philadelphia facility and investing heavily in new and geographically dispersed plants. From 1958 to 1963, the company spent almost $82 million on relocation and new facilities. From 1976 through 1989, Crown had 26 domestic plant locations versus 9 in 1955. The plants were small (usually 2 to 3 lines for two-piece cans) and were located close to the customer rather than the raw material source. Crown operated its plants 24 hours a day with unique 12-hour shifts. Employees had two days on followed by two days off and then three days on followed by three days off.

Crown emphasized quality, flexibility, and quick response to customer needs. One officer claimed that the key to the can industry was "the fact that nobody stores cans" and when customers need them "they want them in a hurry and on time. . . . Fast answers get customers." To accommodate customer demands, some of Crown's plants kept more than a month's inventory on hand. Crown also instituted a total quality improvement process to refine its manufacturing processes and gain greater control. According to a Crown spokesperson, "The objective of this quality improvement process is to make the best possible can at the lowest possible cost. You lower the cost of doing business not by the wholesale elimination of people, but by reducing mistakes in order to improve efficiency. And you do that by making everybody in the company accountable."

Recycling   In 1970, Crown formed Nationwide Recyclers, Inc., as a wholly owned subsidiary. By 1989, Crown believed Nationwide was one of the top four or five aluminum can recyclers in the country. While Nationwide was only marginally profitable, Crown had invested in the neighborhood of $10 million in its recycling arm.

Research and Development (R&D)   Crown's technology strategy focused on enhancing the existing product line. As one executive noted, "We are not truly pioneers. Our philosophy is not to spend a great deal of money for basic research. However, we do have tremendous skills in die forming and metal fabrication, and we can move to adapt to the customer's needs faster than anyone else in the industry."[18] For instance, Crown worked closely with large breweries in the development of the two-piece drawn-and-ironed cans for the beverage industry. Crown also made an explicit decision to stay away from basic research. According to one executive, Crown was not interested in "all the frills of an R&D section of high-class, ivory-towered scientists. . . . There is a tremendous asset inherent in being second, especially in the face of the ever-changing state of flux you find in this industry. You try to let others take the risks and make the mistakes. . . ."

This philosophy did not mean that Crown never innovated. For instance, Crown was able to beat its competitors into two-piece can production. Approximately $120 million in new equipment was installed from 1972 through 1975, and by 1976 Crown had 22 two-piece lines in production—more than any other competitor.[19] Crown's research teams also worked closely with customers on specific customer requests. For example, a study of the most efficient plant layout for a food packer or the redesign of a dust cap for the aerosol packager were not unusual projects.

Marketing and Customer Service   The cornerstone of Crown's marketing strategy was, in John Connelly's words, the philosophy that "you can't just increase efficiency to succeed; you must at the same time improve quality." In conjunction with its R&D strategy, the company's sales force maintained close ties with customers and emphasized Crown's ability to provide technical assistance and specific problem solving at the customer's plant. Crown's manufacturing emphasis on flexibility and quick response to customers' needs supported its marketing emphasis on putting the customer first. Michael J. McKenna, president of Crown's North American Division, insisted, "We have always been and always will be extremely customer driven."[20]

Competing cans were made of identical materials to identical specifications on practically identical machinery, and sold at almost identical prices in a given market. At Crown, all customers' gripes went to John Connelly, who was the company's best salesman. A visitor recalled being in his office when a complaint came through from the manager of a Florida citrus-packing plant. Connelly assured him the problem would be taken care of immediately, then casually remarked that he would be in Florida the next day. Would the plant manager join him for dinner? He would indeed. As Crown's president put the telephone down, his visitor said that he hadn't realized Connelly was planning to go to Florida. "Neither did I," confessed Connelly, "until I began talking."[21]

Financing   After he took over in 1957, Connelly applied the first receipts from the sale of inventory to get out from under Crown's short-term bank obligations. He then steadily reduced the debt/equity ratio from 42% in 1956 to 18.2% in 1976 and 5% in 1986. By the end of 1988, Crown's debt represented less than 2% of total capital. Connelly discontinued cash dividends in 1956, and in 1970 repurchased the last of the preferred stock, eliminating preferred dividends as a cash drain. From 1970 forward, management applied excess cash to the repurchase of stock. Connelly set ambitious earnings goals and most years he achieved them. In the 1976 annual report he wrote, "A long time ago we made a prediction that some day our sales would exceed $1 billion and profits of $60.00 per share. Since then, the stock has been split 20-for-1 so this means $3.00 per share." Crown Cork & Seal's revenues reached $1 billion in 1977 and earnings per share reached $3.46. Earnings per share reached $10.11 in 1988 adjusted for a 3-for-1 stock split in September 1988.

International   A significant dimension of Connelly's strategy focused on international growth, particularly in developing countries. Between 1955 and 1960, Crown received what were called "pioneer rights" from many foreign governments aiming to build up the industrial sectors of their countries. These "rights" gave Crown first chance at any new can or closure business introduced into these developing countries. Mark W. Hartman, president of Crown's International Division, described Connelly as "a Johnny Appleseed with respect to the international marketplace. When the new countries of Africa were emerging, for example, John was there offering crown-making capabilities to help them in their industrialization, while at the same time getting a foothold for Crown. John's true love was international business."[22] By 1988, Crown's 62 foreign plants generated 44% of sales and 54% of operating profits. John Connelly visited each of Crown's overseas plants. (See Exhibit 6 for map of plant locations.)

Crown emphasized national management wherever possible. Local people, Crown asserted, understood the local marketplace: the suppliers, the customers, and the unique conditions that drove supply and demand. Crown's overseas investment also offered opportunities to recycle equipment that was, by U.S. standards, less sophisticated. Because can manufacturing was new to many regions of the world, Crown's older equipment met the needs of what was still a developing industry overseas.

Performance   Connelly's strategy met with substantial success throughout his tenure at Crown. With stock splits and price appreciation, $100 invested in Crown stock in 1957 would be worth approximately $30,000 in 1989. After restructuring the company in his first three years, revenues grew at 12.2% per year while income grew at 14.0% over the next two decades (see Exhibit 7). Return on equity averaged 15.8% for much of the 1970s, while Continental Can and American Can lagged far behind at 10.3% and 7.1%, respectively. Over the period 1968–1978 Crown's total return to shareholders ranked 114 out of the Fortune 500, well ahead of IBM (183) and Xerox (374).

In the early 1980s, flat industry sales, combined with an increasingly strong dollar overseas, unrelenting penetration by plastics, and overcapacity in can manufacturing at home, led to declining sales revenues at Crown. Crown's sales dropped from $1.46 billion in 1980 to $1.37 billion by 1984. However, by 1985 Crown had rebounded and annual sales growth averaged 7.6% from 1984 through 1988 while profit growth averaged 12% (see Exhibits 8 and 9). Over the period 1978–1988 Crown's total return to shareholders was 18.6% per year, ranking 146 out of the Fortune 500. In 1988, *BusinessWeek* noted that Connelly—earning a total of only $663,000 in the three years ending in 1987—garnered shareholders the best returns for the least executive pay in the United States. As an industry analyst observed,

"Crown's strategy is a no-nonsense, back-to-basics strategy—except they never left the basics."[23]

John Connelly's Contribution to Success

Customers, employees, competitors, and Wall Street analysts attributed Crown's sustained success to the unique leadership of John Connelly. He arrived at Crown as it headed into bankruptcy in 1957, achieved a 1,646% increase in profits on a relatively insignificant sales increase by 1961, and proceeded to outperform the industry's giants throughout the next three decades. A young employee expressed the loyalty created by Connelly: "If John told me to jump out the window, I'd jump—and be sure he'd catch me at the bottom with a stock option in his hand."

Yet Connelly was not an easy man to please. Crown's employees had to get used to Connelly's tough, straight-line management. *Fortune* credited Crown's success to Connelly, "whose genial Irish grin masks a sober salesman executive who believes in the eighty-hour week and in traveling while competitors sleep." He went to meetings uninvited, and expected the same devotion to Crown of his employees as he demanded of himself. As one observer remembered:

> The Saturday morning meeting is standard operating procedure. Crown's executives travel and confer only at night and on weekends. William D. Wallace, vice president for operations, travels 100,000 miles a year, often in the company plane. But Connelly sets the pace. An associate recalls driving to his home in the predawn blackness to pick him up for a flight to a distant plant. The Connelly house was dark, but he spotted a figure sitting on the curb under a street light, engrossed in a loose-leaf book. Connelly's greeting, as he jumped into the car: "I want to talk to you about last month's variances."[24]

Avery's Challenge in 1989

Avery thought long and hard about the options available to him in 1989. He considered the growing opportunities in plastic closures and containers, as well as glass containers. With growth slowing in metal containers, plastics was the only container segment that held much promise. However, the possibility of diversifying beyond the manufacture of containers altogether had some appeal, although the appropriate opportunity was not at hand. While Crown's competitors had aggressively expanded in a variety of directions, Connelly had been cautious, and had prospered. Avery wondered if now was the time for a change at Crown.

Within the traditional metal can business, Avery had to decide whether or not to get involved in the bidding for Continental Can. The acquisition of Continental Can Canada (CCC)—with sales of roughly $400 million—would make Canada Crown's largest single presence outside of the United States. Continental's USA business—with estimated revenues of $1.3 billion in 1989—would double the size of Crown's domestic operations. Continental's Latin American, Asian, and Middle Eastern operations

Copenhagen

Rotterdam
Edinburgh
Tredegar
Antwerp
Bedburg
London
Londerzeel
Reinach
Frankenthal/Pfalz
Schwanenstadt
Paris
Milan
Cork
Bilbao
Madrid

Lisbon
Casablanca

Nairobi

Ndola
Harare

Johannesburg

Cape Town

Lagos

Lawrence
North Bergen
Hanover (PA)
Philadelphia
Baltimore
Salisbury (MD)

Aracaju

Victoria Santo Antao
Rio De Janeiro
Sao Paulo
Porto Alegre

Buenos Aires

Santiago

Mississauga

Montreal
Trenton
Toronto
Chatham
Perrysburg
Crawfordsville
Winchester
Arden
Spartanburg (SC)
Cheraw

San Juan

Caracas
Port of Spain

Manaus

Barranquilla
Bogota
Medellin
Caracas

Guayaquil

Pucallpa
Lima

San Jose

Atlanta
Batesville

Minneapolis
Oshkosh (WI)
Lakeville (MN)
Faribault
Milwaukee
Chicago
Kankakee (IL)
Decatur (IL)

Worland

Abilene
Conroe

San Luis Potosi

Guatemala City

Mexico City

Winnipeg

Edmonton
Calgary

Vancouver

La Mirada

Bangkok
Lae
Johore Bahru
Singapore
Jakarta

Exhibit 6   Crown Cork & Seal Facilities, 1989

651

	1956	1961	1966	1971	1973	1975	1977	1979
Net Sales	$115.1	$177.0	$279.8	$448.4	$571.8	$825.0	$1,049.1	$1,402.4
Costs, Expenses and Other Income:								
Cost of products sold	95.8	139.1	217.2	350.9	459.2	683.7	874.1	1,179.3
Sales and administration	13.5	15.8	18.4	21.1	23.4	30.1	34.8	43.9
Depreciation	2.6	4.6	9.4	17.0	20.9	25.4	5.6	16.4
Net interest expense	1.2	1.3	4.6	5.1	4.4	7.4	31.7	40.1
Provision for taxes on income	.1	7.6	12.7	24.6	26.7	34.9	48.7	51.8
Net income	.3	6.7	16.7	28.5	34.3	41.6	53.8	70.2
Earnings per common share (actual)	(6.01)	.28	.80	1.41	1.81	2.24	3.46	4.65
Selected Financial Statistics								
Return on average equity	0.55%	9.66%	16.44%	14.05%	14.46%	15.20%	15.88%	15.57%
Return on sales	0.24	3.76	5.99	6.35	6.00	5.04	5.13	5.00
Return on average assets	0.32	6.00	6.76	7.25	8.00	7.69	9.13	8.93
Gross profit margin	16.76	21.43	22.37	21.76	19.69	17.13	16.68	15.90
Cost of goods sold/sales	83.24	78.57	77.63	78.24	80.31	82.87	83.32	84.29
SGA/sales	11.73	8.65	6.56	4.70	4.09	3.65	3.32	3.13

Crown Cork & Seal Company Consolidated Statement of Financial Position (dollars in millions, year-end December 31)

	1956	1961	1966	1971	1973	1975	1977	1979
Total current assets	$50.2	$66.3	$109.4	$172.3	$223.4	$265.0	$340.7	$463.3
Total assets	86.5	129.2	269.5	398.1	457.5	539.0	631.1	828.2
Total current liabilities	15.8	24.8	75.3	110.2	139.6	170.0	210.8	287.1
Total long-term debt	20.2	17.7	57.9	41.7	37.9	29.7	12.8	12.2
Shareholders' equity	50.3	77.5	110.8	211.8	243.9	292.7	361.8	481.0
Selected Financial Statistics								
Debt/equity	0.40	0.23	0.52	0.20	0.16	0.10	0.04	0.03
Capital expenditures	1.9	11.8	32.7	33.1	40.4	49.0	58.9	55.9
Book value per share of common	1.57	2.74	5.19	10.62	13.13	16.64	23.54	31.84

Source: Adapted from Annual Reports.

Exhibit 8 Crown Cork & Seal Company Consolidated Statement of Income (dollars in millions except earnings per share, year-end December 31)

	1981	1982	1983	1984	1985	1986	1987	1988
Net Sales	**$1,373.9**	**$1,351.9**	**$1,298.0**	**$1,369.6**	**$1,487.1**	**$1,618.9**	**$1,717.9**	**$1,834.1**
Costs, Expenses, and Other Income:								
Cost of products sold	1,170.4	1,175.6	1,116.0	1,172.5	1,260.3	1,370.2	1,456.6	1,569.5
Sales and administrative	45.3	44.2	42.9	42.1	43.0	46.7	49.6	50.9
Depreciation	38.0	39.9	38.4	40.2	43.7	47.2	56.9	57.2
Interest expense	12.3	9.0	9.0	8.9	12.2	6.2	8.9	10.0
Interest income	—	—	—	—	—	—	(15.2)	(14.8)
Total Expenses	1,266.1	1,268.6	1,206.2	1,263.6	1,359.2	1,470.3	1,556.8	1,672.9
Income before taxes	107.8	83.2	91.8	105.9	127.9	148.6	161.1	161.2
Provision for taxes on income	43.0	38.5	40.2	46.4	56.2	69.2	72.7	67.8
Net income	64.8	44.7	51.5	59.5	71.7	79.4	88.3	93.4
Earnings per common share	1.48	1.05	1.27	1.59	2.17	2.48	2.86	3.37

Note: Earnings per common share have been restated to reflect a 3-for-1 stock split on September 12, 1988

Selected Financial Statistics

	1981	1982	1983	1984	1985	1986	1987	1988
Return on Average Equity (%):	11.72%	7.94%	9.34%	11.42%	13.94%	14.34%	14.46%	14.45%
Return on sales	4.72	3.31	3.97	4.35	4.82	4.91	5.14	5.09
Return on average assets	7.38	5.19	6.20	7.31	8.58	8.80	8.67	8.61
Gross profit margin	14.81	13.04	14.03	14.39	15.25	15.36	15.21	14.42
Cost of goods sold/sales	85.19	86.96	85.97	85.61	84.75	84.64	84.79	85.58
SGA/sales	3.30	3.27	3.30	3.07	2.89	2.88	2.89	2.78
Net Sales ($):								
United States	775.0	781.0	749.9	844.5	945.3	1,010.3	985.5	1,062.5
Europe	324.0	304.4	298.7	283.0	282.8	365.6	415.6	444.2
All others	283.6	273.1	259.1	261.3	269.3	269.0	342.5	368.6
Operating Profit ($):								
United States	62.8	58.9	55.0	67.1	88.9	92.8	95.4	70.6
Europe	20.6	19.0	24.0	17.2	17.0	21.9	22.4	33.4
All others	40.0	37.3	33.1	38.3	40.6	39.6	64.9	66.1
Operating Ratio (%):								
United States	8.1	7.5	7.3	7.9	9.4	9.7	9.6	6.6
Europe	6.3	6.2	8.0	6.0	6.0	5.9	5.4	7.5
All others	14.1	13.6	12.7	14.6	15.0	14.7	18.9	17.9

Source: Adapted from Annual Reports.

Note: The above sales figures are before the deduction of intracompany sales.

653

Exhibit 9 Crown Cork & Seal Company Consolidated Statement of Financial Position (dollars in millions, year-end December 31)

	1981	1982	1983	1984	1985	1986	1987	1988
Current Assets:								
Cash	$ 21.5	$ 15.8	$ 21.0	$ 7.0	$ 14.8	$ 16.5	$ 27.6	$ 18.0
Accounts receivables	262.8	257.1	240.6	237.6	279.0	270.4	280.7	248.1
Inventory	206.2	184.4	170.2	174.6	171.9	190.1	228.1	237.6
Total Current Assets	490.6	457.3	431.7	419.2	465.6	477.0	536.4	503.8
Investments	12.4	14.6	26.7	28.8	41.5	43.7	NA	NA
Goodwill	11.2	10.8	9.6	10.3	11.8	14.1	16.7	16.5
Property, plant and equipment	368.4	357.8	353.7	348.0	346.9	404.0	465.7	495.9
Other noncurrent assets	NA	NA	NA	NA	NA	NA	79.1	57.0
Total Assets	882.6	840.6	821.7	806.4	865.8	938.8	1,097.9	1,073.2
Current Liabilities:								
Short-term debt	22.7	21.6	24.4	42.0	16.3	17.2	44.0	20.2
Accounts payable	193.0	165.6	163.1	177.9	197.1	220.1	265.9	277.6
U.S. and foreign taxes	17.3	4.7	11.4	6.0	11.4	11.3	28.4	23.3
Total Current Liabilities	233.0	191.9	198.8	225.8	224.8	248.5	338.2	321.2
Long-term debt	5.8	5.6	2.8	2.7	2.2	1.4	19.7	9.4
Other	14.5	18.5	12.8	15.8	31.2	29.3	0.0	0.0
Total Long-term Debt	20.3	24.1	15.6	18.5	33.5	30.7	19.7	9.4
Deferred income taxes	55.5	57.7	57.8	60.7	71.3	79.2	89.4	93.7
Minority equity in subsidiaries	7.2	7.2	5.2	3.7	4.7	3.8	5.0	0.9
Shareholders' equity	566.7	559.8	544.3	497.8	531.5	576.6	645.6	648.0
Liability and owners' equity	882.6	840.6	821.7	806.4	865.8	938.8	1,097.9	1,073.2

Selected Financial Statistics

	1981	1982	1983	1984	1985	1986	1987	1988
Debt/equity	1.02%	0.99%	0.51%	0.54%	0.42%	0.24%	3.06%	1.45%
Debt/(debt + equity)	3.5%	4.1%	2.7%	3.5%	6.0%	5.0%	3.0%	1.4%
Shares outstanding at year end (M)	14.5	14.0	13.2	11.5	10.5	10.0	9.5	27.0
Capital expenditures ($M)	$ 63.8	$ 50.3	$ 55.5	$ 53.8	$ 50.9	$ 94.0	$ 99.5	$ 102.6
Shares repurchased (000)	75.4	528.3	863.1	1,694.5	1,006.0	677.1	638.7	2,242.9
Stock price: High[a]	$ 12.00	$ 10.00	$ 13.00	$ 15.75	$ 29.62	$ 38.25	$ 46.87	$ 46.72
Stock price: Low[a]	$ 8.00	$ 7.00	$ 10.00	$ 11.75	$ 15.12	$ 25.25	$ 28.00	$ 30.00

Source: Adapted from Annual Reports.

[a]Restated for 9/1998 stock split.

were rumored to be priced in the range of $100 million to $150 million. Continental's European operations generated estimated sales of $1.5 billion in 1989 and included a work force of 10,000 at 30 production sites. Potential bidders for all, or part of Continental's operations, included many of Crown's U.S. rivals in addition to European competition: Pechiney International of France, Metal Box of Great Britain (which had recently acquired Carnaud SA), and VIAG AG, a German trading group, among others.

Avery knew that most mergers in this industry had not worked out well. He also thought about the challenge of taking two companies that come from completely different cultures and bringing them together. There would be inevitable emotional and attitudinal changes, particularly for Continental's salaried managers and Crown's "owner-operators." Avery also knew that the merger of American Can and National Can had its difficulties. That consolidation was taking longer than expected and, according to one observer, "American Can would be literally wiped out in the end."

Avery found himself challenging Crown's traditional strategies and thought seriously of drafting a new blueprint for the future.

Endnotes

1. Salomon Brothers. 1990. *Beverage Cans Industry Report*, March 1.

2. Davis T. 1990. Can do: A metal container update. *Beverage World*, June: 34.

3. Sheehan J. J. 1988. Nothing succeeds like success. *Beverage World*, November: 82.

4. Until 1985, aluminum cans were restricted to carbonated beverages because it was the carbonation that prevented the can from collapsing. Reynolds discovered that by adding liquid nitrogen to the can's contents, aluminum containers could hold noncarbonated beverages and still retain their shape. The liquid nitrogen made it possible for Reynolds to make cans for liquor, chocolate drinks, and fruit juices.

5. Sly, J. 1988. A "can-do crusade" by steel industry. *Chicago Tribune*, July 3: 1.

6. Merrill Lynch Capital Markets. 1991. *Containers and Packaging Industry Report*. March 21, 1991.

7. Salomon Brothers Inc. 1991. *Containers/Packaging: Beverage Cans Industry Report,* April 3.

8. Agoos, A. 1985. Aluminum girds for the plastic can bid. *Chemical Week*, January 16: 18.

9. Oman, B. 1990. A clear choice? *Beverage World*, June: 78.

10. In response to public concern, the container industry developed highly efficient "closed loop" recycling systems. Containers flowed from the manufacturer, through the wholesaler/distributor, to the retailer, to the consumer, and back to the manufacturer or material supplier for recycling. Aluminum's high recycling value permitted can manufacturers to sell cans at a lower cost to beverage producers. The reclamation of steel cans lagged that of aluminum because collection and recycling did not result in significant energy or material cost advantages.

11. Lang, N. 1990. A touch of glass. *Beverage World,* June: 36.

12. Ibid.

13. U.S. Industrial Outlook, 1984–1990.

14. The First Boston Corporation. 1990. *Packaging Industry Report,* April 4.

15. Whalen, R. J. 1962. The unoriginal ideas that rebuilt Crown Cork. *Fortune,* October.

16. Ibid.: 156.

17. In the mid-1960s, growth in demand for soft drink and beer cans was more than triple that for traditional food cans.

18. Hamermesh, R. G., Anderson, M. J. Jr., and Harris, J. E. 1978. Strategies for low market share business. *Harvard Business Review,* May–June: 99.

19. In 1976, there were 47 two-piece tinplate and 130 two-piece aluminum lines in the United States.

20. *One Hundred Years.* Crown Cork & Seal Company, Inc.

21. Whalen, The unoriginal ideas that rebuilt Crown Cork.

22. *One Hundred Years.* Crown Cork & Seal Company, Inc.

23. *Business Week.* 1987. These penny-pinchers deliver a big bang for their bucks. May 4.

24. Whalen, The unoriginal ideas that rebuilt Crown Cork.

Case 12 Growing for Broke*

Look, you've *got* to grow. It's what our economy is all about. Hey, it's what our country is all about! Certainly, it's what drives me. My father, Constantine Anaptyxi, came to America from Greece because he saw big opportunities here. He worked hard, took a few risks, and realized his dreams. I came to this company as CEO five years ago—giving up a senior VP position at a Fortune 500 manufacturer—because I saw big potential for Paragon Tool, then a small maker of machine tools. I didn't make the move so that I could oversee the company's *down*sizing! I didn't intend to create value—for our customers, for our employees, for our shareholders—by thinking small!! I didn't intend to *shrink* to greatness, for God's sake!!!

Okay, so I'm getting a little worked up over this. Maybe I'm just trying to overcome my own second thoughts about our company's growth plans. I know it isn't just about growth; it's about *profitable* growth, as my CFO, William Littlefield, is always happy to remind me. "Nicky," he'll say, "people always talk about getting to the top when they should be focusing on the bottom . . . line, that is." Quite a comedian, that Littlefield. But lame as the quip is, it tells you a lot about Littlefield and what, in my opinion, is his limited view of business. Sometimes you've got to sacrifice profits up front to make *real* profits down the line.

To me, acquiring MonitoRobotics holds just that kind of promise. The company uses sensor technology and communications software to monitor and report real-time information on the functioning of robotics equipment. By adapting this technology for use on our machine tools, we could offer customers a rapid-response troubleshooting service—what consultants these days like to call a "solutions" business. Over time, I'd hope we could apply the technology and software to other kinds of machine tools and even to other kinds of manufacturing equipment. That would make us less dependent on our slow-growing and cyclical machine-tool manufacturing operation and hopefully give us a strong position in a technology market with terrific growth potential. It would also nearly double our current annual revenue of around $400 million—and force Wall Street to pay some attention to us.

What does Littlefield say to this? Oh, he gives a thumbs-down to the acquisition, of course—too risky. But get this: He also thinks we should sell off our existing services division—a "drag on profits," he says. With the help of some outside consultants, the senior management team has spent the last few months analyzing both our services business and the pros and cons of a MonitoRobotics acquisition. Tomorrow, I need to tell Littlefield whether we should go ahead and put together a presentation on the pro-

posed acquisition for next week's board meeting. If we do move forward on this, I have a hunch a certain CFO might start returning those headhunter calls. And I'd hate to lose him. Whatever our differences, there's no denying that he's capable and smart—in fact, a lot smarter than I am in some areas. On this issue, though, I just don't think he gets it.

Mom and Apple Pie

In 1946, when my father was 21, he left the Greek island of Tinos and came to New York City with his new bride. He worked at a cousin's dry-cleaning store in Astoria, Queens, then started his own on the other side of town. When I was seven, he took his savings and bought a commercial laundry in Brooklyn. Over the next several years, he scooped up one laundry after another, usually borrowing from the bank, sometimes taking another mortgage on the three-family home in Bensonhurst where we had moved. By the time I was a teenager, he was sitting on a million-dollar business that did the linens for all kinds of hotels and hospitals around greater New York. "Nikolas, growth is as American as Mom and apple pie," my father would say to me—he loved using all-American expressions like that. "You gotta get bigger to get better."

My mom was somewhat less expansive in her outlook. She kept my father's accounts, having studied book-keeping in night school as soon as her English was good enough. And she had her own saying, one that deftly, if inadvertently, bolted together two other platitudes of American slang. "Keep your shirt on," she would say to my father when, arms waving, he would enthusiastically describe some new expansion plan for his business. "Or else you might lose it." My father was the genius behind his company's growth, but I have no doubt that my mother was the one responsible for its profits.

When I was 15, we moved to a nice suburb in Jersey. I never quite fit in: too small for sports, a little too ethnic for the social set, only a middling student. I worked hard, though, and went to Rutgers, where I majored in economics and then stayed on to get an MBA. Something clicked in business school. I seemed to have a knack for solving the real-world problems of the case studies. And I flourished in an environment where the emphasis was on figuring out what you *can* do instead of what you *can't,* on envisioning how things could go right instead of trying to anticipate how they could go wrong. (Thank God I didn't follow my uncle's advice and become a corporate lawyer!)

When I graduated, I got a job at WRT, the Cleveland-based industrial conglomerate where I'd interned the summer before. Over the next 15 years or so, I moved up through the ranks, mainly because of my ability to spot new market opportunities. And by the time I was 45, I was heading up the machine-tool division, a $2.3 billion business. Both revenues and profits surged in the three years I was there, it's true. But I still found my job frustrating. Every proposed acquisition or new initiative of any substance had to be approved by people at headquarters who were far removed from our business. And whenever corporate profits flagged, the response was mindless across-the-board cost cutting that took little account of individual divisions' performance.

So when I was offered the opportunity to head up a small but profitable machine-tool maker in southern Ohio, I jumped at the chance.

Sunflower Tableau

I still remember driving to work my first day at Paragon Tool five years ago. Winding through the Ohio countryside, I saw a stand of sunflowers growing in a rocky patch of soil next to a barn. "Now *there's* a symbol for us," I thought, "a commonplace but hardy plant that quickly grows above its neighbors, often in fairly tough conditions." I was confident that Paragon—a solid, unexceptional business operating in an extremely difficult industry and economic environment—had the potential to grow with similarly glorious results.

For one thing, Paragon was relatively healthy. The company was built around a line of high-end machines—used by manufacturers of aerospace engines, among others—that continued to enjoy fairly good margins, despite the battering that the machine-tool industry as a whole had taken over the previous decade and a half. Still, the market for our product was essentially stagnant. Foreign competition was beginning to take its toll. And we continued to face brutal cyclical economic swings.

I quickly launched a number of initiatives designed to spur revenue growth. With some aggressive pricing, we increased sales and gained share in our core market, driving out a number of our new foreign rivals. We expanded our product line and our customer base by modifying our flagship product for use in a number of other industries. We also made a string of acquisitions in the industrial signage and electronic-labeling field, aiming to leverage the relationships we had with our machine-tool customers. No question, these moves put real pressure on our margins. Along with the price cuts and the debt we took on to make the acquisitions, we had to invest in new manufacturing equipment and a larger sales force. But we were laying the foundation for what I hoped would be a highly profitable future. The board and the senior management team, including Littlefield, seemed to share my view.

Indeed, the CFO and I had developed a rapport, despite our differing business instincts. Early on in our working relationship, this sixth-generation Yankee started in with the kidding about my alma mater. "Is that how they taught you to think about it at Rutgers?" he'd say if I was brainstorming and came up with some crazy idea. "Because at *Wharton*, they taught us. . . ." I'd just laugh and then tell whoever else was in the room how proud we were

that Littlefield had been a cheerleader for the Penn football team—like that was his biggest scholarly accomplishment. One time he "let it slip" that in fact he was Phi Beta Kappa, and we all just groaned. I said, "Give it up, Littlefield. You may have been Phi Beta Kappa, but, despite those letters on your gold pin, you'll never out-*Greek* me." To tell the truth, our skills are complementary, and between us we manage to do a pretty good job for the company.

As Paragon grew, so did the sense of excitement and urgency among our managers—indeed, among the entire workforce. People who once had been merely content to work at Paragon now couldn't wait to tackle the next challenge. And that excitement spread throughout the small Ohio town where we are based. When I'd go with my wife to a party or speak at the local Rotary Club or even stop to buy gas, people would show a genuine interest in the company and our latest doings—it helped that we always mentioned the job-creation impact when announcing new initiatives. There's no doubt it stoked my ego to be one of the bigger fish in the local pond. But even more important for me was the sense that this was business at its best, providing people with a justified sense of well-being about the present and confidence in the future.

Anyway, my point here is that we've grown fast since I arrived, but we still have a long way to go. I've come to think that the real key to our future is in the company's services division. We currently offer our customers the option to buy a standard service contract, under which we provide periodic machine maintenance and respond to service calls. But we've been developing technology and software, similar to MonitoRobotics', that would allow us to respond immediately if a machine at a customer's site goes down. The division currently accounts for less than 10% of our revenue and, because of the cost of developing the new technology, it's struggling to turn a profit.

But I can see in the services division the seeds of a business that will ultimately transform us from a manufacturing company into a high-tech company. Such a transformation, requiring an overhaul of our culture and capabilities, won't be easy. And it will surely require significant additional investments. But the potential upside is huge, with the promise of sales and profit growth that could make our current single-digit gains seem trivial by comparison. Besides, what choice do we have? A number of our competitors have already spotted these opportunities and have begun moving ahead with them. If we don't ramp up quickly, we might well miss out on the action altogether.

A Company in Play

Just over a month ago, I was sitting at my desk preparing a presentation for the handful of analysts who cover our company. Until recently, most of them have had only good things to say about all our growth moves. But last quarter, when we again reported a year-on-year drop in earnings, a few of them started asking pointed questions about our investments and when they could be expected to bear fruit. As I was giving some thought to how I'd answer their questions in the upcoming meeting, the phone rang. It was our investment banker, Jed Nixon.

"Nicky, I think we should talk," he said. I could tell from the sound of his voice he was on to something big, and then he told me what it was: "MonitoRobotics is in play."

We both did some calendar juggling and managed to get together for lunch the very next day at Jed's office in Cincinnati. The rumor was that one of our direct competitors, Bellows & Samson, was about to launch a hostile takeover bid for MonitoRobotics. As it happened, we had just started a conversation with MonitoRobotics' management a few months before, about collaborating on remote servicing technology for machine tools. But Jed's call had had its intended effect, changing my thinking about the company: Why not acquire it ourselves?

Although MonitoRobotics' technology was designed to detect and report operating failures in robotics equipment, managers there had told us when we met that adapting it for use on other industrial machinery was feasible. Indeed, MonitoRobotics had recently licensed the technology to a company that planned to modify it for use on complex assembly lines that experienced frequent breakdowns. Our engineers had confirmed that a version could be developed for our machines—though in their initial assessment they hadn't been exactly sure how long this would take.

Still, the potential benefits of acquiring MonitoRobotics seemed numerous. It would give us a powerful presence in a fast-growing business while preempting a competitor from staking a claim there. Whatever the time lag in adapting MonitoRobotics' technology for use with our products, we would almost certainly be able to offer our customers this valuable troubleshooting service more quickly than if we continued to develop the technology ourselves. And though our products were different, MonitoRobotics and Paragon potentially served many of the same manufacturing customers. "Think of the cross-selling opportunities," Jed said, as he took a bite of his sandwich. The greatest opportunity, though, lay in the possibility that MonitoRobotics' software technology would become the standard means for machine tools—and ultimately a variety of industrial machines—to communicate their service needs to the people who serviced them and to other machines that might be affected by their shutdown.

This was a fairly speculative train of thought. But a MonitoRobotics acquisition had for me the earmarks of a breakthrough opportunity for Paragon. And our earlier conversations with its management team had been cordial, suggesting the company might welcome a friendly offer from us to counter Bellows & Samson's hostile bid. Of course, even if we were able to get MonitoRobotics at a fair price, an acquisition of this size would further delay our

return to the margins and profit growth we had known in the past. And that, I knew, wouldn't sit well with everyone.

Management Dissension

The day after my meeting with Jed, I called together members of our senior management team. There was a barely suppressed gasp when I mentioned the potential acquisition, particularly given its size. "Boy, that would be a lot to digest with everything we've got on our plate right now," said Joe McCollum, our senior VP of marketing. "It also might represent the chance of a lifetime," countered Rosemary Witkowski, head of the services division. Then Littlefield spoke up. His skepticism wasn't surprising.

"I was just running a few simple numbers on what the MonitoRobotics acquisition might mean to our bottom line," he said. "Besides the costs associated with the acquisition itself, we'd be looking at some significant expenses in the near term, including accelerated software research, hiring and training, and even brand development." He pointed out that these costs would put further pressure on our earnings, just as our profits were struggling to recover from earlier growth-related investments.

Littlefield did concede that a bold acquisition like this might be just the sort of growth move that would appeal to some of our analysts—and might even prompt a few more securities firms to cover us. But he insisted that if our earnings didn't start bouncing back soon, Wall Street was going to pillory us. Then he dropped his bombshell: "I frankly think this is an opportunity to consider getting out of the services business altogether. Eliminating the continued losses that we've been experiencing there would allow us to begin realizing the profit growth that we can expect from the investments we've made in our still-healthy machine-tool business."

Littlefield argued that, whether we acquired MonitoRobotics or not, it wasn't clear we'd be able to dominate the machine-tool services market because a number of our competitors were already flocking there. Furthermore, the market might not be worth fighting over: Many of our customers were struggling with profitability themselves and might not be willing or able to buy our add-on services. "Last one in, turn out the lights" was the phrase Littlefield used to describe the rush to dominate a profitless market.

As soon as she had a chance, Rosemary shot back in defense of her operation. "This is the one area we're in that has significant growth potential," she said. "And we've already sunk an incredible amount of money into developing this software. I can't believe you'd throw all of that investment out the window." But a number of heads nodded when Littlefield argued that we'd recoup much of that investment if we sold the money-losing business.

Several days later, I polled the members of the senior management team and found them split on the issue of the acquisition. And, to be honest, I was beginning to doubt myself on this. I respected Littlefield's financial savvy.

And no one had yet raised the issue of whether Paragon, a traditional manufacturing company, had the management capabilities to run what was essentially a software start-up. We decided to hire two highly regarded consulting firms to do quick analyses of the proposed MonitoRobotics acquisition.

The Sunflowers' Successor

Today, the consultants came back to us with conflicting reports. One highlighted the market potential of MonitoRobotics' technology, noting that we might be too far behind to develop similar technology on our own. The other focused on the difficulties both of integrating the company's technology with ours and of adapting it to equipment beyond the robotics field.

So as I drove home tonight, the dilemma seemed no closer to being resolved. In many ways, I am persuaded by the cautionary message of Littlefield's number crunching. At the same time, I firmly believe the pros and cons of such a complex decision can't be precisely quantified; sometimes you just have to go with your instincts—which in my case favor growth. As I turned the issue over in my head, I looked out the car window, half-consciously seeking inspired insight. Sure enough, there was the barn where the sunflowers had been growing five years before. But the bright yellow blossoms, highlighted by the red timbers of the barn, were gone. Instead, a carpet of green kudzu was growing up the side of the increasingly dilapidated building. This fast-growing vine, which already had ravaged much of the South, was now spreading, uncontrolled and unproductive, into southern Ohio.

My mind started to drift and the image of kudzu—a more sinister symbol of growth than the sunflower—began to merge with thoughts of my father, who had died of lung cancer two years before, and my mother, who these days spends most of her time managing her investments. Suddenly, my parents' favorite phrases came to mind. It occurred to me that kudzu was now becoming as American as Mom and apple pie. Even so, its dense foliage certainly seemed like a place where, if you weren't careful, you could easily misplace your shirt.

Should Paragon Tool further its growth ambitions by trying to acquire MonitoRobotics?

Case 13   Dippin' Dots Ice Cream*

In 2004 Dippin' Dots was a 16-year-old-company with over $36 million in annual sales, 160 employees, and headquartered in Paducah, Kentucky.[1] The company's chief operation is the sale of Dippin' Dots ice cream to franchisees and national accounts throughout the world. Curt Jones is the founder and CEO of Dippin' Dots.[2] So who is Curt Jones and what is Dippin' Dots?

Dippin' Dots is the marriage between old-fashioned handmade ice cream and space-age technology. Dippin' Dots are tiny round beads of ice cream that are made at supercold temperatures, served at subzero temperatures in a soufflé cup, and eaten with a spoon. The supercold freezing of Dippin' Dots ice cream done by liquid nitrogen cryogenically locks in both flavor and freshness in a way that no other manufactured ice cream can offer. Not only had Curt discovered a new way of making ice cream, but many feel his product proved to be much more flavorful and richer than regular ice cream. According to Curt, "I created a way . . . [to] get a quicker freeze so the ice cream wouldn't get large ice crystals. . . . About six months later, I decided to quit my job and go into business."

Jones is a microbiologist by trade with one area of expertise in cryogenics. Curt's first job was researching and engineering as a microbiologist for ALLtech Inc., a bioengineering company based in Lexington, Kentucky. During his days at ALLtech, Curt worked with different types of bacteria to find new ways of preserving them so they could be transported throughout the world. He applied a method of freezing using supercold temperatures with substances like liquid CO_2 and liquid nitrogen—the same method used to create Dippin' Dots.

One method Curt developed was to "microencapsulate" the bacteria by freezing their medium with liquid nitrogen. Other scientists thought he was crazy because nothing like this had ever been done before. Curt, however, was convinced his idea would work. He spent months trying to perfect this method, and continued to make progress in making his idea materialize.

While Curt was working over 80 hours a week in ALLtech's labs to perfect the microencapsulating process, he made the most influential decision of his life when he took a weekend off and attended a family barbeque at his parents' house. It just so happened that his mother was making ice cream the day of the barbeque. Curt began to reminisce about homemade ice cream prepared the slow, old-fashioned way. Then Curt began to wonder if it was possible to flash-freeze ice cream. Instead of using a

bacteria medium, was it possible to microencapsulate ice cream?

The answer was yes to both questions he posed to himself. After virtually reinventing a frozen dessert that had been around since the second century BC,[3] Curt patented his idea to flash-freeze liquid cream and eventually opened the first Dippin' Dots store. Today, the "Ice Cream of the Future" can be found at thousands of shopping malls, amusement parks, water parks, fairs, and festivals worldwide.

Dippin' Dots are transported coast-to-coast and around the world by truck, train, plane, and ship. In addition to specially designed cryogenic transport containers, Dippin' Dots are transported in refrigerated boxes known as Pallet Reefers. Both types of containers ensure the fastest and most efficient method of delivery of these premium products to dealers around the globe. The product is served in 4-, 5-, and 8-ounce cups, and 5-ounce vending prepacks.

Product Specifics

Dippin' Dots are flash-frozen beads of ice cream typically served in a cup or vending package. The ice cream averages 190 calories per serving, depending upon the flavor, and has 9 grams of fat. The ice cream is produced by a patented process that introduces flavored liquid cream into a vat with liquid nitrogen. The liquid cream is flash-frozen in the $-325°$ vat to produce the bead or dot shape. Once frozen, the dots are collected and either mixed with other flavors or packaged separately for delivery to retail locations. The product must be stored in subzero temperatures to maintain the consistency of the dots. Subzero storage temperatures are achieved by utilizing special equipment and freezers, and supplemented with dry ice. To maintain product integrity and consistency, the ice cream must be served at 10 to 20 degrees below zero. A retail location must have special storage and serving freezers. Because the product must be stored and served at such low temperatures, it is unavailable in regular frozen food cases and cannot be stored in a typical household freezer. Therefore, it can only be consumed at or near a retail location, unless stored with dry ice to maintain the necessary storage temperature.

Industry Overview

According to the market research firm Datamonitor, the U.S. ice-cream market experienced a stable growth rate of 0.93 percent from 1999 to 2003, increasing in value by 3.8 percent over the period. The size of the U.S. ice-cream market was $8.8 billion in 2003. According to data from ACNielsen, ice cream and related frozen desserts are consumed by more than 90 percent of households in the United States.[4]

*This case was prepared by graduate student Brian R. Callahan and Professor Alan B. Eisner of Pace University as a basis for class discussion rather than to illustrate either effective or ineffective handling of an administrative situation. Copyright © 2005 Alan B. Eisner.

Only a short while ago, the frozen dairy industry was occupied by family-owned businesses like Dippin' Dots, full-line dairies, and a couple of large international companies that focused on only a single sales region. The past year has been marked by a slight increase in the production and sale of ice cream, as volume in traditional varieties remained flat and new types of ice-cream forms emerged. Despite higher ingredient costs, manufacturers are continually churning out new products ranging from superpremium selections to good-for-you varieties to co-branded packages and novelties. Most novelty ice creams can be found together in a supermarket freezer case, small freezers in convenience stores, and in carts, kiosks, or trucks at popular summertime events. Ice-cream makers have been touched by consolidation trends affecting the overall food and beverage industry that extend beyond their products, as even the big names are folded into global conglomerates.

In 2003 the ice-cream segment became a battleground for two huge international consumer products companies seeking to corner the ice-cream market. Those two industry giants are Nestlé SA of Switzerland, the world's largest food company with more than $46 billion in annual sales, and Unilever PLC, of London and Rotterdam, with over $26 billion in annual revenues. Both have been buying into U.S. firms for quite a while, but Nestlé, which already owns the Häagen-Dazs product line, upped the ante with its June 2003 merger with Dreyer's Grand/Edy's Ice Cream Inc., of Oakland, California.

The reason behind the fierce competition in the frozen dairy industry is the market's potential. A look at the most recent product and sales trends of ice cream shows a category with opportunities for innovation (see Exhibit 1). According to Jay Brigham, executive vice president of a candy and inclusions company in Dallas, "Ice cream has a lot of potential . . . if you look at what milk has done with single serve in the convenience store market, ice cream still has the potential to do something like that. It's a very innovative category, and there's a lot of opportunity to do things like color-changing ingredients, or to try pop-rocks or to develop sugar-free products for instance," Brigham says. Ice cream by its very nature is a source of imaginative flavors and forms.

The estimated total value of the frozen dessert industry grew 3 percent in 2002 to $20.7 billion, attributable in part to higher prices which did not prevent consumers from spending more for ice cream (see Exhibit 2). The International Dairy Foods Association reported that, of that total, $7.7 billion was spent on products for at-home consumption while almost twice that, $13 billion, went toward away-from-home purchases.

The relatively cool summer of 2003 in the United States translated into flat overall sales and unit volume figures. Information Resources Inc. (IRI) of Chicago tallied

Exhibit 1   Top 10 Ice Cream Brands, 2004 (excludes Wal-Mart)

Brand	Sales ($ millions)	Percent Change from 2003
Private label	$1,001.9	−4.20%
Breyers	659.0	2.60%
Dreyer's/Edy's Grand	474.3	1.40%
Blue Bell	241.6	1.40%
Häagen-Dazs	214.6	0.54%
Ben & Jerry's	199.7	0.89%
Wells Blue Bunny	108.4	−.40%
Turkey Hill	107.0	−5.30%
Dreyer's/Edy's Grand Light	100.0	6.90%
Healthy Choice	94.0	−12.60%
Total category	$3,200.5	−1.90%

Source: Information Resources Inc.

total 2003 ice-cream sales in supermarkets, drugstores, and mass merchandisers (excluding Wal-Mart) at $4.51 billion. Ice-cream sales were down 1.2 percent in terms of dollars over 2002, yet unit sales were up 0.3 percent. According to IRI, frozen novelties sales were $2.5 billion during 2003. Novelty sales were up 5 percent over 2002 and unit sales increased by 0.9 percent.

In October 2002, it was announced that Good Humor–Breyers Ice Cream of Green Bay, Wisconsin, and Ben & Jerry's of Vermont had formed a unified retail sales division named Unilever Ice Cream. The new organization brought together both companies and represented the five Unilever North American ice-cream brands, which include

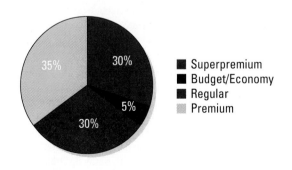

Exhibit 2   Ice-Cream Volume by Price, 2002

Exhibit 3   Top 10 Novelties Brands, 2004
(excludes Wal-Mart)

Brand	Sales (millions)	Market Share (%)
Private label	$ 367.1	14.5%
Klondike	175.8	7.0%
Silhouette	129.2	5.1%
Nestlé Drumstick	118.2	4.7%
Popsicle	108.1	4.3%
Weight Watchers	106.3	4.2%
Carvel	75.9	3.0%
Häagen-Dazs	50.2	2.0%
Dreyer's/Edy's	48.9	1.9%
Fudgsicle	45.4	1.8%
Other Brands	1,301.1	51.5%
Total category	$2,526.2	100.0%

Source: Information Resources Inc.

Ben & Jerry's, Breyers, Good Humor, Popsicle, and Klondike. Good Humor–Breyers has created several new co-branded novelties specifically for convenience store and vending locations. The company also set out to expand the availability of single-serve novelties by placing freezers of its products in Blockbuster video stores and Breyers-branded kiosks in 30 Chicago-area Loew's theaters. In addition to prepackaged products, freshly scooped ice cream is served at the kiosks. The new sales team will focus exclusively on the out-of-home ice cream business and, therefore, exclude grocery channels (see Exhibit 3 for the top 10 novelty brands).

Industry Segmentation   Frozen desserts come in many forms. Each of the following foods has its own definition, and many are standardized by federal regulations:[5]

Ice Cream consists of a mixture of dairy ingredients, such as milk and nonfat milk, and ingredients for sweetening and flavoring, such as fruits, nuts, and chocolate chips. Functional ingredients, such as stabilizers and emulsifiers, are often included in the product to promote proper texture and enhance the eating experience. By federal law, ice cream must contain at least 10 percent butterfat, before the addition of bulky ingredients, and must weigh a minimum of 4.5 pounds to the gallon.

Novelties are separately packaged single servings of a frozen dessert, such as ice-cream sandwiches, fudge sticks, and juice bars, which may or may not contain dairy ingredients.

Frozen Custard or French Ice Cream must also contain a minimum of 10 percent butterfat, as well as at least 1.4 percent egg yolk solids.

Sherbets have a butterfat content of between 1 percent and 2 percent, and a slightly higher sweetener content than ice cream. Sherbet weighs a minimum of 6 pounds to the gallon and is flavored either with fruit or other characterizing ingredients.

Gelato is characterized by an intense flavor and is served in a semifrozen state. Gelato contains sweeteners, milk, cream, egg yolks, and flavoring.

Sorbet and Water Ices are similar to sherbets, but contain no dairy ingredients.

A Quiescently Frozen Confection is a frozen novelty such as a water ice novelty on a stick.

Frozen Yogurt consists of a mixture of dairy ingredients, such as milk and nonfat milk, which have been cultured, as well as ingredients for sweetening and flavoring.

Growth Stages[6]

Initiation   The growth of Dippin' Dots Inc. has been recognized in the United States and the world by industry watchdogs such as *Inc.* magazine, which ranked Dippin' Dots as one of the 500 fastest-growing companies two years in a row in 1996 and 1997. Most recently, Dippin' Dots Franchising, Inc., ranked number four on *Entrepreneur* magazine's 2004 list of the top 50 new franchise companies and achieved the 101st spot on *Entrepreneur's* "Franchise 500" for 2004. Exhibit 4 shows the growth of franchises for Dippin' Dots.

However, the success of Curt Jones and Dippin' Dots has not been without obstacles. Once Curt perfected his idea, he needed to start a company for the new process of flash-freezing ice cream. Like many new entrepreneurs, Curt enlisted the help of his family to support his endeavor. It was essential to start selling his product, but he had no protection for his idea from competitors.

The first obstacle confronting Curt was to locate funding to accomplish his goals. He needed money for the patent to protect his intellectual property and seed money to start manufacturing the ice cream once the patent was granted. At the same time Curt was perfecting the flash-freezing process for his ice cream, he was also working on a small business association (SBA) loan to convert the family farm into one that would manufacture ethanol. However, instead of using the farm to produce the alternative fuel, Curt's parents took out a first, and then a second,

Exhibit 4   Franchise Growth

Year	U.S. Franchises	Canadian Franchises	Foreign Franchises	Company Owned
2004	615	1	0	2
2003	580	0	0	2
2002	580	0	0	2
2001	569	0	0	3
2000	525	0	0	1

Source: Entrepreneur.com.

mortgage to help fund Curt's endeavor. Thus, Curt initiated the entire venture by self-funding his company with personal and family assets.

However, the money from his parents was only enough to pay for the patent and some crude manufacturing facilities (liquid nitrogen tanks in his parents' garage). Curt always believed that his ice cream would sell, but with the patent he felt reassured by the protection it offered from any competitors. He next had to open a store to validate his faith that consumers would buy his product, but opening the store required more money—money that Curt and his family did not have. They were unable to get the SBA loan because, while the product was novel and looked promising, there was no proof that it would sell. So Curt and his newly appointed CFO (his sister) went to an "alternative lender" who lent them cash at an exorbitant interest rate which was tacked onto the principal weekly if unpaid.

With the seed money they needed, Curt Jones and his family opened their first store. Soon after the store opened in the summertime, there was a buzz in the community—and the store was mobbed every night. Dippin' Dots was legitimized by public demand. Through the influx of cash, Curt was able to move his manufacturing operation into a vacant warehouse. There he set up shop and personally made flash-frozen ice cream for 12 hours every day to supply the store.

Development   Once the store had been operating for a few months the Joneses were able to secure small business loans from local banks to cover the expenses of a modest manufacturing plant and office. At the same time, Curt's sister made calls to fairs and events to learn if Dippin' Dots products could be sold there. Luckily for the Joneses, the amusement park at Opryland in Nashville, Tennessee, was willing to have them as a vendor. Unfortunately, the first Dippin' Dots stand was placed in front of a roller coaster and people generally do not want ice cream before they go on a ride. After a few unsuccessful

weeks, they moved the stand and business picked up considerably. Eventually, they were able to move to an inline location, which was similar to a store, where Dippin' Dots had its own personnel and sitting area to serve customers.

Just by word of mouth, the speculation about Curt Jones and Dippin' Dots spread. Soon other entrepreneurs contacted Curt to open up stores to sell Dippin' Dots. In 1991 a dealership network was developed to sell ice cream to authorized vendors and provide support with equipment and marketing. Over the course of nine years, Dippin' Dots grew into a multimillion dollar company with authorized dealers operating in all 50 states and internationally (see Exhibit 5). During that time, Curt employed friends to assume corporate jobs.

Plateau Busting   By the end of the 1990s Curt was happy with his company, but felt as if Dippin' Dots had hit a plateau and needed to reach the "next level" to continue to prosper. He began working with his friend and now controller and director of franchising, Chad Wilson, to develop the franchise system. By January 2000, all existing Dippin' Dots dealers were required to sign a franchise agreement and pay the associated franchise fees for any location they operated or planned to operate. A franchised location is any mall, fair, "national account," or large family entertainment center. The result was a cash flow for Dippin' Dots franchising.

Future Growth

Dippin' Dots is counting on youthful exuberance to expand growth above the $36 million mark of 2003. "Our core demographic is pretty much 8- to 18-year-olds," said Terry Reeves, corporate communications director. "On top of that, we're starting to see a generation of parents who grew up on Dippin' Dots and are starting to introduce the products to their kids."

In 2002 McDonald's reportedly spent $1.2 million on advertising to roll out Dippin' Dots in about 250 restaurants in the San Francisco area. Because the response was good, McDonald's expanded into the Reno, Nevada, and Sacramento, California, areas, believing it would do well. Jones called the deal "open-ended" if it works favorably for both firms. "I think both companies are proceeding with the impression that nothing is going to be overcommitted," he said. "We're growing at a 10 to 15 percent annual rate and we're excited about the potential of McDonald's, but it's too early to tell." By mid-2004 Dippin' Dots was available in 800 western region McDonald's stores. McDonald's was a good fit for Dippin' Dots as a unique ice cream available in an exceptional restaurant for kids. McDonald's generous co-op advertising and promotions

Exhibit 5   Milestones

1988 Dippin' Dots established as a company in Grand Chain, Illinois.

1989 First amusement park account debuts at Opryland USA in Nashville.

1990 Production facility moves to Paducah, Kentucky.

1991 Dealer network established for fair, festival, and commercial retail locations.

1994 First international licensee (Japan).

1995 New 32,000 sq. ft. production facility opens in Paducah.

1997 Production facility expands by 20,000 sq. ft.; earns spot on *Inc.* 500 list of USA's fastest-growing private companies in the United States.

2000 Dippin' Dots Franchising, Inc., established and first franchise offered; initiation of litigation against competitors to protect patent.

2001 Dippin' Dots enlists 30 new franchisees.

  Franchise Times magazine lists Dippin' Dots third nationally behind Baskin Robbins and Dairy Queen in number of franchises.

2002 Dippin' Dots Franchising, Inc., achieves 112th spot on *Entrepreneur* magazine's "Franchise 500" list.

  Dippin' Dots Franchising, Inc., ranked 69th on *Entrepreneur* magazine's list as "Fastest Growing" franchise company.

  Dippin' Dots Franchising, Inc., ranked the number one "New Franchise Company" by *Entrepreneur*.

  Dippin' Dots becomes a regular menu offering on menus at McDonald's restaurants in the San Francisco Bay area.

  Dippin' Dots product and plant featured as one of the world's most unique frozen desserts on the Food Network's new show *Unwrapped*.

  The Paducah plant builds a new freezer to hold 50,000 gallons of product at an average temperature of 55 degrees below zero (Dippin' Dots started with a 19,000-gallon freezer, and added a 45,000-gallon freezer in 1997).

2003 Dippin' Dots Franchising, Inc., achieves 144th spot on *Entrepreneur* magazine's "Franchise 500" list.

  Dippin' Dots Franchising, Inc., ranks number four on *Entrepreneur's* magazine's list of the Top 50 New Franchise Companies.

  Dippin' Dots Franchising, Inc., conducts first nationwide sweepstakes.

  Dippin' Dots Korea Ansong manufacturing plant, a 20,000 sq. ft. facility located 80 miles south of Seoul in South Korea.

2004 Dippin' Dots Franchising, Inc., ranks number four on *Entrepreneur's* list of the Top 50 New Franchise Companies.

  Dippin' Dots Franchising, Inc., achieves 101st spot on *Entrepreneur* magazine's "Franchise 500" list.

  Curt Jones and Dippin' Dots featured on a segment of the *Oprah Winfrey Show* appearing in 110 countries.

  Dippin' Dots featured among the "Top 10 Ice Cream Palaces" on the Travel Channel.

  Curt Jones quoted in Donald Trump's best-selling *The Way to the Top* (p. 131).

made dealing with McDonald's exacting standards, regulations, and inspections worthwhile. Expansion eastward for Dippin' Dots has been delayed by McDonald's efforts to refocus internally.

Second, Dippin' Dots ads have been running in issues of *Seventeen* and *Nickelodeon* magazines, marking the first time the company has purchased national consumer advertising. Reeves said the company has been "inundated with e-mails" since the June 2002 issue of *Seventeen* hit the newsstands. Additionally, Dippin' Dots has hired a Hollywood firm to place its ice cream in the

background of television and movie scenes, including the 2003 hit *Cheaper by the Dozen*. In 2002 the Food Network's "Summer Foods: Unwrapped" showcased Dippin' Dots as one of the most unique and coolest ice cream treats. 'N Sync member Joey Fatone ordered a Dippin' Dots freezer for his home after seeing a Dots vending machine at a theater the band rented in Orlando. Caterers also sought Dippin' Dots for their star clients. A recent birthday party at the home of NBA star Shaquille O'Neal featured Dippin' Dots ice cream. In 2003 Jones, Reeves, and other company officials personally served their products to the band before an 'N Sync show in Memphis. Franchisees must contribute a half-percent of their gross incomes to an advertising fund, which Jones says has greatly enhanced marketing.

Challenges   Dippin' Dots has been in business for 16 years now and has had great success. However, the company has met increased competition in the once infrequent out-of-home ice-cream market. The major threats to Dippin' Dots are Nestlé and Unilever, the industry giants that are now focusing on the out-of-home ice-cream market. In addition, a very similar type of flash-frozen ice cream called Frosty Bites was introduced in the spring of 2000 by disenfranchised former dealers of Dippin' Dots. In 2002 Curt thought that introducing a formal franchising agreement would unify the company's public image—Dippin' Dots was often unrecognizable under a nonstructured dealership network of locations—and put the company on the map with other franchises like Dunkin' Donuts, Baskin Robbins, Häagen-Daaz, and Good Humor.

Terry Reeves, corporate communication director, said:

[T]he stronger and more unified Dippin' Dots retail offering becomes through franchising, the more [franchisees] were able to be considered for better retail properties (high-end malls, better locations, and so on). This obviously strengthens our system and bolsters overall sales for the company and for our franchisees. While franchise fees and royalties are a new income source, much of the profit is put back into the business to promote future growth.[7]

One dealer commented that Dippin' Dots used that money, along with the incoming franchise fees for royalties on sales, for their own corporate means. On the other hand, most dealers did convert to the new franchise system. Dippin' Dots Franchising, Inc., grandfathered existing dealers' locations by issuing a franchise and waiving the franchise fee for the first contract period of five years. Many dealers had to renew their contracts in 2004; while many were initially apprehensive of converting to a franchised system, less than 2 percent left the system, and the firm has shown substantial franchise growth.

Jones, always the inventor, has been back in the lab and investing in R&D to create a conventional ice-cream product that has superfrozen dots embedded in it. He is developing a new product that could withstand conventional

freezers while preserving the superfrozen dots in the ice cream. With this product Dippin' Dots could finally have a take-home ice-cream option. A grocery store product offering might be the ticket to national exposure for Dippin' Dots.

However, the company's experience and resource base are clearly in the ice-cream manufacturing and scoop shop retailing businesses. Dealing with supermarket chains, packaging, and distributors would be a new adventure for this relatively small firm. On the other hand, many opportunities can still be pursued in enlarging the franchise and national accounts businesses for scoop shops. In order to develop the business, Jones will have to choose either a big push with scoop shops or target the grocery store business or some combination of the two. Jones continues to assess his company's situation and then will identify and choose among the best strategic options for Dippin' Dots' growth over the remainder of this decade and beyond.

Endnotes

1. Figures provided by Dippin' Dots, Inc.
2. Information unless otherwise stated is derived from the Dippin' Dots Web site. www.DippinDots.com; the Dippin' Dots 10-year anniversary video; or from the self-published Dippin' Dots Corporate Profile.
3. Ice cream's origins are known to reach back as far as the second century BC, although no specific date of origin or inventor has been indisputably credited with its discovery. We know that Alexander the Great enjoyed snow and ice flavored with honey and nectar. Biblical references also show that King Solomon was fond of iced drinks during harvesting. During the Roman Empire, Nero (AD 54–86) frequently sent runners into the mountains for snow, which was then flavored with fruits and juices. Information from Ice Cream Media Kit, International Dairy Foods Association.
4. Ice cream consists of a mixture of dairy ingredients such as milk and nonfat milk, and ingredients for sweetening and flavoring, such as fruits, nuts, and chocolate chips. Functional ingredients, such as stabilizers and emulsifiers, are often included in the product to promote proper texture and enhance the eating experience. By federal law, ice cream must contain at least 10 percent butterfat, before the addition of bulky ingredients, and must weigh a minimum of 4.5 pounds to the gallon.
5. All definitions taken from the IDFA Web site: www.idfa.org/facts/icmonth/page4.cfm.
6. Dippin' Dots 10th Anniversary Promotional Video.
7. Personal communication with author.

Case 14   Panera Bread Company*

An exciting new segment in the restaurant industry, the fast-casual market, is growing 15–20 percent each year, despite the slowdown in consumer spending, changing economic conditions, and increases in gas prices.[1] The restaurant industry is extremely competitive with existing companies planning major expansion efforts and new concept restaurants opening every day. In addition, media headlines highlight the low-carb trend among consumers. In May 2004 the managers of Krispy Kreme Doughnuts, Inc., a competitor of Panera Bread, announced they were reducing the profit projection for the year because of lower demand for its high-calorie doughnuts. Scott Livengood, chief executive and chairman of Krispy Kreme, stated, "The popularity of low-carb diets has captured the consumer's attention. It's impossible to predict if low-carb is a passing fad or will have a lasting impact."

Panera's management team plans to open between 140 and 150 new bakery-cafes in 2004, expects increases in systemwide sales, and hopes to maintain its leadership position in the very competitive restaurant industry. Can these goals be obtained despite the dynamic characteristics of this industry?

The Restaurant Industry

There are approximately 8 million restaurants in the world and about 300,000 restaurant companies. The industry has two major segments: The full-service segment includes family-style restaurants, dinner houses, and grill/buffet restaurants. The fast-food segment includes sandwiches, hamburgers, Mexican food, pizza, and chicken and is represented by companies such as Burger King, Taco Bell, KFC, Pizza Hut, McDonald's, Popeye's, Subway, and Wendy's.[2] With high competition, a mature market, a decline in the supply of workers age 16 to 24, and low profit margins, this is a difficult industry in which to excel. Overall restaurant sales have been rising about 5 percent annually.

In a recent report on the Top 100 chain restaurant companies, Technomic reported annual growth of 5.1 percent and 2001 systemwide sales of $136.5 billion, an increase of $6.6 billion over 2000.[3] The other sandwich category of the Top 100 chain restaurants grew at 12.8 percent, doughnuts at 12.3 percent, and the full-service, varied menu, Italian, and steak categories each grew more than 8 percent. The 10 fastest-growing chains with sales over $200 million in 2001 were Panera Bread, Krispy Kreme, Quizno's Classic Subs, Culver's, P.F. Chang's China Bistro, Chevys, Carrabba's Italian Grill, Buffalo Wild Wings, Starbucks,

and the Cheesecake Factory. Exhibit 1 shows restaurant chains with the highest three-year sales growth rates as of June 2004.

International sales for the Top 100 chain restaurants increased only 1.8 percent in 2001, down from 6.4 percent in 2000. Technomic analysts suggest that the U.S. restaurant industry is somewhat insulated from economic swings.

There is an exciting new restaurant market segment developing—the fast-casual market—and these restaurants are becoming key players in the industry. The fast-casual market is a combination of the quick service of traditional fast-food restaurants with the higher-quality food products found in sit-down restaurants. The fast-casual market is a $6 billion industry growing 15 to 20 percent each year. It represented about 2 percent of the restaurant market in 2003. Sales growth is expected to double to $12 billion during the next five years and grow to $30 billion by 2010.[4]

What has led to the success of this restaurant segment? Many people are tired of fast food, and the fast-casual restaurant offers a new alternative; baby boomers' children have left home and this group is weary of cooking; young professionals do not want to cook every night; many Americans are concerned about eating more healthy foods; and more individuals want to spend little time eating a

Exhibit 1   Restaurant Chains with Highest Three-Year Sales Growth Rates, June 2004

Restaurant	Three-Year Sales Growth Rate (%)
New World Restaurants (Einstein Bagels)	85.862%
P.F. Chang's	33.527
Buffalo Wild Wings	33.493
Panera Bread	32.965
Krispy Kreme Doughnuts	30.322
Landry's Restaurants	28.513
BUCA Inc.	25.580
Chicago Pizza & Brewery	25.293
Starbucks	23.235
Cheesecake Factory, Inc.	20.864
Industry Average	**11.635%**

Source: Reuters.com.

*This case was prepared by Professors Debora J. Gilliard and Rajendra Khandekar of Metropolitan State College–Denver as a basis for class discussion rather than to illustrate either effective or ineffective handling of an administrative situation. Copyright © 2004 Debora J. Gilliard and Rajendra Khandekar. All rights reserved.

meal. In addition, these restaurants tend to have strong sales in multiple parts of the day and develop a narrow menu focus.[5] Restaurants commonly included in the fast-casual segment include Panera Bread, Moe's Southwest Grill, Firehouse Subs, Chipotle, Sweet Tomatoes, Baja Fresh Mexican Grill, Rubio's Fresh Mexican Grill, Atlanta Bread Company, McAlister's Deli, Wingstop, and Crescent City Beignets. Exhibit 2 shows the leaders in the fast-casual category in 2002.

There are a number of trends that are influencing the restaurant industry:

- Increasing sales of chicken entrees. Many people perceive chicken to be a healthy food. Antonio Swad, founder of Wingstop Restaurants, states, "I was seeing that even people who say, 'I don't eat meat,' really mean that they don't eat red meat or pork. It just shows you what a position poultry has! It's almost the meat that non-meat eaters eat."[6]

- Consumers are showing an increased interest in more healthful foods. Organic foods are becoming more common as are healthy finger foods, such as sushi. Chefs are including more nuts (good sources of protein, fiber, vitamins, and minerals) in salads and entrees.

- Low-carb diets are affecting restaurant sales. The National Bread Leadership Council reported that U.S. consumers are eating 63 percent less bread in 2003 than they did in 2002. The council predicts this number will increase in 2004. Many restaurants are reporting changes in consumer eating habits: fewer bread requests and greater numbers of meat and vegetable requests. A Harris Poll conducted in the summer of 2003 indicated that 32 million Americans reported they were on a high-protein, low-carb diet.[7]

- More restaurants are allowing customers to customize their meals. For example, Peninsula Grill offers four steaks and five fish that guests can

Exhibit 2   Leading Fast-Casual Concepts

		2002 Estimates		
	Sales ($ Millions)	$ Change 2001–2002 %	Total Units	Unit Change 2001–2002 %
Panera Bread	$ 755	42%	478	29%
Boston Market	650	4	662	1
Fazoli's	430	6	401	2
Baja Fresh	249	41	210	39
Chipotle	225	55	232	31
Buca di Beppo	240	37	82	21
Sweet Tomatoes/Souplantation	214	8	97	3
Taco Cabana	175	(1)	126	2
Atlanta Bread Company	160	59	153	27
Corner Bakery	138	17	81	17
La Madeleine	125	3	62	3
Rubio's Fresh Mexican Grill	119	6	143	6
McAlister's	107	34	103	34
Cosi	84	20	91	28
Pick Up Stix	75	15	75	32
Noodles & Company	59	69	58	61
Wolfgang Puck Express	52	53	39	105
Qdoba	58	13	85	13
Est. All Others	823	28	686	25
Total	$4,738	23%	3,864	17%

Source: Hale Group, Ltd.

customize by choosing from 10 sauces. Executive Chef Robert Carter stated, "People can choose what they want to go together. What it creates is the ability for someone to be able to create their own dish. We wanted to have some options and give people what they wanted. . . . I think that the biggest trend is giving customers some options. . . . Restaurants that aren't willing to give customers choices are being perceived as stuffy or snooty."[8]

- Decor sets a restaurant apart from its competition and can be a defining aspect and enhances a restaurant's theme. A majority of restaurant owners/managers indicated they had remodeled their dining areas at least once since 1996 when responding to a National Restaurant Association survey.
- Today's customer is demanding better-quality food, better service, and better food safety. Restaurateurs must meet these demands with innovative food preparation and service.
- About half of 18- to 34-year-olds, who represent 37 percent of fast-food customers, are also eating at fast-casual chains.[9]

Restaurant and Institutions reported that in the rapidly changing restaurant environment, it is imperative for restaurants to engage in brand reengineering.[10] Restaurants do this by changing their name to reflect changes in concepts, changes in menus, new signage, and new decor. Lee Peterson, executive director of the design group at WD Partners, a firm that works with chain restaurants, said that restaurants do not have set shelf lives, but they do have life cycles. He further indicated that concepts are destined to die out, but they do require refurbishing to survive. Peterson stated, "Birth of the fast-casual segment made the quick-service industry realize it was aging. But that is healthy because it spurs reflection and improvement."

The quick-services restaurants are responding to trends by refreshing their menus and expanding into fast-casual concepts. The Hale Group reported that McDonald's and Jack in the Box have introduced premium salads, Burger King has "fire-grilled" burgers, Arby's has been successful with its Market Fresh Sandwiches, Subway is repositioning itself as a provider of healthy foods, and Schlotzsky's has introduced a healthy menu. Casual dining restaurants are also responding by offering convenient options such as Chili's To Go service, Outback's and Applebee's curbside delivery, and Applebee's fast-lunch menus. TGI Friday's, Ruby Tuesday's, and Chili's are adding low-carb options to their menus, and the Don Pablo's chain of Mexican restaurants added Low-Carb Lettuce Wrap Fajitas to its menu.[11]

History of Panera Bread Company

Ron Shaich cofounded Au Bon Pain Co. in 1981 with the opening of three bakery-cafes and one cookie store. The company continued to grow throughout the 1980s and 1990s. By the end of 1997, the company had 160 bakery-cafes in the United States, mostly located on the East Coast, and 96 bakery-cafes outside the country in Chile, the Philippines, Indonesia, Thailand, Brazil, and the United Kingdom. The company had bakery-cafes located in 9 domestic airports and 14 DoubleTree Hotels.

Twenty-five years ago Ken Rosenthal first tasted the sourdough bread that would become a vital part of Panera Bread. He was so taken by the bread's texture and flavor that he persuaded the family that made it to sell him the sourdough starter. In October 1987 Ken packed the starter in a cooler and brought it back to St. Louis where he started the St. Louis Bread Co. The handcrafted bread became a favorite among local citizens and the concept soon evolved to include other breads, bagels, pastries, sandwiches, salads, and espresso beverages.

On December 22, 1993, Au Bon Pain Co. purchased the St. Louis Bread Co. At the time, the St. Louis Bread Co. consisted of 19 company-owned bakery-cafes and one franchised bakery-cafe located primarily in the St. Louis area. Au Bon Pain Co. consisted of over 300 quick-service bakeries in the East. In 1998 Au Bon Pain Co.'s CEO, Ron Shaich, decided to build St. Louis Bread Co. into a national brand under the name Panera Bread. Panera, derived from Latin, means "time of bread" and the name change reflected the vision and focus of expanding the company: "The time of bread was dawning in America."[12] In May 1999 all of Au Bon Pain Co.'s business units were sold except the bakery-cafe business unit, which was officially renamed Panera Bread Company. Today the Panera bakery-cafes produce among the highest average retail unit volumes of any concept outside of casual dining. In 2003 the company reported company bakery-cafe sales of $265.9 million and franchise bakery sales of $711.0 million. As of December 2003 the company had over 602 bakery-cafes with average unit volumes of $1.85 million. It is ranked as one of the top growth companies in the food service industry.

Company Concept and Strategy

The Panera Bread Company brings the tradition of freshly baked bread to neighborhoods. Only the highest-quality ingredients are used—only fresh dough and no preservatives—and the bread is baked fresh everyday. Panera Bread bakes more fresh bread each day than any other bakery-cafe operation in the United States, which helps fulfill the company's mission of putting "a loaf of bread in every arm."

Panera Bread serves 18 kinds of breads, bagels, muffins, scones, rolls and sweet goods, made-to-order sandwiches, hearty soups, custom-roasted coffees, and cafe beverages such as espresso and cappuccino drinks. The company regularly reviews its product offerings to ensure it is satisfying changing customer preferences. Two customer groups have been identified: the "bread-loving trendsetters" who embrace new and nutritional items, and the "bread-loving traditionalists." In 2002 the company introduced a new artisan bread that is an all-natural, hand-crafted bread baked on a stone deck. In spring of 2003 the company introduced a line of ciabatta bread sandwiches. Kevin Ament, a company spokesperson, stated, "People want high-quality handcrafted foods that are made with the best ingredients and that are fresh. What Panera is doing with bread is similar to what Starbucks did with coffee: educating customers about a staple people took for granted."[13] Ron Shaich announced in August 2003 that the company was in the process of equipping its bakery-cafes with free Wi-Fi access. He stated, "Panera is the first national chain to take substantial steps forward in meeting growing consumer demand for high-speed Internet access without charging for the service. By offering this extra amenity, we hope to more fully meet the needs of our sophisticated and diverse consumer base." In December 2003 Panera Bread and Viking Culinary Arts Centers announced they were teaming up to offer monthly classes on how to prepare fresh baked breads at home. Panera artisan bakers will conduct classes at Viking Culinary Arts Centers in Atlanta, Cleveland, Dallas, Long Island, Philadelphia, and St. Louis. Other initiatives the company is introducing in an effort to increase sales growth are: Via Panera, an off-premises sales concept to improve convenience to customers; new and seasonal food items; and a debit card program similar to that offered by Starbucks.

Shaich indicated that consumer interest in the low-carbohydrates diets "served to temper our comparable stores' sales' increases, which totaled a modest 0.2 percent systemwide in 2003."[14] He indicated that Panera's diverse menu has always offered choices to customers. However, to address the low-carb trend, Panera introduced a new line of low-carb breads, bagels, and breadsticks in June 2004.

The menu, operating system, and design allow Panera Bread to operate in several successful times of the day: breakfast, lunch, and daytime "chill out" (between breakfast and lunch and between lunch and dinner when customers take a break from their daily activities to visit bakery-cafes). In addition, the company sells bread to take home.

The bakery-cafes are primarily located in suburban, strip mall, and regional mall locations. As of December 27, 2003, the company operated 602 Panera Bread bakery-cafes in 35 states (see Exhibit 3).

The company has been successful because of its unit economies, its fine premium food, and its loyal customer base. Panera Bread serves its food on China, has well-spaced tables, and the decor reflects that of a French cafe. The environment is very important since about half of its customers eat on-site. Kevin Ament recently stated, "It's

Exhibit 3   Panera Bread/St. Louis Bread Co. Bakery-Cafes

State	Company Bakery-Cafes	Franchise-Operated Bakery-Cafes	Total Bakery-Cafes
Alabama			4
Arkansas		2	2
California		5	5
Colorado		14	14
Connecticut	1	4	5
Delaware		1	1
Florida	5	43	48
Georgia	8	6	14
Iowa		13	13
Illinois	34	32	66
Indiana	3	15	18
Kansas		14	14
Kentucky	4	1	5
Massachusetts	2	18	20
Maryland		18	18
Maine		2	2
Michigan	32	8	40
Minnesota		20	20
Missouri	36	16	52
North Carolina	1	17	18
Nebraska		7	7
Nevada		2	2
New Hampshire		7	7
New Jersey		25	25
New York	5	3	8
Ohio	6	55	61
Oklahoma		15	15
Pennsylvania	7	27	34
Rhode Island		3	3
South Carolina	2		2
Tennessee	1	9	10
Texas	2	9	11
Virginia	20	1	21
West Virginia		2	2
Wisconsin		15	15
Totals	169	429	598

Source: Panera Bread Co. 2003. Annual Report.

very much a gathering place where people can go and relax and enjoy the food."[15] The company also delivers what its sophisticated customers desire: fresh sandwiches, bagels, salads, soups, pastries, and alternatives to fast food.[16]

In order to achieve the goals for this business, Chairman Ron Shaich indicated the company must:[17]

- Ensure the concept remains special.
- Deliver spectacular execution every day.
- Effectively execute a growth strategy through committed franchisees/area development partners, company operators, and joint venture partners.
- Evolve the information systems, management practices, and culture to drive focus, accountability, and transparency.
- Encourage evolution and change consistent with our commitment to bread leadership and our concept essence.

Throughout 2003 Panera Bread Company's breads, bakery products, soups, and sandwiches were often voted "best of" in many regional markets. A few of the awards Panera received include: "Best Bakery" in Chattanooga, Franklin (Massachusetts), Kansas City, Knoxville, Sarasota, Boulder, and Highlands Ranch (Colorado); "Best Bread" in Cincinnati, Cleveland, Hyde Park, and St. Louis; "Best Bagels" in Columbus, Iowa City, Sarasota, and Oak Ridge (Tennessee); and "Best Sandwiches" in Minneapolis/St. Paul, Rochester, and Milwaukee.[18] In the spring of 2003, Panera was ranked as the top-performing company in Standard & Poor's Small Cap 600 Index.[19] Also in that year, Panera Bread received, for the second consecutive year, top ranking in the "Choice of Chains" awards sponsored by *Restaurant and Institutions* magazine. The award is based on consumer rankings of food quality, menu variety, value, service, atmosphere, cleanliness, and convenience. Panera was also ranked number one for food quality among all 95 competitors. *Nation's Restaurant News* announced Panera Bread was ranked number one in a national consumer satisfaction survey of more than 71,000 consumers.[20]

In 1992 the company established Operation Dough-Nation, a program that allows Panera Bread to contribute back to the community. The cash donations received at the bakery-cafes are matched with bread and cash and distributed to local food pantries. At the end of each day, any unsold loaves of bread are taken to a local hunger relief agency. The company has also developed a Dough for Funds program that allows nonprofit groups to sell special coupons for Panera Bread products and keep half the proceeds for their causes.

Management

The management team at Panera Bread Company is filled with individuals with a great deal of food service experience (see Exhibit 4).

Company Operations

Management Information Systems
The cash registers at each bakery-cafe collect point-of-sale transaction data that is used to generate marketing information, product mix, and average check amount. The in-store system is designed to assist managers in scheduling labor, managing food costs, and providing access to retail data. The sales, bank deposit, and variance data for each bakery-cafe are submitted to the company's accounting department daily and the information is then used to generate weekly reports and monthly financial data.

Distribution
Independent distributors are used to distribute sweet goods products and other materials to the bakery-cafes. This allows Panera to eliminate an investment in distribution systems and focus on its retail operations. Fresh dough products are provided by the commissaries, and all other products and supplies (e.g., paper goods and coffee) are contracted for by the company and delivered by vendors to the independent distributors.

Franchise Operations
Panera Bread began its franchising program in 1996. The company prefers to establish area development agreements (ADAs) rather than individual franchises. The ADA requires a franchise to develop a specified number of bakery-cafes on or before specific dates as designated in each agreement. Franchisee-owned bakery-cafes must meet the same standards for product quality, menu, site selection, and construction as company-owned bakery-cafes. Franchisees are required to purchase all dough products from company-approved sources and the company's commissary supplies all fresh dough products. The franchise fee is $35,000 with the total investment in a bakery-cafe ranging from $564,000 to $910,725. A royalty fee of 4 percent to 5 percent on gross sales is payable each week. As of December 28, 2003, the company was working with 32 franchisee groups, had 429 franchised bakery-cafes open, and had commitments to open 409 additional franchised bakery-cafes. The manager and head baker of each franchise are required to attend Panera Bread's training program. The classroom portion of the management training course lasts five days and the in-store training portion lasts four to six weeks. Topics discussed during the training program include area and shift management, administration, customer service, quality assurance, company history, safety procedures, and human resources.

Bakery Supply Chain
All bakery-cafes use fresh dough for the sourdough bread, artisan breads, and bagels which is supplied daily by a regional commissary of the company. As of December 27, 2003, the company had 17 regional fresh dough facilities. Although the distribution system requires a major commitment of capital, it provides cost efficiencies and assures consistent quality and supply of dough to the bakery-cafes. These give Panera Bread a

Exhibit 4   Panera Bread Company Officers

Name and Title	Background
Ronald Schaich Chairman and Chief Executive Officer	Cofounder of Au Bon Pain Co., 1981 MBA, Harvard Business School
Paul E. Twohig Executive Vice President and Chief Operating Officer; joined Panera in January 2003	30 years' experience in food industry; Starbucks, 9 years; Burger King
Neal Yanofsky Executive Vice President, Chief Administrative and Corporate Staff Officer, joined Panera in June 2003	Graduate of Harvard College and Harvard Business School; research fellow, London School of Economics; independent business consultant
Scott G. Davis Senior Vice President and Chief Concept Officer	Started with Au Bon Pain in 1987
Mike J. Kupstas Senior Vice President and Chief Franchise Officer; joined Panera in January 1996	Long John Silver's Inc. and Red Lobster
John Maguire Senior Vice President, Chief Company and Joint Venture Operations Officer; joined Panera in 1994	15 years of bakery experience
Michael J. Nolan Senior Vice President and Chief Development Officer; joined Panera in 2001	
Mark Borland Senior Vice President and Chief Supply Chain Officer	With Au Bon Pain since 1986
Mark E. Hood Senior Vice President and Chief Financial Officer; joined Panera in August 2002	U.S. Loyalty Corp. and Saks Holding Inc.

competitive advantage. Product consistency enhances brand identity. The company distributes the dough using a leased fleet of temperature-controlled trucks. The optimal distribution limit is within 200 miles of the commissary and the average distribution route delivers dough to six bakery-cafes.

In May 2003 Panera opened its first bakery-cafe in Las Vegas using a new concept. In addition to the 5,600-square-foot bakery-cafe, a 500-square-foot fresh dough facility was included. This on-site commissary will produce fresh dough daily and customers are able to observe the baking process.

Other baked goods served at the bakery-cafes are prepared with frozen dough. In 1996 a state-of-the-art production facility was built in Mexico, Missouri, which the company sold to Bunge Food Corporation in 1998 for $13 million. At the time of sale, the company entered into a five-year (1998–2003) supply agreement with Bunge for the supply of its frozen dough needs. The sale of the pro-

duction facility provided economies of scale in plant production and allowed the company to take advantage of Bunge's significant purchasing power.

In April 2003 the company signed an agreement with Dawn Food Products, Inc., to provide sweet goods for the 2003–2008 period. The company believes cost savings will be achieved by making the switch from Bunge to Dawn.

Financial Information

Exhibits 5 and 6 provide income and expense figures, and a consolidated balance sheet, respectively, for the most recent 12-month period.

Exhibit 7 provides key statistics for Panera Bread for the 12 months ended April 30, 2004.

For the 52-week period from May 2003 to May 2004 the stock price reached a high of $47.79 and a low of $32.65.

First quarter 2004 net income increased 26 percent over the same period in 2003. By April 17, 2004, the

Exhibit 5   Panera Bread Company, Income and Expenses

	For the Fiscal Years Ended[1]				
	December 27, 2003	December 28, 2002	December 29, 2001	December 30, 2000	December 25, 1999[2]
	(in thousands, except per share and bakery-cafe data)				
Costs and expenses:					
Bakery-cafe expenses:					
Cost of food and paper products	$ 73,727	$ 63,255	$ 48,253	$ 40,998	$ 52,362
Labor	81,152	63,172	45,768	36,281	45,167
Occupancy	17,990	14,619	11,345	9,313	15,552
Other operating expenses	36,804	27,971	20,729	16,050	18,740
Total bakery-cafe expenses	209,673	169,017	126,095	102,642	131,821
Fresh dough cost of sales to franchisees	47,151	33,959	21,965	12,261	6,490
Depreciation and amortization	19,487	13,965	10,839	8,412	6,379
General and administrative expenses	28,140	24,986	19,589	16,381	17,104
Pre-opening expenses	1,531	1,051	912	414	301
Nonrecurring charge[3]	—	—	—	494	5,545
Total costs and expenses	305,982	242,978	179,400	140,604	167,640
Operating profit	49,904	34,774	21,717	10,785	3,719
Interest expense	48	32	72	164	2,745
Other expense (income), net	1,227	287	213	(409)	735
Loss from early extinguishment of debt[4]	—	—	—	—	579
Minority interest	365	180	8	—	(25)
Income (loss) before income taxes and cumulative effect of accounting change	48,264	34,275	21,424	11,030	(315)
Provision for income taxes	17,616	12,510	8,272	4,177	314
Income (loss) before cumulative effect of accounting change	30,648	21,765	13,152	6,853	(629)
Cumulative effect to December 28, 2002, of accounting change, net of tax benefit	239	—	—	—	—
Net income (loss)	$ 30,409	$ 21,765	$ 13,152	$ 6,853	$ (629)

(*continued*)

company had 637 bakery-cafes. During the 16 weeks ended April 17, 2004, Panera Bread opened 36 new bakery-cafes and closed one.

The company expects price increases in 2004 of about 2 percent for major ingredients such as butter, milk, hard cheeses, and cream cheese. Some of the price increases will be passed along to consumers, but company leaders also expect their margins to experience pressure.

In a press release on May 13, 2004, Ron Shaich, chairman and CEO, reported: "We are very pleased with our performance to date and are enthusiastic about the company's prospects. Sales in both new and mature bakery-cafes are robust and new store development is proceeding at a record pace. These two leading indicators of our performance indicate the stability of our business and the depth of consumer demand for the brand."

Exhibit 5   Income and Expenses (*continued*)

	For the Fiscal Years Ended[1]				
	December 27, 2003	December 28, 2002	December 29, 2001	December 30, 2000	December 25, 1999[2]
	(in thousands, except per share and bakery-cafe data)				
Per common share:					
Basic:					
Income (loss) before cumulative effect of accounting change	$ 1.03	$ 0.75	$ 0.47	$ 0.27	$ (0.03)
Cumulative effect of accounting change	(0.01)	—	—	—	—
Net income (loss)	$ 1.02	$ 0.75	$ 0.47	$ 0.27	$ (0.03)
Diluted:					
Income (loss) before cumulative effect of accounting change	$ 1.01	$ 0.73	$ 0.46	$ 0.26	$ (0.03)
Cumulative effect of accounting change	(0.01)	—	—	—	—
Net income (loss)	$ 1.00	$ 0.73	$ 0.46	$ 0.26	$ (0.03)
Weighted average shares of common stock outstanding:					
Basic	29,733	28,923	27,783	25,114	24,274
Diluted	30,423	29,891	28,886	26,267	24,274
Comparable bakery-cafe sales percentage increases for:					
Company-owned bakery-cafes	1.7%	4.1%	5.8%	8.1%	3.3%
Franchise-operated bakery-cafes	(0.4)%	6.1%	5.8%	10.3%	(7)
Systemwide	0.2%	5.5%	5.8%	9.1%	(7)
Consolidated balance sheet data:					
Cash and cash equivalents	$ 42,402	$ 29,924	$ 18,052	$ 9,011	$ 1,936
Total assets	$245,943	$188,440	$143,934	$111,689	$91,029
Stockholders' equity	$195,937	$153,656	$119,872	$ 91,588	$73,246
Bakery-cafe data:					
Company-owned bakery-cafes open	173	132	110	90	81
Franchise-owned bakery-cafes open	429	346	259	172	100
Total bakery-cafes open	602	478	369	262	181

[1]Fiscal year 2000 consists of 53 weeks. Fiscal years 2003, 2002, 2001, and 1999 were comprised of 52 weeks.

[2]Includes the results of the Au Bon Pain Division (ABP) until it was sold on May 16, 1999.

[3]In 1999 the company recorded a $5.5 million impairment charge to reflect the May 1999 sale of ABP. In 2000 the company received a payment of $0.9 million as consideration for amending the ABP sale agreement to permit a subsequent sale. This nonrecurring gain was offset by a $0.9 nonrecurring charge related to the sale and a $0.5 million charge for asset impairment relating to closure of four Panera Bread bakery-cafes.

[4]Loss from extinguishment of debt was reclassified from an extraordinary item in accordance with the provisions of SFAS No. 145, "Rescission of FASB Statements No. 4, 44, and 64, Amendment of FASB Statement No. 13, and Technical Corrections."

Exhibit 6   Panera Bread Company, Balance Sheet

Consolidated Balance Sheets
(in thousands, except share and per share information)

	December 27, 2003	December 28, 2002
Assets		
Current Assets:		
Cash and cash equivalents	$ 42,402	$ 29,924
Investments in government securities	5,019	4,102
Trade accounts receivable, less allowance		
of $53 in 2003 and $33 in 2002	9,646	7,462
Other accounts receivable	2,748	2,097
Inventories	8,066	5,191
Prepaid expenses	1,294	1,826
Deferred income taxes	1,696	8,488
Other	—	172
Total current assets	70,871	59,262
Property and equipment, net	132,651	99,313
Other assets:		
Investments in government securities	4,000	5,047
Goodwill	32,743	18,970
Deposits and other	5,678	5,554
Deferred income taxes	—	294
Total other assets	42,421	29,865
Total assets	$245,943	$188,440
Liabilities and Stockholders' Equity		
Current liabilities:		
Accounts payable	$ 8,072	$ 5,987
Accrued expenses	35,552	24,935
Current portion of deferred revenue	1,168	1,403
Total current liabilities	44,792	32,325
Deferred income taxes	328	—
Other long-term liabilities	1,115	262
Total liabilities	46,235	32,587
Minority interest	3,771	2,197
Commitments and contingencies		
Stockholders' equity:		
Common stock, $.0001 par value:		
Class A, 75,000,000 shares authorized; 28,296,581		
issued and 28,187,581 outstanding in 2003; and		
27,446,448 issued and 27,337,448 outstanding in 2002	3	3
Class B, 10,000,000 shares authorized; 1,847,221		
issued and outstanding in 2003 and 1,977,363 in 2002	—	—
Treasury stock, carried at cost	(900)	(900)
Additional paid-in capital	121,992	110,120
Retained earnings	74,842	44,433
Total stockholders' equity	195,937	153,656
Total liabilities and stockholders' equity	$245,943	$188,440

Exhibit 7   Panera Bread Company: Key Statistics for the 12-Month Period Ended April 30, 2004

	$ in millions except per share data
Profitability	
Profit margin (ttm):	8.41%
Operating margin (ttm):	14.02%
Management Effectiveness	
Return on assets (ttm):	14.78%
Return on equity (ttm):	18.12%
Income Statement	
Revenue (ttm):	387.15
Revenue per share (ttm):	12.692
Revenue growth (lfy):	28.10%
Gross profit (ttm):	99.06
EBITDA (ttm):	69.39
Net income* (ttm):	32.57
Diluted earnings per share (ttm):	1.07
Earnings growth (lfy):	39.70%
Balance Sheet	
Total cash (mrq):	47.42
Total cash per share (mrq):	1.57
Total debt (mrq):	0
Total debt/equity (mrq):	0
Current ratio (mrq):	1.582
Book value per share (mrq):	6.524
Cash Flow Statement	
From operations (ttm):	68.53
Free cash flow (ttm):	27.34

ttm = trailing 12 months

mrq = most recent quarter

lfy = last fiscal year

*Net income available to common shareholders

Source: Yahoo Finance, 2003–2004, http://biz.yahoo.com.

To date, Panera Bread's performance has been above industry averages. How can the company continue to achieve high growth rates in the future with the low-carb diet gathering momentum, new restaurants opening in the fast-casual segment, changes in the economic environment, and changes in the demographic market?

Endnotes

1. Zganjar, L. 2003. "Quick-casual" restaurants gain healthy ground. *Birmingham Business Journal*, April 21.
2. Hoover's Online, 2003–2004. www-2.hoovers.com.
3. Technomic Annual Report shows solid performance among the top 100 chain restaurant companies, 2002, www.technomic.com/news, May 22.
4. Zganjar, "Quick-casual" restaurants; Rothstein, Kim. 2003. Fast casual sends a strategic signal. *Strategic Initiative* 18(3); www.halegroup.com.
5. Franchise Help Online 2003, online newsletter; Hamaker, S. S., & Panitz, B. 2002. In vogue: What's hot in the restaurant industry. *Restaurants USA,* May; www.restaurant.org/rusa/magArticle.
6. Hamaker & Panitz, 2002, In vogue.
7. www.cyberflexing.com, 2004; Mexican restaurants capitalize on the low-carb craze. 2004. Maiden Name Press, www.restmex.com.
8. Hamaker & Panitz, 2002, In vogue.
9. Fast casual, 2004, Trendscape; 222.trendsetters.com/food-trend/8001,1,fast-casual.html.
10. Hume, Scott. 2004. Reinventing the wheels: Impact of fast casual. *Restaurants and Institutions,* April 1; www.keepmedia.com/jsp/article.
11. Rothstein, 2003. Fast casual; Nelson, R. 2004. Is the low-carb craze affecting bakeries, restaurants? *Minneapolis Star Tribune,* February 12; www.startribune.com/stories/438/4362434.html; Mexican restaurants capitalize on the low-carb craze, 2004.
12. Panera Bread Company. 2003 Annual report, www.panerabread.com.
13. Zganjar, 2003. "Quick-casual" restaurants.
14. Panera Bread Company, 2003. Annual report.
15. Zganjar, 2003. "Quick-casual" restaurants.
16. Suhr, J. 2003. Panera food not fast; its growth is. *Denver Post,* April 6: 16.
17. Panera Bread Company, 2003. Annual report.
18. Panera Bread Company, 2003. www.panerabread.com.
19. Suhr, 2003. Panera food not fast.
20. Yahoo Finance, 2003–2004. http://biz.yahoo.com; Panera Bread Company, 2003. Annual report.

Case 15   Wal-Mart's Strategy for the 21st Century: Sustaining Dominance*

By the turn of the century, Wal-Mart had been named Retailer of the Century by *Discount Store News,* made *Fortune* magazine's lists of the Most Admired Companies in America and the 100 Best Companies to Work For, and was ranked on the *Financial Times'* list of the Most Respected Companies in the World. In 2002 Wal-Mart became number one on the Fortune 500 list and was presented with the Ron Brown Award for Corporate Leadership, a presidential award that recognizes companies for outstanding achievement in employee and community relations.

By the end of 2003, Wal-Mart was the world's largest corporation with a market valuation of more than $400 billion, 1.4 million employees, and 4,700 store locations in the United States and abroad (see Appendixes 1A, 1B, and 2A on pages 683–685). Operating the world's biggest private satellite communications system, the firm tracked sales, replenished inventory, processed payments, and regulated individual store temperatures in real-time. Wal-Mart's Retail Link-System was the largest civilian database in the world, slightly smaller than that of the Pentagon, and three times the size of the Internal Revenue Service's database.

The company's combined annual growth rate during 1999–2003 was 15 percent in revenue and 14 percent in earnings before interest and taxes (EBIT). Similar growth rates over the next decade, if sustained, would result in a $1 trillion business generating well over $50 billion EBIT with a workforce in excess of 4 million people (see Appendix 2B). Virtually everybody—industry experts, market analysts, consumers, special interest groups, competitors, and suppliers—questioned not only the sustainability, but also the desirability, of such current or projected growth rates and consequent dominance. Global 24-hour visibility and exposure were two things that Sam Walton had strived to avoid. His legacy could no longer hope to escape these.

Wal-Mart's leadership was primarily concerned with sustainability. How do you sustain a projected $40 billion growth in revenue and $20 billion growth in EBIT per year? Aware that the past did not always predict the future reliably, top management must have wondered if the firm's formula for success and its current resource allocation strategy would be sufficient to ensure such astronomical growth. How many more Super Centers could be built in the Americas? Could Wal-Mart build a distinctive competency in international operations to fuel growth when neither it nor any other major retailer had yet succeeded in doing so? Could it transport its distinctive competency

in logistics to Europe and China along with its corporate culture? With its increased global presence, the firm was being attacked from all sides. Human resource practices, supplier relationships, and purchasing practices along with community relations were increasingly being targeted. A small group of old-timers in Bentonville, Arkansas (the company's headquarters), reminisced over simpler times when Sam would have just advised them to "Manage one store at a time, respect the individual, and create value with our customers."

Company History—Sam Walton's Era, 1962–1992[1]

With previous retailing experience and expertise, Sam Walton and his brother Bud Walton opened their first Wal-Mart Discount City store in 1962 (the same year that Kmart and Target were founded) in Rogers, Arkansas. They opened 15 department-sized stores in small rural towns throughout the Midwest by the end of the 1960s (see Appendix 3, page 686).

While Wal-Mart's huge stores and variety of branded merchandising resembled Kmart and other competitors, Sam's "every day low price" (EDLP) and limited promotional budgets proved unique in the industry. A hub-and-spoke distribution system with wholly owned warehousing and transportation together propelled Wal-Mart to *Forbes*'s number one ranking among U.S. discounters in 1977 (the ranking was based on return on equity, return on capital, sales growth, and earnings growth).

Sam Walton's Four Basic Beliefs and Three Pricing Philosophies[2]   At the heart of Sam Walton's philosophy and Wal-Mart's corporate culture were four basic beliefs: excellence in the workplace, respect for the individual, customer service, and always having the lowest prices. The company had stayed true to these principles since 1962. Sam envisioned customers who trusted Wal-Mart's pricing philosophy and the ability to find the lowest prices with the best possible customer service. Years ago, Sam Walton challenged associates to practice what he called "aggressive hospitality." He said "Let's be the most friendly—offer a smile of welcome and beyond what our customers expect. Why not? You can do it and do it better than any other retailing company in the world . . . exceed your customers' expectations and they'll come back over and over again."

Perhaps the most unique belief Walton had was that each store should reflect the values of its customers and support the vision they hold for their community. As a result, Wal-Mart's community outreach programs were guided by local associates who grew up in the area and understood its needs.

*This case was prepared by Professor Michael D. Oliff with the support of research assistant Isil Kosdere as the basis for class discussion. It was developed within the scope of Enterprise 2020, a development program conducted with global enterprises. The School of Management, University of Texas, Dallas, © 2004.

Sam's initial pricing policies permeated the Wal-Mart culture. His every day low price (EDLP) strategy flew in the face of another competitor's "blue-light specials." Not considered as a "sale," an ongoing process at Wal-Mart would ensure EDLP. Another strategy, the "special buy," resulted from the continuous pressure on costs and the global search for merchandise of exceptional value.

Growth and Increased Visibility   Sam's Clubs, established in 1983, marked the entrance into the cash-and-carry discount membership market. It also led to expansion into cities and population centers. Within eight years, 150 clubs would be opened in the United States. Format innovations continued as Sam experimented with France's hypermarket concept—stadium-sized stores with groceries, general merchandise, and a host of satellite services. These ultimately gave way to Wal-Mart Super Centers (a 150,000-square-foot format with foods, more items, and more accessible merchandise) with hundreds built in the 1990s.

Wal-Mart enjoyed a 12-year stretch of 35 percent annual profit growth through 1987. Its internal reengineering of the supply chain did not come without external consequences. The firm's buying and distribution practices and general competitive impact on small, independent businesses repeatedly came under fire. Vendor-direct purchasing led to an "uprising" of more than 100,000 independent sales representatives in 1987. Wal-Mart was accused of "excluding them from the selling process." In towns where it had operated for eight or more years, small businesses—drugstores, hardware, clothing, sporting goods—found it virtually impossible to compete with the firm's economies of scale.

In a public relations effort motivated by good business sense, Wal-Mart sent an open letter to U.S. manufacturers in March 1985, inviting them to take part in a "Buy American" program. The company offered to work with them in producing products that could compete against imports. "Our American suppliers must commit to improving their facilities and machinery, remain financially conservative, and work to fill our requirements and, most importantly, strive to improve employee productivity," Walton told American Business in April 1988.

During the same period, Wal-Mart developed a record for community service that began with awarding $1,000 scholarships to high school students in each community it served. At the same time, the company's refusal to stock dozens of widely circulated adult and teen magazines had some critics claiming that Wal-Mart was willfully narrowing the choices of the buying public and in essence bowing to pressure from conservative special interest groups.

Purchases of upstream businesses—Western Merchandise and the McLane Company—increased economies of scale. The merger of the Wholesale Club (adding 28 stores to the Sam's Clubs) and the introduction of Sam's American Choice, the company's own brand of products, signaled the firm's aggressive posture with regard to both current competitors and suppliers.

In 1991 Wal-Mart expanded outside the United States for the first time when it entered into a joint venture with Mexico's largest retailer, Cifra. The venture developed a price club called Club Aurrera, a store that required an annual membership fee of $25. Shoppers could choose from 3,500 products ranging from frozen vegetables to fur coats.

Founder Sam Walton died of bone cancer on April 5, 1992. At the time of his death, he was the second richest man in the world, after the sultan of Brunei, having built a personal fortune in 30 years based solely on creating value with customers. David Glass, CEO, handpicked as Sam's successor, had led a smooth management transition since 1988 and now began to focus on the decade of challenges ahead.

Wal-Mart after Sam

Glass and his management team accelerated growth immediately. From 1992 to 1993, Wal-Mart opened 161 stores, and closed only one. Another 48 Sam's Clubs and 51 Bud's Warehouse Outlets were also opened with expansions or relocations at 170 existing Wal-Mart stores and 40 Sam's Clubs (the company's 2,138 stores included 34 Wal-Mart Super Centers and 256 Sam's Clubs with a net addition of 34.5 million square feet of retail space).

In January 1993 Wal-Mart's reputation was assaulted when NBC-TV's *Dateline* news reported on child laborers in Bangladesh producing merchandise for Wal-Mart stores. The program showed children working for pennies per hour in a country that lacked child labor laws. The program further alleged that items made outside the United States were being sold under "Made in USA" labels as part of the company's "Buy American" campaign started in 1985. Glass appeared on the program saying that he did not know of any child exploitation by the company, but he apologized for some of the incorrect signage.

In April 1993 Wal-Mart expanded further upstream and introduced its private-label "Great Value," which included a line of 350 packaged food items. In the same year Wal-Mart purchased 91 Pace Membership Warehouse clubs from Kmart and converted the new units into Sam's Clubs. Concurrently, the formation of PriceCostco Inc., later renamed Costco Cos., signaled the emergence of Sam's Clubs' only viable rival—a competitor that would challenge the firm's dominance in the cash-and-carry market over the next decade.

Slowdown in the Mid-1990s   Wal-Mart's double-digit comparable store sales rates began falling in 1994 and varied between 4 and 7 percent, which was closer to the retail industry average. The Wal-Mart discount store chain, which reached a peak of 1,995 units in 1996, was reduced to 1,921 units by 1998. Instead, the company staked its domestic future on the Wal-Mart Super Center chain, expanded from 34 units in 1993 to 441 units in 1998. Most of the new Super Centers—377 in total—were converted Wal-Mart discount stores, as the company sought the additional per store revenue that could be gleaned from selling groceries. Meanwhile, the Sam's Club chain was struggling and not as profitable as the company overall. As it attempted to turn this business around, Wal-Mart curtailed its expansion in the United States; only 17 more Sam's Clubs were opened between 1995 and 1998.

International Expansion Continues[3]   Faced with lagging domestic sales, an aggressive international expansion ensued. Following its 1991 move into Mexico, Wal-Mart entered into the other North American Free Trade Agreement (NAFTA) market, Canada, three years later, when it purchased 122 Woolco stores from Woolworth Corporation. Over the next six years, Wal-Mart became the largest retailer in both Mexico and Canada and made additional entries into Puerto Rico, Argentina, and Brazil. The firm ventured into Japan and Korea in the late 1990s.

Wal-Mart entered China in August 1996 with the opening of its first Super Center and Sam's Club in Shenzhen, near Hong Kong. As a harbinger of China's economic reform and the fastest-growing coastal city in China, Shenzhen proved to be the best location for Wal-Mart's investment. Four years later Wal-Mart had 28 stores and employed more than 15,000 associates in Shenzhen. Wal-Mart subsequently opened 26 additional joint venture stores including 21 Super Centers and 5 Sam's Club units in China's coastal cities.

ASDA, Britain's best-value food and clothing superstore, became part of the Wal-Mart family in July 1999. The company had 247 stores and 21 depots across the United Kingdom employing 125,000 associates. The Wal-Mart name appeared on a U.K. store for the first time in 2000, when the first ASDA–Wal-Mart Super Center opened in Bristol. ASDA–Wal-Mart Super Centers brought a unique shopping experience to British customers, offering the best products of both organizations. By 2003 the company operated 14 ASDA–Wal-Mart Super Centers throughout the U.K.

International sales accounted for approximately 16.7 percent of total company sales in fiscal 2003, the same percentage as in 2001. During 2003 Wal-Mart International opened 120 units in existing markets. The announced units included two restaurant formats, specialty apparel retail stores, and supermarkets in Mexico. Overall, however, the international division's profitability lagged well behind that of domestic operations.

Germany and Wal-Mart's First International "War"[4]   By the year 2000, Germany accounted for 15 percent of Europe's $2 trillion a year retail market. Yet it suffered from a shrinking percentage of consumer spending. In conditions of near oligopoly, the top five German retailers alone accounted for over 60 percent of market share (see Appendixes 4A, 4B, 4C, and 4D for data on the European and, specifically, German retail markets). With average profits of 0.8 percent of sales, this was the least profitable retail market in the industrial world. Such lackluster profitability could be attributed in part due to the family ownership of a majority of German retailers; zoning regulations that imposed severe limits on the construction of large-scale stores; the euro conversion on January 1, 2002, and subsequent confusion among consumers; and the apparent preponderance of price/value versus service/quality expectations held by much of the population.

The acquisition of the 21-unit Wertkauf hypermarket chain in Germany in December 1997 marked not only Wal-Mart's entry into Europe but also into the most competitive retail battleground in the world. The German chain had annual sales of $1.4 billion and was the eighth largest hypermarket operator in the country. The takeover of Spar and its 74 domestic locations (revenues: $1.1 billion) marked the second wave of Wal-Mart's attack. By many accounts, Wal-Mart Germany was not a success from its inception until the beginning of 2004. Pundits argued that the firm chose wisely with the Wertkauf acquisition but poorly with Spar. The latter, considered by Germans to be the weakest player in the market, posed significant brand and quality challenges from the beginning.[5] Knorr and Arndt claimed Wal-Mart Germany's operations had also suffered from:[6]

- A "hubris and clash of cultures" approach by management to labor relations.
- A failure to deliver on its legendary "we sell for less—always," "every day low prices," and "excellent service" value proposition.
- Bad publicity from its repeated infringement of some important German laws and regulations.

Regardless of the reasons, Wal-Mart Germany had clearly not met top management's profit expectations as 2004 began and it continued to pose both significant challenges and opportunities.

The Global Retail Industry   Retailing, the second-largest industry in the United States both in the number of establishments and number of employees, was also one of the largest worldwide. In 2003 the retail industry employed over 23 million Americans and generated more than $3 trillion in sales annually. Single-store businesses accounted for over 95 percent of all U.S. retailers, but generated less than 50 percent of all retail store sales. Wal-Mart was by far the largest retailing entity not only in the United States but in the world, equaling the combined sales of the next four largest global players (see Exhibit 1).

An unstable business environment, weak economic growth, and nervous consumers contributed to minimal growth among the world's 100 largest retailers. The average

Exhibit 1   Economic Concentration of the Top 10 Retail Companies in the World, 2002

Company	Home Country	Sales (US$ millions)
Wal-Mart Stores, Inc.	U.S.	$229,617.0
Carrefour Group	France	64,762.3
Home Depot, Inc.	U.S.	58,247.0
Kroger Co.	U.S.	51,760.0
Metro AG	Germany	48,124.4
Royal Ahold	Netherlands	47,114.3
Target Corporation	U.S.	42,722.0
Tesco PLC	U.K.	39,517.2
Costco Companies	U.S.	37,993.1
ITM Enterprises	France	36,183.7

growth rate for the top 100 retailers from 2001 to 2002 dropped to less than 4 percent, with both the "largest" and "smallest" operators struggling to replicate prior-year growth.[7] While Wal-Mart had held the top spot since 1990, there was significant movement among other leading players—both up and down the list—as tough competitive, political, and economic factors took their toll. Further, unlike in prior years, retailers in the U.K., not the United States, were the strongest performers overall.[8] Metro, Carrefour, and Royal Ahold were all focused on new store sales and continued expansion internationally while grappling with growth in existing markets.

As of January 2004, the retail industry was still fragmented globally with no single player yet able to prove it could dominate across several continents. Industry experts agreed retailers that could successfully develop China, Southeast Asia, and the former Soviet Republics (in that order) would reap long-term benefits for decades to come.

It was also clear that traditional internationalization strategies that relied on "exports" (of products, processes, or services) across borders had not fared well in an environment characterized by small, immobile, and uninformed consumers. To succeed internationally, Wal-Mart would have to pick its way carefully. What vehicles—joint ventures, strategic alliances, franchising, shareholdings in local retailers, mergers, or acquisitions—and capabilities would it invest in?

The North American Retail Industry

Target Corporation, the number two discounter in the United States, had carved out a niche by offering more upscale, fashionable merchandise than rivals Wal-Mart and struggling Kmart. Target had distinguished itself by employing a strategy that relied on exclusive private-label offerings from big-name designers. The nation's number two discounter was number one when it came to corporate giving. Target topped the *Forbes* list of America's Most Philanthropic Companies in 2001, donating 2.5 percent of its 2000 income (nearly $86 million). By comparison, Wal-Mart gave away $116.5 million in 2001, less than 1 percent of its income in 2000.

In 2003 Kroger was the number one pure grocery chain in the United States. The grocery chain planned to spend $120 million by the end of 2004 to open as many as nine new stores and remodel older ones in Tennessee, where Wal-Mart was introducing its Neighborhood Market stores. Also in response to intense competition from Wal-Mart Super Centers, which captured 13.0 percent of the U.S. grocery market in 2002 compared to Kroger's 7.2 percent share, Kroger had been cutting prices to hang onto customers. Wal-Mart operated Super Centers in more than half of Kroger's markets. Lured by the growing popularity of dollar stores, Kroger was experimenting with the concept in two of its Houston supermarkets.

During the same period, Sears was developing a freestanding off-mall format—Sears Grand—to compete directly with the big discounter chains by selling consumables, health and beauty aids, housewares, and toys, among other offerings. The first store (twice the size of an average Sears store) opened in Utah in September 2003. The second Sears Grand shop was set to open in Chicago in the spring of 2004, followed by a third in Las Vegas in the fall. (See Exhibit 2 for a financial comparison of these three North American competitors.)

Exhibit 2   The North American Competitors (In $ millions)

		2002	2001	2000
Target	Revenues	$43,917	$39,826	$36,903
	Net income	1,654	1,410	1,264
Sears	Revenues	41,366	40,990	40,848
	Net income	1,376	735	1,343
Kroger	Revenues	51,760	50,098	49,000
	Net income	1,205	1,043	877

The Wal-Mart Culture and Distinctive Competencies

As Wal-Mart continued to grow into new areas and develop new formats, much of its success was attributed to its corporate culture and distinctive competencies (see Appendix 5). Walton wanted all his managers and workers to have a hands-on approach to their jobs and to be totally committed to Wal-Mart's main goal, which he defined as total customer satisfaction. To motivate his employees, Walton created a strategic control system that gave employees at all levels continuous feedback about their performance and the company's.[9]

The culture pushed decision-making authority down to store managers, department managers, and individual employees. Wal-Mart was renowned for treating its employees well, but at the same time, demanding commitment and excellent performance. This culture was backed up with profit-sharing and stock ownership plans for all employees, including associates, to make every employee "think and behave like an owner of the company." No wonder Wal-Mart had higher employee productivity, less shrinkage (employee theft), and lower costs than industry rivals.

Wal-Mart's Distinctive Competencies   As the number of stores grew, Wal-Mart pioneered the development of a hub-and-spoke distribution system, where central distribution warehouses were strategically located to serve clusters of stores. This system allowed Wal-Mart to rapidly replenish stock in its stores and to keep the amount of unproductive space to a minimum.

The results included higher sales per square foot and more rapid inventory turnover. This combination helped to increase store sales and drive down inventory and logistics costs (see Exhibit 3). The firm was also one of the first to utilize computer-based information systems to track in-store sales and transmit this information to suppliers. This information was used to determine pricing and stocking strategies that optimized inventory management. The combination of state-of-the art information systems and the hub-and-spoke distribution system allowed Wal-Mart to build the leanest supply chain in the industry.[10]

The firm's brand and market management, supply chain management, and customer value focus distinguished it in the industry. These corporate abilities or distinctive competencies, coupled with locational assets and unique cultural attributes, served it well throughout the 1990s. Insiders wondered whether these historical strengths alone were sufficient to build a trillion-dollar enterprise over the next decade—with $200 to $500 billion in sales outside the Americas. Furthermore, how could Wal-Mart appease external stakeholders as its influence magnified? For example, concerns with Wal-Mart's purchasing practices resurfaced in December 2003.[11]

> There is no question that doing business with Wal-Mart can give a supplier a fast, heady jolt of sales and market share. But that fix can come with long-term consequences for the health of a brand and a business.
>
> Wal-Mart is legendary for forcing its suppliers to redesign everything from their packaging to their computer systems. It is also legendary for quite straightforwardly telling them what it will pay for their goods.
>
> Many companies and their executives frankly admit that supplying Wal-Mart is like getting into the company version of basic training with an implacable army drill sergeant. The process may be unpleasant. But there can be some positive results.

Future Questions

CNN described the coming extinction of American malls as the "Death of an American Icon." In 2000 PricewaterhouseCoopers and the Center for the New Urbanism first identified "grey fields," or dying malls, as those with annual sales of less than $150 per square foot—less than a third of sales at successful malls. Their study found that 7 percent of existing regional malls qualified as grey fields, and another 12 percent were headed in that direction. Increasingly, these grey fields were being redeveloped into lifestyle centers or "main street centers," which mimicked traditional villages of the past—with lots of open-air space, attractive landscaping, outdoor sound systems, park

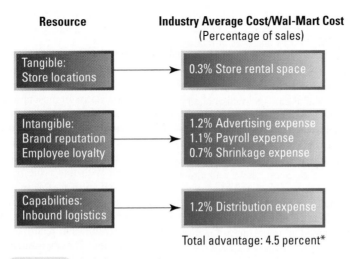

Resource	Industry Average Cost/Wal-Mart Cost (Percentage of sales)
Tangible: Store locations	0.3% Store rental space
Intangible: Brand reputation Employee loyalty	1.2% Advertising expense 1.1% Payroll expense 0.7% Shrinkage expense
Capabilities: Inbound logistics	1.2% Distribution expense

Total advantage: 4.5 percent*

Exhibit 3   Wal-Mart's Competitive Advantage

*Wal-Mart's cost advantage as a percentage of sales. Each percentage point advantage is worth $500 million in net income to Wal-Mart.

Source: Pankaj Ghemawat, "Wal-Mart Stores' Discount Operations," Harvard Business School case 9-387-018.

benches, artistic fountains, and attractive building facades. Regardless of the fate of American malls, Wal-Mart and its rivals wondered:

- What would the retail industry look like by the year 2010?
- Would the economy return to the growth rates of the mid-'90s?
- Would consumers worry about inflation or deflation?
- Would aging baby boomers still be driving consumer spending or would they be tapped out by their overextended credit card debt and devastated retirement accounts?
- By 2010 would Wal-Mart take a larger share in existing product categories, or leap into new categories like banking and auto retailing?

The five dominant trends that could alter the face of the retailing industry in the remaining years of the decade were:[12]

1. Removal of the "one size fits all" premise which would be replaced by a system in which individual retailers employed a more robust multiformat or portfolio strategy.
2. A very unique concept of "Wal-Mart always smiling" would be even more successful by 2010, with the company's continued focus on the customer shopping experience, customer care, customer intimacy, and customer value.
3. As consumers searched for greater shopping efficiency, their preferences would shift away from

traditional supermarkets and discount department stores toward Super Centers. Some supermarkets would expand their one-stop shopping appeal while others would tap into emerging trends such as natural/organic, ethnic, gourmet, and health food products.

4. The days of mass-merchandised specialty chains with multitudes of outlets delivering the same narrow and deep assortment of goods to the market, regardless of location, would be over. Specialty retailers would manage a portfolio of different concepts, each operating a small chain of stores in order to address multiple market opportunities.
5. Customers would embrace technologies that gave them more control over the shopping process. These would include Web-enabled store kiosks which give shoppers access to a retailer's full inventory; wireless technology that provides shoppers with product information on handheld devices; smart carts that draw on shoppers' buying history to alert them to products and promotions; radio frequency identification (RFID)–enabled checkout where all items in a cart are scanned at once; and contactless payment solutions that use RFID-enabled smart cards or transponders.

Other Retail Industry Trends

By 2003 the consolidation wave that started in the United States had caught on in Europe too. With the largest retail space per capita, the U.S. market was a prime candidate for consolidation owing to the proliferation of retailers in the previous two decades that led to the paring down of margins and intense undercutting of prices. The inevitable shakeout was precipitated by Wal-Mart's takeover of many small retailers.

Wal-Mart's acquisition of the U.K. food retailer ASDA in 2002 marked the international entry of American retailers into the United Kingdom. Until then, U.S. retailers had concentrated on domestic expansion only. However, globalization had hit Europe much earlier and the French firm Carrefour had long ago struck roots in South America and Mexico. Similarly, Royal Ahold struck firm roots in the U.S. retail arena with its Stop & Shop chain and the takeover of the ailing Peapod.com.

Many retailers had started vending fuel adjacent to their outlets. This not only came as a boon to the time-starved customer but also provided an opportunity for retailers to cross-subsidize merchandise sales with fuel sales. A similar phenomenon happened at gasoline stations where convenience stores catered to the basic needs of customers. "Buying the product from the cheapest and most efficient source" was the retailer credo.

To reduce time in queues, retailers had given self-checkout authorization to customers. Initially, this was done only for frequent shoppers or loyalty cardholders. The reduction of cycle time (between ordering and physical arrival of the merchandise) was a critical cost driver in the retailing industry. Retailers looked for ways to cut inventories. The most common facilitator was an accurate demand and sales forecast as well as rapid replenishment.

Technology Trends

Enterprise integration, or linking all the different systems used by a retailer to provide seamless information flow and better resource management, was an important trend emerging in the retail industry.

Smart cards that contained detailed customer information provided a wealth of information to the retailer about customers' buying habits and patterns. Also, they helped in tailoring the offering to specific needs. They integrated many operations and one card could be used across locations and functions. To avoid the risk of obsolescence, many retail software vendors provided Web-based packages updated in real-time.

Radio frequency data communication had become a standard in the retail fulfillment industry. Handheld radio frequency devices provided an excellent tool to perform inventory tracking and order-picking activities.

Large retailers had relied on intranets and extranets for information sharing within the organization and with external entities, respectively. Extranets had long been a preferred way of carrying out electronic data interchange with suppliers. However, with the Internet becoming omnipresent, their efficacy would decrease, and virtual private networks that offered a secure pipeline for information flow using the Internet would become increasingly employed for the exchange of information.

Consumer Trends[13]

Single-serve, "easy-pour," and portable packaging had all been on the scene for a while. However, these were expected to become the norm for most products in addition to required enhancements in temperature-control, spill-proof, lifestyle, and alternative-usage packaging.

Obesity and the problems associated with it were expected to increase. Manufacturers and retailers would have to deal with this issue by offering healthier foods and increased information relating to health and nutrition. Products oriented toward wellness and an improved life would continue to emerge in numerous categories beyond the traditional health and beauty aid (HBA) and drug categories. These products made numerous claims and required significant communication with the consumer to ensure their success. This trend began with the aging population, but was fueled by manufacturers seeking any avenue available to develop and market new products ahead of the continued growth of store-controlled brands.

Shoppers continued to decrease the amount of time they spent on each shopping trip. Grocery shopping continued to be viewed as "need to do" instead of "want to do." As such, consumers desired to travel fewer aisles on any one shopping trip and ultimately spend less time in the store. The implications of these views would be continued modification of store layouts and limits on the absolute size of new stores built.

In future, loyalty card programs and, more importantly, the processing of related data would be performed by third-party companies. These dedicated research firms focused on linking databases across industries. The result would be far more valuable marketing information, both within and outside the grocery industry. Due to the inability of most retailers to provide truly individualized services to loyalty cardholders, their future use would be questioned, if not eliminated, by some retailers and refocused by others. This trend would be exacerbated by consumer privacy concerns or plain indifference.

Wal-Mart's Future

In January 2004 Wal-Mart was at the top of the business world. By anyone's reckoning, it had dominated an industry for two decades and grown into one of the most influential corporate enterprises in history. To maintain its phenomenal growth in the future, it needed to sustain growth in the Americas and address development and profitability issues internationally.

With market saturation looming in the United States and the absence of any truly international retailer, how would Sam's successors allocate future resources to ensure Wal-Mart's global dominance across disparate markets?

Appendix 1A *Fortune* Rankings of the World's Largest Companies

Rank	Fortune 1992	Value	Rank	Fortune 2003	Value
1	ExxonMobil	$75,800.00	1	Wal-Mart Stores	$246,525.00
2	General Electric	73,900.00	2	General Motors	186,763.00
3	Wal-Mart Stores	73,500.00	3	ExxonMobil	182,466.00
4	Royal Dutch Shell	71,800.00	4	Ford Motor	163,630.00
5	Nippon Telephone & Telegraph	71,400.00	5	General Electric	131,698.00
6	Philip Morris	69,300.00	6	Citigroup	100,789.00
7	AT&T	68,000.00	7	ChevronTexaco	92,043.00
8	Coca-Cola	55,700.00	8	Intl. Business Machines	83,132.00
9	Mitsubishi Bank	53,500.00	9	American Intl. Group	67,722.80
10	Merck	50,300.00	10	Verizon Communications	67,625.00
11	IND Bank of Japan	46,500.00	11	Altria Group	62,182.00
12	Sumitomo Bank	45,600.00	12	Conoco Phillips	58,394.00
13	Toyota Motor	44,100.00	13	Home Depot	58,247.00
14	Fuji Bank	41,800.00	14	Hewlett-Packard	56,588.00
15	Dai-Ichi Kangyo Bank	41,800.00	15	Boeing	54,069.00
16	Sanwa Bank	37,900.00	16	Fannie Mae	52,901.10
17	British Telecom	37,800.00	17	Merck	51,790.30
18	Procter & Gamble	36,400.00	18	Kroger	51,759.50
19	Glaxo Holdings	36,100.00	19	Cardinal Health	51,135.70
20	Bristol-Myers Squibb	35,100.00	20	McKesson	50,006.00

Amounts in $ millions.

Appendix 1B   Wal-Mart Stores: Five-Year Financial Summary

	(Dollar amounts in millions except per share data) Fiscal Years Ending January 31				
	2004	2003	2002	2001	2000
Net sales	$256,329	$229,616	$204,011	$180,787	$156,249
Net sales increase	12%	13%	13%	16%	20%
Domestic comparative store sales increase*	4%	5%	6%	5%	8%
Cost of sales	$198,747	$178,299	$159,097	$140,720	$121,825
Operating, selling, general, and administrative expenses	44,909	39,983	35,147	30,822	26,025
Interest expense, net	832	927	1,183	1,196	840
Effective tax rate	36%	35%	36%	36%	37%
Income from continuing operations	$ 8,861	$ 7,818	$ 6,448	$ 6,087	$ 5,394
Net income	9,054	7,955	6,592	6,235	5,324
Per share of common stock:					
Income from continuing operations, diluted	2.03	1.76	1.44	1.36	1.21
Net income, diluted	2.07	1.79	1.47	1.39	1.19
Dividends	0.36	0.3	0.28	0.24	0.2
Financial Position					
Current assets of continuing operations	$ 34,421	$ 29,543	$ 26,615	$ 25,344	$ 23,478
Inventories	26,612	24,401	22,053	20,987	19,296
Property, plant and equipment, and capital leases, net	58,530	51,374	45,248	40,461	35,533
Total assets of continuing operations	104,912	92,900	81,549	76,231	68,983
Current liabilities of continuing operations	37,418	32,225	26,795	28,366	25,525
Long-term debt	17,102	16,597	15,676	12,489	13,653
Long-term obligations under capital leases	2,997	3,000	3,044	3,152	3,000
Shareholders' equity	43,623	39,461	35,192	31,407	25,878
Financial Ratios					
Current ratio	0.9	0.9	1	0.9	0.9
Return on assets**	9%	9%	8%	9%	10%
Return on shareholders' equity***	21%	21%	19%	21%	23%

Source: Wal-Mart. 2004. Annual Report.

*Comparative store sales are considered to be sales at stores that were open as of February 1 of the prior fiscal year and have not been expanded or relocated since February 1 of the prior fiscal year.

**Income from continuing operations before cumulative effect of accounting change divided by average assets.

***Income from continuing operations divided by average shareholders' equity.

Financial information for all years has been restated to reflect the sale of McLane Company, Inc. ("McLane") that occurred in fiscal 2004. McLane is presented as a discontinued operation.

All years have been restated for the adoption of the expense recognition provisions of Financial Accounting Standards Board Statement No. 123, "Accounting and Disclosure of Stock-Based Compensation." Fiscal 1994 and 1995 were not affected by the adoption.

In fiscal 2003, the company adopted Financial Accounting Standards Board Statement No. 142, "Goodwill and Other Intangible Assets."

In years prior to adoption, the company recorded amortization expense related to goodwill.

684

Appendix 2A   Number of Wal-Mart Stores

Year	2001		2002		2003	
Store Type	**Domestic**	**International**	**Domestic**	**International**	**Domestic**	**International**
Regular discount stores	1,736	612	1,647	648	1,568	942
Super Centers	888	405	1,066	455	1,258	238
Sam's Club	475	53	500	64	525	71
Neighborhood markets	19	0	31	6	49	37
Total	3,118	1,070	3,244	1,173	3,400	1,288

Appendix 2B   Wal-Mart's EBIT and Net Income, 1987–2003

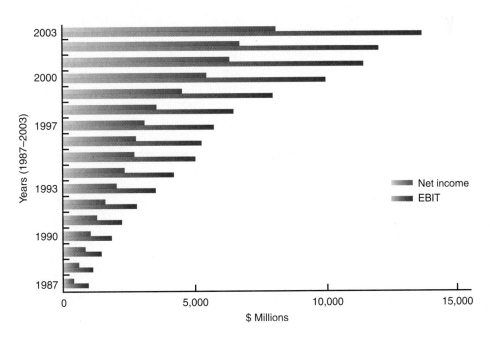

Appendix 3   Wal-Mart Timeline

1962	Sam Walton and his brother opened their first Wal-Mart Discount City in Rogers, Arkansas.
1969	Brothers had opened 18 Wal-Mart stores throughout Arkansas, Missouri, Kansas, and Oklahoma. They still owned 15 Ben Franklin franchises.
1970	Wal-Mart went public.
1972	Company was listed on the New York Stock Exchange for the first time.
1976	The Waltons phased out Ben Franklin Stores.
1977	The company made its first significant acquisition when it bought 16 Mohr-Value stores in Missouri and Illinois.
1977	Based on data from the previous five years, *Forbes* ranked the nation's discount and variety stores. Wal-Mart ranked first in return on equity, return on capital, sales growth, and earnings growth.
1978	Wal-Mart began operating its own pharmacy, auto service center, and jewelry divisions, and acquired Hutchinson Wholesale Shoe Co.
1979	With 276 stores in 11 states, sales rose to $1.25 billion.
1983	The company opened its first three Sam's Wholesale Clubs and began its expansion into markets in larger towns.
1985	"Buy American" program was launched.
1987	Wal-Mart's first Hypermart USA store was opened.
1987	Prices were reduced as much as 40% below full retail level; sales volume averaged $1 million per week.
1987	100,000 independent representatives initiated a public campaign to fight Wal-Mart's effort to remove them from the selling process, claiming that their elimination jeopardized a manufacturer's right to choose how it sells its products.
1988	Concentrated in the South and Midwest, Wal-Mart operated in 24 states.
1990	The first stores opened in California, Nevada, North Dakota, South Dakota, Pennsylvania, and Utah.
1990	Wal-Mart agreed to sell its nine convenience store–gas station outlets to Conoco Inc.
1990	Acquired the McLane Company, Inc., a distributor of grocery and retail products based in Temple, Texas.
1991	A new store brand, Sam's American Choice, was introduced.
1991	The company owned 148 Sam's Clubs.
1992	April 5: Founder Sam Walton died.
1992	The company opened 150 new Wal-Mart stores and 60 Sam's Clubs. Some of these stores represented a change in policy for the company, opening near big cities with large populations.
1992	Wal-Mart entered into a joint venture with Cifra in Mexico.
1993	A television show revealed child laborers in Bangladesh producing merchandise for Wal-Mart for five cents an hour. The program further alleged that foreign-made products were being sold under "Made in USA" labels.
1993	Wal-Mart introduced another private label called Great Value and channeled the proceeds from its American Choice label into the Competitive Edge Scholarship Fund.
1993	Wal-Mart's 1,914 stores included 40 Super Centers in 45 states and Puerto Rico, 208 Sam's Clubs in 42 states, and four Hypermart USAs. Retailers Dayton Hudson, Kmart, and Meijer complained about Wal-Mart's misleading price comparisons.
1994	Purchased 122 Woolco stores in Canada from Woolworth Corporation.
1994	Wal-Mart signed an agreement with the State of Michigan promising various changes in the way it compares prices to those of its competitors.
1994	Announced plans to expand into Argentina and Brazil.
1994	A joint venture was formed to open three to four stores in Hong Kong and to operate discount stores in China.
1995	David Glass received *Chief Executive* magazine's 1995 Chief Executive of the Year Award.

(continued)

(*continued*)

1996   Tested the sale of stock items on the Internet.

1996   Wal-Mart opened its first Super Center and Sam's Club in Shenzhen, China.

1997   Wal-Mart entered Europe for the first time when it acquired the 21-unit Wertkauf hypermarket chain in Germany.

1998   In an effort to accelerate growth, Wal-Mart began testing a new format, the Wal-Mart Neighborhood Market.

1998   Opened 32 Super Center stores, bringing the total number in operation to 542; opened two stores in New Hampshire. Operations spanned 29 states.

1998   Wal-Mart entered Korea through its acquisition and conversion of four Makro stores.

1998   A Wal-Mart expansion under a franchise agreement into a troubled Indonesia appeared to have stalled.

1999   Purchased the 230-store ASDA Group PLC, the third-largest food retailer in the United Kingdom. Named one of the Most Admired Companies in America by *Fortune*.

2000   Glass stepped down as CEO and president, and was succeeded by H. Lee Scott, Jr.

2000   Became the largest retailer in Mexico and acquired full ownership of 194 stores and 205 restaurants from its former partner Cifra SA.

2000   Became union-free in North America and converted the last of its remaining Hypermarket USA stores to a Wal-Mart Super Center.

2002   Wal-Mart purchased at 34% stake in Seiyu, Ltd., a leading Japanese retailer. Seiyu operated over 400 supermarkets in Japan and employed 30,000 associates.

2002   When fiscal year sales reached $220 billion, Wal-Mart became the largest company in the world.

2002   Planned to invest $2 billion in international expansion.

2003   Was announced No. 1 in *Fortune* magazine's annual survey of Most Admired Companies in America.

Appendix 4A   Store Hours in Selected European Union Countries

Country	Mon.–Fri.	Sat.	Sun./Holidays	Hours per Week
United Kingdom	0000–2400	0000–2400	0000–2400	168
Netherlands	0600–2200	0600–2200	Closed	96
Spain	0000–2400	0000–2400	Closed	144
France	0000–2400	0000–2400	Open*	144
Germany	0600–2000	0600–2000	Closed	84

*Only store owners and their family members, but no employees, are permitted to work on Sundays and holidays.

Source: *KPMG/EHI*, 2001: 10.

Appendix 4B Germany's Top 15 Retailers, 2002

Rank	Company	Revenues in Germany (€ billions)
1	Metro AG	€32.0
2	Rewe Group	28.6
3	Edeka/AVA Group	25.2
4	Aldi Group	25.0
5	Schwarz Gruppe	17.2
6	KarstadtQuelle	16.1
7	Tengelmann Group	12.5
8	Lekkerland-Tobaccoland	8.2
9	Spar Group	7.5
10	Schlecker	5.3
11	Globus	3.4
12	Dohle Group	2.9
13	Wal-Mart Germany	2.9
14	Norma	2.4
15	Bartels-Langness	2.1

Source: *KPMG/EHI*, 2001.

Appendix 4C German Retailers: Productivity per Unit of Sales Floor

Rank	Company	Sales in € per Sq. Meter
1	Aldi Group	€7,500
2	Rewe Group	5,850
3	Globus	5,250
4	Schwarz Group	4,900
5	Metro	4,000
6	Edeka Group	3,600
7	Tengelmann Group	3,600
8	Wal-Mart	3,500
9	Spar Group	3,000

Source: *KPMG/EHI*, 2001: 15.

Appendix 4D German Retailers: Overall Customer Satisfaction

Rank	Company	Satisfaction Index (Maximum: 100)
1	Aldi Group	73.45
2	Globus	71.42
3	Kaufland	71.01
4	Lidl	69.09
5	Norma	68.52
6	Marktkauf	66.96
7	Wal-Mart	64.39
8	Metro	63.97
9	Penny	63.32
10	Real	62.50

Source: *KPMG/EHI*, 2001: 15.

Appendix 5 Sam's Rules for Building a Business

Sam's 10 Rules for Building a Business

People often ask, "What is Wal-Mart's secret to success?" In response to this ever-present question, Sam Walton compiled a list of 10 key factors that unlock the mystery in his 1992 book *Made in America*. These factors are known as "Sam's Rules for Building a Business."

Rule 1: Commit to Your Business. Believe in it more than anybody else. I think I overcame every single one of my personal shortcomings by the sheer passion I brought to my work. I don't know if you're born with this kind of passion, or if you can learn it. But I do know you need it. If you love your work, you'll be out there every day trying to do it the best you possibly can, and pretty soon everybody around will catch the passion from you—like a fever.

Rule 2: Share Your Profits with all Your Associates, and Treat Them as Partners. In turn, they will treat you as a partner, and together you will all perform beyond your wildest expectations. Encourage your Associates to hold a stake in the company. Offer discounted stock, and grant them stock for their retirement. It's the single best thing we ever did.

Source: The official Wal-Mart Web site, www.walmart.com.

Rule 3: Motivate Your Partners. Money and ownership alone aren't enough. Constantly, day by day, think of new and more interesting ways to motivate and challenge your partners.

Rule 4: Communicate Everything You Possibly Can to Your Partners. The more they know, the more they'll understand. The more they understand, the more they'll care. Once they care, there's no stopping them.

Rule 5: Appreciate Everything Your Associates Do for the Business. A paycheck and a stock option will buy one kind of loyalty. But all of us like to be told how much somebody appreciates what we do for them. We like to hear it often, and especially when we have done something we're really proud of. Nothing else can quite substitute for a few well-chosen, well-timed, sincere words of praise.

Rule 6: Celebrate Your Successes. Find some humor in your failures. Don't take yourself so seriously. Loosen up, and everybody around you will loosen up. Have fun. Show enthusiasm—always.

Rule 7: Listen to Everyone in Your Company. And figure out ways to get them talking. The folks on the front lines—the ones who actually talk to the customer—are the only ones who really know what's going on out there. You'd better find out what they know. This really is what total quality is all about.

Rule 8: Exceed Your Customers' Expectations.

If you do, they'll come back over and over. Give them what they want—and a little more. Let them know you appreciate them. Make good on all your mistakes, and don't make excuses—apologize.

Rule 9: Control Your Expenses Better than Your Competition.

This is where you can always find the competitive advantage. For 25 years running—long before Wal-Mart was known as the nation's largest retailer—we ranked No. 1 in our industry for the lowest ratio of expenses to sales.

Rule 10: Swim Upstream.

Go the other way. Ignore the conventional wisdom. If everybody else is doing it one way, there's a good chance you can find your niche by going in exactly the opposite direction.

Other Important Rules and Policies

The Sundown Rule: One Sunday morning, Jeff, a pharmacist at a Wal-Mart store in Harrison, Arkansas, received a call from his store. A store associate informed him that one of his pharmacy customers, a diabetic, had accidentally dropped her insulin down her garbage disposal. Knowing that a diabetic without insulin could be in grave danger, Jeff immediately rushed to the store, opened the pharmacy and filled the customer's insulin prescription. This is just one of many ways your local Wal-Mart store might honor what is known by our Associates as the Sundown Rule.

The Ten-Foot Rule: One of Wal-Mart's secrets to customer service is our "10-foot attitude," handed down to us by Wal-Mart Founder, Sam Walton. During his many store visits, he encouraged associates to take a pledge with him: ". . . I want you to promise that whenever you come within 10 feet of a customer, you will look him in the eye, greet him, and ask him if you can help him."

Pricing Policy: Sam's adherence to this pricing philosophy was unshakable, as one of Wal-Mart's first store managers recalls:

> Sam wouldn't let us hedge on a price at all. Say the list price was $1.98, but we had paid only 50 cents. Initially, I would say, "Well, it's originally $1.98, so why don't we sell it for $1.25?" And, he'd say, "No. We paid 50 cents for it. Mark it up 30 percent, and that's it. No matter what you pay for it, if we get a great deal, pass it on to the customer." And of course that's what we did.

Endnotes

1. Wal-Mart Stores, Inc. 1999. *International Directory of Company Histories,* vol. 26 (St. James Press). Reproduced in Business and Company Resource Center, 2003 (Farmington Hills, MI: Gale Group), www.galenet.com/servlet/BCRC.
2. The material in this section is based on information from the official Wal-Mart Web site, www.walmart.com.
3. The material in this section comes largely from the official Wal-Mart Web site, www.walmart.com.
4. Knorr, Andreas, & Arndt, Andreas. 2003. Why did Wal-Mart fail in Germany? *IWIM,* University of Bremen, June 24.
5. *KPMG/EHI.* 2001. 15.
6. Knorr & Arndt, 2003. Why did Wal-Mart fail in Germany?: 18.
7. Retail Forward, comp., The top 100 retailers worldwide 2002.
8. "The world's largest retailers cannot expect a stable business environment going forward," commented Geoff Wissman, vice president with Retail Forward. "Slow economic recovery in the U.S. combined with weak economies in Japan, Latin America, and Western Europe, are forcing many retailers to seek alternative outlets for growth outside their home countries. . . . Retailers will find themselves battling for market share rather than relying on growing markets," Wissman stated. "The recent difficulties faced by some of the world's largest retailers—including Kmart, Royal Ahold, and Sears—reinforce the fact that retailers of any size can experience serious financial strain."
9. Sam Walton's approach to implementing Wal-Mart's strategy, in Walton, Sam. 1992. *Made in America.* New York: Doubleday.
10. The case "Wal-Mart's Mexican Adventure."
11. Fishman, Charles. 2003. The Wal-Mart you don't know (Why low prices have a high cost). *Fast Company,* December.
12. 2003, *Retail Merchandiser,* 43(5): 4.
13. The material in this section is provided in large part by MJH & Associates, July 2003.

Case 16   Edward Marshall Boehm, Inc.*

Edward Marshall Boehm—a farmer, veterinarian, and nature lover living near New York City—was convinced by his wife and friends to translate some of his clay animal sculptures into pieces for possible sale to the gift and art markets. Boehm recognized that porcelain was the best medium for portraying his creations because of its translucent beauty, permanence, and fidelity of color as well as form. But the finest of the porcelains, hard paste porcelain, was largely a secret art about which little technical literature existed. Boehm studied this art relentlessly, absorbing whatever knowledge artbooks, museums, and the few U.S. ceramic factories offered. Then, after months of experimentation in a dingy Trenton, New Jersey, basement, Boehm and some chemist friends developed a porcelain clay equal to the finest in the world.

Next Boehm had to master the complex art of porcelain manufacture. Each piece of porcelain sculpture is a technical as well as artistic challenge. A 52-step process is required to convert a plasticine sculpture into a completed porcelain piece. For example, one major creation took 509 mold sections to make 151 parts, and consumed 8 tons of plaster in the molds. Sculptural detail included 60,000 individually carved feather barbs. Each creation had to be kiln-fired to 2400° where heat could change a graceful detail into a twisted mass. Then it had to be painted, often in successive layers, and perhaps fired repeatedly to anneal delicate colors. No American had excelled in hard paste porcelains. And when Boehm's creations first appeared no one understood the quality of the porcelain or even believed it was hard paste porcelain.

But Boehm began to create in porcelain what he knew and loved best—nature, particularly the more delicate forms of animals, birds, and flowers. In his art Boehm tried "to capture that special moment and setting which conveys the character, charm, and loveliness of a bird or animal in its natural habitat." After selling his early creations for several years during her lunch hours, his talented wife, Helen, left an outstanding opthalmic marketing career to "peddle" Boehm's porcelains full time. Soon Mrs. Boehm's extraordinary merchandising skills, promotional touch, and sense for the art market began to pay off. People liked Boehm's horses and dogs, but bought his birds. And Boehm agreeably complied, striving for ever greater perfection on ever more exotic and natural bird creations.

By 1968 some Boehm porcelains (especially birds) had become recognized as collector's items. An extremely complex piece like "Fondo Marino" might sell for $28,500 at retail, and might command much more upon resale. Edward Marshall Boehm, then 55—though flattered by his products' commercial success—considered his art primarily an expression of his love for nature. He felt the ornithological importance of portraying vanishing species like U.S. prairie chickens with fidelity and traveled to remote areas to bring back live samples of rare tropical birds for study and later rendering into porcelain. A single company, Minton China, was the exclusive distributor of Boehm products to some 175 retail outlets in the United States. Boehm's line included (1) its "Fledgling" series of smaller, somewhat simpler pieces, usually selling for less than $100, (2) its profitable middle series of complex sculptures like the "Snowy Owl" selling from $800 to $5,000, and (3) its special artistic pieces (like "Fondo Marino" or "Ivory Billed Woodpeckers") which might sell initially for over $20,000.

Individual Boehm porcelains were increasingly being recognized as outstanding artistic creations and sought by some sophisticated collectors. Production of such designs might be sold out for years in advance, but it was difficult to anticipate which pieces might achieve this distinction. Many of the company's past policies no longer seemed appropriate. And the Boehms wanted to further position the company for the long run. When asked what they wanted from the company, they would respond, "to make the world aware of Mr. Boehm's artistic talent, to help world wildlife causes by creating appreciation and protection for threatened species, and to build a continuing business that could make them comfortably wealthy, perhaps millionaires." No one goal had great precedence over the others.

---

*Republished with permission from H. Mintzberg and J. B. Quinn, *The Strategy Process,* Prentice Hall, New York, 1996.

Case 17   McDonald's*

On April 19, 2004, James R. Cantalupo, the chairman and CEO of McDonald's, died unexpectedly of a heart attack on his way to a biennial meeting of the firm's executives, franchisees, and suppliers in Orlando, Florida. Cantalupo had come out of retirement only a year before to try to improve upon McDonald's lackluster performance. During his brief tenure, he had started to turn things around, as reflected in strong growth in sales over the last three quarters. Reflecting on Cantalupo's performance, Peter Oakes, an analyst at Piper Jaffrey, stated, "His impact over the 16-month period was as meaningful as any chief executive at McDonald's who preceded him and that includes the big guy, Ray Kroc."[1]

The turnaround at McDonald's could be attributed partly to some new additions that Cantalupo had made to its menu. The chain had received a positive response to its increased emphasis on healthier foods, led by a revamped line of fancier salads. But its bigger success came in the form of the McGriddles breakfast sandwich which was launched nationwide in June 2003. A couple of syrup-drenched pancakes, stamped with the Golden Arches, acted as the top and bottom of the sandwich to hold eggs, cheese, sausage, and bacon in three different combinations. McDonald's has estimated that the new breakfast addition has been bringing in about 1 million new customers every day.

However, Cantalupo's efforts were not limited to changes in the firm's product offerings. He understood that unless he could address more fundamental issues, McDonald's might be at the end of a long run as a growth company. In fact, Cantalupo was attempting to lay the groundwork for the revival of this growth by tackling some of the firm's more pressing problems. He had cut back on McDonald's expansion plans, trying instead to concentrate on improving the firm's relationships with existing franchisees. He had also forced the firm to focus on its core hamburger business and to get rid of the other underperforming subsidiaries.

It was clear to Cantalupo that the problems at McDonald's went way beyond cleaning up restaurants and revamping the menu. The chain has been squeezed by long-term trends that threaten to leave it marginalized. It is facing a rapidly fragmenting market, where changes in the tastes of consumers have made once-exotic foods like sushi and burritos everyday options. Furthermore, competition has been coming from quick meals of all sorts that can be found in supermarkets, convenience stores, and even vending machines.

Amid these changes, McDonald's may be facing its greatest challenge from the "fast-casual" restaurant category. This fast-growing segment includes several newcomers such as Cosi, a sandwich shop, or Quizno's, a gourmet sub sandwich chain, where customers find the food healthier and better tasting. According to Mats Lederhausen, recently appointed to revamp the menu at McDonald's, "We are clearly living through the death of the mass market."[2]

Experiencing a Downward Spiral

Since it was founded more than fifty years ago, McDonald's has been defining the fast food business. It provided millions of Americans their first jobs even as it changed their eating habits. It rose from a single outlet in a nondescript Chicago suburb to become one of the largest chains of outlets spread around the globe. But it had been stumbling over the past decade. (See Exhibit 1 for milestones in the history of McDonald's.)

The decline in McDonald's once-vaunted service and quality can be traced to its expansion in the 1990s, when headquarters stopped grading franchises for cleanliness, speed, and service. By the end of the decade, the chain ran into more problems because of the tighter labor market. McDonald's began to cut back on training as it struggled hard to find new recruits, leading to a dramatic falloff in the skills of its employees. According to a 2002 survey by market researcher Global Growth Group, McDonald's came in third in average service time behind Wendy's and sandwich shop Chick-fil-A Inc.

McDonald's also began to fail consistently with its new product introductions, such as the low-fat McLean Deluxe and Arch Deluxe burgers, both of which were meant to appeal to adults. It did no better with its attempts to diversify beyond burgers, often because of problems with the product development process. Consultant Michael Seid, who manages a franchise consulting firm in West Hartford, pointed out that McDonald's offered a pizza that didn't fit through the drive-through window and salad shakers that were packed so tightly that dressing couldn't flow through them.

In 1998, after McDonald's posted its first-ever decline in annual earnings, CEO Michael R. Quinlan was forced out and replaced by Jack M. Greenberg, a 16-year veteran of the firm. Greenberg did try to cut back on McDonald's expansion as he tried to deal with some of the growing problems. But his efforts to deal with the decline of McDonald's were slowed down by his acquisition of other fast food chains such as Chipotle Mexican Grill and Boston Market Corporation.

On December 5, 2002, after watching McDonald's stock slide 60 percent in three years, the board ousted Greenberg. He had lasted little more than two years. His short tenure had been marked by the introduction of 40 new menu items, none of which caught on big, and the

*This case was prepared by Professor Jamal Shamsie of Michigan State University. This case was developed from published sources as a basis for class discussion rather than to illustrate either effective or ineffective handling of an administrative situation. Copyright © 2005 Jamal Shamsie.

Exhibit 1   McDonald's Milestones

1948	Brothers Richard and Maurice McDonald open the first restaurant in San Bernardino, California, that sells hamburgers, fries, and milk shakes.
1955	Ray A. Kroc, 52, opens his first McDonald's in Des Plaines, Illinois. Kroc, a distributor of milk shake mixers, figures he can sell a bundle of them if he franchises the McDonald's business and install his mixers in the new stores.
1961	Six years later, Kroc buys out the McDonald brothers for $2.7 million.
1963	Ronald McDonald makes his debut as corporate spokesclown using future NBC-TV weatherman Willard Scott. During the year, the company also sells its 1 billionth burger.
1965	McDonald's stock goes public at $22.50 a share. It will split 12 times in the next 35 years.
1967	The first McDonald's restaurant outside the United States opens in Richmond, British Columbia. Today there are 31,108 McDonald's in 118 countries.
1968	The Big Mac, the first extension of McDonald's basic burger, makes its debut and is an immediate hit.
1972	McDonald's switches to the frozen variety for its successful french fries.
1974	Fred L. Turner succeeds Kroc as CEO. In the midst of a recession, the minimum wage rises to $2 per hour, a big cost increase for McDonald's, which is built around a model of young, low-wage workers.
1975	The first drive-through window is opened in Sierra Vista, Arizona.
1979	McDonald's responds to the needs of working women by introducing Happy Meals. A burger, some fries, a soda, and a toy give working moms a break.
1987	Michael R. Quinlan becomes chief executive.
1991	Responding to the public's desire for healthier foods, McDonald's introduces the low-fat McLean Deluxe burger. It flops and is withdrawn from the market. Over the next few years, the chain will stumble several times trying to spruce up its menu.
1992	The company sells its 90 billionth burger and stops counting.
1996	To attract more adult customers, the company launches its Arch Deluxe, a "grownup" burger with an idiosyncratic taste. Like the low-fat burger, it also falls flat.
1997	McDonald's launches Campaign 55, which cuts the cost of a Big Mac to 55¢. It is a response to discounting by Burger King and Taco Bell. The move, which prefigures similar price wars in 2002, is widely considered a failure.
1998	Jack M. Greenberg becomes McDonald's fourth chief executive. A 16-year company veteran, he vows to spruce up the restaurants and their menu.
1999	For the first time, sales from international operations outstrip domestic revenues. In search of other concepts, the company acquires Aroma Cafe, Chipotle, Donatos, and, later, Boston Market.
2000	McDonald's sales in the United States peak at an average of $1.6 million annually per restaurant, a figure that has not changed since. It is, however, still more than at any other fast-food chain.
2001	Subway surpasses McDonald's as the fast-food chain with the most U.S. outlets. At the end of the year it has 13,247 stores—148 more than McDonald's.
2002	McDonald's posts its first-ever quarterly loss—$343.8 million. The stock drops to around $13.50, down 40 percent from five years ago.
2003	James R. Cantalupo returns to McDonald's in January as CEO. He immediately pulls back from the company's 10 to 15 percent forecast for per-share earnings growth.
2004	Charles H. Bell takes over the firm after the sudden death of Cantalupo. He states he will continue with the strategies that have been developed by his predecessor.

Source: McDonald's.

Exhibit 2 Number of McDonald's Outlets

	Total	Company Owned	Franchised	Affiliated
2003	31,129	8,959	18,132	4,038
2002	31,108	9,000	17,864	4,244
2001	30,093	8,378	17,395	4,320
2000	28,707	7,652	16,795	4,260
1999	26,309	6,059	15,949	4,301

Source: McDonald's.

purchase of a handful of nonburger chains, none of which helped the firm to sell more burgers. Indeed, his critics say that by trying so many different things and executing them poorly Greenberg allowed the burger business to continue its decline. According to Los Angeles franchisee Reggie Webb, "We would have been better off trying fewer things and making them work."[3]

Managing a Troubled Franchise

Up until a few years ago, franchisees had clamored to become part of McDonald's growing empire. But during 2002, in an exodus that had been unheard of in the past, 126 franchisees left the system, with 68 of these, representing 169 restaurants, having been forced out for poor performance. The rest left because they were unhappy with the profits that they were making. Since then, as many as 20 franchisees have been leaving McDonald's every month according to Richard Adams, a former franchisee and a food consultant. The firm buys back franchises if they cannot be sold, so forcing out a franchisee can be quite expensive. McDonald's recently took a pretax charge of $292 million last quarter to close 719 restaurants during 2002 and 2003 (see Exhibit 2).

In many cases, franchisees that have seen the chain as stuck in a rut have been jumping ship to faster-growing rivals. Paul Saber, a McDonald's franchisee for 17 years, sold his 14 restaurants back to the company in 2000 when he realized that eating habits were shifting away from McDonald's burgers to fresher, better-tasting food. He moved to rival Panera Bread Company, a fast-growing national bakery cafe chain. "The McDonald's-type fast food isn't relevant to today's consumer," said Saber.[4]

One of the biggest sore points for franchisees has been the top-down manner in which Greenberg and other past CEOs have attempted to fix pricing and menu problems. Many owner-operators still grumble over the $18,000 to $100,000 they had to spend in the late 1990s to install company-mandated "Made for You" kitchen upgrades in each restaurant. The new kitchens were supposed to speed up orders and accommodate new menu items. But in the end, they actually slowed service.

Reggie Webb, who operates 11 McDonald's restaurants in Los Angeles, claimed that his sales have dipped by an average of $50,000 at each of his outlets over the past 15 years. "From my perspective, I am working harder than ever and making less than I ever had on an average-store basis," said Webb.[5] Most franchisees have, in fact, seen their margins dip to a paltry 4 percent, from 15 percent when McDonald's was at its peak.

Franchisees have also complained about McDonald's addiction to cutting prices in order to drive up sales. When McDonald's cut prices in a 1997 price war, sales actually fell over the next four months. "Pulling hard on the price lever is dangerous. It risks cheapening the brand," said Sam Rovit, a partner at Chicago consultant Bain & Company.[6] Yet McDonald's has been sticking with the $1 menu program that it had introduced in 2002. Although the tactic has been squeezing the sales of its rivals, the $1 menu has done little to improve McDonald's results.

Pinning Hopes on a New Team

By the beginning of 2003, consumer surveys were indicating that McDonald's was headed for serious trouble. Measures of the chain's service and quality were beginning to lag far behind those of its rivals. To deal with its deteriorating performance, the firm decided to bring back retired Vice Chairman James R. Cantalupo, 59, who had overseen McDonald's successful international expansion in the 1980s and 1990s. Cantalupo, who had retired only a year earlier, was perceived to be the only candidate with the necessary qualifications, despite shareholder sentiment for an outsider. The board had felt that it needed someone who knew the company well and could move quickly to turn things around.

A few weeks after Cantalupo had taken control, he had to announce the first quarterly loss in its 47-year history. There were clear indications that sales at outlets open at least a year were continuing to drop after showing a decline of 2.1 percent in 2002. Cantalupo clearly realized he had no time to lose. (See Exhibits 3 and 4 for the company's income statements and balance sheets.)

One of the first steps that Cantalupo took was to assemble a fresh team to help McDonald's work itself out of its rut. He chose to bring up younger McDonald's executives, who he felt would bring energy and fresh ideas to the table. "Any company today has to be very vigilant about their business model and willing to break it, even if it's successful, to make sure they stay on top of the changing

Exhibit 3   McDonald's Income Statement
(All numbers in $ thousands)

	Period Ending		
	December 31, 2003	December 31, 2002	December 31, 2001
Total Revenue	17,140,500	15,405,700	14,870,000
Cost of Revenue	11,943,700	10,746,700	10,253,900
Gross Profit	5,196,800	4,659,000	4,616,100
Selling General and Administrative	2,048,400	2,546,100	1,719,100
Nonrecurring	316,200	—	200,000
Operating Income or Loss	2,832,200	2,112,900	2,697,000
Income from Continuing Operations	—	—	—
Total Other Income/Expenses Net	(97,800)	(76,700)	85,100
Earnings Before Interest and Taxes	2,734,400	2,036,200	2,782,100
Interest Expense	388,000	374,100	452,400
Income Before Tax	2,346,400	1,662,100	2,329,700
Income Tax Expense	838,200	670,000	693,100
Net Income from Continuing Ops	1,508,200	992,100	1,636,600
Effect of Accounting Changes	(36,800)	(98,600)	—
Net Income	1,471,400	893,500	1,636,600

Source: McDonald's annual report.

trends," said Alan Feldman, who had just quit as COO for domestic operations at McDonald's.[7]

For starters, Cantalupo appointed as chief operating officer Charles Bell, 42, an Australian whom he also designated as his successor. Bell had become a store manager in his native Australia at age 19 and then had risen through the ranks. He eventually launched a coffeehouse concept called McCafe that did attain considerable success. When he became president of McDonald's Europe, he similarly abandoned McDonald's cookie-cutter orange-and-yellow stores for individualized ones that offered local fare like the ham-and-cheese Croque McDo. (See Exhibits 5, 6, and 7 for a breakdown of McDonald's operations around the globe.)

The second top executive Cantalupo recruited was a bona fide outsider, at least by company standards. Mats Lederhausen, a 39-year-old Swede, held an MBA from the Stockholm School of Economics and worked with Boston Consulting Group for two years. However, he jokes that he grew up in a french-fry vat because his father introduced

McDonald's to Sweden in 1973. Lederhausen was given charge of growth and menu development.

Besides assembling a management team with a fresh perspective, Cantalupo also searched for new ideas from some of the better performing franchisees. McDonald's best hope for revival may lie with its most innovative franchisees. One of these, Irwin Kruger, recently opened a 17,000-square-foot showcase unit in New York's Times Square with video monitors showing movie trailers, brick walls, and theatrical lighting. "We're slated to have sales of over $5 million this year and profits exceeding 10 percent," said Kruger.[8]

Scrambling for a New Strategy

Cantalupo realized that McDonald's often tended to miss the mark on delivering the critical aspects of consistent, fast and friendly service and an all-around enjoyable experience for the whole family. He understood that its franchisees and employees alike needed to be inspired as well as retrained in their role of putting the smile back into the

Exhibit 4   McDonald's Balance Sheet
(All numbers in $ thousands)

	Period Ending		
	December 31, 2003	December 31, 2002	December 31, 2001
Assets			
Current Assets			
Cash and Cash Equivalents	492,800	330,400	418,100
Net Receivables	734,500	855,300	881,900
Inventory	129,400	111,700	105,500
Other Current Assets	528,700	418,000	413,800
Total Current Assets	**1,885,400**	**1,715,400**	**1,819,300**
Long-Term Investments	1,089,600	1,037,700	990,200
Property, Plant, and Equipment	19,924,700	18,583,400	17,289,500
Goodwill	1,665,100	1,559,800	1,419,800
Other Assets	960,300	1,074,200	1,015,700
Total Assets	**25,525,100**	**23,970,500**	**22,534,500**
Liabilities			
Current Liabilities			
Accounts Payable	2,097,800	2,146,800	2,070,700
Short/Current Long-Term Debt	388,000	275,500	177,600
Total Current Liabilities	**2,485,800**	**2,422,300**	**2,248,300**
Long-Term Debt	9,342,500	9,703,600	8,555,500
Other Liabilities	699,800	560,000	629,300
Deferred Long-Term Liability Charges	1,015,100	1,003,700	1,112,200
Total Liabilities	**13,543,200**	**13,689,600**	**13,046,100**
Stockholders' Equity			
Miscellaneous Stocks Options, Warrants	—	—	500,800
Common Stock	16,600	16,600	16,600
Retained Earnings	20,172,300	19,204,400	18,608,300
Treasury Stock	(9,318,500)	(8,987,700)	(8,912,200)
Capital Surplus	1,837,500	1,747,300	1,591,200
Other Stockholder Equity	(726,000)	(1,699,700)	(1,815,500)
Total Stockholder Equity	**11,981,900**	**10,280,900**	**9,488,400**
Net Tangible Assets	**$10,316,800**	**$8,721,100**	**$8,068,600**

Source: McDonald's annual report.

Exhibit 5   Distribution of McDonald's Outlets

	2003	2002
United States	13,609	13,491
Europe	6,186	6,070
Asia/Pacific	7,475	7,555
Latin America	1,578	1,605
Canada	1,339	1,304
Other	942	1,082

Source: McDonald's.

Exhibit 6   McDonald's Breakdown of Revenues
(In millions of dollars)

	2003	2002
United States	6,039	5,423
Europe	5,875	5,136
Asia/Pacific	2,447	2,368
Latin America	859	814
Canada	778	633
Other	1,142	1,032

Source: McDonald's.

Exhibit 7   McDonald's Breakdown of Net Income
(In millions of dollars)

	2003	2002
United States	1,982	1,673
Europe	1,339	1,022
Asia/Pacific	226	64
Latin America	(171)	(133)
Canada	163	125
Other	(295)	(66)

Source: McDonald's.

McDonald's experience. When Cantalupo and his team laid out their plan for McDonald's in the spring of 2003, they stressed getting the basics of service and quality right, in part by reinstituting a tough "up or out" grading system that would kick out underperforming franchisees. "We have to rebuild the foundation. It's fruitless to add growth if the foundation is weak," said Cantalupo.[9]

New product additions to the menu were one of the key elements of Cantalupo's new strategy for McDonald's. His new team began to add new items such as the McGriddles breakfast sandwich that would draw in new customers and lure back old ones. Lederhausen was working on other possible items that could be added to the chain's menu. The revamped menu was promoted through a new worldwide ad slogan, "I'm loving it," which was delivered by pop idol Justin Timberlake through a set of MTV-style commercials.

But Cantalupo also had been keen to build upon the ideas that Bell had tried out in Australia and Europe. The chain had been developing plans to test some outlets in Coral Gables, Florida with much fancier contemporary décor. Modeled after the stores that Bell had opened in Paris, the seats would have cushions and tabletops would be of wood composite instead of plastic. The walls were to be decorated with colorful art instead of Ronald's face. "This is all part of becoming more relevant to our consumers," said company spokesman Walt Riker. "When a customer enters our restaurant, they enter our brand."[10]

Cantalupo was also thinking about trying out some local variations on the McDonald's theme. Based on the success that Bell had with McCafe in Australia, he wanted to adapt some of McDonald's outlets to the local themes. An example of this would be the Arch Bistro, complete with chandeliers, leather couches, and soft lighting that McDonald's had recently opened in downtown New Orleans. The menu offered everything from Louisiana shrimp to panini bread filled with chicken Cordon Bleu.

McDonald's was also planning to exploit its brand name by globally relaunching its marginally successful McKids line and expanding it well beyond kids clothing and toys into interactive videos and books. Under Cantalupo, the firm was in the process of making deals to get some royalties off these items from Mattel, Hasbro, and Creative Designs. While McDonald's was expected to make some money on these offerings, they were designed to keep the brand prominent in the minds of kids. "McDonald's wants to be seen as a lifestyle brand, not just a place to go to have a burger," said Marty Brochstein, executive editor of the *Licensing Letter*.[11]

As the firm moves into these new areas that build upon its brand, Cantalupo was thinking of divesting the nonburger chains that his predecessor had acquired. Collectively lumped under the Partner Brands, these have consisted of Chipotle Mexican Grill, Donatos Pizza, and Boston Market. The purpose of these acquisitions had been to find new growth and to offer the best franchises new expansion opportunities. But these acquired businesses had not fueled much growth and actually had posted considerable losses in recent years.

Continuing with Its Turnaround

During his 16-month tenure, Cantalupo had attempted to turn McDonald's around by cutting back on expansion plans, reducing operating costs, and making new product introductions. By taking these steps, he had managed to boost the firm's financial performance, particularly in the domestic market. But McDonald's was still working hard to improve on the basics of providing tastier burgers, faster service, and cleaner restaurants. "We haven't made as much progress as we could on service," Cantalupo recently acknowledged.[12]

Just months before he died, Cantalupo announced one of McDonald's most controversial changes. In response to concerns about growing obesity among Americans, Cantalupo had stated that the firm would phase out supersizing by the end of 2004. The supersizing option allowed customers to get a larger order of french fries and a bigger soft drink by paying a little bit extra.

Within hours of the announcement of Cantalupo's unexpected death, McDonald's announced the appointment of Bell as the new CEO. As president and chief operating officer, he had been selected by Cantalupo as his successor. A 43-year-old native of Australia, Bell was the youngest and the first non-American to ever head the firm. He generally shared Cantalupo's focus on customer experience and stated that he intended to stick closely to the strategy that had been developed by his predecessor.

Above all, Bell must try to build on the moves that Cantalupo was making in McDonald's core burger business. Winning back customers for its burgers may even be getting harder as a result of increased competition from newer entrants such as the California-based In-N-Out chain. The long-term success of the firm may depend on its ability to compete with rival burger chains. "The burger category has great strength," added David C. Novak, chairman and CEO of Yum! Brands, parent of KFC and Taco Bell. "That's America's food. People love hamburgers."[13]

At the same time, Bell must deal with some of the other critical issues facing the firm. He must figure out how to continue to build sales after the initial excitement that had been generated by new products such as the McGriddles sandwich has worn off. Some franchisees are also upset that recent steps taken by McDonald's have had little effect on the steady decline in their profit margins. Finally, McDonald's efforts to move into kids' clothing and toys is risky, given that the firm did not achieve much success with its previous attempt to launch the McKids line.

Like Cantalupo, Bell realizes that McDonald's may not have many shots at trying to get its strategy working. The firm needs to figure out what steps it needs to take to get its sales and profits growing again. "They are at a critical juncture and what they do today will shape whether they just fade away or recapture some of the magic and greatness again," said Robert S. Goldin, executive vice president at food consultant Technomic Incorporated.[14]

Endnotes

1. Day, Sherri. 2004. McDonald's moves quickly to cover its loss. *New York Times,* April 20: C8.
2. Gogoi, Pallavi, & Arndt, Michael. 2003. Hamburger hell. *BusinessWeek,* March 3: 104.
3. Ibid.: 108.
4. Ibid.: 106.
5. Ibid.
6. Ibid.
7. Ibid.: 108.
8. Ibid.
9. Ibid.: 105.
10. Horovitz, Bruce. 2003. You want ambiance with that? *USA Today,* October 30: 3B.
11. Horovitz, Bruce. 2003. McDonald's ventures beyond burgers to duds, toys. *USA Today,* November 14: 6B.
12. Leung, Shirley. 2003. McDonald's net increases 12.5%, bolstered by strong U.S. sales. *Wall Street Journal,* October 23: A3.
13. *BusinessWeek,* March 3: 108.
14. Ibid.

Case 18   Microsoft's Battle for the Living Room: The Trojan Horse—The Xbox*

On March 10, 2000, Microsoft's chairman Bill Gates stepped onto a stage in the San Jose, California, Convention Center to give the most anticipated speech of the Game Developers Conference. Thousands of people packed the room, and the event was televised all over the world. Gates, dressed in a leather jacket with a large green "X," talked about the future of gaming as he prepared to unveil what he called a "secret, a very deep secret":

> It's very exciting to be here today and have the opportunity to announce a whole new platform. A platform that all of you are going to take in directions that we can't even imagine. Thanks to months of rumors, everyone was in the know: The secret was the Xbox, Microsoft's new video game console.

After this dramatic speech, Gates invited Jonathan "Seamus" Blackley, the chief Xbox technical officer, to the stage to demonstrate the excellent performance of this brand-new machine. Blackley offered several 3-D animation demonstrations to excite the crowd, who roared with applause. In developing the Xbox, Blackley said that "the Xbox was Microsoft's weapon to take on the Japanese in the video game business and make gaming the premier entertainment medium."

Due to the prosperity of its software business, Microsoft had a lock on the PC market to such an extent that "Microsoft" became nearly synonymous with "computer software" in many consumers' minds. As an ambitious entrepreneur, however, Gates was never satisfied with the status quo. He wanted to use the television as he had used the personal computer to sell his products and services, and by doing so, expand his Microsoft kingdom from the den to the living room. The Xbox was the console that Gates needed in order to create a new era of Microsoft.

However, manufacturing and selling this brand-new console became a larger-than-anticipated challenge for both Gates and Microsoft for two reasons. First, without any experience in manufacturing family video game consoles, how could Microsoft integrate its business and capital resources in order to introduce the Xbox successfully? Second, since Japanese firms had dominated the video game market since the 1980s, how would Microsoft's rivals respond to its late entry into the video game industry?

Third, how would Microsoft's investors respond to its entry into an industry that promised sustained short-term losses as development costs were recouped, not to mention uncertain long-term profitability?

Since Microsoft had neither the arcade gaming expertise of Nintendo and SEGA, nor the extensive consumer electronics experience possessed by Sony, many industry analysts questioned its motive in entering such an unfamiliar territory. Did Bill Gates view the video game console as a threat to Microsoft's PC operating system business? After all, Microsoft's major competitors had engineered their consoles to enable Internet access. Due to the decreasing cost of computer memory chips and other devices, the idea of incorporating operating systems other than Microsoft's into their consoles to also serve as personal computers was not inconceivable.

Early Attempts to Enter the Game Business

Microsoft was founded in 1975 by Paul Allen and Bill Gates as a partnership and was incorporated in 1981 (Exhibit 1). The company had a clear mission: "to enable people and businesses throughout the world to realize their full potential." Microsoft also had a company vision, to empower people through great software—any time, any place, and on any device.

Microsoft had begun its business by developing personal computer software. The world famous DOS and Windows series became the backbone of Microsoft's business. Riding the success of its Windows and Office tools, Microsoft quickly expanded its products and services to cover and compete in a wide variety of areas under its seven major business divisions (Exhibit 2). Microsoft now stands as one of the largest companies in the world, enjoying sales exceeding $32 billion and profits approaching $10 billion in fiscal year 2003 (Exhibits 3 and 4).

The history of Microsoft's games business could be tracked to 1983. Although Microsoft's games business had grown modestly from year to year, it was never profitable, especially compared with other successful divisions within the corporation. Despite repeated attempts, Microsoft's games business failed to meet expectations.

In 1983 Microsoft teamed up with several consumer electronics companies to launch its own hybrid PC-console, which was called MSX, in Asian markets. Unfortunately, because it lacked appealing games, MSX quickly failed.

To increase revenue in the mid-1990s, Microsoft's games division designed games for Sony's PlayStation. Although the initial PlayStation product sold more than 5 million units in the U.S. market, the games published by Microsoft did not become as popular as other PlayStation games, nor meet expected revenue goals.

*This case study was prepared by Professors Armand Gilinsky, Jr., and Zachary Wong at Sonoma State University, with the research assistance of MBA student Yu-Bin Chiou, as a basis for class discussion rather than to illustrate the effective or ineffective handling of an administrative situation.

Exhibit 1   Microsoft's History

Year	Event
1975	Founded by Paul Allen and Bill Gates.
1978	Fiscal reports showed annual sales exceeded $1 million dollars.
1981	IBM introduced its PC, which used Microsoft's 16-bit operating system, MS-DOS 1.0.
1983	Unveiled the first version of Microsoft Windows.
1984	Formed a partnership with IBM.
1986	Moved its headquarters to Redmond, Washington. Went public at $21 per share. The initial offering raised approximately $61 million. Employed 1,442 workers at the end of this year.
1989	Created a new multimedia division dedicated to developing and producing multimedia systems software and consumer products.
1990	Annual sales exceeded $1 billion.
1992	The new version Windows 3.1 was available worldwide. Merger with Fox Software Inc.
1994	Acquired SOFTIMAGE Inc., the leading developer of high-performance computer animation software and digital video.
1995	Launched Windows 95. Established MSNBC with NBC as an all-news cable TV channel. Established DreamWorks Interactive with DreamWorks SKG.
1996	Formed Interactive Media Group.
1997	Invested $150 million in Apple. Bought Hotmail for $650 million. Launched Internet Explorer 4.0.
1998	Bought Firefly Network.
1999	Invested $5 billion in AT&T.
2000	Bill Gates stepped aside as Microsoft chief executive.
2001	Announced the Xbox entertainment system. Purchased Great Plains software.
2002	Purchased Navision for $1.34 billion.

Sources: Microsoft Web site—www.microsoft.com—and ketupa.com.

In 1995 Microsoft expanded its games division. After the reorganization, the games department was a 150-person division with four development teams. At the same time, Ed Fries, the current vice president of games at Microsoft and one of the Xbox creators, was named head of the games department.

In 1997 Gates convinced Japan's SEGA Corporation to put Microsoft's Windows CE operating system into the SEGA Dreamcast console. The move was intended to help enter Microsoft the console business by partnering with a seasoned video game company. If the Dreamcast console succeeded, Microsoft could dominate the video game market indirectly by capitalizing on its sophisticated technology in software design. However, by the fall of 2000 the Dreamcast market share in the United States was barely 25 percent and started to decrease exponentially beginning in November when Sony launched its much anticipated PlayStation 2. SEGA eventually discontinued

Exhibit 2   Microsoft's Products and Services

Divisions	Product (Service)	Business Content
Client	Windows XP	Microsoft launched Windows XP in October 2001 as the newest version of the Windows family. XP extends the personal computing experience by uniting PCs, devices, and services, while enhancing reliability, security, and performance. Currently, the Windows operating system is the standard desktop application for PC users worldwide.
	Windows 2000 Professional	The new generation of Windows NT Workstation. Windows 2000 Professional operating system combines features to create a mainstream operating system for desktop and notebook computing in all organizations.
	Windows CE	A robust real-time embedded operating system targeted at mobile 32-bit devices. This embedded operating system offers integrated tool sets to enable embedded system developers to quickly create sophisticated embedded device and application solutions.
	Other OSs	Includes Windows NT Workstation, Windows Millennium Edition, and Windows 98.
	Hardware	The Hardware Group develops and markets several PC accessories including the Microsoft IntelliMouse family of handheld pointing devices using IntelliEye optical technology.
Server and Tools	Server Licenses	A client access license gives its holder the legal right to access a computer that runs a Microsoft server product and access to the services supported by the server.
	SQL Server	A comprehensive data management and analysis platform that enables rapid delivery, dependable performance, and secure operation of connected applications.
	Exchange Server	A messaging and collaboration server that provides e-mail, group scheduling, task management, contact management, and document routing capabilities.
Information Worker	Microsoft Office	A software product that features commonly used desktop functionality. The product is based upon a document-centric concept, with common commands and extensive use of cross-application capabilities.
	Other Desktop Applications	Offers other stand-alone desktop application products. Microsoft Project is a project management program for scheduling, organizing, and analyzing tasks, deadlines, and resources. Visio is a diagramming program that helps people visualize and communicate ideas, information, and systems.
Microsoft Business Solutions	Great Plains	Great Plains offers a range of integrated business and accounting products, including Dynamics, Solomon, and eEnterprise. These products provide Internet-ready accounting and business management capabilities, a full range of e-business and accounting applications, and a collaborative environment for information management and sharing for any size company.
	bCentral	Includes Site Manager, a Web site management and hosting service which empowers small businesses to easily create and manage their own Web sites.

Sources: Microsoft's Web site and 2003 Annual Report.

(*continued*)

Exhibit 2   Microsoft's Products and Services (*continued*)

Divisions	Product (Service)	Business Content
MSN	MSN Internet Access	MSN Internet access is Microsoft's service for accessing the Web and experiencing a wide range of rich online services and content. MSN Internet access subscribers can access their account from multiple sources, including a computer, television, Internet appliances, and personal digital assistants.
	MSN Network Service	The MSN network provides services, content, and advertising on the Internet, including MSN Search, Messenger, eShop, Hotmail, Money, and Music, as well as other services and content. MSN Search makes Web searches more useful by providing users with the most relevant results for the most popular search queries on the Web. MSN Messenger is a free Internet messaging service that enables users to see when others are online and exchange instant messages with them. MSN eShop is a one-stop online shopping resource. MSN Hotmail is the world's leading free Web-based e-mail service. MSN Money is a complete online personal financial service that combines finance tools and content from Microsoft with exclusive investment news and analysis from CNBC. MSN Music provides consumers with one place online to find old favorites, as well as discover new music, and delivers a high-quality listening experience.
Mobile and Embedded Devices	CarPoint online automotive service	The CarPoint online automotive service is the leading online automotive marketplace, visited by more than 7 million consumers each month. With details on more than 10,000 car models and 100,000 used vehicles, users can research and compare cars of virtually every make and model, identify local dealers, and receive instructions for post-purchase service and maintenance.
	Pocket PC	Licensed the right to manufacture the handheld device with a Windows CE OS.
Home and Entertainment	PC and Online Games	Microsoft offers a line of entertainment products from classic software games to online games, simulations, sport products, and strategy games. Zone.com is a gaming community on the Internet, which allows multiplayer gaming competitions of Microsoft's popular CD-ROM games and classic card, board, and puzzle games.
	Xbox	Microsoft's next-generation video game console system delivers high-quality graphics and audio gameplay experiences. Games for the Xbox are developed by Microsoft Game Studios and by third-party game development partners. Xbox Live, an online service available to owners of Xbox systems, was launched in the forth quarter of 2002 and allows online game play among users of online-enabled Xbox games.
Other	Expedia, Inc.	Expedia, Inc., operates Expedia.com, a leading online travel service. Expedia.com provides air, car, and hotel booking, vacation packages and cruise offerings, destination information, and mapping.
	Microsoft Press	Microsoft Press offers comprehensive learning and training resources to help new users, power users, and professionals get the most from Microsoft technology through books, CDs, self-paced training kits, and videos that are created to accommodate different learning styles and preferences.

Exhibit 3   Microsoft Corporation's Income Statements, 2001–2003
($ millions)

	2003	2002	2001
Revenue	$32,187.0	$28,365.0	$25,296.0
Cost of goods sold	4,247.0	4,107.0	1,919.0
Gross profit	27,940.0	24,258.0	23,377.0
Gross profit margin	86.8%	85.5%	92.4%
SG&A expense	13,284.0	11,264.0	10,121.0
Depreciation & amortization	1,439.0	1,084.0	1,536.0
Operating income	13,217.0	11,910.0	11,720.0
Operating margin	41.1%	42.0%	46.3%
Nonoperating income	1,509.0	(397.0)	(195.0)
Nonoperating expenses	0.0	0.0	0.0
Income before taxes	14,726.0	11,513.0	11,525.0
Income taxes	4,733.0	3,684.0	3,804.0
Net Income after taxes	$ 9,993.0	$ 7,829.0	$ 7,721.0

Source: Microsoft annual reports.

Exhibit 4   Microsoft's Revenue and Operating Income by Division, 2002–2003
($ millions)

	Revenue		Operating Income	
Division	2003	2002	2003	2002
Client	$10,394	$ 9,360	$ 8,400	$ 7,576
Server and Tools	7,140	6,157	2,457	2,048
Information Worker	9,229	8,212	7,037	6,448
Business Solutions	567	308	(254)	(176)
MSN	1,953	1,571	(299)	(641)
Mobile and Embedded Devices	156	112	(157)	(157)
Home and Entertainment	2,748	2,453	(924)	(874)
Other	—	192	(3,043)	(2,314)
Consolidated	$32,187	$28,365	$13,217	$11,910

Source: Microsoft 2003 Annual Report.

the Dreamcast console in 2001, adding to Microsoft's failed attempts to expand its games business.

In October 1997 Microsoft's games business received encouraging news. Its new real-time strategy game, *Age of Empires,* sold millions of copies in the United States, and earned more than $40 million for Microsoft. Spokesperson Ed Fries said, "*Age of Empires* helped us finance our growth, but what's been good about the growth was that it

Exhibit 5   Acquisition of Game Companies by Microsoft

Year	Company Name	Location	Game Concentration
1995	Ensemble Studio	Dallas, TX	Real-time strategy games
1998	Virtual House	San Jose, CA	Action games
	Digital Anvil	Austin, TX	Flying and shooting games (Created *Wing Commander* in 1990)
1999	Fasa Interactive	Chicago, IL	Robot games
	Access Software	Seattle, WA	Sports games (*Golf*)

Source: Takahashi, D. 2002. *Opening the Xbox.* Roseville, CA: Prima Publishing.

is mostly organic." *Age of Empires* gave Microsoft respect among hard-core gamers and developers. It became a vehicle Gates and Fries could build upon to continue expanding Microsoft's games business.

In 1999 Gates approached Sony's CEO Nobuyuki Idei before Sony's PlayStation 2 announcement. Gates wanted Idei to use Microsoft's programming tools, which would make it easier to develop games for the upcoming PlayStation 2. Idei turned Gates down because he preferred to use (and protect) Sony's proprietary programming tools.

Approaching Sony's CEO unsuccessfully turned out to be Gates's final attempt to make his games dream come true through partnerships with other game platform manufacturers. Gates then made the determination that Microsoft had sufficient capital, technology, human resources, and experience to launch its own video game console. He then decided to capitalize on a series of recent acquisitions (Exhibit 5).

The development and deployment of Microsoft's own game console, the Xbox, was enabled by the creation of a new division, Home and Entertainment, headed by senior vice president Robert Bach. The Home and Entertainment division was designed from the start to be autonomous, and it had its own functional units in marketing, operations, and technical deployment.

The U.S. Video Game Industry

The Dawn. Video games had a long history in the United States. In 1961 an MIT student named Steve Russell created *Spacewar,* the first interactive computer game in U.S. video game history. From 1965 to 1980, many famous video game companies, including Service Games (SEGA), Nintendo, Midway, and Namco, began releasing arcade games.

The most well-known arcade games, like *Pac-Man, Donkey Kong,* and *Pong,* also appeared during these 15 years. The first period of the U.S. video game history focused on commercial arcade games.

The Warring States. The first family console emerged in the middle of the 1980s. In 1986 Nintendo of America released the Nintendo Entertainment System (NES or Famicom, Family Computer) nationwide. The NES was the first game console designed for family use. The appearance of the NES not only advanced video game evolution to the next stage, but introduced a new style of home entertainment. This evolution formed a new profitable industry.

After the introduction of the NES, more companies devoted themselves to developing new consoles to attract consumers into this fantasy world (see Exhibit 6). Nintendo maintained the lead position and earned considerable revenue from the growing home video game market until a strong competitor, SEGA, joined the arena. SEGA unveiled its high-performing Mega Drive Genesis (MD) in 1989. This 16-bit console had much higher capability in game and sound performance than the NES, which meant that more exciting game factors could be added into this new system. Soon, the sales of the SEGA MD rose sharply in the United States and the MD caught the eye of many Nintendo players. By the summer of 1990, MD had taken more than 55 percent of new console sales, effectively eroding Nintendo's share by as much as 20 percent. Many third-party game developers also started dropping their Nintendo accounts to begin working with SEGA. In order to survive SEGA's severe competition, Nintendo devoted its business to a new video game niche, the pocket game system. Nintendo created the Game Boy, a pocket game system and the most popular console in gaming history, selling more than 115 million units worldwide. With the success of the Game Boy, Nintendo raised the funds needed to allow it to redevelop its new family console.

Nintendo was very ambitious in the home video game market that it had created. In 1991 Nintendo announced the Super NES, the second generation of its original console. Although the Super NES was a 16-bit console like the SEGA MD, with more game developers and therefore more games available with the system,

Exhibit 6   Video Game Console Evolution in the United States, 1986–2001

Year	Console Name	Company	Console Introduction
1986	NES	Nintendo	NES had an 8-bit performance. Also adopted the famous Super Mario Brother as its Mascot.
1989	PC Engine	NEC	The first console with CD-ROM medium.
1989	Mega Drive Genesis	SEGA	Helped SEGA take control of the U.S. console market in 1992.
1989	Game Boy	Nintendo	The most successful pocket console. Sold more than 115 million worldwide.
1990	NeoGeo	SNK	The first 24-bit console.
1991	Super NES	Nintendo	Helped Nintendo take control of the U.S. console market in 1994.
1991	Game Genie	Galoob Toys	Discontinued in 1993.
1993	3DO Multiplayer	Panasonic	The first 32-bit console. Without good software support, discontinued in 1994.
1993	Jaguar	Atari	Discontinued in 1994.
1995	Saturn	SEGA	The first 64-bit console. Discontinued in 1997.
1995	PlayStation	Sony	Established Sony's foundation in the video game business.
1995	Virtual Boy	Nintendo	Discontinued in 1996.
1996	Nintendo 64	Nintendo	Nintendo's first 64-bit console. The last console that used cartridges as the medium.
1999	NeoGeo Pocket	SNK	The Japanese-owned SNK was bought by a Korean company in 2000.
1999	Dreamcast	SEGA	The first console that came with DVD medium.
2000	PlayStation 2	Sony	Took the major market share of console business since its introduction.
2001	Game Boy Advance	Nintendo	The new generation pocket console with a color screen.
2001	GameCube	Nintendo	Nintendo's first step to change its console into mainstream DVD medium.
2001	Xbox	Microsoft	Microsoft's first 128-bit video game console.

Source: Kent, Steven L. 2001. *The ultimate history of video games.* Roseville, CA: Prima Publishing.

Nintendo dominated the U.S. console market again by 1994. The competition between Nintendo and SEGA escalated again in 1995 when SEGA introduced its new 64-bit console, the Saturn, in the U.S. market. Because the Super NES had less than half of the performance quality and capacity of the brand new Saturn, most people believed SEGA would beat Nintendo quickly and take control of the video game market. SEGA was confident that it could take the market leader position back; however, a video game novice smashed SEGA's gaming dream.

New Competitors Enter.   A previously ignored new entrant was Sony, a manufacturer that focused on consumer electronics. Sony entered the video game market in 1995 with its secret weapon—the PlayStation. Like the SEGA Saturn, the PlayStation was a 64-bit console with a CD-ROM game medium. Although there was no obvious difference in the hardware sections of these two systems, the volume of available game software became the advantage Sony needed to beat its powerful rival. Sony positioned its PlayStation as a software provider. Before unveiling this new console, Sony contracted with game developers, so that when the PlayStation premiered, it came with more than a hundred games, approximately half the number of games that Saturn offered. One year later, in 1996, the PlayStation had more than 250 games, exceeding Saturn's titles. Without the competitive advantage of having more games than its competitor, SEGA gradually lost its market share and discontinued the Saturn in 1997, recognizing that it had lost the console war again.

Having high-performing hardware and plenty of supporting software, the PlayStation became unbeatable in the U.S. video game market. The original video game giant, Nintendo, reentered this market in 1996 with its well-designed 64-bit console, Nintendo 64, and attempted to compete against the PlayStation, which was the market leader. With the assistance of some famous game series, like *Super Mario Brothers* and *Pokémon,* the Nintendo 64 sold very well in the beginning. However, the Nintendo 64 had a fatal design flaw. Nintendo used its familiar high-cost cartridges as the game medium instead of adopting the new cheaper CD-ROM game format. The high-cost cartridge became a heavy burden for both developers and consumers and because of this design flaw, Nintendo quickly lost both its game developers and its market share. Nintendo discontinued this console in 1999 and became another victim of Sony's PlayStation.

In 1999 SEGA invested considerable capital in creating the state-of-the-art console—Dreamcast. SEGA was aware of Sony's pending next-generation console, so it introduced the first console of the 21st century before other companies could. The Dreamcast, a high-performance console, earned lots of applause and praise at the Game Developers Conference in 1999. Many TV programs and gaming professional magazines introduced and reviewed the Dreamcast console. However, the thousands of positive reports did not generate the sales that SEGA anticipated. Since the Dreamcast provided higher capacity for software conducting, it was expensive to produce and difficult for developers to design its games. The available software was limited and expensive. Most consumers were still willing to purchase the cheaper PlayStation games with more titles rather than buy the more expensive Dreamcast console and games. The Dreamcast's market share never exceeded 10 percent of the U.S. console market. In 2001 SEGA admitted the failure of Dreamcast, and announced that it was leaving the console business. Since then, SEGA has only been a game-developing company and not a console manufacturer.

After beating SEGA twice, Sony stood alone as the market leader of the U.S. video game industry. Sony did not rest on its laurels, however, and in 2000 it announced its brand-new console, the PlayStation 2. Able to support the games made for the original PlayStation, PlayStation 2 sold more than 10 million units in the United States in November 2001, before the Xbox became available.

Exhibit 7   Video Game Sales in the United States, 1998–2003

Year	Sales ($ billions)	Change in Sales Volume (%)	Change in Units Sold (%)
2003	$14.0		
2002	10.3	+9.57%	+8.21%
2001	9.4	+9.30	+6.33
2000	8.6	+4.88	+3.42
1999	8.2	+6.49	+4.17
1998	7.7		

Sources: The NPD Group/NPD Funworld.

In 2001 Nintendo rejoined the video game race with Sony by introducing the new family console, GameCube, and the new pocket system, Game Boy Advance, in the United States.

After several lessons in failure from SEGA and its own history, Nintendo decided to enter the video game market through a niche market rather than competing directly with Sony's PlayStation 2. While most game companies had chosen not to compete directly with Sony, Microsoft introduced its Xbox to challenge Sony's stable market position and profit from this consistently growing industry (Exhibit 7).

Entering the new millennium, the number of U.S. households with a video game console had risen by 13 percent since 1995—from 31.4 million to 35.5 million in 2001. Video games have also penetrated urban areas and became popular among minorities and homes without children. Contrary to popular belief regarding the demographics of video game players, studies showed that video gaming was primarily an adult-oriented form of entertainment. Video games were no longer child's play; gamers were predominantly adults, both male and female. Research conducted by the Entertainment Software Association in 2004 revealed that 75 percent of console game players were male and 25 percent were female, 46 percent were under 18 years old, 35 percent were 18 to 35, 11 percent were 36 to 45 years old, and 8 percent were over 46.

Competition

Microsoft's Xbox had two competitors: the major one was Sony's PlayStation 2, and the minor one was Nintendo's GameCube. (See Exhibits 8 and 9 for the financial statements of Sony and Nintendo.) Since SEGA had withdrawn from the video game console market, it would not be a major competitor for Microsoft's Xbox.

Exhibit 8   Sony Corporation Income Statements, 2001–2003
($ millions)

	2003	2002	2001
Revenue	$63,264.0	$57,117.0	$58,518.0
Cost of goods sold	40,672.0	34,993.0	38,901.0
Gross profit	22,592.0	22,124.0	19,617.0
Gross profit margin	35.7%	38.7%	33.5%
SG&A expense	15,402.0	16,612.0	13,071.0
Depreciation & amortization	5,621.0	4,498.0	4,743.0
Operating income	1,569.0	1,014.0	1,803.0
Operating margin	2.5%	1.8%	3.1%
Nonoperating income	379.0	(301.0)	79.0
Nonoperating expenses	231.0	275.0	344.0
Income before taxes	1,717.0	438.0	1,771.0
Income taxes	684.0	491.0	924.0
Net income after taxes	$ 1,033.0	$ (53.0)	$ 847.0

Source: Sony Corporation annual reports.

Exhibit 9   Nintendo Corporation Income Statements, 2001–2003
($ millions)

	2003	2002	2001
Revenue	$4,206.5	$4,183.3	$3,661.2
Cost of goods sold	2,574.3	2,522.7	2,204.3
Gross profit	1,632.2	1,660.6	1,456.9
Gross profit margin	38.8%	39.7%	39.8%
SG&A expense	796.8	762.3	786.4
Depreciation & amortization	—	—	—
Operating income	835.4	898.3	670.5
Operating margin	19.9%	21.5%	18.3%
Nonoperating income	312.9	527.7	867.1
Nonoperating expenses	202.8	46.2	202.5
Income before taxes	945.5	1,379.8	1,335.0
Income taxes	383.6	560.5	572.7
Net income after taxes	$ 561.9	$ 819.3	$ 762.3

Source: Nintendo Corporation annual reports.

Nintendo   Nintendo introduced two new gaming systems in 2001, a console and a pocket system. The GameCube, the console, had games that appealed to young players who were less than 20 years old through cute graphics and rich content. Every published game was subject to strict quality control by Nintendo Corporation. Although the GameCube had only one-sixth the number of titles of PlayStation 2, each game was high quality. Nintendo's pocket system was Game Boy Advance, a portable console that appealed to school students. Most of Game Boy Advance's games were easy to play and contained less violence than the games of other consoles. Both of Nintendo's consoles were successful in their own niche markets, the youth market. On average, Nintendo's major consumers were much younger than those of PlayStation 2. After unsuccessfully competing with Sony for six years, Nintendo had decided not to compete directly with this new giant. It focused instead on the young consumer and did well in this niche market. Compared with PlayStation 2's games for teenagers, most of Nintendo's games were easier to design. Nintendo also saved significant cost by developing both the system and the software. Thus, Nintendo made considerable profits in the niche segment, and monopolized the portable console market.

Sony   Sony Entertainment Corporation America (SECA) used a "Trojan horse" strategy to release the moderately priced PlayStation 2. This new console would be the hub of a complete entertainment concept that merged television viewing, movie watching, video game playing, and Internet surfing into one device. In order to fulfill this strategy, Sony designed a new console that was not simply a video game player.

PlayStation 2 was the first console in the 21st century that could play DVD movies. In November 2000 the PlayStation 2 was available for $349.99, a low price compared with other DVD players. Thus, by the end of 2000, only two months after the new console was launched, PlayStation 2 had already sold more than 1 million units in the U.S. market. According to research by NPD FunWorld in December 2000, 32 percent of PlayStation 2 buyers treated this new system as only a DVD player. The DVD player function, part of Sony's Trojan horse strategy, helped Sony sell its video game console to nongaming players.

PlayStation 2 was launched in the United States in November 2000, a year before the official launch of the Xbox. Unlike the launch of the original PlayStation, Sony offered only 19 games for its game console; however, the new PlayStation 2 was completely compatible with the original PlayStation. This meant that PlayStation 2 could not only play the 19 new games, but also play more than 700 original PlayStation games. Original PlayStation users were willing to purchase this new system because they didn't have to abandon their favorite old games. This backward-compatible design became another

selling point for PlayStation 2, adding to PlayStation 2's unique competitive advantage.

PlayStation 2 was also the first console with the ability to work with a hard drive and access a dial-up or broadband Internet connection. This design was one part of the Trojan horse concept. With the capability to expand this system, PlayStation 2 could do much more than other consoles. However, since both the hard drive and Internet access were optional accessories instead of built-in functions, they were not commonly applied. By the end of 2001, less than 3 percent of games supported the hard drive function. In addition, before the launch of Xbox, only 8 of 372 PlayStation 2 games could be played through the Internet.

The launch of PlayStation 2 was thought by industry observers to be well timed and well planned. One timing factor was seasonality; console sales more than tripled during November and December in the United States compared to other months of the year. According to research implemented by NPD FunWorld, PlayStation 2 was the top Christmas present that parents in North America wanted to buy for their children in 2000. Because of PlayStation 2's well-timed introduction during the holiday shopping season, by the end of the year its sales exceeded 1 million units and the console took 24 percent of the market share.

The second timing factor was competition. After SEGA's Dreamcast failed, there were no new products on the video game market for a long time. The appearance of PlayStation 2 offered consumers a chance to renew their gaming life with a new generation of video games. The emergence of PlayStation 2 was like a light in the darkness, and it caught everyone's eye.

The third timing factor was game development. Gaming developer companies depended on a good console in order to survive, and PlayStation 2 was the most attractive console. After selling for five years, the Nintendo 64 was already out of date, and no programmers wanted to develop new games for an old system. With sales of only 0.3 million units, the newcomer, SEGA Dreamcast, didn't sell well in the U.S. console market. There were no economies of scale for the unpopular consoles. PlayStation 2 was the only popular system at that time. Most gaming development companies believed that there were many potential business opportunities behind the PlayStation 2, since they had already had successful experiences with the PlayStation. Thus, PlayStation 2 won considerable contracts with gaming developers, and the number of its games quickly increased in the first quarter of 2001. The variety of games increased the sales of PlayStation 2 more than ever.

Although Sony's PlayStation 2 was largely successful, it had two significant shortcomings. The first was the Trojan horse strategy. The idea of selling a console as a home entertainment hub was a good one. However, Sony was a consumer electronics corporation and did not have many internal resources it could apply to capitalize on its Trojan horse plan. If Sony really wanted to make PlayStation 2 the home entertainment hub, it needed cooperation and resources from a third party, which would increase Sony's cost and risk. Since Sony was the current leader of the U.S. video game industry, it didn't put much effort into transforming PlayStation 2 from a video game console into a home entertainment hub. The second shortage was game development. Many game programmers complained that Sony had created insufficient tools to support PlayStation 2. Shinji Mikami, a seasoned game designer who created best-selling games for Dreamcast, Saturn, Nintendo 64, and PlayStation, said that PlayStation 2 was the most difficult system he had ever worked with. While most game developers recognized the powerful performance capability of the PlayStation 2, they also complained that the PlayStation 2 game-creation process was a nightmare for them.

Entry Wedges and Alternatives

In order to introduce the Xbox into the console market, Microsoft invested $300 million to design the console, $500 million in marketing, and $200 million to build the machines. For Bill Gates, the Xbox was the real "Trojan horse" for Microsoft. By selling the Xbox, Gates not only anticipated considerable profits in the growing video game industry, but expected to sell extra products and services related to the home entertainment industry.

Although Microsoft was not the first company to use the Trojan horse strategy to sell its console, Microsoft had more related products and services that could be added.

Release Timing   The idea of the Xbox had been initially proposed in March 1999, and was quickly approved by Bill Gates and Microsoft's board of directors within three months. According to Kevin Bachus, one of the Xbox creators, the Xbox could be released before the end of 2000, when Sony's PlayStation 2 was released. However, the Xbox was the first console that Microsoft designed and sold in the video game market, and top management teams believed that Microsoft required more time to evaluate the market, consumers, and competitors. Finally, they decided to postpone the release date until November 2001, a year after the release of PlayStation 2.

Another reason for the delay was the cost of the hardware. After evaluating the performance of PlayStation 2, the Xbox development team realized they needed a console with newer graphics technology and a higher capability processor to beat their strong competitor. In order to create an ultimate gaming system, the Xbox developers decided to put the most advanced units into the console. Since they had just been developed, these new units were expensive. However, after a few months, the price of the units could fall significantly due to economies of scale or the maturity of unit technology. For this reason, Microsoft decided to postpone the release date of the Xbox in order to possibly lower the cost of the units.

Price   In the U.S. console market, price alone was not a critical factor for consumers when making their purchasing decisions. Since video games were recreational products, most console buyers were less sensitive to the console's price than its features, quantity and quality of games, and their confidence in the products. For example, at the end of 2000 and the first three quarters of 2001, PlayStation 2 monopolized the family console market. Pricing was not important during this period in which one product, PlayStation 2, was clearly superior to its competitors. Consumers could only choose to buy it or not, rather than choose between PlayStation 2 and a different product.

On the other hand, price became a deciding factor for consumer purchasing decisions when there were two or more similar products existing in the same market. For example, since the market segment of Xbox was very similar to that of PlayStation 2, focusing on male consumers from age 15 to 35 and appealing to the concept of a home entertainment hub, the Xbox was sold with a price similar to the price of the PlayStation 2. To compete with the powerful newcomer, Sony cut the price of PlayStation 2 from $349.99 to $299.99 one month before the Xbox's official release. In response, Microsoft had no choice but to sell its Xbox for $299.99. According to Microsoft, the initial cost of the Xbox was estimated to be approximately $400. This meant that for each console sold, Microsoft incurred a $100 loss on its income statement. Microsoft understood this situation; however, it hoped to make the Xbox as popular as possible without worrying about the losses. As Nat Brown, one of the four Xbox creators, said:

> The goals of the Xbox are to make money, expand Microsoft's technology into the living room, and create the perception that Microsoft is leading the charge in the new era of consumer appliances. We are looking for long-term benefits, thus, we know that painful short-term money losses are inevitable.

Hardware   The Xbox was as outstanding as the developers expected. More than just a video game console, the Xbox could be used as another personal computer. The machine used a 733MHz microprocessor from Intel, which made the Xbox the first console containing a computer processor. The Xbox had a graphics chip from Nvidia that had three times more capacity than the graphics processing unit in PlayStation 2 and an 8-gigabyte hard drive from IBM, which was an add-on component for PlayStation 2. In addition, the Xbox had twice as much memory as PlayStation 2 and a built-in Ethernet card and DVD ROM. As many of these components were made by Microsoft's PC manufacturing partners—including Intel, Nvidia, and IBM—this tended to strengthen Microsoft's bargaining position in negotiations for component costs.

DVD Player   The Xbox had a DVD ROM which played the games and, like PlayStation 2, offered a DVD player kit. However, unlike PlayStation 2, the DVD player of the Xbox was not a default function, and Xbox owners had to spend an additional $29.99 to buy a DVD playback kit in order to play DVD movies on their Xbox. Microsoft cut the built-in DVD player function because it saved $25 in each Xbox produced. However, many Xbox purchasers later complained about the DVD design, feeling that the built-in DVD player function should be a basic part of new consoles. Therefore, the Xbox's DVD design frustrated some consumers.

Internet Connection   Microsoft believed that playing games through the Internet was the future trend of the video game industry, so it made the Ethernet card a built-in part of the Xbox. However, since it did not support a dial-up connection, the Xbox became a device that was designed only for users with broadband Internet access. The Xbox developers had three reasons for this broadband-only design. First, this design simplified the process for game developers, who would not have to worry about designing games for play over both phone lines and high-speed Internet connections such as cable modems or DSL. Second, it was a concept issue. As Ted Hase, one of the Xbox creators, said, "Putting a 56k modem on the Xbox would be akin to putting cloth seats in a Ferrari." Third, since PlayStation 2 provided both dial-up and Ethernet adapters, this was an important way to make the Xbox different from its competitors and prove the high performance of the Xbox. For these reasons, the developers did not add the phone-line modem in the Xbox. Unfortunately, at the end of 2002 only 15 percent of U.S. households had broadband Internet connections. However, Dataquest reported that the rate of broadband Internet use nearly tripled from 2001 to 2002. As of December 2003, about 21 percent of U.S. homes already had high-speed access. This figure translated to approximately 43 percent of the Internet-connected households in the United States. About 57 percent of the Internet-connected households remained dependent on narrowband connections of 56.6 kb/s or lower. According to a report by cNet, the number of U.S. homes with a broadband connection was forecasted to reach 33.5 million by the end of 2004, adding another 8.5 million households. Microsoft, which also operated the MSN Internet service business, believed that after some "blockbuster" online Xbox games became available, it could benefit from both online gaming and add-on Internet services such as e-mail, Web site hosting, and licensed downloads of music and other digital entertainment. (See Exhibit 10 for a comparison of online gaming platforms.)

Direct X   Although developing games for PlayStation 2 had been a nightmare for many programmers, the development process was easier for the Xbox because it involved the use of Microsoft's well-developed program Direct X as the major programming tool. Direct X was a collection of applications programming interfaces, or APIs, that enabled software developers to write code to exploit any type of PC hardware. The technology was crucial to the games business because it allowed software developers to standardize game programs. With the application of Direct X, it was easier for game programmers to design games for the Xbox than for PlayStation 2. Also, since Direct X became the programming standard for PC gaming developers, it was not very difficult for these companies to convert PC games into Xbox games. By using Direct X, Microsoft expected to attract plenty of software developers to design Xbox games or even change their developing platform from PlayStation 2 to the Xbox.

Expanding the Xbox's game titles would be a critical method for increasing Xbox sales. However, since PlayStation 2 had sold more than 8 million units and took more than 50 percent of the market share before the Xbox even joined the race, most game developers could not neglect this huge market. Thus, many developers designed games for PlayStation 2, and then transferred the same title into the Xbox's easier-designed platform. The number of the Xbox's games increased, but most of them were also published for the PlayStation 2 console with the same title and the same content. In addition, since these games were primarily designed for PlayStation 2, they tended not to be optimized for the Xbox platform in terms of performance and features.

Product Launch and Aftermath
On the night of November 14, 2001, Microsoft successfully launched the Xbox in New York City's Times Square. With the success of this first step, Bill Gates realized that the toughest and severest competition was just beginning between the three horses (PlayStation 2, the GameCube, and the Xbox) and the pony (the Game Boy Advance).

Since the launch of the console, the award-winning lineup of software for the Xbox had reached a number of key sales milestones. According to independent data from the NPD Group, the definitive source of sales and market data on the video game industry, the Xbox had sold more than 10 million units of software in the first eight months the console had been on the market in the United States. That's the most software ever sold for a new video game system in the United States in the same period of time.

In May 2002 all three major game console manufacturers announced price cuts. The Xbox, with a cut of $100, experienced the largest percentage gains, with sales having spiked approximately 131 percent in the United States within the first two months, according to NPD. However, initial market enthusiasm in the Xbox soon died down.

Although the Xbox offered the state-of-the-art of what game consoles could deliver and would pleasantly surprise its customers, the features were not the keys for Microsoft

Exhibit 10   Comparison of Online Gaming Platforms

Features	Xbox	PlayStation 2
Built-in Ethernet port	Yes	No—add-on, $40 or $20 with a console purchase
Built-in hard disk for content downloads and multiplayer games	Yes	No—add-on, $80 to $100
All online games under one service	Yes	No
One unique identity	One password for all games	Varies by publisher
Connection	Broadband	Broadband or 56k modem
Find friends across service	Yes	No
Worldwide matchmaking	Yes	Yes
Voice in all games	All games	SOCOM only
Single list for all games	Yes	No
Invite friends to your game	Yes	No
Find and join your friends	Yes	No
Parental controls	Yes	No
Content downloads	Yes	HDD required
Hardware price	Ethernet adapter included with Xbox hardware. Xbox Communicator (free with Xbox *Live* subscription)	Network adapter: $40 Headset: $10 when gamers purchase SOCOM ($59.99)
Service charge	Initial starter kit: $49.95 for one-year subscription, minigame(s) and an Xbox Communicator	Service pricing options determined by each publisher Pricing options determined by each publisher
Ranking against friends	Yes	Not available
Third-party developers	61	16
Number of launch titles	7	5

Source: Gamespot.com.

to attract consumers and beat opponents. During the second half of 2002, sales of the Xbox were well short of the launch team's forecasts. Microsoft announced that sales barely hit the bottom end of its previous forecast, and the company alerted suppliers that it was lowering sales projections for 2003 and, as a result, would buy fewer parts. Microsoft informed its Xbox parts suppliers not to expect any orders in the first half of 2003 so that the company could deplete existing console supplies. Nvidia, a key partner of Microsoft that made the Xbox's video controller, suffered the most. Adding to the soured relationship,

Microsoft and Nvidia were in court over a disagreement regarding the price Microsoft was supposed to pay per unit for the video controllers.

As of June 2003 Sony's PlayStation 2 had captured 74 percent of the market, leaving Nintendo's GameCube to split the remainder of the market with console newcomer Microsoft and its Xbox at 13 percent each. It was now a nearly $30 billion industry, which made it larger than the film entertainment business upon which most of its best-selling titles were based! As of May 2004, PlayStation 2 continued to dominate the market, with more than 70 million consoles sold worldwide, maintaining its market share lead of five times that of the Xbox or GameCube.

Looking Forward

Although the video game industry by 2004 was dominated by only a few major players, Microsoft remained keenly aware that the video gaming console business would be highly competitive and continue to be characterized by limited platform life cycles, frequent introductions of new hit titles, and the development of new technologies. (See Exhibit 11 for the best-selling game titles in the first quarter of 2004.) Industry observers felt that Microsoft would have to outdistance its competitors in terms of price, product quality and variety, timing of releases, and effectiveness of distribution and marketing.

As announced at the 10th Annual E3 Video-Game Convention in Los Angeles in May 2004, Sony cut the price of its PlayStation 2 console to under $150, matching Microsoft's earlier reduction in the price of its Xbox console. By contrast, Nintendo had been selling its GameCube console for $99 since 2003. To mark the 10th anniversary of its founding, the Entertainment Software Association (ESA), an industry trade group representing video and computer game manufacturers, asked gamers what they considered to be the three biggest advancements made by the game industry in the past 10 years. Ninety-one percent said the increased quality of game graphics represented the biggest advancement. Respondents also indicated that the following milestones were significant: the increase in the variety of content (37 percent); the introduction of multiplayer game playing (27 percent); and the introduction of better story lines and more character development into games (28 percent). Over half (53 percent) of all game players expressly stated they were currently playing games as much as or more than they did 10 years ago.

The ESA also asked respondents to pick the three most important goals for the industry in the coming decade. Not surprisingly, most often mentioned (87 percent) was to reduce the price of games. Other goals included offering additional levels, characters, and other content in games (53 percent); creating more games for women (42 percent); decreasing reliance on licensed content (i.e., from films) and increasing reliance on original stories (36 percent); offering more games for purchase via download (21 percent); and making more games playable online (17 percent). The three major video game platform manufacturers also announced that they intended to introduce new consoles in 2005 or 2006.

Microsoft's supreme capital resources, unsurpassed reputation, and immense dominance in the software industry may have a significant influence on its ability to enlist third-party game developers and equipment manufacturers for the Xbox and acquire some video game development companies. However, unlike its past ventures, battling for the living room has been a fundamentally different kind of business for Microsoft. Would Bill Gates and his team be able to dominate the video game industry as they had previously done in their operating systems and software application markets? The answer seemed to depend on their future capability to set industry standards, dictate future strategic moves, and continue to manage "outside the box."

Exhibit 11   Best-Selling Video Game Titles Ranked by Total U.S. Units, 1st Quarter 2004

Rank	Title	Platform	Publisher	Release Date	ARP*
1	*NFL Street*	PlayStation 2	Electronic Arts	Jan. 04	$49
2	*Need Speed: Underground*	PlayStation 2	Electronic Arts	Nov. 03	49
3	*Ninja Gaiden*	Xbox	Tecmo	Mar. 04	50
4	*Pokémon Colosseum*	GameCube	Nintendo	Mar. 04	48
5	*Sonic Heroes*	GameCube	SEGA	Jan. 04	49
6	*MVP Baseball 2004*	PlayStation 2	Electronic Arts	Mar. 04	49
7	*Final Fantasy Crystal*	GameCube	Nintendo	Feb. 04	49
8	*Halo*	Xbox	Microsoft	Nov. 01	30
9	*Mario Kart: Double*	GameCube	Nintendo	Nov. 03	49
10	*Bond 007: Everything*	PlayStation 2	Electronic Arts	Feb. 04	49

*ARP = Average retail price

Source: NPD.com.

Endnotes

Alexander & Associates. 2001. Comparing generations of console gaming, www.alexassox.com.

Bishop, T. 2004. Video game console wars getting hotter, http://seattlepi.nwsource.com.

Boulding, A. 2002. State of the Xbox interview: Ed Fries, http://xbox.ign.com.

Chiu, B. 1998. *Microsoft Internet gaming zone: Fighter ace: Inside moves.* Redmond, WA: Microsoft Press.

DeMaria, R., & Wilson, J. L. 2002. *High score! The illustrated history of electronic games.* New York: McGraw-Hill Osborne Media.

Entertainment Software Associates. 2004. Demographic information, www.theesa.com.

Frederick, J. 2003. The console wars: Game on, www.time.com.

Games-Advertising.com. 2000. Gaming demographics: Gaming is an adult thing, www.games-advertising. com.

Gameinfowire.com. 2004. Americans playing more games, watching less movies and television, www.gameinfowire.com.

GIGnews.com. 2001. U.S. video game industry ahead of its game despite recession, www.gignews.com.

Herman, L. 1994. *Phoenix: The fall & rise of home videogames.* Union, NJ: Rolenta Press.

Herz, J. C. 1997. *Joystick nation: How videogames ate our quarters, won our hearts, and rewired our minds.* New York: Little, Brown.

Hesseldahl, A. 2001. Xbox success? Not so fast, www.forbes.com.

Hopkins, J. 2004. Other nations zip by USA in high-speed net race, www.usatoday.com.

Kent, S. L. 2001. *The ultimate history of video games.* Roseville, CA: Prima Publishing.

Ketupa.com. 2002. Media profiles of Microsoft, www.ketupa.net.

Kovsky, S. 2002. High-tech toys for your TV. Indianapolis: Que Publishing.

Microsoft. 2002. Microsoft's solution for Internet business helps build early Xbox success, www.microsoft.com.

NPD Group. 2004. The NPD Group reports console video games industry sales fall slightly in first quarter 2004 over same period last year, www.npd.com.

NPD Group. 2003. Annual 2002 U.S. video game sales break record, www.npd.com.

Poole, S. 2000. *Trigger happy: Videogames and the entertainment revolution.* New York: Arcade Publishing.

Redmond, W. 2002. Xbox hits major sales milestones for console and games, www.microsoft.com.

Redmond, W. 2002. New price is expected to expand market for world's most powerful video game console, www. microsoft.com.

Redmond, W. 2003. Xbox live bursts through 350,000-subscriber mark as players rush for fresh downloadable content, www.microsoft.com.

Sheff, D. 1993. *Game over: How Nintendo zapped an American industry, captured your dollars, & enslaved your children.* Collingdale, PA: Diane Publishing.

SINA.com. 2004. US broadband connection to reach 33.5 million homes in 2004, http://english.sina.com.

Takahashi, D. 2002. *Opening the Xbox.* Roseville, CA: Prima Publishing.

TeamXbox.com. 2002. Xbox sales soaring, http://news. teamxbox.com.

Thurrott, P. 2003. Xbox sales worse than expected, www. winnetmag.com.

Underdahl, B. 2002. *Xbox: Blow the lid off!* New York: McGraw-Hill Osborne Media.

Case 19   Schoolhouse Lane Estates*

The supply of grapes crushed in California's 2003 harvest was an all-time record and it followed a record 2002 harvest. Quality is excellent—yet thousands of acres of vines are being pulled up across California with replanting of fruit trees. The *Santa Rosa Press Democrat* reported that Mondavi was cutting 10 percent of its workforce due to a reduced demand for wines selling above $25.00 per bottle at retail and to a projected quarterly operating loss for the first time since they became a public company in 1993. Several small wineries here in Sonoma County, notably DeLoach and Roshambo, have gone bankrupt in the last year. How are things going for you on the East Coast, Jan?

Janess (Jan) Thaw had trouble responding to the information she had just received from her cousin, Stan White, during their telephone conversation in late May 2004. She had recently prepared a business plan for the expansion of her Schoolhouse Lane Estates winery, located in Cutchogue on the North Fork of Long Island. Her plans included the purchase of grape-growing acreage as well as expansion of the winery and construction of a retail store, new tasting room, and renovation of a special events facility. The estimated cost of these initiatives was $2.4 million and new construction would take approximately a year to complete. Her cousin Stan's information created a wave of uncertainty concerning not only these plans, but also the outlook for her current business strategy. Regardless of the financing options available to her, Jan knew that she'd first have to get the strategy right.

Company History

Jan and her twin brother Nick grew up on a 35-acre potato farm adjacent to Schoolhouse Lane, located on the North Fork of Long Island. Owned by her parents, the farm barely provided for family living expenses. While her father Harry plowed the fields, her mother Suzanne taught fourth grade at a nearby public school.

The experience of growing up on a farm had a very different impact on the adult lifestyles of the children. Jan loved the land. She enjoyed walking the fields with her Dad and seeing the animals that lived on the land, especially the birds nesting in the tall oaks on the periphery of the family property.

Jan attended the agricultural school at Cornell University. She worked during the summer at small wineries in

the Finger Lakes region in upstate New York. Upon graduation in 1985, she was offered an assistant winemaker position at the Glenora Winery in Hammondsport, New York. For three years she experienced all aspects of the winemaking process and saw a chance to combine her love for the land with a career path in this industry.

By contrast, her brother Nick, an avid reader and athlete, could not wait to leave the farm for college. With a full athletic scholarship to Yale, Nick thrived in what he thought was a "big city" (New Haven, Connecticut). After completing his BA in economics, he then went on to Columbia University for an MBA with a concentration in finance.

A few years later Harry and Suzanne told their children that they were ready to retire and move to Sedona, Arizona. They sold their farm to Jan and Nick for one dollar in 1988 and headed west.

In January 1989 Jan and Nick each unexpectedly inherited $3 million after the death of their uncle Garry. They had very different uses for these funds. Jan paid off her student loans and immediately embarked on a long-held plan to convert the potato fields to the growing of wine grapes. Nick paid off his loans and started a financial consulting firm for private equity investors in Manhattan. Although they spoke often on the phone, Nick had not been out to the farm for more than three years. Jan would occasionally meet him for dinner in Manhattan.

During the spring of 1989 Jan planted 20 acres of grapevines on the property and named her new business Schoolhouse Lane Estates. By fall 1994 her first harvest was completed and the grapes were crushed at a local winery. Production was 60 tons of grapes, resulting in 5,000 cases of bottled wine. Within six months, they were all sold locally to restaurants, catering firms, and local businesses for gifts and promotions. Revenues from cases sold were just over $250,000. The business seemed poised for growth.

Schoolhouse Lane Estates' wines—Cabernet Sauvignon, Merlot (red varietals), Meritage (a blend of red varietals), and Chardonnay (white wine)—were well received on their introduction to the local marketplace. Jan sold her wines at retail prices ranging from $10 per bottle for Merlot ($120 per 12-bottle case) to $36 per bottle for the Meritage ($432 per case). As demand grew, Jan decided to operate her own winery. There was a small winery on six acres of land just east of her vineyards. She had been speaking with the owner and sensed that he was ready to retire and move to Weaverville, North Carolina. After only three meetings, they agreed upon the terms of a sale and in the fall of 1996, Jan was now the proud owner of a winery. She invested $2.2 million, financed with a mortgage from a local Long Island bank, and was ready to oversee her first wine production in the fall of 1997. Having expanded its

*This case was prepared by Professors Raymond H. Lopez of Pace University and Armand Gilinsky, Jr., at Sonoma State University as a basis for class discussion rather than to illustrate either effective or ineffective handling of an administrative situation. All individuals and events have been disguised at the request of the host organization.

acreage, producing quality grapes, and using grape purchases from other vineyards, the renamed Schoolhouse Lane Estates generated just over $1.5 million in revenue.

Over the next five years through 2002, Schoolhouse Lane Estates expanded its presence in the local wine markets. About 35 percent of sales were to off-premises accounts, such as wholesalers and retailers, and 45 percent to on-premises accounts, such as restaurants and caterers. These trade intermediaries handled her products before they were resold to the final consumer, with a retail markup of 100 percent. Direct sales to consumers at retail prices by way of the tasting room accounted for the remaining 20 percent of Schoolhouse Lane's sales. Product acceptance translated into growing net revenues (Exhibit 1). Although her operating expenses for marketing and sales had grown rapidly, Jan felt that these expenditures were needed to differentiate her portfolio of fine wines from competitors' offerings and to stimulate demand from trade intermediaries.

Schoolhouse Lane's balance sheets (Exhibit 2) and statements of cash flow (Exhibit 3) reflected her efforts as well as the challenges of growing her business. Most significant among these challenges was the rapid and

continuing expansion of inventories, as premium red wines and red wine blends require longer aging periods in oak barrels. Growing inventories were financed with an expanding line of credit from Goose Creek Savings, a local lending bank. Goose Creek Savings, however, maintained a lending limit for a business her size of up to $3 million based on the replacement value of fixed assets. Goose Creek Savings was also financing a small percentage of her inventories through a revolving line of credit. Either a larger bank would be needed within the year, or perhaps a more permanent source of financing would be needed. Laurel Durst, Jan's accountant and financial manager, had recently been exploring a number of working capital financing options with the North Fork Bancorp.

Evolution of Long Island's Wine Industry

How did it all begin? A small band of hesitant artisans and amateurs had pioneered the wine industry in converted barns and potato fields in the 1970s, in many cases because they sought a simpler agrarian lifestyle, or so they thought. In less than a third of a century, the profile of Long Island

Exhibit 1   Schoolhouse Lane Estates Income Statements, 1999–2003

($ thousands)

	2003	2002	2001	2000	1999
Net Sales	$5,416.4	$4,924.7	$4,296.6	$3,646.5	$3,040.4
Cost of Goods Sold	3,566.2	3,152.6	2,744.5	2,318.8	1,788.6
Gross Profit	1,850.2	1,772.1	1,552.1	1,327.7	1,251.8
Operating Expenses					
Marketing & Advertising	145.2	130.9	116.6	101.2	89.1
Selling & Administration	935.0	811.8	711.7	572.0	358.6
Total Operating Expenses	1,080.2	942.7	828.3	673.2	447.7
Operating Income (EBIT)	770.0	829.4	723.8	654.5	804.1
Interest Expense[a]	376.2	326.7	295.9	282.7	259.6
Net Income before Taxes	393.8	502.7	427.9	371.8	544.5
Income Taxes[b]	157.3	201.3	171.6	148.5	217.8
Net Income (Loss)	$ 236.5	$ 301.4	$ 256.3	$ 223.3	$ 326.7
Number of cases sold	36,109	32,831	28,644	24,310	20,269
Average wholesale FOB price per 12-bottle case	$150.00	$150.00	$150.00	$150.00	$150.00
Average retail price per 12-bottle case	$300.00	$300.00	$300.00	$300.00	$300.00

[a]Prime + 2% on average balance for a line of credit.

[b]Federal and state income tax rate of 40%.

Exhibit 2   Schoolhouse Lane Estates Balance Sheets, 1999–2003
($ thousands)

	2003	2002	2001	2000	1999
Assets					
Current Assets					
Cash	$ 244.2	$ 218.9	$ 231.0	$ 216.7	$ 210.1
Accounts Receivable	268.4	277.2	294.8	269.5	235.4
Inventories	3,279.1	2,839.1	2,568.5	2,183.5	1,925.0
Prepaid and Other Expenses	48.4	44.0	46.2	41.8	40.7
Total Current Assets	3,840.1	3,379.2	3,140.5	2,711.5	2,411.2
Property, Plant and Equipment	3,578.3	3,440.8	3,291.2	3,254.9	3,172.4
Less: Accumulated Depreciation and Amortization	216.7	191.4	183.7	191.4	216.7
Net Property, Plant and Equipment	3,361.6	3,249.4	3,107.5	3,063.5	2,955.7
Other Assets (Net)	16.5	15.4	16.5	15.4	13.2
Total Assets	$7,218.2	$6,644.0	$6,264.5	$5,790.4	$5,380.1
Liabilities and Capital					
Current Liabilities					
Accounts Payable	$ 298.1	$ 256.3	$ 217.8	$ 194.7	$ 170.5
Accrued Expenses	268.4	222.2	193.6	169.4	150.7
Line of Credit (bank)[d]	1,282.6	999.9	955.9	757.9	565.4
LTD (current portion)	33.0	33.0	33.0	33.0	33.0
Total Current Liabilities	1,882.1	1,511.4	1,400.3	1,155.0	919.6
Long-Term Debt Mortgage[c]	2,288.0	2,321.0	2,354.0	2,381.5	2,429.9
Equity					
Class A Common[a]	1,661.0	1,661.0	1,661.0	1,661.0	1,661.0
Class B Common[b]	0.0	0.0	0.0	0.0	0.0
Retained Earnings (Loss)	1,387.1	1,150.6	849.2	592.9	369.6
Total Equity	3,048.1	2,811.6	2,510.2	2,253.9	2,030.6
Total Liabilities and Equity	$7,218.2	$6,644.0	$6,264.5	$5,790.4	$5,380.1

[d]Class B Common Stock—1 vote.
[c]Class A Common Stock—10 votes.
[a]Prime + 2% on average balance for line of credit.
[b]Long-term debt (mortgage) at 7%.

wine moguls had morphed to that of self-assured professionals backed by deep-pocketed investors who were also seeking a different lifestyle.

The migration to become owners of Long Island wineries was not unlike the one followed by "refugees" from the high-tech world of Silicon Valley, who bought or developed new Napa and Sonoma wineries in California in the late 1990s. Similar to what their California counterparts had accomplished in the prior decade, the showcase Long Island wineries of the early 2000s burst on the New York culinary scene by making prize-winning and sought-after wines. While the production of world-class

Exhibit 3   Schoolhouse Lane Estates Statements of Cash Flow, 2000–2003
($ thousands)

	2003	2002	2001	2000
Cash Flows from Operating Activities				
Net Income	$236.5	$301.4	$256.3	$223.3
Depreciation	25.3	7.7	34.1	24.2
Increase in Receivables (Net)	8.8	17.6	(25.3)	(34.1)
Increase in Inventories	(440.0)	(270.6)	(385.0)	(258.5)
Increase in Prepaid and Other Expenses	(4.4)	2.2	(4.4)	(1.1)
Increase in Accounts Payable	41.8	38.5	23.1	24.2
Increase in Accrued Expenses	46.2	28.6	24.2	18.7
Net Cash Provided (Used) by Operating Activities	(85.8)	125.4	(77.0)	(3.3)
Cash Flows from Investing Activities				
Purchase of Property, Plant and Equipment	(137.5)	(149.6)	(78.1)	(132.0)
Other Assets (Net)	(1.1)	1.1	(1.1)	(2.2)
Net Cash Used for Investing Activities	(138.6)	(148.5)	(79.2)	(134.2)
Cash Flows from Financing Activities				
Increase (Decrease) from Bank Line of Credit	282.7	44.0	198.0	192.5
Increase (Decrease) in Long-Term Debt (current portion)	0.0	0.0	0.0	0.0
Increase (Decrease) in Mortgage	(33.0)	(33.0)	(27.5)	(48.4)
Net Cash Provided (Used) in Financing Activities	249.7	11.0	170.5	144.1
Net Increase in Cash	25.3	(12.1)	14.3	6.6
Cash at the Beginning of the Year	218.9	231.0	216.7	210.1
Cash at the End of the Year	244.2	218.9	231.0	216.7

wines was still said to be some years away, the money, the wine-making talent, and the will to make them were now in place. It seemed just a matter of time before Long Island winemakers were regarded with the same status as their California counterparts, according to the Long Island Wine Council.

The land of the North Fork, where most wineries were located, was flat to slightly rolling, planted not only with grapes but also with potatoes, sod, and fruit trees. Craggy oaks shaded the villages of Greenport, Southold, and Cutchogue, small and quaint with 200-year-old houses and 100-year-old churches and plaques to show where the Pilgrims' punishment stocks used to stand on the village green. The water was never more than a few miles away, as the Long Island Sound lay to the north, and Peconic Bay and the Atlantic Ocean to the south.[1]

From its humble beginnings in 1973, the Long Island wine industry had developed steadily with growing numbers of vineyards, wineries, and acreage to produce quality wine products. Long Island wineries produced a broad variety of red varietals including Cabernet Sauvignon, Cabernet Franc, Merlot, Pinot Noir, and Shiraz, as well as white varietals such as Chardonnay, Gewürztraminer, Riesling, and Sauvignon Blanc. A few wineries, like Schoolhouse Lane, produced a Bordeaux-style blend of red wines called Meritage. All Long Island winery owners and their trade association, the Long Island Wine Council, anticipated continued growth and expansion into the 21st century.

Grape growing and wine production were located primarily on the eastern end of Long Island, which jutted more than 100 miles into the Atlantic Ocean, parallel to the coastlines of Connecticut and Rhode Island. The North and South Forks of eastern Long Island were a maritime region with a unique combination of climate, soil characteristics, and growing conditions ideal for quality wine production.

Bays bordering the North and South Forks insulated the vineyards and trapped moist warm air. Along with rich sandy glacial soil, this combination created the perfect environment for growing grapes. Growing seasons were quite long (averaging approximately 200 days) and relatively mild winters encouraged the planting of Europe's noble vinifera grapes on almost all acres planted.

The Long Island wineries represented three appellations (American Viticultural Areas or AVA) approved by the Bureau of Alcohol, Tobacco and Firearms (BATF)—the North Fork of Long Island, the Hamptons, and, as of April 2001, Long Island AVA. This latest designation allowed for further expansion beyond the two forks of Long Island's east end, while at the same time protecting the overall integrity of the region's wines.[2]

New York State ranked third nationally in wine production. According to the New York Farm Bureau, the state had almost 1,000 family-owned vineyards that produced 175,000 tons of grapes annually—a $40 million industry. There were 160 wineries in the four main wine-producing regions of the state: the Finger Lakes, the Lake Erie region, the Hudson River Valley, and the Long Island region. All told, these regions produced over 100 million bottles of wine each year and attracted approximately one million tourists.[3]

Long Island wines were sold primarily in the New York metropolitan region. Products were found at most vineyards and in local wine retail stores, as well as in a broad variety of restaurants and catering establishments. Quality had been enhanced, resulting in higher ratings by wine magazines and in national taste tests, and the market broadened up and down the East Coast. Large regional distributors had in recent years shown a growing interest in carrying these wines. Several wineries already distributed their products in Florida, California, and Texas.

Anticipating that this trend would accelerate as knowledge spread of the rising quality of Long Island wines, the Long Island wine producers hoped that recent support from a New York U.S. congressional delegation would help to overturn the ban on direct shipments outside the state.[4] New York remained the nation's largest wine producing state that did not allow direct shipments. Current law prohibited wine producers from shipping wine directly to consumers in other states. Thirteen states already had reciprocal wine shipment laws enabling out-of-state shipments of wine, and eight had laws allowing the direct shipment of wine to customers.

Recent Developments and Industry Maturation

By 2003 Long Island boasted 56 vineyards and 30 wineries.[5] The remaining 26 vineyard owners who lacked production capacity either sold their grapes to other wineries or contracted with other wineries to produce wine.

A sure sign of the maturation of the industry on Long Island came with the announcement of a custom-crush facility to be constructed in Mattituck. This facility would cater to independent vineyard owners and grape buyers who lacked their own wine-making facilities.[6] The new custom-crush venture was led by Russell Hearn, the winemaker at Pellegrini Vineyards, along with investors Mark Lieb, a Connecticut money manager and owner of the 50-acre Lieb Vineyard, and Bernard Sussman, also a money manager and an associate of Lieb. The partners expected to fund 40 to 50 percent of the new winery with equity, borrowing the rest from a Long Island bank.

"The primary purpose of this venture is to make wines for a number of small and large producers which choose not to, or are unable to, build their own wineries," Hearn said. "Our service would allow someone to have small amounts of wine made and bring in their own consultant [winemaker] to set the style. The number of wineries that offered custom services in the past are approaching their maximum," Hearn added. Moreover, vineyards for commercial wine production in Long Island were expected to double in the next two decades, further expanding the customer base.[7]

The Long Island wineries drew more than 500,000 visitors in 2003 for wine tours. Although traffic congestion was increasing on the two roads that fed the North Fork, some locals felt that the trade-off was worth the price. Several local residents credited the vineyards as having preserved open space that might otherwise have been developed for housing.[8]

Wine Production in the United States

The internal structure of the U.S. wine industry similarly underwent fundamental changes after the early 1980s. In terms of product, the most significant developments were observed in table wine. After 1992, table wines represented the largest segment of production and value of shipments, and accounted for more than 85 percent of total shipments annually. At the same time, table wine products responded to changes in the tastes and preferences of consumers for higher-quality premium wines.

Grapes used in the production of table wines were of varying quality. Varietals were delicate thin-skinned grapes whose vines usually took approximately four years to begin bearing fruit. As defined by the "truth in labeling" standards of the Bureau of Alcohol, Tobacco, and Firearms, one varietal—the name of a single grape—had to be used if more than 75 percent of the wine was derived from grapes of that variety, and the entire 75 percent was grown in the labeled appellation of origin. Appellation denoted that "at least 75 percent of a wine's volume was derived from fruit or agricultural products and grown in the place or region indicated."[9] Developing the typical varietal characteristics that resulted in enhanced flavor, taste, and finish could take another two to three years after the four years required for newly planted vines to bear fruit. These additional growing periods, in the pursuit of enhanced quality and value, increased both investment levels and operating expenses.

The wine industry was capital intensive. In addition to land and vineyards, a fully integrated firm needed investments in crushing facilities, fermentation tanks, barrels for aging their product, and warehouses to store the bottled and cased wine. Ownership was not essential for any of these activities. However, to control the quality and quantity of production, these investments became essential as a firm developed its brands and expanded its markets.

Since the wine industry was inherently capital intensive, as well as seasonal and cyclical, winery owners generally experienced low profit margins and limited options for outside capital, according to Dan Aguilar of Silicon Valley Bank, a major lender to the wine industry in Napa and Sonoma counties in California. Even under the best of conditions, working capital was under some pressure. Winery owners typically sought to fund continuing operations and business growth/inventory growth from limited retained earnings and bank debt, while at the same time satisfy the voracious appetites of their wineries for funds to finance some mixture of vineyards, production facilities, equipment, barrels, and tasting room and visitor facilities.[10]

Business risks were also substantial. Weather conditions could affect the quality and quantity of grape production. Insect damage and disease could affect the vines. Replanting of new vines required four to five years before commercial quantities of grapes could be expected.

In the fall of the year, usually late September to early November, depending on the weather, grapes were picked and carefully brought from the fields to the crushing facility. There was only one crop per year and crushing took from one to two months. Consequently, the investment in this facility stood idle at least 10 months of the year. Since all the grapes in a region matured at approximately the same time, there was no way to rent out crushing capacity to other wineries at other times of the year.

After crushing, the juice was pumped into the fermentation tanks. These stainless steel vessels were temperature controlled to balance the heat generated by the natural fermentation process. Fermentation lasted only a few weeks after the crush, so this investment was also idle more than 85 percent of the time.

From the fermentation tanks, the wine was pumped into oak barrels for aging. These barrels were expensive, costing $600 to $700 each. Due to quality concerns, they were used for only four or five years at which time their value was negligible (some were cut in half and sold as planters). A barrel-aging facility was a large open space that also had to be climate controlled. During the aging process, some wine was lost due to evaporation through the

porous oak barrel. Every two weeks each barrel was refilled up to 3 inches from its top. For premium red wines that aged in barrels for two years or longer, about 5 percent of the original wine was typically lost to evaporation.

Table wines were defined as those with 7 to 14 percent alcohol content by volume and were traditionally consumed with food. In contrast, other wine products such as sparkling wine (champagnes), wine coolers, pop wines, and fortified wines were typically consumed as stand-alone beverages. Table wines that retailed for less than $3 per 750 ml bottle were generally considered to be generic or "jug" wines, while those selling for more than $3 per bottle were considered premium wines.

Premium wines generally had a vintage date on their labels. This designation signified that the product had been made with at least 95 percent of the grapes harvested, crushed and fermented in the calendar year shown on the label, and used grapes from an appellation of origin (i.e., Napa Valley, Sonoma Valley, Central Coast in California; North Fork, the Hamptons, or Long Island AVA on Long Island). Within the premium wine category, a number of market segments emerged based on retail price points. "Popular premium" wines generally sold for $3 to $7 per bottle, while "super premium" wines retailed for $7 to $14. The "ultra premium" category sold for $14 to $20 per bottle, while any retail price above $20 per bottle was considered by the industry to be "luxury premium."

Changing Dynamics of the U.S. Wine Market

The value of alcoholic and nonalcoholic beverages consumed by Americans grew modestly from 1995 to 2002, according to figures compiled in *Adams' Wine Handbook, 2003*. For purposes of comparison, the largest beverage category was soft drinks, which in 2002 achieved almost double the dollar value of the next largest category, coffee. The consumption of wine produced domestically, as well as imports, grew steadily over the same period, but its volume remained significantly smaller, at less than 4 percent of soft drink volume in 2002. Wine consumption increased by 2.8 percent per year since 1996, trailing only bottled water at 10.8 percent per year and hard cider (an alcoholic beverage) at 8.8 percent per year. By contrast, overall beverage consumption grew at only 1.8 percent per year from 1996 to 2002. On a per capita basis, wine consumption rose steadily from 1.8 gallons per person per year in 1996, to just over 2.0 gallons in 2002.

Total wine consumption in the United States also reached an all-time high in 2002. At 595 million gallons, it exceeded the record consumption of 587 million gallons reached in 1986 (Exhibit 4). From those peak years in the mid-1980s, total consumption as well as per capita consumption trended downward for more than a decade. Since the early 1990s growth rebounded to record consumption and sales levels for table wine (Exhibit 5).

Exhibit 4   U.S. Wine Consumption, 1980–2002 (estimated)

Years	Total Wine (millions of gallons)[1]	Total Wine (per capita)[3]	Total Table Wine (millions of gallons)[2]	Total Table Wine (per capita)[3]
2002 (est.)	595	2.06	532	1.84
2001	561	1.96	503	1.76
2000	558	1.97	498	1.76
1999	551	2.02	482	1.76
1998	526	1.95	466	1.72
1997	520	1.94	461	1.72
1996	505	1.90	443	1.67
1995	469	1.79	408	1.56
1994	459	1.77	395	1.52
1993	449	1.74	381	1.48
1992	476	1.87	405	1.59
1991	466	1.85	394	1.56
1990	509	2.05	423	1.70
1989	524	2.11	432	1.74
1988	551	2.24	457	1.86
1987	581	2.39	481	1.98
1986	587	2.43	487	2.02
1985	580	2.43	378	1.58
1984	555	2.34	401	1.69
1983	528	2.25	402	1.71
1982	514	2.22	397	1.71
1981	506	2.20	387	1.68
1980	480	2.11	360	1.58

[1]All wine types including sparkling wine, dessert wine, vermouth, and other special natural and table wines.

[2]Table wines include all "still" wines not over 14% alcohol content.

[3]Per capita consumption in gallons based on the resident population of the United States.

Sources: The Wine Institute, www.wineinstitute.org; Gomberg, Fredricksen & Associates.

Reflecting the changing tastes and preferences of the American consumer, the growth performance of table wine sales by color also underwent dramatic changes. In 1991 white wine volume accounted for almost one-half of all wine sold in supermarkets, which sold 78 percent of all wine purchased in the United States (the remaining 22 percent of wine shipments were sold through specialty wine shops, tasting rooms, the Internet, or on-premises accounts such as hotels and restaurants). Approximately one-third of total wine sales by dollars in 1991 were blush/rosé, while only 17 percent were red (Exhibit 6). By 2003 the market share of white wine and blush/rosé had declined to about 40 percent and 21 percent of total sales, respectively, but red wine grew to nearly 40 percent. Still, most red wines were more expensive to produce and thus sold for higher prices than either white or blush/rosé. The net result was that revenues at the wholesale and consumer levels had grown more rapidly than the increase in case wine volume that was produced and then sold.

The latest forecasts from *Impact Databank 2003* indicated that strong advances from imported wine could be

Exhibit 5 Wine Sales in the United States (Millions of gallons): Domestic Shipments and Foreign Producers Entering U.S. Distribution Channels, 1991–2003 (estimated)

Year	Table Wine[1]	Dessert Wine[2]	Champagne, Sparkling Wine	Total Wine	Total Retail Value (in $ billions)
2003 (est.)	558	41	28	627	$21.6
2002	532	37	27	595	21.1
2001	503	34	25	561	19.8
2000	499	32	28	558	19.0
1999	475	31	37	543	18.1
1998	466	31	29	526	17.0
1997	461	29	29	519	16.1
1996	439	31	29	500	14.3
1995	404	30	30	464	12.2
1994	394	33	31	458	11.5
1993	381	35	33	449	11.0
1992	405	37	33	476	11.4
1991	394	39	33	466	10.9

[1]Includes all still wines not over 14% alcohol; excludes Canadian Coolers (made from malt).

[2]Includes all still wines over 14% alcohol.

Source: The Wine Institute, http://www.wineinstitute.org.

Exhibit 6 Table Wine Volume Share by Color (in U.S. supermarkets)

Color	1991	1995	2002	2003
Red	17%	25%	39%	40%
White	49	41	40	40
Blush/Rosé	34	34	21	20
Total	100%	100%	100%	100%

Source: U.S. supermarket data from ACNielsen Beverage Alcohol Team.

expected to drive much of the growth for the U.S. wine market through 2010. Forecast growth in consumption of domestic wines was 3.3 percent to 193 million cases in 2003, 198 million cases in 2005, and about 211 million cases by 2010. For imports, a 12 percent increase to 65 million cases was projected for 2003, and case volume was projected to reach 90 million cases by 2010. California's dominant U.S. market share of domestic table wines was forecast to slip from 67 percent in 2003 to 63 percent in 2010, due in part to strong growth from imported varietals such as Shiraz/Syrah, Chardonnay, and Pinot Grigio. *Impact Databank* also forecast that the share of red wine in the U.S. market was expected to continue to gain at a more rapid pace than white or blush wine. Late projections held that red wine consumption would grow to 98 million cases in 2003 and 128 million cases by 2010. Projected annual compound growth rates for red wines were 5.9 percent for 2000–2005, and 3.5 percent for 2005–2010. White wine consumption was forecast to grow to 90 million cases by 2003 and 100 million cases by 2010. This translated into annual compound growth rates for white wines of 4.3 percent for 2000–2005, and further 1 percent annual increases from 2005 to 2010.

Competition

Since the 1960s there had been a substantial increase in the number of firms producing wine products in the United

States. From hundreds of companies in the 1970s, the number exceeded 1,800 wineries by the turn of the century. Most were relatively small, each of the 50 states already had at least one winery, and about 800 were located in California. By 2004 the 20 largest firms produced approximately 90 percent of all American wines by volume and 85 percent by value at wholesale.[11]

The competitive structure of the industry could be classified into 3 types of stand-alone wineries: public conglomerates, private conglomerates, and multi-industry firms (primarily public). The largest publicly traded winery was Robert Mondavi, along with Chalone, a much smaller firm. Privately held wineries included the industry giant E&J Gallo, Kendall-Jackson, The Wine Group, and more than a thousand small- to medium-size wineries. The final group of competitors consisted of large publicly traded multi-industry firms. These included Allied Domecq, Brown Forman (Wine Estates Division), Foster's Group (Beringer Blass), Constellation Brands (Canandaigua Division), Diageo (Chateau and Estates Division), Fortune Brands, Louis Vuitton Moët Hennessey (LVMH), and UST (formerly known as U.S. Tobacco).

In addition to domestic competition, a growing percentage share of the U.S. wine market had been gained by imports. In addition to the traditional "Old World" supplies from France, Italy, Germany, Spain, and Portugal, a new group of countries had experienced growing acceptance of their wine production. Australia, Chile, and Argentina (the "New World" suppliers) increased their market share in the last decade, offering high-quality wines at very competitive prices.

Consolidation among wineries began to accelerate in the early 1990s, as larger producers decided to purchase smaller ones in order to achieve greater economies of scale in marketing and economies of scope in gaining access to more varied channels of distribution. These larger wineries could then become more effective in negotiating favorable selling terms with an increasingly small number of large regional distributors.[12] The "consolidators" were generally public firms that were able to offer predominantly family-run wine businesses a means to greater liquidity of their investment in larger, more diversified firms. Concurrently, the attractiveness of wine production across the United States resulted in a growing number of entrepreneurs purchasing or starting new, small operations.

Jan Meets with Her Team

The day after her conversation with cousin Stan, Jan set up a meeting with her operations manager Dan Henning and her accountant Laurel Durst. She also invited the executive director of the 14-year-old Long Island Wine Council, Nanette Hansen, to get her broader perspective of local conditions.

Jan began the meeting by presenting her plans for the expansion:

We have an opportunity to purchase additional grape-producing acreage across Schoolhouse Lane from our vineyard, that is, to buy 28 acres for $900,000. We have been farming that land and now have the opportunity to purchase it. The winery needs expanded capacity, and I have estimates between $800,000 and $900,000 for the land. Our tasting room is overcrowded—even on weekdays—and its expansion would require $250,000. Finally, many of our neighboring competitors already have facilities for special events (weddings, birthday parties, anniversaries, business meetings, etc.), but I have a design in mind that is expected to cost $450,000. I estimate another $700,000 to $800,000 in working capital will be necessary as well, bringing the total investment up to about $2.4 million.

Dan supported Jan's plans:

The winery is operating at 100 percent capacity and I still had to ship some grapes over to the custom-crush facility in Mattituck. I'd like to bring all our production back here under our complete control.

The Schoolhouse Lane team was eager to hear Nanette's perspective, as she represented a broader regional industry viewpoint. Nanette was prepared for their questions, distributing copies of the information on Long Island wineries (see Exhibits 7 and 8) to the rest of the group.

At the Long Island Wine Council, our prime focus is the local producers and their markets. I can't tell you much about conditions in California such as how long the "glut" of grapes will last, but we have studied the markets extensively in the East Coast.

On the supply side, acreage and production have grown steadily over the last seven years through the harvest of 2003. Grape quality has risen consistently and yields per acre have grown slowly. A number of new owners have come to the area, bringing strong financial support to many vineyards and wineries. On the demand side, a major segment is event driven—celebrations of either a personal or business nature. For many local wineries, this represents 40 percent or more of their revenues and any weakness in pricing or volume will be felt quickly on cash inflows.

There has been a weakening in the last three years in business spending for events. While volume has held up reasonably well, the price points have deteriorated—moderately priced premium products ($10–$15 per bottle) have been substituted for deluxe premium wines ($25 and up per bottle). Corporate and business budgets have been tightened and it is unlikely that this

Exhibit 7   Long Island Wine Industry Statistics
(Selected years)

Year	Number of Vineyards	Number of Wineries	Planted Acres	Total Acres Owned	Value Per Acre ($)	Wine Production (Cases)
2004	56	30				
2002	52	29	3,000	4,000		500,000
2000		21	2,200	2,800	$20,000	400,000
1999		21	2,100			
1998		21				200,000
1996	40			1,800		
1995		23	1,055		15,000	200,000
1989		14				
1987		12				
1985	16	7	600			
1984	12	4	700			
1975		1				
1973	1		17		4,000	

Sources: *The Wine Press, Underground Wine Journal, Wine East, Long Island Business News, Newsday,* and the Long Island Wine Council.

Exhibit 8   Estimated Values of Vineyards and Wineries on Long Island
(Selected years)

Year	Name	Location	Winery Capacity (cases)	Total Planted Acres	Estimated Value ($)
2001	Raphael	Peconic	10,000	70	$6,000,000
2000	Gristina	Cutchogue	10,000	44	5,200,000
	Bedell Cellars	Cutchogue	8,000	50	5,000,000
	Pindar Vineyards	Peconic	80,000	42.5	
	Comtesse Thérèse	Mattituck		40	400,000
1999	Hargrave	Cutchogue	7,000	84	4,000,000
	Laurel Lake Vineyards	Laurel	5,500	23	2,000,000
	Corey Creek	Southold	4,000	30	2,500,000
	Peconic Bay Vineyards	Cutchogue		35	2,200,000
	Bidwell Vineyards	Cutchogue	15,000	34	2,900,000
1997	Laurel Lake Vineyards	Laurel		23	3,000,000
1993	Dzugas-Smith Vineyards	Cutchogue		29	245,000

Sources: *The Wine Press, Underground Wine Journal, Wine East, Long Island Business News, Newsday,* and the Long Island Wine Council.

trend will be reversed in the next few years. On a brighter note, on-premises sales have finally begun to rise this spring, as restaurant patrons are spending more on fine wine.

Will the Long Island wine industry be adversely or positively affected by these national trends? Will the regional extent of our markets shelter us from cyclical slowdowns in demand? From conversations with our members, the next few years are still likely to be quite challenging for our industry here on the East End.

Since 2001 New York City's financial services industry had experienced some of the largest declines in employment as well as reductions in salaries and bonuses. Special events sales volumes had also slowed, due to cost containment at parties and declining expenditures for high-end wines at restaurants. Still, overall volume and revenues had been rising due to expansion of the geographic market for Long Island wines on the East Coast and growth westward through New York, Pennsylvania, Maryland, and Virginia. This geographic expansion, it was hoped by many local producers, could help offset the local trend toward lower prices to bolster sagging sales.

In response to Nanette's overview, Jan mentioned that she'd come across a *BusinessWeek* article concerning the consumption profile of wine drinkers in the United States.[13] Forecasted trends for growth in U.S. wine consumption were hardly spectacular:

> One statistic I picked up was that in many European countries such as France, Germany, Italy, and Spain, wine is almost a necessity with meals—this is not the case here in the United States. Just over 10 percent of American adults account for 86 percent of wine consumed annually! We have not yet been successful at stimulating wine consumption to broader segments of the population. Until this occurs, perhaps our market strategy should be directed towards those consumers who are already drinking wine on a *regular* basis.

Ending the meeting, Jan thanked all present for sharing their ideas and expertise. She knew that she would have to prioritize each projected cost item and defend these expenditures when making a formal proposal for financing. Financing the proposed expansion as well as incremental working capital might have to be sourced by some form of equity, meaning that Jan would no longer own 100 percent of the Schoolhouse Lane Estates!

Jan Seeks Help

Jan decided it was time to call her brother Nick. Although he hadn't visited the North Fork in years, he had been to the Hamptons each summer, driving to his family's summer home on the beach. Jan began the call by saying, "Nick, how has your business and career been going this last year?

I heard about all the reductions in financial services employment. Have you been affected?"

"My firm has maintained its competitiveness in these uncertain times," Nick assured her. "We are also diversifying our clients' portfolios from real estate and annuities into private and public equity positions. If you know of any interesting investment opportunities, we would examine the financial data."

Somewhat surprised, Jan responded, "Nick, did you know that at Schoolhouse Lane Estates, we have a financial proposal on the table? We need an equity investment of approximately $2 million. Although the equity in the business is currently low, I will not be willing to give up control."

"Send me your business plan and financial statements," Nick replied, "and I'll contact you in two weeks with a proposal. The amount you are looking for is well within the range of my clients."

"Thanks, Nick," said Jan. "I'll fax you the documents tomorrow."

Two Weeks Later

"Jan, this is your brother. I received your materials and have a proposal for an investment of $2 million. Can we meet for lunch this Wednesday and I'll present the details? I also would like my wife to be at our meeting. As an equity strategist for a large investment banking house in Manhattan, Monica can provide some insight into the workings of the private equity market. She would also like to visit the winery."

Jan agreed and the three met for a long lunch at the Old Mill House in Peconic. After the salad, Nick presented details of his $2 million proposal to Jan.

"Although investment returns are low these days for fixed-income instruments, venture capital is still expensive. I could offer you a 10-year convertible note with interest at 6 percent," Nick began.

Sipping a glass of locally produced Gallucio Reserve Merlot, Monica added, "The note would provide the investor with potential capital gains up to his or her required return of between 20 and 25 percent per year, and then be converted into common stock with a par value of $1 per share. The holder would have the option over the next five years to convert the note into company stock at today's book value. If conversion did not occur, the note would be amortized from year 6 through year 10."

"Thanks," replied Jan, "I will have to speak with my accountant concerning the number of shares that would be granted should the note be converted, so that the required rate of return will be realized by your investor. By the way, who is this investor and when can I meet her or him?"

Nick smiled as Monica said, "Jan, you have known him all your life!"

The Bank Responds

The next day, Jan's accountant Laurel took Jan's projected capital expenditures of $2.4 million for expansion of the Schoolhouse Lane Estates operations, along with the business plan for the next five years, to the North Fork Bank. The projections included two scenarios: a "best case" for a revenue growth rate of 20 percent and a "base case" at a 15 percent growth rate. Both forecasts assumed enhanced operating efficiencies and expanded profit margins with no changes in prices and no introduction of new wine products.

The bank officer was skeptical of the most optimistic case, especially after speaking with a number of other winery operators in the area. North Fork's initial proposal was for a maximum $400,000 term loan with a small increase in the revolving line of credit to $3 million. The banker's implications and position were clear—Schoolhouse Lane needed permanent equity capital to sustain its growth plans. While the longer-term outlook for the industry was quite favorable, the banker was cautious about the trading conditions for wine over the next two years (2005 and 2006).

As she walked through the parking lot at North Fork Bank, Laurel relayed this disappointing news to Jan on her mobile phone. Although Jan understood why permanent capital was needed to support her growth strategy, she was not able to add to her personal investment in the business. Her husband, Tom, a professor of history at Stony Brook University, also believed that too large a percentage of the family's assets were already tied up in the business.

Nick's Position

After receiving Jan's fax, Nick responded by e-mail with some questions concerning the timing of the expenditures outlined in Jan's proposal. He was concerned about the "grape glut" and its impact on product pricing. In addition, the economic outlook in the near term appeared to be neither clearly defined nor strong. Therefore, could Jan construct forecasts using average annual growth rates in revenues of between 5 and 10 percent (less optimistic than Jan's 15 to 20 percent)? Nick did, however, agree with his sister that enhanced efficiencies could generate faster growth in net income than the growth in revenues.

With respect to Jan's concerns over maintaining ownership control, Nick was nevertheless very understanding. Monica had gently but firmly reminded him that the "last thing he should ever do was take over the operations of Schoolhouse Lane Estates." He thus approached this deal from a strictly financial point of view. Nick was looking for a viable and profitable investment of $2 million that would fit nicely into his portfolio. A current return of 6 percent, with a total expected return of 20 percent over at least a five-year holding period, was quite acceptable to him. While he might have expected a 25 percent total return on an investment with this risk profile some years ago, equity risk premiums had been trending downward in late May 2004, so a 20 percent return would meet or exceed his current portfolio needs.

Nick was aware of the lack of liquidity of an investment in Schoolhouse Lane Estate's operations. This investment would definitely have a "buy-and-hold" profile. Selling a private equity investment was traditionally accomplished through an initial public offering or an acquisition by another wine business, often years after the venture had developed into a viable, competitive, and profitable business. In evaluating his potential position in Schoolhouse Lane Estates, he was not confident that either of these scenarios would occur in the near term.[14] His only hope for monetizing his investment in the next five years would be to sell his shares back to Jan at a reasonable value or try to sell them to another private investor.

One More Meeting

After receiving her brother's proposal, Jan again met with Dan and Laurel. She opened the meeting by saying:

> I can't believe how expensive this funding could be even under the lowest cost presentation. Even given my most optimistic forecast of earnings growth for Schoolhouse Lane Estates and Nick's "cheapest" financing alternative, I will lose more than one-half ownership in the company. I surely do not want that to happen! Maybe we should defer our expansion plans or explore other options.

Dan countered by reiterating his desire to purchase the vineyard across the road and expand the winery's capacity:

> . . . that property has been owned by the O'Reilly family for 55 years. We may never get an opportunity to purchase it again if it is bought by another winery. We have managed it for the last six years and know the quality of grape production.

Laurel had planned what she would recommend. An integral component of her presentation was a summary of an appraisal report that had been prepared for Schoolhouse Lane Estates by a local firm specializing in wine industry asset valuations on Long Island (Exhibit 9). The appraisal clearly showed that the current value of the firm's two largest asset categories was considerably higher than their book values (approximately $9.5 million versus book values of $6.6 million). Adding the difference of nearly $2.9 million to the firm's equity value would surely enhance Jan's bargaining position in negotiating for new funds, possibly with other investors besides her brother. Laurel then summarized and prioritized the three components of the Schoolhouse Lane Estates' expansion plans:

> I agree with Dan that our highest priority at this time is the land purchase. We can produce larger volumes of wine, if the market so demands, at the new custom-crush

Exhibit 9   Report of the Appraisal of Assets of the Schoolhouse Lane Estates

In response to the request of Ms. Janess Thaw, sole owner of the Schoolhouse Lane Estates, we hereby enclose our estimates of current market values for the firm's wine inventory as well as its fixed-asset position. Our personnel have carefully examined your inventories, land, winery building, and equipment and compared these assets with current market values that we have observed over the last six months. We are pleased to report to you that the quality of your inventory is excellent and your assets are in top operating condition.

With your firm's growing emphasis on the production of premium red wines (Meritage, Cabernet Sauvignon, and Merlot), our appraisal estimates that 30 percent of wine in barrels by volume has been stored for more than two years, resulting in a doubling of its book value at the time fermentation was completed in early 2003. Another 40 percent, also red wine and mostly from the 2003 harvest, has been in barrels for 14 months. Remaining wine volumes are a mixture of younger reds and white Chardonnay. We conclude that as of May 2004 the value of inventory, if sold in the local wholesale market, would result in receipts of $5.12 million.

In a separate analysis of property, plant, and equipment, our real estate expert on current market conditions estimates the value of company-owned land at $1,088,000 or $32,000 per acre on the 34 acres under cultivation by Peconic Bay. This is in contrast to $720,000, which is the current book value of this land on a historical cost basis.

The remaining $2,641,600 of depreciated book value of the winery plant and equipment has also increased in value since its original purchase. Its current replacement value is $3.35 million, according to our appraiser.

In summary, upon a sale of these three major asset categories, it is estimated that they would bring to the firm a total of $9,550,233, or $2,909,533 more than their current book value of $6,640,700. This additional value could be added to the firm's equity account of $3,048,100 at year-end 2003, bringing its total up to $5,957,633.

	Summary Data		
Asset	Book Value December 31, 2003	Adjusted Market Value April 30, 2004	Appraisal Difference
Land—34 planted acres	$ 720,000	$1,088,000	$ 368,000
Plant & Equipment	2,641,600	3,347,233	705,633
Inventory	3,279,100	5,115,000	1,835,900
Totals	$6,640,700	$9,550,233	$2,909,533
Less: Liabilities	4,170,100	4,170,100	—
Equity Value	$2,470,600	$5,380,133	$2,909,533

It was a pleasure to provide you with the above data. If there is any additional information or clarifications that you may require, do not hesitate to contact us.

Respectfully submitted,

Sharon Brown, President

East End Associates

May 4, 2004

facility. By postponing the other projects, Jan, you would reduce the volume of funds needed from your brother and, consequently, the dilution of your ownership position. If you really want to spend the entire $2.4 million in the next year, remember you can sell the Class B common stock that you already carry on the balance sheet.

After the meeting ended, Jan walked slowly back to her office. Almost there, she abruptly turned around, walked out of the building, and proceeded toward the vineyard. Strolling leisurely past the old oak trees with birds perching in the branches, she then ambled all the way down Schoolhouse Lane to the shore of Peconic Bay. Sitting on a large rock near the shore, she spent the next hour considering her alternatives. Should she continue the current strategy and focus on internal growth, borrow some money from the North Fork Bank, sell equity, and complete the expansion in order to sell the winery later down the road, or maybe sell all of Schoolhouse Lane Estates now? Jan knew that when she returned to the office, Dan and Laurel would be awaiting her decision.

Endnotes

1. *New York Times.* 2000. On the North Fork, dreams of Napa. July 26: F1.
2. To put this information in perspective, the California wine industry has been in business for more than 200 years and currently has 86 AVAs, www.wineinstitute.org.
3. States News Service. 2004. Washington, DC, February 5.
4. On January 29, 2004, U.S. Senators Hilary Rodham Clinton and Charles Schumer, along with U.S. Representatives Louise Slaughter, Tim Bishop, Maurice Hinchey, Sherwood Boehlert, Jack Quinn, and Arno Houghton, signed a letter calling on Governor Pataki and the New York State Legislature to overturn the direct shipping ban.
5. Canavor, N. 2003. Long Island continues to gain notoriety as wine-making region. *Long Island Business News,* April 4.
6. In contrast, nine custom-crush facilities served California's wine industry.
7. Walzer, R. 1999. Hearn pressing for $2M winery. *Long Island Business News,* October 1: 5A.
8. Johnson, K. 2003. Success is in the grapes; from a scruffy past, a winemaking capital emerges. *New York Times,* August 30: B1.
9. Bureau of Alcohol, Tobacco and Firearms, Regulatory Agency, U.S. Department of the Treasury, Title 27, Part 4 of the Code of Federal Regulations.
10. Aguilar, D. 2003. Working capital analysis for wine industry clients, working paper. Silicon Valley Bank Wine Group, December 26.
11. The Wine Institute, www.wineinstitute.org.
12. According to Vic Motto of Motto Kryla Fisher, a Napa, California, consultant to the wine industry, there were 10,940 distributors of wine in 1990 and 5,134 in 2000, but only two to three major distributors per state. The top 10 distributors accounted for 33 percent of wine sales in 1993 and 60 percent in 2003.
13. Himelstein, L. 2002. This Merlot's for you. *BusinessWeek,* September 30: 65–68.
14. Nick had recently read a *New York Times* article about the Gallucio Family Cellars in Cutchogue. That winery had been on the market for $7.5 million in the fall of 2003 with no takers. Gallucio had 82.5 acres, about 44 of them under vines, and had a 10,000-case annual production capacity. The Gallucios had purchased the property from Gristina Vineyards for $5.2 million in 2000. Vincent and Judy Gallucio had announced an ambitious expansion plan but in 2002 reversed their plan to transform the property from a boutique to a larger-scale winery. See Goldberg, H. G. 2004. Winery to feature state wines. *New York Times,* March 21: sec. 14LI, 12.

Case 20   Atari and Infogrames Entertainment SA*

Bruno Bonnell, CEO of Infogrames Entertainment SA (IESA), announced officially in May 2003 that it had renamed all of its U.S. operations from "Infogrames Inc." to "Atari Inc." This achievement was over three years in the making. During the summer of 2000, Bonnell worked on ways to prevent his company from falling victim to an acquisition or becoming prey to a larger company seeking to consolidate and gobble up smaller software gaming publishers. Later that year, Bonnell and IESA announced plans to purchase Hasbro Interactive, Inc., and along with it the rights to the name of Atari. The deal was concluded in January 2001, by which time the video gaming industry was on the cusp of surpassing Hollywood in total annual revenues. It was obvious to Bonnell that IESA required a significant move if the company was to remain a major player in the gaming industry.

In 2000 Bonnell and most software gaming publishers recognized the incredible growth and potential of the industry, which was then defining itself as the most lucrative of entertainment industries.

> Our business has grown from a niche market for young boys and teenagers to a much broader audience, with many more adults playing. People will play games as simply as they watch TV.[1]

Perhaps the connection between Atari and IESA was evident: taking a classic game company and resurrecting it in the new millennium as a way to market games to adults who were once the quarter-feeding teenagers from the 1980s. Atari was an eighties icon for computer nerds and video game geeks, who eventually became the parents of the interactive entertainment, multimedia, AI and CGI special effects generation.

The gaming industry went from $1 billion annually in video-console sales in 1982 to $10 billion almost 20 years later. It was clear to Bonnell that video games were fast becoming the central source for interactive home entertainment and would soon supplant digital video disks (DVDs), videocassette recorders (VCRs), cable, and satellite TV programming. IESA bought the Atari brand name in hopes of leapfrogging other industry stalwarts Activision and Take 2, and ultimately knocking off Electronic Arts (EA) from the top perch of the gaming industry.

Background

To understand the full story of Atari, it is necessary to realize that the Atari name has a two-part history. The first part of Atari's history covered the "Atari classic"—the company that created old-school video games such as Asteroids; the

second part commenced with IESA's acquisition of the Atari name in 2001.

Atari Classic   Atari classic's life began in the early 1970s when a computer programmer named Nolan Bushnell created *Pong*. As one may recall, *Pong* was an early, two-dimensional video game that involved two players volleying a dot back and forth on-screen between parallel rectangular paddles. Pong debuted in 1972 as an arcade machine in a tavern in Sunnyvale, California, and included a simple instruction: "Avoid missing ball for high score." With this simple format and objective, imaginations were ignited and the gaming industry was officially born. Bushnell progressed from *Pong* by making a $500 investment as the cofounder of a new computer game company named Atari (the origin of *atari* derives from the term for "check" in the Japanese game of Go).[2] Only a few years later, in 1976, Warner Communications purchased Atari from Bushnell for $28 million. A year later, the Atari company took its first step toward pop culture fame when it launched the 2600 Video Computer System (also known as 2600). The system realized only fair success until three years later when Midway's *Space Invaders* game arrived and propelled the 2600 into the mainstream household market in the United States. The 2600 realized incredible success in the early 1980s, despite stiff competition from Mattel's Intellivision and Colleco's CollecoVision systems. During this period Atari also broadened their product selection by creating cartridge versions for smash hit arcade games like Centipede, Asteroids, and Missile Command.

Atari classic enjoyed a fairly rapid rise to the top, but beginning around 1982 entered a period of downturn. Bushnell left the company because of a feud with Warner Communications over the continuing development philosophy of the 2600. At that time, the hot project for Atari programmers was the conversion of the arcade game *Pac-Man* into a cartridge version. Atari gambled and decided to manufacture the game with a cheaper 4k chip instead of 8k as suggested by the project manager. It launched prematurely and proved a failure because of the gross simplification of its graphics and technology. *Pac-Man* never took off with the 2600 and fell flat. Atari grossly miscalculated and overforecasted the *Pac-Man* project and suffered as a result: the number of company employees fell from 10,000 in December 1982 to only 200 by July 1984.[3]

This marked the beginning of the end for Atari classic. Japanese-based companies Nintendo and Sega soon became the pioneers that took over the gaming industry from the 1980s to the 1990s. Atari classic petered out and slowly withered away in 1996 when it posted a $13.5 million third-quarter loss due to its fledgling 64-bit Jaguar game system. Layoffs at Atari ensued and the resignation of the president of North American operations, Ted Hoff, signaled the end of

*This case was prepared by graduate student Carlito Cabelin and Professor Alan B. Eisner of Pace University as a basis for class discussion rather than to illustrate either effective or ineffective handling of an administrative situation. Copyright © 2004 Alan B. Eisner.

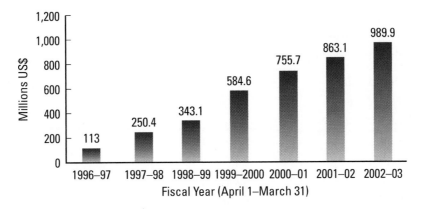

Exhibit 1   Atari/Infogrames Gross Revenues

Atari classic. That same year Atari merged with JTS, a disk drive company, which eventually folded too. In 1998 Hasbro bought the rights to Atari's home titles.

Atari's disintegration was not a reflection of the game industry's health. While Atari was suffocating, Sony's PlayStation and Nintendo's 64 were catching on fire. Those within the industry knew there was still plenty of consumer pie to be consumed; they just needed the right strategy to claim a significant piece.

Atari, Inc.—Infogrames Entertainment SA

Infogrames Entertainment SA was founded in 1983 by Bruno Bonnell and Christopher Sapet as a software game company based in Lyon, France. Both Bonnell and Sapet were in their twenties and invested only $10,000 to start their new company. In 1987 the average age of the company's employees was only 27—an obvious reflection of the youthful vigor of the founders. The company grossed $113 million in revenues in 1996 and by 2002 it grossed $863.1 million to become Europe's largest video game maker. See Exhibit 1.

Infogrames started out offering a wide range of entertainment and educational games, and developing artificial intelligence and online service software.[4] The company made a string of key acquisitions from the mid-1990s through 2000 (see Exhibit 2). Of particular importance was the purchase in 2002 of Shiny Entertainment studios, which held the rights to develop a game based on the movie *The Matrix Reloaded* and *Matrix Revolutions.* (Details of this strategy will be examined later in this case.) Infogrames eventually produced several quality hit games like *Dragon Ball Z, Unreal Championship, Monopoly,* and *Backyard Sports,* to name a few; it also distributed franchise labels in movie games such as *Mission Impossible, Men in Black, Stuart Little,* and of course *The Matrix.*

The acquisition of key interest here is Atari by way of Hasbro Interactive, Inc., in 2000. This marked the end of the first part of Atari's history, and the beginning of a new history as part of the IESA family.

The series of acquisitions that cost about $300 million from 1999 through 2000, combined with the development of high-stakes projects such as the *Enter the Matrix* game, all weighed heavily on the future profitability of Infogrames. The issue at hand in the early 2000s was whether IESA, the parent company, could maximize the biggest bang for every dollar spent on the Atari brand. "It can't hurt them," said Michael Pachter, who covered Atari for Wedbush Morgan Securities. According to Goldman, Sachs & Co., Infogrames was on track to book a net loss for the fiscal year ending June 30, 2003, on revenues of $1 billion while carrying a debt of more than $550 million.[5] Could the *Atari* name help bail IESA out of debt and launch it into its next growth phase? And equally unknown was how long it would take for IESA to become profitable again after the costly purchase of the *Matrix* movie sequels.

The Video Gaming Industry

In 1982 *Time* magazine ran a cover story on video games titled, "Games that Play People."[6] The article reported how the arcade game frenzy took the nation by storm as video games found their way into a variety of public domains besides the local arcade parlor: pizza shops, doctors' offices, airports, restaurants, and even beauty salons.

Market Demographics   In the 1980s the ideal arcade game addict was simply a teenager with a pocket full of quarters. Back then, record high scorers of games like *Defender* needed only a quarter to play 16 hours' worth of entertainment. Now fast-forward 20 years to the article "The (R)evolution of Video Games" in the November 2002 issue of *Siliconindia,* which describes an industry still made up of those teenagers from the 1980s who, now in their thirties, were still buying video games for home entertainment.

Its market no longer consists only of kids and teenagers, though they still comprise a large part of sales, but now the same youngsters from twenty years ago are adults with careers and money of their own.[7]

Exhibit 2   Acquisition History of Infogrames Entertainment SA

Year	Company Acquired	Country	Activity
1996	Ocean Software	U.K.	Publishing
1997	Philips Media	Netherlands	Distribution
1998	ABS Multimedia	Portugal	Distribution
1998	Arcadia	Spain	Distribution
1998	Gremlin	U.K.	Development and publishing
1998	Game City	Switzerland	Distribution
1998	Psygnosis	France	Development
1999	Accolade	U.S.	Development and publishing
1999	Beam Software	Australia	Development
1999	Ozisoft	Australia	Distribution
1999	GT Interactive	U.S.	Development/publishing/distribution
1999	Den-O-Tech	Canada	Development
2000	Hasbro Interactive	U.S.	Publishing
2000	Paradigm Entertainment	U.S.	Development
2002	Shiny Entertainment	U.S.	Development
2002	Eden Studios	France	Development

The consumer demographics for video games had changed quite a bit from 1980 to 2003. Primarily, the market had expanded in its consumer age bracket. "The kids who fell in love with Mario when they were 6, they're now 26," said marketing director Perrin Kaplan of Nintendo.[8] According to the Interactive Digital Software Association, the average American gamer in 2000 was 28 years old, 58 percent of the consumers were over 18, and 21 percent were 35 or older.[9] The older the gamer became, the more likely the gamer was to spend some disposable income on entertainment. Teenagers, preteens, and kids in general didn't have as much luxury nor were they normally allowed such luxury from their parents.

The breadth of ages in video game consumers required companies in the gaming industry to broaden their appeal to a larger demographic profile. Gaming companies had always been challenged with providing the proper age-appropriate content in the games they produced. How to make the games age-appropriate became a tug-of-war battle between management and designers. Ratings such as "M" for mature, "T" for teens, and "E" for everyone was the game industry's equivalent of motion picture ratings "R," "PG-13," and "G." In the early 2000s the hottest-selling title games were rated M. For instance, Take 2's *Grand Theft Auto: Vice City* was all about being a mobster, shooting

cops, killing drug dealers, and consorting with prostitutes. Although the game went on to become the fastest-selling video game in history, it also carried a huge risk of receiving backlash from consumer advocacy groups such as the National Institute on Media and the Family, which campaigned against excessive sex and violence in entertainment. Even family-friendly Nintendo, with the *Donkey Kong* and *Mario Bros.* mascots, received negative feedback when it developed, under a separate label called Rare, an M-rated game titled *Perfect Dark*. According to Bruno Bonnell of Atari, "Nintendo is the light balancing the darkness of teenage games."[10] Gaming companies were forced to respond to the threat of outside consumer advocacy groups tarnishing their brand image.

Gaming Relationship with Motion Pictures

The video game industry built a structure that was very similar to the motion picture industry. When a blockbuster video game was on the drawing board, large production teams were assembled with fat and costly budgets, and the teams worked separately to create an entirely new and profitable product. This Hollywood-like trend of video game production helped make this a large-scale industry—$10.5 billion in 2002. For example, *Enter the Matrix* cost a whopping $80 million, which included all of its marketing expenses and the $50 million needed to acquire Shiny Entertainment. In comparison, the average video game cost $2.5 million to $4 million to produce in 2002.[11] In the early 2000s the sale of 1 million units became the industry benchmark for game title success. Through May 2003, *Enter the Matrix* surpassed 1 million units sold and through June it passed 2.5 million. In comparison, Activision's *Spiderman* sold 2 million units in 2002.

During the early years of the 21st century, mergers and acquisitions activity was commonplace whenever software developers needed to secure franchise rights to blockbuster movies. They would spend millions to purchase smaller entertainment studios with the philosophy that if a movie was a blockbuster the success would carry over to the planned release of its video game. The same was also true with DVDs, and gaming companies started packaging multimedia product launches. For example, the trailer for the movie would run on the DVD and vice versa. In the case of *Enter the Matrix,* scenes were shot specifically for the game and not the movie, so that the consumer could play through the game while using it as a continuum for the movie. In essence, the movie just continued to live on in the game even after the end credits rolled. Examples of this cross-pollination were Take 2's purchase of Rockstar games and Atari's acquisition of Shiny Entertainment. The gaming industry had strong, established relationships between independent software publishers and hardware platform companies, especially among the top market leaders (e.g., licensing arrangements between Electronic Arts and Microsoft or between Atari and Sony). Under the terms of agreement between the software company and the hardware company, the gaming company was authorized to develop and distribute software-compatible games for the respective hardware platform.

Hardware Platform   After Atari classic paved the way for hardware gaming companies, Atari, Nintendo, and Sega were the only companies remaining from the 1980s that still continued in production during the 1990s. In 1996 two significant events occurred: Atari went out of business and Sony launched its PlayStation console game. Through 2002 Sony was the leading hardware console gaming company with its PlayStation and PlayStation 2 systems. Sony's video game division contributed 53 percent to the company's bottom line in 2001. Microsoft entered the console market in 2001 with the launch of its Xbox system, but the software giant remained a remote second.

Nintendo was more diversified in its product offerings with the Nintendo 64, Gamecube's 128-bit system, and the handheld gaming devices Game Boy Advance and Game Boy Advance SP. Despite diversification, the company still ranked a distant third in overall sales in the early years of the 21st century.

Hardware companies realized that to be the market leader and gain market share they also had to participate in the software publishing segment. Besides licensing their hardware to software developers and collecting fees, they also needed to develop in-house software titles. All three top hardware companies did so in the early 2000s, but to successfully continue to develop in-house software, a company needed a supply of high quality in-house talent. Recognizing this need, Sony and Microsoft continually tried to recruit top talent away from independent software developers.

Software engineers were often recruited from smaller firms to the ranks of industry leaders. And while keeping the talent in-house was a real trick, managing the team of programmers was even more challenging. Getting the right mix of talent, personality, and team chemistry was vital for the development of a title game. If the chemistry or the personalities of the software developers conflicted, then a project could be compromised.[12] Atari went overseas to Vietnam to hire subcontractors to assist in providing additional components to some of its games. The cost savings from outsourcing were enormous; a programmer's average annual salary in Vietnam was $4,000 versus $70,000 to $100,000 in the United States.

Industry Ebb and Flow   The video gaming industry was cyclical but nonetheless independent of the overall performance of the economy; if the economy was in a recession, the video gaming industry would not necessarily decline too. The gaming industry cycle was driven first by the launches of the hardware platform. Whenever a next-generation system came to market, the industry began a three- to five-year cycle. Many software companies immediately went into production to meet demand quotas forecasted for the new hardware platform. The initial two years following the launch of next-generation hardware saw software company sales at their highest and inventory flying off the shelves. As the third year approached, the industry reached optimal output where profits were maximized and diminishing returns began to kick in. When a newer, more advanced hardware platform was rolled out, the cycle would begin again.

As suggested above, the video gaming sector was an intensely competitive industry. Through 2002, Electronic Arts (EA) was still the industry top dog with annual sales of $1.7 billion for fiscal 2002. Of the top five software publishers, two were hardware platform companies—Nintendo and Sony—who recognized they had to increasingly position gaming software as a top core strategy (see Exhibit 3). Notice how Microsoft didn't even penetrate the top 10, but understood clearly that developing its own software for its console was industrywide.

However, other gaming software vendors like EA and Activision rivaled Atari in very similar strategies: planning,

Top 10 Video Game Software Publishers (Includes Console & Portable Software) Ranked on Dollars Annual 2003

Rank	Publisher
1	Electronic Arts
2	Nintendo of America
3	THQ
4	Sony
5	Activision
6	Take 2 Interactive
7	Atari
8	Konami of America
9	Vivendi Universal
10	NAMCO

© 2003 NPD Group, Inc. All rights reserved.

developing, publishing, and distributing software game titles. During 2003, Atari maintained a top-ten position for all video game titles (see Exhibit 4).

Historically, game titles went up and down the ranks and were very unpredictable after the initial sales launch. Atari's *Enter the Matrix* was expected to be the top seller for the month after it was released simultaneously with its movie counterpart. Game titles performed similarly to major motion pictures during the summer season: A blockbuster might go from the top-grossing film during the Memorial Day weekend to number five within a month. For example, Take 2's *Grand Theft Auto: Vice City* dropped from number 5 in March 2003 to number 20 just three months later. During the April to June 2003 period EA's *NBA Street Vol. 2* remained at number five and Atari's *Dragon Ball Z* held the number nine spot; this perhaps reflected the fanfare for the NBA's playoff season for the former, and a strong franchise label for the latter. In any event, chart busters could go up and down the ranks within months, always vulnerable to the next hot title.

Gaming History Summary   The 1970s could be seen as the video gaming industry's infancy stage with the invention of *Pong,* Atari's 2600, and, closing out the decade, *Space Invaders.* At that point the industry went through growing pains, which continued through the 1980s. Companies like Atari, Colleco, Mattel, and Magnavox all experienced some failures with their respective hardware systems. During the '80s arcade games raked in billions annually and reached critical mass; throughout

the '90s hardware console companies Nintendo and Sony began to take root as the industry goliaths; and at the beginning of the new millennium, the gaming industry mimicked Hollywood with blockbuster movie tie-ins and projects with gigantic budgets. One could speculate that the future of the gaming industry might be in online entertainment.

Atari's Growth Strategy

After concluding a one-year survey of brand recognition around the world (Asia, Europe, South America), Bonnell announced in May 2003 that the U.S. subsidiary of IESA would be rebranded Atari Inc. In September 2003 shareholders were scheduled to vote to approve a name change for the parent company IESA. Going forward, management expected Atari Inc. to contribute 60–70 percent of the bottom-line profits for IESA.

According to Bonnell, the name-change strategy shouldn't have been a surprise; a survey found that people over 30 tended to remember Atari and many under 15 had their own associations with the venerable brand. "Even if they have never played on an Atari machine, they know what *Pong* is about . . . older people still associate the brand with innovation," said Bonnell.[13] For Bonnell, a recreational marathon runner, the Atari acquisition was the equivalent of the moment in a race when a runner would "break away" from the competition in order to separate from the rest of the pack. In the fall of 2001 Atari Inc. was inaugurated under new management with three games: *Splashdown* and *MXRider* for PlayStation 2, and *Transworld Surf* for the Xbox.

Mission   Atari's mission was to lead mass-market demand for interactive entertainment (see Exhibit 5). This mission was not at all contrary to Bonnell's original founding goal for IESA in 1983: to bring interactive entertainment to consumers around the world across every available distribution platform.

Atari's vision and overall mission were clearly stated in its corporate Web site in contrast to the lack of clarity among the competing top five software game publishers (see Exhibit 3). In order not to divulge any trade secrets, Sony remained silent when probed about what strategy it would take with its next-generation PlayStation 3.[14] Only Activision had an equally thorough and detailed explanation of its corporate objectives and goals as Atari's.

Products   Atari's core offerings included kids/family games, action/adventure games, and sports/racing games. From its founding in 1983, Bonnell and his partner Sapet built Infogrames on an educational software game—*Le Cube Informatique.* It sold 60,000 copies, setting the standard for educational titles.

By the beginning of the new century Atari was consistently a top 10 software gaming company worldwide and

Exhibit 4   Top 20 Video Game Titles Ranked by Total U.S. Units Annual 2003

Rank	Title	Platform	Publisher	Release Date	Average Retail Price $
1	Madden NFL 2004	PS2	Electronic Arts	Aug '03	$49
2	Pokemon Ruby	GBA	Nintendo of America	Mar '03	31
3	Pokemon Sapphire	GBA	Nintendo of America	Mar '03	31
4	Need Speed: Underground	PS2	Electronic Arts	Nov '03	49
5	Zelda: The Wind Waker	GCN	Nintendo of America	Mar '03	47
6	Grand Theft Auto: Vice City	PS2	Rockstar Games	Oct '02	41
7	Mario Kart: Double Dash	GCN	Nintendo of America	Nov '03	49
8	Tony Hawk Underground	PS2	Activision	Oct '03	47
9	Enter the Matrix	PS2	Atari	May '03	46
10	Medal Honor Rising	PS2	Electronic Arts	Nov '03	49
11	NCAA Football 2004	PS2	Electronic Arts	Jul '03	49
12	Halo	XBX	Microsoft	Nov '01	38
13	True Crime: Streets LA	PS2	Activision	Nov '03	48
14	Final Fantasy X-2	PS2	Square ENIX USA	Nov '03	50
15	NBA Live 2004	PS2	Electronic Arts	Oct '03	49
16	SOCOM II: Navy Seals	PS2	Sony Computer Ent.	Nov '03	49
17	Grand Theft Auto 3	PS2	Rockstar Games	Oct '01	21
18	NBA Street Vol. 2	PS2	Electronic Arts	Apr '03	48
19	The Getaway	PS2	Sony Computer Ent. (Sony)	Jan '03	40
20	Mario Bros 3: Mario 4	GBA	Nintendo of America	Oct '03	29

Source: The NPD Group/NPD Funworld ®/Point-of-Sale. David Riley 516-625-2277.

the leading software company in Europe. Although the company described itself as "one of the top 5 third-party publishers of interactive entertainment software in the world," the description was a modest one indeed, considering industry analysts ranked Atari the top software publisher in Europe, and according to NPD, it had the following rankings in the United States.

- No. 1 publisher of Children's Entertainment games for the PC.
- No. 1 publisher of Arcade and Fighting games for the PC.
- No. 2 publisher of Role Playing Games for the PC.
- No. 2 publisher of Family Entertainment games for the PC.[15]

Atari offered the masses a wide variety of titles, franchises, and brand labels covering three major categories: movie tie-in hits, television version games, and general strategy games. In movie tie-ins, Atari had licenses to Warner Brothers' *Looney Tunes, Mission Impossible* and *MI2, Men in Black, Stuart Little 2, The Matrix* sequels, and *Terminator 3*. For its television franchise games, Atari had developed software for the hit series *Survivor* and for the Japanese animation series *Dragon Ball Z,* which was rated the number one animation program in many countries. In the general strategy category, Atari offered such strong brand name titles as *Monopoly* and *Unreal Tournament,* which in 1992 won the "game of the year" award and in the fall of 2002 was ranked as the number one game for the personal computer. For the sports genre, Atari got high

Exhibit 5   Atari's Corporate Philosophy

> Atari will lead mass-market demand for interactive entertainment.
>
> —**Bruno Bonnell,** Chairman and CEO, Atari

Atari's vision is to be the premier global source of digital interactive entertainment, transporting people of all ages and interest levels to a world of wonder and imagination by drawing from next-generation technologies.

While entertainment is at the heart of Atari's products, the company also believes that games must reward players by allowing them to follow their imagination and become immersed in new worlds and fantasies. By adapting next-generation technologies, and cultivating the imagination, innovation, and energy of its people, Atari designs products that facilitate growth in the person who is playing, whether that growth is hand-eye coordination, logic skills, or simply a sense of wonder and inspiration.

Source: www.atari.com.

Exhibit 6   Atari's Senior Management

- *Bruno Bonnell, chief executive officer.* Prior to founding Infogrames, Bonnell was involved in the launch of the Thomson TO7, one of the first computers designed for domestic use.

- *Harry Ruin, senior vice president.* From 1988 to 1993, Rubin worked at NBC, where he served as vice president and general manager of its domestic and international Home Video Divisions.

- *Thomas Heymann, director of Digital Cost Partners.* Heymann was formerly president of The Disney Stores, Inc.

- *Nancy Bushkin, vice president, corporate communications.* Bushkin was vice president, corporate communications, for Spelling Entertainment in Los Angeles from 1997 through 1999. Prior to Spelling, she spent eight years in corporate relations at Viacom Inc. as an integral member of the communications team handling the company's acquisitions of Paramount Communications and Blockbuster.

- *Jason Bell, senior vice president, creative development, Atari Inc.* Bell spent a year at Electronic Arts as producer and senior producer on various multiplayer and online games with responsibility for product design, service quality, and development planning.

- *David Perry, president and founder, Shiny Entertainment.* At age 17, Perry spent four years working for key publishers like Virgin Games. He developed such hits as Teenage Mutant Ninja Turtles and The Terminator for Orion Pictures.

marks for its *Backyard Sports* franchise. *Backyard Sports* received positive remarks and numerous awards from parenting magazines and parenting organizations. The games, which offered customized products for children, allowed a child to play sports—baseball, hockey, or football—with the kid versions of the games played by professional athletes.

IESA used the brand name "Atari" in rolling out some vintage Atari games to connect the adult consumer to the company that started the whole video game craze in the 1980s. Atari had a "10-in-1" TV games product that provided the consumer with a single joystick modeled after the classic 2600 joystick; built into the hardware were 10 classic games such as Centipede, Asteroids, Missile Command,

and Battlezone—essentially, a turnkey lightweight plug-in and play system.

Top Management   There was no doubt that Atari had assembled some of the brightest and most talented senior management teams in the industry. Much of the assembly came by way of the series of acquisitions in the late 1990s (see Exhibit 2). Exhibit 6 lists the executives and senior management at Atari in 2002 and their prior accomplishments.

Atari had indeed created a formidable management team by gathering executives from the "best in class" of companies that were leaders in the interactive entertainment world: Disney, Viacom, EA, Virgin Games, and NBC. Bonnell founded his computer games industry start-up on

Exhibit 7   Selected Five-Year Net Revenues
(in thousands)

	2003	2002	2001	2000	1999	1998
EA[1]	$2,482,244	$1,724,675	$1,322,273	$1,420,011	$1,211,863	
Take 2	N/A	$ 793,976	$ 448,801	$ 364,001	$ 304,714	$194,052
Activision	$ 864,116	$ 786,434	$ 620,183	$ 572,205	$ 436,526	$312,906
Atari[2]	$ 989,900	$ 863,100	$ 755,700	$ 584,600	$ 343,100	$250,400

[1]EA fiscal year ends March 31.
[2]USD at exchange rate as of March 31, 2004.
Source: Various company annual reports.

the energy and youth of whiz kids of the eighties, but he built IESA into an industry titan on the solid foundation of experience provided by a collection of executives with impressive resumés from the greatest and most successful U.S. entertainment businesses.

However, the foundation of experience was not without its cracks. Bonnell was successful in surrounding himself with top-level talent, but over time some of his top management was sneaking out the back door and walking across the street to the competitors. Dawn Paine, senior executive in charge of marketing, left in 2002 to join Nintendo; Matt Woodley joined Sega in 2003 as European marketing director; and Larry Sparks, vice president of European marketing, left just two weeks after Woodley.

Additional Information   Atari's global distribution in 2002 was in excess of 50,000 retail outlets. In Europe alone it had a network of 30,000 retail outlets and in North America it encompassed more than 22,000. Atari also distributed for its affiliate labels such as Strategy First, Xicat, and Codemasters. These affiliates outsourced their outbound logistics to Atari, which ultimately gave Atari a firmer hold on the overall worldwide distribution of the video gaming industry. Atari then set itself up to compete for the same distribution network used by EA: mass merchants and superstores such as Wal-Mart, electronics specialty stores like Best Buy, and software specialty stores such as Electronics Boutique.

In a manner similar to the way motion picture firms outsourced advertising for films, Atari chose to outsource all of its advertising. This practice had become increasingly common among the leading gaming companies. Advertising budgets for Atari were estimated in the $20 million range for 2002.[16]

Selected Competitor Information
Consider the licensing arrangements and brand name titles among the competitors in the early 2000s: Activision had Marvel's *Spiderman,* Disney's *Toy Story 2,* and *Star Trek*

from television; Eidos had *Lara Croft Tomb Raider;* and EA owned the Harry Potter franchise and endless titles of sports games, including the cash cow *Madden NFL.*

EA Sports had an "It's in the Game" motto. This helped its young athletic-minded audience to identify with catchphrases such as Nike's "Just Do It" signature. EA's products, like *Madden NFL,* had become annuities, with the company re-releasing the titles every year with updated versions of the players, teams, and stadiums. Fans bought it year in and year out, as if the older versions were annual trends that went out of style. Thus, every year these products produced a consistent stream of revenue for EA.

Take 2's *Grand Theft Auto* series was also a smash hit. Take 2 did not have as much product diversification in its offerings as Atari or EA and it received a great deal of adverse feedback from the parent population.

> Take 2 made two strategic bets that paid off big . . . decided in 1999 to focus its development dollars on harder-edged, mature-content games . . . All is not rosy, to be sure. Game marketers have come under attack from groups like the National Institute on Media and the Family.[17]

Despite the negative feedback from parents for its sex, drugs, and rock-and-roll image, Take 2 stock continued to perform positively. In 2002 Take 2 generated gross revenues second only to EA (see Exhibit 7). But while Take 2's stock rose, stock in EA, Activision, and Atari all fell.[18] Analysts claimed this was due in part to the expanding consumer age group.

The Future of Atari
Could IESA take the Atari brand name and use it to leapfrog industry stalwarts Activision and Take 2, and ultimately knock off Electronic Arts from its top perch? Could the Atari name help bail IESA out of debt and launch the company into its next growth phase? How long would it take for IESA to become profitable again after the costly purchase of *The Matrix* movie sequels?

Exhibit 8   Atari, Inc., and Subsidiaries Consolidated Statements of Operations
(in $ thousands, except per share data)

	Nine Months Ending Dec. 31	
	2002 (unaudited)	2003 (unaudited)
Net revenues	$ 449,564	$ 402,540
Cost of goods sold	218,062	202,712
Gross profit	**231,502**	**199,828**
Selling and distribution expenses	81,122	71,270
General and administrative expenses	30,904	25,157
In-process research and development	7,400	—
Research and development	60,461	72,734
Gain on sale of development project to a related party	—	3,744
Depreciation and amortization	5,850	6,757
Operating income	**45,765**	**20,166**
Interest expense, net	10,678	7,215
Other (expense) income	(2,844)	(2,297)
Income before provision for income taxes	32,243	18,142
Provision for income taxes	2,167	63
Net (loss) income	**30,076**	**18,079**
Dividend to parent	—	(39,351)
Net (loss) income attributable to common shareholders	**30,076**	**(21,272)**
Basic and diluted net (loss) income per share	0.43	(0.24)
Basic weighted average shares outstanding	69,847	88,891
Diluted weighted average shares outstanding	80,078	88,891
Net Income	**$ 30,076**	**$ 18,079**

Source: Atari annual reports.

Atari was more recognized as a worldwide brand name than IESA. Family-friendly products were one of Atari's core strategies; Atari offered customized sports games for children such as *Backyard Sports*. However, if Atari wanted to gain market share from EA's sports division, licensing some big household names in sports may have been a wise strategic move.

Atari's diverse portfolio ranging from family-friendly products to blockbuster movie games similarly reflect EA's model. Bonnell took a large gamble in 2002 and spent an enormous amount on the Shiny Entertainment acquisition to gain *Enter the Matrix,* but the short-run results showed the gamble was a good one. Within months of its May 15,

2003, release the game sold more than 3 million units worldwide (see Exhibit 8 for financials).

The future of Atari depended on many things, including whether Atari could retain its in-house talent by keeping its existing design team, or if it would be forced to compete with industry rivals who insisted on luring them away with higher compensation packages. Also in question was whether Atari could continue to afford the trend in huge blockbuster movie games that ran short-term budgetary deficits. But the biggest question that created uncertainty around IESA's acquisition of the Atari name was whether Bonnell would succeed long term in his rebranding efforts of adopting Atari as the new company name for Infogrames.

Could the '80s legacy carry IESA to an iconoclastic position in the new millennium?

Endnotes

1. *BusinessWeek.* 2000. Europe's no. 1 video-game player. June 12.
2. *US News & World Report.* 1999. B.I.K.: How Pong invented geekdom. December 27: 67.
3. Driscoll, Edward B., Jr. 2002. The Atari 2600: The cartridge family rides again. *Poptronics,* August.
4. Gross, Daniel. 1987. Infogrames: A French connection. *Information Today,* December.
5. Reinhardt, Andy, & Grover, Ronald. 2003. Will Enter the Matrix save Infogrames' skin? Europe's top video-game maker badly needs a blockbuster. *BusinessWeek,* May 26.
6. Skow, John. 1982. Games that play people. *Time,* January 18.
7. Ridlen, Richard. 2002. The (r)evolution of video games. *Siliconindia,* November.
8. Ibid.
9. Croal, N'Gai. 2000. The art of darkness. *Newsweek,* June 12.
10. Ibid.
11. Delaney, Kevin. 2003. A game maker's big gamble. *Wall Street Journal,* May 14: B1.
12. Judd, James. 2000. Add more quarters. *Upside,* October.
13. *Wall Street Journal.* 2003. Digits. May 8.
14. Brown, Eryn. 2002. Sony's big bazooka. *Fortune,* December 30.
15. Atari, Corporate profile, www.atari.com.
16. Flass, Rebecca, & van der Pool, Lisa. 2002. Infogrames in play. *Adweek,* March 25.
17. Brull, Steven. 2003. Gamers II—magazine platinum. *Institutional Investor,* February.
18. Ibid.

Case 21   FreshDirect*

Company Profile

Operating out of its production center in Long Island City, Queens, FreshDirect offered online grocery shopping and delivery service to Manhattan's East Side and Battery Park City. When it was launched in July 2001 by Joe Fedele and Jason Ackerman, FreshDirect announced to the New York area that it was "the new way to shop for food." This was a bold statement given that the previous decade had witnessed the demise of numerous other online grocery ventures. However, the creators of FreshDirect were confident in the success of their business because their entire operation had been designed to deliver on one simple promise to grocery shoppers: "higher quality at lower prices."

While this promise was an extremely common tagline used within and outside the grocery business, FreshDirect had integrated numerous components into its system to give real meaning to these words. To offer the highest-quality products to its customers, FreshDirect had created a state-of-the-art production center and staffed it with top-notch personnel. The 300,000-square-foot production facility located in Long Island City was composed of 12 separate temperature zones, ensuring that each piece of food was kept at its optimal temperature for ripening or preservation. Each department of the facility, including the coffee roaster, butcher, and bakery, was staffed by carefully selected experts, enabling FreshDirect to offer premium fresh coffees, pastries, breads, meats, and seafood. Further quality management was achieved by the SAP manufacturing-software system that controlled every detail of the facility's operations. All of the thermometers, scales, and conveyor belts within the facility were connected to a central command center. Each specific setting was programmed into the system by an expert from the corresponding department, including everything from the ideal temperature for ripening a cantaloupe to the amount of flour that went into French bread. The system was also equipped with a monitoring alarm that alerted staff to any skew from the programmed settings.

Another quality control element that had been made an integral part of the FreshDirect facility was an extremely high standard for cleanliness, health, and safety. The facility itself was kept immaculately clean and all food-preparation areas and equipment were bathed in antiseptic foam at the end of each day. Incoming and outgoing food was tested in FreshDirect's in-house laboratory, which was managed by a 32-year veteran U.S. Department of Agriculture inspection supervisor, who ensured the facility adhered to USDA guidelines and the Hazard Analysis and Critical Control Point food safety system, and that all food passing through FreshDirect met the company's high safety standards.

System efficiency had been the key to FreshDirect's ability to offer its high-quality products at such low prices. FreshDirect's biggest operational design component for reducing costs had been the complete elimination of the middleman. Instead of going through an intermediary, both fresh and dry products were ordered from individual growers and producers, and shipped directly to FreshDirect's production center where FreshDirect's expert staff prepared them for selling. In addition, FreshDirect did not accept any slotting allowances. This unique relationship with growers and producers allowed FreshDirect to enjoy reduced purchase prices from its suppliers, enabling them to pass even greater savings on to their customers.

The proximity of FreshDirect's processing facility to its Manhattan customer base was also a critical factor in its cost-effective operational design. The processing center's location in Long Island City put approximately 4 million people within a 10-mile radius of the FreshDirect facility, allowing the firm to deliver a large number of orders in a short amount of time.[1] Further cost controls had been implemented through FreshDirect's order and delivery protocols. Orders had to be a minimum of $40.00 with a delivery charge of $3.95 per order. FreshDirect prohibited tipping the delivery person. Delivery was made by one of FreshDirect's 23 trucks and was available only during a prearranged two-hour window on weekdays after 4:30 p.m. and all day on the weekends, which kept delivery trucks out of the heaviest New York City traffic, thus reducing FreshDirect's delivery-related costs.

Founding Partners

FreshDirect was launched in July 2001. CEO Joe Fedele was able to bring a wealth of experience with New York City's food industry to FreshDirect. In 1993 he cofounded Fairway Uptown, a 35,000-foot supermarket located on West 133rd Street in Harlem. Many critics originally scoffed at the idea of a successful store in that location, but Fairway's low prices and quality selection of produce and meats made it a hit with neighborhood residents, as well as many downtown and suburban commuters.

CFO Jason Ackerman had gained exposure to the grocery industry as an investment banker with Donaldson Lufkin & Jenrette, where he specialized in supermarket mergers and acquisitions.

Fedele and Ackerman first explored the idea of starting a large chain of fresh-food stores, but realized maintaining a high degree of quality would be impossible with a large enterprise. As an alternative, they elected to pursue a business that incorporated online shopping with central distribution.

FreshDirect acquired the bulk of its $100 million investment from several private sources, with a small contribution coming from the State of New York. By locating FreshDirect's distribution center within the state border, and promising to create at least 300 new permanent, full-time private sector jobs in the state, FreshDirect became eligible for a $500,000 training grant from the Empire State Development Jobs Now Program. As its name implied, the purpose of the Jobs Now program was to create new, immediate job opportunities for New Yorkers.

Business Plan

While business started out relatively slow, Fedele had hoped to capture around 5 percent of the New York grocery market, with projected revenues of about $100 million in the first year and $225 million by 2004. As of March 2003, FreshDirect had reached the milestone of 2,000 orders a day and was attracting around 3,000 new customers a day, for a total customer base of around 40,000.[2] FreshDirect service was originally slated for availability citywide by the end of 2002. However, in order to maintain its superior service and product quality, FreshDirect had chosen to slowly expand its service area. Services were expected to cover New York City and parts of Suffolk and Nassau counties by the end of 2004, and possibly start up in several other metropolitan regions nationwide by 2005.

The company had employed a relatively low-cost marketing approach, which originally consisted mainly of billboards, public relations, and word of mouth to promote its products and services. In 2003 FreshDirect hired Trumpet, an ad agency that promoted FreshDirect as a better way to shop by emphasizing the problems associated with traditional grocery shopping. For example, one commercial stressed the unsanitary conditions in a supermarket by showing a grocery shopper bending over a barrel of olives as she sneezed, getting an olive stuck in her nose, and then blowing it back into the barrel. The advertisement ended with the question, "Where's your food been?" Another ad showed a checkout clerk morph into an armed robber, demand money from the customer, and then morph back into a friendly checkout clerk once the money was received. The ad urged viewers to "stop getting robbed at the grocery store."[3]

Another innovative marketing approach that had been very successful was the offer of free food. FreshDirect offered $50 worth of free groceries to any first-time service user, believing that once people saw the quality of the food and the convenience of the service they would return as paying customers.

Operating Strategy

FreshDirect's operating strategy had employed a make-to-order philosophy, eliminating the middleman in order to create an efficient supply chain.[4] By focusing its energy on providing produce, meat, seafood, baked goods, and coffees that were made to the customer's specific order, FreshDirect offered its customers an alternative to the standardized cuts and choices available at most brick-and-mortar grocery stores. This strategy had created a business model that was unique within the grocery business community.

A typical grocery store carried about 25,000 packaged goods, which accounted for around 50 percent of its sales, and about 2,200 perishable products, which accounted for the other 50 percent of sales. In contrast, FreshDirect offered around 5,000 perishable products, accounting for about 75 percent of its sales, but only around 3,000 packaged goods, which comprised the remaining 25 percent of sales.[5] While this stocking pattern enabled a greater array of fresh foods, it severely limited the number of brands and available sizes of packaged goods, such as cereal, crackers, and laundry detergent. However, FreshDirect believed customers would accept a more limited packaged good selection in order to get lower prices, as evidenced in the success of wholesale grocery stores which offered bulk sales of limited items. Jason Ackerman identified the ideal FreshDirect customers as those who bought their bulk staples from Costco on a monthly basis and bought everything else from FreshDirect on a weekly basis.[6]

FreshDirect's Web Site

FreshDirect's Web site not only offered an abundance of products to choose from, but also provided a broad spectrum of information on the food that was sold and the manner in which it was sold. Web surfers could take a pictorial tour of the FreshDirect facility; get background information on the experts who managed each department; get nutritional information on food items; compare produce or cheese based on taste, price, and usage; specify the thickness of meat orders and opt for one of several marinades or rubs (see Exhibit 1); search for the right kind of coffee based on taste preferences; and read nutritional information for a variety of fully prepared meals.

For example, if you wanted to purchase chicken, you were first asked to choose from Breasts & Cutlets, Cubes & Strips, Ground, Legs & Thighs, Specialty Parts, Split & Quartered, Whole, or Wings. Once your selection was made—let's say you chose Breasts & Cutlets—you were given further options based on your preference for skin, bone, and thickness. The final selection step offered you a choice of rubs and marinades, including Teriyaki, Sweet & Sour, Garlic Rosemary, Poultry Seasoning, Lemon Herb Rub, and Salt & Pepper Rub. All along the way, the pages offered nutritional profiles of each cut of meat as well as tips for preparation and storage.

FreshDirect employed two different delivery models, one for its urban customers and another for those in the suburbs. Customers within the city were attracted to the FreshDirect service because it eliminated the need to carry groceries for possibly a substantial distance from the closest grocery store, or to deal with trying to park a car near their apartment to unload their purchases. Orders made by

Exhibit 1   Example of FreshDirect Meat Selection Options

customers within the city were delivered directly to their homes by a FreshDirect truck during a prearranged two-hour delivery window (see Exhibit 2).

Suburban customers were serviced in a slightly different manner. Most suburban residents had the convenience of automobile access and easy parking, but were looking for a time-saving device. The widespread congregation of these residents in train station parking lots or office parks made these areas perfect central delivery stations. FreshDirect would send a refrigerated truck, large enough to hold 500 orders, to these key spots during designated periods of time. Suburbanites could then exit the train or their office building, return to their cars, swing by the FreshDirect truck, pick up their order, and head home.

The Retail Grocery Industry

In 2003 the U.S. retail grocery industry was a $682.3 billion business, according to the U.S. Department of Commerce, with almost $362.4 billion of sales made by supermarket chains.[7] The top 10 supermarket chains in the United States commanded more than 44 percent of the market share for the grocery industry (see Exhibit 3).

In 2003 no single supermarket chain had an industry market share above 10 percent. The typical supermarket store carried an average of 32,000 items, averaged 44,000 square feet in size, and averaged $18 million in sales annually.

The supermarket business had traditionally been a low-margin business, with net profits of only 1 to 2 percent of revenues. Store profits depended heavily on creating a high volume of customer traffic and rapid inventory turnover, especially for perishables such as produce and fresh meat. Competitors had to operate efficiently to make money, so tight control of labor costs and product spoilage was essential. Because capital investment costs were modest—involving mainly the construction of distribution centers and stores—it was not unusual for supermarket chains to realize 15 to 20 percent returns on invested capital.

Exhibit 2   FreshDirect Delivery Options

Supermarket Chain	Market Share (%)
Wal-Mart Super Centers	9.6%
Kroger	7.3
Albertson's	5.6
Safeway	5.0
Royal Ahold	3.4
Supervalu	3.1
Costco Wholesale Corp.	3.0
Sam's Club	2.7
Fleming	2.3
Publix Super Markets	2.2
Total Market Share	44.2

Source: *Advertising Age.*

Exhibit 3   Market Share for Top 10 Supermarket Chains

The Online Grocery Segment   The online-grocery shopping business was still in the early stages of development in 2004. Analysts believed that this segment accounted for less than 1 percent of total grocery sales in 2004. Total online sales were about $2.4 billion, but were expected to reach $6.5 billion by 2008.[8] Online grocery shopping had been slow to catch on, and industry newcomers had encountered high start-up and operating costs. Sales volumes and profit margins remained too small to cover the high costs. The problem, according to industry analysts, was that consumers had been largely disappointed in the service, selection, and prices they had gotten from industry members.

However, some analysts expected online grocery sales to grow at a rapid pace as companies improved their service and selection, PC penetration of households rose, and consumers became more accustomed to making purchases online.[9] An article in *Computer Bits* examined the customer base for online grocers, looking specifically at the types of consumers that would be likely to shop online and the kinds of home computer systems that were required for online shopping. An Anderson Consulting report, cited in

Exhibit 4   Types of Online Shoppers and Their Propensity to Be Attracted to Online Grocery Shopping

Types of Online Shoppers	Comments
Traditionals	Might be older technology-avoiders, or simply shoppers who like to sniff-test their own produce and eyeball the meat selection.
Responsibles	Feed off the satisfaction of accomplishing this persistent to-do item.
Time Starved	Find the extra costs associated with delivery fees or other markups a small price to pay for saving them time.
New Technologists	Use the latest technology for any and every activity they can, because they can.
Necessity Users	People with physical or circumstantial challenges that make grocery shopping difficult. Likely to be the most loyal group of shoppers.
Avoiders	Dislike the grocery shopping experience for a variety of reasons.

Source: Anderson Consulting study cited in Sherry Anderson. 2001. Is online grocery shopping for you? *Computer Bits,* 11, April.

Computer Bits, identified six major types of online shoppers (see Exhibit 4) and estimated that by 2007, 15 to 20 million households would order their grocers online.[10] A MARC Group study concluded that "consumers who buy groceries online are likely to be more loyal to their electronic supermarkets, spend more per store 'visit,' and take greater advantage of coupons and premiums than traditional customers."[11]

One of the problems with online grocery shopping was that consumers were extremely price sensitive when it came to buying groceries, and the prices of many online grocers were above those at supermarkets. Shoppers, in many cases, were unwilling to pay extra to online grocers for the convenience of home delivery. Consumer price sensitivity meant that online grocers had to achieve a cost structure that would allow them to (1) price competitively, (2) cover the cost of selecting items in the store and delivering individual grocery orders, and (3) have sufficient margins to earn attractive returns on their investment. Some analysts estimated that to be successful, online grocers had to do 10 times the volume of a traditional grocer.[12]

Supermarket Chains as Potential Competitors in the Online Grocery Segment   When online grocers started appearing within the industry, many established brick-and-mortar grocers began offering online shopping in an attempt to maintain and expand their customer base. Two basic models had been used for online order fulfillment: (1) to pick items from the shelves of existing stores within the grocer's chain, and (2) to build special warehouses dedicated to online orders. The demand for home delivery of groceries had been increasing, but in many market areas the demand had not yet reached a level that would justify the high cost of warehouses dedicated to the fulfillment of online orders.[13]

Safeway began an ambitious online grocery venture by establishing Grocery Works, an online shopping system that included a series of warehouses dedicated to filling online orders. Unfavorable returns forced Safeway to reevaluate its system, and it eventually chose to form a partnership with Tesco, a U.K.–based grocer. Tesco filled its online orders from the shelves of local stores in close proximity to the customer's home. Safeway and Tesco worked together on GroceryWorks in Portland, Oregon, where they received a positive initial response from customers.[14]

Online Grocery Industry

YourGrocer.com   FreshDirect's most geographically significant competitor in the online grocery industry was YourGrocer.com. (See Exhibit 5 for profiles of online grocers. Exhibit 6 compares prices of selected items at these same online grocers.) YourGrocer was launched in New York City in 1998 with the goal of being the leading online grocery service for the New York metropolitan area. By November 2001 the company ran out of money and was forced to shut down. In the spring of 2002 new capital resources were found and the company reopened for business. However, the second time around YourGrocer's approach was a little different.

YourGrocer was created with a bulk-buying strategy, believing that customers would order large, economical quantities of goods from the Web site and the company would make home deliveries in company trucks. During

Exhibit 5   Profiles of Selected Online Grocers

Name	Area Covered	Minimum Order	Delivery Charge	Delivery Method	Specialization
FreshDirect	Manhattan's East Side, Battery Park City	$40	$3.95, no tipping	Trucks; avail. weeknights after 4:30 p.m. and all day on weekends	♦ Mostly perishables: fresh produce, meats, baked goods ♦ Low prices because there is no middleman
YourGrocer	Manhattan, Bronx, Westchester, Greenwich	$75	$9.95	Rented vans; avail. on select days and times, depending on location	♦ Bulk orders of packaged goods
Peapod	Chicago, Boston, DC, southern Connecticut, Long Island	$50	$4.95 for order greater than $75; $9.95 for order less than $75; tipping optional	Truck; avail. 7 a.m.–1 p.m. and 4 p.m.–10 p.m. weekdays, 7 a.m.–1 p.m. weekends	♦ Partner with Giant Foods and Stop & Shop; items picked from shelves of local store near customer's home
NetGrocer	Lower 48 states, DC	None	$3.99–$601.99, depends on order size and destination	FedEx; will receive order within 1 to 4 business days	♦ Only nonperishables; no fresh produce

Source: Company Web sites.

Exhibit 6   Comparison of Prices for Selected Online Grocers, February 2003

Grocery Item	FreshDirect's Price	YourGrocer's Price	PeaPod's Price	NetGrocer's Price
Tide laundry detergent	$7.99 / 100 oz.	$21.99 / 300 oz. ($7.33 / 100 oz.)	$8.79 / 100 oz.	$9.99 / 100 oz.
Wish-Bone Italian dressing	$1.49 / 8 oz.	$4.69 / 36 oz. ($1.04 / 8 oz.)	$1.69 / 8 oz.	$1.79 / 8 oz.
Cheerios	$3.69 / 15 oz.	$7.49 / 35 oz. ($3.21 / 15 oz.)	$3.89 / 15 oz.	$4.29 / 15 oz.
Ragu spaghetti sauce	$1.99 / 26 oz.	$7.99 / 135 oz. ($1.54 / 26 oz.)	$1.99 / 26 oz.	$2.49 / 26 oz.
Granny Smith apples	$1.29 / lb.	$5.99 / 5 lb. bag ($1.20 / lb.)	$2.99 / 3 lb. bag ($1.00 / lb.)	Fresh produce not available

Source: Company Web sites.

YourGrocer's first life, the ambitious business plan covered a large service area and included the acquisition of another online grocery company, NYCGrocery.com.[15] But the business plan was modified in the second life. The company reduced the size of its staff, got rid of warehouses, decided to rent instead of owning its delivery vans, and scaled down its delivery routes.[16] Queens, Nassau County, and New Jersey were eliminated from the service area, leaving only Manhattan, the Bronx, Westchester County, and Fairfield County (Connecticut).

YourGrocer offered a limited selection of items that could only be purchased in bulk. Deliveries were made in

Exhibit 7   YourGrocer.com Web site

varied time slots, depending on the customer's location in the New York area. There was a $75 minimum order with a $9.95 delivery charge (see Exhibits 7 and 8).

Peapod   Founded in 1989 by brothers Andrew and Thomas Parkinson, Peapod (see Exhibits 9 and 10) was an early pioneer in e-commerce, inventing an online home-shopping service for grocery items years ahead of the commercial emergence of the Internet. With its tagline "Smart Shopping for Busy People," the company began providing consumers with a home-shopping experience in the early 1990s, going so far as to install modems in customer homes

Exhibit 8   YourGrocer's Service Focus

New YourGrocer will focus on providing the three benefits that families in the area most value:

1. Easy ordering over the Internet or on the phone, which saves hours of thankless shopping time.
2. Delivery right to the home or office, which eliminates the burden of lifting and transporting heavy and bulky items each month.
3. Meaningful savings everyday, which reduces the prices paid for stock-up groceries and supplies by 20–30%, on average, below local supermarkets.

Exhibit 9   Peapod Web site

to provide an online connection. From its founding in 1989 until 1998, the company's business model involved filling customer orders by forming alliances with traditional grocery retailers. The company chose a retail partner in each geographic area where it operated and used the partner's local network of retail stores to pick and pack orders for delivery to customers. Peapod personnel would cruise the aisles of a partner's stores, selecting the items each customer ordered, pack and load them into Peapod vehicles, and then deliver them to customers at prearranged times. Peapod charged customers a fee for its service and collected fees from its retail supply partners for using their products in its online service. Over the next several years, Peapod built delivery capabilities in eight market areas: Chicago; Columbus, Ohio; Boston; San Francisco/San Jose; Houston, Dallas, and Austin, in Texas; and Long Island, New York.

In 1997, faced with mounting losses despite growing revenues, Peapod management shifted to a new order fulfillment business model utilizing a local company owned and operated central distribution warehouse to store, pick, and pack customer orders for delivery. By mid-1999 the company had opened new distribution centers in three of the eight markets it served—Chicago, Long Island, and Boston; a fourth distribution center was under construction in San Francisco.

In the late spring of 2000, Peapod created a partnership with Royal Ahold, an international food provider based in the Netherlands. At the time, Ahold operated five supermarket companies in the United States: Stop & Shop, Tops Market, Giant-Landover, Giant-Carlisle, and BI-LO. In September 2000 Peapod acquired Streamline.com, Inc.'s operations in Chicago and the Washington, D.C., markets, and announced that it planned to exit its markets in Columbus, Ohio, and Houston, Dallas, and Austin, Texas. All of these moves were made as a part of Peapod's strategic plan for growth and future profitability.

Under Peapod's initial partnership agreement with Ahold, Peapod was to continue as a stand-alone company,

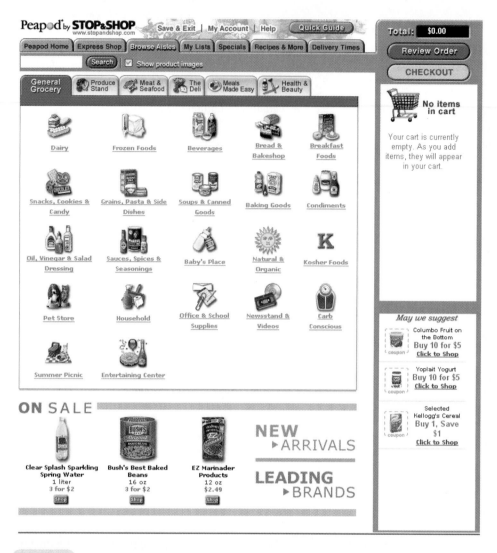

Exhibit 10   Peapod Product Selection

with Ahold supplying Peapod's goods, services, and fast-pick fulfillment centers. However, in July 2001 Ahold acquired all the outstanding shares of Peapod and merged Peapod into one of Ahold's subsidiaries.

In 2003 Peapod provided online shopping and delivery service in five metropolitan areas: Chicago, Boston, southern Connecticut, Long Island, and Washington, D.C. Peapod employed a centralized distribution model in every market: in large markets, orders were picked, packed, loaded, and delivered from a freestanding centralized fulfillment center; in smaller markets, Peapod established fast-pick centralized fulfillment centers adjacent to the facilities of retail partners.[17] Peapod's proprietary transportation routing system ensured on-time delivery and efficient truck and driver utilization.

Netgrocer   Netgrocer.com was founded in 1996 and advertised itself as the first online grocer to sell nonperishable items nationwide (see Exhibits 11 and 12). Netgrocer serviced all 48 continental U.S. states and the District of Columbia. All customer orders were filled in its single, 120,000-square-foot warehouse in North Brunswick, New Jersey. Orders were shipped by Federal Express and were guaranteed to reach any part of Netgrocer's service area within two to four days.

Netgrocer offered its customers a large selection of brand-name and specialty nonperishable items that were difficult to find in a local supermarket. The key customer segment for Netgrocer's services were busy families, urban dwellers, special-needs groups (e.g., dieters,

Exhibit 11 Netgrocer.com Web site

diabetics), and senior citizens. Customers purportedly enjoyed the benefits of convenient online shopping from home 24 hours a day, access to thousands of products, and delivery of their orders directly to their home. Manufacturers also benefited from Netgrocer, as they were able to distribute their products nationwide, rapidly and easily.

In 2002 Netgrocer became a part of a larger grocery enterprise. A new entity named NeXpansion was created that included the existing Netgrocer service and also a new service called Endless Aisle. Rather than competing with local grocery stores, Endless Aisle offered local grocers a way to greatly expand their product assortment. The program worked through Endless Aisle kiosks in-

stalled in participating brick-and-mortar supermarkets. Shoppers could visit the kiosk to shop online for products that were unavailable in the grocery store, such as specialty products, hard-to-find regional items, and product categories not traditionally carried by grocery stores. The products offered through Endless Aisle were designed to complement, not compete, with the local store's product selection. Consumers enjoyed one-stop shopping for all of their grocery needs while local retailers benefited from the Endless Aisle service because they were able to offer their customers easy access to a much wider range of products, without having to use valuable shelf space for products that had a lower sales velocity.

SHIPPING REGION 2	
ORDER BRACKETS	SHIPPING RATE
$0 - 24.99	$8.99
$25 - 49.99	$12.99
$50 - 74.99	$15.99
$75 - 99.99	$19.99
$100 - 124.99	$23.99
$125 - 149.99	$27.99
$150 - 199.99	$41.99
$200 - 299.99	$66.99
$300 - 499.99	$101.99
$500 - 749.99	$201.99
$750 - 999.99	$301.99
$1000 +**	$601.99

SHIPPING REGION 1	
ORDER BRACKETS	SHIPPING RATE
$0 - 24.99	$5.99
$25 - 49.99	$8.99
$50 - 74.99	$10.99
$75 - 99.99	$12.99
$100 - 124.99	$14.99
$125 - 149.99	$17.99
$150 - 199.99	$21.99
$200 - 299.99	$31.99
$300 - 499.99	$51.99
$500 - 749.99	$111.99
$750 - 999.99	$171.99
$1000 +**	$401.99

Exhibit 12   NetGrocer Shipping Charges

Endnotes

1. Laseter, Tim, et. al. 2003. What FreshDirect learned from Dell. *Strategy+Business* (30), Spring.
2. *Business Wire.* 2003. Five months in Manhattan and FreshDirect passes the 2,000-order-a-day mark and has over 40,000 customers. February 12.
3. Elliot, Stuart. 2003. A "fresh" and "direct" approach. *New York Times,* February 11.
4. Laseter, What FreshDirect learned from Dell.
5. Ibid.
6. Ibid.
7. Food Market Institute. *Supermarket Facts: Industry Overview 2003,* www.fmi.org/facts_figs/superfact.htm.
8. McTaggart, Jenny. 2004. Fresh direction. *Progressive Grocer* 83(4), 58–60.
9. Machlis, Sharon. 1998. Filling up grocery carts online. *Computerworld,* July 27: 4.

10. Anderson, Sherry. 2001. Is online grocery shopping for you? *Computer Bits,* 11, April.
11. Woods, Bob. 1998. America Online goes grocery shopping for e-commerce bargains. *Computer News,* August 10: 42.
12. Fisher, Lawrence M. 1999. On-line grocer is setting up delivery system for $1 billion. *New York Times,* July 10: 1.
13. *Frontline Solutions.* 2002. Online supermarkets keep it simple. 3(2): 46–49.
14. Ibid.
15. Joyce, Erin. 2002. YourGrocer.com wants to come back. *ECommerce,* May 15; http://ecommerce.internet.com/news/news/article/ 0,,10375_1122671,00.html.
16. Fickenscher, Lisa. 2002. Bouncing back from cyber limbo: Resurgence of failed dot-coms after downsizing. *Crain's New York Business,* June 24.
17. Peapod, Inc., Corporate fact sheet, www.peapod.com/corpinfo/peapodFacts.pdf.

Case 22   Robin Hood*

It was in the spring of the second year of his insurrection against the High Sheriff of Nottingham that Robin Hood took a walk in Sherwood Forest. As he walked he pondered the progress of the campaign, the disposition of his forces, the Sheriff's recent moves, and the options that confronted him.

The revolt against the Sheriff had begun as a personal crusade, erupting out of Robin's conflict with the Sheriff and his administration. Alone, however, Robin Hood could do little. He therefore sought allies, men with grievances and a deep sense of justice. Later he welcomed all who came, asking few questions, and only demanding a willingness to serve. Strength, he believed, lay in numbers.

He spent the first year forging the group into a disciplined band, united in enmity against the Sheriff, and willing to live outside the law. The band's organization was simple. Robin ruled supreme, making all important decisions. He delegated specific tasks to his lieutenants. Will Scarlett was in charge of intelligence and scouting. His main job was to shadow the Sheriff and his men, always alert to their next move. He also collected information on the travel plans of rich merchants and tax collectors. Little John kept discipline among the men, and saw to it that their archery was at the high peak that their profession demanded. Scarlock took care of the finances, converting loot into cash, paying shares of the take, and finding suitable hiding places for the surplus. Finally, Much the Miller's son had the difficult task of provisioning the ever-increasing band of Merrymen.

The increasing size of the band was a source of satisfaction for Robin, but also a source of concern. The fame of his Merrymen was spreading, and new recruits poured in from every corner of England. As the band grew larger, their small bivouac became a major encampment. Between raids the men milled about, talking and playing games. Vigilance was in decline, and discipline was becoming harder to enforce. "Why," Robin reflected, "I don't know half the men I run into these days."

The growing band was also beginning to exceed the food capacity of the forest. Game was becoming scarce, and supplies had to be obtained from outlying villages. The cost of buying food was beginning to drain the band's financial reserves at the very moment when revenues were in decline. Travelers, especially those with the most to lose, were now giving the forest a wide berth. This was costly and inconvenient to them, but it was preferable to having all their goods confiscated.

Robin believed that the time had come for the Merrymen to change their policy of outright confiscation of goods to one of a fixed transit tax. His lieutenants strongly resisted this idea. They were proud of the Merrymen's famous motto: "Rob the rich and give to the poor." "The farmers and the townspeople," they argued, "are our most important allies. How can we tax them, and still hope for their help in our fight against the Sheriff?"

Robin wondered how long the Merrymen could keep to the ways and methods of their early days. The Sheriff was growing stronger and better organized. He now had the money and the men, and was beginning to harass the band, probing for its weaknesses.

The tide of events was beginning to turn against the Merrymen. Robin felt that the campaign must be decisively concluded before the Sheriff had a chance to deliver a mortal blow. "But how," he wondered, "could this be done?"

Robin had often entertained the possibility of killing the Sheriff, but the chances for this seemed increasingly remote. Besides, while killing the Sheriff might satisfy his personal thirst for revenge, it would not improve the situation. Robin had hoped that the perpetual state of unrest, and the Sheriff's failure to collect taxes, would lead to his removal from office. Instead, the Sheriff used his political connections to obtain reinforcement. He had powerful friends at court, and was well regarded by the regent, Prince John.

Prince John was vicious and volatile. He was consumed by his unpopularity among the people, who wanted the imprisoned King Richard back. He also lived in constant fear of the barons, who had first given him the regency, but were now beginning to dispute his claim to the throne. Several of these barons had set out to collect the ransom that would release King Richard the Lionheart from his jail in Austria. Robin was invited to join the conspiracy in return for future amnesty. It was a dangerous proposition. Provincial banditry was one thing, court intrigue another. Prince John's spies were everywhere. If the plan failed, the pursuit would be relentless and retribution swift.

The sound of the supper horn startled Robin from his thoughts. There was the smell of roasting venison in the air. Nothing was resolved or settled. Robin headed for camp promising himself that he would give these problems his utmost attention after tomorrow's raid.

*Prepared by Joseph Lampel, City University, London. Copyright Joseph Lampel © 1985, Revised 1991. Reprinted with permission.

Case 23   Johnson & Johnson*

Over the first few months of 2005, Johnson & Johnson (J&J) was putting the finishing touches on its deal to acquire Guidant Corporation for $23.9 billion. The acquisition was by far the largest that the firm had made in its 118-year history. It was expected to allow J&J to expand on its existing line of products to treat heart and circulatory illnesses by giving it a strong presence in the fast growing market for devices that stabilize heart rhythms. William C. Weldon, chairman and chief executive officer of J&J, commented: "Bringing Guidant into the J&J family of companies builds on our history of strategic acquisitions and partnerships that provide a foundation for sustained leadership and growth."[1]

J&J growth has clearly been driven by the acquisitions that it has made over the years. Over the past decade, the firm made 58 acquisitions and mergers of mostly small firms that were working on promising new products. These acquisitions have played a key role in allowing J&J to deliver at least 10 percent earnings growth year in and year out going back nearly two decades (see Exhibit 1). As a result of this steady performance, the firm's stock price had increased from less than $3, split-adjusted, in the mid-1980s to more than 20 times that now.

But Weldon is aware that it is going to be harder to maintain J&J's growth rate through a reliance on acquisitions. The firm has been finding it increasingly difficult to spot smaller firms with promising drugs that could become blockbusters. Even when it is able to identify possible acquisition targets, it has been running up against other firms that are looking to make the same kinds of deals. "You get to a point where finding acquisitions that fit the mold and make a contribution becomes increasingly difficult," warned UBS Warburg analyst David Lothson. "This puts pressure on the sustainability of this strategy, and ultimately it could break down."[2]

Therefore, Weldon is trying to squeeze more growth out of J&J's existing businesses. When he took over the firm in 2002, he was particularly concerned about the prospects of J&J's pharmaceutical division, which has consistently accounted for almost half of the firm's revenues and more than half of its operating profits. Like the rest of the pharmaceutical industry, J&J was looking at declining revenues from its best selling drugs because of expiring patents and growing competition. Weldon also believed that the firm had few new potential blockbuster products that it could fall back upon. Exhibits 2 and 3 illustrate J&J's income statements and balance sheets.

*This case was prepared by Professor Jamal Shamsie of Michigan State University. This case was developed from published sources as a basis for class discussion rather than to illustrate either effective or ineffective handling of an administrative situation. Copyright © 2005 Jamal Shamsie.

Exhibit 1   Johnson & Johnson Segment Information

Johnson & Johnson is made up of 204 different companies, many of which it has acquired over the years. These individual companies have been assigned to three different divisions:

Pharmaceuticals

Share of Firm's Sales: 46 percent

Share of Firm's Operating Profits: 58 percent

The most profitable and the fastest growing division, but its best known drugs are facing increased competition. Further growth could come from the use of drug delivery devices to develop new formulations of existing products.

Devices & Diagnostics

Share of Firm's Sales: 36 percent

Share of Firm's Operating Profits: 31 percent

A growing division that has been successful with some recent product introductions, such as the drug-coated stent. May experience more growth with new gene-based tests.

Consumer Products

Share of Firm's Sales: 18 percent

Share of Firm's Operating Profits: 12 percent

The best known division, but it has been the least profitable and shown the slowest growth. Prospects could improve with over-the-counter versions of drugs whose patents expire.

Source: Johnson & Johnson.

Given the scope of the businesses that J&J manages, Weldon felt that the best opportunities may come from increased collaboration between its different units. The firm has the ability to develop new products by combining its strengths across pharmaceutical products, medical devices, diagnostics, and consumer products. But Weldon is also aware that the success of J&J has been based on the relative autonomy and independence that it has accorded its various business units. Any push for greater collaboration must build upon the entrepreneurial spirit that has been built over the years through this type of organization.

Creating Autonomous Business Units

As it has grown, J&J has developed into an astonishingly complex enterprise, made up of over 200 different businesses

Exhibit 2   Johnson & Johnson's Income Statement
(All numbers in $ thousands)

	Period Ending		
	January 2, 2005	December 28, 2003	December 29, 2002
Total Revenue	47,348,000	41,862,000	36,298,000
Cost of Revenue	13,422,000	12,176,000	10,447,000
Gross Profit	33,926,000	29,686,000	25,851,000
Research Development	5,203,000	4,684,000	3,957,000
Selling General and Administrative	15,860,000	14,131,000	12,216,000
Nonrecurring	18,000	918,000	189,000
Operating Income or Loss	12,845,000	9,953,000	9,489,000
Total Other Income/Expenses Net	180,000	562,000	(38,000)
Earnings before Interest and Taxes	13,025,000	10,515,000	9,451,000
Interest Expense	187,000	207,000	160,000
Income before Tax	12,838,000	10,308,000	9,291,000
Income Tax Expense	4,329,000	3,111,000	2,694,000
Net Income from Continuing Operations	8,509,000	7,197,000	6,597,000
Net Income	8,509,000	7,197,000	6,597,000

Source: Johnson & Johnson.

organized into three different divisions. The most widely known of these is the division that makes consumer products such as Band-Aid adhesive strips, Aveeno skin-care lotions and various baby products. But most of J&J's recent growth has come from its pharmaceutical products and from its medical devices and diagnostics. Drugs alone have consistently accounted for almost half of the firm's sales and well over half of its operating profits over the past five years. With revenues approaching $48 billion, J&J has already become one of the largest health care companies in the United States. Its competitors in this field are well aware of J&J's rare combination of scientific expertise and marketing savvy that have helped it to gain a leading position.

To a large extent, however, J&J's success across its three divisions and many different businesses has hinged on its unique structure and culture. Each of its far-flung business units has operated pretty much as an independent enterprise. The firm has been able to turn itself into a powerhouse precisely because each of the businesses that it either buys or starts has always been granted near total autonomy. That independence has fostered an entrepreneurial attitude that has kept J&J intensely competitive as

others around it have faltered. The relative autonomy that is accorded to the business units provides the firm with the ability to respond swiftly to emerging opportunities.

In other words, the business units have been given considerable freedom to set their own strategies. Besides developing their strategies, these units are allowed to plan for their own resources. Many of the businesses even have their own finance and human resources departments. While this degree of decentralization makes for relatively high overhead costs, none of the executives that have run J&J, including Weldon, has ever thought that this was too high a price to pay. "The company really operates more like a mutual fund than anything else," commented Pat Dorsey, director of equity research at Morningstar.[3]

In spite of the benefits that J&J has derived from giving its various enterprises considerable autonomy, there is a growing feeling that they can no longer operate in near isolation. Weldon has begun to realize, as do most others in the industry, that some of the most important breakthroughs in 21st-century medicine are likely to come from the ability to apply scientific advances from one discipline to another. J&J should, therefore, be in a strong position to

Exhibit 3   Johnson & Johnson's Balance Sheet
(All numbers in $ thousands)

	Period Ending		
	January 2, 2005	December 28, 2003	December 29, 2002
Assets			
Current Assets			
Cash and Cash Equivalents	9,203,000	5,377,000	2,894,000
Short-Term Investments	3,681,000	4,146,000	4,581,000
Net Receivables	8,568,000	8,100,000	6,818,000
Inventory	3,744,000	3,588,000	3,303,000
Other Current Assets	2,124,000	1,784,000	1,670,000
Total Current Assets	**27,320,000**	**22,995,000**	**19,266,000**
Long-Term Investments	46,000	84,000	121,000
Property Plant and Equipment	10,436,000	9,846,000	8,710,000
Goodwill	5,863,000	5,390,000	4,653,000
Intangible Assets	5,979,000	6,149,000	4,593,000
Other Assets	3,122,000	3,107,000	2,977,000
Deferred Long-Term Asset Charges	551,000	692,000	236,000
Total Assets	**53,317,000**	**48,263,000**	**40,556,000**
Liabilities			
Current Liabilities			
Accounts Payable	13,647,000	12,309,000	9,332,000
Short/Current Long-Term Debt	280,000	1,139,000	2,117,000
Total Current Liabilities	**13,927,000**	**13,448,000**	**11,449,000**
Long-Term Debt	2,565,000	2,955,000	2,022,000
Other Liabilities	4,609,000	4,211,000	3,745,000
Deferred Long-Term Liability Charges	403,000	780,000	643,000
Total Liabilities	**21,504,000**	**21,394,000**	**17,859,000**
Stockholders' Equity			
Common Stock	3,120,000	3,120,000	3,120,000
Retained Earnings	35,223,000	30,503,000	26,571,000
Treasury Stock	(6,004,000)	(6,146,000)	(6,127,000)
Other Stockholder Equity	(526,000)	(608,000)	(867,000)
Total Stockholder Equity	**31,813,000**	**26,869,000**	**22,697,000**
Net Tangible Assets	**$19,971,000**	**$15,330,000**	**$13,451,000**

Source: Johnson & Johnson.

Exhibit 4   Synergies within Johnson & Johnson

Improved Drugs

J&J's pharmaceutical operation is working with the company's drug-delivery operation, Alza, to come up with a new formulation of the epilepsy drug Topamax. The drug also has been shown to promote weight loss, and this would make it a more tolerable obesity treatment.

New Medical Tests

A new diagnostic unit is working with data generated by drug researchers; they could, for example, develop a gene-based test to identify patients who are most likely to respond to experimental cancer treatments.

Cutting-edge Consumer Products

In 2002 J&J rolled out the new Band-Aid Brand Liquid Bandage, a liquid coating that is applied to cuts on hard-to-cover areas like fingers and knuckles. The product is based on a material used in a wound-closing product sold by J&J's hospital products company, Ethicon.

Source: *BusinessWeek.*

---

exploit new opportunities by drawing on the diverse skills of its various business units across the three divisions.

Pushing for Synergies

Weldon strongly believes that J&J is perfectly positioned to profit from this shift toward combining drugs, devices, and diagnostics, since few companies can match its reach and strength in these basic areas (see Exhibit 4). According to Weldon, "There is a convergence that will allow us to do things we haven't done before."[4] Indeed, J&J has top-notch products in each of those categories. It has been boosting its research and development budget by more than 10 percent annually for the past few years, which puts it among the top spenders, and it now employs over 9,000 scientists in 40 research laboratories around the world.

But Weldon feels that J&J can profit from this convergence only if its fiercely independent businesses can be made to work together. By pushing these units to pool their resources, Weldon believes that the firm could become one of the few that may actually be able to attain that often-promised, rarely delivered idea of synergy. Some of the firm's new products, such as the new drug-coated stent, have clearly resulted from the collaborative efforts and sharing of ideas between its various far-flung divisions.

Weldon's vision for the new J&J may well have emerged from the steps that he took to reshape the pharmaceutical operation shortly after he took it over in 1998. At the time, J&J's drug business had been making solid gains as a result of popular products such as the anemia drug Procrit and the antipsychotic medication Risperdal. But the pipeline of new drugs was beginning to sputter after several potential treatments had failed in late-stage testing.

The solution that Weldon came up with was to create a new post to oversee all of the pharmaceutical division's R&D efforts. He also formed a divisional committee that brought together executives from R&D with those from sales and marketing to decide which projects to green-light. Previously, the R&D group had made these critical decisions on their own. No one had thought it might be beneficial to involve any other departments in these decisions. "Some people may have thought Bill curtailed their freedom," said Dr. Per A. Peterson, who oversees all pharmaceutical research and development. "But we've improved the decision making to eliminate compounds that just won't make it."[5]

To promote this idea of synergy, however, Weldon has to try to create this kind of cooperation throughout the company. He needs to push for this collaboration between J&J's units without quashing the entrepreneurial spirit that has spearheaded most of the growth of the firm to date. Jerry Caccott, managing director of consulting firm Strategic Decisions Group, emphasized that cultivating those alliances "would be challenging in any organization, but particularly in an organization that has been so successful because of its decentralized culture."[6]

Shifting the Company Culture

Weldon, like every other leader in the company's history, has worked his way up through the ranks. His long tenure within the firm has turned him into a true believer in the J&J system. He certainly does not want to undermine the entrepreneurial spirit that has resulted from the autonomy given to each of the businesses. Consequently, even though Weldon may talk incessantly about synergy and convergence, he has been cautious in the actual steps he has taken to push J&J's units to collaborate with each other.

For the most part, Weldon has confined himself to the development of new systems to foster better communication and more frequent collaboration among J&J's disparate operations. Among other things, he has worked with James T. Lenehan, vice chairman and president of J&J, to set up groups that draw people from across the firm to focus their efforts on specific diseases. Each of the groups is expected to report every six months on potential strategies and projects.

Although most of the changes that Weldon has instituted at J&J are not likely to yield real results for some time, there is already evidence that this new collaboration is working. Perhaps the most promising result of this approach has been J&J's drug-coated stent, called Cypher. The highly successful new addition to the firm's lineup resulted from the efforts of teams that combined people from the drug business with others from the device business. They collaborated on manufacturing the stent, which props open arteries after angioplasty. Weldon claims that if J&J had not been able to bring together people with different types of expertise, it could not have developed the stent without getting assistance from outside the firm.

Even the company's fabled consumer brands have been starting to take on a scientific edge. Its new liquid Band-Aid is based on a material used in a wound-closing product sold by one of J&J's hospital supply businesses. And J&J has used its prescription antifungal treatment, Nizoral, to develop a dandruff shampoo. In 2004 the firm was able to launch 300 new products, pushing sales of consumer products up by 12 percent. In fact, products that have developed in large part due to such cross-fertilization have allowed the firm's consumer business to increase its operating margins from around 14 percent to over 18 percent over the last four years.

Some of the projects that J&J is currently working on could produce even more significant results. Researchers working on genomic studies in the firm's labs were building a massive database using gene patterns that correlate to a certain disease or to someone's likely response to a particular drug. Weldon encouraged them to share this data with the various business units. As a result, the diagnostics team has been working on a test that the researchers in the pharmaceutical division could use to predict which patients would benefit from an experimental cancer therapy.

Maintaining the Pressure

Even as Weldon moves carefully to encourage collaboration between the business units, he has continued to push for the highest possible levels of performance. Those who know him well would say that he is compulsively competitive. As Weldon has been known to state on more than one occasion, "It's no fun to be second."[7] He is such an intense athlete that he was just a sprint away from ruining his knee altogether when he finally decided to give up playing basketball.

To make J&J more competitive, Weldon has made some aggressive moves. Two years ago, he pushed for the company's biggest acquisition ever with the $13.2 billion purchase of drug-delivery player Alza Corporation. But Weldon has been trying to let his managers get more

involved in J&J's dealings with other firms. For example, he made sure that he closely followed the negotiations that led up to the recent acquisition of Guidant. But Weldon usually took a back seat and allowed his managers to take the lead through most of these talks.

It is not always easy, however, for Weldon to keep a respectable distance from his managers. For example, he has entrusted the drug business to Christine A. Poon, whom he recruited from Bristol-Myers Squibb Company. Nevertheless, when several senior executives were hammering out details on the $2.4 billion acquisition of Scios Incorporated, a biotech company that has a drug for congestive heart failure, Weldon showed up to join the group. Weldon says he wanted to make an appearance because it was Poon's first major acquisition. "I wanted to be there, if nothing else, to give her some moral support," he said.[8]

Weldon is also letting his managers make their own decisions when forming the teams that are working on various projects. He usually does like to get briefed once a month on the progress that is being made on these projects. Beyond that, Weldon claims that he likes to trust his people. "They are the experts who know the marketplace, know the hospitals, and know the cardiologists," Weldon said about the team that has been working on the Cypher stent. "I have the utmost confidence in them."[9]

Even as Weldon tries to let his managers handle their own affairs, he clearly expects them to seek results with the same tenacity that he displayed in his climb to the top. As he rose through the ranks at J&J, Weldon became famous for setting near-impossible goals for his people and holding them to those goals. And for those executives who may fall short, Weldon does not usually have any difficulty making it clear that he does not like to be disappointed. When a new J&J drug business, Centocor Incorporated, failed to meet the aggressive sales goals set for it in 2000, Weldon was at its headquarters before the week was out. Everyone at the firm knew they could not allow their performance to fall below the targeted level for the next year.

Is There a Cure Ahead?

Weldon will need to draw on all of his competitive spirit to maintain J&J's growth trajectory. At this point, most of J&J's important drugs are under assault from competitors. The recent expiration of the patent on the firms' blockbuster pain drug, Duragesic, is expected to lead to a significant drop in its sales. Generic versions of Concerta, J&J's top-selling drug for the treatment of attention deficit disorders, are also expected to hit the market later in 2005. Its well-known rheumatoid arthritis drug, Remicade, has also been dealing with a strong challenge from competing products launched by Amgen and Abbott Laboratories. Even J&J's successful drug-coated coronary stent, called Cypher, has been struggling to compete with a rival offering from Boston Scientific Corporation, which some experts have claimed to be better.

To respond to such growing competition, Weldon has boosted spending on the development of new products. J&J may have as many as seven new drugs in the pipeline for 2005, including potential blockbusters to treat pain, cancer, sexual dysfunction, and schizophrenia. The firm has also embarked on a $1 billion cost-cutting plan at the end of 2004. A company spokesman emphasized that the cuts were not leading to any significant elimination of jobs but were being sought to search for ways to share technology, marketing, and distribution activities. According to Vice Chairman Poon, who leads the firm's pharmaceutical group, "We'll deal with these external challenges as we have always."[10]

Besides, Weldon hopes for strong results from his efforts to get different business units to work together across different divisions of J&J. Already a team of employees has been combining the slow-release technology from Alza Corporation with an antipsychotic drug from Centocor Corporation. Other cross-divisional teams are working on possible new treatments for diabetes and stroke.

But Weldon and his team are also trying to reduce the heavy reliance of his firm on pharmaceuticals by building up more sales for medical devices. The acquisition of Guidant will allow the firm to expand sales in this growing area. Jeremy Zhou, a health care analyst for Revere Data, a San Francisco–based research firm, said that the company has developed a presence in every subsector of medical devices and is positioned to become a leader in cardiology and orthopedic devices, two high-growth sectors catering directly to aging baby boomers.

Above all, as Weldon searches for various avenues to maintain J&J's growth record, he realizes that he must encourage its businesses to work more closely together than they have ever done in the past. The firm can tap into many more opportunities when it tries to bring together the various skills that it has managed to develop across different divisions. At the same time, Weldon is acutely aware that much of the firm's success has resulted from the relative autonomy that it has granted to each of its business units. Weldon knows that even as he strives to push for more collaborative effort, he does not want to threaten the entrepreneurial spirit that has served J&J so well.

Endnotes

1. Anonymous. Johnson & Johnson acquires Guidant for $24 billion. *New Jersey Business*: 79.
2. Barrett, Amy. 2003. Staying on top. *BusinessWeek,* May 5: 61.
3. Preston, Holly Hubbard. 2005. Drug giant provides a model of consistency. *International Herald Tribune,* March 12–13: 12.
4. *BusinessWeek,* May 5: 62.
5. Ibid.: 63.
6. Ibid.: 62.
7. Ibid.
8. Ibid.: 68.
9. Ibid.: 66.
10. Barrett, Amy, 2004. Toughing out the drought. *BusinessWeek,* January 26: 85.

Case 24 General Motors*

G. Richard Wagoner, Jr., chairman and chief executive officer (CEO) of General Motors, announced on April 19, 2005, that the world's biggest carmaker would report a $1.1 billion first-quarter loss, its worst quarterly performance since 1992. Shares for the firm had already dropped to a 12-year low of around $26 in anticipation of these results. The loss represented a significant decline from the $1.2 billion profit that the firm had made in the first quarter of 2004. Wagoner also announced that General Motors was no longer certain enough of its outlook to provide earnings guidance for the year, given that various projections that had been made over the last three months had proved to be considerably off the mark. He explained, "We have to address some long-standing fundamental problems with the company."[1]

For the most part, General Motors' reported loss could be attributed to a stark reversal in its North American automobile operations. It was clear that these operations, which have provided nearly two-thirds of the firm's automotive revenue, have hit a wall. Unsold cars have been piling up on dealers' lots even though General Motors has been offering some of the highest rebates in the industry. Its share of the U.S. market fell to 27.2 percent in 2004 from 28.0 percent in 2003. The firm's North American automotive operations reported a net loss of $1.3 billion in the first quarter of 2005 compared to a profit of $401 million during the same period in 2004. Even as it made smaller margins on fewer vehicles, GM continued to face soaring health care costs—as much as $6 billion in 2005—for its current and retired employees.

These results indicated that General Motors was slipping again in its bid to regain leadership of the Big Three U.S. car companies after it had made some gains during 2002 and 2003. Wagoner had already worked hard over the past decade, during his years as the firm's chief financial officer and later as its chief operating officer, to slash costs, cut payroll, and overhaul aging plants. After he took over as CEO in May 2000, Wagoner had accelerated his efforts to bring the firm in line with most of its rivals. As a result of his efforts, GM has been able to come much closer to Japanese firms such as Honda and Toyota by making tremendous increases in productivity and attaining significant improvements in quality (see Exhibits 1 and 2).

In spite of these achievements, General Motors was still struggling to turn things around. Wagoner did realize that mistakes that the firm's management had made over the last 30 years would make progress slow and cumbersome. Former chief executives from Frederic Donner to Roger Smith had built up a bloated bureaucracy that had cranked out boring, low-quality cars for many years. Turf battles at headquarters had sapped resources and diverted attention away from a rising threat posed by competitors from Asia and Europe. At the same time, Wagoner was well aware that he did not have much more time to turn things around. Aggressive foreign competitors, such as Toyota, Nissan and Honda, who had already made formidable inroads into the car market, were beginning to attack the market for the higher margin sport-utility vehicles and trucks (see Exhibits 3 and 4 on GM's market share in the United States and abroad).

Allocating Responsibilities

As a long-time GM insider, Wagoner did possess some distinct advantages that he brought to his job as CEO. He knew what brutal facts needed to be confronted, and he was aware of the specific veterans who could handle key jobs. To begin with, Wagoner broke with GM tradition by recruiting respected outsiders for key positions. He recruited John Devine as vice chairman and chief financial officer and Robert A. Lutz as head of the firm's product development. Lutz had sparked Chrysler's resurgence during the 1990s with cars such as the Dodge Viper and PT Cruiser.

Against all odds, Wagoner has also made real progress in energizing GM's torpid culture. Toward this end, he has begun to tear down the boundaries between the firm's free wheeling fiefdoms operating around the world (see Exhibit 5). For most of its history, GM has been run as a collaboration of relatively autonomous geographical divisions that have catered to different markets. But many regions have seen a sharp decline in profits, as they have had to respond to stronger competitors that have competed on a more global basis. The European division, in particular, has lost $3 billion since 2000.

Wagoner has been working with Lutz to restructure GM's four different geographical units to get them to collaborate with each other on designing, manufacturing, and marketing cars. Gradually, key decisions about the firm's product development are being made at GM's headquarters rather than at various far-flung subsidiaries. A global council in Detroit now decides how to allocate GM's $7 billion annual spending on new model development and serves as a check on units whose plans veer off course.

Furthermore, Wagoner and Lutz also have tried to get the various functional areas to work more closely with each other. GM used to have different studios for each division working on car designs that would get passed on to marketing, then engineering, then manufacturing. Lutz has formed one committee to cover the entire process. Every Thursday, he hashes out what vehicles should look like and which division will build them, along with a small group that includes key top managers from design and engineering.

*This case was prepared by Professor Jamal Shamsie of Michigan State University. This case was developed from published sources as a basis for class discussion rather than to illustrate either effective or ineffective handling of an administrative situation. Copyright © 2005 Jamal Shamsie.

Exhibit 1   GM's Income Statement
(Dollars in millions except per share amounts)

	Period Ending		
	December 31, 2004	December 31, 2003	December 31, 2002
Total Net Sales and Revenues	$193,517	$185,837	$177,867
Cost of Sales and Other Expenses	159,951	152,435	147,192
Selling, General, and Administrative Expenses	20,394	20,957	20,834
Interest Expense	11,980	9,464	7,503
Total Costs and Expenses	192,325	182,856	175,529
Income from Continuing Operations before Income Taxes, Equity Income, and Minority Interests	1,192	2,981	2,338
Income Tax (Benefit) Expense	(911)	731	644
Equity Income and Minority Interests	702	612	281
Income from Continuing Operations	2,805	2,862	1,975
(Loss) from Discontinued Operations	—	(219)	(239)
Gain on Sale of Discontinued Operations	—	1,179	—
Net Income	2,805	3,822	1,736
Dividends on Preference Stocks	—	—	(46)
Earnings Attributable to Common Stocks	$ 2,805	$ 3,822	$ 1,690

Source: General Motors.

Although Wagoner may have a low-key style, this does not mean that he does not get involved. His executives may be able to make the day-to-day decisions on various matters, but Wagoner reserves final say. During one trip through the design studio last year, he expressed his interest in a sexy two-door version of the Cadillac CTS sports sedan. Although he left the job to the designers, Wagoner kept himself well informed of the progress that the design team was making on the new car. "Rick trusts my judgment implicitly," Lutz said, "but if I came up with some wacky product proposals, he'd pull me back."[2]

Wagoner also exerts control by imposing tough performance standards. As he rose up through GM's finance division, Wagoner developed a reputation as a legendary number-cruncher who holds top managers to strict measures. Although GM, like most big companies, had performance goals, they never went nearly as deep or into as much detail. Says GM North America President Gary L. Cowger: "Everything can be measured."[3] Lutz was judged on 12 criteria last year, from how well he used existing

parts to save money in new vehicles to how many engineering hours he cut from the development process.

Speeding Up Product Development

Since Wagoner delegated product development to Lutz, he has moved to reorganize the design-by-committee system and cut the time it takes to develop a new car to 20 months from nearly four years. In the past, even if a bold design made it off a drawing board, it had little chance of surviving to the showroom. A concept would go from a designer to the marketing staff, which would try to tailor it to consumers. Then it would go to engineers, who would try to figure out how to build it, and so on. Separate teams worked with suppliers, factories, and parts suppliers on their individual slice of the process, with little interaction.

This change resulted in a very slow and expensive development process. The SSR (Super Sport Roadster) concept vehicle, started a few months after Wagoner had taken over, exposed the problems that GM faced in developing new cars. By the time that the $42,000 SSR finally hit the

Exhibit 2   GM's Balance Sheet
(Dollars in millions)

	December 31, 2004	December 31, 2003
	Period Ending	
Assets		
Cash and Cash Equivalents	$ 35,993	$ 32,554
Other Marketable Securities	21,737	22,215
Total Cash and Marketable Securities	57,730	54,769
Finance Receivables—net	199,600	174,769
Loans Held for Sale	19,934	19,609
Accounts and Notes Receivable (Less Allowances)	21,236	20,532
Inventories (Less Allowances)	12,247	11,602
Deferred Income Taxes	26,241	27,190
Net Equipment on Operating Leases (Less Accumulated depreciation)	34,214	32,751
Equity in Net Assets of Nonconsolidated Affiliates	6,776	6,032
Property—net	39,020	37,972
Intangible Assets—net	4,925	4,760
Other Assets	57,680	58,521
Total Assets	$479,603	$448,507
Liabilities and Stockholders' Equity		
Accounts Payable (Principally Trade)	$ 28,830	$ 25,422
Notes and Loans Payable	300,279	271,756
Postretirement Benefits Other than Pensions	28,111	36,292
Pensions	9,455	8,024
Deferred Income Taxes	7,078	7,508
Accrued Expenses and Other Liabilities	77,727	73,930
Total Liabilities	451,480	422,932
Minority Interests	397	307
Stockholders' Equity		
$1–2/3 Par Value Common Stock (Outstanding, 565,132,021 and 561,997,725 Shares)	942	937
Capital Surplus (Principally Additional Paid-In Capital)	15,241	15,185
Retained Earnings	14,428	12,752
Subtotal	30,611	28,874
Accumulated Foreign Currency Translation Adjustments	(1,194)	(1,815)
Net Unrealized Gains on Derivatives	589	51
Net Unrealized Gains on Securities	751	618
Minimum Pension Liability Adjustment	(3,031)	(2,460)
Accumulated Other Comprehensive Loss	(2,885)	(3,606)
Total Stockholders' Equity	27,726	25,268
Total Liabilities and Stockholders' Equity	$479,603	$448,507

Source: General Motors.

Exhibit 3 GM's U.S. Market Share

	Cars	Trucks	Total
2004	24.9%	29.0%	27.2%
2003	25.7%	30.0%	28.0%
2002	25.4%	31.0%	28.3%
2001	26.9%	29.2%	28.1%
2000	28.6%	27.0%	27.8%
1999	29.8%	27.8%	28.8%
1998	30.2%	27.4%	28.8%

Source: General Motors.

Exhibit 4 GM's Global Market Share

2004	14.5%
2003	14.6%
2002	14.9%
2001	15.0%
2000	15.0%
1999	15.6%
1998	15.5%

Source: General Motors.

showrooms in the summer of 2003, it had taken much longer than planned and the costs had risen from the original $300 million to almost $500 million. Since then, Wagoner and Lutz have smoothed things out a bit. Lutz works with other members of the top management team to decide which ideas for new car models from the design studios will be considered for funding by GM's Automotive Strategy Board, chaired monthly by Wagoner. Now the vast majority of the engineering work has already been finished when a program manager sits down to build a car.

Furthermore, GM is trying to improve its product development process by adopting a practice that the Japanese have perfected over many years. In past decades, only a small percentage of parts were reused from one generation of cars to the next. Now Lutz is trying to raise that to 40 to 60 percent, which is about on par with the Japanese. As GM develops the next generation Chevy Silverado and GMC Sierra pickups for 2008, it aims to reuse much of the existing platform. That should cut development costs by almost half.

The firm is trying to imitate the Japanese by developing several models that share a similar chassis or frame parts. The new Chevy Malibu, for instance, uses the same platform and many of the same parts as the Saab 9-3 sedan. GM is now planning to reuse the skeleton beneath the sleek body of its Pontiac Solstice for its upcoming Saturn coupe and possibly for the sporty Chevrolet wagon called the

Nomad. "GM is managing its product development more efficiently than ever," Lutz recently declared.[4]

But GM still tends to be slow in adopting new technologies in the development of their new models. For years, the firm ignored the efforts of the Japanese carmakers to develop gasoline–electric hybrid automobiles. Hybrid vehicles save on gasoline by supplementing internal combustion with electrical power. Instead, GM's engineers have worked on cars that would run on hydrogen fuel cells, although it may take many years for this technology to become viable. In December 2004, GM finally teamed up with DaimlerChrysler to try to rush out some hybrid versions of their cars and SUVs. By the time they launch these in 2007, they will need to catch up on the progress that Toyota and Honda will have made with the use of hybrid technology.

Building Better Cars

GM, along with its U.S.-based rivals, has been putting a renewed emphasis on sedans, coupes, and station wagons, a category in which they have been struggling against foreign competition. Many of GM's divisions have been struggling to make profits with their offerings. Wagoner has been relying on Lutz to push GM to develop cars that will have more appeal for buyers. A few years ago, Lutz had derided many of the automobile designs that were coming out of Detroit, claiming that they lacked the emotional appeal of classic American cars. He had commented: "One critically bad thing at GM has been the subordination of design. People who rent our cars at airports look at them and say 'Isn't this depressing?'"[5]

Sales of Saturn, the much heralded division that was created to revive the firm's fortunes, have been particularly disappointing. In 2004, sales had fallen to their lowest level since 1992. With only three models to offer, Saturn has

Exhibit 5 Quality Rankings (Defects per 100 vehicles during first 90 days of ownership)

	2003	1999
Toyota	115	132
Honda	126	137
Industry Average	133	170
General Motors	134	179
Ford	136	172
DaimlerChrysler	139	183
Volkswagen	141	215

Source: J. D. Power & Associates.

drained billions of dollars from GM over the past decade. In January 2005, GM finally announced that it would try to turn Saturn into a more upscale brand with more European styling and interiors. The Sky, a new sports car, would be the first of a new crop of Saturns to be introduced in 2006, along with a midsized sedan and a midsized sport-utility vehicle. Under the new plan, however, Saturn will lose its quasi-independence, with many of its operations being combined with those of GM's German Opel brand.

Lutz has also been trying to generate more excitement with his new models for some of the other struggling GM divisions, such as Buick and Pontiac. His plan is to push Buick as the low-priced alternative to Toyota's posh Lexus brand and to use Pontiac to target buyers who yearn for the performance of a BMW without having to deal with the hefty price tag. Toward this end, GM has recently introduced the Buick LaCrosse and the Pontiac G6, neither of which have generated the anticipated interest. GM's hopes are now riding on the Pontiac Solstice that will be introduced later in 2005 as a small sports car for baby boomers.

GM has had more success with reviving interest in its Chevrolet and Cadillac brands. In 2004, Chevrolet had its best sales since 1990, narrowly missing Ford as the best-selling U.S. car brand. Lutz is now pushing the newly launched Chevrolet Cobalt to compete with pricey small cars such as the Honda Civic and the Volkswagen Golf. Cadillac also has continued its resurgence, generating more revenues in 2004 than it has done since 1990. The recent Cadillac STS represents GM's latest move to firm up the brand's position as a credible competitor to European and Japanese luxury carmakers.

Although GM is trying to improve upon its offering of cars, the bulk of its profits have been coming from its larger pickups and sports-utility vehicles. But the firm has not been replacing them as quickly as its growing competition. Lutz has approved a highly stylized 2007 replacement for the Chevy Silverado and Suburban models and GMC Yukon and Sierra pickups, which hold a commanding lead of the pickup market. These will be based partly on the slick Cheyenne concept truck that was recently unveiled by GM, which has improved driver and passenger room and doors on each side of the pickup bed to provide easier cargo access.

On the whole, Lutz has been slow in turning around the image of GM cars. His first crop of car models has only managed to generate a tepid response. Some of the analysts have complained that the new cars have been noticeably devoid of the charm that he had promised to deliver, while others have insisted that his renovation of GM's sprawling product line needs more time to show results. It is possible that Lutz may be running into trouble trying to overcome the firm's bureaucracy. Art Spinella, president of CNW Marketing Research, states, "He's starting to be corralled to some degree by the old, staunch, conservative management style at General Motors."[6]

Dealing with the Benefits Crunch

Wagoner's biggest challenge lies in dealing with the lavish health and retirement benefits that GM had accorded to its workers. The firm had agreed to these terms during the days when it was more profitable as a way to buy peace with the United Auto Workers (UAW). GM pays its UAW workers only slightly more per hour than Toyota, Honda, and Nissan pay their American factory workers (see Exhibit 6). But the cost of pension and health care benefits has escalated, increasing by $1.8 billion from 2002 to 2004. They are expected to rise by another $1 billion during 2005.

In 2004, these benefits added more than $2,000 to the cost of each car that GM rolls off the assembly line. Many Japanese competitors that build their cars in a new, nonunion U.S. plant are paying considering less. Costs for retirees also have escalated as a result of other recent decisions by GM's management. Underestimating the speed of its decline, GM agreed to pay workers for years after a furlough. As losses mounted, GM resorted to early-retirement offers, avoiding billions in unemployment benefits but adding thousands of retirees. Since GM was shrinking faster than Ford, its pension rolls grew more quickly, to 2.5 retirees per worker today, compared to Ford's 1-to-1 ratio.

Those huge legacy costs explain why Wagoner has kept the heat on his competition with the rock bottom financing deals he rolled out aggressively in the wake of the attacks on September 11, 2001. Closing plants and accepting a smaller chunk of the U.S. market would have given GM fewer vehicles over which to spread those big pension and health care costs. Wagoner said, "We have a huge fixed-cost base. It's 30 years of downsizing and 30 years of increased health care costs. It puts a premium on us running this business to generate cash. Our goal is to grow. We don't care who we take it from."[7]

All that would make the outlook for GM pretty bleak. But Wagoner estimates that these legacy costs will eventually start to diminish. Starting around 2008, the ranks of

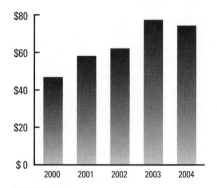

Exhibit 6   Labor Costs (Average cost per hour, including benefits)

Source: General Motors, Automotive News.

GM's elderly retirees will begin to drop, relieving some of the burden. After that, more of the incremental gains Wagoner has been achieving will fall to the bottom line rather than to retirees. The results could be dramatic. Nevertheless, he has to keep up cash flow to cover those benefit costs until they start to shrink. At the same time, he must continue to rack up improvements in quality, efficiency, design, and brand appeal.

Moving beyond Past Problems

Wagoner has been concerned about the declining financial position of General Motors. The Standard and Poor's rating agency has already issued a warning about GM's poor outlook. A decision by the agency to downgrade GM's credit rating is likely to raise its borrowing costs, cutting into the lucrative profits of its lending business. In response to this threat, Wagoner is thinking of creating a new holding company for the mortgage lending portion of General Motors Acceptance Corporation, the firm's highly profitable financing division. Such a move would preserve the credit rating of a portion of its financing operations even if the floundering automobile business is downgraded to junk status (see Exhibits 7 and 8).

In the longer run, however, Wagoner knows that he must take whatever steps that he can to make sure that GM's future lineups of cars and trucks would be good enough to sell on merit, not price. The firm made only $213 on average on each of the 5.4 million cars and trucks it sold in North America during 2004. Toyota, by comparison, has been able to generate more than $1,500 for each of the vehicles that it sells. Wagoner must be able to cut back on the incentives that GM presently offers in order to generate enough profits to place it back on a sound financial footing.

Wagoner insists that GM will do much better in 2006 when it introduces the new models of its more profitable pickups and SUVs. Lutz is also optimistic about the prospects for the cars that the firm is planning to launch

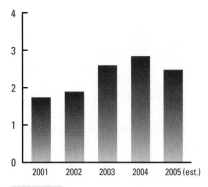

Exhibit 8   GMAC Earnings (Billions of dollars)

Source: General Motors, UBS Securities.

over the next three years. Wagoner tried to reassure GM's investors, saying, "We are making some progress and we are enthused about the growth that we continue to see."[8]

But GM may still have a long way to go before it can win back customers who will pay higher prices for its cars. With the assistance of Lutz, Wagoner and his team are trying hard to develop a steady stream of consistently competitive, reliable and stylish offerings. Even if they are successful with this task, GM may still have to work hard to get customers on board. The image of most of its brands has been damaged by decades of cars that fell apart, lost their value quickly, or were just plain ugly. UBS Warburg analyst Saul Rubin believes that GM, like its U.S. counterparts, faces an uphill battle in changing the perceptions of consumers about their cars and trucks.

But Wagoner clearly realizes that GM has no choice. It has to try to turn things around to survive against the growing competition. "This is one major last-ditch effort to save themselves in the car market," said Joseph Phillippi, a former Wall Street analyst who consults for the industry.[9]

Endnotes

1.   Welch, David. 2005. Running out of gas. *BusinessWeek,* March 28: 29.
2.   Welch, David, & Kerwin, Kathleen. 2003. Rick Wagoner's game plan. *BusinessWeek,* February 10: 56.
3.   Ibid.
4.   Ibid.: 54.
5.   Welch, David, & Kerwin, Kathleen. 2004. Detroit tries it the Japanese way. *BusinessWeek,* January 26: 76.
6.   Hakim, Danny. 2004. Can General Motors design a better Future? *New York Times,* November 7: BU4.
7.   Taylor, Alex III. 2002. Finally GM is looking good. *Fortune,* April 1: 51–52.
8.   Mackintosh, James. 2005. GM casts doubt on earnings target. *Financial Times,* January 10: 21.
9.   *BusinessWeek,* February 10: 55–56.

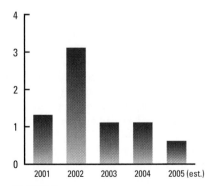

Exhibit 7   North American Automobile Earnings (Billions of dollars)

Source: General Motors, UBS Securities.

Case 25   Heineken*

During the first few months of 2005, Heineken was trying to respond to changes that have been occurring within the global beer industry. Although it has been holding onto its position as one of the world's five largest brewers, the Dutch firm has been concerned about the growth of many of its most formidable competitors. Consequently, Heineken has been trying to increase its stake in some breweries in China, which represents one of the fastest growing markets for beer. At the same time, it has been planning to launch a light version of its flagship brand in the United States to try to strengthen its position in the world's largest beer market.

The push to strengthen Heineken's position across global markets is being spearheaded by Anthony Ruys, who took over the helm of the firm in 2002. Prior to his appointment, the firm had been run by three generations of Heineken ancestors, whose portraits still adorn the dark-paneled office of the CEO in its Amsterdam headquarters. The last of these was Alfred H. "Freddy" Heineken, a hard-nosed businessman with a zest for life, whose recent death created the opportunity for Ruys to take over.

Although the management of Heineken has moved for the first time to an individual who is not a member of the family, Ruys has been well aware of long-standing and well-established traditions that would be difficult to change. "There's a long tradition," he said about the family legacy that he has inherited.[1] Even as he contemplates changes that he must make, Ruys would not dare to dishonor Freddy's memory by claiming that anything as radical as a revolution was in the making at Heineken.

Yet it is not hard to sense that the firm is definitely in the midst of making some changes that have been long overdue. With over $12 billion a year in sales, Heineken can lay claim to a brand that may be the closest thing to a global beer brand. But it may no longer be able to take for granted the strengths that have made its squat green bottle the envy of the business. In fact, there have been plenty of signs to indicate that Heineken may have to double its efforts to maintain its momentum. Its growth has been slowing down, after a six-year streak of double-digit growth in profits (see Exhibits 1 and 2). Furthermore, its core brand has been losing ground in many markets. In the United States, Heineken has lost its leading position among imported beers to Corona, the Mexican beer that is often served with a garnish of lime.

Ruys understands that to build on its previous successes, Heineken needs to prepare itself for widespread changes that are occurring in the global beer market. Beer consumption has been declining in key markets as a result

of tougher drunk-driving laws and a growing appreciation for wine. At the same time, the beer markets around the world have become even more competitive, as the largest brewers have been expanding across the globe through acquisitions of smaller regional and national players. As a result of these changes, Ruys believes that Heineken's future success depends on preserving Freddy's spirit, while trying to meet challenges that Freddy may never have anticipated.

Competing in a Global Industry

The beer industry has been relatively fragmented, with an abundance of smaller regional or national brewers that have dominated each market. Few firms have had significant operations across different countries. Even in 2004, the top four brewing companies controlled a little more than one-third of the global market for beer. Furthermore, many of the leading firms, such as Anheuser-Busch and Miller, have continued to draw most of their revenues from their home markets (see Exhibit 3).

But the industry has been undergoing significant change due to a furious wave of consolidation. Most of the bigger brewers have begun to acquire or merge with their competitors in foreign markets to become global players. In 2004, Belgium's Interbrew combined with Brazil's AmBev, to rise to the position of the largest global brewer with operations across most of the continents. Earlier, South African Breweries Plc acquired U.S.-based Miller Brewing to become the second largest global brewer. Over the past few months, U.S.-based Coors has linked with Canadian-based Coors, and their combined operations make it one of the five biggest brewers.

Many brewers also have expanded their operations without such acquisitions. For example, Anheuser-Busch bought equity stakes and struck partnership deals with Mexico's Grupo Modelo, China's Tsingtao, and Chile's CCU. Such cross-border deals have provided significant benefits to the brewing giants. To begin with, they have given them ownership of local brands and propelled them into a dominant position in various markets around the world. Beyond this, acquisitions of foreign brewers can provide firms with the manufacturing and distribution capabilities that they could use to develop a few global brands. "The era of global brands is coming," said Alan Clark, Budapest-based managing director of SABMiller Europe.[2]

InBev, the combination of Interbrew and AmBev, has been pushing to develop Stella Artois, Brahma, and Becks as its three global flagship brands. Each of these three brands originated in different locations, with Stella Artois coming from Belgium, Brahma from Brazil, and Becks from Germany. Similarly, the newly formed SAB Miller has been attempting to develop the Czech brand Pilsner Urquell into a

*This case was prepared by Professor Jamal Shamsie of Michigan State University. This case was developed from published sources as a basis for class discussion rather than to illustrate either effective or ineffective handling of an administrative situation. Copyright © 2005 Jamal Shamsie.

Exhibit 1   Heineken's Turnover and Profit
(In millions of euros)

	2004	2003	2002	2001	2000	1999	1998
Net Turnover	10,005	9,255	8,482	7,637	6,766	5,973	5,347
Operating Profit	1,248	1,222	1,282	1,125	921	799	659
Operating Profit BEIA[1]	1,329	1,327	1,282	1,125	921	799	659
as % of Net Turnover	13.3	14.3	15.1	14.7	13.6	13.4	12.3
as % of Total Assets	12.8	12.2	16.4	15.6	14.6	13.3	12.4
Interest Cover Ratio	11.2	13.3	16.6	22.5	21.0	30.1	92.7
Net Profit Including Extraordinary Income	537	798	795	767	621	516	445
Net Profit BEIA[1]	791	806	795	715	621	516	445
as % of Shareholders' Equity	23.4	25.4	30.1	25.9	25.9	19.7	19.4
Dividend	173	157	157	157	125	125	100
as % of Net Profit	32.2	19.7	19.7	20.5	20.1	24.2	22.4

Source: Heineken.

[1]Before exceptional items and amortization

global brand. Exports of this pilsner have doubled since SAB acquired it in 1999. John Brock, the CEO of InBev, commented, "Global brands sell at significantly higher prices, and the margins are much better than with local beers."[3]

Heineken has been a pioneer of this global strategy, using cross-border deals to extend its operations to 170 countries around the globe. In fact, the Heineken brand ranked second only to Budweiser in a global brand survey jointly undertaken by *BusinessWeek* and Interbrand earlier this year. Heineken has achieved worldwide recognition according to Kevin Baker, director of alcoholic beverages at British market researcher Canadean Ltd. Its success as a global brand has been remarkable. A U.S. wholesaler recently asked a group of marketing students to identify an assortment of beer bottles that had been stripped of their labels. The stubby green Heineken container was the only one that incited instant recognition among the group.

Maintaining a Strong Brand

Heineken had long enjoyed a leading position among the beers in many markets around the world. It had been the best-selling imported beer in the United States for several decades, giving it a steady source of revenues and profits from the world's biggest market. But Heineken's appeal has been difficult to maintain as consumers in many of its markets have been turning away from beer and those sticking with beer are being offered many more choices. Beer consumption in the United States has declined slightly since 2000, while the number of imports that are available to consumers has risen by almost one-fifth over the same period.

In fact, Ruys has been especially concerned about the decline in sales of its flagship Heineken brand. By the late 1990s, Heineken had lost its 65-year-old leadership among imported beers in the United States to Group Modelo's Corona. In early 2004, Corona had been able to develop about 29 percent of the U.S. imported beer market, which was far ahead of Heineken's 19 percent share. The Mexican beer has been able to reach out to the growing Hispanic American population, which represents one of the fastest-growing segments of beer drinkers. Other Americans also have developed a taste for Corona while vacationing on Mexican beaches.

Heineken's managers have been trying to deal with this loss of leadership by working hard to increase awareness of their flagship brand. While the core Heineken brand has become quite well known on the East Coast, it has been lagging behind other foreign beers in the West. Consequently, the firm has been spending about $51 million per year to market the brand throughout the United States—a much higher figure than the $35 million per year that is being spent by the Mexican firm that sells Corona. "Heineken has one of the best marketing machines in the industry, but it has been around a long time so it has to work hard to stay relevant with young, hip consumers," said Nicole van Putten, beer analyst at Fortis Bank in Amsterdam.[4]

In particular, Ruys and his U.S. managers have been trying hard to liven up the image of Heineken through tie-ins with big-budget youth films, such as the *Austin Powers* and *The Matrix* sequels. In a spot based on *The Matrix Reloaded*, when an obnoxious customer smacks a waitress's

Exhibit 2   Heineken's Financing
(In millions of euros)

	2004	2003	2002	2001	2000	1999	1998
Share Capital	784	784	784	784	711	711	711
Reserves	2,595	2,383	1,853	1,974	1,685	1,907	1,588
Shareholders' Equity	3,379	3,167	2,637	2,758	2,396	2,618	2,299
Minority Interest	483	732	393	381	124	248	256
Group Equity	3,862	3,899	3,030	3,139	2,520	2,866	2,555
Provisions	568	1,367	981	1,024	976	770	733
Employee Benefits	680	—	—	—	—	—	—
Long-Term Debts	2,642	2,721	1,215	797	875	490	522
Current Liabilities	2,666	2,910	2,555	2,235	1,892	1,860	1,460
Liabilities	5,308	5,631	3,770	3,032	2,767	2,350	1,982
Total Equity and Liabilities	**10,418**	**10,897**	**7,781**	**7,195**	**6,263**	**5,986**	**5,270**
Employment of Capital (In millions of euros)							
Intangible Fixed Assets	1,720	1,151	39	13	—	—	—
Tangible Fixed Assets	5,127	4,995	4,094	3,592	3,250	2,964	2,605
Financial Fixed Assets	779	1,122	835	531	615	422	490
Fixed Assets	7,626	7,268	4,968	4,136	3,865	3,386	3,095
Stocks	779	834	765	692	550	490	452
Accounts Receivable	1,309	1,379	1,270	1,192	1,024	903	775
Cash and Securities	704	1,416	778	1,175	824	1,207	948
Current Assets	2,792	3,629	2,813	3,059	2,398	2,600	2,175
Total Assets	**10,418**	**10,897**	**7,781**	**7,195**	**6,263**	**5,986**	**5,270**

Source: Heineken.

behind, she throws a tray of *Heineken* beer in the air, where it remains suspended. She then uses a Matrix-style kick to knock the customer against the wall. More recently, Heineken has hired actors such as John Travolta and Brad Pitt to promote their flagship brand.

The efforts have started to pay off in the United States. Steve Davis, the firm's senior vice president of marketing, has seen a significant shift in the brand's image. "We pretty much reinvented the brand, injected some energy, some vitality, some excitement into it," he said.[5] As a result of this makeover, the average age of a Heineken drinker has dropped from about 40 in the mid-1990s to the early 30s today. Ruys's goal is to push that age down into the high-20s in coming years. But he wants to be careful that in reaching out to younger customers he does not alienate the middle-aged beer drinkers who have been Heineken's core customers.

Even as Ruys and his marketing team have been working hard to maintain Heineken's relevance in the changing market, they want to maintain a fair degree of consistency across global markets. "The cliché 'think global, act local' is applicable to our situation," said Frans van der Minne, president and CEO of Heineken USA. But he added, "We wouldn't do anything with the brands that would be totally different from the initiatives that are taken by our colleagues in other parts of the world. We have global brand managers and they are gatekeepers so that all of our commercial initiatives are consistent with the integrity and quality of the brand."[6]

Building a Stronger Portfolio

In large part, Heineken's decline in the United States could be attributed to growing problems with its reliance on one

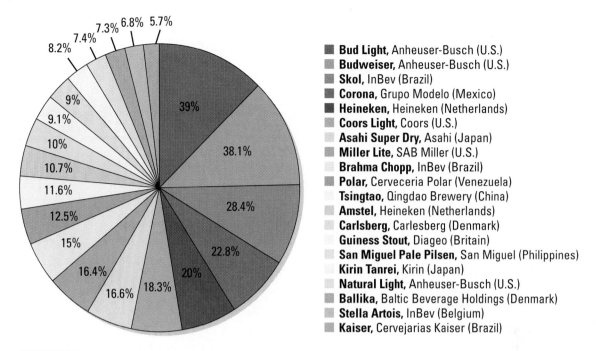

Bud Light, Anheuser-Busch (U.S.)
Budweiser, Anheuser-Busch (U.S.)
Skol, InBev (Brazil)
Corona, Grupo Modelo (Mexico)
Heineken, Heineken (Netherlands)
Coors Light, Coors (U.S.)
Asahi Super Dry, Asahi (Japan)
Miller Lite, SAB Miller (U.S.)
Brahma Chopp, InBev (Brazil)
Polar, Cerveceria Polar (Venezuela)
Tsingtao, Qingdao Brewery (China)
Amstel, Heineken (Netherlands)
Carlsberg, Carlesberg (Denmark)
Guiness Stout, Diageo (Britain)
San Miguel Pale Pilsen, San Miguel (Philippines)
Kirin Tanrei, Kirin (Japan)
Natural Light, Anheuser-Busch (U.S.)
Ballika, Baltic Beverage Holdings (Denmark)
Stella Artois, InBev (Belgium)
Kaiser, Cervejarias Kaiser (Brazil)

Exhibit 3   Leading Beer Brands (Millions of barrels)
Source: Impact Databank.

core brand, which has posed a challenge for the firm as the overall market for beer has begun to show signs of maturity and younger consumers have continued to show a greater degree of divergence. The risks that stem from these developments are likely to be higher because Heineken also tends to be regarded as an obsolete brand by many young drinkers. John A. Quelch, a professor at Harvard Business School who has studied the beer industry, said of Heineken, "It's in danger of becoming a tired, reliable, but unexciting brand."[7]

Ruys was aware that his firm may have to offer more different beers to gain back some of the market share that it had lost in the United States to more aggressive competitors. Heineken has already achieved considerable success with Amstel Light, which has become the leading imported light beer. It has also managed to develop a relatively small but loyal consumer base for certain specialty brands, such as Murphy's Irish Red and Moretti (see Exhibit 4).

But Heineken also may be ready to try to draw a broader base of consumers to its flagship brand. It was widely speculated that the firm was planning to launch Heineken Premium Light to tap into one of the largest sources of growth in a maturing U.S. beer industry. Beers that contain fewer calories and lower carbohydrates have grown in popularity, accounting for more than half of the 200-million-barrel U.S. beer market. Commenting on the anticipated move, Bryan Spillane, an analyst with Banc of America Securities, stated, "They need to do something to inject some enthusiasm for the consumer back behind the Heineken brand."[8]

The new version, which will initially be launched only within the United States, is expected to have a lighter flavor than the original version. Industry analysts have reacted with cautious optimism. They believe that Heineken will have to be careful not to steal volume from its Amstel Light, the leading imported light beer. At the same time, it must try not to alienate the loyal consumer base that regards Heineken as a premium import beer with a well-refined taste.

Finally, Ruys and his management team have been stepping up its marketing to Hispanics, who account for one-quarter of U.S. sales. Besides trying to target more of this population with Spanish-language advertising for Heineken, the firm concluded a deal in 2004 with a leading Mexican brewer to market and distribute its five popular brands within the United States. The three-year agreement with the Fomento Economico Mexicana, or Femsa, covers their best selling brands, Tecate and Dos Equis, along with its other brands, Sol, Carta Blanca, and Bohemia. Benj Steinman, publisher and editor of the *Beer Marketer's Insight* newsletter, claims that the deal will give a tremendous boost to Heineken. "This gives Heineken a commanding share of the U.S. import business and . . . gives them a bigger presence in the Southwest . . . and better access to Hispanic consumers," he stated.[9]

Exhibit 4   Heineken Brands (Significant Heineken brands in various markets)

Markets	Brands
United States	Heineken, Amstel Light, Paulaner,[1] Moretti
Netherlands	Heineken, Amstel, Kylian, Lingen's Blond, Murphy's Irish Red
France	Heineken, Amstel, Buckler,[2] Desperados[3]
Germany	Paulaner,[1] Kulmbacher, Thurn, und Taxis
Italy	Heineken, Amstel, Birra Moretti
Poland	Heineken, Zywiec
China	Tiger, Reeb*
Singapore	Heineken, Tiger
Kazakhstan	Tian Shan, Amstel
Egypt	Fayrouz[2]
Israel	Maccabee, Gold Star*
Nigeria	Amstel Malta, Maltina
Panama	Soberana, Panama

*Minority interest
[1]Wheat beer
[2]Nonalcoholic beer
[3]Tequila-flavored beer

Picking Up on Its Global Efforts

Ruys well understands the need to expand globally by making deals with or acquiring brewers in various parts of the world. In fact, Heineken was actually one of the first brewers to recognize the value of cross-border deals. For years, Freddy had been picking up small brewers from several countries to add more brands and to get better access to more markets.

But Freddy had been reluctant to spend heavily on making big ticket acquisitions. For the most part, therefore, Heineken has limited itself to snapping up small national brewers, such as Italy's Moretti to Spain's Cruzcampo, that have provided it with small but profitable avenues for growth. In 1996, for example, Heineken had acquired Fischer, a small French brewer, whose Desperados brand has been quite successful in niche markets. Similarly, Paulaner, a wheat beer that the firm picked up in Germany a few years ago, has been making inroads into the U.S. market.

But as other brewers have been reaching out to make acquisitions from all over the globe, Heineken runs the risk of falling behind its more aggressive rivals. To deal with this growing challenge, Ruys has been pushing Heineken to break out of its play-it-safe corporate culture.

Already, he has managed to pull off some of Heineken's biggest deals in some time. In 2003, Ruys spent $2.1 billion to acquire BBAG, a family-owned company based in Linz, Austria. Because of BBAG's extensive presence in Central Europe, Heineken has become the biggest beer maker in seven countries across Eastern Europe. More recently, Heineken has begun an aggressive push into Russia with the acquisition of a couple of mid-sized brewing concerns.

At the same time, Ruys does not plan to stop acquiring smaller brewers that show promise. During his short tenure, he has already added several labels to Heineken's shelf, pouncing on brewers in places like Panama, Egypt, and Kazakhstan. In Egypt, Ruys bought a majority stake in Al Ahram Beverages Co. and hopes to use the Cairo-based brewer's fruit-flavored, nonalcoholic malts as an avenue into other Muslim countries.

However, Ruys believes that his firm should try to get much more growth out of their cross-border deals. He wants to use these to make his managers more knowledgeable of different markets. In fact, Heineken's boss has been resorting to tough tactics to stir his troops out of their complacency. Ruys and his top lieutenants have been traveling to places like Madrid and Shanghai to down a cold one with groups of randomly selected young people to find out more about their tastes. They meet regularly to think about the steps that they need to take to win over customers across different markets that have not yet developed a strong loyalty to a particular beverage.

Transitioning from the Past into the Future

Even as Ruys tries to develop Heineken into a major global player, he must appear to adhere to the core values and traditions that have guided the family-controlled firm. With Freddy gone, control has passed to his only child and heir, Charlene de Carvalho, a housewife and mother of five who resides in London. She has insisted on having a say in all of the major decisions, but she has left Ruys with the responsibilities of the day-to-day running of the firm. Her husband, Michel de Carvalho, can also exert considerable influence as a prominent member of the board. Speaking on behalf of the family, he emphasized the need to maintain a strong sense of continuity, "We won't deviate from the old man's principle."[10]

If that extends to Heineken's financially conservative style of running the business, it may not allow much room for Ruys to find avenues of growth. Heineken needs to spend heavily to build its presence in various markets if it does not want to lose out to its more aggressive global rivals. But it has been constrained in its ability to either buy out or merge with other firms due to concerns about diluting the family's control.

Ruys may gain more flexibility if Freddy's family decides to sell off their stake. However, it is not clear what he can do to persuade the family members to sell off their controlling shares. A hostile takeover would be almost impossible to pull off under the current ownership structure. Publicly, de Carvalho has stated that the family remains committed to the firm's past, present, and future. "Our mission is to hand a healthy company to the next generation,"

she recently announced.[11] Nevertheless, there has been considerable speculation that the family might sell if they get the right price.

If the family grip is loosened, Ruys may be able to take more aggressive steps to build Heineken into a more formidable global competitor. "This could be Heineken unchained," said Michael Kraland, the Dutch president of Trinity Capital Partners, a Paris investment firm.[12] But the firm will have to work hard if it wants to catch up with the recent moves of the other major global players. Karel Vuursteen, who retired in 2002 from a top management post at the firm, acknowledged that "in the long run, nobody knows what will happen."[13]

Endnotes

1. Ewing, Jack, & Khermouch, Gerry. 2003. Waking up Heineken. *BusinessWeek,* September 8: 68.
2. Ibid.: 70.
3. Tomlinson, Richard. 2004. The new king of beers. *Fortune,* October 18: 238.
4. Bilefsky, Dan. 2003. Heineken brews comeback plans for U.S. market. *Wall Street Journal,* May 27: B1.
5. Theodore, Sarah. 2002. Rising star. *Beverage Industry,* July: 39.
6. Ibid.: 40.
7. *BusinessWeek,* September 8: 69.
8. Lawton, Christopher. 2005. Heineken to enter light beer fray; thirsting for sales growth, Dutch brewer will extend its flagship brand in U.S. *Wall Street Journal,* March 11: B3.
9. Kaplan, Andrew. 2004. Border crossings. *Beverage World,* July 15: 6.
10. Baker, Stephen, White, Christina, & Khermouch, Gerry. 2002. Freddy Heineken's recipe may be scrapped. *BusinessWeek,* January 28: 56.
11. *BusinessWeek,* September 8: 70.
12. *BusinessWeek,* January 28: 56.
13. Ibid.: 56.

Case 26   Procter & Gamble*

Procter & Gamble (P&G), the nation's largest consumer products firm, announced on January 27, 2005, that it had reached a deal to acquire the Gillette Company, the shaving products company, for about $55 billion in stock. The merger would create the world's largest consumer products conglomerate, combining some of the world's best-known billion-dollar brands like Tide, Crest, and Pampers with Gillette, Right Guard, and Duracell. The merger of P&G with Gillette would create a firm that would have annual sales of more than $60 billion.

The acquisition represented the latest move by CEO Alan G. "A.G." Lafley, a 23-year veteran, to help P&G reclaim its previous status as the premier consumer goods firm. He believed that his firm would derive substantial benefits from its merger with another company that was operating in similar markets and using complementary skills. "The combination of these two recognizes the pressures from strengthening retail customers, variety-seeking consumers and the investment necessary to build scale in the developing market," said Ann Gillin-Lefever, an equity analyst for Lehman Brothers who follows both P&G and Gillette.[1]

Lafley had begun to restructure P&G even before he took over the helm in June 2000. He was asked to take the reins from Durk I. Jaeger, whose attempts to rip apart P&G's insular culture and remake it from the bottom up during his 17-month tenure had failed to stop the firm's decline. Like many of its competitors, the firm was being squeezed by slowing sales, growing costs and waning pricing power. P&G had become saddled with old and tired brands, as the Swiffer dust mop represented the only successful new brand that it had managed to develop over the previous 15 years. At the same time, big-box retail chains such as Wal-Mart, Costco, and Carrefour had begun to use their growing clout with consumers to negotiate for better pricing deals from their suppliers.

Under Lafley, P&G has begun to strip away much of the bureaucracy to speed up its product development and build upon its well-known brands. By divesting its weaker brands, the firm has been investing in extending the reach of brands that exhibit greater potential. Lafley wants to focus the firm on building a small number of "superbrands," each with annual sales of over $1 billion. The purchase of Gillette would allow P&G to increase the number of such brands from 16 to 21. According to Clayton C. Daley Jr., the firm's chief financial officer, "We will have more $1 billion brands, more opportunities to bring product

innovation to the market because that's what retailers want."[2]

But Lafley has many more ideas about how to make P&G relevant in the 21st century, during which time he believes that speed and agility will become essential for competitive advantage. Even as president of North American operations, he had spoken with CEO Jaeger about the need to remake the company. Now that he has taken charge, Lafley has been pushing for the most sweeping transformation of the company since it was founded by William Procter and James Gamble in 1837 as a maker of soap and candles.

An Attempted Turnaround

For most of its long history, P&G has been one of America's preeminent companies. The firm has developed several well-known brands such as Tide, one of the pioneers in laundry detergents, which was launched in 1946, and Pampers, the first disposable diaper, which was introduced in 1961. P&G built its brands through its innovative marketing techniques. In the 1880s, it was one of the first companies to advertise nationally. Later on, P&G invented the soap opera by sponsoring *Ma Perkins* when radio caught on and *Guiding Light* when television took hold. In the 1930s, P&G was the first firm to develop the idea of brand management, setting up marketing teams for each brand and urging them to compete against each other.

But by the 1990s, P&G was in danger of becoming another Eastman Kodak or Xerox—a once-great company that might have lost its way. Sales on most of its 18 top brands were slowing as it was being outhustled by more focused rivals such as Kimberly-Clark and Colgate-Palmolive. The only way P&G kept profits growing was by cutting costs, which would hardly work as a strategy for the long term. At the same time, the dynamics of the industry were changing as power shifted from manufacturers to massive retailers. Retailers such as Wal-Mart were starting to use their size to try to get better deals from P&G, further squeezing its profits.

In 1999, P&G decided to bring in Durk I. Jaeger to try to make the big changes that were obviously needed to get P&G back on track. But the moves that he made generally misfired, sinking the firm into deeper trouble. He introduced expensive new products that never caught on, while letting existing brands drift. He also put in place a companywide reorganization that left many employees perplexed and preoccupied. During the fiscal year when he was in charge, earnings per share showed an anemic rise of just 3.5 percent, much lower than in previous years. And during that time, the share price slid 52 percent, cutting P&G's total market capitalization by $85 billion. The effects were widely felt within the firm, where employees and retirees hold about 20 percent of the stock (see Exhibits 1, 2, and 3 for income statements, balance sheets and share prices).

*This case was prepared by Professor Jamal Shamsie of Michigan State University. This case was developed from published sources as a basis for class discussion rather than to illustrate either effective or ineffective handling of an administrative situation. Copyright © 2005 Jamal Shamsie.

Exhibit 1   Procter & Gamble's Income Statement
(All numbers in $ thousands)

	Period Ending		
	June 30, 2004	June 30, 2003	June 30, 2002
Total Revenue	51,407,000	43,377,000	40,238,000
Cost of Revenue	25,076,000	22,141,000	20,989,000
Gross Profit	26,331,000	21,236,000	19,249,000
Selling General and Administrative	16,504,000	13,383,000	12,571,000
Operating Income or Loss	9,827,000	7,853,000	6,678,000
Income from Continuing Operations			
Total Other Income/Expenses Net	152,000	238,000	308,000
Earnings before Interest and Taxes	9,979,000	8,091,000	6,986,000
Interest Expense	629,000	561,000	603,000
Income before Tax	9,350,000	7,530,000	6,383,000
Income Tax Expense	2,869,000	2,344,000	2,031,000
Net Income from Continuing Operations	6,481,000	5,186,000	4,352,000
Net Income	6,481,000	5,186,000	4,352,000

Source: Procter & Gamble Co. annual reports.

But Jaeger's greatest failing was his scorn for the family. Jaeger, a Dutchman who had joined P&G overseas and worked his way to corporate headquarters, pitted himself against the P&G culture. Susan E. Arnold, president of P&G's beauty and feminine care division, said that Jaeger tried to make the employees turn against the prevailing culture, contending that it was burdensome and insufferable. Some go-ahead employees even wore buttons that read "Old World/New World" to express disdain for P&G's past.

A New Style of Leadership

On June 6, 2000, the day of his 30th wedding anniversary, Alan G. Lafley received a call from John Pepper, a former CEO who was now a board member. He was asked to take over the reins of P&G from Jaeger, representing a boardroom coup unprecedented in the firm's history. In a sense, Lafley had been preparing for this job his entire adult life. He never hid the fact that he wanted to run P&G one day. Recruited as a brand assistant for Joy dish detergent in 1977, Lafley rose quickly to head P&G's soap and detergent business, where he introduced Liquid Tide in 1984. A decade later, he moved to Kobe, Japan, to head the Asian

division. Lafley returned to Cincinnati in 1998 to run the company's entire North American operations.

By the time he had taken charge of P&G, Lafley had developed a reputation as a boss who steps back to give his staff plenty of responsibility and who helps shape decisions by asking a series of keen questions. As CEO, Lafley has refrained from making any grand pronouncements on the future of P&G. Instead, he has been spending an inordinate amount of time patiently communicating to his employees about the types of changes that he would like to see at P&G.

Lafley did begin his tenure by breaking down the walls between management and the employees. Since the 1950s, all of the senior executives at P&G used to be located on the eleventh floor at the firm's corporate headquarters. Lafley changed this setup, moving all five division presidents to the same floors as their staff. Then he turned some of the emptied space into a leadership training center. On the rest of the floor, he knocked down the walls so that the remaining executives, including himself, would share open offices.

Lafley chose to place his office next to the two people he talks to the most, which, in true P&G style, was officially established by a flow study. They are Ricard L.

Exhibit 2   Procter & Gamble's Balance Sheet
(All numbers in $ thousands)

	Period Ending		
	June 30, 2004	June 30, 2003	June 30, 2002
Assets			
Current Assets			
Cash and Cash Equivalents	5,469,000	5,912,000	3,427,000
Short-Term Investments	423,000	300,000	196,000
Net Receivables	5,020,000	3,881,000	3,611,000
Inventory	4,400,000	3,640,000	3,456,000
Other Current Assets	1,803,000	1,487,000	1,476,000
Total Current Assets	**17,115,000**	**15,220,000**	**12,166,000**
Property Plant and Equipment	14,108,000	13,104,000	13,349,000
Goodwill	19,610,000	11,132,000	10,966,000
Intangible Assets	4,290,000	2,375,000	2,464,000
Other Assets	1,925,000	1,875,000	1,831,000
Total Assets	**57,048,000**	**43,706,000**	**40,776,000**
Liabilities			
Current Liabilities			
Accounts Payable	13,860,000	10,186,000	8,973,000
Short/Current Long-Term Debt	8,287,000	2,172,000	3,731,000
Total Current Liabilities	**22,147,000**	**12,358,000**	**12,704,000**
Long-Term Debt	12,554,000	11,475,000	11,201,000
Other Liabilities	2,808,000	2,291,000	2,088,000
Deferred Long-Term Liability Charges	2,261,000	1,396,000	1,077,000
Total Liabilities	**39,770,000**	**27,520,000**	**27,070,000**
Stockholders' Equity			
Preferred Stock	1,526,000	1,580,000	1,634,000
Common Stock	2,544,000	1,297,000	1,301,000
Retained Earnings	13,611,000	13,692,000	11,980,000
Capital Surplus	2,425,000	2,931,000	2,490,000
Other Stockholder Equity	(2,828,000)	(3,314,000)	(3,699,000)
Total Stockholder Equity	**17,278,000**	**16,186,000**	**13,706,000**
Net Tangible Assets	**($6,622,000)**	**$2,679,000**	**$276,000**

Source: Procter & Gamble.

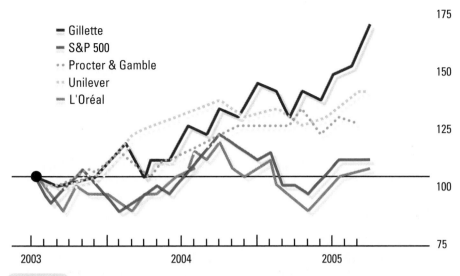

- Gillette
- S&P 500
- Procter & Gamble
- Unilever
- L'Oréal

Exhibit 3   Procter & Gamble Share Prices (In U.S. dollars, January 1, 2003: 100)

Source: Thomas Datastream.

Antoine, head of Human Resources, and Vice Chairman Bruce Byrnes. In fact, Lafley has established a tradition of meeting with Antoine every Sunday evening to review the performance of the firm's 200 most senior executives. This reflects Lafley's determination to make sure the best people rise to the top. And Byrnes, whom Lafley refers to as "Yoda," the sagelike Star Wars character, gets a lot of face time because of his marketing expertise. As Lafley says, "The assets at P&G are what? Our people and our brands."[3]

Lafley's leadership style has been particularly visible in P&G's new conference room, where he and the firm's 12 other top executives meet every Monday at 8 a.m. to review results, plan strategy, and set the drumbeat for the week. The table is now round instead of rectangular. Instead of sitting where they are told, the executives now sit where they like. True to his character, Lafley maintains a low profile at most of these meetings. He occasionally joins in the discussion, but most of the time the executives talk as much to each other as to Lafley.

Indeed, Lafley's charm offensive has so disarmed most P&Gers that he has been able to make drastic changes within the company. He has replaced more than half of the company's top 30 officers, more than any P&G boss in memory, and trimmed its workforce by as many as 9,600 jobs. And he has moved more women into senior positions. In fact, Lafley skipped over 78 general managers with more seniority to name 42-year-old Deborah A. Henretta to head P&G's then-troubled North American baby care division. "The speed at which A.G. has gotten results is five years ahead of the time I expected," said Scott Cook,

founder of software maker Intuit Incorporated, who joined P&G's board shortly after Lafley's appointment.[4]

A New Strategic Focus

Lafley is intent on shifting the focus of P&G back to its consumers. At every opportunity, he has tried to drill his managers and employees to not lose sight of the consumer. He feels that P&G has often let technology dictate its new products rather than consumer needs. He would like to see the firm work more closely with retailers, the place where consumers first see the product on the shelf. And he would like to see much more concern with the consumer's experience at home. At the end of a three-day leadership seminar, Lafley was thrilled when he heard the young marketing managers declare, "We are the voice of the consumer within P&G, and they are the heart of all we do."[5]

To better focus on serving the needs of its consumers, Lafley is putting a tremendous amount of emphasis on the firm's brands. When he described the P&G of the future, he said, "We're in the business of creating and building brands."[6] (See Exhibit 4 for P&G's product segments.) Since Lafley has taken over P&G, the firm has updated all of its 200 brands by adding innovative new products. It has begun to offer devices that build on its core brands, such as Tide StainBrush, a battery powered brush for removing stains, and Mr. Clean AutoDry, a water pressure–powered car cleaning system that dries without streaking. "We are growing market share in 70 percent of our businesses," commented Clayton Daley, the firm's chief financial officer. "That doesn't happen unless you have strong innovation."[7]

Exhibit 4   Procter & Gamble Segment Information

Beauty Care

Net Sales:	2004: $17.1 billion		*Net Earnings:*	2004: $2.4 billion
	2003: $12.2 billion			2003: $2.0 billion
	2002: $10.7 billion			2002: $1.6 billion

Core Brands: Olay, Wella, Head & Shoulders, Pantene

Fabric & Home Care

Net Sales:	2004: $13.0 billion		*Net Earnings:*	2004: $2.2 billion
	2003: $12.6 billion			2003: $2.1 billion
	2002: $11.6 billion			2002: $1.8 billion

Core Brands: Tide, Downey, Ariel

Baby & Family Care

Net Sales:	2004: $10.7 billion		*Net Earnings:*	2004: $1.0 billion
	2003: $9.9 billion			2003: $0.9 billion
	2002: $9.2 billion			2002: $0.7 billion

Core Brands: Pampers, Always, Charmin, Bounty

Health Care

Net Sales:	2004: $7.0 billion		*Net Earnings:*	2004: $1.0 billion
	2003: $5.8 billion			2003: $0.7 billion
	2002: $5.0 billion			2002: $0.5 billion

Core Brands: Crest, Iams, Actonel

Snacks & Beverages

Net Sales:	2004: $3.5 billion		*Net Earnings:*	2004: $0.4 billion
	2003: $3.2 billion			2003: $0.3 billion
	2002: $3.2 billion			2002: $0.3 billion

Core Brands: Pringles, Folgers

Source: Procter & Gamble.

Lafley has fostered this innovative spirit by pushing everyone at P&G to approach its brands more creatively. Crest, for example, which used to be marketed as a toothpaste brand, is now defined as an oral care brand. The firm now sells Crest-branded toothbrushes and tooth whiteners. There's even an electric toothbrush, SpinBrush, which was added to the Crest line after P&G acquired it in January 2001. The inexpensive, fun-to-use brush has created a new and positive vibe around the whole Crest brand. "People remember experiences," Lafley explained. "They don't remember attributes."[8]

A key element of Lafley's strategy also has been to move P&G away from basic consumer products such as laundry detergents, which can be knocked off by private labels, to higher-margin products. This has led him to focus more strongly on the firm's beauty care business. Under Lafley, P&G has made some of its costly acquisitions to complement its Cover Girl and Oil of Olay brands. He purchased Clairol in 2001 for $5 billion, and followed this up by acquiring German beauty firm Wella in 2003 for $6.9 billion. With the acquisition of Gillette, Lafley is trying to move P&G into the men's market for personal care products.

P&G is also willing to work with other firms to develop its products and get them to the marketplace. The firm has been partnering with appliance makers who make hardware to support its unique products. Applica Inc. recently launched the Home Café, a one-cup coffee maker that uses distinctive Folgers and Millstone coffee pads from P&G. It joined with Clorox Company, maker of Glad Bags, last October to share a food-wrap technology it had developed. It was unprecedented for P&G to work with a competitor, says licensing head Jeffrey Weedman. The overall effect is undeniable. "Lafley has made P&G far more flexible," said Banc of America's Steele.[9]

A Revolution Still in the Making

Although Lafley has managed to give a tremendous push to P&G to rethink is business model, it is quite clear he has more revolutionary changes in mind. A confidential memo was circulated among P&G's top brass in late 2001 that even drew a sharp response from some of its board members. It argued that P&G could be cut to 25,000 employees, less than a quarter of its current size. Lafley admitted that the memo had drawn a strong reaction, saying, "It terrified our organization."[10]

Even though Lafley did not write this infamous memo, it did reflect the central tenet of his vision that P&G should do only what it does best and nothing more. He clearly wants a more outwardly focused, flexible company, which means that P&G does not have to do everything in house. If there are no clear benefits that stem from doing something within the firm, it should be contracted out. Such a philosophy has serious implications for every facet of P&G's operations from R&D to manufacturing.

Lafley has clearly challenged the supremacy of P&G's research and development operations. He has confronted head-on the stubbornly held notion that everything must be invented within P&G, asserting that half of its new products should come from the outside. Under his tenure, the firm has begun to get about 20 percent of its new product ideas from outside the firm. This is double the 10 percent figure that existed at P&G when he took over.

A variety of other activities are also being driven out of the firm. In April 2003, Lafley turned over all bar soap manufacturing, including Ivory, P&G's oldest surviving brand, to a Canadian contractor. One month later, he outsourced P&G's information-technology operation to Hewlett-Packard Company. While Lafley shies away from saying just how much of P&G's factory and back-office operations he may hand over to someone else, he does admit that facing up to the realities of the marketplace may force some hardships on its employees.

Lafley is well aware that nearly one-half of the firm's 102,000 employees work in its plants. So far, he has taken concrete steps to ease the hardships that may be caused by cutting back on P&G's operations. At the bar soap operations, based entirely in Cincinnati, 200 of the 250 employees went to work for the Canadian contractor. Similarly, all 2,000 of the information-technology workers were moved over to HP. "Lafley has deftly handled the outsourcing deals, which has lessened fear within P&G," said Roger Martin, a close adviser of Lafley's who is dean of the University of Toronto's Joseph L. Rotman School of Management.[11]

Such moves to outsource some of the activities may also create more flexibility for the firm over the longer term. It could decide how much it wants to invest in particular brands, products or even lines of businesses. No one would dispute that these moves are clearly revolutionary for a firm such as P&G. "He's absolutely breaking many well-set molds at P&G," said eBay's CEO, Margaret C. "Meg" Whitman, whom Lafley had recently appointed to the board.[12]

Daunting Challenges

Precisely because of his achievements, Lafley has come under enormous pressure to restore P&G to a company that is admired, imitated, and uncommonly profitable. Nowhere are those expectations more apparent than on the second floor of headquarters, where three of its former chief executives are still active. John Pepper, a popular former boss who returned briefly as chairman when Jaeger left, stated, "It's now clear to me that A.G. is going to be one of the great CEOs in this company's history."[13]

But Lafley still faces daunting challenges. He has been pushing the firm to build on its most promising brands, partly by creating new product forms and even new forms of devices such as the Tide StainBrush and Mr. Clean AutoDry. It is still unclear whether these new introductions can generate the level of sustained demand that will allow P&G to maintain its higher margins. Sales of the firm's Dawn Power Dish Brush, for example, have eased considerably since its launch in 2003. P&G's managers are also worried about the quality of these devices, which can ultimately hurt the overall brand. The firm recently recalled its Swiffer Vac because of electrical problems. Lafley has acknowledged that they have to be careful with their new devices: "We have to be careful we don't push it too far."[14]

The reliance on external sources for new products can also be problematic. As any scientist will attest, decisions to purchase a new product idea often tend to be extremely hard to make. The process of picking winners from other labs is likely to be both difficult and expensive. P&G already missed a big opportunity by passing up the chance to buy water-soluble strips that contain mouthwash. Listerine managed to grab the product and has profited handsomely from the deal.

But finding new avenues to grow could be the only way to balance P&G's growing reliance on Wal-Mart. Former and current P&G employees say the discounter could account for one-third of P&G's global sales by the end of the decade. Meanwhile, the pressure from consumers and competitors to keep prices low will only increase. "P&G has improved its ability to take on those challenges, but those challenges are still there," said Lehman analyst Ann Gillin.[15]

The biggest risk, though, is that Lafley will lose the people at P&G. The firm's insular culture has been famously resistant to new ideas. Employees form a tightly knit family because most of them started out and grew up together at P&G, which only promotes from within. Over the years, these people have gradually adopted the culture of the firm and have come to believe in it. Lafley is well aware of his predicament. He recently admitted, "I am worried that I will ask the organization to change ahead of its understanding, capability, and commitment."[16]

Endnotes

1. Dash, Eric. 2005. A merger in search of a home. Yours. *New York Times,* January 29: B3.

2. Grant, Jeremy. 2005. P&G starts on integration plan. *Financial Times,* January 31: 17.

3. Berner, Robert. 2003. P&G: New and improved. *BusinessWeek,* July 7: 62.

4. Ibid.: 55.

5. Ibid.: 62.

6. Ibid.: 63.

7. Berner, Robert, Byrnes, Nanette, & Zellner, Wendy. 2004. P&G has rivals in a wringer. *BusinessWeek,* October 4: 74.

8. Berner, Robert, & Symonds, William C. 2005. Welcome to Procter & gadget. *BusinessWeek,* February 7: 77.

9. *BusinessWeek,* July 7: 63.

10. Ibid.: 55.

11. Ibid.: 63.

12. Ibid.: 58.

13. Ibid.: 55.

14. *BusinessWeek,* February 7: 77.

15. *BusinessWeek,* July 7: 63.

16. Ibid.: 58.

Case 27   Sun Life Financial: Entering China*

Introduction

In early 2000, Dikran Ohannessian, Sun Life Financial's vice president, China, was flipping through piles of consultants' reports on the plane from Toronto, Canada, to Beijing, China.

As Ohannessian got up to stretch, he thought about what had been achieved: a representative office in Beijing, valuable contacts with the Chinese government and business people, and an agreement to partner with a well-established Chinese financial services group. He knew there were many major milestones ahead, such as forming an entry strategy, choosing the geographical market area in which to operate, while keeping an eye on the financial viability as well as all the necessary hurdles to obtain a business license in China.

History of Sun Life Financial

Sun Life Financial of Canada began in 1865, in Montreal, selling insurance policies to Canadians in the process of the country's creation. By the 1890s, Sun Life Financial had begun an internationalization process, by expanding into Nicaragua, Ecuador, Peru, and Chile and later into Asia, including Japan, India, and China. At the turn of the century, Sun Life Financial looked to diversify its investments and began expanding through growing industries, such as electric utilities, gas, telephone, and transport. Sun Life Financial maintained private ownership and staved off a take-over attempt by a U.S. firm in the 1950s, allowing it to strengthen its roots within Canada.

In 1999, Sun Life Financial posted revenues of $14.7 billion,[1] of which $3.3 billion was life insurance premiums, $1.2 billion was health insurance, $3.5 billion was annuities, $4.1 billion was net investment income, and $2.6 billion was fee income. Sun Life Financial's net income was $164 million in 1999, up from $54 million realized on revenues of $12.9 billion in 1998. Net income in 1998 and 1999 had been negatively impacted by the costs associated with pensions sales practices reviews and increased reserves for guaranteed annuity rates in the U.K. business, as

well as a significant increase in reserves in the discontinued accident and health reinsurance business. By early 2000, Sun Life Financial was a month away from a $2.1 billion initial public offering (IPO) in Toronto, New York, London, and the Philippines. Although there was pent-up demand for Sun Life Financial's shares in the Canadian marketplace, executives of Sun Life Financial and their advisers (RBC Dominion Securities and Morgan Stanley) had two tensions to balance—not letting the stock rise too quickly for those policy holders who had decided to take cash instead of becoming shareholders, while giving the investment community and those policy holders who were to become shareholders a strong initial stock price increase. The IPO would be the fifth in a string of Canadian life insurance companies that had gone public since the summer of 1999.[2]

Sun Life Financial had a six-pronged approach to its strategy:

1. Aggressively expand the wealth management business
2. Strategically grow higher return protection business lines
3. Achieve superior shareholder returns while maintaining financial discipline
4. Leverage strong brands across multiple product offerings
5. Capitalize on distribution strengths
6. Pursue expansion in key strategic markets

Exhibit 1 shows Sun Life Financial's sales by country. By early 2000, the majority of sales for Sun Life Financial were generated by sales in Canada and the United States. Although Sun Life Financial was not profitable in every country in which it operated, the company was not committed to any business that was not able to meet 15 percent after-tax return on equity in the future.[3] This low return on equity was the case in the country's U.K. operations, which some industry observers believed Sun Life Financial would sell off. Sun Life Financial believed that it would drive revenue growth through its 80 percent ownership of the Boston-based MFS wealth management business and, in the longer term, its foray into China.

Product and Services

Sun Life Financial's two principal businesses were wealth management and protection. Wealth management included all asset management, mutual funds, pensions, annuities, trusts, and banking operations. The wealth management business primarily was based in Canada, the United States and the United Kingdom and made up 52 percent of the company's revenues with $7.7 billion and 89 percent of its assets ($268.9 billion) in 1999. The complete wealth management business served 2.9 million individual investors and 7,000 institutional investors around the world. Almost

*Ken Mark and Jordan Mitchell prepared this case under the supervision of Professor Paul W. Beamish solely to provide material for class discussion. The authors do not intend to illustrate either effective or ineffective handling of a managerial situation. The authors may have disguised certain names and other identifying information to protect confidentiality.

Revenue by Business 1999

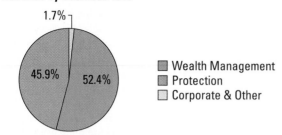

Wealth Management
Protection
Corporate & Other

Revenue by Geography 1999

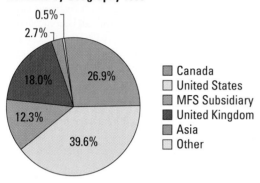

Canada
United States
MFS Subsidiary
United Kingdom
Asia
Other

Exhibit 1   Sun Life Financial Revenue by Business and Geography

Source: Sun Life Financial Initial Public Offering Booklet, Introduction, March 23, 2000.

all of the company's wealth management products (97 percent) were sold through independent third parties.

The protection business included Sun Life Financial's insurance products, including individual insurance, group life insurance, and health insurance, making up 46 percent or $6.8 billion of the company's revenues in 1999. Principally, the group life and health insurance was based in Canada, the United States, and the United Kingdom, whereas the individual insurance business was in all the company's markets. Sun Life Financial was ranked second for group and health insurance in Canada and third in the United Kingdom. For individuals, Sun Life Financial offered whole life, term life, universal life, unit-linked life, and corporate-owned life insurance products. For groups, life, health, and disability insurance were available. Exhibit 2 shows definitions of insurance terms.

Sun Life Financial believed it had a winning formula in its protection business, due to its wide range of products backed by the company's financial strength and the effectiveness of it customer service and underwriting ability. In North America, Sun Life Financial was competing in a mature industry; however, the company needed to respond to the mounting pressures from banks that had entered the insurance industry, often undercutting prices. Due to deregulation in the marketplace, direct marketers and

telemarketers were becoming more common in insurance sales. With greater emphasis on retirement planning in the mature markets, traditional life insurance products were losing ground against universal life in Canada and the United States and unit-linked life insurance in the United Kingdom. This trend was not necessarily the case in Asia or South America, where traditional life insurance products were still popular.

Sun Life Financial's focus in the United States was on high net worth individuals with tailored packages for executive benefit plans. The company had restructured its United States sales force in 1997 by moving away from a career agency sales force to general agents selling a wide variety of products. In 1999, 65 percent of U.S. insurance sales were through general agents, and 35 percent were through third parties, such as banks and investment advisers. The general shift of sales approach caused a decrease in the number of policies, but through focusing on the high net worth segment, Sun Life Financial was able to increase total premium revenues.

In Canada, Sun Life Financial believed that it had expertise in selling group life and health insurance to large businesses as it had more than 7,000 policies representing more than 3 million individuals. Sun Life Financial marketed and distributed its group life and health insurance through its own sales representatives and career agents, independent brokers and consultants, Canadian associations, such as professional and alumni organizations, and through the Internet.

For individual life insurance, Sun Life Financial had 627,000 individual life insurance policies in force with 450,000 policyholders. Sun Life Financial had experienced an increase in premium income, despite a decreasing number of policies, due to success in selling through independent agents who tended to focus on high net worth individuals, increasing the average size of the policy. Although Sun Life Financial increasingly sold through independent life insurance brokers, such as financial planners and investment dealers, it still distributed a large portion through career agents, meaning that costs of distributing the insurance were moving from fixed to variable costs. Four years prior, in 1996, third-party distributors accounted for seven percent of sales for new individual life insurance, whereas in 1999, 30 percent were created through independents. In March 1999, Sun Life Financial formed a distribution alliance with Great-West Life, London Life, and Investors Group, where each organization could sell each other's universal life and term life insurance products.

History of Sun Life Financial's Involvement in China

In 1992, China opened two geographical market areas in the country to foreign investment—Shanghai and Guangzhou. To create a presence in China, a country that

Exhibit 2   Definitions of Insurance Types

Actuary

A person professionally trained in the technical aspects of pensions, insurance, and related fields. The actuary estimates how much money must be contributed to an insurance or pension fund in order to support the benefits that will become payable in the future.

Life Insurance

Insurance providing for payment of a specified amount on the insured's death, either to his or her estate or to a designated beneficiary; or in the case of an endowment policy, to the policy holder at a specified date.

Premium

The sum paid by a policyholder to keep an insurance policy in force.

Nonparticipating Policy

One that does not provide for the payment of a dividend.

Participating Policy

One under which the policy owner is entitled to receive shares of the divisible surplus of the insurer. Such shares are commonly called dividends.

Reinsurance

The purchase of insurance by an insurance company from another insurance company (reinsurer) to provide it protection against large losses on cases it has already insured.

Term Insurance

Life or health insurance protection during a limited number of years but expiring without value if the insured survives the stated period.

Unit-linked Life Insurance

An insurance product linked to a particular investment fund in which the policy holder would combine tax advantages with protection. Common in Europe and the United Kingdom.

Universal Life Insurance

A flexible premium life insurance policy under which the policyholder may change the death benefit from time to time (with satisfactory evidence of insurability for increases) and vary the amount or timing of premium payments. Premiums (less expense charges) are credited to a policy account from which mortality charges are deducted and to which interest is credited at a rate that may change from time to time.

Source: www.haskayne.ucalgary.ca/rmin/rmin_glossary_a.html, accessed December 16, 2003.

Sun Life Financial had operated in nearly a century earlier, Sun Life Financial opened a representative office in Beijing. (By 1920, Sun Life Financial had grown to be the largest foreign insurance company, but like all other foreign-owned insurance firms, it was forced to leave China in 1949, when the Communist party took power.)[4] The purpose of the office was to establish a presence, provide information to the Canadian headquarters, stay abreast of Chinese regulatory policies and lobby the local and national governments to acquire a license. In May 1999, the Chinese government granted the right for Sun Life Financial to apply for a license. Seven months later, Sun Life Financial signed a memorandum of understanding for a joint venture with China Everbright Group. Joint venture agreements were required by the Chinese government to maintain domestic involvement in business expansion within the country.

Sun Life Financial's strategy was to partner with a respected and prestigious firm that had clout with the national and local authorities. The company wanted to create an entity that was "Chinese in operation in spirit with Western business practices, management and technology." Sun Life Financial aimed to enter into the "strategically higher return protection business lines," followed by plans to enter the wealth management business. This plan would mean creating a mutual fund and starting a fee-based asset management business. In the future, Sun Life Financial felt that the pensions business would be attractive. However, both wealth management and pensions domains were not yet open to foreign companies.[5]

China Everbright Group and the Joint Venture Agreement   China Everbright Group was founded in 1983, as part of China's open economic policy. It was a state-owned entity with direct control coming from the State Council. The group's primary business was financial services with several divisions, including Everbright Bank (the sixth largest bank on a national level) and Everbright Securities, considered to be the premier brokerage company in the country. China Everbright Group controlled $40 billion in assets and posted profits of $675 million in 1999.

In making the decision to partner with Everbright, Sun Life Financial had to consider other alternatives. An executive from the insurance company Winterthur gave his opinion between one alternative and Everbright:

> Given a choice, I would prefer the alternative to Everbright. We know [the alternative] well and have done business with them for many years. We like them very much. They are very sophisticated and professional—and that is hard to find in China. Of course, [they] have ongoing business in financial services that may compete with you later, and given [their] high-level political relations, you have to go forward assuming confidentiality is impossible. But, those high-level political relations could be very useful.[6]

An executive with AXA believed Everbright to be a better choice:

> Everbright is the best partner, bar none. Its management is tops, and even this recent blip with the chairman [his removal] does not change that. They want to be in the insurance business, and they want a foreign partner to manage. They are aggressive, and not as bureaucratic as [some others]. Also not as arrogant. They are easier to deal with. AXA, in my view, made a serious mistake going with Minmetals. . . .[7]

The decision to partner with Everbright was made and a memorandum of understanding with China Everbright was signed in December 1999. The working name for the joint venture was Guang Da Yong Ming, or Sun Life Everbright in English. The agreement called for both sides to own 50 percent, with each partner contributing $18 million as an initial capital start-up. In year four, it was predicted that each partner would need to contribute an additional $3 million. Each side split decision-making duties, with four board members being appointed from each partner. All board-level decisions required their parent partners to give the nod. Everbright had the right to appoint the first chairman, with partners making the decision on an alternating three-year basis.

For the first five years of the venture, Sun Life Financial was responsible for the day-to-day operations. The foreign partner under Chinese regulations was required to provide its technology knowledge for free during the start-up period. Sun Life Financial had planned on providing insurance software for free, negotiating for the new entity to cover the costs of non-insurance software and hardware outlays. In addition to technology, Sun Life Financial was poised to provide management direction and the sales agent training. In doing so, any expatriate costs over the cost of a comparable local Chinese employee were required to be covered outside of the partnership by the foreign partner. Everbright was expected to share its distribution network and its management's local expertise and ability to deal with the governments in seeking approvals.

Sun Life Financial projected that the operation would show a profit in seven years. In the circumstance that profits were 10 percent lower than expected, both sides would need to provide an additional $1.5 million in capital, with the first profit year being pushed back one year.

China[8]

China was geographically the fourth largest country with 9.6 million square kilometres across 23 provinces and had the largest population in the world with 1.3 billion people. The average age was 31.7 years, and the population comprised 23.1 percent aged zero to 14 years, 69.5 percent aged 15 to 64 years, and 7.4 percent aged 65 years and older. On average, the country's residents were expected to live to 72.2 years, with the average life expectancy being 70.33 years for men and 74.28 years for women. The total fertility rate was estimated at 1.7 children born per woman. The population growth rate was estimated at 0.6 percent.

China's communist system had been put in place under Mao Zedong in 1949, and it placed tight controls on the country through political, social, and economic policies. Eventually, some of the economic policies were relaxed in the late 1970s, allowing for some decentralized economic decision making and greater foreign trade. China was seen as a market with untapped potential due to its population size and underdeveloped business in some industries. Although its gross domestic product (GDP) per capita was wedged between Ukraine and Swaziland, ranked at 129th at US$4,400, the country was considered to be second to the United States on purchasing power parity basis. Ten percent of the population was considered to be living below the poverty line.

China had quadrupled its GDP since 1978, driven through industry and construction (51.2 percent of GDP), agriculture (15.2 percent of GDP), and services (33.6 percent of GDP) gains, some of which were attributed to the involvement of foreign enterprises helping to increase domestic goods and exports. The current GDP was estimated to be more than $5 trillion, second to the United States, and growing at approximately eight percent. The exchange rate for China's currency, the yuan or reminibi (RMB), was pegged at 8.28 to US $1, and inflation was slightly negative at −0.8 percent. China was criticized for its bureaucracy as well as the growing disparity in income, due to the influx of new business. The government was seen to periodically loosen and retighten its controls, making for uneven operating conditions. The government had made progress but was not always successful at reducing corruption in business or keeping its state-owned enterprises in check. Missing payments or not providing full pension amounts were not uncommon. Approximately 80 million to 120 million rural workers were considered to be surplus, moving freely between small towns and large cities, and this movement was seen to add to problems of maintaining the country's living standards. While unemployment in urban areas was estimated to be 10 percent, unemployment rates of migrant or rural workers was seen to be much higher. It was estimated that the workforce was 744 million people of whom 50 percent worked in agriculture, 22 percent in industry, and 28 percent in services.

Risks of Doing Business in China   Due to the country's population size and growing economy, management of many foreign firms were excited about the possibilities of benefiting from a largely untapped marketplace. However, many foreign business people were critical of China for the level of bureaucracy in obtaining the appropriate licenses and being heavily restricted as to the types of products and services allowed to be offered for sale. Corruption and piracy still existed as well.

China's Pending WTO Membership   As of early 2000, China was not yet a member of the World Trade Organization (WTO). The WTO comprised 145 countries, with the responsibility to set up standards for international trade and commerce. Through its pending membership, expected to take place in 2001, observers felt that China would be further opened up, where potential growth could be harnessed. However, the membership also meant pressure on the country's tight political controls.

Chinese Life Insurance Market

China's life insurance market was widely considered to have one of the largest growth rates over the next 10 years, due to low penetration (an estimated 1.69 percent of the population had life insurance, and general insurance was 0.63 percent).[9] China was valued at US$16.8 billion per year in premium income in 1999. Exhibit 3 shows growth and penetration rates of both life and nonlife insurance in China, and Exhibit 4 shows comparative data for six cities. Industry analysts believed that low insurance penetration coupled with economic growth could produce annual compounded growth of 15 percent over a 10-year period.[10] Within Asia, China was the fourth largest market in premium revenues behind Japan (US$279 billion), Korea (US$56 billion) and Taiwan (US$28 billion).

The Chinese insurance market was divided into life insurance and general insurance. Under life insurance, options were open to group insurance or individual. Group insurance was open to domestic firms only, while individual insurance was open to both foreign and domestic companies. Thus far, foreign firms were only permitted to operate in Shanghai (China's largest city with a population of 14 million), with the exception being American International Assurance (AIA), which was licensed to do business in Guangzhou as well. Foreign enterprises were able to open

Exhibit 3   China: Premium Income 1990 to 1999
(US$ millions)

	Life Growth			Nonlife Growth			Total Growth		Penetration (%)		
	Premium	%	% of Total	Premium	%	% of Total	Premium	%	Life	General	Total
1990	1,088.8		32.0	2,311.3		68.0	3,400.1		0.3	0.7	1.0
1991	1,316.1	25.8	30.0	3,069.1	38.2	70.0	4,385.3	34.2	0.3	1.2	1.6
1992	1,829.6	47.1	27.9	4,734.5	63.3	72.1	6,564.1	58.4	0.4	1.1	1.5
1993	1,721.6	(5.1)	19.0	7,338.6	56.3	81.0	9,060.1	39.2	0.3	1.2	1.5
1994	2,802.9	137.1	38.0	4,572.3	(9.3)	62.0	7,375.2	18.5	0.5	0.8	1.3
1995	3,086.1	8.4	35.0	5,730.8	23.4	65.0	8,816.9	17.7	0.4	0.8	1.3
1996	4,319.0	39.8	42.0	5,965.1	4.0	58.0	10,284.1	16.5	0.5	0.7	1.3
1997	7,332.1	69.4	56.0	5,760.5	(3.6)	44.0	13,092.7	27.0	0.8	0.6	1.5
1998	9,037.4	22.8	60.0	6,025.0	4.2	40.0	15,062.4	14.6	0.9	0.6	1.6
1999	10,538.1	16.6	62.6	6,296.3	4.5	37.4	16,834.3	11.8	1.1	0.6	1.7

Source: Global Insurers in China, Nomura, April 3, 2003, p. 4.

Exhibit 4   Comparative Data—Six Cities

City	Population (in millions)	Number of Households (millions)	Total GDP (RMB billions/ US$ billions)	GDP % Increase over Previous Year	GDP per Capita (RMB '000s/ US$ 000s)
Chongqing (+ region)	30	2.9	143.5/17.3	8.5	4.8/0.6
Shanghai	14	4.6	368.8/44.3	10.1	26.3/2.5
Tianjin	9	2.8	134.1/16.2	9.3	14.9/1.8
Guangzhou	6.6	1.9	184.4/21.1	13	28.0/3.8
Dalian	5.4	1.7	93.5/11.3	12.2	17.3/2.1
Shenzhen	3.8	0.3	128.9/15.5	14.5	34.0/4.1
Average	11.5	2.4	175.5/21.1	11.3	20.8/2.5

representative offices to investigate, research, and make contacts with government officials. It was expected in early 2000 that, in addition to Shanghai and Guangzhou, four more cities would open: Tianjin, Shenzhen, Dalian and Chongqing. However, if no foreign company showed interest in opening up an office in those markets, the government was not likely to open it up. Furthermore, if a foreign insurer could make a strong case to open up in a particular city, it could enlist the help of the municipal government with a possibility that it would be granted a license.

China's entry into the World Trade Organization (WTO) called for the government to completely open up the market by 2005, permitting foreign companies to operate in any city or province. Some speculators believed that the Chinese government would ultimately control that decision, even after 2005. Domestic competitors were permitted to operate in 14 cities, other than the state-owned People's Insurance Company of China (PICC), which was not restricted. An industry analyst talked about the WTO and the benefits for local firms:

> We believe existing insurance companies will benefit from the WTO. We do see foreign companies introducing a dose of competition, but, actually, quite a mild one. There are five significant national domestic insurance groups and around 25 foreign insurers in operation in China. Despite the competition, the five national players have a near-complete lock on market share, at about 98 percent of the market. Foreign insurers still face restriction expansions. Nonetheless, their entry to the market should boost local standards.[11]

The insurance regulator was the People's Bank of China until November 1998, when the CIRC (China Insurance Regulatory Commission) was established. The aim of the CIRC was to approve new regulations and police insurance activity within the country. With just over one year of being in operation, the CIRC was still formulating its identity. One foreign insurance representative was complimentary of the new organization:

> The CIRC is receptive to new ideas. They may like the concept of limiting agency force and using the Internet to distribute products—if you show them how you are going to create jobs for Chinese.[12]

Another foreign insurance representative had a different view:

> I was chief representative in Beijing for more than five years, and in that time, China's regulators have not changed. No, maybe they have gotten worse, more bureaucratic. The new regulators just say "no" to requests, especially if they are about something that PICC does not want to change. [Note: the CIRC is led by former PICC officials.] That said, I think the CIRC wants to implement regulation "by the book" but PICC does not want that if it encourages competition. Our strongest competitor is PICC.[13]

Foreign firms participating in life insurance sales were permitted to own up to a maximum of 50 percent of the venture, forcing them to seek a partnership with a domestic organization. In the general insurance category, foreign enterprises would be allowed to own up to 100 percent in 2004.[14]

Chinese Consumers for Insurance   Generally, as a country's GDP per capita increases, a broader base of its population is more likely to have insurance.[15] China's consumers in the US$1,000 to US$10,000 GDP per capita bracket did not have enough to take a risk in the equity market, but they still had disposable income, making China a ripe ground for insurance. By avoiding risk in playing the equity markets, Chinese consumers would typically increase savings in deposits or guaranteed return instruments (usually at 2.5 percent). Although sometimes offering lower returns, insurance offered an alternative to these vehicles through greater protection to its policy holders.[16] Throughout the mid-1990s, the composition of an average Chinese household's financial assets were: savings deposits 67 percent to 77 percent, securities 9 percent to 11 percent, cash 12 percent to 21 percent, and insurance less than one percent.[17]

The other major change that was occurring was the decreasing dependence on lifelong security through state-operated organizations. Known as the "iron rice bowl," this security was fading fast from the employer and moving into the direction of private enterprise. A study performed in Shanghai by Watson Wyatt in 1996 showed that 84 percent of respondents purchased insurance for reasons of protection, 10 percent purchased it for savings, 5 percent because it was trendy, and 1 percent for other reasons.[18]

Types of Insurance Products   There were six general classifications for insurance products in China: personal life, property, liability, agricultural, reinsurance, and foreign insurance (to cover persons or objects outside of China). The types of insurance products sold varied greatly depending on the area within the country. For example, Shanghai sold extensive individual life insurance, while group life made up less than 10 percent of the total life insurance market there. In contrast, Guangzhou's group life policies represented more than 60 percent of its total life insurance market.[19]

Competition

There were several hungry foreign firms that had signed agreements with Chinese domestic firms or were looking for partnerships to enter the insurance market. One of the differentiating factors would be the channel of distribution—the method of sale of insurance products via door-to-door sales, force, telephone sales, or through companies.

There were two distinct camps in the Chinese insurance market: domestic firms or joint-ownership between domestic and foreign companies. All the market leaders in life insurance in 1999 were domestic firms. PICC had 68.63 percent of market share followed by Ping An with 20.24 percent, China Pacific with 7.48 percent, New China Life with 1.20 percent, and Tai Kang with 0.71 percent. PICC was the oldest insurance firm in the country (established in 1949), was government-owned and provided its policy owners with the perception of stability and history. Its closest competitor, Ping An, was regarded to have strong business practices, a good asset base (30 percent in cash and deposits), and was able to retain the right to offer financial services and insurance services, a feat that few other insurance firms were able to achieve. It was also the first Chinese insurance company to comply with international accounting standards. Although it was considered to be a domestic firm, Morgan Stanley and Goldman Sachs each owned six percent of Ping An. China Pacific was attempting to prepare for international competition by signing a joint-venture agreement with Aetna for life insurance, as well as developing a specialty in insurance for large-scale projects.

Out of the five major established foreign firms, the estimated combined market share was under two percent. The most established foreign life insurance firm was American International Assurance (AIA), founded in 1992, with 4,850 sales agents and RMB 1,406 million in premium revenues. The following table depicts the other foreign firms operating joint ventures or companies with representative offices.

Company	Foreign Country Involved	License	Premiums US$ million	Number of Agents
AIA	U.S.	Shanghai, 1992 Guangzhou, 1995	170.0	4,850
Manulife Sinochem	Canada	Shanghai, 1996	33.0	3,089
China Pacific-Aetna	U.S.	Shanghai, 1997	25.0	5,168
Allianz Dazhong	Germany	Shanghai, 1998	6.6	934
AXA-minmetal	France	Shanghai, 1999	7.7	1,334
China Life Colonial Mutual	Australia	Expected in 2000		
John Hancock—Tian An	U.S.	Rep Office		
Prudential CITIC	U.K.	Rep Office		
Sun Life Financial Everbright	Canada	Rep Office		

With licenses taking several years, the process of establishing an insurance business for a foreign firm was arduous. Companies needed to also engage in the difficult task of contracting qualified individuals, as the insurance market in China was less than 20 years old. As such, companies were enacting training programs to attract strong agents. Actuary work could be outsourced, but selling insurance was seen to be a combination of understanding the products and having the personal ability to sell with the appropriate cultural manner.

As an employee from Aetna stated, "Under the current environment, Aetna may never make money for 20 years—but it does not matter because Aetna is limiting costs and waiting for change, and anyway, Aetna is really in China for the chairman's ego."[20] Opinions from the French firm, Axa, were not much different: "There is no profit to be made in China for decades or more, unless the regulations change."[21]

What Do the Consultants Think Sun Life Financial Should Do?

A consultant's report dated in September 1999 talked about the business opportunity for Sun Life Financial in China:

> Our starting hypothesis was that market constraints and other environmental factors make China a significant

Target Population by Age Segment

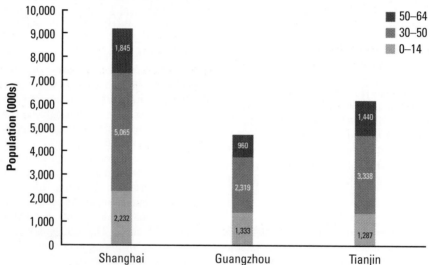

Life Insurance Density 1987 to 1998 (in RMB per head)

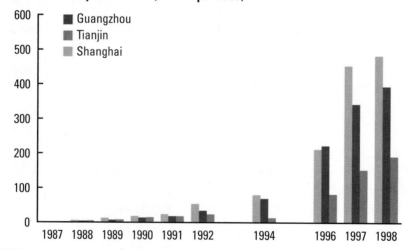

Exhibit 5   Comparative Data—Three Cities

challenge to success for Sun Life Financial [as] the main business is currently the type we want to exit, market access and freedom of action are largely restricted, short-term rewards and economic success are illusionary and operating risks are high and difficult to control. While we believe that by and large our hypothesis still holds true today, in particular with respect to timing, signs of sustained and favourable change are evident:

- continued attempts to break the regulatory product gauntlet with indications that the product licensing approach may be abandoned within the coming two years
- two large and distinct segment markets are growing rapidly and offer opportunities in almost every location
- large-scale social asymmetry and lack of long-term security are propelling selectively the health and pension businesses
- distribution alternatives are being recognized by a number of players supported by solid growth in Internet users

We still have to recognize that the industry as a whole [is developing], but governmental and business pressure indicate a move towards better trained, qualified, and rational participants. This trend does favorably support a

player like Sun Life Financial with its ethical business approach.

In the same consultant's report, three different strategies were outlined for Sun Life Financial's entry into China: the "Minimalist" approach, the "Full Speed" development or the "Model Citizen." The minimalist approach called for the selection of a less advanced city, focusing on traditional insurance products and containing the capital investment. The idea with this approach was to maintain a presence and "shift gears" when restrictions were dropped and the marketplace became more favorable. The full speed strategy involved selecting a high-growth city, building a large agency force and developing a full portfolio of products in the eventuality that regulations would change. The model citizen plan called for selecting a city based more on co-operation, with a focus on building government relations. This option also called for capital containment and the slow development of new insurance products beginning with the traditional portfolio.

City Selection   There were six cities about to be opened for foreign insurers: Guangzhou, Shenzhen, Tianjin, Dalian, Shanghai, and Chongqing. Exhibit 5 shows comparisons of some of the cities. A consultant's report defined each market in terms of the foreign companies currently involved on the following grid:[22]

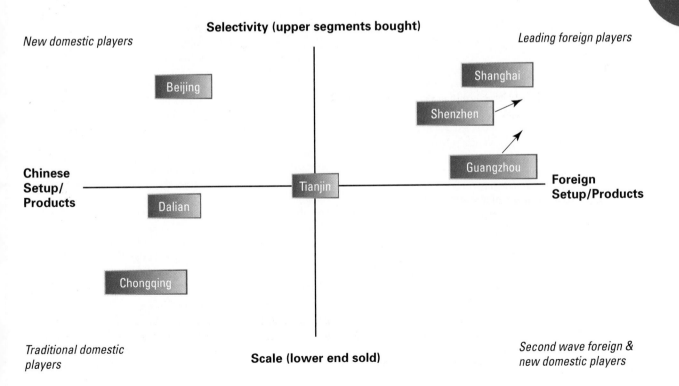

Based on government relations and market attractiveness, Sun Life Financial narrowed its options down to Shanghai, Guangzhou, and Tianjin in order to start its insurance sales operations. The city selection was seen to be important for several reasons. Once the market opened, the Chinese government required that insurers have a minimum of RMB 100 million (US$12 million) in premium revenues in its entry city before applying for a second license. Also, if the insurer was not successful in its city of choice, it would risk disappointing its partner, the municipal government, and its headquarters. A poor city selection would also put the company further behind in its break-even targets.

Sun Life Financial had hired another consulting company to do a complete investigation of Shanghai, Gaungzhou, and Tianjin. Along with the consultants, Sun Life Financial had established the criteria of the city, based on market size, purchasing potential, market growth, and market development. The consultants gave a greater weighting to market size and purchasing potential as they believed that a bigger market would provide a greater opportunity to carve out a niche. Shanghai had the largest market and strong market growth. Along with Gaungzhou, both were estimated to lead China's economic growth, while Tianjin would be in line with the national average. Shanghai and Guangzhou were equal in terms of market development, and Guangzhou was the clear leader for purchasing potential.

With the results of the findings, the consultants' report suggested that Sun Life Financial enter into the Shanghai market with the following explanations:

Shanghai appears to enjoy significantly higher political support from the central government than does Guangzhou: Their closely knit group of senior advisors includes many former bureaucrats in the Shanghai Municipal Government. Shanghai's cosmopolitanism should not be underrated. The city was Asia's financial services centre before WWII, and governments and consumers clearly intend for Shanghai to regain that stature. This desire manifests itself in a much more cosmopolitan attitude in Shanghai, which translates into a greater willingness to experiment with foreign products and services.

We also believe that a market presence in Shanghai is more replicable in other cities than if Sun Life Financial began in Guangzhou. Cultural differences are greater than those between Shanghai and other provinces: Key staff trained in a Shanghai operation are more likely to be able to hit the ground running in other cities in the future. While there is far greater competition in the insurance industry in Shanghai, this could prove to be a benefit for the company. Competition focuses business strategy, promotes innovation, increases efficiencies, leads to greater tolerance of risk, and potentially leverages higher returns.

There is no major cost differential between Shanghai and Guangzhou: Rents in both cities for Grade A office space are US$40 to $60/m2/day, operating costs are about the same, local business taxes (eight percent), and salary costs (US$300 to US$500 for administrative staff, $600 to $1,200 for department managers, and $1,000 to $2,000/month for senior managers) are also likely to be at par.

The same report assessed Tianjin, the lower cost alternative:

We do not believe that Tianjin is a suitable point for market entry into China. Market conditions, underinvestment, and structural economic problems will continue to drag the urban and regional economy of Tianjin with serious unemployment looming as a major challenge. In such a context, we do not believe that a significant number of consumers will divert comparatively lower discretionary incomes to purchase of insurance products. While establishment and operational costs will certainly be lower than in Shanghai or Guangzhou, we suggest that, ultimately, the purchasing power of regional markets should dictate the selection of market entry point. In establishing in Tianjin, Sun Life Financial would admittedly have a low-cost operation in a city with little competition; this is fully understandable given the inherent weakness in the Tianjin market.

Another consultant's report had a different view of the attractiveness of each market:

From a supply side point of view, there is ample opportunity for a new player to gain market share in either city although the large incumbent agency base in Shanghai reduces the outlook for a new entrant. Under almost any growth scenario Tianjin quickly outpaces Shanghai in attractiveness. This can be explained by Tianjin still being on the "steep" part of the development curve while Shanghai is already on the "flatter" part. Guangzhou is a distant third given the Hong Kong offshore market factor. Even without a privileged position, Tianjin becomes the first choice under a balanced growth scenario.

Because Tianjin was on the "steep" part of the development curve, the consultant's report above argued that Tianjin's life insurance market would grow at a much faster rate than Shanghai's or Guangzhou's. The other part of the equation was the growth of GDP per capita, which was calculated based on historical figures for the next five years: Shanghai 15 percent, Guangzhou 23 percent, and Tianjin 12 percent. Exhibit 6 shows comparative data for the three cities.

Conclusion

Now in a taxi amongst the hectic Beijing traffic, Ohannessian had a lot of information to digest about the Chinese market and the opportunity to sell life insurance products. He wondered about the best way to organize his company's entry into the country, the first city to choose,

	Average Salary (RMB)	Life Insurance Premium Spending (RMB)	Retail Sales Consumer Goods (RMB)	% of Salary Spent on Life Premiums	% of Salary Spent on Retail Sales
Shanghai	11,425	478	1,325	4%	12%
Tianjin	8,238	188	535	2%	6%
Guangzhou	13,118	384	803	3%	6%

Projections—Total Life Insurance Market 1999 to 2005

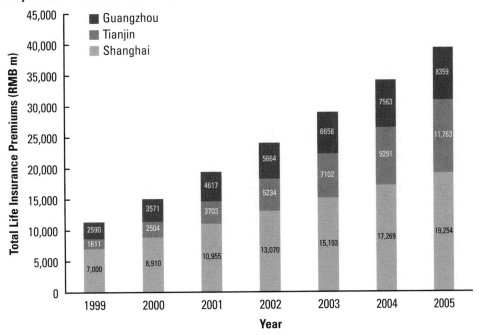

Exhibit 6 Comparative Data—Three Cities

and the strategy that would provide long-term viability while not exhausting Sun Life Financial's or Everbright's resources.

Endnotes

1. All monies in Cdn$ unless otherwise specified.
2. Andrew Willis, "Tension surrounds Sun Life Financial IPO," *Report on Business,* March 24, 2000.
3. John Patridge, "Sun Life Financial IPO Shines Brightly in TSE Trading," *Report on Business,* March 24, 2000.
4. August Chow et al., *A Guide to the China Insurance Market,* 1st ed., Watson Wyatt Worldwide, Hong Kong, 1996, p. 5.
5. "Board of Directors' Meeting," Sun Life Financial Company documents, April 13, 2000, pp. 3–6.
6. *Creating a Winning Vision,* Riddell Tseng, September 9, 1999, p. 62.
7. Ibid.
8. *CIA Factbook,* available at www.cia.org, accessed November 15, 2003.

9. "Global Insurers in China," Global Equity Research, Nomura, April 1, 2003, p. 4.
10. Ibid., p. 5.
11. Ibid., p. 14.
12. "Creating a Winning Vision," Riddell Tseng, September 9, 1999, p. 48.
13. Ibid.
14. Ibid., p. 14.
15. Ibid., p. 6.
16. Ibid.
17. *Creating a Winning Vision,* Riddell Tseng, September 9, 1999, p. 11.
18. August Chow et al., *A Guide to the China Insurance Market,* 1st ed., Watson Wyatt Worldwide, Hong Kong, 1996, p. 175.
19. *Creating a Winning Vision,* Riddell Tseng, September 9, 1999, p. 13.
20. China Insurance Yearbook 1998.
21. Ibid.
22. *Creating a Winning Vision,* Riddell Tseng, September 9, 1999, p. 14.

Case 28   The Casino Industry*

In April 2005, legendary casino mogul Steve Wynn launched the most expensive casino resort ever built. Located on the Las Vegas Strip, the new $2.7 billion Wynn Las Vegas property was designed to offer the highest conceivable level of luxury. Each of the 2,700 rooms offers floor-to-ceiling windows, 320-thread count European linens, flat screen televisions, and marble bathrooms. The 18 restaurants located inside the resort are all run by chefs who have won the James Beard award for their cooking. The shopping arcades provide the feel of a walk down New York City's Fifth Avenue with outlets such as Chanel, Dior, and Cartier. If that is not enough, the property includes a Ferrari and Maserati dealership. "No expense has been spared," said Anthony Curtis, publisher of the newsletter that covers Las Vegas. "It's not a matter of 'Will it be great?' but 'Just how great will it be?'"[1]

The new resort represents the triumphant return of Wynn, who is widely credited with the development of the theme-driven resort casinos that have begun to increasingly characterize the look and feel of modern Las Vegas. Wynn's previous venture, Mirage Resorts, was snatched up by Kirk Kerkorian's MGM a little over five years ago. Worries about the profitability of the expensive new casinos that Wynn was developing, such as the $1.6 billion Bellagio, had pushed Mirage's stock prices down, making it an attractive acquisition target.

Refusing to be discouraged by the loss, Wynn had been planning for some time to make his comeback. His new Wynn Las Vegas was even splashier than the Bellagio to target high-end gamblers who would wager as much as $10,000 per hand. Commenting on Wynn's desire to create a luxurious casino that stands above all others, Anthony Curtis, publisher of *Las Vegas Advisor,* stated, "He has put everything into showing he's the guy who makes the best resorts in the world."[2]

However, in attempting to outdo his rivals, Wynn is taking considerable risks. Gaming revenues in the casino industry have shown little recent growth, even in centers of gambling such as Las Vegas and Atlantic City (see Exhibit 1). This decline in growth can be attributed to a variety of factors such as the expansion of Native American casinos and the emergence of online gaming. To deal with the slower growth in gaming revenues, casinos have felt the need to spend more and more to entice more gamblers.

Even as the newly completed Wynn resort was opening its doors to gamblers, several of its rivals had started to work on casinos that would match if not surpass it. Las Vegas Sands, which owns the Venetian, has already started construction of a $1.5 billion casino hotel to be called the

*This case was developed by Jamal Shamsie of Michigan State University.
This case was developed from published sources as a basis for class discussion rather than to illustrate either effective or ineffective handling of an administrative situation. Copyright © 2005 Jamal Shamsie.

Palazzo. Not to be outdone, MGM Mirage is working on several projects, including a $4.7 billion luxury complex of hotels, condominiums, and shopping centers called Project Center City. "We think it will be the hub of Las Vegas," said MGM Mirage CEO Terry Lanni.[3]

Riding the Growth Wave

Although some form of gambling has been traced back to colonial times, the recent advent of casinos can be traced back to the legalization of gaming in Nevada in 1931. For many years, this was the only state in which casinos were allowed. As a result, Nevada still retains its status as the state with the highest revenues from casinos, with gambling revenues reaching $10.3 billion in 2004. More than half of these revenues came from casinos that are located in Las Vegas, which drew more than 37 million visitors in 2004.

After New Jersey passed laws in 1976 to allow gambling in Atlantic City, this gave the large population on the east coast easier access to casinos. However, the further growth of casinos has only occurred since 1988, as more and more states have begun to legalize the operation of casinos because they help generate more commercial activity and create more jobs, in large part through the growth of tourism. However, several states may still restrict the number of casino licenses that they issue and may also impose tough requirements for any casinos that are granted licenses. The greatest growth has come in the form of water-borne casinos that have begun to operate in six states and have allowed casinos to develop at waterfronts such as rivers and lakes. As of 2004, about 85 such casinos generated almost $10.5 billion in revenues.

Along with this increased access to casinos, there has also been a growing tendency to regard casino gambling as an acceptable form of entertainment. Although casinos have tended to draw players from all demographic segments, a recent national survey found that their median age was 47 and their median household income was around $50,000. On the whole, casino gamblers tended to be better educated and more affluent than those who bought lottery tickets. In fact, the bigger casinos attracted a high-roller segment, which could stake millions of dollars and included players from all over the world. Many of the casinos worked hard to obtain the business of this market segment, despite the risk that the sustained winning streak of a single player could significantly weaken the earnings for a particular quarter.

The growth of casino gambling has also been driven by the significantly better payouts that they give players compared with other forms of gambling. Based on industry estimates, casinos typically keep less than $5 of every $100 that is wagered. This compares favorably with racetrack betting, which keeps over $20 of every $100 that is

Exhibit 1   U.S. Casino Industry Gaming Revenues*

	Revenues ($ millions)			
	2003	2002	2001	2000
Nevada, total	9,625	9,447	9,469	9,600
Las Vegas Strip	4,760	4,654	4,704	4,806
Atlantic City, total	4,489	4,382	4,303	4,301
Western towns, total	768	786	735	685
Deadwood, SD	70	66	58	53
Colorado	698	720	677	632
Other land-based, total	1,412	1,400	1,257	989
New Orleans	282	275	250	245
Detroit	1,130	1,125	1,007	744
Riverboats, total	10,232	10,156	9,714	9,038
Iowa	694	656	615	598
Illinois	1,710	1,832	1,784	1,658
Mississippi	2,700	2,717	2,701	2,649
Louisiana	1,566	1,610	1,633	1,447
Missouri	1,332	1,279	1,138	997
Indiana	2,230	2,062	1,843	1,689
Native American casinos	15,055	13,290	11,400	9,700
Total	**41,581**	**39,461**	**36,878**	**34,313**

Sources: Casino Journal's National Gaming Summary; Standard & Poor's estimates.

*Gaming revenues include the amount of money won by casinos from various gaming activities, such as slot machines, table games, and sports betting.

wagered, and with state run lotteries, which usually keep about $45 of every $100 that is spent on tickets. Such comparisons can be somewhat misleading, however, because winnings are put back into play in casinos much faster than they are in other forms of gaming. This provides a casino with more opportunities to win from a customer, largely offsetting its lower retention rate.

Finally, most of the growth in casino revenues has come from the growing popularity of slot machines. These coin-operated slot machines typically account for more than 60 percent of all casino gaming revenues. A major reason for their popularity is that it is easier for prospective gamblers to feed a slot machine than learn the nuances of various table games. New slot machines tend to be based on familiar games such as *Monopoly* and *Wheel of Fortune* or TV shows such as *Star Trek* or *The Munsters*. With the advent of new technology, these slot machines are being replaced by electronic gaming devices that have video screens instead of spinning wheels, buttons to push instead of handles to pull, and use prepaid tickets rather than coins for payment.

Betting on a Few Locations

Although casinos have spread across much of the country, two cities have dominated the casino business. Both Las Vegas and Atlantic City have seen a spectacular growth in casino gaming revenues over the years. Although Las Vegas has far more hotel casinos, each of the dozen casinos in Atlantic City typically generate much higher revenues. By 2004, these two locations accounted for almost a quarter of the total revenues generated by all forms of casinos throughout the U.S. (see Exhibit 2).

Las Vegas clearly acts as a magnet for the overnight casino gamblers, offering more than 120,000 hotel rooms and many choices for fine dining, great shopping, and top-notch entertainment. It is linked by air to many major cities

Exhibit 2   Comparitive Statistics

	Las Vegas	Atlantic City
Year Gambling Legalized	1931	1976
Annual Visitors	35 million	33 million
Average Stay	3.4 days	1.5 days
Number of Casinos	197	12
Casino Revenue	$7.8 billion	$4.4 billion
Hotel Rooms	130,000	120,000
Largest Hotel	MGM Grand 5,035 rooms	Borgata 2,002 rooms

Sources: Nevada Casino Control Board; Las Vegas News Bureau; New Jersey Casino Control Commission; Atlantic City Convention & Visitors Bureau.

both in the U.S. and around the world. During the 1990s, Las Vegas tried to become more receptive to families with attractions such as circus performances, animal reserves, and pirate battles. But the city has been very successful with its recent return to its sinful roots with a stronger focus on topless shows, hot night clubs, and other adult offerings that have been highlighted by the new advertising slogan "What happens in Vegas, stays in Vegas." Paul Cappelli, who creates advertising messages, believes that Las Vegas lost its way with the effort to become family friendly. "People don't see Vegas as Jellystone Park. They don't want to go there with a picnic basket," he explained.[4]

For the most part, Las Vegas has continued to show a consistent pattern of growth in visitors (see Exhibit 3).

Exhibit 3   Las Vegas Visitors (In millions)

2004	37.2
2003	35.5
2002	35.1
2001	35.0
2000	35.8
1999	33.8
1998	30.6
1997	30.5
1996	29.6
1995	29.0

Source: Las Vegas Convention & Visitors Authority.

"We still compete with Orlando and New York," said Terry Jicinsky, head of marketing for the Las Vegas Convention and Visitors Authority. "But based on overnight visitors, we're the top destination in North America."[5] In order to accommodate this growth, several of the major resorts such as Bellagio, the Venetian, and Mandalay Bay did add new wings during 2003 and 2004, leading to the opening of Steve Wynn's brand new casino resort in the spring of 2005. Even some of the older properties, such as Caesers Palace has been given an expensive renovation and

expanded to include a new Colosseum and a new Roman Plaza. According to Tom Graves, stock analyst at Standard & Poor's, "There's a perception among gamblers that Las Vegas is still the foremost gaming market."[6]

By comparison, Atlantic City cannot compete with Las Vegas in terms of the broad range of dining, shopping and entertainment choices. It does, however, offer a beach and a boardwalk along which its dozen large casino hotels are lined. Atlantic City attracts gamblers from various cities in the Northeast, many of whom arrive by charter bus and stay for less than a day. Atlantic City officials point out that one-quarter of the nation's population lives sufficiently close so that they can drive there on just one tank of gas.

The opening of the much-ballyhooed Borgata Hotel Casino in 2003 has started a drive to try to make Atlantic City much more competitive with Las Vegas. As the first new casino to open in the city in 13 years, the Borgata is at the center of a $2 billion makeover of Atlantic City that might make it a hotter destination. "There's no question that this is a Las Vegas-style mega-resort," said Bob Boughner, CEO of the Borgata.[7] Two of the town's older casinos are adding expensive new wings to accommodate more overnight visitors. Other casino hotels such as Caesars, Trump Plaza, and Hilton have also added outdoor bars on the beach that have helped to turn the waterfront into one big party zone. "Borgata is the catalyst for a new Atlantic City," said Mike Epifanio, the editor of *Atlantic City Weekly*. "There's been a major change of thinking in town."[8]

Raising the Stakes

The gradual rise in the number of casinos, including those on riverboats, has led each of them to compete more heavily with each other to entice gamblers. Casinos have had to continuously strive to offer more to stand out and gain attention. This is most evident in Las Vegas and Atlantic City, the two destinations where most of the largest casinos are located next to each other. Potential gamblers have more choices when they visit either of these cities than they have anywhere else.

In Las Vegas, each of the casinos has tried to deal with this competition by differentiating itself in several different ways. A large number of them have tried to differentiate on the basis of a special theme that characterizes their casino, such as a medieval castle, a pirate ship, or a movie studio. Others have tried to incorporate into their casinos the look and feel of specific foreign destinations. Luxor's pyramids and columns evoke ancient Egypt, Mandalay Bay borrows looks from the Pacific Rim, and the Venetian's plazas and canals recreate the Italian resort.

Each of the casinos also tries to offer more lavish settings and more exciting attractions. The newly opened $2.7 billion Wynn Las Vegas features a man-made mountain of imported coniferous trees with waterfalls that are illuminated by a nightly music-and-light show. It also boasts an 18-hole, Tom Fazio–designed golf course. If that is not enough, the Wynn also hosts a $121-a-seat aquatic show created by Franco Dragone, who was the inspiration behind many of the creations of Cirque de Soleil. The show takes place in a 1 million gallon pool that is encircled by a 2,087 seat amphitheater and features 75 performers, including water-ballet chorines, scuba divers, comedians, aerialists, and death defying high divers.

Aside from ramping up the appeal of their particular properties, most casinos must also offer incentives to keep their customers from moving over to competing casinos. These incentives can be particularly helpful in retaining those high rollers who come often and spend large amounts of money. Casinos try to maintain their business by providing complimentary rooms, food, beverage, shows and other perks each year that are worth billions of dollars. Gamblers also can earn various types of rewards through the loyalty programs that are offered by the casinos, with the specific rewards being tied to the amount that they bet on the slot machines and at the tables.

Some of the larger casinos in Las Vegas are also trying to fend off competition by growing through mergers and acquisitions. In 2004, Harrah's announced that it was buying casino rival Caesars, allowing it to become the nation's leading operator of casinos, with several properties in both Las Vegas and Atlantic City. This deal came just a month after MGM Mirage had stated that it was buying the Mandalay Resort Group, allowing it to double the number of casinos it held on the Las Vegas strip. Firms that own several casinos can also pitch each of their properties to a different market and allow all of their customers to earn rewards on the firm's loyalty program by gambling at any of these properties (see Exhibit 4).

Such a trend towards consolidation, however, does not seem to have a serious effect on smaller firms that operate just one or two resorts that appeal to particular types of customers. Wynn's new casino hotel is expected to attract up to 8 million customers each year, which represents about 60 percent of the annual attendance of Disneyland. Las Vegas Sands also has been drawing hordes of visitors to the luxury suites that it offers at its opulent Venetian Resort. In fact, the recently opened 455-room Palms Casino Resort has already become one of the hottest and most profitable properties in Las Vegas. "There will always be a market for a person who doesn't feel comfortable in a big casino setting," said George Maloof, a co-owner of the Palms Casino Resort.[9]

Responding to Growing Threats

Even though the traditional casinos have been working hard to maintain and build upon their sizable market, they are facing growing competition from a variety of sources. Foremost among these is the rise in the number of Native American casinos. The Indian Gaming and Recreation Act of 1988 authorized Native Americans to offer gaming on tribal lands as a way to encourage their self-sufficiency. Of the approximately 550 Native American tribes in the United States, more than 65 have negotiated agreements with states to allow gaming on tribal land. Native American casinos are exempt from federal regulations and are not required to pay any taxes on their revenues, but they generally pay a percentage of their winnings to the state in which they are located.

The National Indian Gaming Commission reported that in fiscal 2003, Native American casinos generated slightly more than $15 billion of gaming revenues, representing almost 60 percent of the total gaming revenues that were generated by all other casinos, including riverboats. At two high-volume casinos in southern Connecticut, one owned by the Mashantucket Pequot tribe and the other by the Mohegan tribe, total gaming revenues were expected to exceed $1.8 billion in 2004. Each of these facilities is likely to have higher winnings than any of the 12 casinos located in Atlantic City.

The impact of Native American casinos over the traditional casino industry is likely to increase over the next few years. Several states are reaching agreements to allow the introduction or expansion of Native American casinos because of the additional revenues that they can provide. This has created fears that the growth of these Native American casinos is likely to draw gamblers away from the other types of casinos. In particular, the growth of these casinos in states such as California and New York may reduce the number of gamblers who make trips to gambling destinations such as Las Vegas and Atlantic City.

The casino industry is also facing growing competition as a result of the move to introduce gaming machines at racetracks. Several states are passing legislation that would allow racetracks to raise their revenues by providing slot machines to their visitors. The introduction of gaming machines at racetracks—sometimes referred to as "racinos"—has being growing in popularity in the six

Exhibit 4 Leading Casino Operators

Harrah's Entertainment*

2004 Revenue: $4.55 billion (almost $9 billion with Caesars Entertainment)
2004 Income: $367.7 million

Operates 26 casinos in 12 different states, including riverboats and casinos on Indian reservations. Properties include Harrah's and Rio in Las Vegas and Harrah's and Showboat in Atlantic City.

MGM Mirage**

2004 Revenue: $4.67 billion (over $7 billion with Mandalay Resort Group)
2004 Income: $412.3 million

Operates 26 casinos throughout the country, including MGM Grand, Bellagio, New York, Mirage, Treasure Island, and Monte Carlo in Las Vegas and the Borgata in Atlantic City.

Boyd Gaming

2004 Revenues: $1.73 billion
2004 Income: $111.4 million

Operates 18 casinos across the United States. Its purchase of Coast Casinos in 2004 expanded its Las Vegas properties to include the more modestly priced Stardust, Barbary Coast, Orleans, and Sams Town. Runs the newly opened Borgata in Atlantic City.

Trump Entertainment Resorts

2004 Revenues: $1.46 billion
2004 Income: ($191.3 million)

Operates 3 casinos in Atlantic City, a riverboat in Indiana, and an overseas casino in the Grenadines. Atlantic City properties consist of Trump Taj Mahal, Trump Plaza, and Trump Marina. Operating under bankruptcy law since November 2004.

Las Vegas Sands

2004 Revenues: 1.26 billion
2004 Income: $495.2 million

Operates a single casino in Las Vegas called the Venetian. Also operates a single casino overseas in Macau.

Penn National Gaming

2004 Revenues: $1.14 billion
2004 Income: $71.5 million

Operates 8 casinos spread over the United States. No properties in Las Vegas or Atlantic City. Also operates several racetracks.

Argosy Gaming

2004 Revenues: $1.04 billion
2004 Income: $61.5 million

Operates 6 riverboats in several different states. No properties in Las Vegas or Atlantic City.

Ameristar Casinos

2004 Revenues: $1.02 billion
2004 Income: $61.9 million

Operates 7 casinos across the United States, including a couple of riverboats. No properties in Las Vegas or Atlantic City.

Aztar Corporation

2004 Revenues: $816 million
2004 Income: $28.5 million

Operates 5 casinos, including 2 riverboats. Runs the moderately priced Tropicana in both Las Vegas and Atlantic City.

Station Casinos

2004 Revenues: $987 million
2004 Income: $66.4 million

Operates 10 lower-end casinos in Las Vegas under the State and Fiesta brands. Leading casino in Las Vegas is Palace Station.

Wynn Resorts

2004 Revenues: N/A
2004 Income: N/A

Recently started with one newly opened casino called Wynn Resort in Las Vegas. Also starting an overseas casino in Macau. It has yet to produce any significant revenues or income.

*Acquired Caesars Entertainment in 2004, which operates 13 casinos around the United States and 5 casinos in overseas locations. Caesars runs Caesars Palace, Ballys, Paris, and Flamingo hotels in Las Vegas and Ballys and Caesars in Atlantic City. It produced revenues of almost $4.5 billion in 2004, which are not included in the revenues that have been reported above for Harrah's. Combined operations would have resulted in almost $9 billion in revenue for 2004.

**Acquired Mandalay Resort Group in 2004, which operates 12 casinos around the United States. Major properties in Las Vegas include Mandalay Bay, Luxor, Excalibur, and Circus Circus. It generated revenues of over $2.5 billon in 2004, which are not included in the revenues for MGM Mirage reported above. Combined operations would have resulted in over $7 billion in revenue for 2004.

Source: Company Web sites.

states where they are presently allowed. According to the American Gaming Association, gaming activity at these racetracks generated $2.2 billion in revenue during 2003.

Finally, all casinos are closely observing the growth of gambling on the Internet. Although the United States has been trying to ban Internet gambling, some 2,000 offshore sites generated about $10 billion in revenue in 2004. Electronic payment systems have made it possible for gamblers in the United States to make bets on these sites without cash, checks, or credit cards. Most casino operators believe that Internet gambling could represent both a threat and an opportunity for them. Placing bets through home computers offers convenience for prospective gamblers and a potentially low-cost business model for firms that already operate casinos. It is widely believed that gambling on the Internet will soon be legalized, regulated and taxed. "We frankly find attempts at prohibition to be very short-sighted," said Alan Feldman, senior vice president of MGM Mirage in Las Vegas.[10]

Gambling on the Future

Even as the competition from both rivals and substitutes continues to grow, all of the firms in the casino industry have little choice but to keep spending to survive and grow. In many cases, the heavy spending can burden the firm with large amounts of debt that must be serviced through profits from the casino. The debt can be harder to manage if demand for casino gambling does not stay strong and even show some growth.

Of the 14 hotel casinos that have opened in Atlantic City since 1978, at least five have faced bankruptcy proceedings and a few have closed. Even in Las Vegas, where demand has been relatively strong, a few casinos have been pushed to the verge of bankruptcy. Most recently, Aladdin, one of the newest casinos to open on the strip, entered into such proceedings, resulting in its sale to a partnership of Planet Hollywood and Starwood Resorts.

Realizing that casinos must continue to offer more, Wynn has already announced plans for a $1.4 billion, 2,300 suite sister casino next door to his newly opened casino. The extravagant budget for the planned casino resort represents a significant increase from the $900 million figure that had been announced just a few months ago. Dubbed Encore at Wynn Las Vegas, it is expected to open its doors sometime in 2008. Marc Falcone at Deutsche Bank, who has been following Wynn's return to casinos, commented, "There's significant growth ahead."[11]

Endnotes

1. Sloan, Gene. 2005. Wynn plunks down $2.7 billion on Vegas strip. *USA Today,* April 22: D1.
2. Palmeri, Christopher. 2005. The revenge of Steve Wynn. *BusinessWeek,* April 11: 74.
3. Woodyard, Chris. 2004. MGM Mirage plans hotel-condo complex that would be Las Vegas "hub." *USA Today,* November 11: B3.
4. McCarthy, Michael. 2005. Vegas goes back to naughty roots; ads trumpet return to adult playground. *USA Today,* April 11: B6.
5. *USA Today,* April 11: B6.
6. Woodyard, Chris, & Krantz, Matt. 2004. Latest Vegas marriage: Harrah's, Caesars tie knot; $5 billion deal marks strategy to reach more gamblers. *USA Today,* July 16: B1.
7. Sloan, Gene. 2003. Atlantic City bets on glitz: Down-at-the-heels resort rolls the dice, wagering a cool $2 billion that it will one day rival Las Vegas. *USA Today,* August 29: D1.
8. *USA Today,* August 29: D1.
9. Palmeri, Christopher. 2004. Little guys with big plans for Vegas. *BusinessWeek,* August 2: 49.
10. Woellert, Lorraine. 2004. Can online betting change its luck? *BusinessWeek,* December 20: 67.
11. Krantz, Matt. 2005. Investors wild for Wynn Resort; gaming stocks soar as opening draws near. *USA Today,* March 31: B4.

Case 29   Yahoo!*

In January 2005, Yahoo! announced that its strong performance in the fourth quarter should result in profits of $839.6 million for 2004, representing an almost four-fold increase from the $237.9 million that it had earned during 2003. Total revenues showed a similar increase to $3.57 billion, up from $1.63 billion during the previous year. The growth was driven, in large part, by the sharp increase in advertising revenues resulting from the recent resurgence of online advertising.

However, the Sunnyvale, CA–based Internet firm also drew 8.4 million subscribers by the end of 2004, representing a sharp increase from the 2.2 million subscribers that it had in 2002. The fees that these subscribers paid for various offerings provided over 15 percent of the firm's total revenues. The growth in the number of paying subscribers could be attributed to the basic strategy that Chief Executive Officer (CEO) Terry S. Semel has been pursuing to build the Web site into digital Disneyland—a souped-up theme park for the Internet Age. His goal is to build the Yahoo! site into a self-contained world of irresistible offerings that will grab and keep surfers glued to it for hours at a time.

When Semel was persuaded by Yahoo! cofounder Jerry Yang to come out of retirement to take over the floundering firm, he faced an unenviable task. As a retired Hollywood executive, he did not really know much about Internet technology, and he looked stiffly out of place at Yahoo!'s playful, egalitarian headquarters. Yet less than four years after taking control as chairman and CEO, Semel has silenced the doubters. During the short time he has been there, he has done nothing less than remake the culture of the quintessential Internet company. The spontaneity that drove the firm's decisions during its go-go days has been replaced by a strong sense of order. By imposing his buttoned-down management approach on Yahoo!, the 61-year-old has engineered one of the most remarkable revivals of a beleaguered dot-com.

Once paralyzed by management gridlock and written off as another overhyped has-been, Yahoo! has been roaring back. Semel's new strategy for Yahoo! has also been gaining fans on Wall Street and stoking new fears of a mini-Internet bubble. The company drew 119 million unique visitors in December 2004, more than any other site, according to comScore Networks, an Internet research firm. Its shares have soared to almost $38, representing a significant jump from the lows of around $15 at the time that Semel took over. Exhibits 1 and 2 show Yahoo! Inc.'s income statements and balance sheets.

Semel's efforts clearly have been successful in turning around the performance of an Internet firm that was in

trouble. "What he has done is just phenomenal," said Barry Diller, CEO of USA Interactive, a Yahoo! competitor.[1] Yet there are some nagging questions about Yahoo!'s future. Will Semel be able to maintain the momentum that he has generated? Can Yahoo! continue to make gains against established rivals such as AOL, MSN, and Google? Are Semel's ambitions to make Yahoo! a digital theme park realistic?

Remaking the Culture

Like many other Internet firms, Yahoo! had attracted visitors by developing a site that would offer a variety of services for free. Those who logged on were able to obtain, among other things, the latest stock quotes and news headlines. The firm relied on online advertising for more than 90 percent of its revenue. Yahoo! founders Koogle and Yang were confident that advertisers would continue to pay to reach its younger and more technologically savvy surfers. In fact, Yahoo! often came across as arrogant to most of its advertisers at the height of the Net bubble. Its attitude, recalls Jeff Bell, a marketing vice president at DaimlerChrysler, was "Buy our stuff and shut up."[2]

By the spring of 2001, Yahoo!'s advertising revenue was falling precipitously, its stock was losing most of its value, and some observers were questioning the firm's business model. With the collapse of the dot-com advertisers, the firm's revenue was down almost one-third from the previous year. Semel was asked to help turn the firm around by cofounder Jerry Yang but he agreed to take on the task only after cofounder Timothy Koogle had agreed to step down as chairman. Semel's style was in stark contrast to Koogle's relaxed, laid-back approach. With the cofounder Koogle out of the way, Semel started on work on replacing Yahoo!'s freewheeling culture with a much more deliberate sense of order.

The changes that Semel has made may not be evident to the casual observer. Visitors to Yahoo!'s headquarters will still see the purple cow in the lobby, be confronted with acres of cubicles, and meet workers who are clad in jeans. But Semel has dispensed with the hype that once vaulted companies such as Yahoo! into the stratosphere. He moved swiftly to chop down the 44 business units he inherited to 5, stripping many executives of pet projects. He did not care much for the firms' "cubicles only" policy, finally locating his own office into a cube adjacent to a conference room so he could make phone calls in private.

Semel has even changed Yahoo!'s old freewheeling approach to decision making. When Koogle was in charge, executives would brainstorm for hours, often following hunches with new initiatives. Under Semel, managers have to make formal presentations to bring up their new ideas in weekly meetings for a group called the Product Council. Championed by Semel and his chief operating officer,

*This case was prepared by Professor Jamal Shamsie of Michigan State University. This case was developed from published sources as a basis for class discussion rather than to illustrate either effective or ineffective handling of an administration situation. Copyright © Jamal Shamsie.

Exhibit 1   Yahoo! Income Statement
(All numbers in thousands)

	Period Ending		
	December 31, 2004	December 31, 2003	December 31, 2002
Total Revenue	3,574,517	1,625,097	953,067
Cost of Revenue	1,298,559	358,103	162,881
Gross Profit	2,275,958	1,266,994	790,186
Operating Expenses			
Research Development	368,760	207,285	143,468
Selling General and Administrative	1,072,921	709,669	537,344
Others	145,696	54,374	21,186
Operating Income or Loss	688,581	295,666	88,188
Income from Continuing Operations			
Total Other Income/Expenses Net	496,443	95,158	91,588
Earnings Before Interest and Taxes	1,185,024	384,903	178,225
Income Before Tax	1,185,024	384,903	178,225
Income Tax Expense	437,966	147,024	71,290
Minority Interest	(2,496)	(5,921)	(1,551)
Net Income from Continuing Operations	839,553	237,879	106,935
Effect of Accounting Changes	—	—	(64,120)
Net Income	839,553	237,879	42,815

Source: Yahoo!

Daniel Rosensweig, the Product Council typically includes nine managers from all corners of the company. The group sizes up business plans to make sure all new projects bring benefits to Yahoo!'s existing businesses.

"We need to work within a framework," said Semel. "If it's a free-for-all . . . we won't take advantage of the strengths of our company."[3] With the focus and discipline that he has imposed on the firm, Semel appears to be making some progress in getting Yahoo! to grow again. Most of the employees, who have been anxious to see the value of their stock rise again, have begun to support Semel in his efforts to remake Yahoo! "People don't always agree with the direction they're getting, but they're happy the direction is there," said a current Yahoo! manager who requested anonymity.[4]

Rethinking the Business Model

Semel began turning Yahoo! around by wooing traditional advertisers, making gestures to advertising agencies that it had angered with its arrogance during the boom.

Traditional advertisers such as Coca-Cola, General Motors, and the Gap have been flocking to Yahoo!'s sites. They say they have gravitated to Yahoo because it has been using technology to move beyond static banner advertising, offering eye-catching animation, videos and other rich-media formats. As a result of these efforts, Yahoo! has drawn more advertisers with the recent resurgence in online advertising. Exhibit 3 shows Internet advertising revenues from 1998 to 2004.

Semel has also used the deal-making skills that made him a legend in the movie business to land crucial acquisitions and partnerships that would allow Yahoo! to tap into new sources of advertising revenue. Of all of his deals, none shines brighter than the $1.8 billion deal for Overture Services, whose "pay per click" lets advertisers buy placement next to search results. The move has provided Yahoo! with a substantial new stream of revenue from a new form of search-related advertising. If a user searches for "cookware," for instance, advertisers ranging from Macy's to Sur

Exhibit 2   Yahoo! Balance Sheet
(All numbers in thousands)

	Period Ending		
	December 31, 2004	December 31, 2003	December 31, 2002
Assets			
Current Assets			
Cash and Cash Equivalents	823,723	713,539	310,972
Short-Term Investments	2,688,252	595,978	463,204
Net Receivables	483,951	282,415	113,612
Other Current Assets	94,549	129,777	82,216
Total Current Assets	**4,090,475**	**1,721,709**	**970,004**
Long-Term Investments	1,295,370	1,452,629	914,207
Property Plant and Equipment	531,696	449,512	371,272
Goodwill	2,550,957	1,805,561	415,225
Intangible Assets	480,666	445,640	96,252
Other Assets	33,121	56,603	23,221
Deferred Long-Term Asset Charges	195,916	—	—
Total Assets	**9,178,201**	**5,931,654**	**2,790,181**
Liabilities			
Current Liabilities			
Accounts Payable	901,320	515,518	276,313
Other Current Liabilities	279,387	192,278	135,501
Total Current Liabilities	**1,180,707**	**707,796**	**411,814**
Long-Term Debt	750,000	750,000	—
Other Liabilities	136	516	—
Deferred Long-Term Liability Charges	101,646	72,374	84,540
Minority Interest	44,266	37,478	31,557
Negative Goodwill	—	—	—
Total Liabilities	**2,076,755**	**1,568,164**	**527,911**
Stockholders' Equity			
Common Stock	1,416	678	611
Retained Earnings	1,069,939	230,386	(7,493)
Treasury Stock	(159,988)	(159,988)	(159,988)
Capital Surplus	5,682,884	4,288,816	2,430,222
Other Stockholder Equity	507,195	3,598	(1,082)
Total Stockholder Equity	**7,101,446**	**4,363,490**	**2,262,270**
Net Tangible Assets	**$4,069,823**	**$2,112,289**	**$1,750,793**

Source: Yahoo!

Exhibit 3   Internet Advertising Revenues (in billions of dollars)

2004	8.5*
2003	7.3
2002	6.2
2001	7.3
2000	8.2
1999	4.1
1998	2.1

*Estimated

Source: Interactive Advertising Bureau.

La Table are able to bid to showcase their links near the results. While Yahoo! had debated such a partnership for years under Koogle, Semel managed to push it through in little more than a year.

But Semel does not want Yahoo! to rely primarily on advertising revenues. He has been trying to add services that consumers would be willing to pay for. The strategy will require some time to put into place. When Semel took over, he was shocked to find out that Yahoo! did not have the technology in place to handle surging demand for paid services such as online personals, say two former executives. He had to crack down on the firm to whip it into shape to handle the addition of such premium services.

With the capabilities in place, Semel has also been making acquisitions that would allow Yahoo! to offer more premium services. The most significant of these was the buyout of HotJobs.com in 2002, which moved the firm into the online job-hunting business. The addition of this premium service has provided a significant boost to the firm's revenue. In 2004, Semel followed up with another significant acquisition. He paid $160 million for online music service Musicmatch, Inc., hoping that its music offerings would bring more subscribers into the Yahoo! fold.

By making such smart deals, Semel has built Yahoo! into a site that can offer surfers many different services, with several of them requiring the customer to pay a small fee. The idea has been to coax Web surfers to spend hard cash on everything from digital music and online games to job listings and premium e-mail accounts with loads of extra storage. Semel hopes that the contribution from such paid services will continue to rise over the next few years, allowing the firm to rely less heavily on advertising. He talked about the opportunities that will be provided by premium services, "We planted a lot of seeds . . . and some are beginning to grow."[5]

An Internet Theme Park

To build upon the foundation that he has already laid, Semel envisions building Yahoo! into a digital Disneyland, a souped-up theme park for the Internet Age. The idea is that Web surfers logging on to Yahoo!'s site, like customers squeezing through the turnstiles in Anaheim, should find themselves in a self-contained world full of irresistible offerings. Instead of Yahoo! being an impartial tour guide to the Web, it should be able to entice surfers to stay inside its walls as long as possible.

This vision for Yahoo! represented a drastic change from the model that had been developed by its original founders. Koogle had let his executives develop various offerings that operated relatively independently. Managers had built up their own niches around the main Yahoo! site. No one had thought about developing the portal as a whole, much less how the various bits and pieces could work together. "Managers would beg, borrow, and steal from the network to help their own properties," said Greg Coleman, Yahoo!'s executive vice president for media and sales.[6]

Semel has been pushing to stitch it all together. He has demanded that Yahoo!'s myriad of offerings from e-mail accounts to stock quotes to job listings interact with each other. Semel has called this concept "network optimization" and regards this as a key goal for his firm. To make this concept work, every initiative should not only make money but also should feed Yahoo!'s other businesses. Most of the focus of the Product Council meetings has been on the painstaking job of establishing these interconnections between the various services that are offered on the site.

With these constraints, it has become much harder for new projects to get approved. Semel has been determined to have any new offerings tied in with what is already being offered on Yahoo!. He claims this makes them easier for customers to find, increasing their chances of success. Although many different ideas are always under consideration, only a few are eventually offered by Yahoo!.

A key element of Semel's strategy to build Yahoo into a digital theme park also lies in his ability to push customers into broadband. Lots of the services that he is banking on, such as music and interactive games, are data hogs that appeal mostly to surfers who have high-speed links. Furthermore, since broadband is always on, many of Yahoo!'s customers are more likely to be be lingering in Semel's theme park for hours on end, day after day. "The more time you spend on Yahoo!, the more apt you are to sample both free and paid services," he says.[7]

Semel is, therefore, trying to make deals with various providers of broadband service. He started out with a deal with phone giant SBC Communications to launch the firm into the business of selling broadband access to millions of American homes. Under the terms of the deal, SBC pays Yahoo! about $5 out of the $40 to $60 customers pay each month for service. In January 2005,

Yahoo! also announced a partnership with Verizon Communications to develop a portal for high-speed Internet services to obtain far greater access to customers around the country.

Vying for Search Customers

But Yahoo! is not the only player with aspirations to becoming a digital theme park. Both Time Warner's AOL and Microsoft's MSN have the same goal in mind, and they can boast of substantial advantages over Yahoo!. AOL, despite its merger headaches, can tap into popular content from the world's largest media company, from CNN to Warner Music. MSN can derive substantial benefits from the software muscle and cash reserves of Microsoft, as well as several broadband partnerships.

Furthermore, Semel's dream of a digital theme park may be tied to the growing popularity of search engines (see Exhibit 4). He clearly sees a strong search operation as a way to keep users inside Yahoo!'s group of Internet properties such as Yahoo! Finance or Yahoo! Shopping. "What's at stake is the starting point for many people's Internet experience," said Charlene Li, a principal analyst with Forrester Research.[8]

In this regard, Yahoo! may have to deal with the recent rise of a newer competitor, Google. In less than five years, Google has turned into a global sensation and is now widely regarded as the most prominent search engine in most parts of the world. The firm, which recently went public, has continued to attract more users, although its growth seems to be slowing. Internet surfers may be inclined to rely on Google's uncluttered search offerings to find everything they need instead of flocking to flashy theme parks such as the one Yahoo! is attempting to develop.

Semel has understood the importance of attracting surfers who have been turning to Google and MSN for their Internet searches. He was concerned that Yahoo! had been relying on Google for the searches that were carried out on its site. Semel therefore closed a $290 million deal for search company Inktomi in March 2003 because he realized that it was important to own the technology behind this and to manage it internally. Analysts claim that in terms of technology, Inktomi offers a search engine that is better than most others.

With its own Inktomi–driven search capabilities in place, Semel and the rest of his team have been trying to push Yahoo! as a search engine. The firm has been trying, like most of its competitors, to offer new ways to search through more information. Yahoo! has been making significant gains in this area, with a growing array of new features. The firm has been moving swiftly to beef up Yahoo!'s search capabilities, including the ability to incorporate more and more information such as weather forecasts into search results, eliminating the need to jump to additional Web pages.

Exhibit 4   Share of Internet Searches

Global	
Google	
November 2004	47%
November 2003	44%
Yahoo!	
November 2004	27%
November 2003	25%
MSN	
November 2004	12%
November 2003	14%
AOL	
November 2004	5%
November 2003	9%
United States	
Google	
November 2004	38%
November 2003	37%
Yahoo!	
November 2004	35%
November 2003	29%
MSN	
November 2004	18%
November 2003	17%

Source: comScore Networks.

Fulfilled or Shattered Dreams?

It is hard to dispute that Semel has clearly pulled off a stunning revival of a floundering firm by cutting costs, imposing discipline, and making deals. Yahoo! is clearly back in the running along with the other leaders that have survived from the Internet-driven era. Its accomplishments under Semel have attracted considerable attention. "Yahoo! has reemerged as a potent force," said Derek Brown, an analyst at Pacific Growth Equities. "It's well-positioned to leverage its massive global user base and dominant brand."[9]

To build on its existing strengths, Yahoo! is also trying to develop a strong broadband presence. Semel is trying to make the dozens of services that his site offers, such as digital music, instant messaging, and streaming video, more widely available not just on personal computers but also on any device connected to the Internet. Towards this end, Yahoo! has expanded its alliance with SBC Communications to bring new services onto mobile phones and digital video recorders.

Semel is also trying to pursue his broadband strategy through acquisitions. Towards the end of 2004, Yahoo! acquired WUF Networks Inc., a small start-up whose technology aims to let consumers move their songs, photographs and other digital content from their computers to devices such as mobile phones. Charlene Yi of Forrester Research stressed the growing emphasis on this new strategy: "Mobile is a very big part of their strategy because it allows them to extend beyond the Web and to touch the customer offline."[10]

But Yahoo! still has a long way to go before it can become the digital Disneyland that Semel has envisioned. In particular, critics have been worried that under Semel's careful and laborious screening process for new projects, Yahoo! may run the risk of losing its innovative edge. Semel has responded by pointing to the advantages that he has provided Yahoo! by the reduction of clutter and the focus on a handful of high-performance services that feed each other.

Semel has pointed to the company's recently relaunched search capabilities as one of the several areas in which Yahoo! has achieved considerable success. For example, consumers who search for "pizza" and type in their area code end up on Yahoo!'s Yellow Pages, which provide them with return addresses and driving maps to nearby pizza joints. Semel boasts that Yahoo! is the only heavyweight portal that integrates content this deeply with its search features.

In fact, most of Semel's team have shown growing confidence in their ability to build Yahoo! into a brand that will be able to hold its own against formidable rivals. "We are a healthy paranoid company," said Dan Rosenweig, the firm's chief operating officer. "We are appropriately focused on the fact that this is a fluid market, but we're a company born out of competition."[11]

Endnotes

1. Elgin, Ben, & Grover, Ronald. 2003. Yahoo!: Act two. *BusinessWeek*, June 2: 71.
2. Ibid.: 76.
3. Ibid.: 74.
4. Ibid.: 74.
5. Ibid.: 72.
6. Ibid.: 74.
7. Ibid.: 72.
8. Gaither, Chris. 2004. Yahoo! drops Google search engine in U.S. *Los Angeles Times,* February 19: C5.
9. *BusinessWeek,* June 2: 73.
10. Gaither, Chris. 2004. Yahoo! aims to move beyond PC with deal. *Los Angeles Times,* December 7: C2.
11. Zeller, Tom Jr. 2005. Yahoo!'s profit soars in quarter on ad spending and investments. *New York Times,* January 19: C5.

Case 30 Enron: On the Side of the Angels*

"We're on the side of angels. We're taking on the entrenched monopolies. In every business we've been in, we're the good guys."

—**Jeffrey Skilling**, President and CEO,
Enron Corporation

On the day he was elected CEO, Enron's president, Jeffrey Skilling, was pictured on the front cover of the February 12, 2001 edition of *BusinessWeek* dressed in a black turtle-neck and holding an electrified orb in his right hand, appearing more sorcerer than executive. Enron was charging into the deregulated energy markets. Skilling defended Enron's activities, saying;

> We're on the side of angels. We're taking on the entrenched monopolies. In every business we're in, we're the good guys.[1]

By August 2001, the charge would be over and Skilling would resign after only six months as CEO. In September 2000, Enron's stock price was in the $85 to $90 region; by November 2001 it had declined to less than a dollar. In January 2002, John Clifford Baxter, an Enron executive, died, an apparent suicide. Timothy Belden, an Enron trader in the California markets, would plead guilty to conspiracy to manipulate markets in the California energy market[2] and another, John Forney, would be arrested for conspiracy and wire fraud in the same California market.[3] The angels, it seems, had come back to earth.

From Pipelines to Commodity Trader

In June 1984, the board of Houston Natural Gas (HNG), a natural gas distribution firm, hired Kenneth Lay as Chair and CEO. His first task was to defend HNG from a takeover bid by refocusing HNG on its core business. In a 1990 speech, Lay characterized his leadership:

> In carrying out that assignment, between June 1984 and January 1985, $632 million of non-natural gas operations were sold and $1.2 billion of natural gas operations were purchased. As one director was heard to quip at the time, the Board gave me unlimited authority, and I exceeded it.[4]

Lay created Enron, a natural gas and oil company, in 1986, through the merger of HNG with InterNorth, a natural gas pipeline company and other acquistions.[5] Lay, the merger's architect and Enron's first CEO, appeared to be one of the few individuals who recognized the opportunities of deregulation in the U.S. and privatization abroad. By the early 1990s, Enron owned an interest in a 4,100 mile pipeline in Argentina, and commenced its power marketing business worldwide.

In 1994, *Fortune* ranked Enron first in a new category, pipelines, and 39th overall as one of "America's Most Admired Companies." By 1996 Enron had climbed to 22nd overall. In the 1990s, Enron busily expanded its business structure into other areas, such as energy generation, broadband, and financial markets. Yet Enron maintained its dominance of the pipeline industry's ranking and was ranked in the top 20 firms overall through February 2001. In that year, *Fortune* named Enron the most innovative firm in the U.S. for the second consecutive year. It first won the category in 1997. From 1994 to 2001 the firm steadily climbed in *Fortune*'s "America's Most Admired Company" list. Its stock price rose as dramatically: on December 31, 1996, Enron's stock listed at $21\frac{7}{16}$ (adjusted for a 1999 split), and on December 31, 2000, its price was $83\frac{1}{8}$. In the entry foyer, a huge banner was placed, reading, "World's Leading Company."[6] Skilling's license plate, which had once read "WLEC" (World's Leading Energy Company) changed to "WMM" (We Make Markets).[7]

Throughout 2001, as Enron's stock declined, its rankings dropped from first to last in its industry. Enron was ranked 523 (of 530) in wise use of corporate assets and quality of management and 521 in fiscal soundness.

"Get It Done. Get It Done Now. Reap the Rewards."

Lay built a management team, not of gas and energy people, but primarily of MBAs. Rebecca Mark, an energy professional who rose from part-time trader to president of Enron International and Azurix Water, characterized Enron employees as ex-military, Harvard Business School, and ex-entrepreneurship types. A *Fortune* article described the employees as "aggressive, well-compensated traders."[8] Enron had developed from an oil and gas exploration and pipeline company to a derivatives trading company. In its office tower, the executive offices on the seventh floor overlooked the sixth floor, an expansive derivatives trading operation.[9]

Enron's management saw creativity and human capital as the real resource behind its future growth. In the 1999 Annual Report Letter to Shareholders, Lay wrote:

> Creativity is a fragile commodity. Put a creative person in a bureaucratic atmosphere, and the creative output will die. We support employees with the most innovative

*This case was prepared from published materials by Professors Donald Schepers and Naomi A. Gardberg from Baruch College, City University of New York, to provide a basis for class discussion. Copyright © 2003 by the *Journal of Business and Applied Management*. Reprinted with permission of *Journal of Business and Applied Management*. Readers may find the two Appendices at the end of the case helpful in reading the case. Appendix A is a timeline of major events in this case. Appendix B is a glossary of various financial terms used in the case.

culture possible, where people are measured not by how many mistakes they make, but how often they try.[10]

Every employee received a copy of the *Code of Ethics,* and with it a memo from Lay dated July 1, 2000 that read in part:

> As officers and employees of Enron Corp. . . . we are responsible for conducting the business affairs of the Company in accordance with all applicable laws and in a moral and honest manner. . . . An employee shall not conduct himself or herself in a manner, which directly or indirectly would be detrimental to the best interests of the Company or in a manner which would bring the employee financial gain separately derived as a direct consequence of his or her employment with the Company. . . . We want to be proud of Enron and to know that it enjoys a reputation for fairness and honesty that is respected. . . . **Let's keep that reputation high.**[6]

In April 2002 Lay described Enron's culture:

> One of our greatest successes at Enron was creating a culture, an environment, where people could try to achieve their God-given potential. But certainly I wanted it to be a highly moral and highly ethical environment. I have done the best job I can of following that everywhere I have been.[11]

Skilling put his own mark on Enron's culture. Extravagance was celebrated. At one meeting, Mark rode onto the stage with another executive on a Harley. At another, an adult elephant was brought in. One executive arrived at an employee gathering with a tractor-trailer full of expensive sports cars. The floors of the parking garage were marked by words to remind employees of valued attributes: bold, innovative, smart, united, ambitious, accomplished, resourceful, creative, confident, adventurous, adaptable, and undaunted.[6]

Two realities of life existed at Enron: stock price and the Peer Review Committee (PRC).[12] Nothing else mattered. Michael J. Miller, a manager in Enron's failed high-speed Internet service venture described the atmosphere as "Get it done. Get it done now. Reap the rewards." An acrylic paperweight from the legal department stated its mission as "To provide prompt and first-rate legal service to Enron on a proactive and cost-effective basis."[13] Below that was "Translation: We do big, complex, and risky deals without blowing up Enron." Employees were rewarded for earnings that could be quickly booked, regardless of the long-term consequences. Two of the Enron executives who closed the deal on the doomed Dabhol power project in India received bonuses in the range of $50 million just for closing the deal.[14]

Like many dot-coms in the 1990s, Enron had a high reward structure. More than 2000 Enron employees were millionaires. Employees received free laptops and hand-held devices, expensive ergonomic chairs and lunches at Houston's finest restaurants. Enron's Board of Directors was also well compensated. Chosen by management, Enron directors received cash and stock worth $300,000 a year.[14]

Recruitment took place both in long, intense interviews and visits to topless bars and strip clubs.[6] Once past an initial interview, candidates were invited to a "Super Saturday" session of 8, 50-minute interviews. Offers would go out within a few days, and candidates that declined would be offered signing bonuses or other financial inducements.[12]

Central to Enron's human resource policy was Skilling's PRC, or what became known as the "rank and yank" process.[6] Every six months, each person would choose five individuals (four plus the immediate supervisor) to provide feedback on his or her performance. This feedback went to the PRC's ratings meeting where employees were rated on a scale from 1 (excellent) to 5 (worst performing). The PRC took place behind closed doors, but in plain sight, since interior walls on the trading floors were glass. The picture of the individual being discussed would appear on a slide show, visible to all on the floor, while management discussed the evaluations. The PRC was a forced ranking system, where 15% of those reviewed had to receive 5s. These would then be "redeployed," meaning they had to search for a job in the organization or find themselves unemployed.

On the trading floor, men rated women as potential calendar models. When one of the "candidates" would walk onto the floor, someone would yell the name of the month to alert others of her presence.[6] Gambling was also prevalent. One year, the NCAA basketball pool supposedly reached almost $90,000.[15]

This culture spilled out of the doors and into Enron's relationships with others. On one occasion, Andy Fastow, the Chief Financial Officer (CFO), was asked by a Citigroup banker if he understood the equations on the whiteboard in the conference room next to his office. Fastow replied, "I pulled them out of a book to intimidate people."[16]

Analysts who listened to the quarterly earnings report conference calls would be derided if they had questions about the details. During the April 17, 2001, conference call, Skilling had finished presenting the numbers and was responding to questions when Richard Grubman, a managing director of Highlands Capital Management, asked about Enron's balance sheet and cash-flow statement after earnings. Enron had failed to provide either. When Grubman commented that Enron was the only financial institution that never provided such statements for these calls, Skilling shot back, "Well, thank you very much. We appreciate that, [expletive]."[6]

Enron and the Capital Markets

Prior to his employment at Enron, Skilling served as consultant to Enron for McKinsey & Co. In 1989, Enron launched GasBank at Skilling's urging for the purpose of hedging risk for natural gas producers and wholesale suppliers.[12] Both parties could arrange forward contracts (contracts to purchase or sell commodities at a future date) at set prices, and Enron would sell financial derivative contracts to sell the risk of the forward contracts to other interested investors. In 1990, Enron became a market maker, a financial clearinghouse, for natural gas, selling swaps and futures on the New York Mercantile Exchange. In that same year, Lay hired Skilling as CEO of Enron Gas Services (EGS), and Skilling hired Fastow as CFO. EGS was ultimately renamed Enron Capital and Trade Resources (ECT).

ECT provided financial and risk management services for Enron and its trading partners. The process, asset securitization, involves selling the rights to future cash flow streams. Corporations, such as mortgage companies, would take their risky investments and sell them to another financial institution, such as an investment bank. The investment bank, in turn, would bundle a number of such investments together, separate the cash flows by level of risk, and put the result into securities they would then sell. In the case of mortgage-backed securities, investment banks might offer two securities, one based on the principal and the second on the interest payments. Each would have a different yield, based on the level of risk. Asset securitization is attractive to the originating corporation on two counts: it transfers risk of default to the investment bank and lowers cost of capital by providing immediate cash inflow.

ECT fulfilled two functions. First, it provided asset securitization services for Enron's natural gas and oil entities, making those entities much more profitable. Second, it moved Enron further toward Lay's vision of the company as a market maker for a variety of commodities. With the attainment of risk management and capital flow-through, Enron could in principle trade anything. Through the 1990s, Enron was rapidly becoming a commodities market based in Houston. Even weather risk was commoditized and traded.[6] This was supplemented with what Skilling would term "asset-lite": the hard assets Enron originally controlled in such deals would be sold, in many cases to special-purpose entities (SPEs) that were created by Enron.

Two Critical Elements: Mark-to-Market and the SPEs
Enron funded its growth as a financial services firm using very sophisticated financial practices, mark-to-market accounting, and SPEs. Originally termed mark-to-model, the mark-to-market accounting method was intended to assist investors in obtaining some reference point in valuing a security. A model was constructed using a number of assumptions, and the security was then valued using that model. In reality, these prices were generated by computers, not by market process. Enron relied on this procedure

to establish prices (sometimes unrealistically high) in its new commodities (for example, weather) where there were no reference prices.[9]

The second mechanism Enron used was the creation of special-purpose entities. SPEs are financial devices designed to give companies greater flexibility in finance and risk management. There are two requirements for SPEs to be legitimate: first, there must be a 3 percent outside equity position; and second, the outside capital must clearly be at risk.

Fastow set up a number of SPEs for Enron. Among the more famous were partnerships named Chewco, JEDI, LJM1, and LJM2, and four investments named Raptors. In 1993, Joint Energy Development Investment (JEDI), a $500 million partnership between Enron and the California Public Employees Retirement System (CalPERS), was the first SPE created. This partnership would continue until 1997, when CalPERS sold its position to Chewco, another SPE created specifically by Enron to purchase the CalPERS shares in JEDI. Enron hoped that this buyout would then encourage CalPERS to invest in JEDI II, a proposed $1 billion venture.

SPEs would be used to solve Enron's financial problems. Enron not only brokered commodities contracts, but actually bought and sold natural gas. High default risk on Enron's part would ruin the swap business. SPEs provided Enron the opportunity to continually move debt from its balance sheet, keeping its high credit rating and its swap business.

As Enron expanded the use of SPEs, new investors were required to satisfy the SEC requirement of 3 percent outside equity investment. Fastow and Michael Kopper (managing director, Enron Global Finance, and a direct report to Fastow) established the "Friends of Enron." These "friends" were actually relatives or friends of Enron's executives. Fastow and Kopper funneled monies through these people to finance the "outside equity" in the SPEs.

Enron's need for a high credit rating drove the creation of over 3,000 SPEs to keep debt off the balance sheet.[9] Maturing markets meant decreasing profits, but profits were necessary to continue Enron's trading mechanism. The only way to create more profits was to open new commodity markets, exploit them quickly, and then create newer markets. The SPEs were critical to this strategy, keeping debt from the books and providing capital. Enron's stock price soared dramatically, unburdened by the debt that was accumulating in the SPEs.

The SPEs presented Enron with the opportunity to disguise debt and loss as revenue, but did not necessarily result in cash flow.[9] Enron would establish an SPE by issuing Enron stock to collateralize the SPE, and then engage other entities such as banks to invest in the SPE. Enron would then "sell" the SPE deal that it had set up to handle in return for either cash or a promissory note, which Enron would then book as revenue. In one case, it was a forward contract on shares of an Internet company in which Enron had invested. Another case was "dark fiber"; that is, fiber optic cable that was already laid but as yet unusable. In both cases, Enron had a "make whole" contract with the SPE, insuring that the SPE would not lose money. However, even as the dot-com bubble burst, the shares in the Internet company declined, and the value of the dark fiber likewise dropped, Enron was able to shield its balance sheet from these losses.

Constructed on Enron stock, these SPE arrangements contained triggers, that is, valuation points where these deals would need infusions of either more Enron stock or other collateral. For example, in an SPE named Osprey, if Enron's stock fell below $59.78, Enron was obligated to either issue new stock or provide cash sufficient to bring the value of Osprey up to cover its debt obligations.[17] In another instance, Enron's stock price decline forced restructuring of four SPEs named Raptor I, II, III, and IV in December 2000, and then requiring an additional infusion of stock in the first quarter of 2001 to shore up their falling credit capacity. By the end of the restructuring, Raptors II and IV owed an additional $260 million to Enron.[18]

The Investment Bank Connection   Enron's need for a high credit rating influenced its relationships with investment banks as well. In return for its business, Enron sought short-term deals that allowed it to disguise loans as sales revenue, and in turn unload (for brief periods of time) unprofitable entities from Enron's balance sheet. Between 1992 and 2001, Enron borrowed $8 billion from Citigroup and J.P. Morgan Chase & Co. in transactions that had the appearance of gas trades rather than loans, understating Enron's debt by $4 billion, and overstating its $3.2 billion cash flow from operations by 50 percent.[19] An independent bank examiner, Neal Batson, found that Enron had recorded profit of $1.4 billion through similar transactions with six investment banks.[20]

The Enron Control System

> Our philosophy is not to stand in the way of our employees, so we don't insist on hierarchical approval. We do, however, keep a keen eye on how prudent they are, and rigorously evaluate and control the risk involved in each of our activities.[10]

The Enron culture was not without its system of checks and balances, particularly in the financial dealings. The Board turned to those checks and balances when approving the deals with the SPEs, as well as Fastow's role in the various SPEs. It was the task of Risk Assessment and Control (RAC) to examine each deal and perform due diligence. RAC had the responsibility to oversee and

approve all deals in which Enron engaged, over 400 each year. Each deal was accompanied by a Deal Approval Sheet (DASH) assembled by the business unit responsible for the deal. Each DASH had a description of the deal, origination information, economic data, a cash-flow model, risk components, financial approval sheet, and authorization page.[6] Corporate policy required approval from the relevant business unit, legal department, RAC, and senior management. Many of the DASH forms for SPEs had incomplete authorizations. In particular, Skilling's signature is blank on many of the DASH forms associated with the LJM deals.[18]

As the number of deals with LJM increased, a separate LJM approval sheet was added as a control procedure. This approval sheet was printed with check marks already in the boxes. No third-party documentation was required to substantiate claims made on the document. Conclusions were used as questions ("Was this transaction done strictly on an arm's-length basis?"), while others revealed low standards ("Was Enron advised by any third party that this transaction was not fair, from a financial perspective, to Enron?").[18]

Enron formed 20 deals with LJM1 and LJM2. In setting up the LJM entities, the Board had waived Enron's Code of Ethics and allowed Fastow to be named general partner, with a $1 million investment in LJM1 alone. When Fastow presented the option of creating the LJM entities to the Board, he portrayed them as alternative purchasers for Enron assets, providing perhaps better valuations for assets Enron was in the process of selling. In fact, there were no alternative buyers for most of what was sold to the SPEs.

The Board made two critical assumptions. First, it assumed that, since the operational results of each division were at stake, each division would therefore aggressively market assets. Second, it assumed that Andersen's counsel on the LJM deals would be independent. The Board relied on the reviews by Richard Causey (Chief Accounting Officer) and Richard Buy (Chief Risk Officer) as a first level of control. In addition, the Board's Audit and Finance committees were assigned the task of reviewing all the previous year's transactions. The Board also required Skilling to review and approve all LJM transactions, as well as to review Fastow's economic interest in Enron and LJM.

Skilling, as COO and later CEO, did not sign many of the DASH forms for the LJM transactions. No evidence exists that Skilling knew how much money Fastow was making through LJM. Skilling, in one note, simply said that Fastow's first duty was to Enron because he received more compensation through salary and options than he might be making through LJM.

Neither stockholders nor analysts found it easy to monitor Enron's overall performance. Information on the financial dealings, particularly those with the SPEs, was difficult to find. The information on the SPE deals was disclosed either through proxy statements or in footnotes on the 10-Ks and 10-Qs. At one level, accounting standards required adequate information for management to assert the related-party transactions were at least comparable with those that would have taken place with unrelated parties. Second, details were often omitted. In the 2000 10-K, Enron stated, "Enron paid $123 million to purchase share-settled options from the [Raptor] entities on 21.7 million shares of Enron common stock." What Enron had actually purchased were put options, thereby betting that its stock would decline.[18]

Three International Deals

Rebecca Mark served as president of Enron Development Corporation. The power plant at Dabhol, India, was one of her achievements, though its overall value to Enron faded over time. Mark finalized the $3 billion deal in 1995, partnering Enron with General Electric and Bechtel (Enron's share was 65 percent; GE and Bechtel each owned 10 percent). The remaining 15 percent was owned by the state of Maharashtra electric utility. In addition to the partners, four lenders (the Industrial Development Bank of India, Citibank, Bank of America, and the Overseas Private Investment Corporation, a U.S. government agency) lent $2 billion.[21]

The Dabhol plant was troubled from the beginning with local and state authorities. The Clinton administration, at Lay's request, sent Ron Brown, secretary of commerce, to India in 1995 to keep the deal afloat. During construction, there were reports of human rights violations by guards.[22] Enron distanced itself from such instances, noting that it was only leasing the property, though it also paid the guards.

There were local benefits. Roads were constructed, and the local economy benefited both from increasing levels of employment and consumption. But when the plant opened in 1999, opposition exploded as energy bills rose as much as 400 percent. Maharashtra annulled its contract, and the plant was shuttered.

Mark also negotiated the Cuiaba project in Brazil. Enron had a 65 percent share in a gas-fired power generating plant and its associated pipelines. Construction exceeded the budget by over $120 million and showed no signs of profit. In 1999, LJM1 bought a 13 percent interest in the project for $11.3 million, enabling Enron to shield the associated debts from its balance sheet. In addition, the sale allowed Enron to mark to market a related power supply contract. With the sale and recognition of this contract, Enron booked a total of $65 million profit in the last half of 1999. Enron had a secret agreement with LJM1 to buy the interest back, should it be necessary for LJM1's profit. This buyback occurred in 2001, for $13.725 million.[23]

Azurix was a 1998 spin-off from Enron. Mark was named chair and CEO, with the mandate to create deals in the water supply industry. Enron's strategy was to assert itself as an international market maker in water. With Azurix divorced from Enron, these deals could be done under Enron oversight without the debt accruing to the balance sheet. Azurix went public in 1999, amassing $695 million in capital in the process.[12]

In 1999, Azurix acquired Wessex Water in the UK for $2.4 billion in cash and $482 million in debt.[24] Following that, Azurix bought the rights to an Argentinian water utility. These two acquisitions quickly undid Azurix, Mark, and any remaining Enron strategy involving hard assets. The Argentinian utility was plagued with contaminated water and labor union issues. The British government reduced the price Wessex could charge for its water. Mark was forced to resign in the summer of 2000, and she left Enron. Wessex Water was sold in 2002 to YTL Power International, a Malaysian firm, for $777 million in cash, with YTL also assuming $991 million in Wessex debt.[24]

It Comes Undone   Six months after taking the reins as CEO on February 12, 2001, Skilling abruptly resigned effective August 14, 2001. His 15 years at Enron were over, but Enron would haunt him long after. Skilling cited "personal reasons" as the cause, but there was widespread speculation that more was behind it.

Exhibit 1 provides a quick glance at Enron's profit and loss from 1998 to 2000. The declining gross margin indicates that Enron's nonderivatives business was losing money. Any profitability was coming from derivatives. In fact, Enron's derivative profits were roughly equivalent to Goldman Sachs, Inc.'s annual net revenue.[9]

Exhibit 1   Enron Corp. and Subsidiaries 2000 Consolidated Income Statement (in $ millions)

	2000	1999	1998
Nonderivative revenues	$93,557	$34,774	$27,215
Nonderivative expenses	94,517	34,761	26,381
Nonderivatives gross margin	(960)	13	834
Gain (loss) from derivatives	7,232	5,338	4,045
Other expenses	(4,319)	(4,549)	(3,501)
Operating income	1,953	802	1,378

Source: Testimony of Frank Partnoy in Hearings before the United States Senate Committee on Governmental Affairs, January 24, 2002.

In the Raptor restructurings from late 2000 to early 2001, a series of promissory notes from the Raptors had been recorded as increases in shareholders' equity, eventually totaling $1 billion. In August 2001, Andersen accountants declared that Raptors I, II, and IV were improperly accounted for, and revisions were required. On November 8, 2001, Lay announced a $1.2 billion reduction to shareholders' equity, with the additional $200 million write-down resulting from a difference in contracts between the Raptors and Enron. In addition to the $1.2 billion write-down in shareholders' equity, Enron consolidated the SPEs back to 1997. Hence, the balance sheets of Chewco, JEDI, and LJM were now part of Enron's balance sheet. These adjustments reduced Enron's income by $591 million, and increased its debt by just less than $2.6 billion. And some feared that the restatements were insufficient.

In the midst of this restructuring, Milberg Weiss Bershad Hynes & Lerach, LLP filed a class-action suit on behalf of Enron shareholders on October 22, 2001. As part of its filing the lawsuit disclosed the names and amounts of stock sold by Enron insiders, both senior management and directors (see Exhibit 2).[6]

During this time, Enron's one hope was a proposed merger with Dynegy, a corporation once viewed by Enron employees as an insignificant competitor. This merger also died of the same problems that had plagued Enron: fear of what was not disclosed. The merger was announced on November 9, the day after the restatements. On November 28, Standard & Poor's downgraded Enron debt to junk status, Dynegy declared the merger dead, and Enron's share price dropped from $3.69 at opening to $0.61 at close. On December 2, 2001, Enron filed for Chapter 11 bankruptcy protection. Jeff McMahon (Executive Vice President, Finance, and Treasurer, Enron Corp.) was named president and CEO following Ken Lay's resignation on January 23, 2002. McMahon would in turn resign in April 2002.

The Aftershocks

Criminal Actions   In addition to a number of Congressional hearings, the Enron bankruptcy also brought criminal actions by the government. David Duncan, Arthur Andersen's lead auditor for Enron, pleaded guilty to obstruction of justice in April 2002 for document shredding in connection with the Enron account. Kopper pleaded guilty in August 2002 to conspiracy to commit wire fraud and money laundering, losing almost approximately $12 million that he admitted he had improperly acquired through various SPE deals. Fastow was indicted in October 2002 on 78 counts for his role at Enron and in the various SPEs, and his accounts were frozen. On January 13, 2004, Fastow pled guilty to two counts, one for covering up financial problems and one for defrauding

Exhibit 2   Senior Management and Board of Director Members Accused of Insider Trading

Senior Management and Board Members	Proceeds from Enron Stock Traded between October 1998 and November 2001
J. Clifford Baxter[a]	$ 34,734,854
Robert A. Belfer[b]	$111,941,200
Norman P. Blake Jr.[b]	$ 1,705,328
Richard B. Buy[a]	$ 10,656,595
Richard A. Causey[a]	$ 13,386,896
James V. Derrick Jr.[a]	$ 12,563,928
John H. Duncan[b]	$ 2,009,700
Andrew S. Fastow[a]	$ 33,675,004
Mark A. Frevert[a]	$ 54,831,220
Wendy L. Gramm[b]	$ 278,892
Kevin P. Hannon[a]	"Unknown but substantial"
Ken L. Harrison[a]	$ 75,416,636
Joseph M. Hirko[a]	$ 35,168,721
Stanley C. Horton[a]	$ 47,371,361
Robert K. Jaedicke[b]	$ 841,438
Steven J. Kean[a]	$ 5,166,414
Mark E. Koenig[a]	$ 9,110,466
Kenneth L. Lay[a,b]	$184,494,426
Rebecca P. Mark[a,b]	$ 82,536,737
Michael S. McConnell[a]	$ 2,506,311
Jeffrey McMahon[a]	$ 2,739,226
Cindy K. Olson[a]	$ 6,505,870
Lou L. Pai[a]	$270,276,065
Kenneth D. Rice[a]	$ 76,825,145
Jeffrey K. Skilling[a,b]	$ 70,687,199
Joseph W. Sutton[a]	$ 42,231,283
Lawrence Greg Whalley[a]	"Unknown but substantial"

[a]Employee, Enron Corp.

[b]Member, Enron Board of Directors

Source: Cruver, B. 2002. *Anatomy of Greed: The unshredded truth from an Enron insider.* New York: Carroll and Graf Publishers: 132–133.

the company, and was sentenced to 10 years in a federal prison.[25] His wife, Lea, pled guilty to one count of tax fraud and received a 1-year sentence. On February 21, 2004, Jeff Skilling and Rick Causey were indicted for their roles, and on July 7, 2004,[26] Ken Lay was indicted for his.[25]

The Retirement Vanishes   Enron had been a significant holding in many large funds, particularly pension funds that sought to invest by industry segment. Enron employees' 401(k)s were primarily Enron, and they were barred from selling their shares until they turned 55. Many were solely invested in Enron. As late as the summer of 2001, Ken Lay was predicting that Enron would regain much of its loss in stock price. His e-mail announcing the resignation of Skilling as CEO, and his own resumption of that post, ends with this:

> Our performance has never been stronger; our business model has never been more robust; our growth has never been more certain; and most importantly, we have never had a better nor deeper pool of talent throughout the company. We have the finest organization in American business today. Together, we will make Enron the world's leading company.[12]

At the same time, however, Lay was busy selling much of his Enron stock. During 2001, Lay is reported to have sold $70 million in Enron shares. For almost an entire year, he was selling between 3,000 and 4,000 shares each workday.[27] He sold some shares back to the company to repay a loan from Enron. By doing so, he not only disposed of the stock, but also circumvented disclosure laws that would have required him to report insider stock sales.

The pension funds of every state were invested, to some extent, in Enron stock. The estimated loss to these funds was $1.5 billion. Florida lost $328 million, California $142 million, and Georgia $122 million.[28]

The Accounting Profession   Fallout spread throughout the accounting profession as well, as reports of inadequate oversight continued throughout the fall of Enron. In the fall of 2001, the Houston office of Arthur Andersen shredded documents associated with the Enron account. Nancy Temple, a lawyer associated with Arthur Andersen's Chicago offices, e-mailed David Duncan, the lead Enron auditor for Andersen, a reminder of the corporate policy on memo retention leading to massive document shredding efforts at Andersen's Houston offices. Duncan later pleaded guilty to criminal obstruction of justice, and Temple was named by a grand jury as one of four or five "corrupt persuaders" who encouraged the destruction of documents.[29]

Andersen itself was stripped of its license to audit public corporations in the U.S. and ceased to do business.

A major feature of the Sarbanes-Oxley Act was aimed at the conflicts that some thought brought about Enron: the mix of consulting and audit business. Andersen had both audit and consulting relationships with Enron, earning $52 million in 2001, split almost equally between consulting and audit fees. Enron was Andersen's largest client.[9] Audit firms would no longer be allowed to offer consulting services to audit clients. In addition, a number of other services were also proscribed, such as actuarial services, expert witnessing, and investment banking services, to name a few. In short, many of the services rendered by audit firms in attempts to generate extra revenue are now banned.

The Charity Fallout   Enron and its executives were very generous to not only their hometown of Houston but to educational institutions nationwide and the favorite causes of its board members. Initiatives included sponsorship of Enron Field (home to the Houston Astros), college scholarships, United Way, and university endowments.

Enron also generously contributed to the causes of several of its directors.[30] For instance, when the president of M.D. Andersen Cancer Center, John Mendelsohn, became an Enron director and member of its audit committee, Enron and Lay donated $332,150 to the center. Of $60,000 donated to a think tank at George Mason University, $45,000 was contributed after Wendy Lee Gramm (wife of then Senator Phil Gramm, R-TX, and an associate of the center), became an Enron board member. Concerned with an appearance of conflict of interest and a threat to independence, the U.S. House of Representatives passed a bill dubbed the "Enron Bill" to require disclosure of certain contributions and non-cash gifts to organizations associated with board members.

Conclusion   This case is still writing its own ending. Many of the stakeholders will never recover from their losses. Criminal actions have resulted in some going to jail, and others being indicted and waiting for trial. Two of the investment banks, Citigroup and J.P. Morgan Chase, have settled investor lawsuits for $2.575 billion and $2.2 billion, respectively. Other investment banks still face civil actions.[31] And federal lawmakers are debating the cost of some provisions of the Sarbanes-Oxley Act. This case will evolve for years to come.

Appendix A Enron Timeline

1984		Ken Lay becomes CEO of Houston Natural Gas (HNG).
1985		HNG merges with Internorth. Lay becomes CEO of the new company.
1986		Company changes name to Enron, and moves to Lay's hometown, Houston.
1990		Skilling leaves McKinsey & Co. to join Enron as executive officer of Enron Gas Services. Skilling hires Andrew Fastow from banking industry.
1991		Enron adopts mark-to-market accounting strategy, reporting income and value of assets at their replacement cost. Fastow forms first legitimate SPEs.
1993		Deregulation of worldwide energy markets. Enron begins marketing power and forms first SPE, JEDI, with CalPERS to invest in natural gas projects.
1994		As deregulation in the U.S. grows, Enron begins trading electricity.
1996		Enron commences construction of the Dabhol power plant in India. Lay promotes Skilling to Enron's president and COO.
1997		Enron buys first electric utility, Portland General Electric. Fastow promoted to head new finance department. Enron applies energy-trading model to new commodities markets such as weather derivatives, coal, pulp and paper, and bandwidth capacity. Chewco (another SPE) created to purchase CalPERS' shares of JEDI1 so that CalPERS could participate in a larger partnership, JEDI2. Chewco never meets the 3 percent outside ownership and is never a legitimate SPE.
1998		Fastow named CFO. Enron begins power trading in Argentina, becoming first power marketer, and gains control of Brazilian utility. Enron acquires UK utility Wessex Water and forms Azurix, a global water business. It then takes Azurix public, retaining a 69 percent stake. Enron trades most of Enron Oil & Gas for cash and its properties in India and China.
1999		New Houston Astros baseball stadium named Enron Field. Skilling and Fastow present LJM partnerships to board of directors.
2000		
	February	*Fortune* names Enron "the most innovative company in America" for the fifth consecutive year.
	April	Enron creates the first Raptor SPE.
	August	Rebecca Mark resigns due to poor results at Azurix and tension with Skilling. Stock hits all-time high of $90 and revenue surpasses $100 billion making it the seventh largest company in the *Fortune* 500.
2001		
	February	Lay steps down as CEO. President and COO Skilling replaces Lay as CEO.
	August	Skilling resigns and Lay becomes CEO again. Sherron Watkins, an Enron accountant, sends anonymous memo to Lay warning of potential accounting scandal.
	September	Arthur Andersen compels Enron to change an aggressive accounting action, causing a $1.2 billion reduction in Enron's equity.
	October	SEC launches investigation of Enron's off-balance-sheet partnerships. Enron changes its 401(k) pension plan administrator, preventing employees from selling Enron stock for 30 days. Fastow is put on leave. Enron establishes special committee to investigate third-party transactions to be known as the Powers Report. Enron's stock drops to $11.

(*continued*)

(*continued*)

November	Enron strikes deal with Dynegy, its largest energy-industry rival. Dynegy backs out of the deal once more details of Enron's finances are available. Enron trades at less than $1 per share.
December	Enron files for Chapter 11 bankruptcy protection and lays off 4,000 employees.

2002

January	Watkin's memo leaked to Congress. U.S. Justice Department launches a criminal investigation into Enron's fall. Enron fires Arthur Andersen LLP. Enron sells its energy trading business to UBS's investment banking unit. Sells Wessex Water to a Malaysian firm, and shuts down its broadband unit. Lay resigns, and McMahon becomes CEO. Former Enron Vice Chairman Cliff Baxter is found dead as government investigation deepens.
February	Skilling testifies before Congress. Lay pleads the Fifth Amendment. Watkins testifies before Congress about her memo to Lay.
April	Andersen lays off 7,000 employees. McMahon resigns as of June 1.
August	Kopper pleads guilty to money laundering and wire-fraud conspiracy. Cooperates with authorities.
October	Fastow indicted on 78 counts of federal fraud, conspiracy, and money laundering.

2003

May	Federal prosecutors file new charges against Fastow and two others. Indict Fastow's wife and seven other former Enron officials for fraud and other criminal investigations.

2004

January	Fastow pleads guilty on two counts and receives 10 years in federal prison. Lea Fastow pleads guilty to one count of tax fraud and receives a 1-year sentence.
February	Skilling and Causey indicted on 42 counts, including securities fraud, wire fraud, and insider trading.
July	Lay indicted on 11 counts, including wire and bank fraud, as well as making false statements.

Appendix B   Glossary of Terms

Adjustments	A deduction made to financial statements to charge off a loss, as with a bad debt.
Asset-lite	Enron jargon for short-term or noncapital-intensive assets.
CalPERS	California Public Employees Retirement System
DASH	Deal Approval Sheet
Derivative	A financial instrument whose characteristics and value depend upon the characteristics and value of an underlier, typically a commodity, bond, equity or currency.
Downgrade	A negative change in an analyst's ratings for a security.
Hedge	An investment made in order to reduce the risk of adverse price movements in a security, by taking an offsetting position in a related security.
Insider stock sales	Selling of a company's stock by individual directors, executives or other employees.
JEDI	Joint Energy Development Investment—an Enron SPE
Mark-to-Market	Recording the price or value of a security, portfolio, or account on a daily basis to calculate profits and losses or to confirm that margin requirements are being met.
Off-balance sheet	Financing from sources other than debt and equity offerings, such as joint ventures, R&D partnerships, and operating leases.
Options	The right, but not the obligation, to buy (for a call option) or sell (for a put option) a specific amount of a given stock, commodity, currency, index, or debt, at a specified price (the strike price) during a specified period of time.

Premium	The amount by which a bond or stock sells above its par value.
Privatization	The process of moving from a government-controlled system to a privately run, for-profit system.
Put options	An option contract that gives the holder the right to sell a certain quantity of an underlying security to the writer of the option, at a specified price (strike price) up to a specified date (expiration date); also called put.
RAC	Risk Assessment & Control, an Enron department.
Rank and Yank	Employee jargon for Enron's employee review process.
Securitization	The process of aggregating similar instruments, such as loans or mortgages, into a negotiable security.
SPEs	Special Purpose Entities
Write-down	Make a downward adjustment in the accounting value of an asset.
Yields	The annual rate of return on an investment, expressed as a percentage.

Endnotes

1. BusinessWeek Online, February 12, 2001.
2. Eichenwald, K. 2002. A powerful, flawed witness against Enron. *New York Times,* October 21: C1.
3. Eichenwald, K. 2003. Ex-trader at Enron is charged in California power case. *New York Times,* June 4: C6.
4. Lay, K. 1990. The Enron story. Speech delivered on October 9, 1990 in New York to Newcomen Society of the United States.
5. A more detailed history of the origin of Enron can be found at www.hoovers.com.
6. Cruver, B. 2002. *Anatomy of greed: The unshredded truth from an Enron insider.* New York: Carroll & Graf Publishers.
7. Preston, R., & Koller, M. 2000. *Enron feels the power.* Internetweekonline: October 30.
8. O'Reilly, B. 1997. The secrets of America's most admired corporations: New ideas, new products. *Fortune,* 135(4): 60–64.
9. Testimony of Frank Partnoy in Hearings before the United States Senate Committee on Governmental Affairs, January 24, 2002.
10. 1999 Annual Report, Enron Corp.
11. Grulye, B., & Smith, R. 2002. Anatomy of a fall: Keys to success left Kenneth Lay open to disaster—From rural Missouri to helm of Enron to ignominy—Trust and willfull optimism—"The American dream is alive." *Wall Street Journal,* April 26: A1.
12. Fusaro, P. C., & Miller, R. M. 2002. *What went wrong at Enron: Everyone's guide to the largest bankruptcy in U.S. History.* Hoboken, NJ: John Wiley & Sons.
13. Schwartz, J. 2002. As Enron purged its ranks, dissent was swept away. *New York Times,* February 4.
14. Levin, C. 2002. After Enron: Government's role and corporate cultures. *Mid-American Journal of Business,* 17(2): 7–10.
15. Banerjee, N., Berboza, D., & Warren, A. 2002. Enron's many strands: Corporate culture; at Enron, lavish excess often came before success. *New York Times,* February 26: C1.
16. Raghavan, A., Kranhold, K., & Barriounuevo, A. 2002. Full speed ahead: How Enron bosses created a culture of pushing limits—Fastow and others challenged staff, badgered bankers; Porsches, Ferraris were big—A chart to "intimidate people." *Wall Street Journal,* August 26: A1
17. Note 8, Q3 SEC filing, 2001.
18. Report of Investigation by the Special Investigative Committee of the Board of Directors of Enron Corp. (the Powers Report).
19. Reason, CFO.com, 2002.
20. Berger, E., & Fowler, T. 2002. The fall of Enron; Enron masked loans as sales, report says; deals inflated bottom line by $1.4 billion. *Houston Chronicle,* September 22: A1.
21. Rai, S. 2002. Seeking ways to sell Enron's plant in India. *The New York Times,* April 11: W1.
22. Kolker, C., & Fowler, T. 2002. The fall of Enron; roots of discontent; dead Enron power plant affecting environment, economy and livelihoods in India. *The Houston Chronicle,* August 4: B1.
23. Criminal Complaint, United States Securities and Exchange Commission v. Andrew S. Fastow, October 1, 2002, #s 15–22.
24. Goldberg, L. 2002. Enron's Azurix to well Wessex Water at a loss. *The Houston Chronicle,* March 26: B4.
25. Eichenwald, K. 2004. Enron ex-chief indicted by U.S. in fraud case. *New York Times,* July 8: A1.
26. Carr, R. 2004. Former Enron chief indicted. *Atlanta Constitution,* February 20: 1A.
27. Flood, M., & Fowler, T. 2002. The fall of Enron; grand jurors eye Lay; $70 million in stock sales focus of probe. *Houston Chronicle,* October 24: A1.
28. Healy, B. 2002. Shared pain: Bay State isn't alone in taking a hit from Enron. *Boston Globe,* September 10: C1.
29. Fowler, T. 2002. Andersen attorney may be next. *The Houston Chronicle,* June 27: B1.
30. Weber, J., & McNamee, M. 2002. Boardroom charity: Reforms don't go far enough. *BusinessWeek,* June 10: 128.
31. Creswell, J. 2005. J.P. Morgan Chase to pay Enron investors $2.2 billion. *New York Times,* June 15: C1.

In the quarter ending on January 28, 2005, World Wrestling Entertainment (WWE) posted a profit of $10.9 million, up sharply from the $8.8 million profit that it had made in the same period a year earlier. Although the firm had shown a relatively smaller growth in its revenues, it had managed to generate a stronger profit. This resulted from its ability to tap into several sources of revenue even as it found ways to cut costs. "We continue to see the distribution of our creative content through various emerging channels," stated WWE's President and Chief Executive Officer (CEO) Linda McMahon. "As an integrated media company, we are well positioned to take advantage of these new avenues in order to distribute our content on a global basis."[1]

The results could indicate that WWE was clearly pulling out of a three-year period when its performance had slumped after several years of strong growth. During the 1990s, WWE's potent mix of shaved, pierced, and pumped-up muscled hunks; buxom, scantily clad, and sometimes cosmetically enhanced beauties; and body-bashing clashes of good versus evil had resulted in an empire that claimed over 35 million fans. Furthermore, the vast majority of these fans were males between the ages of 12 and 34, the demographic segment that makes most advertisers drool. And these guys had driven up WWE's revenues by their insatiable appetite for tickets, broadcasts, books, CDs, games, and other merchandise. (See Exhibits 1 and 2 for the company's income statements and balance sheets.)

By the end of 1999, WWE had managed to draw on its surge in popularity to raise $170 through an initial public offering. The husband-and-wife team of Vince and Linda McMahon decided to use these new funds to aggressively push for further growth by moving the firm beyond its wrestling roots. However, most of WWE's efforts to build on its success with wrestling led to significant losses. The failure of the firm's effort to create a football league folded after just one season, resulting in a $57 million loss.

As WWE stumbled in its efforts to diversify, it also began to see a drop in revenues from its core wrestling businesses. Its attendance began to drop off at its live shows and advertising revenues for its television shows started to decline. WWE struggled with its efforts to build new wrestling stars and to introduce new characters into its shows. Some of its most valuable younger viewers were also turning to new reality-based television shows such as *Survivor, Fear Factor,* and *Jackass.*

Over the last couple of years, however, things seem to be finally turning around for WWE. Vince gained a lot of publicity from the show that his crew performed for the U.S. troops in Iraq over the 2003 Christmas holidays. The 2004 version of its annual premier live show, Wrestlemania XX, sold out almost immediately after its tickets went on sale at Madison Square Garden in New York City. And new wrestling stars such as rapper John Cena and Randy Orton are beginning to draw back audiences to WWE's live events and are drawing more viewers to its television shows, including pay-per-view events.

Developing a Wrestling Empire

Most of the success of the WWE can be attributed to the persistent efforts of Vince McMahon. He was a self-described juvenile delinquent who went to military school as a teenager to avoid being sent to a reformatory institution. Around 1970, Vince joined his father's wrestling company, Capital Wrestling Corporation. He did on-air commentary, developed scripts, and otherwise promoted wrestling matches.

Vince brought Capital Wrestling from his father in 1982, eventually renaming it World Wrestling Federation. At that time, wrestling was managed by regional fiefdoms where everyone avoided encroaching on anyone else's territory. Vince began to change all that by paying local television stations around the country to broadcast his matches. His aggressive pursuit of audiences across the country gradually squeezed out most of the other rivals. "I banked on the fact that they were behind the times, and they were," said McMahon.[2]

Soon after, Vince broke another taboo by admitting to the public that wrestling matches were scripted. Although he had made this admission to avoid the scrutiny of state athletic commissions, wrestling fans appreciated the honesty. The WWF began to draw in more fans through the elaborate story lines and the captivating characters of its wrestling matches. The firm turned wrestlers such as Hulk Hogan and Andre the Giant into mainstream pop culture icons. By the late 1980s, the WWF's *Raw is War* had become a top-rated show on cable, and the firm had also begun to offer pay-per-view shows.

Vince faced his most formidable competition after 1988, when Ted Turner brought out World Championship Wrestling, one of the few major rivals that was still operating. He spent millions luring away WWF stars such as Hulk Hogan and Macho Man Randy Savage. He used these stars to launch a show on his own TNT channel to go up against WWF's major show, *Raw is War*. Although Turner's new show caused a temporary dip in the ratings for WWF's shows, Vince fought back with pumped-up scripts, mouthy muscle-men and lyca-clad women. "Ted Turner decided to come after me and all of my talent," growled Vince, "and now he's where he should be . . ."[3]

*This case was prepared by Professor Jamal Shamsie of Michigan State University. This case was developed from published sources as a basis for class discussion rather than to illustrate either effective or ineffective handling of an administrative situation. Copyright © 2005 Jamal Shamsie.

Exhibit 1   World Wrestling Entertainment Income Statement
(All numbers in $ thousands)

	Period Ending		
	April 30, 2004	April 30, 2003	April 30, 2002
Total Revenue	$374,909	$374,264	$425,026
Cost of Revenue	207,121	237,343	260,218
Gross Profit	167,788	136,921	164,808
Operating Expenses			
Selling General and Administrative	81,845	99,349	109,571
Others	12,363	10,965	13,113
Operating Income or Loss	73,580	26,607	42,124
Total Other Income/Expenses Net	7,181	1,114	18,202
Earnings Before Interest and Taxes	80,761	27,721	60,326
Interest Expense	767	783	784
Income Before Tax	79,994	26,938	59,542
Income Tax Expense	30,421	10,836	21,947
Net Income from Continuing Operations	49,573	16,102	37,595
Nonrecurring Events			
Discontinued Operations	(1,381)	(35,557)	4,638
Net Income	48,192	(19,455)	42,233

In 2001 Vince was finally able to acquire WCW from Turner's parent firm AOL Time Warner for a bargain price of $5 million. Because of the manner in which he eliminated most of his rivals, Vince has earned a reputation for being as aggressive and ambitious as any character in the ring. Paul MacArthur, publisher of *Wrestling Perspective,* an industry newsletter, praised his accomplishments, saying, "McMahon understands the wrestling business better than anyone else. He's considered by most in the business to be brilliant."[4]

Creating a Script for Success

Since taking over the WWF, Vince began to change the entire focus of the wrestling shows. He looked to television soap operas for enhancing the entertainment value of his live events. Vince reduced the amount of actual wrestling and replaced it with wacky yet somewhat compelling story lines. He began to develop interesting characters and create story lines by employing techniques that were quite similar to those being used by many successful television shows. There was a great deal of reliance on the "good versus evil" or the "settling the score" themes in the development of the plots for his wrestling matches. The plots and subplots ended up providing viewers with a mix of romance, sex, sports, comedy, and violence against a backdrop of pyrotechnics.

Over time, the scripts for the matches became tighter, with increasingly intricate story lines, plots, and dialogue. All the details of every match were worked out well in advance, leaving the wrestlers themselves to decide only the manner in which they would dispatch their opponents to the mat. Vince began to refer to his wrestlers as "athletic performers" who were selected on the basis of their acting ability in addition to their physical stamina.

Vince's use of characters was well thought-out. He was able to exploit the stage characters that he created for each of his wrestlers to develop and sell various kinds of merchandise. Vince also ensured that his firm owned the rights to the characters that the wrestlers played.

Exhibit 2 World Wrestling Entertainment Balance Sheet
(All numbers in $ thousands)

	Period Ending		
	April 30, 2004	April 30, 2003	April 30, 2002
Assets			
Current Assets			
Cash and Cash Equivalents	$ 48,467	$128,473	$ 86,659
Short-Term Investments	224,824	142,641	207,407
Net Receivables	62,703	49,729	63,835
Inventory	856	839	1,851
Other Current Assets	14,718	39,572	15,935
Total Current Assets	**351,568**	**361,254**	**375,687**
Property Plant and Equipment	71,369	59,325	91,759
Goodwill	—	—	11,588
Intangible Assets	4,492	4,625	—
Other Assets	26,915	7,447	8,407
Total Assets	**454,344**	**432,651**	**487,441**
Liabilities			
Current Liabilities			
Accounts Payable	59,355	49,179	64,076
Short/Current Long-Term Debt	700	777	601
Other Current Liabilities	25,913	36,216	24,024
Total Current Liabilities	**85,968**	**86,172**	**88,701**
Long-Term Debt	7,955	9,126	9,302
Other Liabilities	7,316	—	—
Total Liabilities	**101,239**	**95,298**	**98,003**
Stockholders' Equity			
Common Stock	684	730	729
Retained Earnings	102,766	69,634	93,435
Treasury Stock	—	(30,569)	(1,139)
Capital Surplus	250,775	297,315	296,938
Other Stockholder Equity	(1,120)	243	(525)
Total Stockholder Equity	**353,105**	**337,353**	**389,438**
Net Tangible Assets	**$348,613**	**$332,728**	**$377,850**

Source: World Wrestling Entertainment.

This would allow him to continue to exploit the characters that he developed for his television shows, even after the wrestler that played that character had left his firm.

By the late 1990s Vince had two weekly shows on television. Besides the original flagship program on the USA cable channel, WWF had added a *Smackdown!* show on the UPN broadcast channel. He developed a continuous story line using the same characters so that his audience would be driven to both the shows. But the acquisition of the WCW resulted in a significant increase in the number of wrestling stars under contract. Trying to incorporate more than 150 characters into the story lines for WWF's shows proved to be a challenging task.

To deal with this challenge, Vince began to develop different plots using a different set of characters for his cable television show *Raw* and his broadcast television show *Smackdown!*. He also moved *Raw* from USA's cable channel to Viacom's cable channel. The combination of these changes resulted in a significant drop in viewers for both of WWF's television shows. Attendance at the firm's live events was also hurt by the absence of key wrestling stars such as "Stone Cold" Steve Austin and "The Rock" Dwayne Johnson, who were either out with injuries or taking time off to make movies.

Managing a Road Show

A typical work week for the WWF can be grueling for the McMahons, for the talent, and for the crew. The organization is now putting on more than 300 live shows a year, requiring everyone to be on the road most days of the week. The touring crew includes over 200 crew members, including stage hands. All of WWF's live events, including those that are used for its two weekly shows *Raw* and *Smackdown!,* are held in different cities. Consequently, the crew is always packing up a dozen 18-wheelers and driving hundreds of miles to get from one performance to the other. The live shows also provide material for WWF specials or for pay-per-views. Since there are no repeats of any WWF shows, the live performances must be held all year round.

In fact, the live shows form the core of all of WWF's businesses (see Exhibit 3). They give the firm a big advantage in the entertainment world. Most of the crowd shows up wearing WWF merchandise and scream throughout the show. Vince and his crew pay special attention to the response of the audience to different parts of the show. The script for each performance is not set until the day of the show and sometimes changes are even made in the middle of a show. Vince boasted: "We're in contact with the public more than any entertainment company in the world."[5]

Although the live shows usually fill up, the attendance fee, which averages around $35, barely covers the cost of the production. But these live performances provide content for nine hours of original television programming as well as additional footage for the WWF Web site. The shows also create strong demand for WWF merchandise. In addition, WWF cuts most of its own advertising deals, offering spots on its television shows, its Internet site, or even at the live shows. "It's really one content being re-purposed over and over again," explained August Liguori, the firm's chief financial officer.[6]

This road is managed not only by Vince, but by all of his family. Vince's efforts notwithstanding, the development of the WWF has turned into a family affair. While the slick and highly toned Vince could be regarded as the creative muscle behind the growing sports entertainment empire, his wife Linda began to quietly manage its day-to-day operation. Throughout its existence, she helped to balance the books, do the deals, and handle the details that were necessary for the growth and development of the WWF franchise.

One of Vince and Linda's greatest pleasures has been to see their kids also move into the business. Their son, Shane, heads wwf.com, the firm's streaming-media site, and their daughter, Stephanie, has just become part of the creative writing team. "This business is my heart and soul and passion and always has been," Stephanie commented.[7] The family's devotion lies behind much of the success of WWF. "If they are out there giving 110 percent, it's a lot easier to get it from everyone else," said wrestler Steve Blackman.[8]

Pursuing New Opportunities

Flush with this success, WWF raised some $170 million through an initial public offering in late 1999. In its prospectus, the firm stated that it would use the proceeds to expand into a variety of other businesses, some of which would move it away from its heavy dependence on wrestling. Under the expert guidance of Linda, WWF had already branched out into merchandise such as action figures, CDs, home video, books, magazines, and games (see Exhibits 4 and 5.)

The most ambitious of WWF's diversification efforts was the attempt to create an eight-team football league called the XFL. Promising full competitive sport unlike the heavily scripted wrestling matches, Vince tried to make the XFL a faster-paced, more fan-friendly form of football than the NFL's brand. Emphasizing that the X stands for extreme, Vince stated: "This will not be a league for pantywaists or sissies. The XFL will take you places where the NFL is afraid to go because, quite frankly, we are not afraid of anything."[9] He also introduced several technological enhancements to its telecasts, such as wiring coaches with live microphones, placing cameras in the locker rooms, and using plenty of helmet cameras.

Vince was able to partner with NBC, which was looking for a lower-priced alternative to the NFL televised games. The XFL kicked off with great fanfare in February

Exhibit 3   Wrestlemania's Five Best Bouts

Andre the Giant vs. Hulk Hogan
WrestleMania III, March 29, 1987

- **The Lowdown:** A record crowd of 93,173 witnessed Andre the Giant, undefeated for 15 years, versus Hulk Hogan, wrestling's golden boy.
- **The Payoff:** Hogan body-slammed the 500-pound Giant, becoming the sport's biggest star and jump-starting wrestling's first big boom.

The Rock vs. Stone Cold Steve Austin
WrestleMania X-7, April 1, 2001

- **The Lowdown:** The two biggest stars of wrestling's modern era went toe-to-toe in the culmination of a two-year-long feud.
- **The Payoff:** Good-guy Austin aligned with "evil" WWE owner Vince McMahon and decimated the Rock to win the title in front of a shocked crowd.

Hulk Hogan vs. The Ultimate Warrior
WrestleMania VI, April 1, 1990

- **The Lowdown:** The most divisive feud ever—fan favorite Hulk Hogan defended his title against up-and-coming phenom the Ultimate Warrior.
- **The Payoff:** Half the crowd went into cardiac arrest (the other half were in tears) when Hogan missed his patented leg drop and the Warrior won.

Bret Hart vs. Shawn Michaels
WrestleMania XII, March 31, 1996

- **The Lowdown:** Two men who didn't like each other outside the ring locked up in a 60-minute Iron Man match for the title.
- **The Payoff:** After an hour, neither man had scored a pinfall. Finally, Michaels, aka the Heartbreak Kid, pinned Hart in overtime to win the belt.

Kurt Angle vs. Brock Lesnar
WrestleMania XIX, March 30, 2003

- **The Lowdown:** Olympic medalist Angle squared off against former NCAA wrestling champ Lesnar in a punishing bout.
- **The Payoff:** The 295-pound Lesnar landed on his head after attempting a high-flying attack. But he recovered to pin Angle and capture the championship.

Source: *TV Guide.* March 13, 2004.

2001. Although the games drew good attendance, television ratings dropped steeply after the first week. The football venture was folded after just one season, resulting in a $57 million loss for WWF. Both Vince and Linda insist that the venture could have paid off if it had been given enough time. Vince commented, "I think our pals at the NFL went out of their way to make sure this was not a successful venture."[10]

WWF also failed to generate much business with the $40 million theme restaurant that was opened in New York's Times Square. Seating more than 600 patrons, the restaurant was expected to showcase the firm's talent, who would make occasional guest appearances. It was also expected to drive up sales of WWF merchandise. There were also plans to hold some wrestling matches at the restaurant. But the enterprise has racked up losses of about $8 million over the last year.

The firm, now known as WWE, is currently focusing more heavily on television and film. "Television is our base," Linda said.[11] WWE now has as many as seven regular shows on television, including two in syndication. It is excited about the launch of WWE 24/7, a subscriber

Exhibit 4   World Wrestling Entertainment Revenue
Breakdown (All figures in $ millions)

	2004	2003	2002
Live Events	70.2	72.9	74.5
Television Shows	71.0	58.5	53.3
Television Advertising	59.5	72.9	83.6
Pay-Per-View	95.3	91.1	112.0
Branded Merchandise	78.8	78.9	86.1

Source: World Wrestling Entertainment.

Exhibit 5   World Wrestling Entertainment Profit
Breakdown (All figures in $ millions)

	2004	2003	2002
Live Events	17.8	16.1	21.9
Television Shows	20.5	8.3	3.7
Television Advertising	37.0	37.8	46.7
Pay-Per-View	59.4	54.4	69.6
Branded Merchandise	42.6	32.1	29.2

Source: World Wrestling Entertainment.

video-on-demand service that deliver highlights from old shows as well as exclusive new programming. Meanwhile, WWE also has become involved in movie production with action-adventure or horror films, many of which have its wrestlers, such as The Rock or Stone Cold, as stars. Linda insisted that they will continue to explore new ventures, although they will be paying much more attention to their potential bottom-line implications.

Poised for a Resurgence?

In 2002, WWF was also hit with a ruling by a British court that their original WWF acronym belonged to the World Wildlife Fund. The firm had to undergo a major branding transition, changing its well-known name and triple logo from WWF to WWE. Although the name change has been costly, it is not clear that this will hurt the firm in the long run. "Their product is really the entertainment. It's the stars. It's the bodies," said Larry McNaughton, managing director and principal of CoreBrand, a branding consultancy.[12] Linda stated that the new name might actually be beneficial for the firm. "Our new name puts the emphasis on the 'E' for entertainment," she commented.[13]

Vince and his crew are using the name change to try to re-create the buzz that had surrounded his firm a few years ago before it hit some serious bumps. The firm had launched a new campaign with the message "Get the 'F' out." Linda rejects any suggestion that the fortunes of WWE may be driven by a fad that is unlikely to last. She maintains that the interest in their shows will survive in spite of growing competition from newer sources of entertainment such as reality-based television shows. In fact, there are signs that WWE's new wrestling stars are beginning to catch on and fans are being drawn back to the different characters such as The Undertaker and Triple Hand. It is creating fresh story lines for all of its television shows, including the two major weekly series, *Raw* and *Smackdown! Raw* still continues to be one of the top weekly cable television shows. *Smackdown!* has maintained its status as the leading show for UPN network. It draws about 25 percent more viewers than the network's next most popular shows.

Furthermore, Vince and Linda McMahon claim that their attempts to diversify were never meant to convey any loss of interest in wrestling. In fact, they believed that it was their experience with staging wrestling shows over the years that had provided them with the foundation to move into other areas of entertainment. After all, it was their ability to use wrestling to create a form of mass entertainment that had made the WWF such a phenomenal success. In response to critics who question the value of wrestling matches whose outcomes are rigged, James F. Byrne, senior vice president for marketing, had stated; "Wrestling is 100 percent entertainment. There's no such thing as fake entertainment."[14]

With more characters at their disposal and different characters being used in each of their shows, WWE is planning to ramp up the number of live shows, including more in overseas locations. An increase in the number of shows may also boost the revenues that the firm is able to generate from its merchandise. Andy Rittenberry, an analyst with Gabelli Asset Management who has been following WWE, stated: "Maybe you think it's idiotic, and you don't like the typical wrestler and the people who watch it. But they have built a good brand."[15] Moreover, unlike many other media firms, WWE has little debt and over $270 million in cash. "We make money when we are not hot," remarked Vince. "When we are hot, it's off the charts."[16]

Those who understand don't need an explanation. Those who need an explanation will never understand.

—**Marty,** a 19-year-old wrestling addict quoted in *Fortune,* October 6, 2000.

Endnotes

1. WWE. World Wrestling Entertainment, Inc. reports Q3 results. Press release, February 23, 2005.
2. McLean, Bethany. 2000. Inside the world's weirdest family business. *Fortune,* October 16: 298.
3. Bradley, Diane. 2000. Wrestling's real grudge match. *BusinessWeek,* January 24: 164.
4. Mooradian, Don. 2001. WWF gets a grip after acquisition. *Amusement Business,* June 4: 20.
5. *Fortune,* October 16: 304.
6. Ibid.
7. Ibid.: 302.
8. Ibid.
9. Fisher, Eric. 2000. A perfect marriage: Football, WWF? *Washington Times,* February 4: B2.
10. Bradley, Diane. 2004. Rousing itself off the mat? *BusinessWeek,* February 2: 73.
11. McConville, Jim. 2000. Taking the WWF off the beat-'em-up path. *Electronic Media,* January 24: 42.
12. Oestricher, Dwight, & Steinberg, Brian. 2002. WW . . . E it is, after fight for F nets new name. *Wall Street Journal,* May 7: B2.
13. Finnigan, David. 2002. Down but not out, WWE is using a rebranding effort to gain strength. *Brandweek,* June 3: 12.
14. Wyatt, Edward. 1999. Pro wrestling tries to pin down a share value. *New York Times,* August 4: C11.
15. Beatty, Sally. 2002. Unusual executive couple fights to save World Wrestling Federation. *Wall Street Journal,* February 21: B1.
16. *BusinessWeek,* February 2: 74.

Case 32   ZARA: Fast Fashion*

Fashion is the imitation of a given example and satisfies the demand for social adaptation. . . . The more an article becomes subject to rapid changes of fashion, the greater the demand for cheap products of its kind.

—Georg Simmel, "Fashion" (1904).

Inditex (Industria de Diseño Textil) of Spain, the owner of Zara and five other apparel retailing chains, continued a trajectory of rapid, profitable growth by posting net income of €340 million on revenues of €3,250 million in its fiscal year 2001 (ending January 31, 2002). Inditex had had a heavily oversubscribed Initial Public Offering in May 2001. In the next 12 months, its stock price increased by nearly 50%—despite bearish stock market conditions—to push its market valuation to €13.4 billion. The high stock price made Inditex's founder, Amancio Ortega, who had begun to work in the apparel trade as an errand boy half-a-century earlier, Spain's richest man. However, it also implied a significant growth challenge. Based on one set of calculations, for example, 76% of the equity value implicit in Inditex's stock price was based on expectations of future growth—higher than an estimated 69% for Wal-Mart or, for that matter, other high-performing retailers.[1]

The next section of this case briefly describes the structure of the global apparel chain, from producers to final customers. The section that follows profiles three of Inditex's leading international competitors in apparel retailing: The Gap (U.S.), Hennes & Mauritz (Sweden), and Benetton (Italy). The rest of the case focuses on Inditex, particularly the business system and international expansion of the Zara chain that dominated its results.

The Global Apparel Chain

The global apparel chain had been characterized as a prototypical example of a buyer-driven global chain, in which profits derived from "unique combinations of high-value research, design, sales, marketing, and financial services that allow retailers, branded marketers, and branded manufacturers to act as strategic brokers in linking overseas factories"[2] with markets. These attributes were thought to distinguish the vertical structure of commodity chains in apparel and other labor-intensive industries such as footwear and toys from producer-driven chains (e.g.,

in automobiles) that were coordinated and dominated by upstream manufacturers rather than downstream intermediaries (see Exhibit 1).

Production   Apparel production was very fragmented. On average, individual apparel manufacturing firms employed only a few dozen people, although internationally traded production, in particular, could feature tiered production chains comprising as many as hundreds of firms spread across dozens of countries. About 30% of world production of apparel was exported, with developing countries generating an unusually large share, about one-half, of all exports. These large cross-border flows of apparel reflected cheaper labor and inputs—partly because of cascading labor efficiencies—in developing countries. (See Exhibit 2 for comparative labor productivity data and Exhibit 3 for an example.) Despite extensive investments in substituting capital for labor, apparel production remained highly labor-intensive so that even relatively large "manufacturers" in developed countries outsourced labor-intensive production steps (e.g., sewing) to lower-cost labor sources nearby. Proximity also mattered because it reduced shipping costs and lags, and because poorer neighbors sometimes benefited from trade concessions. While China became an export powerhouse across the board, greater regionalization was the dominant motif of changes in apparel trade in the 1990s. Turkey, North Africa, and sundry East European countries emerged as major suppliers to the European Union; Mexico and the Caribbean Basin as major suppliers to the United States; and China as the dominant supplier to Japan (where there were no quotas to restrict imports).[3]

World trade in apparel and textiles continued to be regulated by the Multi-Fiber Arrangement (MFA), which had restricted imports into certain markets (basically the United States, Canada, and West Europe) since 1974. Two decades later, agreement was reached to phase out the MFA's quota system by 2005 and to further reduce tariffs (which averaged 7% to 9% in the major markets). As of 2002, some warned that the transition to the post-MFA world could prove enormously disruptive for suppliers in many exporting and importing countries, and might even ignite demands for "managed trade." There was also potential for protectionism in the questions that nongovernmental organizations and others in developed countries were posing about the basic legitimacy of "sweatshop trade" in buyer-driven global chains such as apparel and footwear.

Cross-Border Intermediation   Trading companies had traditionally played the primary role in orchestrating the physical flows of apparel from factories in exporting countries to retailers in importing countries. They continued to be important cross-border intermediaries, although the complexity and (as a result) the specialization of their operations seemed to have increased over time. Thus, Hong

*HBS Professor Pankaj Ghemawat and IESE Professor José Luis Nueno prepared this case. Copyright 2004 by the President and Fellows of Harvard College. Harvard Business School Case No. 703–492. This case was prepared as a basis for class discussion rather than to illustrate either effective or ineffective handling of an administrative situation. Reprinted by permission of Harvard Business School. No part of this publication may be reproduced, stored in a retrieval system, used in a spreadsheet, or transmitted in any form or by any means—electronic, mechanical, photocopying, recording, or otherwise—without the permission of Harvard Business School.

Exhibit 1   Buyer-Driven vs. Producer-Driven Global Chains

	Buyer-Driven Global Chains (e.g., Apparel)	**Producer-Driven Global Chains (e.g., Automobiles)**
Upstream Structure	Fragmented, locally owned, dispersed, and often tiered production	Global oligopolies
Downstream Structure	Relatively concentrated intermediaries	Relatively fragmented intermediaries
Key Cross-Border Links	Retailers, branded marketers, and branded manufacturers	Producers
Rent Concentration	Downstream	Upstream
Types of Rents	Relational Trade policy Brand name	Technology Organizational
Typical Industries	Labor-intensive consumer products	Capital- and technology-intensive products

Source: Casewriter compilation of data from Gereffi, Gary. 1999. International trade and industrial upgrading in the apparel commodity chain. *Journal of International Economics* 48 (June): 37–70.

Kong's largest trading company, Li & Fung, derived 75% of its turnover from apparel and the remainder from hard goods by setting up and managing multinational supply chains for retail clients through its offices in more than 30 countries.[4] For example, a down jacket's filling might

Exhibit 2   Average Labor Costs and Productivity in Apparel ($/hour, 1998)

	Labor Cost	**Value Added**
EU Countries		
Germany	18	23
Spain	7	11
Italy	14	20
Portugal	4	6
UK	11	13
Major Suppliers		
Turkey	2	12
China	0.4	na
India	0.4	2
Egypt	0.7	2
Other Major Markets		
U.S.	10	20
Japan	14	na

Source: Casewriter compilation of data from Stengg, Werner. 2001. The textile and clothing industry in the EU. Enterprise Papers No. 2, June; and http://europa.eu.int/comm/enterprise/textiles/statistics.htm accessed: 12/17/2002.

come from China, the outer shell fabric from Korea, the zippers from Japan, the inner lining from Taiwan, and the elastics, label, and other trim from Hong Kong. Dyeing might take place in South Asia and stitching in China, followed by quality assurance and packaging in Hong Kong. The product might then be shipped to the United States for delivery to a retailer such as The Limited or Abercrombie & Fitch, to whom credit risk matching, market research, and even design services might also be supplied.

Branded marketers represented another, newer breed of middlemen. Such intermediaries outsourced the production of apparel that they sold under their own brand names. Liz Claiborne, founded in 1976, was a good example.[5] Its eponymous founder identified a growing customer group (professional women) and sold them branded apparel designed to fit evolving workplace norms and their actual shapes (which she famously described as "pear-shaped"), that was presented in collections within which they could mix and match in upscale department stores. Production was outsourced from the outset, first domestically, and then, in the course of the 1980s, increasingly to Asia, with a heavy reliance on OEM or "full-package" suppliers, and was organized in terms of six seasons rather than four to let stores buy merchandise in smaller batches. But after a performance decline in the first half of the 1990s, Liz Claiborne restructured its supply chain to reduce the number of suppliers and inventory levels, shifted half of production back to the Western Hemisphere to compress cycle times, and simultaneously cut the number of seasonal collections from six to four so as to allow some reorders of merchandise that was selling well in the third month of a season.

Exhibit 3 Landed Costs of a Large Men's Shirt in Spain: Illustrative (in Euros €)

Manufactured in Spain		Manufactured in Asia	
Fabric Costs	17.20	Purchasing costs	25.32
Other Input Costs	13.25	Transportation costs	1.49
Labor Costs	11.79	Rehandling costs	2.28
Total	42.24	Total	29.09

Source: Confidential industry sources.

Other types of cross-border intermediaries could be seen as forward or backward integrators rather than as pure middlemen. Branded manufacturers, like branded marketers, sold products under their own brand names through one or more independent retail channels and owned some manufacturing as well. Some branded manufacturers were based in developed countries (e.g., U.S.-based VF Corporation, which sold jeans produced in its factories overseas under the Lee and Wrangler brands) and others in developing countries (e.g., Giordano, Hong Kong's leading apparel brand). And in terms of backward integration, many retailers internalized at least some cross-border functions by setting up their own overseas buying offices, although they continued to rely on specialized intermediaries for others (e.g., import documentation and clearances).

Retailing   Irrespective of whether they internalized most cross-border functions, retailers played a dominant role in shaping imports into developed countries: thus, direct imports by them accounted for half of all apparel imports into West Europe.[6] The increasing concentration of apparel retailing in major markets was thought to be one of the key drivers of increased trade. In the United States, the top five chains came to account for more than half of apparel sales in the course of the 1990s, and concentration levels elsewhere, while lower, also rose during the decade. Increased concentration was generally accompanied by displacement of independent stores by retail chains, a trend that had also helped increase average store size over time. By the late 1990s, chains accounted for about 85% of total retail sales in the United States, about 70% in West Europe, between one-third to one-half in Latin America, East Asia, and East Europe, and less than 10% in large but poor markets such as China and India.[7]

Larger apparel retailers had also played the leading role in promoting quick response (QR), a set of policies and practices targeted at improving coordination between retailing and manufacturing so as to increase the speed and flexibility of responses to market shifts, that began to diffuse in apparel and textiles in the second half of the 1980s.[8] QR required changes that spanned functional, geographic, and organizational boundaries but could help retailers reduce forecast errors and inventory risks by planning assortments closer to the selling season, probing the market, placing smaller initial orders and reordering more frequently, and so on. QR had led to significant compression of cycle times (see Exhibit 4), enabled by improvements in information technology and encouraged by shorter fashion cycles and deeper markdowns, particularly in women's wear.

Retailing activities themselves remained quite local: the top 10 retailers worldwide operated in an average of 10 countries in 2000—compared with top averages of 135 countries in pharmaceuticals, 73 in petroleum, 44 in automobiles, and 33 in electronics—and derived less than 15% of their total sales from outside their home markets.[9] Against this baseline, apparel retailing was relatively globalized, particularly the fashion segment. Apparel retailing chains from Europe had been the most successful at cross-border expansion, although the U.S. market remained a major challenge. Their success probably reflected the European design roots of apparel, somewhat akin to U.S.-based fast food chains' international dominance, and the gravitational pull of the large U.S. market for U.S.-based retailers. Thus, The Gap, based on its sales at home in the United States, dwarfed H&M and Inditex combined. The latter two companies were perhaps the most pan-European apparel retailers but had yet to achieve market shares of more than 2%–3% in more than two or three major countries.

Markets and Customers   In 2000, retail spending on clothing or apparel reached approximately €900 billion worldwide. According to one set of estimates, (West) Europe accounted for 34% of the total market, the United States for 29%, and Asia for 23%.[10] Differences in market size reflected significant differences in per capita spending on apparel as well as in population levels. Per capita spending on apparel tended to grow less proportionately with increases in per capita income, so that its share of expenditures typically decreased as income increased. Per capita spending was also affected by price levels, which were influenced by variations in per capita income, in costs, and in the intensity of competition (given that competition continued to be localized to a significant extent).

There was also significant local variation in customers' attributes and preferences, even within a region or a country. Just within West Europe, for instance, one study concluded that the British sought out stores based on social affinity, that the French focused on variety/quality, and

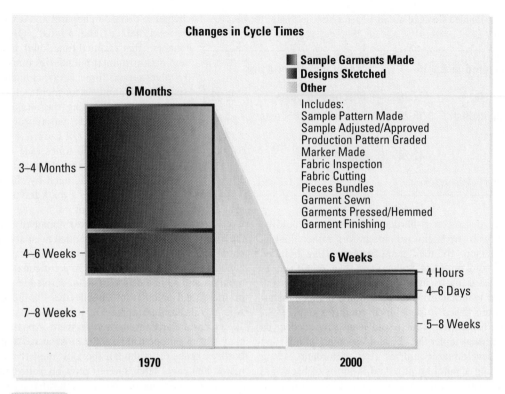

Changes in Cycle Times

Exhibit 4   Cycle Time Compression through Quick Response
Source: Inditex.

that Germans were more price-sensitive.[11] Relatedly, the French and the Italians were considered more fashion-forward than the Germans or the British. Spaniards were exceptional in buying apparel only seven times a year, compared with a European average of nine times a year, and higher-than-average levels for the Italians and French, among others.[12] Differences between regions were even greater than within regions: Japan, while generally traditional, also had a teenage market segment that was considered the trendiest in the world on many measures, and the U.S. market was, from the perspective of many European retailers, significantly less trendy except in a few, generally coastal pockets. There did, however, seem to be more cross-border homogeneity within the fashion segment. Popular fashion, in particular, had become less of a hand-me-down from high-end designers. It now seemed to move much more quickly as people, especially young adults and teenagers, with ever richer communication links reacted to global and local trends, including other elements of popular culture (e.g., desperately seeking the skirt worn by the rock star at her last concert).

Attempts had also been made to identify the strategic implications of the changing structure of the global apparel chain that were discussed above. Some reduced to "get big fast"; others, however, were more sophisticated. Thus, an article by three McKinsey consultants identified five ways for retailers to expand across borders: choosing a "sliver" of value instead of competing across the entire value chain; emphasizing partnering; investing in brands; minimizing (tangible) investments; and arbitraging international factor price differences.[13] But Inditex, particularly its Zara chain, supplied a reminder that strategic imperatives depended on how a retailer sought to create and sustain a competitive advantage through its cross-border activities.

Key International Competitors

While Inditex competed with local retailers in most of its markets, analysts considered its three closest comparable competitors to be The Gap, H&M, and Benetton. All three had narrower vertical scope than Zara, which owned much of its production and most of its stores. The Gap and H&M, which were the two largest specialist apparel retailers in the world, ahead of Inditex, owned most of their stores but outsourced all production. Benetton, in contrast, had invested relatively heavily in production, but licensees ran its stores. The three competitors were also positioned differently in product space from Inditex's

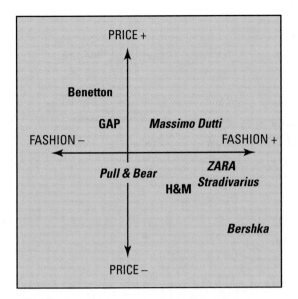

Exhibit 5   A Product Market Positioning Map

Source: Adapted from Morgan Stanley Dean Witter. 1998. Inditex.

Note: Zara, Massimo Dutti, Pull & Bear, Bershka, and Stradivarius were separate Inditex chains, as described in the "Inditex: Structure" section within the main case text.

chains (see Exhibit 5 for a positioning map and Exhibit 6 for financial and other comparisons).[14]

The Gap   The Gap, based in San Francisco, had been founded in 1969 and had achieved stellar growth and profitability through the 1980s and much of the 1990s with what was described as an "unpretentious real clothes stance," comprising extensive collections of T-shirts and jeans as well as "smart casual" work clothes. The Gap's production was internationalized—more than 90% of it was outsourced from outside the United States—but its store operations were U.S.-centric. International expansion of the store network had begun in 1987, but its pace had been limited by difficulties finding locations in markets such as the United Kingdom, Germany, and Japan (which accounted for 86% of store locations outside North America), adapting to different customer sizes and preferences, and dealing with what were, in many cases, more severe pricing pressures than in the United States. And by the end of the 1990s, supply chains that were still too long, market saturation, imbalances, and inconsistencies across the company's three store chains—Banana Republic, The Gap, and Old Navy—and the lack of a clear fashion positioning had started to take a toll even in the U.S. market. A failed attempt to reposition to a more fashion-driven assortment—a major fashion miss—triggered significant write-downs, a loss for calendar year 2001, a massive decline in the Gap's stock price, and the departure, in May 2002, of its long-time CEO, Millard Drexler.

Hennes and Mauritz   Hennes and Mauritz (H&M), founded as Hennes (hers) in Sweden in 1947, was another high-performing apparel retailer. While it was considered Inditex's closest competitor, there were a number of key differences. H&M outsourced all its production, half of it to European suppliers, implying lead times that were good by industry standards but significantly longer than Zara's. H&M had been quicker to internationalize, generating more than half its sales outside its home country by 1990, 10 years earlier than Inditex. It also had adopted a more focused approach, entering one country at a time—with an emphasis on northern Europe—and building a distribution center in each one. Unlike Inditex, H&M operated a single format, although it marketed its clothes under numerous labels or concepts to different customer segments. H&M also tended to have slightly lower prices than Zara (which it displayed prominently in store windows and on shelving), engaged in extensive advertising like most other apparel retailers, employed fewer designers (40% as many as Zara, although Zara was still 40% smaller), and refurbished its stores less frequently. H&M's price-earnings ratio, while still high, had declined to levels comparable to Inditex's because of a fashion miss that had reduced net income by 17% in 2000 and a recent announcement that an aggressive effort to expand in the United States was being slowed down.

Benetton   Benetton, incorporated in 1965 in Italy, emphasized brightly colored knitwear. It achieved prominence in the 1980s and 1990s for its controversial advertising and as a network organization that outsourced activities that were labor-intensive or scale-insensitive to subcontractors. But Benetton actually invested relatively heavily in controlling other production activities. Where it was investment-light was downstream: it sold its production through licensees, often entrepreneurs with no more than $100,000 to invest in a small outlet that could sell only Benetton products. While Benetton was fast at certain activities such as dyeing, it looked for its retailing business to provide significant forward order books for its manufacturing business and was therefore geared to operate on lead times of several months. Benetton's format appeared to hit saturation by the early 1990s and profitability continued to slide through the rest of the 1990s. In response, it embarked on a strategy of narrowing product lines, further consolidating key production activities by grouping them into "production poles" in a number of different regions, and expanding or focusing existing outlets while starting a program to set up much larger company-owned outlets in big cities. About 100 such Benetton megastores were in operation by the end of 2001, compared with a network of approximately 5,500 smaller, third-party–owned stores.

Inditex

Inditex (Industria de Diseño Textil) was a global specialty retailer that designed, manufactured, and sold apparel, footwear, and accessories for women, men, and children through Zara and five other chains around the world. At the

Exhibit 6   Key Competitors and Inditex, 2001

	Gap	H&M	Benetton	Inditex
Operating Results (€ Millions)				
Net Operating Revenues	15,559	4,269	2,098	3,250
Cost of Goods Sold	10,904	2,064	1,189	1,563
Gross Margin	4,656	2,204	909	1,687
Operating Expenses	4,276	1,615	624	982
Operating Profits	379	589	286	704
Non-operating Expenses	108	−28	43	209
Pre-tax Income	272	617	243	495
Income Tax	280	206	92	150
Minority Interests	0	0	2	5
Net Income	−9	410*	148	340
Financial Position (€ Millions, except where noted otherwise)				
Current Assets	3,436	1,468	1,558	854
Property, Plant, and Equipment	4,695	661	720	1,228
Other Noncurrent Assets	435	54	543	523
Total Assets	8,566	2,183	2,821	2,605
Current Liabilities	2,320	432	956	834
Noncurrent Liabilities	2,850	101	625	285
Total Liabilities	5,170	532*	1,580	1,119
Equity—Book Value	3,396	1,650	1,241	1,486
Equity—Market Value[a]	12,687	15,564	2,605	13,433
One Year Change in Market Value (%)[b]	−60%	8%	−20%	47%
Other Statistics				
Employees	166,000	22,944	6,672	26,724
Number of Countries of Operation	6	14	120	39
Sales in Home Country (%)	87%	12%	44%	46%
Sales in Home Continent (%)	NA	96%	78%	77%
Number of Store Locations[c]	3,097	771	5,456	1,284
Stores in Home Country (%)	87%	15%	40%	60%
Stores in Home Continent (%)	92%	96%	80%	86%
Average Store Size (sq. meter)	632	1,201	279	514

Sources: Compiled from Annual reports; analyst reports; Bloomberg; Standard & Poor's Research Insight; J. P. Morgan, "Hennes & Mauritz," Company Report, February 10, 1999, p. 89, Compustat.

*Totals off due to rounding.

[a]On May 22, 2002.

[b]In-home currency.

[c]Includes franchised stores.

end of the 2001 fiscal year, it operated 1,284 stores around the world, including Spain, with a selling area of 659,400 square meters. The 515 stores located outside Spain generated 54% of the total revenues of €3,250 million. Inditex employed 26,724 people, 10,919 of them outside Spain. Their average age was 26 years and the overwhelming majority were women (78%).

Just over 80% of Inditex's employees were engaged in retail sales in stores, 8.5% were employed in manufactur-

ing, and design, logistics, distribution, and headquarters activities accounted for the remainder. Capital expenditures had recently been split roughly 80% on new-store openings, 10% on refurbishing, and 10% on logistics/maintenance, roughly in line with capital employed. Operating working capital was negative at most year-ends, although it typically registered higher levels at other times of the year given the seasonality of apparel sales (see Exhibit 7 for these and other historical financial data).

Exhibit 7   Inditex Historical Financials (millions of euros)

Year	2001	2000	1999	1998	1997	1996
Net Operating Revenues	3,249.8	2,614.7	2,035.1	1,614.7	1,217.4	1,008.5
Cost of Goods Sold	1,563.1	1,277.0	988.4	799.9	618.3	521.0
Gross Margin	1,686.7	1,337.7	1,046.7	814.8	599.1	487.5
Operating Expenses	982.3	816.2	636.2	489.2	345.5	285.4
Operating Profits	704.4	521.5	410.5	325.6	253.6	202.1
Non-Operating Expenses	209.3	152.7	118.1	96.7		
Pre-Tax Income	495.1	368.8	292.4	228.9		
Income Tax	149.9	106.9	86.2	76.1		
Minority Interest	4.8	2.7	1.5	−0.2		
Net Income	340.4	259.2	204.7	153.0	117.4	72.7
Net Margin	**10.47%**	**9.91%**	**10.06%**	**9.48%**	**9.64%**	**7.21%**
Inventories	353.8	245.1	188.5	157.7		
Accounts Receivable	184.2	145.2	121.6	75		
Cash and Cash Equivalents	315.7	210	171.8	158.8		
Total Current Assets	853.7	600.3	481.9	391.5	274.0	190.3
Property, Plant, and Equipment	1,336.8	1,339.5	1,127.4	880.4	635.7	
Other Non-Current Assets	414.5	167.8	163.6	54.4	67.5	
Total Assets	2,605	2,107.6	1,772.9	1,326.3	977.2	820.3
Asset Turnover	**1.25**	**1.24**	**1.15**	**1.2**	**1.2**	**1.2**
ROA	**13.07%**	**12.30%**	**11.54%**	**11.54%**	**12.01%**	**8.86%**
Accounts Payable	426.3	323.0	276.1	215.6	131.4	
Other Current Liabilities	407.9	347.3	275.6	229.1	141.5	
Total Current Liabilities	834.2	670.3	551.7	444.7	272.9	234.1
Non-Current Liabilities	284.5	1,437.7	1,221.3	881.6	704.3	586.2
Total Liabilities	1,118.7	2,108	1,773	1,326.3	977.2	820.3
Equity	1,486.2	1,170.9	893.2	673.4	529.9	414.9
Leverage	**1.75**	**1.80**	**1.98**	**1.97**	**1.84**	**1.98**
ROE	**22.9%**	**22.1%**	**22.9%**	**22.7%**	**25.0%**	**20.0%**

Source: Inditex.

Plans for 2002 called for continued tight management of working capital and €510–560 million of capital expenditures, mostly on opening 230–275 new stores (across all chains). The operating economics for 2001 had involved gross margins of 52%, operating expenses equivalent to 30% of revenues, of which one-half were related to personnel, and operating margins of 22%. Net margins on sales revenue were about one-half the size of operating margins, with depreciation of fixed assets (€158 million) and taxes (€150 million) helping reduce operating profits of €704 million to net income of €340 million. Despite high margins, top management stressed that Inditex was *not* the most profitable apparel retailer in the world: that stability was perhaps a more distinctive feature.

The rest of this section describes the pluses and minuses of Inditex's home base, its foundation by Amancio Ortega and subsequent growth, the structure of the group in early 2002, and recent changes in its governance. (A timeline, Exhibit 8, summarizes key events over this period chronologically.)

Exhibit 8   Inditex Timeline

Year	No. of Stores	Event
1963		• Establishment of Confecciones Gao, S.A. Beginning of the company's activities
1975	2	• Opening of 1st Zara store in La Coruña
1976	2	• Establishment of Goasam as the owner of the Zara chain stores
		• Purchase of first computer
1985	37	• Reorganization of group structure with Inditex at the apex
1988	71	• Formation of Zara B.V. in the Netherlands as holding company for international activities
1989	88	• International rollout begins with opening of a Zara store in Portugal
1990	105	• Opening of fully automated 130,000 square meter central warehouse
		• Joint venture with Toyota (Japan) introduces just-in-time system at one of the factories
1991	218	• Establishment of commercial office in Bejing to handle purchase of supplies in Asia
		• Diversification into new segments
		• Acquisition of 65% of Massimo Dutti
		• Implementation of telecommunications system between headquarters and the supply, production, and sales centers
		• Launch of the Pull & Bear chain
1993	369	• Preparation/implementation of expansion plan for Zara in the French market
1995	508	• Acquisition of all of the share capital of Massimo Dutti
1996	541	• Expansion of central warehouse to cope with the increase in the number of points of sale
1998	748	• Creation of the Amancio Ortega Foundation
		• Alliance with Otto Versand to enter the German market
		• Launch of the Bershka chain, targeting the younger female market
1999	922	• Acquisition of Stradivarius makes it the fifth chain of the Group
2000	1,080	• Opening of new Inditex headquarters complex in Arteixo, near La Coruña
2001	1,284	• Initial public offering of 26% of Inditex's shares
		• Launch of the Oysho lingerie chain
2002		• Alliance with Percassi results in opening of first Italian store

Source: Inditex.

Exhibit 9   Map of Spain

Source: Adapted from *The encyclopedia of world geography.* 1996. New York: Barnes and Noble.

Home Base   Inditex was headquartered in and had most of its upstream assets concentrated in the region of Galicia on the northwestern tip of Spain (see Exhibit 9). Galicia, the third-poorest of Spain's 17 autonomous regions, reported an unemployment rate in 2001 of 17% (compared with a national average of 14%), had poor communication links with the rest of the country, and was still heavily dependent on agriculture and fishing. In apparel, however, Galicia had a tradition that dated back to the Renaissance, when Galicians were tailors to the aristocracy, and was home to thousands of small apparel workshops. Galicia lacked a strong base upstream in textiles, sophisticated local demand, technical institutes and universities to facilitate specialized initiatives and training, and an industry association to underpin these or other potentially cooperative activities. And even more critical for Inditex, as CEO José Maria Castellano put it, was that "Galicia is in the corner of Europe from the perspective of transport costs, which are very important to us given our business model."

Some of the same characterizations applied at a national level, to Inditex's home base of Spain compared, for example, to Italy. Spanish consumers demanded low prices but were not considered as discriminating or fashion-conscious as Italian buyers—although Spain had advanced rapidly in this regard, as well as many others, since the death of long-time dictator General Francisco Franco in 1975 and its subsequent opening up to the world. On the supply side, Spain was a relatively productive apparel manufacturing base by European standards (see Exhibit 2), but lacked Italy's fully developed thread-to-apparel vertical chain (including machinery suppliers), its dominance of high quality fabrics (such as wool suiting), and its international fashion image. For this reason, and because rivalry among them had historically been fierce, Italian apparel chains had been quick to move overseas. But Spanish apparel retailers had followed suit in the 1990s, and not just Inditex. Mango, a smaller Spanish chain that relied on a franchising model with returnable merchandise, was already present in more countries around the world than Inditex.

Early History   Amancio Ortega Gaona, Inditex's founder, was still its president and principal shareholder in early 2002 and still came in to work every day, where he could often be seen lunching in the company cafeteria with employees. Ortega was otherwise extremely reclusive but reports indicated that he had been born in 1936 to a railroad worker and a housemaid, and that his first job had been as an errand boy for a La Coruña shirtmaker in 1949. As he moved up through that company, he apparently developed a heightened awareness of how costs piled up through the apparel chain. In 1963, he founded Confecciones Goa (his acronym reversed) to manufacture products such as housecoats. Eventually, Ortega's quest to improve the manufacturing/retailing interface led him to integrate forward into retailing: the first Zara store was opened on an up-market shopping street in La Coruña, in 1975. From the beginning, Zara positioned itself as a store selling "medium quality fashion clothing at affordable prices." By the end of the 1970s, there were half-a-dozen Zara stores in Galician cities.

Ortega, who was said to be a gadgeteer by inclination, bought his first computer in 1976. At the time, his operations encompassed just four factories and two stores but were already making it clear that what (other) buyers ordered from his factories was different from what his store data told him customers wanted. Ortega's interest in information technology also brought him into contact with Jose Maria Castellano, who had a doctorate in business economics and professional experience in information technology, sales, and finance. In 1985, Castellano joined Inditex as the deputy chairman of its board of directors, although he continued to teach accounting part-time at the local university.

Under Ortega and Castellano, Zara continued to roll out nationally through the 1980s by expanding into adjoining markets. It reached the Spanish capital, Madrid, in 1985 and, by the end of the decade, operated stores in all Spanish cities with more than 100,000 inhabitants. Zara then began to open stores outside Spain and to make quantum investments in manufacturing logistics and IT. The early 1990s was also when Inditex started to add other retail chains to its network through acquisition as well as internal development.

Structure   At the beginning of 2002, Inditex operated six separate chains: Zara, Massimo Dutti, Pull & Bear, Bershka, Stradivarius, and Oysho (as illustrated in Exhibit 10). These chains' retailing subsidiaries in Spain and abroad were grouped into 60 companies, or about one-half the total number of companies whose results were consolidated into Inditex at the group level; the remainder were involved in textile purchasing and preparation, manufacturing, logistics, real estate, finance, and so forth. Given internal transfer pricing and other policies, retailing (as opposed to manufacturing and other activities) generated 82% of Inditex's net income, which was roughly in line with its share of the group's total capital investment and employment.

The six retailing chains were organized as separate business units within an overall structure that also included six business support areas (raw materials, manufacturing plants, logistics, real estate, expansion, and international) and nine corporate departments or areas of responsibility (see Exhibit 11). In effect, each of the chains operated independently and was responsible for its own strategy, product design, sourcing and manufacturing, distribution, image, personnel and financial results, while group management set the strategic vision of the group, coordinated the activities of the concepts, and provided them with administrative and various other services.

Coordination across the chains had deliberately been limited but had increased a bit, particularly in the areas of real estate and expansion, as Inditex had recently moved toward opening up some multichain locations. More broadly, the experience of the older, better-established chains, particularly Zara, had helped accelerate the expansion of the newer ones. Thus, Oysho, the lingerie chain, drew 75% of its human resources from the other chains and had come to operate stores in seven European markets within six months of its launch in September 2001.

Top corporate managers, who were all Spanish, saw the role of the corporate center as a "strategic controller" involved in setting the corporate strategy, approving the business strategies of the individual chains, and controlling their performance rather than as an "operator" functionally involved in running the chains. Their ability to control performance down to the local store level was based on standardized reporting systems that focused on (like-for-like) sales growth, earnings before interest and taxes (EBIT) margin, and return on capital employed. CEO José Maria Castellano looked at key performance metrics once a week, while one of his direct reports monitored them on a daily basis.

Recent Governance Changes   Inditex's initial public offering (IPO) in May 2001 had sold 26% of the company's shares to the public, but founder Amancio Ortega retained a stake of more than 60%. Since Inditex generated substantial free cash flow (some of which had been used to make portfolio investments in other lines of business), the IPO was thought to be motivated primarily by Ortega's desire to put the company on a firm footing for his eventual retirement and the transition to a new top management team.

Second, Inditex also made progress in 2001 toward implementing a social strategy involving dialogue with employees, suppliers, subcontractors, non-governmental organizations, and local communities. Immediate initiatives included approval of an internal code of conduct, the establishment of a corporate responsibility department, social audits of supplier and external workshops in Spain and Morocco, pilot developmental projects in Venezuela and Guatemala, and the joining, in August 2001, of the Global Compact, an initiative headed by Kofi Annan, Secretary General of the United Nations, that aimed to improve global companies' social performance.

Zara

- 500 stores in 30 countries
- Created in 1975
- Continuous innovation based on customer desires
- For women, men, and youth, from infants to age 45
- Web link: www.zara.com

Massimo Dutti

- 200 stores in 12 countries
- Acquired by Inditex in 1995
- Fashion variety, from sophisticated to sporty
- For men & women, age 25-45
- Web link: www.massimodutti.com

Bershka

- Founded by Inditex in 1998
- 170 stores in 8 countries
- Trendy clothing for a younger female target audience, age 13-23
- Stores are designed as a social hot-spot, highlighting fashion, music, and street art
- Web link: www.bershka.com

Pull and Bear

- 225 stores in 9 countries
- Founded by Inditex in 1991
- Casual clothing at affordable prices
- For men and women, ages 14-28
- Web link: www.pullbear.com

Stradivarius

- Acquired in 1999
- 100 stores in 7 countries
- Youthful urban fashion
- For young men & women, ages 15-25
- Web link: www.e-stradivarius.com

Oysho

- Inditex's newest chain
- 25 stores in 6 European countries
- Latest trends in lingerie
- Quality products at reasonable prices
- Web link: www.oysho.com

Exhibit 10   Inditex Chains
Source: Inditex.

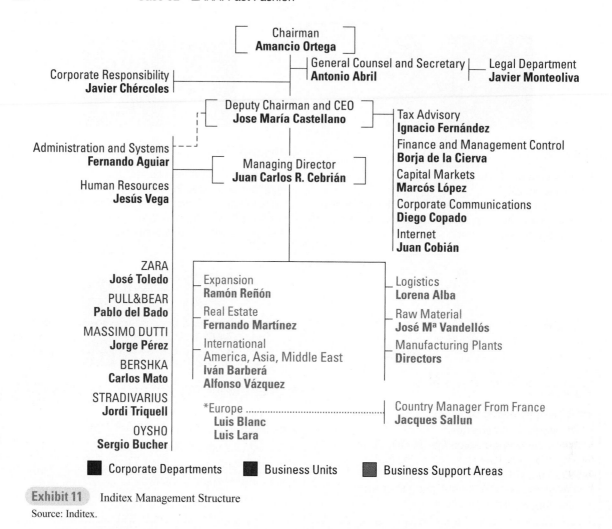

Exhibit 11   Inditex Management Structure
Source: Inditex.

Zara's Business System

Zara was the largest and most internationalized of Inditex's chains. At the end of 2001, it operated 507 stores around the world, including Spain (40% of the total number for Inditex), with 488,400 square meters of selling area (74% of the total) and employing €1,050 million of the company's capital (72% of the total), of which the store network accounted for about 80%. During the course of fiscal year 2001, it had posted EBIT of €441 million (85% of the total) on sales of €2,477 million (76% of the total). While Zara's share of the group's total sales was expected to drop by two or three percentage points each year, it would continue to be the principal driver of the group's growth for some time to come, and to play the lead role in increasing the share of Inditex's sales accounted for by international operations.

Zara completed its rollout in the Spanish market by 1990, and began to move overseas around that time. It also began to make major investments in manufacturing logistics and IT, including establishment of a just-in-time

manufacturing system, a 130,000 square meter warehouse close to corporate headquarters in Arteixo, outside La Coruña, and an advanced telecommunications system to connect headquarters and supply, production, and sales locations. Development of logistical, retail, financial, merchandising, and other information systems continued through the 1990s, much of it taking place internally. For example, while there were many logistical packages on the market, Zara's unusual requirements mandated internal development.

The business system that had resulted (see Exhibit 12) was particularly distinctive in that Zara manufactured its most fashion-sensitive products internally. (The other Inditex chains were too small to justify such investments but generally did emphasize reliance on suppliers in Europe rather than farther away.) Zara's designers continuously tracked customer preferences and placed orders with internal and external suppliers. About 11,000 distinct items were produced during the year—several hundred thousand

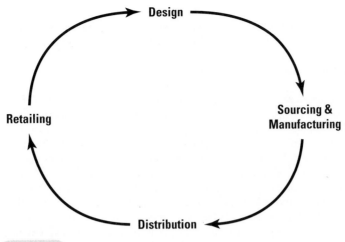

Exhibit 12   Zara's Business System
Source: Casewriter.

SKUs given variations in color, fabric, and sizes—compared with 2,000–4,000 items for key competitors. Production took place in small batches, with vertical integration into the manufacture of the most time-sensitive items. Both internal and external production flowed into Zara's central distribution center. Products were shipped directly from the central distribution center to well-located, attractive stores twice a week, eliminating the need for warehouses and keeping inventories low. Vertical integration helped reduce the "bullwhip effect": the tendency for fluctuations in final demand to get amplified as they were transmitted back up the supply chain. Even more importantly, Zara was able to originate a design and have finished goods in stores within four to five weeks in the case of entirely new designs and two weeks for modifications (or restocking) of existing products. In contrast, the traditional industry model might involve cycles of up to six months for design and three months for manufacturing.

The short cycle time reduced working capital intensity and facilitated continuous manufacture of new merchandise, even during the biannual sales periods, letting Zara commit to the bulk of its product line for a season much later than its key competitors (see Exhibit 13). Thus, Zara undertook 35% of product design and purchases of raw

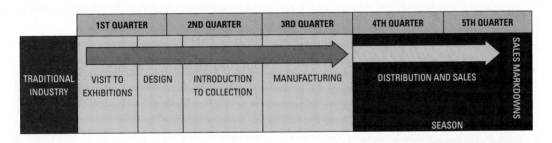

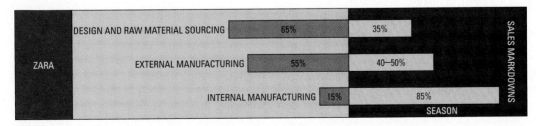

Exhibit 13   Product Precommitments: Zara vs. Traditional Industry
Source: Inditex.

material, 40%–50% of the purchases of finished products from external suppliers, and 85% of the in-house production *after* the season had started, compared with only 0%–20% in the case of traditional retailers.

But while quick-response was critical to Zara's superior performance, the connection between the two was not automatic. World Co. of Japan, perhaps the only other apparel retailer in the world with comparable cycle times, provided a counterexample. It too had integrated backward into (domestic) manufacturing, and had achieved gross margins comparable to Zara's.[15] But World Co.'s net margins remained stuck at around 2% of sales, compared with 10% in the case of Zara, largely because of selling, general, and administrative expenses that swallowed up about 40% of its revenues, versus about 20% for Zara. Different choices about how to exploit quick-response capabilities define these differences in performance. World Co. served the relatively depressed Japanese market, appeared to place less emphasis on design, had an unprofitable contract manufacturing arm, supported about 40 brands with distinct identities for use exclusively within its own store network (smaller than Zara's), and operated relatively small stores, averaging less than 100 square meters of selling area. Zara had made rather different choices along these and other dimensions.

Design   Each of Zara's three product lines—for women, men, and children—had a creative team consisting of designers, sourcing specialists, and product development personnel. The creative teams simultaneously worked on products for the current season by creating constant variation, expanding upon successful product items and continuing in-season development, and on the following season and year by selecting the fabrics and product mix that would be the basis for an initial collection. Top management stressed that instead of being run by maestros, the design organization was very flat and focused on careful interpretation of catwalk trends suitable for the mass-market.

Zara created two basic collections each year that were phased in through the fall/winter and spring/summer seasons, starting in July and January respectively. Zara's designers attended trade fairs and ready-to-wear fashion shows in Paris, New York, London, and Milan, referred to catalogs of luxury brand collections, and worked with store managers to begin to develop the initial sketches for a collection close to nine months before the start of a season. Designers then selected fabrics and other complements and, simultaneously, the relative price at which a product would be sold was determined, guiding further development of samples. Samples were prepared and presented to the sourcing and product development personnel, and the selection process began. As the collection came together, the sourcing personnel identified production requirements, whether an item

would be insourced or outsourced, and a timeline to ensure that the initial collection arrived in stores at the start of the selling season.

The process of adapting to trends and differences across markets was more evolutionary, ran through most of the selling season, and placed greater reliance on high-frequency information. Frequent conversations with store managers were as important in this regard as the sales data captured by their IT system. Other sources of information included industry publications, TV, Internet, and film content, trend-spotters who focused on venues such as university campuses and discotheques, and even Zara's young, fashion-conscious staff. Product development personnel played a key role in linking the designers and the stores, and were often from the country in which the stores they dealt with were located. On average, several dozen items were designed each day, but only slightly more than one-third of them actually went into production. Time permitting, very limited volumes of new items were prepared and presented in certain key stores and produced on a larger scale only if consumer reactions were unambiguously positive. As a result, failure rates on new products were supposed to be only 1%, compared with an average of 10% for the sector. Learning by doing was considered very important in achieving such favorable outcomes.

Overall, then, the responsibilities of Zara's design teams transcended design, narrowly defined. They also continuously tracked customer preferences and used information about sales potential based, among other things, on a consumption information system that supported detailed analysis of product life cycles, to transmit repeat orders and new designs to internal and external suppliers. The design teams thereby bridged merchandising and the back-end of the production process. These functions were generally organized under separate management teams at other apparel retailers.

Sourcing & Manufacturing   Zara sourced fabric, other inputs, and finished products from external suppliers with the help of purchasing offices in Barcelona and Hong Kong, as well as the sourcing personnel at headquarters. While Europe had historically dominated Zara's sourcing patterns, the recent establishment of three companies in Hong Kong for purposes of purchasing as well as trend-spotting suggested that sourcing from the Far East, particularly China, might expand substantially.

About one-half of the fabric purchased was "gray" (undyed) to facilitate in-season updating with maximum flexibility. Much of this volume was funneled through Comditel, a 100%-owned subsidiary of Inditex, that dealt with more than 200 external suppliers of fabric and other raw materials. Comditel managed the dyeing, patterning, and finishing of gray fabric for all of Inditex's chains, not just Zara, and supplied finished fabric to external as well as in-house manufacturers. This process, reminiscent of Benetton's, meant that it took only one week to finish fabric.

Further down the value chain, about 40% of finished garments were manufactured internally, and of the remainder, approximately two-thirds of the items were sourced from Europe and North Africa and one-third from Asia. The most fashionable items tended to be the riskiest and therefore were the ones that were produced in small lots internally or under contract by suppliers who were located close by, and reordered if they sold well. More basic items that were more price-sensitive than time-sensitive were particularly likely to be outsourced to Asia, since production in Europe was typically 15%–20% more expensive for Zara. About 20 suppliers accounted for 70% of all external purchases. While Zara had long-term ties with many of these suppliers, it minimized formal contractual commitments to them.

Internal manufacture was the primary responsibility of 20 fully owned factories, 18 of them located in and around Zara's headquarters in Arteixo. Room for growth was provided by vacant lots around the principal manufacturing complex and also north of La Coruña and in Barcelona. Zara's factories were heavily automated, specialized by garment type, and focused on the capital-intensive parts of the production process—pattern design and cutting—as well as on final finishing and inspection. Vertical integration into manufacturing had begun in 1980, and starting in 1990, significant investments had been made in installing a just-in-time system in these factories in cooperation with Toyota—one of the first experiments of its kind in Europe. As a result, employees had had to learn how to use new machines and work in multifunctional teams.

Even for the garments that were manufactured in-house, cut garments were sent out to about 450 workshops, located primarily in Galicia and across the border in northern Portugal, that performed the labor-intensive, scale-insensitive activity of sewing. These workshops were generally small operations, averaging about 20–30 employees, although a few employed more than 100 people apiece, that specialized by product type. As subcontractors, they generally had long-term relations with Zara, which accounted for most if not all of their production, provided them with technology, logistics, and financial support, and paid them prearranged rates per finished garment, carried out inspections onsite, and insisted that they comply with local tax and labor legislation.

The sewn garments were sent back from the workshops to Zara's manufacturing complex, where they were inspected, ironed, folded, bagged, and ticketed before being sent on to the adjoining distribution center.

Distribution   Like each of Inditex's chains, Zara had its own centralized distribution system. Zara's system consisted of an approximately 400,000 square meter facility located in Arteixo and much smaller satellite centers in Argentina, Brazil, and Mexico that consolidated shipments from Arteixo.

All of Zara's merchandise, from internal and external suppliers, passed through the distribution center in Arteixo, which operated on a dual-shift basis and featured a mobile tracking system that docked hanging garments in the appropriate barcoded area and carrousels capable of handling 45,000 folded garments per hour. As orders were received from hand-held computers in the stores (twice a week during regular periods, and thrice weekly during the sales season), they were checked in the distribution center and, if a particular item was in short supply, allocation decisions were made on the basis of historical sales levels and other considerations. Once an order had been approved, the warehouse issued the lists that were used to organize deliveries.

Lorena Alba, Inditex's director of logistics, regarded the warehouse as a place to move merchandise rather than to store it. According to her, "The vast majority of clothes are in here only a few hours," and none ever stayed at the distribution center for more than three days. Of course, the rapidly expanding store network demanded constant adjustment to the sequencing and size of deliveries as well as their routing. The most recent revamp had been in January 2002, when Zara had started to schedule shipments by time zone. In the early morning while European store managers were still taking stock, the distribution center packed and shipped orders to the Americas, the Middle East, and Asia; in the afternoon, it focused on the European stores. The distribution center generally ran at half its rated capacity but surges in demand, particularly during the start of the two selling seasons in January and July, boosted utilization rates and required the hiring of several hundred temporary workers to complement close to 1,000 permanent employees.

Shipments from the warehouse were made twice a week to each store via third-party delivery services, with shipments two days a week to one part of the store network and two days a week to the other. Approximately 75% of Zara's merchandise by weight was shipped by truck by a third-party delivery service to stores in Spain, Portugal, France, Belgium, the United Kingdom, and parts of Germany. The remaining 25% was shipped mainly by air via KLM and DHL from airports in Santiago de Compostela (a major pilgrimage center in Galicia) and Porto in Portugal. Products were typically delivered within 24–36 hours to stores located in Europe and within 24–48 hours to stores located outside Europe. Air shipment was more expensive, but not prohibitively so. Thus, one industry participant suggested that air freight from Spain to the Middle East might cost 3%–5% of FOB price (compared with 1.5% for sea freight) and, along with a 1.5% landing charge, a 1% finance charge, miscellaneous expenses and (generally) a 4% customs duty, bring the landed markup on FOB price to

12% or so. In the case of the United States, a 20%–25% landed markup seemed a better approximation because of tariffs of up to 12% as well as other added cost elements.

Despite Zara's historical success at scaling up its distribution system, observers speculated that the centralized logistics model might ultimately be subject to diseconomies of scale—that what worked well with 1,000 stores might not work with 2,000 stores. In an attempt to increase capacity, Zara was beginning construction of a second distribution center, at Zaragoza, northeast of Madrid. This second major distribution facility, to be started up in summer 2003, would add 120,000 square meters of warehouse space at a cost of €88 million close to the local airport and with direct access to the railway and road network as well.

Retailing Zara aimed to offer fresh assortments of designer-style garments and accessories—shoes, bags, scarves, jewelry and, more recently, toiletries and cosmetics—for relatively low prices in sophisticated stores in prime locations in order to draw masses of fashion-conscious repeat customers. Despite its tapered integration into manufacturing, Zara placed more emphasis on using backward vertical integration to be a very quick fashion follower than to achieve manufacturing efficiencies by building up significant forward order books for the upstream operations. Production runs were limited and inventories strictly controlled even if that meant leaving demand unsatisfied. Both Zara's merchandising and store operations helped reinforce these upstream policies.

Merchandising Zara's product merchandising policies emphasized broad, rapidly changing product lines, relatively high fashion content, and reasonable but not excessive physical quality: "clothes to be worn 10 times," some said. Product lines were segmented into women's, men's, and children's, with further segmentation of the women's line, considered the strongest, into three sets of offerings that varied in terms of their prices, fashion content, and age targets. Prices, which were determined centrally, were supposed to be lower than competitors' for comparable products in Zara's major markets, but percentage margins were expected to hold up not only because of the direct efficiencies associated with a shortened, vertically integrated supply chain but also because of significant reductions in advertising and markdown requirements.

Zara spent only 0.3% of its revenue on media advertising, compared with 3%–4% for most specialty retailers. Its advertising was generally limited to the start of the sales period at the end of the season, and the little that was undertaken did not create too strong a presence for the Zara brand or too specific an image of the "Zara Woman" or the "Zara Girl" (unlike the "Mango Girl" of Spanish competitor Mango). These choices reflected concerns about overexposure and lock-in as well as limits on spending. Nor did Zara exhibit its merchandise at the ready-to-wear fashion shows: its new items were first displayed in its stores. The Zara name had nevertheless developed considerable drawing power in its major markets. Thus by the mid-1990s, it had already become one of the three clothing brands of which customers were most aware in its home market of Spain, with particular strengths among women between ages of 18 and 34 from households with middle to middle-high income.

Zara's drawing power reflected the freshness of its offerings, the creation of sense of scarcity and an attractive ambience around them, and the positive word of mouth that resulted. Freshness was rooted in rapid product turnover, with new designs arriving in each twice-weekly shipment. Devout Zara shoppers even knew which days of the week delivery trucks came into stores, and shopped accordingly. About three-quarters of the merchandise on display was changed every three to four weeks, which also corresponded to the average time between visits given estimates that the average Zara shopper visited the chain 17 times a year, compared to an average figure of 3 to 4 times a year for competing chains and their customers. And attractive stores, outside and inside, also helped. Luis Blanc, one of Inditex's international directors, summarized some of these additional influences:

> We invest in prime locations. We place great care in the presentation of our storefronts. That is how we project our image. We want our clients to enter a beautiful store, where they are offered the latest fashions. But most important, we want our customers to understand that if they like something, they must buy it now, because it won't be in the shops the following week. It is all about creating a climate of scarcity and opportunity.[16]

For the customers who did walk in through the door, the rapid turnover obviously created a sense of "buy now because you won't see this item later." In addition, the sense of scarcity was reinforced by small shipments, display shelves that were sparsely stocked, limits of one month on how long individual items could be sold in the stores, and a degree of deliberate undersupply.

Of course, even though Zara tried to follow fashions instead of betting on them, it did make some design mistakes. These were relatively cheap to reverse since there was typically no more than two to three weeks of forward cover for any risky item. Items that were slow to sell were immediately apparent and were ruthlessly weeded out by store managers with incentives to do so. Returns to the distribution center were either shipped to and sold at other Zara stores or disposed of through a small, separate chain of close-out stores near the distribution center. The target was to minimize the inventories that had to be sold at marked down prices in Zara stores during the sales period that ended each season. Such markdowns had a significant impact on apparel retailers' revenue bases: in the United

States, for example, women's apparel stores averaged markdowns of 30%-plus of (potential) revenues in the mid-1990s.[17] Very rough estimates for West Europe indicated markdowns that were smaller but still very significant. Zara was estimated to generate 15%–20% of its sales at marked down prices, compared with 30%–40% for most of its European peers. Additionally, since Zara had to move less of its merchandise during such periods, the percentage markdowns on the items affected didn't have to be as large—perhaps only half as much as the 30% average for other European apparel retailers, according to Zara's management.

Store Operations   Zara's stores functioned as both the company's face to the world and as information sources. The stores were typically located in highly visible locations, often including the premier shopping streets in a local market (e.g., the Champs Elysées in Paris, Regent Street in London, and Fifth Avenue in New York) and up-scale shopping centers. Zara had initially purchased many of its store sites, particularly in Spain, but had preferred long-term leases (for 10 to 20 years) since the mid-1990s, except when purchase was necessary to secure access to a very attractive site. Inditex's balance sheet valued the property that it owned (mostly Zara stores) at about €400 million on the basis of historical costs, but some analysts estimated that the market value of these store properties might be four or five times as high.

Zara actively managed its portfolio of stores. Stores were occasionally relocated in response to the evolution of shopping districts and traffic patterns. More frequently, older, smaller stores might be relocated to and updated (and typically expanded) in new, more suitable sites. The average size of the stores had gradually gone up as Zara improved the breadth and strength of its customer pull. Thus, while the average size of Zara stores at the beginning of fiscal year 2001 was 910 square meters, the average size of the stores opened during the year was 1,376 square meters. In addition, Zara invested more heavily and more frequently than key competitors in refurbishing its store base, with older stores getting makeovers every three or four years.

Zara also relied on significant centralization of store window displays and interior presentations in using the stores to promote its market image. As the season progressed and product offerings evolved, ideas about consistent looks for windows and for interiors in terms of themes, color schemes, and product presentation were prototyped in model window and store areas in the headquarters building in Arteixo. These ideas were principally carried to the stores by regional teams of window dressers and interior coordinators who visited each store every three weeks. But some adaptation was permitted and even planned for in the look of a store. For example, while all

Zara in-store employees had to wear Zara clothes while working in the stores, the uniforms that the sales assistants were required to wear might vary across different Zara stores in the same city to reflect socio-economic differences in the neighborhoods in which they were located. Uniforms were selected twice a season by store managers from the current season's collection and submitted to headquarters for authorization.

The size, location, and type of Zara store affected the number of employees in it. The number of sales assistants in each store was fixed on the basis of variables such as sales volume and selling area. And the larger stores with the full complement of stores-within-stores—Women's, Men's, and Children's—typically had a manager for each section, with the head of the Women's section also serving as store manager. Personnel were selected by the store manager in consultation with the section manager concerned. Training was the responsibility of the section manager and was exclusively on-the-job. After the first 15 days, the trainee's suitability for the post was reviewed. Personnel assessment was, once again, the job of the store manager.

In addition to overseeing in-store personnel, store managers decided which merchandise to order and which to discontinue and also transmitted customer data and their own sense of inflection points to Zara's design teams. In particular, they provided the creative teams with a sense of latent demand for new products that could not be captured through an automated sales tracking system. The availability of store managers capable of handling these responsibilities was, according to CEO Castellano, the single most important constraint on the rate of store additions. Zara promoted approximately 90% of its store managers from within and had generally experienced low store manager turnover. Once an employee was selected for promotion, his or her store, together with the human resources department, developed a comprehensive training program that included training at other stores and a two-week training program, with specialized staff, at Zara's headquarters. Such off-site training fulfilled important socialization goals as well, and was followed up by periodic supplemental training.

Store managers received a fixed salary plus variable compensation based primarily on their store's performance, with the variable component representing up to one-half of the total, which made their compensation very incentive-intensive. Since prices were fixed centrally, the store managers' energies were primarily focused on volume and mix. Top management tried to make each store manager feel as if she were running a small business. To this end, clear cost, profit, and growth targets for each store were set, as were regular reporting requirements—with stores' volume metrics being tracked particularly closely at the top of the (relatively flat) managerial hierarchy.

Zara's International Expansion

At the end of 2001, Zara was by far the most international-ized as well as the largest of Inditex's chains. Zara operated 282 stores in 32 countries outside Spain (55% of the inter-national total for Inditex) and had posted international sales of €1,506 million (86% of Inditex's international sales) during the course of the year. Of its international stores, 186 were located in Europe, 35 in North America, 29 in South America, 27 in the Middle East, and 5 in Japan. Overall, in-ternational operations accounted for 56% of Zara's stores and 61% of its sales in 2001, and had been steadily increas-ing their shares of those totals. The profitability of Zara's operations was not disaggregated geographically but, ac-cording to top management, was roughly the same in (the rest of) Europe and the Americas as in Spain. Approxi-mately 80% of the new Zara stores slated to be opened in 2002 were expected to be outside Spain, and Inditex even cited the weight of Zara in the group's total selling area as the principal reason Inditex's sales were increasingly inter-national. But over a longer time frame, Zara faced several important issues regarding its international expansion.

Market Selection   Zara's international expansion be-gan in 1988 with the opening of a store in Oporto in north-ern Portugal. In 1989, it opened its first store in New York and in 1990, its first store in Paris. Between 1992 and 1997, it entered about one country per year (at a median distance of about 3,000 kilometers from Spain), so that by the end of this period, there were Zara stores in seven European countries, the United States, and Israel. Since then, countries had been added more rapidly: 16 countries (at a median distance of 5,000 kilometers) in 1998–1999, and 8 countries (at a median distance of less than 2,000 kilometers) in 2000–2001. Plans for 2002 included entry into Italy, Switzerland, and Finland. Rapid expansion gave Zara a much broader footprint than larger apparel chains: by way of comparison, H&M added eight countries to its store network between the mid-1980s and 2001, and The Gap added five. (Exhibit 14 tracks aggregate store addi-tions across all of Inditex's chains.)

Inditex's management sometimes described this pat-tern of expansion as an "oil stain" in which Zara would first open a flagship store in a major city and, after developing some experience operating locally, add stores in adjoining areas. This pattern of expansion had first been employed in Spain and had been continued in Portugal. The first store opened in New York was intended as a display window and listening post but the first store in Paris anchored a pattern of regional—and then national—expansion that came to encompass about 30 stores in the Paris area and 67 in France by the end of 2001. CEO José Maria Castellano explained the approach:

> For us it is cheaper to deliver to 67 shops than to one shop. Another reason, from the point of view of the

awareness of the customers of Inditex or of Zara, is that it is not the same if we have one shop in Paris compared to having 30 shops in Paris. And the third reason is that when we open a country, we do not have advertising or local warehouse costs but we do have headquarters costs.

Similarly, Zara's entry into Greece in 1993 was a spring-board for its expansion into Cyprus and Israel.

Zara had historically looked for new country mar-kets that resembled the Spanish market, had a minimum level of economic development, and would be relatively easy to enter. To study a specific entry opportunity, a commercial team from headquarters conducted both the macro and micro analysis. Macro analysis focused on lo-cal macroeconomic variables and their likely future evo-lution, particularly in terms of how they would affect the prospects for stores (e.g., tariffs, taxes, legal costs, salaries, and property prices/rents). Micro analysis, per-formed onsite, focused on sector-specific information about local demand, channels, available store locations, and competitors. The explicitly competitive information gathered included data on levels of concentration, the formats that would compete most directly with Zara, and their potential political or legal ability to resist/retard its entry, as well as local pricing levels. According to Castellano, Zara—unlike its competitors—focused more on market prices than on its own costs in forecasting its prices in a particular market. These forecasts were then overlaid on cost estimates, which incorporated consider-ations of distance, tariffs, taxes, and so forth, to see whether a potential market could reach profitability quickly enough (often within a year or two of opening the first store).

The actual application of this template for market analysis varied somewhat from country to country. The opening of the first store in New York for informational purposes was an early example. Germany provided a more recent case: while Zara usually conducted market analysis at the country level, it had made an exception by sepa-rately analyzing seven large German cities. And some-times, specific opportunities or constraints overshadowed market-level analysis. Castellano characterized the early entry into Greece in such terms: "The obvious next step [after France] was to open in Belgium. But Greece offered, to us at least, a unique real estate opportunity. From the point of view that it was not a very competitive market there in the early 1990s, we decided to open in Greece. But now our strategy is to be in all the advanced countries [of Europe]."

Market Entry   If the commercial team's evaluation of a particular market was positive, the logical next step was to assess how to enter it. In contrast to Spain, where all of Zara's stores were company-owned and managed, three

Exhibit 14   Globalization of Inditex

	1987	1988	1989	1990	1991	1992	1993	1994	1995	1996	1997	1998	1999	2000	2001	Zara Stores Only (2001)
Europe																
Spain	57	70	85	99	201	266	323	350	391	399	433	489	603	692	769	225
Portugal		1	2	4	11	17	28	38	49	60	74	87	97	104	140	38
France				1	3	5	13	20	30	36	47	55	59	64	68	67
Greece							1	6	8	10	14	17	17	19	29	20
Belgium								4	8	11	13	17	20	21	28	14
Sweden								1	3	3	4	6	6	5	3	0
Malta									1	1	1	1	2	2	2	0
Cyprus										1	2	4	5	8	9	2
Norway												1	1	1	1	0
Great Britain												1	3	7	11	11
Germany													2	7	17	15
Netherlands													2	2	6	3
Poland													2	2	2	2
Andorra														1	2	1
Austria														3	3	3
Denmark														1	2	2
Czech Rep.															1	1
Iceland															1	1
Ireland															2	0
Italy															3	0
Luxembourg															2	1
Subtotal	*57*	*71*	*87*	*104*	*215*	*288*	*365*	*419*	*490*	*521*	*589*	*678*	*819*	*939*	*1101*	*406*
Americas																
United States			1	1	3	3	3	4	6	6	7	7	6	6	8	8
Mexico						1	1	7	12	14	20	25	29	41	55	27
Argentina												4	8	8	8	8
Venezuela												1	3	4	20	7
Canada													1	3	4	4
Chile													2	2	3	3
Brazil													3	5	7	7
Uruguay													2	2	2	2
Subtotal	*0*	*0*	*1*	*1*	*3*	*4*	*4*	*11*	*18*	*20*	*27*	*37*	*54*	*71*	*107*	*66*
Middle East/Asia																
Israel											6	16	22	23	24	9
Lebanon												1	3	4	4	2
Turkey												3	3	4	5	5
Kuwait												1	2	4	4	2
United Arab Emirates												1	3	5	15	4
China												1	1	0	0	0
Japan												10	11	17	5	5
Saudi Arabia													3	11	14	6
Bahrain													1	1	2	1
Qatar														1	2	1
Jordan															1	0
Subtotal	*0*	*0*	*0*	*0*	*0*	*0*	*0*	*0*	*0*	*0*	*6*	*33*	*49*	*70*	*76*	*35*
TOTAL	**57**	**71**	**88**	**105**	**218**	**292**	**369**	**430**	**508**	**541**	**622**	**748**	**922**	**1080**	**1284**	**507**

Source: Inditex.

different modes of market entry were used internationally: company-owned stores, joint ventures, and franchises. Zara usually employed just one of these modes of market participation in a particular country, although it did sometimes shift from one to another. Thus, it had entered Turkey via franchising in 1998, but had acquired ownership of all its Turkish stores in 1999.

Zara had originally expanded internationally through company-owned stores and, at the end of 2001, operated 231 such stores in 18 countries outside Spain. Zara typically established company-managed stores in key, high-profile countries with high growth prospects and low business risk. Company-owned stores did, however, entail the most commitment of resources, including management time. As a result, Zara had used two other modes of market entry, franchises, and joint ventures, in about half the countries it had entered since 1998.

Zara first used franchising to enter Cyprus in 1996 and, at the end of 2001, had 31 franchised stores in 12 countries.[18] Zara tended to use franchises in countries that were small, risky, or subject to significant cultural differences or administrative barriers that encouraged this mode of market participation: examples included Andorra, Iceland, and Poland in Europe and the Middle Eastern countries that the chain had entered (where restrictions on foreign ownership ruled out direct entry). Franchise contracts typically ran for five years, and franchisees were generally well-established, financially strong players in complementary businesses. Franchisees were usually given exclusive, countrywide franchises that might also encompass other Inditex chains but Zara always retained the right to open company-owned stores as well. In return for selling its products to franchisees and charging them a franchise fee that typically varied between 5% and 10% of their sales, Zara offered franchisees full access to corporate services, such as human resources, training, and logistics at no extra cost. It also allowed them to return up to 10% of purchased merchandise—a higher level than many other franchisers permitted.

Zara used joint ventures in larger, more important markets where there were barriers to direct entry, most often ones related to the difficulty of obtaining prime retail space in city centers. At the end of 2001, 20 Zara stores in Germany and Japan were managed through joint ventures, one in each country. Interests in both ventures were split 50:50 between Zara and its partners: Otto Versand, the largest German catalog retailer and a major mall owner, and Bigi, a Japanese textile distributor. The agreements with these partners gave Zara management control, so that it grouped stores in both countries with its corporate-owned stores as "company-managed." Nevertheless, the split ownership did create some potential complexities: thus, the agreement with Otto Versand contained put and call options under which Zara might be required to buy out its partner's interest or elect to do so.

In addition, Zara had been presented with opportunities to acquire foreign chains but had rejected them because of overlapping store networks, physical and cultural impediments to retrofitting its model on to them, and the difficulty of meeting profitability targets after paying acquisition premiums. Some of Inditex's smaller chains, in contrast, *had* been acquired and, partly because of that heritage, relied much more heavily on franchising. Overall, nearly one-third of the international stores of Inditex's other chains were franchised.

Marketing   While management emphasized that Zara used the same business system in all the countries in which it operated, there was some variation in retailing operations at the local level. The first store(s) opened in each market—often a flagship store in a major city—played a particularly critical role in refining the marketing mix by affording detailed insights into local demand. The marketing mix that emerged there was applied to other stores in the country as well.

Pricing was, as described earlier, market-based. However, if a decision *was* taken to enter a particular market, customers effectively bore the extra costs of supplying it from Spain. Prices were, on average, 40% higher in Northern European countries than in Spain, 10% higher in other European countries, 70% higher in the Americas, and 100% higher in Japan. (Exhibit 15 provides more information for

Exhibit 15   The Price of a T-shirt at Zara

Country	Relative Price Level
Spain	100%
United Kingdom	151%
Denmark	153%
Poland	158%
Cyprus	136%
Lebanon	152%
Kuwait	171%
Saudi Arabia	170%
Bahrain	170%
Qatar	160%
Canada	178%
USA	209%
Mexico	164%
Venezuela	147%
Japan	231%

Source: Inditex.

a representative product.) Zara had historically marked lo-cal currency prices for all the countries in which it operated on each garment's price tag, making the latter an "atlas" as its footprint expanded. (See Exhibit 16 for an old, multi-country price tag.) As key West European markets switched to the Euro at the beginning of 2002, Zara simplified its price tags to list only the prices in the local markets in which a particular garment might be sold, even though this complicated logistics.

The higher prices outside Spain did imply a somewhat different positioning for Zara overseas, particularly in emerging markets. Castellano explained the situation with an example:

> In Spain, with the prices we have and the information available to the public, about 80% of Spanish citizens can afford Zara. When we go to Mexico, for cultural reasons, for informational reasons, for economic reasons—because the average income in Mexico is $3,000 com-pared to $14,000—our targeted customer base is narrower. Who buys from us in Mexico? The upper class and the middle class. That is the class that knows fashion, that is accustomed to buying in Europe, or in the United States, in New York or Miami. In Mexico we are targeting 14 million inhabitants, compared to 35–36 million in Spain [out of populations of 100 million and 40 million respec-tively]. But 14 million is more than enough to put in a network of stores there.

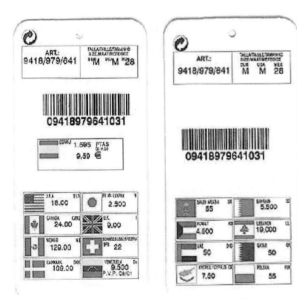

Exhibit 16   Sample Garment Price Tag

Source: Inditex.

Differences in positioning also affected the stores in which products were sold and Zara's overall image. For ex-ample, in South America, Zara products had to present a high-end rather than a mid-market image and it was em-phasized that they were "made in Europe." The image pre-sented was never one of "made in Spain," however. Thus, according to a survey by *Vogue*, young Parisiennes—who voted Zara to be their favorite apparel chain—generally thought it was of French origin.[19]

Zara's promotion policies and product offerings varied less internationally than did its prices or positioning. Adver-tising and other promotional efforts were generally avoided worldwide except during the sales periods, which were typi-cally biannual, in line with West European norms. And while product offerings catered to physical, cultural, or climate differences (e.g., smaller sizes in Japan, special women's clothes in Arab countries, different seasonality in South America), 85%–90% of the basic designs sold in Zara stores tended to be common from country to country. This commonality was facilitated by the frequent interactions between the creative team in La Coruña and local store man-agers. Furthermore, the 10%–15% of products that did vary from country to country were selected from the same broad menu of offerings: Zara did not develop products to meet just one country's requirements. Management thought that the implementation of this relatively standardized strategy had become easier over time as tastes converged across national boundaries. And residual differences permitted products that didn't sell well in one market to be sold in others.

Management   Zara's international activities were organized primarily under a holding company created in 1988, Zara Holding, B.V. of the Netherlands. Zara Hold-ing's transactions with international franchisees were de-nominated in Euros (Inditex's official currency). Sales in other currencies to subsidiaries in the Americas roughly offset dollar-denominated purchases from the Far East.

Under Zara Holding were the country operations through which managerial control of the downstream por-tions of the value chain—particularly the real estate and personnel costs associated with store operations—was ac-tually exercised. Country management teams typically consisted of a country general manager, a real estate man-ager, a human resource manager, a commercial manager, and an administrative and financial manager. Such man-agement teams sometimes served clusters of neighboring countries (e.g., Belgium and Luxembourg) if individual countries were too small. Country general managers played a particularly important role bridging between top manage-ment at headquarters and store managers at the local level: they were key conduits, for example, in propagating best practices through the organization. A committee of sub-sidiaries that met every two to three months was of partic-ular help in this regard. Country managers each received four to six months of training at headquarters. The country managers in key European markets were all locals, but some in the Americas were expatriates.

Corporate as well as country managers' ability to control local store operations was enhanced by the use of standardized reporting systems. Persistently subpar performance generally triggered extensive analysis followed by attempts to fix the problem(s) identified rather than market exit. However, a Pull & Bear franchised store in China had shut down during 2000 and, in early 2002, the prospects for the Argentine operation—struggling because of 35% tariffs and advance tax payment requirements even before the country's acute macroeconomic crisis—looked grim.

Growth Options   Inditex's plans for 2002 called for the addition of 55 to 65 Zara stores, 80% of them outside Spain.[20] But the geographic focus of Zara's store additions over a longer time frame remained to be determined. Since Zara had accounted for two-thirds of the total selling area added by Inditex across all its chains in 2001, decisions about Zara's expansion would have important group-level implications. The growth options for Zara within its home market of Spain seemed somewhat limited. Zara still had only a 4% share there, but Inditex's total share amounted to 6%. And the experience of H&M—which had undergone like-for-like sales declines after its share in its home market, Sweden, hit 10%—hinted that there might be relatively tight constraints on such an approach. Also of possible relevance was H&M's entry into Spain in 2001.

Castellano and his top management team saw the rest of Europe as offering the brightest prospects for significant, sustained growth over the medium term. Italy was thought to be a case in point. Italy was the largest single apparel market in Europe, partly because Italians spent more than €1,000 per capita on apparel (versus less than €600 per capita for Spaniards). Italian consumers visited apparel stores relatively frequently and were considered relatively fashion-forward. Apparel retailing in Italy was dominated by independent stores, which accounted for 61% of the market there (vs. 45% in Spain and 15%–30% in France, Germany, and the United Kingdom). Relatedly, concentration levels were lower in Italy than in any of the four other major European markets. (See Exhibit 17 for data on European markets along some of these and other dimensions.)

Both of Zara's attempts to enter the Italian market had been orchestrated through joint ventures given planning and retailing regulations that made it hard to secure the location and the multiple licenses required to open a new store. An initial joint venture agreement with Benetton, formed in 1998, failed to overcome this difficulty and was later dissolved. Over roughly the same timeframe, Benetton apparently secured a large bank loan and launched an aggressive campaign, particularly in Italy, to open up directly managed megastores of its own that were much larger than the third-party stores that it had traditionally

licensed. In 2001, Inditex formed a 51:49 joint venture with Percassi, an Italian group specializing in property and fashion retail premises and one of Benetton's largest licensees to enable expansion in Italy. This second joint venture resulted in the opening of Zara's first store in Milan in April 2002—at 2,500 square meters, the largest Zara store in Europe and a major media event. Inditex and Percassi reportedly planned to add 70–80 Zara stores in Italy over the next 10 years.

Of course, expansion within Europe was only one of several regional options. Zara could conceivably also deepen its commitment to a second region by investing significantly in distribution and even production there. North America and Asia seemed to be the two other obvious regional possibilities. South America was much smaller and subject to profitability pressures that were thought likely to persist; the Middle East was more profitable on average, but even smaller. However, the larger regions presented their own challenges. The U.S. market, the key to North America, was subject to retailing overcapacity, was less fashion-forward than Europe, demanded larger sizes on average, and exhibited considerable internal variation. Benetton had had to retreat after a disastrous attempt to expand in the United States in the 1980s. And in early 2002, H&M had slowed down its ambitious expansion effort there because of higher-than-expected operating costs and weak demand—despite the fact that its prices there were pegged at levels comparable to those that it posted in its large markets in North Europe. Asia appeared to be even more competitive and difficult to penetrate than North America.

Outlook

While the issues surrounding Zara's future geographic focus were important, top management had to consider some even farther-reaching questions. One immediate set concerned the non-Zara chains, which had recently proliferated, but at least some of which were of subcritical scale. Could Inditex cope with the complexity of managing multiple chains without compromising the excellence of individual ones, especially since its geographic scope was also relatively broad? And looking farther out, should it start up or acquire additional chains? The questions were sharpened by Inditex's revenue growth rate requirements, which top management pegged at 20%+ per annum. While like-for-like sales growth had averaged 9% per year recently, it might fall to 7% or even 5%, so a 15% annual increase in selling space seemed to be a minimal requirement. And of course, margins had to be preserved as well—potentially a challenge given some of the threats to the sustainability of Inditex's competitive advantages. A roundtable video of Inditex's top management sheds additional light on some of these issues as well as others discussed in this case.

Exhibit 17 European Markets for Apparel, 1999

	Total Sales (€ billion)	Apparel Outlets per Million Inhabitants	Specialist Share of Apparel Sales (%)	Specialist Sales (€/sq. meter)	Total GNP (€ billion)	Population (million)	GNP per Capita (€)	Distance from Spain (km)
Austria	8	416	40	2,500	229	8	28,280	1,809
Belgium	8	845	50	3,500	283	10	27,489	1,314
Denmark	4	702	25	3,100	192	5	36,183	2,072
Finland	3	493	33	2,100	145	5	27,822	2,949
France	41	640	56	3,400	1,603	59	27,217	1,053
Germany	61	725	69	4,500	2,308	82	28,073	1,870
Greece	8	1,416	36	1,700	142	11	13,357	2,366
Ireland	3	934	30	2,500	98	4	25,708	1,458
Italy	63	1,725	70	5,600	1,295	58	22,435	1,377
Netherlands	11	1,049	64	4,000	449	16	28,234	1,480
Poland	na	906	na	na	182	39	4,700	2,289
Portugal	5	na	25	1,900	124	10	12,412	503
Spain	25	1,599	57	3,100	662	40	16,756	na
Sweden	6	na	76	4,000	307	9	34,461	2,592
Switzerland	7	800	39	1,400	307	7	42,631	1,148
United Kingdom	55	560	67	5,600	1,641	60	27,492	1,263
Total	**308**	**915**			**9,965**	**422**		
Average	**21**		**49**	**3,260**	**623**	**26**	**25,203**	**1,703**

Source: Compiled from Verdict, Retail Intelligence, and UBS Warburg estimates. na = not available

Endnotes

1. Catoni, Luciano, Larssen, Nora F., Naylor, James, & Zocchi, Andrea. 2002. Travel tips for retailers. *The McKinsey Quarterly* 3: 126–133.

2. Gereffi, Gary. 1999. International trade and industrial upgrading in the apparel commodity chain. *Journal of International Economics* 48: 37–70.

3. Gereffi, Gary. 2002. Outsourcing and changing patterns of international competition in the apparel commodity chain. Paper presented at the Responding to Globalization: Societies, Groups and Individuals Conference, Boulder, Colorado, April 4–7.

4. McFarlan, F. Warren, & Young, Fred. 2000. Li & Fung (A): Internet issues. HBS Case No. 9-301-009. Boston: Harvard Business School Publishing: 3.

5. Siggelkow, Nicolai. 2001. Change in the presence of fit: The rise, the fall, and the renaissance of Liz Claiborne. *Academy of Management Journal* 44: 838–857.

6. Scheffer, Michel. 1994. *The changing map of European textiles: Production and sourcing strategies of textile and clothing firms.* Brussels: L'Observatoire Eureopeen du Textile et de l'Habillement.

7. A. T. Kearney data as reported in MacKinnon, Ian. 2001. Mall rush? *Newsweek,* April 2: 48.

8. Hammond, Janice, & Kelley, Maura G. 1991. Quick response in the apparel industry. HBS Case No. 690-038. Boston: Harvard Business School Publishing.

9. Catoni et al. Travel Lips for refailers.

10. Euromonitor data as reported in Murray, Carol Pope. 2001. Crossing the pond: European growth strategies. Salomon Smith Barney Equity Research (Apparel/Footwear/Textiles), October 23.

11. Child, Peter N., Heywood, Suzanne, & Kliger, Michael. 2002. Do retail brands travel? *The McKinsey Quarterly* 1: 11–13.

12. *Trends International* (English Edition). 2001. Euro Consumers: Survey. November 19.

13. Incandela, Denise, McLaughlin, Kathleen L., & Shi, Christina Smith. Retailers to the world. *The McKinsey Quarterly* 3: 84–97.

14. The template for applying the Du Pont formula to Inditex's and key competitors' financials was suggested by Professor Guillermo D'Andrea of I.A.E., Universidad Austral, Argentina.

15. Raman, Ananth, & Fisher, Marshall. 2001. Supply chain management at World Co. Ltd. HBS Case No. 9-601-072. Boston: Harvard Business School Publishing.

16. Crawford, Leslie. 2001. Allzarage. *Report on Business Magazine,* March 30, available from Factiva, http://www.primark.com, accessed September 23, 2002.

17. National Retail Federation. 1996. Merchandise and operating results for department and specialty stores.

18. Sales to franchises were made at lower prices than retail sales to final customers, limiting their contribution to international sales to 6% of the total even though they accounted for 11% of the number of international stores.

19. Crawford. Allzarage.

20. Aggregating across all its chains, Inditex anticipated opening a total of 230 to 275 stores during 2002, slightly over half of them outside Spain, and budgeted for €510–560 million of capital expenditures.

Case 33 Kmart–Sears Merger of 2005*

"Unless this new retail giant proves that it's capable of creating stronger customer connections, there will be no real value to this merger."

—**William J. McEwen,** Gallup Management Journal

"As a retailer, we really have not grown at all for the last 35 years."

—**Alan Lacy,** Vice Chairman of SHC, Ex-Chairman of Sears

"The idea is to form 'one great culture.'"

—**Edward Lampert,** Chairman of SHC, Ex-Chairman or Kmart

The Merger

In late 2004, two giant U.S. retail corporations—Sears, Roebuck and Co. and Kmart Holding Corporation—announced that they would merge operations to form the Sears Holding Company (SHC). In terms of how the new entity's name was selected, the Sears name was apparently held in higher esteem by consumers than the Kmart name. Based on a survey of 1,050 U.S. adults conducted by Rivkin & Associates, Opinion Research Corp., 75 percent of Americans preferred the "Sears" name over "Kmart."

Under the terms of the merger, SHC became the third largest retailer in the United States with approximately $55 billion in annual revenues and 2,350 full-line and off-mall stores and 1,100 specialty retail stores in the United States. Kmart shareholders received one share of SHC common stock for each Kmart share. Sears shareholders had the right to elect $50 in cash or 0.5 of a share of SHC for each share of Sears's common stock. At the time of the merger, it was estimated that the former shareholders of Kmart would have an approximate 63 percent interest in SHC and former shareholders of Sears would hold a 37 percent interest in SHC. On the morning of March 24, 2005, the merger approval date, Sears shares fell $6.06 (about 11 percent) to $50.74 (NYSE) and Kmart shares rose $1.19 (about 1 percent) to $126.02 (NASDAQ).

Twelve teams—composed of members from both companies—were created to ease the merger process. According to Alan Lacy, former president and chief executive officer of Sears and new vice chairman of SHC, one post-merger goal is that "Kmart will benefit from the planned cost sharing of several of Sears leading proprietary brands" as well as present opportunities "to capture significant revenue and cost synergies, including merchandise and non-merchandise purchasing, distribution and other SG&A expenses." Ultimately, the goal of the merger, according to Edward S. Lampert, former chairman of Kmart and new chairman of SHC, was to "seek to leverage the combined strengths of Sears and Kmart to obtain greater long-term value than either could have generated on a stand-alone basis. SHC plans to offer customers a new, more compelling experience with a differentiated and expanded product range."[1]

These changes are the first of many for these historic and somewhat disparate companies, both of which were founded in the late 1800s and are woven in American culture. The newly merged entity—SHC—will face challenges of marrying two distinct retail entities in terms of their unique cultures to create requisite synergies to keep pace with (or surpass) the competition. Before looking on to the future, it is important to look at the historical evolution of Sears and Kmart to better understand the respective organizations' strategies and cultures.

Background of Companies

Sears, Roebuck & Co. Richard W. Sears found the R.W. Sears Watch Co. in 1886. The early days of the organization were filled with changes in structure and partnership—moving to Chicago, taking on Alvah Roebuck (an Indiana watchmaker) as a partner, and publishing the company's first mail-order catalog (which contained 80 pages) in 1888. The watch business was sold in 1889, and by 1891, Sears had developed the nation's first mail-order business. In 1893, the company's name changed to Sears, Roebuck and Co. At that time, the company's sales had exceeded $400,000. By 1895, the 532-page Sears catalog offered a variety of merchandise, including apparel, shoes, china, saddles, musical instruments, firearms, buggies, wagons, fishing tackle, watches, and jewelry.

In 1911, when banks did not lend to consumers, Sears opted to offer credit services to its customers. Around this time, Sears also established a research lab to ensure product standards and conduct merchandise quality-control checks. In February 1925, Sears opened its first retail store. In terms of retail history making, Richard Sears is credited with creating the modern department store; he also came up with the idea of the "unconditional money back guarantee."

Like most other U.S. companies, Sears struggled during the great depression. After the depression, the company continued its growth in terms of number of retail locations, business line diversification (e.g., Sears introduced a line of tires, "Allstate," which was ultimately expanded into an automobile insurance and life insurance company), international expansion (e.g., early expansions included Cuba in 1942 and Mexico in 1947), acquisitions of several other organizations (e.g., Simpsons Ltd. of Canada and Coldwell Banker Co.), and the erection of the Sears Tower in Chicago in the 1970s (at the time, the tallest building in the world).

*This case was prepared by Professor Noushi Rahman, Professor Alan B. Eisner, and Graduate student Pamela Monastero of Pace University as a basis for class discussion rather than to illustrate either effective or ineffective handling of an administrative situation. Copyright © 2005 Noushi Rahman and Alan B. Eisner.

By 1963, Sears was the number one retailer in the United States and one in five consumers shopped at Sears regularly.

Early success ultimately made Sears complacent. By the 1970s, competition became stiff, and other discounters (e.g., S. S. Kresge Co., which later became Kmart) started cutting into Sears' profits. In 1974 alone, Sears experienced a $170 million drop in profits. In an effort to continue its growth, Sears attempted to further diversify its businesses. Despite diversification in the 1980s (e.g., purchase of Coldwell Banker, then the nation's largest real estate broker; Dean Witter Reynolds, a securities firm; the launch of Prodigy, an online service with IBM and CBS; the launch of the Discover Card; and ultimately the transformation of Sears into a collection of specialty stores), profits continued to decline through the 1990s. In 1992, Sears slashed jobs and suffered a year-end loss of almost $2.3 billion. This outcome prompted Sears to sell off several of its businesses (e.g., Coldwell Banker and Dean Witter Reynolds).

As a strategic response to declining revenue in the 1990s, Sears made an effort to target female consumers, introducing the "softer side of Sears." To support this strategy, Sears restructured its stores by moving appliances, hardware, and furniture from mall stores to their own freestanding retail outlets. By 1995, profits hit $1 billion again, and in 1997, Sears stock reached an all-time high of $65.25 per share. By 1998, however, Sears again saw downturns in business, and many executives, including the chief executive officer, departed. In October 2000, current President Alan Lacy took the reins and created "The Great Indoors" store concept. Another strategic move made by Lacy was to transfer Sears

account holders to MasterCard, as Sears had come to rely too heavily on its credit card financing operations. This move resulted in many consumer defaults because of the higher interest rates. Sears in-store sales also continued to falter. In 2003 sales were slumping and staff layoffs were instituted again. In addition, the credit card business was sold for $3 billion to Citigroup. The "softer side of Sears" was ultimately considered to be "too soft" as witnessed by the eleven consecutive months of declining sales seen in 2004 (see Exhibits 1 and 2 for Sears' revenues and net income).

In general, Sears' retail business had been weak, consistent with its declining store sales. Sears' in-mall locations had been a major impediment to its sales of home-related categories because the majority of home goods are sold in off-mall locations. Indeed, Sears was able to retain some of its charisma in small-town America where its off-mall stores were located.

Kmart Holding Corporation   Kmart was founded as S. S. Kresge Co. in 1899 by Sebastian Spering Kresge as a five-and-dime retail store in downtown Detroit. It then expanded into chain stores, similar to Woolworth, and ultimately acquired Mount Clemens Pottery, which manufactured inexpensive, popular dinnerware sold in the stores. By 1912, Kresge stores were the second largest five-and-dime chain in the United States with 85 stores and annual sales of over $10 million. By 1924, there were 257 stores with annual sales of $90 million.

Similar to Sears, Kresge stores struggled through the Great Depression. Unlike Sears, Kresge stores did not offer

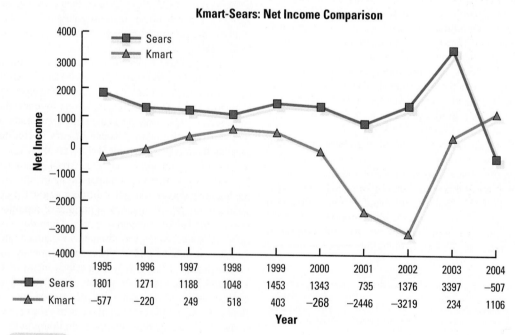

Kmart-Sears: Net Income Comparison

	1995	1996	1997	1998	1999	2000	2001	2002	2003	2004
Sears	1801	1271	1188	1048	1453	1343	735	1376	3397	−507
Kmart	−577	−220	249	518	403	−268	−2446	−3219	234	1106

Exhibit 1   Net Income of Kmart and Sears, 1995–2004

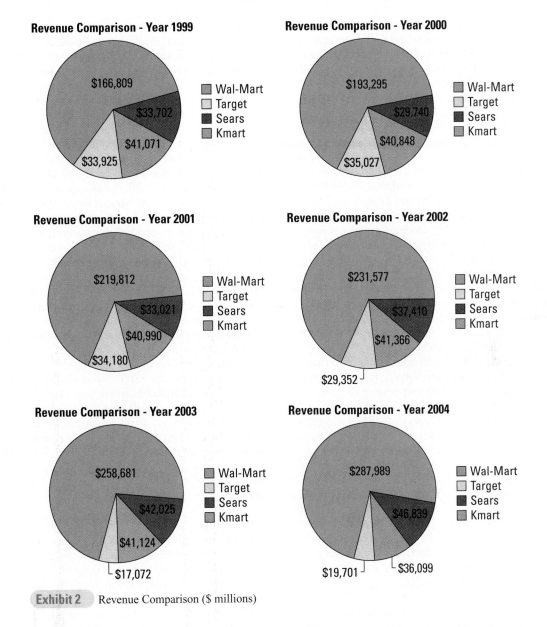

Revenue Comparison - Year 1999

$166,809
$33,702
$41,071
$33,925

- Wal-Mart
- Target
- Sears
- Kmart

Revenue Comparison - Year 2000

$193,295
$29,740
$40,848
$35,027

- Wal-Mart
- Target
- Sears
- Kmart

Revenue Comparison - Year 2001

$219,812
$33,021
$40,990
$34,180

- Wal-Mart
- Target
- Sears
- Kmart

Revenue Comparison - Year 2002

$231,577
$37,410
$41,366
$29,352

- Wal-Mart
- Target
- Sears
- Kmart

Revenue Comparison - Year 2003

$258,681
$42,025
$41,124
$17,072

- Wal-Mart
- Target
- Sears
- Kmart

Revenue Comparison - Year 2004

$287,989
$46,839
$19,701
$36,099

- Wal-Mart
- Target
- Sears
- Kmart

Exhibit 2   Revenue Comparison ($ millions)

credit to its customers in the early years. Although Kresge offered layaway payment plans, this approach hurt the company because customers were more attracted to credit offerings.

In the late 1950s, food grew into the single largest department in Kresge stores and in-store luncheonettes were created. Consequently, Kresge acquired various food companies (e.g., Furr's Cafeterias and Bishop Buffets), created a fast food drive-through called Kmart Chef, and ultimately entered grocery retailing in the 1970s. Kmart Chef was discontinued in 1974.

In 1962, Kresge's president, Harry Cunningham, conducted a research study on discounters and competition. Cunningham found that discount stores were the main

competition for Kresge stores. As a strategic response, Kmart was born in Garden City, Michigan.

Kmart's first year sales reached $483 million and plans were made to open 32 additional Kmart locations that were geographically isolated from the competition. Through the 1960s, Kmart and Kresge continued to evolve and older Kresge stores were converted to Jupiter Discount. By 1976, Kmart became the second largest general merchandise retailer in the United States with annual sales of $8.4 billion. The corporation controlled the stock, holding 1,206 out of 1,647 shares, and maintained 271 stores. The S. S. Kresge name was officially changed to Kmart Corp. in 1977.

In the mid-1970s, Kmart expanded internationally into Australia. However, Kmart sold its stake in the Australian Kmart in 1978. In the 1980s, Kmart expanded into Mexico, where the stores were operated by a prominent Mexican retailer; the company also formed a joint venture with Japan's top retailer.

By 1981, Kmart had 2,000 worldwide stores and continued expanding through acquisitions of Penske Auto, Walden Books, and Home Centers America (renamed Builders Square). By 1987, sales were up to $25.6 billion. To continue its growth, from 1980 through the 1990s, Kmart Corp. acquired Sports Authority, OfficeMax, and Borders Inc.; merged with PayLess Drug Stores; launched the Jaclyn Smith Collection; and opened Super Kmart Centers (1,200 sites by 1997). During this time, Kmart also enjoyed the growth of its apparel business, which was the store's fastest growing business.

In 1994, Kmart streamlined operations in response to shareholder displeasure. The company closed 110 stores, laying off 6,000 staff members and managers. It also sold off several of its previously acquired businesses, including OfficeMax, Borders/Walden bookstores, PayLess Drugs, Penske Auto, and Sports Authority.

Facing tremendous competition from other major retailers (mainly Wal-Mart and Target), Kmart continued to change throughout the 1990s by selling its stake in the Rite Aid Corp.; partnering with Salton/Maxim Housewares, giving Kmart exclusive distribution rights to Salton/Maxim's small electrical appliances, consumer electronics, kitchen housewares, and personal care products and other White Westinghouse brands; introducing the highly successful Martha Stewart line of home fashion products that neared $1 billion in sales; creating Blue-Light.com, an independent e-commerce company formed in 1999; and entering the food retailing segment. However, all this shuffling proved futile, as Kmart continued to lose market share (see again Exhibits 1 and 2 for Kmart's revenues and net income). Kmart Corp. filed for Chapter 11 bankruptcy protection in January 2002.

Edward Lampert, former chairman of Kmart, turned around Kmart from bankruptcy in less than two years. By the end of 2004, Kmart reported three consecutive profitable quarters and operated 1,511 Kmart discount stores and SuperCenters. Such expedited recovery sent Kmart's stock price above $100 per share in late 2004. Despite the turnaround orchestrated by Lampert, Kmart's market share continued to shrink. Some suggested that Lampert pumped Kmart to generate cash rather than to build the business.[2]

The New Entity: Sears Holdings Corporation

As indicated in the comparison chart (see Exhibit 3), there is common territory among the products offered by the Sears and Kmart stores, with the primary overlaps being in the home goods and apparel arenas. Some major differences in product offerings exist too. Sears sells lawn, garden, tools, large appliances, automotive, hardware and window/siding products, which are not offered by Kmart. Kmart's retail food line and pharmacy operations are not common to Sears. Differences in product lines need to be exploited by SHC, as the new entity "will feature a powerful home appliance franchise with strong positions in tools, lawn and garden, home electronics and auto repair and maintenance." The new company expects that these product lines, in addition to the combined strengths of the apparel lines previously offered by both Sears and Kmart, the strength of the Martha Stewart Home line, and the predicted extra traffic generated by the retail food line, will result in a realization of approximately $200 million in incremental gross margin from revenue synergies capitalized by these cross-selling opportunities and by the conversion of off-mall Kmart stores to Sears. According to an SHC Press Release, "The company expects to achieve annual costs savings of $300 million principally through improved merchandising and non-merchandising purchasing scale as well as improved supply chain, administrative and other operational efficiencies."[3]

Lampert believes that the anticipated $200 million in additional revenue, the $300 million in cost savings, and Kmart's $3.8 billion in tax credits, which will shield profits for a number of years, will help SHC's per share price to rise. As a result, SHC should be able to accumulate cash and be in a strong market position. His vision for SHC is to build a broader customer base and to increase sales to achieve profits of 10 percent EBITDA-to-sales ratio, similar to successful retailers like The Gap and Home Depot. This will be accomplished using several strategies.

First, SHC will convert Kmart stores to the Sears name in markets where existing Kmart stores better fit Sears' demographic of slightly higher-income shoppers. Second, given its huge real estate portfolio, SHC will benefit from the flexibility of switching stores between chains and selling stores as necessary, although this can be limited by mall owners, because 74 percent of mall owners followed by Merrill Lynch have a Sears store.

Third, SHC will expand on the Sears Grand concept (off-mall stores which carry consumables) to counter the "loss of consumers to savvier rivals." Plans are already in place to open 60 Sears Grand stores by 2006. Sears Grand expectations should benefit from Kmart's experience in the consumables and apparel markets. Consumables are viewed by the SHC as "traffic builders."

Fourth, SHC will expand the Sears Essentials stores (relatively smaller convenience-driven stores) by converting approximately 400 existing Kmart locations. Sears Essentials will offer products such as appliances, lawn and garden tools, home electronics, apparel and home fashions as well as convenience goods such as health and beauty aids, a pharmacy, pantry items, household products, paper products, pet supplies, and toys. These stores will benefit from Kmart's position as one of the nation's largest pharmacy and health care retailers with 1,150 in-store pharmacies, 2,400 staff pharmacists, and significant expertise in disease management. The Kmart stores slated for conversion are located in key urban and high-density suburban markets with customer demographics and income levels matching those of the typical Sears shopper. The first 25 Sears Essential stores will open in Spring 2005.

Fifth, SHC will cross-sell products by having Kmart and Sears carry each other's lines. For example, Kmart will carry Kenmore appliances, Craftsman tools, and DieHard batteries, while Sears will carry some of Kmart's brands in the future.

Lastly, SHC will be able to emphasize apparel labels that appeal to a multicultural audience. Latinos and African Americans make up a significant share of Sears' shoppers and this group also represents large share of the shoppers at Kmart's inner-city locations.

Overall, management's strategy for the restructuring is aimed at better supporting existing Sears stores, although both stores will continue to operate separately under their respective names for quite some time after the merger. The new structure creates eight regions that cover 110 districts, each composed of six to nine stores. There will be a new position entitled "director of stores" to manage each district. This position will report to a regional vice president. Since SHC will operate under at least six different formats, a challenge for the new leadership will be to determine how the retail formats would fit in each market and how they should be named (e.g., Sears Grand, Sears Essentials, etc.). Therefore, to avoid the inherent confusion that will result among stakeholders (e.g., consumers, SHC employees, shareholders, and analysts), it will be critical for the leadership of SHC to clearly define the organization's identity, image, and direction. This is even more important because, historically, both Sears and Kmart were accused of having an ill-defined media image caused by frequently changing strategies. Both firms were also deficient in strategy execution and employee training. Because of this, the new SHC executive staff, in particular Aylwin Lewis, the former president and CEO of Kmart, is focused on team building and staff training.[4]

Equally important in terms of strategy is retaining and building customer loyalty. A former Kmart executive, Gary Ruffing, who now serves as senior director of retail consulting for BBK, Ltd, has advice for the SHC management team: "You can fix a lot of things, but if you can't get the customer back, it doesn't matter . . . . My advice to the new CEO is to listen to the customer and keep the team focused on four or five critical points of the shopping experience . . . the keys are the in-stock position, the touch points at checkout, the friendly service and keeping the pricing

within the value range." Ruffing also underscored the importance of strategically placing Aylwin Lewis.

> [H]is ability to understand and bring brands and positions together to drive the success of Sears Holding Co. and Kmart's ability to fit outside of discounting . . . where they fit has always been an issue . . . . [E]ventual success could lie in the chains' combining of product lines rather than that of the retail brands. Many people say the retailers are two losers. The brand equity is not the Sears or Kmart name . . . brands are brands . . . you have to understand who they are and put together a marketing program and the ambient features that go with that. You need somebody who has done that.

Aylwin Lewis is credited with the successful transformation of Kentucky Fried Chicken from a sleepy Southern brand touted by an aged colonel to the hip and urban KFC.[5]

In terms of changes for stakeholders as a result of the merger, one glaring difference will be the loss of dividend payments to former Sears shareholders. Another change, which will directly affect employees, is the reduction by SHC of the number of employees eligible for stock options (Sears had already reduced the number from 17,000 to 2,000 in early 2004 and further reductions are expected). In addition, there will be the inherent management changes and organizational policy changes. According to a March 14, 2005, article in *Home Textiles Today,* "there will be seismic shifts among senior executives and middle managers immediately following the merger." Importantly, in April 2005 SHC announced the first of a series of staff layoffs (which will directly affect employees and management at the Sears Chicago headquarters) as well as salary and benefits changes to take effect in 2006.

Management   The new Board of Directors consists of seven directors from the former Kmart Board and three directors from the former Sears Board. The executive team is also a blend of former Kmart and Sears staff members, as follows:

- Edward S. Lampert, chairman (formerly chairman of Kmart)
- Alan J. Lacy, vice chairman (formerly chairman of Sears)
- Aylwin B. Lewis, president of Sears Holdings and CEO of Sears Retail (formerly president and CEO of Kmart)

In addition, two other previous Sears executives and five Kmart executives were appointed to SHC.

Retail Industry and Competition

Retail Industry   The retail industry is the second largest industry in the United States when ranked by number of establishments (20 percent of all establishments) and number of employees (18.3 percent of all employment covered by

Exhibit 3 Premerger Operations and Financial Comparisons of Sears and Kmart
(data as of 1/1/05)

Item	Sears	Kmart
1/1/05 Revenue	$36,099,000,000	$17,072,000,000
Full-time employees	247,000	158,000
Number of shares outstanding	253,824	89,629
Dividends per share	$0.92	$0
Earnings per share	$1.53	$2.52
Price per share	52 Week High: $50.49	52 Week High: $99.64
	52 Week Low: $49.81	52 Week Low: $97.35
Stockholder's equity	$6,092,000,000	$2,192,000,000
Long-term debt	$3,473,000,000	$477,000,000
Total assets	$22,474,000,000	$6,084,000,000
Total liabilities	$16,382,000,000	$3,892,000,000
Return on equity	5.45%	11.31%
Return on assets	1.48%	4.08%
Return on investment	(1.36)	106.77
Net profit margin	(1.40%)	1.45
Total debt to equity ratio	0.57	0.22
Fortune 2005 "America's Most Admired Companies" —General Merchandisers	Overall score: 6.67; ranked third behind Wal-Mart (7.86) and Kohl's (6.71) and moved from fourth to third place from last year	Overall score: 4.22; ranked tenth following Wal-Mart, Kohl's, Sears, JC Penney, Federated Dept. Stores, Target, Dollar General, May Dept. Stores, and Dillard's and moved from eleventh to tenth place from last year
Number of stores in United States	873 full-line department stores, 1,307 specialty-format stores (auto, neighborhood hardware) and 15 Lands' End retail stores	1,511 (includes Puerto Rico, Guam and the U.S. Virgin Islands) and 60 Kmart Supercenters
Fortune 500	Ranked 32 in 2004; was 30 in 2003.	Ranked 67 in 2004; was 39 in 2003.
Analysis	*In 2004*, total revenue decreased 12.2% from 2003 (attributable to the decline in credit and financial products revenues as a result of the sale of the domestic Credit and Financial Products business).	*In 2004*, Kmart did not have a 10K filing. In 2003, Kmart was in the midst of reorganizing from its 2002 Chapter 11 filing, which resulted in the closing of 284 stores and the elimination of 22,000 jobs and a charge of more than $1 billion.
	In 2003, total revenue decreased 0.6% from 2002.	*In 2003*, total revenue decreased 15.4% from 2002.
Business Description	*Home group:* Includes appliances, electronics, home fashions, home improvement products (e.g., tools, fitness equipment, lawn and garden equipment), and the Kenmore, Craftsman and WeatherBeater brands.	*Home group:* Includes appliances, electronics, home fashions, fitness and sports equipment, and the Martha Stewart Everyday brand.
	Apparel/Accessories: Includes apparel and footwear, jewelry and accessories, and the Lands' End, Covington, Canyon River Blues, Apostrophe, and TKS Basics brands.	*Apparel/Accessories:* Includes apparel and footwear, jewelry and accessories, and the Disney, Jaclyn Smith, Joe Boxer, Route 66, Thalia Sodi, Sesame Street, and Kathy Ireland brands.

	Sears	Kmart
	Sears Auto Centers: Includes automotive services and sales of tires and batteries, including the DieHard brand. Has 1,000 specialty stores in off-mall locations, an Internet retail site (sears.com), 792 dealer stores (which are primarily independently owned), 245 hardware stores (Sears Hardware and Orchard Supply Hardware), 18 The Great Indoors stores (specializing in home decorating and remodeling interiors), and 45 Sears Outlet stores (carrying overstocks and discount merchandise).	Kmart Supercenters: 60 stores that combine a grocery, deli, and bakery along with general merchandise.
Significant International Presence	Sears Canada: Similar to U.S. operations with 122 department stores, 42 furniture and appliance stores, 144 dealer stores, 14 outlet stores, 53 floor covering stores, 49 automotive centers, 110 travel offices, and 2,200 catalog pick-up locations. Sells brands similar to those sold in the United States.	No significant presence outside the United States.
Motto and Business Model	Motto: "Satisfaction guaranteed or your money back." Their vision is to be the preferred and most trusted resource for products and services that enhance their customers' home and family life.

Business Model: To offer a compelling customer value proposition through the combination of high-quality products and services at competitive prices. This is affected by low pricing and promotional activities and minimization of product and service costs. This is achieved through economies of scale, centralized overhead expense structure, reinvestment of operating cash flows into capital projects, and quality improvements in proprietary brands. The goal is to return profits to shareholders, issue dividends, repurchase shares, and increase share price.

Differentiation: To offer high-quality national brands as well as Sears proprietary brands, which enjoy high levels of consumer awareness, trust, and integrity (Kenmore, Craftsman, DieHard, and Land's End brands are offered exclusively at Sears stores) and retail-related services such as delivery, installation, product repair, product warranty, and protection services.

Premerger challenges: Consumers do not prefer retail stores within a mall-based format. Sears has been challenged by competitors that specialize in certain types of consumer goods and has focused on being the lowest cost provider in those categories. | Motto: Unclear. No reference of a formal motto can be traced.

Business Model: The historical core competency of Kmart is in designing and sourcing apparel and in its merchandising and marketing approach on quality brand names.

Differentiation: To design and source its apparel.

Premerger challenges: Kmart has been challenged by competitors like Wal-Mart and Target and was forced to close stores, eliminate jobs, and declare Chapter 11 bankruptcy in 2002 due to a rapid decline in liquidity which resulted from below-plan sales and earnings performance in the fourth quarter of fiscal 2001, the evaporation of the surety bond market, erosion of supplier confidence, intense competition, unsuccessful sales and marketing initiatives, and the continuing recession and capital market volatility. After emerging as Kmart Holding Corp., the focus was to generate profitable sales, control costs, streamline overhead, increase asset productivity, and improve customer service. |

unemployment insurance). The retail industry expanded at unprecedented rates from the late 1990s to 2000, before the recession resulted in a manufacturing slowdown, job losses, high consumer debt, and retail bankruptcies. The industry was further plagued by the dot-com bust, uncertainty following the September 11, 2001 terrorist attacks, and global unrest. The rise of Wal-Mart and other big box discount retailers (or "mass merchandisers") and the economic recovery in the mid-2000s changed the retail landscape. Retailers responded to these market pressures by restructuring stores, reorganizing internal operations, and marketing patterns and by taking advantage of technology to assist with e-commerce, inventory issues, point-of-sale systems, and data analysis. In 2004 (which is considered by analysts to be the most "stable" retail year in quite some time), the top 10 U.S. general merchandise retailers based on 2004 sales figures were: (1) Wal-Mart ($285 billion), (2) Sears Holding Corp. (recently merged with a combined $55 billion), (3) Target ($48 billion), (4) Federated/May (recently merged with a combined $30 billion), (5) JCPenney ($18 billion), (6) Gap Inc. ($16 billion), (7) TJX Cos. ($15 billion), (8) Limited Brands ($9 billion), (9) Dillard's ($8 billion), and (10) Saks ($6 billion). Home Depot, the number two retailer in the United States, is not considered a department store. While retail sales were strong in the luxury and discount sector in 2004, department stores and other retailers struggled to make their numbers. In early 2005, the gross domestic product (GDP) had risen 4.4 percent, which was the fastest pace in five years, and was led by consumer and capital spending.[6]

The architecture of the retail industry has drastically changed from the introduction of catalogs and general trading stores, to department stores, to the rise of indoor malls, to the growth of discounters and big box stores, to Internet-based selling, to changing demographics (more single parent households, double income households, geographic shifts and increased catalog sales due to busy lifestyles). In addition, catalogs and e-commerce have globalized the retail market.

Several other notable changes are taking place in the 2000s. For example, as enclosed malls are falling out of favor with consumers, new open-air "lifestyle centers" are becoming increasingly popular. These centers have plenty of outdoor space—fountains, plazas, and walking paths—designed to attract customers and keep them there for longer periods of time. Because retailers generally pay less rent for these open air arenas, profits are higher. In addition, consumers can park very close to the store entrance, unlike traditional mall setups.[7]

More mega-mergers (such as the Sears–Kmart combination and Federated–May stores) will result in the closing of more stores, which in turn will propel even more mergers and acquisitions in retail and closely related industries. Because of this activity, suppliers may be forced to merge to survive the huge bargaining clout created by these mega-mergers. Suppliers potentially face fewer orders, higher pressure for markdowns, discounts, and promotions from the shrinkage wave following these mergers. Ultimately, smaller suppliers will be swallowed up by larger, healthier entities as they will be unable "to meet the demands and prices of the newly emerging retail behemoths."[8]

Another recent trend is that clothing vendors, such as Ralph Lauren, are opening their own stores, which has created somewhat of a backlash on major retailers. In retaliation, chain operators like Federated are opening a series of ministores (mini-Macys, mini-Bloomingdales and other specialty ministores such as Charter Club and INC.) throughout the country to accommodate consumers' varied tastes.[9]

In the current retail economy, consumer trends lean toward value and frugality, leading to a movement away from department stores and to the rise of discount retailers warehouse and wholesale clubs such as Costco and Sam's Club. Warehouse shopping outlets are currently growing at a rate of 10 percent per year—twice as fast as the rest of the retail industry. The long-term forecast for department stores in the United States suggests a continued slow growth rate into the next century as the industry continues to battle online retailing, direct marketing, and home shopping networks.

Competition Wal-Mart was established in 1962 in Arkansas and is currently the largest retailer in the United States and in the world. Wal-Mart is also considered to be the low-price leader. The company went public in 1970 and has 4,800 stores worldwide with 75 percent of those located in the United States. Annual sales in the United States in 2004 were $256.3 billion, and their sales were higher than the combined total of the nine second-largest stores (Target, Sears, Kmart, J.C. Penney, Federated, Mays, TJX, Kohl's, and Dillards). Wal-Mart is planning to open 500 new stores by the end of 2005, which will result in an 8 percent expansion of total square footage to 55 million square feet. Wal-Mart also has entered the grocery market, which has been strategic to its growth in recent years. In 2005, Wal-Mart will add 240 to 250 Supercenters (stores that sell both general merchandise and groceries), 30 to 40 Sam's Clubs (large warehouse stores), and 25 to 30 Neighborhood Markets (smaller grocery-store formats designed to accommodate zoning in metropolitan areas).

Wal-Mart has significant power over its suppliers and has been accused of unfair labor practices for years (they maintain a strict anti-union position). It has a 44 percent turnover rate in its hourly workforce and, in 2001, the average Wal-Mart employee's salary was below the poverty level. Wal-Mart is also accused of putting many small town department stores and individual establishments out of business and has been criticized for limiting the public's choices by catering to conservative special interest groups. Wal-Mart accounts for 2.3 percent of the gross national product (GNP). By comparison, General Motors contributed

3 percent to the GNP in 1955, and U.S. Steel contributed 2.8 percent in 1917 at their respective peaks. In 2003, Wal-Mart was plagued by class-action employment suits (sexual discrimination against women, with nearly 1.5 million potential plaintiffs, and employees forced to work off-the-clock to avoid overtime payments) and use of illegal immigrants in cleaning companies.

Target is now the fourth-largest retailer in the United States (due to the Sears–Kmart merger, Target moved from third to fourth place) with 1,275 stores and 2004 annual U.S. sales of $48.16 billion. Target has its roots in the J.L. Hudson company, which was established in 1881 in Michigan and was the largest retailer of men's clothing by 1891. They opened their first Target store in 1962. Target is considered an upscale discounter with better brands and is very attractive to chic, hip, young consumers.

JCPenney is ranked fifth in the retail category for 2004 with total revenues of $18 billion. JCPenney stands to suffer from the Sears–Kmart merger because the move gives SHC an opportunity to increase its off-mall locations at a rapid pace. Although it appears that SHC may be positioned more as a discount retailer, which would not directly compete with JCPenney, which is known for its value fashions for moderate consumers, the indirect result for JCPenney could be problematic if SHC pulls their stores out of malls (the absence of Sears mall anchor stores would reduce foot traffic to malls which could ultimately hurt JCPenney's bottom line).[10]

Clearly, there is no shortage of retail competition between Wal-Mart, Target, Federated–May Department Stores, JCPenney, and others. If SHC were to focus exclusively on the strength of the Sears brand lines of Kenmore, Craftsman, DieHard, and other home services, then their competitors would include Home Depot and Lowe's. At the moment, however, it appears that SHC may be aiming to become more of a mass merchandiser by cross-selling both hard and soft product lines in various formats such as Sears Grand, Sears Essentials and mall/off-mall locations. In this category, Wal-Mart is the undisputed leader. Competing head-on with Wal-Mart will prove to be a daunting task as noted by Howard Davidowitz, chairman of consulting and investment banking firm Davidowitz & Associates: "All the dead retailers had grandiose plans . . . there's been more than 100 casualties. Nobody has ever taken on Wal-Mart and lived."

The Future of the Sears Holding Company   To be successful, SHC's business strategy must specifically address the issues of competition, culture, and synergy in a very focused way. "Four out of five companies that have attempted to change business strategies have failed to meet the new strategy's objectives,"[11] and "employees resisting change may make implementing a strategic change difficult or impossible."[12] In terms of competition, the mere combination of the Sears and Kmart retail empires does not propose any significant threat to competitors (e.g., Wal-Mart,

Target, Home Depot, etc.), because their consumer messages are more consistent and they continue to grow by building market share. With regard to culture, both organizations come from distinct, historic, and proud pasts, and it will be a challenge to combine these disparate entities to form one unique forward-driven culture. And, finally, while there are countless opportunities to combine brands, product lines, operations, and systems, corporate history books are filled with failed mergers (e.g., AOL-Time Warner) that underscore the difficulty of creating synergies on such a large scale.[13]

It should be noted that 70 percent of mergers fall short when it comes to achieving their targets for revenue synergies, while 40 percent lead to cost-synergy disappointment. Other mergers are "dis-synergy disasters," such as the aforementioned AOL-Time Warner merger, which resulted in $99 billion in write-downs by January 2003.

Miscalculations of revenue synergies can be attributed to unexpectedly high consumer defection levels, poor assumptions about market growth and competitive realities, and overly optimistic prospects for cross-selling opportunities in a deal's wake. It is also important to make efforts to retain employees from both companies. Bad assumptions, such as overly optimistic projections, simplistic predictions and assumptions, and poor time projections, "will lead to substantial over-estimates of synergy net present value by making cash flow accretion and other deal metrics look unrealistically positive."[14]

The question looming over the top management of Sears Holding Company is whether they can create a distinct brand image and identity to outperform fierce competitors like Wal-Mart and Target. To take on the competition successfully, key goals will be to create a culture of success among the disparate organizations of Sears and Kmart, to generate consumer loyalty, and to appropriately position SHC based on its identity in the general merchandise market.

Analyst Reviews

Analysts' reviews of the merger are mixed, ranging from optimism and faith in the leadership and vision of Lampert to ultimate failure of SHC (see Exhibit 4). There is, however, much speculation among analysts about whether Lampert can successfully accomplish the stated goals without selling off real estate. Hailed by *BusinessWeek* as the next Warren Buffet, Lampert closely mirrors Buffet's strategy of investing in cash-rich, old-line companies, and he stands to benefit enormously from the merger via his private investment fund and ESL Investments, which held 52.6 percent of Kmart and 14.6 percent of Sears premerger. As of March 2005, many industry analysts and insiders remained skeptical as to Lampert's motives—whether they would build a successful retail empire or merely generate cash.

Exhibit 4 Analysts' Reviews

Date	Positive Reviews	Negative Reviews	Source
November 18, 2004		There are "two threats immediately for the merged firms: debt will be more expensive because bond-rating firms are downgrading Sears' credit-worthiness, and the power and growth of Web shopping are weak areas for both firms . . . neither Sears nor Kmart have strong Internet sales . . . Walmart.com and Target.com have seen significant growth in sales but this merger is not likely to improve the Internet presence for Kmart or Sears."—Cynthia Jeffrey, Associate Professor, Iowa State College of Business	*Ascribe Newswire.* Iowa State sources offer expertise, perspective on Sears/Kmart merger
November 22, 2004	They will provide a compelling power brand statement in both fashion and home categories that will drive shoppers to the stores. If they pool their war chest of brand names and become one, they may solve the "brand image" problem that has eluded both. Sears Grand expectations should benefit from Kmart's experience in the consumables market.		*Retail Merchandiser.* Consultants question success of Sears/Kmart merger
November 22, 2004	Sears has long offered ethnic-specific programs . . . Kmart has just begun to "officially" target Hispanics . . . Perhaps bringing the benefits of big box retailing combined with these power brands to inner city, lower income, ethnic shoppers will provide the right niche for a still underserved audience.		*Retail Merchandiser.* Consultants question success of Sears/Kmart merger
November 22, 2004	"Long-term, the combined entity's success will hinge on execution, where neither company had a particularly good track record. . . . In our view, neither management team brings a significant track record of operating success to the transaction. . . . Still, better real estate locations will give them access to greater customer traffic, so we think it would be rash to discount the deal entirely."—Danielle Fox, Merrill Lynch analyst		*Business and Industry,* HFN, "The big deal: S-Mart?" by Barbara Thau, p. 1, ISSN: 1082-3010

Date		Source
November 22, 2004	"We do not believe that adding Sears appliances to Kmarts or Joe Boxer apparel to Sears will turn either company around."—George Strachan, Goldman Sachs analyst	*Business and Industry, HFN.* "The big deal: S-Mart?" by Barbara Thau, p. 1, ISSN: 1082-3010
November 29, 2004	Overall, Kmart brings stronger soft home goods to the merger . . . the Martha Stewart brand will be re-energized and become the focus private-label brand for the merged chain.	*Business and Industry, HFN.* Battle of the brands for Kmart and Sears, p. 4
November 30, 2004	Most analysts are skeptical the combination of two struggling retail brands that will continue to operate separately will thrive in a sector dominated by Wal-Mart.	*Retail Merchandiser.* How Kmart–Sears merger affects suppliers
February 10, 2005	"You have two retailers who are doing badly right now. . . . It's hard to fathom how combining them is suddenly going to produce a new entity that will do better."—Stephen Hoch, The Wharton School	*Gallup Management Journal.* Merger myopia: Two retail giants join forces. But how will the customer benefit? by William J. McEwen
March 24, 2005	"It's about profitability, not about sales. It may get smaller, but . . . it's going to be more profitable, more stable, with a better strategy. And it'll be more competitive with Wal-Mart and Target."—Richard Hastings, independent retail analyst	*The Associated Press.* Kmart buyout of Sears gets final approval; changes loom, by Dave Carpenter
March 24, 2005	"For the short term, it's very exciting. But for the long term, watch out." Davidoff forecasts a "bleak outlook" for Sears unless the move away from malls is successful.—Howard Davidoff, Davidoff and Associates	*The Associated Press.* Kmart buyout of Sears gets final approval; changes loom, by Dave Carpenter

Endnotes

1. SHC press release, March 24, 2005, www.searsholdings.com.

2. Garbato, Debby. 2004. Team Grit. *Retail Merchandiser,* February 1; *BusinessWeek,* November 2004; Thau, Barbara. 2004. The Big Deal: S-mart? *Business and Industry, HFN,* November 22: 1.

3. SHC press release, November 17, 2004, www.searsholdings.com.

4. Guy, Sandra. 2005. Brands a key in success of merger. *Chicago Sun-Times,* March 22; Berner, Robert, & Weber, Joseph. 2004. Eddie's master stroke. *BusinessWeek,* November 29: 34.

5. Clark, Ken. 2004. Kmart orders out. *Chain Store Age,* December, 80(12): 39.

6. Sway, Roxanne, & Mussleman, Faye. 2005. 2004, a very good year. *Display & Design Ideas,* March, 17(3): 34.

7. Kennedy, Kim. 2005. Retailing changes create opportunities. *FDM,* March, 77(3):18.

8. Ostroff, Jim. 2005. Store mergers to roil suppliers. *Kiplinger Business Forecasts,* March 8.

9. Ibid.

10. *DSN Retailing Today.* 2004. J. C. Penney merchandised itself better than Sears. December 13: 3.

11. Porter, Michael E. 1996. What is strategy? *Harvard Business Review,* 74(6): 61.

12. Lewin, Kurt. 1952. Group decision and social change. In Swanson, G. E., Newcombe, T. M., & Harley, E. L. *Readings in Social Psychology, 2nd Ed.,* pp. 459–473. New York: Holt.

13. Sway & Musselman. 2004, a very good year.

14. Frieswick, Kris. 2005. Acquirers seeking synergies would do well to shrink their expectations. *CFO Magazine,* February.

Case 34   Kroger Company*

Introduction

When Barney Kroger and his partner opened their first store in 1883, Kroger probably had no idea what the company that bears his name would look like 120 years later. From that first store the company has evolved into an operation consisting of 2,532 grocery retail stores in 32 states as of May 2005. This includes supermarkets, price-impact warehouse stores, and multi-department stores similar to supercenters. In addition, Kroger operates 795 convenience stores in 16 states and 436 fine jewelry stores. To complete the one-stop shopping strategy, Kroger also operates 536 fuel centers and 1,898 pharmacies. Besides the retail operations, Kroger also operates 42 food processing or manufacturing facilities producing high-quality, private-label products that provide value for customers and enhance profit margins. Kroger is the only U.S. supermarket that operates an economical three-tier distribution system.[1]

With all these operations, Kroger has positioned itself as a leader in the grocery retail industry. However, there is no time to relax and rest on past accomplishments. The grocery retail industry has entered the mature stage, so companies are looking for ways to innovate and revitalize their operations. With the addition of new competitors like Wal-Mart, Costco, and BJ's, the traditional supermarkets are being challenged to compete in this new industry environment of a flat market and stiff competition.[2] David B. Dillon, Kroger chairman and chief executive officer, indicates that Kroger is "off to a good start in 2005. Across the organization, our associates are working together to deliver the best possible shopping experience to our customers every day. Yet we also recognize that a lot of work remains. In this competitive environment, we must do an even better job of understanding and delivering what our customers need so that we can drive profitable sales growth and create the value that our shareholders expect from their investments."[3]

Company History

The first store was opened in 1883 in Cincinnati, Ohio. By 1884, Barney Kroger had bought out his partner on the initial store and opened a second location. The first bakeries were introduced in grocery stores in 1901 by Kroger, and by 1902 the Kroger Grocery and Baking Company was incorporated with 40 stores. When Kroger bought 14 Nagel meat markets and packaging houses in 1904, meat and groceries were sold under the same roof for the first time. By 1929 Kroger was operating a total of 5,575 stores, the most in its history. The Kroger Grocery and Baking

Company officially became the Kroger Company in 1946 and by 1952 sales topped 1 billion dollars.

During the 1970s Kroger listened to its customers through extensive market research and introduced ultra-modern stores featuring old-fashioned values and trendsetting specialty shops including cheese, delis, bakeries, and flowers among other items. By the end of the 1970s Kroger had become the nation's second-largest food retailing company. By 1980 Kroger had sales over 10 billion dollars, and during the decade introduced more specialty departments, including fresh seafood and fine fragrances. In 2000 Kroger was named "Grocery Distributor of the Year" by America's Second Harvest, the nation's largest food bank network. During the year Kroger donated 19 million pounds of product valued at $32 million. Kroger was named one of America's "100 Best Corporate Citizens" in 2001 by *Business Ethics,* a national publication honoring corporate social responsibility, and for the first time sales topped 50 billion dollars.[4]

Mergers and Acquisitions

Dillon Companies   Started in the early 1900s by J. S. Dillon, Dillon Companies, Inc., had grown to 24 stores in Kansas when it merged with King Soopers of Denver, Colorado, in 1957. Also in 1957, the company purchased the Wichita division of the Kroger Company. Through the years, Dillon continued to grow and prosper. Operating under the Dillon umbrella are many supermarket chains, convenience stores, and dairies in various states:[5]

Supermarkets:

- Dillon Stores: Arkansas, Oklahoma, Missouri, Kansas, and Nebraska
- King Soopers: Colorado
- Fry's Food Stores: Arizona
- City Markets: Colorado, Wyoming, Utah, and New Mexico

Convenience Stores:

- Turkey Hill Mini Markets: Pennsylvania
- Tom Thumb: Florida and Alabama
- Kwik Shop: Kansas, Nebraska, Iowa, Illinois, and Oklahoma
- Loaf & Jug: Colorado, New Mexico, Montana, Nebraska, South Dakota, North Dakota, and Wyoming

Dairies and Other:

- Turkey Hill Mini Markets: Pennsylvania
- Jackson's Ice Cream: Kansas and Colorado
- Wells Aircraft (Charter Air Transportation): Kansas

In 1983 Dillon Companies became a wholly owned subsidiary of the Kroger Company. With this merger Kroger

*This case was prepared by Debora J. Gilliard, Ph.D. of Metropolitan State College–Denver as a basis for class discussion rather than to illustrate either effective or ineffective handling of an administrative situation. Copyright © 2005 Debora J. Gilliard. Thank you to Donna Weins, a student at Metropolitan State College–Denver who wrote the initial version of this case for a class.

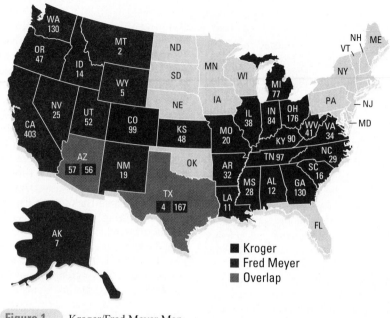

Figure 1 Kroger/Fred Meyer Map

began a new era as a coast-to-coast operator of food, drug, and convenience stores, and the manufacturer of more than four thousand food and nonfood products.[6]

Fred Meyer   In 1998 the Kroger Company and Fred Meyer, Inc. announced a strategic merger that created the nation's largest supermarket company. Freddy's—as the chain is known—is a supercenter pioneer providing food and general merchandise to cost-conscious consumers mainly in the Northwest. Earlier in 1998 the company increased its grocery store chains by acquiring Quality Food Centers, Ralph's Grocery, and Food 4 Less.[7] Fred Meyer is headquartered in Portland, Oregon, operating food and general merchandise stores in 12 western states from Alaska to Texas. The Kroger/Fred Meyer combination created the broadest geographic coverage and widest spectrum of retail formats, offering substantial economies of scale and increased purchasing power (see Figure 1).[8]

Current Acquisition Strategy   Kroger's current acquisition strategy focuses on existing markets, which decreases the company's risk and produces a higher incremental return because the stores require very little investment. The company acquired 48 stores in 2000, 31 stores in 2001, 42 stores in 2002, and 23 stores in 2003.[9]

Corporate Mission, Strategy, Strategic Growth Plan, and Technology

The Kroger Mission Statement reads as follows:

> Our Mission is to be a leader in the distribution and merchandising of food, health, personal care, general merchandise, and related consumable products and services.

By achieving this mission, we will satisfy our responsibilities to shareowners, associates, customer, suppliers, and the communities we serve.

We will conduct our business to produce financial returns that reward investment by shareowners and allow the Company to grow. Investments in retailing, distribution, and food processing will be continually evaluated for their contribution to our corporate return objectives.

We will constantly strive to satisfy the needs of customers as well as, or better than, the best of our competitors. Operating procedures will increasingly reflect our belief that the organization levels closest to the customer are best positioned to serve changing consumer needs.

We will provide all associates and customers with a safe, friendly work and shopping environment and will treat each of them with respect, openness, honesty, and fairness. We will solicit and respond to the ideas of our associates and reward their meaningful contributions to our success.

We value America's diversity and will strive to reflect that diversity in our work force, the companies with which we do business, and the customers we serve. As a Company, we will convey respect and dignity to all individuals.

We will encourage our associates to be active and responsible citizens and will allocate resources for activities that enhance the quality of life for our customers, our associates, and the communities we serve.[10]

Kroger recognizes the importance of investing in the communities where their customers and associates live and work, as reflected in the final paragraph of the mission statement. Charitable giving is focused around five key areas: hunger relief, education, advancement of women and minorities, "good neighbor" grassroots service organizations, and women's health. In 2003 the Company contributed nearly $120 million to local communities and nonprofit organizations. These contributions included donations made by Kroger retail divisions and the company's three foundations, employees, and funds raised through in-store events and promotions. The company worked with more than 40 regional food banks to donate 26 million pounds of food, donated $23 million to local schools and charitable organizations, and through employee donations and in-store fundraising generated $16 million in contributions to support local campaigns that included disaster relief agencies, children's hospitals, and breast cancer research.[11]

Kroger's fundamental operating strategy is: "To achieve competitive responsiveness and flexibility through the decentralized management of merchandising and operations combined with the economies of scale available from coordinating or consolidating volume-based activities and support systems."[12] With a decentralized structure, substantial authority for merchandising and operating decisions is placed in the retail divisions. Divisional managers are able to respond quickly to changes in competition and customer preferences within each local market. For processes that offer economies of scale, the company leverages its size to create value for customers and better returns for shareholders. The merger with Fred Meyer was consistent with this fundamental strategy because it generated tremendous opportunities for economies in purchasing, manufacturing, information systems, logistics, and support systems.[13]

The Kroger Company has identified four key strengths to set it apart from its competitors:

1. A high-quality asset base that holds leading market shares in many of the nation's largest and fastest-growing metro areas.
2. Broad geographic diversity and multiple retail formats that allow Kroger to meet the needs of virtually every customer.
3. A successful track record of competing against supercenters.
4. Industry-leading corporate brand products.

Since there is such a strong relationship between market share and return on assets (basically the higher the market share the greater the ROA), Kroger's fundamental operating philosophy is to grow market share in order to increase shareholder value.[14]

In December 2001 Kroger's management team announced a Strategic Growth Plan in response to the current economic and competitive environment. Three key elements of the plan include: reduce operating and administrative costs; leverage Kroger's size to achieve greater economies of scale; and reinvest in their core business to increase sales and

market share. In 2003, Kroger continued implementation of the plan by further narrowing the retail price gap with major discounters and widening its price advantage over traditional supermarket competitors. Identical food-stores sales, excluding stores affected by labor disputes, increased 0.7% in 2003. The company continued to achieve cost savings through improved labor productivity, lower product costs, energy conservation, and administrative efficiencies.[15] In addition to the price reductions, Kroger continues to differentiate the stores by offering customers a convenient shopping experience for pharmacy, natural foods, high-quality perishable, expanded general merchandise, and outstanding private-label products. The company continues to identify additional opportunities to operate more efficiently.

Kroger continues to invest in technology in order to have an efficient and cost effective information system and logistics network. Some recent technology investments include: self-checkout technology, time and attendance systems, labor and management scheduling technology, pharmacy systems, HR self-serve, customer loyalty, manufacturing planning and control systems, and shrink management applications. The distribution centers have state-of-the- art racking and product handling systems; refrigeration, temperature, and humidity controls; and space for cross-docking seasonal and promotion merchandise. Kroger has outsourced much of its distribution centers and store delivery fleets in order to gain flexibility and access to new approaches to distribution.

Kroger is the only major supermarket with a three-tier distribution system. The first tier consists of regional dry grocery, perishables, and freezer buildings that service stores within a 200 mile radius. The second tier consists of consolidation centers that service retail stores within a 350 mile radius for slower moving products such as pharmaceuticals, health and beauty care, and dry grocery merchandise. By using consolidation centers Kroger can purchase in larger quantities at the lowest possible prices. The third tier ships seasonal and promotional products to stores in large geographic ranges. To fully utilize the tiered network system, Kroger has invested in new technology. One new technology is "demand forecasting" which uses store-specific and market data to enhance each store's order system capabilities. Voice-pick technology uses wireless communication and voice instructions for picking product. A new real-time warehouse management system is increasing the speed and accuracy of product assembly and shipping. A Web-based freight management system is used to eliminate "empty" trucking miles and reduce freight expense.[16]

Company Operations

Kroger is headquartered in Cincinnati, Ohio. In 2004, Kroger was still one of the nation's largest retail grocery chains and was ranked number 19 on the Fortune Five Hundred list. The company was also the world's largest florist with 2,167 floral shops around the country. Either directly

Table 1   Store Formats

Store Formats	# of Stores	% of Stores	% of Revenue
Combination Stores	1,839	73%	
Superstores	285	11%	
Conventional Stores	127	5%	
Multi-department Stores	145	6%	
Price-Impact Warehouse Stores	136	5%	
Subtotal Food Store Count	**2,532**		**95%**
Convenience Stores	802		3%
Jewelry Store	440		1%
Other Sales (manufacturing sales to outside customers)			1%
Total	**3,774**		

Source: Kroger Fact Book 2003.

or through its subsidiaries, Kroger operated 2,532 super-markets, price impact, or multi-department stores in 32 states under almost two dozen banners in 2004 (see Table 1). Kroger has grown through acquisition and believes strongly in maintaining local banners where appropriate. Kroger also operated 802 convenience stores under six banners, 440 fine jewelry stores under four banners, 466 supermarket fuel centers, and 42 manufacturing plants.[17] Approximately 290,000 full- and part-time associates were employed by the company at the end of 2002.[18]

Supermarkets   The Supermarket format has been divided into three categories. The combination store is Kroger's primary format. The strategy here is to offer customers the advantages of one-stop shopping, in convenient locations, for a wide selection of consumables. They feature a complete supermarket and pharmacy with expanded perishable, health care, and general merchandise departments. More and more are featuring a supermarket fuel center. Combination stores average 55,000 square feet, but superstores are usually somewhat smaller. They generally do not include pharmacies, and have fewer specialty departments than combination stores. Conventional stores offer a broad selection of grocery items and operate in less than 25,000 square feet. The small size limits the perishable and general merchandise departments.[19]

Multi-Department Stores   Multi-department stores operate under the Fred Meyer and Fry's Marketplace banners.

Fred Meyer stores operate an average of 140,000 square feet and offer over 225,000 food and nonfood items. These stores offer food, apparel, home fashion and furnishings, outdoor living, electronics, automotive, toys, fine jewelry and fuel. This unique combination of merchandise allows Fred Meyer to sell a diverse selection of top national brands in all departments. In February 2004, Kroger converted five Fred Meyers stores in the Salt Lake area to a new Smith's Marketplace. These stores average 154,000 square feet and will offer new bakery and service delis in addition to grocery, produce, frozen food, and dairy products.[20]

Price-Impact Warehouse Stores   Price-impact warehouse stores operate under the Food 4 Less and Foods Co banners. These stores average 53,000 square feet in size and offer budget-conscious shoppers everyday low prices, superior quality of perishables, and a wide selection of national brand groceries, health and beauty care items, meat, dairy products, baked goods, and fresh produce. The high-quality produce in these stores is unique in the warehouse format and provides these stores with a key competitive advantage.

At year-end 2003, Kroger operated in 52 major markets. A major market is one in which Kroger operates nine or more stores. Kroger held the number one or two position in 43 of those major markets. Thirty-nine of Kroger's major markets are located among the nation's top one hundred Metropolitan Statistical Areas ranked by population.[21] See Tables 2 and 3 on major markets and competitors and retail food operations by state.

Table 2   Major Markets and Competitors

Major Markets	# Stores	Division	#1 or #2?	Major Competitors	
1 Los Angeles CA	199	Ralphs/Food 4 Less	Yes	Vons	Albertsons
2 Atlanta GA	128	Atlanta	Yes	Publix	Wal-Mart SC
3 Houston TX	100	Southwest	Yes	Wal-Mart SC	Randalls
4 Seattle WA	87	Fred Meyer/QFC	Yes	Safeway	Albertsons
5 Phoenix AZ	82	Fry's	Yes	Safeway	Albertsons
6 Detroit MI	71	Great Lakes	Yes	Farmer Jack	Meijer
7 Orange County CA	68	Ralphs/Food 4 Less	Yes	Albertsons	Vons
8 Denver CO	67	King Soopers	Yes	Safeway	Albertsons
9 Riverside CA	60	Ralphs/Food 4 Less	Yes	Stater Bros.	Albertsons
10 Cincinnati OH	56	Cincinnati	Yes	Bigg's	Meijer
11 Columbus OH	55	Great Lakes	Yes	Meijer	Big Bear
12 Dallas TX	50	Southwest	No	Albertsons	Wal-Mart SC
13 Indianapolis IN	48	Central	Yes	Marsh	Meijer
14 Las Vegas NV	48	Smith's/Food 4 Less	Yes	Albertsons	Vons
15 Nashville TN	41	Mid-South	Yes	Wal-Mart SC	Food Lion
16 Portland OR	41	Fred Meyer/QFC	Yes	Safeway	Albertsons
17 San Diego CA	41	Ralphs/Food 4 Less	Yes	Vons	Albertsons
18 Salt Lake City UT	38	Smith's/Fred Meyer	Yes	Albertsons	Harmons
19 Memphis TN	34	Delta	Yes	Wal-Mart SC	Schnuck's
20 Louisville KY	33	Mid-South	Yes	Wal-Mart SC	Meijer
21 Fort Worth TX	30	Southwest	No	Albertsons	Wal-Mart SC
22 San Francisco CA	28	Ralphs	No	Safeway	Albertsons
23 Dayton-Springfield OH	27	Cincinnati	Yes	Meijer	Cub
24 Wichita KS	25	Dillon	Yes	Wal-Mart SC	Food4Less (A)
25 Toledo OH	24	Great Lakes	Yes	Meijer	Farmer Jack
26 Little Rock AR	20	Delta	Yes	Wal-Mart SC	Harvest Food
27 Knoxville TN	19	Atlanta	Yes	Food City	Wal-Mart SC
28 Lexington KY	18	Mid-South	Yes	Wal-Mart SC	Meijer
29 Raleigh-Durham NC	18	Mid-Atlantic	No	Food Lion	Harris Teeter
30 Tucson AZ	17	Fry's	Yes	Safeway	Albertsons
31 Albuquerque NM	16	Smith's	Yes	Wal-Mart SC	Albertsons
32 Omaha NE	16	Dillon Stores	Yes	Hy Vee	Wal-Mart SC
33 Oxnard-Ventura CA	15	Ralphs/Food 4 Less	No	Vons	Albertsons
34 Tacoma WA	15	Fred Meyer/QFC	Yes	Safeway	Albertsons
35 Richmond VA	14	Mid-Atlantic	No	Ukrops	Food Lion
36 Flint MI	13	Great Lakes	Yes	Meijer	Farmer Jack
37 Roanoke VA	12	Mid-Atlantic	Yes	Food Lion	Wal-Mart SC
38 Sacramento CA	12	Ralphs/Food 4 Less	No	Albertsons	Bel Air Mkts
39 Wheeling WV-Steubenville OH	12	Great Lakes	Yes	Wal-Mart SC	Riesbecks
40 Charleston WV	11	Mid-Atlantic	Yes	Wal-Mart SC	Foodland
41 Peoria IL	11	Central	Yes	Wal-Mart SC	Cub
42 Savannah GA	11	Atlanta	Yes	Wal-Mart SC	Publix
43 Ann Arbor MI	10	Great Lakes	Yes	Meijer	Busch

(*continued*)

Table 2 (*Continued*)

Major Markets	# Stores	Division	#1 or #2?	Major Competitors	
44 Fort Wayne IN	10	Central	No	Scotts	Wal-Mart SC
45 Macon GA	10	Atlanta	Yes	Wal-Mart SC	Brunos
46 Saginaw MI	10	Great Lakes	Yes	Meijer	Farmer Jack
47 Augusta GA	9	Atlanta	Yes	Bi-Lo	Food Lion
48 Boulder-Longmont CO	9	King Soopers	Yes	Safeway	Albertsons
49 Colorado Springs CO	9	King Soopers	Yes	Safeway	Wal-Mart SC
50 Hamilton OH	9	Cincinnati	Yes	Meijer	Jungle Jim's
51 Hampton Roads VA	9	Mid-Atlantic	No	Food Lion	Farm Fresh
52 Jackson MS	9	Delta	Yes	Wal-Mart SC	Winn-Dixie
TOTAL	**1,825**		**43**		

(A)   Not owned or operated by Kroger.
____ Denotes supercenter operator.

Source: Kroger Fact Book 2003.

Convenience Stores   Kroger operates five convenience store divisions under six banners. The c-stores benefit from synergies with Kroger food stores by offering a limited selection of private label products. Convenience stores continue to concentrate on small to medium sized towns located near interstate highways. Two-thirds of the stores are located in towns with fewer than 75,000 residents. Of the 802 stores in 2003, 717 also sell gasoline. Average store size is 2,700 square feet. During 2003 the company opened 25 convenience stores and closed 7 stores. The new stores feature a large gasoline offering with 4 to 8 pumps and a well-lit canopy covering the pumps.[22]

Jewelry Stores   With 440 fine jewelry stores in 35 states at the end of 2003, the Kroger Co. ranked as the fourth-largest fine jewelry retailer in the nation. There are 119 jewelry locations inside Fred Meyer stores and another 321 located in shopping malls. The stores operate primarily under the banners of Fred Meyer Jewelers, Littman Jewelers, and Barclay Jewelers.[23]

Pharmacies   Kroger is the seventh largest pharmacy operator in the United States. In fiscal year 2003, the company operated 1,800 retail pharmacies in its stores and filled 111 million prescriptions at a retail value of about $5.5 billion.[24]

Corporate Brands and Manufactured Products   Corporate brand products play a central role in the company's merchandising strategy and provide a key competitive advantage to Kroger. In addition to the grocery category, Kroger carries a wide selection of products in meat, seafood, deli, floral, produce, health and beauty care, and general merchandise. Kroger brand products are produced and sold in three quality tiers.

1. Private Selections is the premium quality brand designed to meet or beat "gourmet" or "upscale" national or regional brands or can be unique items. Kroger offers about 625 Private Selection Items and 13 of the products have earned the Good Housekeeping Seal.

2. Banner Brands represents the majority of the corporate brand items. They are designed to be equal to or better than the national brand and carry the "Try it, Like it, or Get the National Brand Free" guarantee in most divisions. Before Kroger will carry a banner brand private label it must meet three tests:

   - Quality must be equal to or better than the national brand.
   - It must be able to sell at a retail price lower than the national brand equivalent.
   - It must be able to make more pennies profit per item.

3. For Maximum Value (FMV) is the value brand that is designed to deliver good quality at a very affordable price.

In April 2003, Kroger announced the official launch of "Naturally Preferred," its own brand of premium-quality natural and organic products. Baby food, pastas, cereals, snacks, milk, and soy items are among the 140 items available. The Naturally Preferred products are minimally processed using natural/organic ingredients and they do not contain artificial color, preservatives, or flavors.

Table 3   Retail Food Operations By State

State	Banner	Y/E 2002	Y/E 2003
California	Ralphs, Food 4 Less, Cala, Bell, Foods Co.	457	458
Texas	Kroger	202	209
Ohio	Kroger	200	207
Georgia	Kroger	169	173
Indiana	Kroger, Jay C, Pay Less, Owens, Food 4 Less	137	137
Washington	QFC, Fred Meyer	136	137
Colorado	King Soopers, City Market	122	130
Tennessee	Kroger	118	117
Michigan	Kroger, Kessel	116	121
Arizona	Fry's, Smith's	109	112
Kentucky	Kroger	98	99
Kansas	Dillon	75	76
Virginia	Kroger	65	67
Oregon	Fred Meyer, QFC	55	54
Nevada	Smith's, Food 4 Less	50	52
Utah	Smith's, Fred Meyer, City Market	52	54
Illinois	Kroger, Hilander, Food 4 Less	49	53
West Virginia	Kroger	47	46
Arkansas	Kroger, Dillon	41	41
Mississippi	Kroger	28	28
New Mexico	Smith's, City Market, Price Rite	26	26
Missouri	Kroger, Dillon, Gerbes	24	24
Nebraska	Baker's, Food 4 Less	16	16
Idaho	Fred Meyer, Smith's	14	14
South Carolina	Kroger	14	14
Alabama	Kroger	11	11
Louisiana	Kroger	11	11
Wyoming	Smith's, King Soopers, City Market	9	9
Alaska	Fred Meyer	9	10
Montana	Smith's	7	5
Oklahoma	Dillon	1	1
Total		**2,468**	**2,512**

Source: 2003 Kroger Fact book.

Table 4   The Kroger Co. Consolidated Balance Sheets
(In $ millions)

	Years Ended	
	January 29, 2005	January 31, 2004
Assets		
Current assets		
Cash and temporary cash investments	$ 144	$ 159
Deposits in-transit	506	579
Receivables	661	674
Receivables—taxes	167	66
FIFO inventory	4,729	4,493
LIFO credit	(373)	(324)
Prefunded employee benefits	300	300
Prepaid and other current assets	272	251
Total current assets	6,406	6,198
Property, plant and equipment, net	11,497	11,178
Goodwill, net	2,191	3,134
Fair value interest rate hedges	—	6
Other assets	397	247
Total Assets	$20,491	$20,763
Liabilities		
Current liabilities		
Current portion of long-term debt including obligations under capital leases and financing obligations	$ 71	$ 248
Accounts payable	3,778	3,637
Accrued salaries and wages	659	547
Deferred income taxes	267	138
Other current liabilities	1,541	1,595
Total current liabilities	6,316	6,165
Long-term debt including obligations under capital leases and financing obligations		
Face value long-term debt including obligations under capital leases and financing obligations	7,830	8,012
Adjustment to reflect fair value interest rate hedges	70	104
Long-term debt including obligations under capital leases and financing obligations	7,900	8,116
Deferred income taxes	939	974
Other long-term liabilities	1,796	1,523
Total Liabilities	16,951	16,778
Commitments and Contingencies		

(*continued*)

Table 4   (*Continued*)

	Years Ended	
	January 29, 2005	January 31, 2004
Shareowners' Equity		
Preferred stock, $100 par, 5 shares authorized and unissued	—	—
Common stock, $1 par, 1,000 shares authorized: 918 shares issued in 2004 and 913 shares issued in 2003	918	913
Additional paid-in capital	2,432	2,382
Accumulated other comprehensive loss	(202)	(124)
Accumulated earnings	3,541	3,641
Common stock in treasury, at cost, 190 shares in 2004 and 170 shares in 2003	(3,149)	(2,827)
Total Shareowners' Equity	3,540	3,985
Total Liabilities and Shareowners' Equity	$20,491	$20,763

The accompanying notes are an integral part of the consolidated financial statements.

Source: Kroger Form 10-K.

Highly efficient manufacturing plants produce approximately 55 percent of the 7,800 private-label products sold by Kroger. The remaining items are produced to strict Kroger specifications by outside manufacturers. Management performs a "make or buy" analysis on private-label products and decisions are based on a comparison of market-based transfer prices adjusted for plant profit versus open-market purchases. By manufacturing their own products, Kroger lowers their costs and passes on the saving to their customers. Kroger has 15 dairy and 3 ice cream plants that produce milk, yogurt, cottage cheese, ice cream, novelty treats, and non-carbonated beverages. The 7 bakeries provide cakes, donuts, cookies, bagels, muffins, snacks and crackers to the retail stores. The 5 grocery plants produce items such as pet foods, sugar-based products, coffee, spices, salad dressings, and peanut butter. In addition, Kroger also operates 2 cheese plants, 3 meat plants, and 3 beverage plants.[25]

Financial Recap

A major event in Kroger's financial history happened in 1988 when a hostile takeover was attempted. To fend off the takeover Kroger restructured, borrowing more than five billion dollars. They also issued stockholders a $40 per share dividend and a five-year note valued at $8.69 at the

time. After the restructuring, stock traded at $9 per share.[26] With this huge debt burden, Kroger was prohibited from paying stockholders any cash dividends. Since the 1988 restructure Kroger has attempted to restructure the debt burden whenever possible.

At least three items are having a significant impact on Kroger's operating results. First are costs related to the mergers including expenses recognized as a consequence of the continued integration of the company's divisions. Integration primarily resulted from the company's merger with Fred Meyer and relates to severance agreements, enterprise system and banner conversions, and inventory write-downs. Second, with the implementation of the Strategic Growth Plan in December of 2001, the company began incurring restructuring charges. While these actions did produce some additional costs, they also reduced expenses by approximately $306 million. Finally, accounting changes also impacted the reported financials for 2004.[27]

For fiscal year ending January 29, 2005, sales rose five percent to $56.43 billion and the company experienced a net loss of $100 million. The net loss is largely due to the company's goodwill impairment charge which is determined through analysis of the carrying value of a division, including goodwill, and fair value of a division. Impairment loss is recognized for any excess of the carrying

Table 5   The Kroger Co. Consolidated Statements of Operations
(In $ millions, except per share amounts)

	Years Ended		
	January 31, 2004 (52 weeks)	**February 1, 2003 (52 weeks)**	**February 2, 2002 (52 weeks)**
Sales	$56,434	$53,791	$51,760
Merchandise costs, including advertising, warehousing, and transportation, excluding items shown separately below	42,140	39,637	37,810
Operating, general and administrative	10,611	10,354	9,618
Rent	680	657	660
Depreciation and amortization	1,256	1,209	1,087
Goodwill impairment charges	900	444	—
Asset impairment charges	—	120	—
Restructuring charges	—	—	15
Merger-related costs	—	—	1
Operating Profit	847	1,370	2,569
Interest expense	557	604	619
Earnings before income tax expense and cumulative effect of accounting change	290	766	1,950
Income tax expense	390	454	732
Earnings (loss) before cumulative effect of accounting change	(100)	312	1,218
Cumulative effect of an accounting change, net of income tax benefit of $10 in 2002	—	—	(16)
Net earnings (loss)	$ (100)	$ 312	$ 1,202
Earnings (loss) per basic common share			
Earnings (loss) before cumulative effect of accounting change	$ (0.14)	$ 0.42	$ 1.56
Cumulative effect of an accounting change, net of income tax benefit	—	—	(0.02)
Net earnings (loss)	$ (0.14)	$ 0.42	$ 1.54
Average number of common shares used in basic calculation	736	747	779
Earnings (loss) per diluted common share:			
Earnings (loss) before cumulative effect of accounting change	$ (0.14)	$ 0.41	$ 1.54
Cumulative effect of an accounting change, net of income tax benefit	—	—	(0.02)
Net earnings (loss)	$ (0.14)	$ 0.41	$ 1.52
Average number of common shares used in diluted calculation	736	754	791

Source: Kroger Annual 10-K FYE January 29, 2005.

value of the division's goodwill over the implied fair value.[28] In addition, the company repurchased approximately 4.2 million shares of stock in the fourth quarter of 2004 for a total investment of $69.2 million. In a March 8, 2005, press release Kroger CEO David B. Dillon stated,

> We are very pleased with our sales performance in the fourth quarter. Kroger's identical food-store sales, without the effect of fuel and southern California, have shown sequential improvement for seven of the past eight quarters. This is a clear sign that Kroger's strategic focus on fulfilling the needs of our customers continues to generate positive results. This momentum has continued in fiscal 2005, with identical food-store sales through the first five weeks running ahead of our fourth-quarter results.[29]

In identifying its 2005 guidance, Mr. Dillon states, "Kroger's growth strategy is squarely focused on consistently meeting the needs of our customers through our associates providing improved service, selection, and value. We have made considerable progress, and in 2005, the successful execution of our strategy will be clearly evident in our financial performance."[30]

Goals for 2005 include:[31]

- To achieve in excess of 2.0% identical food-store sales growth. This figure includes southern California and excludes fuel sales.
- To generate cost savings and productivity improvements which will be invested to improve our customers' shopping experiences.
- To invest $1.6–$1.8 billion in capital project, excluding acquisitions, as the company focuses on remodels, merchandising, and productivity improvements.
- To use one-third of cash flow for debt reduction and two-thirds for stock repurchase or payment of a cash dividend.

- To adopt expensing of stock options during the year. Kroger currently estimates the effect of this adoption will be $0.04–$0.05 per diluted share.

Kroger's stock price has ranged from $14.65–$18.36 for the 52-week period ending May 15, 2005.[32]

Industry Background

Over the past decade there has been a steady consolidation of supermarket chains. In 2000 this movement was slowed slightly by some objections from the Federal Trade Commission, which was trying to keep some geographical areas competitive. It is not easy to separate grocery sales from other interests of these companies, particularly in drug stores and in many nongrocery items sold. The five top chains in the U.S. (Kroger, Albertson's, Safeway, Winn Dixie, and Ahold) account for nearly 50 percent of all grocery sales (see Table 6).

As companies have worked to eliminate competition by restricting the ownership of supermarkets, they have been challenged by new, and to some extent unexpected, competition outside the industry. The biggest is Wal-Mart, which has aggressively expanded its grocery efforts, followed by Target and Meijer's. Second are major drug chains, such as Walgreen's and CVS, who now sell many grocery items as well. A third area is convenience store chains, of which Southland (Seven Eleven) is by far the biggest. Some of these chains are migrating up with a wide variety of grocery products, sometimes termed "mega-mini" stores. A fourth set of competitors comes from super discount and club stores like BJs, Sam's Club (Wal-Mart), and Costco. The supermarket industry in the U.S. is still competitive and diverse. Further consolidation seems inevitable, with the new number one grocery company, Wal-Mart, making life hard for the chains and independents alike.[33]

Leading industry players are looking for ways to break the mold in an effort to strengthen market share, increase profitability potential, and defend against fierce competitive

Table 6	Top Five U.S. Food Retailers—by 2003 Grocery Sales		
Name	**Headquarters**	**Sales—2003**	**# of Stores**
Wal-Mart	Bentonville, AR	$103,200,000,000	1,427
Kroger Co.	Cincinnati, OH	$ 53,600,000,000	3,313
Albertson's	Boise, ID	$ 35,718,000,000	2,315
Safeway	Pleasanton, CA	$ 35,552,700,000	1,805
Ahold USA, Inc.	Chantily, VA	$ 26,660,000,000	1,475

Source: Food Marketing Institute.[34]

| Table 7 | Supermarket Facts—Industry Overview 2004 |

Number of employees—2002	3.4 million
Total supermarket sales—2004	$457.4 billion
Number of supermarkets ($2 million or more in annual sales)	34,352
Net profit after taxes, 2003/2004	0.88%
Percentage of disposable income spent on food—USDA figure 2003	
Food-at-home	6.1%
Food away-from-home	4.0%
Weekly sales per square foot of selling area—2004	$8.68
Sales per customer transaction—2004	$24.64
Average trips per week consumers make to the supermarket	2.2

Source: Food Marketing Institute.

pressures. The number of market leaders contemplating divesting underperforming businesses is likely to rise. A certain amount of retrenching is possible, with chains closing underperforming stores and pulling out of non-core markets to focus resources in stores with the greatest potential and highest market share. More companies will review pricing strategies and take advantage of emerging technologies in an effort to maintain price parity with low-price competitors. Efforts to differentiate on nonprice measures will escalate, including fresh foods, micro-merchandising, creative partnerships, online retailing, and technology advancements. Finally, traditional supermarkets will emphasize convenience, growing their one-stop appeal with bigger nonfoods offers, more "grab-and-go" meal options, and adding fuel centers.[35]

Major Competitors

Wal-Mart   Wal-Mart Stores is an irresistible (or at least unavoidable) retail force that has yet to meet any immovable objects. It is the world's number one retailer. The company organizes its business into three segments: Wal-Mart, Sam's Club, and International, with the Wal-Mart segment providing 67.3 percent of sales and Sam's Club providing 13 percent of sales. The International segment operates in eight countries and Puerto Rico and has provided 19.7 percent of sales in fiscal 2005.[36] Nearly 75 percent of its stores are in the U.S., but Wal-Mart is expanding internationally.[37] Wal-Mart is the big disrupter in the supermarket industry. The company has come from nowhere in the grocery market to a position that really threatens supermarket chains, winning big on comparative pricing. Wal-Mart is

the highest grossing food retailer. Several factors contribute to Wal-Mart's lower prices. First it has tough labor tactics and does not have to meet union wages. Another reason is its tough negotiation with its suppliers. On the technology side, Wal-Mart has perfected the art of managing and evaluating shelf space. These factors give it a cost advantage over the many rival grocers that use third-party wholesalers.[38]

Safeway   In 1915 M.B. Skaggs, an ambitious young man in the small Idaho town of American Falls, purchased a grocery store from his father. His business strategy, to give customers value and to expand by keeping a narrow profit margin, proved spectacularly successful. By 1926 he was operating 428 Skaggs stores in 10 states. That year his business almost doubled when Skaggs merged with Safeway. In 1928, M.B. Skaggs listed Safeway on the New York Stock exchange. Today, Safeway operates approximately 1,800 stores across the U.S. and Canada. They operate under the banners of: Safeway, Vons, Dominick's, Randalls, Tom Thumb, Genuardi's, and Carrs. Safeway has over 1,800 stores in 22 states and Canada and owns a 49 percent interest in 115 Casa Ley Stores in western Mexico. A key ingredient in Safeway's success has been the introduction of one of the most extensive private label programs in North America. Safeway has always made giving back to the community a priority. Even with Safeway's community leadership and growth to one of the largest food and drug retailers in North America, it has not come at the expense of M.B. Skaggs's vision. His strong sense of customer value that proved so innovative in American Falls in 1915 continues to work successfully in a new century.[39] Safeway reported a 12% increase in total revenues in its first quarter 2005 report. Safeway has also announced its intent to change its strategy by improving the shopping environment, updating the fresh areas of the stores, and offering higher quality prepared meals and remodeling stores into a "lifestyle" format. The company estimates it will convert 25 percent of its stores by the end of 2005.[40]

Alberston's   In 1939 Joe Alberston opened a small grocery store in Boise, Idaho. Joe changed the rules in the grocery business by introducing services like a scratch bakery, magazine racks, homemade ice cream, popcorn, nuts, and an automatic doughnut machine. He based his store on providing high quality, good value and excellent service. It was the beginning of what is now one of the largest retail food and drug chains in the United States. The original philosophy of giving the customers the merchandise they want, at a price they can afford, in clean stores with great service from friendly personnel, still applies today. Albertson's strives to continue to offer consumers new and exciting one-stop shopping ideas.[41] Currently, Albertson's operates approximately 2,500 stores in 37 states, employing about 200,000 associates.[42]

Ahold USA   On May 27, 1887, Mr. Albert Heijn laid the foundations for what was to become a truly global food retailing company when he took over his father's small grocery store close to the Dutch town of Zaandam. Mr. Heijn, with a fine nose for the needs of his customers, soon opened more stores and started to offer his own private label products, including among others, coffee. Now, over 100 years later, entrepreneurial skills, a precise sense of what customers want and an excellent value-for-money private label policy, are still very much the pillars of Royal Ahold's global retailing strategy.[43] In the United States, Ahold has food retail and e-commerce activities. Ahold operates over 1,600 stores grouped in six retail operating companies along the U.S. eastern seaboard. The retail stores combined serve approximately 20 million customers every week. They also operate Peapod, an e-commerce business headquartered in Chicago. Ahold USA employs over 200,000 people. Almost 60 percent of Ahold worldwide sales are generated in the United States. Banners under the Ahold umbrella include The Stop & Shop Supermarket Company, Giant Food, Inc., Tops Markets, BI-LO, and Bruno's Supermarkets.[44] First quarter 2005 consolidated sales were 13.0 billion euro which is a one percent decline compared to the same period last year. On April 25, 2005, Ahold announced it had reached an agreement to divest its chain of 198 convenience stores of its U.S. subsidiary Tops Markets LLC ("Tops") to WFI Acquisition, Inc., a corporation formed by Nanco Enterprises, Inc. and Bruckmann, Rosser, Sherrill & Co, Inc. These were Ahold's remaining convenience stores in the United States.[45]

Tables 8 and 9 provide comparative information for the major competitors in the industry.

Table 8   Direct Competitor Comparison—May 2005

	Kroger	Albertson's	Safeway	Wal-Mart	Industry
Market Cap:	12.33B	7.78B	9.89B	198.95B	827.60M
Employees:	289,000	241,000	191,000	1,700,000	9.00K
Rev. Growth (ttm):	4.90%	12.60%	0.80%	11.30%	6.50%
Revenue (ttm):	56.43B	39.90B	36.76B	294.43B	3.85B
Gross Margin (ttm):	25.33%	28.04%	29.36%	22.99%	26.05%
EBITDA (ttm):	2.10B	2.33B	2.22B	21.93B	109.68M
Oper. Margins (ttm):	1.50%	3.08%	3.57%	5.92%	2.15%
Net Income (ttm):	−100.00M	474.00M	648.40M	10.56B	17.12M
EPS (ttm):	−0.152	1.274	1.443	2.486	0.96
PE (ttm):	N/A	16.57	15.29	18.91	17.31
PEG (ttm):	1.50	1.89	1.82	1.11	1.64
PS (ttm):	0.21	0.19	0.26	0.68	0.20

Source: finance.yahoo.com.

(ttm = trailing twelve months)

| Table 9 | Competitor Information |

	Kroger	**Albertson's**	**Safeway**	**Wal-Mart**	**Industry**
Key Numbers					
Annual Sales ($ mil)	56,434.0	39,897.0	35,822.9	285,222.0	
Employees	289,000	241,000	191,000	1,700,000	
Profitability					
Gross Profit Margin	25.33%	30.80%	31.92%	24.48%	31.42%
Net Profit Margin	(0.18%)	1.11%	1.76%	3.60%	0.13%
Return on Equity	—	8.2%	14.6%	20.8%	1.3%
Return on Assets	(0.5%)	2.4%	4.2%	8.5%	0.3%
Operations					
Inventory Turnover	9.9	9.0	9.4	7.7	10.8
Financial					
Current Ratio	1.01	1.05	.84	.90	1.09
Quick Ratio	0.2	0.2	0.2	0.2	0.5
Leverage Ratio	5.79	3.38	3.45	2.43	3.77
Total Debt/Equity	2.25	1.27	1.53	.64	1.48
Interest Coverage	1.50	2.50	3.30	14.40	1.50

Source: Hoovers Online.[46]

Endnotes

1. Kroger Company. 2005. Available at www.kroger. com; Yahoo Finance. 2005. Available at www.finance.yahoo.com.
2. Otte, Timothy M. 2005. Safeway slides into first. *Motley Fool*. May 3. Available at www.biz.yahoo. com/fool/.
3. Press release, June 21, 2005.
4. Kroger Company. 2004/2005. Available at www.kroger.com/operations.htm.
5. Career Builder. 2004. Available at www.careerbuilder.com/JobSeeker/Companies/CompanyDetails.
6. Kroger Company. 2004/2005. Available at www.kroger.com/operations.htm.
7. Hoovers On-line. 2004. Available at www.hoovers.com/fred-meyer-stores/factsheet.xhtml.
8. Fred Meyer Company. 2004. Available at www.fredmeyer.com/pressreleases&speeches/pr_archive.
9. Kroger Fact Book. 2003. Available at http://www.kroger.com/financialinfo_reportsandstatements.htm.
10. Ibid.
11. Ibid.
12. Ibid.
13. Kroger Fact Book. 2002. Available at www.kroger. com/financialinfo_reportsandstatements.htm.
14. Kroger Fact Book. 2003. Available at http://www.kroger.com/financialinfo_reportsandstatements.htm.
15. Ibid.
16. Ibid.
17. Kroger Company. 2005. Available at www.kroger.com.
18. Kroger Fact Book. 2003. Available: http://www.kroger.com/financialinfo_reportsandstatements.htm.
19. Ibid.
20. Ibid.
21. Ibid.
22. Ibid.
23. Ibid.
24. Ibid.
25. Ibid.
26. Kroger Company. 2004/2005. Available at www.kroger.com/operations.htm.
27. Edgar. 2004. Available at www.sec.gov/Achives/ edgar/data.
28. Kroger Company. 2005. Available at www.kroger.com.
29. Press release, March 8, 2005.
30. Ibid.
31. Ibid.
32. Yahoo Finance. 2005. Available at www.finance.yahoo.com.
33. Oligopoly Watch. 2004. Available at www.oligopolywatch.com.

34. Food Marketing Institute. 2005. Available at www.fmi.org/facts_figs/faq/top_retailers.htm.

35. Retail Forward. 2004. Available at www. retailforward.com/freecontent/pressreleases/ press65.asp.

36. Yahoo Finance. 2005. Available at www.finance. yahoo.com.

37. Yahoo Business. 2004. Available at www.biz.yahoo.com.

38. Oligopoly Watch. 2004. Available at www. oligopolywatch.com.

39. Safeway Company. 2004, 2005. Available at www.safeway.com/OurCompany.asp.

40. Otte, Timothy M. 2005. Safeway slides into first. *Motley Fool,* May 3. Available at www.biz.yahoo. com/fool/.

41. Albertson's Company. 2004, 2005. Available at www. albertsons.com/abs_aboutalbertsons/albertsonsfacts/ default.asp.

42. Yahoo Finance. 2005. Available at www.finance. yahoo.com.

43. Ahold Company. 2004, 2005. Available at www.aholdusa.com/history.cfm.

44. Ibid.

45. Ibid.

46. Hoover's. 2005. Available at www.premium.hoovers.com.

Case 35   QVC*

Nail clippers that catch clippings, bicycle seats built for bigger bottoms, and novelty items shaped like coffins were among the nearly 600 products trying out for a spot on the QVC home shopping channel. The products were pitched to QVC buyers in the St. Louis area in one of the six try-outs that had been scheduled across the country for the home shopping channel's Decades of Discoveries Tour. The tour, designed to commemorate 10 years of QVC's national product searches, was launched on January 31, 2005. Buyers from the channel were expected to select the top 100 products that would be featured on special broadcasts during the summer of 2005.

Thousands of entrepreneurs have used QVC's product searches over the past decade to try to sell their products on the popular home shopping channel. A chance to display their offerings to QVC's national TV audience can transform a one-person operation into a multibillion-dollar business. "The vendors who are our success stories for this past decade have done over $1 billion in sales on QVC over the past 10 years," said Marilyn Montross, the channel's director of vendor relations.[1]

QVC has used its product searches to find products that are not readily available through other channels. Its success with such exclusive offerings has helped to establish the network as the most popular home shopping network. QVC has attained this leading position although it was launched in 1986, a couple of years after the debut of rival Home Shopping Network. By 2004, its reach had extended to 95 percent of all U.S. cable homes as well as over 23 million satellite homes. It had shipped 137 million units to customers around the world during 2004 as the result of 192 million telephone calls, resulting in more than $5.7 billion in sales (see Exhibit 1).

In spite of this stellar performance, Donald S. Briggs, president and CEO of QVC, was concerned about the opportunities for further growth for the world's largest television home shopping channel. He has been turning to higher-margin product categories such as beauty, apparel, and cooking. QVC also has been pitching its products to more customers by expanding to countries outside the United States and through the development of a Web-based operation. In fact, much of the firm's recent growth has come from product categories that are relatively new to QVC and from recently introduced television shopping channels in the United Kingdom, Germany, and Japan.

At the same, QVC may find it challenging to maintain its growth rate. Despite a significant annual increase in the number of units sold, the firm has been struggling to demonstrate a comparable increase in total revenues or net

*This case was prepared by Professor Jamal Shamsie of Michigan State University. This case was developed from published sources as a basis for class discussion rather than to illustrate either effective or ineffective handling of an administrative situation. Copyright © 2005 Jamal Shamsie.

Exhibit 1   Sales Growth

Year	Sales
2004	$5.7 billion
2001	3.8 billion
1998	2.4 billion
1995	1.6 billion
1992	0.9 billion
1989	0.2 billion

Source: QVC, Liberty Media.

profit (see Exhibit 2). For the most part, this can be attributed to the difficulties it has been facing in developing a greater share of sales from higher-margin product categories. The firm continues to derive most of its sales from popular categories such as home electronics and appliances, which carry much lower margins.

Developing a Leading Shopping Network

QVC was founded by Joseph Segel in June 1986 and began broadcasting by November of the same year. In early 1986, Segel had tuned into the Home Shopping Network, which had been launched just two years earlier. He had not been particularly impressed with the crude programming and the down-market products of the firm. But Segel was convinced that another televised shopping network would have the potential to attract a large enough client base. He also felt that such an enterprise should be able to produce significant profits, because the operating expenses for a shopping network could be kept relatively low.

Over the next few months, Segel raised $30 million in start-up capital, hired several seasoned television executives, and launched his own shopping network. Operating out of headquarters that were located in West Chester, Pennsylvania, QVC offered 24-hour-a-day, seven-day-a-week television shopping to consumers at home. By the end of its first year of operation, QVC had managed to extend its reach to 13 million homes by satellite and cable systems. Three million orders were shipped to 700,000 viewers who had already become customers. Its sales had already topped $100 million and the firm was actually able to show a small profit.

Segel attributed the instant success of his company to the potential offered by television shopping. "Television's combination of sight, sound, and motion is the best way to sell a product. It is more effective than presenting a product in print or just putting the product on a store shelf," he stated. "The cost-efficiency comes from the cable distribution system. It is far more economical than direct mail, print advertising, or traditional retail store distribution."[2]

Exhibit 2 Income Statement

	2004	2003	2002
	(Years ended December 31)		
	(Amounts in millions)		
Net Revenue	$5,687	$4,889	$4,362
Cost of Sales	(3,594)	(3,107)	(2,784)
Gross Profit	2,093	1,782	1,578
Operating Expenses*	(497)	(447)	(413)
S, G, & A Expenses	(366)	(322)	(304)
Operating Cash Flow	1,230	1,013	861
Stock Compensation	(33)	(6)	(5)
Depreciation & Amortization**	(437)	(222)	(119)
Operating Income	$ 760	$ 785	$ 737

*Operating expenses consist of commissions and license fees, order processing and customer service, credit card processing fees, and provision for doubtful accounts.

**Depreciation & amortization includes amortization of intangible assets recorded in connection with the purchase of QVC by Liberty Media.

Source: Liberty Media, QVC.

In the fall of 1988, Segel acquired the manufacturing facilities, proprietary technology, and trademark rights of the Diamonique Corporation, which produced a wide range of simulated gemstones and jewelry that could be sold on QVC's shows. Over the next couple of years, Segel expanded QVC by acquiring its competitors such as the Cable Value Network Shopping channel.

By 1993, QVC had overtaken Home Shopping Network to become the leading televised shopping channel in terms of sales and profits. Its reach extended to over 80 percent of all cable homes and to 3 million satellite dishes. Segel retired during the same year, passing control of the company to Barry Diller. Since then, QVC's sales have continued to grow at a substantial rate. As a result, it has consistently widened the gap between its sales and those of Home Shopping Network, which has remained its closest competitor.

Achieving Efficiency in Operations

Over the years, QVC has managed to establish itself as the world's preeminent virtual shopping mall that never closes. Its televised shopping channel has become a place where customers can, and do, shop at any hour at the rate of two customers per second. It sells a wide variety of products, using a combination of description and demonstration by live program hosts. Each of the products is presented by QVC in a format where it is attractively modeled and carefully explained by the hosts of the show and by representatives from the vendor. QVC works hard to develop descriptions for each of their offerings that have been carefully crafted to resonate with its viewing audience. If necessary, complete on-air instructions are also provided for the use of every product that it sells.

In addition, most of the products are offered on regularly scheduled shows, each of which is focused on a particular type of product and a well-defined market. Each of these shows typically lasts for one hour and is based on a theme such as Now You're Cooking or Cleaning Solutions. QVC has enticed celebrities such as clothing designers or book authors to appear live on special program segments to sell their own products. On some occasions, customers are able to call in and have on-air conversations with program hosts and visiting celebrities (see Exhibit 3).

QVC's themed programs are telecast live 24 hours a day, seven days a week to over 87 million households in the United States. Announcements for the channel's programming are sent out by mail to established customers and advertised on the stations themselves. QVC transmits its programming live from its central production facilities in Pennsylvania through uplinks to a satellite. Consumers receive the programming at home either through a local cable television company or through their own satellite dishes.

Exhibit 3 QVC Programming Typical Weekly Schedule

Eastern Standard Time	Monday	Tuesday	Wednesday	Thursday	Friday	Saturday	Sunday
4–5 a.m.	Turquoise Jewelry	14K Gold Jewelry	CAROLE HOCHMAN HEAVENLY SOFT SLEEPWEAR	Savings on Style	Silver Marketplace	Royal Palace Handmade Rugs	Smashbox Cosmetics
5–6 a.m.	Around the House	Make Life Easier	ELECTRONICS TODAY	Savings on Style	Problem Solvers	Denim & Co	Smashbox Cosmetics
6–7 a.m.	Now You're Cooking	Beauty by Tova	DECOR...DEWBERRY STYLE	Savings on Style	Marcel Drucker Watches	Pilates Home Studio	Kitchen Ideas
7–8 a.m.	The QVC Morning Show	The QVC Morning Show	THE QVC MORNING SHOW	The QVC Morning Show	The QVC Morning Show—Fashion Friday	Bracelet Showcase	Silver Style
8–9 a.m.	The QVC Morning Show	The QVC Morning Show	THE QVC MORNING SHOW	The QVC Morning Show	The QVC Morning Show—Fashion Friday	AM Style	Silver Style
9–10 a.m.	Joan Rivers Classics Collection	14K Gold Jewelry	SILVER JEWELRY	Susan Graver Style	Diamonique Jewelry	AM Style	Silver Style
10–11 a.m.	Joan Rivers Classics Collection	14K Gold Jewelry	BODIPEDIC MEMORY FOAM SYSTEM	Susan Graver Style	Clarks Footwear	Tracy Porter's Home Style	Silver Style
11 a.m.–12 p.m.	Joan Rivers Classics Collection	Denim & Co	CLEANING SOLUTIONS	Citrine Jewelry	Take Care of Yourself	Tracy Porter's Home Style	QVC Sampler
12–1 p.m.	Family Time	Fine Jewelry Collection	CAROLE HOCHMAN HEAVENLY SOFT SLEEPWEAR	Clothes Out	Silver Marketplace	Eternagold	In the Kitchen with Bob
1–2 p.m.	Quacker Factory with Jeanne Bice	Beauty by Tova	THE MASTER BEDROOM	Victorian Home	Silver Marketplace	Royal Palace Handmade Rugs	In the Kitchen with Bob
2–3 p.m.	Quacker Factory with Jeanne Bice	Beauty by Tova	BIRTHSTONE COLLECTION	Victorian Home	Easy Solutions	Royal Palace Handmade Rugs	Ross-Simons Jewelry
3–4 p.m.	Outdoor Toys & Fun	Bracelet Showcase	BIRTHSTONE COLLECTION	Victorian Home	Philosophy—Beauty	14K Gold Jewelry	Local Flavors
4–5 p.m.	Turquoise Jewelry	Kitchen Ideas	PROBLEM SOLVERS	Statements on Style	Philosophy—Beauty	Easy Solutions	Smashbox Cosmetics
5–6 p.m.	QVC Sampler	Jewelry Showcase	LOW-CARB GOURMET FOOD	Suspicion Marcasite Jewelry	Philosophy—Beauty	Pilates Home Studio	Smashbox Cosmetics

Source: QVC.

QVC has eight phone centers worldwide for a total of more than 7,000 phone lines and the capacity to handle well over 120,000 calls per hour. Of all the orders placed with QVC, more than 90 percent are shipped within 48 hours from one of their distribution centers. Paul Day, a logistics manager for QVC, explained how they can ensure such fast delivery to their customers, "The whole supply chain has to be working, from how the buyers buy and set up dates on their orders to how we receive the orders."[3] The distribution centers have a combined floor space of 4.6 million square feet, which is equivalent to the size of 103 football fields.

To make it easier for viewers to purchase products that they may see on their home shopping channel, QVC also provides a credit program to allow customers to pay for goods over a period of several months. Everything it sells is also backed by a 30-day unconditional money-back guarantee. Furthermore, QVC does not impose any hidden charges, such as a restocking fee, for any returned merchandise. These policies help the home shopping channel attract customers for products that they can view but are not able to either touch or feel.

Searching for Profitable Products

More than 100 experienced, informed buyers comb the world on a regular basis to search for new products to launch on QVC. The shopping channel concentrates on unique products that can be demonstrated on live television. Furthermore, the price of these products must be high enough for viewers to justify the additional shipping and handling charge. Over the course of a typical year, QVC carries more than 50,000 products. Almost 1,700 items are typically offered in any given week, of which about 15 percent, or 250, are new products for the network. QVC's suppliers range from some of the world's biggest companies to small entrepreneurial enterprises.

All new products must, however, pass stringent tests that are carried out by QVC's in-house Quality Assurance Lab. In many cases, this inspection process is carried out manually by the firm's employees. Only 15 percent of the products pass the firm's rigorous quality inspection on first try, and as many as one-third are never offered to the public because they fail altogether. Everyone at QVC works hard to make sure that every item works as it should before it is shipped and that its packaging will protect it during the shipping process. "Nothing ships unless it is quality-inspected first," said Paul Day, the logistics manager for QVC. "Since our product is going business-to-consumer, there's no way to fix or change a product-related problem."[4]

About one-third of QVC's sales come from broadly available national brands. The firm has been able to build trust among its customers in large part through the offering of these well-known brands. QVC also relies upon promotional campaigns with a variety of existing firms for an-

other third of its sales. It has made deals with firms such as Dell, Target, and Bath & Body Works for special limited-time promotional offerings. But QVC has been most successful with products that are exclusively sold on QVC or that are not readily available through other distribution channels. Although such products account for another one-third of its sales, the firm has been able to earn higher margins with these proprietary products, many of which come from firms that are either start-ups or new entrants into the U.S. market.

Apart from searching for exclusive products, QVC also has been trying to move away from some product categories, such as home appliances and electronic gadgets, which offer lower margins. It has been gradually expanding into many new product categories that have higher margins such as cosmetics, apparel, food, and toys. Several of these new categories also have displayed the strongest rates of growth in sales for the shopping channel over the past couple of years. At the same time, QVC continues to rely on some of its older higher margin staples. Jewelry, for example, still accounts for almost 30 percent of the shopping network's airtime.

QVC has been struggling, however, to develop more sales from higher margin product categories. It has been hard to keep finding new products that carry higher margins and to sell them in sufficient quantity. The shopping channel has relied in part, over the years, on products by various fashion designers such as Arnold Scassi and Calvin Klein. Many designers have been attracted to QVC because of its access to a much broader market. More recently, the firm has been offering apparel and accessories by exclusive designers that have been specifically created for the mass market. In late 2004, QVC contracted with Marc Bouwer to develop an M collection to be sold exclusively on its home shopping channel. Bouwer's initial products included a $50 kimono blouse, $50 matte jersey pants with side slits, and a $149 silk dress with a ruffled front. "Where else can you sell thousands of units in virtually minutes?" Bouwer explained.[5]

Expanding upon the Customer Base

By 2005, QVC's shopping channel had penetrated almost all of the cable television and broadcast satellite homes in the United States. The firm was, therefore, aware that any further growth would have to come from an increase in sales to its existing customers. In this respect, it has been helped by surveys indicating that QVC has established a reasonably strong reputation among a large majority of its current consumers. By its initials alone, QVC had promised that it would deliver Quality, Value, and Convenience to its viewers. More than three-quarters of the shopping channel's customers have given it a score of 7 out of 7 for trustworthiness. This has led most of its customers to demonstrate a strong tendency to purchase often from the channel and to recommend it to their friends.

But the shopping channel also was trying to use its reputation to attract new customers, both in its existing markets and in new markets. Over the last decade, QVC has expanded to the U.K., Germany, and Japan, giving it access to about 66 million new households in these three countries. Partly as a result of this expansion into new markets, a large part of the shopping network's strong growth in sales over the past few years has come from the regular addition of new customers. In a typical month, QVC can gain as many as 194,000 new customers worldwide and many of them stay on to become repeat customers. The firm's total customer file has surpassed 42 million customers that are spread over four countries (see Exhibit 4).

QVC also has benefited from the growing percentage of women entering the workforce, resulting in a significant increase in dual-income families. Although the firm's current customer base does span several socioeconomic groups, it is led by young professional families who have above average disposable income. They also enjoy various forms of "thrill-seeking" activities and rank shopping relatively higher as a leisure activity when compared to the typical consumer.

In 1995, QVC launched its own retail Web site to complement its television home shopping channel. Called iQVC, the 24-hour service has provided the firm access to more than 100 million households in the United States that have Internet connections. The Web site also has allowed the firm to perform well with some product categories that have not done as well on the television channel. For example, its Books, Movies and Music link offers more than 500,000 books, 100,000 movies, and 150,000 compact discs. Although the Internet operations have emerged as a critical secondary source of growth, it still accounts for less than one-fifth of QVC sales.

Finally, QVC rolled out an interactive shopping service in June 2004 that allows its customers to purchase whatever QVC is offering on its shopping channel with a single click of the remote. The interactive shopping service that the firm was offering in partnership with Charter Communications and Open TV represented yet another step to increase the attractiveness of its home shopping channel. The service initially was being offered to more than 1.3 million homes that subscribe to Charter's cable service. "There is quite a bit of momentum building behind ITV," said James Ackerman, CEO of Open TV, the firm that had partnered with QVC on the interactive service.[6]

Positioning for Future Growth

QVC's rapid growth had attracted the attention of Comcast and Liberty Media, both of which had jointly taken control of the shopping network in 1995. During 2003, Liberty Media took everyone by surprise when it decided to buy out Comcast's stake. In establishing the price that

Exhibit 4 Geographical Breakdown

Revenue ($ millions)			
	2004	**2003**	**2002**
	(Years ended December 31)		
U.S.	$4,141	$3,845	$3,705
U.K.	487	370	296
Germany	643	429	275
Japan	416	245	86

Homes (millions)		
	2004	**2003**
	(Years ended December 31)	
U.S.	88.4	85.9
U.K.	15.6	13.1
Germany	35.7	34.6
Japan	14.7	11.8

Source: Liberty Media, QVC.

Liberty Media's John Malone paid, he put a value of $14.1 billion on QVC. It was clear that Malone felt that the home shopping network would continue to grow in spite of the development of competing forms of home shopping. QVC's sales have actually grown to match that of Internet giant Amazon.com. But while the Internet firm has struggled to show strong profits, QVC has been generating tons of cash.

To date, QVC certainly looks like it is well positioned for continued growth in sales. Since the launching of its Web site, the firm has taken steps to become an innovative practitioner of electronic retailing. Its Web site has moved well beyond its initial capabilities, when it simply offered supplementary information on the products that were featured on the television shopping channel. The recent introduction of the interactive service for the shopping channel represents one of the first launches of on-screen interactivity, the kind in which viewers can interact with television content simply through the remote control. Looking towards the future, QVC is already focusing on new avenues for growth, such as those that might be offered through retailing on the mobile telephone.

Regular technological developments may, in fact, allow QVC to continue to offer much higher margin products to both existing and new markets. Doug Rose, vice president of merchandising brand development, claims that interactivity in all aspects of the firm's business, including its television shopping channel, will only become more pronounced in the future, making it easier for customers to act on what they see. QVC believes that it still has a lot of room to grow, since only about 2 percent to 3 percent of its television viewers currently purchase at any given time.

"I was at an anniversary for employees last month, and they were showing clips of what QVC looked like 10 years ago," Rose said. "I was just stunned at how, by my reckoning, it looked so primitive. I fully expect that in 10 years, I'll be looking at clips of what we are doing now and think, 'How primitive.' So much has changed here, and yet we are taking baby steps. We're very much in our infancy."[7]

Endnotes

1. Feldstein, Mary Jo. 2005. Investors, entrepreneurs vie for QVC appearance. *Knight Ridder Tribune Business News*, February 11: 1.

2. QVC Annual Report, 1987–1988.

3. Gilligan, Eugene. 2004. The show must go on. *Journal of Commerce,* April 12: 1.

4. Journal of Commerce, April 12: 1.

5. Feitelberg, Rosemary. 2004. Bouwer prime for QVC. *WWD,* November 23: 8.

6. Whitney, Daisy. 2004. Charter, QVC premiere interactive shopping. *TelevisionWeek,* May 3: 74.

7. Duff, Mike. 2005. QVC turns up the volume. *DSN Retailing Today,* March 14: 2.

Case 36 Philips versus Matsushita: A New Century, a New Round*

Throughout their long histories, N.V. Philips (Netherlands) and Matsushita Electric (Japan) had followed very different strategies and emerged with very different organizational capabilities. Philips built its success on a worldwide portfolio of responsive national organizations while Matsushita based its global competitiveness on its centralized, highly efficient operations in Japan.

During the 1990s, both companies experienced major challenges to their historic competitive positions and organizational models, and at the end of the decade, both companies were struggling to reestablish their competitiveness. At the turn of the millennium, new CEOs at both companies were implementing yet another round of strategic initiatives and organizational restructurings. Observers wondered how the changes would affect their long-running competitive battle.

Philips: Background

In 1892, Gerard Philips and his father opened a small lightbulb factory in Eindhoven, Holland. When their venture almost failed, they recruited Gerard's brother, Anton, an excellent salesman and manager. By 1900, Philips was the third largest light-bulb producer in Europe.

From its founding, Philips developed a tradition of caring for workers. In Eindhoven it built company houses, bolstered education, and paid its employees so well that other local employers complained. When Philips incorporated in 1912, it set aside 10% of profits for employees.

Technological Competence and Geographic Expansion While larger electrical products companies were racing to diversify, Philips made only light-bulbs. This one-product focus and Gerard's technological prowess enabled the company to create significant innovations. Company policy was to scrap old plants and

*This case derives from an earlier case, "Philips versus Matsushita: Preparing for a New Round," HBS No. 399-102, prepared by Professor Christopher A. Bartlett, which was an updated version of an earlier case by Professor Bartlett and Research Associate Robert W. Lightfoot, "Philips and Matsushita: A Portrait of Two Evolving Companies," HBS Case No. 392-156. The section on Matsushita summarizes "Matsushita Electric Industrial (MEI) in 1987," HBS Case No. 388-144, by Sumantra Ghoshal (INSEAD) and Christopher A. Bartlett. Some early history on Philips draws from "Philips Group—1987," HBS Case No. 388-050, by Professors Frank Aguilar and Michael Y. Yoshino. This version was also prepared by Professor Bartlett. HBS cases are developed solely as the basis for class discussion. Cases are not intended to serve as endorsements, sources of primary data, or illustrations of effective or ineffective management.

use new machines or factories whenever advances were made in new production technology. Anton wrote down assets rapidly and set aside substantial reserves for replacing outdated equipment. Philips also became a leader in industrial research, creating physics and chemistry labs to address production problems as well as more abstract scientific ones. The labs developed a tungsten metal filament bulb that was a great commercial success and gave Philips the financial strength to compete against its giant rivals.

Holland's small size soon forced Philips to look beyond its Dutch borders for enough volume to mass produce. In 1899, Anton hired the company's first export manager, and soon the company was selling into such diverse markets as Japan, Australia, Canada, Brazil, and Russia. In 1912, as the electric lamp industry began to show signs of overcapacity, Philips started building sales organizations in the United States, Canada, and France. All other functions remained highly centralized in Eindhoven. In many foreign countries Philips created local joint ventures to gain market acceptance.

In 1919, Philips entered into the Principal Agreement with General Electric, giving each company the use of the other's patents. The agreement also divided the world into "three spheres of influence": General Electric would control North America; Philips would control Holland; but both companies agreed to compete freely in the rest of the world. (General Electric also took a 20% stake in Philips.) After this time, Philips began evolving from a highly centralized company, whose sales were conducted through third parties, to a decentralized sales organization with autonomous marketing companies in 14 European countries, China, Brazil, and Australia.

During this period, the company also broadened its product line significantly. In 1918, it began producing electronic vacuum tubes; eight years later its first radios appeared, capturing a 20% world market share within a decade; and during the 1930s, Philips began producing X-ray tubes. The Great Depression brought with it trade barriers and high tariffs, and Philips was forced to build local production facilities to protect its foreign sales of these products.

Philips: Organizational Development

One of the earliest traditions at Philips was a shared but competitive leadership by the commercial and technical functions. Gerard, an engineer, and Anton, a businessman, began a subtle competition where Gerard would try to produce more than Anton could sell and vice versa. Nevertheless, the two agreed that strong research was vital to Philips' survival.

During the late 1930s, in anticipation of the impending war, Philips transferred its overseas assets to two trusts, British Philips and the North American Philips Corporation; it also moved most of its vital research laboratories to Redhill in Surrey, England, and its top management to the United States. Supported by the assets and resources transferred abroad, and isolated from their parent, the individual country organizations became more independent during the war.

Because waves of Allied and German bombing had pummeled most of Philips' industrial plant in the Netherlands, the management board decided to build the postwar organization on the strengths of the national organizations (NOs). Their greatly increased self-sufficiency during the war had allowed most to become adept at responding to country-specific market conditions—a capability that became a valuable asset in the postwar era. For example, when international wrangling precluded any agreement on three competing television transmission standards (PAL, SECAM, and NTSC), each nation decided which to adopt. Furthermore, consumer preferences and economic conditions varied: in some countries, rich, furniture-encased TV sets were the norm; in others, sleek, contemporary models dominated the market. In the United Kingdom, the only way to penetrate the market was to establish a rental business; in richer countries, a major marketing challenge was overcoming elitist prejudice against television. In this environment, the independent NOs had a great advantage in being able to sense and respond to the differences.

Eventually, responsiveness extended beyond adaptive marketing. As NOs built their own technical capabilities, product development often became a function of local market conditions. For example, Philips of Canada created the company's first color TV; Philips of Australia created the first stereo TV; and Philips of the United Kingdom created the first TVs with teletext.

While NOs took major responsibility for financial, legal, and administrative matters, 14 product divisions (PDs), located in Eindhoven, were formally responsible for development, production, and global distribution. (In reality, the NOs' control of assets and the PDs' distance from the operations often undercut this formal role.) The research function remained independent and, with continued strong funding, set up eight separate laboratories in Europe and the United States.

While the formal corporate-level structure was represented as a type of geographic/product matrix, it was clear that NOs had the real power. NOs reported directly to the management board, which Philips enlarged from 4 members to 10 to ensure that top management remained in contact with and control of the highly autonomous NOs. Each NO also regularly sent envoys to Eindhoven to represent its interests. Top management, most of whom had careers that included multiple foreign tours of duty, made frequent overseas visits to the NOs. In 1954, the board established the International Concern Council to formalize regular meetings with the heads of all major NOs.

Within the NOs, the management structure mimicked the legendary joint technical and commercial leadership of the two Philips brothers. Most were led by a technical manager and a commercial manager. In some locations, a finance manager filled out the top management triad that typically reached key decisions collectively. This cross-functional coordination capability was reflected down through the NOs in front-line product teams, product-group-level management teams, and at the senior management committee of the NOs' top commercial, technical, and financial managers.

The overwhelming importance of foreign operations to Philips, the commensurate status of the NOs within the corporate hierarchy, and even the cosmopolitan appeal of many of the offshore subsidiaries' locations encouraged many Philips managers to take extended foreign tours of duty, working in a series of two- or three-year posts. This elite group of expatriate managers identified strongly with each other and with the NOs as a group and had no difficulty representing their strong, country-oriented views to corporate management.

Philips: Attempts at Reorganization

In the late 1960s, the creation of the Common Market eroded trade barriers within Europe and diluted the rationale for maintaining independent, country-level subsidiaries. New transistor- and printed circuit-based technologies demanded larger production runs than most national plants could justify, and many of Philips' competitors were moving production of electronics to new facilities in low-wage areas in East Asia and Central and South America. Despite its many technological innovations, Philips' ability to bring products to market began to falter. In the 1960s, the company invented the audiocassette but let its Japanese competitors capture the mass market. A decade later, its R&D group developed the V2000 videocassette format—superior technically to Sony's Beta or Matsushita's VHS—but was forced to abandon it when North American Philips decided to outsource, brand, and sell a VHS product which it manufactured under license from Matsushita.

Over three decades, seven chairmen experimented with reorganizing the company to deal with its growing problems. Yet, entering the new millennium, Philips' financial performance remained poor and its global competitiveness was still in question. (See Exhibits 1 and 2.)

Van Riemsdijk and Rodenburg Reorganizations, 1970s   Concerned about what one magazine described as "continued profitless progress," newly appointed CEO

Exhibit 1 Philips Group Summary Financial Data, 1970–2000
(millions of guilders unless otherwise stated)

	2000	1995	1990	1985	1980	1975	1970
Net sales	F83,437	F64,462	F55,764	F60,045	F36,536	F27,115	F15,070
Income from operations (excluding restructuring)	NA	4,090	2,260	3,075	1,577	1,201	1,280
Income from operations (including restructuring)	9,434	4,044	−2,389	N/A	N/A	N/A	N/A
As a percentage of net sales	11.3%	6.3%	−4.3%	5.1%	4.3%	4.5%	8.5%
Income after taxes	12,559	2,889	F−4,447	F1,025	F532	F341	F446
Net income from normal business operations	NA	2,684	−4,526	N/A	328	347	435
Stockholders' equity (common)	49,473	14,055	11,165	16,151	12,996	10,047	6,324
Return on stockholders' equity	42.8%	20.2%	−30.2%	5.6%	2.7%	3.6%	7.3%
Distribution per common share, par value F10 (in guilders)	F2.64	F1.60	F0.0	F2.00	F1.80	F1.40	F1.70
Total assets	86,114	54,683	51,595	52,883	39,647	30,040	19,088
Inventories as a percentage of net sales	13.9%	18.2%	20.7%	23.2%	32.8%	32.9%	35.2%
Outstanding trade receivables in month's sales	1.5	1.6	1.6	2.0	3.0	3.0	2.8
Current ratio	1.2		1.4	1.6	1.7	1.8	1.7
Employees at year-end (in thousands)	219	265	273	346	373	397	359
Wages, salaries and other related costs	NA	NA	F17,582	F21,491	F15,339	F11,212	F5,890
Exchange rate (period end; guilder/$)	2.34	1.60	1.69	2.75	2.15	2.69	3.62
Selected data in millions of dollars:							
Sales	$35,253	$40,039	$33,018	$21,802	$16,993	$10,098	$4,163
Operating profit	3,986	2,512	1,247	988	734	464	NA
Pretax income	5,837	2,083	−2,380	658	364	256	NA
Net income	5,306	1,667	−2,510	334	153	95	120
Total assets	35,885	32,651	30,549	19,202	18,440	11,186	5,273
Shareholders' equity (common)	20,238	8,784	6,611	5,864	6,044	3,741	1,747

Source: Annual reports; Standard & Poors' *Compustat*; Moody's Industrial and International Manuals.

Note: Exchange rate 12/31/00 was Euro/US$: 1.074

Exhibit 2 Philips Group, Sales by Product and Geographic Segment, 1985–2000
(millions of guilders)

	2000		1995		1990		1985	
Net Sales by Product Segment:								
Lighting	F11,133	13%	F 8,353	13%	F 7,026	13%	F 7,976	12%
Consumer electronics	32,357	39	22,027	34	25,400	46	16,906	26
Domestic appliances	4,643	6	—		—		6,644	10
Professional products/systems	—		11,562	18	13,059	23	17,850	28
Components/semiconductors	23,009	28	10,714	17	8,161	15	11,620	18
Software/services	6,679	8	9,425	15	—		—	
Medical systems	1,580	2	—		—		—	
Origin	—		—		—		—	
Miscellaneous	4,035	5	2,381	4	2,118	4	3,272	5
Total	83,437	100%	64,462	100%	F55,764	100%	F 64,266	100%
Operating Income by Sector:								
Lighting	1,472	16%	983	24%	419	18%	F 910	30%
Consumer electronics	824	9	167	4	1,499	66	34	1
Domestic appliances	632	7	—		—		397	13
Professional products/systems	—		157	4	189	8	1,484	48
Components/semiconductors	4,220	45	2,233	55	−43	−2	44	1
Software/services	372	4	886	22	—		—	
Medical systems	2,343	25	—		—		—	
Origin	—		—		—		—	
Miscellaneous	−249	−3	423	10	218	10	200	7
Increase not attributable to a sector	−181	−2	(805)	(20)	−22	−1	6	0
Total	9,434	100%	4,044	100%	2,260	100%	F 3,075	100%

Source: Annual reports.

Notes:

Conversion rate (12/31/00): 1 Euro: 2.20371 Dutch Guilders

Totals may not add due to rounding.

Product sector sales after 1988 are external sales only; therefore, no eliminations are made; sector sales before 1988 include sales to other sectors; therefore, eliminations are made.

Data are not comparable to consolidated financial summary due to restating.

Hendrick van Riemsdijk created an organization committee to prepare a policy paper on the division of responsibilities between the PDs and the NOs. Their report, dubbed the "Yellow Booklet," outlined the disadvantages of Philips' matrix organization in 1971:

> Without an agreement [defining the relationship between national organizations and product divisions], it is impossible to determine in any given situation which of the two parties is responsible. . . . As operations become increasingly complex, an organizational form of this type will only lower the speed of reaction of an enterprise.

On the basis of this report, van Riemsdijk proposed rebalancing the managerial relationships between PDs and NOs—"tilting the matrix" in his words—to allow Philips to decrease the number of products marketed, build scale by concentrating production, and increase the flow of goods among national organizations. He proposed closing the least efficient local plants and converting the best into International Production Centers (IPCs), each supplying many NOs. In so doing, van Riemsdijk hoped that PD managers would gain control over manufacturing operations. Due to the political and organizational difficulty of closing local plants, however, implementation was slow.

In the late 1970s, his successor CEO, Dr. Rodenburg, continued this thrust. Several IPCs were established, but the NOs seemed as powerful and independent as ever. He furthered matrix simplification by replacing the dual commercial and technical leadership with single management at both the corporate and national organizational levels. Yet the power struggles continued.

Wisse Dekker Reorganization, 1982   Unsatisfied with the company's slow response and concerned by its slumping financial performance, upon becoming CEO in 1982, Wisse Dekker outlined a new initiative. Aware of the cost advantage of Philips' Japanese counterparts, he closed inefficient operations—particularly in Europe where 40 of the company's more than 200 plants were shut. He focused on core operations by selling some businesses (for example, welding, energy cables, and furniture) while acquiring an interest in Grundig and Westinghouse's North American lamp activities. Dekker also supported technology-sharing agreements and entered alliances in offshore manufacturing.

To deal with the slow-moving bureaucracy, he continued his predecessor's initiative to replace dual leadership with single general managers. He also continued to "tilt the matrix" by giving PDs formal product management responsibility, but leaving NOs responsible for local profits. And he energized the management board by reducing its size, bringing on directors with strong operating experience, and creating subcommittees to deal with difficult issues. Finally, Dekker redefined the product planning process, incorporating input from the NOs, but giving global PDs the final decision on long-range direction. Still sales declined and profits stagnated.

Van der Klugt Reorganization, 1987   When Cor van der Klugt succeeded Dekker as chairman in 1987, Philips had lost its long-held consumer electronics leadership position to Matsushita, and was one of only two non-Japanese companies in the world's top ten. Its net profit margins of 1% to 2% not only lagged behind General Electric's 9%, but even its highly aggressive Japanese competitors' slim 4%. Van der Klugt set a profit objective of 3% to 4% and made beating the Japanese companies a top priority.

As van der Klugt reviewed Philips' strategy, he designated various businesses as core (those that shared related technologies, had strategic importance, or were technical leaders) and noncore (stand-alone businesses that were not targets for world leadership and could eventually be sold if required). Of the four businesses defined as core, three were strategically linked: components, consumer electronics, and telecommunications and data systems. The fourth, lighting, was regarded as strategically vital because its cash flow funded development. The noncore businesses included domestic appliances and medical systems which van der Klugt spun off into joint ventures with Whirlpool and GE, respectively.

In continuing efforts to strengthen the PDs relative to the NOs, van der Klugt restructured Philips around the four core global divisions rather than the former 14 PDs. This allowed him to trim the management board, appointing the displaced board members to a new policy-making Group Management Committee. Consisting primarily of PD heads and functional chiefs, this body replaced the old NO-dominated International Concern Council. Finally, he sharply reduced the 3,000-strong headquarters staff, reallocating many of them to the PDs.

To link PDs more directly to markets, van der Klugt dispatched many experienced product-line managers to Philips' most competitive markets. For example, management of the digital audio tape and electric-shaver product lines were relocated to Japan, while the medical technology and domestic appliances lines were moved to the United States.

Such moves, along with continued efforts at globalizing product development and production efforts, required that the parent company gain firmer control over NOs, especially the giant North American Philips Corp. (NAPC). Although Philips had obtained a majority equity interest after World War II, it was not always able to make the U.S. company respond to directives from the center, as the V2000 VCR incident showed. To prevent replays of such experiences, in 1987 van der Klugt repurchased publicly owned NAPC shares for $700 million.

Exhibit 3   Philips Research Labs by Location and Specialty, 1987

Location	Size (staff)	Specialty
Eindhoven, The Netherlands	2,000	Basic research, electronics, manufacturing technology
Redhill, Surrey, England	450	Microelectronics, television, defense
Hamburg, Germany	350	Communications, office equipment, medical imaging
Aachen, W. Germany	250	Fiber optics, X-ray systems
Paris, France	350	Microprocessors, chip materials, design
Brussels	50	Artificial intelligence
Briarcliff Manor, New York	35	Optical systems, television, superconductivity, defense
Sunnyvale, California	150	Integrated circuits

Source: Philips. 1998. *BusinessWeek*, March 21: 156.

Reflecting the growing sentiment among some managers that R&D was not market oriented enough, van der Klugt halved spending on basic research to about 10% of total R&D. To manage what he described as "R&D's tendency to ponder the fundamental laws of nature," he made R&D the direct responsibility of the businesses being supported by the research. This required that each research lab become focused on specific business areas (see Exhibit 3).

Finally, van der Klugt continued the effort to build efficient, specialized, multi-market production facilities by closing 75 of the company's 420 remaining plants worldwide. He also eliminated 38,000 of its 344,000 employees—21,000 through divesting businesses, shaking up the myth of lifetime employment at the company. He anticipated that all these restructurings would lead to a financial recovery by 1990. Unanticipated losses for that year, however—more than 4.5 billion Dutch guilders ($2.5 billion)—provoked a class-action law suit by angry American investors, who alleged that positive projections by the company had been misleading. In a surprise move, on May 14, 1990, van der Klugt and half of the management board were replaced.

Timmer Reorganization, 1990   The new president, Jan Timmer, had spent most of his 35-year Philips career turning around unprofitable businesses. With rumors of a takeover or a government bailout swirling, he met with his top 100 managers and distributed a hypothetical—but fact-based—press release announcing that Philips was bankrupt. "So what action can you take this weekend?" he challenged them.

Under "Operation Centurion," headcount was reduced by 68,000 or 22% over the next 18 months, earning Timmer the nickname "The Butcher of Eindhoven." Because European laws required substantial compensation for layoffs—Eindhoven workers received 15 months' pay, for example—the first round of 10,000 layoffs alone cost Philips $700 million. To spread the burden around the globe and to speed the process, Timmer asked his PD managers to negotiate cuts with NO managers. According to one report, however, country managers were "digging in their heels to save local jobs." But the cuts came—many from overseas operations. In addition to the job cuts, Timmer vowed to "change the way we work." He established new performance rules and asked hundreds of top managers to sign contracts that committed them to specific financial goals. Those who broke those contracts were replaced—often with outsiders.

To focus resources further, Timmer sold off various businesses including integrated circuits to Matsushita, minicomputers to Digital, defense electronics to Thomson and the remaining 53% of appliances to Whirlpool. Yet profitability was still well below the modest 4% on sales he promised. In particular, consumer electronics lagged with slow growth in a price-competitive market. The core problem was identified by a 1994 McKinsey study that estimated that value added per hour in Japanese consumer electronic factories was still 68% above that of European plants. In this environment, most NO managers kept their heads down, using their distance from Eindhoven as their defense against the ongoing rationalization.

After three years of cost-cutting, in early 1994 Timmer finally presented a new growth strategy to the board. His plan was to expand software, services, and multimedia to become 40% of revenues by 2000. He was betting on Philips' legendary innovative capability to restart the growth engines. Earlier, he had recruited Frank Carrubba,

Hewlett-Packard's director of research, and encouraged him to focus on developing 15 core technologies. The list, which included interactive compact disc (CD-i), digital compact cassettes (DCC), high definition television (HDTV), and multimedia software, was soon dubbed "the president's projects." But his earlier divestment of some of Philips' truly high-tech businesses and a 37% cut in R&D personnel left the company with few who understood the technology of the new priority businesses.

By 1996, it was clear that Philips' HDTV technology would not become industry standard, that its DCC gamble had lost out to Sony's Minidisc, and that CD-i was a marketing failure. While costs were lower, so too was morale, particularly among middle management. Critics claimed that the company's drive for cost-cutting and standardization had led it to ignore new worldwide market demands for more segmented products and higher consumer service.

Boonstra Reorganization, 1996

When Timmer stepped down in October 1996, the board replaced him with a radical choice for Philips—an outsider whose expertise was in marketing and Asia rather than technology and Europe. Cor Boonstra was a 58-year-old Dutchman whose years as CEO of Sara Lee, the U.S. consumer products firm, had earned him a reputation as a hard-driving marketing genius. Joining Philips in 1994, he headed the Asia Pacific region and the lighting division before being tapped as CEO.

Unencumbered by tradition, he immediately announced strategic sweeping changes designed to reach his target of increasing return on net assets from 17% to 24% by 1999. "There are no taboos, no sacred cows," he said. "The bleeders must be turned around, sold, or closed." Within three years, he had sold off 40 of Philips' 120 major businesses—including such well known units as Polygram and Grundig. He also initiated a major worldwide restructuring, promising to transform a structure he described as "a plate of spaghetti" into "a neat row of asparagus." He said:

> How can we compete with the Koreans? They don't have 350 companies all over the world. Their factory in Ireland covers Europe and their manufacturing facility in Mexico serves North America. We need a more structured and simpler manufacturing and marketing organization to achieve a cost pattern in line with those who do not have our heritage. This is still one of the biggest issues facing Philips.

Within a year, 3,100 jobs were eliminated in North America and 3,000 employees were added in Asia Pacific, emphasizing Boonstra's determination to shift production to low-wage countries and his broader commitment to Asia. And after three years, he had closed 100 of the company's 356 factories worldwide. At the same time, he replaced the company's 21 PDs with 7 divisions, but shifted day-to-day operating responsibility to 100 business units,

each responsible for its profits worldwide. It was a move designed to finally eliminate the old PD/NO matrix. Finally, in a move that shocked most employees, he announced that the 100-year-old Eindhoven headquarters would be relocated to Amsterdam with only 400 of the 3,000 corporate positions remaining.

By early 1998, he was ready to announce his new strategy. Despite early speculation that he might abandon consumer electronics, he proclaimed it as the center of Philips' future. Betting on the "digital revolution," he planned to focus on established technologies such as cellular phones (through a joint venture with Lucent), digital TV, digital videodisc, and web TV. Furthermore, he committed major resources to marketing, including a 40% increase in advertising to raise awareness and image of the Philips brand and de-emphasize most of the 150 other brands it supported worldwide—from Magnavox TVs to Norelco shavers to Marantz stereos.

While not everything succeeded (the Lucent cell phone JV collapsed after nine months, for example), overall performance improved significantly in the late 1990s. By 1999, Boonstra was able to announce that he had achieved his objective of a 24% return on net assets.

Kleisterlee Reorganization, 2001

In May 2001, Boonstra passed the CEO's mantle to Gerard Kleisterlee, a 54-year-old engineer (and career Philips man) whose turnaround of the components business had earned him a board seat only a year earlier. Believing that Philips had finally turned around, the board challenged Kleisterlee to grow sales by 10% annually and earnings 15%, while increasing return on assets to 30%.

Despite its stock trading at a steep discount to its breakup value, Philips' governance structure and Dutch legislation made a hostile raid all but impossible. Nonetheless, Kleisterlee described the difference as "a management discount" and vowed to eliminate it. The first sign of restructuring came within weeks, when mobile phone production was outsourced to CEC of China. Then, in August, Kleisterlee announced an agreement with Japan's Funai Electric to take over production of its VCRs, resulting in the immediate closure of the European production center in Austria and the loss of 1,000 jobs. The CEO then acknowledged that he was seeking partners to take over the manufacturing of some of its other mass-produced items such as television sets.

In mid-2001, a slowing economy resulted in the company's first quarterly loss since 1996 and a reversal of the prior year's strong positive cash flow. Many felt that these growing financial pressures—and shareholders' growing impatience—were finally leading Philips to recognize that its best hope of survival was to outsource even more of its basic manufacturing and become a technology developer and global marketer. They believed it was time to recognize that its 30-year quest to build efficiency into its global operations had failed.

Matsushita: Background

In 1918, Konosuke Matsushita (or "KM" as he was affectionately known), a 23-year-old inspector with the Osaka Electric Light Company, invested ¥100 to start production of double-ended sockets in his modest home. The company grew rapidly, expanding into battery-powered lamps, electric irons, and radios. On May 5, 1932, Matsushita's 14th anniversary, KM announced to his 162 employees a 250-year corporate plan broken into 25-year sections, each to be carried out by successive generations. His plan was codified in a company creed and in the "Seven Spirits of Matsushita" (see Exhibit 4), which, along with the company song, continued to be woven into morning assemblies worldwide and provided the basis of the "cultural and spiritual training" all new employees received during their first seven months with the company.

In the post-war boom, Matsushita introduced a flood of new products: TV sets in 1952; transistor radios in 1958; color TVs, dishwashers, and electric ovens in 1960. Capitalizing on its broad line of 5,000 products (Sony produced 80), the company opened 25,000 domestic retail outlets. With more than six times the outlets of rival Sony, the ubiquitous "National Shops" represented 40% of appliance stores in Japan in the late 1960s. These not only provided assured sales volume, but also gave the company direct access to market trends and consumer reaction. When postwar growth slowed, however, Matsushita had to look beyond its expanding product line and excellent distribution system for growth. After trying many tactics to boost sales—even sending assembly line workers out as door-to-door salesmen—the company eventually focused on export markets.

The Organization's Foundation: Divisional Structure   Plagued by ill health, KM wished to delegate more authority than was typical in Japanese companies. In 1933, Matsushita became the first Japanese company to adopt the divisional structure, giving each division clearly defined profit responsibility for its product. In addition to creating a "small business" environment, the product division structure generated internal competition that spurred each business to drive growth by leveraging its technology to develop new products. After the innovating division had earned substantial profits on its new product, however, company policy was to spin it off as a new division to maintain the "hungry spirit."

Exhibit 4   Matsushita Creed and Philosophy (Excerpts)

Creed

Through our industrial activities, we strive to foster progress, to promote the general welfare of society, and to devote ourselves to furthering the development of world culture.

Seven Spirits of Matsushita
- Service through Industry
- Fairness
- Harmony and Cooperation
- Struggle for Progress
- Courtesy and Humility
- Adjustment and Assimilation
- Gratitude

KM's Business Philosophy (Selected Quotations)

"The purpose of an enterprise is to contribute to society by supplying goods of high quality at low prices in ample quantity."

"Profit comes in compensation for contribution to society. . . . [It] is a result rather than a goal."

"The responsibility of the manufacturer cannot be relieved until its product is disposed of by the end user."

"Unsuccessful business employs a wrong management. You should not find its causes in bad fortune, unfavorable surroundings or wrong timing."

"Business appetite has no self-restraining mechanism. . . . When you notice you have gone too far, you must have the courage to come back."

Source: Matsushita Electric Industrial (MEI) in 1987. Harvard Business School Case No. 388-144.

Under the "one-product-one-division" system, corporate management provided each largely self-sufficient division with initial funds to establish its own development, production, and marketing capabilities. Corporate treasury operated like a commercial bank, reviewing divisions' loan requests for which it charged slightly higher-than-market interest, and accepting deposits on their excess funds. Divisional profitability was determined after deductions for central services such as corporate R&D and interest on internal borrowings. Each division paid 60% of earnings to headquarters and financed all additional working capital and fixed asset requirements from the retained 40%. Transfer prices were based on the market and settled through the treasury on normal commercial terms. KM expected uniform performance across the company's 36 divisions, and division managers whose operating profits fell below 4% of sales for two successive years were replaced.

While basic technology was developed in a central research laboratory (CRL), product development and engineering occurred in each of the product divisions. Matsushita intentionally underfunded the CRL, forcing it to compete for additional funding from the divisions. Annually, the CRL publicized its major research projects to the product divisions, which then provided funding in exchange for technology for marketable applications. While it was rarely the innovator, Matsushita was usually very fast to market—earning it the nickname "Manishita," or copycat.

Matsushita: Internationalization

Although the establishment of overseas markets was a major thrust of the second 25 years in the 250-year plan, in an overseas trip in 1951 KM had been unable to find any American company willing to collaborate with Matsushita. The best he could do was a technology exchange and licensing agreement with Philips. Nonetheless, the push to internationalize continued.

Expanding through Color TV   In the 1950s and 1960s, trade liberalization and lower shipping rates made possible a healthy export business built on black and white TV sets. In 1953, the company opened its first overseas branch office—the Matsushita Electric Corporation of America (MECA). With neither a distribution network nor a strong brand, the company could not access traditional retailers, and had to resort to selling its products under their private brands through mass merchandisers and discounters.

During the 1960s, pressure from national governments in developing countries led Matsushita to open plants in several countries in Southeast Asia and Central and South America. As manufacturing costs in Japan rose, Matsushita shifted more basic production to these low-wage countries, but almost all high-value components and subassemblies were still made in its scale-intensive Japanese plants. By the 1970s, protectionist sentiments in the West forced the company to establish assembly operations in the Americas and Europe. In 1972, it opened a plant in Canada; in 1974, it bought Motorola's TV business and started manufacturing its Quasar brand in the United States; and in 1976, it built a plant in Cardiff, Wales, to supply the Common Market.

Building Global Leadership through VCRs   The birth of the videocassette recorder (VCR) propelled Matsushita into first place in the consumer electronics industry during the 1980s. Recognizing the potential mass-market appeal of the VCR—developed by Californian broadcasting company, Ampex, in 1956—engineers at Matsushita began developing VCR technology. After six years of development work, Matsushita launched its commercial broadcast video recorder in 1964, and introduced a consumer version two years later.

In 1975, Sony introduced the technically superior "Betamax" format, and the next year JVC launched a competing "VHS" format. Under pressure from MITI, the government's industrial planning ministry, Matsushita agreed to give up its own format and adopt the established VHS standard. During Matsushita's 20 years of VCR product development, various members of the VCR research team spent most of their careers working together, moving from central labs to the product divisions' development labs and eventually to the plant.

The company quickly built production to meet its own needs as well as those of OEM customers like GE, RCA, and Zenith, who decided to forego self-manufacture and outsource to the low-cost Japanese. Between 1977 and 1985, capacity increased 33-fold to 6.8 million units. (In parallel, the company aggressively licensed the VHS format to other manufactures, including Hitachi, Sharp, Mitsubishi and, eventually, Philips.) Increased volume enabled Matsushita to slash prices 50% within five years of product launch, while simultaneously improving quality. By the mid-1980s, VCRs accounted for 30% of total sales—over 40% of overseas revenues—and provided 45% of profits.

Changing Systems and Controls   In the mid-1980s, Matsushita's growing number of overseas companies reported to the parent in one of two ways: wholly owned, single-product global plants reported directly to the appropriate product division, while overseas sales and marketing subsidiaries and overseas companies producing a broad product line for local markets reported to Matsushita Electric Trading Company (METC), a separate legal entity. (See Exhibit 5 for METC's organization.)

Throughout the 1970s, the central product divisions maintained strong operating control over their offshore production units. Overseas operations used plant and equipment designed by the parent company, followed manufacturing procedures dictated by the center, and used materials from Matsushita's domestic plants. Growing trends toward local sourcing, however, gradually weakened the

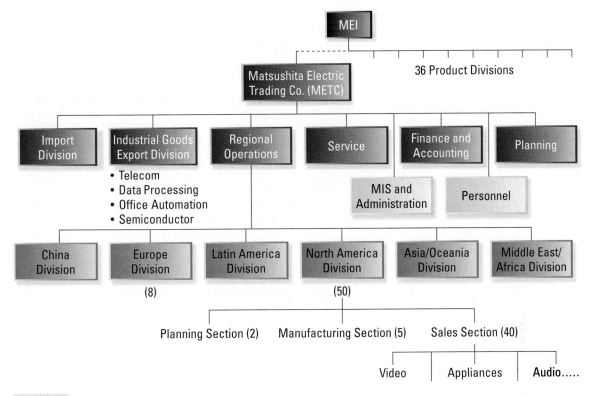

Exhibit 5   Organization of METC, 1985

Source: Harvard Business School Case No. 388-144.

Note: ( ) = number of people.

divisions' direct control. By the 1980s, instead of controlling inputs, they began to monitor measures of output (for example, quality, productivity, inventory levels).

About the same time, product divisions began receiving the globally consolidated return on sales reports that had previously been consolidated in METC statements. By the mid-1980s, as worldwide planning was introduced for the first time, corporate management required all its product divisions to prepare global product strategies.

Headquarters-Subsidiary Relations   Although METC and the product divisions set detailed sales and profits targets for their overseas subsidiaries, local managers were told they had autonomy on how to achieve the targets. "Mike" Matsuoko, president of the company's largest European production subsidiary in Cardiff, Wales, however, emphasized that failure to meet targets forfeited freedom: "Losses show bad health and invite many doctors from Japan, who provide advice and support."

In the mid-1980s, Matsushita had over 700 expatriate Japanese managers and technicians on foreign assignment for four to eight years, but defended that high number by describing their pivotal role. "This vital communication role," said one manager, "almost always requires a manager from the parent company. Even if a local manager speaks Japanese, he would not have the long experience that is needed to build relationships and understand our management processes."

Expatriate managers were located throughout foreign subsidiaries, but there were a few positions that were almost always reserved for them. The most visible were subsidiary general managers whose main role was to translate Matsushita philosophy abroad. Expatriate accounting managers were expected to "mercilessly expose the truth" to corporate headquarters; and Japanese technical managers were sent to transfer product and process technologies and provide headquarters with local market information. These expatriates maintained relationships with senior colleagues at headquarters, who acted as career mentors, evaluated performance (with some input from local managers), and provided expatriates with information about parent company developments.

General managers of foreign subsidiaries visited Osaka headquarters at least two or three times each year—some as often as every month. Corporate managers reciprocated these visits, and on average, major operations hosted at least one headquarters manager each day of the year. Face-to-face meetings were considered vital: "Figures are important," said one manager, "but the meetings are necessary to develop judgment." Daily faxes and nightly phone calls between headquarters and expatriate colleagues were a vital management link.

Yamashita's Operation Localization   Although international sales kept rising, as early as 1982 growing host country pressures caused concern about the company's highly centralized operations. In that year, newly appointed company President Toshihiko Yamashita launched "Operation Localization" to boost offshore production from less than 10% of value-added to 25%, or half of overseas sales, by 1990. To support the target, he set out a program of four localizations—personnel, technology, material, and capital.

Over the next few years, Matsushita increased the number of local nationals in key positions. In the United States, for example, U.S. nationals became the presidents of three of the six local companies, while in Taiwan the majority of production divisions were replaced by Chinese managers. In each case, however, local national managers were still supported by senior Japanese advisors, who maintained a direct link with the parent company. To localize technology and materials, the company developed its national subsidiaries' expertise to source equipment locally, modify designs to meet local requirements, incorporate local components, and adapt corporate processes and technologies to accommodate these changes. And by the mid-1980s, offshore production subsidiaries were free to buy minor parts from local vendors as long as quality could be assured, but still had to buy key components from internal sources.

One of the most successful innovations was to give overseas sales subsidiaries more choice over the products they sold. Each year the company held a two-week internal merchandising show and product planning meeting where product divisions exhibited the new lines. Here, overseas sales subsidiary managers described their local market needs and negotiated for change in features, quantities, and even prices of the products they wanted to buy. Product division managers, however, could overrule the sales subsidiary if they thought introduction of a particular product was of strategic importance.

President Yamashita's hope was that Operation Localization would help Matsushita's overseas companies develop the innovative capability and entrepreneurial initiatives that he had long admired in the national organizations of rival Philips. (Past efforts to develop such capabilities abroad had failed. For example, when Matsushita acquired Motorola's TV business in the United States, its highly innovative technology group atrophied as American engineers resigned in response to what they felt to be excessive control from Japan's highly centralized R&D operations.) Yet despite his four localizations, overseas companies continued to act primarily as the implementation arms of central product divisions. In an unusual act for a Japanese CEO, Yamashita publicly expressed his unhappiness with the lack of initiative at the TV plant in

Cardiff. Despite the transfer of substantial resources and the delegation of many responsibilities, he felt that the plant remained too dependent on the center.

Tanii's Integration and Expansion   Yamashita's successor, Akio Tanii, expanded on his predecessor's initiatives. In 1986, feeling that Matsushita's product divisions were not giving sufficient attention to international development—in part because they received only 3% royalties for foreign production against at least 10% return on sales for exports from Japan—he brought all foreign subsidiaries under the control of METC. Tanii then merged METC into the parent company in an effort to fully integrate domestic and overseas operations. Then, to shift operational control nearer to local markets, he relocated major regional headquarters functions from Japan to North America, Europe, and Southeast Asia. Yet still he was frustrated that the overseas subsidiary companies acted as little more than the implementing agents of the Osaka-based product divisions.

Through all these changes, however, Matsushita's worldwide growth continued generating huge reserves. With $17.5 billion in liquid financial assets at the end of 1989, the company was referred to as the "Matsushita Bank," and several top executives began proposing that if they could not develop innovative overseas companies, they should buy them. Flush with cash and international success, in early 1991 the company acquired MCA, the U.S. entertainment giant, for $6.1 billion with the objective of obtaining a media software source for its hardware. Within a year, however, Japan's bubble economy had burst, plunging the economy into recession. Almost overnight, Tanii had to shift the company's focus from expansion to cost containment. Despite his best efforts to cut costs, the problems ran too deep. With 1992 profits less than half their 1991 level, the board took the unusual move of forcing Tanii to resign in February 1993.

Morishita's Challenge and Response   At 56, Yoichi Morishita was the most junior of the company's executive vice presidents when he was tapped as the new president. Under the slogan "simple, small, speedy and strategic," he committed to cutting headquarters staff and decentralizing responsibility. Over the next 18 months, he moved 6,000 staff to operating jobs. In a major strategic reversal, he also sold 80% of MCA to Seagram, booking a $1.2 billion loss on the transaction.

Yet the company continued to struggle. Japan's domestic market for consumer electronics collapsed—from $42 billion in 1989 to $21 billion in 1999. Excess capacity drove down prices and profits evaporated. And although offshore markets were growing, the rise of new competition—first from Korea, then China—created a global glut of consumer electronics, and prices collapsed.

With a strong yen making exports from Japan uncompetitive, Matsushita's product divisions rapidly shifted production offshore during the 1990s, mostly to low-cost Asian countries like China and Malaysia. By the end of the decade, its 160 factories outside Japan employed 140,000 people—about the same number of employees as in its 133 plants in Japan. Yet, despite the excess capacity and strong yen, management seemed unwilling to radically restructure its increasingly inefficient portfolio of production facilities.

In the closing years of the decade, Morishita began emphasizing the need to develop more of its technology and innovation offshore. Concerned that only 250 of the company's 3,000 R&D scientists and engineers were located outside Japan, he began investing in R&D partnerships and technical exchanges, particularly in fast emerging fields. For example, in 1998 he signed a joint R&D agreement with the Chinese Academy of Sciences, China's

leading research organization. Later that year, he announced the establishment of the Panasonic Digital Concepts Center in California. Its mission was to act as a venture fund and an incubation center for the new ideas and technologies emerging in Silicon Valley. To some it was an indication that Matsushita had given up trying to generate new technology and business initiatives from its own overseas companies.

Nakamura's Initiatives In April 2000, Morishita became chairman and Kunio Nakamura replaced him as president. Profitability was at 2.2% of sales, with consumer electronics at only 0.4%, including losses generated by one-time cash cows, the TV and VCR divisions. (Exhibits 6 and 7 provide the financial history for Matsushita and key

Exhibit 6   Matsushita, Summary Financial Data, 1970–2000[a]

	2000	1995	1990	1985	1980	1975	1970
In billions of yen and percent:							
Sales	¥7,299	¥6,948	¥6,003	¥5,291	¥2,916	¥1,385	¥932
Income before tax	219	232	572	723	324	83	147
As % of sales	3.0%	3.3%	9.5%	13.7%	11.1%	6.0%	15.8%
Net income	¥100	¥90	¥236	¥216	¥125	¥32	¥70
As % of sales	1.4%	1.3%	3.9%	4.1%	4.3%	2.3%	7.6%
Cash dividends (per share)	¥14.00	¥13.50	¥10.00	¥9.52	¥7.51	¥6.82	¥6.21
Total assets	7,955	8,202	7,851	5,076	2,479	1,274	735
Stockholders' equity	3,684	3,255	3,201	2,084	1,092	573	324
Capital investment	355	316	355	288	NA	NA	NA
Depreciation	343	296	238	227	65	28	23
R&D	526	378	346	248	102	51	NA
Employees (units)	290,448	265,397	198,299	175,828	107,057	82,869	78,924
Overseas employees	143,773	112,314	59,216	38,380	NA	NA	NA
As % of total employees	50%	42%	30%	22%	NA	NA	NA
Exchange rate (fiscal period end; ¥/$)	103	89	159	213	213	303	360
In millions of dollars:							
Sales	$68,862	$78,069	$37,753	$24,890	$13,690	$4,572	$2,588
Operating income before depreciation	4,944	6,250	4,343	3,682	1,606	317	NA
Operating income after depreciation	1,501	2,609	2,847	2,764	1,301	224	NA
Pretax income	2,224	2,678	3,667	3,396	1,520	273	408
Net income	941	1,017	1,482	1,214	584	105	195
Total assets	77,233	92,159	49,379	21,499	11,636	4,206	2,042
Total equity	35,767	36,575	20,131	10,153	5,129	1,890	900

Source: Annual reports; Standard & Poors' *Compustat;* Moody's Industrial and International Manuals.

[a]Data prior to 1987 are for the fiscal year ending November 20; data 1988 and after are for the fiscal year ending March 31.

product lines.) The new CEO vowed to raise this to 5% by 2004. Key to his plan was to move Matsushita beyond its roots as a "super manufacturer of products" and begin "to meet customer needs through systems and services." He planned to flatten the hierarchy and empower employees to respond to customer needs, and as part of the implementation, all key headquarters functions relating to international operations were transferred to overseas regional offices.

But the biggest shock came in November, when Nakamura announced a program of "destruction and creation," in which he disbanded the product division structure that KM had created as Matsushita's basic organizational building block 67 years earlier. Plants, previously controlled by individual product divisions, would now be integrated into multi-product production centers. In Japan alone 30 of the 133 factories were to be consolidated or closed. And marketing would shift to two corporate marketing entities, one for Panasonic brands (consumer electronics, information and communications products) and one for National branded products (mostly home appliances).

They were radical moves, but in a company that even in Japan was being talked about as a takeover target, observers wondered if they were sufficient to restore its global competitiveness.

Exhibit 7   Matsushita, Sales by Product and Geographic Segment, 1985–2000 (billions of yen)

	FY 2000		FY 1995		FY 1990		FY 1985	
By Product Segment:								
Video and audio equipment	¥1,706	23%	¥1,827	26%	¥2,159	36%	¥2,517	48%
Home appliances and household equipment	1,306	18	—	—	—	—	—	—
Home appliances	—	—	916	13	802	13	763	14
Communication and industrial equipment	—	—	1,797	26	1,375	23	849	16
Electronic components	—	—	893	13	781	13	573	11
Batteries and kitchen-related equipment	—	—	374	4	312	5	217	4
Information and communications equipment	2,175	28	—	—	—	—	—	—
Industrial equipment	817	11	—	—	—	—	—	—
Components	1,618	21	—	—	—	—	—	—
Others	—	—	530	8	573	10	372	7
Total	¥7,682	100%	¥6,948	100%	¥6,003	100%	¥5,291	100%
By Geographic Segment:								
Domestic	¥3,698	51%	¥3,455	50%	¥3,382	56%	¥2,659	50%
Overseas	3,601	49	3,493	50	2,621	44	2,632	50

Source: Annual reports.

Notes: Total may not add due to rounding.

Case 37   UPS/FedEx Package Wars*

In February of 2005, Mike Eskew, chairman and CEO of the United Parcel Service, talked about the need for transformation:

> Think about how UPS was when you first met us. We had one kind of service: a reliable ground delivery business engineered for the masses. We had one way of doing things. Now we're going to be a one-to-one company—treating every package as if it's the only one we have, every customer as if he or she is the only one we have, every transaction as if it's the only one we have. UPS is also moving from satisfying the customer's small package needs to enabling global commerce.

In order to do this, Eskew believed UPS had to acquire assets to add capabilities, update the brand, upgrade technology, and get the message about change out to the employees. When asked about the competition posed by FedEx and DHL, Eskew replied, "They're aggressive. We've got to be better."[1]

John Beystehner, UPS chief operating officer (COO), underscored Eskew's beliefs by saying, "Our future rests on our continued ability to innovate and compete in a heated global economy."[2] It was time to undertake an unbiased analysis of UPS's corporate strategy. UPS, although by all reports still one of the major players both in air and ground package delivery and supply chain solutions, had recently lost ground in the U.S. market to FedEx.[3,4] DHL and parent Deutsche Post AG, with its recent purchase of Airborne, were making a big push worldwide, and several other strong niche competitors based in Europe, such as TNT and Exel, were announcing major growth plans and posting impressive operating statistics (see Exhibit 1: 2005 Growth, 2004 Market Share; see Exhibits 2 and 3 for further financial and operational comparisons).

There had been many changes in the package industry over the last 10 years. Emery Air Freight used to be a case study example of efficiency, but Emery had stopped doing parcel deliveries in the early 1990s, shortly after being acquired by CNF Inc., the former owner of Consolidated Freightways. (Emery became a subsidiary of the CNF logistics company Menlo Worldwide Forwarding, and stopped doing business under the Emery name in 1996.) Menlo, although a money-loser for CNF, was subsequently purchased by UPS in 2004 to add the capability of guaranteed heavy air freight in North America, supply chain solutions in ocean shipping, and customs brokerage services. What a journey for Emery!

Industry consolidation through acquisition in the delivery arena appeared to be accelerating, with FedEx acquiring RPS and Viking Freight in 1998 and American Freight in 2001, DHL acquiring Airborne in 2003, and UPS acquiring Overnite Transportation in 2005. On the retail side, UPS bought out the Mailboxes Plus franchise in 2001 and FedEx acquired Kinkos in 2004. And these were only the headlines most people were aware of. What other activity was out there?

According to the *Financial Times,* certain analysts feared UPS had "not responded quickly enough to the shift in manufacturing to China and other low-cost countries, leaving it with too much infrastructure and cost in its slow-growing U.S. market and too little capacity in the fast-expanding international markets."[5] UPS probably needed to do an overview of the industry as a whole before focusing in on specific questions such as: What business sectors should UPS consider as major opportunities over the next three years and how should they position themselves to become the primary competitor in those sectors? What were the areas of concern, if any, in UPS's current portfolio of business units? What should UPS do to continue to define their unique attributes and fulfill their value proposition to their customers?

Additional and probably more important questions became: What *was* the nature of UPS's original industry? Who *were* the customers? *Where* was the competition coming from?[6] (See Appendix A for a glossary of industry terms.) A general search for some answers revealed information that was readily available, starting with UPS.

What Can Brown Do for You?

Founded by James E. Casey in 1907 as a messenger company in Seattle, Washington, as of 2005, UPS was the world's largest package delivery company and one of the global leaders in supply chain services, offering an extensive range of options for synchronizing the movement of goods, information, and funds.[7] Headquartered in Atlanta, Georgia, UPS serves more than 200 countries and territories worldwide. Since 1999, UPS's stock has traded on the New York Stock Exchange (UPS).

UPS's vision was to synchronize "the flow of goods, information, and funds—the three flows of commerce."[8] UPS claimed to be the only company in the industry that had one operation network for all types of shipments: domestic, international, air, ground, commercial, and residential, making for economies of scope and scale that improved operating efficiency as well as customer service.

UPS's 97-year-old company culture was based on the owner/management philosophy through which over 30,000 active management employees had significant investments in UPS stock. With a large percentage of full-time non-management employees also having stock ownership, UPS claimed a decision-making mentality that had a

Exhibit 1   2005 Growth, 2004 Market Share

Quarterly Growth 2005	UPS	FedEx	DHL	USPS
Ground Shipments Volume	+1.5%	+15%		
Air Shipments Volume	+4.1%	+6.1%		
2004 U.S. Market Share[52]	47%	31%	8%	13%

long-term focus, centered on achieving strong returns on invested capital, and maintained a work ethic that was characterized by dedication, aligning employees' interests with the interests of public shareowners'.

However, employee–management relations have been shadowed by uncertain union relationships, with the pilot union contract negotiations in 2004–2005 and driver negotiations starting in 2007. The 15-day strike by UPS's Teamster drivers in 1997 cost an estimated $750 million in revenue and caused previously loyal customers to search out and perhaps switch to competitors like FedEx and the United States Postal Service (USPS), among others. The 2001 union contract with drivers negotiated for wages, benefits and new jobs that were estimated to increase UPS costs by $9 billion over the six years of the contract, which might contribute to larger increases in delivery rates over time.[9]

Overnite Transportation Company, acquired by UPS in 2005, was not unionized, and remained so because it was run as a separate operating company. Before acquisition, Overnite was a subsidiary of Union Pacific (UP), having been purchased by UP in 1986, and it was one of the 10 largest U.S. trucking carriers, operating from over 200 terminals, consolidating pallet-sized shipments in the labor-intensive sector of trucking known as less-than-truckload or LTL. LTL freight was "dramatically different from UPS small package operations," partly because it operated dock-to-dock.[10]

Although originally founded as a "common carrier" parcel post delivery service, since going public in 1999 UPS has expanded into retail shops with the purchase of Mail Boxes Etc., into logistics and freight forwarding, and then into heavy freight (see Appendix B: UPS Milestones, and Appendix C: Selected Awards Given UPS and FedEx). UPS has also focused a lot of attention on their Supply Chain Solutions Business Segment. In a 2005 Harris poll, 70 percent of executives surveyed believed that effective management of their supply chains would have "a large impact" on the ability of their companies to achieve their strategic goals; however, at the time, only 33 percent of these executives outsourced their supply chain solutions. The remaining 66 percent admitted various problems with effective supply chain management, and only 16 percent were comfortable extending their existing infrastructure to include China. This confirmed UPS's belief that having a supply chain

solution (SCS) was a strategically vital part of their business model.[11,12]

According to their 2004 Annual Report, SCS enables UPS to move any type of freight, by any mode, anywhere in the world. Through this business UPS manages warehouses and distribution networks and handles complexities of customs brokerage, frequently relying on UPS's small package network for package delivery.

UPS Supply Chain Solutions and other nonpackage businesses offer more than 60 products and services in transportation and freight management, logistics and distribution, international trade, financial services, and consulting. The infrastructure includes facilities that oversee global freight shipments, fill orders, perform technical repairs, deploy critical parts, and manage customs brokerage.

Examples of Supply Chain Solutions' business include:[13]

- In 2004, repairing and returning laptop computers in as little as 24 hours from the Louisville, Kentucky hub, helping Toshiba distinguish its repair service from its competitors, saving on repair costs, and providing better customer service. This repair program utilized The UPS Store retail network for professional packaging and convenient drop-off of laptops from customers; UPS's package delivery network for movement of customer computers, and the UPS Supply Chain Solutions for parts management and technical repair. The specially designed repair center is a 2-million square foot campus adjacent to the UPS Worldport global air hub where certified repair technicians have access to parts to repair the entire laptop.

- Consolidating distribution of Honeywell automotive aftermarket products from five distribution centers into two facilities using sophisticated IT systems and automation that significantly reduces order cycle time and provides real-time order tracking from order entry to final delivery, with order accuracy near 100 percent on an annual total of about 400 million units. The facility includes built-in flexibility to accommodate seasonal swings in demand as well as growth in business. UPS Supply Chain Solutions integrates the Honeywell Consumers Products Group information systems with advanced logistics software. Orders are sent through the UPS transportation management system, generating carrier options and consolidation opportunities for each order, minimizing transportation costs, and raising reliability of service. Customers consistently receive orders on the requested dates, and the average number of shipments per purchase order have dropped from three to one.

Exhibit 2   Operational and Customer Rate Comparisons

Overview of Assets (2003–2004 estimates)	UPS	FedEx	DHL	TNT	USPS
Number of employees	384,000	195,838	381,492	162,244	770,000
Number of vehicles	88,000	41,200	75,000	22,387	215,000
Number of aircraft	582	663	275	42	0

Rate Comparisons

Woodbury, CT 06798 — **Wimberley, TX 78676**
3 lbs   12 × 12 × 12 box   **Business to Business**

Carrier	Overnight	Next Day	2nd Day	Ground	Comments
DHL	$65.42		$33.36	$ 7.22	3 day total
FedEx	$65.08	$56.44	$32.92	$ 6.56	4 day total
UPS		$64.06	$33.89	$ 8.66	7 day total
USPS		$22.80	$10.50	$ 5.77	5 day total
TNT		$58.23	$38.14	$25.83	unknown

Woodbury, CT 06798   **Kiev, Ukraine 04208**   **$90 value**
3 lbs   12 × 12 × 12 box   **Business to Business International**

Carrier	Document	Priority Dutiable	Comments
DHL	$79.15	$249.95	3 day total
FedEx	$63.28	$219.24	5 day total
UPS	$81.58	$260.06	5 day total
USPS	$32.00	$206.00	3 day total
TNT	$42.85	$237.11	6 day total

Woodbury, CT 06798   **Xiamen, China 361004**   **$90 value**
3 lbs   12 × 12 × 12 box   **Business to Business International**

Carrier	Document	Priority Dutiable	Comments
DHL	$58.19	$161.27	3 day total
FedEx	$56.10	$139.36	5 day total
UPS	$40.52	$148.65	9 day document, 13 day box
USPS	$ 5.90	$116.00	3 day total
TNT	$42.85	$197.38	6 day total

Woodbury, CT 06798   **Tustin, CA 92780**
1.5 lbs   6 × 6 × 6   **Business to Consumer, residential**

Carrier	Overnight	Next Day	2nd Day	Ground	Comments
DHL	$39.93	$34.82	$17.14	$7.15	6 day total
FedEx	$40.19	$35.73	$17.28	$6.73	4 day total
UPS	$39.69	$36.14	$17.47	$8.82	6 day total
USPS		$19.60	$ 8.40	$7.24	7 day total
TNT	no residential delivery				

Exhibit 3 Financial Comparisons
(from Annual Reports)

UPS

	Revenue ($ millions)					
	2004	**2003**	**2002**	**2001**	**Q1 2005**	**Q1 2004**
U.S. domestic package	$26,960	$25,362	$24,280	$24,391	$ 6,811	$6,625
International package	6,809	5,609	4,720	4,280	1,842	1,630
Supply chain solutions	2,813	2,514	2,272	1,650	1,233	664
Total revenue	36,582	33,485	31,272	30,321	9,886	8,919

	Profit ($ millions)					
U.S. domestic package	$ 3,702	$ 3,657	$ 3,925	$ 3,969	$ 1,028	$ 912
International package	1,149	732	338	139	348	277
Supply chain solutions	138	56	(167)	(146)	9	28
Total operating profit	4,989	4,445	4,096	3,962	1,385	1,217
Net income	$ 3,333	$ 2,898	$ 3,182	$ 2,399	$ 882	$ 759
Percentage growth	7.9%	−8.9%	32.6%		16.2%	

FedEx

	Revenue ($ millions)					
	2004	**2003**	**2002**	**2001**	**Q1 2005**	**Q1 2004**
Express*	$14,365	$16,467	$15,438	$15,645	$ 4,616	$4,137
Ground**	3,447	3,581	2,918	2,565	1,073	914
Freight	2,374	2,443	2,253	993	807	367
Kinkos	1,513	—	—	—	490	—
Total revenue	24,710	22,487	20,607	19,629	6,975	5,687

	Profit ($ millions)					
Express*	$ 629	$ 783	$ 801	$ 836	$ 310	$ 23
Ground**	522	494	337	113	147	116
Freight	244	193	185	61	103	61
Kinkos	39	—	—	—	19	—
Total profit	1,440	1,471	1,321	1,071	579	200
Net income	$ 838	$ 830	$ 710	$ 584	$ 330	$ 128
Percentage growth	1.0%	16.9%	21.6%		157.8%	

*Includes Trade Networks **Includes Supply Chain Services

DHL

	Revenue ($ millions)			
	2004	**2003**	**Q1 2005**	**Q1 2004**
Mail	$15,164	$14,864	$ 3,684	$ 3,703
Express	21,165	18,193	4,981	5,063
Logistics	8,073	6,992	1,960	1,813
Financial services	8,742	9,114	1,877	1,970
Total revenue	51,353	47,604	12,522	12,575

(*continued*)

Exhibit 3   (DHL *Continued*)

	Profit ($ millions)			
Mail	$ 2,480	$ 2,477	$ 765	$ 887
Express	437	434	44	(17)
Logistics	334	245	71	40
Financial services	823	676	220	190
Total operating profit	3,541	3,160	1,036	1,008
Net income	$ 2,578	$ 2,963	$ 531	$ 541
Percentage growth	3.5%		−2.0%	

TNT

	Revenue ($ millions)				
	2004	**2003**	**2002**	**Q1 2005**	**Q1 2004**
Mail	$ 3,900	$ 3,915	$ 4,005	$ 981	$ 976
Express	4,696	4,251	4,175	1,206	1,094
Logistics	4,081	3,735	3,610	1,100	920
Total revenue	12,677	11,901	11,790	3,287	2,990

	Profit ($ millions)				
Mail	$ 833	$ 765	$ 774	$ 216	$ 225
Express	322	223	194	96	65
Logistics	90	(202)	85	15	20
Total operating profit	1,245	786	1,053	327	310
Net income	$ 667	$ 301	$ 604	$ 194	$ 186
Percentage growth	121.6%	−50.2%		4.3%	

UPS estimated supply chain spending around the world at over $3 trillion in 2004, of which only about 10 percent was outsourced. Anticipated growth in this market was part of the reason that UPS purchased Menlo Worldwide Forwarding in 2004. Menlo was a subsidiary of CNF, formerly Consolidated Freightways, Inc., another major freight and supply chain management company, and had been losing money. But it was a well-established global air freight forwarder with international trade capabilities, providing ocean services and international customs brokerage in more than 175 countries and territories around the world, with customers in pharmaceuticals, apparel, high tech and consumer goods.[14] Menlo included the entity formerly known as Emery Air Freight, one of the dominant carriers of heavyweight air cargo in North America.

UPS's abilities in their supply chain solutions business had gained them a top 10 rating in 2004 as one of an elite group of 3PLs increasingly dominating logistics outsourcing around the world. Expectations are that this "closed club" will become even more exclusive in years ahead as acquisitions concentrate the power among fewer but larger third-party logistics providers[15] (see Appendix D: Top 25 Third-Party Logistics (3PL) Providers).

Some of the factors that might affect the package delivery and expedited service industry as a whole include the following:

- Fuel charges, both in airline and truck (ground) segments, currently offset by an indexed fuel surcharge for both domestic and international air products
- Potential U.S. union contract negotiations, regarding funding for pensions and other benefits
- Fluctuating volume of U.S. mortgage refinancing activity, affecting overnight and next day air letter demand
- Percentage of residential deliveries versus commercial deliveries, currently cost adjusted by an additional delivery area surcharge to certain U.S. zip codes
- Worldwide currency fluctuations
- Governmental laws and regulations worldwide, including possible regulations resulting from increased security concerns related to 9/11

- Aircraft and other asset impairment, repair, and maintenance charges
- Various allegations of violations of state wage-and-hour laws
- Increasing consolidation in the industry, with combining entities competing aggressively for business
- Growing e-commerce business worldwide, and keeping up with technology innovations, both internally and in customer interface applications
- Practicing systematic cost control
- In addition to Asia and Africa, reaching out to be more of a force in the growing markets of Brazil, India, and Eastern Europe

For UPS, its conservative culture and regimented work style might also become a hindrance. Knowing that, in the U.S. at least, UPS faced FedEx as its biggest rival, an overview of the FedEx operation was needed.

When It Absolutely, Positively Has to Be There Overnight

Federal Express was founded in 1971, inspired by its now-famous CEO, Frederick W. Smith's, undergraduate term paper about the need for a different distribution system for time-sensitive air shipments. It has traded on the NYSE as FDX since 1978.[16] FedEx was the first company to offer the overnight letter; the first to offer next-day delivery by 10:30 a.m.; the first to offer Saturday delivery; the first to offer time-definite service for freight; the first to offer money-back guarantees; and in 1990; the first service category company to win the Malcolm Baldrige National Quality Award.

In January 1998 Federal Express, the express delivery company, acquired the small package, freight, forwarding, logistics, and technology resources of Caliber System Inc., and in 2000, FDX Corp. was renamed FedEx Corporation. From its headquarters in Memphis, Tennessee, FedEx provided the following services. With a slightly different segmentation than UPS, it was interesting to note how the divisions were organized.

FedEx Express: The mother of overnight, time-critical service provided time-guaranteed express shipping of small packages up to 150 pounds to every U.S. address and to more than 220 countries and territories. Express delivery of freight weighing from 151 to 2,200 pounds was delivered to any U.S. location and to 50 countries within one to three business days.

FedEx Ground: Using the automated sorting system introduced to the industry by Roadway Package System (RPS) in 1985, the ground segment of the business, initiated in 1998, handled 2.8 million packages on a typical day. Dan Sullivan, president of the FedEx Ground division, believed it was "critically important" to really create a work force that was entrepreneurial. Avoiding the threats of unionization, FedEx Ground drivers were independent contractors who purchased their white trucks with the FedEx logo and were paid by the stop and number of packages. This was part of FedEx Home Delivery, a business-consumer service designed to give catalog and online retailers evening and Saturday deliveries. FedEx SmartPost, which used the USPS Parcel Select program to give price breaks to large-volume retail customers who ship lightweight items that don't need expedited delivery, augmented this service. These packages were delivered by FedEx to bulk mail centers or post offices, and the USPS delivered them the "last mile" to the customer.[17]

FedEx Freight: American Freightways, a northeastern regional carrier acquired by FedEx in 2001, combined with Caliper System's Viking Freight, a regional, less-than-truckload (LTL) carrier serving the western U.S., and Caribbean Transportation Services, an airfreight forwarding provider. This service offers coverage to the 40 contiguous United States and, via airfreight forwarding, to Puerto Rico and Dominican Republic for LTL shipments.

FedEx Custom Critical: Based on the Roberts Express expedited model acquired in 1998, Custom Critical provides exclusive-use shipping via either air or ground for critical freight such as custom race cars, priceless art pieces, emergency equipment, temperature-sensitive items, and hazardous goods, door-to-door internationally.

FedEx Trade Networks: Tower Group International and World Tariff Ltd., acquired in 2000, handles customs brokerage; global ocean and air cargo distribution; and trade information on duties, tariffs, and taxes for 118 countries, providing customer clearance solutions for international shippers.

FedEx Supply Chain Services and FedEx Services: Augmented by the acquisition of Caliper Systems Logistics and Technology solutions in 1998, this segment provides logistics management, consulting services, and data management and technology support for the package tracking capabilities of FedEx Express, Ground, and Freight services.

In 2003 FedEx CEO Fred Smith acknowledged that UPS had something FedEx did not: 3,300 branded full-service retail stores. As Smith said then, "It is an area we are keenly interested in."[18] Therefore, it was no surprise that in 2004, FedEx acquired Kinkos, allowing them to provide copying, printing, film processing, shipping, and other services to residential and commercial customers at more than 1,500 locations in 11 countries, many with 24-hour 7-day-a-week operation. (For other milestones in FedEx history, see Appendix E.)

Donald Broughton, analyst for A.G. Edwards, believed there was a shift in momentum from UPS to FedEx, giving the advantage to FedEx, saying, "It's more entrepreneurial, more willing to take risk. And the model it's employing should produce better operating margins for it and steal the premium yield from UPS."[19]

Looking forward, FedEx CEO Fred Smith was interviewed on the occasion of FedEx's ranking on *Business-Week's* 2004 Global 1,000 list and stressed the importance of expanding to provide service in Brazil, India, China, and Eastern Europe.[20] FedEx had some of the same operational challenges as UPS, plus these additional ones:

- Legal challenges to the FedEx Ground independent contractor status
- Competition for the "worksharing" arrangements FedEx had with the USPS
- Anticipation of additional capital spending for FedEx's extensive air fleet
- "Rightsizing" at FedEx Express in 2004, reflecting cost squeeze concerns
- The need to expand FedEx capabilities in logistics and supply chain management
- Complaints from customers about unreliable and inconsistent service from the FedEx Ground delivery contract drivers[21]

Much has been written about the differences between the FedEx and UPS cultures. FedEx, which is nonunion except for pilots, is known for having an entrepreneurial culture, being innovative and quick to respond, and providing lots of training opportunities for employees. Creativity is encouraged, and employees are given latitude to make decisions on their own.[22] Risk-taking behavior is also reflected in aggressive expansion activity and sometimes heavy borrowing, but this has also paid off, especially in FedEx technology investments. FedEx differentiated itself with many firsts in its first 20 years. UPS's culture emphasizes accountability and engineered efficiency with fairly rigid operational guidelines. This, plus a tradition of promoting from within, has given UPS one of the lowest historical turnover rates in the industry, and has generally pleased the union, which has also helped maintain service reliability.[23] UPS also has historically been fiscally conservative, rejecting debt, and subsequently has been the industry's cost leader. (See Appendix F: UPS Mission and Appendix G: FedEx Mission). FedEx and UPS are basically neck and neck in the U.S. market, but how do they compare in global competition?

Turning to the International Players, DHL Delivers

When considering rivals, UPS's Eskew had to consider DHL, especially since it had acquired U.S. rival Airborne in 2004 to gain a ground delivery unit and access to the former Airborne air delivery operations, which were frugally run by original aircraft management company ABX Air, Inc.,[24] out of their private airport complex in Wilmington, Ohio. From Albania to Zimbabwe, the DHL Worldwide Network delivers.

This subsidiary of Deutsche Post World Net is the world leader in cross-border express deliveries, ahead of both FedEx and UPS, and is a major provider of logistics and freight forwarding services. Overall, DHL's express service links 120,000 destinations in more than 220 countries and territories. The company maintains about 5,000 offices, and it operates a fleet of some 75,000 vehicles.

The DHL brand has a powerful history.[25] Founded in San Francisco in 1969 by Adrian Dalsey, Larry Hillblom, and Robert Lynn, DHL quickly turned its focus to the Far East and the Pacific Rim, providing expedited document services there by 1972, and initiating service in Europe in 1974. By 1979, when DHL began delivering packages in addition to documents, DHL had offices in Frankfurt, Germany, and London, with service to Latin America, the Middle East, and Africa. In 1983, DHL became the first international air express company to serve Eastern Europe, and in 2005 it was still many customers' preferred provider for inbound deliveries to that area.

In 1985 DHL opened a major hub in Brussels, and in 1986 it entered into a joint venture with China, becoming the first company to provide express services there. In 2005, DHL won the Best Express Operator Asia-Pacific award from *Asia Freight & Supply Chain* for the 19th year in a row. By 1998, DHL had a hub in Bahrain, a gateway facility in Moscow, a global IT facility in Kuala Lumpur, and an alliance with Japan Airlines. DHL also had had an alliance with Lufthansa Air Cargo since 1990. In 2001 DHL invested $34 million in a new hub in Singapore. In 2002 DHL was fully acquired by Germany's Deutsche Post World Net.

DHL continued to invest in the Pacific and Oceania regions, with initiatives in India, New Zealand and Australia and a joint venture with Cathay Pacific air cargo. In 2004, DHL acquired U.S. companies SmartMail Services and QuikPak Inc., providing catalog fulfillment and flat mail transporting and sorting services, and extending DHL's "workshare" program with the USPS. Unique in the U.S. market, in 2005 DHL announced Import Express for U.S. customers, where, with one phone call, customers could move documents or packages of any size, weight, or value to and from over 210 countries and pay for delivery in the U.S. on one invoice and in one currency, greatly reducing frustration and confusion.[26] UPS needed to take notice of this.

With its somewhat exotic story, you wouldn't think this American company founded by three guys from California could become such a powerhouse. DHL Worldwide Network S.A./N.V. was headquartered in Brussels, Belgium. Headquartered in Bonn, Germany, its parent company, Deutsche Post World Net, had some 380,000 employees in more than 220 countries and territories worldwide, and generated revenue of €43 billion (approximately $58 billion) in 2004.[27] The divisions of Deutsche Post World Net were DHL Express/Logistics, Mail, and Finance. Once again, it's interesting to see how the business segments are organized under the overall Deutsche Post brand.

DHL Express was the result of the consolidation of the former DHL Worldwide Express business and the Deutsche Post Euro Express parcels business. It offers Same Day, Express, Parcel and Freight services, both by air and ground.

DHL Freight offers international and national transport solutions for part- and full-load shipments in Europe, moving goods by ground, rail, and a combination of the two. DHL Freight covers the former DHL's nondocuments and nonparcels business as well as the former Danzas Eurocargo road transport business.

DHL Danzas Air & Ocean offers customized worldwide logistics solutions for air and sea freight, regardless of size and weight. It also provides specialist services such as integrated turnkey project forwarding for industry segments and cargo management services.

DHL Solutions provides tailor-made contract and industry-specific logistics solutions ranging from consulting to supply chain design and including storage and sales logistics to production and order management. Logistics solutions are customized to meet the needs of special industry sectors such as electronics/telecommunications, fast-moving consumer goods, textiles/fashion, automotive, and pharma/healthcare and includes the handling of dangerous goods.

Deutsche Post and DHL Global Mail delivers an average of 70 million letters throughout Germany each working day and offers international mail services, providing expertise in international direct marketing services and publication solutions.

Deutsche Postbank AG provides the whole spectrum of banking services to retail customers, including payment transaction services and selective finance solutions.

The history of Deutsche Post World Net proves that large enterprises with a long history do not need to be stuck in the past. On the contrary, from 1995 to 2005 the company had gone through an unparalleled transformation. In a short period of time Deutsche Post evolved from a government-controlled, debt-ridden national agency into a highly profitable Global Player (see Appendix H: Deutsche Post World Net Mission).

In 1995 shares in the former government entity Deutsche Post were offered to private shareholders, and with that investment, Deutsche Post began to modernize its mail and parcel centers, rebuilding its entire infrastructure in Germany. In 1997 Deutsche Post pursued acquisitions and alliances with postal services in Poland, Belgium, and Switzerland, and by 1998 had a Europewide distribution network in place under the Euro Express brand, becoming the European market leader in parcel and express services for business customers. Also in 1998, Deutsche Post acquired a 25 percent share in DHL and acquired rights to handle U.S. Global Mail international distribution. By 1999 Deutsche Post had acquired all the government-held shares of Postbank and also had acquired the Swiss logistics company Danzas and Air Express International.

In 2000 Deutsche Post AG, now Deutsche Post World Net, made its public offering to considerable success, and Postbank merged with DSL Bank, becoming public itself as Deutsche Postbank AG in 2004. By the end of 2002, Deutsche Post had completed the acquisition of DHL and consolidated all of Danzas logistics and express business under the DHL brand. Airborne Express was added to this group in late 2003, and DHL then made a move to acquire a stake in Asian logistics company Sinotrans, paving the way for more expansion into China.

A formidable world player that UPS had so far seemed to have ignored, Deutsche Post World Net was a German behemoth with a complex structure, but significant worldwide potential for further growth, especially in Asia Pacific and India. With lots of work still to do in the U.S. market, the Bonn, Germany-based parent, still partly held by the German government (7 percent share ownership), had access to capital and a strict sense of fiscal responsibility.

Spokespeople for the DHL division had said that, in spite of their splashy and aggressive-sounding 2004 ad campaign, ambitions in North America were actually rather modest, with the most urgent objective being to improve service quality and continue to work to integrate the Airborne infrastructure.[28,29] Analysts in the United States believed that, although UPS had its competitive problems, DHL had a ways to go. Arthur Hatfield, at Morgan Keegan, said, "DHL has certainly spent a lot of money on ads, and they've said they're going to spend a billion or so to compete against FedEx and UPS, but I think to get the kind of network they're going to need to be on par with FedEx and UPS, they're going to have to spend a lot more than that. More like $3 billion or $5 billion."[30]

Looking Further in Europe: Fulfilling Ambitions

Similar to Deutsche Post, but more focused on specific strategic segments of the industry, TNT is a company that UPS might consider for study, especially regarding international logistics. TNT N.V., headquartered in Amsterdam, is part of the TNT Post Group (TPG) of companies, including Royal TPG Post, TNT Express, and TNT Logistics.[31] It is the Netherlands' largest private employer. The group employs over 162,000 people in 63 countries and serves over 200 countries. The company is known for its caring culture, obtaining top rank in the 2004 Hewitt Associates Best Employer in Europe survey. Consistently, from 2000 to 2005, TNT has also ranked highly in *Fortune*'s delivery industry category (see the TNT CEO's leadership statement in Appendix I). For 2004 the company reported sales of €12.6 billion. TNT N.V. was publicly listed on the stock exchanges of Amsterdam, New York, London, and Frankfurt.

TNT has made a journey similar to Deutsche Post's. In 1799, the small individual postal services in the Netherlands were brought together to form the first Dutch national postal service. PTT Post remained a state-owned company until its incorporation on January 1, 1989, which allowed PTT Post to undertake new commercial activities. In addition to conventional postal services, the company developed national and international express-delivery and logistics services. In December 1996, PTT Post acquired the Australian company TNT and thus became a key player in the world market. In 1998 TNT and PTT Post became TNT Post Group. TPG was the first mail company to go public under the stock listing of TNT N.V.

TPG Post processes 17 million postal items addressed to more than 7 million addresses in the Netherlands each day, collecting, sorting, transporting, and delivering letters and parcels. The company also specializes in data and document services, direct mail, e-commerce, and international post. TPG had continuing relationships with the Swiss Post, U.K. Royal Mail, Singapore, and China Post, with the potential for further expansion in Europe after the acquisition in 2003 of Werbeagentur Fischer GmbH, a Bavarian-based unaddressed mail distribution company.

Founded in Australia in 1946, TNT Express was acquired in 1996 and became part of the TNT Post Group in 1998. On April 27, 1998, TNT opened its European Express Centre (EEC) in Liège, Belgium. The EEC contains six state-of-the-art sorting units. It operates three sorting systems: one for documents, one for parcels, and one for aircraft containers. It processes all freight consignments within Europe and forms the link with the rest of the world. It was initially designed to handle 1,000 tons of freight per night, with the ability to add capacity for future growth.

TNT is the world's leading business-to-business express delivery company. The company delivers 3.4 million parcels, documents, and pieces of freight a week to over 200 countries using its network of 857 depots, hubs, and sorting centers. TNT Express operates over 20,000 road vehicles and 42 aircraft and has the largest door-to-door air and road express business-to-business delivery infrastructure in Europe.

TNT Logistics is a leading global logistics company, operating in 39 countries. Carving out a significant niche for itself, TNT Logistics is the number one logistics provider to the automotive industry and the largest foreign investor in the Chinese logistics market. In 2003 TPG signed the largest automotive inbound logistics contract awarded in China to date. TNT Logistics employs approximately 40,000 people who manage over 7 million square meters of warehouse space and operate complex transportation networks. In 2004 TNT Logistics reported sales of €4.1 billion. Over the last six years, revenue had grown an average of 22 percent a year.

Major market segments for TNT Logistics include automotive, tires, electronics, consumer goods, publishing and media, and pharmaceutical and healthcare. TNT Logistics is the world leader in servicing the logistics needs of all major car manufacturers.[32] TNT Logistics has a particular focus on automotive inbound and spare parts, but it also offers the full range of supply chain services for this market sector. In 2005 TNT announced that their logistics business in Asia had grown 900 percent in the last five years, and they expected this sector to grow an additional 20 to 30% from 2005 to 2010. TNT also provides dedicated and managed truckload transportation for Ford Motor Company in both the U.S. and Canada, receiving Ford's Q1 Award, the highest honor for sustained level of excellence in customer satisfaction, in 2003, 2004, and 2005. TNT also won DaimlerChrysler's Gold Award in 2004.

Rounding out the legacy mail providers is a quick look at the United States Postal Service (USPS), which could probably take a few pointers from TNT's and Deutsch Post World Net's stories.

Neither Snow nor Rain nor Heat nor Gloom of Night . . .

The U.S. Postal Service is an independent establishment of the executive branch of the U.S. government.[33] Unlike other federal agencies, it receives no tax dollars for its operations. It is self-supporting, and has not received a public service appropriation since 1982.[34] In 2002 the USPS announced a major transformation plan to carry out its mission of providing affordable universal service, forging "a new and modern business model for an institution that has served this country and evolved with changing times since 1789."[35] General initiatives have included fostering growth, increasing operational efficiency, creating a performance-based culture, and restructuring functions to enable all of these goals. Major goals include a $5 billion savings commitment made in 2002 that was almost achieved in 2004, and a reduction in outstanding debt from $11.3 billion in 2001 to $1.8 billion in 2004, which also has almost been achieved.

The USPS is a competitive force, especially in the overnight express and 2-day priority mail service niches. In fiscal year 2004, the USPS reported total revenue of $69 billion, of which $4.4 billion, or 849 million pieces, was Priority Mail; $2.2 billion, or 1,132 million pieces, was Package Services; $1.7 billion, or 844 million pieces, was International; and $0.9 billion, or 54 million pieces, was Express Mail. The Global Express Mail revenue was up 17.1 percent in 2004, with Global Air Parcel Post revenue up 11.8 percent. FedEx won the contract to provide Global Express Guaranteed Service for the USPS in 2004.

The USPS delivers more than 200 billion pieces of mail each year, but its future role is uncertain because customer needs are changing; electronic alternatives to mail are eroding volume; costs are rising faster than revenues, especially retirement and health benefit liabilities; fixed costs are high; giant private firms, some former national foreign postal services, some privatized, are dominating global parcel and express markets, entering an increasing portion of the postal value chain; and finally, rising security concerns are requiring expensive and sophisticated countermeasures.[36] Although the USPS acknowledges that long-term restructuring of the legislative and regulatory framework is required, and although the USPS presumably has the historical field advantage in price, that advantage is eroding. The USPS is proposing either transforming into a privatized corporation, like TPG Post or Deutsch Post, or into a commercial government enterprise.[37]

The USPS interacted with various private partners such as UPS, FedEx, and DHL, in a worksharing arrangement where these carriers collected parcels from high-volume shippers, such as mail order and Internet retailers, and delivered these packages as deep into the postal stream as possible, and then the USPS carried the merchandise to the customer's door, thereby providing seamless service, but reducing the USPS's opportunity for productivity improvements.[38] However, opportunity for future alliances and innovation at the Postal Service interface has major potential in the future.

Other Players in the Industry as of 2005: CNF, Inc.—Heavy Freight Trucking and More

UPS purchased Menlo Logistics, Menlo Worldwide Freight Forwarding, and the former Emery Air Freight from CNF in 2004. Under CNF, Menlo had been losing money for several years, so this divestiture presumed that CNF was consolidating its strategic focus. On the other hand, UPS Supply Chain Group spokesman Bob Stoffel, felt that the Menlo acquisition was "an ideal strategic and operational fit" for UPS.[39]

Born in 1939 out of now bankrupted Consolidated Freightways, CNF, trading on the NYSE as *CNF,* is a $3.7 billion company and a leading provider of heavy freight, re-builder of transportation equipment, and creator of global supply chain solutions for a wide range of manufacturing, industrial, retail, and government customers.[40]

CNF believes effective supply chain management is increasingly important for businesses worldwide as competition drives them to reduce inventories and speed up cycle times. The potential savings from these efforts is enormous since the value of the U.S. supply chain alone is estimated to be $936 billion, or 8.5 percent of gross domestic product.

While CNF transports freight for many of its customers, like many heavy freight companies it has a much larger role.[41] Like others, CNF assumes total management of the complex transportation and information networks required for companies to get all of the raw materials they need in the door not just on the right day, but at the right time of day. CNF also manages warehouses, completes final configurations, packages products, and distributes the finished goods.

Although CNF's roots are in heavy freight transportation, the nature of moving freight has changed and become so sophisticated that the movement of information is now as important as the movement of the products. CNF has invested heavily in technology, focusing its efforts on conducting customer transactions via the Internet; developing and implementing state-of-the-art dispatch, warehouse management, order fulfillment, and tracking systems; and optimizing the routing of its delivery vehicles to increase efficiency and reduce transit times. Subsidiaries include the following:

Vector SCM is CNF's supply chain management division and is the leading logistics manager worldwide for General Motors, the world's largest vehicle manufacturer. Vector SCM is a joint venture between CNF and GM. Vector SCM leverages the extensive supply chain expertise of all of CNF's operating companies, along with advanced Web-based technologies developed by CNF, to produce visibility of all material and vehicles within GM's supply chain.

Road Systems, Inc., CNF's truck support segment, is a proprietary manufacturer and rebuilder of doubles and semi-freight trailers, converter dollies, and other transportation equipment under contract with CNF. Road Systems processes up to 7,000 trailers per year, both new and reconditioned, and over 1,100 dollies/pallet decks and docks. Construction was completed in 2004 on a facility that doubled both the size and production of existing operations in Arkansas.

Con-Way Transportation Services Inc., the traditional trucking segment of CNF's business, is a $2.6 billion transportation and services company that provides time-definite and day-definite freight delivery services and logistics for commercial and industrial businesses. Within the Con-Way family are the regional less-than-truckload carriers Con-Way in the central, southern, and western United States and in Canada and Mexico; Con-Way NOW, an expedited carrier specializing in emergency shipment service; Con-Way Logistics, a supply chain services provider; Con-Way Air, an airfreight forwarder with service throughout the United States, Canada, and Puerto Rico; and Con-Way Full Load, a truckload brokerage service offered throughout the United States and Canada.

Con-Way's resources include more than 19,000 employees and 27,000 tractors and trailers. Con-Way maintains more than 440 service locations in the United States, Canada, and Puerto Rico and provides contract carriage services to and from Mexico. The company serves more than 400,000 customers, providing them with 98 percent on-time next-day delivery performance. Driven by the Con-Way companies, CNF was named America's Most Admired Trucking Company in 1998, 1999, and 2000 by *Fortune* magazine. Con-Way increased earnings in the first quarter of 2005 by more than 30 percent, primarily from less-than-truckload growth across all regions of North America.

Exel plc: Supply Chain Expert

Even though UPS has been gaining ground after its purchase of Menlo, Exel plc, headquartered in England and with a background in ocean transport, is far and away the global leader in supply chain management and third party logistics support.[42] The origins of what is now Exel plc began in 1865 as the Ocean Steam Ship Company. Acquiring McGregor, Swire Air Services (MSAS) in 1981, it became an international multi-modal freight forwarding unit, including sea-freight and road groups, without having to own any planes or trucks. The Exel logistics brand, which originated in 1982 as Britain's National Freight Company, was launched in 1989, merging with the Ocean Group in 2000. Exel had grown through acquisition to have alliances and significant footholds in countries including Japan, Brazil, Turkey, South Africa, Germany, the United States, China, Asia Pacific, India, Chile, Finland, and Korea.

Exel's comprehensive range of innovative logistics solutions encompasses the entire supply chain from design and consulting through freight forwarding, warehousing, and distribution services to integrated information management and e-commerce support. Exel, a UK listed, FTSE 100 company with 2004 revenue of £6.3 billion (US $11.6 billion/€9.3 billion), employs over 111,000 people in 2,000 locations in more than 135 countries worldwide. Exel's customers include over 75 percent of the world's largest nonfinancial companies.

Exel's contract logistics segment includes warehousing and ground-based distribution, both separately and in combination. These services are charged in two ways over the life of the contract: (1) "open book," with costs passed on to the customer plus a management fee usually linked to performance, or (2) "closed book," with an inclusive price agreed to upfront that is linked to volume and mix. Hybrid contracts use both types of fee, which was of mutual benefit, particularly when using campus and shared-user solutions. Additional value share arrangements could also be included within the contract structure to encourage both parties to work together to deliver cost savings and other areas of value such as lower inventories.

In providing freight management, Exel does not own any planes or ships but is a world leader in the coordination and movement of air, ground, and sea freight. Freight management is the movement of customers' products, using the most efficient mode of transport, whether air, sea, rail or ground, while meeting customers' expectations on delivery time and cost. Rather than shopping around for individual freight providers, customers buy freight capacity from Exel, as their rates are generally cheaper. Exel is able to offer cheaper rates by consolidating the shipments of different customers to the same destination and delivering this to the carrier as a single shipment. Rates charged to customers and margins generated varied according to supply and demand, which was seasonal. In addition, carriers can increase rates to reflect increases in their costs, such as fuel. In general, price and commercial terms with customers and suppliers are less committed in freight management than in contract logistics. Additional services are often added to the basic forwarding service, for example, customs brokering, which enhances seamless transfer of cargos across borders. Exel's sophisticated IT systems enable them to track products at every step of the way.

Integrating Exel's contract logistics and freight management services enables them to provide customers with a one-stop supply chain shop. This is a real area of growth for Exel. They are unique in that they have the geographical presence and operational scale to meet customer demand for a worldwide end-to-end supply chain.

The three biggest market sectors for Exel are consumer products, retail, and technology. Exel's customers include Coca-Cola, General Mills, Heineken, Hershey Foods, P&G, Unilever, Carrefour, Marks & Spencer, Pier 1 Imports, Wal-Mart, Williams-Sonoma, Agilent, Ericsson, Honeywell, HP, IKON, Lanier, Lucent, Motorola, Ricoh, Sony, Sun, Texas Instruments, and Xerox.

As an example, Exel provides supply chain solutions to all of Motorola's business units from 14 different locations around the world. Managing 1.2 million square feet of storage space for Motorola, Exel moves over 12 million kilograms of freight for the customer annually and is its largest global provider of external facilities.

The outlook for medium- to long-term growth in Exel's business is positive. The global supply chain market is relatively fragmented and expanding by 5 to 6 percent each year. Exel's revenue of over £6 billion represents a market share of barely 2 percent. Most importantly, Exel works with more than three-quarters of the world's largest 250 nonfinancial companies and still had a long way to go in terms of business potential with almost every one of these customers. Almost half of the new business Exel won in 2004 came from customers outsourcing for the first time.

Ensenda: Delivery the Last Mile

Outsourced logistics is often associated with the large, global operators that manage vast, multi-modal supply chains for the world's largest manufacturers and retailers; however, niche players have emerged to prove that big isn't always better.[43] Ensenda, based in San Francisco, was formed by two entrepreneurs in 2001 to serve what they perceived as a logistics vacuum: Ensenda is the leading last mile logistics provider in North America.[44] A nonasset company with national reach to oversee local delivery providers, Ensenda puts their network of independent delivery experts—over 300 local delivery firms with 10,000 individual drivers—to work for their customers in over 135 markets across the United States and Canada, providing complete coverage for local domestic delivery needs and moving product between distribution centers and stores or branch locations or from branch locations and stores out to the end buyer.

Unlike the FedEx Ground model, Ensenda uses a certification process to qualify each company, and tracks performance using key performance indicators on a weekly basis. Ensenda has redundant coverage in every market and changes the delivery network frequently, creating healthy competition among drivers. Customers only pay for the services they use on a per-transaction basis. Ensenda buys delivery services wholesale based on economies of scale and marks up the services to sell at retail. Customers could do the same but find it cheaper to use Ensenda rather than trying to manage such a network themselves. For the delivery companies, Ensenda buys unused capacity, making the delivery firm more efficient.[45]

Customers include outbound shipments from industrial supplier W.W. Grainger to restock their retail customers in 24 hours, delivery to residential customers of building supplies from The Home Depot, housewares and furniture from Ikea, and electronic products from Best Buy.[46] Ensenda boasts an average on-time delivery rate of over 99.2 percent.

Their comprehensive software suite of "last mile" local and regional logistics links Ensenda with local drivers and customers, and customers can access delivery information real-time over the Internet. Services have helped shippers reduce shipping costs by 65 percent versus managing a proprietary fleet and have provided a faster, more cost-effective alternative to LTL. Ensenda has created one point of contact and one invoice for all North American last mile deliveries and, therefore, have been able to predict and control local delivery costs and accessorial charges. In summary, Ensenda has been able to respond creatively to customers' special requests.[47]

Final Thoughts

Although the transportation services industry is over 100 years old, for express delivery services it has changed drastically, especially in the last five years (see Exhibit 4: Relative

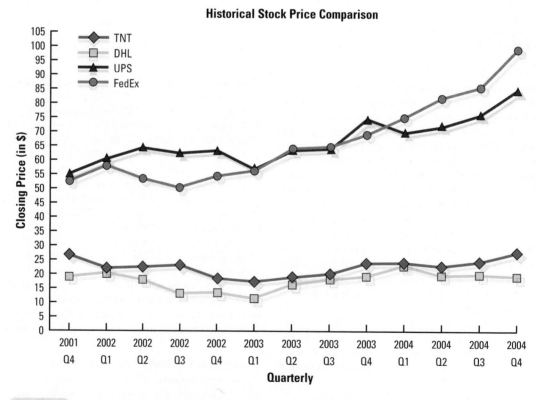

Historical Stock Price Comparison

Exhibit 4   Relative Growth Chart, December 2001–December 2004
Showing the quarterly increase in overall relative stock value for this industry since 2001.

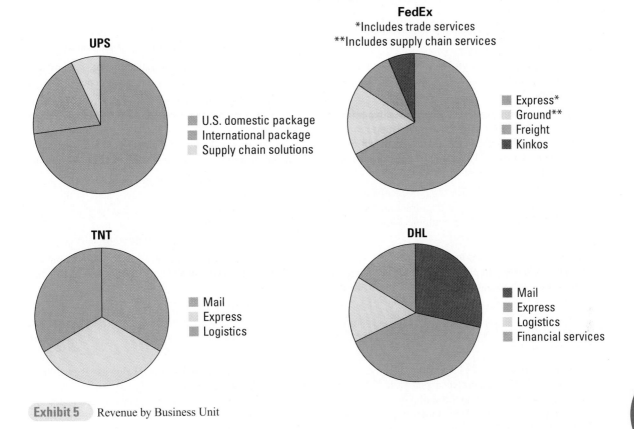

Exhibit 5   Revenue by Business Unit

Growth Chart). Research analysts have been warning since 2003 that a change is on the way, specifically the dominance of the transportation buyer,[48] the decline in average shipment weight, the shift from mode-specific to time-based shipping, and the shortening of the average length of haul, which in 2005 significantly shifted cargo from air to ground transport.[49] This implied that carriers would be expanding regional distribution centers and partnering with logistics firms and LTL transporters. In 2005, for the first time, it was projected that less than 50 percent of FedEx's domestic traffic would move by air,[50] causing more structural changes and shifts in acquisitions among all the major players.

Global competition, customization manufacturing, increasing technology and information needs, expanded trade opportunities, and increased customer expectations have all exerted pressure on providers to make significant adjustments to their business and corporate strategies, so much so that the industry has been difficult to categorize. Other players have emerged all over the world from previously separate niches. Major players have varying business unit structures, making it hard to do direct comparisons within service segments (see Exhibit 5: Revenue by Business Unit).[51] To compete, major players have had to consider many factors before making strategic decisions. What can UPS take from this to help craft competitive strategy? More generally, where will the industry end up, and who will survive and prosper?[52]

Appendix A   Glossary of Industry Terms

Air cargo services—Companies that provide delivery of freight by air.[53]

Express (or expedited) delivery services—Companies that provide express delivery of parcels, letters, and documents.

Freight forwarding services—Companies that arrange the movement of freight by various transportation methods, including air, sea, and land, on behalf of exporters and importers. These companies may or may not own the assets themselves.

Less-than-truckload carriers (LTL)—Companies that provide transportation of less-than-truckload shipments, in which freight from multiple shippers is consolidated into a truckload.

Logistics services—Companies that engage in the process of planning, implementing, and controlling the movement and storage of raw materials, in-process inventory, finished goods, and related information from the point of origin to the point of consumption.

Postal services—Companies that operate post offices and deliver parcels, letters, and documents.

Supply chain management services—Companies that provide services that help companies manage the movement and storage of raw materials, in-process inventory, finished goods, and related information from the point of origin to the point of consumption.

Transportation services (a general industry heading that includes all the other services listed on this page)—Companies that provide transportation of passengers and freight, arrange for transportation of freight, and manage transportation infrastructure.

Warehousing & distribution services—Companies that provide warehousing and distribution of freight.

Appendix B   UPS Milestones

- Founded in 1907. In 1922 UPS was one of the few companies to offer "common carrier" delivery service at rates comparable to those of parcel post, and in 1924 it was the first service to develop a conveyor belt system to handle packages.
- By 1950 UPS was in direct competition with the U.S. Postal Service.
- In 1975 UPS went international to Canada. By 1989 UPS was serving more than 175 countries with its own aircraft, and in 1990 it began flights to Asia.
- In 1998 UPS Capital was founded to provide a comprehensive menu of integrated financial products and services to enable companies to grow their business.
- In 1999 UPS became a publicly traded security on the New York Stock Exchange.
- In 2001 UPS acquired Mail Boxes Etc., and in 2003 it allowed franchisees in the 3,300 U.S. retail centers to convert to The UPS Store brand.
- In 2002 UPS consolidated UPS's Logistics Group, Freight Services, Capital, and Consulting and Mail Innovations companies into UPS Supply Chain Solutions, offering a global IT and physical infrastructure for third-party logistics (3PL) services, including financing through First International Bank, which was acquired in 2001.
- In 2004 UPS was awarded 12 more frequencies to fly to China, and concluded an agreement with its Chinese partner to take full control of international express operations in more than 200 cities in China by the end of 2005.
- In 2004 UPS acquired Menlo Worldwide Forwarding (including what was formerly Emery Air Freight) from CNF, providing the capability of guaranteed heavy air freight in North America, and Supply Chain Solutions in ocean shipping and customs brokerage services.
- Construction continued on UPS's highly automated hub in Cologne, Germany—their largest hub outside the United States.
- In 2004 UPS invested more than $1 billion in technology to support both customer-facing solutions and internal operational systems and processes, including a $600 million investment in package flow technology to be used at package centers and by drivers, including wireless communication in trucks.
- In 2005, to compete with FedEx Freight, UPS bought trucking company Overnite Transportation, expanding its heavy freight capability with more hubs and more trucks and allowing UPS to ship freight weighing more than 150 pounds using more of its own planes.
- By 2006 UPS expanded its main freight hub in Louisville and finished building five regional freight hubs to accommodate the anticipated increase in business from the acquisition of Menlo Worldwide Forwarding.[54]
- In 2004 UPS acquired Japan's Yamato Express Co., and in 2005 it acquired Messenger Service Stolica, one of the leading express delivery companies in Poland.
- A new distribution and logistics hub opened in Singapore in 2006 as a logistics Free Trade Zone (FTZ).

Appendix C   Selected Awards Given to UPS and FedEx

Some of the many awards UPS earned in 2004 included:

- Top Performing Airlines Ranking, *Aviation Week and Space Technology.*
- Number one on World's Most Respected Transport Companies Survey, *Financial Times.*
- Most Valuable Corporate Brand, Best Big Companies in America, *Forbes.*
- Among 50 Best Companies for Minorities, America's Most Admired Company in its Industry (21st consecutive year), World's Most Admired Company in its Industry (6th consecutive year), Fortune 500, Fortune Global 500, Blue-Ribbon Company, *Fortune.*
- Technologies of the Year—Notable Innovations Award for UPS Package Flow Technologies, *Industry Week.*

FedEx's awards included:

- On lists of Most Admired Companies (2002–2005), Best Companies to Work for in America (1998–2005), Best Companies for Minorities (2000–2001, 2003), *Fortune.*
- *Harris Interactive* U.S. Corporation Reputation Top 10 (2003–2004, Top 20 (2001–2002).
- Various awards for technological innovation *InformationWeek, Computerworld, Wired, CIO Magazine.*
- Business Ethics Best Corporate Citizens List (2002–2004).
- Top 3PL Provider listings 1998–2003, *Inbound Logistics, Logistics Management & Distribution Report.*
- Hall of Fame recognition as highest rating for customer service, 10 year top performer in LTL carrier category, 2003, *Logistics Management & Distribution Report.*

Appendix D   Top 25 Third-Party Logistics (3PL) Providers

In 2004 the top 25 3PL providers were:[55]

1. Excel plc, UK & Ohio: 2004 revenue $8.3 billion; major focus—consumer goods.
2. Kuehne & Nagel International, Switzerland: $6.9 billion; major focus—automotive, industrial.
3. Schenker, Germany: $6.4 billion; major focus—automotive.
4. DHL Danzas Air & Ocean, Switzerland/Deutsche Post WorldNet, New Jersey: $5.7 billion; major focus—electronics.
5. P&O Nedlloyd, Netherlands/P&O Nedllloyd Ltd., New Jersey: $4.8 billion; major focus—retail.
6. TPG/TNT, Netherlands/TNT Logistics North America, Florida: $4.7 billion; major focus—automotive.
7. Panalpina, Switzerland: $4.6 billion; major focus—automotive, electronics.
8. UPS Supply Chain Solutions, Georgia: $4.1 billion; major focus—computers & electronics.
9. Nippon Express, Japan & Nippon Express, New York: $4 billion; major focus—automotive, healthcare.
10. C.H. Robinson Worldwide, Minnesota: $3.6 billion; major focus—technology, food & beverage.
11. Menlo Worldwide, California (in late 2004 became part of UPS): $3.1 billion; major focus—computers & electronics.
12. NYK Logistics, Japan: $3 billion; major focus—food & beverage.
13. Expeditors International of Washington, Washington: $2.6 billion; major focus—automotive, electronics.
14. Penske Logistics, Pennsylvania: $2.5 billion; major focus—automotive.
15. Eagle Global Logistics, Texas: $2.2 billion; automotive, aerospace.
16. BAX Global, California: $2 billion; major focus—computers & electronics.
17. Ryder, Florida: $1.9 billion; major focus—automotive, aerospace.
18. Schneider Logistics, Wisconsin: $1.9 billion; major focus—consumer products.
19. Uti Worldwide, California: $1.2 billion; major focus—chemicals.
20. Caterpillar Logistics, Illinois: $1 billion; major focus—automotive, industrial.
21. APL Logistics, California: $990 million; major focus—automotive, retail.
22. Wilson Logistics Group, Sweden/Wilson Logistics, U.S., New Jersey: $860 million; major focus—automotive.
23. FedEx Supply Chain Services, Ohio: $603 million; major focus—apparel, automotive.
24. Maersk Logistics, Denmark: $350 million; major focus—consumer goods.
25. SembCorp Logistics, Singapore & SembCorp Logistics USA, California: $275 million; major focus—automotive.

Appendix E   FedEx Milestones

- Federal Express installs its first drop box in 1975.
- In 1981 Federal Express introduces the Overnight Letter, begins service to Canada, and opens its "SuperHub" adjacent to Memphis International Airport.
- In 1984 Federal Express began shipping to Europe and Asia, and in 1989 it acquired Tiger International, becoming the world's largest full-service, all cargo airline
- FedEx developed an innovative IT infrastructure and in 1986 was the first air express company to provide a highly reliable tracking system.
- RPS was acquired in 1998 and became FedEx Ground in 2000.
- Acquiring Evergreen International Airlines in 1995, Federal Express (now officially FedEx), was the first U.S.-based cargo carrier to obtain authority to service China, opening the Asia Pacific Hub at Subic Bay in the Philippines.
- FedEx opened its European hub at Roissy-Charles de Gaulle airport in France in 1999
- In 2000 FedEx acquired Tower Group's international logistics and trade information technology business and WorldTariff, a customs duty and tax information company, forming the backbone of FedEx Trade Networks.
- In 2001 American Freightways, a leading LTL freight carrier in the eastern U.S., was combined with FedEx's Viking Freight to become FedEx Freight.
- In 2001 FedEx Express and the USPS formed an alliance where FedEx provided air transportation of U.S. mail, and FedEx drop boxes were placed at post offices nationwide; in 2004 FedEx won the contract to be the international carrier for the USPS Global Express Guaranteed Service, winning out over previous carrier DHL.
- In 2004 FedEx acquired Kinko's, providing document management services and shipping options of all sizes to customers, with 400 out of 1,200 stores open 24/7.
- Also in 2004 FedEx acquired Parcel Direct, a leading parcel consolidator, rebranding it as FedEx SmartPost to provide low-weight, less time-sensitive service for e-tailers and catalog companies.
- FedEx Ground planned expansion from 2005 to 2010 in Florida to double the average daily volume, in addition to nine new hubs, and expansion of 30 existing hubs, and relocation of nearly 290 pickup and delivery terminals elsewhere in the U.S.[56]

Appendix F   UPS Mission

The UPS Charter[57]

Our Values—Our Enduring Beliefs

We believe that integrity and excellence are the core of all we do.

We believe that attention to our customers' changing needs is central to the success of UPS.

We believe that people do their best when they feel pride in their contributions, when they are treated with dignity, and when their talents are encouraged to flourish in an environment that embraces diversity.

We believe that innovation fortifies our organization through the discovery of new opportunities to serve our people and our customers.

Our Purpose—Why We're in Business

We enable global commerce.

Our Mission—What We Seek to Achieve

We fulfill our promise to our constituents throughout the world in the following ways:

We serve the evolving distribution, logistics, and commerce needs of our customers worldwide, offering excellence and value in all we do.

We sustain a financially strong company, with broad employee ownership, that provides a long-term competitive return to our shareowners.

We strive to be a responsible and well-regarded employer by providing our people with an impartial, rewarding, and cooperative environment with the opportunity for advancement.

We build our legacy as a caring and responsible corporate citizen through the conduct of our people and company in the communities we serve.

Our Strategy—The UPS Plan of Action

Create the future through One company. One vision. One brand.

We will continue to expand our distribution and supply chain solutions to synchronize the world of commerce—the flow of goods, information, and funds. We will expand our position as a trusted broker between buyers and sellers worldwide. We will harness the appropriate technology to create new services and to strengthen our operations and networks.

We will attract and develop the most talented people whose initiative, good judgment, and loyalty will help realize our company's mission. We will continually study customers' behavior, anticipate their needs, and design our products and services to exceed their expectations.

We will create a practice of innovation that leads to sustainable growth. We will maintain an environment that enables us to treat every customer as if they are our only one; We will leverage the UPS brand to maximize brand loyalty among all constituencies.

Appendix G FedEx Mission

FedEx Mission[58]

FedEx will produce superior financial returns for share-owners by providing high value-added supply chain, transportation, business, and related information services through focused operating companies competing collectively, and managed collaboratively, under the respected FedEx brand. Customer requirements will be met in the highest quality manner appropriate to each market segment served. FedEx companies will strive to develop mutually rewarding relationships with its employees, partners and suppliers. Safety will be the first consideration in all operations. All corporate activities will be conducted to the highest ethical and professional standards.

Strategy

The unique FedEx operating strategy works seamlessly—and simultaneously—on three levels.

Operate independently by focusing on our independent networks to meet distinct customer needs.

Compete collectively by standing as one brand worldwide and speaking with one voice.

Manage collaboratively by working together to sustain loyal relationships with our workforce, customers, and investors.

Values

People—We value our people and promote diversity in our workplace and in our thinking.

Service—Our absolutely, positive spirit puts our customers at the heart of everything we do.

Innovation—We invent and inspire the services and technologies that improve the way we work and live.

Integrity—We manage our operations, finances, and services with honesty, efficiency, and reliability.

Responsibility—We champion safe and healthy environments for the communities in which we live and work.

Loyalty—We earn the respect and confidence of our FedEx people, customers, and investors every day, in everything we do.

Appendix H Deutsch Post World Net Mission

Deutsche Post World Net is the world's leading logistics group.[59] Its integrated Deutsche Post, DHL, and Postbank companies offer tailored, customer-focused solutions for the management and transport of goods, information, and payments through a global network combined with local expertise.

We see ourselves as consultants and service providers, as procurement and process managers, as an interface and information platform between suppliers and consumers. Our mission is to provide the optimal supply, with the best possible quality, at the right time, on target, and taking processing costs into account.

Our new Corporate Culture creates added value and leads us on the way to becoming stronger than our competitors. This is an obligation we also have to fulfill towards our shareholders. Our Corporate Culture unites the excellence of every subsidiary and their unique company cultures to produce a shared strength.

An active, open Corporate Culture enhances our worth as an attractive employer of top talents and strengthens our position as a responsible corporate citizen in this world. We commit ourselves to adhere to the values defined in this Corporate Culture. They constitute both a challenge and a help. They support the evolution of our business while we and they continue to develop. Our seven values are:

To deliver excellent quality and excellent service.

To make our customers successful.

To foster openness and transparency; to make decisions based on facts and analyses.

To act according to clear priorities, with outstanding cooperation between all parties.

To act in an entrepreneurial way, promoting individual responsibility.

To act with integrity internally and externally, creating an atmosphere of mutual trust.

To accept social responsibilities, respecting the traditions, structures and values of the countries where we operate.

Appendix I TNT N.V. Statement of Values

Leadership Vision Statement by Peter Bakker, CEO, TNT N.V., 5/28/05, from http://group.tnt.com/aboutus/introduction fromtheceo/leadershipvision/index.asp

TNT is a global company that offers work to 162,000 men and women of all ages, backgrounds, education, abilities, experience, and cultures. It is estimated further that half a million people are directly related to these employees. If we include our outside suppliers, we believe that almost 1 million people on this globe come into contact with TNT every day. And we are not just talking about our countless valued customers, whether they are worth a million euros or buy just one beautiful stamp.

We at TNT strive to operate as One. Of course, we do different tasks, think different thoughts, and speak many different languages. But when a potential customer thinks of TNT, he or she should see one face. Hopefully one with a smile. And when a potential employee considers joining us, he or she should have one Big Idea of us. Hopefully a positive one.

When the general public turns its attention to us through the media, it should have no doubt what to expect from us: trustworthiness, loyalty, and a hands-on approach are just some of our qualities. And when we, the 162,000 employees of TNT, think about ourselves as a company, we ideally feel at home, at ease, and proud.

A company is not one because it says so. Trust isn't granted on the basis of an advertisement. New talent won't join us on the experience of a showcase. The public will not believe us if we do not walk our talk. And no customer will reward us for not performing, no matter how hard we smile while failing to deliver.

We want to fulfil our ambitions. We want to be at the top, as a company, as people, as professionals, as a service provider in express, logistics, and mail. And we want to be a responsible part of society and the world in which we operate.

Our Ambitions We want to work and live in harmony with the people around us and with our environment. We want to do this by helping people make the best of their abilities. As a company we can offer them an outlook in their current lives. And we do not want to forget the needs of future generations. They too must be able to meet their own needs.

We have therefore signed the Global Compact that was drawn up by the United Nations. This Compact (www.unglobalcompact.org) is a set of principles dealing with human rights, labour standards, and the environment. We are committed to living by the principles of this document. We know that these principles set requirements and standards for us and that we will have to go through a learning process to achieve compliance in all areas of our business. But we will comply because it is the best way to build a future for all of us, all over the world.

In the long term, no big company can operate without the support of the local community. What we decide to do or not to do can have great impact, whether it be on a town, a city, a region, a country, or the world. That's why we want this support to be as positive and sustained as possible. To secure this, we have developed dedicated policies and practices with which we go beyond the demands of the law. In fact, we do everything within our power to deliver best practices.

This Is Our Declaration of Social Leadership

As a corporation in the 21st century we have taken a hard look at the world outside. This has made us realize more than ever that there is only a future for us as a company if there is one for those around us, including the planet itself. Realizing this we pledge to act accordingly. Not for today and tomorrow, but for years to come; not every once in a while, but every day.

Under our Corporate Sustainability policy we strive to live in harmony with the people and the environment around us. Under the umbrella of Corporate Governance we strive to live in harmony with ourselves. Corporate Governance is in essence the set of values and standards that we want to live by as a company of people. Corporate Governance and Corporate Sustainability go hand in hand. One cannot go without the other.

Under Corporate Governance we in our company promise to do everything we can in order to:

- keep our business in good order
- act in a responsible manner
- be accountable towards all our stakeholders

TNT has made those promises. But we have taken on more obligations than those imposed by national and international laws. TNT will do everything it possibly can to act with integrity, objectivity, and transparency.

The overall framework of Corporate Sustainability and Corporate Governance contains many fields, each of which is just as important as the other. They are all links in the same chain. We look at it and work with it as a coherent system of measures, actions, rules, regulations, and initiatives which links our business and our values.

Only if we do it all will we reach our goals. Only if we all do it will we succeed.

It is therefore vital that we feel ourselves to be part of a family. Just like in a family we do not have to agree on each and every single matter and we certainly do not have to be the same. But we must have a firm common ground of basic values.

Who do we want to be? How do we want to act? Which responsibilities do we want to pick up? Business ones only? Or do we deliver more? There is already a set of answers to these important questions. TNT itself is a young and modern multinational, but it is rooted in long and firm traditions. Think of customer loyalty, fair treatment of employees, transparency and trust.

Our Initiatives and Actions   Anyone can say that they have ambitions. Anyone can say they share certain values. Words are easy. So, where's the proof? Which initiatives do we take to support our good intentions? And what actions do we take to implement and secure our values?

Global Approach   TNT has in place a truly global approach to Corporate Sustainability. As a company we want to do more than just comply with the key performance indicators in our sector. On the one hand we are working hard on our unique commitment to corporate citizenship called Moving the World. We aim to exceed international standards for health, safety and the environment. In those fields we give proof of our ambitions through systematic reporting of our measurable, certified results.

All this secures that we make progress in our efforts to organize our work in a way that is best for future social developments and care for the environment. For a company operating worldwide in many different cultures this is no easy task, but we believe it is well worth the effort.

Most importantly, we ask all our employees to be our ambassadors in the field when it comes to caring for people and safeguarding the environment. As a widespread company we depend upon our employees, wherever they are, to walk our talk. Without the added bonus of your personal conviction and commitment we will not reach our goals.

Endnotes

1. A conversation with Mike Eskew. Interview by Walter Klechel, editor-at-large, Harvard Business School Publishing, 2/17/05, from http://www.pressroom.ups.com/execforun/speeches.

2. Driving growth through innovation. Speech at Commerce & Industry Association of New Jersey, 3/32/05, http://www.pressroom.ups.com/execforum/speeches.

3. FedEx gained share across air, truck categories in 2004, 3/1/05, http://www.colography.com/press/2005.

4. Ward, A. 2005. UPS fades as global rivals deliver. *Financial Times,* January 26.

5. Ibid.

6. Also see reports Competition within the United States parcel delivery market at http://www.postcom.org/public/articles/2003articles/parcel_competition.htm and The parcel service industry in the U.S.: Its size and role in commerce, 8/1/00, http://www.seas.upenn.edu/sys/logistics/parcelstudy.html.

7. "What can Brown do for you?" is the tagline for UPS's new branding push in 2004. Hearsay has it that the trucks are brown because that kept the mud from being seen when deliveries were made over the dirt roads in the 1900s.

8. This quote and the following summary are from UPS 2004 Annual Report, http://www.shareholder.com/ups/stock.cfm.

9. Brooks R., & Whelan, C.B. 2002. A tentative 6-year agreement with teamsters stabilizes UPS. *The Wall Street Journal,* July 17.

10. Nguyen, T. 2005. UPS deal sparks Overnite-Teamsters uncertainty. May 19, http://fleetowner.com/news/t.

11. Corporate Execs say supply chains a strategic key to their business future, 4/28/05, from http://ups.com/pressroom/us/press_releases/press_release/0,0,4553,00.html.

12. Thuermer, K.E. 2004. Small package delivery goes global like the big boys. *World Trade Magazine,* July 1, http://www.worldtrademag.com.

13. See http://ups-scs.com/about/PR/04_27_2004_release.html?pr=true.

14. *Supply & Demand Chain Executive.* 2004. UPS to acquire Menlo Worldwide Forwarding, October 5, http://www.sdcexec.com/article_arch.asp?article_id=6172.

15. Foster T.A., & Armstrong, R. 2004.Top 25 third party logistics providers extend their global reach. May; Foster, T.A., & Armstrong, R. 2004. 3PLs on the rise: Smaller firms prove big isn't always better. *Global Logistics & Supply Chain Strategies: SupplyChainBrain.com,* April, http://www.glscs.com.

16. From http://www.fedex.com.

17. Also see McKay, J. 2005. Moon's FedEx Ground is booming and has become fierce rival to UPS. *Pittsburgh Post-Gazette,* March 5, http://www.post-gazette.com.

18. Costello, T. 2003. Arch rivals: FedEx vs. UPS: Package shippers follow very different strategies. *CNBC,* December 18, http://www.msnbc.msn.com.

19. Ibid.

20. See *BusinessWeek Online,* 6/3/05 at http://www.businessweek.com.

21. See http://www.epinions.com, search for "FedEx" and read all reviews.

22. Smith, S. S. 2001. Measuring the people side of FedEx Express. *Journal of Organizational Excellence.*

23. Bowen, D.E., & Lawler, E.E. 1992. The empowerment of service workers: What, why, how and when. *Sloan Management Review,* Spring.

24. See http://www.abxair.com.

25. See http://www.dhl-usa.com.

26. DHL announces Import Express program for U.S. customers, 6/1/05, http://www.dhl.com press release

27. See http://www.dpwn.de.

28. See continuing commentary at http://blog.cmsconsultants. com/blog/Carriers.

29. See, for instance, Who sucks more?? UPS, FEDEX, or DHL??, http://peterdawson.typepad.com/scmv/20/2005/02/ who_sucks_more_.html for comments about DHL delivery service in the U.S.

30. Hesseldahl, A. 2005. DHL presence heats up shipping wars: UPS's no.1 position challenged by FedEx, other competitors. *Forbes,* January 17, from http://www.msnbc.msn.com.

31. From http://www.tpgpost.com/strategy/strategyanddata.html and http://www.tnt.com/tntgroup/en_corporate.html.

32. Bowman, R. J. 2005. "Thinking strategically about outsourcing: 3PLs can do much more than cut costs. *Global Logistics & Supply Chain Strategies, SupplyChainBrain.com,* March, http://www.glscs.com.

33. Long believed to be the slogan of the USPS, "neither snow nor rain nor heat nor gloom of night" is rumored to actually come from Herodotus in 503 B.C.

34. From 2004 Comprehensive Statement of Operations, http:// www.usps.com/strategicplanning/cs04/.

35. See Strategic transformation plan, http://www.usps.com/strategicplanning/.

36. For an insider's view of USPS reform, see Reisner, R.A.F. 2002. When a turnaround stalls. *Harvard Business Review, First Person,* February.

37. For an interesting discussion of the future of the postal market, see Diehl, H.M., & Waller, P. 2001. Competing with Mr. Postman: Business strategies, industry structure and competitive prices in liberalized letter markets, June 13, from http://www.whu.edu/orga/geaba/Papers/2001/ GEABA-DP01-22.pdf.

38. See http://postcom.org/public/articles/2004articles/ USPS.Partner.with.DHL.htm.

39. UPS to acquire Menlo Worldwide Forwarding. *Supply & Demand Chain Executive,* 10/5/05, http://www. sdcexec.com.

40. From http://www.cnf.com.

41. See also Nagarajan, A., Canessa, E., Mitchell, W., & White C.C. 2000. E-commerce and the changing terms of competition in the trucking industry: A study of firm level responses to changing industry structure, August 11, from http://e-conomy.berkeley.edu/conferences/9-2000/ EC-conference2000_papers/mitchelbrie.pdf.

42. From Exel 2004 Annual Report, http://www.exel.com/files/financial%20presentations/ annual_report18-03-05.pdf.

43. Foster, T. A. 2004. 3PLs on the rise: Smaller firms prove big isn't always better, April, *Global Logistics & Supply Chain Strategies, SupplyChainBrain.com,* http://www.glscs.com.

44. From http://www.ensenda.com/why/index.html.

45. Mottley, R. 2004. Going the "last mile." *American Shipper, Journal of International Logistics,* August 1, http://www.ensenda.com/about/gfx/AmericanShipper_ 080104.pdf.

46. Trunick, P. A. 2005. Best practices in transportation: Network in progress. *Logistics Today,* March 15, http://www. logisticstoday.com/.

47. For other "last mile" stories see Siegel, J. 2004. Nouveau niche. *Operations & Fulfillment,* November 1, http:// opsandfulfillment.com/mag/.

48. *J.D. Power & Associates.* 2002. FedEx sweeps customer satisfaction awards for small package delivery service, December 10, http://www.jdpower.com/news/releases/. Reliability in pickup and delivery was most important for ground and international customers and second on the list for air customers; value for price paid was most important for air service and second for international customers. Clear invoicing, driver relationships, reputation, and tracking information were in the second tier for both ground and air service; having access to helpful account executives, driver relationships, and tracking information were second for international customers.

49. Scherck, T.R. 2003. A view of the future for the U.S. expedited transportation industry, November 14, http://www.colography.com/press/2003/futureview.html.

50. Shift in distribution strategies to mute airfreight growth, 4/7/04, U.S. airports must re-think strategies to attract cargo business, 2/8/05, Watershed event, 5/18/05, It's a ground game: Are airports ready to play?, 1/21/05, http://www. colography.com/press.

51. One final note: Qatar Airways, recently voted best cargo carrier, Middle East by *Asian Freight & Supply Chain,* was one of the fastest growing freight handling airlines in the world, in 2004 launching service to South Africa; see http://www.payloadasia.com/Magazine/archives/10_04/ 1004_supplement1.html.

52. Hannon, D. 2005. Small package market changes could benefit buyer. *Purchasing.com,* March 17.

53. See http://www.hoovers.com/transportation-services.

54. Associated Press. 2005. UPS to build five new freight hubs, May 10, from http://news.moneycentral.msn.com

55. Foster, T.A., & Armstrong, R. 2004. Top 25 third party logistics providers extend their global reach, May, *Global Logistics & Supply Chain Strategies: SupplyChainBrain.com,* http://www.glscs.com.

56. *Business Wire.* 2005. FedEx Freight continues strategic expansion and growth throughout U.S., March 28.

57. From http://www.ups.com.

58. From http://www.fedex.com.

59. From http://www.dpwn.de.

Case 38

Reader's Digest: Inform, Enrich, Entertain, and Inspire— Inspire Whom? and for How Much Longer?*

The Reader's Digest Association, Inc. 2004 Annual Report contained the cautionary statement that there were "risks and uncertainties" relating to "our ability to attract and retain new and younger magazine subscribers and product customers in view of the maturing of an important portion of our customer base."[1] When that was written, the Reader's Digest Association's (RDA) net income had yet to rebound from the downturn of 1996 (see Exhibit 1: RDA Stock Prices 1996–2005 and Exhibit 2: RDA Sales 1995–2004). Extensive restructuring, reduction in staffing levels, acquisitions, and development of international ventures initiated by CEO Thomas O. Ryder in 1998 had not produced a significant improvement in earnings.

Would Ryder's strategic initiatives work in the long run? Would the future be able to report that *Readers' Digest,* once named one of the most successful magazines in the Western world,[2] had redefined its product line and found a new generation of customers to "inspire"? Would the implementation of nonpublishing revenue streams, like the online weight loss program, "ChangeOne," help? Now that almost any type of information was available, online for free, what would that mean to a company whose flagship product was a five-by-seven-inch pocket-sized compendium of human interest stories, educational material, humor, and practical advice?

After the November 2004 sale of the 114-acre property in Chappaqua, NY, home of the company's corporate headquarters since 1939, the internal culture change had been inevitable. RDA old timers said the founders, DeWitt and Lila Wallace, "would be turning over in their graves."[3] After significant restructuring in business unit management ranks,[4] could leadership be expected to redefine a culture of quality and commitment and sustain any improvement? Was the overall strategy sound?

Background

In April 1998, Thomas O. Ryder was recruited from American Express as Chairman and CEO of Reader's Digest Association, Inc. With Ryder's appointment came a formidable task of rebuilding and revitalizing the then 75-year-old company. When asked about what changes had to be made, Ryder, an unabashed fan, said he didn't feel the magazine was all that broken to begin with. "Any time magazines are grouped together for sale, the number-one seller is *Reader's Digest.* It ain't *Vanity Fair.* It ain't *Time.* It ain't *People.*

*This case was prepared by Graduate student Pauline Assenza and Professor Alan B. Eisner of Pace University. This case was solely based upon library research and was developed for class discussion rather than to illustrate either effective or ineffective handling of an administrative situation. Copyright © 2005 The Case Association and Pauline Assenza and Alan B. Eisner. Reprinted with permission from Volume 2 Issue 1 of *The Case Journal,* the on-line journal of The Case Association (www.caseweb.org).

That's also true in Brazil, Russia, and Hong Kong. It's true in a lot of places. This is a magazine of the people," he said.[5]

Ryder was to replace the interim CEO, George Grune, who had stepped back into the role of Chairman and CEO after James P. Schadt resigned in 1997. Grune's original tenure in the position lasted from 1984–1994. He was very successful, leading the company through the transition to become public, while doubling revenue and increasing operating profits ninefold. However, Grune's main concern during this stabilization period was to "bring in a successor" to put the company back on track.

Thomas Ryder seemed to be the answer. He came into the role a champion of RDA's flagship title. As Ryder said, he grew up reading *Reader's Digest,* and in his hometown of Alexandria, Louisiana, "*Reader's Digest* is pretty close to the word of the Lord."[6] As of the beginning of 2005, after seven years in charge of some extensive changes to the business, he had tried to improve performance and lead the company back to the success that Grune had established during his first passage as Chairman and CEO. However, the question remained, could Reader's Digest continue to fulfill its stated mission to create "products that inform, enrich, entertain and inspire people of all ages and cultures around the world"?[7] And could it do this by continuing to rely on the *Reader's Digest* magazine?

Reader's Digest Association Business Mix[8]

Reader's Digest Association was a diversified publishing and direct-marketing corporation. They produced and distributed magazines, books, videos, music, and many other products in more than 60 countries throughout the world. The flagship magazine, *Reader's Digest,* was the world's most widely read magazine, reaching almost 100 million readers worldwide each month, delivered in 49 different editions, in 20 different languages. Although much of the business was still in publishing, Ryder had initiated a strategic plan to move away from what was considered the "core" business of the *Reader's Digest* magazine. This was a possible reaction to claims that the core Reader's Digest franchise was in a state of "perpetual decline" and was a possible way to shake the reputation as a "hinterlands magazine read by kindly grandparents."[9]

Reader's Digest's had been known for an extensive line of products, reaching customers on a global scale. The performance of the *Reader's Digest* magazines and other special interest publications had been driven primarily by circulation and subscription revenues and, to a lesser extent, by advertising sales worldwide. The international market segment had been more susceptible to changes in local market financial conditions due to the number of countries in which RDA had operated.

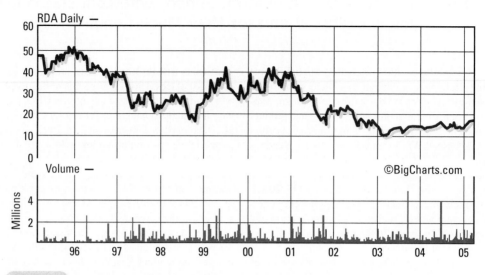

Exhibit 1   The Reader's Digest Association, Inc. Stock Prices—1996–2005
Source: From http://phx.corporate-ir.net/phoenix.zhtml?c=71092&p=irol-stockquotechart.

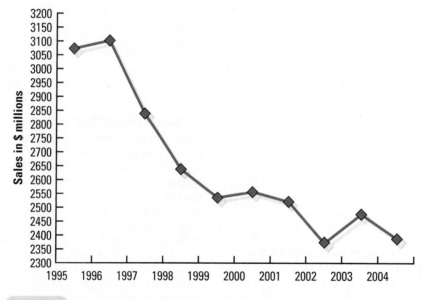

Exhibit 2   RDA Sales 1995–1004 (all products)

Ryder had divided RDA into three business units (see Exhibit 3: 2004 Business Segments and Exhibits 4 & 5: 2004 RDA Business Mix). Reader's Digest North America consisted of the following products distributed in the U.S. and Canada:

Reader's Digest: RDA's flagship magazine publication, the world's largest monthly magazine. In 2004 the U.S. edition had an approximate base rate of 10 million copies reaching approximately 40 million readers. A large-type edition and a Spanish language edition, *Selecciones,* were also published for U.S. distribution.

Reiman Media Group: Acquired in 2002, Reiman publications included 11 magazines catering to "lifestyle topics" such as cooking and travel. *Taste of Home,* in 2004 the largest-selling food magazine in North America, was included in this category.

Illustrated Reference Books: Sold via direct mail and the publishing trade; products in this category

Reader's Digest North America	Consumer Business Services—USA & Canada	Reader's Digest International
Reader's Digest Magazine Reiman's Publications Special Interest Magazines Books & Home Entertainment Select Editions	Books Are Fun QSP Trade Publishing Young Families Financial Services Alliances	Reader's Digest Magazine Special Interest Magazines Books & Home Entertainment Books Are Fun Young Families Financial Services Alliances

Exhibit 3   2004 RDA Business Segments

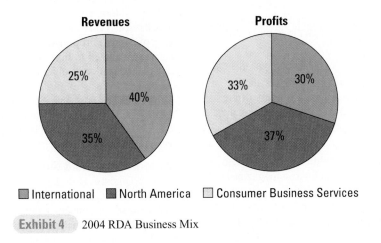

Exhibit 4   2004 RDA Business Mix

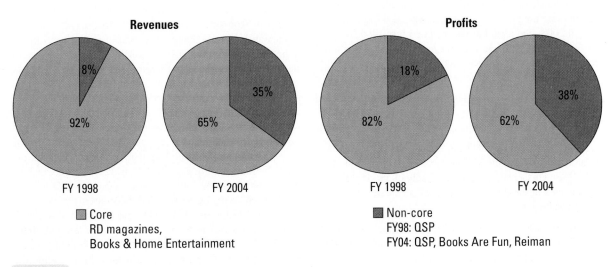

Exhibit 5   2004 RDA Core vs. Noncore Business Mix

included do-it-yourself, computer, travel, and health books.

Reading Series/Select Editions: These books included *Select Editions,* which were specially edited novels by top authors. These volumes were sold worldwide in several countries and languages.

Recorded Music and Videos: Individual box sets and series compilations in several musical and video genres were sold worldwide. Many Gold and Platinum certifications have been awarded to RDA's recorded music.

Special Interest Publications: This category of products included other special interest Reader's Digest magazines. *RD Specials* were one-time publications sold at grocery store checkout counters.

Young Families: Including some trade publishing relationships, this category marketed books and home entertainment products through direct and retail channels.

Nonpublishing Products and Services: Products in this category included noncore ventures such as financial and insurance services that were offered through marketing ventures with other companies.

Reader's Digest International consisted of products sold in more than 60 countries outside the United States and Canada, including Select Editions, music, video, and Young Families products; Special Interest magazines in the Czech Republic; The Family Handyman in Australia; Books Are Fun operations in France, Mexico, and Spain; and financial services marketing partnerships and other nonpublishing initiatives in more than 30 countries. Local editions of *Reader's Digest* magazine in 48 editions and 20 languages were produced in various countries by local staff. *Selecciones,* the Spanish-language edition, was the number one magazine in most Spanish-speaking countries and, in 2003, had a paid circulation of 1.6 million.[10]

Consumer Business Services segment distributed products through nondirect marketing channels and utilized a specialized sales force. Businesses included:

Books Are Fun: This category represented the marketing of books and gifts using product displays in North America. Established in 1999, it also served as an important marketing tool for products created in other parts of the company.

QSP: This organization helped school and youth groups in the United States and Canada in their fundraising efforts.

As reported in 2004, International Business represented 40 percent of RDA's revenue, and Consumer Business Services represented 25 percent—a very different profile than the one presented in 1998.[11]

Thanks to internal development and acquisitions, and as part of the specific strategy put in place by CEO Thomas Ryder, 38 percent of profits came from noncore operations, so that each of the three operating segments produced roughly the same amount of profit. (The financial services portion of the North American business unit was considered noncore.)

Traditional revenues for the magazine, books, and home entertainment businesses had been principally driven by direct mail, and therefore were the most sensitive to changes in payment rates and returns. The Consumer Business Services businesses had been much less susceptible because the largest businesses in this segment collected most of their cash at the point of sale. This was another reason for diversifying away from the magazine core.

After a tough downward slide, RDA's operating profits in 2004 grew slightly by $10 million in North America and by $8 million internationally. However, Consumer Business Services profits declined by $26 million, mainly because of a sharp drop in sales at QSP and Books Are Fun that was attributed to high turnover in the sales force and related distribution problems that were scheduled to be fixed in 2005 (see Exhibits 6–11 for a 10-Year Income Summary, 5-Year Income Statement, Balance Sheet and Cash Flow, a 3-Year Reportable Segment Results Summary, and a 3-Year Revenue by Product and Geographical Area Summary).

Strategies, Goals & Accomplishments   In 2004, Reader's Digest's goals had included reducing operating expenses and improving margins, stabilizing the customer base, expanding consumer acquisition channels and increasing interdivisional selling to drive revenue growth. RDA had launched two new magazines, *Our Canada,* published by Reader's Digest Canada, and *Backyard Living,* produced by Reiman, both exemplifying the Reiman Publications editorial formula. RDA launched new book businesses in Romania, Slovenia, and Croatia and tested or launched Books Are Fun, Young Families, and other products elsewhere in the world. Eastern Europe had proven to be a profitable venture, with completed book product tests in Ukraine and revenue increases in Russia and Hungary. The *Reader's Digest* magazine, under a new publishing team, had created an Indonesian edition and changed to a more prominent license partner in India, in a move to expand circulation further in that populous part of the world.

Children's Publishing had grown through partnerships with Disney, Nickelodeon, Hasbro, Mattel's Barbie, Fisher-Price, and NASCAR. This division was intended to help RDA reach young customers and their parents.

In November of 2004, RDA sold the original Reader's Digest Chappaqua property, including the Georgian mansion built in 1939. This sale resulted in a one-time gain for RDA and reduced operating overhead in future years; the Reader's Digest corporate headquarters would continue to

Exhibit 6   RDA 10-Year Income Summary

Income Statement (In U.S. $ millions)

	Sales	EBIT	Depreciation	Total Net Income	EPS	Tax Rate (%)
06/04	2388.5	121.1	75.3	49.5	0.49	25.10
06/03	2474.9	146.9	64.7	61.3	0.60	38.90
06/02	2368.6	159.2	35.9	91.2	0.89	35.10
06/01	2518.2	187.8	56.8	132.1	1.26	29.70
06/00	2553.7	263.8	47.5	173.8	1.63	34.10
06/99	2532.2	211.7	43.7	126.6	1.15	40.20
06/98	2633.7	41.5	46.2	17.9	0.16	NA
06/97	2839.0	210.2	46.7	133.5	1.24	36.50
06/96	3098.1	137.7	48.8	80.6	0.73	41.50
06/95	3068.5	422.5	44.7	264.0	2.35	37.50

Balance Sheet (In U.S. $ millions)

	Current Assets	Current Liabilities	Long Term Debt	Shares Outstanding
06/04	690.3	892.3	637.7	99.1 Mil
06/03	788.0	881.2	834.7	98.2 Mil
06/02	863.7	980.8	818.0	87.1 Mil
06/01	770.6	859.5	NA	90.2 Mil
06/00	772.5	904.4	NA	90.5 Mil
06/99	1146.5	986.3	NA	86.0 Mil
06/98	972.6	1015.9	NA	85.5 Mil
06/97	925.8	1013.1	NA	84.6 Mil
06/96	1204.1	1113.0	NA	85.6 Mil
06/95	1215.1	1072.1	NA	86.4 Mil

Source: All tables are from http://moneycentral.msn.com/detail/stock_quote?Symbol=rda unless otherwise indicated.

rent space for the approximately 800 corporate staffers who remained.

Analysts in early 2005 were more positive regarding RDA's outlook, with some calling it a "solid pick," mostly encouraged by share prices in the $17 range, and the projected earnings growth in 2005, achieved mostly through expense and overhead cuts. This was the first time since the end of 2002 that the stock showed some positive momentum.[12] RDA also announced an increase in dividend from the $.05/share level in place since 1998 to $.10/share starting in the second quarter of 2005. Was it possible that the turnaround Ryder had worked for since 1998 had

come? A review of how Reader's Digest came to be, and the strategy that drove its initial rise to popularity, might provide some useful information for crafting future strategy. What were RDA's competencies, and how did they develop? What additional information might be helpful?

A Source of "Enormous Popularity" for Over 80 Years

History[13]   In 1920, DeWitt Wallace created a sample magazine containing condensed articles, which were intended to provide lasting interest and enduring significance.

Exhibit 7   RDA 5-Year Income Statement

Annual Income Statement (In U.S. $ millions)	6/2004	6/2003	6/2002	6/2001	6/2000
Sales	2,388.5	2,474.9	2,368.6	2,518.2	2,553.7
Cost of Sales	897.6	977.3	938.5	932.8	904.6
Gross Operating Profit	1,490.9	1,497.6	1,430.1	1,585.4	1,649.1
Selling, General, & Administrative Expense	1,294.5	1,293.8	1,236.5	1,299.6	1,347.8
Other Taxes	0.0	0.0	0.0	0.0	0.0
EBITDA	196.4	203.8	193.6	285.8	301.3
Depreciation & Amortization	75.3	64.7	35.9	56.8	47.5
EBIT	121.1	139.1	157.7	229.0	253.8
Other Income, Net	0.0	7.8	4.0	−41.2	10.0
Total Income Avail for Interest Expense	121.1	146.9	159.2	187.8	263.8
Interest Expense	55.0	46.5	18.6	0.0	0.0
Minority Interest	0.0	0.0	0.0	0.0	0.0
Pre-tax Income	66.1	100.4	140.6	187.8	263.8
Income Taxes	16.6	39.1	49.4	55.7	90.0
Special Income/Charges	0.0	0.0	−2.5	0.0	0.0
Net Income from Total Operations	49.5	61.3	91.2	132.1	173.8
Normalized Income	49.5	61.3	93.7	132.1	173.8
Total Net Income	**49.5**	**61.3**	**91.2**	**132.1**	**173.8**
Dividends Paid per Share	0.20	0.20	0.20	0.20	0.20
Preferred Dividends	1.30	1.30	1.30	0.00	0.00
Basic EPS from Total Operations	0.50	0.61	0.90	1.27	1.63
Diluted EPS from Total Operations	0.49	0.60	0.89	1.26	1.63

Source: From http://moneycentral.msn.com/investor/invsub/results/statemnt.asp?Symbol=RDA.
Financial data presented in a Media General Financial Services proprietary format.

He had long believed that much of currently published American journalistic content was "too verbose" and therefore escaped the attention of the public who didn't have the time to search for good stories. He submitted his sample digest-sized magazine to various publishers. When he was rejected by all of them, he published the magazine himself. In 1921 he established The Reader's Digest Association, selling 1,500 subscriptions to be delivered exclusively by mail. The magazine was intended to provide a reading service with selected material to "inform, enrich, entertain, and inspire." After marrying Lila Acheson in 1921, the two of them opened the first RDA office in their Greenwich Village apartment and published 5,000 copies of Volume 1, No. 1 of the *Reader's Digest* magazine in February of 1922.

Later in 1922, the couple moved to Pleasantville (really Chappaqua), New York and in 1925 started a home and office there. (By 1939 they had finished building the majestic Georgian-style headquarters.) In 1929, *Reader's Digest* began selling at newsstands and the circulation grew to 62,000. By 1935 circulation had passed the 1 million mark. Throughout the next decade, RDA continued to grow and expanded into different languages and countries for distribution. Starting with the United Kingdom edition in 1938, by 1945 the company had issued Brazilian, Swedish, Finnish, Australian, Danish, French-Canadian, English-Canadian, Norwegian, French, Belgian, German, Italian, Swiss-French, Swiss-German, and South African editions. The first foreign language edition was published in Spanish for distribution in America in 1940.

Exhibit 8   RDA Balance Sheet

Annual Balance Sheet (In U.S. $ millions)	6/2004	6/2003	6/2002	6/2001	6/2000
Assets					
Current Assets					
Cash and Equivalents	50.3	51.3	107.6	35.4	49.7
Receivables	229.0	256.5	306.0	305.1	285.3
Inventories	152.0	155.7	156.0	161.6	120.3
Other Current Assets	259.0	324.5	294.1	268.5	317.2
Total Current Assets	690.3	788.0	863.7	770.6	772.5
Noncurrent Assets					
Property, Plant & Equipment, Gross	382.3	391.5	375.4	350.4	419.5
Accumulated Depreciation & Depletion	226.5	229.0	207.3	190.2	267.1
Property, Plant & Equipment, Net	155.8	162.5	168.1	160.2	152.4
Intangibles	1,183.4	1,221.7	1,244.6	409.8	438.8
Other Noncurrent Assets	413.2	427.3	426.3	334.5	395.1
Total Noncurrent Assets	1,752.4	1,811.5	1,839.0	904.5	986.3
Total Assets	**2,442.7**	**2,599.5**	**2,702.7**	**1,675.1**	**1,758.8**
Liabilities & Shareholder's Equity					
Current Liabilities					
Accounts Payable	110.6	97.5	102.8	86.4	146.4
Short-Term Debt	83.9	31.3	132.7	160.3	89.4
Other Current Liabilities	697.8	752.4	745.3	612.8	668.6
Total Current Liabilities	892.3	881.2	980.8	859.5	904.4
Noncurrent Liabilities					
Long-Term Debt	637.7	834.7	818.0	0.0	0.0
Deferred Income Taxes	0.0	0.0	0.0	0.0	0.0
Other Noncurrent Liabilities	449.6	483.3	432.0	359.4	350.1
Minority Interest	0.0	0.0	0.0	0.0	0.0
Total Noncurrent Liabilities	1,087.3	1,318.0	1,250.0	359.4	350.1
Total Liabilities	**1,979.6**	**2,199.2**	**2,230.8**	**1,218.9**	**1,254.5**
Shareholder's Equity					
Preferred Stock Equity	0.0	28.8	28.8	0.0	0.0
Common Stock Equity	463.1	371.5	443.1	456.2	504.3
Total Equity	463.1	400.3	471.9	456.2	504.3
Total Liabilities & Stock Equity	**2,442.7**	**2,599.5**	**2,702.7**	**1,675.1**	**1,758.8**
Total Common Shares Outstanding	99.1 Mil	98.2 Mil	99.5 Mil	102.7 Mil	103.0 Mil
Preferred Shares	288,000.0	288,000.0	288,000.0	0.0	0.0
Treasury Shares	46.9 Mil	47.7 Mil	41.6 Mil	38.5 Mil	23.5 Mil

Exhibit 9   RDA Cash Flow

Annual Cash Flow (In U.S. $ millions)	6/2004	6/2003	6/2002	6/2001	6/2000
Cash Flow from Operating Activities					
Net Income (Loss)	49.5	61.3	91.2	132.1	173.8
Depreciation and Amortization	75.3	64.7	35.9	56.8	47.5
Deferred Income Taxes	0.0	0.0	0.0	0.0	0.0
Operating (Gains) Losses	28.5	−5.4	7.3	39.5	2.2
Extraordinary (Gains) Losses	0.0	0.0	0.0	0.0	0.0
Change in Working Capital					
(Increase) Decrease in Receivables	34.1	55.0	7.4	−27.4	20.9
(Increase) Decrease in Inventories	6.4	6.4	21.8	−45.5	35.2
(Increase) Decrease in Other Curr. Assets	−14.3	0.0	0.0	−0.1	−3.2
(Decrease) Increase in Payables	−6.8	−20.1	24.7	−109.4	−55.8
(Decrease) Increase in Other Curr. Liabs.	0.0	−12.1	−10.1	0.0	0.0
Other Noncash Items	1.7	3.5	−45.7	−29.3	−45.7
Net Cash from Continued Operations	174.4	153.3	132.5	16.7	174.9
Net Cash from Discontinued Operations	0.0	0.0	0.0	0.0	0.0
Net Cash from Operating Activities	**174.4**	**153.3**	**132.5**	**16.7**	**174.9**
Cash Flow from Investing Activities					
Cash Flow Provided by:					
Sale of Property, Plant, Equipment	7.1	5.5	4.6	1.4	16.6
Sale of Short-Term Investments	3.8	5.2	11.6	13.7	23.2
Cash Used by:					
Purchase of Property, Plant, Equipment	−16.1	−15.7	−787.8	−45.8	−428.2
Purchase of Short-Term Investments	−1.3	−10.5	−1.3	0.0	−97.2
Other Investing Changes Net	0.0	0.0	0.0	−24.0	−0.1
Net Cash from Investing Activities	**−6.5**	**−15.5**	**−772.9**	**−54.7**	**−485.7**
Cash Flow from Financing Activities					
Cash Flow Provided by:					
Issuance of Debt	343.9	0.0	950.0	73.1	94.3
Issuance of Capital Stock	2.5	4.3	8.6	19.8	15.1
Cash Used for:					
Repayment of Debt	−488.4	−85.3	−160.4	0.0	0.0
Repurchase of Capital Stock	0.0	−101.7	−64.1	−34.1	−133.5
Payment of Cash Dividends	−20.7	−21.0	−21.3	−21.9	−22.6
Other Financing Charges, Net	−7.1	6.9	2.7	−0.9	5.0
Net Cash from Financing Activities	**−169.8**	**−196.8**	**715.5**	**36.0**	**−41.7**
Effect of Exchange Rate Changes	0.9	2.7	−2.9	−12.3	−11.2
Net Change in Cash & Cash Equivalents	−1.0	−56.3	72.2	−14.3	−363.7
Cash at Beginning of Period	51.3	107.6	35.4	49.7	413.4
Free Cash Flow	137.6	116.6	−676.6	−51.0	−275.9

Exhibit 10   RDA 3-Year Reportable Segment Results Summary

	Years ended June 30		
	2004	**2003**	**2002**
Revenues			
Reader's Digest North America	$835	$854	$649
Consumer Business Services	609	641	668
Reader's Digest International	970	1008	1078
Intercompany Eliminations	(26)	(28)	(26)
Total Revenues	**$2,388**	**$2,475**	**$2,369**
Operating Profit (Loss)			
Reader's Digest North America	$71	$61	$(2)
Consumer Business Services	64	91	88
Reader's Digest International	57	49	106
Magazine Deferred Promotion Charge[1]	(27)	—	—
Corporate Unallocated	(44)	(22)	(7)
Other Operating Items, Net[2]	(15)	(40)	(27)
Operating Profit	**$106**	**$139**	**$158**
Intercompany Eliminations			
Reader's Digest North America	$(1)	$(1)	$(4)
Consumer Business Services	(21)	(24)	(16)
Reader's Digest International	(4)	(3)	(6)
Total Intercompany Eliminations	**$(26)**	**$(28)**	**$(26)**

[1]Magazine deferred promotion charge relates to: 45 percent to Reader's Digest North America and 55 percent to Reader's Digest International.

[2]Other operating items, net in 2004 related to: 12 percent to Reader's Digest North America, 22 percent to Consumer Business Services, 61 percent to Reader's Digest International, and 5 percent to corporate departments that benefit the entire organization. In 2003, these items related to: 13 percent to Reader's Digest North America, 6 percent to Consumer Business Services, 64 percent to Reader's Digest International, and 17 percent to corporate departments that benefit the entire organization. In 2002, these items related to: 22 percent to Reader's Digest North America, 27 percent to Consumer Business Services, 16 percent to Reader's Digest International and 35 percent to corporate departments that benefit the entire organization.

Source: From SEC 10K filing June 30, 2004, retrieved from http://phx.corporate-ir.net/phoenix.zhtml?c=71092&p=irol-sec#3001434.

In the 1950s and 1960s, the Reader's Digest Association expanded into the publishing of condensed books, recorded music, and direct mail sweepstakes. In 1955, RDA accepted its first advertising but did not carry liquor ads until 1978 and has never carried cigarette ads. RDA also began to sponsor several educational funds and in 1963 founded QSP, Inc., an organization created to assist school and youth-group fundraising efforts in the U.S. and Canada. In 1973, the Wallaces gave up active management of the business, and after their passing, George Grune took over as chairman and CEO in 1984.

Under Mr. Grune's leadership RDA continued to thrive. A $15-million data center was opened at the RDA headquarters in Chappaqua. This operation allowed data to be collected and processed from all over the world. RDA entered the video business and had one of their books,

Exhibit 11   RDA 3-Year Revenue by Product and Geographical Area Summary

Net Revenues by Product	2004	2003	2002
Books	$ 968.5	$ 982.9	$ 963.8
Magazines—Subscription & Other	$ 702.7	$ 750.1	$ 610.1
Magazines—Advertising	$ 150.0	$ 151.0	$ 151.4
Music & Videos	$ 240.3	$ 257.4	$ 328.8
Food & Gift	$ 228.7	$ 244.9	$ 256.7
Fees from Financial Services Marketing Alliances	$ 16.9	$ 13.2	$ 20.8
Other	$ 81.4	$ 75.4	$ 37.0
TOTALS	**$2,388.5**	**$2,474.9**	**$2,368.6**
Revenues by Area	**2004**	**2003**	**2002**
United States	$1,291.3	$1,351.8	$1,176.7
International	$1,102.1	$1,124.6	$1,196.3
Interarea	($4.9)	($1.5)	($4.4)
TOTALS	**$2,388.5**	**$2,474.9**	**$2,368.6**

Source: From 2004 10K filing, in $ millions.

Household Hints & Handy Tips, become number one on the General Books best-seller list. In 1990 Reader's Digest became a public company trading on the New York Stock Exchange. The offering price was $21.50 per share.

In 1992, the company undertook its first global advertising campaign. The campaign included ads in 13 languages and appeared in 77 magazines and newspapers worldwide. A television commercial also aired on six continents. RDA established Young Families, Inc. in 1994. This new subsidiary created and marketed children's books and home entertainment products. On August 1, 1994, James P. Schadt succeeded Grune as president and CEO of RDA.

Under Schadt   After assuming the role of president and CEO in 1994, James P. Schadt, former CEO of Cadbury Beverages, initiated a strategy to attract babyboomers to *Reader's Digest* and to transition the company into a new phase. His specific strategy was to "get prices down . . . get a new variety of promotions and a new variety of products." Yet Schadt himself admitted "there's a lot of drama as the company comes face-to-face with the Information Age." He also said that he was "wrestling with a changing external world, and [had] a company that's unaccustomed to change."[14]

Despite the predisposition to "old-school" ways that Schadt felt he had to deal with at RDA, they were able to launch an advanced Web site for *Reader's Digest* in 1996.

The Web site was aimed at exposing new and younger consumers to RDA and to "expand into new channels of distribution."[15] During Schadt's tenure, RDA also launched the Polish and Thai editions of *Reader's Digest* magazine.

However, by this point in time, it was common knowledge throughout the industry that RDA was struggling to move its content into the 21st century. One publishing industry analyst asserted that they had "lost their direction."[16] Some speculated that the largest hurdle for the *Reader's Digest* magazine, whose average reader at the time was 47 years old, was that it could not capture the interest of younger readers.

This same problem was evident with respect to the company's records, videos, and books, resulting in decreased earnings. Between 1994 and 1997, the company's stock price fell by 40 percent. Operating profits had fallen 31 percent, and revenue also decreased by 8 percent. Dividends were cut in half. Fiscal 1997 would not meet initial expectations. This was merely three months after Schadt had announced a $400 million plan for customer research, promotion, and product development.

Acknowledging the difficulties that RDA was facing and his failure to meet promises to attract a younger audience, Schadt said, "We were not successful, and we underachieved our goals." He cited an overabundance of mailings sent to customers, declining response rates, and seemingly stale products as a few of the issues contributing to RDA's problems.[17] James Schadt resigned as chairman and CEO on August 11, 1997.

Grune Returns   After Schadt's resignation in 1997, George Grune was brought out of retirement to return as interim chairman and CEO of Reader's Digest. One of his major goals was to stabilize the struggling company. In one effort to do this, a joint venture between Reader's Digest Music and Warner Resound was established to bring RDA's music products into the $1 billion-a-year Christian bookstore marketplace.[18]

The second major activity under Grune's leadership was making editorial management changes at RDA. A number of senior appointments were made to strengthen the management teams in core business areas and aid in the transition.[19]

Another move toward modernization was a major change to the traditional appearance of *Reader's Digest* magazine. Forty-eight editions of the flagship magazine would replace their traditional front cover table of contents with photography and enhanced graphics. The table of contents was moved inside the magazine and expanded to cover two pages. It was also categorized by theme to make it more reader-friendly, modern in appearance, and hopefully more attractive to advertisers.[20]

Grune's final appointment and act as interim leader of RDA was to help find and appoint a new CEO and Chairman for the company. The Board of Directors, aided by Grune, found what they considered the perfect candidate in Thomas Ryder.[21]

The "Quiet Revolution" 1999–2001[22]

Ryder Steps In   After leaving American Express, where he was President of Travel-Related Services and served on the Policy and Planning Committee, Ryder was excited about the task that lay ahead with RDA. He was not unfamiliar with the type of situation RDA faced. At American Express he had led the effort to strengthen the organization through a global re-engineering program, which helped redefine the organization's strategic direction. This was an experience that he could draw from in leading Reader's Digest.

There were many issues for Ryder to address, including assessing viability of products, broadening the customer base to include younger customers, overhauling the company's work processes and cost structure, addressing underperforming assets, and developing and acquiring growth businesses. He had to reassess overall strategy: an over-reliance on sweepstakes had lulled the company into failing to develop any other substantial means of generating business, and when subscriptions began to drop, there was no ready strategic response. His job would not be easy. One of Ryder's mantras became "no wimpy goals."[23]

After settling into his new role, Ryder's first order of business in July of 1998 was to redesign the corporate structure. He described this as the first step in a long-term strategy to build on the company's fundamental strengths and create new growth opportunities. He would create four domestic strategic business units in Books and Home Entertainment and three geographical units outside the U.S., with each unit organized according to customer and business relationships. They would have specific product development and profit-and-loss responsibility.[24]

In September 1998, after profits and revenues continued to decline due to restructuring costs in the previous year, RDA refocused on gaining younger readers. This second phase of their restructuring included their acquisition of *American Woodworker* magazine from Rodale Press. The company also sold some assets, including part of its art collection and some real estate holdings, for approximately $200 million. Some warehouse jobs were also moved outside the company. As a result, Ryder announced that several hundred employees were to be laid off.

In February 1999, Ryder announced the last phase of the restructuring that would focus the company's assets on five basic growing consumer interests: home, health, family, finance, and faith. The strategy was to expand RDA's nonpublishing products; diversify marketing channels, including the Internet; and broaden global operations.

In 1999, Reader's Digest Music, previously sold only by direct mail, made several instrumental albums by performers such as Henry Mancini available in Wal-Mart stores. Also RDA made an exclusive multi-year deal with CBS Productions to develop television movies and miniseries based on personal dramas that had been reported in *Reader's Digest* magazine. This collaboration would extend RDA's reach and publicity, it would afford them advertising opportunities, and RDA would control print publication and video distribution rights.

Your Family, a new magazine offering insight and emotional support to parents of children from infants to six years old, was also launched. The magazine was intended to promote RDA's values and traditions, yet include new ways of doing things that Baby Boomer parents did not necessarily focus on. It would be sold via newsstands, supermarkets, and mass merchandisers such as Barnes & Noble.

A strong emphasis was placed on marketing and advertising resulting in a 9 percent increase in advertising revenues for fiscal 1998. RDA credited their magazines as the "front door" through which customers come in and become familiar with their products and services.[25]

Books Are Fun, Ltd. (BAF) was acquired by Reader's Digest in August 1999. BAF was the nation's leading display marketer of books and gifts. RDA purchased the privately held company for approximately $380 million. The acquisition was part of RDA's strategy to increase distribution channels for existing products and also add new products to their current offerings.

First USA, a subsidiary of Bank One Corporation and RDA reached an agreement in September of 1999 to launch a co-branded credit card. This agreement would allow the marketing of Reader's Digest credit cards to their customers. This followed an announcement that RDA had established partnerships to sell various insurance products with Torchmark Corporation in North America and with American International Group in 26 other nations.

In 2000, still continuing to pursue the strategies announced the year before, RDA acquired *Receptar,* a special interest do-it-yourself and gardening magazine in the Czech Republic. Their QSP arm also acquired the World's Finest Chocolate sales force. Lastly, the first volume of Select Editions was published in Russia. RDA experienced earnings and revenue growth for the second year in a row, with operating profits increasing 54 percent over fiscal 1999.

In 2001, Reader's Digest made several editorial and design changes to enhance publication and modernize their flagship magazine. In international business, RDA entered China. Also, RDA and Vanguard entered a marketing alliance to offer mutual funds and other financial services to Reader's Digest customers. This built upon RDA's strategy to focus on nonpublishing and financial products.

But in January 2001 the Internet bubble burst and lowered the value of RDA's Web holdings; then in September the 9/11 tragedy and anthrax scares focused the country's attention elsewhere and revenues plunged. Post office slowdowns affected the distribution of products and many direct mail customers never even opened their envelopes. In addition, lawsuits were causing regulatory agreements for all magazine sweepstakes promotions to be challenged, forcing a redefinition of this historic Reader's Digest practice.

How Much Longer? 2002–2003

The year 2002 brought with it two major events for RDA: the purchase of Reiman Publications LLC and approval of the recapitalization of the company. Reiman Publications was purchased for $760 million. Reiman's publications were being sold completely by direct mail and 77 percent of their readership had never purchased an RDA product before. These publications included *Taste of Home,* one of the best-selling food magazines in North America.

This acquisition was also part of RDA's effort to reduce reliance on sweepstakes sales for their magazines, since sweepstakes-generated subscriptions decreased from 92 percent in 1998 to 8 percent in 2002 as a result of regulatory changes and the attorney general's 2001 agreement to "dramatically change the way [RDA promoted] the sale of its products through the use of sweepstakes."[26] From 2001 on, the judgment read, all sweepstakes must provide "a clear and conspicuous" disclosure to recipients indicating that entry is free and a purchase won't help the recipient win sweepstakes prizes. In addition, RDA was to monitor sales and stop sending solicitations to consumers "who have purchased unreasonably high amounts of product."[27] Although this might have been perceived as a blow to RDA's marketing strategy,

Ryder saw it as an opportunity to retool. "There was an overreliance on sweepstakes," Ryder said. "When you overwhelm a limited audience with 50 mailings a year that are similar in all their aspects, you begin to blind them with similarities. You lost your sense of differentiation."[28]

Finally, in December 2002, RDA's class B voting common stock shareholders approved the re-capitalization of Reader's Digest. As a result the RDA's class A (nonvoting) and Class B common stocks became a single class with voting rights.

After four years as Chairman and CEO, Thomas Ryder had made great efforts to get Reader's Digest back to its earlier success. What else needed to be done? With the acquisition of Reiman, RDA now had more than 23 million Gen-X and Baby Boomer readers ages 25 to 54, but attempts to gain younger readers' loyalty were not yet consistently successful. Even though Ryder noted that *Reader's Digest* had "nearly twice as many readers 18 to 34 as *Entertainment Weekly* and more professionals than *The Wall Street Journal, BusinessWeek, Forbes,* and *Fortune* combined," RDA's stock price continued to fall. Net sales, revenues, and shareholder's equity were also lower.[29]

International business units, which accounted for 51 percent of RDA's revenues in 2001, fell to 20 percent in 2003 due to troubled economies in Germany and England. With RDA's reliance on direct mail, anthrax scares in the aftereffects of September 11, 2001, had additionally complicated North American and international business operations.

In 2003, the first full year of revenues for Reiman Publications only increased revenues by 5 percent. Although changes in the Books and Home Entertainment division were beginning to show a turnaround, revenues continued to fall there by 12 percent, reflecting the reduction in U.S. sweepstakes business.[30] Based on an overall revenue reduction of 5.9 percent, Moody's Investors Service cut RDA's bond credit rating to junk status.[31] Were the problems RDA continued to encounter due to outside forces (such as the economy) or were they problems inherent to the Reader's Digest Association itself?

Ryder's stated strategies for 2003 included a two-year plan to "achieve sustainable revenue and profit growth by Fiscal 2005" by, in part, reducing marketing activity in the mature businesses to "'rest' customer bases, lower risk and improve margins," while investing in new products, expanding new customer acquisition channels, and providing more "inter-division selling opportunities to drive growth."

In 2003 RDA launched ChangeOne. With a book, weekly features, and a Web site for interactive support, ChangeOne was a weight loss program designed to improve eating habits over the course of 12 weeks and was meant to "inspire people of all ages."[32]

RDA also reorganized into the three divisions of Reader's Digest North America, Reader's Digest International, and Consumer Business Services to "combine related businesses under common leadership, reduce costs and improve . . . synergies." Noted was a decrease in revenues for *Reader's Digest* magazine, stated as being "due to lower circulation and advertising revenues."[33] (Remember, for the first 35 years of its existence, *Reader's Digest* didn't need to rely on any advertising.) In May 2003, RDA announced its first advertising campaign in 10 years to support the flagship magazine. Meant to attract media buyers, the campaign urged advertisers to "tap into the deep connection" readers have with the magazine.[34]

One analysis concluded that Reader's Digest's products were mature. The revenue reductions in core businesses that were not successful were outpacing the introduction of new and innovative products. The analysis stated that, "We are inclined to believe that the core Reader's Digest franchise is in a state of perpetual decline."[35]

Internal and External Cultural Factors and the Industry

Reader's Digest Cultural Impact   The *Reader's Digest* magazine format and style, the features like "Word Power," "Everyday Heroes," "Life in These United States," and "Humor in Uniform," and the legacy of the Reader's Digest Condensed Books have all become part of the American experience and American culture. The brand name "Reader's Digest" has become the vernacular for a whole category of products. Even Garrison Keeler's Prairie Home Companion references the "reader's digest version" as part of Chatterbox Café lingo for "a condensed report on something or other."[36] Pastor Josh Hunt of the Gospelcom.net Web site encourages use of the Reader's Digest style when communicating an evangelistic message:

> It aims at the reading level of a 13-year old, yet does not talk down to adults. It uses many true real-life stories about people . . . told in a dramatic way . . . with plenty of quoted speech. . . . It addresses practical problems and worries, and offers ideas to help readers improve their quality of life. In other words, it addressees felt needs which is a key strategy in evangelism.[37]

Even though some have wondered about an old-fashioned image, many readers, some in their 40s, like the magazine just the way it is. Reviewers at Epinions in Books rate the magazine 4 stars out of 5, calling it the "King of Magazines," "an enduring American institution and treasure," and a magazine with advertisements that "cover only about 25 percent of the pages . . . about half the saturation rate of most magazines," so your reading isn't "interrupted by constant attempts at marketing persuasion." It calls *Reader's Digest*

> a complete magazine that combines practical advice, humor, words of wisdom, educational material, and human-centered stories about life and all its ups and downs. It

does seem to be geared more toward the older crowd, but there is something here for everyone. It makes for good reading for people of all ages and backgrounds and it's one of the best overall magazines in publication today.[38]

RDA had acknowledged the importance of technology. Their Web site http://www.rd.com provided links to almost all their current products, and included shopping as well as information, citing over 14.5 million visitors to the site from around the world.[39] With that link to technology, even the Web's "bloggers" were realizing that "weblogs are an online reincarnation of the Reader's Digest format."

> Some Wall Street analysts argue that Reader's Digest has reached its limits and can't grow significantly in the future. Others argue just the opposite—that the basic publishing premise is still viable, even more so for today's readers than for their grandparents. [Reader's Digest as a blog?] Time will tell.[40]

Part of Thomas Ryder's "quiet revolution" to draw in "today's readers" was the engineered "subtle revamping process," developing ways to make the editorial content of the magazine younger without turning off loyal, older subscribers. Eric Schrier, hired by Ryder in 2000 to change the look and subtly upgrade the content, said Ryder warned him that it had to be done slowly, and that "this would be like changing the engine while the plane is flying."[41] In order to make that kind of change, employees had to change as well.

Regarding the internal view of the RDA culture, older employees had spoken wistfully about the paternalistic coddling, a legacy from DeWitt Wallace's days of raising salaries just because he was in a good mood;[42] of the "rides home for sick employees in the Wallace's limousine"; of the Georgian renaissance headquarters building's cupola, whose carillon bells would ring at 4 p.m. to signal the end of the work day; of Mr. Wallace walking from office to office "turning off workers' lights, urging them to go home"; and about giving workers Fridays off in May to work in their gardens. Now, thanks in part to Thomas O. Ryder, this is "a far leaner, more profit-oriented company where nobody can count on a lifetime job."[43] And the final blow to the old culture was the 2004 sale of the Wallace's elegant corporate headquarters.

The change of culture was inevitable, and Ryder said "I came at a time when people absolutely knew things had to change if the company was to survive." Some of many changes were the ones made in the executive team. Richard Garvey was hired as a Senior V.P. in 1996 by Schadt, and worked under three CEOs before being fired himself by Ryder in 1998. He is quoted as saying "There must have been 25 vice presidents fired while I was there"[44] (see Exhibit 12: RDA Management Changes 1997–2004 and Exhibit 13: Corporate Officers, 2004).

Exhibit 12   RDA Management Changes 1997–2004

1997

George V. Grune	CEO, President (retired in 1998)
Marcia Lefkowitz	Senior V.P., President Reader's Digest, U.S.A. (gone in 1998)
Richard Garvey	Senior V.P., Corporate Planning (gone in 1998)
Barbara Morgan	Senior V.P., Editor-in-Chief, Books and Home Entertainment (gone in 1998)
Christopher Willcox	Senior V.P., Editor-in-Chief, Reader's Digest Magazine (gone in 2000)
George Scimone	Chief Financial Officer (gone in 2001)
John Bohane	Senior V.P., President International Operations (gone in 2002)
Peter Davenport	Senior V.P., Global Marketing (retired in 2003)
Clifford DuPree	V.P., Corporate Secretary, and Associate General Counsel

1998

Thomas O. Ryder	CEO, President
Thomas Belli	President, QSP, Inc. (gone in 1999)
Gregory Coleman	Senior V.P., President U.S. Magazine Publishing (gone in 2001)
Elizabeth Chambers	V.P., Business Redesign (gone in 2002)
Robert Krefting	Senior V.P., President International Magazine Publishing (gone in 2002)
Michael A. Brizel	V.P. and General Counsel
Gary Rich	Senior V.P. Human Resources, in 2004 became President QSP
Thomas Gardner	V.P. Business Planning, in 2003 became Senior V.P., President, International

1999

Dominic Rossi	V.P., U.S. Publisher of Reader's Digest Magazine (gone in 2003)
Robert Raymond	V.P., Strategic Acquisitions, in 2003 became President, Consumer Business
Albert Perruzza	Senior V.P., Global Operations

2000

Michael Geltzeiler	Senior V.P., Chief Financial Officer
Eric Schrier	Senior V.P., Global Editor-in-Chief
Jeffrey Spar	V.P., Chief Information Officer

2001

Richard Fontana, Jr.	President, QSP, Inc. (gone in 2002)
John Klingel	Worldwide Circulation Director, General Manager, Reader's Digest U.S. Magazines (gone in 2003)

2002

Ian Marsh	Senior V.P., President, Reader's Digest Europe (gone in 2003)
Michael Brennan	Senior V.P., President Latin America and Asia Pacific
Richard Clark	V.P. Investor Relations, Global Communications

2003   No additions

2004

Giovanni di Vaio	V.P., Human Resources, International
Francoise Hanonik	V.P., Human Resources, North America

Source: Information derived from SEC 10K filings for each year.

Exhibit 13   RDA Corporate Officers, 2004

Michael A. Brennan
  Senior V.P., and President, Latin America and Asia-Pacific
Michael A. Brizel
  Senior V.P. and General Counsel
Richard E. Clark
  V.P., Investor Relations and Global Communication
Giovanni de Vaio
  V.P., Human Resources International, Chief Human Resources Officer
Clifford H.R. DuPree
  V.P., Corporate Secretary and Associate General Counsel
Thomas D. Gardner
  Senior V.P. and President, International
Michael S. Geltzeiler
  Senior V.P. and Chief Financial Officer
Francoise Hanonik
  V.P., Human Resources, North America, Chief Human Resources Officer
Albert L. Perruzza
  Senior V.P., Global Operations and Business Redesign
Robert E. Raymond
  Senior V.P. and President, Consumer Business Services
Gary S. Rich
  Senior V.P. and President, QSP, Inc.
Thomas O. Ryder
  Chairman and Chief Executive Officer
Eric W. Schrier
  Senior V.P. and Global Editor-in-Chief, President, North America
Jeffery S. Spar
  Senior V.P. and Chief Information Officer

Part of the culture change, and an overt strategy on the part of Ryder, was to use employee survey feedback, visualization workshops, a reconfigured benefits and retirement plan, and performance-based financial bonuses to create a younger, more ambitious workforce, a company that rewarded risk-taking, not conservatism; "in short, a place where someone like Mr. Wallace would be out of a job."[45] As an indication that this change had worked, Jeffrey Spar, hired by Ryder in 2000 as V.P. and Chief Information Officer, was able to get turnover in IT staff down to 5 percent by 2002, and boasted an employee satisfaction level of 71 percent in 2001, up from 58 percent in 1999.[46]

One of the questions was whether the management team was like-minded enough to continue to redefine a culture of quality and commitment to sustain any improvements. Shake-ups at Reiman Publishing, acquired by RDA for its mission of home-spun, reader-generated content in hopes of injecting new life into the RDA portfolio, caused concern that the highly successful Reiman culture would be harmed by the new, more businesslike approach of RDA.[47] One of the issues was whether or not to add advertising; Reiman's founders had staunchly resisted this. Industry analysts wondered how far Reiman would be able to advance RDA's fortunes given competition from ad-revenue-generating magazines like Time Inc.'s natural foods/rustic living entry *Real Simple.*[48]

In 2005, the *Reader's Digest* flagship magazine still reflected conservative, optimistic values, but with a new look and up-to-date content. For instance, RDA had hired CNBC Maria Bartiromo as a *Reader's Digest* "Money Talks" columnist.[49] In Asia, Reader's Digest English edition had gained the top spot in the Pan Asia cross Media Survey of nine markets, citing readership among affluent adults and business decision-makers. Market share grew in the region from 9 to 11 percent, and some media directors believed that *Reader's Digest* "mix of inspiration, drama and information clearly appealed to a younger and middle- to upper-class audience in Asia."[50] Noelle Chiu, Executive media director for FCB Hong Kong said "if you want to find an escape from the heavy business world, *Reader's Digest* can definitely serve that purpose."[51]

Unfortunately, however, *Reader's Digest* had been fighting for a long time against that image of being a magazine only read by kindly grandparents in Iowa. Even back in 2000, then publisher Dominic Rossi was saying "our median [readership] age is 47. Because we're so large, it pretty much reflects the population in general, which is 44. It's not like we have an ancient reader base." But media buyers weren't convinced, for, after all, how many of them—New York 20-somethings—read the magazine?[52] The median age of *Reader's Digest* readers as of 2004 was 50.3, but the median age of the *Reader's Digest Family Plus* edition readers was 44.2.[53] The challenge was convincing the media buyer to take a look at the statistics. RDA also had not been keeping pace with the overall publishing industry in terms of profit margins and other key ratios (see Exhibit 14: Key Ratio Comparisons to the Industry). However, the entire magazine industry was in trouble, and perhaps RDA's strategy of expanding into nonpublishing areas was an innovative response.

Publishing Industry Issues   In 2002 at the American Magazine Conference in Phoenix, some of the biggest players in the industry declared, "the business model for U.S. magazine publishing is broken and needs to be repaired to ensure the medium's survival." Thomas Ryder, CEO of Reader's Digest Association, said, "We have no choice but to change," citing the industry's overdependence on advertising, unwillingness to charge more for subscriptions, and the uncertain status of the newsstand distribution channel. No executive at the conference spoke of any visible turnaround for the industry, which had seen a major downward slide, especially since the terrorism threats of 2001.[54]

Baird Davis, veteran consumer marketer and publishing consultant, commented on industry market factors affecting the decline in circulation profitability of most mature consumer magazines during the years from 1999 to 2004. He believed the reasons for the decline could be traced to major market factors that drastically altered circulation economics: too many magazines chasing too few readers; the demise of sweepstake generated subscriptions; decrease in newsstand sales accompanied by increase in newsstand marketing costs; the availability of free content, especially on the Internet; and other industry specific concerns such as audit bureau disclosure rule changes and a reduction in publishers' circulation staffs.[55]

Sarah Gonser of *Folio* warned that "publishers face the toughest ad market since the Great Depression, and there is little room for failure." She suggested that publishers were being maybe too cautious about looking for "ancillary revenue streams" that might be perceived as distractions from their core businesses. Citing Thomas Ryder's willingness to expand RDA into nonpublishing areas, she stated, "What might at first glance appear as an overwhelming hodge-podge of initiatives is in fact a highly organized, meticulously researched endeavor." There's no guarantee of success, but RDA appeared to be leveraging their brand strength, their 50-million-person proprietary database, and their direct marketing expertise to try to find hidden profit sources.[56]

RDA raised the *Reader's Digest* cover price from $2.49 to $2.99,[57] then announced it would drastically reduce its circulation beginning in 2004 by a million copies. This caused a stir in media circles: "for some old enough to remember, it was a reminder of the demise of the golden days of mass-circulation magazines, when once-venerable titles like *Life, Look,* and *The Saturday Evening Post* slashed their circulation bases in an effort to survive the onslaught from the insurgent new medium, television."[58] The idea behind the circulation reduction was to follow the advice of Baird Davis to "deliver a higher-quality audience mix to advertisers at lower costs to the company" and therefore appeal to the media buyers by proving the magazine was delivering a more targeted readership.[59]

Regarding the Internet, most magazine publishers, including RDA, had made the shift to delivering timely content online, yet retaining their print product for its indepth approach, its synthesis and analysis, and ability to satisfy the reader with a reliable, permanent, portable, and tactile alternative. Steve Adler of *BusinessWeek* said, "I'd even go so far as to say if the Internet didn't exist, we in this industry would want to invent it," suggesting that the online version further attracts readers to the publisher's brand, to see what else is available in the magazine. As Adler said, "there's still something extremely intimate and extremely powerful about settling down with a magazine and not knowing what you're going to get, page to page, and the experience of reading it."[60]

Even with a multiplatform media mix of products, the major challenge for publishers was to convince retail

Exhibit 14   Key Ratio Comparisons to the Industry (Publishing–Books) and S&P 500
(Data as of 2004)

Growth Rates %	Company	Industry	S&P 500
Sales (Quarter vs year ago quarter)	0.20	8.20	10.20
EPS (YTD vs YTD)	−48.20	7.00	19.00
EPS (Quarter vs year ago quarter)	−13.10	7.30	25.00
Sales (5-Year Annual Average)	−1.29	2.94	4.25
EPS (5-Year Annual Average)	−26.89	10.58	2.18
Dividends (5-Year Annual Average)	0.00	4.54	2.89

Price Ratios	Company	Industry	S&P 500
Current P/E Ratio	74.6	23.3	20.9
P/E Ratio 5-Year High	34.0	33.9	64.8
P/E Ratio 5-Year Low	15.8	14.5	16.9
Price/Sales Ratio	0.72	2.02	1.57
Price/Book Value	3.41	4.61	2.98
Price/Cash Flow Ratio	17.30	13.50	13.10

Profit Margins %	Company	Industry	S&P 500
Gross Margin	62.7	63.1	47.1
Pre-Tax Margin	0.9	13.4	11.3
Net Profit Margin	1.0	8.8	7.6
5-Year Gross Margin (5-Year Average)	62.2	61.2	47.4
5-Year PreTax Margin (5-Year Average)	6.2	12.6	9.3
5-Year Net Profit Margin (5-Year Average)	4.1	8.0	5.8

Financial Condition	Company	Industry	S&P 500
Debt/Equity Ratio	1.08	0.28	1.18
Current Ratio	0.8	1.2	1.5
Quick Ratio	0.4	0.7	1.0
Interest Coverage	1.4	15.9	3.4
Leverage Ratio	5.0	2.3	6.0
Book Value/Share	5.03	11.92	12.30

Investment Returns %	Company	Industry	S&P 500
Return On Equity	4.8	20.1	14.4
Return On Assets	1.0	8.6	2.4
Return On Capital	2.3	15.7	6.6
Return On Equity (5-Year Average)	22.7	20.7	11.9
Return On Assets (5-Year Average)	4.5	7.9	2.0
Return On Capital (5-Year Average)	11.1	14.9	5.5

Management Efficiency	Company	Industry	S&P 500
Income/Employee	6,000	30,000	25,000
Revenue/Employee	555,000	337,000	333,000
Receivable Turnover	6.9	6.5	7.3
Inventory Turnover	5.2	4.2	8.4
Asset Turnover	0.9	1.0	0.3

buyers to create cross-merchandizing opportunities at diverse distribution channels. Pointing to the success Barnes & Noble had had with its placement of do-it-yourself books next to magazines like RDA's *American Woodworker,* the goal of the magazine industry was to "stimulate demand."[61]

Thomas Ryder said he felt the "time was right to go on the offensive." He referred to the weakness in television advertising caused by TiVo and channel surfing. Even though the challenge was daunting, with "continuing circulation woes, looming postal rate hikes of possibly 15 percent by 2006, and the specter of losing more ad dollars to the twin media of cable TV and a resurgent Web," print publishing represented a media in which ads were "bulletproof" from technology.[62] Jack Kliger, CEO of Hachette Fillipacchi Media U.S., said, "Magazines are the original on-demand medium, available on consumers' terms— whenever and wherever they choose to indulge. Magazines engage while other media interrupt."[63] In fact, studies had

shown that the "influential" baby boomers are heavier readers of magazines, lighter viewers of television, and that for advertisers, adding magazine advertising to the marketing mix along with TV and Internet advertising offers a powerful punch. In fact, the "highest percentage of consumers find advertising in magazines to be more acceptable and trustworthy than advertising on network or cable TV or online"[64] (see Exhibit 15: Media Usage Habits of Baby Boomers and Exhibit 16: Incremental Effect of Medium on Brand Metrics).

Where to Go from Here?

In 2000 there had been rumors that Bertelsmann, the German privately held conglomerate with interests in 600 companies in 53 countries, was in informal talks to acquire Readers Digest.[65] At the time, Thomas Ryder's turnaround plan seemed to be on schedule. Since 2001, with the overall dropoff in the publishing industry, these rumors had

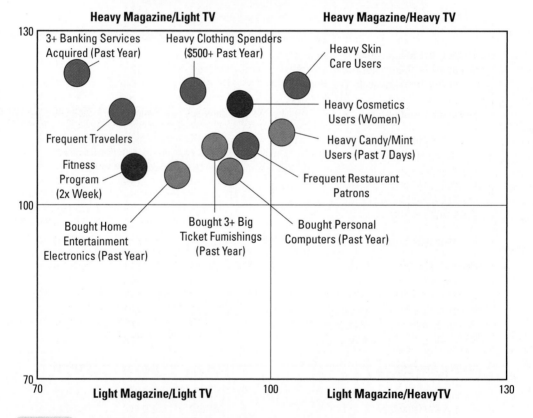

Compared to the average Baby Boomer, those who are most attractive to marketers (heavy users and recent purchasers) are heavier readers of magazines and tend to be lighter viewers of television.

Exhibit 15   Media Usage Habits of Baby Boomers

Source: From Media QuadMaps, retrieved 6/30/2005 from http://www.magazine.org; MRI 2003 Fall.

Base: U.S. adults age 45–54.

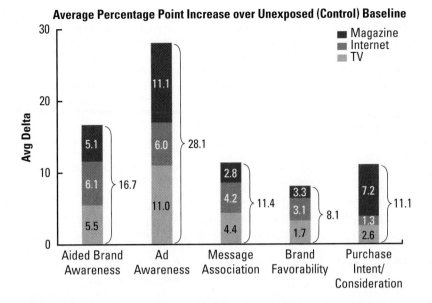

Average Percentage Point Increase over Unexposed (Control) Baseline

Legend:
- Magazine
- Internet
- TV

Metric	Magazine	Internet	TV	Total
Aided Brand Awareness	5.1	6.1	5.5	16.7
Ad Awareness	11.1	6.0	11.0	28.1
Message Association	2.8	4.2	4.4	11.4
Brand Favorability	3.3	3.1	1.7	8.1
Purchase Intent/ Consideration	7.2	1.3	2.6	11.1

Exhibit 16   Incremental Effect of Medium on Brand Metrics

Source: Dynamic Logic Crossmedia Research Studies.
N=8; September 2004; Delta= Exposed − Control

died down, but RDA could still be an attractive takeover option.[66]

In 2000, after being asked why he had taken on such a big challenge at that time in his career, Thomas O. Ryder said, "I grew up reading *Reader's Digest.* The allure of trying to save an American icon was just too great to ignore."[67] RDA's results for the second quarter of 2005 showed a $2 million increase in revenue.[68] Things were looking like they might go in the right direction. It appeared Ryder's strategy of refocusing the business might work after all, assuming RDA could avoid all the "risks and uncertainties" facing most global businesses in 2005. Time will tell.

Endnotes

1. Annual Report. 2004. The Reader's Digest Association, Inc.: 46.
2. Angeletti, N., & Oliva, A. 2004. *Magazines that make history.* Univ. Press of Florida.
3. Rubenstein, C. 2004. As Digest goes the way of older readers. *New York Times,* August 29.
4. Romell, R. 2004. Management turnover at Reiman since sale; several question new approach; new president calls some change inevitable. *Milwaukee Journal Sentinel.* March 8.
5. Kaplan, M. 2000. Reviving Reader's Digest. *Folio,* July 1, 29(8): 70.
6. Ibid.
7. Annual Report 2004. The Reader's Digest Association, Inc.: 2.
8. Ibid.
9. Kaplan, op. cit.
10. Reader's Digest and ECM to develop "Selecciones at the movies." 8/26/03. (RDA Web site www.rd.com.)
11. Pie Charts from Reader's Digest Annual Report 2004, http://media.corporate-ir.net/media_files/irol/71/71092/pdf/2004ar.pdf.
12. Tarsala, M. 2005. "Under the radar—Reader's Digest. Market Report, March 22. Retrieved from http://www.briefing.com on 3/13/05.
13. Information from Reader's Digest Web site "timeline" at http://www.rd.com and from Canning, Peter. 1996. *American Dreamers: The Wallaces and "Reader's Digest."* Simon & Schuster, NY http://syracuseuniversitypress.syr.edu/encyclopedia/entries/readers-digest.html.
14. Leiberman, D. 1997. Reader's Digest wants baby boomers. *USA Today,* July 21: 3B.
15. Oneserver Provides RDA with Advanced Web Site. Telephone IP News, December 1, 1996, 7: 1–8.
16. Berkowitz, H. 1997. Digest chairman out after turnaround fails. *Newsday,* August 12: A49.
17. Leiberman, op. cit.
18. Reader's Digest Music, Warner Bros. announce joint venture in Christian music retailing. *Business Wire,* September 2, 1997.
19. Reader's Digest Announces management changes. *Business Wire,* September 7, 1997.
20. Reader's Digest magazine redesigns editions worldwide; bold cover photography replaces table of contents; eye-opening graphics inside create dynamic new look. *Business Wire,* March 29, 1998.

21. Reader's Digest names Thomas O. Ryder of American Express as chairman and chief executive officer. *Business Wire,* April 4, 1998.
22. Information in this section comes primarily from Annual Reports and 10K filed by Reader's Digest.
23. Kaplan, M. 2000. Reviving Reader's Digest. *Folio,* July 1, 29(8): 70.
24. Ibid.
25. Reader's Digest strengthens publishing arm. *Business Wire,* June 14, 1999.
26. Teague, M. 2001. Pryor reaches settlement with Reader's Digest regarding sweepstakes solicitations. March 9. Retrieved from http://www.ag.state.ar.us/prrecent11.htm.
27. Ibid.
28. Kaplan, op cit.
29. Reader's Digest 2002 Annual Report.
30. Craig Huber, Douglas Arthur, Lisa Monaco, analysis of RDA for Morgan Stanley, January 24, 2003.
31. Reader's Digest credit rating cut to "junk." *Bloomberg News,* June 21, 2003.
32. Reader's Digest groundbreaking program for weight loss. January 7, 2003. RDA Web site.
33. Reader's Digest 2003 Annual Report.
34. Reader's digest launches first ad campaign in 10 years. May 15, 2003. RDA Web site.
35. Mandana Hormozi, Kathryn Mak, analysis of RDA for Lazard Freres & Co., LLC, June 25, 2003.
36. Search the Chatterbox Café postings on http://prairiehome.forum.publicradio.org/.
37. Reader's Digest—A style to follow. Retrieved from http://www.gospelcom.net/guide/resources/readersdigest.php.
38. Various reviews from Keith Pruitt, Bryan Carey and others posted during December 2004 at http://www.dealtime.com/xPR-Reader_s_Digest~.
39. Excerpted from the 10K filed by RDA on 9/9/2004.
40. Hiler, J. 2000. Blogger's Digest: How Weblogs are becoming the new Reader's Digest. October 31, retrieved from http://www.microcontentnewscom/articles/digests.htm.
41. Kilgannon, C. 2000. A workplace like no other painfully enters the real world. *New York Times,* December 24. Retrieved from ProQuest Historical Newspapers.
42. Rubenstein, C. 2004. As Digest goes the way of older readers. *New York Times,* August 29. Retrieved from Lexis/Nexis.
43. Kilgannon, op. cit.
44. Ibid.
45. Ibid.
46. Brandel, M. 2002. Best places to work in IT worldwide 2002 company detail. *Computerworld,* May 6, 2002. Retrieved from http://www.computerworld.com.
47. Romell, R. 2004. Management turnover at Reiman since sale; several question new approach; new president calls some change inevitable. *Milwaukee Journal Sentinel,* March 8. Retrieved from Lexis/Nexis.
48. Rattled at Reiman: A look at Reader's Digest two-year record. *Folio,* October 2004: 33(10): 45.
49. Reader's Digest adds CNBC anchor Maria Bartiromo as columnist. September 7, 2004. RDA Web site.
50. Shaw, S.D. 2003. Reader's Digest's climb to the top of PAX may help it chip away at agency bias. *Media Asia,* January 10: 15.
51. Chiu, N. 2004. Media Choice: Readers Digest. *Media Asia,* July 30: 12.
52. Kaplan, M. 2000. Reviving Reader's Digest. *Folio,* July 1, 29(8): 70.
53. From http://www.rdevents.com/mediakit/rd/circulation.shtml.
54. Fine, J. 2002. Magazines confront flawed business plan. *Advertising Age,* October 28, 73(43): 1.
55. Davis, B. 2004. Can't get no respect? Read this! *Circulation Management,* October.
56. Gonser, S. 2002. Looking inward for outside profits. *Folio,* April 1, 31(4): 54.
57. Kopp, L. 2003. Reader's Digest continues to slim down. *Circulation Management,* June 1.
58. Mandese, J. 2003. Fear and bloating on Mad Ave. *Folio,* June, 32(8):17.
59. Davis, B. 2004. Circ levels: Getting a grip. *Circulation Management,* May: 30.
60. Business Magazine editors identify trends that could affect your bottom line. Magazine Publishers of America, 6/16/2005, http://www.magazine.org.
61. Loughlin, J. 2005. Retail growth initiative update. Magazine Publishers of America Retail Conference, March 1, http://www.magazine.org.
62. Fine, J. 2004. Publishers finally unite to rally behind "engagement." *Advertising Age,* November 1, 75(44): 3.
63. Kliger, J. 2005. Magazine marketing coalition: Creating a movement. World Magazine Congress of the International Federation of the Periodical Press (FIPP), 5/24/2005, from http://www.magazine.org.
64. Ibid.
65. Marcial, G. 2000. Buy Reader's Digest? *BusinessWeek,* June 19.
66. Morais, R. 2003. Takeover bait. *Forbes,* July 7, 172(1): 72.
67. Fine, J. 2000. Ryder pulls "Digest" back from brink. *Advertising Age,* October 23, 71(44): S20.
68. RDA Announces 2Q Fiscal 2005 Results. January 26, 2005. RDA Web site.

Case 39   Southwest Airlines: How Much Can "LUV" Do?*

Southwest Airlines (SWA) did it again in 2005. For eight years in a row, and even four years after its celebrity CEO Herb Kelleher stepped down in 2001, the company retained its grip on the Fortune Top Ten list of America's most admired companies.[1] Also, Southwest posted a profit for the 33rd consecutive year and for 56 consecutive quarters by the first quarter of 2005—both of which were achievements unsurpassed in the airline industry. All this was achieved while the airline industry as a whole was experiencing losses for three straight years and when several larger airlines underwent or continued to restructure their business, gain wage concessions from their employees, and slash costs in efforts to avoid bankruptcy or emerge from bankruptcy.[2]

While these were admirable achievements, there seemed to be some emerging chinks in Southwest's low-cost, fun-culture armor. In 2002, its employee groups started calling for federal mediation for the first time. This was a result of their negotiations for pay raises which represented brewing tension between management and workers over the sharing of the spoils.[3] As the company grew to over 35,000 employees, there were challenges to keep the "LUV" culture intact (LUV was Southwest's ticker symbol on the New York Stock Exchange, signifying the company's operations from Love Field in Dallas as well as its emphasis on "love" to its customers and employees). Further, competition in the discount segment was heating up with the entry of several new low-cost, high-frill carriers such as JetBlue, Song, and Ted, though they were not at that moment direct competitors in Southwest's markets. And the effect of leadership change was too early to gauge with Herb Kelleher still playing a dominant role making strategy for the company. With the spirit of the "underdog" becoming irrelevant, was there a dominant vision for the company to propel it to success in the future?

Background and Growth

The inconvenience and expense of ground travel by bus or automobile between the cities of Houston, Dallas, and San Antonio—the Golden Triangle that was experiencing rapid economic and population growth during the late 1960s—offered an opportunity for an intrastate airline. The idea was suggested by Rollin King, a San Antonio entrepreneur who owned a small commuter air service, when his banker,

*This case study was prepared by Ms. Naga Lakshmi Damaraju of the University of Texas at Dallas, Professor Gregory G. Dess at University of Texas at Dallas, Professor Alan B. Eisner at Pace University, and Vasudev Krishnan, former graduate student at the University of Texas at Dallas. The purpose of the case is to stimulate class discussion rather than to illustrate effective or ineffective handling of a business situation. The authors thank Professor Michael Oliff at the University of Texas at Dallas, for his valuable comments on an earlier version of this case.

John Parker, complained about the issue. King then talked to Herb Kelleher—a New Jersey born, New York University Law School graduate who moved to San Antonio in 1967 to practice law. They soon pooled the seed money to start Southwest Airlines. The infant Southwest Airlines (SWA) fought long-drawn legal battles, primarily engineered by the major airline carriers, for over four years before it got its first flight off the ground in 1971. Later on, the company had to work around a regulation intended to penalize SWA's decision to operate out of Dallas Love Field instead of moving to the new Dallas–Fort Worth (DFW) airport. With Herb's brilliant legal expertise and extensive lobbying with the House of Representatives, the issue was settled and SWA was allowed to operate out of Love Field in 1979. The struggle for existence in the initial years worked to the advantage of the company as it created the esprit de corps for which it became so well known. The employees were caught up fighting for the "SWA cause" that created "the warrior mentality, the very fight to survive," according to Colleen Barrett, who became the president and chief operating officer of SWA in 2001.[4]

Kelleher, however, was not the first chief executive officer of Southwest. Lamar Muse, an airline veteran who worked earlier with Trans Texas, Central and Universal Airlines was brought in to get the company off to a good start. That was followed by the brief tenure of Howard Putnam, another airline veteran hired from United Airlines, from 1978 to 1982. Herb Kelleher served as the chairman of the board during that period, then took the CEO position in 1982 and championed Southwest's expansion (at that time the company had only 27 planes, $270 million in revenues, and flew only to 14 cities).[5] SWA was one of a kind right from its beginning. It was the pioneer of the "low-cost strategy." It flew planes point-to-point—short-haul flights bypassing the expensive hub-and-spoke operations. It chose less popular, less congested airports to achieve quicker turnarounds.

SWA offered airfares so low that it gave the bus and car travel companies a run for their money. It served no meals on its airlines and provided only a snack of peanuts. That saved plenty of money and manpower. There was no assigned seating which reduced boarding times and helped planes turn around faster. The average turnaround time for planes was around 25 minutes. Faster turnaround times and higher aircraft utilization also meant a reduced number of aircraft and gate facilities than would otherwise have been necessary. SWA's attractive flight attendants in hot pants were a source of live entertainment on flights (e.g., the flight attendants made funny presentations of the otherwise routine and boring safety instructions or performed preflight tricks such as popping out of overhead bins).[6] It was the first major airline that introduced ticketless travel and one of the first to put up a Web site and offer online booking.[7] It operated a single aircraft type, Boeing 737, that kept its training costs low and manpower utilization high as it offered great flexibility in manpower deployment. Starting with three Boeing 737s in 1971, the company fleet grew to 388 Boeing 737 aircraft, providing service to 59 airports in 58 cities in 30 states throughout the United States by the end of 2003 (see Exhibits 1, 2, and 3). It topped the monthly domestic passenger traffic rankings for the first time in May 2003. From May through August 2003, Southwest Airlines was the largest carrier in the United States based on originating domestic passengers boarded and scheduled domestic departures.[8]

The SWA Leadership and Culture

There are many stories about Herb Kelleher's flamboyant style for a CEO. He smoked cigars, loved Wild Turkey whiskey, was often seen dressed up as Elvis Presley, and publicly arm-wrestled and won over a rival company CEO to settle a dispute over an advertisement slogan.[9] Kelleher truly believed that business could and should be fun—at too many companies, people put on masks when they came to the office. At work, people were not themselves and would be overly serious, which explained why most business encounters were bland and impersonal. Therefore, SWA tried not to hire people who were humorless, self-centered, or complacent. Not surprisingly, there was no human resources department but a People Department at Southwest. The guiding principle for recruitment at SWA was "Hire for attitude and train for skills." Herb believed that to be the most important principle. When a person from the People Department said to him, "Herb, I'm getting a little embarrassed because I've interviewed 34 people for a ramp agent position in Amarillo," Herb replied, "If you have to interview 134 people to find the appropriate person to be a ramp agent in Amarillo, do it. Because the most important thing is to get the right people, and if you get the wrong ones they start poisoning everybody else."[10]

Kelleher's penchant for laughter and fun became a part of Southwest's culture. Prospective employees were asked how humor helped them out of a difficult situation. Prospective pilots were sometimes asked to pull on shorts and the ones who saw fun in it passed the interview. All people at the company were to be treated with dignity and respect and Herb did not believe in hierarchical barriers. When a vice president complained to the CEO that customers, gate agents, pilots, and baggage handlers had more access to him than he did, Kelleher said to him, "Let me explain this: They're more important than you are." Herb recognized the key to satisfied customers was having satisfied employees. So employees came first and that orientation was embodied in the mission statement (Exhibit 4).

The culture was put into operation through a number of policies and programs. The casual dress policy reinforced the company's desire that people be themselves on the job. Celebrations such as "Spirit Parties," culture parties, and weekly deck parties were organized at headquarters regularly to bring employees together. Activities at the events included gong shows, talent shows, dance contests, limbo contests, and famous person look-alike themes. The culture committee at SWA welcomed new employees with a "New Hire Welcome Kit" that included a bag, T-shirt, badge holder, pen, and a welcome letter. To build solidarity across all departments, there was an employee recognition program in which employees recognized each other's achievements. Such a practice helped community building within and across departments. For example, one work group committee recognized flight attendants 10 times a year with "Hokey Days," named for the broom apparatus used by flight attendants to sweep the cabin after the flights. Committee members chose two locations at which to honor flight attendants, greeted each arriving plane, waited until passengers got off, and then boarded with goodies. Flight attendants were asked to relax while the committee members cleaned the plane for them. There were similar programs to honor other departments as well.[11] There was also a "Walk a Mile Program" designed to foster problem solving and cooperation, in which an employee could do somebody else's job for a day (while operations people obviously could not fly the airplanes, pilots could do the work as operations agents).[12] Further, the company had the "Star of the Month"—outstanding employees would be chosen to appear in *Spirit,* the in-flight magazine of Southwest—which recognized the distinct contributions of employees toward excellence in customer service.[13]

The warmth toward employees was also expressed by other means. At Southwest's headquarters in Dallas, the walls were covered with more than 10,000 picture frames that contained photos of employees' pets, of stewardesses in miniskirts, of Southwest planes gnawing on competitors' aircraft. Also there were teddy bears, jars of pickled hot peppers, and pink flamingos. There was cigarette smoking and lots of chuckling. "To me, it's comfortable," said Colleen Barrett, who was most responsible for nurturing Southwest culture from its early days. "This is an open scrapbook. We aren't uptight. We celebrate everything. It's like a fraternity, a sorority, a reunion. We are having a party!" she said. Barrett also regularly traveled to meet the employees and personally sent them birthday cards, not so much to win their loyalty as to communicate the true spirit of a family. The company celebrated with its employees when good things happened and grieved with them when they had a devastating experience.[14] She said, "What we do is very simple, but it's not simplistic. We really do everything with passion. We scream at each other and we hug each other."[15]

Cost consciousness was another important part of the culture. "Yes, our culture is almost like a religion," said

Exhibit 1 Financial and Operating Data for Southwest Airlines, 2000–2004[*]

	Years Ended December 31,				
	2004	2003	2002	2001	2000
Financial Data					
(In $ millions, except per share amounts)					
Operating revenues	$ 6,530	$ 5,937	$ 5,522	$ 5,555	$ 5,650
Operating expenses	5,976	5,454	5,105	4,924	4,628
Operating income	554	483	417	631	1,022
Other expenses (income) net	65	(225)	24	(197)	4
Income before income taxes	489	708	393	828	1,018
Provision for income taxes	176	266	152	317	392
Net Income	$ 313	$ 442	$ 241	$ 511	$ 626
Net income per share, basic	$ .40	$ .56	$ .31	$ .67	$ .84
Net income per share, diluted	.38	.54	.30	.63	.79
Cash dividends per common share	.0180	.0180	.0180	.0180	.0148
Total assets at period-end	11,337	9,878	8,954	8,997	6,670
Long-term obligations at period-end	1,700	1,332	1,553	1,327	761
Stockholders' equity at period-end	5,524	5,052	4,422	4,014	3,451
Operating Data					
Revenue passengers carried	$70,902,773	$65,673,945	$63,045,988	$64,446,773	$63,678,261
Enplaned passengers	81,066,038	74,719,340	72,462,123	73,628,723	72,566,817
Revenue passenger miles (RPMs) (000s)	53,418,353	47,943,066	45,391,903	44,493,916	42,215,162
Available seat miles (ASMs) (000s)	76,861,296	71,790,425	68,886,546	65,295,290	59,909,965
Load factor	69.5%	66.8%	65.9%	68.1%	70.5%
Average length of passenger haul (miles)	753	730	720	690	663
Average stage length (miles)	576	558	537	514	492
Trips flown	981,591	949,882	947,331	940,426	903,754
Average passenger fare	$ 88.57	$ 87.42	$ 84.72	$ 83.46	$ 85.87
Passenger revenue yield per RPM	11.76¢	11.97¢	11.77¢	12.09¢	12.95¢
Operating revenue yield per ASM	8.50¢	8.27¢	8.02¢	8.51¢	9.43¢
Operating expenses per ASM	7.77¢	7.60¢	7.41¢	7.54¢	7.73¢
Operating expenses per ASM, excluding fuel	6.47¢	6.44¢	6.30¢	6.36¢	6.38¢
Fuel cost per gallon (average)	82.8¢	72.3¢	68.0¢	70.9¢	78.7¢
Number of employees at year-end	31,011	32,847	33,705	31,580	29,274
Size of fleet at year-end	417	388	375	355	344

[*]Refer to the Appendix for a list of terms used in the airline industry.

Source: Southwest Airlines, SEC filings, Form 10-K for 2004, www.sec.gov/.

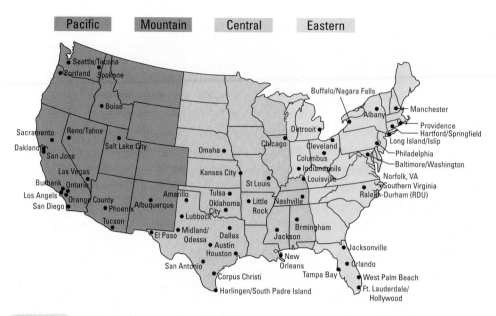

Exhibit 2   Cities Served by Southwest Airlines

Source: Southwest Airlines Web site, with permission from the company; www.southwest.com/swatakeoff/cities_states_airports.html.

Gary Kelly, CFO of Southwest, "but it's a dichotomy. In many ways we are conservative. Financially, for instance."[16] According to Herb Kelleher, close attention to costs had produced the kind of financial success Southwest had seen. He said, "Even in the best of times, we kept our costs low and questioned every expenditure. For years, I used to approve every expenditure over $1,000. Why? To encourage a cost-conscious culture. I couldn't look at all of them, of course. But I would question them selectively, and that kept people paying attention."[17]

Exhibit 3   Growth in the Number of Cities Served by Southwest Airlines, 1994–2005

Year Ended	No. of Cities Served
1994	44
1995	45
1996	49
1997	51
1998	52
1999	56
2000	57
2001	58
2002	58
2003	58
2004	59

Source: Southwest Airlines, Form 10-Ks filed with SEC.

Exhibit 4   The Mission of Southwest Airlines

The mission of Southwest Airlines is dedication to the highest quality of Customer Service delivered with a sense of warmth, friendliness, individual pride, and Company Spirit.

To Our Employees

We are committed to provide our Employees a stable work environment with equal opportunity for learning and personal growth. Creativity and innovation are encouraged for improving the effectiveness of Southwest Airlines. Above all, Employees will be provided the same concern, respect, and caring attitude within the organization that they are expected to share externally with every Southwest Customer.

Source: Southwest Airlines, www.southwest.com/about_swa/mission.html.

Treating employees well at Southwest did not mean that they were paid high salaries. By creating value through intangibles, the company kept wages lower than those of competitors. Officers at Southwest were paid about 30 percent less, on average, than their counterparts at other airlines. But the airline made stock options widely available, so all employees—not just executives—could share in the company's financial success. Southwest even had a policy that its officers received pay increases that were no larger, proportionally, than what other employees received. But employees were also expected to take pay reductions when times were not good. Job security was ensured, however, with a "no-furlough policy" and Southwest did not lay off a single employee during the economic downturn after the terrorist attacks on September 11, 2001, while many of its competitors did.[18] Caring for employee happiness showed positive results. Southwest had less employee turnover than its competitors. For years, Southwest enjoyed the loyalty of its employees despite the high level of employee unionization. "Once labor leaders realize that you're trying to take care of your people, most of the edge [in contract negotiations] is gone," said Kelleher.[19]

Southwest's employees worked more hours than their counterparts at other airlines. Southwest pilots flew nearly 80 hours a month compared to United's 50 hours. Southwest pilots were paid by trip, not per hour, which created a strong interest in keeping flights on schedule. Also, pilots tended to be cost conscious because a big part of their compensation came from stock options. On some occasions, pilots even pitched in to help ground crews move luggage to ensure on-time flights—something virtually unheard of at Southwest's bigger rivals. Flight attendants at Southwest worked about 150 hours a month, compared with 80 hours at many other airlines, according to union president Thom McDaniel. Southwest attendants were required by contract to make a reasonable effort to tidy the airplane between flights, a job performed by maintenance personnel at rival airlines. According to an airline labor expert, senior flight attendants at United got as many as 52 vacation days a year (compared with 35 days for veterans at Southwest) and they never had to clean up after the passengers.[20]

Maintaining focus on the core business was another element for both cost control and pursuing a niche strategy. Kelleher consciously ensured that the company did not diverge into allied businesses such as car rentals or reservations. Most of Southwest's growth had been organic, that is, by adding more flights on its existing routes and by connecting more dots (adding cities). The airline started complementing its short-haul flights with long-haul flights and began transcontinental services. According to Kelleher, the airline did not plan for international flights as it meant a total change in the way it operated and involved training its 35,000 employees to handle that change.[21]

The cost consciousness and employee commitment translated into operational excellence and increased profitability. Southwest's planes flew about 10.9 hours per day, much more than any other airline except for that of JetBlue, which flew close to 13.0 hours per day. Southwest could offer lower fares—as much as 50 percent lower than its major rivals—and still remain profitable. With such low costs, it created what was called the "Southwest effect," an explosion in the traffic and nabbing of customers who would have driven before.[22] The term Southwest effect was coined by the U.S. Department of Transportation to refer to the consistent phenomenon of a decrease in average fares and stimulation of demand that occurred when Southwest Airlines entered any market.[23]

In May 1988 Southwest became the first airline to win the coveted "Triple Crown" for a month: Best On-Time Record, Best Baggage Handling, and Fewest Customer Complaints. Since then, Southwest has won it more than 30 times, as well as five annual Triple Crowns for 1992, 1993, 1994, 1995, and 1996. Southwest crossed its $1 billion revenue mark in 1990 to become a major airline and continued its profitable operations to emerge as number seven among major airlines based on revenue in 2003. Stories of Southwest employees providing excellent customer service abound and Southwest had even set up a direct TV to show how its employees treated customers.[24]

The Changing Times and Challenges

Southwest Airlines had a change in leadership in August 2001 when Herb Kelleher relinquished power to two of his close aides. Colleen C. Barrett, vice president for customers, became the president and chief operating officer; and James F. Parker, general counsel, became the chief executive officer. Barrett and Parker had each worked together for over 22 years and for much longer with Kelleher from the time he was a lawyer. In contrast to Kelleher's obtrusive personality, Parker was a quiet diplomat. He had been the company's lead labor negotiator for years, and his opponents said he pursued the company line quite forcefully, if politely, in talks. "He will surprise you because he doesn't look like he's tough, but he doesn't give anything away," said a former vice president of the airline's pilot association.[25] Unlike Kelleher, Parker was not as fond of celebrations because he didn't see them as contributing to productivity. But he came to realize that the party preparations were a model of teamwork and employee bonding and he started participating in the celebrations in 2002.[26]

Barrett, on the other hand, had been the culture keeper of Southwest since the earliest days of the company. However, she was a reluctant public speaker. Thus, she let Parker take the lead with Wall Street and the media. How far the lieutenants replaced the "rock star" personality of Kelleher, who exuded warmth to his employees, was too early to guess. Kelleher remained chairman of the board and focused on long-range strategy and government affairs. He maintained control of schedule planning and aircraft acquisitions, the backbone of Southwest's strategy during the period of transition.[27] Whether things would be the same after Kelleher left the scene completely was another important question facing Southwest.

The growth of the company and the consequent increase in the number of employees also posed challenges to keeping the culture intact. The distance between the rank-and-file and top management was growing. While Colleen Barrett could reach all the employees through personally signed birthday cards when the company was small, such a task was becoming increasingly unrealistic. Even though she continued to do so, she could reach only a fraction of Southwest's 35,000 employees dispersed over different cities. Keeping in close touch with employees was becoming an increasingly challenging task. In earlier times of difficulty, Herb Kelleher personally addressed and rallied his troops, but such an exercise was no longer easy.

In addition, the otherwise warm employee relations at Southwest seemed to chill over time. Unions were becoming more aggressive in expressing their frustration, in contrast to earlier days when disputes were resolved more amicably and peacefully. In the summer of 2001, ramp workers picketed near company headquarters with signs that read, "Record Profits Empty Pockets." They complained that staff shortages, combined with Southwest's record passenger loads, and a drive to improve on-time performance, meant they had to lift more bags and had to do so more quickly which put them at risk of injury.[28] And for the first time in company history, in July 2002 Southwest's mechanics union asked federal mediators to intervene to break a contract deadlock over pay. While the company was nowhere near a strike, the incident clearly signaled the strains appearing in employee relations.[29]

Since 2002 the company was also engaged without much success in a contract renegotiation with flight attendants. In July 2003 a group of flight attendants staged a demonstration at the headquarters with signs "Spread the LUV" and handed out cards to travelers reading "Give our flight attendants a break." The move was an expression of frustration toward management's idea of increasing their work hours. Also, workers who had been working hard to boost the productivity of the company were not seeing much return from profit sharing and a pummeled stock. After years of hard work, some long-time employees felt that they had no more to give. Karen Amos, a 26-year Southwest veteran, said, "We have been there for them. There comes a time when it becomes too much."[30] The company had to drop the move to increase work hours, but still could not get a deal made with the flight attendants. Some workers perceived that the company had been fairer in its negotiations in past years.

In November 2003, after 11 rounds of talks without success, the flight attendants threw a Thanksgiving party at

Salt Lake City International Airport, primarily as a means of putting pressure on management to accept their demands for holiday pay and better working conditions. Kevin Onstead, a Southwest negotiator and flight attendant, said:

> We are concerned about the culture of the airline. We are fighting for the recognition of our contribution to that culture. We've been key in Southwest Airlines' success. Flight attendants are prepared to strike as a last resort. We are willing to do whatever it takes to get a fair contract.[31]

The negotiations had not borne fruit by early 2004. Thom McDaniel, president of the TWU, said that flight attendants were willing to return to the negotiating table. However, he made the point that the latest management offer fell short of their expectations. "We feel that our culture is at risk because of the actions taken by Southwest's management during these negotiations."[32]

Pressure on Southwest for pay increases was also likely to mount from the pilots' union whose contract was due to expire in 2006. Many of the employee groups started feeling that Southwest Airlines was no longer the underdog and that their pay should match the profitability of the company. Love (LUV) alone no longer seemed to be enough. That meant a twin challenge in terms of culture and costs.

In July of 2004 James Parker abruptly resigned as CEO of Southwest amid strained labor negotiations with flight attendants. Some people said that Parker had spent too much time in the back offices of Southwest and was never really cut out for a job in the limelight.[33] Herb Kelleher stepped into the negotiations, and the flight attendants walked away smiling with a 31 percent pay raise.[34]

Gary C. Kelly, former chief financial officer of Southwest, took the helm. Kelly appears to have some of the aggressiveness and flamboyance of Kelleher. Kelly is certainly energetic, showing up at the office Halloween party in 2004 dressed as Gene Simmons, leader of the rock group Kiss.[35] Kelly audaciously acquired six gates at Chicago's Midway Airport from bankrupt carrier ATA and signed Southwest's first ever code share agreement with ATA.

Southwest was already experiencing cost increases per average seat mile (ASM), a key metric used to measure performance in the industry, primarily due to increases in fuel costs and wages. The cost per ASM went up from 7.07 cents in 1995 to 7.77 cents in 2004, with fuel costs, wages, and benefits as the major contributors (Exhibit 5). Southwest's cost per average seat mile remained below that of the big carriers whose costs ranged between 9.0 and 13.0 cents. The company was already working hard on controlling costs. With more of its customers making reservations online, it closed three call centers in 2003, saving about $20 million annually.[36] Further cost squeezing appeared to be a difficult proposition. Some industry experts, however, believed that even if Southwest raised employee pay, it

Exhibit 5   Southwest Airline's Operating Expenses per Average Seat Mile, 1995–2004 (In cents)

Expense Category	2004	2003	2002	2001	2000	1999	1998	1997	1996	1995
Salaries, wages & benefits (including employee retirement plans)	3.18	3.10	2.89	2.84	2.81	2.75	2.70	2.56	2.45	2.40
Fuel and oil	1.30	1.16	1.11	1.18	1.34	.93	.82	1.11	1.19	1.01
Maintenance materials and repairs	.60	.60	.57	.61	.63	.70	.64	.58	.62	.60
Agency commissions	—	.07	.08	.16	.27	.30	.33	.35	.35	.34
Aircraft rentals	.23	.25	.27	.29	.33	.38	.43	.45	.47	.47
Landing fees and other rentals	.53	.52	.50	.48	.44	.46	.45	.46	.46	.44
Depreciation	.56	.53	.52	.49	.47	.47	.47	.44	.45	.43
Other expenses	1.37	1.37	1.47	1.49	1.44	1.49	1.48	1.45	1.51	1.38
Total	7.77	7.60	7.41	7.54	7.73	7.48	7.32	7.40	7.50	7.07

Source: Southwest Airlines annual reports and 10-K reports.

would still remain profitable because it had the lowest unit labor costs compared to other major airlines.

Intensifying competition in the low-fare segment was another factor that had become difficult to ignore. While the newly launched competitors such as JetBlue, AirTran, Delta's Song, and United's Ted were not a direct threat to Southwest on its existing routes, further expansion of those carriers could bring them head-on with Southwest. JetBlue's intentions, as expressed in early 2004, indicated that it was exploring the possibility of launching a service from Austin (and later from Dallas–Fort Worth) to New York.[37] These new airlines offered far more attractive services such as leather seats and in-flight entertainment systems, for almost the same fare. Therefore, these rivals could make the no-frills approach of Southwest pale before them (Exhibit 6). Whether Southwest's loyal customers

Exhibit 6   A Comparison of Southwest and Its New "Low-Cost" Rivals

Airline	Year Founded	Aircraft Fleet	Hubs	Unions	Assigned Seats	Ticket Change Fee	Food	In-Flight Entertainment	No. of Cities Served*
Southwest	1971	Boeing 737s	No	Yes	No	No	Snacks only	Wisecracking flight attendants	58
AirTran	1993	Varied	Yes	Yes	Yes	$50	Snacks only	Nothing at the time	45
JetBlue	2000	Airbus A320s	No	No	Yes	$25	Snacks only	DirectTV at each seat	27
Song (Delta)	2003	Boeing 757s	No	Pilots only	Yes	$25	Meals for sale	Satellite TV at each seat; pay-per-view movies; videogames	13
Ted (United)	2004	Airbus A320s	Yes	Yes	Yes	$100	Meals for sale	Nothing at the time	13

*Obtained from destinations served as shown on their respective Web sites as of April 2004.

Source: Serwer, B. 2004. Southwest Airlines: The hottest thing in the sky. *Fortune,* March 8: 88–106.

would still stick with the airline when they could get more value for their money elsewhere was another significant question. Southwest's investments to automate and significantly streamline the ticketing and boarding process with computer-generated bag tags, automated boarding passes, self-service boarding pass kiosks, and so forth, and its investments to increase the functionality of its Web site, along with its moves to enhance aircraft interiors with leather seats, can hardly be described as *not* motivated by competition.[38] That JetBlue caught Southwest's attention was clear by the comment that Southwest was studying the possibility of introducing an in-flight entertainment system, though at the moment it was too costly to adopt. Thus, matching amenities with the newly emerging competition could pose additional challenges to the low-cost strategy. Kelleher's reaction to the emerging competition was simple—he had seen that movie before.

Meanwhile, Southwest entered the Philadelphia market, a stronghold of US Air, in May of 2004. The Philadelphia market was one of the most overpriced and underserved. Southwest aimed at capturing the market with its tried and tested low-cost, no frills formula albeit, with leather seats on some of its newer planes. US Air responded, "We will be a vigorous competitor to Southwest in Philadelphia on every route they fly."[39]

In addition to the ATA code share for Chicago's Midway,[40] Kelly added Phoenix to the code share in April of 2005.[41] Then, Kelly directed the entry into Pittsburgh in May of 2005 announcing, "The Pittsburgh International Air-port will be a great addition to our system."[42] In October of 2005 Southwest started new service out of Southwest Florida International Airport in Fort Myers, making it the 61st Southwest city.[43] Robert M. Ball, Executive Director of Florida's Lee County Port Authority, said after courting Southwest for nearly a decade, "We have been working closely with Southwest for many years and are pleased they have selected Southwest Florida as their newest destination."[44] Gary Kelly, Southwest's Chief Executive Officer, was on hand to wave the banner and said, "Now, our Southwest Florida Customers have to look no further than their own backyard for Southwest's legendary low fares and great customer service."

In the in-flight entertainment arena, Southwest still shuns expensive in-flight video systems. However, they struck a deal with online movie rental company, Movielink LLC to allow passengers to "rent" movies by downloading them over the Internet to their laptop computers for viewing in-flight. Southwest customers will receive a voucher for their first movie free and a 20 percent discount thereafter on Movielink movie rentals.[45]

Southwest could perhaps sustain its advantage over its major rivals, but could it face the prospect of sustaining its advantage over its low-cost rivals if they chose to enter the same market? One must ask: Would Southwest's further flight to success be smooth enough given the triple challenge of managing leadership change, maintaining culture in the face of growth, and increasing competition?

Appendix   Key Terms Used

Aircraft utilization. The average number of block hours operated per day per aircraft for the total fleet of aircraft.

Available seat miles. The number of seats available for passengers multiplied by the number of miles the seats are flown.

Average fare. The average one-way fare paid per flight segment by a revenue passenger.

Average stage length. The average number of miles flown per flight.

Breakeven load factor. The passenger load factor that will result in operating revenues being equal to operating expenses, assuming constant revenue per passenger mile and expenses.

Load factor. The percentage of aircraft seating capacity actually utilized (revenue passenger miles divided by available seat miles).

Operating expense per available seat mile. Operating expenses divided by available seat miles.

Operating revenue per available seat mile. Operating revenue divided by available seat miles.

Revenue passenger miles. The number of miles flown by revenue passengers.

Revenue passengers. The total number of paying passengers flown on all flight segments.

Yield per passenger mile. The average amount one passenger pays to fly one mile.

Endnotes

1. Serwer, B. 2004. Southwest Airlines: The hottest thing in the sky. *Fortune,* March 8: 88–106.
2. Southwest Airlines. 2005. SEC filings, Form 10-Q for 2005.
3. Roman, M. 2002. Southwest Air's family feud. *BusinessWeek,* July 15: 48.
4. Freiberg, K., & Freiberg, J. 1996. Nuts! Southwest Airlines' crazy recipe for personal and business success. Austin, TX: Bard Press: 20–27; http://archives.californiaaviation.org/airport/msg15249.html.
5. Ibid.

6. Freiberg, & Freiberg. 1996. Nuts! Southwest Airlines' crazy recipe: 6.

7. Greylock Associates. 2003. Herb Kelleher, chairman, CEO and president, Southwest Airlines.

8. Southwest Airlines, SEC filings, Form 10-K for 2003.

9. McConnell, B. 2001. The wild, flying turkey with wings: Creating customer evangelists—A profile of Herb Kelleher; www.creatingcustomerevangelists.com/resources/evangelists/herb_kelleher.asp.

10. Kelleher, Herb. 2003. Interview with Mark Morrison of *BusinessWeek* at Texas McComb's School of Business, December 23; www.businessweek.com.

11. Southwest Airlines. 2003. Great Place to Work Institute—Innovation Awards; www.greatplacetowork.com/education/innovate/honoree-2003-southwest.htm.

12. Kelleher, Herb. 1997. *Leader to Leader,* No. 4; www.pfdf.org/leaderbooks/L2L/spring97/kelleher.html.

13. Southwest Airlines, www.southwest.com/careers/stars/stars.html.

14. Shinn, S. 2003. LUV, Colleen. *BizEd.,* March–April.

15. Serwer. 2004. Southwest Airlines: The hottest thing in the sky.

16. Ibid.

17. What makes Southwest Airlines fly?; http://knowledge.wharton.upenn.edu/articles.cfm?catid=2&articleid=753.

18. Ibid.; Kelleher. 1997. *Leader to Leader;* Freedman, M. 2002. Non-stop growth? ABCNews.com, July 2.

19. What makes Southwest Airlines fly?

20. Donnelly, S. B. 2002. One airline's magic. *Time,* October 28: 45–47.

21. Kelleher. 2003. Interview with Mark Morrison; McConnell. 2001. The wild, flying turkey with wings.

22. Zellner, W. 2001. Southwest: After Kelleher, more blue skies. *BusinessWeek,* April 2: 45.

23. Southwest Airlines, www.southwest.com/swatakeoff/southwest_effect.html.

24. www.southwest.com; Serwer. 2004. Southwest Airlines: The hottest thing in the sky: 88–106.

25. Freedman. 2002. Non-stop growth?

26. Trotman, M. 2003. Inside Southwest Airlines, storied culture feels strains. *Wall Street Journal Online,* July 11; http://online.wsj.com.

27. Zellner. 2001. Southwest: After Kelleher, more blue skies; Zellner, W., & Arndt, M. 2003. Holding steady. *Business-Week,* February 3: 66–68.

28. Trotman. 2003. Inside Southwest Airlines.

29. Roman. 2002. Southwest Air's family feud, 48.

30. Trotman. 2003. Inside Southwest Airlines.

31. Warchol, G., 2003, Southwest crews rally for their cause. *Salt Lake Tribune,* November 26; www.sltrib.com/2003/Nov/11262003/Business/Business.asp.

32. Southwest flight attendants may resume contract talks. 2004. *AIRwise News,* February 18; www.airwise.com/news/airlines/southwest.html.

33. Economist.com/Global Agenda. London: July 16, 2004: 1. www.economist.com.

34. Gimbel, Barney. 2005. Southwest's new flight plan. *Fortune,* May 16, 151(10):93–97.

35. Zellner, Wendy. 2005. Dressed to kill . . . competitors. *BusinessWeek,* February 21, 39(21): 60.

36. Serwer. 2004, Southwest Airlines: The hottest thing in the sky.

37. Torbenson, E. 2004. Breaking from formation. *Dallas Morning News,* February 22: 1-D.

38. Southwest Airlines, SEC filings of Form 10-K.

39. Serwer. 2004. Southwest Airlines: The hottest thing in the sky.

40. Zellner. 2005. Dressed to kill . . . competitors.

41. Southwest Airlines, press releases, March 7, 2005 and June 28, 2005.

42. Southwest Airlines, press release, May 4, 2005.

43. Southwest Airlines, press release, July 14, 2005

44. Southwest Airlines, press release June 27, 2005.

45. Johnson, Avery. 2005. Travel watch. *Wall Street Journal* (Eastern edition), February: D4.

Case 40   Toys "R" Us*

During 2003, Toys "R" Us and the rest of the specialty toy retailers took a huge bashing from Wal-Mart and other department stores that offered low prices on popular items. Toys sales at toy stores dropped 7.7 percent from 2002, forcing several top stores to file for Chapter 11 protection.[1] FAO Inc., parent of FAO Schwartz toy stores, filed for bankruptcy twice during 2003. After withholding vendor payments in December 2003, KB Toys announced in January 2004 it too had filed for bankruptcy and planned to close almost half of its 1,217 stores. The news wasn't quite as grim for Toys "R" Us, but it also wasn't celebratory. During the first week of January 2004, Toys "R" Us CEO and chairman John Eyler told investors that the company had made a "strategic decision to match Wal-Mart's deep price cuts in order to protect market share," and that the company had suffered as a result of that approach.[2]

One reason Wal-Mart and other discount retailers are able to set their prices so low is because they "use toys as a loss leader, selling them at rock-bottom prices, and making up the profit on sales of other items."[3] This pricing of toys at cost or below cost is destroying the profit margins of stand-alone toy retailers like FAO Inc., KB Toys, and Toys "R" Us.

So what can specialty toy stores do to stay afloat? According to industry analysts they need to differentiate themselves from the discount toy stores. This can be accomplished in several ways, by offering higher-end products, better selection, exceptional service, or a unique "shopping experience." Toys "R" Us has in the past attempted to differentiate itself using several of these methods. *USA Today* observed that "Shoppers go to discounters for price and to Toys "R" Us for broad selection."[4] Recent differentiation strategies have focused on improving the customer service and creating stores that are a destination for fun, not just shopping. However, the pressure from discounters has been immense and, as a result of a greater than expected $38 million loss, Toys "R" Us announced in November 2003 that it planned to close its Kids "R" Us clothing and Imaginarium educational toys stores and cut 3,800 jobs.[5]

Snapshot of Toys "R" Us

Toys "R" Us, Inc., headquartered in Paramus, New Jersey, became a public company in 1978. At the beginning of 2004, it was an $11.5 billion dollar business with approximately 1,500 stores worldwide. The merchandise mix ranged in price from three dollars to three hundred dollars, and included both children's and adults' toys and games,

bicycles, sporting goods, small pools, infant and juvenile furniture, infant and toddler apparel, and children's books, as well as an electronics section, which featured video games, electronic handheld toys, videotapes, audio CDs, and computer software, along with a smattering of small TVs, shelf-stereos, and radios. In early 2004 Toys "R" Us included several divisions: Toys "R" Us—U.S., Toys "R" Us—International, Kids "R" Us, Babies "R" Us, and Toysrus.com. See Exhibit 1 for store types and Exhibit 2 for the company's vision, mission, and goal.

History of Toys "R" Us

Charles Lazarus founded Toys "R" Us in 1948 in Washington, D.C. Lazarus started out in business with a baby furniture store. However, as his customers increasingly requested toys for their children, Lazarus strove to meet their demand and gradually moved into the toy business. In 1957 Lazarus opened the first toy supermarket, during a time when specialty retailing and off-price positioning were revolutionary concepts in the days before malls and discount stores. With the success of these stores, Toys "R" Us became a public company in the late 1970s and by early 2000 had become an $11 billion business. Exhibit 3 provides the company's earnings from January 2000 to January 2005.

In the 1980s Toys "R" Us set out to expand its customer reach to cover not only the greater part of the United States, but also the world market. Toys "R" Us International opened its first stores in 1984 in Singapore and Canada. As of 2004 Toys "R" Us had more than 700 stores in the United States and more than 500 stores elsewhere in 27 countries, including franchised and licensed operations. The company's expansion effort did not stop only at reaching more people, but also endeavored to offer customers a greater variety of items, just as Lazarus had when he first opened his store in 1948. To this end, Kids "R" Us opened its doors in 1983, and offered name-brand children's wear (such as OshKosh B'Gosh) and K.R.U. private-label brands, as well as its own line of "lifestyle products," including fashion accessories, bath and body products, cosmetics, and home decor. Babies "R" Us, which first opened in Westbury, New York, in May 1996, offered baby apparel, furniture, car seats, bedding, strollers, and more. The stores also provided a baby registry system for expecting parents and allowed parents to create, view, and change their personal registry over the Internet. In July 1999 Toys "R" Us, with an interest in the educational and learning toy segment, purchased Imaginarium, the 37th player ranked by sales. Existing stand-alone Imaginarium stores continued, and Toys "R" Us incorporated in-store Imaginarium World sections in 10 to 20 of its stores in time for Christmas 1999. By early 2004 all stand-alone Imaginarium stores had been closed. Imaginarium Worlds could be found in more

---

*This case was prepared by Professor Alan B. Eisner and graduate student Keeley Townsend of Pace University as a basis for class discussion rather than to illustrate either effective or ineffective handling of an administrative situation. Copyright © 2005 Alan B. Eisner.

Exhibit 1   Breakdown of Stores by Divisions

	2005	2004	2003	2002	2001	2000	1999	1998	1997	1996	1995
Number of Stores											
Toys "R" Us—U.S.	681	685	685	701	710	710	704	700	682	653	618
Toys "R" Us—International	601	574	544	507	491	462	452	441	396	337	293
Kids "R" Us—U.S.	—	44*	183	165	198	205	212	215	212	213	204
Babies "R" Us—U.S.	217	198	146	184	145	131	113	98	82	—	—
Imaginarium—U.S.	—	—	37	42	37	40	—	—	—	—	—
Total Stores	1499	1501	1595	1599	1,581	1,548	1,481	1,454	1,372	1,203	1,115

Source: Toys "R" Us, Inc., 10-K report.

*All Kids "R" Us stores were closed by the end of 2004.

than 436 Toys "R" Us stores in the United States. The division continued to operate 185 international locations and guests could shop online.

In the late 1990s convenient online shopping for goods from all Toys "R" Us divisions became one of the company's major objectives. Toysrus.com was founded in 1998 with the goal of becoming a premier online toy, video game, and baby store. However, the division experienced a rocky beginning when, during the 1999 Christmas season, Toysrus.com employees faced a real siege. The company's "Black Sunday" came on November 6, 1999, as 62 million advertising circulars were placed in local newspapers around the country offering free shipping on Christmas toy orders placed over the Internet. When Toysrus.com was unable to fulfill orders in time for Christmas, the firm received numerous consumer complaints and negative publicity from the press and television news about the firm's problems. Toys "R" Us had the toys available in its warehouses, but was unable to pick, pack, and ship customer orders in a timely manner. Toysrus.com gained momentum again when it formed an alliance with Amazon.com in 2000. The alliance proved successful by more than tripling Toysrus.com sales and the number of orders from the prior year and by providing customers with a favorable online toy-buying experience.

Competition

At the same time that Toys "R" Us was creating its online business unit, it was also facing competitive pressures in its traditional brick-and-mortar business. Its market share had dropped from 25 percent in 1990 to 15.6 percent in 1999. In 1998 Wal-Mart dethroned Toys "R" Us as the number one toy seller after more than a decade of being on top.

The $30.7 billion traditional toy industry had undergone significant changes since the early 1990s (see Exhibit 4 for the growth of the toy industry). General mass merchandise retailers had grown, as had their toy departments. Mall retailers like KB Toys managed to channel a great deal of money into shopping malls with the introduction of their small mall-based toyshops. Exhibit 5 shows the changing market share among retailer types. The Toys "R" Us chain suffered and saw its

Exhibit 2   Toys "R" Us: Vision, Mission, and Goal

Vision:	Put joy in kids' hearts and a smile on parents' faces.
Mission:	A commitment to making each and every customer happy.
Goal:	To be the "Worldwide Authority on Kids, Families, and Fun."

Source: Toys "R" Us, Inc., 2000 Annual Report.

Exhibit 3   Consolidated Statements of Earnings: Toys "R" Us, Inc., and Subsidiaries
(In $ millions except per share data)

	January 2005	January 2004	February 2003	February 2002	February 2001	January 2000
Net sales	$11,100	$11,320	$11,305	$11,019	$11,332	$11,862
Cost of sales	7,506	7,646	7,799	7,604	7,815	8,321
Gross Profit	3,594	3,674	3,506	3,415	3,517	3,541
Selling, general, and administrative expenses	2,932	3,026	2,718	2,721	2,832	2,743
Depreciation, amortization, and asset write-offs	354	368	317	308	290	278
Restructuring	4	63		186		
Equity in net earnings, Japan					(31)	
Total Operating Expenses	3,290	3,457	3,035	3,215	3,091	3,021
Operating income	304	217	471	200	426	520
Gain from IPO, Japan					315	
Interest expense	(130)	(142)	(119)	(117)	(127)	91
Interest and other income	19	18	9	8	23	(11)
Interest expense, net	193	93			80	93
Earnings/Loss before Income Taxes	(59)	30	361	91	637	440
Income taxes			132	24	233	161
Net Earnings/Loss	252	63	229	67	404	279
Basic earnings/loss per share	1.17	0.30	1.10	.34	1.92	1.14
Diluted earnings/loss per share	1.16	0.29	1.09	.33	1.88	1.14

market share drop from 25 percent in 1990 to 16.8 percent in 1998 and 17 percent in 2004.[6] Toys "R" Us had been the leader for over a decade until ousted in 1998 by Wal-Mart (see Exhibit 6).

The Toys "R" Us Strategy

One method for Toys "R" Us to regain its competitive edge in the brick-and-mortar business was through qualitative improvements in its traditional stores. To address retail quality, Toys "R" Us set out to improve the customers' shopping experience within its stores. Initially, most U.S. Toys "R" Us stores conformed to a traditional big-box format, with full-size stores averaging about 46,000 square feet and stores in smaller markets ranging between 20,000 and 30,000 square feet. In 1999, however, the company began converting stores to a new layout called the "C3" format store, which was designed to make Toys "R" Us stores easier to shop in, with wider aisles, more feature opportunities

Exhibit 4   U.S. Toy Industry Sales
(In $ billions)

Industry Segments	1993	1994	1995	1996	1997	1998	1999	2000	2001	2002	2003	2004
Total industry (with video games)	$18.7	$20.1	$20.8	$22.7	$25.6	$27.2	$29.9	$29.4	34.1	$31.6	$30.7	$30.0
Traditional toys	14.8	17.0	17.7	19.1	20.6	21.0	23.0	23.0	24.7	21.3	20.7	20.1
Video games	3.9	3.1	3.1	3.6	5.0	6.2	6.9	6.4	9.4	10.3	10.0	9.9

Sources: Toy Manufacturers of America, Inc., New York, and NPD Group, New York.

Exhibit 5   Distribution of Sales by Retailer Type: Percentage of Dollar Share

Type	1995	1996	1997	1998	1999	2000	2001	2002	2003
Discount Stores	41.2	40.7	41.6	41.5	40.0	41.8	45.5	47.3	48.6
National Toy Stores	23.6	23.6	23.2	21.7	20.8	21.0	23.0	26.3	25.1
All Other Outlets	13.8	13.4	12.9	12.8	13.8	11.9	8.2	7.7	9.8
Mail Order	4.4	4.8	4.6	5.3	5.0	5.1	4.0	3.9	3.8
Card/Gift/Stationary	0.9	1.2	1.9	3.1	4.2	2.2	2.0	2.0	2.0
All Other Toy Stores	3.6	4.3	3.9	3.7	3.9	3.4	3.3	3.3	3.2
Food/Drug Stores	3.4	3.4	3.5	3.6	3.4	2.9	2.5	2.6	2.6
Department Stores	4.1	3.8	3.4	4.1	3.3	4.0	3.1	2.1	2.5
E-Tailers*						1.2	2.1	3.5	5.1	4.5
Hobby/Craft Stores	2.9	3.1	3.2	2.7	2.8	3.5	3.3	3.1	3.3
Variety Store	2.1	1.7	1.8	1.5	1.7	2.1	1.9	1.8	1.6

*New category.

Sources: Toy Manufacturers of America, Inc., New York, and NPD Group, New York and author estimates.

and end-caps, more shops, and logical category layouts.[7] To make the stores more shopper-friendly and better able to compete with the more intimate specialty retailers, Toys "R" Us also introduced the merchandise "world" in 1999. Exhibit 7 lists the various "worlds" developed. The company took the quality shopping experience one step further when, in November 2001, Toys "R" Us opened its international flagship store in Times Square in New York City. The multilevel store offered a vast selection of toys and other entertainment, including a 60-foot Ferris wheel, 4,000-

Exhibit 6   Top Toy Sellers: Percent of Annual Industry Sales

Retailer	1995	1996	1997	1998	1999	2000	2001	2002	2003	2004
Wal-Mart	14.6%	15.3%	16.3%	17.4%	17.4%	19.0%	19.3%	19.6%	20.0%	22.0
Toys "R" Us	19.2	18.9	18.3	16.8	15.6	16.5	16.6	16.8	17.0	17.0
Kmart	8.5	8.3	8.2	8.0	7.2	7.4	7.0	6.5	6.0	6.0
Target	6.1	6.4	7.1	6.9	6.8	7.2	7.4	7.8	8.0	18.0
KB Toys/ Toy Works	4.3	4.3	4.9	4.9	5.1	4.7	4.8	4.8	5.0	4.5
Ames	1.2	1.2	1.1	1.3	1.6	1.0	0.8	.4*		
J. C. Penney	1.5	1.7	1.5	1.6	1.2	1.4	1.4	1.2	1.0	0.8
Hallmark					1.0	1.1	0.9	0.9	0.9	0.9
Meijer		1.0	1.1	1.2	1.0	0.9	1.0	1.0	1.0	1.0
Shopko					0.9	0.8	0.8	0.8	0.8	0.8	1.0
Service Merchandise	1.8	1.6	1.1*							
Hills	1.6	1.3	1.2	1.1*						

Sources: NPD Group, New York, and Toy Manufacturers of America, Inc., New York, and author estimates.

*Exited the toy business.

Exhibit 7   Toys "R" Us Merchandise Worlds

World	Description
R Zone	Video, electronics, computer software, and related products
Action and Adventure	Action figures, die-cast cars, etc.
Girls	Dolls, collectibles, accessories, lifestyle products
Outdoor Fun	Bikes, sports, play sets
Preschool	Toys, accessories
Seasonal	Christmas, Halloween, Summer, etc.
Juvenile	Baby products and apparel
Learning Center	Educational and developmental products
Family Fun	Games and puzzles

Source: Toys "R" Us, Inc., 1999 Annual Report.

square-foot Barbie Dollhouse, and a 20-foot tall animatronic Jurassic Park T-Rex that roared.

To help recapture its number one place from Wal-Mart, Toys "R" Us developed a new corporate strategy and marketing plan. Toys "R" Us hired a new marketing vice president, Warren Kornblum, who immediately overhauled the company's entire marketing operation. In the past Toys "R" Us had joined in small vendor promotions and managed scattered marketing efforts. Kornblum changed that around, deciding to do fewer but bigger promotions. The company teamed with Major League Baseball as a sponsor for the Diamond Skills Program, a youth skill competition. Then the firm helped a champion women's soccer team travel to 12 U.S. cities with a tie-in from SFX Entertainment to create the Toys "R" Us Victory Tour. Toys "R" Us also carried out a promotional deal with Fox Kids Network and Walt Disney for the feature film *Toy Story 2*. As a result of these marketing efforts, sales increased from $11.2 billion in 1998 to $11.9 billion in 1999.[8] Warren Kornblum's strategy seemed to be working, yet the company was still unable to unseat Wal-Mart. He set up a "Scan and Win" promotion where shoppers held up Universal Product Code (UPC) game pieces to scanners to see if they had won a prize. More than a million consumers were scanned in with this promotion, making this one of the company's most successful programs for store traffic improvement. The mountains of sweepstakes entries and packed venues, however, began causing inventory shortages in the all-important holiday period of 1999. Inventory mishaps were the main reason why fourth-quarter 1999 sales stayed at a flat $5 billion.

When John Eyler came in as the new CEO of Toys "R" Us in January 2000, he slashed expenses across the board, started efforts to provide better customer service,

increased the number of employees in stores, and expanded store operating hours. All of the marketing activities were aimed at bringing customers into the chain's new store design and layout model—C3: customer-driven, cost-effective concept. This easier-to-shop C3 format allowed for 18 percent more selling space through wider aisles, which were to be installed in 75 percent of the stores by the end of 2000. Toys "R" Us hoped this new strategy would take market share back from Wal-Mart, Kmart, Target, and KB Toys. For 2000–2001 the company restructured its budget to allocate more money toward marketing. Toys "R" Us planned to continue with sports and movie entertainment themes for promotions.

Toys "R" Us saw evidence in 2002 that its strategies for marketing and improving the customer experience were working. The company saw increases in both average transaction size and consumer satisfaction research scores in 2002; it received higher marks from customers for service, in-stock position, knowledgeable associates, and competitive pricing.[9] Despite these successes, Toys "R" Us was not satisfied with the comparable store sales performance of its U.S. toy stores in 2002. Seasonal, video, and juvenile businesses experienced negative comparable store sales, but the core toy sales, which included Boys and Girls, Learning, and Preschool toys, outpaced toy industry performance by 4 percent for the year.[10]

Also in 2002, three company divisions—Babies "R" Us, Toys "R" Us International, and Toysrus.com—enjoyed record performances. Toysrus.com achieved operating profitability in the fourth quarter of 2002, a full year ahead of schedule. The Kids "R" Us division had been struggling in its stand-alone stores, but began seeing positive results from sourcing apparel through the division from the Babies

"R" Us stores and the Toys "R" Us/Kids "R" Us combo stores. At the end of fiscal year 2002, the Toys "R" Us total apparel business represented approximately $900 million in sales, at above-average profit margins, and continued growth was expected.[11] Approximately 65 percent of those sales came from exclusive products that generated higher margins than nationally branded items.

New Directions?

To compete with Wal-Mart and reach potential customers more often, Toys "R" Us began to test a new concept called *Toys "R" Us Toy Box* in a limited number of grocery stores in 2001. Eyler hoped to offer toys at the place where, he believed, potential customers shopped most frequently: grocery stores. The Toy Box concept consists of approximately 40 to 70 feet of space containing smaller toy items with prices generally below $25. In 2003 Eyler inked a multi-year deal with Albertson's, Inc., to become the exclusive toy provider for its supermarkets and drugstores. Toys "R" Us opened approximately 900 toy sections across Albertson's store locations.

Toys "R" Us and Amazon.com became embroiled in a series of lawsuits regarding the exclusivity of Toys "R" Us products on the Amazon.com site. In January 2004 Toys "R" Us implemented the closing of the 36 freestanding Imaginarium and 146 freestanding Kids "R" stores due to continuing declining performance.[12] Office Depot, Inc., agreed to acquire the majority of the former Kids "R" Us stores.

Meanwhile competitive pressure from discounters and other channels was intense. FAO Schwarz filed for bankruptcy for the second time in as many years and closed all of their Zany Brainy stores. Also, KB Toys filed for bankruptcy and closed hundreds of stores and sold its KBToys.com and eToys.com Web site operations.[13] Wal-Mart was still the dominant toy seller and Target was moving into the number two spot. The future of the once dominant Toys "R" Us was in question and John Eyler was searching for solutions.

Endnotes

1. Moore, Angela. 2004. Sad holiday season for toy stores? *Reuters,* January 3; www.reuters.com.
2. Verdon, Joan. 2004. Retailer Toys "R" Us posts disappointing holiday results. *Record—Knight Ridder/Tribune Business News,* January 9; http://news.stockselector.com/newsarticle.asp?symbol=TOY&article=62013210.
3. Moore. 2004. Sad holiday season for toy stores?
4. Grant, Lorrie. 2004. KB Toys files for Chapter 11 after cutthroat holiday season. *USA Today,* January 15.
5. Gatlin, Greg. 2003. Toyshops go own way in Wal-Mart fight. *Boston Herald,* November 25; http://business.boston herald.com.
6. Liebeck, Laura. 1999. TRU follows a new leader. *Discount Store News,* 38(8): 1, 92.
7. C3—customer-driven, cost-effective concept.
8. *Promo.* 2000. The real toy story, 13(5).
9. Toys "R" Us. 2002. Annual Report.
10. Ibid.
11. Ibid.
12. Toys "R" Us Press Release, May 17, 2004.
13. Pereira, J., Tomsho, R., & Zimmerman, A. 2004. Toys "Were" Us. *Wall Street Journal,* August 12: B1.

Case 41   The Lincoln Electric Company, 1996*

It was February 29, 1996. The Lincoln Electric Company, a leading producer of arc welding products, had just celebrated its centennial year by reporting record 1995 sales of over $1 billion, record profits of $61.5 million, and record employee bonuses of $66 million. This performance followed two years of losses—the only losses in the company's long history—stemming from a seemingly disastrous foray into Europe, Asia, and Latin America. (Exhibits 1 and 2 tabulate operating results and ratios for recent years.)

Headquartered in the Cleveland suburb of Euclid, Ohio, Lincoln Electric was widely known for its Incentive Management System. According to the *New York Times,* thousands of managers visited Lincoln's headquarters each year for free seminars on the system, which guaranteed lifetime employment, paid its production people only for each piece produced, and paid profit-sharing bonuses which had averaged 90 percent of annual wages or salary for the sixty years from 1934 to 1994.[1] James Lincoln, the main architect of the Incentive Management System, had been dead 30 years by 1995, but he remained a dominant influence on the company's policies and culture.

Record sales and profits, however, were not of themselves cause for complacence. Lincoln Electric had gone public during 1995 in order to reduce the substantial debts it had run up during its two losing years; now the company was subject to public scrutiny and such publications as the *New York Times* and *BusinessWeek* questioned whether the famous Incentive Management System was consistent with the firm's obligations to its public stockholders. Dividends for 1995 amounted to $9.1 million, while bonuses had totalled $66 million. Even at $66 million, however, bonuses equalled only 56 percent of employees' annual pay. Some workers complained loudly that the average $21,000 payment in December was far short of what it should have been.

Lincoln's hometown newspaper, the Cleveland *Plain Dealer,* saw the worker complaints as a sign of increasing strain between management and workers. Characterizing Lincoln's work pace as ". . . brutal, a pressure cooker in which employees are constantly graded and peer pressure borders on the fanatical," reporter Thomas Gerdel said Lincoln "faces growing discontent in its workforce."[2] *BusinessWeek* said, ". . . Lincoln increasingly resembles a typical public company. With institutional shareholders and new, independent board members in place, worker bonuses are getting more of a gimlet eye." Chairman and CEO Donald F. Hastings had set up a committee and hired Price Waterhouse to study the bonus program and the company's productivity.

"If Lincoln can adapt to new times without sacrificing employee goodwill," said *BusinessWeek,* "another model pay plan may yet emerge."[3]

A Historical Sketch

In 1895, having lost control of his first company, John C. Lincoln took out his second patent and began to manufacture an improved electric motor. He opened his new business with $200 he had earned redesigning a motor for young Herbert Henry Dow (who later founded the Dow Chemical Company). In 1909, John Lincoln made his first welding machine (Exhibit 3 describes the welding process). That year, he also brought in James, his younger brother, as a salesman. John preferred engineering and inventing to being a manager, and in 1914 he appointed James vice president and general manager. (Exhibit 4 shows a condensed history of the firm.)

James Lincoln soon asked the employees to form an "Advisory Board." At one of its first meetings, the Advisory Board recommended reducing working hours from 55 per week, then standard, to 50. This was done. In 1934, the famous Lincoln bonus plan was implemented. The first bonus averaged 25 percent of base wages. By 1940, Lincoln employees had twice the average pay and twice the productivity of other Cleveland workers in similar jobs. They also enjoyed the following benefits:

- An employee stock purchase plan providing stock at book value
- Company-paid life insurance
- An employees' association for athletic and social programs and sick benefits
- Piece rates adjusted for inflation
- A suggestion system with cash awards
- A pension plan
- A policy of promotion from within
- A practice, though not in 1940 a guarantee of lifetime employment
- Base pay rates determined by formal job evaluation
- A merit rating system which affected pay
- Paid vacations

During World War II, the company suspended production of electric motors as demand for welding products escalated. Employee bonuses averaged $2,250 in 1942 (about $20,000 in 1995 dollars). Lincoln's original bonus plan was not universally accepted: the Internal Revenue Service questioned the tax deductibility of employee bonuses,

*By Arthur Sharplin, of Waltham Associates, Austin, Texas, and John A. Seeger, of Bentley College. The authors thank Richard S. Sabo of Lincoln Electric for help in the field research for this case, which is written solely for the purpose of stimulating student discussion. Management exerted no editorial control over content or presentation of the case. All events and individuals are real.

Exhibit 1   Five-Year Operating Results

	Year Ended December 31				
	1995	1994	1993	1992	1991
	(in thousands of dollars, except per share data)				
Net sales	$1,032,398	$906,604	$845,999	$853,007	$833,892
Income (loss) before cumulative effect of accounting change	61,475	48,008	(40,536)	(45,800)	14,365
Cumulative effect of accounting change			2,468		
Net income (loss)	$ 61,475	$ 48,008	$ (38,068)	$ (45,800)	$ 14,365
Per share:					
Income (loss) before cumulative effect of accounting change	$ 263	$ 219	$ (1.87)	$ (212)	$ .67
Cumulative effect of accounting change			.12		
Net Income (loss)	$ 2.63	$ 2.19	$ (1.75)	$ (2.12)	$ .67
Cash dividends declared	$ .42	$ .38	$ .36	$ .36	$ .30
Total assets	$ 617,760	$556,857	$559,543	$603,347	$640,261
Long-term debt	$ 93,582	$194,831	$216,915	$221,470	$155,547

arguing they were not "ordinary and necessary" costs of doing business, and the Navy's Price Review Board challenged Lincoln's high profits. But James Lincoln overcame the objections, loudly refusing to retract the firm's obligations to its workers. Also during World War II, Lincoln built factories in Australia, South Africa, and England.

In 1951, Lincoln completed a new main plant in Euclid, Ohio; the factory remained essentially unchanged in 1995. In 1955, Lincoln again began making electric motors, but they represented only a small percentage of the company's revenue through 1995.

Executive Succession   William Irrgang, an engineer and longtime Lincoln protégé, was president when James Lincoln died in 1965. By 1970, Lincoln's annual revenues had grown to $100 million, and bonuses were averaging about $8,000 per employee each year (about $30,000 in 1995 dollars). Irrgang was elevated to chairman in 1972 and Ted Willis, also an engineer and protégé of James Lincoln, became president. In 1977, Lincoln completed a new electrode plant a few miles from Euclid, in Mentor, Ohio; this doubled the capacity for making welding wire and rods.

Lincoln's net sales were $450 million in 1981, and employee bonuses averaged $20,760 (about $34,000 in 1995 dollars) that year. But sales fell by 40 percent in the next two years owing, Lincoln management said, to "the combined effects of inflation, sharply higher energy costs, and a national recession." By 1983, the firm's net income

and bonuses had collapsed to less than half their 1981 levels. (Table 1 lists bonus amounts from 1981 to 1995.)

But there was no layoff. Many factory workers volunteered to do field sales work and customer assistance. Others were reassigned within the plants, some repairing the roof of the Euclid factory, painting, and cleaning up. The work week, previously averaging about 45 hours, was shortened to 30 hours for most nonsalaried workers. Several new products, which had been kept in reserve for just this kind of eventuality, were brought to market. Sales, profits, and bonuses began a slow recovery.

Bill Irrgang died in 1986. Ted Willis took over as chairman and Don Hastings became president, taking primary responsibility for domestic operations.

The Lincoln Philosophy

Throughout the tenures of these CEOs, the business philosophies first articulated by James Lincoln remained in effect, forming the foundation of the company's culture and providing the context within which the Incentive Management System worked. Lincoln's own father had been a Congregationalist minister, and the biblical Sermon on the Mount, with Jesus' praise of meekness, mercifulness, purity of heart, and peacemaking, governed his attitudes toward business. James never evangelized his employees, but he counseled truthfulness in speech, returning evil with good, love of enemies, secret almsgiving, and quiet trust and confidence.[4]

Exhibit 2   Financial Ratios, 1992–1995

Fiscal Year Ending December 31:	1995	1994	1993	1992
Quick Ratio	0.89	0.95	0.74	0.89
Current Ratio	2.12	2.17	1.85	2.16
Sales/Cash	102.35	86.97	41.51	41.35
SG&A/Sales	0.28	0.29	0.33	0.35
Receivables: Turnover	7.33	7.19	7.66	7.66
Receivables: Days Sales	49.11	50.04	47.02	46.98
Inventories: Turnover	5.65	5.84	5.89	4.98
Inventories: Days Sales	63.77	61.66	61.14	72.27
Net Sales/Working Capital	5.48	5.35	5.65	4.94
Net Sales/Net Plant & Equipment	5.02	4.92	4.99	4.09
Net Sales/Current Assets	2.89	2.89	2.60	2.66
Net Sales/Total Assets	1.67	1.63	1.51	1.41
Net Sales/Employees	172,066	159,249	140,159	134,714
Total Liability/Total Assets	0.46	0.64	0.73	0.64
Total Liability/Invested Capital	0.67	0.92	1.13	0.92
Total Liability/Common Equity	0.87	1.90	3.01	2.13
Times Interest Earned	9.07	6.09	−1.66	−0.84
Long-Term Debt/Equity	0.28	1.00	1.51	1.11
Total Debt/Equity	0.29	1.02	1.58	1.19
Total Assets/Equity	1.87	2.87	3.90	3.04
Pre-Tax Income/Net Sales	0.10	0.09	−0.06	−0.04
Pre-Tax Income/Total Assets	0.16	0.14	−0.08	−0.06
Pre-Tax Income/Invested Capital	0.24	0.21	−0.13	−0.08
Pre-Tax Income/Common Equity	0.31	0.43	−0.35	−0.19
Net Income/Net Sales	0.06	0.05	−0.04	−0.05
Net Income/Total Assets	0.10	0.09	−0.07	−0.08
Net Income/Invested Capital	0.15	0.12	−0.11	−0.11
Net Income/Common Equity	0.19	0.26	−0.28	−0.25
R & D/Net Sales	NA	NA	NA	NA
R & D/Net Income	NA	NA	NA	NA
R & D/Employees	NA	NA	NA	NA

Source: Disclosure, Inc.

Dow-Jones On-Line News Service

Relationships with Customers   In a 1947 speech, James Lincoln said, "Care should be taken . . . not to rivet attention on profit. Between 'How much do I get?' and 'How do I make this better, cheaper, more useful?' the difference is fundamental and decisive." He later wrote, "When any company has achieved success so that it is attractive as an investment, all money usually needed for expansion is supplied by the customer in retained earnings. It is obvious that the customer's interests, not the stockholder's, should come first." He added,

The Christian ethic should control our acts. If it did control our acts, the savings in cost of distribution would be tremendous. Advertising would be a contact of the expert consultant with the customer, in order to give the customer the best product available when all of the customer's needs are considered. Competition then would be in improving the quality of products and increasing efficiency in producing and distributing them; not in deception, as is now too customary. Pricing would reflect efficiency of production; it would not be a selling dodge that the customer may well

Exhibit 3   What Is Arc-Welding?

Arc-welding was the standard joining method in shipbuilding for decades and remained so in 1995. It was the predominant way of connecting steel in the construction industry. Most industrial plants had their own welding shops for maintenance and construction. Makers of automobiles, tractors, and other items employed arc-welding. Welding hobbyists made metal items such as patio furniture and barbecue pits. The popularity of welded sculpture was growing.

Arc-welding employs electrical power, typically provided by a "welding machine" composed of a transformer or solid-state inverter connected to a building's electrical system or to an engine-driven generator. The electrical output may vary from 50 to 1,000 amps at 30–60 volts (for comparison, a hair dryer may use 10 amps at 120 volts) and may be alternating or direct current (AC or DC) of varying wave patterns and frequencies. The electrical current travels through a welding electrode and creates an arc to the item being welded. This melts the actual surface of the material being welded, as well as the tip of the electrode, resulting in deposit of the molten metal from the electrode onto the surface. When the molten metal re-freezes, the pieces being joined are fused into one continuous piece of steel.

Welding electrodes—called "consumables" because they are used up in the welding process—are of two main types: short pieces of coated wire (called "stick" electrodes or "welding rods") for manual welding and coils of solid or tubular wire for automatic and semiautomatic processes. The area of the arc must be shielded from the atmosphere to prevent oxidation of the hot metal. This shielding is provided by a stream of inert gas which surrounds the arc (in "MIG," or metallic-inert gas welding) or by solid material called "flux" which melts and covers the liquefied metal surface. Flux often contains substances which combine with the molten metal or catalyze chemical reactions. The flux may be affixed as a coating on welding rods, enclosed inside tubular welding wire, or funeled onto the weld area from a bin (in "submerged-arc" welding). Arc-welding produces sparks, heat, intense light, and noxious fumes, so operators usually wear face, body, and eye protection and, if ventilation is inadequate, breathing devices.

Other types of welding include oxy-fuel welding, which uses a flame to melt metals together, tungsten-inert gas (TIG) welding, which employs a tungsten electrode to create an arc to melt a welding rod; induction welding, which uses electrical coils to induce currents in the metal being welded, thereby heating it; resistance welding, which heats the weld joint by passing current directly through it; and plasma-arc welding, which is similar to arc-welding but involves higher temperatures and a more tightly constrained arc. Related processes include cutting metals with oxy-fuel torches, laser beams, and plasma-arc systems.

be sorry he accepted. It would be proper for all concerned and rewarding for the ability used in producing the product.

Lincoln's pricing policy, often stated, was "Price on the basis of cost and keep downward pressure on cost." C. Jackson Graham, founder of The American Productivity Institute, said prices of Lincoln products, on average, grew at only one-fifth the rate of inflation in the decades after 1930. Some prices actually went down. For example, Lincoln welding electrodes which sold for $0.16 per pound in 1929 were $0.05 in 1942. And Lincoln's popular SA-200 welder decreased in price from 1958–1965.

Until the 1990s, Lincoln was the dominant U.S. producer of arc-welding products and was able to keep market prices low, especially for consumables. That changed after Miller Welding Co. grew to match Lincoln in U.S. sales of machines, and ESAB became the world's largest supplier of consumables and materials. In 1984, Don Hastings said,

Right now we are paying the price of not having enough capacity in Mentor [Ohio] to supply our customer demand. We are spending money now. But if we had spent it last year, we would not be having the shortages that we're having right now. We're allowing our competition to raise prices because there's nothing we can do about it without more capacity.

Lincoln quality was legendary. In the refinery and pipeline industries, where price was seldom the main consideration in purchasing, Lincoln welders and electrodes were almost universally specified for decades. Warranty costs at Lincoln typically averaged under one-fourth of one percent of sales. A Lincoln distributor in Monroe, Louisiana, said he had sold hundreds of Lincoln welders and had never had a warranty claim.

Lincoln sold its products directly to major customers and indirectly through distributors, most of which were welding supply stores. Lincoln also licensed hundreds of

Exhibit 4   Condensed History of Lincoln Electric Company

1895	Company founded by John C. Lincoln.
1909	James Lincoln joins as salesman. (General Manager, 1914)
1934	Bonus plan implemented, at 25 percent of base earnings.
1940	Employees earning double the area's average wage.
1942–1945	Factories built in South Africa (later closed), England (later sold to employees), and Australia. Motor production discontinued.
1951	Main factory built in Euclid, Ohio.
1955	Motor production resumed.
1958	Historic guaranteed employment policy formalized.
1965	James Lincoln's death. William Irrgang named president.
1970	Annual revenues reach $100 million for the first time.
1972	Irrgang named chairman/CEO. Ted Willis becomes president.
1977	New electrode factory built in Mentor, Ohio.
1982–1983	Recession slashes revenues. Employees on 30-hour weeks. ESAB begins global expansion.
1986	Willis named chairman/CEO. Don Hastings becomes president. International operations include five plants in four countries.
1992	Foreign operations include 21 plants in 15 countries. Long-term debt at $220 million. Hastings named chairman/CEO. Fred Mackenbach named president.
1992–1993	Global recession. First losses in Lincoln's history. International retrenchment begins.
1995	International operations include 16 plants in 11 countries. Public stock issue provides funds for debt reduction. New motor factory built.

service centers and trained their personnel to do maintenance and warranty work on Lincoln machines. The company maintained a system of regional sales offices, which serviced both direct customers and distributors. In keeping with James Lincoln's principle that salespersons should be "expert consultants," sales jobs at Lincoln were open only to graduate engineers until about 1992, when Hastings changed the policy; he began to recruit majors in liberal arts, business, and other disciplines into the sales force.

Hastings instituted Lincoln's Guaranteed Cost Reduction (GCR) program in 1993. Under GCR, Lincoln sent teams of engineers, technical representatives, and distributors to customer facilities with a goal to "find ways to improve the customer's fabrication procedures and product quality as well as methods to increase its productivity." Hastings promised, "The Lincoln Electric Company will guarantee in writing that your company's annual arc welding fabrication costs will be reduced by a specified amount when you use Lincoln products and methods. If you don't save that amount, a check

will be written for the difference." Lincoln cited these "successes" in its literature promoting GCR:

A fabricator of steel buildings found GCR savings of $25,000/year and, as a result of the program, developed an improved welding cost analysis system. A manufacturer of heavy grading equipment verified savings in excess of $50,000/year and productivity gains from 50 to 90 percent. An automotive manufacturer produced productivity increases, in specific welding operations, exceeding 20 percent. Resultant savings totaled over $1,000,000 a year.

Relationships with Employees   The company professed to still adhere to the basic precepts James Lincoln set down early in his development of the incentive system:

The greatest fear of the worker, which is the same as the greatest fear of the industrialist in operating a company, is the lack of income. . . . The industrial manager is

Table 1   The Lincoln Electric Company Bonus History

Year	Total $ Millions	Number Employees	% of Wages	Average Gross Bonus	W-2 Average Earnings Factory Worker
1981	59.0	2684	99.0	22,009	
1982	41.0	2634	80.1	15,643	
1983	26.6	2561	55.4	10,380	
1984	37.0	2469	68.0	15,044	
1985	41.8	2405	73.2	17,391	
1986	37.7	2349	64.8	16,056	
1987	44.0	2349	70.5	18,791	
1988	54.3	2554	77.6	21,264	
1989	54.5	2633	72.0	20,735	47,371
1990	56.2	2701	71.2	20,821	47,809
1991	48.3	2694	65.0	17,935	39,651
1992	48.0	2688	61.9	17,898	40,867
1993	55.0	2676	63.9	20,585	48,738
1994	59.0	2995	60.2	19,659	55,757
1995	64.4	3396	55.9	*21,168	57,758

*Employees with more than 1 year of service

Source: Lincoln Electric Company document

very conscious of his company's need of uninterrupted income. He is completely oblivious, evidently, of the fact that the worker has the same need.

He is just as eager as any manager is to be part of a team that is properly organized and working for the advancement of our economy. . . . He has no desire to make profits for those who do not hold up their end in production, as is true of absentee stockholders and inactive people in the company.

If money is to be used as an incentive, the program must provide that what is paid to the worker is what he has earned. The earnings of each must be in accordance with accomplishment.

Status is of great importance in all human relationships. The greatest incentive that money has, usually, is that it is a symbol of success. . . . The resulting status is the real incentive. . . . Money alone can be an incentive to the miser only.

There must be complete honesty and understanding between the hourly worker and management if high efficiency is to be obtained.

"I don't work for Lincoln Electric; I work for myself," said Lester Hillier in the 1994 *New York Times* article. "I'm an entrepreneur," added Hillier, a welder at Lincoln for 17 years. Other workers, asked in April of 1995 about why people worked so hard and what motivated them, responded:

Joe Sirko, machine operator since 1941:

People want their bonus. And a decent job. No layoffs. I wanted a job where I could spend all the money I make all year and then I get the bonus. I still do that. I go out and live it up. I go to the races. I go everywhere.

When I came here—under James Lincoln—the jobs were given to family. Almost everybody in here was family. My brother got me in. Somebody else's brother got them in or their dad got them in. It was all family. And J.F. backed that a hundred percent. Family, right on down. If you had someone in your family, they were in. Now, they have three different interviewers down there. They all interview.

They hired a lot of people once, to reduce the overtime, remember, and they had all them people when it slowed down. They were sweeping and cleaning—and they didn't know what to do with them. When James Lincoln was alive, he always got up when he gave the bonus and told them—they would be complaining about overtime—he told them that they would either work, because he didn't want to over hire all them extra people. He believed in all the overtime.

Kathleen Hoenigman, wiring harness assembler hired in 1977:

I worked in factories before and the factories I worked at either went out of business or moved to another state. I will have to say that my money is more here, but I did always make good money. This is much more, because of the bonus. I invest. I also bought a house. Right now, I give my mother money.

I feel that people here that are making all this money, they work so hard for it that they don't want to spend it stupidly and what they do is invest, for the future. And they also, you know, take care of their family.

I like the challenge. I also like the money and the fact that the money is tied to my own output. You have to be motivated yourself. You want the company to succeed, so you want to do better. By having guaranteed employment, the company has to be strong. To me, guaranteed employment means if there's a slowdown you always have a job. Like they'll always take care of you. Back in 1982, when sales slumped, they put me on the roof carrying buckets of tar.

Scott Skrjanc, welder hired in 1978:

Guaranteed employment is in the back of my mind. I know I'm guaranteed a job. But I also know I have to work to get paid. We don't come in and punch a card and sit down and do nothing.

Linda Clemente, customer service representative hired in 1986:

Well, I guess the biggest thing is guaranteed employment. And I think most people want to be the best that they can be. For other people, maybe the motivation is the money, because they are putting kids through college and things like that. I mean, it's definitely a benefit and something everybody works for.

Relationships with Unions   There had never been a serious effort to organize Lincoln employees. While James Lincoln criticized the labor movement for "selfishly attempting to better its position at the expense of the people it must serve," he still had kind words for union members. He excused union excesses as "the natural reactions of human beings to the abuses to which management has subjected them." He added, "Labor and management are properly not warring camps; they are parts of one organization in which they must and should cooperate fully and happily."

Several of the plants Lincoln acquired during 1986–1992 had unions, and the company stated its intention to cooperate with them. No major Lincoln operation had a union in 1995, although 25 of the Ohio employees did attend a union presentation by the United Auto Workers in December, after the announcement of the 1995 bonus rate. "The attendance, out of a total of 3,400 workers, was disappointing even to organizers," said the Cleveland *Plain Dealer.* Lincoln spokesman Bud Fletcher said, "The secret to avoiding those types of situations is that management has to work twice as hard to provide all the elements that membership in an organization like a union would have. We've got to listen, we've got to sit down, we've got to take our time."

Relationships with Stockholders   Through 1992, Lincoln shareholders received dividends averaging less than 5 percent of share price per year, and total annual returns averaged under 10 percent. The few public trades of Lincoln shares before 1995 were at only a small premium over book value, which was the official redemption price for employee-owned stock.

"The last group to be considered is the stockholders who own stock because they think it will be more profitable than investing money in any other way," said James Lincoln. Concerning division of the largess produced by Incentive Management, he wrote, "The absentee stockholder also will get his share, even if undeserved, out of the greatly increased profit that the efficiency produces."

Under Hastings, Lincoln Electric gave public shareholders more respect. Dividends, while limited under certain credit agreements, were increased in 1994 in preparation for the public issue, and again in 1995. And the presence of new outside directors on the Lincoln board (see Exhibit 5) seemed to protect public shareholder interests.

The Lincoln Incentive Management System

Lincoln's Incentive Management System was defined by the firm's philosophy and by the rules, regulations, practices, and programs that had evolved over the 60 years since its origination.

Recruitment   Every job opening at Lincoln was advertised internally on company bulletin boards and any employee could apply. In general, external hiring was permitted only for entry-level positions. Often, applicants were relatives or friends of current employees. Selection for these jobs was based on personal interviews—there was no aptitude nor psychological testing and no educational requirement—except for engineering and sales positions, which required a college degree. A committee consisting of vice presidents and supervisors interviewed candidates initially cleared by the Personnel Department. Final selection was made by the supervisor who had a job opening. Out of over 3,500 applicants interviewed by the Personnel

Exhibit 5   Officers and Directors of Lincoln Electric Company

DIRECTORS

Donald F. Hastings, 67, *1980
Chairman of the Board and
Chief Executive Officer

Frederick W. Mackenbach, 65, *1992
Retired President and Chief Operating
Officer

Harry Carlson, 61, *1973
Retired Vice Chairman

David H. Gunning, 53, *1987
Chairman, President and Chief
Executive Officer of Capitol American
Financial Corp.

Edward E. Hood., Jr., 65, *1993
Former Vice Chairman of the Board and
Executive Officer of The General
Electric Co.

Paul E. Lego, 65, *1993
President of Intelligent Enterprises

Hugh L. Libby, 70, *1985
Retired Chairman of the Board and
Chief Executive Officer of Libby Corp

David C. Lincoln, 70, *1958
Retired Chairman of the Board and
Chief Executive Officer of Lincoln
Laser Co. and President of Arizona
Oxides LLC

Emma S. Lincoln, 73, *1989
Retired
Formerly an Attorney in private practice

G. Russell Lincoln, 49, *1989
Chairman of the Board and Chief
Executive Officer of Algan, Inc.

Kathryn Jo Lincoln, 41, *1995
Vice President of The Lincoln
Foundation, Inc. and Vice Chair/
Secretary of The Lincoln Institution
of Land Policy

Anthony A. Messaro, 52, *1996
President and Chief Operating Officer

Henry L. Meyer III, 46, *1994
Chairman of the Board of Society
National Bank and Senior Executive
Vice President and Chief Operating
Officer of KeyCorp

Lawrence O. Selhorst, 63, *1992
Chairman of the Board and
Chief Executive Officer of American
Spring Wire Corporation

Craig R. Smith, 70, *1992
Former Chairman and Chief Executive
Officer of Ameritrust Corporation

Frank L. Steingass, 56, *1971
Chairman of the Board and
President of Buehler/Steingass, Inc.

*Date elected as a director

OFFICERS

Donald F. Hastings, 67, *1953
Chairman and Chief Executive Officer

Anthony A. Massaro, 52 *1993
President and Chief Executive Officer

David J. Fullen, 64, *1955
Executive Vice President,
Engineering and Marketing

John M. Stropki, 45, *1972
Executive Vice President
President, North America

Richard C. Ulstad, 56, *1970
Senior Vice President,
Manufacturing

H. Jay Elliott, 54, *1993
Senior Vice President,
Chief Financial Officer and Treasurer

Frederick G. Stuber, 42, *1995
Senior Vice President,
General Counsel and Secretary

Frederick W. Anderson, 43, *1978
Vice President,
Systems Engineering

Paul J. Beddia, 62, *1956
Vice President,
Government and Community Affairs

Dennis D. Crockett, 53, *1965
Vice President,
Consumable Research and
Development

James R. Delaney, 47, *1987
Vice President
President, Lincoln Electric Latin
America

Joseph G. Doria, 46, *1972
Vice President
President and Chief Executive Officer,
Lincoln Electric Company of Canada

Paul Fantelli, 51, *1970
Vice President,
Business Development

Ronald A. Nelson, 46, *1972
Vice President,
Machine Research and Development

Gary M. Schuster, 41, *1978
Vice President,
Motor Division

Richard J. Seif, 48, *1971
Vice President,
Marketing

S. Peter Ullman, 46, *1971
Vice President
President and Chief Executive Officer,
Harris Calorific Division
of Lincoln Electric

Raymond S. Vogt, 54, *1996
Vice President,
Human Resources

John H. Weaver, 57, *1961
Vice President
President, Lincoln Africa, Middle East
and Russia

*Year joined the Company

Department in 1988, fewer than 300 were hired. The odds were somewhat better in 1995, as Lincoln scrambled to staff its new electric motor factory and to meet escalating demand for its welding products.

Training and Education   New production workers were given a short period of on-the-job training and then placed on a piecework pay system. Lincoln did not pay for off-site education unless specific company needs were identified. The idea behind this policy was that not everyone could take advantage of such a program, and it was unfair to spend company funds for a benefit to which there was unequal access. Recruits for sales jobs, already college graduates, were given an average of six months on-the-job training in a plant, followed by a period of work and training at a regional sales office.

Sam Evans, regional manager for international, described the training program when he joined Lincoln in 1953 as an electrical engineering graduate:

> A few months into the training, I decided to move to sales. During those days, the training program was about a year—several months learning to weld, several months on the factory floor, and in other departments. I got the MBA while I was working in Buffalo as a Sales Engineer.

Merit Rating   Each manager formally evaluated subordinates twice a year using the cards shown in Figure 1. The employee performance criteria—"quality," "dependability," "ideas and cooperation," and "output"—were considered independently of each other. Marks on the cards were converted to numerical scores, which were forced to average 100 for each specified group, usually all the subordinates of one supervisor or other manager. Thus, any employee rated above 100 would have to be balanced off by another rated below 100. Individual merit rating scores normally ranged from 80 to 110. Any score over 110 required a special letter to top management. These scores (over 110) were not considered in computing the required 100 point average for each evaluator. Point scores were directly proportional to the individual's year-end bonus.

Welder Scott Skrjanc seemed typical in his view of the system. "You know, everybody perceives they should get more. That's natural. But I think it's done fairly."

Under Lincoln's early suggestion program, employees were given monetary awards of one-half of the first year's savings attributable to their suggestions. Later, however, the value of suggestions was reflected in merit rating scores. Supervisors were required to discuss performance marks with the employees concerned. Each warranty claim was traced to the individual employee whose work caused the defect, if possible. The employee's performance score was reduced, or the worker could repay the cost of servicing the warranty claim by working without pay.

Compensation   Basic wage levels for jobs at Lincoln were determined by a wage survey of similar jobs in the Cleveland area. These rates were adjusted quarterly in response to changes in the Cleveland Area Wage Index, compiled by the U.S. Department of Labor. Wherever possible, base wage rates were translated into piece rates. Practically all production workers—even some fork truck operators—were paid by the piece. Once established, piece rates were changed only if there was a change in the methods, materials, or machinery used in the job. Each individual's pay was calculated from a daily Piecework Report, filled out by the employee. The payroll department, responsible for paying 3,000 employees, consisted of four people; there was no formal control system for checking employees' reports of work done.

In December of each year, bonuses were distributed to employees. Lincoln reported that incentive bonuses from 1934 to 1994 averaged about ninety percent of annual wages; the total bonus pool typically exceeded after-tax (and after-bonus) profits. Individual bonuses were determined by merit rating scores. For example, if the Board of Directors authorized a bonus equal to 80 percent of total base wages paid, a person whose performance score averaged 95 in the two previous evaluation periods received a bonus of 76 percent (0.80×0.95) of base wages.

Because of company losses in 1992 and 1993, the bonus was about 60 percent of base wages, and management was forced to borrow $100 million to pay it. After Lincoln's turnaround in 1994, the 60-percent bonus rate was continued as $63 million was used to repay principal and interest on the borrowed money. Average compensation of Lincoln's Cleveland employees in 1994 was about $35,000 before bonuses, and the average bonus was $20,000—$12,000 less than if the 90 percent average had applied. Some felt that employees were paying for management's mistakes.

Continuous Employment   In 1958 Lincoln formalized its guaranteed continuous employment policy, which had already been in effect for many years. Starting in 1958, every worker with over two years' longevity was guaranteed at least 30 hours per week, 49 weeks per year. The requirement was changed to three years' longevity in the recession year of 1982, when the policy was severely tested. In previous recessions the company had been able to avoid major sales declines. However, sales plummeted 32 percent in 1982 and another 16 percent the next year. Management cut most of the nonsalaried workers back to 30 hours a week for varying periods of time. Many employees were reassigned, and the total workforce was slightly reduced through normal attrition and restricted hiring. The previous year had set records, and some employees grumbled at their unexpected misfortune, to the surprise and dismay of some Lincoln managers.

Increasing Output ➤

OUTPUT

This card rates *HOW MUCH PRODUCTIVE WORK* you actually turn out.

It also reflects your willingness not to hold back and recognizes your attendance record.

This rating has been done jointly by your department head and the Production Control Department in the shop and with other department heads in the office and and engineering.

Days Absent ◯

B1-629A REV. 1968

Increasing Ideas & Cooperation ➤

IDEAS & COOPERATION

This card rates your Cooperation, Ideas and Initiative.

New ideas and new methods are important to your company in our continuing effort to reduce costs, increase output, improve quality, work safely and improve our relationship with our customers.This card credits you for your ideas and initiative used to help in this direction.

It also rates your cooperation–how you work with others as a team. Such factors as your attitude towards supervision, co-workers and the company: your efforts to share your expert knowledge with others; and your cooperation in installing new methods smoothly, are considered here.

This rating has been done jointly by your department head and the Time Study Department in the shop and with other department heads in the office and engineering.

B1-629B REV. 1968

Increasing Dependability ➤

DEPENDABILITY

This card rates how well your supervisors have been able to depend upon you to do those things that have been expected of you without supervision.

It also rates your ability to supervise yourself including your work safety performance, your orderliness, care of equipment, and the effective use you make of your skills.

This rating has been done by your department head.

B1-629C REV. 1968

Increasing Quality ➤

QUALITY

This card rates the *QUALITY* of the work you do.

It also reflects your success in eliminating errors and in reducing scrap and waste.

This rating has been done jointly by your department head and the Quality Assurance Department in the shop and with other department heads in the office and engineering.

B1-629D REV. 1968

Figure 1 Lincoln's Merit Rating Cards

Among employees with a year or more of service, employee turnover ran only four percent at Lincoln Electric. Absenteeism, too, was extremely low; critics in the press noted this was understandable, since workers were not paid for sick days. They noted, too, that 25 to 30 percent of new hires quit in their first six months of work, in spite of Lincoln's intensive interview process. In 1995, Lincoln's Cleveland workers were averaging over 45 hours a week on the job. Employee turnover after the first year was under 1 percent per year, excluding retirements. "The vast majority that quit do so before their first bonus," said Dick Sabo, director of corporate communications. "Once they see the dollars, they realize they are extremely well paid for their efforts." The average length of service of Lincoln's Cleveland workers in 1995 was about 14 years.

Stock Ownership by Employees   James Lincoln said that financing for company growth should come from within the company—through initial cash investment by the founders, through reinvestment of earnings, and through stock purchases by those who work in the business. He claimed this approach gave the following advantages:

1. Ownership of stock by employees strengthens team spirit. "If they are mutually anxious to make it succeed, the future of the company is bright."
2. Ownership of stock provides individual incentive because employees feel they will benefit from company profitability.
3. "Ownership is educational." Owner-employees "will know how profits are made and lost; how success is won and lost."
4. "Capital available from within controls expansion." Unwarranted expansion would not occur, Lincoln believed, under his financing plan (which did not allow for borrowing capital for growth).
5. "The greatest advantage would be the development of the individual worker. Under the incentive of ownership, he would become a greater man."
6. "Stock ownership is one of the steps that can be taken that will make the worker feel that there is less of a gulf between him and the boss."

Under Lincoln's Employees' Stock Purchase Plan, each employee could buy a specified number of shares of restricted common stock from the company each year, with company financing. The stock was priced at "estimated fair value" (taken to be book value), and the company had an option to repurchase it. Lincoln had always exercised its option to repurchase shares tendered by employees, and many employees felt it was obligated to do so. In 1992, approximately 75 percent of the employees owned over 40 percent of the total stock of the company. Lincoln family members and former Lincoln executives owned about half the remainder.

As Lincoln was preparing to report its first quarterly loss in August 1992, the directors voted to suspend repurchases under the Stock Purchase Plan in order to prevent wholesale tendering of shares by employees at a time when Lincoln was short of cash. The change in policy meant that employees could sell their stock in the open market as unrestricted stock if they wished to convert it to cash. At that time, book value (and therefore market value) was about $19 per share. As it turned out, only 11 percent of the restricted shares were converted.

In preparation for the public issue of stock in 1995, the Employees' Stock Purchase Plan was terminated on March 30, automatically converting all shares issued under it to unrestricted stock. Market value of the shares at that time was about $40. After the public issue, shareholders approved a new stock purchase plan permitting employees to purchase up to $10,000 per year in open-market shares without brokers' commissions.

Vacations   Lincoln's plants were shut down for two weeks in August and two weeks during the Christmas season for vacations, which were unpaid. Employees with over 25 years of service got a fifth week of vacation at a time acceptable to superiors. When Lincoln was unable to meet its customers' orders in 1994, most employees agreed to work overtime through the August vacation period. Some of these employees were given vacations at alternate times.

Fringe Benefits   Lincoln sponsored a medical plan (whose cost was deducted from the annual bonus pool) and a company-paid retirement program. At the main plant, a cafeteria operated on a break-even basis, serving meals at about sixty percent of outside prices. The Employee Association, to which the company did not contribute, provided disability insurance and social and athletic activities. Dick Sabo commented,

> The company maintains traditional fringe benefits which include life insurance, health care, paid vacations, an annuity program (401K), and a variety of employee participation activities. All of these programs, of course, reduce the amount of money which otherwise could be received by the employees as bonus. Each employee is, therefore, acutely aware of the impact of such benefit items on their overall earnings in each year.

He also cautioned,

> When you use "participation," put quotes around it. Because we believe that each person should participate only in those decisions he is most knowledgeable about. I don't think production employees should control the decisions of the chairman. They don't know as much as he does about the decisions he is involved in.

The primary means of employee participation beyond an employee's immediate work environment were the suggestion program and the Advisory Board. Members of the Advisory Board were elected by employees and met with President Fred Mackenbach every two weeks. Unlike

Exhibit 6   Excerpts From Advisory Board Minutes, March 14, 1995

Mr. Mackenbach opened the meeting by welcoming three new members to the Board. He called on Mr. Beddia to inform the Board about the Harvest for Hunger food drive.

Prior Items

1. Could all air-cooled engines be covered when we receive them? Answer: The Material Handling Department will cover the top pallet of each stack when the engines are unloaded.

2. Could the 401K contributions from bonus be included in the year-to-date totals on the remaining regular December pay stubs? Answer: Yes, it will be.

3. An employee was almost hit by a speeding electric cart in Bay 16. Could a slow speed sign be posted? Answer: Signs cautioning pedestrians regarding Towmotor traffic have been installed. Additional changes are being reviewed.

New Business

1. Why was an employee of the Motor Division penalized for a safety issue when he performed his job as instructed? Answer: Referred to Mr. Beddia.

2. Has our total percent of market share increased? Answer: In the past, we could provide a precise answer. Some of our competitors no longer provide the required information to NEMA. However, in our judgment, we are increasing our percent of market share in both consumables and equipment.

3. Could an additional microwave unit be installed in the Bay 24 vending area? Answer: Referred to Mr. Crissey.

4. Could we consider buying an emergency vehicle instead of paying between $300 and $500 per ambulance run to the hospital? Answer: When we use the services of the Euclid Fire and Rescue Squad, there is a charge of approximately $350. While in general this charge is covered by hospitalization insurance, we will ask Mr. Trivisonno to review this with city officials.

5. When will the softball field be completed? Answer: A recreational area on the EP-3 site will become a reality, although certain issues with the city must be resolved first. We will show the preliminary layout at the next meeting.

6. Is a member of the Board of Directors being investigated for fraud? Answer: We are not aware of any investigation of this type.

7. Is our investment in Mexico losing value? Could we have an update as to how our Mexican operation is doing? Answer: Yes. An update will be provided at the next meeting.

8. Could something be done to eliminate the odor created when the septic tank is cleaned? Answer: Referred to Mr. Hellings.

James Lincoln and Bill Irrgang, CEOs Willis and Hastings did not regularly attend these meetings. Responses to all Advisory Board items were promised by the following meeting. Exhibit 6 provides excerpts from minutes of the Advisory Board meeting of March 14, 1995 (generally typical of the group's deliberations).

The Advisory Board could only advise, not direct, although its recommendations were taken seriously. Its influence was shown on December 1, 1995, when Lincoln reversed a two-year-old policy of paying lower wages to new hires. Veteran workers had complained loudly. *BusinessWeek* quoted Joseph Tuck, an inspector with 18 years' service: "If an individual shows he can handle the workload, he should be rewarded" with full pay.[5]

International Expansion

Internationally, the welding equipment industry was highly fragmented but consolidating. No global statistics reported total economic activity or companies' market shares in various countries, but many developed economies had local suppliers. Two U.S. producers—Lincoln and Miller Electric—and one European firm, ESAB (the largest welding firm in the world by 1996), were present in most

Table 2   Financial Results by Geographic Sector, 1993–1995
(in thousands of dollars)

	United States	Europe	Other Countries	Total*
1995				
Net Sales to Unaffiliated Customers**	$711,940	$201,672	$118,786	$1,032,39
Pre-Tax Profit (Loss)	79,737	10,171	10,956	99,584
Identifiable Assets	404,972	194,319	80,921	617,760
1994				
Net Sales to Unaffiliated Customers	$641,607	$156,803	$108,194	$ 906,604
Pre-Tax Profit (Loss)	68,316	7,891	4,062	80,168
Identifiable Assets	350,012	165,722	76,129	556,857
1993				
Net Sales to Unaffiliated Customers	$543,458	$211,268	$ 91,273	$ 845,999
Pre-Tax Profit (Loss)	42,570	(68,865)	(22,903)	(46,950)
Identifiable Assets	389,247	172,136	69,871	559,543

*Totals for Profit/Loss and Identifiable Assets will not cross-add due to elimination of intercompany transactions.

**Net Sales reported for the United States include materials exported to unaffiliated customers, amounting to $81,770 in 1995; $64,400 in 1994; and $58,100 in 1993. Net Sales excludes intracompany sales to Lincoln's overseas branches.

markets. (Table 2, adapted from the 1995 annual report, shows Lincoln's recent sales by region.)

Until 1986, Lincoln Electric held to James Lincoln's original policy toward international ventures, according to Sam Evans, regional manager of international and a 40-year Lincoln veteran. James Lincoln had felt his company could manufacture in any English-speaking country. Otherwise, he let others promote Lincoln products internationally. Evans described the approach:

> We dealt with Armco International, which was a division of Armco Steel. Lincoln licensed Armco to manufacture and market our products in Mexico, Uruguay, Brazil, Argentina, and in France. It was electrodes, but included assembly of machines in Mexico. Armco also marketed Lincoln products along the Pacific Rim and in a few other areas of the world. At one point, we also had a joint venture with Big Three Corporation in Scotland.

In 1986, Lincoln Electric faced a newly aggressive Scandinavian competitor, ESAB Corporation, part of the Swiss-Swedish engineering/energy group Asea Brown Boveri. ESAB had bought up welding products manufacturers throughout the world during the industry downturn of 1982–1985. Starting in 1986, ESAB began to penetrate the U.S. market, buying several U.S. welding products companies (trade names acquired by ESAB included Oxweld, Genuine Heliarc, Plasmarc, Allstate Welding Products, Alloy Rods, and the former Lindy Division of Union Carbide). ESAB opened an electrode plant less than a mile from Lincoln's Cleveland headquarters.

In the global recession of the early 1980s, ESAB's movement toward consolidation threatened to give the firm a volume base large enough to provide economies of scale for research and development programs. Dick Sabo said Lincoln's CEO, Ted Willis, was concerned and met with the chairman of ESAB in 1986, hoping "that we could work together." The relationship soon soured, however, and Willis decided to challenge ESAB internationally.

From 1986–1992, Lincoln purchased controlling interests in manufacturing and marketing operations in 16 countries. It took over most of the operations previously licensed to Armco and Big Three. It put a factory in Brazil, where ESAB had an estimated 70-percent market share. Lincoln expanded into gas welding and cutting by buying Harris Calorific Corporation, which made oxyacetylene cutting and welding equipment in the U.S., Italy, and Ireland. Lincoln's largest new investment was the purchase of Messer Griesheim's welding products business in Germany, considered ESAB's most profitable territory. Altogether, Lincoln opened or expanded plants in England, France, the Netherlands, Spain, Norway, Mexico, Venezuela, and Japan. The expansion required heavy borrowing; for the first time, James Lincoln's conservative financial policies were discarded. Long-term debt rose from zero in 1986 to over $220 million in 1992. (Exhibit 7 summarizes Lincoln financial statements for 1986–1994.)

Exhibit 7   Summaries of Lincoln Financial Statements, 1986–1995*

Balance Sheets	12/86	12/87	12/88	12/89	12/90	12/91	12/92	12/93	12/94	12/95
Assets										
Cash and Equivalents	47.0	61.0	23.9	19.5	15.5	20.3	20.6	20.4	10.4	10.1
Receivables	46.0	61.7	90.9	100.8	127.3	118.0	111.3	110.5	126.0	140.8
Inventories	52.3	74.7	116.3	120.5	164.4	206.3	171.3	143.7	155.3	182.9
Other Current Assets	9.4	9.1	12.0	14.4	14.5	17.5	18.0	51.1	21.7	23.3
Total Current Assets	154.8	206.4	243.1	255.1	321.7	362.1	321.2	325.7	313.4	357.1
Gross Plant	153.2	195.7	274.8	328.2	387.7	422.9	435.2	406.7	444.5	490.6
Accumulated Depreciation	93.4	121.2	148.6	170.2	193.1	213.3	226.8	237.0	260.3	285.0
Net Plant	59.8	74.5	126.3	158.0	194.7	209.6	208.4	169.7	184.2	205.6
Long-Term Investments	11.5	0.3	0.0	0.0	0.0	0.0	0.0	0.0	0.0	0.0
Intangible and Other Assets	13.1	13.4	33.8	42.6	55.9	68.6	73.7	64.1	59.2	55.1
Total Assets	239.2	294.7	403.2	455.8	572.2	640.3	603.3	559.5	556.9	617.8
Liabilities & Equity										
Short-Term Debt	4.6	6.6	39.2	41.6	40.6	50.7	27.1	33.4	18.1	29.8
Accounts Payable	11.2	23.4	36.8	40.0	44.3	46.6	44.2	43.5	54.8	53.9
Other Current Liabilities	25.1	32.7	38.1	41.0	52.4	61.3	77.2	99.0	71.2	85.0
Total Current Liabilities	41.0	62.7	114.2	122.6	137.3	158.6	148.5	175.9	144.1	168.7
Long-Term Debt	0.0	5.7	17.5	30.2	109.2	155.5	221.5	216.9	194.8	93.6
Other Long-Term Liabilities	11.7	9.7	15.3	16.6	24.0	20.3	17.8	15.3	17.0	20.1
Minority Interests	4.0	11.9	31.4	42.6	47.4	41.7	16.8	7.9	6.8	5.5
Total Liabilities	56.7	90.0	178.4	211.9	317.9	376.1	404.6	416.0	218.6	287.9
Common Equity	182.6	204.7	224.8	243.8	254.3	264.1	198.7	143.5	194.1	329.9
Total Equity Capital	182.6	204.7	224.8	243.8	254.3	264.1	198.7	143.5	194.1	329.9
Total Liabilities & Capital	239.2	294.7	403.2	455.8	572.2	640.3	603.3	559.5	556.9	617.8
Income Statements										
Net Sales	370.2	443.2	570.2	692.8	796.7	833.9	853.0	846.0	906.6	1,032.4
Cost of Goods Sold	245.4	279.4	361.0	441.3	510.5	521.8	553.1	532.8	556.3	634.6
Gross Profit	124.8	163.8	209.2	251.5	286.2	312.1	299.9	313.2	350.3	397.8
SG&A Expense	100.3	119.7	165.2	211.1	259.2	270.5	280.3	273.3	261.7	289.8
Operating Profit	24.5	44.1	44.0	40.4	27.0	41.6	19.6	39.9	88.6	108.0
Restructuring Charge	0	0	0	0	0	0	−23.9	−70.1	2.7	0
Non-Recurring Oper. Exp.	0	0	0	0	0	0	−18.9	−3.7	0	0
Other Income	6.1	7.1	14.4	15.7	14.4	8.5	7.5	4.5	4.5	3.9
EBIT	30.6	51.2	58.4	56.1	41.4	50.1	−15.7	−29.4	95.9	111.9
Interest Expense	1.0	1.3	2.6	7.6	11.1	15.7	18.7	17.6	15.7	12.3
Pre-tax Earnings	29.6	49.9	55.9	48.5	30.4	34.4	−34.4	−47.0	80.2	99.6
Income Taxes	13.7	22.3	21.5	21.0	19.3	20.0	11.4	−6.4	32.2	38.1
Accounting Change	0	0	0	0	0	0	0	2.5	0	0
Net Income	15.8	27.6	34.4	27.6	11.1	14.4	−45.8	−38.1	48.0	61.5

*Source of Data, McDonald and Company and SEC reports

Separate Lincoln-type incentive management plans remained in place at the company's factories in Australia, Mexico, and the U.S., but attempts to implement such plans in other countries were largely unsuccessful. Sabo said the main problem was that Europe lapsed into recession. He added, "Germany started to fail within two months after we purchased Griesheim. The country had 27-percent unemployment. So we didn't implement the system at all. We didn't get a chance to." In Brazil, Willis learned that regulations defined incentive bonuses to be part of base salaries, which could not be reduced during downturns, so the Lincoln system was not installed there.

Welder Scott Skrjanc, a 17-year veteran of the production force, had another idea about why the system did not work out overseas:

> Their culture, as I understand it, was so much different from ours. Their work ethic and work habits, I guess, aren't like the United States. They have a saying in German that means, "slowly, slowly, but good." And I guess that's how they perceive it. Here, we do high-quality work, but we work fast—and smart. As you get older, you get wiser and work smarter.

Sam Evans, who had run Lincoln's operations in Eastern Europe until cancer forced his return to Cleveland for successful treatment, gave his view of CEO Willis' performance in the international expansion:

> Ted Willis' belief—and I think it was a very good belief, although he is often criticized by Lincoln people—was that we needed a stronger world organization. The welding industry was consolidating in the world market, much like the steel industry did in the 1930s. He felt we needed this larger sales base so that we could invest in the research and development to maintain our position in the industry. I think that has succeeded. Even though we have had failures internationally, we have grown with our base.
>
> We are coming out with a lot of new items—the new square-wave machines, which control the actual wave form, the new stainless products, the inverter technology in motors and machines. We are moving rapidly ahead of the industry. That was Mr. Willis' vision, and it was a good one. His financial vision wasn't so good—perhaps.

Retrenchment and Turnaround under Hastings

Willis retired in 1992 and Don Hastings became chief executive officer. Hastings set about "consolidating and reorganizing" the foreign operations. He agreed with ESAB to close the Lincoln factory in Brazil and to license ESAB to make Lincoln products there. Similarly, ESAB closed its Spanish electrode plant, and Lincoln used its excess capacity in that country to supply ESAB's needs. Lincoln mothballed its German plant, losing an estimated $100 million there. It also shut down factories in Venezuela and Japan. Practically all Lincoln's international operations which were not closed were scaled back. By 1996 ESAB, now owned by Britain's Charter Group, was recognized as the largest welding vendor in the world, with key markets in East and Western Europe, South America, and the Far East; it had the "leading position in stick electrodes (a declining market) and an even bigger position in fluxed core wires (a rapidly growing market)."[6]

In 1992 and 1993, Lincoln wrote off about $130 million of its foreign assets and reported its first-ever net losses—$46 million and $38 million respectively. Citing the profitable performance of the firm's U.S. workers, Hastings convinced the Board of Directors to give them incentive bonuses averaging $19,000 each year in spite of the overall losses. Dividends were cut by nearly 40 percent from the 1991 level. In 1994, Hastings told the U.S. employees, "We went from five plants in four countries in 1986 to 21 plants in 15 countries in 1992. We did it too fast, we paid too much, we didn't understand the international markets or cultures, and then we got hit by a tremendous global recession." By mid 1995, Lincoln was down to 16 plants in 11 countries. Dick Sabo described the company's new relationship with ESAB:

> So the animosity has ended. We're still competitors, but we are more like the U.S. competitors. In the U.S. we've always had a competitive situation, but we're friendly competitors. So, overall, the strategy that Ted Willis originated was good. The implementation was poor. That's where the problem was.

Rank and file employees commented on the results of the attempt at international expansion. Stenographer Dee Chesko, a 27-year employee, said she had heard no bitterness voiced about the losses:

> What I was hearing was people were disappointed—that they felt upper management should know, per se, what they're doing. You know, how could this happen? Not bitterness . . . a little frustration. But, if companies are to expand and be global, this has to be expected.

Assembler Kathleen Hoenigman, hired in 1977, added:

> They say, "We want to be number one. We want to be number one." So we are going to keep buying and buying and buying. I think we will be investing more overseas. And I think we are going to be number one internationally, not just in the U.S., but the manufacturing will be done here. The expansion helped. We lost money, but I think it helped. You know what, if we didn't do as we did, we wouldn't be known as well as we are right now. Because we were staying just like a little . . . a little pea, while everybody was building up around us.

Sabo said Lincoln expected to continue expanding internationally, "But we're going at it a little differently." He explained,

Under Willis, we bought a manufacturing site with the intent of creating the marketing demand. Under Hastings, we're developing the marketing demand with the anticipation that we'll build the manufacturing site to meet the demand. So what we're trying to do is take the existing facilities that we have and sell a lot of product and create enough demand so that we have to buy—or build—more facilities to service that demand.

We're just getting there in terms of being global. We're global to the extent that we market in 123 countries.

We're global to the extent that we have distributors in 86 different countries. We're global because we have manufacturing sites in ten countries. Are we global in our management style? No. We're just starting to develop that.

The U.S. Welding Products Industry in 1995

The welding products market of the mid 1990s was classified as "mature and cyclical." In the United States, annual sales volume had ranged between $2.5 and $2.7 billion since 1988 (see Exhibit 8). The main arc-welding products were

Exhibit 8   Trends and Forecasts: Welding Apparatus (SIC 3548)
(in millions of dollars except as noted)

	1987	1988	1989	1990	1991	1992[1]	1993[2]	1994[3]
Industry Data								
Value of shipments[4]	2,105	2,498	2,521	2,684	2,651	2,604	2,576	—
Total employment (000)	18.7	19.7	19.0	19.2	19.5	19.4	19.5	—
Production workers (000)	11.5	12.3	11.6	12.0	11.8	11.7	11.7	—
Average hourly earnings ($)	12.10	12.45	12.67	13.15	13.07	—	—	—
Capital expenditures	45.4	49.3	59.1	67.7	50.5	—	—	—
Product Data								
Value of shipments[5]	1,918	2,263	2,298	2,475	2,434	2,374	2,340	—
Value of shipments (1987 $)	1,918	2,135	2,077	2,154	2,034	1,935	1,874	1,954
Trade Data								
Value of imports	—	—	480	365	478	381	458	458
Value of exports	—	—	491	566	597	621	661	671

	Percent Change (1989–1994)					
	88–89	89–90	90–91	91–92	92–93	93–94
Industry Data						
Value of shipments[4]	0.9	6.5	−1.2	−1.8	−1.1	—
Value of shipments (1987 $)	−3.3	2.5	−5.2	−4.1	−3.0	3.9
Total employment (000)	−3.6	1.1	1.6	−0.5	0.5	—
Production workers (000)	−5.7	3.4	−1.7	−0.8	0.0	—
Average hourly earnings ($)	1.8	3.8	−0.6	—	—	—
Capital expenditures	19.9	14.6	−25.4	—	—	—
Product Data						
Value of shipments[5]	1.5	7.7	−1.7	−2.5	−1.4	—
Value of shipments (1987 $)	−2.7	3.7	−5.6	−4.9	−3.2	4.3
Value of exports	747	15.3	5.5	4.0	8.1	11.3

[1]Estimate, except exports and imports.

[2]Estimate.

[3]Forecast.

[4]Value of all products and services sold by establishments in the welding apparatus industry.

[5]Value of products classified in the welding apparatus industry produced b.

Source: U.S. Department of Commerce: Bureau of the Census; International U.S. Industrial Outlook January, 1994

power sources and welding machines; consumable items such as welding electrodes; accessories such as protective clothing; automated wire feeding systems; and devices to manipulate or position the electrodes, such as robots.

After the downturn in 1982–1983, when industry sales fell 30–40 percent, the U.S. welding products industry consolidated. By 1995, at least 75 percent of machine and consumables sales could be attributed to just four companies: Lincoln, Miller Electric Company (which did not sell consumables), ESAB Corporation, and Hobart Brothers, Inc. ESAB was now owned by Britain's Charter Group; both Miller and Hobart had recently been acquired by Illinois Tool Works, Inc. Lincoln and Miller were thought to have about equal unit sales of machines and power supplies, about double Hobart's volume. Hundreds of smaller companies marketed various niche products, and several international firms sold limited lines of transformer- and inverter-based machines in the U.S. and elsewhere. Over 600 exhibitors were registered to show their wares at the 1996 annual Welding Show in Chicago, where 25,000 potential customers would attend.

Starting in the early 90s, Lincoln, Miller, and Hobart each began buying similar articulated-arm robots and adapting them to welding applications. The size of the robotics segment of the welding products market was unclear in 1995, but Chet Woodman, head of Lincoln Automation, said his unit had robotics sales of about $7 million in 1994 and predicted $50 million annual revenue by the year 2000.

ESAB, Lincoln, and Hobart each marketed a wide range of continuous-wire and stick electrodes for welding mild steel, aluminum, cast iron, and stainless and special steels. Most electrodes were designed to meet the standards of the American Welding Society (AWS) and were thus essentially the same as to size and composition from one manufacturer to another. Price differences for similar products among the three companies amounted to only a percent or two. Low-price competitors were well represented in the market, however, as imported consumables that purported to meet AWS standards were commonly available. There was no testing system to confirm a product's conformance to the standards.

Every electrode manufacturer had a limited number of unique products, which typically constituted only a small percentage of its total sales. There were also many producers of specialized electrodes for limited applications, such as welding under water and welding space-age alloys, and several international companies marketed general-purpose electrodes. Wire for gas-shielded welding was thought to be the biggest-selling welding consumable. ESAB claimed to have the largest share of the global welding consumables and materials market.

Lincoln's Manufacturing Processes

Lincoln made about twice as many different products in 1995 as it had ten years earlier. Its net sales per employee in 1994 were $159,248. For U.S. employees only, the number was about $225,000. About two-thirds of net sales was represented by products made in the Cleveland area.

Fortune magazine declared Lincoln's Euclid operation one of America's ten best-managed factories, and compared it to a General Electric plant also on the list:

> Stepping into GE's spanking new dishwasher plant, an awed supplier said, is like stepping "into the Hyatt Regency." By comparison, stepping into Lincoln Electric's 33-year-old, cavernous, dimly lit factory is like stumbling into a dingy big-city YMCA. It's only when one starts looking at how these factories do things that similarities become apparent. They have found ways to merge design with manufacturing, build in quality, make wise choices about automation, get close to customers, and handle their work forces.[7]

As it had for decades, Lincoln required most suppliers to deliver raw materials just as needed in production. James Lincoln had counseled producing for stock when necessary to maintain employment. For many years after his death, however, the firm manufactured only to customer order. In the late 1980s, Hastings decided to resume maintaining substantial finished goods inventories. Lincoln then purchased its finished goods warehouse.

Outsourcing   It was James Lincoln's policy to keep Lincoln as insulated as possible from work stoppages in supplier plants, especially unionized ones. He also felt Lincoln quality was higher than that most suppliers could provide. So instead of purchasing most components from outsiders, Lincoln made them from basic industrial raw materials such as coils of steel sheet and bar, pieces of metal plate, spools of copper and aluminum wire, and pallets of paints and varnishes. Lincoln even made its own electronic circuit boards, to assure their performance in outdoor, cold, dirty conditions; commercial suppliers were accustomed to making circuits boards for warm, clean computers. At one point the firm had contemplated buying its own steel rolling mill. President Ted Willis, however, was concerned over the mill's union affiliation, and the purchase was not completed.

As an exception to on-site manufacture of components, gasoline and diesel engines for the engine-driven machines were purchased. Like its main competitors, Lincoln used Wisconsin-Continental, Perkins, and Deutz engines in 1995.

Welding Machine Manufacture   In the machines area, most engine-driven welders, power supplies, wire feeders, and so forth were assembled, tested, and packaged on conveyor lines. Almost all components were made by numerous small "factories within a factory." Various of these small factories—mostly open work areas—made gasoline tanks, steel shafts, wiring harnesses, and even switches, rheostats, and transformers. The shaft for a certain generator, for example, was made from round steel bar by two men who used five machines. A saw cut the bar to length, a digital lathe machined different sections to varying diameters, a special milling machine cut a slot for the key way, and so forth, until a finished shaft was produced. The operators moved the shafts from machine to machine and made necessary adjustments and tool changes. Nearby, a man punched, shaped and painted sheet metal cowling parts. In another area, a woman and a man put steel laminations onto rotor shafts, then wound, insulated, and tested the rotors. Many machines in the factory appeared old, even obsolete; James Lincoln had always insisted on a one-year payback period for new investments, and it appeared the policy was still in effect.

Consumables Manufacture   The company was secretive about its consumables production, and outsiders were barred from the Mentor, Ohio, plant (which made only electrodes) and from the electrode area of the main plant. Electrode manufacture was highly capital intensive, and teams of Lincoln workers who made electrodes shared group piece rates. To make electrodes, rod purchased from metals producers, usually in coils, was drawn down to make wire of various diameters. For stick electrodes, the wire was cut into pieces, most commonly 14" long, and coated with pressed-powder "flux." Dick Sabo commented,

> The actual production of a stick electrode has not changed for at least forty years. Bill Irrgang designed that equipment. As to the constituents which make up the electrodes, that may change almost daily. There are changes in design from time to time. And every new batch of raw material has a little different consistency, and we have to adjust for that. We make our own iron oxide [a main ingredient of many fluxes]. We have had that powder kiln in operation since about the 1930s. We may have the largest production facility for iron oxide pellets in the world. At first, we contemplated selling the pellets. But we decided not to give our competition an edge.

Stick electrodes were packaged in boxes weighing two to 50 pounds. Continuous-wire electrode, generally smaller in diameter, was packaged in coils and spools, also two to 50 pounds each, and in drums weighing up to half a ton. Some wire electrode was coated with copper to improve conductivity. Lincoln's Innershield wire, like the "cored" wire of other manufacturers, was hollow and filled with a material similar to that used to coat stick electrodes.

The New Electric Motor Factory   In 1992, Lincoln saw an opportunity to become a major factor in the electric motor business by purchasing the assets of General Motors' AC-Delco plant in Dayton, Ohio. New government regulations on motors' energy efficiency made it necessary to re-design whole product lines; GM decided instead to exit the industry. Lincoln's intent was to combine AC-Delco's technology and product line with Lincoln's manu-

facturing expertise and cost structure in the Dayton plant. Don Hastings offered to involve the existing union in its operation of the plant if it were retained. Dick Sabo described the implementation efforts:

> We asked the AC-Delco employees if they wanted to adopt the Lincoln Incentive System and keep their plant open—and their jobs. They voted overwhelmingly not to adopt the system. And they knew all about us. We put a lot of effort into telling them about Lincoln, even brought some employees up here to tour our plant and talk to Lincoln people. What struck Mr. Hastings as odd was that people would vote themselves out of work rather than knuckle down and put in the effort that it takes to be in the motor business. That was sort of an eye opener for Lincoln Electric.

In mid-1995, Lincoln's new electric motor factory, close to the main plant, was near completion and in partial operation. The plant was designed to make motors from one-third to 1,250 horsepower, in custom configurations as well as standard specifications, with shipment six days after customer orders. Lincoln's net sales of electric motors in 1994 totalled about $50 million, and the goal was $100 million in sales by the year 2000.

Robotics   Adjacent to the electric motor factory was a smaller building housing Lincoln's Automation unit. There, work teams of two or three put together robotic welding units that combined Fanuc (Japanese) articulated arms with Lincoln automatic welders. In operation, the robot arm manipulated the wire electrode much as a human operator would, but faster and more accurately. The system, priced at about $100,000, could be purchased with a laser "eye" to track irregular seams and could be programmed to follow any three dimensional path within the arm's reach. Chet Woodman, head of Lincoln Automation, was a former Hobart executive with over a decade of experience in robotics manufacturing and marketing.

Management Organization
James Lincoln stressed the need to protect management's authority. "Management in all successful departments of industry must have complete power," he said, "Management is the coach who must be obeyed. The men, however, are the players who alone can win the game." Examples of management's authority were the right to transfer workers among jobs, to switch between overtime and short time as required, and to assign specific parts to individual workers. As to executive perquisites, there were few—crowded, austere offices, no executive washrooms or lunchrooms or automobiles, and no reserved parking spaces, except for visitors. Even CEO Hastings and President Mackenbach paid for their own meals, normally in the employee cafeteria.

James Lincoln never allowed preparation of a formal organization chart, saying this might limit flexibility.

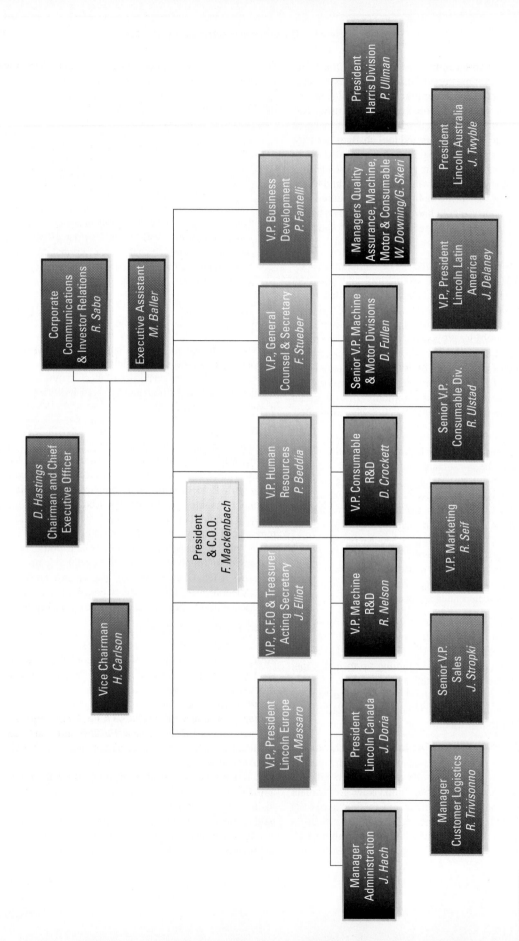

Figure 2 Lincoln Organization Chart, 1995

Irrgang and Willis continued that policy. During the 1970s, Harvard Business School researchers prepared a chart reflecting the implied management relationships at Lincoln. It became available within the company, and Irrgang felt this had a disruptive effect. Only after Hastings became CEO was a formal chart prepared. (Figure 2 shows the official chart in 1995 and Exhibit 5 lists officers and directors.) Two levels of management, at most, existed between supervisors and Mackenbach. Production supervisors at Lincoln typically were responsible for 60 to over 100 workers. Hastings, who was 67, had recruited experienced managers from outside the company and appointed a number of new, young vice presidents, mainly from the field, so they could compete for the top jobs.

Promotion from Within   Until the 1990s, Lincoln had a firm policy of promotion from within and claimed to hire above the entry level "only when there are no suitable internal applicants." In 1990, all senior managers at Lincoln were career Lincoln employees—and all directors were present or former employees or Lincoln family members. However, when Lincoln purchased Harris Calorific in 1992, its CEO, Paul F. Fantelli, was retained and later became vice president, business development of Lincoln. A number of other acquired company officials were integrated into Lincoln's management structure.

Lincoln's CFO in 1996, H. Jay Elliott, came from Goodyear in 1993; General Counsel Frederick Stueber came from a private law firm in 1995; and Anthony Massaro, the nominated successor to Fred Mackenbach as president, joined Lincoln from his position as group president of Westinghouse Electric Co. in 1993. Several outside directors were also elected, including the CEO of Capitol American Financial Corporation, a former vice chairman of General Electric, a former CEO of Westinghouse, and the CEO of Libby Corporation. Still, there were no announced plans to hire more managers from outside. And insiders and Lincoln family members retained a clear majority on the board.

Lincoln managers received a base salary plus an incentive bonus. The bonus was calculated in the same way as for workers. The only exceptions were the three outsiders Hastings hired as managers in 1993–1995 and the chairman and chief executive officer. The former outsiders had special employment contracts. Sabo explained how the CEO was compensated:

> James Lincoln set the chairman's salary at $50,000 plus 0.1 percent of sales. After Willis became chairman, it was based on a percentage of sales plus a percentage of profit. It became apparent that when the company started losing money it was difficult to pay someone based on losses. So they changed the approach for Don Hastings.

> [Through the lean years] Don has made somewhere around $600 thousand base salary plus incentives.

For 1995, Hastings was paid $1,003,901.[8]

Looking to the Future

In the spring of 1995 Lincoln announced plans to raise capital with a public issue of stock. Dick Sabo said, certain Lincoln family members were afraid the family would lose control of the company. "Paranoid, I guess, is the proper term," he remarked. Sam Evans added,

> I hope the public issue is handled in such a manner that those public owners understand that the success of this company is based on the incentive system. For sixty or seventy years, that has been our success—through the contribution of the employees. We have succeeded because we had a good product, good R and D, and excellent management for most of that period. But we've also had great contribution from the employees.

With the public issue accomplished and a record year in the books, noted *BusinessWeek,*

> . . . executives are now considering ways to move toward a more traditional pay scheme and away from the flat percentage-bonus formula. "The bonus is a good program, and it has worked well, but it's got to be modified some," says Director David C. Lincoln, whose father John C. Lincoln founded the company in 1895. Adds Edward E. Lawler, who heads the University of Southern California's Center for Effective Organizations: "One of the issues with Lincoln is how [its pay plan] can survive rapid growth and globalization."

Endnotes

1.   Feder, Barnaby J. 1994. Rethinking a model incentive plan. *The New York Times,* September 5, Section 1: 33.
2.   Gerdel, Thomas W. 1995. Lincoln Electric experiences season of worker discontent. *Cleveland Plain Dealer,* December 10.
3.   Schiller, Zachary. 1996. A model incentive plan gets caught in a vise. *BusinessWeek,* January 22: 89.
4.   Eiselen, F. C., Lewis, E., & Downey, D. G. (Eds.). 1929. *The Abingdon Bible Commentary.* Nashville, TN: The Abingdon Press, Inc.: 960–969.
5.   Schiller, op. cit.
6.   Utley, N., et al. Grieg Middleton & Co., Ltd. Company report number 1674211. Charter 12/12/95. Investext 02/23.
7.   Bylinsky, Gene. 1984. America's best-managed factories. *Fortune,* May 28: 16.
8.   Baltimore, MD, Disclosures, Inc. (Via Dow Jones News Service).

Indexes

IMPORTANT

HERE IS YOUR REGISTRATION CODE TO ACCESS MCGRAW-HILL
PREMIUM CONTENT AND MCGRAW-HILL ONLINE RESOURCES

For key premium online resources you need THIS CODE to
gain access. Once the code is entered, you will be able to
use the web resources for the length of your course.

Access is provided only if you have purchased a new book.

If the registration code is missing from this book, the registration screen on our
website, and within your WebCT or Blackboard course will tell you how to obtain
your new code. Your registration code can be used only once to establish
access. It is not transferable

To gain access to these online resources

1. **USE** your web browser to go to: **http://www.mhhe.com/dess3e**

2. **CLICK** on "First Time User"

3. **ENTER** the Registration Code printed on the tear-off bookmark on the right

4. After you have entered your registration code, click on "Register"

5. **FOLLOW** the instructions to setup your personal UserID and Password

6. **WRITE** your UserID and Password down for future reference. Keep it in a safe place.

If your course is using WebCT or Blackboard, you'll be able to use this code to
access the McGraw-Hill content within your instructor's online course.

To gain access to the McGraw-Hill content in your instructor's WebCT or
Blackboard course simply log into the course with the user ID and Password
provided by your instructor. Enter the registration code exactly as it appears to
the right when prompted by the system. You will only need to use this code the
first time you click on McGraw-Hill content.

These instructions are specifically for student access. Instructors are not required
to register via the above instructions.

The McGraw·Hill Companies

McGraw-Hill
Irwin

Thank you, and welcome to your
McGraw-Hill/Irwin Online Resources.

Dess/Lumpkin/Eisner
Strategic Management, 3/e
ISBN 10-Digit: 0-07-326694-9
ISBN 13-Digit: 978-0-07-326694-7

REGISTRATION CODE

6DAW–CCJX–PW76–4D6A–NBD6

The Reviewer Hall of Fame

We would like to thank the dedicated instructors who have graciously provided their insights since the inception of *Strategic Management: Creating Competitive Advantages* and *Strategic Management: Text and Cases.*

Alessandri, Todd	Syracuse University	Fausnaugh, Carolyn J.	Florida Institute of Technology
Alexander, Larry	Virginia Polytechnic Institute	Ferguson, Tamela D.	University of Louisiana at
Amason, Allen C.	University of Georgia		Lafayette
Antoniou, Peter H.	California State University, San Marcos	Fox, Isaac	University of Minnesota
		Frankforter, Steven A.	Winthrop University
Arnott, Dave	Dallas Baptist University	Fried, Vance	Oklahoma State University
Azriel, Jay	Illinois State University	Gilbertson, Diana L.	California State University, Fresno
Bailey, Jeffrey J.	University of Idaho		
Barringer, Bruce	University of Central Florida	Gilley, Matt	Oklahoma State University
Beal, Brent D.	Louisiana State University	Gilliard, Debora	Metropolitan State College of Denver
Bell DeTienne, Kristen	Brigham Young University		
Bernstein, Eldon	Lynn University	Goel, Sanjay	University of Minnesota, Duluth
Bodie, Dusty	Boise State University		
Bogner, William	Georgia State University	Harrison, Niran	University of Oregon
Calhoun, Mikelle A.	Valparaiso University	Harveston, Paula	Berry College
Cappel, Samuel D.	Southeastern Louisiana State University	Hester, Kim	Arkansas State University
		Hironaka, John	California State University, Sacramento
Carini, Gary	Baylor University		
Carraher, Shawn M.	Texas A&M University, Commerce	Hoffman, Alan	Bentley College
		Holbein, Gordon	Northern Kentucky University
Caruth, Don	Amberton University	Hough, Jill	University of Tulsa
Castrogiovanni, Gary J.	University of Tulsa	Humphreys, John	Eastern New Mexico University
Chaganti, Radha	Rider University	Ibe, James G.	Morris College
Cho, Theresa	Rutgers University	Janney, Jay J.	University of Dayton
Coffey, Betty S.	Appalachian State University	Jauch, Lawrence	University of Louisiana - Monroe
Coggins, Wade	Webster University, Fort Smith Metro Campus		
		Johnson, Dana M.	Michigan Technical University
Coombs, Joseph	University of Richmond	Katzenstein, James	California State University, Dominguez Hills
Cordeiro, James J.	SUNY Brockport		
Covin, Jeffrey	Indiana University	Kellermanns, Franz	Mississippi State University
Datta, Deepak	University of Texas at Arlington	Kelley, Donna	Babson College
Davis, James	University of Notre Dame	Kelley, Craig	California State University, Sacramento
Deresky, Helen	State University of New York, Plattsburgh		
		Ketchen, Dave	Florida State University
DeWitt, Rocki-Lee	University of Vermont	Kilpatrick, John A.	Idaho State University
Dobbs, Michael E.	Arkansas State University	Kowalczyk, Stan	San Francisco State University
Doh, Jonathan	Villanova University	Kraska, Daniel	North Central State College
Douglas, Tom	Clemson University	Kreps, Donald E.	Kutztown University
Down, Jon	Oregon State University	Kulkarni, Subdoh P.	Howard University
Engle, Clare	Concordia University	Lant, Theresa	New York University
Evans, William A.	Troy State University, Dothan	Legatski, Ted	Texas Christian University
Fabian, Frances H.	University of North Carolina, Charlotte	Lengnick-Hall, Cynthia	University of Texas at San Antonio
Fanelli, Angelo	Warrington College of Business	Lester, Wanda	North Carolina A&T State University
Fathi, Michael	Georgia Southwestern University		